The Little Black Book of Neuropsychology

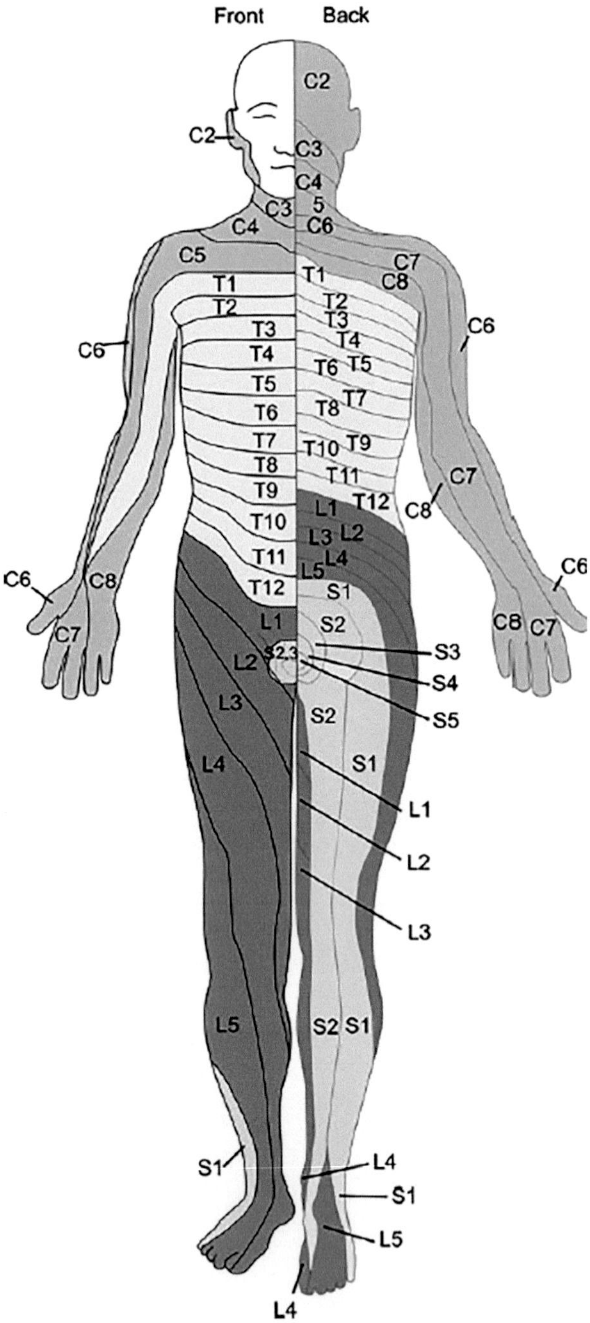

Anterior and Posterior Views of the Human Dermatomes

Michael R. Schoenberg • James G. Scott
Editors

The Little Black Book of Neuropsychology

A Syndrome-Based Approach

Second Edition

Springer

Editors
Michael R. Schoenberg
Departments of Psychiatry and Neurosciences, Neurology, and Neurosurgery, University of South Florida College of Medicine, Tampa, FL, USA

James G. Scott
Department of Psychiatry and Behavioral Sciences, University of Oklahoma Health Sciences Center College of Medicine, Oklahoma City, OK, USA

ISBN 978-3-032-07776-9　　ISBN 978-3-032-07777-6 (eBook)
https://doi.org/10.1007/978-3-032-07777-6

This Springer imprint is published by the registered company Springer Nature Switzerland AG
The registered company address is: Gewerbestrasse 11, 6330 Cham, Switzerland

Preface

The second edition of the Little Black Book of Neuropsychology attempted to stay true to the goals of the first edition and remain a syndrome-based overview and resource for many of the issues faced by neuropsychologists, neurologists and neurosurgeons in serving patients. The second edition provides an overview of the domains of neuropsychology and methods of bedside or office examination of each domain. New to the second edition is an expanded method of brief, acute assessment, which is helpful in acute settings or office settings requiring a brief screening of each cognitive domain or a quick assessment of only a single domain which is symptomatic. The book was designed to offer those interested in neuropsychology a reference guide in the tradition of pocket references in medical subspecialties and we maintain an emphasis on presenting information in tabular form or key point boxes where appropriate. Readers of the first edition will note that the title for these summary boxes has been changed from the previous "Rule of Thumb" to "Key Points," as it was brought to our attention the Old English Law origins of the phrase and its potential insensitivity.

Neuropsychology practice and science has exhibited an exponential growth in the diagnosis and treatment of known or suspected dysfunction of the central nervous system. The clinical application of neuropsychological evaluation has increased in a variety of settings, including primary care offices, acute care (e.g., emergency departments, intensive care centers, acute trauma centers), as well as a multitude of tertiary care and rehabilitation centers. Furthermore, the research application of neuropsychology has continued to expand, with increased emphasis on measures of cognitive, behavioral and emotional functions (attention/executive, memory, language, visuo-perceptual and/or mood/affect) as important endpoints in a variety of treatment and research areas. Assessment of neuropsychological functions continues to be increasingly integrated in the management of patient health care. Furthermore, neuropsychological evaluation has become increasingly important in studies evaluating the effectiveness of pharmacologic and surgical therapies. Measurement of cognitive functions is also being used to assess neuropsychological processes that may be early signs of disease or a marker for a disease course or outcome. In addition to the scientific application of neuropsychological assessment to better understand brain processes, markers of disease, evaluate treatment courses, or predict outcomes, these data guide the emergence of evidence-based clinical neuropsychology practice, and are being increasingly applied to clinical and forensic applications. Over the past decades, neuropsychological evaluations have become increasingly important in legal proceedings to assist in understanding the cause and ramifications of known or suspected central nervous system dysfunction on behavior, emotion and cognition, including decision-making and judgment.

However, the practice of neuropsychology is not limited to clinical psychologists. The assessment of neuropsychological functions is routinely evaluated by various physician specialties, including neurologists, neurological surgeons and psychiatrists. This book aims to address the needs of licensed practitioners and to provide an overview of neuropsychology practice and science to medical and healthcare specialties having an interest in neuropsychology assessment. To continue to meet these goals, the first three chapters provide an overview for understanding referrals from healthcare providers, how to read the medical chart when conducting a neuropsychological evaluation, and a primer for the clinical neuropsychologist for understanding the common shorthand and notations made by physicians and nurses that are so often seen in the medical chart. For physicians in training (medical students, residents and fellows), Chap. 1 provides information about how to understand and interpret a neuropsychological evaluation report, what the qualitative descriptors mean to neuropsychologists and the basic premises and theories underlying clinical neuropsychological assessment and practice. Chapter 2 provides information regarding understanding the medical chart and is geared toward those in neuropsychology who may be less familiar with medical charting and abbreviations. Chapter 3 provides an update and review of functional neuroanatomy for both the neuropsychologist and medical specialist with an emphasis on the relationship of anatomy to function.

Chapters 4 and 5 are designed to be complementary and provide an overview of the neuropsychological assessment process and a comprehensive and brief assessment method for neuropsychological functioning by cognitive domain and subdomain.

A second unique aspect of this book is the presentation of descriptions of syndromes affecting each cognitive domain and brief office assessments that can be used to understand patients in acute settings and office settings where domain-focused assessment can guide treatment and patient management. This approach can also be helpful in guiding and focusing a more thorough, comprehensive evaluation based on normative data and parametric statistics that are traditional in Western neuropsychological practice.

The first section of this book continues to approach neuropsychological evaluations from a presenting-symptoms perspective. We believe the first section is particularly well suited to clinicians faced with common clinical problems. Thus, the clinician may review chapters about attention problems (see Chaps. 5 and 6), language deficits (Chap. 8) and/or memory complaints (Chap. 9). For less common complaints involving visuo-spatial deficits, behavioral or reasoning and judgment deficits or affect/mood symptoms, Chapters 10, 11 and 12 would be helpful in assessing and managing these patients. This provides a neuropsychological method to systematically assess cognitive and behavioral signs and symptoms in order to formulate hypotheses about lesion lateralization, localization and diagnosis within a brief, consultative assessment framework. This, we believe, is the neuropsychological complement to the tradition of neurology in which the question of "Where is the lesion?" leads to differential diagnoses of the etiology of the lesion.

The next section is a more traditional approach to neuropsychology principles and science, in which the diagnosis is specified (e.g., epilepsy, dementia or stroke) and the neuropsychological evaluation attempts to answer questions based on this diagnosis. Thus, these chapters provide an overview of the disease states and how these may present clinically. Special emphasis is given to neuropsychological features of diseases, giving recommendations for assessment procedures and data to assist interpretation. Each chapter is designed with comprehensive neuropsychological evaluations in mind, with the authors providing their clinical pearls, recommendations for the neuropsychological, neurological and psychological domains to assess, as well as helpful clinical information.

The book includes another section for the neuropsychologist, which is also likely to be of interest to both practitioners and consumers of neuropsychological evaluations (e.g., psychologists, physicians, nurses, social workers and our patients). This section includes a practical review of psychometrics, including a clinically focused overview of the measurement of change in cognitive functioning over time and issues regarding validity and common errors in interpreting neuropsychological data. Increasing sophistication in the measurement of neuropsychological processes and associated psychometrics, along with better appreciation for the natural variation in neuropsychological function among healthy individuals, has led to an evolution in the interpretation of neuropsychological data to identify disease. These Chapters explicitly review methods to interpret neuropsychological data founded in psychometric principles and neuropathologic science and subsequently to integrate data to improve the accuracy from making diagnoses from neuropsychological impairment (i.e., cognitive disorders). Collectively, we strongly believe that the material provided in this book provides a foundation for the clinician in evidence-based clinical neuropsychological practice.

Tampa, FL, USA — Michael R. Schoenberg
Oklahoma City, OK, USA — James G. Scott

References

American Board of Clinical Neuropsychology. (2007). American Academy of Clinical Neuropsychology (AACN) practice guidelines for neuropsychological assessment and consultation. *The Clinical Neuropsychologist*, *21*, 209–231.

Bush, S. S., Ruff, R. M., Troster, A. I., Barth, J. T., Koffler, S. P., Pliskin, N. H., Reynolds, C. R., & Silver, C. H. (2005). Symptom validity assessment: Practice issues and medical necessity. NAN Polocy and Planning Committee. *Archives of Clinical Neuropsychology*, *20*, 419–426.

Chelune, G. J. (2003). Assessing reliable neuropsychological change. In R. D. Franklin (Ed.), *Prediction in forensic and neuropsychology: Sound statistical practices* (pp. 65–88). Mahwah, NJ: Lawrence Erlbaum Associates.

Chelune, G. J. (2010). Evidenced-based research and practice in clinical neuropsychology. *The Clinical Neuropsychologist, 24*, 454–467.

Hannay, H. J., Bieliauskas, L. A., Crosson, B. A., Hammeke, T. A., Hamsher, K. DeS., & Koffler, S. P. (1998). Policy statement. Proceedings of the Houston conference on specialty education and training in clinical neuropsychology. *Archives of Clinical Neuropsychology, 13*, 160–166.

Heilman, K. M., & Valenstein, E. (2007). *Clinical neuropsychology* (4th ed.). New York: Oxford University Press.

Jacobson, N. S., & Truax, P. (1991). Clinical significance: A statistical approach to defining meaningful change in psychotherapy research. *Journal of Consulting and Clinical Psychology, 59*(1), 12–19.

Lezak, M. D., Howieson, D. B., & Loring, D. W. (2004). *Neuropsychological assessment* (4th ed.). New York: Oxford University Press.

Miller, W. R., & Rollnick, S. R. (2002). *Motivational interviewing: Preparing people for change* (2nd ed.). New York: Guilford Press.

Miller, W. R., & Rollnick, S. R. (2009). Ten things that motivational Interviewing is not. *Behavioural and Cognitive Psychotherapy, 37*, 129–140.

Reports of the INS-Division 40 task force on education, accreditation, and credentialing (1987). *The Clinical Neuropsychologist, 1*, 29–34.

Strauss, E., Sherman, E. M. S., & Spreen, O. (2006). *A compendium of neuropsychological tests: Administration, norms, and commentary* (3rd ed.). New York: Oxford University Press.

Acknowledgments

The assistance, wisdom and guidance of Jim Scott, my co-editor, allowed me to laugh when things seemed darkest and the book would not have been finished without his friendship and support. I would also like to thank the contributing authors of this book. The breadth and depth of knowledge and expertise brought to this volume frankly astounds me. A special thanks to Grant Iverson who contributed to several substantive areas. A note of gratitude to the many colleagues who have shaped my thinking about neuropsychology, including Russell Adams, Lyle Baade, Darwin Dorr, Kevin Duff, Philip Fastenau, Herman Jones, Jim Scott, Mary Ann Werz and David (DJ) Williamson. A dedication to Bob Maciunas, a true friend, a pinnacle of professional integrity and perhaps the smartest and most genuine individual I have ever known. Continue to conquer the world, my friend! A nod of appreciation to Patrick Marsh, a friend and an expert in handling professional and personal life challenges. Finally, I would like to thank Janice Stern for her unending support, advice, encouragement and nudges to complete the first edition.

Michael R. Schoenberg

Thanks first to my spouse (Vickie) and children (Remi and Logan) who made as many sacrifices in this effort as I did. Also, a big thanks to my co-editor Michael R. Schoenberg, who sowed the seed for the book, weeded, fertilized and made gardening fun. A big thank you to all our contributors, not only for your excellent contributions but for your indulgence of Mike and I as we asked for additions, deletions and re-writes. I also want to thank those behind the scenes who were my mentors, including F. William Black, Oscar Parsons, Russell Adams and Herman Jones. While I have benefited from being taught by many in neuropsychology, your teaching continues to give me inspiration. I would be remiss if I didn't thank all the neuropsychology interns and postdoctoral fellows with whom it has been my pleasure to work over the years (many of whom are represented on the title pages of this volume). You have all reinforced my belief that learning really is a two-way street.

James G. Scott

Contents

Contributors

Vicki A. Anderson Department of Psychology, Australian Centre for Child Neuropsychology Studies, Murdoch Children's Research Institute, Royal Children's Hospital, University of Melbourne, Parkville, Melbourne, Australia

Priyanka Atit University of South Florida Tampa, FL, USA

Michelle A. Babicz-Boston Mental Health Behavioral Science Service, James A. Haley Veteran's Hospital, Tampa, FL, USA

Erin K. Bailey Mental Health Behavioral Science Service, James A. Haley Veteran's Hospital, Tampa, FL, USA

Department of Psychiatry, University of South Florida, Tampa, FL, USA

Selim R. Benbadis Department of Neurology, University of South Florida College of Medicine and Tampa General Hospital, Tampa, FL, USA

Cady Block Emory University, Atlanta, GA, USA

Kyle Boone Independent Practice, Torrance, CA, USA

Joseph J. Boscarino Departments of Psychiatry and Neurosciences, Neurology, and Neurosurgery, University of South Florida College of Medicine, Tampa, FL, USA

Edith N. Botchway Australian Centre for Child Neuropsychology Studies, Murdoch Children's Research Institute, Melbourne, VIC, Australia

Brian L. Brooks Alberta Children's Hospital, University of Calgary, Calgary, AB, Canada

Cathy Catroppa Department of Psychology, Australian Centre for Child Neuropsychology Studies, Murdoch Children's Research Institute, Royal Children's Hospital, University of Melbourne, Melbourne, Australia

Julia Cho Harvard Medical School, Boston, MA, USA

Erica L. Coady MINCEP Epilepsy Care, Minneapolis, MN, USA

Christohper T. Copeland Department of Psychiatry and Behavioral Sciences, University of Oklahoma, Health Sciences Center College of Medicine, Oklahoma City, OK, USA

Louise Crowe Australian Centre for Child Neuropsychology Studies, Murdoch Children's Research Institute, Melbourne, Australia

Luis Cruz-Saavedra Mayo Clinic, Jacksonville, FL, USA

Catherine Dion Department of Psychiatry and Psychology, Mayo Clinic-Jacksonville, Jacksonville, FL, USA

Daniel L. Drane Department of Neurology, Emory University, Atlanta, GA, USA

Department of Neurology, University Washington School of Medicine, Seattle, WA, USA

Kevin Duff Department of Neurology, Oregon Health Sciences University, Portland, OR, USA

Rachel L. Fazio Central Arkansas VA Healthcare System, North Little Rock, AR, USA

Kyle E. Ferguson British Columbia Mental Health & Addiction Services & University of Nevada, Reno, NV, USA

Juliette Galindo Department of Psychiatry and Behavioral Sciences, University of Oklahoma, Health Sciences Center College of Medicine, Oklahoma City, OK, USA

Shelley Gremley Alexian Neurosciences Institute, Elk Grove, IL, USA

Steven A. Gunzler Department of Neurology, The Neurological Institute, University Hospitals Case Medical Center and Case Western Reserve University School of Medicine, Cleveland, OH, USA

Grant L. Iverson Department of Physical Medicine and Rehabilitation, Harvard Medical School, Boston, MA, USA

Department of Physical Medicine and Rehabilitation, Spaulding Rehabilitation Hospital, Boston, MA, USA

Schoen Adams Research Institute at Spaulding Rehabilitation, Boston, MA, USA

Mass General for Children Sports Concussion Program, Boston, MA, USA

Home Base, A Red Sox Foundation and Massachusetts General Hospital Program, Boston, MA, USA

Joel E. Kamper Mental Health Behavioral Science Service, James A. Haley Veteran's Hospital, Tampa, FL, USA

Nicholas Kavish Department of Neurological Sciences, University of Nebraska Medical Center, Omaha, NE, USA

Rael T. Lange British Columbia Mental Health and Addiction Services, Coquitlam, BC, Canada

Alan J. Lerner Department of Neurology, The Neurological Institute, Cleveland, OH, USA

Robert J. Maciunas Department of Neurological Surgery, The Neurological Institute, University Hospitals Case Medical Center and Case Western Reserve University School of Medicine, Cleveland, OH, USA

Julia E. Maietta Department of Physical Medicine and Rehabilitation, Harvard Medical School, Boston, MA, USA

Department of Physical Medicine and Rehabilitation, Spaulding Rehabilitation, Boston, MA, USA

Mass General for Children Sports Concussion Program, Boston, MA, USA

Patrick J. Marsh Department of Psychiatry and Neurosciences, University of South Florida, College of Medicine, Tampa, FL, USA

John W. Miller Department of Neurology, University of Washington School of Medicine, Seattle, WA, USA

Michele Price Department of Neurology, Emory University School of Medicine, Atlanta, GA, USA

David E. Riley Department of Neurology, The Neurological Institute, University Hospitals Case, Cleveland, OH, USA

Medical Center and Case Western Reserve, Unviersity School of Medicine, Cleveland, OH, USA

Angelica Rivera-Cruz University of South Florida, College of Medicine, Tampa, FLA, USA

Scott M. Roye Department of Psychiatry and Behavioral Sciences, University of Oklahoma Health Sciences Center College of Medicine, Oklahoma City, OK, USA

Nicholas P. Ryan Australian Centre for Child Neuropsychology Studies, Murdoch Children's Research Institute, Melbourne, Australia

David S. Sabsevitz Department of Psychiatry and Psychology, Mayo Clinic-Jacksonville, Jacksonville, FL, USA

Michael R. Schoenberg Departments of Psychiatry and Neurosciences, Neurology, and Neurosurgery, University of South Florida College of Medicine, Tampa, FL, USA

James G. Scott Department of Psychiatry and Behavioral Sciences, University of Oklahoma, Health Sciences Center College of Medicine, Oklahoma City, OK, USA

Elisabeth M. S. Sherman Alberta Children's Hospital, University of Calgary, Calgary, AB, Canada

Cathy Sila Department of Neurology, The Neurological Institute, University Hospitals Case, Medical Center and Case Western Reserve University School of Medicine, Cleveland, OH, USA

Daniel J. Slick Alberta Children's Hospital, University of Calgary, Calgary, AB, Canada

Nikita Sood Australian Centre for Child Neuropsychology Studies, Murdoch Children's Research Institute, Melbourne, Australia

Esther Strauss Department of Psychology, University of Victoria, Victoria, BC, Canada

Jennifer A. Sweet Department of Neurological Surgery, The Neurological Institute, University Hospitals Cleveland Medical Center and Case Western Reserve University School of Medicine, Cleveland, OH, USA

Emily N. Vanderbleek Departments of Psychiatry and Neurosciences, Neurology, and Neurosurgery, University of South Florida College of Medicine, Tampa, FL, USA

Heber Varela Department of Neurology, University of South Florida College of Medicine and James A. Haley Veterans Affairs Medical Center, Tampa, FL, USA

Benjamin Walter Department of Neurology, The Neurological Institute, University Hospitals Case Medical Center and Case Western Reserve University School of Medicine, Cleveland, OH, USA

Mary Ann Werz Department of Neurology, University of Iowa Carver School of Medicine, Iowa City, IA, USA

David J. Williamson Ortho-McNeil Janssen Scientific Affairs, LLC, Mobile, AL, USA

Chapter 1
The Neuropsychology Referral and Answering the Referral Question

Michael R. Schoenberg and James G. Scott

Neuropsychological evaluations provide a wealth of information to the referring clinician and patient and has become a highly saught referral source for managing disorders that have cognitive, behavioral and emotional symptoms, offering a host of answers to important diagnostic and treatment-related questions. The range of questions a neuropsychological evaluation can answer are broad, but generally fall under six broad categories (e.g., Lezak et al., Neuropsychological assessment, 4th edn. Oxford University Press, New York, 2004):

1. Diagnoses: Identifying the existence of brain dysfunction [and differentiating brain dysfunction from non-lesional psychiatric diagnosis or otherwise reversible causes of cognitive symptoms (e.g., depression)].
   (a) *Example*: Distinguishing dementia from depression or identifying the presence of mild cognitive impairment (MCI).
2. Describing neuropsychological status: Detailing how a disease or lesion(s) is expressed from cognitive, behavioral and affective perspectives.
   (a) *Example*: Describing how a traumatic brain injury (TBI) has affected a patient's cognitive and emotional functioning, including the severity and extent persistent symptoms.

M. R. Schoenberg (✉)
Department of Psychiatry and Behavioral Sciences, University of South Florida College of Medicine, Tampa, FL, USA
e-mail: mschoenb@health.usf.edu

J. G. Scott
Department of Psychiatry and Behavioral Sciences, University of Oklahoma, Health Sciences Center College of Medicine, Oklahoma City, OK, USA
e-mail: jim-scott@ouhsc.edu

M. R. Schoenberg, J. G. Scott (eds.), *The Little Black Book of Neuropsychology*,
https://doi.org/10.1007/978-3-032-07777-6_1

3. Treatment planning: including risk factor assessment for proposed treatment, post acute placement, quantification of skills necessary for living and occupational/educational planning.
   (a) *Example*: Identifying if a patient meets inclusion/exclusion criteria for placement in a treatment or living facility. An increasing emphasis within neuropsychology is predicting neuropsychological outcome from proposed medical treatment (e.g., temporal lobectomy for intractable epilepsy or DBS for Parkinson's disease, intraoperative cortical brain mapping).
4. Identifying the effects of treatment (often includes measuring change in function over time).
   (a) *Example*: Evaluating post surgical outcomes in cognitive function in Epilepsy, Parkinsons disease or other procedures where cognitive or emotional symptom change might occur.
5. Research evaluation tool: Identifying change or deficits in experimental studies.
   (a) *Example*: Evaluating the neuropsychological effects of a medication to treat epilepsy in a randomized controlled trial.
6. Forensic applications: Neuropsychological evaluations are increasingly being used to assist fact-finding bodies to determine if, or the extent to which, an alleged event resulted in cognitive or emotional sequelae. Another use is to assist courts in evaluating if a defendant is capable of managing his/her affairs independently.

Key Points and Chapter Summary

- Neuropsychology is the study of brain–behavior relationships
- Neuropsychology evaluations provide quantifiable, objective information about a person's cognitive and behavioral functioning that can be essential for (1) diagnosis, (2) describing cognitive and emotional status, (3) treatment planning/program placement, (4) monitoring effect of treatment(s), (5) the identification of underlying processes for cognition and/or effects of treatments/other agents and (6) forensic applications.
- Referring health providers for neuropsychological consult should clearly identify the purpose of the referral (i.e., identify the referral question(s) the neuropsychological study is to answer).
- Neuropsychological report should clearly specify if the neuropsychological study is abnormal (vs normal), recommendations based on referral question(s), and in most cases, diagnosis.
- Neuropsychological consult reports will typically: (1) characterize cognitive and emotional deficits and strengths, (2) relate deficits to functional neuroanatomy, (3) provide diagnostic considerations and (4) offer etiology for neuropsychological deficits.
- Interpretation of the neuropsychological study and study results should be communicated to the patient in most cases.

(continued)

(continued)

- Conclusions as to presence or absence of neuropsychological deficits are based upon deficit measurement which requires that a comparison standard be established. The comparison standard is used as a benchmark against which current performance is compared to determine the presence or absence of neuropsychological deficits.
- Comparison standard may be of two broad types: (1) normative comparison standards (i.e., population based norms or species wide expectations) or (2) individual comparison standards (i.e., comparison to prior level of functioning based on statistical prediction using individual factors such as education, occupation and/or previous indicators of cognitive ability or performance on tests that have known resistence to the current etiology under consideration).
- Neuropsychological studies are increasingly part of medico-legal proceedings, including questions of competence and functional capacity, and evaluation is used to quantify functioning across cognitive, behavioral and emotional domains as they relate to causal issues.

Evidenced Based Neuropsychological Practice

The unique information provided by neuropsychological evaluations identified above has been demonstrated to impact the management of patients (and parties in medico-legal contexts) and improve patient outcomes, an essential component for evidence-based medicine and evidence-based clinical neuropsychology practice (Chelune, 2010).

As a diagnostic tool, the neuropsychological examination can contribute essential information on cognitive and/or behavioral dysfunction that is required to make a diagnosis [e.g., dementia and/or mild cognitive impairment (MCI), learning disorders, intellectual disability, mild traumatic brain injury and toxic encephalopathies]. The description of the type and extent of neuropsychological dysfunction can provide indispensable information to health providers for patient management and/or clinical research. For example, even when the lesion and its etiology are known, the neuropsychological evaluation offers *unique* information as to the type and severity of cognitive or behavioral problems the individual exhibits, and how the patient's functioning may affect his/her ability for self-care, following medical recommendations, and/or completing activities of daily living (ADLs). Thus, while it may be known a patient has a specific disease (e.g., Parkinson's disease, epilepsy or a traumatic brain injury), the impact of the disease or brain lesion on the patient's cognitive functioning and behavior may *only* be objectively quantified through neuropsychological assessment.

Finally, the neuropsychological evaluation can provide predictive information with respect to outcome from a suspected or known condition. As an example, neuropsychological variables are predictive of a variety of functional outcomes (return to work, school, living independently, etc.) following traumatic brain injury (Ponsford et al., 2008; Ruff, 2005; Sherer et al., 2002). Likewise, neuropsychological evaluations can predict cognitive outcome from temporal lobectomy (e.g.,

Chelune, 1995; Chelune & Najm, 2001; Hermann et al., 1999; Lineweaver et al., 2006), contribute unique variance to identifying laterality of seizure focus (Busch et al., 2005; Drane et al., 2006) and to predicting the likelihood a patient will be seizure free following temporal lobectomy (e.g., Sawrie et al., 1999). Indeed, neuropsychological results have provided predictive value beyond other neuroimaging and clinical variables to identify those individuals at increased risk for cognitive decline over time (and disease progression) across a variety of medical conditions, such as epilepsy (e.g., Seidenberg et al., 2007), multiple sclerosis (e.g., Achiron et al., 2005), Parkinson's disease (e.g., Dujardin et al., 2004) and mild cognitive impairment (e.g., Fleisher et al., 2008) to name a few.

Description of Neuropsychological Functioning

Neuropsychological evaluations describe an individual's brain–behavior function. However, the neuropsychological evaluation should generally *not* be limited to describing the neuropsychological scores a patient obtained, or simply a patient's cognitive strengths and weaknesses. Indeed, we argue that providing a detailed description of the patient's neuropsychological functioning, in and of itself, is often the least important aspect of a neuropsychological evaluation. Rather, the clinical neuropsychologist should state whether (or not) there is evidence for brain dysfunction, the degree of impairment, and relate this description to the patient's functional level and limitations (i.e., the individual's level of adjustment, and/or how the individual's needs for care and/or treatment/rehabilitation/educational programming may be affected).

The most important aspect of the neuropsychological evaluation is to relate how the patient's cognitive and emotional functioning is likely to affect their ability to adhere to their treatment, interact within their physical and/or social environment, affect their treatment plan, and/or affect their ability to make decisions, etc. In other words, the neuropsychologist's report answers the consulting clinician's questions by the interpretation, and not just description, of a patient's neuropsychological functions.

Structure and Organization of the Evaluation

At a basic level, the neuropsychological evaluation should provide a written document in which the referral question(s) are clearly answered. We strongly advocate answers to referral questions be clearly specified in a section of the report, often identified as "conclusions" or "diagnostic impressions" (see below). Subsequent recommendations for the patient's care should be clearly specified (see below).

The neuropsychological evaluation report need not be lengthy. In some cases, a single page report is sufficient. While we do not wish to dictate report formats (as these will be guided by the individual needs of the patient, the providers, and institutional/cultural variables), we provide a sample report format of a routine inpatient consultation in Appendix 1 and a more detailed outpatient evaluation in Appendix 2 to illustrate the headings and organization of reports outlined above. In most cases, the neuropsychologist should first identify the neuropsychological study as normal or abnormal, and the reason why the study was abnormal (a study may also be equivocal, see detailed review below). This will generally involve describing which cognitive or functional domains were impaired. However, this statement should be limited to one or two concise sentences (e.g., "The neuropsychological study was abnormal due to mild impairment in memory and visuoconstructional skills."). The etiology and expected course should be identified along with a statement regarding the confidence of these opinions. This information should then be related to functional capacities specific to the referral source such as medication management, safety to live independently, driving, returning to work/school and any accommodations/rehabilitation which may be helpful to the patient.

Key Points: Structure of Neuropsychological Evaluation

- Current complaints and history
- Past medical and psychiatric history
- Psychosocial history
- Medications
- Assessment tests/Procedures
- Results
- Conclusions/Interpretation of the data incorporating referral question, patient complaints, and past medical, psychiatric and psychosocial history
- Diagnosis
- Recommendations, which must answer referral question(s) and incorporate interpretation of data in light of the patient's unique history

Responding to Referrals: Timelines as an Important Variable in the Neuropsychological Referral

There are at least two temporal issues in the neuropsychological referral, each impacting the type of referral questions a clinical neuropsychologist can answer. The first aspect of time reflects when a referral is first made for a patient with known or suspected disease onset (i.e., Is the referral made within days to weeks of onset or after months to years of onset?). The second time issue refers to the duration and course in which symptoms presented (e.g., did symptoms present slowly over months to years, or did the symptoms present over a period of seconds? Did symptom onset appear to wax and wane?).

Both aspects of time have broad implications for the clinical neuropsychologist. As an example, referral for evaluation shortly (within hours, days or in some cases weeks) after the onset of symptoms that presented over several minutes (e.g., embolic stroke) is likely to have different questions and a different assessment approach than the evaluation of a patient having slowly progressive symptoms over several years. The clinical neuropsychologist should carefully consider the likely etiology and course of the condition, designing an assessment appropriately. As an example, a patient sustaining a moderate to severe traumatic brain injury may be assessed with a brief bedside screening to evaluate for post-traumatic amnesia and when declarative memory functions return. Likewise, a referral for neuropsychological evaluation acutely after stroke may be used to guide treatment planning (rehabilitation programming). However, changes in neuropsychological functioning over days, weeks and even hours should be anticipated, and in most cases, the neuropsychologist will be unable to answer questions about stability of deficits with certainty. Alternatively, patients with mild TBI may be administered a more comprehensive assessment within weeks of the injury, as most individuals neuropsychological functioning have returned to baseline within this time frame.

Key Points: Answering Referral Question(s)

- Neuropsychological evaluations must endeavor to answer referral question(s)
- Answers to referral question(s) should be clearly stated in the report
- Time is an important aspect of neuropsychological evaluations in terms of establishing the assessment procedures and the referral question(s) that may be answered by a neuropsychological study
  - Assessment results within days to weeks of acute insult is likely dynamic
  - Assessment results of patient(s) with subacute or chronic loss of function is more stable

Providing Results and Recommendations

We recommend the neuropsychological report/evaluation includes a specific sections on conclusins and recommendations. Often "Conclusions and Recommendations" may be combined, and an example is provided in Appendix 1. Having sections highlighted, particularly the conclusions (and recommendations if separate) will assist the reader quickly identify this crucial information. It is often the only part of the report the referral source will read prior to seeing the patient in follow up, so its importance cannot be overstated.

The "Conclusions (and Recommendations)" section should be short and concise. The neuropsychologist should clearly state his/her interpretation of the obtained data. We advocate a summary sentence specifying if the neuropsychological study was interpreted as "normal," "equivocal" or "abnormal." While this section may include a brief discussion of the neuropsychological scores, this is secondary to interpreting these scores for the intended recipient of the report.

The Conclusions (and Recommendations if combined) section should also include the patient's diagnosis(es). For example, a neurological diagnosis should be provided when the patient has a neurological disorder, while a psychiatric diagnosis is given when the condition is psychiatric in nature. The clinical neuropsychologist should conform to regional and local practices for reporting diagnostic codes.

The "Recommendations" section, whether incorporated with the Conclusions section or not, should be *concise* and *unambiguous*. We recommend providing recommendations in a point by point fashion. Regardless, recommendations should provide the neuropsychologist's opinions as to what interventions may be of benefit to the patient. The neuropsychological recommendations should integrate ongoing medical and/or psychiatric care. Recommendations for rehabilitation, if any, should flow logically from the interpretation of neuropsychological data and diagnosis. We strongly encourage neuropsychologists working with children and adolescents to always consider the impact neuropsychological data may have on the child's learning and academic/vocational performance. Recommendations for school programming (if made) should be clear and follow state and federal guidelines. Diagnosis of a learning disorder or developmental disorder should be clearly specified, and follow the guidelines and/or those of the currently accepted language for state and federal programs. If patients – children and adolescents in particular – meet criteria for accommodations at work or school, we recommend the clinical neuropsychologist specify which program(s) or accommodation(s) the patient is likely to benefit from. Indeed, such operationally specific recommendations can be crucial for a patient to obtain access to services (i.e. tutoring, additional time to complete assignments, access to peer/teacher notes, testing in distraction free environment, etc.).

Key Points: Conclusions and Recommendations

- Conclusions and recommendations should be clearly specified in the body of the report.
- Conclusions section should clearly specify if the study is normal, equivocal or abnormal.
  - Neuropsychological deficits are often associated with functional neuroanatomical correlates.
- Conclusions section general should include diagnosis(es)
- Recommendations, if applicable, should always answer referral question and be concise and clearly state need.

Providing Results to the Patient and Other Users of the Data

In most situations, the patient is the focus of the evaluation, and neuropsychological services are provided to improve the health of the patient. The conclusions (interpretation of the data) of the neuropsychological evaluation should be communicated to the patient's referring provider/entity and to the patient. Without violating HIPAA privacy rules, it is desirable for the neuropsychologist to provide necessary information gained from the neuropsychological evaluation to all those who will be making treatment decisions about the patient. This commonly includes communicating results to the patient's treating physicians and/or other treatment team members. In the case of children (those under the legal age of majority within the neuropsychologist's licensing board or region), results should be communicated to the patient's parents or legal guardian. It is often the case that discussion with the parents about the results will provide a framework in which to provide feedback when the patient is a minor.

When providing results for children to parents (legal guardian), we recommend information be provided that includes:

1. Child's cognitive strengths and weaknesses.
2. Diagnosis(es).
3. Treatment recommendations/treatment plan (if relevant).
4. If other consultation service experts will be recommended to provide additional information and/or clinical correlation to neuropsychological findings.
5. Provide information to parents about short- and long-term potential prognosis.
6. Educate parents about potential local, regional and/or national resources available to their child.
7. Implications of the findings to the child's academic functioning and any recommendations for school programming. These may then be, if desired by the patient's legal guardian, disclosed to the patient's school/teachers. While the neuropsychologist should clearly identify the child's weaknesses/deficits, emphasis on strengths should be made. If the child meets criteria for learning disorder or qualifies for services through Americans with Disabilities Act or other state or federal rule, this should also be specified.
8. Recommended limitations, if any, for the child. This should include potential risks or impact of comorbid conditions on the child's functioning.

Key Points: Providing Recommendations

- In most cases, we advocate the report include a summary of the scores that were used to derive the conclusions and recommendations for care.
  - The inclusion of standardized scores and/or percentile scores can be helpful, while providing raw scores are likely less helpful, except in some cases.
- Evaluations completed as part of independent medical evaluation (IME) and/or court ordered evaluation often may not be released directly to the claimant, but must come from the insurance company or legal entity that requested and paid for the evaluation.

(continued)

(continued)

- In medico-legal contexts, the claimant should be fully informed regarding the confidentiality of information that is provided by him/her, and the restrictions on release of the information, including those parties who will have access to the report. Claimant should also be informed that the usual doctor–patient relationship is not established during the course of an IME.
- The claimant should also be informed regarding procedures for requesting a copy of the results.

Releasing the Report/Data

A copy of the report should be included in the patient's chart, and a copy sent to the referring provider/entity. A copy of the report may (and often is) provided to the patient (and in almost all cases, must be if a patient requests it). As part of routine practice, we ask if the patient would like a copy of the report. Under federal and most state laws, the patient (or the patient's lawful health decision maker, if the patient is under the age of majority or found to be unable to make medical decisions) has access to the neuropsychological report, and in most cases, the test scores. While debate continues with respect to what counts as "raw data," it is generally agreed the patient (and/or health decision maker) have access to the test scores. With appropriate release authorization, the patient's report and his/her scores may be released to the patient and/or someone the patient designates.

In medico-legal contexts, and in cases of independent medical evaluations (IMEs), the individual undergoing the neuropsychological evaluation may *not* be the owner of the data. In these instances, the technical owner of the report is the referring agent, be they an attorney, judge or other agency, and the claimant should be informed before the evaluation that they will not receive a copy of the report from you (assuming no superseding state or federal laws), but rather must solicit a copy from the referring entity/individual. In these cases, a doctor–patient relationship has not been established, and the individual may be denied a copy of the report by the neuropsychologist. Often, the claimant should be directed to the requesting party (e.g., IME business or attorney) to obtain a copy of the report.

Medico-Legal Considerations in Neuropsychological Reports

Neuropsychological evaluations are increasingly requested in legal contexts both criminal and civil. Neuropsychological reports may be requested for the purpose of supporting litigation from the litigant, defense or the court. In these contexts, it is important to remember the goal of evaluation is often greater than providing input into patient care and management, and is used for assignment of damages or attributions of cause of injury or responsibility for criminal behavior. We suggest adopting an approach that considers any neuropsychological evaluation report or consultation possibly becoming an integral part of a legal proceeding, even if it was not expressly so from the initiation of the evaluation. For this reason, we recommend that evaluations address anticipated legal issues in a straightforward and direct manner. We advise asking directly if there are any legal issues pending or anticipated in most cases and, if so, what those issues might be. We caution against going beyond the existing data and/or research literature in making statements regarding the patient's current or expected functioning. The neuropsychologist should be careful to avoid the impression of over reliance on a single piece of data and be considerate of all the data at their disposal when making summary statements and providing recommendations. Issues that may have legal ramifications are considered below.

Key Points: Medico-legal Issues in Neuropsychology

- The claimant should be informed that the usual doctor-patient relationship is not established during the course of an Independent Medical Evaluation (IME) and most other forensic settings.
- In medico-legal contexts, the claimant should be fully informed regarding the limits of confidentiality of information that is provided by him/her, and the restrictions on release of the information, including those parties who will have access to the report.
- The claimant should be advised that evaluations completed as part of an IME and/or court ordered evaluation often may not be released directly to the claimant, and release of results/conclusions and/or test data must come from the insurance company or legal entity that requested and paid for the evaluation.
  - In general, we recommend the claimant be informed regarding procedures for requesting a copy of the results.

Issues of Decision-Making Capacity and Competence

Neuropsychological assessment is frequently used to determine decision-making capacity in several areas of functioning. Unlike in legal proceedings in which competence is an absolute issue (and decided by a judge or jury), in neuropsychological assessment, the clinician can often provide opinions about decision-making capacity, which varies by degree and often by function. While a neuropsychologist can assess overall decision-making capacity, and assist the court in making a determination of competence, the issue for the neuropsychologist is rarely absolute. Neuropsychological assessment can often determine decision-making capacity to manage one's own affairs in a legal, medical or financial context and take into consideration the impact of cognitive, behavioral and emotional factors assessed in the neuropsychological evaluation in determining the ability for decision making. It is often the case that while patients retain the basic understanding necessary to participate in decisions within these realms, their cognitive compromises makes them vulnerable and impacats decision making such that full independence in legal, medical or financial decisions would leave them vulnerable to exploitation or less than full appreciation of the ramifications of their decisions. For example, a patient with no, or relatively minor, reasoning difficulties but severe memory problems may not be able to enter into legal agreements or make medical decisions without the assistance of others, but is able to fully understand the ramifications of such decisions at the time the decision(s) is/are made.

Issues of Functional Capacities

Neuropsychological evaluations are also crucial in determining multiple functional capacities including driving, working, living independently and management of activities of daily living (dressing, meal preparation, hygiene, medication management, etc.) and instrumental activities of daily living (transportation, financial management, budgeting/shopping, scheduling, etc.). These functional capacities are often the predominant reason for evaluation, and can have significant impact on the patient and their family and support network. The functional capacities in any of these realms can be negatively impacted by cognitive, behavioral or emotional factors assessed in the neuropsychological evaluation and these issues should be addressed directly.

The overriding concern in this regard is balancing patient safety, public safety and the rights of the patient to have the least restrictive environment that provides for their needs. The functional capacities of the patient should be evaluated in the context of their available resources and support network. For example, a patient with good insight into their deficits and a compliant history may be able to continue to live independently with only daily supervision and restrictions on travel, cooking and oversight of finances. Similarly, a patient with limited insight and a recent history of poor judgment may need to live in a 24-hours supervised environment with suspension of driving/transportation, provision of meals and assistance with medication compliance and finances. These capacities should be addressed directly and explicitly in the context of the summary and recommendations section of an evaluation. It is often helpful to address these issues categorically as legal, medical, financial, independent living, medication management and driving capacities.

Key Points: Medico-legal Evaluations

- Write reports like you mean it.
- Do NOT offer conclusions (interpretation) and/or recommendations that extend beyond the data
  - Provide conclusions, diagnosis and recommendations which are supported by the obtained data

(continued)

(continued)

- Neuropsychological assessment is increasingly important in medico-legal proceedings and many evaluations that are conducted for clinical purposes eventually become evidence in legal proceedings. It is best to write reports assuming they may eventually become part of a legal proceeding.
- Questions about decision making capacity and functional ability are common.
  - Decision making capacity domains often include the ability to independently make: medical, financial and legal decisions
- Functional capacity often includes questions about living independently, managing medications and driving.
  - Driving is not well correlated with individual neuropsychological measures

    Aspects of driving ability are associated with overall cognitive functioning, attentional/executive functions, processing speed (reaction time), visuoperceptual, and motor skill and neuropsychological assessment is helpful in assessing these domains.

Part II: Perspectives for Physicians, Medical Students/Residents/Fellows: The Neuropsychology Referral

This section is designed to help referring physicians in general, and medical students, residents and fellows in particular, understand the types of information a clinical neuropsychological evaluation provides, optimize how one may request the specialized skills and knowledge set of clinical neuropsychologists and aid in the provision of feedback to patients from results obtained from the neuropsychological consult report.

A prerequisite to understand the scope and power of a neuropsychological evaluation is to present a brief overview of key concepts in neuropsychology (see also Chap. 31 and 32 for additional details). Readers of the chapter will appreciate two things about clinical neuropsychology; (1) neuropsychology is a science and a discipline, and (2) the determination of neuropsychological abnormality is based upon deficit measurement. As a science, neuropsychology is studied by many disciplines of the neurosciences. Aspects of neuropsychological assessment are usually included into a typical patient encounter. For example, when one assesses the orientation and basic mental functions of a patient, this process involves some assessment of neuropsychological functions (e.g., assessing basic receptive and expressive speech functions). However, as a subspecialty, the clinical neuropsychologist assesses neuropsychological function in more detail, often using psychometric-based tests that allow for the quantification of specific neuropsychological deficits. As a discipline, the clinical neuropsychologist is a subspecialist with a doctorate degree in psychology who has specialized training in the science of brain–behavior relationships. The discipline is based on the science of measuring brain–behavior relationships, and incorporates knowledge of neuroanatomy, neuropathology, behavioral neurology, psychometrics/statistics, psychiatry and psychology (e.g., Hannay et al. 1998). Second, neuropsychological evaluation requires establishment of a comparative standard to allow for *deficit measurement*.

Neuropsychology is the science of brain–behavior relationships, and is not limited to the clinical neuropsychologist. Indeed, many health professionals measure neuropsychological function by various means as part of routine patient care. Completing a neurological exam and mental status exam incorporate a screening of basic Neuropsychological functions (e.g., attention/executive, language, visuoperceptual functions and remote and recent memory). However, a clinical neuropsychological evaluation is distinguished from these more cursory reviews of neuropsychological function by the inclusion of a detailed, systematic assessment using psychometric tests with known standardized assessment procedures and normative performance data. Thus, the neuropsychological evaluation can provide a detailed description of a patient's cognitive functioning that is referenced to a comparison standard (see below for details). When integrated with specialized training, the clinical neuropsychologist can provide a unique contribution to the evaluation and management of patients with known or suspected central nervous system dysfunction (see Heilman and Valenstein 2003; Lezak et al. 2004, for reviews).

The concept of *deficit measurement* is an essential principle in neuropsychology. The basic premise in deficit measurement dictates that an observation of a patient's function must be compared against some standard, termed a *comparison standard*, to identify if a change in neuropsychological function has, in fact, occurred. Thus, the comparison standard serves as a benchmark against which current performance is compared against to evaluate if a decline or increase (i.e., deficit or improvement) in neuropsychological functioning has occurred. This same principle also applies in medicine, but the emphasis of the comparison standard is often different. Two general comparison standards are: (1) normative comparison standards, and (2) individual comparison standard.

Normative comparisons include species-specific and population average comparison standards. Species-specific comparison standards reflect species-wide capacities. As an example, in deciding if a deep tendon reflex is abnormal, the comparison standard is a species-based comparison standard. That is, it is known what the normal reflex is for an intact adult human nervous system, and differences from this norm reflect "abnormality." Population averages reflect the average performance of a large sample of individuals on a particular cognitive (or behavioral) test. When using population normative-based information, a patient's performance is compared to standardization data from a known (often healthy) population whose distribution of scores is assumed to approximate a normal curve, but is sometimes negatively skewed (that is, most individuals' performance on a neuropsychological test is close to the highest score possible, with few individuals performing below this level). Using the central limit theorem, we can statistically calculate the position on the normal curve where a patient falls. As a standardized score, the neuropsychologist can provide a percentile score(s) identifying how the particular patient's performance compared against a normative population.

The central limit theorem states many human characteristics in a population are distributed in a manner such that plotting them would represent a normal or bell-shaped curve. This curve would have many people in the average range and fewer and fewer people as we progress farther (higher or lower) from the average (mean). This comparison allows us to more definitively make decisions about the presence of brain dysfunction, the location of brain dysfunction, and gauge the severity of brain dysfunction more precisely. As an example, suppose we measured a male's height as 6′3″ and we want to know how his height compares to the general male population in the U.S. If we know the average male height in the USA is 5′9″ and that the standard deviation for height in males is 3″, then we would know that our 6′3″ person is two standard deviations above average in height, which falls at the 98th percentile (97.72 to be exact) on the normal curve. An example in neuropsychology is an IQ score. This method utilizes statistical properties of the normal population for comparison, while also taking into consideration research findings from patients with specific anatomical lesions and their associated functional deficits. A similar use of population normative comparison standards are used for many laboratory tests in medicine. The laboratory values for identifying abnormal levels are frequently set by a specific laboratory based on reference values obtained within a particular healthy reference population. Therefore, one must either know the laboratory and equipment value or have the laboratory provide the range of normal values and flag an abnormal value within the report. Applying this approach to neuropsychological deficit measurement, if we observe a patient scored two standard deviations below the normal population on a test of verbal memory (second percentile), this score would be considered very unusual. If verbal memory was the patient's only low score(s), and the testing was valid, the pattern might be interpreted as a deficit that reflects brain dysfunction. However, it is important to rule out other explanations for an observed significant weakness in verbal memory for a particular patient.

A population normative comparison does *not* provide information sufficient to identify a specific deficit *within an individual*. To highlight the limitation of population-based normative comparison standards, let us say a neuropsychologist finds that a patient scored at the 25th percentile compared to other healthy adults on a measure of memory. Is this score normal or abnormal? The answer is, such a score may be an abnormal or normal performance, depending upon the patient's original (premorbid) level of function. Thus, the individual comparison standard allows the determination that a particular patient's obtained score represents a deficit (decline from previous ability) or is normal (no decline from previous ability). Developing an individual comparison standard requires one to estimate an individual's premorbid level of ability.

Key Points: Perspective from Referring Providers

- Neuropsychological evaluations provide unique information regarding an individual's cognitive, emotional and behavioral functioning
- Neuropsychological evaluation can be crucial for diagnosis, predicting outcome and patient management for individuals with diseases that affect

(continued)

(continued)

the central nervous system (e.g., brain tumors, epilepsy, dementias, Hepatitis C, etc.)
- Neuropsychological evaluation is often helpful to hospital staff and families in patient management such as level of supervision needed and planning for future care
- Repeated evaluations over time can document improvement or decline in function, assist in evaluating treatment effectiveness and/or monitor for what type and/or power/intensity of an intervention (e.g., educational programming, assisted living, etc.) might be needed.

Establishing Premorbid Cognitive Ability: The Individual Comparison Standard

Individual comparison standards require the person's level of ability before the onset of known or suspected disease (premorbid functioning) be determined, and compared against current performances. The individual comparison standard may be developed from estimates (often derived from various psychometric methods) or obtained from historical records (e.g., previous cognitive testing, academic records or vocational indices) and/or behavioral observations (see Lezak et al. 2004; Strauss et al. 2006, for reviews).

While establishing a comparison standard using historical records (e.g., prior cognitive test scores) reduces the chance for error in determining change, such historical information is rarely available in the time frames necessary for most clinical neuropsychology services. Thus, clinical neuropsychologists often estimate premorbid ability using a variety of methods, often based on demographic variables (age, education level, occupational history) as well as performance at the time of the evaluation (current performance) on various neuropsychological functions thought to be relatively resistant to effects of brain dysfunction and/or aging (e.g., word recognition, vocabulary knowledge, etc.) (see Lezak et al. 2004, for review). Other techniques have endeavored to decrease errors in estimating premorbid cognitive function by combining demographic-based approaches with current performance on cognitive tests (e.g., reading words or evaluation of known vocabulary). A detailed review of methods to predict premorbid functioning is beyond the scope of this book. However, the reader of the neuropsychological report will often identify the level of functioning the neuropsychologist has established for the patient within the body of the report, often labeled as "estimated premorbid functioning" or something similar. By developing an individual comparison standard, the presence of cognitive or behavioral deficits can be appreciated at the individual level [rather than the nomethetic (i.e., group) level]. If for example, our hypothetical person who scores at the 25th percentile had a tenth grade education and was estimated to be functioning in the normal range, no negative change would be inferred; however, if the person's ability was estimated to be at the 99th percentile of ability, a decline in function is inferred.

Key Points: Deficit Measurement and Comparison Standard

- Neuropsychological evaluation is based on deficit measurement using an established comparison standard
- Comparison standard may be established by normative comparisons or individual comparisons
  - Normative comparison standard based on species-wide performance (e.g., development of language, bipedal gait) or population averages (i.e., cognitive and behavioral functions that develop through childhood such as attentional capacity or memory)

    A patient's performances (test scores) would be compared to normative data generated from a demographically representative sample of.
  - Individual comparison standard based on individual history, characteristics or other data (e.g., educational/occupational history, school records, previous cognitive test scores, etc.). For efficiency, premorbid level sometimes estimated by a variety of demographic variables and/or functional abilities thought to be resistant to effects of aging and brain disease (e.g., word reading ability)

    A patient's performance (test scores) would be compared to a premorbid estimate of that particular individual's level of cognitive functioning thought to be present before onset of known or suspected neurological dysfunction

What Can You Ask a Neuropsychologist About a Patient?

The neuropsychological referral can provide crucial information to assist in the health care of individuals as reviewed at the beginning of this chapter. As some practical examples, common referral questions might involve the following: (1) identifying the existence of brain dysfunction (e.g., differentiating brain dysfunction from psychiatric diagnosis); (2) describing cognitive and behavioral status for treatment planning or resource utilization decisions; (3) predicting outcome from medical or surgical treatments; (4) identifying change in cognitive function over time (often to monitor status of known or suspected disease or syndrome or to monitor the effect of treatment on a disease or syndrome); (5) evaluating cognitive capacity to make medical, financial or legal decisions; and/or (6) assist the trier of fact (e.g., a judge or, more often, a jury) in legal proceedings in which the existence, proximate cause, decision-making capacity and/or likely functional outcome from a known or suspected brain injury is being evaluated. The more detailed referral question(s) you ask, the more likely you will be provided with direct and useful answers from the clinical neuropsychologist.

Neuropsychological data can be crucial to the early diagnoses of cognitive disorders (e.g., Mild Cognitive Impairment), identify presence of cognitive dysfunction in diseases (e.g., systemic lupus erythematosus, movement disorders, etc.), plan and evaluate treatments (medical, behavioral, surgical, etc.) and to predict recovery patterns. The importance of specificity in referral questions cannot be understated (see common referral domains earlier in this chapter). Review of this chapter establishes how neuropsychological evaluations can provide important diagnostic and treatment information. Perhaps more importantly, however, regardless of the sophistication of future neuroimaging technologies, the neuropsychological evaluation is uniquely able to provide the health provider(s) with information about *how* a particular disease, lesion or treatment is affecting the cognitive and behavioral functions of the individual. The determination of cognitive or behavioral effects of diseases, lesions or treatments has been shown to be related to quality of life, and can be helpful in understanding how the patient is likely to perform activities of daily living(e.g., Heilman and Valenstein 2003; Lezak et al. 2004, for reviews).

Overview and Description of Neuropsychological Evaluation Procedures

From the patient's perspective, the neuropsychological evaluation will typically involve meeting with the licensed neuropsychologist for some period of time to discuss problems/symptoms and provide history. In some cases, a spouse, family member or close friend may also be requested to interview with the neuropsychologist to provide collateral information. The patient will then complete neuropsychological testing. The patient may be tested by the clinical neuropsychologist and/or a psychometrician. The psychometrician is a technician having training in how to administer and score tests under the supervision of the neuropsychologist. Neuropsychological tests include administration of paper-and-pencil tests, answering questions presented orally and/or responding using a computer interface.

The time duration of a neuropsychological evaluation can vary substantially based on the referral question(s), the patient's presenting symptoms and the neuropsychologists' training. In our experience, patients will generally spend 3–6 hours at the clinic to complete a typical outpatient neuropsychological evaluation. This includes time registering in the clinic, interviewing with the neuropsychologist as well as time actually taking the neuropsychological tests. Shorter evaluations lasting less than an hour (some taking less than 30 min) and longer evaluations that may require 2 days of testing may be conducted. The duration of the evaluation is determined by the referral question(s)/needs [i.e. immediate patient management, pre-surgical planning, differential diagnosis (MCI vs Dementia), competency determination, etc.] and patient variables (i.e. age, fatigue, comorbid medical conditions, acuity of injury, questions patient may have regarding their health). There is a trade-off in terms of the depth and breadth of an evaluation and the time it takes to administer, score and analyze data. Longer evaluations allow for more in-depth study of neuropsychological functions, while shorter evaluations limit the detail in which some neuropsychological functions can be assessed.

Depending upon referral question(s), practice patterns of the referring provider, neuropsychologist's practice pattern, institutional practices and state licensing laws; the neuropsychologist may provide initial results to the patient on the same day of the evaluation. Alternatively, results may be conveyed to the patient after the evaluation report is completed, which, in our experience, is usually in 3–10 working days. The feedback may include discussion of strengths and weaknesses of cognitive/neuropsychological functions, mood, diagnosis and opinions to answer the referral question(s) and provide recommendations for the patient's care.

In most cases, the neuropsychological evaluation is a procedure that is covered (paid for) by insurance companies. Some exceptions do, however, occur; and some evaluations must be self-paid. This is more common for educational/learning disability evaluations. Pre-authorization for the neuropsychological evaluation from the patient's insurance company (if available) is often obtained by the neuropsychologist's office.

Making the Referral for a Neuropsychological Evaluation

The manner in which the physician (or other health care provider) makes a referral for neuropsychological evaluation can have important implications. There are three issues: (1) specify the referral question(s) you would like answered (see above); (2) providing any previous medical records of the patient documenting or summarizing other evaluation(s) to diagnose and treat the patient's symptoms; and (3) establishing expectations for the patient regarding the neuropsychological evaluation. As detailed above, clarifying the referral question(s) is (are) essential. Like any other specialist in medicine, the neuropsychologist will benefit from the referral accompanied by previous medical records of any other studies completed to evaluate the patient's symptoms (e.g., neuroimaging results, laboratory studies, results of electroneurophysiology studies). The third aspect of the referral can be crucial. A sound referral is one wherein the *referring* clinician provides the patient with a brief explanation of the purpose of the evaluation, what to expect as part of a neuropsychological evaluation, how the information will be used for the patient's care and the potential risks and benefits of the evaluation. For the clinical neuropsychologist, the referral will be received, and the patient you referred may receive an informational letter, history form or other information as provided by any other specialty physician. Once you make a referral, you will receive a neuropsychological evaluation report, to which we now turn.

Key Points: Making a Referral for Neuropsychological Evaluation

- Specify, as detailed as possible, questions desired to be answered by neuropsychological evaluation
- Provide previous medical and psychiatric history and/or laboratory study results when available
- Review purpose of neuropsychological referral to patient, and importance of the study in assisting in managing the health care of the patient

Understanding the Neuropsychological Report

The neuropsychological report can be somewhat confusing to physicians not accustomed to clinical neuropsychology consult services. While there is considerable variability, the neuropsychological report will often include the typical information of most consultations (e.g., referral question, patient complaints, relevant history, list of medications, mental status exam and conclusions and recommendations). The more unique aspect of the neuropsychological evaluation is typically the inclusion of a list of either scores (may be standard or percentiles, sometimes raw scores) or description of neuropsychological test scores. Test scores are based on a normative comparison standard, with the 50th percentile being the population average. Multiple different normative groups have been developed, such that normative comparisons are often provided for individuals of similar age, level of education, and in some cases, gender and ethnicity. Then these are adjusted for individual level comparisons, and evaluation of performances are provided in terms of descriptors (low average, average, high average, etc.) and/or percentiles or, in some cases, standardized scores. A brief summary is provided below for convenience in Table 1.1.

The clinical neuropsychologist will summarize the cognitive and behavioral data, answer the referral question(s), provide diagnostic data and, if indicated, provide recommendations for the patient's care. In general, the report will typically make recommendations for the patient's based on the diagnosis, cognitive compensatory strategies or therapies and emotion al functionign. Recommendations may include initiating pharmacological treatment (if otherwise medically indicated), obtaining further clinical correlation for identified neuropsychological deficits, along with other important components of treatment planning (i.e., psychological treatment, rehabilitation, surgical candidacy, educational programming, driving cessation, etc.) Examples of neuropsychological evaluation reports are provided in the Appendices below. If you are unable to find desired information quickly in the neuropsychological consult report, we encourage you to call or email the consulting clinical neuropsychologist for clarification (Table 1.2).

Table 1.1 Typical descriptors and percentiles in neuropsychological reports

Descriptor	Typical referent percentile range
"Superior"	Scores between 91st and 99th percentiles
"High average"	Scores between 75th to 90th percentiles
"Average"	Scores between 25th to 74th percentiles May also describe obtained scores above the average score of the normative group (i.e., scores 51st percentile or greater)
"Below average"	Term describing scores 16th to 24th percentiles.
"Low average or Low normal"	Typically, scores between 16th to 24th percentiles
"Extremely low"	Scores less than or equal to second percentile
"Moderately impaired"	Typically, scores between first and fifth percentiles.
	Can be subdivided into "mild-to-moderately impaired" and "moderate-to-severely impaired"
"Moderately-to-severely impaired"	Scores between 0.13 to 0.59 percentiles
"Severely impaired"	Typically, scores less than first percentile
	More recently, defined as at or below 0.12 percentile.
	However, has been used for scores equal to, or less than, first percentile
"WNL or Within normal limits"	Typically scores falling within expectations for the individual or equal to or above the 16th percentile (e.g., 16th percentile or greater)

Table 1.2 Common neuropsychological terminology in neuropsychological evaluations

Phrase or term in neuropsychological report:	Neuropsychological term/phrase means:
Attention/executive dysfunction	Impairment in attention/concentration as well as problem solving, sequencing, planning, reasoning, insight, judgment and inhibition. Localization frequently refers to frontal lobe function and/or fronto-striatal impairment
Below expectations	Test performance is impaired based on determination of patient's likely premorbid level of ability
Data *not* consistent with neurological dysfunction	Study is normal. Often followed by explanation the study quality was either poor due to lack of adequate patient effort and/or psychiatric overlay
Data consistent with [focal, diffuse or lateralized] brain dysfunction	Phrase describing the domains of neuropsychological function that were impaired. Can be followed by determination of localization or lateralization of brain dysfunction
Phrase to describe where dysfunction occurs. Frequently followed by opinion as to where neurological dysfunction is present and/or etiology	
Neuropsychological impairments were found in [attention, memory, language, visuoperceptual/visuoconstructional and/or executive functions]	

(continued)

Table 1.2 (continued)

Phrase or term in neuropsychological report:	Neuropsychological term/phrase means:
Data consistent with expectations	Study is normal
Data [most] consistent with brain dysfunction	Study is abnormal. Complaints not due to psychiatric function
Insufficient [effort, task engagement, attention to testing, etc.]	Insufficient patient effort on testing procedures. Quality of study is poor. Question (or diagnosis) of malingering, dissimulation or somatoform disorder frequently raised/made
Language	Refers to expressive and receptive language skills, inclusive of repetition, writing, reading and prosody. Not limited to "speech" per se, which is a term to describe the quality of a patient's ability to speak
Memory (and/or learning)	Most commonly refers to declarative memory systems
Neuropsychological deficits present. Etiology unknown, but most likely are/is [presented in order]	Abnormal study. Likely disease or condition is specified. Other possibilities are often provided
No clear deficits	Study is normal. Complaints due to psychiatric variables and/or lack of adequate patient effort
No significant neuropsychological impairment	Study is normal
Overlay of [depression, anxiety, mood, worry, psychiatric disease, etc.]	Study is normal. Complaints due to psychiatric variables
Quality of study is poor [sometimes followed by description of why study quality was poor]	Frequently, this identifies insufficient patient effort on testing procedures. Question (or diagnosis) of malingering, dissimulation or somatoform disorder frequently raised/made
Task engagement was [poor, inadequate, variable, below criteria, etc.]	Insufficient patient effort on testing procedures. Quality of study is poor. Question (or diagnosis) of malingering, dissimulation or somatoform disorder frequently raised/made
Validity (or symptom validity) was [descriptor term here] May also be summarized as "The study is valid."	Refers to patients' effort to perform at his/her best ability. Validity may be interpreted to be adequate or good or poor or insufficient. Frequently also incorporates testing environment information and procedures which can adversely affect the validity of the test data, such as insufficient lighting, noise level, participation of third party observers, etc
Visuoperceptual, Visuoconstructional, Visuospatial	Cortical visuoperceptual and visuoconstructional functions such as accurately perceiving objects, visual organization and synthesis of visual material and being able to accurately draw or reconstruct viewed models (2 or 3 dimensional)

Appendix 1

Key Points: Understanding the Neuropsychological Report

- Neuropsychological reports are often detailed and include a description of how a patient is functioning across many neuropsychological domains (i.e. attention/executive, learning/memory, language, visuoperceptual/visuo-constructional as well as behavior/personality/psychological functions).
- Interpretation is typically given in the summary/conclusions/recommendations section where the test performance results previously described are used to answer the referral question(s) and often providing a diagnosis, neuroanatomic correlates of neuropsychological findings, expected disease course, determination of change in function over time (if applicable), and/or answer questions about functional capacity (i.e., driving, living independently, managing medications and decisional capacity).
- Qualitative description of neuropsychological function follow general guidelines, but variability exists.
- Neuropsychological conclusions are often stated in terms of supporting or refuting a diagnosis/etiology.
  - If conclusions not clear, contact clinical neuropsychologist for clarification

Example of Inpatient/Screening Neuropsychological Consult Report

NEUROPSYCHOLOGY SERVICE
Neuropsychological Consultation

NAME: XXX, XXXX	**PATIENT #:**
BIRTH DATE:	**EDUCATION:** X years
EXAM DATE: [Must document date and time of evaluation and time spent with patient]	
REFERAL SOURCE:	
REFERRAL INFORMATION AND RELEVANT HISTORY:	

[Brief summary of presenting history and reason for referral. Should include symptoms/diagnosis warranting neuropsychological consult]

[Brief summary of presenting patient complaints, if any. The history of complaints, when the symptoms started, severity, and course should be specified].

Example might be: "Patient is a 30-year-old right handed Caucasian male status-post left middle cerebral artery ischemic stroke (date) with mild right hemiparesis and language problems referred to assist with diagnosis and treatment planning. The patient may be a candidate for a community re-integration program. Patient complained of memory and language problems and symptoms of depression."

MENTAL STATUS AND [BEHAVIORAL OBSERVATIONS OR GENERAL CONSTITUTION]

[Detail the patient's mental status. At a minimum, the patient's level of arousal and orientation should be noted along with behavioral observations (gait, tremor, etc.). Quality of speech should be reviewed along with mood and affect. Presence/absence of suicidal and/or homicidal ideation, intent or plan along with hallucinations or delusions should be specified. The patient's cooperation with the evaluation should be noted. Example provided below.]

"Patient was AAOx3 and appropriately groomed. Made good eye contact. Speech articulation, rate, rhythm and prosody was WNL. Speech content was appropriate. Speech process was linear. Mood was euthymic and effect was full. No suicidal/homicidal ideation, plan or intent (no SI/HI, plan or intent). No delusions or hallucinations. Insight and judgment WNL. Study is valid."

ASSESSMENT PROCEDURES

[Specified the assessment procedures including what tests were administered. We advise the clinician to specify inclusion of symptom validity measures as such, and not identify specific test names in keeping with recent recommendations.]

NEUROPSYCHOLOGICAL FINDINGS

[Provide results of test scores here. May be separated into major domains or a brief summary. See examples below. We recommend results provided as advised in Chelune (2010).

Examples

Paragraph Format

The patient exhibited deficits in areas of attention/executive functions, verbal memory and language functions. Specifically, the patient exhibited mild to moderate deficits in complex focused and divided attention tasks. Verbal immediate and delayed memory scores were mildly impaired. Language screening was functional, but there were deficits in confrontation naming and verbal fluency. Strengths were basic span of attention, gross receptive and expressive language functions and visuoperceptual skills. Discrepancy among scores were rare in a normal population.

Bulleted Format

Attention: Intact for basic functions. Impaired for complex attention

Memory: Impaired verbal memory. Intact visual memory.

Language: Impaired confrontation naming and verbal fluency. Unable to follow 3-step instructions. Otherwise receptive and expressive speech grossly intact. Repetition intact. No alexia or agraphia.

Visuoperceptual/visuoconstructional: Grossly intact. No constructional apraxia

Executive functions (insight, judgment, reasoning): Insight and judgment [intact, poor, etc.]. Sequencing, set-shifting, problem solving scores were normal.

Personality/psychological/emotional functioning: [brief summary of results of any personality/psychological functioning. May also include quality of life variables, as well as any behavioral apathy and other neurovegetative symptoms.

CONCLUSIONS AND RECOMMENDATIONS

[Interpretation of neuropsychological results. Statement(s) to answer the referral question(s) should be clearly specified. Diagnoses should be listed. If combined with recommendations, recommendations should flow from interpretation.] See example below, and Chelune (2010).

Neuropsychological study was [abnormal, equivocal, normal].

[If relation to neuroanatomical function is needed, specify here. For example: Data suggest left frontotemporal dysfunction, and consistent with reported left MCA stroke.]

[If surgical candidacy is a referral question. For example: *Surgical candidacy*: From a neuropsychological standpoint, the patient is a (poor, fair, good, excellent) candidate for (left, right, extratemporal, multilobar, corpus callosotomy, DBS, VNS, CABG, renal/hepatic transplantation, spinal fusion, morphine pump, etc.…). The patient is at (low, medium, high) risk for post-surgical (language, memory, attention/executive, psychiatric, etc.) problems.

[If feedback notation is included in same report. For example: Initial results of the neuropsychological evaluation were reviewed with ________ [as much detail as is necessary].

Diagnostic impressions: [List diagnostic conditions here. Should follow ICD-9 or DSM-IV diagnostic codes].

Recommendations

[List recommendations here].We recommend including time spent with patient completing neuropsychological evaluation. Example may be "A total of __ hours of neuropsychological services (including interviewing, administering, scoring, interpretation and report writing) completed by Dr. ____.

Appendix 2

Example of Outpatient Comprehensive Evaluation Report

NEUROPSYCHOLOGY SERVICE
Neuropsychological Evaluation

NAME: XXX, XXXX	**PATIENT #:**
BIRTH DATE:	**ETHNICITY:**
EXAM DATE:	**EDUCATION:** X years
REPORT DATE:	**OCCUPATION:**
REFERAL SOURCE:	
REFERRAL INFORMATION	

[One or two sentences describing reason for referral. Should include symptoms/diagnosis warranting neuropsychological consult]

[OPTIONAL SECTION – RESULTS SUMMARY: [one or two sentences summarizing findings of neuropsychological evaluation. For example: Neuropsychological evaluation was abnormal with deficits in memory and language. (if surgical patient: Patient is a (fill in appropriate descriptor – poor/fair/good surgical candidate) (if dementia patient: Data consistent with (fill in likely etiology)]

CURRENT COMPLAINTS AND HISTORY

[Specify where data was obtained, e.g., patient and spouse]

[Brief summary of presenting complaints, if any. The history of complaints, when the symptoms started, severity, and course should be specified].

Example—bullet format:

1. Seizures/Epilepsy. Patient has a history of seizures since childhood. Seizures medication refractory. Seizures occur 2/month on average. Last known seizure was _____.
2. Attention, memory and language problems past 2 years. Increasing problems concentrating the past 2 years. Forgets details of recent events, appointments, and repeats self. Increasing dysnomia the past 2 years. Speech problems past ____.
3. Depression for past year. Symptoms of depression more often than not the past year. Denied anxiety symptoms. Sleep and appetite were _____. Difficulty falling asleep and his/her appetite has decreased with loss of 15 pounals past 6 months without dealing. Energy level was _____.

MEDICAL AND PSYCHIATRIC HISTORY: [Relevant medical and psychiatric history specified. This may only be noted as "unremarkable" or "noncontributory" but may also include information about neurological exam, laboratory studies, EEG, MRI, CT, surgical/operative notes, consulting notes of other health care providers, previous diagnosis(es) and treatments (successful or unsuccessful). Allergies may also be stated.).

[Review of developmental, social, educational, occupational history provided. One may also make a statement about patient's ability to complete activities of daily living (ADLs). Can be brief, for example "Patients medical and psychiatric history was reviewed and detailed in chart. Otherwise unremarkable. Developmental history unremarkable. Patient worked as an engineer and retired in 2003. Patient is independent in ADLs and is driving.]

CURRENT MEDICATIONS: [list medications and dosages]

MENTAL STATUS AND GENERAL CONSTITUTION

[Detail the patient's mental status. At a minimum, the patient's level of arousal and orientation should be noted along with observations about gait and station, stature and hygiene. Quality of speech should be reviewed along with mood and affect. Presence/absence of suicidal and/or homicidal ideation, intent or plan along with hallucinations or delusions should be specified. The patient's cooperation with the evaluation should be noted.]

[A comment about task engagement or validity of the study may be made here or in the neuropsychological results section. An example is given below.]

Appearance: well groomed. Appeared stated age. Of normal height and build.

Gait/station: normal.

Tremor: No obvious tremor observed.

AAOx4: Yes

Speech: articulation and rate, rhythm, intonation and prosody WNL.

Speech Content: generally appropriate to context.

Speech Process: organized and goal-directed.

Mood: euthymic

Affect: consistent with mood

Suicidal/Homicidal Ideation Plan or Intent: denied

Hallucinations/Delusions: None

Judgment: within normal limits

Insight: within normal limits

Test Taking Behavior: Cooperative and appeared to give adequate effort. *Study is valid.*

ASSESSMENT PROCEDURES

[Specified the assessment procedures including what tests were administered. We advise the clinician to specify inclusion of symptom validity measures as such, and not identify specific test names.]

SENSORY/MOTOR AND PERCEPTUAL FUNCTIONING

[Results from sensorimotor and perceptual testing, if completed, specified here. This may also include results from neurological exam, if completed. Presence of finger agnosia, visual field defects, etc. and motor exam (motor speed, dexterity and/or grip strength.] Example is below.

Sense of smell: intact to several common scents.

EOM: appeared grossly intact.

Visual fields: grossly full to confrontation.

Light touch: Sensation intact in face and hands, and no extinction with bilateral simultaneous stimulation.

Auditory: intact, bilaterally

Ideomotor apraxia: None (or Yes, present)

Agraphasthesia: None (or Yes, present)

Finger agnosia: None (or Yes, present)

R/L orientation: Intact (or Impaired)

Grip strength: [description of performance. Example "Average, bilaterally."]

Finger tapping speed: [description of performance]

Manual dexterity: [description of performance]

NEUROPSYCHOLOGICAL FUNCTIONING [OR RESULTS]

[Provide results of test scores here. May be separated into major domains or a summary of performances provided]. See examples below. We recommend the inclusion of a summary table of neuropsychological scores (including standardized scores) be included in most neuropsychological reports either imbedded or as an appendix. Base rate information regarding the frequency in which score differences are observed in healthy samples and/or if results exceed reliable change scores (if known) may be included. No references needed. [Note: the reporting base rate and/or discrepancy information provided following recommendations for evidenced-based neuropsychology practice (Chelune, 2010)].

Paragraph format

Premorbid functioning estimated to be high average to superior. General cognitive functioning was average. The patient exhibited deficits in areas of attention/executive functions, verbal memory and language functions. Specifically, the patient exhibited mild to moderate deficits in complex focused and divided attention tasks. Verbal immediate and delayed memory scores were mildly impaired. Language screening was grossly functional, but there were deficits in confrontation naming and verbal fluency. Strengths were basic span of attention, receptive and expressive language functions and visuoperceptual skills.

Bulleted format

Premorbid functioning: Estimated to be high average to superior in general cognitive ability.

General Cognitive: High average compared to age-matched peers. Indices of verbal and nonverbal abilities were high average and average, respectively (Verbal Comp. = 115, 84th %; Perceptual Reasoning = 100, 50th %).

Processing Speed: WNL.

Attention: Intact for basic functions. Impaired for complex attention

Memory: Impaired verbal memory. Intact visual memory. Differences in scores infrequent in healthy sample.

Language: Impaired confrontation naming and verbal fluency. Unable to follow 3-step instructions. Otherwise receptive and expressive speech grossly intact. Repetition intact. No alexia or agraphia.

Visuoperceptual/visuoconstructional: Grossly intact. No constructional apraxia

Executive functions (insight, judgment, reasoning): impaired. Insight and judgment [intact, impaired, etc.]

Brief Results Section Example

The patient exhibited deficits in areas of attention/executive functions, verbal memory and language functions. Specifically, the patient exhibited mild to moderate deficits in complex focused and divided attention tasks. Verbal immediate and delayed memory scores were borderline to impaired compared to age-matched peers. Language screening was functional, but the patient exhibited deficits in confrontation naming (BNT = 38/60) and phonemic and semantic verbal fluency scores.

Strengths were in basic attention functions, general cognitive (intellectual) functioning was average, and visuoperceptual and visuoconstructional skills were entirely intact.

PSYCHOLOGICAL AND PERSONALITY FUNCTIONING

[Provide results of any psychological or personality testing done. See example below]

The patient completed the BDI-2 and STAI. He reported mild to moderate symptoms of depression and anxiety. The patient denied rumination and appeared well adjusted.

CONCLUSIONS AND DIAGNOSTIC IMPRESSIONS

[Interpretation of neuropsychological results. Statement(s) to answer the referral question(s) should be clearly specified. Diagnoses should be listed. If combined with recommendations, recommendations should flow from interpretation.] See example below.

Neuropsychological study was [abnormal, equivocal, normal]. [If abnormal, describe what was abnormal].

For example: The study was abnormal due to deficits in attention/executive functions, verbal memory and language functions. There were mild to moderate symptoms of depression. Strengths included the patient's basic span of attention, nonverbal "visual" memory, visuoperceptual and visuoconstructional skills.

[If relation to neuroanatomical function is needed, specify here. For example: Assuming normal neuroanatomical functional organization, data suggest left frontotemporal dysfunction, and consistent with history of left temporal mesial temporal scelrosis.] [In dementia example. Neuropsychological data are generally consistent with a dementia of the Alzheimer's type. A less likely possibility is a frontotemporal dementia (FTD) process. History of symptoms argues against FTD].

[If surgical candidacy is a referral question, clearly specify neuropsychological opinion. For example: *Surgical candidacy*: From a neuropsychological standpoint, the patient is a (poor, fair, good, excellent) candidate for (left, right, extratemporal, multilobar, corpus callosotomy, DBS, VNS, CABG, renal/hepatic transplantation, spinal fusion, morphine pump, etc.]. The patient is at (low, medium, high) risk for post-surgical (language, memory, attention/executive, psychiatric, etc.) problems. The patient is likely a good candidate for [additional diagnostic/laboratory procedures to further evaluate for potential risks to the patient.].

[If feedback notation is included in same report. For example: Initial results of the neuropsychological evaluation were reviewed with the patient, and all questions were answered to his/her/their satisfaction. As much detail as is necessary is appropriate here.].

Diagnostic Impressions: [List diagnostic conditions here. Should follow ICD-9 or DSM-IV diagnostic codes].

RECOMMENDATIONS

[List recommendations for the patient's care here.] These will vary widely depending upon the individual patient. However, some common domains for recommendations are provided below:

1. Referral for further work-up of condition.
2. Recommend consultation by another specialist/subspecialist
3. Initiate treatment for psychiatric/psychological symptoms
4. Initiate treatment/rehabilitation for cognitive deficits
5. Cognitive ability to make medical, legal and/or financial decisions (capacity is a legal term and decided by a court – not a neuropsychologist).
6. Cognitive and/or behavioral prognosis based on available data
7. Rehabilitation/treatment recommendations

   (a) Summary of deficits with prognosis for recovery
   (b) Participate in medical treatment
   (c) Behavioral management
   (d) 1:1 Supervision/therapies
   (e) Suicide precautions
   (f) Escort to and from all activities

(g) Relaxation
(h) Minimal stimulation
(i) Shortened therapy sessions
(j) Cognitive rehab.
(k) Neglect training
(l) Attentional training
(m) Orientation group/training
(n) Memory notebook training
(o) Problem solving training

8. Occupational recommendations/driving restrictions

    (a) Capacity to return to work (school if child)
    (b) Schedule to return if unable to return to full time work
    (c) Accommodations necessary for successful re-integration

9. Reference of local, state, regional, national or international support and advocacy groups of any known disorders/conditions.
10. Specify diagnosis for Americans with Disabilities Act (ADA) and/or Individuals with Disabilities Education Act (IDEA, 2004).

    (a) Specify need for IEP (based on diagnosis/diagnoses)
    (b) Specify what accommodations and/or adaptations may be helpful to the patient academically, socially, emotionally and/or vocationally.

11. [If appropriate, make statement(s) about return to work/school. If not return to work/school now, when, and if accommodations (as above) are likely to be needed.].
12. [Specify if follow-up is needed].

[Closure of report and include information, if appropriate, for further contact and information if desired. Include information about services provided [Services included: Neuropsychological evaluation (_____ hours including administering, scoring, interpretation and report writing). Psychometrician-based neuropsychological assessment (____ hours).]

References

Achiron, A., Polliack, M., Rao, S. M., Barak, Y., Lavie, M., Appelboim, N., et al. (2005). Cognitive patterns and progression in multiple sclerosis: Construction and validation of percentile curves. *Journal of Neurology, Neurosurgery, and Psychiatry, 76*, 744–749.

Busch, R. M., Frazier, T. W., Haggerty, K. A., & Kubu, C. S. (2005). Utility of the Boston Naming Test in predicting ultimate side of surgery in patients with medically intractable temporal lobe epilepsy. *Epilepsia, 46*, 1773–1779.

Chelune, G. J. (1995). Hippocampal adequacy versus functional reserve: Predicting memory functions following temporal lobectomy. *Archives of Clinical Neuropsychology, 10*, 413–432.

Chelune, G. J. (2010). Evidenced-based research and practice in clinical neuropsychology. *The Clinical Neuropsychologist, 24*, 454–467.
Chelune, G. J., & Najm, I. (2001). Risk factors associated with postsurgical decrements in memory. In H. O. Luders & Y. Comair (Eds.), *Epilepsy surgery* (2nd ed., pp. 497–504). Lippincott Williams & Wilkins.
Drane, D. L., Lee, G. P., Cech, H., Huthwaite, J. S., Ojemann, G. A., Ojemann, J. G., et al. (2006). Structured cueing on a semantic fluency task differentiates patients with temporal versus frontal lobe seizure onset. *Epilepsy and Behavior, 9*, 339–344.
Dujardin, K., Defbvre, L., Duhamel, A., Lecouffe, P., Rogelet, P., Steinling, M., et al. (2004). Cognitive and SPECT characteristics predict progression of Parkinson's disease in newly diagnosed patients. *Journal of Neurology, 251*, 1432–1459.
Fleisher, A. S., Sun, S., Taylor, C., Ward, C. P., Gamst, A. C., Petersen, R. C., et al. (2008). Volumetric MRI vs clinical predictors of Alzheimer disease in mild cognitive impairment. *Neurology, 70*, 191–199.
Heilman, K. M., & Valenstein, E. (2003). *Clinical neuropsychology* (4th ed.). Oxford University Press.
Hermann, B., Davies, K., Foley, K., & Bell, B. (1999). Visual confrontation naming outcome after standard left anterior temporal lobectomy with sparing versus resection of the superior temporal gyrus: A randomized prospective clinical trial. *Epilepsia, 40*(8), 1070–1076.
Individuals with Disabilities Act (IDEA). (1990). Pub. L. No 101–336, S2, 104 Stat. 328.
Lezak, M. D., Howieson, D. B., & Loring, D. W. (2004). *Neuropsychological assessment* (4th ed.). Oxford University Press.
Lineweaver, T. T., Morris, H. H., Naugle, R. I., Najm, I. M., Diehl, B., & Bingaman, W. (2006). Evaluating the contributions of state-of-the-art assessment techniques to predicting memory outcome after unilateral anterior temporal lobectomy. *Epilepsia, 47*(11), 1895–1903.
Ponsford, J., Draper, K., & Schonberger, M. (2008). Functional outcome 10 years after traumatic brain injury: Its relationship with demographic, injury severity, and cognitive and emotional status. *Journal of the International Neuropsychological Society, 14*, 233–242.
Ruff, R., (2005). Two Decades of of advances in understanding mild traumatic brain injury. *Journal of Head Trauma Rehabilitation, 20*(1), 5–18.
Sawrie, S. M., Martin, R. C., Gilliam, F. G., Roth, D. L., Faught, E., & Kuzniecyk, R. (1999). Contribution of neuropsychological data to the prediction of temporal lobe epilepsy surgery outcome. *Epilepsia, 39*, 319–325.
Seidenberg, M., Pulsipher, D. T., & Hermann, B. (2007). Cognitive progression in epilepsy. *Neuropsychology Review, 17*(4), 445–454.
Sherer, M., Novack, T. A., Sander, A. M., Struchen, M. A., Alderson, A., & Thompson, R. N. (2002). Neuropsychological assessment and employment outcome after traumatic brain injury: A review. *The Clinical Neuropsychologist, 16*, 157–178.

Chapter 2
Deconstructing the Medical Chart

Alan J. Lerner and Michael R. Schoenberg

Key Points and Chapter Summary

- The medical chart has several components, and familiarity with the basic structure of each section is important to both effective patient management and quality care.
- The History and Physical (H&P) is the initial evaluation of a patient upon admission to a hospital, service or transfer, and is often the most comprehensive source of current patient information.
- While the basic structure of a H&P is similar across medical disciplines/specialties, elaboration within different sections is often discipline/specialty-specific

The Medical Chart

Good assessment and consultation often start with a review of the existing medical chart and records. In this chapter, a practical method for extracting information from often complex, chaotic medical records is reviewed with particular emphasis

A. J. Lerner (✉)
Department of Neurology, The Neurological Institute,
Cleveland, OH, USA
e-mail: Alan.Lerner@UHhospitals.org

M. R. Schoenberg
Departments of Psychiatry and Neurosciences, Neurology, and Neurosurgery,
University of South Florida College of Medicine, Tampa, FL, USA
e-mail: mschoenb@health.usf.edu

M. R. Schoenberg, J. G. Scott (eds.), *The Little Black Book of Neuropsychology*,
https://doi.org/10.1007/978-3-032-07777-6_2

on information relevant for neuropsychological evaluation (see also Lezak et al., 2004; Victor & Ropper, 2001; Zaidat & Lerner, 2008, for review).

Inpatient Chart

The admission note is often the most detailed source of information available in an entire chart, and therefore bears special scrutiny in helping with neuropsychological assessment. The basic form of the admission History and Physical includes the following subsections:

Chief complaint. This is usually in the form of a succinct sentence often or ideally in the patient's own words such as "shortness of breath" or "change in mental status" or "admitted for elective cardiac surgery." The chief complaint encapsulates the reason for admission, at least on the initial basis.

1. *History of present illness*. This forms the main narrative of the admission history and physical and often starts with a brief review of past medical history. The History of Present Illness often contains additional important information such as who provided the history; whether it was the patient or family or other medical personnel. It may also contain cross-references to other portions of the medical chart such as records obtained from the Emergency Medical Services. More importantly, one should be aware of data that is critical to neuropsychological evaluation which may not be commonly present in medical records such as education, occupation and psychological and social factors that will need to be considered in the interpretation of the consultation or evaluative report.
2. *Past medical history*. Typically, this is a listing of medical conditions, frequently abbreviated. Regulatory agencies such as JCAHO have rightly criticized the practice of abbreviations in medical charts as they can be confusing or ambiguous, and this may impact patient quality of care. Caution should be given in considering the source of medical history and confirming the list of critical past illnesses, as these can be in error and, if so, may lead to erroneous conclusions about contributing factors in the patient's current condition. For example, a patient with an erroneously reported history of diabetes, hypertension or coronary artery disease may be evaluated differently when presenting with stroke symptoms only to find out they have blood clots (phlebitis) after a long journey in a sedentary position.
3. *Family and social history*. Although this is usually a very truncated section of the history and physical, it is of importance in interpretation of any neuropsychological testing. It will frequently contain information such as marital status or gender, tobacco, alcohol and drug abuse. It may also contain information about the number of children, although in an inpatient setting this is often not specified. Of special importance is the patient's educational history and primary language (if specified), as many neuropsychological skills and test performances vary considerably with education, and consideration should be given to evaluate a patient in his/her primary language. If not a Fluent English speaker, performances and expectations should be altered. For practitioners who do not speak the language of the patient, options may include identifying another practitioner who does speak

the language or finding an interpreter (caution should be taken if a family member or friend of the patient is used as this may introduce bias). If unavailable basic cognitive testing using nonverbal tasks/tests may provide some useful information, but interpretation and conclusions should acknowledge appropriate caution.

4. *Review of systems*. The review of systems should ideally complement previous medical history. A complete review of systems encompasses constitutional symptoms as well as up to about 15 bodily systems. This commonly includes systems such as general appearance/constitution, head/ears/eyes/nose/throat, skin, respiratory, cardiovascular, gastrointestinal, gastrourinary, musculoskeletal, neurologic, psychiatric, endocrine, hematologic/lymphatic, allergic/immunologic, but the depth of each system is often expanded or abbreviated to accommodate the reason for the examination.
5. *Vital signs*. Typically, this would include temperature (recorded either in centigrade or Fahrenheit), pulse (per minute), respirations (per minute) and blood pressure with systolic recorded over diastolic. In charting, these are often abbreviated as T, P, R, B/P, and often noted as numbers in that order. Caution is again warranted as the information provided here may be duplicated from a prior admission note or delayed from the time of their actual collection to producing the History and Physical.

The following subsections of the Review of Systems are common:

HEENT. This stands for Head, Eyes, Ears, Nose and Throat. A frequent abbreviation is NC/AT which stands for Normocephalic, Atraumatic. Ideally, this section will identify any observed defects and state of the skin, oral mucosa, dentition, use of hearing aids or glasses. However, this information is often omitted. Again, cross-reference with the history as described above is often useful. Gross vision problems may be noted here (or in CN exam section), including strabismus, exotropia, esotropia or amblyopia. Strabismus is the lack of muscle coordination between the eyes. Exotropia refers to an eye being deviated away from midline (deviated outward), and is a form of strabismus. Esotropia refers to an eye being deviated toward the midline (deviated inward), and is a form of strabismus. Amblyopia refers to when the brain does not process visual signals of a misaligned eye (the eye that is exotropic or esotropic), resulting in vision being based on one eye and a patient losing depth perception. Strabismus refers to the condition of misaligned eyes when looking ahead.

Neck. This is often described as supple, a rigid neck being a concerning finding regarding the possibility of meningitis in a patient particularly who is febrile. There may be referral to nuchal (neck) rigidity which may be accompanied by a Brudzinski's sign (raising of the legs toward the chest when the head is bent forward at the neck) often associated with meningeal irritation or inflammation. Other abbreviations seen here would be JVD, standing for jugular venous distention, which may be increased with right heart failure as with pulmonary hypertension, for example. There may also be references to the size of the thyroid as well as the presence or absence of carotid bruits (an abnormal sound made by blood in the carotid arteries when it swirls past a stenotic or ulcerative plaque).

Respiratory. This may or may not include a breast examination. A variety of maneuvers are taught to medical students to describe chest findings. The most common abbreviation here is CTA (Clear To Auscultation) meaning the quadrants of the chest do not demonstrate any abnormal (i.e., different or atypical) sound when thumped or listened to (auscultated). It is less likely, particularly with more senior clinicians, to have a detailed chest examination unless they are performed by a pulmonologist or a cardiologist. Other findings of note may include findings suspicious for a pleural effusion such as dullness at the base or evidence for pneumonia such as crackles or decreased breath sounds. The presence of wheezes suggestive of obstructive airway disease is sometimes noted as well. These comparisons are often reported by chest or lung quadrant indicating a more precise area of abnormal findings.

Cardiovascular. This refers primarily to the heart sounds on auscultation, but may also contain information regarding peripheral arterial disease. Most commonly, it may say normal S_1 S_2 (S refers to sound and S_{1-4} refers to the first through fourth heart sounds in a normal heart beat) referring to the normal opening heart sounds. The presence of additional heart sounds which are nonspecific findings includes the possibility of an abnormal S_3 or $S_{4.}$ The presence of murmurs is often noted, and this may be abbreviated as an M. Pulses may also be included under cardiovascular. The dorsalis pedis pulse (or pedal pulse) is abbreviated as DP and often will be marked as +/+; the initial + referring to their right side and the second + to the left side.

Gastrointestinal/genitourinary. Frequently abbreviated as GI/GU. The most common abbreviations here are BS for bowel sounds and NT for non-tender. Also noted is focal tenderness or masses, and sometimes the presence of an aortic or femoral bruit may be located here rather than under the cardiovascular examination. Rectal examination may be included under the abdominal examination or it may be deferred. Often times, abbreviations here refer to the presence or absence of occult blood such as determined with the guaiac screening card or the presence of normal rectal reflexes indicative of normal sacral spinal cord function. Genitourinary would include vaginal or external male genitalia examination including the penis, scrotum and testes. This examination may also be deferred in inpatient evaluations.

Musculoskeletal. This includes examination of any skeletal deformities and muscle tone and any asymmetry that may be present. The most common abbreviation is C/C/E standing for cyanosis, clubbing or edema. The presence of osteoarthritic changes may be noted here, as may be congenital or acquired deformities such as an amputation. This is sometimes accompanied by a drawing of an affected or infected extremity. Frequently, the pulse is recorded and relevant here, and may be obtained from two extremities (e.g., the dorsalis pedis pulses may be recorded here rather than under the cardiovascular examination). Evaluation is based not only on recording abnormalities but also symmetry. Differences in symmetry in either palor, size or functionality may be noted here. Limitations in movement, such as inability to abduct or adduct a limb may be noted here. Abduct(ion) is an action that moves a body part away from the midline or center axis along an horizontal plane. Adduct(ion) is an action moving a body part toward the midline or center axis. A common abbreviation is CVA or costovertebral angle (this refers to the angle of the spine and ribs) or CVAT for costovertebral angle tenderness which may or may not be present. The presence of scoliosis or kyphosis may also be noted here. Also noted here may be any complaints of pain and the distribution of the region of the pain, which may be helpful in differentiating central and peripheral from referred pain that may be associated with organ dysfunction.

Neurological/Psychiatric. The neurologic examination is frequently replete with abbreviations. The importance of the neurologic examination to neuropsychological evaluation cannot be overstated and is considered in greater detail below. The most important piece of information available to the consulting neurologist or neuropsychologist is a prior neurological examination noted in sufficient depth to reassure the examiner that it was performed with more than cursory inspection. The components of the neurologic examination are elaborated below.

Mental status. This is frequently abbreviated as AO × 3 standing for alert, oriented to person, place and time. Occasionally one may see orientation described as AO × 4 with the "4" referring to situation or circumstances. A more detailed listing of specific findings such as a score obtained for the Mini-Mental State Exam (MMSE; Folstein et al., 1975) may be found (e.g., 30/30), as well as descriptions of which items the patient failed. This section should include observations regarding attention, language, memory and insight/awareness of any current problems. Notation of defects in orientation, language problems (dysarthria, expressive/receptive aphasia, paraphasias) may be reported here. This section may also report about the patient's mood and affect along with presence of hallucinations or delusions and risk of harm to self or others.

Cranial nerves. These are often summarized as "CN II-XII intact." Cranial nerve I (olfactory nerve) is generally not tested. As with mental status, it is not always clear when this is a cursory evaluation versus a summation of a detailed examination. See Chap. 3 for review of anatomy of Cranial Nerves, and Chap. 4 for list of the Cranial Nerves and methods for assessment.

Motor examination. This includes muscle tone (resistance to passive movement), bulk, strength, often expressed according to the 0–5 Medical Research Council (MRC) grading scale. Deep tendon reflexes (DTRs) should be noted here (see Tables 2.1 and 2.2; Fig. 2.1 for detailed examination). Frequently, these are provided along with a stick drawing of a person with reflexes noted (see Fig. 2.1 and Table 2.1). Plantar responses may also be provided here, and may be noted along with DTRs (see Fig. 2.1). Figure 2.2 illustrates how the plantar response can be elicited.

Table 2.1 Grading of deep tendon reflexes (DTRs)

Grading of DTRs	Qualitative descriptor of reflex grading
0	Not present, even with facilitatory procedure
1	Present but reduced or weak
2	Normal
2+	Normal, but somewhat brisk (high normal)
3	Brisk
3 + 4 (or 3+)	Very brisk, but no clonus
4	Pathologically brisk with clonus

Reflex grading of 2+ throughout is discussed as "reflexes were 2+ throughout"

Table 2.2 Grading of muscle strength (MRC scale)

Grading of muscle strength	Qualitative descriptor of muscle grading
0	No palpable muscle contraction
1	A flicker or trace of contraction
2	Active movement with gravity eliminated
3	Movement against gravity but not resistance
4–	Active movement against gravity and slight resistance
4	Active movement against gravity and resistance
4+	Active movement against gravity and strong resistance
5	Full active range of motion and normal muscle resistance

A muscle grading of 0 is verbally discussed as "muscle strength is/was zero or zero out of five".

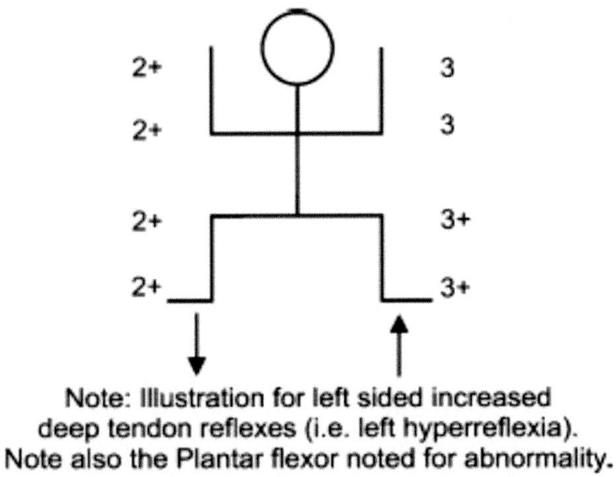

Fig. 2.1 Common notation used to record reflexes as part of a neurological exam

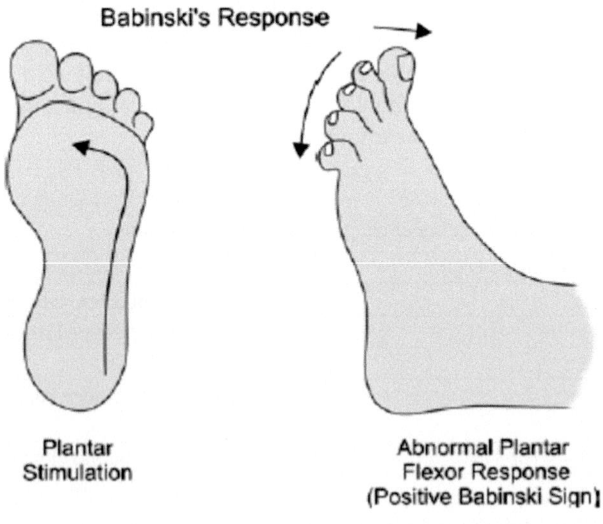

Fig. 2.2 Illustration of the plantar (Babinski) reflex

The presence of an abnormal movements/movement disorder (e.g., tremor, jerks, incoordination), apraxia, ataxia, hypertonicity (rigidity), hypotonicity (flaccidity) or other abnormalities of gait and station are also often noted here. Tremor description should indicate where the tremor is present (e.g., upper extremity, lower extremity, head), when it is present (i.e., continuous, under stress, only at rest) and the severity of the tremor (see Fig. 2.3 for illustration of tremors). A variety of terms may be used to describe when it is present, but the most common will be *action tremor* (including postural, kinetic, physiological and intention tremors) or *resting tremor* (classically, Parkinsonian tremor). When exaggerated, termed Enhanced Physiological tremor, by fright, anxiety, extreme exertion, withdraw from alcohol, toxic effects from some chemicals (caffeine, lithium, etc.) or metabolic dysfunction (e.g., hyperthyroidism or hypoglycemia), the physiological tremor increases to be seen and to disrupt routine activities.

Other abnormal movements, such as chorea, athetosis, dystonias, ballismus (often hemiballismus) or akinesia, are often noted here.

Motor abnormalities of hypertonicity/rigidity [e.g., spasticity, cogwheel rigidity, lead pipe rigidity, paratonia (gegenhalten), etc.] or hypotonicity are also frequently noted here. Hypertonicity refers to excess motor tension, presence of spasticity, lead pipe rigidity (rigidity of a limb maintained during and after passive movement of muscle), cogwheel rigidity (passive movement results in a cogwheel or ratchet like catching and quickly releasing as limb moves) and paratonia (involuntary variable

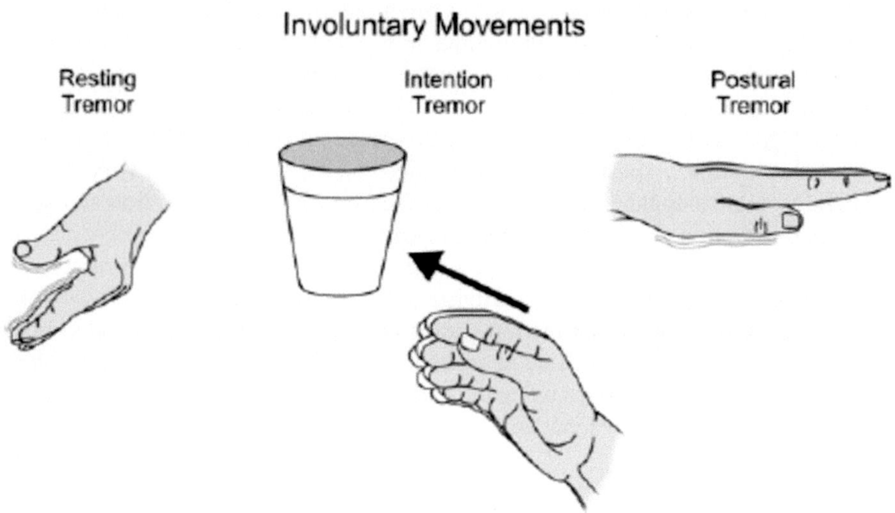

Fig. 2.3 Illustration and descriptions for common types of tremors

resistance to efforts at passive movement of a muscle, like a limb) (see Chaps. 10 and 19, this volume, for more details).

The presence of apraxia, ataxia and/or disorders associated with cerebellar function, such as dysmetria or dysdiadochokinesia, may be identified here or in the Gait and Balance section below. Examples include ideomotor and ideational apraxia. Ataxia refers to inability to coordinate muscle movements that is not due to motor weakness. Muscle movements will appear clumsy or "jerky." Ataxia is typically associated with lesions to the cerebellum leading to gait abnormalities (see below), but may also occur due to sensory ataxia from damage to proprioception sensory pathways. Optic ataxia is the inability to coordinate eye–hand motor movements and is observed with Balint's syndrome (see Chap. 9, this volume). Ataxic respiration is the poor coordination of muscles in chest and diagram, related to damage of the respiratory centers in the medulla oblongata or associated pathways.

Gait and balance. Sometimes included under the motor system, this includes rapid alternating movements (RAM), finger-to-nose testing (FTN), Romberg testing and other gait and balance descriptions. Observations of ataxia (e.g., dysmetria, dysdiadochokinesia) may be noted here. Dysmetria is abnormal movements associated with cerebellar damage and involves dysfunction in the ability to accurately control the range of movement needed for a muscular action. Dysmetria is commonly tested with finger-to-nose testing. The individual with dysmetria will be unable to guide his/her finger to the examiners finger or nose, in which the target is under- or overshot, with attempts at corrections which have a "jerky" quality and overcorrection is often present. Dysdiadochokinesia is the inability to complete rapid alternating movements associated with cerebellar ataxia, and is often tested by having a patient rapidly alternate slapping the palm of each hand and back of the hand on a stable surface (i.e., pronation/supination test). Gait may be described with various terms, but some of the more common include: normal, spastic, apraxic (wide-based), ataxic (also wide-based), Parkinsonian, steppage or scissored gait (see Fig. 2.4 for illustration and summary description of common gait abnormalities).

Sensory. Basic sensory modalities include light touch, pain sensation, vibratory sensation and joint position testing. "Higher order" sensory testing such as two point discrimination, sensory extinction and/or graphesthesia may be included here. Figure 2.5 illustrates a bedside neurological examination to assess for graphesthesia. While this illustrates using the patient's palm, it may also be tested on the patient's finger tips. Presence of agraphasthesia is associated with contralateral parietal lobe damage.

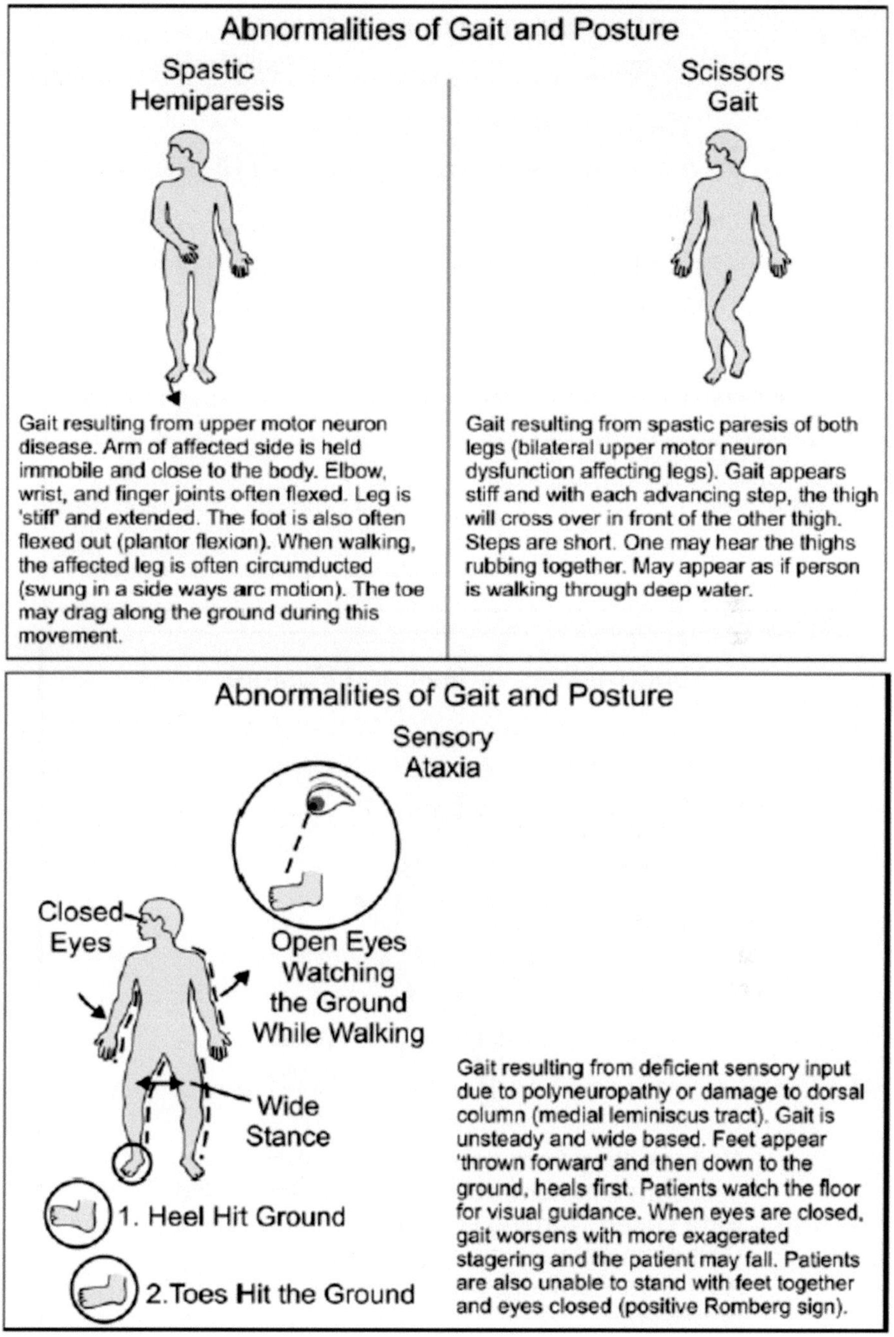

Fig. 2.4 Illustration and description of common gait abnormalities

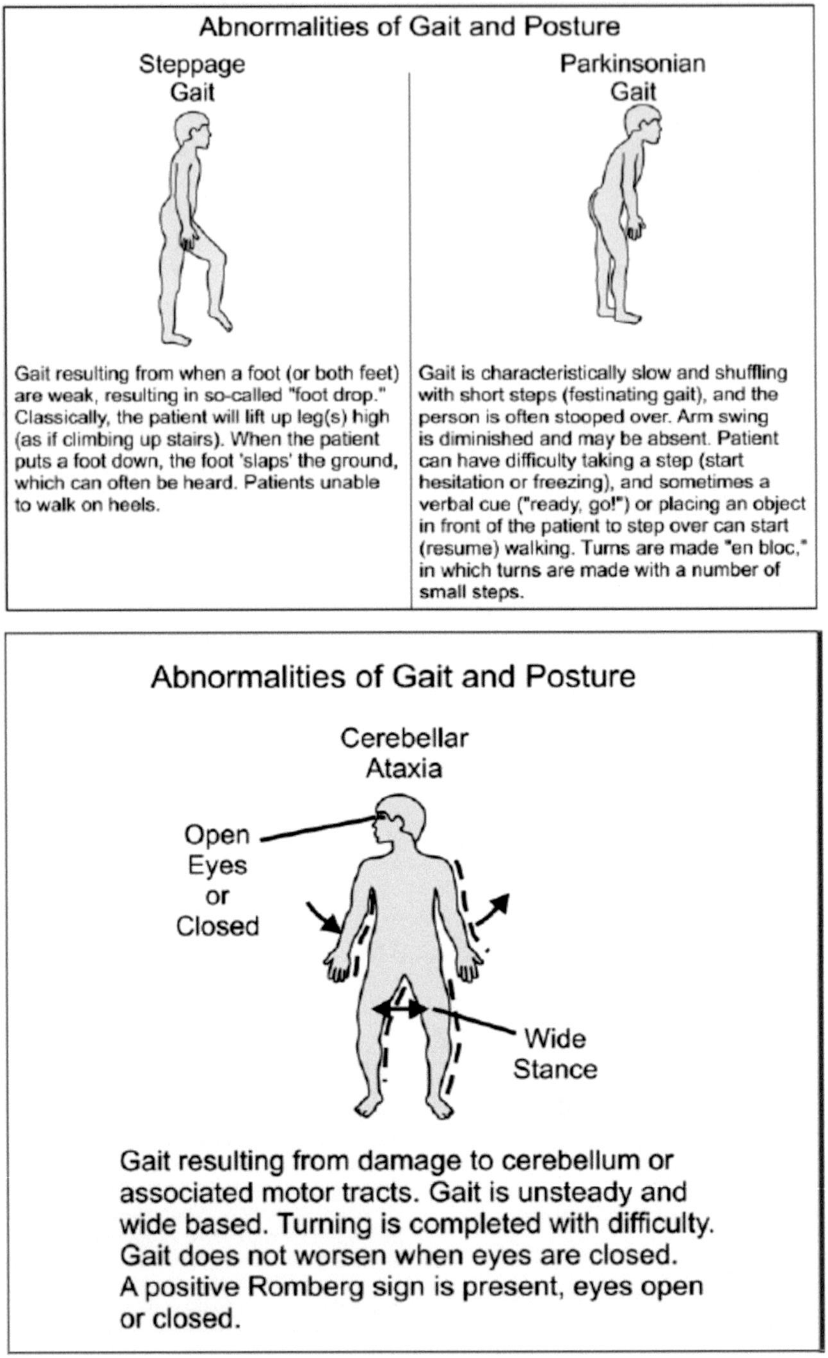

Fig. 2.4 (continued)

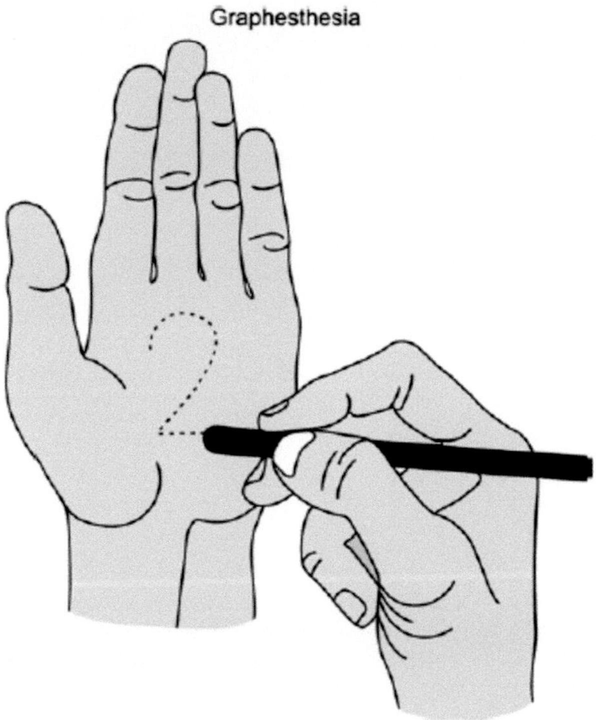

Fig. 2.5 Bedside procedure to assess graphesthesia

References

Folstein, M. F., Folstein, S. E., & McHugh, P. R. (1975). "Mini-mental state". A practical method for grading the cognitive state of patients for the clinician. *Journal of Psychiatric Research, 12*, 189–198.

Lezak, M. D., Howieson, D. B., & Loring, D. W. (2004). *Neuropsychological assessment* (4th ed.). Oxford.

Victor, M., & Ropper, A. H. (2001). *Adams and Victor's principals of neurology* (7th ed.). McGraw-Hill.

Zaidat, O. O., & Lerner, A. J. (2008). *The little black book of neurology* (5th ed.). Elsevier Health Sciences.

Chapter 3
Neuroanatomy Primer: Structure and Function of the Human Nervous System

Michael R. Schoenberg, Patrick Marsh, Joseph J. Boscarino, Emily N. Vanderbleek, and Alan Lerner

Chapter Summary

- Central nervous system includes the brain and spinal cord.
- Neurons process information by an electrochemical process in which "communication" between neurons (and some glial cells) occurs with the release of neurotransmitters.
- Neurotransmitters are small molecules (ex. glutamate, GABA), and facilitate action potentials that excite or inhibit synapsing neurons.
- Peripheral nervous system includes cranial nerves, spinal nerves (motor and sensory) and autonomic nervous system.
- Autonomic nervous system includes the parasympathetic and sympathetic divisions. Parasympathetic nervous system is associated with "rest and digest" functions, arises from cranial nerves and sacral (S2-S4) spinal levels, and uses acetylcholine neurotransmitter on end organs. Sympathetic nervous system is associated with "flight or fight" functions, arises from

(continued)

M. R. Schoenberg (✉)
Department of Psychiatry and Neurosciences, University of South Florida, Tampa, FL, USA
e-mail: Emily.vanderbleek@va.gov

P. Marsh
Departments of Psychiatry and Neurosciences, Neurology, and Neurosurgery, Morsani College of Medicine Tampa, University of South Florida, Tampa, FL, USA
e-mail: Mschoenb@health.usf.edu; Pmarsh@health.usf.edu

J. J. Boscarino
Departments of Psychiatry and Neurosciences, Neurology, and Neurosurgery, University of South Florida College of Medicine, Tampa, FL, USA
e-mail: Joseph.Boscarino@va.gov

M. R. Schoenberg, J. G. Scott (eds.), *The Little Black Book of Neuropsychology*,
https://doi.org/10.1007/978-3-032-07777-6_3

(continued)

thoracic and upper lumbar (T1 to L2) spinal levels, and uses norepinephrine neurotransmitter on end organs.

- Major afferent (sensory) system is the dorsal (posterior) column-medial lemniscus (vibration, two-point discrimination, proprioception) and spinothalamic tracts (pain, temperature and deep/crude touch).
- Major efferent (motor) system is corticospinal (corticobulbospinal) pathway.
- Cerebrovascular supply originates from paired internal carotid arteries for anterior blood supply and paired vertebral arteries for the posterior supply.
- Major regions of the brain include medulla, pons, cerebellum, midbrain, thalamus, basal ganglia and cerebral cortex.
- Medulla and pons are associated with basic life functions.
- Cerebellum is associated with balance, posture, motor coordination and implicit learning.
- Cerebral hemispheres are divided into frontal, parietal, temporal, occipital lobes, and insular cortex (lobe).
- Frontal lobe is associated with motor functions, expressive language, "executive" functions (e.g., behavioral planning, monitoring/regulation, inhibition, motivation, judgment) and mood/affect (emotional regulation). It also includes olfactory cortex.
- Parietal lobe is associated with somatosensory functions, spatial awareness/attention and complex visuoperceptual processing (reading and shape orientation/direction).
- Temporal lobe is associated with receptive language, primary auditory cortex, declarative memory, visuoperceptual processing (form/shape integration), mood/affect and olfactory cortex.
- Occipital lobe is associated with primary and secondary visual processing.
- Two of the main large-scale functional brain networks are the default-mode network (medial frontoparietal) and salience network (midcingulo-insular).
- Neuropsychological functions involve distributed networks of cortex involved in processing one stimuli along with cortex involved in integraded functions.

E. N. Vanderbleek
Departments of Psychiatry and Neurosciences, Neurology, and Neurosurgery, University of South Florida College of Medicine, Tampa, FL, USA
e-mail: Emily.vanderbleek@va.gov

A. Lerner
Department of Neurology, Case Western University School of Medicine, Cleveland, OH, USA
e-mail: Alan.Lerner@UHospitals.org

Overview

This chapter is provided as a general primer for the neuropsychologist and others interested in functional neuroanatomy. This chapter is not meant as a detailed examination of the nervous system, and readers are encouraged to review comprehensive texts in the area for further detail (e.g., Blumenfeld, 2021; Brodal, 2016; Gould & Brueckner-Collins, 2016; Heilman & Valenstein, 2011; Kolb & Whishaw, 2021; Lezak et al., 2012; Martin, 2020; Mesulam, 2000; Ropper et al., 2023).

The primer is organized into two sections. Section 1 provides an overview of the anatomical structure of the human nervous system. Section 2 provides a primer on functional neuroanatomy. While neuropsychologists are generally well versed in aspects and organization of the central nervous system, particularly the cerebral cortex, less attention is given to the spinal cord, brain stem, diencephalon and peripheral nervous system. This chapter will also provide a brief overview of gross pathology of the skull, meninges, cerebrospinal fluid and important afferent and efferent pathways of the human nervous system. We begin with a review of some important terms and definitions.

Definitions and Important Terms

Action potential—A transient voltage change that occurs when excitatory synaptic inputs combine with endogenous transmembrane currents to sufficiently excite a neuron, which lasts about 1 ms and can travel rapidly throughout the length of a neuron at rates of up to around 60 meters per second. Classically, they travel from the dendritic end of a neuron along its axon to reach presynaptic terminals, and are often coupled to neurotransmitter release from the presynaptic terminal.

Afferent (see also efferent)—Pathway carrying signals *to* a Central Nervous System (CNS) structure. For example, sensory pathways are afferent, sending sensory information to the brain. Often termed as afferents or afferent (fibers, pathways or tracts).

Basal Ganglia—A term used to describe a cluster of nuclei lying in the deep white matter under the cerebral cortex. Key structures include the caudate nucleus, putamen and globus pallidus.

Cingulum (cingulate gyrus)—It means "girdle" or "belt," and is a medial cortical gyrus which is immediately superior to the corpus callosum.

Commissure—White matter pathway connecting analogous structures between the right and left hemispheres of the brain. Commissural pathways include the anterior commissure and posterior commissure.

Corpus Callosum—Main commissure between the two cerebral hemispheres. The divisions of the corpus callosum, anterior to posterior, are: rostrum, genu, body, splenium.

Cuneus ("wedge")—Portion above the calcarine fissure in the visual cortex.

Decussate/decussation—A term used to describe the "crossing" of a fiber tract. Most of the motor tracts and some of the sensory pathways decussate in the pyramids of the brainstem and give the CNS its "crossed" (right brain-left body; left brain-right body) characteristic.

Efferent (see also afferent)—Pathway carrying signals *away* from a CNS structure. Classically, motor pathways are thought of as taking motor signals from the brain to muscles, and are termed efferents or efferent (fibers, pathways or tracts).

Fascicle/fasciculus (see also fiber)—White matter tract connecting areas within a hemisphere. May connect neighboring gyri (arcuate or U-fibers) or more distal areas (e.g., arcuate fasciculus connects expressive and receptive language areas in the left hemisphere and is considered part of the superior longitudinal fasciculus, which runs from the frontal to occipital lobes).

Fiber (also termed bundle, fascicle, lemniscus or tract)—Names for white matter pathways. Fibers have been classified as association, commissural or projection. Association fibers connect cortical areas in each hemisphere. Commissural fibers connect homologous areas between hemispheres. Projection fibers connect cortical areas with deep brain nuclei.

Ganglia—A cluster of neuronal cell bodies often applied to "basal ganglia" (see above).

Gyri—Bumps or ridges between sulci, giving the cortex its characteristic wrinkled appearance. The folding of tissue allows for more surface area.

Gyrus rectus ("straight gyrus")—Located inferomedially on the frontal lobe, adjacent to the longitudinal fissure.

Insular cortex—Cortical structure located between the temporal and frontal lobe deep within the lateral fissure.

Lemniscus (see also tract, fascicle, fiber and bundle)—Name for white matter pathways.

Lingula ("little tongue")—Portion of the medial occipital lobe below the calcarine fissure.

Longitudinal fissure (or interhemispheric fissure)—Midline fissure separating the two hemispheres.

Myelin sheath—Insulating lipid layer of an axon formed by specialized glial cells; speeds the rate of action potential conduction.

Nodes of Ranvier—Short exposed segments of axon where voltage-gated ion channels are concentrated; conduction from node to node occurs rapidly by a process called *salutatory (sodium) conduction.*

Nuclei—Large cluster of neurons within the CNS.

Oligodendrocytes—Myelin-forming glial cells in the CNS; in the PNS myelin is formed by Schwann cells.

Operculum—"Lip," the folds from the frontal, parietal and temporal lobes of the cerebrum overlying the insular cortex.

Schwann cells—A specialized cell in the peripheral nervous system (PNS) which supports the neurons. Schwann cells wrap around the axons of neurons to form the myelin sheath for nerves which increases speed of neuronal transmission via salutatory conduction.

Somatotopic—Related to point-to-point correspondence between a body part (finger) and its representation in the brain. The primary motor and sensory cortices of the brain are arranged somatotopically, but inverse, with functions of the tongue represented on the inferior lateral portion while the trunk is at the superior sagittal area, and the legs are in the medial area of the pre- and post-central gyrus.

Sulci—Crevices/infolds of brain. Sulci that are deep/pronounced are termed fissures.

Synapse—Gap or space between two neuron structures in which neurotransmitter substances are transferred and cellular communication occurs.

Tract (see also fascicle, fiber, lemniscus and bundle)—Names for white matter pathways.

Introduction to Human Nervous System

The human nervous system is grossly organized into the central and peripheral nervous systems (see Fig. 3.1). The Central Nervous System (CNS) is defined as the brain and the spinal cord. The brain is a three pound organ encased in the skull while the spinal cord is located in the spinal canal within the vertebrae. The Peripheral Nervous System (PNS) includes the nerves of the body that are not the brain or spinal cord. Another more technical definition for the PNS is the nerves outside of the

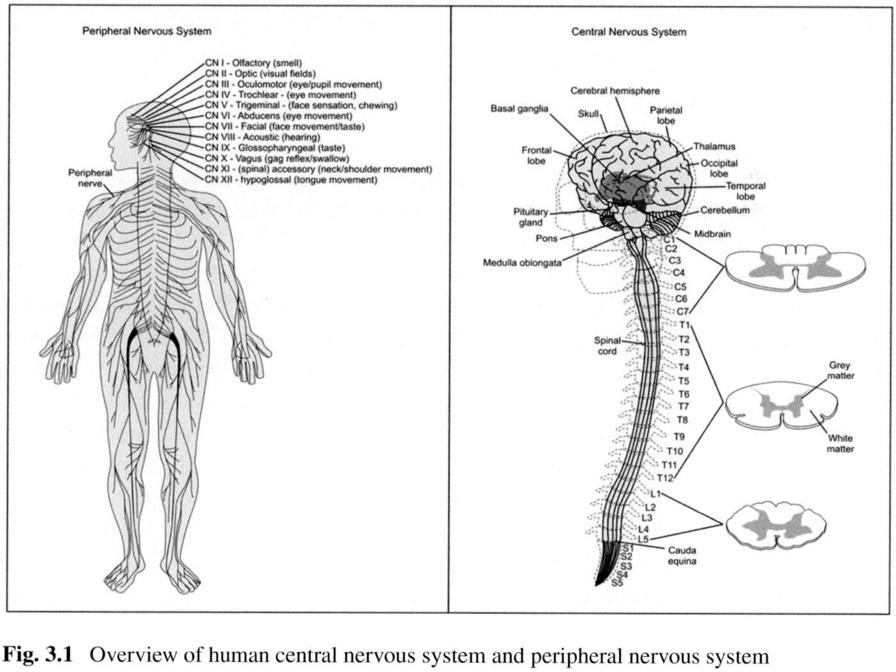

Fig. 3.1 Overview of human central nervous system and peripheral nervous system

dura mater or the nerves that are covered by Schwann cells. The PNS has three main components: (1) somatosensory (afferent) nerves, (2) motor (efferent) nerves and (3) autonomic nervous system. The autonomic nervous system is composed of three systems: (a) the sympathetic nervous system, (b) the parasympathetic nervous system and (c) enteric nervous system (see PNS description below for more details). The PNS includes the paired twelve cranial nerves (i.e., two of each of the cranial nerves, one for the right side and one for the left side). The cranial nerves include somatosensory and motor functions, and a description of the function and assessment of each cranial nerve is provided in Chap. 4.

Key Points: Human Nervous System

- Central Nervous System
  - Brain
  - Spinal cord (cervical, thoracic, lumbar, sacral and coccyx)
- Peripheral Nervous system
  - 12 paired cranial nerves
  - Spinal nerves (sensory and motor)
  - Autonomic nervous system

    Parasympathetic—"Rest and digest"
    Sympathetic—"Fight or flight"
    Enteric—Controls peristalsis and gastrointestinal secretion

The Central Nervous System

The brain is encased in the skull, which consists of 22 individual bones. Fourteen of the bones make up the facial structures of the skull and 8 cranial bones house the brain. The cranial bones include: Parietal, Temporal, Occipital, Frontal and right and left Ethmoid and Sphenoid bones (see also Fig. 3.9). Figure 3.2 illustrates a cut-away view of the anatomy from the scalp to the brain, inclusive of the skin layers, skull, layers of meninges and brain surface. The meninges surround the entire brain and spinal cord and are composed of three different membranes: Dura mater, Arachnoid mater and Pia mater. Adherent to the inside of the cranial bones and surrounding the entire brain is the Dura mater. The dura is a somewhat shiny, inelastic membrane. In addition to surrounding the brain, the dura folds to divide the cranium into separate compartments and create the venous sinuses which drain blood from the brain. The dura creates three named falx. The falx cerebri divides the cranium vertically into right and left compartments housing the right and left hemispheres of the brain. The tentorium cerebelli supports the occipital lobes horizontally and separates them from the cerebellum. The falx cerebelli is analogous to the falx cerebri and separates the left and right hemispheres of the cerebellum. The next layer is the arachnoid, which is an elastic and fibrous two-layered membrane lining the inner surface of the Dura mater. Between the dura and the arachnoid mater is a noncommunicating space called the subdural space. Subdural veins with very little mechanical support traverse the subdural space and are susceptible to mechanical injury (subdural hemorrhage). Because the subdural space is noncommunicating (closed space), bleeding from a subdural vein accumulates to create a subdural hematoma. Subdural hematomas can become large and exert pressure on brain structures necessitating external drainage through the skull (see Chap. 25 for more details of traumatic hemorrhages). Inferior to the arachnoid mater is a fine membrane rich in blood supply called the pia mater. The pia mater is intimately associated with the brain surface, following all the sulci, gyri and conformations of the brain surface. Between the arachnoid mater and the pia mater is the subarachnoid space. The subarachnoid space is a spongy area containing subarachnoid fluid. Damage to blood vessels here results in subarachnoid hemorrhages, which may result in blood products entering the spaces of the cerebrospinal fluid. Internal to the pia mater is the brain.

Key Points: Layers of Meninges (Skull to Brain)
- Dura mater
- Arachnoid mater
- Pia mater

Brain Anatomy Overview

The brain is divided into the Hindbrain (Rhombencephalon), Midbrain (Mesencephalon) and Forebrain (Prosencephalon) based on anatomic location and embryologic origin of the tissues which make up each division (See Fig. 3.3). The hindbrain and midbrain contain nuclei essential for sustaining life and homeostasis.

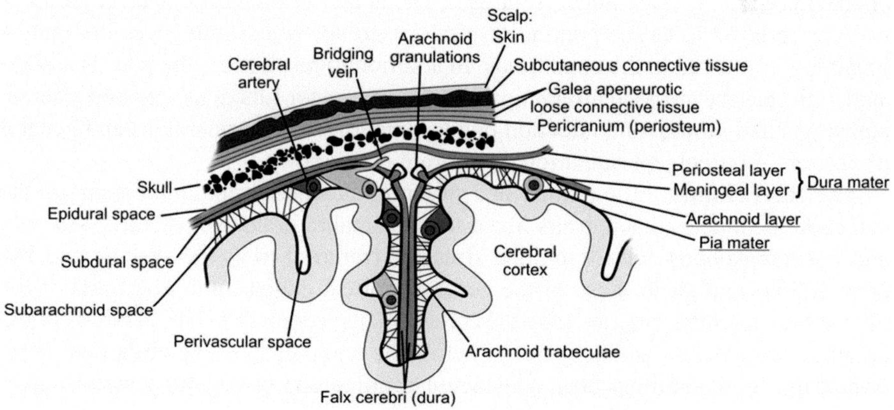

Fig. 3.2 Illustration of components of dura matter and falx cerebri

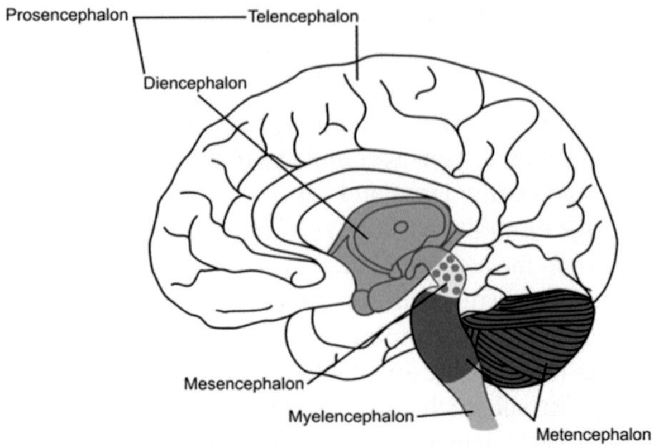

Fig. 3.3 Illustration of the embryonic divisions of the brain

The forebrain includes the basal ganglia, white matter and neocortex traditionally associated with complex behaviors and cognition. The neocortex is divided into four "lobes" or areas: frontal, parietal, temporal and occipital. We now turn to reviewing the anatomy of functions of the major components of the central nervous system.

The **Hindbrain (Rhombencephalon)** is composed of the medulla oblongata, pons and cerebellum. The **medulla oblongata** is the most caudal portion of the brain and continues to form the spinal cord as it exits the skull. It mainly functions as a functional center for the crossing of motor fibers between the spinal cord and the brainstem. The medulla contains the nuclei of the cranial nerves 9–12 (see Fig. 3.1 and Chap. 5 for review of function and bedside assessment): Glossopharyngeal, Vagus, Accessory and Hypoglossal. Medulla also houses the centers for respiration, vasomotor and cardiac control, as well as many mechanisms for controlling reflex activities such as coughing, gagging, swallowing and vomiting.

The **pons** is a bridge-like structure which links the medulla and midbrain. The large body of the pons is made up of axons entering the cerebellum. These axons or fiber tracts are referred to as the cerebellar peduncles. The pons contains nuclei for cranial nerves 5–8: Trigeminal, Abducens, Facial and Vestibulocochlear. A group of neurons referred to as the pontine respiratory group, which influences the rate of breathing, is located in the upper pons. In addition to respiration, the pons is associated with sensory (crossed afferent pathways) and motor functions (crossed efferent pathways) and arousal and attention due to function of locus coeruleus and general projection of norepinephrine throughout brain (see below).

The **cerebellum** ("little brain") is a structure attached to the brain stem via the cerebellar peduncles that appears like a second smaller brain. It is divided into right and left hemispheres with a midline structure (referred to as the vermis) and has convolutions similar to those of the cerebral cortex, called folia. The folds of the cerebellum are much smaller. Like the cerebrum, the cerebellum has an outer cortex, an inner white matter and deep nuclei below the white matter. The traditional function of the cerebellum has been considered coordination of voluntary motor movement, balance and equilibrium and muscle tone. However, more recently, the cerebellum has shown to be involved in emotional and cognitive functions including types of learning (nondeclarative or implicit learning) and executive functions. The cerebellum receives input from the cerebral cortex, including information from: (1) sensory areas of the cerebral cortex, (2) motor areas and (3) cognitive/language/ emotional areas of the cortex and thalamic nuclei.

Key Points: Hindbrain (Rhombencephalon)

- Medulla (oblongata)—Life support functions (heart rate, blood pressure, gag reflex, etc.) and area where afferent (sensory) and efferent (motor) pathways decussate
- Pons—Life support (sleep, heart rate, breathing), arousal (Reticular Activating System) and crossed afferent (sensory) and efferent (motor) pathways.
- Cerebellum—Motor control and coordination, balance, posture/equilibrium as well as implicit learning and memory (motor actions).

The **Midbrain (Mesencephalon)** is composed of the tectum, cerebral peduncle, tegmentum, pretectum and mesencephalic duct (aka aqueduct of Sylvius) (see Figs. 3.1 and 3.3).

The dorsal surface of the midbrain forms the **tectum**, meaning "roof." It consists of the superior colliculi and inferior colliculi. The superior colliculus is involved in preliminary visual processing and control of eye movements (automatic/unconscious visual orientation). The inferior colliculus is involved in automatic/unconscious orientation to auditory stimuli and receives auditory input from various brain stem nuclei. Afferent fibers than project to the thalamus to relay auditory information to the primary auditory cortex.

Key Points: Mnemonic for Superior Colliculus
Superior Colliculus is for See

The term **cerebral peduncle** denotes the white matter tracts, which contain the efferent axons of the cerebral cortex that project to the brainstem and spinal cord. The cerebral peduncles are the part of the midbrain that links the remainder of the brainstem to the thalami. They are the most anterior structure in the midbrain and form the walls of the fourth ventricle. The cerebral peduncles contain the large ascending and descending tracts that run to and from the cerebrum.

The midbrain **tegmentum** is the part of the midbrain extending from the substantia nigra to the cerebral aqueduct in a horizontal section of the midbrain, and forms the floor of the midbrain which surrounds the cerebral aqueduct. The midbrain tegmentum contains cranial nerve nuclei III, IV, and two important nuclei complexes of the motor system, the red nucleus and the substantia nigra. In the core of the midbrain tegmentum is the reticular formation, which is integrally involved in maintenance of arousal and a conscious state. The ventral tegmental area has a concentration of dopaminergic neurons that project to the nucleus accumbens, limbic structures and frontal lobes. This structure and dopaminergic pathway associated with feelings of pleasure, and is the so-called pleasure center of the brain along with nucleus accumbens and other limbic structures.

Key Points: Midbrain

Associated with afferent (sensory) and efferent (motor) pathways, motor control (part of basal ganglia and substantia nigra), eye movements, auditory relay area, arousal/attention (superior part of Reticular Activating System) and "pleasure center" of brain (ventral tegmental area)

- Inferior colliculus—Auditory attention
- Superior colliculus—Visual attention/reflexes
- Cerebral peduncles/red nucleus—Projections to and from cerebrum to cerebellum
- Tegmentum—Arousal and ventral tegmentum area part of "pleasure center" of brain

The midbrain **Pretectum** is a group of neurons found at the border of the midbrain and the thalamus. The Pretectum receives input from retinal cells and is responsible for the pupillary light reflex. The **Mesencephalic Duct** (*aqueduct of Sylvius)*, connects the third and fourth ventricles.

Forebrain (Prosencephalon). Embryonic term referring to the Diencephalon and Telencephalon.

Diencephalon. A term to describe a part of the brain that includes the epithalamus, thalamus, hypothalamus, subthalamus, pituitary gland, pineal gland and the third ventricle (see Figs. 3.1, 3.5 and 3.8).

Thalamus. The thalamus is a roughly football shaped pair of structures at the top of the midbrain. All afferent somatosensory neurons, except olfaction (smell), synapse at thalamic nuclei prior to reaching the cerebral cortex. Efferent motor commands are processed by thalamic nuclei as well prior to being acted on. The thalamus is roughly divided into three regions: the principle body of the thalamus, the hypothalamus and the epithalamus.

The thalamus serves as a major "relay" station for sensory input into the brain (see Fig. 3.4). In addition to senses, the thalamus receives input from the cerebral cortex, basal ganglia, brain stem/cerebellum nuclei (see Fig. 3.4) and is involved in motor behaviors as well as cognitive/emotional processes. The thalamus has been divided into five nuclear groups, based partly on a "Y" shaped white matter tract through the thalamus called the internal medullary lamina. The "Y" shaped white matter tract divides the thalamus into three broad areas: anterior, lateral and medial. The fourth nuclear group is a series of nuclei that lie within the internal medullary lamina termed the intralaminar nuclei. The fifth thalamic nuclear group, a thin wall of neurons covering the lateral aspect of the thalamus is termed the reticular nucleus.

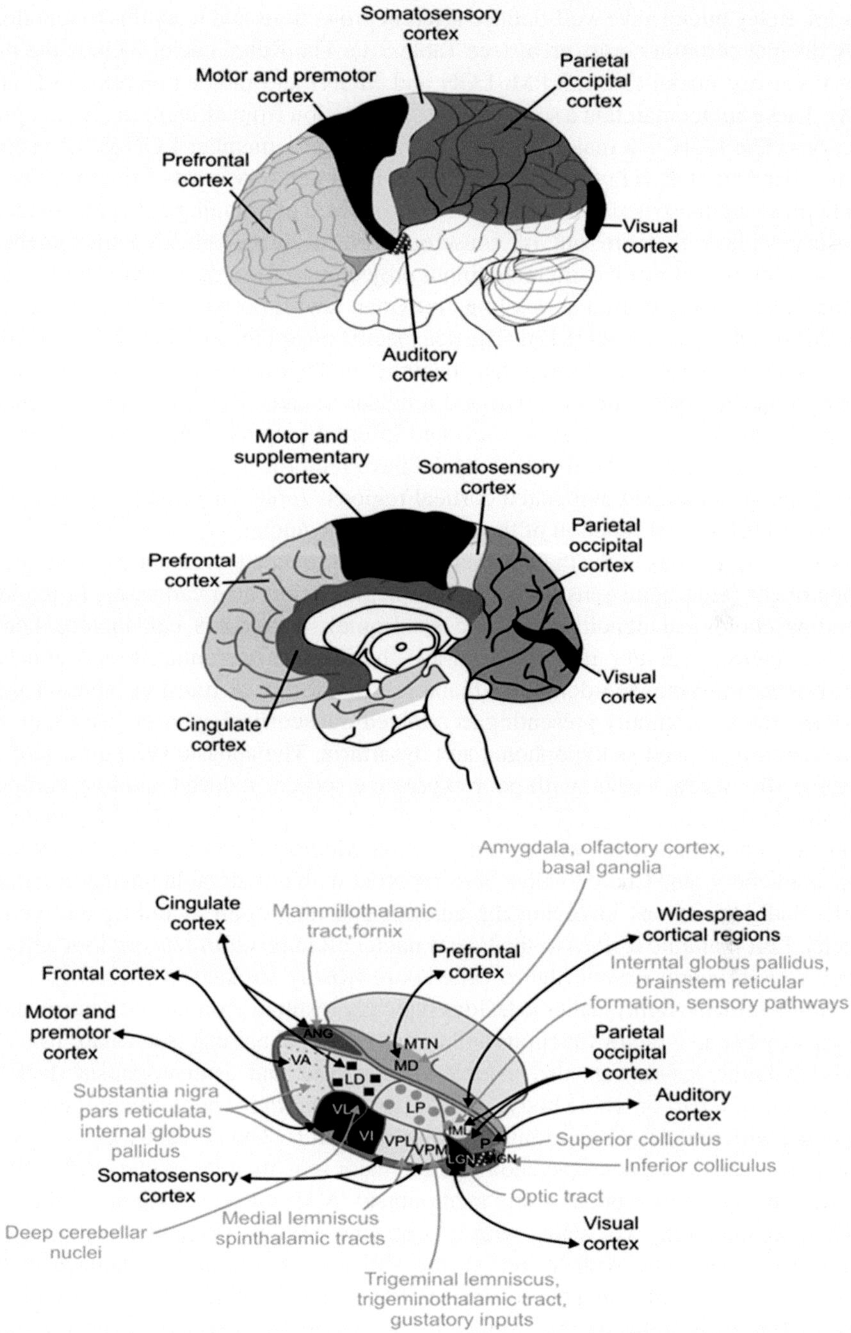

Fig. 3.4 Major thalamic nuclei with afferent and efferent pathways identified with associated cerebral cortex projection areas

The nuclei of the thalamus are of three types: Relay, Association and Nonspecific nuclei. Relay nuclei have well-defined afferent projections and relay this to functionally distinct cerebral cortex areas (see Table 3.1). The Relay nuclei include the primary sensory nuclei (VPL, VPM, LGN and MGN) and motor functions (VL and VA). These nuclei maintain a somatotopic organization from afferent to efferent projections. The LGN is a major pathway for vision (to remember LGN is for vision, remember *L* in *LGN* = *Look*), while the MGN is for auditory inputs from the inferior colliculus, and these nuclei are thought to be involved in orienting behaviors to these sensory stimuli that are out of conscious control (e.g., reflexive movements). Association nuclei receive afferents (input projections) from the cerebral cortex and project back to association cortex [e.g., pulvinar, lateral posterior (LP), medial dorsal (MD) and lateral dorsal (LD)]. The nonspecific nuclei receive diffuse inputs from the ARAS, cerebral cortex and other thalamic nuclei, and have diffuse projections throughout the cortex (intralaminar and reticular nuclei). Review of Fig. 3.4 highlights the afferent/input (gray arrows) and efferent/outputs (black arrows) for the major thalamic nuclei. All thalamic nuclei have reciprocal projections to and from the reticular nuclei and associated cortical regions. Table 3.1 provides a list of the presumed behavioral function of the major thalamic nuclei.

Clinically, lesions to the thalamus is typically associated with marked neurologic impairment (e.g., hemi-sensory loss, hemi-neglect), but also can result in marked neuropsychological deficits (amnestic syndrome). Symptoms can include hemi-neglect (sensory and/or motor), hemi-anesthesia, apraxia, amnesia and aphasia. Lesions to the language-dominant thalamus can result in transient aphasia syndromes, most commonly presenting as a mixed transcortical aphasia (see Chap. 8), but stuttering as well as hypophonia and dysarthria. The aphasic symptoms tend to resolve after a few weeks, with poor expressive speech, reduced auditory comprehension (although reading is often preserved), intact repetition (and writing to dictation, but poor spontaneous writing) and anomia. Memory deficits limited to impaired verbal memory (see Chap. 9) have been reported with unilateral language-dominant (left) thalamic lesions involving the anterior and also often including the medial nuclei. Left thalamic lesions to the lateral nuclei often result in sensory loss without gross cognitive impairment (the so-called pure sensory stroke, see Chap. 14).

Nondominant (right) thalamic lesions typically result in pronounced hemi-neglect to sensory but also motor functions and a constructional apraxia (see Chap. 10). The right thalamic lesion can also exhibit anosognosia and asomatognosia (lack of awareness of a part or whole body). Visual (spatial) memory impairments have been reported with unilateral nondominant thalamic infarcts. The clinically most relevant thalamic nuclei to the neuropsychologist are major sensory relay nuclei (VPL, VPM) as well as the anterior nucleus and mediodorsal (MD) nucleus. Lesions of the sensory relay nuclei are associated with loss of sensory function (and sometimes thalamic pain syndrome with lesions to the VPL). As noted above, damage to the anterior nucleus results in a dense amnestic syndrome, in which episodic memory is lost (anterograde amnesia) but semantic knowledge and implicit memory remain intact. Damage limited to the MD nucleus results in a clinical presentation of severe inattentiveness, confusion (disorientation to time and place) and lethargy. Memory

Table 3.1 Thalamic nuclei, afferents, efferents and function

Nuclei	Afferent (Input)	Efferent (output)	Function
Anterior nuclei group			
• Anterior nucleus	Hippocampus/fornix, mammillary bodies	Cingulate gyrus	Explicit memory
Intralaminar nuclei			
• Centromedian	Globus pallidus, ARAS, sensory pathways	Striatum, cerebral cortex	Motor function. Relay for basal ganglia to cerebral
Lateral nuclei group			
• Lateral geniculate nucleus (LGN)	Retina	Primary visual cortex	Visual input to primary visual cortex
• Medial geniculate nucleus (MGN)	Inferior colliculus	Primary auditory cortex	Auditory inputs to primary auditory cortex
• Pulvinar	Tectum (extra lateral geniculate visual pathway)	Parietal, occipital, temporal heteromodal association cortex	Behavioral orientation to visual (and other sensory) stimuli
• Ventral anterior nucleus (VA)	Substantia nigra pars reticulata, globus pallidus interna, deep cerebellar nuclei	Frontal cortex, particularly pre-motor/ supplementary motor and prefrontal regions	Relay loop of basal ganglia and cerebellar inputs to cortex. Awareness and control of body movements/ coordination?
• Ventral lateral nucleus (VL)	Globus pallidus interna, substantia nigra pars compacta, deep cerebellar nuclei	Motor, premotor and supplementary motor cortex	Relay loop for basal ganglia and cerebellum to cortex
• Ventral posterior lateral nucleus (VPL)	Medial lemniscus/ dorsal columns, spinothalamic tract	Parietal somatosensory cortex	Somatosensory inputs to cortex
• Ventral posteromedial nucleus (VPM)	Trigeminal lemniscus, trigeminothalamic tract, gustatory inputs	Parietal somatosensory cortex	Somatosensory cranial nerve inputs (including taste) to cortex
• Lateral dorsal nucleus (LD)	Substantia nigra pars reticulata, globus pallidus interna, deep cerebellar nuclei	Frontal cortex, particularly pre-motor/ supplementary motor and prefrontal regions	Relay loop of basal ganglia and cerebellar inputs to cortex. Awareness and control of body movements/ coordination?
• Lateral posterior nucleus (LP)	Tectum (extra lateral geniculate visual pathway)	Parietal, occipital, temporal heteromodal association cortex	Behavioral orientation to visual (and other sensory) stimuli
• Ventral medial nucleus (VM)	Reticular formation (midbrain)	Diffuse afferents to cortex	Likely involved in maintaining awake conscious state

(continued)

Table 3.1 (continued)

Nuclei	Afferent (Input)	Efferent (output)	Function
Medial nuclear group			
• mediodorsal (MD)	Amygdala, limbic basal ganglia, olfactory cortex	Frontal cortex	Cognition (attention/memory), emotional functions. Major limbic/frontal relay pathway
Midline nuclei			
• internio-medial, internio-dorsal, paraventricular, parataenial, etc.	Amygdala, basal forebrain, hippocampus, hypothalamus	Amygdale, hippocampus, limbic cortex	Limbic pathways
Reticular nucleus			
• Reticular nucleus	Cerebral cortex, thalamic, all other thalamic nuclei, ARAS	All thalamic nuclei	Appears to regulate other thalamic nuclei

ARAS ascending reticular activating system

loss can also be present, but may or may not improve, depending upon the extent of the lesion. Damage to the MD nucleus results in EEG changes similar to that seen in Wernicke's encephalopathy (inability to generate EEG sleep patterns). In addition, damage to the intralaminar and/or reticular thalamic nuclei results in lethargy and coma, thought to reflect the diffuse reciprocal projections from the ascending reticular activating system (ARAS) and the cortex.

Key Points: Thalamic Nuclei

- Anterior nuclei group
  - Anterior nucleus—Memory input from hippocampus/mammillary body to cingulate gyrus
- Lateral nuclei group
  - LGN—Visual input from retina to primary visual cortex
  - MGN—Auditory input from inferior colliculus to auditory cortex
  - Pulvinar—Visual input from tectum to diffuse association cortex
  - VPL—Sensory from dorsal (posterior) column-medial lemniscus to primary sensory cortex
  - VPM—Sensory from trigeminal lemniscus/taste to primary sensory cortex
  - VL—Motor from basal ganglia and cerebellum to motor cortex
  - VA—Motor from basal ganglia and cerebellum to diffuse frontal cortex
- Medial nuclei group
  - Affective/mood and cognition input from amygdale, olfactory (piriform) cortex and nucleus basalis of Meynert to frontal cortex.

(continued)

(continued)

- Intralaminar nuclei group
  - Centromedian nucleus—Motor, arousal, sensory input to basal ganglia and cortex
- Reticular nuclei
  - From diffuse thalamic relay to cortex

Hypothalamus. The hypothalamus is located at the most inferior portion of the thalamus. The hypothalamus, together with the pituitary and adrenal glands, plays a major role in whole-body homeostasis and control and regulation of the autonomic nervous system. The hypothalamus is involved in the regulation of behavior which pertains to homeostatic functions, such as appetite and thirst as well as the body's efforts to regulate temperature. The hypothalamus is also involved in regulating sexual arousal as well as behaviors associated with fear and rage reactions. Together, the hypothalamus–pituitary–adrenal (HPA) axis (described in detail below) has also been implicated in the development and maintenance of mood disorders. Secretions from hypothalamic neurons regulate a number of physiological functions (see Table 3.2). The hormones involved in the HPA are detailed in Table 3.3.

Pituitary Gland. The pituitary gland is about the size of a pea and located inferior (underneath) to the hypothalamus. A small funnel shaped fiber tract called the infundibulum or infundibular stalk connects the pituitary gland to the base of the hypothalamus. The pituitary gland is referred to as "the master gland," because of its control of other endocrine organs. Hormones released from the pituitary gland regulate endocrine organs and processes throughout the body. See Table 3.3 for a summary of the hormones and function excreted by the pituitary gland.

Table 3.2 Major hypothalamic nuclei and associated hormone with function

Hypothalamic nucleus	Releasing hormone	Presumed function
Supraoptic	Oxytocin, vasopressin	
Paraventricular	Oxytocin, vasopressin, CRH	
Preoptic, septal	GnRH	
Arcuate	GnRH, GHRH, PRIH	
Periventricular	TRH, GHIH	

Table 3.3 Hormone and related function of the pituitary gland

Hormone	Function
Growth hormone	Stimulates cell production and growth
Prolactin	Stimulates milk production after giving birth
ACTH (adrenocorticotropic hormone)	Adrenal glands—released during arousal or stress. Causes production/release of adrenalin to increase metabolic availability.
TSH (thyroid-stimulating hormone)	Thyroid gland—causes release of thyroid hormone and affects metabolism rate.
FSH (follicle-stimulating hormone)	Ovaries and testes—regulates hair growth.
LH (luteinizing hormone)	Ovaries and testes.
Melanocyte-stimulating hormone	Control skin pigmentation
ADH (antidiuretic hormone)	Increase absorption of water into the blood by the kidneys
Oxytocin	Contract the uterus during childbirth and stimulate milk production

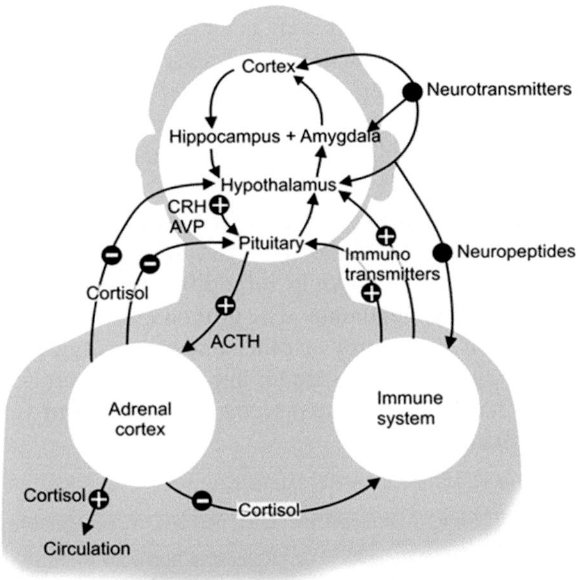

Fig. 3.5 Illustration of the hypothalamus–pituitary–adrenal axis function. *ACTH* adrenocorticotropic hormone, *AVP* vasopressin, *CRH* corticotropin releasing hormone

Stress and the Hypothalamus–Pituitary–Adrenal Axis

The hypothalamic–pituitary–adrenal (HPA) axis is a neuroendocrine control system for initiating, regulating and terminating the secretion of glucocorticoids in response to physical and psychological stressors. Glucocorticoids are cholesterol-derived hormones which travel through the blood stream and interact with glucocorticoid receptors to influence metabolic and inflammatory processes. Figure 3.5 summarizes the major afferent and efferent pathways of the HPA axis. The paraventricular nucleus (PVN) of the hypothalamus receives input from ascending brain systems in response to stress. Input to the PVN comes from brainstem aminergic and peptidergic systems in the nucleus of the solitary tract and the ventrolateral medulla and limbic system associated regions including the prefrontal cortex, the hippocampus and the amygdala. The hippocampus projections to the PVN are inhibitory while projections from the amygdale are excitatory. In addition, local hypothalamic interactions influence hormone release (see Table 3.3). These inputs trigger the release of corticotrophin releasing hormone (CRH) and vasopressin. These hormones act on the pituitary gland causing the release of adrenal corticotropic hormone (ACTH) which, in turn, travels through the blood and acts on the adrenal cortex causing the rapid release of corticosteroids (glucocorticoids) such as cortisol into the bloodstream. Cortisol affects various organ systems to promote homeostasis, but also provides negative feedback to the hypothalamus and the pituitary gland. The net effect of the cortisol inhibitory effect on the hypothalamus and pituitary gland is a reduction in the production of CRH, vasopressin (AVP) and ACTH. Chronic stress has been shown in animals and some human experiments to result in chronically elevated cortisol levels. Chronic stimulation of the HPA axis in response to stress has been argued to adversely affect the function of the HPA axis as well as associated interconnected brain areas (neocortex, hippocampus and amygdala). This dysfunction is thought to play a role in the development of symptoms in depressive and anxiety disorders (Tsigos & Chrousos, 2002).

Epithalamus. The epithalamus includes the **Pineal Gland** and the habenular nuclei. The function of the pineal gland in humans is not entirely clear, but is thought to be associated with the regulation of the circadian rhythm.

Third ventricle. Ventricle located between the lobes of the thalamus (see Fig. 3.8). It is connected to the lateral ventricles via the foramen of Monro (Interventricular Foramen) and with the fourth ventricle via the aqueduct of Sylvius (cerebral aqueduct).

Key Points: Hypothalamus, Pituitary and HPA axis

- Hypothalamus—Regulation of thirst, appetite, temperature, sexual arousal and fear/rage behaviors as well as affect activity of pituitary gland
- Pituitary gland—Regulation of endocrine functions

Telencephalon. Embryonic term that includes the following structures of the brain: Rhinencephalon, amygdala, hippocampus, basal ganglia, neocortex and the lateral ventricles (See Figs. 3.3 and 3.8).

The **Rhinencephalon** (also called piriform, pyriform or olfactory cortex) in humans is responsible for olfaction and includes the olfactory nerve, bulb, stria and tract and a portion of the amygdala.

Amygdala. Almond-shaped groups of nuclei located deep within the medial temporal lobes and just anterior to the hippocampi (see also Fig. 9.3). The amygdala receives input from somatosensory areas as well as limbic structures and is thought to be primarily involved in processing emotional states and associates memory with emotional functioning [i.e., involved in state-dependent learning (see Kandel et al., 2021 for review)].

Hippocampus. The hippocampi structures make up part of the mesial temporal lobes and are located beneath the cortical surface of the parahippocampal gyrus and just posterior to the amygdala. The hippocampus takes the form of an elongated tube thicker at its anterior end and becoming thin at its posterior (tail) end (see Fig. 9.3). The hippocampus plays a significant role in long-term memory formation and spatial navigation (see Sect. II below, and Chap. 9 for more details).

Basal Ganglia. A term to describe a group of nuclei beneath the cortex white matter, and include: caudate nucleus, putamen, globus pallidus external and internal (GPe and GPi), substantia nigra pars reticulata and pars compacta (SNr and SNc) and subthalamic nucleus (STN). The nucleus accumbens is also generally included in the basal ganglia (see Chap. 21 for detailed review of the structure and function of the basal ganglia). In general, the basal ganglia reflect a system of control and mediation of motor function between the cortex, thalamus and cerebellum. The major input to the basal ganglia is the striatum (caudate nucleus, putamen and nucleus accumbens). The SNr and GPi are the major output nuclei. The basal ganglia have two traditional "pathways" for processing information, a "direct" and "indirect" pathway. The "direct" pathway, which serves to increase (excite) the activity the thalamus, thereby increasing cortical motor activity. Alternatively, the "indirect" pathway, which serves to decrease activity of the thalamus, inhibits cortex activity (indirect inhibits). Once considered limited to purely motor control, the basal ganglia is recognized as having at least five (5) major channels that are parallel but also intermix: (1) Motor, (2) ocular motor, (3) dorsolateral, (4) orbitofrontal and (5) anterior cingulate/limbic/affective. Each component or channel maintains a somatotopic organization through the basal ganglia along with input and output cortices. The motor channel is the traditionally recognized function of the basal ganglia, and receives inputs from somatosensory and motor cortex to the putamen which project to the GPi/SNr (direct pathway) or projects to the GPe then STN and then the GPi/SNr (indirect pathway). Projections of the GPi/SNr go to the VL/VA of the thalamus and then to motor cortex (primary, pre and supplementary). The ocular motor channel receives input from frontal and parietal cortex to the caudate nucleus (body) to the direct and indirect pathways and the GPi/SNr to the MD and VA thalamic nuclei to the frontal eye fields. The dorsolateral prefrontal channel receives inputs from dorsolateral prefrontal as well as some motor and parietal cortex to the caudate nucleus (head) with the primary outputs (GPi/SNr) projecting to the MD and VA thalamic nuclei which projects to the dorsolateral prefrontal cortex. The orbitofrontal component is similar to the dorsolateral, except the input fibers are mostly from the lateral orbitofrontal region as well as some from the anterior temporal lobes. These cortical areas project to the caudate nucleus (head) and project to MD and VA thalamic nuclei, which projects back to the orbitofrontal regions. The anterior cingulate/limbic channel receives inputs from the anterior cingulate and temporal cortices (amygdala and hippocampus) to the nucleus accumbens and ventral caudate nucleus. Output from the basal ganglia is via the ventral pallidum that projects to the MD thalamic nuclei. This information is then projected to the anterior cingulate and orbital frontal cortex.

Key Points: Basal Ganglia

- Basal ganglia include the major input nuclei of the striatum (caudate nucleus, putamen and nucleus accumbens), the globus pallidus externa and substantia nigra pars compacta and major output nuclei (globus pallidus interna and substantia nigra pars compacta)
- Two major pathways: Direct and indirect
  - Direct end effect is to excite activity of cortex
  - Indirect "inhibits" and main effect is to inhibit activity of cortex
- Major channels of basal ganglia
  - Motor
  - Ocular motor
  - Dorsolateral prefrontal
  - Lateral orbitofrontal
  - Anterior cingulate/limbic/affective

Neocortex. A term defining the six outermost layers (see below) of neurons and underlying white matter. The neocortex is the newest part of the nervous system to develop and serves as the center of all higher mental functions such as speech and language, declarative memory (see Chap. 9), visuoperceptual/visuospatial skills and conscious thought. The neocortex is divided into right and left cerebral hemispheres by the longitudinal cerebral fissure. Information is passed directly between the two hemispheres via a massive collection of axons called the corpus callosum. The embryologic development of the cerebral hemispheres results in a wrinkled or folded appearance. The convex portions of the cerebral cortex are referred to as gyri, and the concave portions are referred to as sulci. While there are no two brains that have the exact same pattern of gyri and sulci, there are some gyri and sulci that are consistently maintained (central sulcus, Sylvian fissure), and form the basis for named landmarks that are used to divide the cerebral cortex into the frontal, parietal, temporal and occipital lobes. The region between the frontal and temporal operculum (a series of gyri and sulci lying underneath the frontal and temporal lobes) is identified as the insular cortex or lobe (see Figs. 3.1, 3.3, 3.6 and 3.7).

Each hemisphere of the neocortex is divided into four traditional "lobes": frontal, parietal, temporal and occipital. The insular region (or cortex) is cerebral cortex underlying the frontal and temporal operculum (making the "floor" of the Sylvian fissure) and is sometimes referred to as a "fifth" lobe of the human brain (see below). The frontal cortex is divided from the parietal by the central sulcus. The frontal lobe

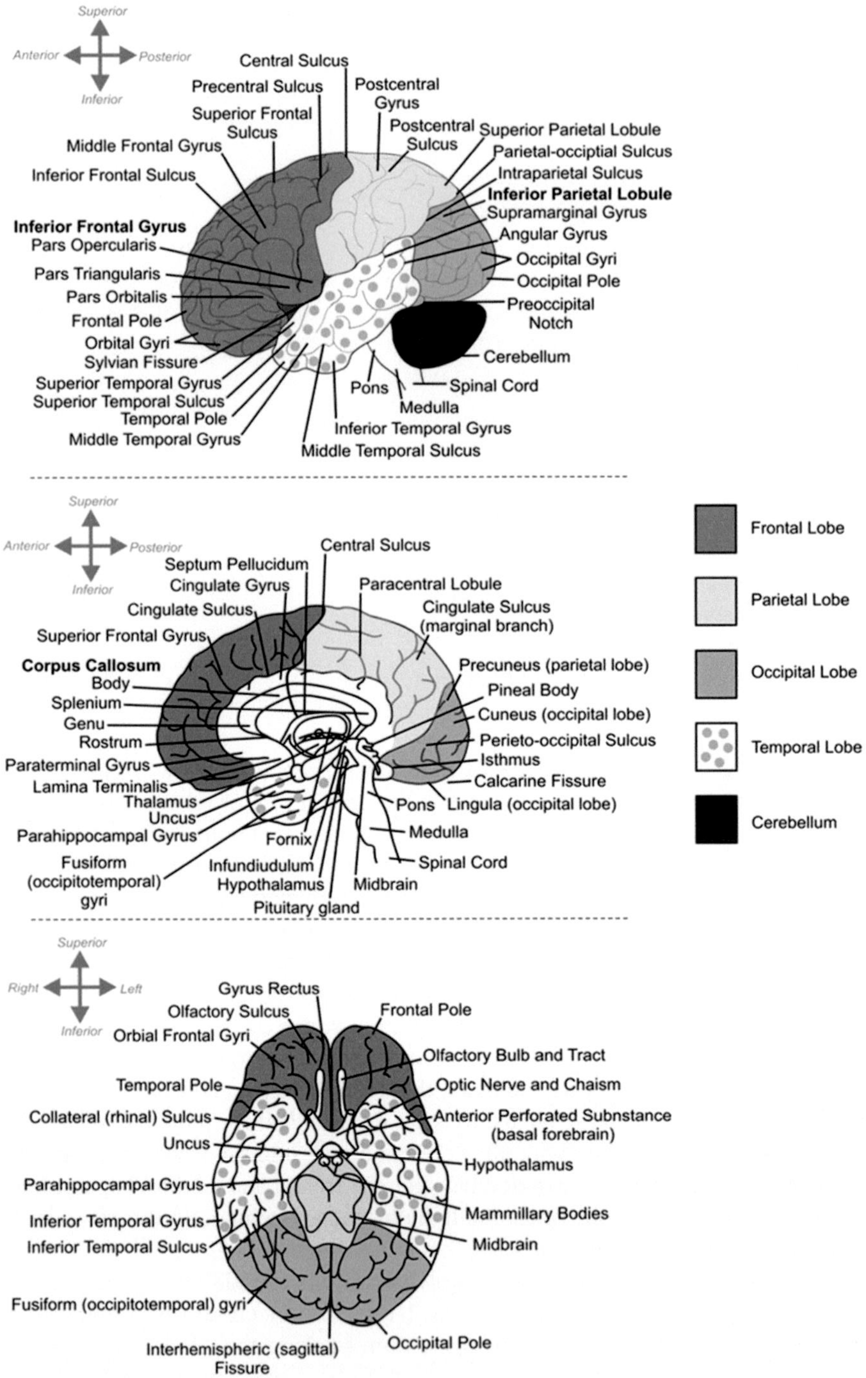

Fig. 3.6 Surface anatomy of the lateral, midsagittal and inferior views of the brain

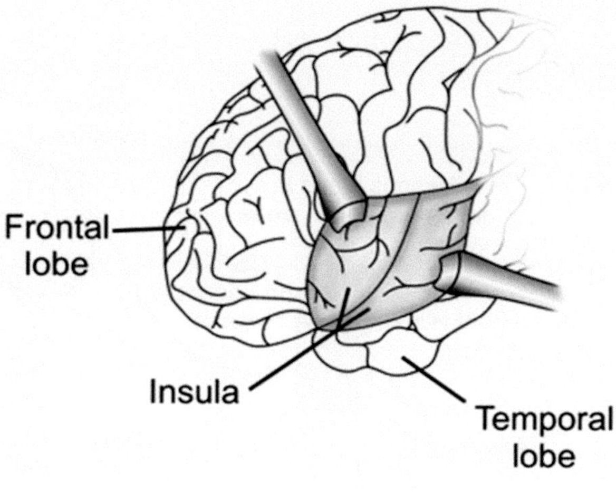

Fig. 3.7 Frontal and temporal operculum pulled back to show the underlying insular cortex (lobe)

is separated from the temporal lobe by the Sylvian fissure. The parietal and occipital lobes are separated by the parieto-occipital sulcus. The inferior portion of the parietal cortex is divided from the temporal cortex by the posterior portion of the Sylvian fissure (see Fig. 3.6).

Cerebrospinal Fluid

The entire central nervous system is bathed and suspended in a clear colorless fluid called Cerebrospinal Fluid (CSF). The CSF occupies the space between the arachnoid matter and pia matter surrounding the brain, and also fills the spaces within the brain formed by the ventricles, cisterns, sulci and the central canal of the spinal cord (see Fig. 3.8). The total volume of CSF in an adult human is about 125–150 ml. While the weight of the brain is anywhere from 1100–1400 g, the weight of the brain while suspended in CSF encased in the skull is decreased to about 50 g. CSF is produced by the choroid plexus in the lateral, third and fourth ventricles at a rate of about 400–700 ml/day (average is 500 ml/day) or about 20–22 ml/h, allowing for the "turnover" of all CSF 4 to 5 times per day. Figure 3.8 illustrates the circulation of CSF beginning in the lateral ventricles, through the Foramen of Monro to the third ventricle then through the aqueduct of Sylvius to the fourth ventricle and the foramens of Magendie (medial) or Luschka (lateral) to the subarachnoid space where it flows around brain stem and spinal cord and is reabsorbed by the arachnoid granulations that contain the arachnoid villus. Because the brain and spinal cord are encased in a closed skull and spinal canal surrounded by the meninges, changes in the volume of the brain, blood or cerebrospinal fluid will result in increased intracranial pressure (ICP). In adults, normal CSF pressure is 150–180 mm H_2O (or 8–14 mmHg) and is lower in children (30–60 mm H^2O). There are several common mechanisms of increased intracranial pressure, including (1) space occupying lesion, (2)

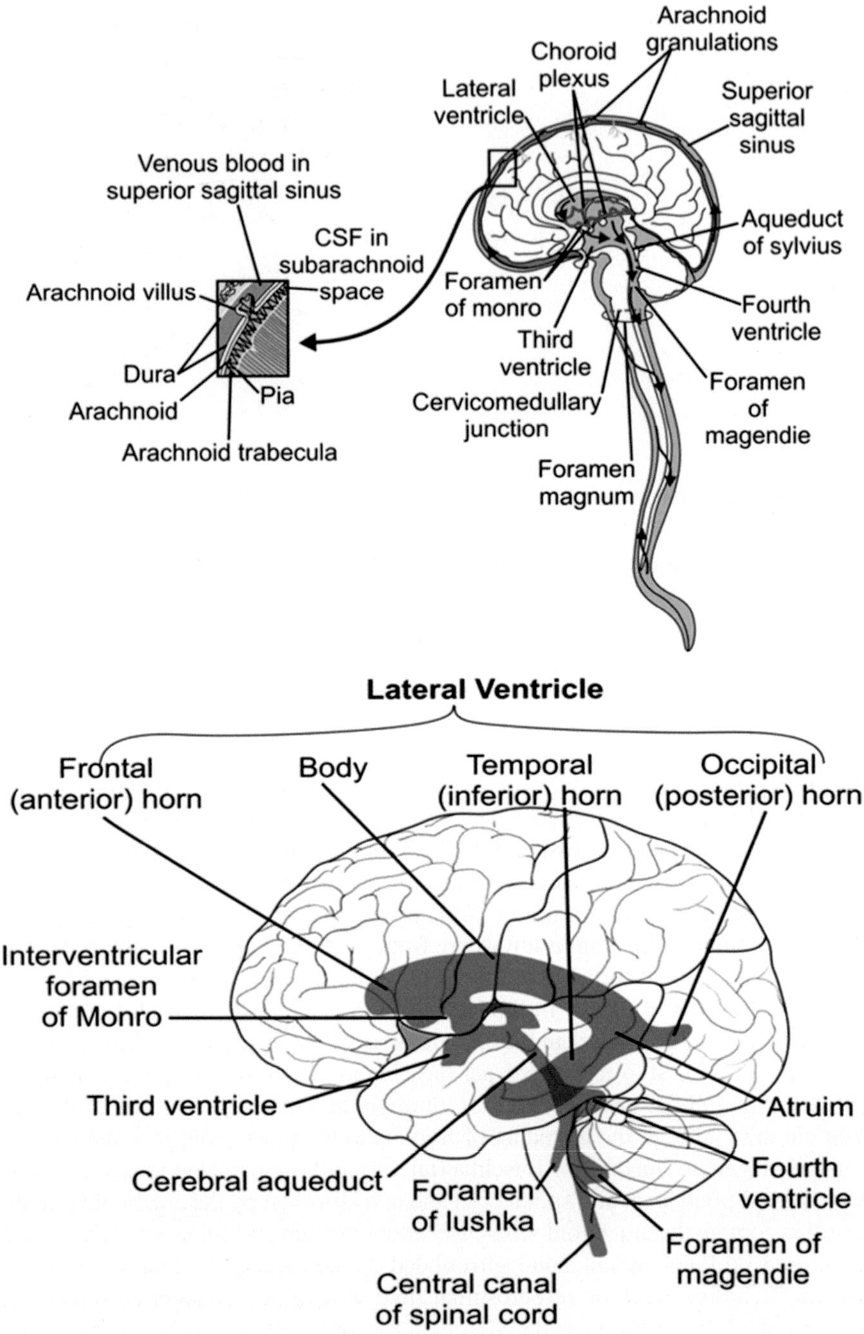

Fig. 3.8 Cerebral ventricles, cerebrospinal fluid production and flow

generalized brain swelling, (3) increased venous pressure (e.g., cerebral venous thrombosis or obstruction of jugular vein), (4) obstruction of the flow or absorption of CSF or (5) process increasing CSF volume (e.g., tumor increasing CSF production). The aspects of increased intracranial pressure due to the first three mechanisms mentioned above are reviewed in Chaps. 14 and 25. Interruptions in the flow or re-absorption of CSF can result in increased CSF pressure termed hydrocephalus. There are two general types of hydrocephalus, communicating and noncommunicating (obstructive) hydrocephalus. Communicating hydrocephalus is a term used to describe hydrocephalus not due to blockage of the CSF flow through the brain, but rather due to disrupted re-absorption of CSF. Noncommunicating (obstructive) hydrocephalus is a term used to describe increased CSF pressure when the flow of CSF fluid is obstructed. Common areas for obstructed flow are the foramen of Monro (between lateral and third ventricle) and the aqueduct of Sylvius (between third and fourth ventricles). It may be the result of meningitis or subarachnoid hemorrhage (see also Chap. 14).

Key Points: Cerebrospinal Fluid (CSF)
- Produced by choroid plexus in lateral, third and fourth ventricles
- CSF produced 20–22 ml (20–22 cc) per hour
- Total CSF volume is 125–150 ml (125–150 cc)
- Provides buoyancy to brain

Spinal Cord

The bony skull attaches to the spinal cord at the base of the skull by means of a series of dense fibrous ligamentous attachments. There are 33 vertebrae which make up the spinal column, and are divided into seven cervical, twelve thoracic, five lumbar, five fused sacral and four fused coccygeal vertebrae (see Figs. 3.1 and 3.10). The bony spinal column houses the spinal cord. The spinal cord begins at the base of the skull where it is the continuation of the brain stem, medulla oblongata. The spinal cord exits the skull through the foramen magnum (Fig. 3.9). Thirty-one pairs of spinal nerve roots exit the spine at each vertebral level between vertebral processes. The nerve roots derived from the dorsal aspect of the spinal cord make up the spinal **sensory nerve roots**. The nerve roots derived from the ventral aspect of the spinal cord make up the spinal **motor nerve roots**. The body of the spinal cord terminates at the lower border of the first lumbar vertebrae, L1, into the conus medularis. The conus medularis terminates as the cauda equina, a filamentous structure which gives rise to the lumbar, sacral and coccygeal spinal nerve roots. The spinal cord itself generally ends around the L1 vertebral body, so one needs to distinguish between spinal cord level and the vertebral level.

Fig. 3.9 Skull base and foramen magnum

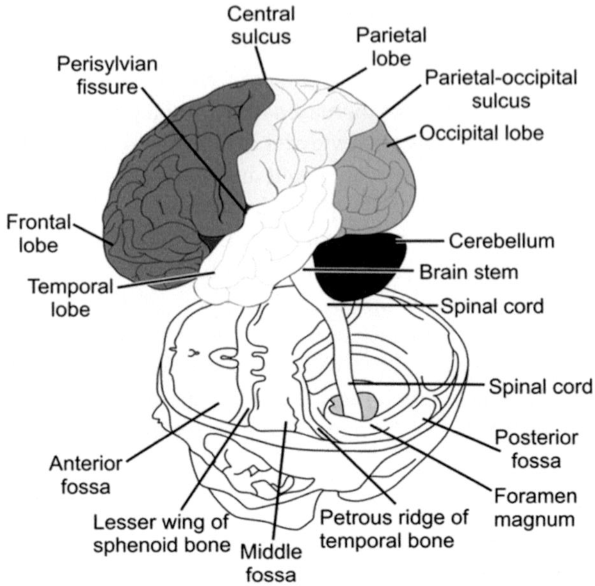

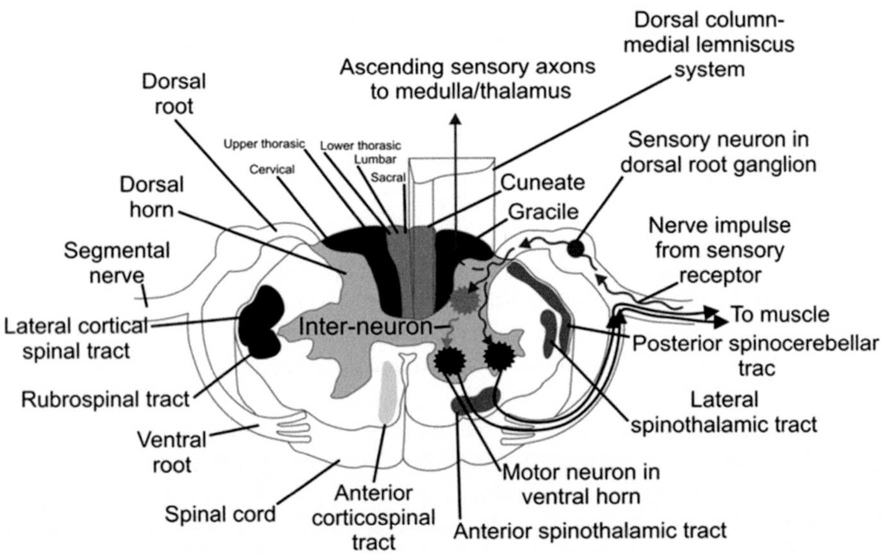

Fig. 3.10 Location of major afferent and efferent pathways in spinal cord including dorsal and ventral roots

Figure 3.10 provides an overview for the organization of the spinal cord. Unlike the brain with gray matter (neurons) on the exterior and white matter on the interior, the organization of the spinal cord has gray matter (neurons) on the interior and white matter (axons) on the periphery. The major afferent (sensory) and efferent (motor) pathways are discussed in detail below. For now, we direct the reader to appreciate that the sensory pathways are generally in the dorsal (posterior) aspect of the spinal cord while the motor afferents are generally in the ventral (anterior) area of the spinal cord.

Key Points: Spinal Cord
- Dorsal (toward back) root is sensory
- Ventral (toward stomach) root is motor
- Clinically Important Reflex levels
  - C5/6—Biceps and Brachioradialis
  - C7—Triceps
  - C8—Finger flexors
  - L3—Knee
  - S1—Ankle
- Clinically Important Dermatomes
  - C2/3—Posterior head and neck
  - C5—Anterior shoulder
  - C6—Thumb
  - C7—Index and middle fingers
  - C7/8—Ring finger
  - C8—Pinky (little finger)
  - T1—Inner forearm
  - T2—Upper inner arm
  - T4/5—Nipple
  - T10—Umbilicus
  - L2—Anterior upper thigh
  - L3—Knee
  - S1—Toes fourth toe and pinky

Peripheral Nervous System (PNS)

The peripheral nervous system innervates the organs and muscles of the body and is classically divided into the motor and sensory components, which applies both to segmental nerve roots from the spinal cord as well as the cranial nerves (see Fig. 3.11). The sensory and motor components incorporate what is termed the autonomic nervous system.

Components of the Peripheral Nervous System

Cranial Nerves are part of the PNS. There are 12 paired cranial nerves. These are illustrated in Fig. 3.1 with respect to the overall organization of the PNS. The function and assessment of the 12 cranial nerves are reviewed in Chap. 2.

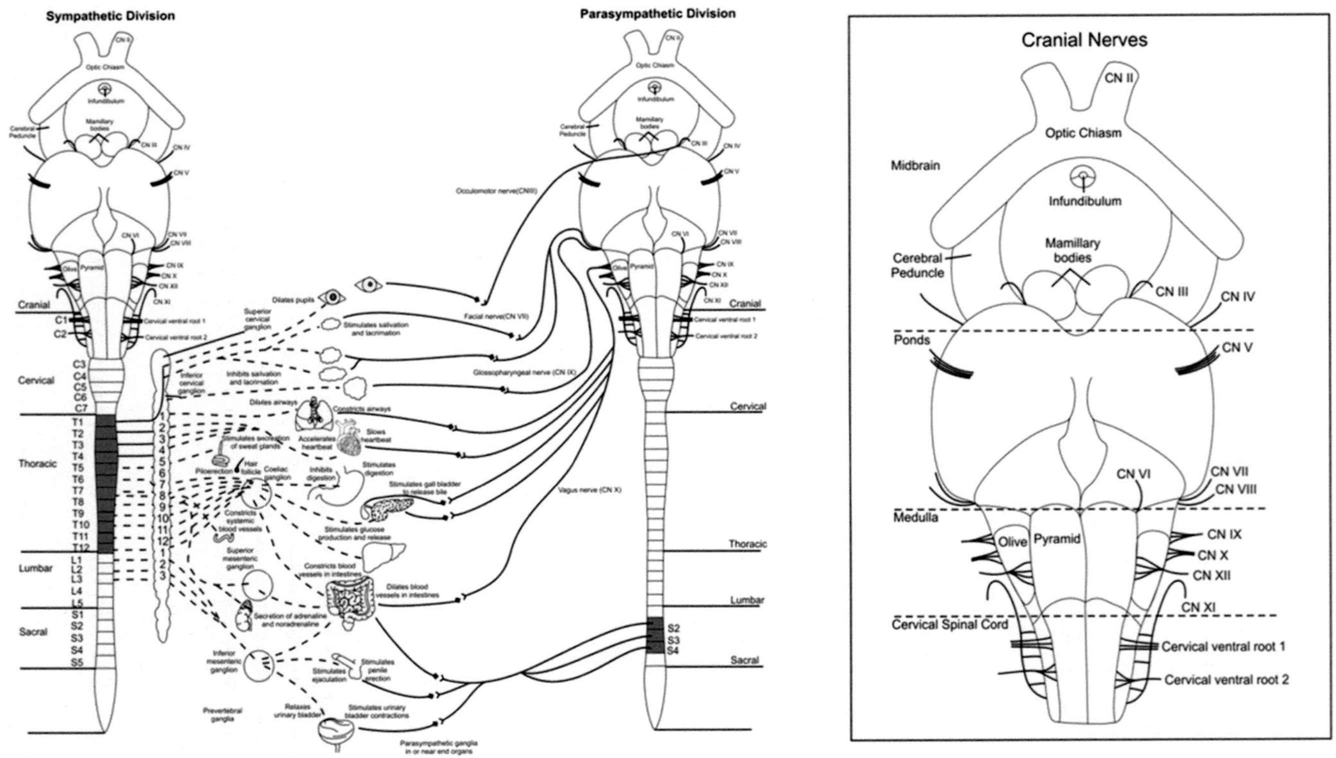

Fig. 3.11 Sympathetic and parasympathetic divisions of the peripheral nervous system. *Note*: The sympathetic nervous system is mostly associated with "flight or fight" responses, while the parasympathetic nervous system is involved in "rest and digest" functions

Dorsal nerve roots carry afferent sensory information from the peripheral nervous system to the sensory neurons of the spinal cord (CNS). The neurons that make up the dorsal root ganglia, the primary sensory neurons, are outside of the CNS, but have axon processes that enter and ascend in the spinal cord to synapse with secondary sensory neurons (see Fig. 3.26).

Ventral nerve roots carry efferent motor information from the upper motor neurons (e.g., corticospinal tract) to the endings in skeletal muscle.

Plexus is a term that refers to an elaborate meshwork of peripheral nerves [e.g., brachial plexus (arm) or lumbosacral plexus (leg)] where axons from several adjacent nerve roots (e.g., C5 to T1 in the brachial plexus) are recombined into named peripheral nerves, such as the median nerve which contains motor axons from several nerve roots.

Autonomic Nervous System

The autonomic nervous system is divided into the **sympathetic** and **parasympathetic** nervous system. The sympathetic nervous system arises from thoracic and lumbar spinal levels and releases *norepinephrine* onto end organs. The sympathetic nervous system is involved in "fight or flight" functions. The parasympathetic nervous system is the "counterpart" to the sympathetic nervous system. The parasympathetic nervous system is associated with "rest and digest" functions, such as increasing gastric secretions and peristalsis, slowing heart rate and decreasing pupil size. The parasympathetic nervous system arises from the cranial nerves and from the sacral spinal levels (S2 – S4) and primarily utilizes the neurotransmitter *acetylcholine* for its actions on the end organs. While a comprehensive description of the actions of the parasympathetic and sympathetic nervous system is beyond the scope of this chapter, Fig. 3.11 provides a detailed illustration of the actions of the parasympathetic and sympathetic systems on organs and tissues.

Key Points: Peripheral Nervous System

- Cranial Nerves
  - 12 pairs (eyes, vision, face, hearing, tongue, larynx, pharynx, heart)
- Spinal Nerves
  - Sensory (dorsal) component
  - Motor (ventral) component
- Autonomic Nervous system (ANS)
  - Sympathetic nervous system

    "Rest and digest" functions
    Arises from cranial nerves and sacral (S2-S4) spinal levels
    Acetylcholine neurotransmitter on end organs.

(continued)

(continued)

- Sympathetic nervous system

  "Flight or fight" functions
  Arises from thoracic and upper lumbar (T1 to L2) spinal levels
  Norepinephrine neurotransmitter on end organs

- Enteric nervous system

  Innervates walls of digestive tract
  Controls peristalsis and gastrointestinal secretion with other ANS

Cerebrovascular System Overview

Blood supply to the brain is provided by two paired sets of arteries, forming an anterior and posterior circulatory system to the brain (see Fig. 3.12; see also Chap. 14 for further details). The paired internal carotid arteries (ICA) arise from the common carotid artery on each side. The ICA enters the skull through the carotid canal and supplies blood to the anterior portion of the brain and intracranial structures. The major arteries providing vascular supply to the brain derived from the ICA include the anterior cerebral artery, middle cerebral artery and the posterior communicating artery (see Chap. 14 for further details). The MCA provides blood to most of the basal ganglia through a variety of small penetrating arteries termed lenticulostriate arteries (see Fig. 3.13). The ophthalmic artery and the anterior choroidal also originate from the ICA.

The *vertebral artery* supplies the posterior portion of the brain (see Fig. 3.14). The vertebral artery is a branch of the subclavian artery which ascends through the foramina of the transverse processes of the upper six cervical vertebrae, winds behind the articular process of C1 and enters the skull through the foramen magnum. The paired vertebral arteries traverse across the anterior surface of the medulla oblongata and join at the pontomedullary junction (base of the pons) to form the single basilar artery. Along the course the vertebral arteries give off three primary branches which provide blood supply to the brain stem and cerebellum: (1) posterior spinal artery, (2) anterior spinal artery and (3) posterior inferior cerebellar artery (PICA). The posterior spinal

Key Points: Mnemonic for Arteries That Originate from the Internal Carotid Artery (Proximal to Distal): OPAAM

Ophthalmic artery
  Posterior communicating artery (PCoA)
  Anterior choroidal artery
  Anterior cerebral artery (ACA)
  Middle cerebral artery (MCA)

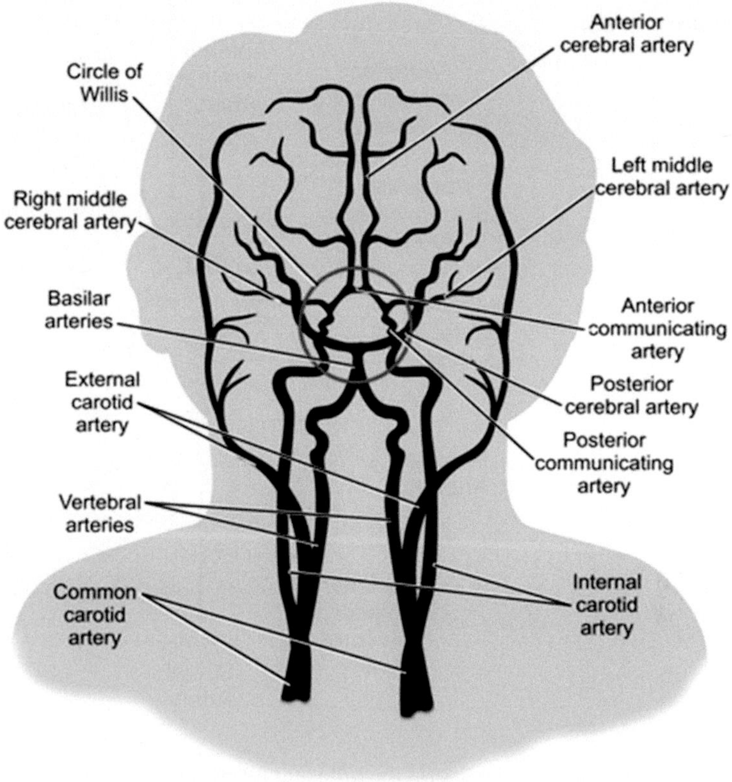

Fig. 3.12 Blood supply to the brain

Fig. 3.13 Coronal view of MCA inferior and superior divisions and lenticulostriate arteries

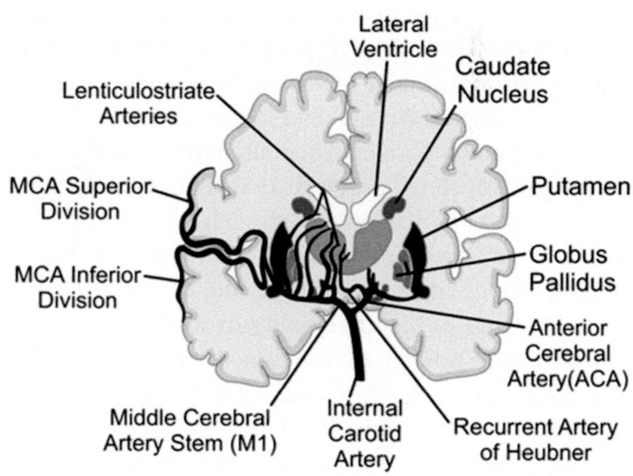

arteries (not shown) provide blood supply to the posterior 1/3 of the spinal cord (one side of the cord for each posterior spinal artery). The anterior spinal artery runs along the ventral midline of the spinal cord and supplies the anterior 2/3 of the spinal cord.

Fig. 3.14 Cerebral vasculature and the circle of Willis

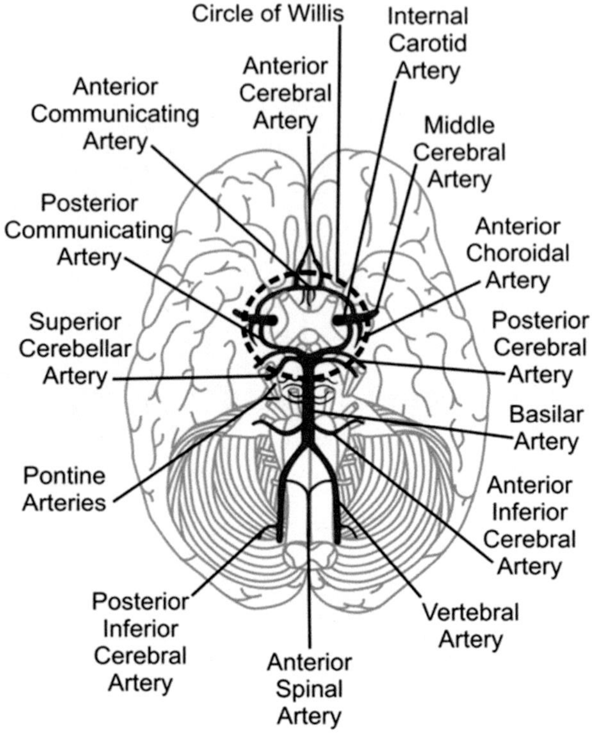

The PICA provides blood to the lateral medulla and inferior surface of the cerebellum. The basilar artery gives rise to short paramedian arteries as well as the Anterior Inferior Cerebellar artery (AICA) and the Superior Cerebellar artery (SCA) before bifurcating to form the two Posterior Cerebral arteries (PCAs). The two AICAs supply the anterior portions of the ventral surface of the cerebellum (e.g., flocculus) and the caudal pons. The SCAs profuse the remaining superior surface of the cerebellum, rostral pons and caudal midbrain. The PCA's perfuse primarily the mesial temporal lobes and occipital (mesial and lateral) lobes. The PCAs can also provide blood flow to the occipitotemporal and occipitoparietal cortices. Branches of the PCA perfuse the subthalamic nucleus, posterior thalamus, hypothalamus and splenium of the corpus callosum (see Fig. 3.12 and Chap. 14).

The major branches of the internal carotid artery and the basilar artery combine to form a structure referred to as the *Circle of Willis* (see Fig. 3.14). The circle of Willis is a ring of blood vessels surrounding the optic chiasm and pituitary stalk. It consists of the posterior communicating arteries which arise from the ICA and connect the posterior cerebral arteries to the anterior circulation. The anterior communicating artery connects the right and left anterior cerebral arteries. The posterior cerebral arteries are connected at the bifurcation of the basilar artery. A complete circle of Willis allows collateral blood flow to the posterior and anterior cerebrovascular systems. However, there is substantial variability to the circle of Willis, and a hemodynamically complete circle of Willis is found in only 21%–52% of healthy subjects.

Venous System of the Brain

The veins of the brain carry away deoxygenated blood and flow into a series of sinuses formed by spaces left between the meninges (dura). Cortical veins drain into the superior sagittal sinus, which flow to paired transverse sinuses. The transverse sinuses are at the junction of the tentorium cerebelli and the dura. The transverse sinuses flow along the occipital bone to the petrous bone. At the petrous bone, the two transverse sinuses form the sigmoid sinus which makes an “S” shape through the skull to form the internal Jugular vein (see Fig. 3.15). The inferior sagittal sinus lies at the inferior edge of the falx cerebri, and drains the mesial brain structures. The flow of the inferior sagittal sinus is anterior (rostral) to posterior (caudal) and then forms the straight sinus which runs directly posterior and connects with the superior sagittal sinus and the two transverse sinuses at the sinus confluence (Torcula). The superior sagittal sinus lies in the interhemispheric fissure and flows posteriorly to the sinus confluence. The straight sinus also receives blood from the great vein of Galen, which drains blood from the basal ganglia and thalamus. The cavernous sinus is at the base of the brain (anterior portion) and lies in the sella turcica. The cavernous sinus drains blood posterior to the superior and inferior petrosal sinuses which then drain into the transverse sinus.

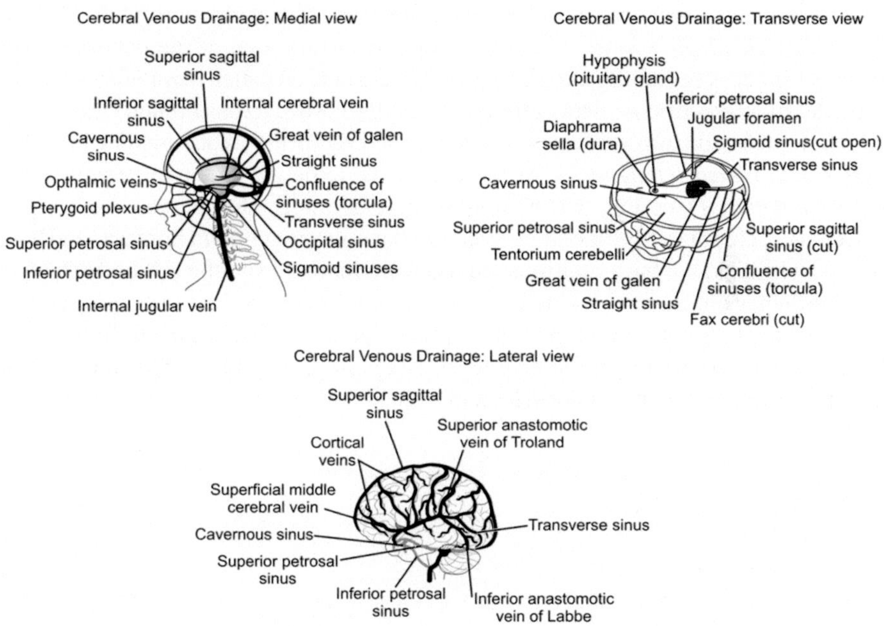

Fig. 3.15 Venous system of brain including sinuses

Key Points: Venous System of Brain
- Reflects the network of veins and sinuses to carry venous blood to heart
- Sinuses formed by spaces in dura.
- Sinuses drain both midsagitally (superior sagittal sinus) and laterally (transverse sinuses)
- Transverse sinuses form sigmoid sinus which forms the Jugular vein

Microanatomic Organization and Function of Nervous System

It has been estimated the human brain consists of about 100 billion neurons, which have unique characteristics allowing the cells to alter their function and activity in response to stimuli from other neurons and supporting cells called glial cells. A neuron consists of (1) cell body (soma), (2) dendrites and (3) an axon (see Figs. 3.16 and 3.17). The *soma* contains the nucleus of the cell, which houses the genes and chromosomes of the cell. The soma also includes the *endoplasmic reticulum* where proteins are synthesized by the cell, and the *Golgi bodies* that package proteins for transportation via *microfilaments* (tiny microtubules making up a "transportation" network) to all areas of the cell. The powerhouse of neurons, like all cells, is the *mitochondria. Dendrites* are branchlike processes of the neuron that receive most electrochemical inputs into a neuron. Dendrites have tiny protrusions along the surface called *dendritic spines*, which increase the surface area of the dendrites. The *axon* is a process beginning as a slight swell in the neuron called *axon hillock*, which provides most electrochemical output of the neuron. Most axons branch extensively, which are termed *axon collaterals*. Toward the end of the axon, smaller branches may occur, called *telodendria*. At the end of the axon are the axon terminals (or *terminal buttons)* (see Fig. 3.16). Neurons may be multipolar, bipolar or, rarely in vertebrates, unipolar. Multipolar neurons are the most common in humans, and have one axon hillock, but have multiple dendrites originating from the cell body. A bipolar neuron has one axon and only one primary dendrite extending in opposite directions and are typically found in sensory processes (e.g., vision, olfaction, hearing). Unipolar neurons are mostly in invertebrates and have only one extension from the cell body (soma) which is a dendrite and axon.

Key Points: Neurons
- ~100 billion neurons in brain
- ~300 billion glial cells
- Neuron cells made of soma, axon and dendrites

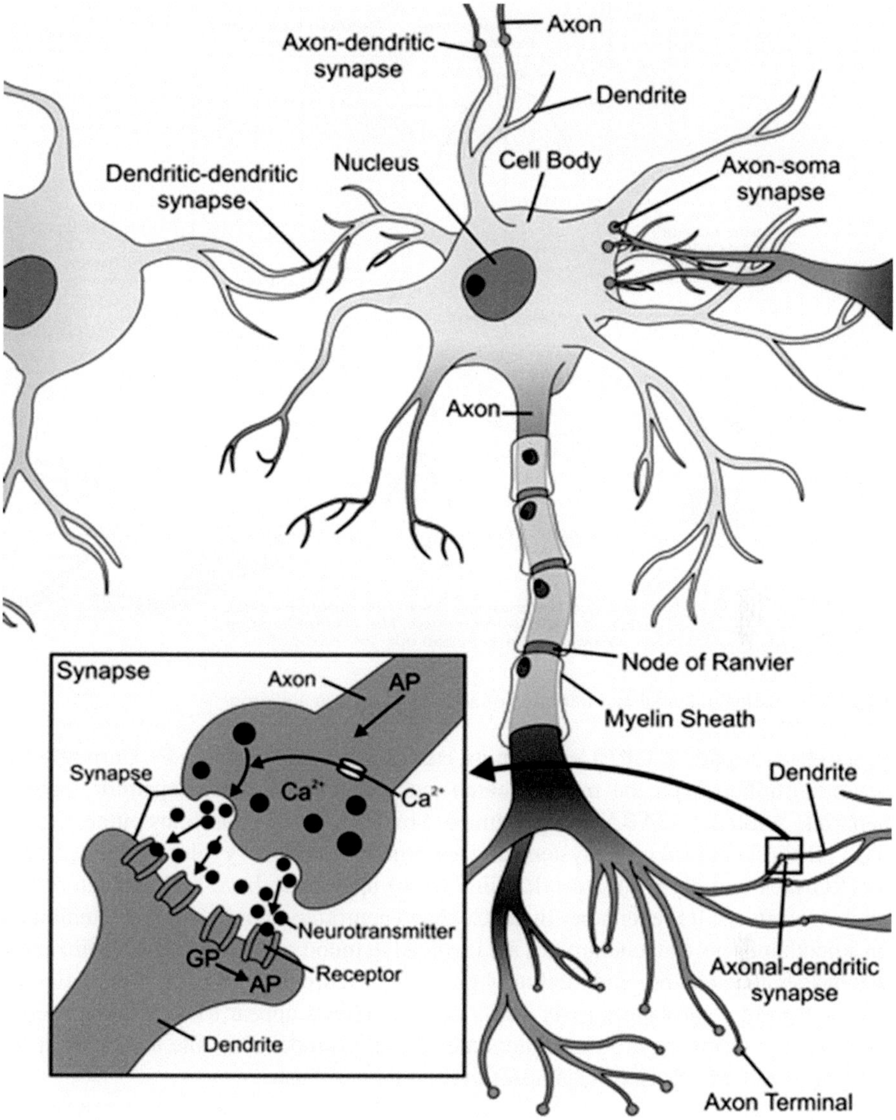

Fig. 3.16 Components of neuron and common types of synapses

Major Neurotransmitter Systems of the CNS

Hundreds of chemicals have been identified which satisfy the definition of a neurotransmitter; however, some are much more abundant and have had more research as playing a significant role in cognitive and mood/behavioral functions. Common neurotransmitters can be classified into those of small molecules [acetylcholine, Gamma Aminobutyric Acid (GABA), glutamate and glycine), catecholamines [e.g., dopamine, epinephrine, histamine, norepinephrine and serotonin] and neuropeptides [e.g., calcitonin

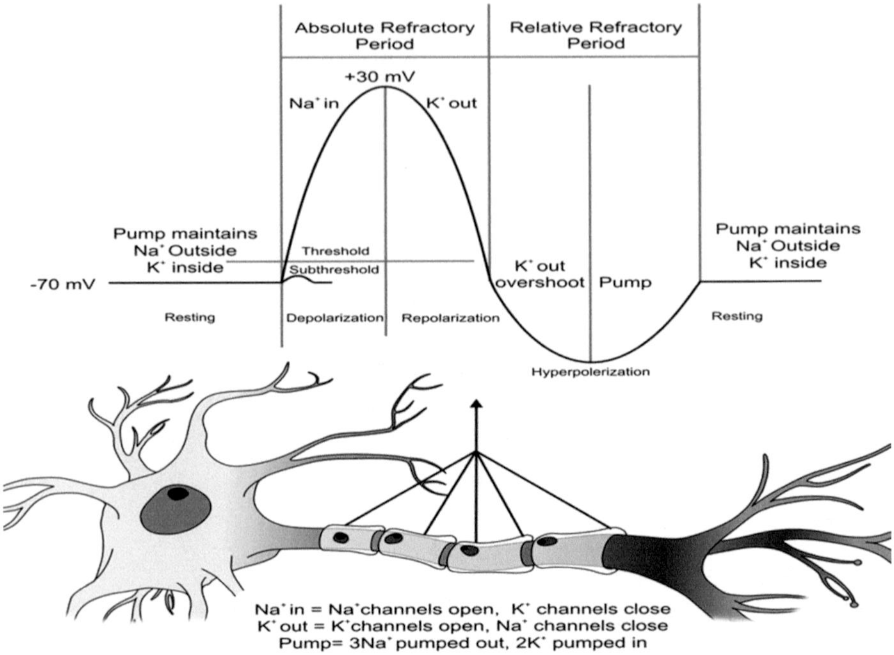

Fig. 3.17 Resting potential and initiation of action potential in a neuron

gene-related peptide (CGRP), endorphins, enkephalins and Substance P). Currently, the neurotransmitters with the most research include: acetylcholine, dopamine, norepinephrine, serotonin, GABA and glutamate. Small molecule neurotransmitters are the most plentiful in the nervous system, and are primarily excitatory (glutamate) or inhibitory (GABA and glycine). Acetylcholine (Ach) appears to have both excitatory and inhibitory effects. It is excitatory in the CNS and neuromuscular junction and inhibitory on smooth muscle. Catecholamines are involved in mood modulation and stabilization, and have both excitatory and inhibitory processes. Neuropeptides form a large class of neurotransmitter substances (over 100), but their effects appear to be through second messenger systems. Neurotransmitters are typically produced in the soma (or at the terminals) and are released at synapses to exert their influence.

Key Points: Neurotransmitter Actions

- Neurotransmitters "Communicate" between neurons by binding to receptors
- Receptors are located in chemical synapses
- Chemical synapses are where many clinical disorders are expressed either in abnormalities in the receptor binding or the production or release of neurotransmitters
- Chemical synapses are site of action for the behavioral effects of drugs
- Receptors may have multiple binding sites for multiple neurotransmitters

(continued)

(continued)

- Neurotransmitter actions are either "fast acting" or neuromodulatory
  - Fast acting is binding that generally results in EPSP or IPSP within milliseconds via ligand-gated ion channels
  - Neuromodulatory effects occur within seconds to minutes of binding, and can alter the structure, function and expression of the neuron, often via G-protein-coupled receptors and activation of second messenger systems

Small Molecule Neurotransmitters

Acetylcholine acts as a neuromodulator in the CNS, generally having an inhibitory influence. Acetylcholine also is thought to play a major role in memory functioning, with reduced concentration of acetylcholine thought to account for some of the cognitive loss associated with Alzheimer's disease. Furthermore, medications with an anticholinergic affect (e.g., tricyclic medications) are known to adversely affect learning and memory, particularly among older adults. The Nucleus Basalis of Meynert is a major source of acetylcholine producing neuronal projections to the neocortex. It is a collection of neuronal cell bodies located within the substantia innominata. (See Fig. 3.18).

GABA is the primary inhibitory neurotransmitter in the human CNS, and is found in all brain regions (see Fig. 3.19). GABA is synthesized from neuronal bodies throughout the brain. GABA action tends to be "fast" inhibition, most commonly through the $GABA_A$ receptors but also through $GABA_B$ receptors. Activation of the GABA receptor leads to an influx of Cl- and other anions which hyperpolarize the neuron (reduce the negative charge) such that action potential generation is unlikely (IPSP). The action of GABA can be thought of as counteracting the principle excitatory neurotransmitter *glutamate* (see below). There are 20 subtypes of $GABA_A$ receptors identified, and can be found in the synapse and postsynaptic membranes on dendrites.

Fig. 3.18 Acetylcholine system

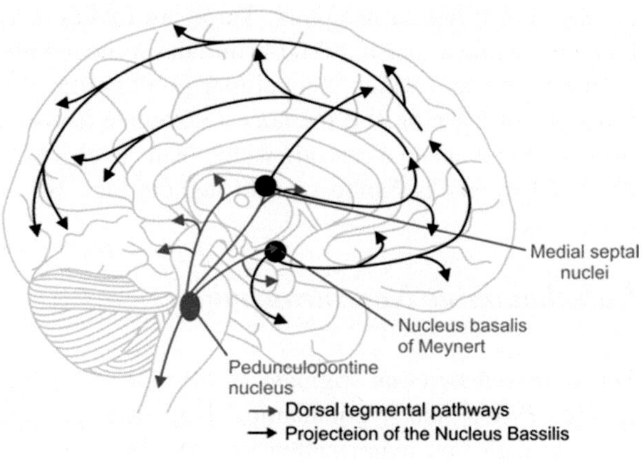

Fig. 3.19 GABA system

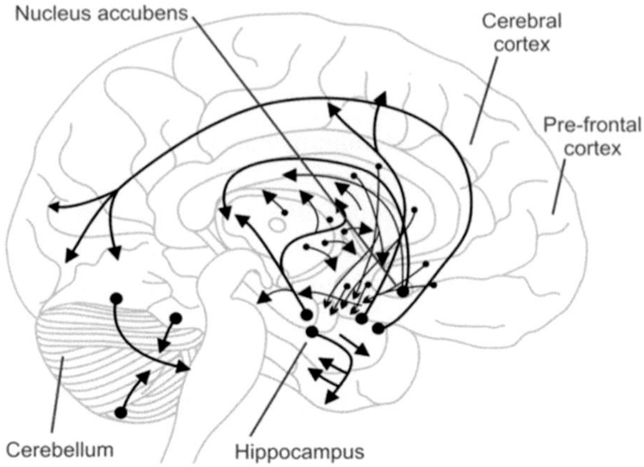

Fig. 3.20 Glutamate system

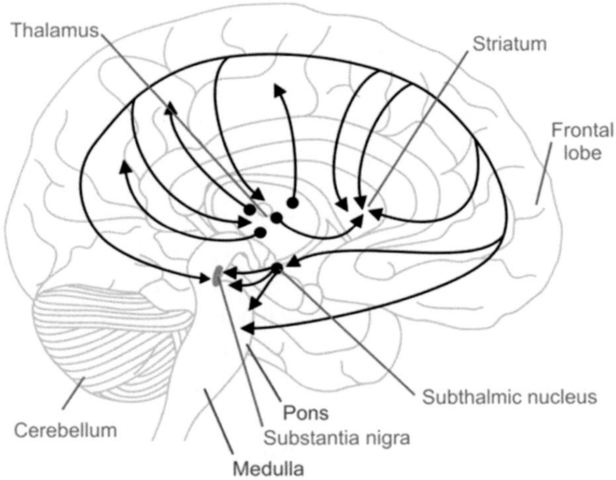

Glutamate is always excitatory in the human nervous system and plays a central role in long-term potentiation in the hippocampus and neocortex. Glutamate binds to at least four different receptors. Three are traditionally described as shorter acting receptors while a fourth, NMDA, initiates a second messenger system termed long-term potentiation, which is a cellular process thought to account for the cognitive functions of learning and memory. Glutamate is also a neurotoxin when in excess, believed to be due to a cascade which leads to excess Ca^{+2} ions and lead to neuronal death. Glutamate is synthesized throughout the CNS (see Fig. 3.20).

Catecholamine Neurotransmitters

Dopaminergic neurons originate in substantia nigra pars compacta, ventral tegmental area (VTA) and hypothalamus. Dopaminergic neurons project throughout the CNS through four major pathways; the mesocortical and mesolimbic pathway, the

Fig. 3.21 Dopamine system

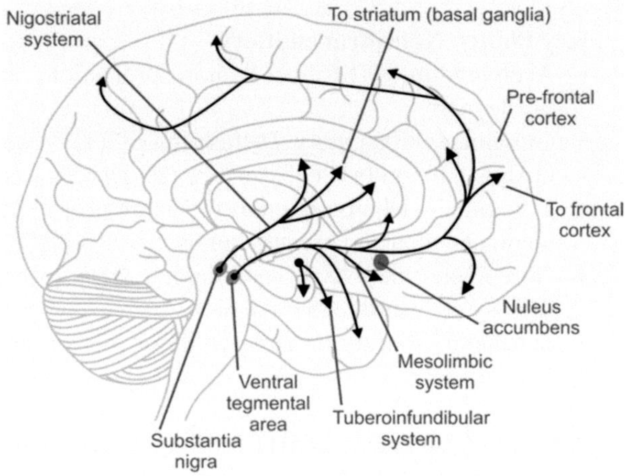

Fig. 3.22 Norepinephrine system

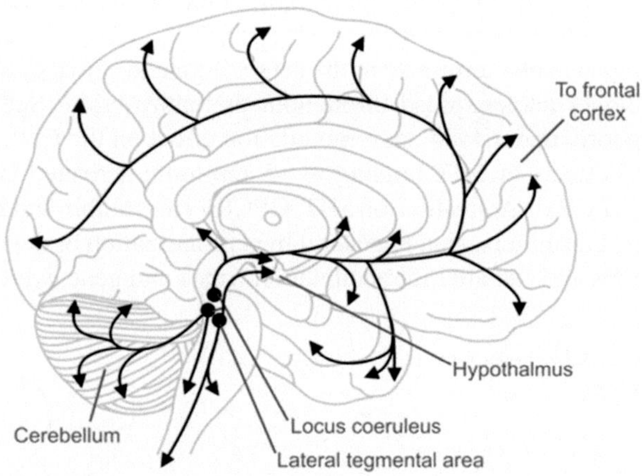

nigrostriatal pathway, and the tuberoinfundibular pathway (see Fig. 3.21). Mesocortical dopamine neurons project from the ventral tegmental area to the pre-frontal cortex. Mesolimbic dopamine neurons project from the ventral tegmental area to the nucleus accumbens via the hippocampus and amygdala. The nigrostriatal pathway consists of neurons in the substantia nigra that project to the caudate and putamen. The tuberoinfundibular dopamine neurons project from the hypothalamus to the pituitary gland.

Norepinephrine (noradrenergic) neurons originate both in the locus coeruleus and the lateral tegmental area (see Fig. 3.22). The noradrenergic neurons in the locus coeruleus project to many areas of the brain. The lateral tegmental noradrenergic neurons mainly project to the hypothalamus. The noradrenergic system in the brain effects alertness and arousal and influences the reward system.

Key Points: Neurotransmitters
- Acetylcholine—Diffuse. Major projection area is nucleus basalis of Meynert
- Glutamate—Excitatory. Diffuse through nervous system
- GABA—Inhibitory. Diffuse through nervous system
- Dopamine—Neuromodulatory. Major projection areas are SNc, ventral tegmental area and hypothalamus
- Norepinephrine—Neuromodulatory. Major projection areas are locus coeruleus and lateral tegmental area
- Serotonin—Neuromodulatory. Major projection area is raphe nuclei.

Serotonin (also known as 5HT for 5-hydroxytryptamine) is a monoamine synthesized from tryptophan. A major source of 5HT is from the neurons of the raphe nuclei. The raphe nuclei are centered around the reticular formation, grouped and distributed along the entire length of the brainstem. Axons from these neurons reach almost every part of the central nervous system. Neuron projections in the lower raphe nuclei terminate in the cerebellum and spinal cord while the projections of the higher nuclei spread throughout the entire brain (See Fig. 3.23). Serotonin has a poorly understood neuromodulation effect on the CNS, which appears to be related to effects of 5HT binding to 15 serotonin-activated G-Protein-Coupled Receptors (GPCRs). Activation of 5HT GPCRs can inhibit and/or excite the release of neurotransmitters, lead to general hyperpolarization or depolarization of associated neurons and can alter intracellular enzymes and gene expression.

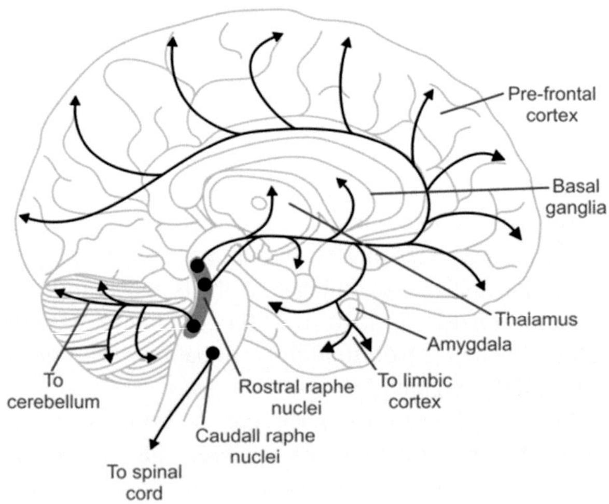

Fig. 3.23 Serotonin system

Cellular Organization of the Cortex

The outer layer of the cerebral cortex is composed of six quite distinct layers identified by the different density and type of neurons that make up each cell layer (see Fig. 3.24). The principle neuronal cell type found in the gray matter is the pyramidal cell. Pyramidal cells extend axons out of the gray matter to remote portions of the nervous system forming the white matter projection fibers making up the subcortical white matter. The neurocortical cell layers are labeled from the surface of the brain inward, and are as follows:

- **Layer I** (molecular layer) Dendrites and axons from other layers.
- **Layer II** (small pyramidal layer) Cortical–cortical connections.
- **Layer III** (medium pyramidal layer) Cortical–cortical connections.
- **Layer IV** (granular layer) receives inputs from thalamus.
- **Layer V** (large pyramidal layer) sends outputs to subcortical structures (other than thalamus).
- **Layer VI** (polymorphic layer) sends outputs to the thalamus.

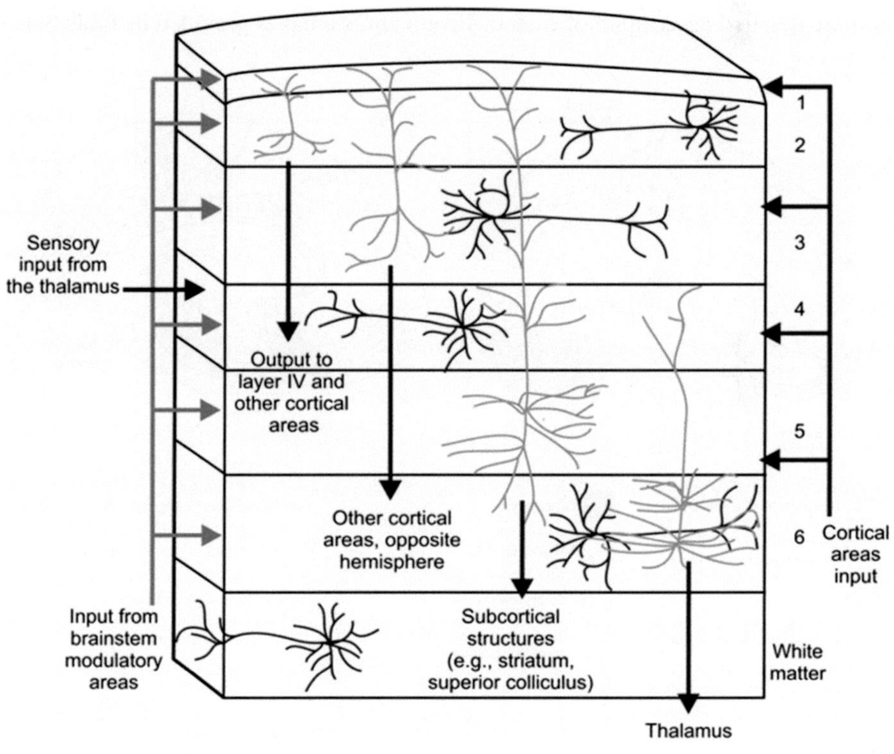

Fig. 3.24 Cellular organization of neocortex

- The thickness of the cell layers varies according to the function of that area of the cortex. Primary motor cortex has a thicker layer V, because there are many more cell bodies than, say, layer IV. However, layer IV is thicker in a sensory area, such as primary visual cortex.

Structural Classification of the Neocortex: Cytoarchitecture

The regions of the cerebral cortex were divided into discrete regions by Korbinian *Brodmann* in 1909 based on *cytoarchitectonic areas* (areas based on the microscopic appearance of different regions of the cerebral cortex) reviewed above. Often referred to as "Brodmann's Areas" (BA), the areas identified by Brodmann are sometimes used to describe specific functional regions of the brain (e.g., Brodmann's area 44 is often used to identify Broca's area, although Broca's area includes BA 45 as well). While potentially useful, the structural designation of areas is problematic in variation from individual to individual. Figure 3.25 provides a lateral and midsagittal view of the brain that identifies the location of each of Brodmann's areas as well as a general description of its function (e.g., motor, sensory, cognition, emotion, etc.). A more detailed description of each of Brodmann's areas is provided in Table 3.4.

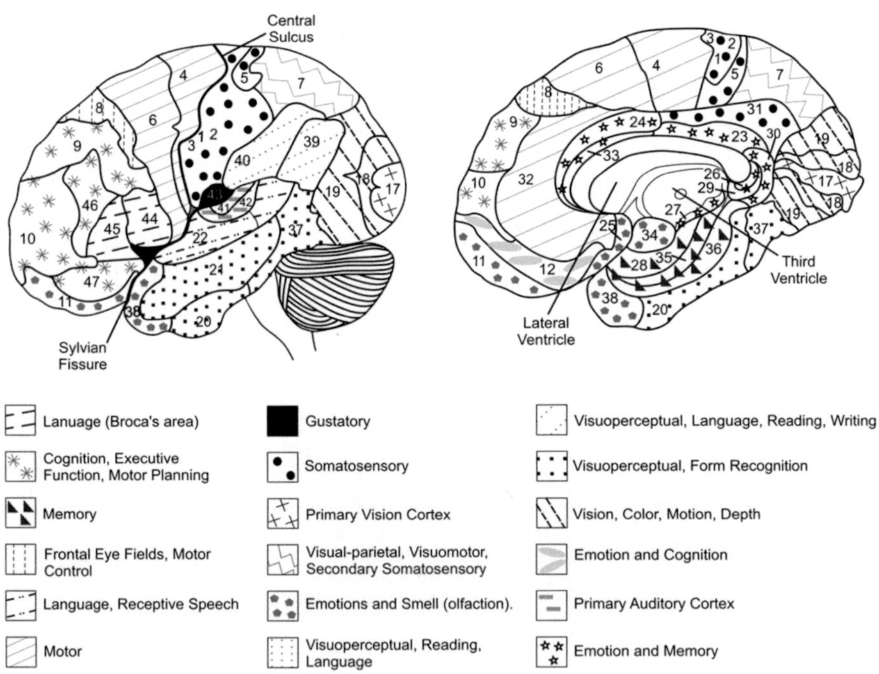

Fig. 3.25 Brodmann's areas and associated function

Table 3.4 Brodmann's area, presumed function and functional area

Brodmann's area	Function	Functional area	Location
1, 2, 3	Two-point discrimination, vibration sense/light touch	Primary somatosensory area	Postcentral gyrus
4	Voluntary motor movement	Primary motor cortex	Precentral gyrus
5	Stereognosis, tactile agnosia, apraxia	Secondary somatosensory cortex (posterior parietal association area). Part of visual dorsal stream.	Superior parietal lobule
6	Motor planning and movement (limb and eyes)	Supplementary motor cortex, premotor cortex, frontal eye fields	Precentral gyrus and rostral cortices.
7	Visuomotor function and visuoperceptual skills	Posterior parietal association area. Part of visual dorsal stream.	Superior parietal lobule
8	Eye movements (saccades)	Frontal eye fields	Superior frontal (middle) gyrus (medial frontal lobe)
9, 10, 11, 12	Planned movement, problem-solving, organization	Prefrontal association cortex	Superior and middle frontal lobe (rostral to frontal eye fields)
13, 14, 15, 16	Psychic awareness of viscero-sensory feelings, stomach/gastric sensations, emotional aspect to sensory feelings, heart rate/blood pressure perception, psychic evaluation of temperature and body states	Limbic cortex, heteromodal association cortex	Insular cortex
17	Visual perception	Primary visual cortex (V1)	Calcarine fissure
18	Depth perception, vision	Secondary visual cortex (V2)	Medial and lateral occipital gyri
19	Color, depth perception, motion	Associative visual cortex (V3)	Medial and lateral
20, 21	Visual naming, auditory naming, visual perception of form	Inferotemporal cortex	Inferior and middle temporal gyrus
22	Auditory perception/speech sounds	Auditory association cortex (Wernicke's area)	Superior temporal gyrus

(continued)

Table 3.4 (continued)

Brodmann's area	Function	Functional area	Location
23–27	Emotional regulation/ perception, memory	Limbic association cortex, subgenual cingulate, part of hippocampal formation	Cingulate gyrus, BA 25 in caudal orbitofrontal area, Rostral parahippocampal gyrus (presubiculum)
28	Memory, emotional experience, smell	Limbic cortex, olfactory cortex	Parahippocampal gyrus (entorhinal cortex)
29–33	Emotional experience, memory	Limbic association cortex	Cingulate gyrus retrosplenial area,
34–36	Memory, emotions, olfactory (smell)	Limbic cortex, olfactory cortex	Parahippocampal gyrus
37	Reading, speech, vision	Parietal-temporal-occipital association cortex	Middle and inferior temporal gyri at temporo-occipital junction
38	Smell, emotions, speech/ naming	Primary olfactory cortex, limbic association cortex	Anterior temporal pole
39	Reading, speech, vision, dysgraphia, dyscalculia, visual working memory	Parietal-temporal-occipital heteromodal association cortex	Inferior parietal lobule (angular gyrus)
40	Reading, speech, vision, dysgraphia, dyscalculia, visual working memory	Parietal-temporal-occipital heteromodal association cortex	Inferior parietal lobule (supramarginal gyrus)
41	Perception of sound	Primary auditory cortex	Heschl's gyrus and superior temporal gyrus
42	Hearing of speech sounds	Secondary auditory cortex	Medial Heschl's gyrus and superior temporal gyrus
43	Taste	Gustatory association cortex	Insular cortex, frontoparietal operculum
44	Expressive speech	Broca's area, lateral premotor cortex	Inferior frontal gyrus (frontal operculum)
45	Expressive speech, planning, reasoning	Prefrontal association cortex	Inferior frontal gyrus (frontal operculum)
46	Planning, reasoning, sequencing, abstraction	Frontal heteromodal association cortex	(Middle frontal gyrus) Dorsolateral prefrontal cortex
47	Judgment, insight, reasoning, altering behavior with feedback	Ventrolateral prefrontal cortex	Inferior frontal gyrus (frontal operculum)
48	?	Association cortex	Medial surface of temporal lobe
52	?	Association cortex	Parainsular area between temporal lobe and insula

Key Points: Brodmann's Areas Important in Neuropsychological Evaluations

- 1–3 (primary somatosensory cortex of postcentral gyrus)
- 4, 6 (primary motor and supplemental motor)
- 5 (tertiary somatosensory area)
- 7 (heteromodal visuomotor, visuoperceptual function)
- 8 (frontal eye fields)
- 9–12 (prefrontal association areas)
- 17–19 (primary and secondary visual cortex)
- 20–21 (visual inferior temporal area for recognition of visual forms)
- 22 (Wernicke's area/higher-order auditory cortex)
- 23–27 (limbic/emotional functions)
- 39 (parietal-temporal-occipital heteromodal association cortex for higher order vision/reading/speech)
- 41 (Primary auditory cortex/Heschl's gyrus)
- 44 (Broca's area/motor speech area)
- 45–47 (prefrontal heteromodal association cortex for behavioral planning, reasoning, etc.).

Functional Classification of the Neocortex

The areas of the cerebral cortex can also be divided in terms of functional subtype areas. While several different terms have been used, these generally reflect efforts to describe regions of the brain in terms of the behaviors or level of processing that may occur within the region. Five main functional subtypes have been identified: Limbic, paralimbic, primary sensory-motor, primary association and heteromodal (multi-modal) association cortex.

Limbic cortex includes cortical zones termed corticoid and allocortex. The limbic cortex zone includes portions of the basal forebrain and amygdala, piriform (or pyriform) cortex (also identified as olfactory cortex). The basal forebrain structures (septal region, substantia innominata) and amygdala, and part of the olfactory cortex are designated corticoid since the organization of neurons is not well differentiated, and no clear layers can be identified. The hippocampus and piriform/pyriform (also known as paleocortex) cortex are the two areas of the cortex having two bands of neurons and has been termed allocortex. The piriform/pyriform cortex is localized to the most rostral part of the parahippocampal gyrus and the dorsal part of the uncus. The hippocampus complex is posterior (caudal) to the piriform cortex in the parahippocampal gyrus. The limbic zone is associated with function of the hypothalamus and is associated with regulation of autonomic functions, emotions, hormonal balance, and memory, and motivation.

Paralimbic cortex (also known as mesocortex) has an increased structural complexity over the limbic cortex (corticoid and allocortex) but does not have the 6 layer cortical organization of the neocortex. The paralimbic cortex reflects a "transition area" of cortex between limbic and associative cortex and involves five regions: (1) orbitofrontal cortex, (2) insula cortex/lobe, (3) temporal pole, (4) parts of the parahippocampal gyrus (e.g., entorhinal area) and (5) the cingulate gyrus. The functional aspects of the paralimbic cortex are associated with primary limbic functions, including bridging autonomic function perception, emotions, hormonal functions, memory and motivation.

Primary sensory-motor cortex refers to the cortex where primary auditory, motor and somatosensory functions occur. Primary auditory cortex refers to Heschl's gyrus in the Sylvian fissure. Primary motor refers to cortex of the precentral gyrus. Primary somatosensory cortex is cortex of the postcentral gyrus. Primary visual cortex (striate or calcarine cortex) refers to the cortex on the sides of the calcarine fissure in the occipital lobe. These primary sensory-motor cortex areas project to unimodal and heteromodal (multimodal) cortex areas.

Unimodal cortex is composed of six-layered cortex that is modality specific. This area of the cortex has neurons that respond to stimulation of a single sensory modality, and afferents to this cortex only come from primary sensory (or motor) cortex and/or other unimodal cortex.

Heteromodal cortex refers to cortex that receives afferent (input) from multiple sensory (or motor) unimodal (or other heteromodal) cortex. Neurons in heteromodal cortex respond to multiple sensory (and/or motor) stimuli. Damage to heteromodal cortex results in disruptions of functions not confined to one sensory (or motor) modality (e.g., not just deafness or blindness).

Functional Neuroanatomy: Structural and Functional Networks

Below we provide a brief overview of the functional neuroanatomy of the central nervous system. We first review the major afferent (sensory) and efferent (motor) systems. We then review the major divisions of the neocortex (frontal, occipital, parietal and temporal lobes). The reader is also directed to review chapters that identify neuropsychological functions for more detailed description of the functional neuroanatomy.

*Major Afferent (Sensory) and Efferent (Motor) Pathways of the CNS*The spinal cord has afferent (sensory) and efferent (motor) pathways. In general, motor pathways are anterior or lateral. Sensory pathways are lateral and ventral (see Fig. 3.9). Below, we summarize the major efferent (sensory) pathways, followed by afferent (motor) pathways through the central nervous system.

Major Sensory (Afferent) Pathways

There are two principle somatosensory pathways: the rapidly conducting and highly localized dorsal column- medial lemniscus system and the slowly conducting and diffuse, anterolateral system. Both convey information from a peripheral receptor to the cortex via three neurons. The primary afferent has a specialized peripheral termination which is the sensor. The soma of the primary afferent is located in the dorsal root ganglion and makes a synaptic connection with a secondary neuron in the ipsilateral spinal cord. The secondary neuron axon crosses the midline and terminates in the thalamus. The tertiary neuron makes synaptic connection with the secondary neuron in the thalamus and projects to layer IV of the cortex.

Dorsal column-medial lemniscus. The dorsal column is the rapidly conducting system which carries fine tactile sensation (e.g., two-point discrimination), vibration and proprioception (see Fig. 3.26). The dorsal columns can be divided into the cuneate and gracile pathways. The gracile pathway carries information from the legs and

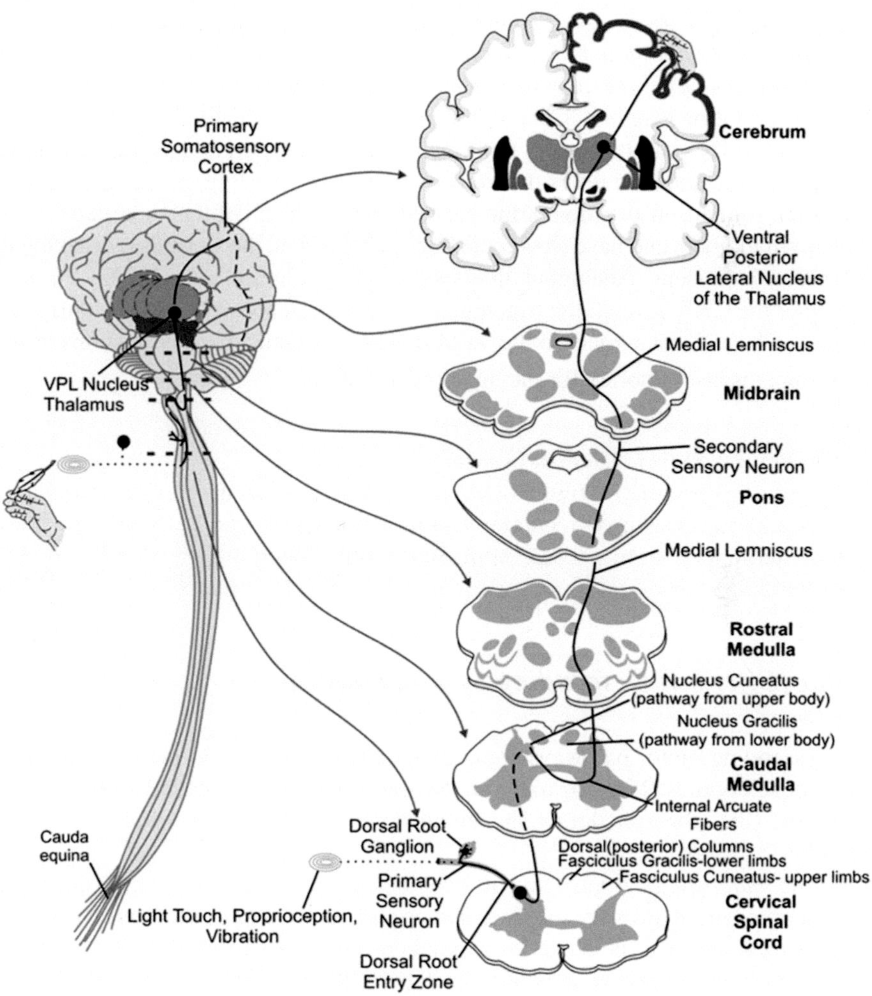

Fig. 3.26 Dorsal (posterior) column-medial lemniscus pathway

trunk, while the cuneate tracts carry signals from the upper extremities (see Fig. 3.10). The primary afferent neurons form synaptic connections with the second-order neuron in the gracile and cuneate nuclei in the dorsal medulla. The second-order neurons then cross the midline as the internal arcuate fibers and become the medial lemniscus. The medial lemniscus continues anterior toward the ventral posterior lateral (VPL) nucleus of the thalamus. Fibers of facial sensation from the trigeminal nerve join the medial lemniscus and project to the thalamic ventral posterior medial (VPM) nucleus. From the thalamus, sensory information is projected to somatosensory cortex (Brodmann's areas 3, 1 and 2, where area 3 gets most of the projections). Projects to cerebral cortex are primarily to level IV (granular layer).

Anterolateral system. The sensory neurons in the joints, muscles, organs and skin project to the lateral and anterior tracts (spinothalamic tract, spinomesenthalamic and spinoreticular tract) in the spinal cord, carrying information about *pain, temperature and "crude" touch.* These pathways project primarily to ventral posterior lateral (VPL) nuclei of the thalamus, but also to intralaminar thalamic nuclei, and the reticular formation (see Fig. 3.27). While many of the anterolateral sensory fibers do *not* project to the parietal cortex, terminating in the basal ganglia, midbrain and/or thalamus; some thalamic fibers do project via the posterior limb of the internal capsule to the somatosensory area of the parietal cortex. Fibers of the anterolateral system are small fibers and have slower conduction rates than the large fibers making up the medial lemniscus. Analogous fibers subserving pain and temperature from the face enter the CNS through the trigeminal nerve, then descend in the spinal trigeminal tract. These fibers project to the VPM thalamic nucleus, with projections to primary somatosensory cortex for the third-order neurons.

Key Points: Major Afferent (Sensory) Pathways

- Dorsal (Posterior) Column/Medial Lemniscus—Decussates at medulla. Vibration sense, proprioception and light touch
- Anterolateral—Pain, temperature and "crude" touch

Motor (Efferent) Descending System Pathways

The descending motor pathways are organized into four sets of tracts based on the origin of cell bodies. The four tracts are the corticospinal (also called corticobulbospinal) tract, the rubrospinal tract, the reticulospinal tract and the vestibulospinal tract (see Figs. 3.28 and 3.29).

Corticobulbospinal tract. The corticobulbospinal (corticospinal) tract originates from neurons in the primary motor cortex as well as from some neurons in the supplementary motor and the posterior parietal cortex. Axons from these neurons project to the brainstem and spinal cord (see Fig. 3.28). This tract comprises the entire voluntary cortical drive to brainstem and spinal motor systems. The system is traditionally divided into a corticospinal (limbs) and corticobulbar (head) tract. Axons

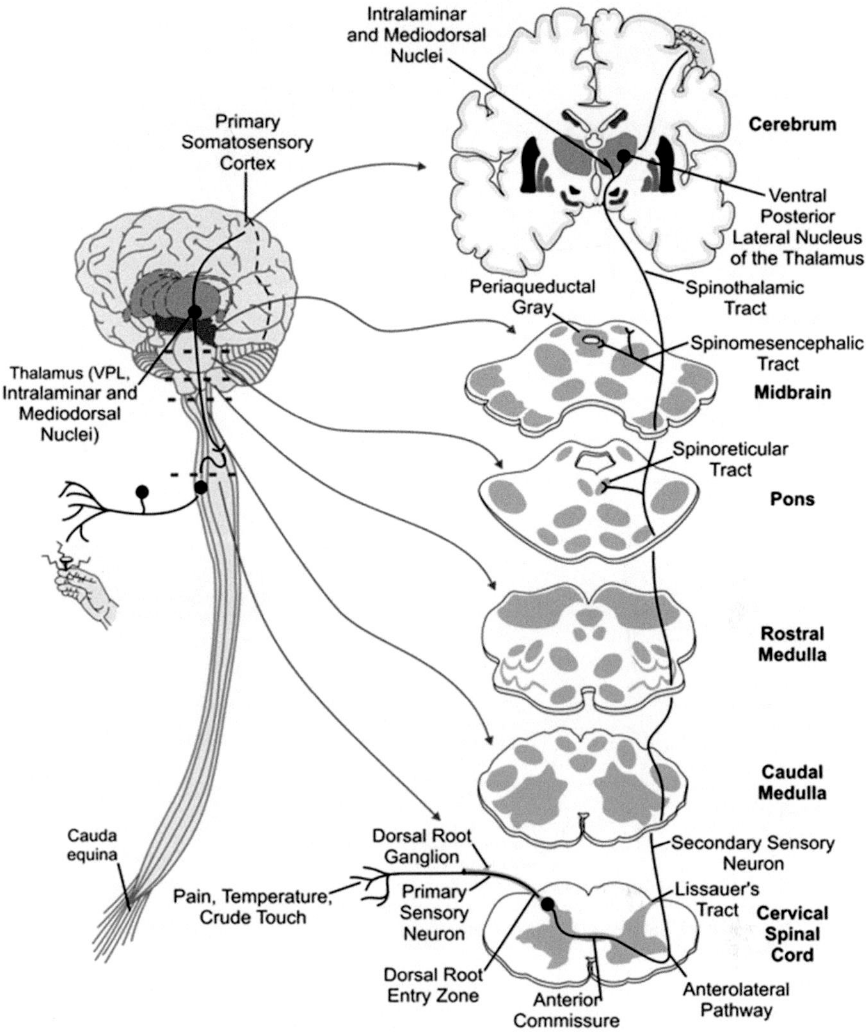

Fig. 3.27 Anterolateral (spinothalamic) pathway

collect together forming the corona radiata and then become increasingly closely bundled forming part of the posterior limb of the internal capsule. Axons of the corticobulbar division synapse in the red nucleus and the various motor nuclei of the cranial nerves. The majority of the axons of the corticospinal division cross at the pyramidal decussation, becoming the *lateral corticospinal tract*. About 10% of the corticospinal neurons continue uncrossed as the *anterior corticospinal* tract but cross the midline at the level of their termination. Corticospinal neurons terminate primarily on interneurons of the spinal cord.

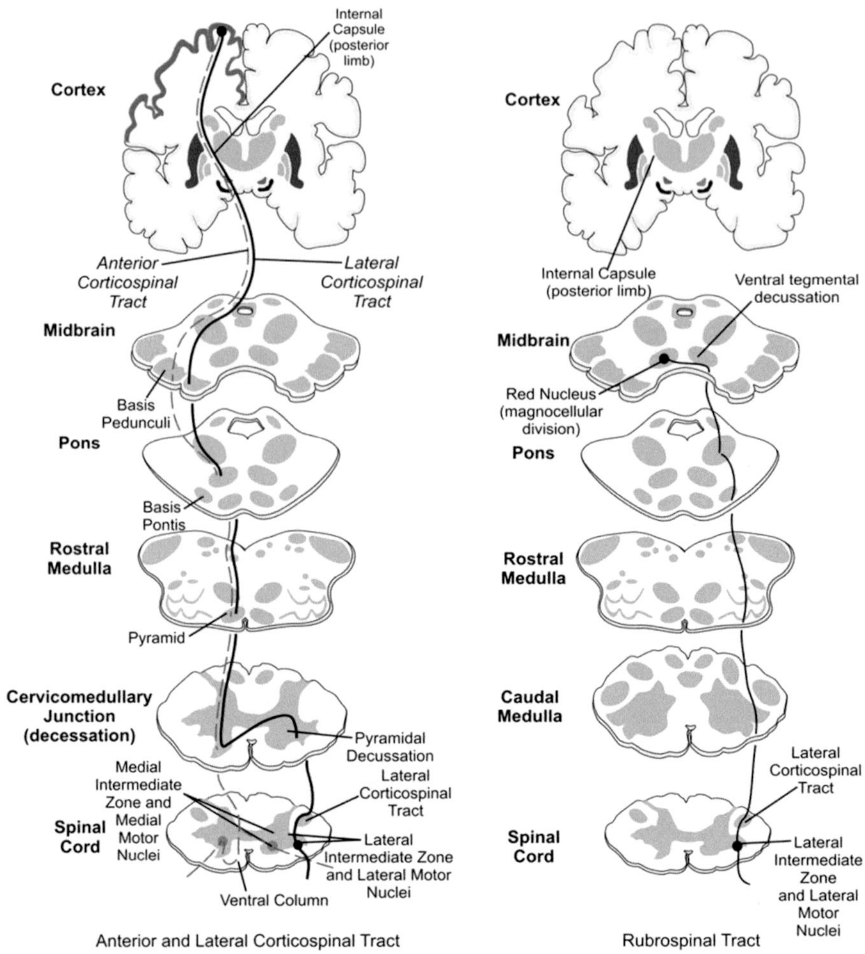

Fig. 3.28 The lateral corticospinal (corticobulbospinal) and rubrospinal pathways. *Note*. The lateral corticospinal illustration incorporates the anterior corticospinal tract as a subsystem of the lateral corticospinal tract that does not decussate

Rubrospinal tract. Beginning with axons in the red nucleus, axons cross the midline immediately after leaving the red nucleus and descend through the brainstem and form a pathway just ventral to the corticospinal tract (see Fig. 3.28). The rubrospinal tract mediates mainly voluntary control of large muscles in the upper extremities.

Reticulospinal tract. The reticulospinal tract has two subdivisions: the pontine and medullary reticulospinal tracts (see Fig. 3.29). The pontine division descends in the medial cord to facilitate extensor motor neurons and inhibit flexor motor neurons

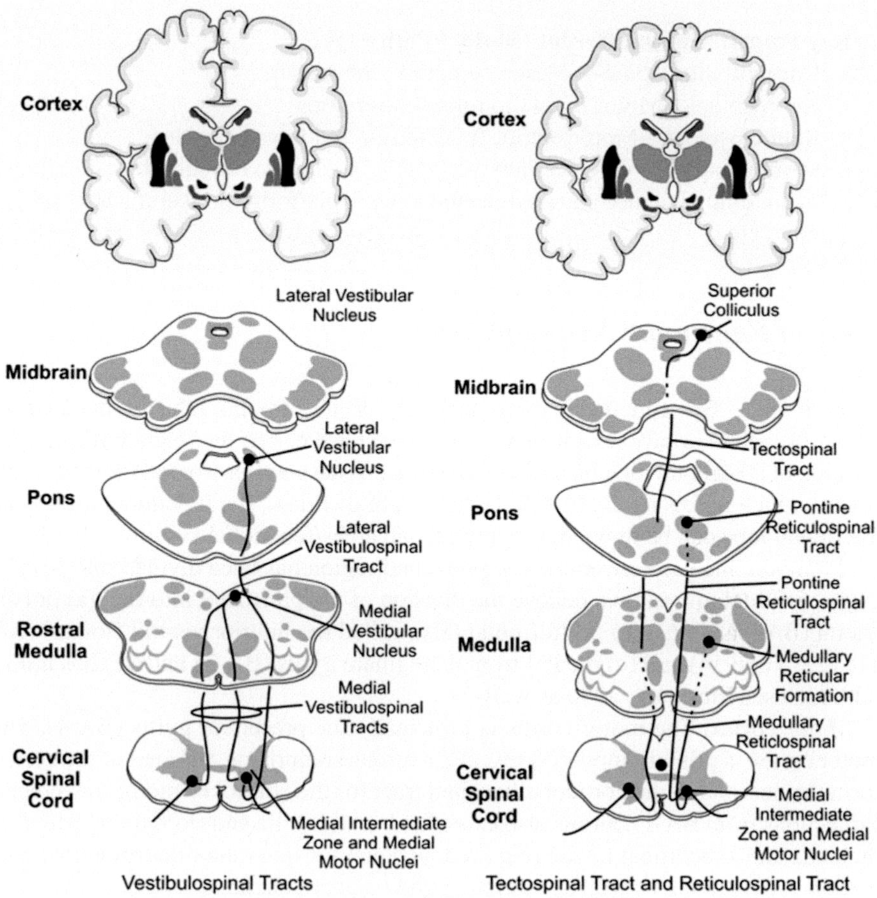

Fig. 3.29 Vestibulospinal, tectospinal and reticulospinal motor pathways

of the limbs. The medullary division descends in the anterolateral column of the spinal cord. It functions to inhibit extensor and facilitate flexor motor neurons.

Vestibulospinal tracts. Four tracts originating from the superior, lateral, medial and inferior vestibular nuclei, all of which receive afferent connections from the vestibular nerve. The lateral and medial vestibulospinal tracts are descending motor tracts (Fig. 3.29). The medial vestibulospinal tract descends only to cervical and high thoracic levels and synapses on neurons innervating the muscles of the head and neck. The principle function is to provide a stable platform for the eyes. The lateral vestibulospinal tract descends to all levels of the spine in the ipsilateral ventral medial funiculus. The lateral vestibulospinal tract primarily regulates posture and balance.

Key Points: Major Efferent (Motor) Pathways
- Cortico(bulbo)spinal—Motor output to limb muscles
- Rubrospinal—Motor output to upper extremities
- Reticulospinal—Motor output for extensor and flexor muscles
- Vestibulospinal—Divided into four subdivisions for vestibular function for maintaining balance and posture and a stable platform for vision when running, etc.

Cortical Functional Neuroanatomy

Frontal lobe. The functional neuroanatomy of the frontal lobe is detailed in Chap. 11, and is briefly reviewed here for convenience. The neuroanatomical organization of the frontal lobe includes all the brain tissue anterior (rostral) to the central sulcus, which makes up about 40% of the cerebral cortex. The functional aspects of the frontal lobe can be divided into three broad areas/functional systems: (1) Motor, (2) Premotor and (3) Prefrontal. The prefrontal region has been divided into several distinction regions, and we believe the division of the prefrontal into the: (a) dorsolateral (BA 9 and 46), (b) orbitofrontal (also called the inferior ventral frontal) (BA 11, 12, 13 and 14) and (c) medial frontal/cingulate gyrus (BA 25 and 32) has utility (although see Mesulam, 2000 as well).

Motor cortex. The motor cortex is principally the precentral gyrus (BA 4). The motor cortex is primary motor cortex, and neurons comprising this area of the cortex form the neurons of the corticobulbospinal tract for the control of motor movement. Projections from BA 4 neurons also extend to basal ganglia and from there extend to thalamic and subcortical nuclei (e.g., red nucleus) for fine motor coordination, correction and planning as well as vestibular and balance functions.

Premotor cortex. The premotor cortex includes the regions anterior (rostral) to the precentral gyrus and includes BA 6 and 8. The areas of BA 6 and 8 have been further subdivided into the premotor and supplementary motor cortices. Lateral BA 6 is a premotor cortex while medial BA 6 is a supplementary motor cortex. BA 8 is the frontal eye fields while the more lateral aspects are supplementary eye fields. The premotor areas are heteromodal cortex, receiving inputs from parietal association cortex (BA 5 and 7), and projecting axons to the primary motor cortex as well as directly to the corticobulbospinal (corticospinal) pathways. The premotor and supplementary motor cortices are involved in motor planning.

Prefrontal cortex. In general, the prefrontal cortex is involved in planning, organizing, executing, initiation, inhibiting, organizing and/or selecting behaviors. In addition, areas of the frontal lobe are also associated with processes of speech production, maintaining vigilance, working memory, as well as learning and memory. Each of the three prefrontal regions has classic characteristics that are summarized below.

Dorsolateral Prefrontal (dysexecutive syndrome). The dorsolateral prefrontal area is involved in reasoning, problem-solving, sequencing and maintenance of behaviors (persistence). Problem-solving and reasoning is concrete with patients having more difficulty with divergent reasoning tasks (requiring many solutions to a problem) than convergent reasoning tasks (drawing similarities or solutions from two or more things). Furthermore, insight and judgment are often poor. Patients may exhibit environmental dependency and memory problems. Learning rate is often slow, and the patient may not remember some things due to reduced working memory/attention but also reduced retrieval. Additionally, deficits in remembering the temporal sequence of when events occurred (as opposed to forgetting something occurred altogether) may be present. Finally, disruption in emotional functioning can also occur, in which affect is generally blunted/apathetic, but intermixed with episodes of anger outbursts when emotionally aroused. Expressive aphasia with involvement of BA 44/45, but spontaneous speech can be generally reduced.

Orbitofrontal or inferior ventral frontal (pseudopsychopathy or pseudodepressed syndrome): The orbitofrontal (inferior ventral) part of the prefrontal cortex is involved in behavioral inhibition and emotional regulation as well as olfaction. In general, patients with orbitofrontal lesions often appear disorganized, behaviorally disinhibited, impulsive and emotionally dysregulated. Anosmia is not uncommon. Behavior inhibition is reduced, so individuals will behave hedonistically, often appearing to have no concern for the feelings or rights of other people. The orbitofrontal region is associated with conscious control of behavior through the evaluation of punishment (lateral orbitofrontal) and reward value of reinforcing (desirable) stimuli (medial orbitofrontal). Memory is *only* disrupted *if* the basal forebrain/septal area is damaged, which results in a dense anterograde amnesia (poor declarative memory) and a temporally graded retrograde amnesia. *Witzelsucht*, a term to describe "hollow" or inappropriate jocularity (laughing at a funeral) may be present.

- *Mesial Frontal/Anterior Cingulate (akinetic syndrome).* The medial frontal/anterior cingulate cortex is associated with attention, behavioral inhibition, initiation and motivation, motor function (lower extremities), social cognition, including Theory of Mind, memory, mood and autonomic (visceral) systems. Damage to the orbitofrontal/anterior cingulate can result in akinesia, lethargy, lack of self-initiation of behavior and a dense antegrade amnesia (impaired explicit memory). Bilateral lesions can result in an akinetic and mute state. Unilateral lesions are less devastating, and the patient may engage in some self-initiated behaviors. Lesions affecting the language-dominant hemisphere can result in a transcortical motor aphasia. Emotional functioning is generally blunted, with little insight or judgment. Damage to the medial motor cortex results in a contralateral hemiparesis of the lower extremity (extremities if bilateral lesions).

Insular Cortex (lobe). The insular cortex is a small area of cortex underlying the frontal and temporal operculum and lies deep within the Sylvian (lateral) fissure (see Fig. 3.7). The insular cortex is divided into two regions, a larger anterior region and a smaller posterior region. Less is known about the functional neuroanatomy of the insular cortex (lobe), but structurally, the insular cortex (lobe) has an extensive network of pathways with connections to auditory cortex (primary and secondary), amygdala, entorhinal cortex, hippocampus, motor cortex, prefrontal cortex (anterior cingulate gyrus, dorsolateral and orbitofrontal), frontal operculum, olfactory cortex/bulb, parietal operculum, the temporal pole and superior temporal gyrus and somatosensory association cortices (primary and secondary).

While details remain to be delineated, the insular cortex appears to be involved in: motor control, homeostasis, interoceptive awareness and association with somatosensory experiences, cognitive functions including self-awareness and social-emotional processing, as well as complex somatosensory association experiences. Motor control function includes association with the coordinated movement of hand and eyes, swallowing, speech articulation and motor activities of the gastrointestinal (GI) tract. Homeostasis functions include the control and monitoring of the autonomic nervous system. Interoceptive awareness refers to being aware of internal body states, and the insular cortex (lobe) appears to be a center for the conscious appreciation of cardiovascular function (heartbeat and blood pressure), pain, temperature and GI sensations. Indeed, the insular cortex has a "command center" for increasing heart rate and blood pressure with exercise. Right (nondominant) insular cortex has been associated with conscious perception of heart rate. Judgment of pain severity as well as the subjective grading of nonpainful coldness or warmth involves the insula. Conscious perception of visceral organs (dissention of stomach or bladder) is also associated with the insular cortex. Relatedly, the insular cortex (lobe) is associated with the limbic system and involved in the integration of sensory inputs with limbic and body visceral states for higher cognitive order processing and perception. This process is thought to associate limbic and sensory processes to memories and associate these with interpersonal relationships and events (e.g., stomach in knots when thinking about a particular person or event). The insular cortex (lobe) appears to have an important role as an area for integrating multiple sensory (auditory, gustatory, olfactory, tactile, vestibular and visual) information. Recently, it was found that synesthesia (perception of one sensory modality as another, for example, hearing colors or seeing music) is associated with disruptions of the insular cortex. Food and drug craving has been associated with the insular cortex. Emotionally, the insular cortex is involved in processes for anger, fear, disgust, happiness and sadness. The insular cortex is involved in the association of disgust to both olfactory inputs and/or visual images of mutilation and contamination or putrefaction. Imagination of these inputs is sufficient for similar brain activation and insular cortex activity. Finally, emotional salience, that is attending to, and making decisions about, the subjective importance of stimuli is associated with the insular cortex and also cingulate gyrus and connected orbitofrontal cortex.

Occipital lobe. The occipital cortex is traditionally identified as associated with visual processing. Visual processing is a distributed hierarchical organized process. Grossly, primary visual processing begins in the calcarine sulcus (striate cortex or BA 17 or V1) and more complex visual processing occurs in associated anterior (rostral) areas (e.g., BA 18 and 19 or V2). The lateral geniculate nucleus (of the thalamus) projects to V1. Neurons of V1 project to other visual unimodal and heteromodal cortex (V2, V3, etc.). Neurons in V2 also project to other visual unimodal and heteromodal cortex. Beginning after V2, there are three distinct visual processing systems: (1) dorsal stream, (2) ventral stream and (3) a superior temporal sulcus (STS) stream. The dorsal stream and the ventral stream have been well described while the third stream, the STS stream is less well described (see Fig. 10.4).

The region of V4 is specialized to appreciate color, although cells here also respond to color/form combinations. Lesions to V4 result in inability to see color and are unable to "think" in color. This reflects loss of not color perception but color knowledge. The area described as area V3 appears to be sensitive to processing the object of shapes in motion (Kolb & Whishaw, 2021). Area V5 is also concerned with the perception of objects in motion. Lesions to area V5 can result in the inability to see objects when they are moved, but able to see the objects when they are stationary.

In summary, the dorsal pathway is primarily involved in identifying where objects are in space and the relative distances from one another and the person as well as guiding body movements by vision, which runs from the occipital cortex to the parietal cortex. The ventral pathway processes the object forms and the associated semantic network for recognized objects in space. This system runs from the occipital cortex to the temporal cortex (see Chap. 9 this volume for more details). The STS pathway appears to be specialized for the categorization of stimuli as well as the detection of motion of body parts (e.g., hands) thought to be involved in the perception of social nonverbal communication cues. Table 3.5 summarizes the cerebral region and proposed function as well as some neuropsychological deficits associated with lesions of these areas.

Table 3.5 Visual processing regions of the posterior neocortex

Pathway	Function	Cerebral localization
Dorsal (where)		
	Eye movements (voluntary)	Lateral intraparietal sulcus
	Visual motor guidance and grasping	Ventral and anterior intraparietal sulcus
	Visually guided reach	Parietal reach region
Ventral (what)		
	Body analysis	Extrastriate and fusiform body areas
	Face analysis	Fusiform face area
	Landmark analysis	Parahippocampal place area
	Object analysis	Lateral occipital
STS (specialized where/what)		
	Analysis of body movements for nonverbal communication	Superior temporal sulcus
	Analysis of moving body	Superior temporal sulcus

Adapted from Kolb and Whishaw (2021)

Parietal lobe. The parietal cortex is demarcated by the cortex posterior to the central sulcus and anterior to the parieto-occipital sulcus and ventral (superior) of the Sylvian (lateral) fissure. It also includes the cortex and underlying white matter from the interhemispheric fissure to the cingulate gyrus. The parietal lobe includes BA 1, 2 and 3 (postcentral gyrus), BA 5 and 7 (superior parietal lobule), BA39 (angular gyrus), BA 40 (supramarginal gyrus) and BA 43 (parietal operculum).

Functionally, the parietal cortex may be divided into two broad functions: somatosensory processing and sensory integration for motor control. The anterior parietal areas (BA 1, 2, 3 and 43) and is primarily involved in somatosensory processing and includes primary sensory and unimodal association cortex in the postcentral gyrus. The posterior parietal cortex includes BA 5, 7, 39 and 40 are involved in the dorsal pathway of visual processing (see Occipital lobe above).

The anterior parietal area reflects primary and unimodal somatosensory cortex, and processes information about tactile, muscle, joint, vibration, vestibular and two-point discrimination information. The primary and unimodal association cortex projects to posterior parietal regions in BA 5 and 7 as well as supplementary and premotor areas, which are unimodal and heteromodal cortex. Projections of BA 5 go to posterior parietal regions (BA 7) as well as supplementary and premotor areas. Additionally, BA 7 receives input from primary somatosensory cortex, motor and premotor cortex and some inputs from visual occipitoparietal regions. There are reciprocal connections between areas of BA 7 and the dorsolateral prefrontal cortex (BA 8 and 46). The posterior parietal cortex is involved in the integration of sensory inputs (somatosensory, visual, auditory, etc.) for the control of movement and processing of visual word information (reading). As discussed in the occipital lobe functional neuroanatomy, the visual pathway of where objects are in space (dorsal pathway) is processed in heteromodal cortex of the superior parietal lobe (BA 5 and 7), making a part of the *dorsal visual stream* (see Chap. 10, this volume). Together, BA 5 and 7 are involved in guiding movement and some processing of spatial working memory. BA 39 and 40 are involved in high level integration of visual stimuli and language functions in association with reading. In addition, arithmetic functions, particularly those involved in more complex arithmetic requiring "borrowing" or other mathematical operations requiring a spatial aspect, have been associated with posterior parietal regions, particularly the inferior parietal lobule.

Lesions of the postcentral gyrus that disrupt the connections between primary and unimodal association cortex areas result in *astereognosia* (inability to recognize objects by feel/palpitating them but not seeing them). Damage frequently also results in *agraphesthesia*, which is the inability to identify letters or numbers written on the palm of the hand or fingertips. Other associated agnosias include *atopognosia* (inability to localize touch) and *abarognosia* is the inability to discriminate weights. Lesions to the medial parietal area [medial parietal region (MPR)] and posterior cingulate gyrus result in poor spatial navigation. Spatial rotation appears to include the interparietal sulcus.

Temporal lobes. The temporal lobe is most commonly associated with receptive language functions (BA 41, 42 and 22) and memory (parahippocampal gyrus, BA 28, 35 and 36). However, the temporal lobe is also involved in considerable visual processing, and makes up the ventral visual pathway (BA 20, 21, 37 and 38), which allows for the processing of "what" visual percepts are and associating these with a semantic memory network that is thought to include portions of the temporal lobe, including the anterior tip. In fact, the temporal lobe has (at least) five distinct neuroanatomic pathways: (1) Sensory pathways of auditory and visual information; (2) auditory dorsal pathway; (3) polymodal/heteromodal processing/STS visual processing pathway; (4) memory/mesial temporal pathway; and (5) affect/emotional processes and movement control/frontal lobe pathway. We briefly summarize the functional anatomy of each below.

Sensory pathways of auditory and visual information. The temporal lobe includes primary sensory and association cortex for auditory stimuli as well as association cortex for visual information. These are discussed separately below.

Auditory processing. The dorsal (superior) aspect of the temporal lobe includes Heschel's gyrus (BA 41 and 42), which lies in the Sylvian fissure and is primary auditory cortex. Cells in the left (language dominant) hemisphere within Heschel's gyrus are disproportionately sensitive to sound frequencies associated with human speech, while cells in the right (nonlanguage dominant) hemisphere are sensitive to the pitch, timbre and melodies of music. The primary auditory sensory cortex projects to hierarchical auditory association cortex (Wernicke's area, BA 22) classically associated with verbal comprehension (or spoken and written language) in the language-dominant hemisphere. Projections from BA 22 radiate anteriorly along the superior aspect of the temporal lobe toward the temporal pole. There is also a dorsal projection of BA 22 posteriorly to the angular gyrus in the temporoparietal region (described below).

Visual processing. The temporal lobe includes visual association cortex receiving projections from primary visual cortex (BA 17, 18, 19) involved in the ventral visual processing pathway for object recognition. In addition, the temporal lobe includes (at least) two special visual perception regions, the fusiform face area (FFA) and the parahippocampal place area (PPA). The FFA is differentially active while viewing faces and reflects a unique processing area and pathway for the perception of faces. The activation of this region is specific to faces and is active despite variability in the presentation of faces (having glasses, a beard, a hat, etc.). The FFA is active regardless if the face is directly "facing" the viewer or is it some other angle (e.g., from the side). However, the FFA is *not* active if a face is viewed "upside down." The right hemisphere is more sensitive to facial perception than the left hemisphere. Additionally, the unique pathway for processing of human faces also includes input from the STS pathway, which provides input as to facial movements important for conveying nonverbal communication cues as to mood/affect and social-emotional functioning. The PPA is preferentially active when the visual stimuli is a geographic scene (e.g., picture of your town or Central Park in New York, NY).

The neurons making up the cortex of the inferior temporal lobe activate to complex visual features and that cells having similar but not identical selectivity for activation to particular complex visual stimuli are organized together in columns. The columnar organization of neurons responding to similar, but not identical, complex visual features allows these areas to activate despite slight variations in the visual properties of the stimuli. In so doing, this organization allows for learning visual categorization based on similarity of a complex series of features.

Auditory dorsal pathway. A processing pathway projecting posterior and dorsally to the parietal cortices thought to be involved in semantic knowledge of words, word reading, and related to aspects of directing movements that is related to auditory sensory information. Since BA 39 is involved in reading, some aspects of discerning the visual aspects of language or perhaps semantic knowledge of words (e.g., word identification and meaning) has been associated with processing of the superior temporal lobe and angular gyrus.

Polymodal/heteromodal processing/STS visual processing pathway. Described above briefly as part of the occipital lobe, the STS visual processing pathway includes a series of parallel projections from visual and auditory association cortices converging largely in the superior temporal sulcus and running posterior toward the temporal pole. It is a complex heteromodal/multimodal association cortex and has a role in associating visual and auditory information for categorization (associating sounds with certain objects). This region is also involved in the perception of different facial features and body movements with nonverbal communication cues and social behaviors (e.g., recognizing a smirk while telling a joke).

Memory/mesial temporal pathway. The projections of the auditory, visual and other somatosensory information are projected toward the parahippocampal gyrus where information is "funneled" to the perirhinal cortex and then entorhinal cortex along to the hippocampal formation and/or amygdala. Efferent projections from the hippocampus form the perforant pathway which form part of the Papez circuit involving the limbic cortex. The mesial temporal lobe structures (perirhinal and entorhinal cortices and hippocampus) are involved in declarative memory, particularly episodic (time and person specific) memory (see Chap. 8 for details) for objects, spatial information and verbal/auditory information.

Affect/emotional aspects to memory and movement control/frontal lobe pathway. The temporal lobe has projections to the frontal lobe, both the dorsolateral and the orbitofrontal lobe based on fibers from the inferior longitudinal fasciculus and the uncinate fasciculus that is primarily involved in affective/emotional processing, short-term memory and aspects of movement control. The emotional processing is associated with connections of the amygdala and orbitofrontal connections, inclusive of olfactory processing and emotional/affective processing. One function of the amygdala is to "tag" emotional/affective features to visual and/or auditory information, which increases the encoding (learning) of material and provides a neuroanatomic pathway for state-dependent learning such that being in a similar affective state can enhance memory. The associative information of the temporal lobe with respect to categorizing information, including the body movements that have implications for emotional/social communication is processed in the STS pathway and also areas of the frontal lobe, including the dorsolateral and orbitofrontal lobes, and is thought to be involved in the "theory of mind" (see Chap. 11). Briefly, theory of mind refers to the ability to theorize about other people's feelings, thoughts and the intentions of their behaviors.

After summarizing the five different neuroanatomic projection pathways in the temporal lobe, there are nine (9) neuropsychological symptoms frequently associated with temporal lobe lesions, which include impaired:

1. Auditory sensation or perception (cortical deafness to receptive aphasia)
2. Perception of visual features (visual object agnosias, prosopagnosia, alexia and appreciation of social facial/body part cues). Alexia has been associated with lesions to BA 39 (angular gyrus) as well as a region on the inferior occipitotemporal gyrus. Patients with right temporal resections fail to exhibit the left visual field bias in viewing faces that is normal.
3. Perception of music (amusia)
4. Auditory and/or visual selective attention
5. Categorization of visual or auditory stimuli (poor semantic organization)
6. Use of contextual information
7. Declarative (particularly episodic) memory
8. (Changed) personality and affective behavior. Patients may exhibit an increased focus on minutia, particularly details of personal problems, have religious preoccupation, paranoia and increased aggressiveness associated with the so-called temporal lobe or Geschwind personality. However, these features are rarely all present, and there is no consistent data supporting the temporal lobe personality. Nonetheless, personality change has been associated with temporal lobe damage, more often with right temporal lobe injury.
9. (Changed) sexual behavior (associated with Kluver–Bucy syndrome)

Distributed and Parallel Processing Networks: Structural and Functional Components

In the discussion above, we provided an overview of functions traditionally associated with a region of the cerebral cortex (e.g., frontal lobe), however, the discussion of cytoarchitecture and functional divisions of the cortex highlights the function of the nervous system (and production of behaviors) is based on complex systems of distributed and parallel processing networks that can be demonstrated both in terms of structural neuroanatomy as well as functionally in terms of neurophysiological mechanisms and effectors acting on associated brain areas (e.g., neurotransmitter actions). The neuroanatomic organization of the brain into networks can be appreciated at a cellular level, discussed above in terms of the extensive connections of each neuron with other neurons (one neuron may synapse to a 1000 or more other neurons via axons and dendrites) as well as the hierarchical and integrative networks displayed by the cytoarchitecture or the functional cortical areas organized hierarchically to process single sensorimotor stimuli projecting to more complex heteromodal/multimodal association cortex. At a larger neuroanatomical level, the complex processing networks of the brain can be readily appreciated by the intricate network of white matter tracts (bundles, fibers and fasciculi) projecting throughout the cortex and to other regions of the CNS. Fibers (bundles of axons) may project from one closely associated region to another (neighboring gyri) with arcuate fibers (also called U-fibers) or to regions quite distanced from each other via fasciculi. Figure 3.30

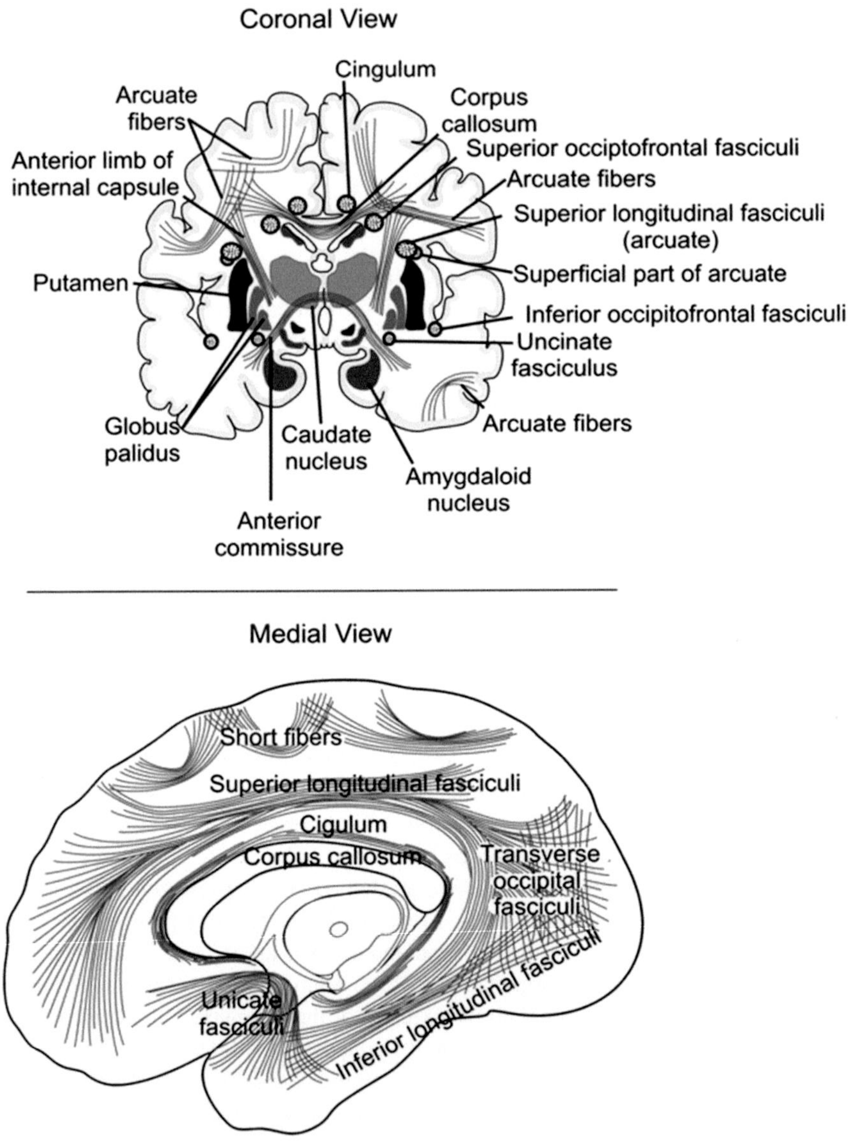

Fig. 3.30 Fasciculi and fibers of cerebral cortex

Table 3.6 Major fasciculi of the brain with associated connected areas

Fasciculus name	Areas connected	Function
Arcuate fasciculus (now considered part of superior longitudinal fasciculus)	Temporal and frontal lobes	Language functions associating receptive and expressive areas
Inferior longitudinal (occipitotemporal)	Occipital and temporal lobes	Semantic language, memory, visual processing
Superior longitudinal	Occipital, parietal, temporal and frontal lobes	Regulate motor movement, spatial orientation, spatial perception, working memory, language
Inferior occipitofrontal	Occipital, temporal and frontal lobes	Visual processing, semantic memory, language processes
Superior occipitofrontal	Occipital, parietal, temporal and frontal lobes. Fibers project to thalamus	Visual processing, motor control, language functions, semantic memory
Uncinate	Orbitofrontal regions to anterior temporal	Affective (emotion), memory, cognition
Anterior commissure	Left and right anterior temporal/olfactory bulb/basal frontal areas	Olfactory functions, emotion/affective processing
Cingulum (bundle)	Cingulate gyrus to frontal lobe, amygdala, nucleus accumbens and thalamus	Cognition (including alertness/attention) and affective/emotional processes
Corpus callosum	Left and right hemispheres	Broad connections for motor, sensory and cognitive processes
Posterior commissure	Left and right pretectal nuclei	Pupil light reflex

illustrates some of the major fasciculi of the neocortex. Table 3.6 identifies the major fasciculi and the association areas connected.

The multiple processing networks involved in many behaviors/cognitions that may not seem complex on the surface are illustrated by two examples. Figure 3.31 illustrate a complex widely diffuse distributed network thought to account for semantic memory (conceptual knowledge). Recall that semantic memory (conceptual knowledge) refers to one's memory for facts and knowledge and is not specific to time or place (autobiographical) and is cultural in nature (e.g., knowing the capital cities of the 50 states in the United States of America) (see also Chap. 9). The two theories accounting for semantic memory reflect a distributed network model and a distributed network-plus-hub model. The latter model includes a distributed network of modality-specific cortex processing areas (e.g., visual form, movement, language, tactile features, etc.) as in the distributed network model, but also includes a nondomain specific processing center (or perhaps more correctly a multimodal processing center) which processes the many different domain-specific information by a common set of neurons. The distributed network-plus-hub model is garnering increasing support, but there remains debate as to the location and importance of these

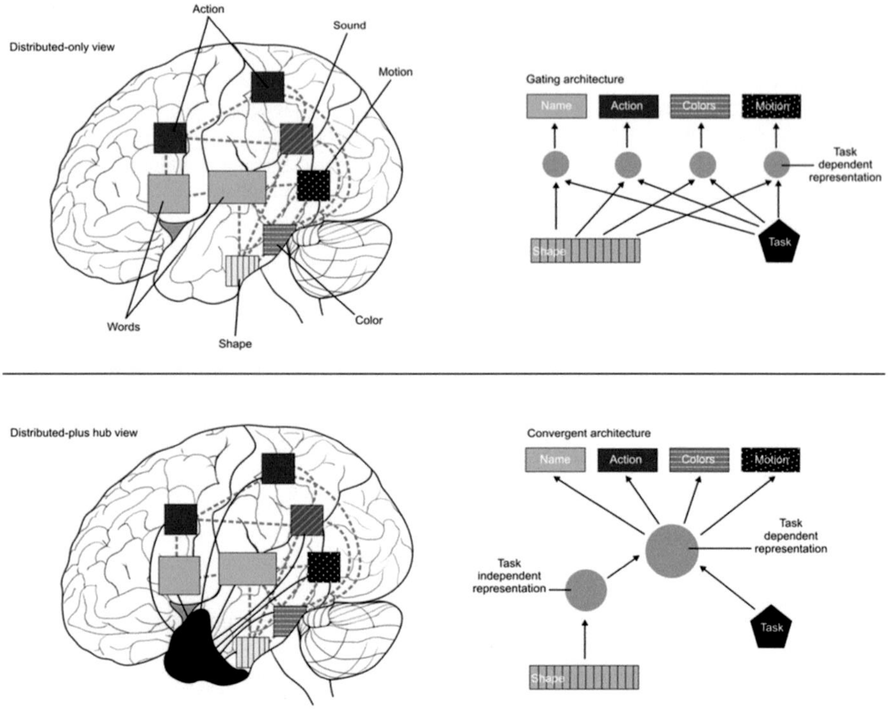

Fig. 3.31 Models of distributed network and distributed network-plus-hub for semantic memory

nondomain specific hub area(s). While the debate continues, neuropsychological processes clearly involve a distributed network of areas, many with "hub" areas which are highly efficient at integrating stimuli for the neuropsychological functions reviewed in this book.

The second example is the complex parallel distributed network needed for speech, which is presented in detail in Chap. 7 (see Fig. 7.1). The distributed network includes hubs for expressive (BA 44/45) and receptive language (BA 22, 41/42), which network with other regions of the frontal (e.g., BA 6), temporal (BA 38, 20, 21 and 37), parietal (BA 39 and 40) and occipital (BA 17, 18, 19) cortices to allow for effortless language functions. Note the production of speech requires activation of brain regions outside the traditional language areas (BA 44/45; Broca's area), such as the facial area of the premotor cortex (BA 6, inferior portion). Similarly, reading involves primary and associative visual cortex (BA 17/V1, BA18/V2, BA19/V3) in processing letters/words. The semantic association of words (i.e., mental representation of a "canary," which is a unit of the semantic class of birds) involves areas of the occipital, occipitotemporal and inferior parieto-temporal cortices (BA 19, 21, 37 and 39) and left frontal regions (note these areas are part of the semantic memory network reviewed above). In addition, motor and premotor areas are involved in reading and writing, respectively, along with the corticobulbar tracts and cranial nerves. Chapter 8 also reviews the analogous areas in the nondominant hemisphere involved in language prosody functions. Clearly, there is a distributed network to read, understand or produce speech. Similarly, there are distributed and parallel networks involved in the neuropsychological functions reviewed in this book, including alertness/arousal (Chap. 6), attention/concentration (Chap. 7), visuoperceptual/visuoconstructional skills (see above and Chap. 10), memory (see Chaps. 9 and 11), motor control (above and Chaps. 11 and 21), executive (Chap. 11) and emotion/affective functions (Chaps. 11 and 12). The distributed networks include cortical areas involved in more integrative functions and interconnected with cortical areas that are highly specialized and efficient at processing specific types of information. We know turn to further evaluating the cerebral and cortical specializations in behavior.

Cerebral Asymmetry

While the brain has two hemispheres that, on gross exam, appear very similar, years (100 or more years) of research has documented asymmetry in the structure and function of the human brain. Below we summarize some anatomic and functional differences.

Anatomic cerebral asymmetry. As early as the 1860s, the asymmetry of the cerebral cortex has been appreciated (Kolb & Whishaw, 2021 for review). Some common anatomical asymmetries of the cerebral hemispheres are summarized below:

Asymmetry favoring the dominant (Left) hemisphere

- Left hemisphere is denser and has more gray matter relative to amount of white matter.
- Frontal operculum total area larger due to more surface area in sulcus.
- Inferior parietal lobule larger.
- Insula is larger.
- Medial temporal lobe larger.
- Neocortex is thicker.
- Occipital lobe wider.
- Occipital horn of lateral ventricle longer.
- Planum temporale (Wernicke's area/BA 22) larger.
- Sylvian fissure is longer.
- Temporoparietal cortex larger in some areas.
- *Asymmetry favoring the non-dominant (right) hemisphere*
- Right hemisphere is larger and slightly heavier
- Heschl's gyrus is larger
- Convexity of frontal operculum (due to larger gyrus) larger
- Frontal lobe wider
- Medial geniculate nucleus larger (auditory)

Functional cerebral asymmetry. Study of the asymmetry of the brain has a long history, predominately with patients whom suffered lateralized lesions (Kolb & Whishaw, 2021; Lezak et al., 2012). Some functional asymmetries of the cerebral hemispheres are provided in Table 3.7.

Table 3.7 Functional asymmetries of the human brain

Function	Left dominant	Right dominant
Attention	Speech sounds (see below)	Left hemispace for visual, auditory, somatosensory stimuli
Auditory system	Language/speech related sounds	Music Nonlanguage sounds
Language/speech	Expressive and receptive speech: • Verbal comprehension • Spontaneous speech • Repetition • Reading • Writing	Prosody of speech • Comprehension of prosody • Expressive prosody • Repetition of prosody
Memory	Verbal memory • Word lists • Stories • Word-pairs	Spatial/ "visual" memory[a] • Faces • Spatial locations
Motor/movement	Right side of body Mouth movements	Left side of body
Visual/spatial processing	Printed letters/words	Faces Geometric patterns Geometry Mental rotation of shapes Spatial orientation

[a]Determination of right hemisphere material specific memory dominance for "spatial/visual memory" has not been consistent

Large-Scale Brain Networks

Large-scale brain networks represent an increasingly important area of clinical and research interest. Early theoretical perspectives posited that these neural pathways synthesize information in a parallel distributed fashion to explain the dissociable yet interactive nature of their functional correlates (Mesulam, 1990). The dorsal and ventral visual streams illustrate this phenomenon of emergent properties comprised both discrete and interlinked subcomponents—the individual features (e.g., shape, size, spatial arrangement) obtained from networks of object identification ("what" or ventral stream) and location perception ("where" or dorsal stream) are superimposed to inform visuomotor and visuospatial processing that require concurrent integration of information and ongoing feedback. The advent of functional neuroimaging has led to a broader understanding of the larger dynamic interplay and interconnectivity of large-scale brain networks, which continue to undergo further refinement.

Recent efforts have focused on advocating for consensus guidelines surrounding both nomenclature and anatomical bounds of macro-scale brain networks. Regarding terminology, some authors have advocated for naming networks by neuroanatomical hubs involved as opposed to by name of their associated functions (e.g., medial frontoparietal network for default-mode network) given the variability of how phenotypic terms such as salience are defined, but ultimately no definitive guidance has been offered at the time of this publication. In support of this notion, recent brain-wide association studies (Marek et al., 2022) found that establishing reliable brain–behavior correlations with adequate effect sizes necessitates including thousands of subjects. Alternatively, it is the syndromes that ultimately define and distinguish these distributed networks from each other, as some network hubs are involved in multiple, interconnected neuroanatomical pathways.

Tremendous strides have been made toward elucidating the cognitive underpinnings and clinical relevance of large-scale brain networks through a variety of functional neuroimaging techniques, namely functional magnetic resonance imaging (fMRI) and positron emission tomography (PET). Resting state functional MRI (rsfMRI) has unveiled critical discoveries distinct from past studies that focused solely on overlapping sites of "activation" during tasks (e.g., BOLD, glucose metabolism, etc.). Indeed, literature has supported both correlations and anti-correlations of activity in large-scale brain networks that fluctuate based on the task at hand and environmental stimuli (Fox et al., 2005).

Recent advances in improved demarcation of brain regions have been made by combining multimodal imaging techniques and various structural, connective, functional and cellular characteristics from both structural MRI and task-based, resting state and myelin fMRI. Leveraging data from the Human Connectome Project, Glasser et al. (2016) developed a machine-learning algorithm that, combined with empirically based anatomical bounds delineated by neuroscientists, more accurately and reliably parcellated 180 brain areas in each hemisphere with 97 novel regions. This method better accounted for interindividual variability in terms of neuroanatomical bounds of each region and functional correlates with multimodal agreement. The authors then validated this algorithm in their sample of 210 adult controls by overlaying imaging modalities into a topographical representation of regions involved in somatosensory, auditory and visual processing superimposed on task-negative versus task-positive areas. By defining each brain area through this amalgamation of various cortical features, this paradigm may enable more tailored surgical mapping and improve neuropsychological predictive utility.

The clinical applications of large-scale brain networks are hard to overstate. For instance, epilepsy research has implicated some of these distributed pathways in playing a large role in predicting seizure freedom and neuropsychological outcomes post-operatively (Neal et al., 2020). Subsequent research further reinforced the importance of these large-scale brain networks by demonstrating the selective vulnerabilities of specific networks implicated in particular syndromes of neurodegenerative diseases. While there are several other macro-scale functional networks detailed elsewhere, this section will provide an overview of two large-scale brain networks, namely the default-mode network and the salience network, and their relation to clinical settings as well as their putative anatomical hubs and functional correlates.

Default-Mode Network

The Default-Mode Network (DMN) was first coined by Raichle et al.'s seminal paper (2001) describing the network's metabolic activity and negatively correlated activity with goal-directed tasks. Originally termed the task-negative network, owing to its increase in activity during resting states and deactivation during externally driven tasks, it was postulated to solely represent the baseline state of the brain, hence its name. However, further investigation revealed increasing nuance in this network as research has illustrated that the DMN is increasingly activated by internalizing and conceptual tasks (Spreng & Grady, 2010), which may overlap with certain goal-directed behaviors that involve self-referential processing (Spreng, 2012). Additional research has implicated the DMN's roles across a myriad of functions, including daydreaming, mind-wandering, autobiographical memory and theory of mind (Raichle, 2015). In general, connectivity and efficiency of the DMN has been shown to be lowest at the beginning and end points of the lifespan (e.g., children and elderly) while its highest peak occurs during adulthood (Mak et al., 2017). Clinical populations that DMN dysfunction has been investigated in include epilepsy, Alzheimer's disease, anxiety, depression and schizophrenia.

Anatomically, the DMN has been mapped out to contain certain medial frontoparietal regions that can be divided into its primary hubs broadly speaking and its subsystems, varying in their regional connectivity and functional correlates (Raichle, 2015). In general, the main hubs of the DMN include the posterior cingulate cortex (PCC), angular gyrus and medial prefrontal cortex (mPFC). Andrews-Hanna et al. (2010) have proposed subdivisions of the DMN based on hierarchical clustering of ROI-based functional connectivity, namely the dorsal DMN or the dorsal medial DMN (dmDMN), and the ventral DMN or the medial temporal lobe DMN (MTL DMN). The dorsal DMN has been posited to play a role in theory of mind and metacognition and contains the dorsal medial prefrontal cortex, temporal pole, lateral temporal cortex and temporoparietal junction. On the other hand, the ventral DMN comprised the retrosplenial cortex, hippocampus, parahippocampus cortex, medial orbitofrontal cortex and posterior parietal cortex and has been hypothesized to be implicated in memory retrieval and prospective thinking. More broadly, extant literature has illustrated a positive association between cognitive functioning and DMN connectivity (Mak et al., 2017). Figure 3.32 depicts the neuroanatomical primary hubs, secondary areas and white matter tracts that comprise the DMN.

In terms of clinical relevance, there is vast empirical evidence implicating the DMN's selective vulnerability in Alzheimer's disease (AD) (Seeley et al., 2007). It is thought that dysfunction in the DMN may contribute to the amnestic profile that is prototypical of AD. While the exact mechanism for this is not fully understood, some researchers have hypothesized that consolidation of memories occurs via increased DMN while the mind is not engaged in a particular task; thus, any disruption of the DMN could conceivably lead to memory storage loss. Anatomically, the

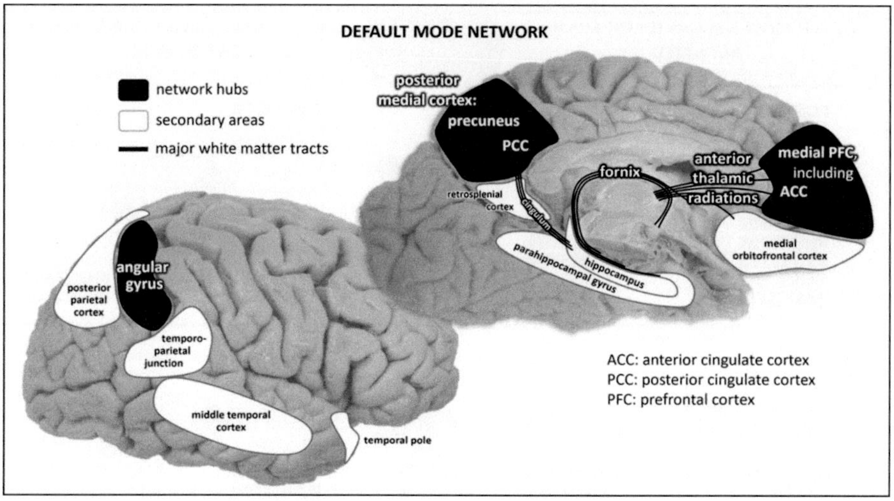

Fig. 3.32 Default-mode network anatomical overview

DMN's functional connectivity to areas implicated in verbal memory including the PCC and bilateral hippocampi likely at least partially account for its link to this function (Cook et al., 2019), and such areas are often implicated in AD neuropathology. Indeed, functional neuroimaging has consistently identified posterior cingulate cortex and inferior parietal lobes hypometabolism early in the disease course, which in turn is thought to adversely impact connected structures, namely the mesial temporal lobes; thus, disrupted DMN activity in these hub regions has been demonstrated to demarcate healthy aging from AD (Greicius et al., 2004). Other more recent research has suggested that subcortical structures implicated in memory related DMN activity have received less attention, including the thalamus and basal forebrain (Alves et al., 2019). Dysfunction to these related circuits could also account for the aforementioned amnestic deficits that are associated with DMN disruption. Moreover, DMN connectivity has also been shown to be decreased in normal aging, which tends to follow a pattern in line with the posterior-anterior shift in aging (PASA) (Davis et al., 2008; Jones et al., 2011). In particular, age-related changes have been associated with less inhibition of the PCC but more inhibition of DMN anterior hubs relative to younger controls when performing attentionally demanding tasks and a lower overall intensity of DMN activity while a person is at rest. Disease states, such as AD, more significantly disrupt DMN functional connectivity than normal aging (Mevel et al., 2011). Figure 3.33 displays the differences in DMN activity levels across the above-mentioned clinical spectrum.

The DMN has also been often implicated as a network susceptible to dysfunction in epilepsy, especially in temporal lobe epilepsy (TLE). To date, the precise underlying mechanism for this selective vulnerability, however, is not entirely clear. Putative models indicate chronic neuronal overexcitation from seizures may spread via

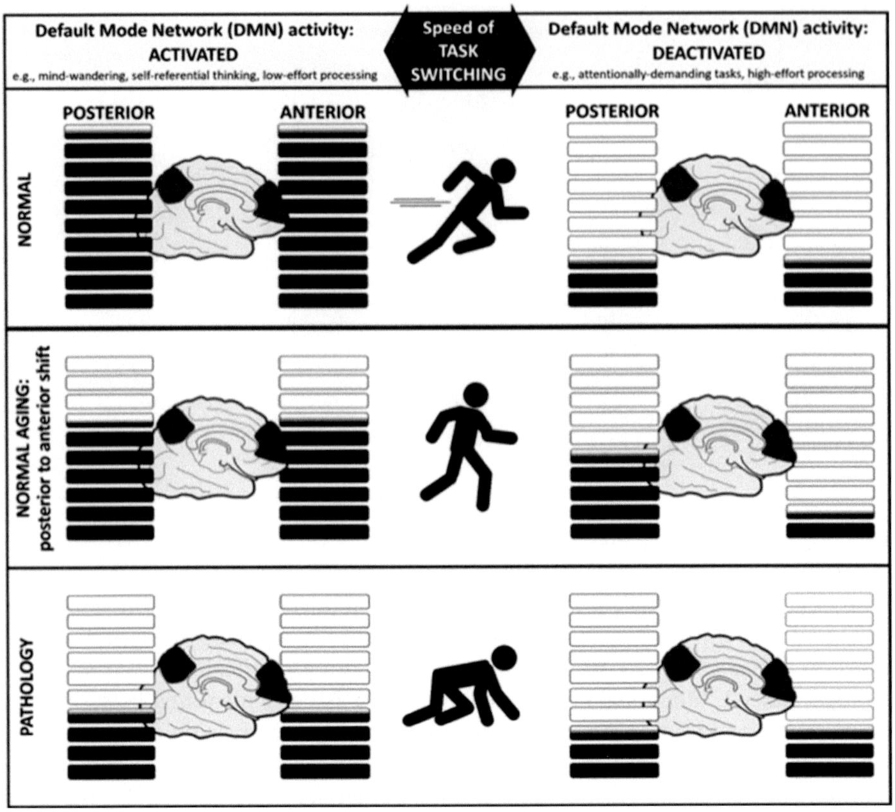

Fig. 3.33 Default-mode network activity levels in healthy controls, normal aging and brain pathology

functional networks and in turn impede DMN connectivity, with increasing length of time afflicted by TLE being positively correlated with increased DMN dysconnectivity (Cook et al., 2019), while durations of interictal spike-free periods have been shown to augment DMN connectivity (Hsiao et al., 2015). McCormick et al. (2013) found that the degree of DMN functional connectivity, particularly between the PCC and mesial temporal lobes, better predicted post-surgical memory outcomes than other clinical metrics, such as mesial temporal structural integrity and baseline memory performance in patients with lateralized mesial TLE. In particular, PCC connectivity to the contralateral mesial temporal lobe was positively associated with post-operative memory scores, likely suggestive of cognitive reserve, while the same connectivity to the ipsilateral mesial temporal lobe was negatively associated with post-operative memory scores (McCormick et al., 2013). Indeed, the functional connectivity of the DMN has demonstrated robust potential toward optimizing the assessment and treatment of patients with TLE.

Key Points: Default-Mode Network (DMN)

- Originally termed the "task negative" network, the DMN is associated with autobiographical memory, mind-wandering and theory of mind.
- Decreased DMN activity ➔ increased network inhibition ➔ focused attention.
- Network hubs include PCC, angular gyrus and mPFC.
- DMN dysfunction associated with a variety of disorders including AD, epilepsy, ASD and depression.
- Subdivisions include dorsal and ventral DMN.

Salience Network

The salience network (SN), comprised mainly midcingulo-insular structures, was initially described by Seeley et al. (2007) as being involved in dynamic switching between brain networks and shifting attention to goal-related tasks associated with homeostasis and survival, especially as it relates to social functioning. As such, the SN plays an important role in helping to attend to what is critical for safety and health maintenance. It has also been posited to be related to the synthetization of affective and sensory input, including social cognition tasks such as interpreting emotional expressions from faces, other forms of nonverbal communication and related autonomic functions. The functional connectivity of the network bears clinical relevance, as decreased connectivity has been associated with apathy, while conversely hyperconnectivity of the SN has been suggested to lead to anxiety (Menon, 2011). Aberrant SN activity also may diminish the perceived relevance of certain tasks and leverage mental faculties to focus on other extraneous stimuli, which in turn can impair higher-order goal-oriented behavior.

The SN comprised two primary anatomical hubs, namely the anterior insula and dorsal anterior cingulate cortex (dACC). In this particular network, the anterior insula has been posited to be a bottom-up relay center responsible for allocating attention/working memory resources to tasks deemed most critical. The insula additionally functions as a somatosensory gauge and interprets autonomic signals in conjunction to their affective counterparts, as well as accurately monitoring interoceptive information more broadly (e.g., tracking heartbeat), thought to add the visceral component to our emotional responses. As such, any disruption could conceivably lead to problems judging emotions and self-monitoring. Other subcortical nodes involved in the SN include amygdala, ventral striatum and ventral tegmental area (Menon, 2015). The uncinate fasciculus has been identified as one of the central white matter tracts that connects the SN to the medial aspects of the frontal lobes, as well as runs along from the anterior insula to the anterior temporal lobes and amygdala (Menon, 2015). The role of the dACC in the SN has been associated with filtering the importance of stimuli, reinforcement of behaviors, decision-making and task initiation. Aside from these neuroanatomical delineations of the SN, aspects of the dACC and

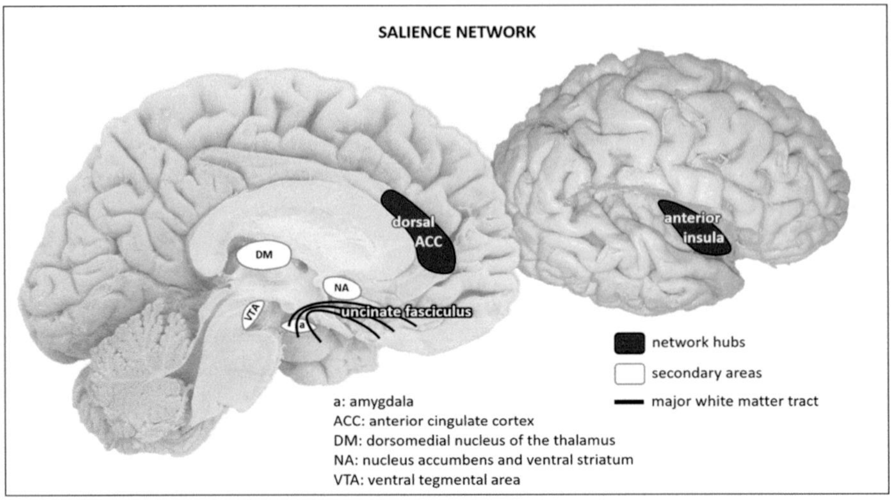

Fig. 3.34 Salience network anatomical overview

anterior insula also contain unique cytoarchitecture, namely von Economo neurons, which are able to engage in faster neurotransmission owing to their larger axons, allowing for more expedient communication surrounding saliency (Menon, 2015). Figure 3.34 presents the primary neuroanatomical hubs, secondary regions and white matter tract associated with the SN.

Clinically, the SN has been implicated as a selectively vulnerable network early in the disease stages of frontotemporal dementia (FTD). The importance ascribed to social cues is attenuated due to SN dysfunction, leading to inattention to important facets of communication that underlie impaired social functioning in FTD. Spread of neuropathological changes and atrophy patterns have been found to spread across the network hubs of the SN at the earliest disease stages of FTD. Resting state functional connectivity of the SN, especially in the insula, has been shown to be predictive of disease progression in FTD (Day et al., 2013). The SN has also been demonstrated to be aberrant in individuals with autism spectrum disorder (ASD), which is thought to potentially underlie nonverbal social communication deficits that are prototypical of the disorder. Aberrant functional changes to the SN have also been associated with excessive attention to internally generated stimuli in schizophrenia, which is consistent with structural neuroimaging studies that have associated volume loss in anterior insula and ACC with delusions and hallucinations in schizophrenia (Menon, 2011). While further validation and replication of the above findings are needed prior to clinical application, the SN offers a potential marker of disease severity and therapeutic target for a variety of psychiatric and neurologic conditions.

Key Points: Salience Network (SN)

- Functional network correlates include goal-oriented attention shifting, motivation, internetwork switching, empathy and nonverbal communication.
- Hypoactive SN ➔ apathy, but hyperactive SN ➔ anxiety.
- Network hubs include anterior insula and dorsal anterior cingulate cortex (dACC), while main white matter tract is uncinate fasciculus.
- SN dysfunction associated with a variety of disorders including FTD, schizophrenia and ASD.

Summary

The nervous system is composed of the central nervous system (brain and spinal cord) and the peripheral nervous system (motor and sensory nerves outside the CNS, including the cranial nerves). There are about 100 billion neurons and about 300 billion supporting glial cells, allowing for 60 to 240 trillion synapses in the adult human brain. The trillions of synapses form complex distributed, parallel and hierarchical networks to process sensory stimuli in order to affect behavior. The complex neurochemical process involving neurotransmitters provides the neurophysiological basis in the function of the nervous system. The major afferent (sensory) and efferent (motor) pathways maintain a somatotopic organization in which sensory functions tend to be caudal/dorsal/posterior (toward the back) while motor functions tend to be rostral/ventral/anterior (toward the nose). Lesions produce well-defined clinical syndromes. The thalamus is a major relay station for sensorimotor and cognitive based pathways, and is interconnected with the basal ganglia to have extensive interconnections with both afferent (sensory) and efferent (motor) functions of the brain and spinal cord. While the review of functional neuroanatomy suggested some localized areas important in sensory or motor functions, the complex organization of the brain cannot be overstated. These networks should be appreciated when evaluating each patient's neuropsychological functioning, and the determination of neuropsychological (brain) dysfunction is best made when the identified patterns of neuropsychological deficits can be appreciated in the context of functional neuroanatomy and known neuropathology. That is, recognition of the patterns of neuropsychological deficits that can be expected to present together versus a distribution of poor neuropsychological test scores that can*not* be reasonably associated with known functional neuroanatomy. Other chapters in this book provide more detailed functional neuroanatomical reviews when appropriate.

Key Points: Cortical Functional Neuroanatomy

- Frontal Lobe—"Executive functions" planning, organizing, monitoring, inhibiting behavior, motor function, motor speech area, orbital and mesial frontal areas involved in affect and personality
- Temporal lobe—Memory, affect/mood, olfactory and gustatory process
- Parietal lobe—Somatosensory perception, spatial awareness/attention and complex visuoperceptual processing (letter/word identification and shape orientation/direction)
- Occipital lobe—Primary and secondary visual processing
- Insular cortex (lobe)—Emotions and association with sensory information, homeostasis, motor control, self-awareness, cognitive function and social-emotional experiences

References and Suggested Readings

Alves, P. N., Foulon, C., Karolis, V., Bzdok, D., Margulies, D. S., Volle, E., & Thiebaut de Schotten, M. (2019). An improved neuroanatomical model of the default-mode network reconciles previous neuroimaging and neuropathological findings. *Communications Biology, 2*(1), 1–14.

Andrews-Hanna, J. R., Reidler, J. S., Sepulcre, J., Poulin, R., & Buckner, R. L. (2010). Functional-anatomic fractionation of the brain's default network. *Neuron, 65*(4), 550–562.

Blumenfeld, H. (2021). *Neuroanatomy through clinical cases* (3rd ed.). Sinauer Associates.

Brodal, P. (2016). *The central nervous system* (5th ed.). Oxford University Press.

Cook, C. J., Hwang, G., Mathis, J., Nair, V. A., Conant, L. L., Allen, L., et al. (2019). Effective connectivity within the default mode network in left temporal lobe epilepsy: Findings from the epilepsy connectome project. *Brain Connectivity, 9*(2), 174–183.

Davis, S. W., Dennis, N. A., Daselaar, S. M., Fleck, M. S., & Cabeza, R. (2008). Que PASA? The posterior-anterior shift in aging. *Cerebral Cortex (New York, N.Y. : 1991), 18*(5), 1201–1209.

Day, G. S., Farb, N. A., Tang-Wai, D. F., Masellis, M., Black, S. E., Freedman, M., et al. (2013). Salience network resting-state activity: Prediction of frontotemporal dementia progression. *JAMA Neurology, 70*(10), 1249–1253.

Fox, M. D., Snyder, A. Z., Vincent, J. L., Corbetta, M., Van Essen, D. C., & Raichle, M. E. (2005). The human brain is intrinsically organized into dynamic, anticorrelated functional networks. *Proceedings of the National Academy of Sciences, 102*(27), 9673–9678.

Glasser, M. F., Coalson, T. S., Robinson, E. C., Hacker, C. D., Harwell, J., Yacoub, E., et al. (2016). A multi-modal parcellation of human cerebral cortex. *Nature, 536*(7615), 171–178.

Gould, D. J., & Brueckner-Collins, J. K. (2016). *Neuroanatomy* (5th ed.). Wolters Kluwer.

Greicius, M. D., Srivastava, G., Reiss, A. L., & Menon, V. (2004). Default-mode network activity distinguishes Alzheimer's disease from healthy aging: Evidence from functional MRI. *Proceedings of the National Academy of Sciences, 101*(13), 4637–4642.

Heilman, K. M., & Valenstein, E. (2011). *Clinical neuropsychology* (5th ed.). Oxford University Press.

Hsiao, F. J., Yu, H. Y., Chen, W. T., Kwan, S. Y., Chen, C., Yen, D. J., et al. (2015). Increased intrinsic connectivity of the default mode network in temporal lobe epilepsy: Evidence from resting-state MEG recordings. *PLoS One, 10*(6), e0128787.

Jones, D. T., Machulda, M. M., Vemuri, P., McDade, E. M., Zeng, G., Senjem, M. L., Gunter, J. L., Przybelski, S. A., Avula, R. T., Knopman, D. S., Boeve, B. F., Petersen, R. C., & Jack, C. R., Jr. (2011). Age-related changes in the default mode network are more advanced in Alzheimer disease. *Neurology, 77*(16), 1524–1531. https://doi.org/10.1212/WNL.0b013e318233b33d

Kandel, E. R., Koester, J. D., Mack, S. H., & Siegelbaum, S. A. (2021). *Principals of neural science* (6th ed.). McGraw-Hill.

Kolb, B., & Whishaw, I. (2021). *Fundamentals of human neuropsychology* (8th ed.). Worth Publishers.

Lezak, M. D., Howieson, D. B., Bigler, E. D., & Tranel, D. (2012). *Neuropsychological assessment* (5th ed.). Oxford University Press.

Mak, L. E., Minuzzi, L., MacQueen, G., Hall, G., Kennedy, S. H., & Milev, R. (2017). The default mode network in healthy individuals: A systematic review and meta-analysis. *Brain Connectivity, 7*(1), 25–33.

Marek, S., Tervo-Clemmens, B., Calabro, F. J., Montez, D. F., Kay, B. P., Hatoum, A. S., et al. (2022). Reproducible brain-wide association studies require thousands of individuals. *Nature, 603*(7902), 654–660.

Martin, J. H. (2020). *Neuroanatomy text and Atlas* (5th ed.). McGraw Hill.

McCormick, C., Quraan, M., Cohn, M., Valiante, T. A., & McAndrews, M. P. (2013). Default mode network connectivity indicates episodic memory capacity in mesial temporal lobe epilepsy. *Epilepsia, 54*(5), 809–818.

Menon, V. (2011). Large-scale brain networks and psychopathology: A unifying triple network model. *Trends in Cognitive Sciences, 15*(10), 483–506.

Menon, V. (2015). Salience network. In A. W. Toga (Ed.), *Brain mapping: An encyclopedic reference* (Vol. 2, pp. 597–611). Academic Press; Elsevier.

Mesulam, M. M. (1990). Large-scale neurocognitive networks and distributed processing for attention, language, and memory. *Annals of Neurology: Official Journal of the American Neurological Association and the Child Neurology Society, 28*(5), 597–613.

Mesulam, M. M. (2000). *Principles of behavioral and cognitive neurology* (2nd ed.). Oxford University Press.

Mevel, K., Chételat, G., Eustache, F., & Desgranges, B. (2011). The default mode network in healthy aging and Alzheimer's disease. *International Journal of Alzheimer's Disease, 2011*, 535816.

Neal, E. G., Maciver, S., Schoenberg, M. R., & Vale, F. L. (2020). Surgical disconnection of epilepsy network correlates with improved outcomes. *Seizure, 76*, 56–63.

Raichle, M. E. (2015). The brain's default mode network. *Annual Review of Neuroscience, 38*, 433–447.

Raichle, M. E., MacLeod, A. M., Snyder, A. Z., Powers, W. J., Gusnard, D. A., & Shulman, G. L. (2001). A default mode of brain function. *Proceedings of the National Academy of Sciences, 98*(2), 676–682.

Ropper, A. H., Samuels, M. A., Klein, J. P., & Prasad, S. (2023). *Adam and Victor's principles of neurology* (12th ed.). McGraw-Hill.

Spreng, R. N. (2012). The fallacy of a "task-negative" network. *Frontiers in Psychology, 3*, 145.

Spreng, R. N., & Grady, C. L. (2010). Patterns of brain activity supporting autobiographical memory, prospection, and theory of mind, and their relationship to the default mode network. *Journal of Cognitive Neuroscience, 22*(6), 1112–1123.

Tsigos, C., & Chrousos, G. P. (2002). Hypothalamic-pituitary-adrenal axis, neuroendocrine factors and stress. *Journal of Psychosomatic Research, 53*, 865–871.

Chapter 4
Components of the Neuropsychological Evaluation

James G. Scott

Key Points and Chapter Summary

- Neuropsychological evaluation uses a Biopsychosocial model in assessing Brain–Behavior Relationships.
- Assessment progresses from simple sensory and motor functions to complex integrative cognitive skills and/or behaviors such as attention, language, memory, visuoperceptual/visuoconstructional, executive (reasoning, problem-solving, insight, judgment, etc.) and mood/personality functioning.
- The foundations of Neuropsychological Assessment include a knowledge of neuropsychology, psychology, functional neuroanatomy, neuropathology and psychometric principles of tests and measurements.
- Neuropsychological assessment of cognitive skills can range from rapid repeatable bedside qualitative assessment in consultation and acute care settings to lengthy formal psychometric evaluation in outpatient settings.
- The decision regarding the assessment method, whether brief qualitative evaluation or detailed psychometric assessment is determined by the neuropsychologist with consideration of factors including: (1) the purpose and nature of the referral, (2) the hypothesized etiology of the known or suspected neuropsychological dysfunction and (3) the time and course of symptoms.

J. G. Scott (✉)
Department of Psychiatry and Behavioral Sciences, University of Oklahoma, Health Sciences Center College of Medicine, Oklahoma City, OK, USA
e-mail: jim-scott@ouhsc.edu

M. R. Schoenberg, J. G. Scott (eds.), *The Little Black Book of Neuropsychology*,
https://doi.org/10.1007/978-3-032-07777-6_4

Overview

Neuropsychological evaluation at its core examines brain–behavior relationships as they pertain to cognitive, emotional and behavioral manifestations of central nervous system developmental delay, trauma, disease or dysfunction. Neuropsychological evaluation includes examination of sensory, motor and perceptual functioning as a prerequisite for evaluation of increasingly complex cognitive, emotional and behavioral functions. Evaluation is typically on an ordinal scale (i.e., impaired/non-impaired) for sensory and perceptual skills and progresses to an integral scale for more complex functions (i.e., percentile relative to normative group). Rapid bedside or interview assessment of functions such as attention, language and memory can be done; however, it is important to note that a brief evaluation will yield less precise information than more psychometrically based formal testing. In Neuropsychology, there is an axiom of the tradeoff between the brevity of the examination and the precision of the findings, and determining the appropriate depth and detail of the examination is about pragmatically balancing this tradeoff.

Brief evaluations have several advantages. These evaluations are quick to perform and can be repeated as necessary to mark progress or suspected deterioration. Information from such evaluations are typically used to assist in patient management, set immediate goals and assist in treatment planning. In later chapters, we discuss brief assessment methods in each domain of cognition and include a chapter with one method of organizing brief assessment across multiple domains of a Neuropsychological examination.

Further details regarding the interpretive process, prerequisite knowledge base for adequate neuropsychological evaluations, psychometric principals guiding interpretation of neuropsychological psychometrically derived data, and common errors to interpretation can be found throughout this book, but particularly in Chaps. 1, 5 and 30–32. Sample neuropsychological reports are provided in Chap. 1 Appendix A.

Basics of the Neuropsychology Evaluation

The clinical neuropsychologist will integrate the patient's current complaints and history (medical, psychiatric, educational, etc.), with available imaging, laboratory data, knowledge of brain–behavior relationships, functional neuroanatomy, neuropathology, cognitive psychology, psychometrics and test theory, psychopathology and neurodevelopment. The obtained assessment data are compared against a comparison standard to identify relative neuropsychological deficits. The patterns of deficits are associated with brain function, which guides the answers to the referral questions. This information is integrated into a consultation or more lengthy formal report. This information is helpful to acutely assess the functioning of the patient, assist in guiding medical staff (Physicians and Nurses) and hospital staff (i.e.,

Physical therapists, Occupational therapists, Speech pathologists, etc.) in their expectations and care of the patient. This detailed consultation or formal assessment can also help family in recognizing deficits, adjusting to change in the patient and beginning to set expectations for the future functioning and accommodations which may be necessary.

Below we review critical patient history and medical information to be obtained followed by a sequential evaluation process of skills and behaviors of increasing complexity which are essential in evaluating brain function. This sequential process is necessary because each previous process or skill is an essential prerequisite to successful and accurate evaluation of subsequent skills of a higher, more complex level. It does us no good to evaluate memory functioning when arousal is impaired or taken to its absurd, everyone in a coma is aphasic.

Key Points: Neuropsychological Assessment

- Assessment must be sequential and assure integrity of prerequisite skills
- Assessment must take a biopsychosocial perspective including integration of all available information (i.e., etiology, course, medical history, social history and psychiatric history) in the analysis and interpretation of assessment results
- Assessment should be tailored to meet the specific purpose and goals for the assessment and may range from brief consultative assessment to lengthy psychometrically based evaluation

Factors Affecting Neuropsychological Functioning

The clinical neuropsychologist will conduct a review of the patient's records, including medical, psychiatric and personal history. In addition, basic demographic information is important to obtain to assist in interpretation of any subsequently obtained neuropsychological data. Important demographic information is reviewed first, followed by medical and psychiatric history.

Several patient-specific demographic factors are critical for accurate interpretation of assessment results and must be considered prior to the evaluation. These demographic factors include age, education, gender, socioeconomic status, employment history and social history such as alcohol use/abuse and other substance use/abuse. In addition, English language proficiency must be considered in persons fluent in another language or who have acquired English as a second language. This is true whether assessment is conducted briefly or with more formal psychometric test instruments.

A thorough understanding of the medical history is also essential. A review of the medical history should be obtained via the patient, collateral informant and, if at all possible, medical records (as medical records can differ from patient's report).

These issues should cover developmental history, medical history, family medical (and psychiatric) history, social history, developmental history as well as factors such as lateral dominance (i.e., handedness, ocular dominance and pedal dominance). Psychiatric history is important to consider, as chronic and acute psychiatric symptoms can influence test or assessment results and have important implications for any interventions or treatments being considered.

A thorough history of the present illness is also critical and will guide evaluation regarding the diagnostic possibilities, cause and expected outcome. This examination should also include current medical factors which may contribute to the present illness such as medication change, toxic exposure, electrolyte imbalances, hormonal deficiencies, previous major surgeries and other medical factors which may be risk factors for the current illness (e.g., diabetes, hyperlipidemia, hypertension, cardiac arrhythmia, sleep apnea, genetic abnormality, etc.)

Time: An Important Variable in the Neuropsychological Evaluation

Creating a timeline including symptom onset and course is critical in understanding current functioning and expectations for future recovery and functioning. The duration of symptoms is an important factor the neuropsychologist should consider when designing the assessment (or treatment program). Time refers not only to the elapsed time since the onset of the injury, but also to the course of the injury and any complications that have arisen. Acute onset or chronic course may result in a neuropsychological evaluation. This should be considered when deciding the type of evaluation to conduct. The neuropsychologist should consider the likely source of the onset of problems and design an evaluation appropriately. For example, a patient sustaining a moderate to severe TBI (Traumatic Brain Injury) may be assessed acutely and /or repeatedly with a brief bedside screening to evaluate severity of their current deficits and gauge recovery. This same patient may need a more formal and thorough evaluation to measure more precisely their functioning when they have stabilized in their recovery and allow for better understanding of long-term deficits and functional capacities. In the case of ischemic or hemorrhagic stroke, acute neuropsychological assessment may be used to gauge recovery, but recognize changes in neuropsychological functioning over days, weeks and even hours may occur. When the presentation is progressive or insidious onset, more comprehensive neuropsychological evaluations may be conducted. Duration of complaints, knowledge of the recovery process and the timing of the assessment thus have profound impacts on the selection of neuropsychological procedures and interpretation of the neuropsychological data obtained.

Hierarchical Assessment of Basic Nervous System Functions (Cranial Nerves, Sensory and Motor Functions)

Prerequisite Function

Examination of cranial nerve function is important for establishing prerequisite functioning for the remainder of the evaluation. This is especially true in acute hospital settings. The cranial nerves, associated functions and methods to assess cranial nerve function are provided in Table 4.1.

Cranial nerves consist of 12 pairs of nerves that emanate from the brain stem (Medulla, Pons and Midbrain) and basal forebrain. Cranial nerves project ipsilaterally and produce deficits on the same side as the injury. Anatomically, Cranial Nerves (CN) I–IV originate from the basal forebrain and midbrain, CN V–VIII originate from the pons, and CN IX–XII originate from the medulla. Both the laterality and anatomical origination of cranial nerves are important for differentiation of cortical and subcortical injuries and localization of injury. Examination of Cranial Nerve function is a critical part of the neurologic evaluation and establishes the integrity of functions that are prerequisite for any accurate evaluation of subsequent cortical functioning.

Cranial nerve function can be grouped into sensory associations such that smell is attributable to the olfactory nerve (CN I), vision is associated with the Optic (CN II). Eye movement is associated with the Occulomotor (CN III), Trochlear (CN IV) and Abducens (CN VI). Similarly, taste is associated with the Facial nerve (CN VII) and Glossopharyngeal (CN IX). Specifically, the Facial Nerve innervates the tip of the tongue and the perception of predominately sweet taste while the Glossopharyngeal Nerve innervates the posterior aspect of the tongue and perception of sour tastes. (Now you know the secret to sweet and sour sauce.) Auditory function is associated with the Acoustic nerve (CN VIII).

It should be noted that Cranial Nerve functions are considered part of the peripheral nervous system and that similar deficits can be obtained from cortical or other central nervous system lesions. Lesions produced centrally (cortically) are distinguished by the contralateral nature of the deficit they produce (with the exception of olfaction). For example, deficits to primary auditory cortex on the right will produce primarily auditory deficits in the left ear, while a lesion to the left acoustic nerve (CN VIII) would produce a primary auditory deficit in the left ear.

Sensory Functioning

Sensory testing involves establishing thresholds for vibratory, tactile and position sensations. In neurological examinations, sensation is established for each level of the spinal cord and cranial nerves involving sensation. In neuropsychological evaluations, sensation is typically examined only for the cranial nerves, and cervical

Table 4.1 Cranial nerve

	Cranial nerve	Function	Abnormality	Assessment
I.	Olfactory	Smell	Anosmia	Test each nostril independently for smell (i.e., Coffee) (Note: Smell is the only uncrossed sense)
II.	Optic	Vision	Pre-chiasmic: monocular blindness Post-chiasmic: hemi-visual field loss	Test Visual Fields in each eye and for both eyes simultaneously
III.	Oculomotor	Eyelid retraction Pupillary constriction Medial eye movement	Drooping eyelid Enlarged pupil Deviation of affected eye laterally (outward)	Note Ptosis, check pupillary asymmetry and reaction to light and accommodation. Note downward and lateral eye deviation upon fixed forward gaze
IV.	Trochlear	Rotation of eye with head tilt	Compensatory head tilt to reduce diplopia	Note diplopia produced with head tilt. Note which eye does not demonstrate appropriate rotation upon head tilt (note: often difficult to test without specialized equipment)
V.	Trigeminal	Mastication muscles Facial sensations	Weakness in bite Loss of sensation	Note asymmetry in mastication musculature or facial sensation threshold
VI.	Abducens	Lateral eye movement	Deviation of eye medially (outward)	Note inward deviation of affected eye upon fixed forward gaze
VII.	Facial	Musculature of facial expression Anterior tongue taste	Weakness of facial muscles Loss of taste on anterior tongue (Ageusia)	Note weakness of facial muscles or asymmetry in facial expression. Inquire about loss of sense of taste, particularly sweet sensitivity
VIII.	Acoustic	Hearing	Decreased auditory sensation	Assess symmetry of auditory threshold
IX.	Glossopharyngeal	Taste on posterior tongue Gag reflex	Ageusia Poor gag reflex	Inquire about loss of sense of taste, particularly sour/bitter. Assess gag reflex
X.	Vagus	Motor movement of soft palate Vocal cord innervation	Decreased palate movement Hoarse voice	Assess elevation symmetry of soft palate. Inquire about change in vocal quality
XI.	Spinal accessory	Neck muscles	Weakness of trapezia	Assess symmetry of strength in shoulder shrug
XII.	Hypoglossal	Muscle of the tongue	Weakness or deviation upon tongue protrusion	Assess tongue weakness via sustained tongue thrust and note deviation.

distributions through C8 which captures sensory function of the hands, as well as integrated sensory perception requiring cortical processing (i.e., graphesthesia, astereoagnosia and bilateral simultaneous stimulation).

In neuropsychological examination, primary sensory testing involves touch and vibratory sensation thresholds, established for each hand (recall sensation above the neck is governed by CN function) as well as examination for laterality of extinction or suppression in double simultaneous sensory stimulation which would be indicative of contralateral cortical sensory strip lesion or a hemisensory neglect syndrome. Sensation from the cervical spinal region (C2–C8) includes the upper chest and arms. The thoracic region (T1–T12) innervates from the chest to just below the umbilicus; whereas the lumbar spine (L1–L5) innervates the genitalia and legs with the exception of the dorso-lateral aspect and sole of the foot, which is innervated by the sacral region (S1–S2) of the spinal cord (see inside front cover for anterior and posterior dermatome map).

Secondary sensation involves examination of sensory functions requiring cortical processing beyond basic perception. Such functions involve bilateral simultaneous processing of stimuli, which may indicate a subtle lesion in the sensory cortex of the hemisphere contralateral to the body side on which the sensation was suppressed. In addition, tactile identification of objects (stereognosis) or the inability to identify tactile information (numbers or letters) written on the palms (graphesthesia) may be impaired and typically represents right hemisphere parietal lobe lesions. In addition, examination of position sense and joint pressure can be evaluated by manipulation of joint position (toe or finger up or down) and by asking the patient to judge weight held in the hands.

Motor Testing

"Motor Testing" may refer to two different types of assessing the function of a patient's motor system: (1) a neurological-based approach utilizing species-wide normative reference information for motor strength, tone and deep tendon reflexes, and (2) a clinical neuropsychological approach using population normative information to assess motor speed, dexterity and strength.

Neurological-Based Assessment

This assessment approach is not routinely administered by clinical neuropsychologists, but if available, the clinician can (and should) incorporate this information into the more quantitative motor assessment often completed as part of a neuropsychological evaluation. As part of the neurological evaluation, motor function is graded in terms of motor strength, tone and deep tendon reflexes. In addition, cerebellar functioning and praxis are often evaluated. Motor strength is graded on a 1–5 scale where 1 is paralysis and 5 is full normal strength. Scores of 2–4 represent graded degrees of paresis (weakness) (see Chap. 2, Table 2.1 for description of anchor points). Motor strength is evaluated both in lateral plane (right-left) and in terms of proximal-distal (moving from the center of the body to distal parts of the limb). While the lateral plane is indicative of the side of the lesion (contralateral), the proximal-distal and extensor-flexors comparisons often are related to the degree of recovery. Specifically, motor recovery after an injury often progresses from proximal to distal with large muscle groups such as shoulders and hips regaining function before hands and feet. Motor function also typically recovers in a pattern of flexor muscles returning before extensor muscles. This is important for ambulation in the ability of patients to raise the foot (dorsiflexion) and for manual functioning in the extension of the hand, which are often the last motor functions to return following cerebral damage.

Motor tone is graded on a continuum of flaccid to spastic, with muscle wasting and flaccidity being associated with peripheral (lower motor neuron) injury and spasticity being associated with central nervous system (upper motor neuron) injury. While initial response to both peripheral and central nervous system injury results in flaccidity, as time progresses, flaccidity remains in peripheral injury but over time is replaced by hyper-tonicity in central nervous system injury. These distinctions give the clinician insight into the location of the injury, but also the expected recovery pattern and potential long-term issues in functional capacity to expect.

Tone is graded on a scale of 1–4, determined subjectively by muscle stretch reflexes (See Chap. 2, Table 2.1). Hyper-tonicity (i.e., spastic muscle tone) is associated with central nervous system damage whereas hypo-tonicity (decreased muscle stretch reflex) is associated with peripheral nerve injury. Reflex rating of 2 is normal, with ratings of 3 indicating hyper reflexia and ratings of 4 indicating hyper reflexia with clonus (repeated elicitation of stretch receptor reflex after single stimulation). These ratings are sometimes denoted with a plus sign (i.e., 2^+ or 3^+) if they are considered to be in the high end of normal (2+) or the high end of abnormal but do not elicit clonus (3+) (see Chap. 2, Table 2.1).

Neuropsychological-Based Assessment

Evaluation of motor function is often completed as part of the neuropsychological examination. Clinical neuropsychologists will frequently assess motor function using a hand dynamometer, rate of finger oscillations within a specified time and/or performance completing a timed task of fine motor dexterity [e.g., Grooved Pegboard Test or Purdue Pegboard Test]. Unlike neurological examination of motor strength, the comparison standard for these tests is population based, such that age-, education- and gender-demographic based norms are available. The normative-based motor function assessment often completed as part of a neuropsychological evaluation should be incorporated with global ratings of motor function and muscle tone. Patient's with clear hemiparesis (e.g., flaccid hemiplegia) often will not require further neuropsychological-based assessment of motor function. Alternatively, patients completing rehabilitation who have good recovery of motor function to a cursory neurological exam will often continue to exhibit clear deficits on more detailed neuropsychological-based assessment of motor function, providing helpful information for diagnosis and treatment planning (see Lezak et al., 2004 for review).

Cerebellar and Praxis Examination

Examination of cerebellar functions involves performing tasks of smooth motor pursuit and balance. This is most typically evaluated by having the person perform such tasks as finger to nose in which they alternatingly touch the examiner's finger and their nose rapidly in succession. Heal-to-toe walking, walking on a straight line and raising the heal along the shinbone while seated are other common methods of assessing cerebellar function. Each activity is evaluated subjectively on a pass/fail basis.

Praxis evaluation involves performing complex, sequenced motor movements both to command and imitation (see also Chap. 10, this volume for more details). Cortical damage to left parietal association area often disrupts such overlearned complex motor tasks and may affect such tasks as grooming, dressing or feeding behaviors. Damage to the right parietal lobe often is associated with constructional praxis. Praxis is typically evaluated by asking patients to simulate blowing out a match, unlocking a door, using a hammer or sucking a straw. Patients who are unable to easily simulate these acts spontaneously are then asked to mimic the examiner performing these acts. Individuals suspected of constructional praxis are typically asked to draw a simple object (i.e., house, face, tree) and if they are unable to draw spontaneously, they are given a design to copy. Failure to spontaneously perform commands or draw is indicative of deficits and should prompt further, more detailed assessment.

"Higher Order" Neuropsychological Function Examination

We now turn our attention to higher level cognitive processing. These skills involve arousal, processing speed, attention and concentration, language, memory, visuospatial/visuoperceptual executive skills (i.e., reasoning, sequencing, problem-solving, judgment and insight) and mood/affect. In addition, a thorough neuropsychological evaluation will evaluate a patient's effort or motivation to perform to his/her best ability using a variety of methods that can include stand-alone measures of task engagement (e.g., performance or symptom validity testing) as well as various algorithms and comparison within and across neuropsychological measures to assess for consistency and adherence to known neuropathological patterns of performance (see Chaps. 19 and 20, this volume for details). Evaluation of mood is typically completed using a variety of psychological measures, which may be based on patient's report, the report of collateral informants (i.e., family members, teachers and perhaps friends or coworkers) and/or ratings by a clinician. In general, we recommend a screening assessment of emotional functioning include symptoms of anxiety and depression at a minimum. More detailed psychological assessment may be needed depending upon the nature of the referral, patient variables and clinician variables. Finally, the neuropsychological evaluation will establish a premorbid level of cognitive functioning as an additional comparison standard.

The neuropsychological functions assessed as part of a comprehensive evaluation are discussed throughout the rest of this book. However, as a process of neuropsychological evaluation, they are mentioned here to highlight the sequential nature of each as an integral part of the assessment of increasingly complex functions. As measurement of cognitive functions get increasingly complex, the lateralizing and localizing nature of them becomes less certain. For example, the areas that can result in an expressive aphasia are well established, but damage almost anywhere in the brain can produce complex attentional and information processing deficits. As a process however, accurate neuropsychological evaluation is dependent on the adequacy of a hierarchical series of prerequisite skills. These skills are presented graphically in a Neuropsychological Evaluation Process Pyramid, with prerequisite skills on the bottom and subsequently more complex skills at the top (Fig. 4.1).

Assessment of these functions may be brief or extensive. In brief examinations, these areas of more complex and integrative cognitive functioning are assessed at basic levels. Individuals who have acquired these skills are expected to demonstrate very good function on these brief and often simple assessment tasks. In younger patients or those with developmental delays or intellectual disability, expectations must be adjusted accordingly. These brief evaluations are limited in that they yield results that allow only ordinal data such as impaired vs. normal or a mild-moderate-severe impairment continuum. While brief evaluation has the benefit of repeatability, rapid assessment and targeting specific deficits, it also has the drawback of being less thorough in the assessment of any given higher cognitive function as well as not providing a finer delineated psychometrically based measurement of the higher cognitive function or integrative skill being assessed.

More formal neuropsychological assessment involves measurement of these "Higher Cognitive" functions and comparisons to both known populations that are matched as closely as possible to the patient in age, education, gender and other demographic factors which might have an influence on the function being measured. The patient's performance is also typically evaluated in light of an individual-level comparison standard that is derived from estimates of the individual's premorbid level of cognitive function. Further details of psychometrics and interpretation are covered in Chaps. 1 and 30–32 in this volume (see also Lezak et al., 2004 for detailed discussion of interpretation in neuropsychology).

Key Points: Deficit Measurement

- Assessment of change requires comparison standard be established
- Comparison standards include normative comparison standards or individual comparison standards
  - Normative comparison standard may be species-wide behaviors/skills or population-based normative information on cognitive skills and behaviors
  - Individual comparison standards can include historical information (previous test scores before onset of known or suspected brain dysfunction) or, most commonly, estimated premorbid ability level(s)
- A comparison standard establishes a benchmark against which an individual's performance is compared to determine if change (deficit or improvement) in neuropsychological function has occurred
- Patterns of neuropsychological deficits are associated with functional neuroanatomy and neuropathology to associate behavior deficits to brain dysfunction

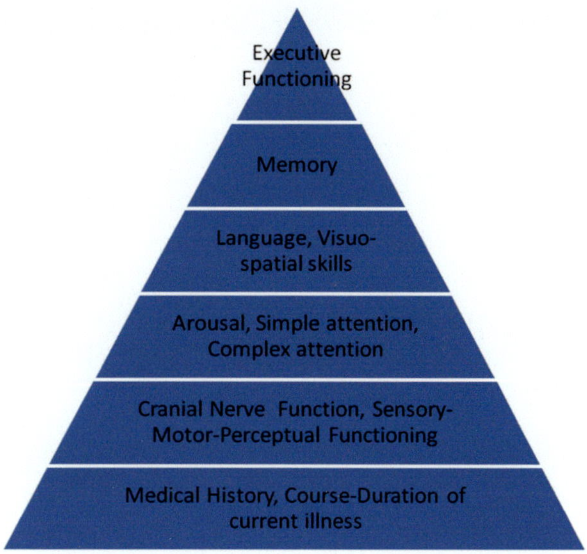

Fig. 4.1 Pyramid perspective for assessment of prerequisite neuropsychological functioning

References and Suggested Further Readings

Bonner, J. S., & Bonner, J. J. (1991). *The little black book of Neurology* (2nd ed.). Mosby.

Lezak, M. D., Howieson, D. B., & Loring, D. W. (2004). *Neuropsychological assessment* (4th ed.). Oxford University Press.

Chapter 5
Brief Cognitive Assessment

Scott M. Roye and James G. Scott

> **Key Points and Chapter Summary**
> - Bedside assessments are conducted using brief, repeatable, neuropsychological tests that are less sensitive than the standardized measures used in a comprehensive evaluation.
> - Results from a bedside evaluation can be used to acutely assess and monitor cognition, as well as inform providers if more comprehensive, follow-up testing is necessary.
> - Although bedside testing measures lack diagnostic precision, brief forms of sensory, motor and cognitive testing can help localize significant impairments.
> - Prior to administering even brief cognitive measures, clinicians should ensure that basic functioning capabilities are present.
> - The BBRAT is a bedside screening measure designed to briefly evaluate specific aspects of sensory, motor and cognitive functioning for clinically significant deficits/impairments.
> - BBRAT forms, along with instructions for administering, scoring and interpreting results of the measure, can be found toward the end of this chapter.

S. M. Roye (✉) · J. G. Scott
Department of Psychiatry and Behavioral Sciences, University of Oklahoma Health, Health Sciences Center College of Medicine, Oklahoma City, OK, USA
e-mail: scott-roye@ouhsc.edu; jim-scott@ouhsc.edu

M. R. Schoenberg, J. G. Scott (eds.), *The Little Black Book of Neuropsychology*,
https://doi.org/10.1007/978-3-032-07777-6_5

Bedside Evaluations

In an acute medical setting, neuropsychologists are often called upon for multiple roles, including providing psychoeducation and conducting bedside evaluations. Unlike a comprehensive, outpatient neuropsychological evaluation, a bedside evaluation is a targeted, brief assessment of acute cognitive changes, often utilized to offer diagnostic clarity, address issues related to capacity and independent living, offer insight about a patient's baseline functioning and monitor symptom progression over time (Kessler, 2006; Pavol, 2019). Although the brief nature of such an evaluation limits diagnostic sensitivity, they provide prompt information that is often necessary for patient care.

Bedside evaluations are not without their restrictions though. Limitations and challenges to these assessments include providing diagnostic impressions in both a limited timeframe and with limited data. Assessment measures used in these settings often have reduced sensitivity and, while they can effectively identify areas of impairment, they should not be used to formulate diagnoses beyond identifying acute impairment. Therefore, given these limitations, the importance of receiving specific referral questions cannot be understated. Neuropsychologists working in these settings are encouraged to communicate the strengths and limitations of these evaluations with referral providers, and ensure that impressions based on the findings are not overgeneralized or interpreted as being comparable to more comprehensive, outpatient neuropsychological evaluations.

Evaluation of Individual Domains

Cranial Nerve Exam

The importance of demographic factors, review of a patient's records and thorough history of the present illness cannot be overstated and should be considered with every case. Once that information has been obtained and thoroughly reviewed, an evaluation of sensory, behavioral and cognitive functioning can begin. An assessment of arousal, orientation and basic language functioning is an important prerequisite to establish prior to beginning a bedside evaluation and can be observed starting with introducing yourself to your patient. Examiners should make note of the patient's ability to communicate basic information (e.g., their name, where they are and why they are here), as limitations in these areas can alter the trajectory of an examination. Once these prerequisite functions have been established, evaluating cranial nerve functions can begin. Examination of cranial nerve functions is important for establishing prerequisite sensory functioning for the remainder of the evaluation and can be particularly important within an acute hospital setting. The cranial nerves, associated functions and methods to assess cranial nerve function are provided in Table 5.1 as well as in the Brief Bedside Repeatable Assessment Test (BBRAT).

Table 5.1 Cranial nerves

Cranial nerve	Function	Assessment	Abnormality
CN I olfactory	Smell	Test each nostril independently for smell (e.g., coffee)	Anosmia
CN II optic	Vision	Test visual fields of each eye, as well as both simultaneously	Pre-chiasmic: Monocular defect Post-chiasmic: Contralateral hemianopia or quadrant anopsia
CN III oculomotor	Eyelid retraction, pupillary constriction, medial eye movement	Assess for ptosis, pupillary asymmetry, reaction to light and accommodation, downward and lateral eye deviation upon fixed forward gaze	Enlarged pupil, ptosis, downward and lateral gaze deviation; diplopia on upward contralateral gaze
CN IV trochlear	Rotation of eye with head tilt	Note diplopia with head tilt or compensatory head tilt. Assess eye rotation on head tilt	Decreased eye rotation with head tilt; diplopia reported with head tilt (difficult to detect)
CN V trigeminal	Mastication muscles, facial sensations	Note asymmetry in V1, V2 and V3 with unilateral stimulation	Bite weakness; loss of tactile facial sensation
CN VI abducens	Lateral eye movement Eyelid protractions	Note inward gaze deviation of affected eye. Proptosis of eyelid.	Deviation of eye medially (inward); increased diplopia with lateral gaze in affected eye
CN VII facial	Musculature of facial expression, anterior tongue taste	Note facial asymmetry (particularly in nasolabile fold), note loss of sweet taste	Facial muscle weakness, Loss of taste on anterior tongue
CN VIII vestibulocochlear	Hearing	Test acuity with unilateral stimulation	Decreased auditory acuity
CN IX glossopharyngeal	Taste on posterior tongue, gag reflex)	Assess gag reflex, inquire about loss of sour or bitter taste	Ageusia, decreased gag reflex
CN X vagus	Motor movement of soft palate, vocal cord innervation	Assess elevation symmetry of soft palate, inquire about change in vocal tone/quality	Decreased soft palate movement, vocal cord innervation, hoarse voice
CN XI spinal accessory	Neck muscles	Assess strength and symmetry of shoulder shrug	Trapezius weakness
CN XII hypoglossal	Muscle of the tongue	Assess tongue thrust, noting deviation and sustainability	Weakness or deviation upon unsupported protrusion

Cranial nerves consist of 12 pairs of nerves that emanate from the brain stem (medulla, pons and midbrain) and basal forebrain. Cranial nerves project ipsilaterally and produce deficits on the same side of the body as the injury. This should not be confused with non-cranial nerve examinations of sensory and motor functions which are contralateral to the site of the cerebral lesion (olfaction being the exception to this rule). Anatomically, cranial nerves (CN) I–IV project from the inferior frontal lobe and midbrain, CN V–VIII project from the pons, and CN IX–XII project from the medulla. Both the laterality and anatomical origination of cranial nerves are important for differentiating cortical and subcortical injuries, as well as localizing injuries. Note that while cranial nerve functions are ipsilateral, similar cortical sensory and motor functions are contralaterally organized. Examination of cranial nerve function is a critical part of the neurologic evaluation and establishes the integrity of functions that are prerequisite for any accurate evaluation of subsequent cortical functioning.

Cranial nerve function can be grouped into sensory associations such that smell is attributable to the olfactory nerve (CN I) and vision is associated with the optic nerve (CN II). Eye movement is associated with the occulomotor nerve (CN III), trochlear nerve (CN IV) and abducens (CN VI). The trigeminal nerve (CN V) is associated with physical sensations for the face, mouth, tongue, sinuses and meninges, as well as muscles of mastication. Taste is associated with the facial nerve (CN VII) and glossopharyngeal nerve (CN IX). Specifically, the facial nerve innervates the tip of the tongue and the perception of predominately sweet taste, while the glossopharyngeal nerve innervates the posterior aspect of the tongue and perception of sour tastes. (Now you know the secret to sweet and sour sauce.) Auditory function is associated with the vestibulocochlear nerve (CN VIII).

It should be noted that CN functions are considered part of the peripheral nervous system and that similar deficits can be obtained from cortical or other central nervous system lesions. Lesions produced centrally (cortically) are distinguished by the contralateral nature of the deficit they produce (with the exception of olfaction). For example, deficits to the primary auditory cortex in the right hemisphere will primarily produce auditory perceptual deficits predominantly in the left ear, while a lesion to the left vestibulocochlear nerve (CN VIII) would primarily produce primary auditory deficits in the left ear. See the Brief Bedside Repeatable Assessment Test below regarding methods of assessment and notable abnormalities associated with individual cranial nerve function.

Somatosensory Functioning

Sensory testing involves establishing thresholds for vibratory, tactile and position sensations. Sensation is evaluated for each level of the spinal cord, as well as sensation requiring cortical processing (i.e., graphesthesia, asteroagnosia and bilateral simultaneous stimulation).

Primary sensory testing involves touch and vibratory sensation thresholds, established for each level of the body from feet to neck (recall sensation above the neck is governed by CN function). Sensation from the cervical spinal region (C2–C8) is in the upper chest and arms. The thoracic region (T1–T12) innervates from the chest to just below the umbilicus; whereas the lumbar spine (L1–L5) innervates the genitalia and legs with the exception of the dorsolateral aspect and sole of the foot, which is innervated by the sacral region (S1–S2) of the spinal cord (see front inside cover for Sensory and Motor Dermatome diagram).

Secondary sensation involves examination of sensory functions requiring cortical processing beyond basic threshold perception. Such functions involve bilateral simultaneous processing of stimuli, which may indicate a subtle lesion in the sensory cortex of the hemisphere contralateral to the body side on which the sensation was suppressed. In addition, tactile identification of objects (stereognosis) or the inability to identify tactile information (numbers or letters) written on the palms (graphesthesia) may be impaired and typically represents right hemisphere parietal lobe lesions. In addition, examination of position sense and joint pressure can be evaluated by manipulation of joint position (toe up or down) and by asking the patient to judge weight held in the hands. Unique to other sensory functions, basic hearing can be evaluated by whispering or rubbing your fingers next to a patient's ear, with observed deficits suggesting ipsilateral cranial nerve or contralateral primary auditory cortex dysfunction.

Motor Testing

"Motor Testing" in Neuropsychology may refer to two types of assessment: (1) a neurological-based approach utilizing species-wide universal reference information for motor strength, tone and deep tendon reflexes, and (2) a clinical neuropsychological approach using population normative information to assess motor speed, dexterity and strength.

Neurologically Based Assessment

This assessment approach is not routinely administered by clinical neuropsychologists in an outpatient setting, but if available, the clinician can (and should) incorporate this information into the more quantitative motor assessment often completed as part of a neuropsychological evaluation. As part of the neurological evaluation, motor function is graded in terms of motor strength, tone and deep tendon reflexes. In addition, cerebellar functioning and praxis are often evaluated. Motor strength is graded on a 1–5 scale where 1 is paralysis and 5 is fully normal strength. Scores of 2–4 represent graded degrees of paresis (weakness) (Table 5.2 for descriptive anchor points for each rating 2–4). Motor strength is evaluated both in lateral plane (right-left) and in terms of proximal-distal (moving away from the center of the body). While the lateral plane is indicative of the side of the lesion (contralateral), the proximal-distal and extensor-flexors comparisons are often related to the degree of

Table 5.2 Grading of deep tendon reflexes (DTRs)

Grading of DTRs	Qualitative descriptor of reflex grading
0	Not present, even with facilitatory procedure
1	Present but reduced or weak
2	Normal
2+	Normal, but somewhat brisk (high normal)
3	Brisk
3 + 4 (or 3+)	Very brisk, but no clonus
4	Pathologically brisk with four beat clonus

recovery or help to medial-lateral spinal cord impairment/involvement. Specifically, motor recovery after an injury often progresses from proximal to distal with large muscle groups such as shoulders and hips regaining function before hands and feet. Motor function also typically recovers in a pattern of flexor muscles returning before extensor muscles. This is important for ambulation in the ability of patients to raise the foot (dorsiflexion) and for manual functioning in the extension of the hand, which are often the last motor functions to return following cerebral damage.

Motor tone is graded on a continuum of flaccid to spastic, with muscle wasting and flaccidity being associated with peripheral (lower motor neuron) injury and spasticity being associated with central nervous system (upper motor neuron) injury. Although both peripheral and central nervous system injuries present initially with flaccidity, over time, flaccidity only persists in a peripheral injury, as it is replaced by hyper-tonicity in central nervous system injuries.

Muscle tone is graded on a scale of 1–4, determined subjectively by muscle stretch reflexes (See Table 5.2). Hyper-tonicity (i.e., spastic muscle tone) is associated with central nervous system damage, whereas hypo-tonicity (decreased muscle stretch reflex) is associated with peripheral nerve injury. Reflex rating of 2 is normal, with ratings of 3 indicating hyper reflexia and ratings of 4 indicating hyper reflexia with clonus (repeated elicitation of stretch receptor reflex after a single stimulation). These ratings are sometimes denoted with a plus sign (i.e., 2^+ or 3^+) if they are considered to be in the high end of normal (2+) or the high end of abnormal but do not elicit clonus (3+) (Table 5.2).

Cerebellar and Praxis Examination

Examination of cerebellar functions involves performing tasks of smooth motor pursuit and balance. This is typically evaluated by asking the patient to alternate between touching the examiner's finger and the patient's nose in rapid succession, as well as heal-to-toe walking, walking on a straight line and raising the heel along the shinbone while seated. Each activity is evaluated subjectively on a pass/fail basis.

Praxis evaluation involves performing complex, sequenced motor movements both to command and imitation (see also Chap. 10, this volume for more details). Cortical damage to left parietal association area often disrupts such overlearned complex motor tasks and may affect such tasks as grooming, dressing or feeding behaviors. Damage to the right parietal lobe is often associated with ideomotor praxis, and is typically evaluated by asking patients to simulate blowing out a match, unlocking a door, using a hammer or sucking a straw. Patients who are unable to easily simulate these acts spontaneously are then asked to mimic the examiner performing these acts. Individuals suspected of constructional praxis are typically asked to draw a simple object (i.e., house, face, tree) and, if they are unable to draw spontaneously, they are given a design to copy. Failure to spontaneously perform commands or draw is indicative of a deficit, and should prompt a more detailed assessment.

Neuropsychological Perspective

Patients with frontal lobe damage often have difficulty with fine motor skills and sequencing motor skills. They may exhibit difficulty both with tasks requiring sustained rapid motor responses and sequenced, novel motor skills. Patients may also have difficulty with simple sequencing tasks, which may be detected through perseverative responding. To test these deficits, patients can be asked to rapidly tap their thumb and index finger. They should be instructed to perform this after being shown the examiner performing the task. Observations should be made regarding their ability to sustain their fine motor speed for 15 seconds to ensure that there is no gross slowing or increasing rigidity as indicated by progressively smaller taps (note: Parkinsons Disease and other movement disorders can produce this deficit as well). A second task involves asking them to perform a novel three-step sequenced task (Sequencing Hands task) after being shown through modeling. In this case, the examiner places his hand on a table first making a fist, then with palm flat (slap), then on the side (i.e., Karate chop). The patient is asked to mimic this "fist-palm-side" sequenced movement. After success or failure with one hand, the other hand should be tested. While it is not unusual for some patients (especially elderly) to require repeated modeling to acquire the appropriate sequence, if more than two trials are necessary, a sequencing deficit should be suspected. The patient should be able to complete three complete motor sequences without error.

Motor persistence and perseveration can be assessed using tasks requiring rapid alternation of hand movements. Rapid alternating motor sequencing can be assessed by asking patients to rapidly alternate hands from palm up to palm down (Alternating Hands task). The examiner first models the task and then requests that the patient mimic the hand motions. The examiner places both hands down on a surface (typically a table or top of legs if seated) and then alternatingly lifts and rotates hands to be palm up and then palm down. Each hand is rotated palm up and palm down and then the alternate hand is rotated. The alternate rotating is then increased in speed and should be sustained in rapid succession for 10–15 seconds. Patients should be expected to master the sequence of movements rapidly within one or two modeling trials and sustain the sequence for the duration of the task. If patients have difficulty, the examiner may try to teach the task by adding the verbal label, "all the way over, all the way back," to their demonstration to gauge if verbal cueing or prompting assists in acquiring or maintaining the task performance. If labeling the examiner's modeling of the behavior is unsuccessful, the examiner can take the patient's hands and rotate them and verbalize, "all the way over, all the way back," to see if kinetic cueing is effective in allowing them to master the task. In general, patients are expected to master the task after observing a demonstration. Failure to perform or sustain rapid alternations over a 10–15 seconds timeframe should be considered an abnormal performance and reason for further psychometric investigation.

"Higher Order" Neuropsychological Function Examination

We now turn our attention to higher level cognitive processing. These skills involve sustained arousal, processing speed, attention and concentration, language, memory, visuospatial/visuoperceptual, and executive skills (i.e., reasoning, sequencing, problem-solving, judgment and insight) Although a more detailed description of these processes can be found in later chapters, in this section, we describe how to measure individual cognitive abilities in the context of a brief assessment and discuss the importance of a lower- to higher-order sequential assessment process when evaluating cognition. As measurement of cognitive functions becomes increasingly complex, the lateralizing and localizing nature of each function can become less certain as these level skills often require integrative cortical communication. For example, areas that can result in an expressive aphasia are well established, but damage almost anywhere in the brain can produce attentional and information processing deficits. As a process however, accurate neuropsychological evaluation is dependent on the adequacy of a hierarchical series of prerequisite skills. These skills are presented graphically in a Neuropsychological Evaluation Process Pyramid, with prerequisite skills on the bottom and subsequently more complex skills at the top.

During brief examinations, areas of more complex and integrative cognitive functioning are assessed at basic levels. Individuals with intact cognitive abilities are expected to demonstrate adequate functioning on these brief, and sometimes simpler, tasks. In younger patients, as well as in those with developmental delays or intellectual disability, expectations must be adjusted accordingly. Additionally, while brief evaluations have the benefits of being completed quickly and being easily repeated, they also have the drawback of being less thorough, and do not typically provide a psychometric based measurement for higher cognitive functions or integrative skills being assessed. More specifically, brief evaluations are often nominal or ordinal scale, which can only result in gross descriptions or performance levels such as intact-impaired, present-absent or normal-mild-moderate or severe impairment. Nominal and ordinal scales restrict the range of performance evaluation to these less specific terms noted above and, as such, limit our understanding of the magnitude of deficit in the function being assessed.

Bedside Assessment of Arousal

Arousal is the most basic cognitive function, and therefore, needs to be largely intact for a patient to engage in a cognitive evaluation. Several aspects of arousal can be evaluated during an initial assessment within both inpatient or outpatient settings. Minimal assessment of arousal should include qualitative observation of arousal over time and fluctuations in arousal level across time through serial assessment. At a basic level, patients with arousal deficits have difficulty orienting to changes in visual, tactile or auditory stimuli within their environment, and often require redirection to interview and assessment processes. Several instruments have been designed to assess arousal and have applications for serial assessment in acute settings such as the Galveston Orientation and Amnesia Test (GOAT; Levin et al., 1979), the Glasgow Coma Scale (GCS; Teasdale & Jennett, 1974) and Confusion Assessment Method (CAM; Inouye et al., 1990). The GOAT, GCS and CAM are presented in Tables 5.3, 5.4 and 5.5. Further evaluation can be provided through periodical, observational ratings of the patient's arousal throughout the day (see Table 5.6). Finally, the clinical neuropsychologist observing a patient with disrupted arousal should also assess for the possibility of acute stroke including cranial nerve abnormalities, hemiparesis, tremor or signs of decorticate or decerebrate posturing. If not already under a physician's care, we strongly recommend the neuropsychologist immediately refer the patient with suspected altered or fluctuating arousal to a physician or hospital emergency department for further evaluation.

Bedside Assessment of Attention

General Assessment Issues

Directed and sustained attention is a critical prerequisite involved in nearly all objective performance measures used during a cognitive assessment. For example, patients with frontal lobe impairment often present with attention related concerns, ranging from subtle to grossly overt. The complexity of the frontal lobe's involvement in many tasks, both directly and indirectly, means that cognitive deficits due to frontal lobe dysfunction may range from only noticeable to those familiar with the patient, to more overt and easily recognizable signs of impairment. Additionally, attention deficits can have implications for other aspects of cognitive testing. While frontal lobe impairment can produce simple, sustained and complex voluntary attention deficits, from an objective testing perspective, these deficits can have a discernible impact on seemingly unrelated tasks, such as object naming, geometric figure copy or even holding a conversation without becoming tangential or circumloquacious (Table 5.7).

Table 5.3 The Galveston Orientation and Amnesia Test (GOAT) (* entered by examiner)

*Name: ______________	*Date of test / / /	
*Gender:______________	*Time: ______________	
*Day of the week: _____	*Date of injury / / /	
*Date of birth: / / /		
*Diagnosis: ___________		
1. What is your name? (2) ______	Error	Points
When were you born? (4) ______	______	______
Where do you live? (4) ______	______	______
2. Where are you now? (5) city ______	______	______
(5) hospital ______ (Unnecessary to state name of hospital)	______	______
3. On what date were you admitted to this hospital? (5) ______	______	______
4. What is the first event you can remember after the injury? (5) ______	______	______
Can you describe in detail (e.g., date, time and companions) the first event you can recall after the injury? (5) ____________	______	______
5. Can you describe the last event you recall before the accident? (5) ____________	______	______
Can you describe in detail (e.g., date, time and companions) the first event you can recall before the injury? (5) ____________	______	______
6. What time is it now? ______ (−1 for each ½ hour removed from correct time to maximum of −5)	______	______
7. What day of the week is it now? ______ (−1 for each day removed from the correct day to a maximum of −5)	______	______
8. What day of the month is it now? ______ (−1 for each day removed from correct date to maximum of −5)	______	______
9. What is the month? ______ (−5 for each month removed from correct one to maximum of −15)	______	______
10. What is the year? ______ (−10 for each year removed from correct one to maximum of −30)	______	______
Total error points:	______	
Total GOAT Score (100 points minus total error points)		

Source: Reprinted from Levin HS, O'Donnell VM, Grossman RG: The Galveston Orientation and Amnesia, Test: a practical scale to assess cognition after head injury. *J Nerv Ment Dis* 167:675–684, 1979. Copyright 1979 by Williams & Wilkins. Used with permission

Simple Attention

Simple attention can be evaluated by asking a patient to watch your finger as you move it slowly back and forth horizontally. They should be informed to keep their head still and track the examiner's finger with their eyes. This should be sustained for 15 seconds. The examiner can then add distraction to the task by prompting a discussion or purposefully diverting their gaze away from the patient. If the patient fails to maintain their voluntary gaze on the examiner's finger under either circumstance, the instructions can be repeated that the examiner wants them to maintain

Table 5.4 Glasgow Coma Scale (GCS)

Eye response	**Circle Score**	
None	1	Not attributable to ocular swelling
To pain	2	Pain stimulus is applied
To speech	3	Nonspecific eye opening to speech; does not imply the patient obeys commands
Spontaneous	4	Eyes are open, but this does not imply intact awareness
Motor response	**Circle Score**	
No response	1	Flaccid
Extension	2	"Decerebrate"; extended arms, internal rotation of shoulder and pronation of the forearm
Abnormal flexion	3	"Decorticate"; contracted arms, abnormal flexion of wrists and hands
Withdrawal	4	Normal flexor response; generalized withdrawal (non-specific) to pain
Localizes pain	5	Localized withdrawal to painful stimuli, attempts to remove pain source
Obeys commands	6	Follows simple commands
Verbal response	**Circle Score**	
No response	1	(Self-explanatory)
Incomprehensible	2	Moaning and groaning, but no recognizable words
Inappropriate	3	Intelligible speech (e.g., shouting or swearing), but no sustained or coherent conversation
Confused	4	Responds to questions, but the responses indicate varying disorientation and confusion
Oriented	5	Normal orientation to time, place and person
	Total Score ________/15	

Source: Adapted from Teasdale and Jennett 1974

attention on the moving finger no matter what distractions are present. Individuals with attention deficits will often demonstrate difficulty with persistent voluntary attention and either lose attention to the task or have difficulty sustaining attention when confronted with verbal or visual competing environmental stimuli.

Although attention can be measured from an auditory or visual perspective, it is often easier to assess auditory attention during a bedside evaluation. Forward digit span is a common auditory attention task that involves orally stating random, single-digit numbers (0–9) to a patient at one per second (e.g., 6-4-9-7-2). The numbers are repeated by the patient and assessed for accuracy. While education does have an impact on performance, age appears to have a minimal effect on digit-span forward (Lezak et al., 2012). The range of repetition of digits forward is traditionally considered to be 7 with an approximate standard deviation of 2 (e.g., correctly repeating 5 to 9 digits forward is considered normal). Test presentation data and descriptions of performance are presented in Table 5.8. For those patients older than 65, a reduction of 1 digit is appropriate (e.g., 4 to 8 digits forward). Individuals who have speech production problems can be presented with a page of numbers arranged from 0–9

Table 5.5 Confusion Assessment Method (CAM) diagnostic algorithm (*Diagnostic criteria for scale in measure footnote)

Feature 1	**Acute onset and fluctuating course**
	This feature is usually obtained from a family member or nurse and is shown by positive responses to the following questions: Is there evidence of an acute change in mental status from the patient's baseline? Did the (abnormal) behavior fluctuate during the day, that is, tend to come and go, or increase and decrease in severity?
Feature 2	**Inattention**
	This feature is shown by a positive response to the following question: Did the patient have difficulty focusing attention, for example, being easily distractible or having difficulty keeping track of what was being said?
Feature 3	**Disorganized thinking**
	This feature is shown by a positive response to the following question: Was the patient's thinking disorganized or incoherent, such as rambling or irrelevant conversation, unclear or illogical flow of ideas or unpredictable switching from subject to subject?
Feature 4	**Altered level of consciousness**
	This feature is shown by any answer other than "alert" to the following question: Overall, how would you rate this patient's level of consciousness? (alert [normal], vigilant [hyper alert], lethargic [drowsy, easily aroused], stupor [difficult to arouse] or coma [unarousable])

* The diagnosis of delirium by CAM requires the presence of features I and 2 and either 3 or 4

Table 5.6 Observational Assessment of Arousal

Feature	Assessment	Grading[a]			
Adaptation to environmental change	Response to new person, verbal or visual stimulation	0	1		
Activity level	Maintenance of appropriate response, avoidance of fluctuations	0	1	2	3
Response latency	Similar reaction time, response latency across tasks and time	0	1	2	3
Task persistence	Persistence on task through completion, minimal redirection needed	0	1	2	3

[a]0—No response/severely impaired
1—Hypo arousal, minimal impairment
2—Fluctuations hypo–hyperarousal, normal/impaired
3—Normal performance

and test stimuli either presented aurally or by pointing to numbers. Similar performance levels should be expected as with aural presentation and verbal response.

Reverse digit span is a slightly more difficult task requiring patients to listen (or view as in the case of visually presented stimuli) to digits presented at a rate of one per second and then report the sequence of numbers in reverse order. This task is more demanding in that it not only requires short-term attention, but also storage and manipulation of this information prior to repetition of the digits. This task has been shown to be much more sensitive to the effects of acute and chronic cortical compromise. In a normal population, the average person should perform one digit less in digits backward than forward (i.e., 6 ± 2). Serial 7 is another complex

Table 5.7 Interview assessment of frontal lobe changes

Area	Change	Frequency/ duration/severity[a]
Activity/energy	Hypoactive	
	Hyperactive	
Initiation	Hypo initiative (Abulic)	
	Disinhibited	
Social function	Decreased social skill	
	Social imperturbability	
	Social avoidance	
	Social disinhibition	
Emotional responsiveness	Overreactive	
	Underreactive	
	Rapidly variable	
Attention	Poor sustained attention	
	Difficulty switching attention	
	Perseveration	
Language	Disorganized	
	Unresponsive to questions asked	
	Lapses from attentional difficulty	
Memory	Increased variability/inconsistency	
	Poor detail recall	
	Difficulty with temporal order in recall	
Reasoning/ sequencing	Difficulty sequencing tasks such as cooking, repair or other frequent activities	
	Concrete understanding, inability to see from others perspective	
	Knows conceptually, but can't problem-solve the solution, step or steps to resolve novel problem	

[a]Column can be used as part of a working guide to note extent of change in domains listed. We have used percentile change, ranging from no change (around 0%) to total change (100%) in that function/behavior. In some situations, it may be appropriate to not ask percent change, but rather a qualitative description, such as "no, small, medium or large" change in function has occurred

Table 5.8 Digit span forward and reverse[a]

Digits	Forward	Reverse
2–6	Severely impaired	Moderately impaired
9–3 – 1	Moderately impaired	Mildly impaired
5–7 – 4 – 8	Mildly impaired	Borderline
3–9 – 6 – 2 – 5	Borderline	Low normal
8–3 – 1 – 2 – 9 – 4	Low normal	Normal
7–6 – 4 – 1 – 3 – 5 – 2	Normal	High normal
3–9 – 4 – 6 – 8 – 2 – 5 – 1	High normal	High performance
5–6 – 9 – 2 – 8 – 3 – 5 – 1 – 7	High performance	Superior

[a]For patients age 65 or older, add one digit to obtained performance to derive normative descriptor

attention task, where patients are instructed to continuously subtract 7 from a previous number, starting at 100. Individuals are expected to complete at least 4 correct subtractions throughout this process (see Arousal/Attention section in BBRAT). For those interested, descriptions of other forward and reverse attention span tasks (e.g., letter span and visual span) can be found in Lezak et al. (2012).

Assessment of Vigilance

Vigilance, or the ability to sustain attention voluntarily, is also critical for successful performance on bedside assessment tasks and a prerequisite skill in making meaningful interpretation of subsequent performance. It is especially important to assess vigilance periodically in patients who are acutely injured or otherwise believed to experience fluctuations in attentional capacity.

The most direct way to assess vigilance is to ask the patient to perform a task that requires sustaining attention. Vigilance should be sustainable for at least 60–90 s without interruption. During the interview, a patient can be asked to point to a series of objects in the room either by mimicking the examiner or by following verbal commands. Such commands can be repeated to ensure that vigilance can be sustained for 60–90 s. Such commands or mimicking can include pointing to the ceiling, floor, walls, windows, furniture or personal objects in the room. The individual could also be asked to count to 100, recite the alphabet or read aloud for 60 s. The critical element is that the task involves overlearned stimuli which require minimal cognitive processing.

More formal bedside assessment of vigilance can be conducted using a letter or digit vigilance task (see Table 5.9 for example). Such tasks require the patient to listen to a series of numbers or letters and respond only to a target letter or number by raising a finger or tapping a table. In such tasks, each number or letter is read at a rate of one per second and performance is evaluated based on omissions errors (failing to detect a target), commission errors (falsely reporting a target as presented) and perseverative responding. These tests typically have a one-to-four response items-to-distracter ratio, and minimal total errors are expected in normally functioning patients aged 6 years and older. Performances with greater than three total errors should be considered impaired. Test stimuli are presented in Table 5.9 for both letter and digit vigilance tasks. While the assessment of attention should be conducted at bedside or during interview, assessment of more complex attention and a quantitative assessment of attentional capacities are best done in a formal assessment setting which can control environmental factors and make statistical comparisons to normal population data. The interested reader is referred to Lezak et al. (2012) for a thorough review of attention assessment measures.

Table 5.9 Letter and number vigilance assessment tasks[a]

Digits	Letters
5 3 9 1 5 5 6 7 **4** 1 8 2 5 6 5	**A** C R P **A A** M D Q S D T **A** B **A**
5 5 8 3 1 6 **4 4** 2 7 1 9 **4** 5 1	**A A** Z P T M N N E F G B S **A** L
5 8 6 3 9 5 5 5 2 7 6 1 5 **4** 2	**A** S P L R **A A A** G M C D **A** D B
2 7 6 5 **4** 9 3 8 6 **4** 8 2 5 1 **4**	B G F **A** D S T P Z R F T **A** C F

[a]Patients should be informed to tap their hand when they hear "4" or "A." Digits and letters should be read at one per second. Errors should be noted as commission (c) omission (o) or perseveration (p). Total errors exceeding three indicate impairment. After a patient understands directions, no further assistance is provided during testing

Bedside Assessment of Language

For most clinical evaluations, language assessment serves two functions—first as a screening for language impairment and secondly as an assessment of prerequisite skills necessary for language-dependent aspects of the bedside neuropsychological examination. Language assessments should be conducted systematically to evaluate for deficits in reception (aural comprehension and reading), expression (speech output and writing), repetition and naming. In addition, careful observation of word finding deficits, semantic or phonemic paraphasic errors and articulation difficulties should be noted. The quality of language organization and completeness of responses in reciprocal conversation should be evaluated relative to common expectations or in conjunction with collateral confirmation of a change.

The brief assessment below begins with receptive language in both auditory and written modalities. Auditory comprehension begins with simple yes/no questions and progresses to more complex yes/no questions, along with multi-step commands in both congruent and reversed sequence. Note that comprehension need not be illustrated by the patient speaking or writing. Indeed, questions should be posed such that responses can be elicited by movement of eyes, eye blink, etc., among patients who have expressive language deficits, are intubated or have motor paresis. Basic comprehension testing may then be followed by increasingly more complex receptive language skills involving both aural and reading skill. Questions such as "Is my hair on fire?", "Do airplanes eat their young?" and "Does two pounds of sugar weigh more than one pound of sugar?" are sensitive to mild deficits in comprehension. This provides a brief understanding of comprehension in both aural and written modalities, which is essential in managing patient care. Additionally, receptive prosody can be assessed by making statements that emphasize different emotions using the same words. Patients should have little difficulty identifying the emotional tone implied within a phrase so long as the examiner speaks in an exaggerated fashion. Phrases such as "I'm going home" can be stated using angry, sad or questioning tones, and patients should be able to tell from the prosody of the statement if it displays a particular emotion or question. When assessing prosody, the examiner may wish to have the patient close his/her eyes to avoid providing visual emotional cues about the prosody stimulus (e.g., accidently displays a facial expression along with the auditory stimuli).

Expressive language is subsequently assessed by asking the patient to name objects and subparts of objects of increasing detail. For example, a patient could be asked to name a shirt, followed by subparts of the shirt, such as sleeves, cuffs or a collar. While patients are often able to name whole objects (pen), requesting them to name parts of objects (clip) often elicits naming deficits which might otherwise go undetected. Additionally, patients are asked to repeat words and phrases of increasing complexity to assess repetition; a function that can be impaired from damage to the arcuate fasciculus and spare receptive and expressive language functions. When found in isolation, repetition deficits usually represent isolated subcortical deficit involving the arcuate fasciculus, sparing the overlying cortex. Expressive prosody is assessed by asking patients to make statements as if they were mad, happy or sad.

Lastly, language should be assessed for organizational quality and discourse. Any suspected tangentiality, circumloquaciousness or halting or incomplete expression patterns should be noted. This is typically done by providing stimuli, such as a picture or scenario, and asking open-ended questions requiring the patient to organize and structure a response that is reasonably complete. Qualitative descriptions should address organization, completeness of responses and the patient's ability to both expect and respect reciprocal conventions during communication, such that a conversation occurs naturally, and speech is not pressured in a way that might belie great effort in getting words out before they are lost.

While language deficits typically involve left hemisphere structures, these types of impairments are rarely isolated to a single language modality. For example, Broca's aphasia (or Expressive Aphasia) is caused by impairment within the left posterior frontal region and is often associated with speech production, writing and object naming deficits. On the other hand, Wernicke's aphasia (or Receptive Aphasia) derives from impairment in the left posterior temporal/parietal region and is characterized by nonsensical speech, impaired reading and comprehension and repetition deficits that typically include paraphasic errors. Those interested in a more detailed description about language are referred to Chap. 8 which provides additional language related deficits and their associated neuroanatomical origins.

Bedside Assessment of Memory

An initial assessment of memory can be done in an interview format as part of an extended mental status examination. This type of assessment relies on environmental factors and is intended to gather information about current memory functioning. Specific accident and/or illness factors are likely to be large, influential considerations and statements about functioning garnered from this type of assessment must acknowledge the possibility of rapid change. This assessment yields information about remote and recent memory as well as memory across visual, semantic and verbal domains. Items presented during this type of evaluation should be recalled with nearly complete accuracy. While it is not appropriate to assign quantitative levels of performance to such an examination, results can be useful in evaluating current functioning, including baseline abilities, a need for future assessment and the degree to which supervision may be necessary to meet their current needs. Table 5.10 lists methods for an acute assessment.

Several methods can be used to briefly assess memory in a systematic and structured manner. These methods focus on list-learning, semantic memory and visual memory tasks. The following, three-component assessment is offered as an expedient memory measure, with guidelines provided for interpretation. Importantly, applying such interpretations is intended for clinical purposes, as many factors, such as age and education, influence memory performance. This type of memory assessment is not intended to substitute for a more comprehensive evaluation of memory, but rather is offered to assess memory in an acute or medical office setting, and determine if further assessment is indicated. With these cautions in mind, the following 6-item test of memory is included within the Memory section of the BBRAT provided below. Patients are read a list of items at a rate of one word per second and asked to recall as many words as possible following the completion of each list. Following the third recall trial, a 10-min delay ensues, after which the patient is asked to freely recall as many of the previously administered words as they can remember. Next, the patient is provided three categorical cues (i.e., animals, colors, utensils), and asked to recall words from the list that fall within each category. For example, "Tell me all of the words from the list that are animals?" Lastly, recognition memory is assessed by asking the patient to respond either "Yes" or "No" to whether the presented word was on the original list. Additionally, frequencies of phonemic and semantic errors should be noted, as this information may provide insight about the patient's approach and clinical presentation. Again, caution should be used when interpreting performance, as these descriptors are offered as guidelines and should not be considered an equivalent substitute for statistical comparison to a normative group. More information about memory formation processes and associated neuroanatomical structures can be found in Chap. 9.

Bedside Assessment of Visuospatial (Visuoconstructional) Skills

An initial screening of visuospatial deficits can be conducted on interview by asking questions related to visual acuity, as well as problems completing activities of daily living. Assuming that sensory deficits and neglect in other sensory modalities have been ruled out by assessing sensory thresholds and unilateral suppressions across tactile, auditory and visual modalities, a bedside assessment of visuospatial skills should progress from simple to more integrated skills. These skills should include assessment of perception, scanning, inattention/neglect, visual recognition, facial recognition, visual form discrimination, construction (drawing) and visual synthesis skills.

Table 5.10 Acute/interview assessment of memory

	Item	Example	Area assessed	Record response/ accuracy
1.	Self-introduction	I'm Dr. Herman Jones	Auditory registration	
	• Ask them to repeat.		• Repetition	
	• Give multiple cues.	• My name sounds like ________. • I look like _______. • Touch my pretty face. • How many pretty Hermans do you know?	• Auditory, visual and tactile sensory facilitated learning • Semantic elaborative facilitated learning	
	• Tell them you will ask them your name later.		• Intentional recall	
2.	Ask why they are here.	• What happened? • Last memory prior… • First memory after …	• Remote memory/ Orientation • Retrograde amnesia • Anterograde amnesia	
	• Provide info if necessary	• You are here because … • You have been here …		
3.	Ask about family	• Who lives with you? • Describe your family. • Who lives in the area, where, when?	• Autobiographical information • Personal facts • Remote memory	
4.	Contemporary information	• How about X (recent news item)? • What can be done about X, etc.?	• Recent memory • Intentional semantic memory	
	Tell them you will ask about these topic later.	• What issues are politicians focused on?		
5.	Intervening conversation	• What is your doctor's name? • Are they (Is this??) your regular doctor? • What medications do you take? • What do you do to stay healthy?	• Recent memory	
6.	Close your eyes and tell me		• Incidental visual memory	
	a. Items patient is wearing	• Item, color, description		
	b. What you (the interviewer) are wearing	• Shirt or other prominent item		
	c. Where items are in room	• Furniture, door, window, TV		
7.	Show them 3 items and ask patient to remember them.	• Cup, paper clip, coins, pen	• Immediate intentional visual memory	

(continued)

Table 5.10 (continued)

	Item	Example	Area assessed	Record response/ accuracy
	• Tell patient you will ask again later.			
8.	Ask them to recall your name.	• I'm Dr. ___________.	• Intentional verbal recall	
		• Provide previous cues as necessary.	• Cued facilitation	
9.	Ask patient to recall items previously shown.	• Coins, paper clip, pen	• Intentional visual recall	
		• Provide cues if necessary • Office supply • In my pocket		
10.	Ask patient to recall topic previously discussed.	• Babies, politics, terrorism • Recall accident facts	• Intentional verbal semantic recall	

Perception, at a basic level, involves the patient's ability to appropriately perceive angles of straight and curved lines. Using a sheet with both curved and straight lines, patients can be asked to match or point to the lines that are most similar. Patients can also be asked to identify colors across blue-green and red-purple spectrums within their immediate environment to ensure correct color perception.

Scanning and assessment of neglect should involve the use of both behavioral assessment and cancellation tasks. Behaviorally, the examiner should present a different finger count on each hand and ask the patient to report the sum of the fingers displayed. Another method requires the patient to focus their gaze centrally (i.e., look at my nose), while the examiner alternates between flashing multiple (2–3) fingers with one hand and one finger with the other hand to each visual hemifield and quadrant field. The patient should respond with the total number of fingers shown indicating appropriate perception in all tested visual fields. To confirm a request, fingers from both hands can be presented in the same visual field and should assure perceptual skills in a unilateral visual field. If neglect is present, similar further presentation can be done in the upper and lower visual field quadrants (both unilaterally and bilaterally) to discern between quadrant inattention or neglect. Visual scanning can be readily assessed by drawing letters at various orientations on a page in a random array. The patient is asked to cross off all of a specific letter and the examiner notes any items that are omitted, as well as the side or quadrant in which these items are omitted. Similarly, patients can be shown horizontal lines in a random array on a sheet of paper and asked to draw a vertical line that bisects each horizontal line as close to the middle as possible. Patients should not distort or bias their responses consistently to the left or right, as these errors may be pathognomonic.

Visual recognition and facial perception can be assessed quickly by asking patients to recognize and name objects and individuals in their environment. The examiner can facilitate this process by pointing to objects within the room, including a door, shirt, pants and shoes. Faces can include family members or well-known cultural figures; although identification of cultural figures varies considerably among individuals depending on age, gender and exposure to presented cultural icons.

Visual form discrimination, construction and visual synthesis skills can be assessed by showing patients common objects that have been drawn as separate parts and asking them to mentally rotate and assemble into a single object. Common objects may include a cross or addition sign, square or circle. Additionally, patients should be asked to copy and draw objects that require appropriate relational elements, with regard to size and shape of an object. For example, patients can copy a pentagon or ramparts, where each drawing is evaluated based on the size, shape and number of sides included within each drawing. The patient can also draw an analog clock, where they are told to include all numbers in their correct positions and accurate clock hand placement to indicate a particular time. Interpreting the clock hands can further evaluate the patient's visuospatial skills, as well as their ability to inhibit and plan. For example, ask the patient to set the clock hands to read 11:10. Evaluation of a patient's performance can be judged not only on the correct position of the numbers, but the patient's understanding of the need to draw hands pointing at 11 and 2 in representing 11:10.

More information regarding the neuroanatomy of visuospatial functioning can be found in Chap. 10.

Bedside Assessment of Executive Functioning

Assessing Impulsivity/Disinhibition

The ability to initiate or inhibit a behavior is integrally linked to frontal lobe integrity. Patients with frontal lobe injuries often demonstrate changes in their ability to spontaneously initiate appropriate behavior or inhibit the enacting of overlearned or high frequency behavior. These deficits are most frequently observed soon after a traumatic or acute injury and can progressively worsen in neurodegenerative diseases involving the frontal lobes. There are several ways to test this during an evaluation. Perhaps the easiest way is to use contradictory verbal commands and physical gesture. In such a circumstance, the examiner can present an object or their hand and tell the patient not to take the object or shake their hand. For example, the examiner would offer an object to the patient such as a pen, cup or paper while simultaneously telling them, "Don't take this." A patient who spontaneously takes the object should be asked to repeat what the instructions were and then given a second trial. Failure on a second trial would indicate difficulty with inhibiting the behavior.

A second task, which emphasizes more subtle disinhibition, is referred to as the "*go-no go*" task. In this task, the examiner first instructs the patient to hold up one finger when the examiner holds up one finger and hold up two fingers when the examiner holds up two fingers (checking for cooperation and sufficient motor/sensory function). Complete a minimum of two trials in random order of holding up one and then two fingers. Once this is mastered, the examiner then instructs the patient to hold up two fingers when the examiner holds up one finger, and to display one finger when the examiner displays two fingers. The examiner alternates between presenting one and two fingers at an increasing rate. The patient is evaluated on accuracy of their responses, the consistency of accuracy (i.e., can they maintain response set), how quickly they respond (should be decreasing delay as task is learned) and their spontaneous recognition and correction of errors. Once their responses have stabilized with several correct responses, the examiner randomly alternates holding up one or two fingers and assesses the patient's ability to respond correctly. This sequence of trials should include at least one series in which the same number of fingers are held up repeatedly, in order to establish a habitual response from the patient, at which point, the examiner switches the number of fingers displayed. Patient responses following this change demonstrates their ability to suppress what has become an overlearned response. To establish this overlearned response, four to five trials with display of the same number by the examiner are typically required. Patients are typically expected to make some errors early in learning this task, but quick mastery is expected, along with rapid recognition and correction of errors.

Perseverations and deficits in set-shifting may also be identified by asking patients to complete an alternating sequence rampart (see Fig. 5.1) between flat or pointed ramparts or cursive m's and n's. The examiner should first demonstrate the pattern and then ask the patient to begin where the pattern stopped. The task is evaluated based on the patient's ability to appropriately alternate between figures or letters. For example, impaired performances due to perseverative responding would include failing to alternate between rectangles and triangles (often making linked triangles or linked rectangles only) or between cursive m's and n's (see Fig. 5.1). A final task requires the examiner to draw (outside of the examinee's vision) a series of large "3" shaped figures with 3 loops each. The patient is asked to replicate the looped figures until reaching the horizontal edge of the page. Failure reflects having more or less than exactly three loops for each figure. It is not unusual for patients with frontal lobe damage to make the figures with more successive loops in the "3" shaped figures (see Fig. 5.1). Similarly, errors suggestive of frontal dysfunction may also be observed aurally, when asking patients to count forward or backward, or when asking them to identify obvious patterns. For example, you can ask the patient to complete the following patterns, "2, 4, 6" or "1A, 2B, 3C." Errors on these tasks, such as perseverative responding or an inability to recognize the presented patterns, may indicate some degree of frontal dysfunction.

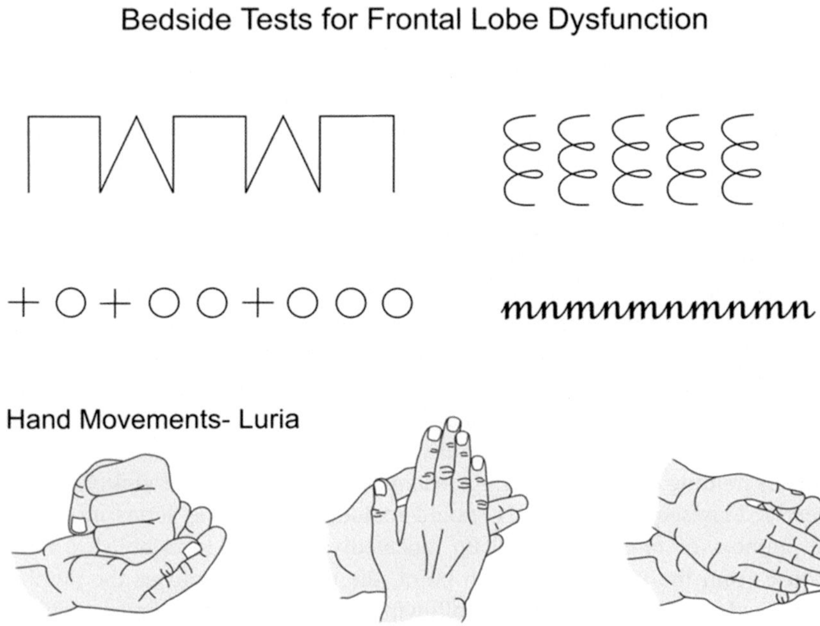

Fig. 5.1 Luria's figures and sequencing tasks ("3 s" and xoxooxooo)

Abstract Reasoning

Both verbal and nonverbal abstract reasoning can be impaired by frontal lobe injury. These patients tend to have greatest difficulty with divergent abstract reasoning tasks compared to relatively intact convergent reasoning. The conceptual difference between the two being the increased demand in divergent reasoning tasks to escape a single, sometimes concrete (right/wrong) answer of convergent reasoning and attempt to enact a creative, multi-solution divergent response to a stated problem. For example, patients may be asked to identify similarities between a list of items, followed by an explanation of their differences. Both the similarities and differences should demonstrate an understanding of multiple ways the two are similar and different. The examiner can prompt for other ways in which the objects are similar or different but should not provide answers. Examples may include a dog and a wolf, a shark and a whale, a house of representatives and a senate or a house and a hotel (see Table 5.11). The patient should be able to provide 2–3 examples of how each pair is similar and different and is evaluated on the quantity, organization and the quality of their responses. Again, frontal lobe patients would be expected to have difficulty switching between similarities and differences and are likely to provide fewer and/or less organized responses.

Table 5.11 Verbal Convergent/Divergent Reasoning Examples

Object pairs	Similarities	Differences
Dog—wolf	Canine Social Physical characteristics (legs, fur) Carnivores Mammals Multiple pups	Domesticated—Wild Geographically widespread—restricted Size variable—Typically large Seeks human contact—Avoids human contact
Shark—whale	Live in water Alive (breath oxygen) Swim Widespread Similar physical characteristics (i.e., fins, skin, organs, teeth)	Size Fish–mammal Bones—cartilage Lungs—gills Horizontal swimming motion—vertical swimming motion
House of Representatives—Senate	Part of Congress Legislative branch Elected Represent constituencies Work at capital Pass bills	Population proportioned—two per state 2-year term – 6-year term 435 House representatives—100 senators Rules and procedures differ

Problems	Solutions
Refrigerator repair	Check power supply Secure alternate food storage Call repairman Check breaker box/circuit breaker Inspect power cord, electrical outlet Check with neighbors about power supply
Pet behavior	Check food supply Check for injuries Check temperature Recall past routine (diet, interactions, elimination) Inspect physically Call vet Call knowledgeable friend Offer desired object (treat, toy)

Object	Alternative uses
Coat hanger	Hang clothes Probe Fastener Toothpick Guide wire Skewer Open car door lock Holder, extender Sculpting Form for object (i.e., lamp shade) Made into tongs or a rod for reaching/grabbing objects Scraping tool

(continued)

Table 5.11 (continued)

Object	Alternative uses
Brick	Building material Water saver device for commode tank Message delivery system Door stop Paper weight Hammer Stepping stone Landscaping Art object Motor vehicle chock Speed bumps Self-defense

Similarly, patients with frontal lobe dysfunction may have difficulties solving novel, everyday problems. Deficits within this domain can be assessed by asking questions like, "what would you do if your refrigerator stopped working?" or "what would you do if you notice a change in your pet's behavior?". Correct responses should include recognition that these situations may have multiple causes and/or that certain ideas can be systematically ruled out but ultimately, an adequate solution likely requires seeking additional help. Additionally, evaluating a patient's ability to interpret nonliteral language can suggest potential higher-order deficits related to abstract reasoning. This can be accomplished by asking a patient to explain common proverbs such as, "What does the saying, 'A bird in the hand is worth two in the bush' mean?" Responses that reference a known gain being better than a risk of losing everything would suggest intact reasoning abilities, while more concrete responses may indicate dysfunction.

One method for assessing visual divergent reasoning is to ask the patient to list multiple uses for a common object, such as a coat hanger, knife or brick. The patient should be able to generate at least 3–4 non-traditional uses for each object. Responses are not judged for the quality of the object as a substitute for another purpose or object, but rather for the presence of divergent abstraction and creativity. For example, a brick might be used as a paper weight, a door stop, a water-saving or displacement device (e.g., in a commode tank), an exercise device, etc. Another task designed to measure visual divergent reasoning involves constructing as many shapes/designs as possible by using four straight lines of similar length. Responses may include drawing a sequence, two Xs, a series of crosses, a series of triangles, etc. Again, the quality of the designs should not be judged, but rather the diversity and frequency of responses. Patients should be able to spontaneously draw 4–6 designs in less than a minute. Following the completion of the test, process questioning (e.g., "What did you find to be difficult about this task?") can also provide clinically relevant information. Possible solution sets for a bedside figure fluency task are presented in Fig. 5.11.

Brief Bedside Repeatable Assessment Test

The Brief Bedside Repeatable Assessment Test (BBRAT) is a neuropsychological screener designed specifically for brief repeatable assessment. This abbreviated measure is intended to provide a snapshot of a patient's sensory, motor and neurocognitive functioning, at both global and domain-specific levels. Individual test items have been adapted from empirically supported, standardized measures. When given in its entirety, the BBRAT takes approximately 40 min to administer, including 10–15 min for the cranial nerve exam and approximately 25-min for cognitive testing, which includes a 10-min delay for memory. Importantly, for clinicians who administer the memory portion, they are encouraged to use nonverbal tasks between immediate and delayed recall trials to mitigate task interference. The BBRAT measure, instructions for administering and scoring and a scoring summary sheet can be found at the end of this chapter.

Caveats for Administering and Interpreting the Bedside Assessment Measure

Qualitative interpretations describing a patient's objective testing performance, as well as their subjective presentation, are provided for each testing subdomain. Qualitative interpretations include: "Severely Impaired," "Moderately Impaired," "Mildly Impaired" and "Within Normal Limits." Interpretations about an individual's performance are considered within the context of empirically supported research conducted using similar measures. For example, most people are capable of recalling 7 ±2 numbers in their working memory. Therefore, individuals unable to repeat at least 5 numbers forward would suggest an abnormal performance that may require a more thorough examination of their attention. It is worth noting that the interpretive labels associated with this measure are intended to highlight the presence of current deficits and evaluate change over time, but may require more formal testing to establish the magnitude of a deficit or change over time.

Individual subdomains are designed to assess minimal functional capabilities using items of increasing difficulty. It is anticipated that examinees are capable of answering every question, and any incorrect responses may indicate a potential deficit. Given that item difficulty increases within each series of questions, evaluators are expected to administer questions in order, starting with the easiest item. Additionally, receiving an incorrect response terminates that series of questions, as patients would be unlikely to correctly answer more difficult questions that follow. For example, if the examinee is unable to repeat four digits forward, they would be unlikely to repeat five digits forward. Although the most difficult questions within a given subdomain could be asked first, and a correct response would suggest that the patient's ability is largely intact, if the patient does not understand the instructions, an incorrect response could lead to misinterpreting results. Therefore, administering the easiest items first provides the patient a chance to better understand what the task requires. Overall subdomain performances can be interpreted using the qualitative descriptors associated with the examinees' most recent correct response.

A comprehensive set of instructions for administering and scoring each item can be found at the end of this chapter. Additionally, brief guides for administering and scoring individual items are also included in the BBRAT Administration Form, as well. For example, scoring Serial 7's requires the administrator to sum the frequency of correct responses and pair that total with a corresponding qualitative interpretation. If the patient provides four or five correct answers, their performance is considered within normal limits (WNL). However, if they only provide one correct response, this would suggest moderate impairment. Notably, correct answers on the Serial 7's task do not need to be provided consecutively and, if an incorrect response is provided, correct responses going forward must be calculated based on the patient's incorrect response. For example, if the patient says "93 - 7 = 87" instead of "86," the next correct response would be "80" instead of "79." Similarly, frequency-related scoring can be observed on the Vigilance, Visual Cancellation of A's, Clock Drawing and the presidents naming tasks, where error scoring interpretations are provided within the measure.

Unique to most tasks within the BBRAT, patients receive more autonomy when completing visuospatial tasks, and capturing any response variability can, at times, provide clinically relevant information. Therefore, visuospatial performances include spaces for examiners to record qualitative descriptors, along with an overall interpretation regarding the patient's performance. For example, interpretations about Line Bisection performances should note whether bisecting lines are largely centered, or if they contain left-right biases, as visuospatial neglect may suggest an underlying pathology. Similarly, the quality and quantity of errors committed on the Rampart copy task can also offer clinically relevant information suggestive of varying pathologies.

Lastly, regarding the Verbal Memory task, patients are exposed to three semantically related pairs words (6 words total) for three learning trials. While it is expected that most individuals should be capable of learning all six words within three trials, not doing so is less important than how much a patient can recall after a 10-min delay, or their ability to recognize and discern between previously presented words. It is anticipated that most patients will recall up to at least one less than their highest learning trial. For example, if a patient's best learning trial is four words, they should be able to freely recall at least three of those four words on the delay trial. Similarly, individuals are expected to perform equally well or better on cued recall and recognition trials. Patients who recall fewer than one minus their highest learning trial would suggest some degree of impairment.

Brief Bedside Repeatable Assessment Test (BBRAT): Instructions

The Brief Bedside Repeatable Assessment Test (BBRAT) is designed as a bedside measure that can be administered as individual subtests or in its entirety, depending on the presenting concern. This measure is intended to screen multiple subdomains within aspects of cognition, including motor functioning, arousal/attention, language, memory, visuospatial abilities and abstraction/reasoning/judgement. Time to administer is variable, depending on the areas of functioning being assessed.

Arousal/orientation

Orientation

1. Administration:
   (a) "Tell me the [date, month, year, day] today."
   (b) "Tell me the name of [building, city] we are currently in."
      (i) The patient should provide the exact name of hospital/clinic to receive credit.
2. Scoring:
   (a) 6 correct responses = Oriented
   (b) 1–5 correct responses = "Some Disorientation"
   (c) 0 correct responses = "Fully Disoriented"

Gross awareness/attention

1. Observation:
   (a) Observations should be used to answer if the patient orients when someone enters the environment, if they are capable of answering direct questions, and if they can hold a conversation.

Working memory

1. Digits forward
   (a) Administration:
      (i) Read the number sequence at a rate of one digit per second.
      (ii) "I am going to say some numbers, and when I'm through, I want you to repeat these numbers back to me in the same order that I say them."
      (iii) Administration should cease following any errors.
   (b) Scoring:
      (i) Patients receive a check if they provide accurate numbers in order.
2. Digits backward
   (a) Administration:

    (i) Read the number sequence at a rate of one digit per second.
    (ii) "Now I am going to say some more numbers, only this time when I'm finished, I want you to repeat these numbers backwards."

  (b) Scoring

    (i) Patients receive a check if they provide accurate numbers in order.

3. Serial 7's

1. Administration:

   (a) "For this task, I want you to start with the number 100. I then want you to subtract 7 from that, and continue to subtract 7, until I tell you to stop."

2. Scoring

   (a) Record the number of responses that correctly subtract 7.
   (b) If the individual provides an incorrect response, but then correctly subtracts 7 from that response, this would be considered on incorrect response and one correct response. For example, if the patient says "93 - 7 = 87" instead of "86," the next correct response would be "80" instead of "79."

4. Sustained attention/vigilance

1. Administration

   (a) Read letters at a rate of one per second
   (b) Record when patient omits a hand tap "A" or taps on the wrong letter.

2. Scoring

   (a) See Administration form

Language

1. *Simple/complex/discourse*

   (a) Administration: "I'm going to ask you some questions and I want you to tell me the answer."
   (b) Scoring: Record a "✓" for correct responses and "X" for incorrect responses.

2. *Command*

   (a) Administration: "I am going to give you some commands. I'd like you to do what I say, and then relax."
   (b) Scoring: Record a "✓" for correct responses and "X" for incorrect responses.

      (i) If the patient correctly points to the floor and ceiling during the final trial, but does so in an incorrect order, this is considered incorrect.

3. *Repetition*

   (a) Administration: "I am going to say a word or phrase, and I want you to repeat what I say. Say …"

(b) Scoring: Record a "✓" for correct responses and "X" for incorrect responses.

4. *Naming*

   (a) Administration:

      (i) Choose one of the three lists provided on the sheet to follow (e.g., Shirt, Sleeve, Collar, Cuff).
      (ii) "I am going to point to some objects, and I want you to tell me what I am pointing to."

   (b) Scoring: Record a "✓" for correct responses and "X" for incorrect responses.

5. *Reading*

   (a) Administration

      (i) Fold the BBRAT form where it says "Reading" before presenting to the patient.
      (ii) "I want you to read this aloud and do what it says."

   (b) Scoring

      (i) If the patient either reads the statement aloud but does not raise their hand or raises their hand but does not read the statement aloud, it should be recorded as "Incomplete."

6. *Writing*

   (a) Administration

      (i) Fold the BBRAT form where it says "Writing" before presenting to the patient.
      (ii) Ask the patient to write their full name in the "Name" box

      If they are unable to do this, discontinue.

      (iii) If they can write their name, ask them to write any sentence.

      If they cannot think of something to write about, ask them to write about how they are feeling.

   (b) Scoring

      (i) Individuals should receive full credit if they accurately write their full name following an initial request or prompting.

      If they only write their first or last name even after being prompted, this should be considered incomplete.

      (ii) If the individual writes a sensible, full sentence, including a subject and a verb, they should receive full credit.

      Full credit may still be provided even if punctuation is incorrect.

(iii) If the individual writes a word or a non-coherent group of words, this should be considered incomplete.

Memory

1. *Remote memory*
   (a) Administration:
      (i) "Can you tell me, who is currently the president of the United States?"
      (ii) Next, ask them, "Can you name 4 United States Presidents since 1961?"
   (b) Scoring
      (i) See Administration form
2. *Verbal memory*
   (a) Administration:
      (i) Read each word at a rate of one per second.
      (ii) Do not correct the patient if they provide an incorrect word.
      (iii) There is a 10-min delay between Trial 3 and Delay Trial

      During the delay trial, attempt to fill

      (iv) After you administer the Delay Trial, administer Cued Recall

      See Cued Recall instructions below

      (v) After you administer Cued Recall, administer Recognition

      See Recognition instructions below
   (b) Instructions to patient
      (i) *Trial 1*: "For this next test, I am going to read you a list of words, and when I'm through, I want you to tell me as many words as you can remember. You do not have to tell me the words in the same order, just tell me as many as you can remember, in any order."
      (ii) *Trial 2*: "I am going to read these same words again. Again, when I finish, I want you to tell me as many words as you can, in any order, even if you said them before."
      (iii) *Trial 3*: "I am going to read this same list, one more time. Again, when I finish, I want you to tell me as many words as you can, in any order, even if you said them before."

      After they finish providing responses for Trial 3, say, "Now, I want you to try to remember these words because I am going to ask you to repeat them again in a few minutes."

      (iv) *Delay trial*: "Do you remember that list of words that I read to you earlier? I want you to tell me as many words as you can remember, in any order."

(v) *Cued recall*: "I'd like you to tell me how many words from the list I read to you are [animals, colors, utensils]."
(vi) *Recognition*: "I am going to read some more words to you and after I read each one, I want you to tell me if that word was on the list I read to you earlier. Was [recognition word] on the list?"

After "Fish" can just read the word listed without asking if it was on the list.
For example, "Was Spoon on the list? Was Fish on the list? Home? Pig?" etc.

(c) Scoring

(i) Record a "✓" next to each word that was recalled during their respective trials.
(ii) Total the number correct at the bottom of each trial.
(iii) When scoring the recognition trial, correct responses, phonemic errors and semantic errors are indicated based on their fonts (e.g., correct responses are bolded, phonemic errors are italicized, and semantic errors are in normal print).

(d) Interpretations

(i) Initial learning trials should be recorded, though level of potential impairment will be reflected during recall and recognition trials. It is anticipated that most patients will recall up to at least one less than their highest learning trial.

For example, if a patient's best learning trial is four words, they should be able to freely recall at least three of those four words on the delay trial.

(ii) Similarly, individuals are expected to perform equally well or better on cued recall and recognition trials. Patients who recall fewer than one minus their highest learning trial would suggest some degree of impairment.

Equal or greater than their highest learning trial = WNL
1 fewer than their highest learning trial = Mild impairment
> 1 fewer than their highest learning trial = Moderate impairment

(iii) Although phonemic and semantic errors may improve clinical impressions, a quantitative interpretation of error frequency is not expected.

Visuospatial

1. *Prior to administering the visuospatial tasks, fold the paper on the dotted line, to ensure the patient is unable to see questions from the Memory section.
2. *Visual Cancellation of A's*

(a) Administration:

   (i) Hand the patient a pen/pencil and say, "Here, you are going to see some letters. I want you to cross out all of the "A's" in this area without missing any. Go ahead."

(b) Scoring:

   (i) Frequency of omission and commission errors should be summed.
   (ii) Qualitative interpretations should be made based on the sum of total errors.

3. *Visual closure recognition*

   (a) Administration:

      (i) Hand the patient a pen/pencil, point to the visual closure recognition area and say, "Here are some figures that have been separated. I want you to put them together in your mind and tell me the names of each figure."
      (ii) Record responses verbatim on the lines provided under each figure.

   (b) Scoring:

      (i) Acceptable responses for each figure include:

      Figure 1: square; rectangle; quadrilateral
      Figure 2: heart
      Figure 3: arrow

      (ii) If an individual provides an incorrect response on an earlier item, but provides a correct response on a later item, qualitative interpreted should be made based on the patient's highest correct response.

      Example 1: If an incorrect response is made for Figure 1, but correct responses are provided for Figures 2 and 3, the overall performance should be interpreted as within normal limits.
      Example 2: If incorrect responses are provided for Figures 1 and 3 and a correct response is provided for Figure 2, this should be interpreted as mildly impaired.

4. *Line bisection*

   (a) Administration:

      (i) Hand the patient a pen/pencil, point to the line bisection area, and say, "Look at these lines. I'd like you to use your pen/pencil to draw a vertical line through the middle of each of the horizontal lines in this box."

   (b) Scoring:

      (i) Total the frequency of "Off-Center" lines, which include all lines that deviate more than 6 mm from the center of a horizontal line.

(ii) Right-left bias is calculated by totaling the directional bias of each off-center line.
(iii) Multiple off-center lines with consistent directional biases should be considered impaired.

5. *Rampart copy*

(a) Administration

(i) Hand the patient a pen/pencil, point to the image of the ramparts, and say, "I want you to copy this entire design in the space provided below."

(b) Scoring

(i) Total the frequency of perseverative, omission and commission errors.
(ii) A perseverative error should be counted each time a shape is repeated in the drawing sequence.
(iii) Overall performance on this task is considered impaired if any errors occur.

6. *Pentagons*

(a) Administration

(i) Hand the patient a pen/pencil, point to the image of the pentagons, and say, "I want you to copy this design exactly in the space provided next to it."

(b) Scoring

(i) To receive full credit, the drawing must include: 1) two pentagons with sides that are mostly equal in length and 2) the two pentagons should overlap one another, with less than one full side overlapping the other figure.

7. *Clock drawing*

(a) Administration:

(i) Hand the patient a pen/pencil, point to the image of the clock drawing area, and say, "I would like you to draw a clock and set the time to 11:10."

(b) Scoring

(i) Patient can receive 1 point for each of the three criteria:

1. ***Contour:*** The clock needs to be drawn as a circle with minimal distortion.

2. ***Numbers:*** Clock numbers 1–12 need to be included and in their correct locations. Patients can receive credit if the numbers are accurately placed outside of the clock's perimeter.
3. ***Hands:*** Two hands must be included to receive credit. There must be an hour hand that is clearly shorter than the other and the two hands must originate from the center of the clock.

Abstraction/reasoning/judgement

1. *Convergent & divergent reasoning*

   (a) Administration

      (i) Questions can be repeated if requested.
      (ii) If a patient provides multiple answers, ask them to select their best answer.

   (b) Scoring

      (i) Convergent reasoning

      While not all possible responses could be included on the BBRAT form, additional abstract responses should receive full credit, while concrete responses should be considered as indicating mild impairment.

      (ii) Divergent reasoning

      Responses unique to those provided on the BBRAT form indicating distinct, categorical differences, should receive full credit.

2. *Sequencing*

   (a) Simple

      (i) Administration

      Ask the patient to, "Count from 1 to 25."
      Ask the patient to, "Count backwards from 10."
      Follow-up attempts may be made on these tasks if requested by the examiner/examinee.

      (ii) Scoring

      Tasks should be completed without error.
      Examinees should receive full credit if they complete the task successfully, even if this is accomplished on follow-up attempts.

   (b) Complex

      (i) Administration

      Read each number or number/letter combination at a rate of one per second.

Say, "For this task, I am going to begin a pattern and, when I stop, I want you to say the next two sequences of the pattern."

(ii) Scoring

Record a "✓" for correct responses and record incorrect responses verbatim.

3. *Judgement*

(a) Administration

(i) Questions can be repeated if requested.
(ii) Responses should be directly recorded on the BBRAT form.
(iii) Say to the patient, "I am going to ask you some questions and I want you to answer each question as best you can."

(b) Scoring

(i) Criteria for interpreting responses can be found on the BBRAT form.

BRIEF BEDSIDE REPEATABLE ASSESSMENT TEST (BBRAT)

Name:________________	DOB (Age):__________( )	Education:____	Gender:_______	Date:______________

CRANIAL NERVE	FUNCTION	ASSESSMENT	ABNORMALITY
CN I Olfactory: __R __L	Smell	Test each nostril independently for smell (e.g., coffee)	Anosmia
CN II Optic: __R __L	Vision	Test visual fields of each eye, as well as both simultaneously	Pre-chiasmic: Monocular defect Post-Chiasmic: Contralateral hemianopia or quadrant anopsia
CN III Oculomotor: __R __L	Eyelid retraction, pupilary constriction, medial eye movement	Assess for ptosis, pupillary asymmetry, reaction to light and accommodation, downward and lateral eye deviation upon fixed forward gaze	Enlarged pupil, ptosis, downward and lateral gaze deviation; diplopia on upward contralateral gaze
CN IV Trochlear: __R __L	Rotation of eye with head tilt	Note diplopia with head tilt or compensatory head tilt. Assess eye rotation on head tilt	Decreased eye rotation with head tilt; diplopia reported with head tilt (difficult to detect)
CN V Trigeminal: __V1 __V2 __V3	Mastication muscles, facial sensations	Note asymmetry in V1, V2, and V3 with unilateral stimulation	Bite weakness; loss of sensation
CN VI Abducens: __R __L	Lateral eye movement Eyelid protractions	Note inward gaze deviation of affected eye. Proptosis of eyelid.	Deviation of eye medially (inward); increased diplopia with lateral gaze in effected eye
CN VII Facial: __R __L	Musculature of facial expression, anterior tongue taste	Note facial asymmetry (particularly in nasolabile fold), note loss of sweet taste	Facial muscle weakness, Loss of taste on anterior tongue
CN VIII Vestibulocochlear: __R __L	Hearing	Test acuity with unilateral stimulation	Decreased auditory acuity
CN IX Glossopharyngeal: __R __L	Taste on posterior tongue, gag reflex)	Assess gag reflex, inquire about loss of sour or bitter taste	Ageusia, decreased gag reflex
CN X Vagus: __R __L; Voice___	Motor movement of soft palate, vocal cord innervation	Assess elevation symmetry of soft palate, inquire about change in vocal tone/quality	Decreased soft palate movement, vocal cord innervation, hoarse voice
CN XI Spinal Accessory: __R __L	Neck muscles	Assess strength and symmetry of shoulder shrug	Trapezius weakness
CN XII Hypoglossal: __R __L	Muscle of the tongue	Assess tongue thrust, noting deviation and sustainability	Weakness or deviation upon unsupported protrusion

MOTOR EXAMINATION

	Finger Tapping	Grip	Finger To Nose	Heel/Shin	Oral Motor
Right	__WNL __Slow __Decreasing	__WNL __Mild Impairment __Mod. Impairment	__WNL __Dysmetria	__WNL __Dysmetria	Labial __WNL __Impaired Lingual __WNL __Impaired Oral Praxis __WNL __Impaired
Left	__WNL __Slow __Decreasing	__WNL __Mild Impairment __Mod. Impairment	__WNL __Dysmetria	__WNL __Dysmetria	Labial __WNL __Impaired Lingual __WNL __Impaired Oral Praxis __WNL __Impaired

FRONTAL MOTOR SYSTEMS

Alternating Hand Movements	Sequential Hand Movements	Behavioral Inhibition
Right __WNL __Impaired Cue (Y/N) Left __WNL __Impaired Bilateral __WNL __Impaired	Right __WNL __Impaired Cue (Y/N) Left __WNL __Impaired Bilateral __WNL __Impaired	Right __WNL __Impaired Left __WNL __Impaired Bilateral __WNL __Impaired

SENSORY EXAMINATION

Auditory (Unilateral Stim.)	Right__ Left__	Suppressions (Bilateral Stim.)	Right__ Left__
Visual Fields (Unilateral Stim.)	OD__ OS__	Neglect (Bilateral Stim.)	Right__ Left__
Tactile (Unilateral Stim.)	Right__ Left__	Suppressions	Right__ Left__
Tactual Form Recognition			
Circle	Right__ Left__	Square	Right__ Left__
Triangle	Right__ Left__	Cross	Right__ Left__

*See Little Black Book 2nd Edition: Bedside Assessment chapter for full instructions

BRIEF BEDSIDE REPEATABLE ASSESSMENT TEST (BBRAT)

Name:______________	DOB (Age):________( )	Education:___	Gender:______	Date:____________

AROUSAL/ATTENTION						
Orientation	Date__	Month__	Year__	Day__	Place__	City__
Gross Awareness	Orients to persons entering environment or speaking; focuses attention appropriately ___*Moderate*					
Gross Attention	Answers Questions __*Mild*			Holds Conversation __*WNL*		

Working Memory				**Sustained Attention** (Target A's; one second intervals)
Digits Forward		**Digits Backwards**		**Vigilance**
3-9-5	__Mod.	8-3	__Mod.	L T P E A O A I C T D A L A A A N A I B F
7-2-1-4	__Mild	7-4-9	__Mild	S A J R Z E O A D P A K L A U C J T O E A
4-1-0-6-3	__WNL	2-6-5-1	__WNL	Total Errors__ (>3 errors__Mod. or ≤3 errors__WNL)
Serial 7's	93__ 86__ 79__ 72__ 65__			Total: __/5 **Scoring** 4 or 5 = WNL; 2 or 3 correct = Mild; 1 correct = Moderate; 0 correct = Severe

LANGUAGE

Receptive Language

Simple		**Complex**		**Command**	
Do you have brown eyes?	__Mod.	No Answer Provided	__Mod.	Point to yourself.	__Mod.
Is it winter?	__Mild	Is high school before college?	__Mild	Point to me and the wall.	__Mild
Is it July?	__WNL	Is North Dakota south of South Dakota?	__WNL	After you point to the ceiling, point to the floor.	__WNL

Expressive Language

Repetition ("Say…")		**Discourse Speech**		**Naming (pick one column)**			
...Bed"	__Sev.	What is your first name?	__Mod.	Shirt	Watch	Hand	__Sev.
...Hospital"	__Mod.	*What is your address?	__Mild	Sleeve	Face	Finger	__Mod.
...I want to sleep"	__Mild	Why are you here?	__WNL	Collar	Band	Nail	__Mild
...No if's, and's, or but's"	__WNL			Cuff	Clasp	Knuckle	__WNL

Reading		**Write your name.**		**Write any sentence.**	
No Answer Provided	__Mod.	No Answer Provided	__Mod.	No Answer Provided	__Mod.
Incomplete	__Mild	Incomplete	__Mild	Incomplete	__Mild
Complete	__WNL	Complete	__WNL	Complete	__WNL

Writing

NAME

SENTENCE

Reading

RAISE YOUR HAND

*See Little Black Book 2nd Edition: Bedside Assessment chapter for full instructions

BRIEF BEDSIDE REPEATABLE ASSESSMENT TEST (BBRAT)

Name:___________	DOB (Age):_________( )	Education:___	Gender:______	Date:___________

MEMORY

Remote Memory

Current U.S. President:	__/1 (1 = WNL; 0 = Mod.)	Name 4 presidents since 1961: (Kennedy, Johnson, Nixon, Ford, Carter, Reagan, Bush, Clinton, Bush Jr., Obama, Trump, Biden)	__/4 (4 = WNL; 2-3 = Mild; 1-0 = Mod.)

Verbal Memory

List	Trial 1	Trial 2	Trial 3	Delay (10-min)	Cued Recall (after Delay)			Recognition (after cued recall and non-verbal tasks)					
Horse	___	___	___	___	Animals	______	______	**Spoon**	_	**Horse**	_	**Fork**	_
Spoon	___	___	___	___		______	______	Fish	_	*Blend*	_	*Spill*	_
Green	___	___	___	___	Colors	______	______	*Home*	_	Cow	_	White	_
Fork	___	___	___	___		______	______	**Pig**	_	Plate	_	**Green**	_
Pig	___	___	___	___	Utensils	______	______	*Grave*	_	**Blue**	_	*Pit*	_
Blue	___	___	___	___		______	______	*Forum*	_	Knife	_	Red	_
Total	___	___	___	___	**Total Corr.** ______			**Total Corr.**	_	*Phon. Err.*	_	Sem. Err.	_

VISUOSPATIAL

Visual Cancellation of A's

A	C	D	E	A	F	E	B	C	R	D	A
C	E	A	F	R	A	C	D	R	P	F	E
M	A	C	R	K	P	C	D	R	A	M	F
T	P	A	C	P	R	D	E	A	D	R	D

Score:____ (>3 errors = Mod. or ≤3 errors = WNL) Ommissions:___ Comissions:___

Visual Closure Recognition

Response (Mod.):___________ Response (Mild):___________ Response (WNL):___________

*See Little Black Book 2nd Edition: Bedside Assessment chapter for full instructions

BRIEF BEDSIDE REPEATABLE ASSESSMENT TEST (BBRAT)

Name:______________	DOB (Age):________( )	Education:____	Gender:______	Date:____________

ABSTRACTION/REASONING/JUDGEMENT		
Convergent Reasoning	**Answers (circle interpretation)**	
How are an **apple** & **banana** similar?	Does not know or does not provide response	*Moderate*
	*Eat, food, peel	*Mild*
	*Fruit	*WNL*
How are a **boat** & **automobile** similar?	Does not know	*Moderate*
	*Move, metal, ride inside	*Mild*
	*Transportation or methods of travel	*WNL*
Divergent Reasoning	**Answers (circle interpretation)**	
How are an **apple** & **banana** different?	Does not know or does not provide response	*Moderate*
	*Shape, size, color, taste, seeds	*WNL*
How are a **boat** & **automobile** different?	Does not know or does not provide response	*Moderate*
	*Operate on land vs. water; propeller vs. wheels	*WNL*
Sequencing	**Answers (circle impairment if errors occur)**	
Simple Sequencing	Count from 1 to 25	*Severe*
	Count backwards from 10	*Moderate*
Complex Sequencing (Say: "Complete this pattern…)	"2 – 4 – 6" __8 __10	*Mild*
	"1A – 2B – 3C" __4D __5E	*WNL*
Judgement	**Answers (circle interpretation)**	
What should you do if you cut yourself and you are bleeding a lot?	Does not know or does not provide response	*Moderate*
	*Includes appropriate and inappropriate response; or only one of two correct responses	*Mild*
	*Need for temporary remedy and follow-up response (e.g., stop bleeding and seek help)	*WNL*
Response:		
What should you do if you smell smoke?	Does not know	*Moderate*
	*Includes appropriate and inappropriate response	*Mild*
	*Recognizes danger and need for immediate response (e.g., fire dept.)	*WNL*
Response:		

*Additional responses may fulfill category requirements.
See Little Black Book 2nd Edition: Bedside Assessment chapter for full instructions

BRIEF BEDSIDE REPEATABLE ASSESSMENT TEST (BBRAT)

Name:____ DOB (Age):____ ( ) Education:____ Gender:____ Date:____

Line Bisection

Scoring: Centered:___ Off-Center:__ (R-bias/L-bias) Interpretation (circle): Impaired or WNL

Rampart Copy

Scoring: Perseverative:___ Errors:__ (Omissions/Commissions) Interpretation: (circle): Impaired or WNL

Pentagons "Please copy these pentagons in the space below"	**Clock Drawing** "I would like you to draw a clock and set the time to 11:10."
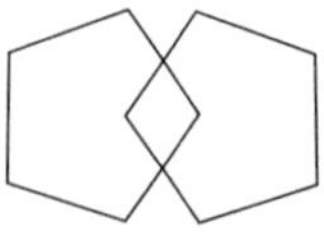	
Scoring: WNL__ Impaired__	**Scoring:** ____Contour ____Number ___Hands ___Total (0 = Sev.; 1 = Mod.; 2 = Mild; 3 = WNL)

*See Little Black Book 2nd Edition: Bedside Assessment chapter for full instructions

BRIEF BEDSIDE REPEATABLE ASSESSMENT TEST (BBRAT)

PERFORMANCE SUMMARY SHEET				
Arousal/Attention	**WNL**		**Impaired**	
Orientation	Oriented	Some Disorientation		Disoriented
Awareness/Attention	WNL	Mild	Moderate	
Digits Forward	WNL	Mild	Moderate	
Digits Backward	WNL	Mild	Moderate	
Sustained Attention	WNL	Mild	Moderate	
Serial 7's	WNL	Mild	Moderate	Severe
Language	**WNL**		**Impaired**	
<u>Receptive</u>				
Simple	WNL	Mild	Moderate	Severe
Complex	WNL	Mild	Moderate	Severe
Command	WNL	Mild	Moderate	Severe
<u>Expressive</u>				
Repetition	WNL	Mild	Moderate	Severe
Discourse	WNL	Mild	Moderate	
Naming	WNL	Mild	Moderate	Severe
Reading	WNL	Mild	Moderate	
<u>Writing</u>				
Name	WNL	Mild	Moderate	
Sentence	WNL	Mild	Moderate	
Memory	**WNL**		**Impaired**	
<u>Remote</u>				
Current President	WNL		Moderate	
Past Presidents	WNL	Mild	Moderate	
<u>Verbal</u>				
Total (Trials 1-3)	Highest Recall	< 5	5	6
Total Delay	WNL	Mild	Moderate	
Total Cued	WNL	Mild	Moderate	
Recognition	WNL	Mild	Moderate	
Visuospatial	**WNL**		**Impaired**	
Cancellation	WNL	Mild	Moderate	Severe
Closure Recognition	WNL	Mild	Moderate	Severe
Abstraction/Reasoning/Judgement	**WNL**		**Impaired**	
Convergent	WNL	Mild	Moderate	Severe
Divergent	WNL	Mild	Moderate	Severe
<u>Sequencing</u>				
Simple	WNL	Mild	Moderate	Severe
Complex	WNL	Mild	Moderate	Severe
Judgement	WNL	Mild	Moderate	Severe

References

Inouye, S. K., Van Dyke, C. H., & Alessi, C. (1990). Clarifying confusion: The confusion assessment method (CAM). *Annuals of Internal Medicine, 113*, 941–948.

Kessler, H. R. (2006). The bedside neuropsychological examination. In P. J. Snyder, P. D. Nussbaum, & D. L. Robins (Eds.), *Clinical neuropsychology: A pocket handbook for assessment* (2nd ed., pp. 75–101). American Psychological Association. https://doi.org/10.1037/11299-005

Levin, H. S., O'Donnell, V. M., & Grossman, R. G. (1979). The Galveston Orientation and Amnesia Test (GOAT): A practical scale to assess cognition after head injury. *Journal of Nervous and Mental Disease, 167*, 675–684.

Lezak, M. D., Howieson, D. B., Bigler, E. D., & Tranel, D. (2012). *Neuropsychological assessment* (5th ed.). Oxford University Press.

Pavol, M. A. (2019). Inpatient neuropsychological assessment in older adults. In L. D. Ravid & H. L. Katzen (Eds.), *Handbook on the neuropsychology of aging and dementia* (pp. 89–103). Springer. https://doi.org/10.1007/978-3-319-93497-6_7

Teasdale, G. M., & Jennett, B. (1974). Assessment of coma and impaired consciousness. *Lancet, 2*, 81–84.

Chapter 6
Arousal: The Disoriented, Stuporous, Agitated or Somnolent Patient

James G. Scott

Arousal refers to the maintenance of an appropriate level of cerebral activity to successfully complete the task in which one is engaged. Arousal occurs on a continuum from hypoarousal to hyperarousal and may fluctuate over minutes to hours to days. From a neurologic perspective, appropriate arousal is a necessary prerequisite for consciousness. Arousal is anatomically mediated through the ascending reticular activating system (RAS), which has projections arising from the medulla and pons, projecting to the midbrain, thalamus and hypothalamus (see Chap. 3 for more details). Stimulation of the RAS is essential for maintaining consciousness at a basic neurophysiologic level. Hyperarousal produces states of agitation. States of arousal vary from coma to normal and are typically classified or categorized clinically as below. Table 6.1 presents categorical classification of arousal, response to attempts to influence arousal and course of arousal with varying stimulation.

Key Points and Chapter Summary

- Maintenance of appropriate arousal is a critical prerequisite for assessment of cognition in patients with difficulty attaining, sustaining or consistently maintaining arousal invalidating assessment of cognition
- Arousal level should be assessed at several points in time as it may fluctuate considerably over time
- Delirium is common in many hospitalized groups and should be monitored frequently
- Delirium in outpatient populations should be an initial focus if acute cognitive and behavioral changes or fluctuations are suspected during examination

J. G. Scott (✉)
Department of Psychiatry and Behavioral Sciences, University of Oklahoma, Health Sciences Center College of Medicine, Oklahoma City, OK, USA
e-mail: jim-scott@ouhsc.edu

M. R. Schoenberg, J. G. Scott (eds.), *The Little Black Book of Neuropsychology*,
https://doi.org/10.1007/978-3-032-07777-6_6

Table 6.1 Categorization of arousal states

Arousal state	Arousal response	Course
Coma	No response to stimuli	No change
Stupor	Sleepy—awakens to arousal but unable to maintain without stimulation	Fluctuations build or fall as stimulation varies with return to sleep with decreased stimulation
Delirium	Awake with fluctuations in arousal, vacillations from hypo-to hyperarousal	Fluctuations based on environmental factors and medical factors. Fluctuations may be rapid or prolonged.
Normal	Awakens to stimulation, maintains arousal	Normal sleep–wake cycle established

Arousal Problems: A Behavioral Guide

A symptomatic guide for how problems in arousal typically present is provided below. This is then followed by a list of possible diagnostic or syndromic explanations for the observed problems in arousal (see also Chap. 16, this volume). In general, alterations in a patient's arousal should be considered a serious acute concern to the clinical neuropsychologist. It often reflects a serious medical condition which can become life threatening if left undiagnosed and untreated.

There are three general patterns of disrupted arousal:

1. Hypoarousal–hypoactive problems

   The patient appears stuporous, sleepy, "hypoalert" or somnolent. The patient may react to auditory or other somatic stimuli (touch, mild pain) by appearing to wake up, may look around the environment and then fall back asleep. If not "sleeping," the patient will appear "sleepy," often will complain of being tired, may yawn frequently, appear confused and is easily irritated. Speech may be slurred and/or often of short phrase length (often one- or two-word answers to questions). If phrase length is longer, speech content may not be consistent with the situation, with the patient being tangential or incomprehensible. Patients with hypoarousal generally do not exhibit spontaneous speech. The patient may only eat with encouragement and the patient's sleep–wake cycle is likely disrupted. Management of other basic activities of daily living, toileting, bathing, etc., is also likely to be disrupted. Arousal in these patients may be solicited with constant stimulation (i.e., interacting or physical movement), but they quickly revert to hypo-aroused when external stimulation is reduced or withdrawn.

   The patient exhibits difficulty with sustained simple attention, and assessing higher cortical functions at this point is not valid. Unlike a patient with problems in attention, but not in arousal (see Chap. 7, this volume), patients with poor arousal have difficulty maintaining arousal long enough to complete any assessment task. More subtle disruptions in arousal can appear as a problem with attention, but close observation will demonstrate fluctuations in arousal rather than deficits in efforts to sustain or focus attention.

2. Hyperarousal–hyperactive problems

   The patient will appear "hyperactive," and may present with delusions, hallucinations and extreme irritability and agitation. The patient's high energy level is unable to be effectively directed to any sustained task or focused activity. The patient is likely to be agitated and anger outbursts or episodes of aggression may occur. Affective labiality is also probable, with patients crying or laughing inappropriately. While the patient may appear aroused enough to complete testing of higher-order cognitive functions, frequently the impairment in arousal will manifest as extreme disruption of attention.
3. Mixed arousal problems

   The patient will appear to present with alternating periods of hypoarousal-hypoactivity and hyperarousal-hyperactivity. The fluctuating course can occur over periods of minutes to hours and may be the most frequently seen pattern of arousal deficit seen in acute hospitalization.

Below, diagnostic considerations for altered arousal are provided. In general, there are four broad categories resulting in disrupted arousal: intracranial disease, systemic disease affecting CNS, toxins/metabolic and drug withdrawal. Other factors such as age, general health, chronic illnesses and chronic psychiatric illness should be considered ongoing risk factors to developing arousal deficits.

1. **Primary intracranial disease (stroke, seizure, intracranial mass).** Primary intracranial disease affects the RAS by compression on the brain stem. Frequent causes are uncal herniation or central (foramen magnum) herniation, diffuse increased intracranial pressure or bilateral diffuse frontal lobe damage.
2. **Systemic disease affecting the CNS**. Some of the more common are urinary tract infections, sepsis, hepatic failure and cardio-pulmonary diseases. Included in this category are medical procedures which place the patient at high risk such as those resulting in high volume blood loss (i.e., orthopedic surgery) or those requiring extensive time on cardio-pulmonary support (i.e., Cardiac Artery Bypass Grafting, CABG). In addition, those procedures that require extended periods of general anesthesia also place patients at risk for subsequent deficits in arousal.
3. **Toxins/metabolic conditions**. Exposure to exogenous toxins and drugs (e.g., ETOH) as well as metabolic dysfunction (e.g., hypoglycemia, hyponatremia, etc.).
4. **Drug withdrawal. Drug exposure and/or withdrawal**. Many stimulant, sedative or hallucinogenic substances can induce alterations in arousal, and a delirium (e.g., narcotics, sedatives, muscle relaxers, etc.).

Key Points: Assessment of Arousal

- Arousal deficits and delirium are significant risk factors for mortality and should not be dismissed as a normal course of recovery or normal individual behavior
- Arousal may fluctuate rapidly and necessitates serial assessment
- Causes of arousal deficits and delirium are numerous and complex and require a thorough medical workup to identify contributing factors

Stuporous Conditions Mimicking Coma

Several conditions may present as coma-like with restricted responses to environmental stimuli or attempted arousal. These conditions include akinetic mutism and decorticate state or persistent vegetative state (see also locked-in syndrome below). A triad of symptoms distinguish the first two from stuporous conditions, including akinesia, mutism and decreased consciousness. Akinetic mutism and persistent vegetative state result from incomplete disturbance of the reticular activity system and produce varying states of disturbances of arousal. There is controversy regarding these states and whether it is better to categorize them as a continuum of coma states or separate entities. The distinction lies in the presence of visual alertness with spontaneous eye opening and sporadic tracking of auditory, tactile and visual stimulation in the environment. Akinetic mutism results from damage to the sub-thalamic region and septal nucleus, or from bilateral extensive frontal lobe lesions. While some response to arousal occurs, this arousal is not maintained and a return to an akinetic-mute state quickly results. When akinetic mutism is due to bilateral frontal lobe damage, the patient presents as severely abulic with extreme amotivation. Unlike patients with damage to areas around the third ventricle, patients with bilateral frontal lobe lesions are aware of surroundings and can encode new information. In persistent vegetative states, following a period of coma, diurnal rhythms often re-establish and the individual exhibits spontaneous eye opening and sporadic eye tracking of visual, auditory or tactile stimulation of their environment. Individuals with diffuse cortical lesions often exhibit eye opening to stimulation with frequently intact brain stem reflexes. These states often are the result of acute diffuse causes such as anoxia/hypoxia, toxic/metabolic or drug-induced states.

Locked-In Syndrome

In locked-in syndrome, a lesion in the pontine level (tegmental area) effectively blocks descending pathways (complete transaction of the corticospinal and corticobulbar pathways) while the ascending pathways remain intact. These lesions are often the result of a circumscribed hemorrhagic or occlusive lesion and spare the cortex and cranial nerves I–III, sparing smell, sight and some aspects of eye movement. Thus, a patient with locked-in syndrome may appear in a coma, but these patients' mental status and awareness is generally preserved. Locked-in syndrome can be distinguished from stuporous condition or coma in careful examination utilizing eye movements to demonstrate responses to stimuli. These patients are able to communicate only with eye movements, but remain very much conscious, perceive stimulation throughout their bodies, and are aware, despite their inability to speak or produce voluntary movement.

Delirium

Delirium refers to an acutely developing and fluctuating deficit in arousal (see also Chap. 16 for a discussion of confusional states generally, including encephalopathy and delirium). Delirium is common in acute medical settings with estimates of prevalence raging from 10% to 15% of hospital admissions. Increasing risks for delirium are closely associated with the reason for hospitalization and associated demographic factors. Specifically, individuals undergoing cardiac or orthopedic procedures are especially vulnerable, as are the chronically ill, aged or demented. In addition, these procedures are often associated with high blood volume losses, high use of pain medication and potential hypoxia associated with length of time on heart/lung bypass equipment. Table 6.2 lists the DSM-V diagnostic criteria for delirium. Table 6.3 lists some of the common medical and demographic risk factors in delirium. The diagnosis of acute delirium is critical as mortality rises dramatically as delirium is prolonged. A useful mnemonic of I WATCH DEATH is presented in Yudofsky and Hales (1992) and adapted below.

Mnemonic for medical conditions associated with delirium (I WATCH DEATH)

Category	Medical factors
Infection	Encephalitis, meningitis, sepsis
Withdrawal	Alcohol, sedatives, analgesics
Acute metabolic	Electrolyte, renal-hepatic failure, acidosis, alkalosis
Trauma	Post-surgical, hypo- or hyperthermia
CNS pathology	Hemorrhage, hydrocephalus, seizure, tumor, vasculitis
Hypoxia	Carbon monoxide poisoning, hypotension, cardiac arrest
Deficiencies	B12, thiamin, severe nutritional deficiency
Endocrinopathies	Hyper- or hypoadrenocorticism, hyper- or hypoglycemia
Acute vascular	Hypertension, occlusive stroke
Toxins or drugs	Medication reaction/change/overdose, toxic exposure
Heavy metals	Manganese, mercury

Adapted from Wise and Brandt in Yudofsky and Hales (1992) (p. 368)

Table 6.2 Diagnostic and Statistical Manual (DSM), fifth edition: criteria for delirium

Criteria A	Disturbance of attention and awareness
Criteria B	Disturbance develops over a short period of time, represents a change from baseline and fluctuates in severity over the course of a day
Criteria C	An additional disturbance in cognition (i.e., memory, perception, language, etc.)
Criteria D	Disturbances in criteria A and C are not better explained by a preexisting disorder or occur in the context of severe arousal reduction or coma
Criteria E	There is evidence that the condition is a direct physiological consequence of another medical condition or combination of conditions

Table 6.3 Demographic and medical risk factors associated with increased occurence of delirium

• Increased age (particularly over 65)
• Previous cognitive compromise (stroke, dementia, trauma)
• Chronic medical condition (diabetes, hypertension, cardio-pulmonary deficit)
• Prolonged hospitalization
• Sensory deprivation, sleep–wake disturbance
• Medical procedures with high blood volume loss/exchange (transplant, etc.)
• Cardiac procedures with necessary prolonged cardio-pulmonary bypass
• Occupational exposure to toxins
• Use of, or change in, dose of sedative, analgesic medications or reaction to new medication

Table 6.4 Observational assessment of arousal

Feature	Assessment	Grading [a]
Adaptation to environmental change	Response to new person, verbal or visual stimulation	0 1
Activity level	Maintenance of appropriate response, avoidance of fluctuations	0 1 2 3
Response latency	Similar reaction time, response latency across tasks and time	0 1 2 3
Task persistence	Persistence on task through completion, minimal redirection needed	0 1 2 3

[a]0, No response/severely impaired; 1, Hypo arousal, minimal impairment; 2, Fluctuations hypo–hyperarousal, normal/impaired; 3, Normal performance

Assessment of Arousal

Several aspects of arousal can be evaluated in the initial assessment in inpatient and outpatient settings (Table 6.4). Minimal assessment of arousal should include qualitative observation of arousal over time and fluctuations in arousal level across time through serial assessment. Several instruments have been designed to assess arousal and have applications for serial assessment in acute settings such as the Galveston Orientation and Amnesia Test (GOAT; Levin et al., 1979), the Glasgow Coma Scale (GCS; Teasdale & Jennett 1974) and Confusion Assessment Method (CAM; Inouye et al., 1990). The GOAT, GCS and CAM are presented in Tables 6.5, 6.6 and 6.7. In addition, arousal can be assessed by evaluating the patient periodically throughout the day by observation and rating aspects of arousal (see Table 6.4). Finally, the clinical neuropsychologist observing a patient with disrupted arousal should also observe for cranial nerve abnormalities, hemiparesis, tremor or signs of decorticate or decerabrate posturing. If not already under a physician's care, we strongly recommend the neuropsychologist immediately refer the patient with suspected altered arousal to a physician or hospital Emergency Department for further evaluation.

Table 6.5 The Galveston Orientation and Amnesia Test (GOAT)

Name: ____________	Date of test: ___/___/___	
Gender:____________	Time: ___________	
Day of the week: _____	Date of injury: ___/___/___	
Date of birth: ____/____/____		
Diagnosis: ___________	Error	Points
1. What is your name? (2)___________	_____	_____
When were you born? (4)___________	_____	_____
Where do you live? (4)___________	_____	_____
2. Where are you now? (5) city_____	_____	_____
(5) Hospital___________	_____	_____
(unnecessary to state name of hospital)		
3. On what date were you admitted to this hospital? (5) ______	_____	_____
4. What is the first event you can remember after the injury? (5)	_____	_____
____		
Can you describe in detail (e.g., date, time and companions) the first event you can recall after the injury? (5)	_____	_____
____		
5. Can you describe the last event you recall before the accident? (5)	_____	_____
____		
Can you describe in detail (e.g., date, time and companions) the first event you can recall before the injury? (5)	_____	_____
____		
6. What time is it now?___________	_____	_____
(−1 for each ½ hour removed from correct time to maximum of −5)		
7. What day of the week is it now?_____	_____	_____
(−1 for each day removed from the correct day to a maximum of −5)		
8. What day of the month is it now?_____	_____	_____
(−1 for each day removed from correct date to maximum of −5)		
9. What is the month?___________	_____	_____
(−5 for each month removed from correct one to maximum of −15)		
10. What is the year?___________	_____	_____
(−10 for each year removed from correct one to maximum of −30)		
Total error points:	_____	_____
Total GOAT score (100 points minus total error points)		

Source. Reprinted from Levin HS, O'Donnell VM, Grossman RG: The Galveston Orientation and Amnesia, Test: a practical scale to assess cognition after head injury. J Nerv Ment Dis 167:675–684, 1979. Copyright 1979 by Williams & Wilkins. Used with permission

Table 6.6 Glasgow coma scale (GCS) (1974)

Eye opening	
1. None	Not attributable to ocular swelling
2. To pain	Pain stimulus is applied
3. To speech	Nonspecific eye opening to speech; does not imply the patient obeys commands
4. Spontaneous	Eyes are open, but this does not imply intact awareness
Motor response	
1. No response	Flaccid
2. Extension	"Decerebrate"; extended arms, internal rotation of shoulder, and pronation of the forearm
3. Abnormal flexion	"Decorticate"; contracted arms, abnormal flexion of wrists and hands
4. Withdrawal	Normal flexor response; generalized withdrawal (nonspecific) to pain
5. Localizes pain	Localized withdrawal to painful stimuli, attempts to remove pain source
6. Obeys commands	Follows simple commands
Verbal response	
1. No response	(self-explanatory)
2. Incomprehensible	Moaning and groaning, but no recognizable words
3. Inappropriate	Intelligible speech (e.g., shouting or swearing), but no sustained or coherent conversation
4. Confused	Responds to questions, but the responses indicate varying disorientation and confusion
5. Oriented	Normal orientation to time, place and person

Table 6.7 The confusion assessment method (CAM) diagnostic algorithm

Feature 1.	Acute onset and fluctuating course
	This feature is usually obtained from a family member or nurse and is shown by positive responses to the following questions: Is there evidence of an acute change in mental status from the patient's baseline? Did the (abnormal) behavior fluctuate during the day, that is, tend to come and go, or increase and decrease in severity?
Feature 2.	Inattention
	This feature is shown by a positive response to the following question: Did the patient have difficulty focusing attention, for example, being easily distractible or having difficulty keeping track of what was being said?
Feature 3.	Disorganized thinking
	This feature is shown by a positive response to the following question: Was the patient's thinking disorganized or incoherent, such as rambling or irrelevant conversation, unclear or illogical flow of ideas or unpredictable switching from subject to subject?
Feature 4.	Altered level of consciousness
	This feature is shown by any answer other than "alert" to the following question: Overall, how would you rate this patient's level of consciousness? (alert [normal], vigilant [hyper alert], lethargic [drowsy, easily aroused], stupor [difficult to arouse] or coma [unarousable])

The diagnosis of delirium by CAM requires the presence of features 1 and 2 and either 3 or 4

References

Inouye, S. K., Van Dyke, C. H., & Alessi, C. (1990). Clarifying confusion: The confusion assessment method (CAM). *Annuals of Internal Medicine, 113*, 941–948.

Levin, H. S., O'Donnell, V. M., & Grossman, R. G. (1979). The Galveston Orientation and Amnesia Test (GOAT): A practical scale to assess cognition after head injury. *Journal of Nervous and Mental Disease, 167*, 675–684.

Teasdale, G. M., & Jennett, B. (1974). Assessment of coma and impaired consciousness. *Lancet, 2*, 81–84.

Yudofsky, S. C., & Hales, R. E. (1992). *Textbook of neuropsychiatry* (2nd ed.). American Psychiatric Press.

Further Reading

Lipowski, Z. J. (1990). *Delirium: Acute confusional states*. Oxford University Press.

Chapter 7
Attention/Concentration: The Distractible Patient

James G. Scott

Attention and concentration are simple concepts on the surface but become complex when asked to assess or differentiate among attentional capacities. While, at its most basic, attention refers to an organism's ability to recognize and respond to changes in its environment. The concept of attention when applied in neuropsychology represents a range of behavior which is dependent on functional integrity of many anatomical regions. The range of behavior includes everything from autonomic and reflexive auditory and visual orientation to sound and movement, to the ability to process several stimuli simultaneously or alternate back and forth from competing stimuli rapidly (see Kolb & Whishaw, 2009 for review). While a universally accepted definition of attention and concentration would be broad, the models of attention typically have common features including orienting, selecting stimuli and maintenance for a necessary time or successful completion of a task. These factors are represented in Fig. 7.1. Attention is typically viewed as a sequence of processes that occur in several different regions of the brain, which are involved with the acquisition and sustaining of attention. Attention is organized hierarchically, usually modality-specific at its origin and then multi-modality or multi-cortically mediated as in rapid alternation or switching of attention or maintenance of concentration.

In addition to attention, concentration refers to two elements: the capacity to sustain attention on relevant stimuli and the capacity to ignore irrelevant competing stimuli. Again, while simple, the concept of concentration is objectively difficult to differentiate in an orthogonal manner, several models of attention and concentration have been proposed and the interested reader is referred to Posner (1990) for elaboration.

J. G. Scott (✉)
Department of Psychiatry and Behavioral Sciences, University of Oklahoma, Health Sciences Center College of Medicine, Oklahoma City, OK, USA
e-mail: jim-scott@ouhsc.edu

M. R. Schoenberg, J. G. Scott (eds.), *The Little Black Book of Neuropsychology*,
https://doi.org/10.1007/978-3-032-07777-6_7

Initial Attention		Selective Attention		Concentration
Automatic or voluntary orientation to sensory stimuli	→→→	Selection of stimuli from array of competing sensory stimuli	→→→	Maintenance of focus on stimuli to complete task

Fig. 7.1 Common elements in cognitive models of attention and concentration

Key Points and Chapter Summary

- Attentional capacity is a prerequisite skill for accurate assessment of more complex neuropsychological functions
- Damage to the frontal lobes is most detrimental to attentional skills, but damage in any part of the brain can compromise attention
- Attention should be assessed at many levels including:
  - Autonomic attention (orienting to visual, tactile or auditory stimuli in the environment)
  - Voluntary attention
  - Focused attention
  - Divided attention
  - Sustained attention (concentration)
  - Alternating attention

Anatomy of Attention/Concentration

Attention and concentration are multiply determined from an anatomical perspective and involve many regions of the brain. Broadly speaking, attention and concentration deficits can arise from compromise in virtually any region of the brain; however, certain regions contribute different aspects to the attentional process. Table 7.1 outlines anatomical areas involved in different aspects of attention. For additional review of neuroanatomic correlates of attention, see Chap. 3, this volume (see also Kolb & Whishaw, 2009; Lezak et al., 2004 for a thorough review of functional neuroanatomy for attention and concentration).

Table 7.1 Localization and lateralization of attentional deficits

Area	Attentional function
Superior colliculus	Regulates automatic orientation to visual stimuli
Inferior colliculus	Regulates automatic orientation to auditory stimuli
Ascending reticular activating system	Provides activating stimulation to cortex to initiate and maintain arousal necessary for initial and sustained attention
Thalamus	Lesions can produce contralateral inattention, or interfere with transmission of sensory input necessary for sustained or alternated attention
Limbic system (amygdala, cingulate gyrus and hippocampus)	Determines saliency of increasing stimuli, provides emotional tone thus facilitating attention and memory, involved with stimuli detection and appropriate alternation of attentional focus
Parietal lobes	Cross-modality hemispatial attention, with right parietal dominance for hemispace attention
Pre-frontal cortex	Responsible for voluntary initiation and sustaining attention, rapid alternation of attentional focus and shifting of attention
Dorsolateral frontal cortex	Initiation of attentional focus
Orbital frontal cortex	Sustaining of attentional focus

Attention Problems: A Behavioral Guide

Below, we provide a behavioral description of some common types of attention problems followed by a possible diagnostic or syndromic explanation for the observed attention deficits. It is important to note that attention problems may not be apparent in one-on-one situations and/or in highly structured settings where distracting stimuli are minimized and the environment and task are novel. Common symptoms of attention deficits and hyperactivity and impulsivity as listed by the DSM-V are summarized in Table 7.2.

A. Problems in Attention Without Hyperactivity

Patients often present as being easily distractible and may have difficulty with compliance to complete some testing due to attention problems. Patients may be distracted by efforts to examine visual fields with confrontation, and will have difficulty maintaining a task if the examiner or environment is distracting. While common in the general population, these patients frequently report difficulty completing projects they start and start another project before finishing the current project. Patients may also complain of memory problems such as forgetting to do school or work projects. However, the forgetfulness often reflects a secondary effect of varying attention on consolidation of memory rather than a direct memory failure. These individuals often appear disorganized and inefficient or scattered due to the effect of their attentional difficulties in gathering the necessary prerequisite materials or completing tasks. While overt hyperactivity and impulsivity may not be present, these patients often appear fidgety, restless or anxious.

Table 7.2 Common symptoms of attention deficits, hyperactivity and impulsivity as listed by the DSM-V

Neuropsychological deficit	Clinical presentation/symptoms
Attention	For DSM-V diagnostic criteria, must have six (6) or more of the symptoms below for six (6) months in duration of severity that is maladaptive and inconsistent with the patient's developmental level
	• Avoids engaging in tasks that require sustained mental effort
	• Does not listen when spoken to directly
	• Does not follow through on instructions
	• Has difficulty sustaining attention in activities
	• Fails to give close attention to details
	• Has difficulty organizing tasks
	• Loses things necessary for activities
	• Is easily distracted by extraneous stimuli
	• Is forgetful in daily activities
Hyperactivity and impulsivity	For DSM-V diagnosis of hyperactivity/impulsivity type (or combined type) ADHD, patient must have six (6) or more of the following symptoms persisting for at least six (6) months in duration of severity that is maladaptive and inconsistent with the patient's developmental level.
	Hyperactivity
	• Acts as if "driven by a motor."
	• Has difficulty playing quietly
	• Is fidgety
	• Leaves seat when expected to remain seated
	• Runs about in situations in which it is inappropriate
	• Talks excessively
	Impulsivity
	• Blurts out answers before questions have been completed
	• Has difficulty taking turns
	• Interrupts or intrudes on others

B. Problems Primarily with Impulsivity and/or Hyperactivity

Patients often present with a history of rash decisions and impulsive behaviors that can often threaten their safety. These patients are clearly overactive relative to their peers and are often perceived as disruptive, non-compliant and unruly. They are also often perceived by peers as intrusive or annoying. Patients may complain of difficulty maintaining vigilance (focus) on tasks across environments (home, school and/or work). Patients often have difficulty keeping still, and will fidget in their chairs or when trying to stand still. Younger patients may exhibit symptoms of conduct disorder and/or mood symptoms of anxiety or depressive symptoms. These patients may describe themselves as "class clowns" and may over-use alcohol and/or drugs as coping mechanisms as they age. They are often avoidant of situations that require restricted movement or sustained attention (i.e., long travel, classrooms/lectures/meetings).

C. Problems in Attention with Impulsivity/Hyperactive

Patients present with a combination of inattentiveness and impulsivity and hyperactivity. Patients present with being easily distracted, and go from one project to another without finishing the first. Patients also exhibit high energy levels and make rash and impulsive decisions. They often have difficulty learning from past mistakes and appear to impulsively make the same judgment errors repeatedly, despite good ability to verbalize alternative or correct responses and often display true remorse subsequent to their repeated mistakes. Like patients with primarily hyperactive-based attention problems, patients with both attention and hyperactivity/impulsivity may describe themselves as "class clowns" and may over-use alcohol and/or drugs as coping strategies.

D. Problems in Maintaining Vigilance

Patients having trouble maintaining vigilance may readily engage in a task and indicate an interest in completing the task. Span of attention (e.g., digit span) can be entirely intact, potentially even above average. However, for tasks taking longer times to complete, these patients lose interest in the task and become distracted. Patients typically begin to fidget and can daydream or are susceptible to even minor distractions in their environment. Novel stimuli present in the area will frequently distract a patient to move or stop engaging in the task. Patients with deficits in vigilance often avoid and/or complain about engaging in repetitive tasks.

Patients with deficits in vigilance often develop compensatory behaviors and fidget by playing with writing instruments, doodling, shifting position frequently (sitting or standing), and may "tap" their foot or fingers.

While appearing to be entirely inattentive, often when these patients are asked about recent events or details, they can usually respond correctly. Child patients with problems in vigilance deficits are often able to respond correctly to questions posed to them about what had recently transpired in the classroom, despite seemingly attending to doodling, talking to neighbors and/or fidgeting in their desks.

E. Adult Presenting with Primary Attention Problems

The adult patient presenting to the neuropsychology clinic for predominate attention problems poses a significant challenge to the diagnosis and treatment of attention deficits. The diagnosis of Attention Deficit Disorder and Attention Deficit with Hyperactivity Disorder (ADD/ADHD) retrospectively requires a careful and detailed analysis of when symptoms of attention and/or impulsivity/hyperactivity problems began. DSM-V criteria require onset of attention problems before the age of 12 years old. Onset of attention problems and/or hyperactivity/impulsivity in adulthood (after age 18) generally precludes a diagnosis of ADHD. While changes in attentional capacity are both common in the general population and expected with age, they may be a secondary symptom of developing neurologic or psychiatric disease. Attentional difficulties are a very common symptom across multiple neurologic and psychiatric disorders and thus it is critical that an acute cause be ruled out. In patients complaining of attention and/or hyperactivity/impulsivity symptoms with an onset in adulthood, the diagnosis is neurological disease or psychiatric mood disorder until proven otherwise.

Assessment of Attention

The clinical assessment of attention ranges from tasks requiring simple attentional capacities to complex attentional functions involving selection, sustaining and alternating attention as well as inhibiting distraction or avoiding unwanted attentional switching to automatic or overlearned processes (i.e., reading or semantic processing rather than color naming or stating the case a word is printed in). Assessment of attention typically involves assessment of attentional capacity including *focused attention, sustained attention, divided attention and rapid alternating attention.* In addition, assessment of attention frequently includes an evaluation of ability to inhibit automatic or overlearned responses. Assessment proceeds from the simplest tasks of attentional capacity to more complex tasks of focused, sustained, divided and rapid attentional alternation. A brief summary is provided below, and bedside assessment examples are discussed in more detail below.

- Simple attentional capacity is a prerequisite skill which must be considered both in the assessment of more complex attentional factors in addition to other higher-order cognitive skills (memory, language, visual-spatial reasoning, abstraction, etc.) that are assessed later in the neuropsychological evaluation. Digit span forward is an example of this ability in which patients are asked to repeat a series or random numbers.
- Focused attention (selective attention) refers to the ability to "tune out" or attend to chosen (consciously targeted information) stimuli while simultaneously ignoring other stimuli that are judged less important (i.e., not becoming distracted by competing stimuli). Examples of this are the Wechsler Intelligence tests digit symbol/coding and symbol search tasks and cancelation tasks. Among researchers, there is debate as to whether there is a difference between focused and sustained attention.
- Sustained attention (or vigilance) is the ability to maintain attention to stimuli over an extended period of time, even when stimuli may not be constant. Some would consider sustained attention as *concentration*. Examples include the various continuous performance tests in which attention must be sustained on a computer screen looking for a specified target over an extended time.
- Divided attention (some consider this to reflect working memory) refers to the ability to process more than one (multiple) stimuli (information) at the same time or maintain involvement in more than one task at a time (keeping information from multiple stimuli or tasks "on line" and respond appropriately to several operations of a task simultaneously). An example of this is mental arithmetic and letter–number sequencing tasks.
- Rapid alternating attention refers to the ability to rapidly shift attentional ability between stimuli or tasks. This type of attention is more difficult to evaluate

without psychometric instruments. Examples include the Wechsler Intelligence tests digit symbol/coding subtest and symbol search subtest. These tests require rapid alternation of attentional focus, usually for short periods of time (ex. 90 seconds).

Before discussing the assessment of attention, several factors should be considered which could produce detrimental effects on immediate attention and distort the assessment of attention. These factors include the general medical condition of the patient, with acute patients and those immediately post-procedure likely to display attentional deficits that are varying and transient. Medication can also have a detrimental effect, and it is critical to be aware of the medication the patient is taking, the dosing schedule of medication that potentially affects attention, and any recent change in medication, dose or dosing schedule. It is also important to assess the patient's level of fatigue, the extent of previous activity on the day of assessment and to account for the potentially fatigue-inducing effect in the current assessment as it progresses. In noting fatigue, it is important to consider the time of day in which the assessment occurs, as in many individuals (especially the young and elderly) fatigue effects occur rapidly as the day progresses. An assessment of the environment is also necessary to rule out any extraneous distractions prior to assessing attention. Table 7.3 provides a checklist of pre-testing factors that can affect measured attentional skills.

Table 7.3 Factors which can negatively affect assessment of attention

Factor	Assessment
Establish sensory thresholds	Assure adequate auditory, visual and tactile sensory thresholds, provide compensation if necessary (i.e., amplifier, large print, etc.)
Medication	Rule out sedative, hypnotic, analgesic, anxiolytic or other medication that affects attention (i.e., antihistamines).
	Examine dose schedules to minimize negative post dose effect.
	Examine medication and dose changes that may indicate magnified effect due to ineffectual habituation.
Fatigue	Examine the individual's activity level on the day of assessment; ask about changes in sleep/wake cycle and quality of rest on previous evening.
	Note the age and general health condition of the individual; examine individual level of fatigue as testing progresses, and note time of day the assessment of attention is occurring.
Environmental factors	Note auditory and visual distractions.
	Note presence of others or any change in environmental stimuli and the individual's response to these changes.

Methods to Assess Attention and Concentration

As previously discussed, attention varies in complexity from simple to complex attentional abilities. Simple components of attention can be assessed in the interview both informally and formally. Attention should be assessed through observation by noting such behaviors as reciprocal conversation skill, time on task, response time and susceptibility to distraction or environmental change. Assuming that these behaviors are noted to be within normal limits, assessment of attention should progress from simple attention to auditory and visual tasks to more demanding tasks requiring sustained attention, rapid shifting of attention and dual processing of information. Many of these tasks can be administered at the bedside for patient screening or brief assessment while other components of attention are better evaluated in a controlled testing environment. This chapter will focus on brief/bedside evaluation of attention and concentration, but for more structured and elaborate attentional assessment, the interested reader is referred to Lezak et al. (2004).

Brief/Bedside Assessment of Attention

Auditory Attention Span. Forward digit span involves the presentation of random single-digit numbers (0–9) to the patient at one per second (e.g., 6—4—9—7—2). The numbers are repeated by the patient and assessed for accuracy. While education does have an impact on performance, age appears to have a minimal effect on digit-span forward (Lezak et al., 2004). The range of repetition of digits forward is traditionally considered to be 7 with an approximate standard deviation of 2 (e.g., correctly repeating 5–9 digits forward is considered normal). Test presentation data and descriptions of performance are presented in Table 7.4. For those patients older than 65, a reduction of 1 digit is appropriate (e.g., 4–8 digits forward). Individuals who have speech production problems can be presented with a page with numbers

Table 7.4 Digit span forward and reverse [a]

Digits	Forward	Reverse
2—6	Severely impaired	Moderately impaired
9—3—1	Moderately impaired	Mildly impaired
5—7—4—8	Mildly impaired	Borderline
3—9—6—2—5	Borderline	Low normal
8—3—1—2—9—4	Low normal	Normal
7—6—4—1—3—5—2	Normal	High normal
3—9—4—6—8—2—5—1	High normal	High performance
5—6—9—2—8—3—5—1—7	High performance	Superior

[a] For patients age 65 or older, add one digit to obtained performance to derive normative descriptor

arranged from 0–9 and test stimuli either presented aurally or by pointing to numbers. Similar performance levels should be expected as with aural presentation and verbal response.

Reverse digit span is a slightly more difficulty task requiring patients to listen to digits presented at a rate of one per second (or view as in the case of visually presented stimuli) and then report the sequence of numbers in reverse order. This task is more demanding in that it not only requires short-term attention, but the storage and manipulation of this information prior to repetition of the digits. This task has been shown to be much more revealing as to the effects of acute and chronic cortical compromise. In a normal population, the average person should perform one digit less in digits backward than forward (i.e., 6 ± 2). Test data are presented in Table 7.4.

Many other attention span tasks are available that include assessing forward and reverse span including letter span and visual span, and the interested reader is referred to Lezak et al. (2004) for a description of these tests.

Key Points: Bedside Assessment of Attention

- Adequate and sustained arousal is a prerequisite for assessment of attention
- Attentional deficits produce a pattern of variable performance across neuropsychological assessment
- Attention assessment should include:
  - Sustained attention/vigilance
  - Attention under distraction
  - Divided attention
  - Rapid alternation of attention focus

Assessment of Sustained Attention and Impulsivity

Vigilance, or the ability to sustain attention voluntarily, is also critical for successful performance on neuropsychological tests and a prerequisite skill in making meaningful interpretation of subsequent neuropsychological test data. It is especially important to assess vigilance periodically in patients who are acutely injured or otherwise believed to experience fluctuations in attentional capacity.

The most direct way to assess vigilance is to ask the patient to perform a task that requires sustaining attention. Vigilance should be sustainable for at least 60–90 seconds without interruption. In the interview, a patient can be asked to point to a series of objects in the room either by mimicking the examiner or by following verbal commands. Such commands can be repeated to ensure that vigilance can be sustained for 60–90 seconds. Such commands or mimicking can include pointing to ceiling, floor, walls, windows, furniture or personal objects in the room. The individual could also be asked to count to 100 or recite the alphabet or read aloud for 60 seconds. The critical element is that the task involves overlearned stimuli which require minimal cognitive processing.

Table 7.5 Brief bedside letter and number vigilance assessment tasks[a]

Digits	Letters
5 3 9 1 5 5 6 7 4 1 8 2 5 6 5	A C R P A A M D Q S D T A B A
5 5 8 3 1 6 4 4 2 7 1 9 4 5 1	A A Z P T M N N E F G B S A L
5 8 6 3 9 5 5 5 2 7 6 1 5 4 2	A S P L R A A A G M C D A D B
2 7 6 5 4 9 3 8 6 4 8 2 5 1 4	B G F A D S T P Z R F T A C F

[a]Digits and letters should be read at one per second. Errors should be noted as commission (c) omission (o) or perseveration (p). Total errors exceeding three indicate impairment. After a patient understands directions, no further assistance is provided during testing

More formal bedside assessment of vigilance can be conducted using a letter or digit vigilance task (see Table 7.5 for example). Such tasks require the patient to listen to a series of numbers or letters and respond only to a target letter or number by raising a finger or tapping a table. In such tasks, each number or letter is read at a rate of one per second and performance is evaluated based on omissions errors (failing to detect a target), commission errors (falsely reporting a target as presented) and perseverations of response. These tests typically have a one-to-four response items-to-distracter ratio, and minimal total errors are expected in normally functioning patients aged 6 years old and older. Patients with greater than three total errors should be considered to be impaired. Test stimuli are presented in Table 7.5 for both letter and digit vigilance tasks (Target letter A and number 5 in this example). While the assessment of attention should be conducted at the bedside or during interview, assessment of more complex attention and a quantitative assessment of attentional capacities are best done in a formal assessment setting which can control environmental factors and make comparisons to standardized data. The interested reader is referred to Lezak et al. (2004) for a thorough review of attention assessment measures. Common measures to assess for vigilance include continuous performance tests, which require the patient to respond to various stimuli on the screen while not responding to others.

References

Kolb, B., & Whishaw, I. Q. (2009). *Fundamentals of human neuropsychology* (6th ed.). Worth Publishers.

Lezak, M. D., Howieson, D. B., & Loring, D. W. (2004). *Neuropsychological assessment* (4th ed.). Oxford University Press.

Posner, M. I. (1990). Hierarchical distributed networks in the neuropsychology of selective attention. In A. Caramazzo (Ed.), *Cognitive neuropsychology and neurolinguistics: Advances in models of cognitive function and impairment*. Erlbaum.

Further Reading

Strub, R. L., & Black, R. W. (1993). *The mental status examination in neurology* (3rd ed.). F.A. Davis.

Chapter 8
Language Problems and Assessment: The Aphasic Patient

James G. Scott and Michael R. Schoenberg

The singular most unique human attribute is language. Such a bold statement is difficult to make, but profoundly true. Many species possess communication skill and communication among some species is elaborate and facilitates complex social relationships and interactions; however, the extent and sophistication of human use of representational language is truly unique. Language is so intertwined into what it is to be human that its complexity is often overlooked as a prerequisite skill in neuropsychological assessment.

At its simplest, language can be conceptualized as expressive and receptive language functions. While typically residing in the left hemisphere (referred to as the dominant hemisphere because of the propensity of language to develop even if damage occurs to normal language centers), bilateral representation and right hemisphere representation of language occur both naturally and secondarily in response to early cerebral injury that affects the typically dominant left hemisphere (see Table 8.1 for relative frequencies of hemispheric language dominance). See also Chaps. 3 and 13.

The evaluation of the patient with language deficits first requires a review of the assessment of language and the definition of some terms. We will first review the basic aspects to evaluate speech and define terms describing different types of speech problems. We will then return to evaluating various speech problems commonly encountered in the clinic.

J. G. Scott (✉)
Department of Psychiatry and Behavioral Sciences, University of Oklahoma, Health Sciences Center College of Medicine, Oklahoma City, OK, USA
e-mail: jim-scott@ouhsc.edu

M. R. Schoenberg
Departments of Psychiatry and Neurosciences, Neurology and Neurosurgery, University of South Florida College of Medicine, Tampa, FL, USA
e-mail: mschoenb@usf.edu

M. R. Schoenberg, J. G. Scott (eds.), *The Little Black Book of Neuropsychology*,
https://doi.org/10.1007/978-3-032-07777-6_8

Table 8.1 Percent of individuals with hemispheric language dominance by handedness

	Hemispheric language dominance		
Handedness	Left	Right	Bilateral
Left	70	15	15
Right	96	4	<.5

Note: Numbers are percentages

Key Points and Chapter Summary

- The hemisphere that controls language is referred to as the dominant hemisphere
  - The left hemisphere controls language in the vast majority of people (but not all)
  - Anterior dominant hemisphere cortex controls expressive language (including written language)
  - Posterior dominant cortex controls receptive language (including reading)
- The right hemisphere plays a significant role in prosodic aspects of language
  - Expressive prosody is controlled by the nondominant anterior cortex
  - Receptive prosody is controlled by the nondominant posterior cortex
- Language deficits are most commonly produced by focal lesions, but more diffuse lesions and neurodegenerative disease can produce language deficits typically in high-level language skills such as rapid fluency, organization and discourse

Overview of Language

Assessment of language can be complex and detailed with many aspects of language being parceled out, but most clinical assessment of language includes basic aspects of expressive language (including writing), receptive language (including reading), repetition, naming and verbal fluency. The acquired inability to read is termed alexia and the acquired inability to write is called agraphia. Developmental deficits in reading (that is, difficulty learning to read, when reading had not been acquired, is termed dyslexia). Another domain frequently assessed is termed language prosody. Prosody refers to the ability to express and interpret vocal tone, inflection and other nonlanguage auditory cues and extract meaning that facilitates communication. The presence of an increased tone at the end of the sentence, "Here he comes," distinguishes that it was a question rather than an affirmative statement.

Similar auditory cues are used in detecting sarcasm, irony, innuendo and many other aspects of communication.

Assessment of language functions should differentiate deficits in the language process from articulation and other oral motor deficits that may significantly impact speech production. For example, patients can develop oral apraxias which reflect inability to appropriately move the musculature of the mouth, tongue and larynx. The motor apraxias can be distinguished from aphasias by the fact that difficulty in moving the musculature of the mouth, tongue and larynx will also be present with tasks other than talking, such as swallowing, using a straw, trying to whistle or chewing. Patients with oral apraxias may also have difficulty smiling appropriately to conscious effort (a good joke, however, will allow the patient to smile spontaneously). Note, however, there may be motor weakness (e.g., hemiparesis) associated with a contralateral cortical lesion or ipsilateral lesion of the cranial nerves innervating the face, lips and tongue. Likewise, evaluation of basic hearing and vision functions should precede any evaluation to assess for language comprehension.

Anatomical Correlates

We briefly review anatomic correlates for language below for convenience. Readers are also directed to Chaps. 3 and 13 for additional review.

Language function is traditionally described as inclusive of the perisylvian area (cortex around the Sylvian fissure or lateral fissure) of the dominant (left) hemisphere. Analogous representation of prosodic language function has been proposed for the nondominant hemisphere (e.g., Ross, 1997). Language function can be divided into two broad neuroanatomical zone, an anterior expressive language zone and posterior receptive language zone. Expressive language is strongly associated with function of the left posterior frontal cortex, typically referred to as Broca's area, and corresponds to Brodmann's area (BA) 44 (along with BA 45) (see Fig. 8.1). Receptive language (comprehension) is associated with the left posterior temporal–parietal area, in which Wernicke's area (BA 22) is classically identified as the neuroanatomic localization for receptive language (see Chap. 3, Fig. 3.25 for detailed cortical map of Brodmann's areas).

Figure 8.1 highlights the cortical regions involved in expressive (spoken and writing) and receptive (aural and reading) language functions. The numbers correspond to Brodmann's areas involved in the left hemisphere. The illustration includes areas of the cortex not traditionally considered to be involved in language (e.g., visual cortex of BA 17, 18 and 19), but are included here to provide the reader with a better appreciation for the complex distributed network involved in language processes (see also Chap. 3). Broca's area is the expressive language hub, and integrally involved in expressive language (speech and writing). In addition, BA 6 (premotor area) is also involved in expressive language, including motor planning in speech articulation of the face, tongue, lips, pharynx/larynx, etc. The production of speech includes the corticobulbar tracts and cranial nerves involving

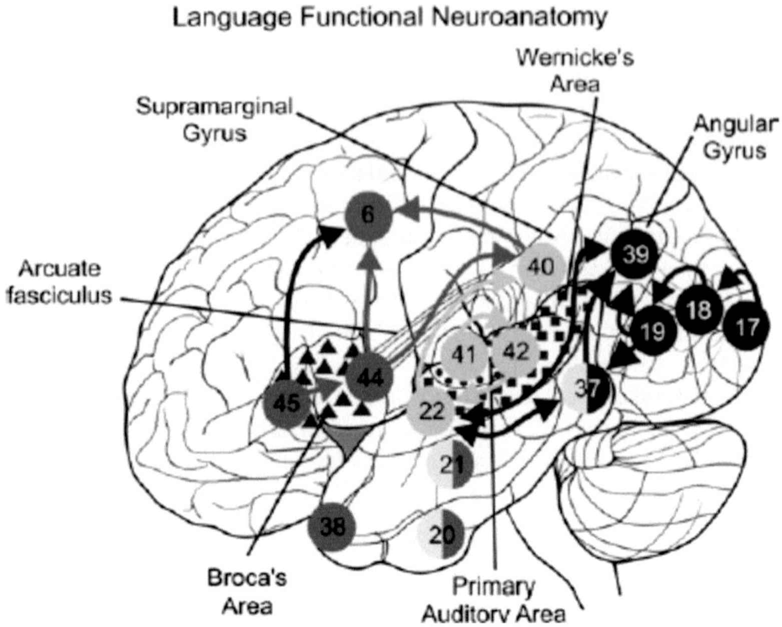

Fig. 8.1 Neuroanatomy of language

the motor/sensory function of the mouth, tongue and larynx as well as control of the diaphragm in order to produce speech. Receptive language (comprehension and reading) is strongly associated with BA 22 (Wernicke's area), BA 41 and 42 (primary auditory sensory cortex) and BA 39 (angular gyrus). Primary auditory cortex anatomically corresponds to Heschl's gyrus, which is a part of the temporal lobe located adjacent to the Sylvian fissure. The projections from BA 41 and 42 to BA 22 (Wernicke's area) are integral in the perception of auditory sensory stimuli. Wernicke's area (BA 22) is identified as the central receptive language area, which is involved in comprehension of oral and written language. Brodmann's area 39 (angular gyrus) is a central area in the processing of written language. Semantic association of words (i.e., mental representation: canary is a bird) involves the occipitotemporal cortex (BA 21 and 37). Note that reading involves visual stimuli projected first to primary and associative visual cortex (BA 17/V1, BA18/V2, BA19/V3), which is then projected to language areas (BA 37, 22 and 39). The arcuate fasciculus (part of the superior longitudinal fasciculus) underlying BA 39 and 40 and projecting to BA 44/45 is necessary for intact language, traditionally associated with the ability to repeat what is heard. Naming functions have been associated with the anterior, superior and middle temporal gyri (BA 38, 21 and 22) as well as the left anterior cingulate, left ventral frontal lobe and left medial occipital regions (not shown).

Large lesions in the left hemisphere frequently produce both verbal expressive and auditory receptive language deficits such that reading and writing are also impaired (see Fig. 8.2). Focal damage to BA 44/45 produces a gross decrease in

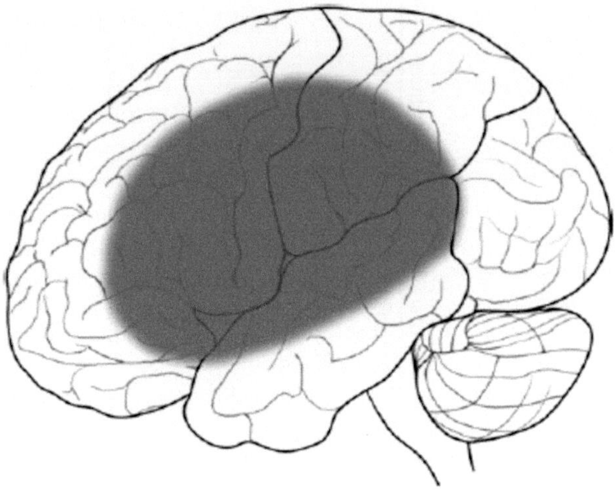

Fig. 8.2 Large left hemisphere damage resulting in global aphasia

expressive language. However, lesions to BA 6 also result in impaired speech production beyond motor paresis, and BA 6 is involved in expressive speech (see Chap. 13). Lesions affecting primary auditory cortex (BA 41 and 42) result in deficits in auditory sensory perception (e.g., cortical deafness, auditory verbal agnosia, etc.; see Chap. 13). Injury to BA 22 results in deficits of language comprehension, including reading. The basic aphasias are presented in Table 8.2 along with their typical lesion location. See Chap. 13 for detailed review of aphasic syndromes.

Prosodic functions are similarly represented as Expressive and Receptive language functions in the left hemisphere, with expressive prosody functions being associated with right anterior (frontal) areas and receptive prosody being associated with right posterior (temporoparietal) regions. The effect of prosody deficits in communication can be profound, leading to literal, inefficient communication, which has a significant impact on communication of emotional information. Individuals with expressive aprosody are often viewed by others as dull, emotionless and lacking compassion and empathy. Their verbal output is frequently monotone, flat and lacking the tone and inflection that communicates a corresponding appropriate emotional state. When asked directly, they are often able to verbalize the internal experience of emotional states that they are not able to display adequately in their verbal tone and inflection. Similarly, individuals with receptive aprosodies are often viewed as emotionally unavailable, lacking insight into others' emotional states or uncaring. They often miss verbal cues that would communicate the emotional states of others. This in turn leads to a decrease in appropriate emotional responsiveness and a generally literal interpretation of what is verbally said with little appreciation for the way it was verbalized or the context in which it occurred. Table 8.3 lists the major Aprosodies and their anatomical correlates. See Chap. 13 for a detailed review of common aphasia and aprosody syndromes.

Table 8.2 Types of aphasias and associated deficits

	Anatomical association	Speech	Comprehension	Reading	Writing	Repetition
Expressive (Broca's) aphasia	Left posterior frontal (Broca's area)	Impaired	Grossly intact	Grossly intact	Impaired	Impaired
Receptive (Wernicke's) aphasia	Left posterior temporal/ parietal (Wernicke's area)	Fluent, but nonsensical	Impaired	Impaired	Grossly intact	Mildly impaired, paraphasic
Global aphasia	Left anterior and posterior	Impaired	Impaired	Impaired	Impaired	Impaired
Mixed transcortical aphasia	Left anterior and posterior sparing Broca's and Wernicke's areas	Impaired	Impaired	Impaired	Impaired	Intact
Transcortical motor aphasia	Left anterior frontal with relative sparring of Broca's area	Impaired	Typically intact	Typically intact	Impaired	Typically intact
Transcortical sensory aphasia	Posterior parietal/temporal cortical lesion with sparring of Wernicke's area	Impaired	Impaired	Impaired	Typically intact	Typically intact
Conduction aphasia	Lesion of the arcuate fasiculus which connects Broca's and Wernicke's areas	Mildly impaired—frequent paraphasias	Intact	Intact—for comprehension. Oral reading poor due to paraphasias	Typically impaired. Poor spelling/ paraphasias	Impaired, even for single words

Table 8.3 Types of aprosodies and associated deficits

	Anatomical location	Verbal (expressive) prosody	Aural (receptive) prosody	Gestural receptive prosody	Gestural expressive prosody
Expressive aprosody	Right lateral frontal lobe, superior anterior temporal lobe	Severely impaired	Grossly intact	Grossly intact	Moderately impaired
Receptive aprosody	Right posterior temporal lobe, inferior parietal/temporal lobe juncture	Grossly intact	Severely impaired	Moderately impaired	Grossly intact
Global aprosody	Right anterior and posterior lesion	Severely impaired	Severely impaired	Moderately impaired	Moderately impaired

Key Points: Language Anatomical Correlates

- Broca's area (Brodmann area 44) is twice Wernicke's area (Brodmann area 22)
- Language arcculate fasiculus Connection of Wernicke's area to Broca's area via Arcuate fasciculus
- Written language needs Brodmann area 39 (angular gyrus)

Receptive Language and Receptive Aprosodies

Examination of receptive language includes aural and written receptive communication as well as examination of receptive prosody. These basic functions are prerequisite skills to the assessment of both higher and more difficulty aspects of language (phonemic or semantic fluency) and verbal reasoning. The appendix demonstrates items which assess a progression of receptive language skills from simple to complex. Each item should be passed easily by intact individuals, but additional items of similar complexity can be administered to assess degree and consistency of deficit in the assessed area of functioning.

Expressive Language and Expressive Aprosodies

Expressive language should be assessed both verbally and in writing. Similarly, expressive language should be assessed in both simple and gradually more complex functions. Appendix A includes a section for assessing expressive language functions. Assessment should include both responses to simple questions and responses to more unstructured, open-ended questions. Again, emphasis should be taken to note any paraphasic errors of either phonemic or semantic type as well as any articulation or oral motor deficits.

Recovery of Language Function

It is important to note that lesions that result in language deficits acutely may resolve substantially over the course of the first few weeks to months post-injury. In most cases, the most recovery occurs in the first 3 months after insult. Thus, assessment must consider the time since injury carefully as a critical factor in expected future functional language deficits and treatment programming (see also Chap. 1 for related issues in symptom onset timing). Often, individuals having acquired broad language deficits (receptive and expressive speech is impaired) will exhibit recovery, but less recovery of language function than individuals with less disrupted language functions. As an example, individuals with language deficits in which receptive speech remains intact while expressive speech and repetition are impaired (Broca's aphasia) will often have recovery of language function such that repetition improves, and expressive language improves to include consistent simple one- or two-word utterances that enhance functional communication. A patient with pronounced acute expressive deficits may present in the neuropsychology clinic months later with subtle deficits of reduced phrase length, dysnomia and dysgraphia. Conversely, patients with moderate to severe receptive language deficits may recover concrete receptive language skills, with only subtle residual deficits. Global aphasias recovery is generally to a Broca's (expressive) aphasia while Wernicke's (receptive) aphasias will recover to a conduction or anomic aphasia. Recovery may be so complete that deficits remain only in complex receptive language and are only detectible with detailed, in-depth testing of language skills. Unfortunately, patients with global deficits acutely often do not have good functional language outcomes and remain profoundly impaired.

We turn now to descriptions of various language problems one might encounter in the clinic setting. For the sake of description, subtle impairments which may be present are not reviewed, and the following is limited to description of language problems that may be readily identified by a detailed bedside evaluation of language functions.

Key Points: Recovery of Language

- Lesions in the dominant hemisphere are much more likely to produce permanent language deficits
- The size of the lesion is significantly related to the extent and persistence of the language deficit
- Most language recovery occurs rapidly in the first 1–3 months following an injury
- Expressive, receptive and repetition language deficits are anatomically separate
- Expressive deficits generally include written and spoken modalities equally
- Receptive deficits generally include auditory and reading modalities equally

Language Problems: A Behavioral Guide

Below, we provide a symptomatic description of various common language problems followed by a possible diagnostic or syndromic explanation for the observed language deficits. Further details of the identified aphasia syndrome and associated neurological and neuropsychological deficits can be found in Chap. 13.

Nonfluent Speech Problems

The patient is unable to speak or speech is halting or limited to a few words and/or may be of shorter phrase length in less severe cases.

1. The patient is unable to speak, repeat what he/she hears or comprehend speech. The patient is unable to read or write. The patient is observed to be able to swallow and eat without choking. Naming is impaired. The tongue is not significantly weak, although some weakness of the lower face and limbs is to be expected.

   - Suggests a *global aphasia*. Commonly associated with large left hemisphere lesions affecting left frontal, parietal and temporal lobes (MCA stem infarct). A lesion affecting the left frontal lobe that extends mesially to insular region and basal ganglia can result in global aphasia, which may improve to a Broca's aphasia.

2. The patient is unable to speak, repeat or comprehend speech. The patient is able to write. The patient is able to read. Weakness may or may not be present.

   - This pattern is not associated with known neurological etiology and reflects a psychiatric syndrome.

3. The patient is unable to speak, or speech is labored with a few words (telegraphic) that are typically nouns. Prosody and intonation impaired (dysprosody). Repetition is disrupted. Comprehension is grossly intact. The patient is able to follow basic commands and understand simple sentences, but some difficulty with grammatically complex sentences. Writing impaired with poorly formed letters and few if any words. Frequently has right hand hemiparesis, forcing patient to hold pen with nondominant (left) hand. The patient can comprehend simple words as indicated by motor or gestural responses and reading comprehension is often intact for simple commands. There are paraphasias. While nearly mute, patients may be able to blurt out words of profanity when upset or irritated. Patients may also be able to sing well-known songs. Naming generally impaired. Improved with phonemic cues.

   - Suggests a *Broca's aphasia*. Commonly associated with left inferior frontal lobe lesions. More extensive lesions affecting the left inferior gyrus and extending beyond central sulcus along the Rolandic fissure in which underlying white matter is affected results in more extensive and long-lasting Broca's aphasia features. Smaller lesions, affecting only left inferior frontal gyrus area (Broca's area), results in temporary mutism followed by mild transcortical motor aphasia (see below). Lesions limited to precentral gyrus result in aphemia.

4. The patient is unable to speak, or speech is labored and effortful with few words and/or paraphasias. Echolalia can be present. Less telegraphic speech (speech grammar is better than in Broca's aphasia). Speech prosody is poor (dysprosody). Repetition is grossly intact, and patient able to repeat single words and short sentences. Comprehension is intact. Writing is impaired with poorly formed letters. Reading comprehension is intact. Reading out loud is disrupted, effortful, and paraphasias and echolalia may be present. Naming is variable, but may be intact.

   - Suggests a *transcortical motor aphasia*. Commonly associated with left frontal lesions anterior and superior to Broca's area, which is spared. Generally, involves anterior dorsolateral cortex, but may also occur with mesial frontal lesions affecting anterior cingulate and supplementary motor area fibers. Lesions affecting basal ganglia of the left (dominant) hemisphere also associated with this aphasia syndrome. The patient is likely able to blurt out words of profanity when upset or irritated. Patients may also be able to sing overlearned songs (e.g., "Happy Birthday").

5. The patient's speech is mildly disrupted with short phrase length (commonly less than 6–7 words per sentence). Phonemic paraphasias often present. Repetition is grossly intact. The patient is able to repeat short phrases. Comprehension is intact. The patient can follow basic commands. Reading may be intact for simple words. Writing may be mildly disrupted, with misspelling and frequently short sentences. Naming grossly intact.

   - Suggests a resolving *transcortical motor aphasia*.

6. The patient is unable to speak, or speech is labored and effortful with few words and/or paraphasias. Repetition is intact. The patient may be able to repeat surprisingly long sentences accurately. Comprehension is impaired, and frequently unable to follow basic commands. Writing is impaired. Reading comprehension is impaired. Reading aloud is impaired. Naming is impaired.

   - Suggests a *mixed transcortical aphasia*. Commonly associated with diffuse left hemisphere lesions that spare the perisylvian fissure with lesions affecting both anterior and posterior regions. Most often caused by watershed infarcts of the ACA–MCA and MCA–PCA territories.

Key Points: Nonfluent Speech Problems
Nonfluent speech is generally effortful and labored, and can consistent of no spoken or written words. Words of profanity may be elicited when upset. May be able to sing secondary to melodic intonation facilitation.

- *Global aphasia*: Often mute (but may have few words and is effortful). Repetition impaired. Comprehension impaired. Reading impaired. Writing impaired.
- *Broca's aphasia*: May be mute or speech is limited with few words and effortful. Repetition impaired. Comprehension intact. Reading comprehension intact. Writing impaired.
- *Transcortical motor aphasia*: Speech is limited with few words and effortful. Repetition grossly intact. Comprehension intact. Reading comprehension intact. Writing impaired.
- *Mixed transcortical aphasia*: Speech is limited with few words and effortful. Repetition intact for even complex sentences. Comprehension impaired. Reading impaired. Writing impaired (can copy written sentence).

Fluent Speech Problems: Speech Is Fluent, but Is Unintelligible

The extent of unintelligibility will vary from extensive to mild. At the extreme, the patient may emit sounds fluently, but speech sounds do not correspond to recognized words. Mild cases will reflect fluent speech in which paraphasias and/or neologisms are present and/or speech (writing) grammar and syntax structure is poor.

1. The patient's speech is fluent but unintelligible. Words are paraphasias or neologisms (e.g., "whifel da pora at da sefa be fod the no…"). Prosody and intonation intact. Repetition is impaired. Comprehension is impaired. Patient is unable to follow basic commands. Reading is impaired. Writing is impaired, consisting of well-formed letter(s) and paraphasias and/or neologisms that do not make sense. Few if any real words. Naming is impaired.

- Suggests a *Wernicke's aphasia*. Commonly associated with left posterior lesions affecting Wernicke's area and superior temporal lobe (e.g., superior temporal gyrus) and, often, extending to left parietal supramarginal and/or angular gyrus while anterior perisylvian fissure remains intact. Underlying white matter damage results in more classic Wernicke's aphasia symptoms and more persistent aphasia.

2. The patient's speech is fluent, but generally unintelligible. Some distinct words may be appreciated, but most words are paraphasias and/or neologisms (e.g., "why da pora at be thing over the tretka…"). Words of profanity can be blurted out when upset or irritated. Prosody and intonation intact. Repetition may be surprisingly intact, even for long and complex sentences. Comprehension is impaired, but patient may be able to respond correctly to simple yes/no questions and/or follow simple one-step commands ("close your eyes"). Reading is impaired. Writing is nonsensical, and composed of well-formed letters and frequent paraphasias and neologisms. Some real words may be present. Naming is impaired.

   - Suggests a *transcortical sensory aphasia*. Commonly associated with left posterior hemisphere lesions typically including left temporo-occipital or left temporo-parietal. Brain structures of Wernicke's area and forward are persevered.

3. The patient's speech is generally fluent and grossly intelligible, although frequent phonemic paraphasias are usually present, which does decrease ability to understand the patient. Some pauses for naming (dysnomia) may also be present. Repetition is markedly impaired, and the patient may have difficulty repeating even single words. Comprehension is intact. Reading comprehension is generally intact, but reading aloud is somewhat impaired, with frequent phonemic paraphasias. Writing is generally impaired with frequent phonemic paraphasias (poor spelling) and confused word order. Naming is mild to moderately impaired.

   - Suggests a *conduction aphasia*. Commonly associated with lesion of the left (dominant) temporoparietal area, particularly the supramarginal area and underlying white matter. Arcuate fasciculus is classically involved; however, damage to arculate fasciculus itself need not occur, as conduction aphasia is possible with damage to left insular region and associated white matter. Overlying cortex of arcuate fasciculus damage can also lead to conduction aphasia symptoms.

4. The patient's speech is generally fluent and intelligible. Some paraphasias or pauses in speech are present when the patient appears to be searching for a word. Phonemic cues often help the patient retrieve the word during a pause in speech. Repetition is intact, even for long phrases. The patient's comprehension is intact. Able to follow three-step commands without difficulty. Reading is intact. Writing is intact. Naming is impaired.

   - Suggests an *anomic aphasia*. Can be associated with residual deficit from a previous left hemisphere stroke that had resulted in more extensive aphasia syndrome. Acute anomia associated with small inferior temporal or angular gyrus dysfunction of dominant (left) hemisphere. However, is also frequently found among patients with neurodegenerative disorders with more diffuse brain dysfunction, such as Alzheimer's disease, fronto-temporal dementia and Parkinson's disease dementia. Damasio et al. (1996) found anterior temporal tip most associated in naming famous faces/people. The inferior temporal lobe was most strongly associated with inferior temporal lobe, while tool naming was associated with left posterior lateral temporal lobe.

Key Points: Fluent Dysphasic Problems

Speech is rapid and effortless, but speech will not make sense with paraphasias and neologisms.

- Wernicke's aphasia: Fluent speech that does not make sense. Repetition impaired. Comprehension impaired. Reading impaired. Writing impaired.
- Transcortical sensory aphasia: Fluent speech that does not make sense. Comprehension impaired. Repetition intact. Reading is impaired. Writing somewhat impaired.
- Conduction aphasia: Fluent speech that makes some sense, but frequent phonemic paraphasias and some neologisms decrease intelligibility. Repetition impaired. Comprehension intact. Reading comprehension intact. Writing impaired.
- Anomic aphasia: Speech effortful with pauses and some paraphasias. Repetition intact. Comprehension intact. Reading intact. Writing intact.

Other Types of Speech/Language Problems

1. The patient's speech is generally fluent and intelligible. Some paraphasias or pauses in speech are present. Repetition is intact, even for long phrases. Comprehension is intact. Able to follow three-step commands. Reading is markedly impaired (alexia). Writing is impaired (agraphia). Naming is frequently reduced, but no frank impairment.

    - Suggests an *alexia with agraphia*. Commonly associated with discrete lesion of the left (dominant) temporoparietal angular gyrus or underlying white matter.

2. The patient's speech is generally fluent and intelligible. Some paraphasias or pauses in speech may be present or may not be. Repetition is intact, even for long phrases. Comprehension is intact. Able to follow three-step commands. Reading is markedly impaired (alexia). Writing is intact. Naming is generally intact.

    - Suggests *alexia without agraphia.* Classically associated with discrete lesion of the dominant (left) hemisphere involving the white matter of the posterior corpus collosum which underlies the occipital lobe. Can also be associated with discrete lesion involving the posterior dominant (left) inferior temporal gyrus.

3. The patient is unable to speak or speech is effortful with few words. Speech articulation can be poor or the patient may sound as if he/she is speaking with an unusual accent. Repetition is intact, even for long phrases. Comprehension is intact. Able to follow three-step commands. Reading is intact. Writing is intact. Naming is poor, but patient able to accurately write out objects. This condition may be acquired or it may be present since early development.

    - Suggests *aphemia* (verbal apraxia in childhood). Commonly associated with discrete lesion of the dominant (left) frontal lobe affecting precentral gyrus involving primary motor and premotor areas.

4. The patient's speech articulation is poor. Speech may sound as if the patient is mumbling, slurring, and/or has "marbles in his/her mouth." Speech rate is often slowed and may have a labored aspect. Paraphasias can be present. Repetition is intact. Comprehension is intact. Able to follow three-step commands. Reading is intact. Writing is intact (however, writing size may be very small in some cases). Naming is reduced secondary to poor articulation or slurring and/or mumbling.

    - Suggests speech *dysarthria*. May be due to Parkinson's disease but also found following lesions to the corticobulbar tracts, including brain stem lesions.

5. The patient's speech is fluent and articulate. Comprehension is impaired for words presented orally (can repeat written words and sentences). Repetition is impaired for materials presented orally (but can repeat written words and sentences). Reading is intact. Writing is intact. Naming is intact. The patient is unable to respond appropriately to other sounds (appears deaf).

    - Suggests *cortical deafness*. Classically associated with bilateral lesions to Heschl's gyrus.

6. The patient's speech is fluent and articulate. Comprehension is impaired for words presented orally (can repeat written words and sentences). Repetition is impaired for materials presented orally (but can repeat written words and sentences). Reading is intact. Writing is intact. Naming is intact. The patient is able to respond appropriately to other sounds (does not appear deaf to other sounds).

    - Suggests *pure word deafness* (also known as *verbal auditory agnosia*). Classically associated with discrete lesion of the dominant (left) temporal lobe Heschl's gyrus that extends to the underlying white matter to prevent input from the contralateral hemisphere primary auditory cortex.

7. The patient's speech is fluent and articulate. Comprehension is intact. Repetition is intact. Reading is intact. Writing is intact. Naming is intact. The patient is unable to respond appropriately to other sounds (appears deaf to sounds, except for spoken words).

    - Suggests *nonverbal auditory agnosia*. Rare, but classically associated with discrete lesion of the nondominant (right) Heschl's gyrus. Recovery is often complete in days to weeks.

Prosodic Speech Problems

In general, the description below describes patients with intact basic speech. That is, the patient can both follow directions and speech is articulate and reasonably fluent. The deficits in language may only be appreciated with an examiner's appreciation of a speaker's monotone by careful evaluation for prosody, intonation and inflection. The patient's speech may be monotone voice (almost robotic in quality), and with careful assessment for difficulties in appreciating the nonverbal aspects of speech (prosody, intonation and inflection).

1. The patient is unable to appreciate or express mood in speech. While speech production and comprehension are generally intact, the patient's speech output is monotone. Repetition for prosodic inflection is impaired. Able to follow three-step commands. Reading, writing and naming are intact.
   - Suggests a *global aprosody*. Commonly associated with large lesion involving the right (nondominant) hemisphere.
2. Receptive prosodic deficits. Inflection and tonal quality of emotions can be expressed. However, the patient is unable to appreciate tonal inflections in speech. Repetition for prosodic inflection may be impaired.
   - Suggests *receptive aprosody*. Classically associated with lesion of the nondominant (right) hemisphere involving the temporoparietal area and/or underlying white matter.
3. Expressive prosodic deficits. Inflection and tonal quality of emotions cannot be expressed. Speech is likely to sound monotone (although rate can vary). Repetition for prosodic inflection and intonation may be impaired. The patient is able to appreciate prosodic inflection and intonation of other's speech.
   - Suggests an *expressive aprosody*. Commonly associated with lesion of the nondominant frontal region homologous to the left hemisphere Broca's area, including underlying white matter.

Bedside Assessment of Language

For most clinical evaluations, language assessment serves two functions—first as a screening for language impairment and secondly as an assessment of prerequisite skills necessary for language-dependent aspects of the remainder of the neuropsychological examination. Language assessment should be conducted systematically to evaluate for deficits in receptive (comprehension and reading), expressive (speech output and writing), repetition and naming. In addition, careful observation of word finding deficits, semantic or phonemic paraphasic errors and articulation difficulties should be noted. The quality of language organization and completeness of responses in reciprocal conversation should be evaluated relative to common expectations or in conjunction with collateral confirmation of a change. We have included a bedside-based screening form for the assessment of language in Appendix A.

The brief assessment below begins with receptive language in both auditory and written modalities. Auditory comprehension starts initially with simple yes/no questions and progresses to more complex yes/no questions and multi-step commands in congruent sequence and reversed sequence. Note that comprehension need *not* be illustrated by the patient speaking or writing. Indeed, questions should be posed such that responses can be elicited by movement of eyes, eye blink, etc., among patients who have expressive language or motor paresis. Basic comprehension testing may then be followed by increasingly more complex receptive language skills involving both auditory and reading skill. Questions such as "Is my hair on fire?", "Do airplanes eat their young?" and "Does two pounds of sugar weigh more than one pound of sugar?" are sensitive to mild deficits in comprehension. This gives us a brief understanding of comprehension in both auditory and written modalities, which is essential in managing patient care. Additionally, receptive prosody is assessed by making statements emphasizing different emotions which use the exact same words. Patients should be able to identify the emotional tone implied in the way the phrase was spoken with little difficulty as long as they are presented in exaggerated fashion by the examiner. When assessing for prosody, the examiner may wish to have the patient close his/her eyes and/or turn from the patient to prevent the examiner from providing visual cues as to the emotional content of the prosody stimulus if the examiner accidently exhibits a facial expression along with the auditory stimuli.

Key Points: Language Assessment
Language assessment should include

- Expressive skills
  - Fluency
  - Articulation
  - Organization
  - Writing
- Receptive skills
  - Naming
  - Aural comprehension
  - Reading
- Repetition
- Prosody
  - Expressive prosody
  - Receptive prosody

Expressive language is subsequently assessed by asking the patient to name objects of increasing detail from general objects such as a shirt to parts like sleeve, cuff or collar. While patients are often able to name whole objects (pen), requesting them to name parts of objects (clip) often elicits naming deficits which might otherwise go undetected. Additionally, patients are asked to repeat words and phrases of increasing complexity to assess repetition which may be impaired independently from both receptive and expressive language functions. Expressive prosody is assessed by asking patients to make statements as if they were mad, happy or sad.

Lastly, language should be assessed for organizational quality and discourse. Any suspected tangentiality, circumloquaciousness or halting or incomplete expression patterns should be noted. This is typically done by providing stimuli such as a picture or scenario and asking an open-ended question requiring the patient to organize and structure a response that is reasonably complete. Note should be taken to describe the quality of organization, completeness of the response and the patient's ability to both expect and respect reciprocal conventions in communication such that a conversation occurs naturally and speech is not pressured in a way that might belie great effort in getting words out before they are lost.

Psychometric-Based Assessment of Language

Many excellent comprehensive batteries are available for the assessment of language such as the Boston Diagnostic Aphasia Examination—3 (Goodglass et al., 2000), Neurosensory Center Comprehensive Examination for Aphasia (Spreen & Strauss, 1991), Multilingual Aphasia Examination (Benton & Hamsher, 1989) and the Western Aphasia Battery (Kertesz, 1982) (see Strauss et al., 2006 or Lezak et al., 2004, for detailed review and description of these and other language tests.) These batteries examine aspects of language in greater depth than conventional bedside clinical evaluations, and offer a more comprehensive quantification and description of language deficits.

In general, the advantage of detailed neuropsychological assessment of language functions allows for quantification of language function in terms of performance compared to population normative data, which may be expressed in terms of percentiles. Such a detailed assessment allows for the identification of subtle expressive and/or receptive language deficits that may not be appreciated in a bedside assessment. We recommend an outpatient neuropsychological evaluation to assess expressive and receptive speech along with repetition and naming. Common measures of expressive speech include carefully listening to the patient describe his/her problems or history, and various oral or written verbal fluency tests. Typical measures include phonemic verbal fluency and semantic verbal fluency tests. Naming is commonly assessed with visual or auditory confrontation naming tests. Comprehension can be assessed with measures assessing increasing complex directions. See Chap. 13 this volume and Heilman & Valenstein, 2003; Lezak et al., 2004; Mesulam, 2000; and/or Strauss et al., 2006 for detailed reviews.

Appendix: Acute Assessment of Language and Prosody

Receptive language and prosody	Response	Correct
Simple receptive language		
Simple yes/no question		
Is it winter?	_____	_____
Are you in a hospital?	_____	_____
Complex yes/no question		
Are cows carnivorous?	_____	_____
Would a nice person express complements?	_____	_____
Receptive comprehension of commands		
Simple		
one step Point to the door	_____	_____
two step Look up and then look down	_____	_____
Complex		
Sequenced Touch your arm and then touch your ear	_____	_____
Reversed Point to the door after you point to the chair	_____	_____
Reading (read and/or comply)		
I feel good today	_____	_____
Point to each person in the room	_____	_____
Prosody		
Simple prosody (statement or question)		
I'm going to town! (spoken as a statement)	_____	_____
I'm going to town? (spoken as a question)	_____	_____
Emotional prosody (expressed emotion)		
That is wrong. (spoken angrily)	_____	_____
That is wrong. (spoken sadly)	_____	_____
That is wrong. (spoken happily)	_____	_____
Expressive language and prosody can we eliminate this line...it is redundant		
Naming		
Simple objects		
What is this? (point to shirt)	_____	_____
What is this? (point to pen)	_____	_____
Complex naming		
What is this? (point to sleeve or cuff of shirt)	_____	_____
What is this? (point to point or tip of pen)	_____	_____
Repetition		
Single word		
Desk, chair, light	_____	_____
Simple statement		
I would like some ice cream	_____	_____

Receptive language and prosody	Response	Correct
Complex statement	________	________
No ifs, ands, or buts		
Writing		
Simple		
Write his/her name	________	________
Write name of watch	________	________
Write a sentence	________	________
Verbal fluency (60 seconds, record number)		
Phonemic fluency (i.e., words beginning with the letter r)	________	________
Semantic fluency (i.e., animals)	________	________
Expressive prosody		
Say, "I'm going to work."		
Phrase as if sad	________	________
Phrase as if angry	________	________
Discourse/spontaneous expressive speech		
Structured		
Show a picture; ask patient to describe what is happening	________	________
Unstructured		
Ask patient what he/she did/does		
for work and give the details.	________	________

References

Benton, A. L., & Hamsher, K. (1989). *Multilingual aphasia examination*. AJA Associates.

Cermack, L. (2000). *Language and the brain: Representation and processing*. Academic.

Damasio, H., Grabowski, T. J., Tranel, D., Hichwa, R. D., & Damasio, A. R. (1996). A neural basis for lexical retrieval. *Nature, 380*, 499–505.

Goodglass, H., Kaplan, E., & Barresi, B. (2000). *The Boston Diagnostic Aphasia Examination (BDAE-3)* (3rd ed.). Lippincott Williams & Wilkins.

Heilman, K. M., & Valenstein, E. (2003). *Clinical neuropsychology* (4th ed.). Oxford University Press.

Kertesz, A. (1982). *Western aphasia battery*. Psychological Corporation.

Lezak, M. D., Howieson, D. B., & Loring, D. W. (2004). *Neuropsychological assessment* (4th ed.). Oxford University Press.

Mesulam, M. M. (2000). *Principles of behavioral and cognitive neurology* (2nd ed.). Oxford University Press.

Ross, E. D. (1997). The aprosodies. In T. E. Feinberg & M. J. Farah (Eds.), *Behavioral neurology and neuropsychology* (pp. 699–717). McGraw-Hill.

Spreen, O., & Strauss, E. (1991). *A compendium of neuropsychological tests: Administration, norms, and commentary*. Oxford University Press.

Strauss, E., Sherman, E. M. S., & Spreen, O. (2006). *A compendium of neuropsychological tests: Administration, norms, and commentary* (3rd ed.). Oxford University Press.

Chapter 9
Memory and Learning: The Forgetful Patient

James G. Scott and Michael R. Schoenberg

The capacity to encode, retain and retrieve information is essential to the evolution of all living animals. From the amoeba to ourselves, learning from interaction with our environment is critical to adaptation to the stimuli that influence our well-being. The human brain is masterful at recognizing patterns of recurrence, be they sensory, motor or cognitive. This process of pattern recognition produces engrams which are the building blocks of concepts and organization which facilitate retrieval. Through this chapter, we will discuss models of processing and outline the essential elements for memory. Several syndromic patterns of memory loss are reviewed below and common possible etiologies for these observed memory deficits. Finally, in this chapter, we will discuss how to perform an assessment of memory functions which will allow the clinician to determine if problems in memory are present and if more detailed assessment of memory functions is indicated.

As with many cognitive functions beyond the basic sensory, perceptual and motor systems, memory is dependent on prerequisite skills for accurate assessment and determination of the etiology of a deficit. Accurate assessment of memory hinges on the adequacy of sensory input, perceptual skill, motor output and attentional capacity. Factors which influence these prerequisite skills can produce a profound impact on memory. In addition, some internal cognitive aspects of

J. G. Scott (✉)
Department of Psychiatry and Behavioral Sciences, University of Oklahoma, Health Sciences Center College of Medicine, Oklahoma City, OK, USA
e-mail: jim-scott@ouhsc.edu

M. R. Schoenberg
Departments of Psychiatry and Neurosciences, Neurology, and Neurosurgery, University of South Florida College of Medicine, Tampa, FL, USA
e-mail: mschoenb@usf.edu

M. R. Schoenberg, J. G. Scott (eds.), *The Little Black Book of Neuropsychology*,
https://doi.org/10.1007/978-3-032-07777-6_9

functioning such as reasoning and organization produce secondary effects on measured memory skills. In addition to these factors, assessment of memory must consider the emotional functioning of the person being assessed. Severe psychopathology such as schizophrenia or bipolar disorder can have an obvious and profound effect on memory; however, even mild depression and situational anxiety can produce subtle but predictable effects on memory performance which may be detrimental or enhancing.

Key Points and Chapter Summary

- Memory includes encoding, storage and retrieval and memory deficits can be caused by impairment at any level in the process
- Intact sensory, motor, arousal and attentional skills are prerequisite for memory assessment
- Memory capacities change considerably with aging and assessment must consider age in evaluating performance to improve accuracy in detecting deficits or change
- There are many individual- (i.e., age, education), anatomical- (i.e., temporal, frontal, and somatosensory) and material (i.e., verbal, visual)-specific factors that affect memory performance and these factors must be taken into consideration in assessing individual's memory performance
- Memory assessment should include evaluation of recent memory and remote memory as the pattern of memory impairment is related to the anatomy and etiology of impairment

A Model of Memory

The act of turning an experience into a memory appears simple at first glance, but involves a complicated series of processes, which are dependent on the integrity of many brain functions. While there are several models, common themes include three stages involving encoding, storage and retrieval. The process by which information is transferred from encoding to storage depends on the nature of the material which is to be recalled. There are three basic memory stages: sensory storage, short-term memory and long-term memory. Each has been subdivided into more refined aspects of memory systems, and briefly reviewed below.

Key Points: General Memory Functioning

- Memory processes can be divided into encoding, recall and recognition phases
- Recognition should almost always be better than encoding and recall unless motivational factors are responsible
- The number of repetitions in learning trials (overlearning) improves recall for almost all people, but does not facilitate delayed recall in persons with neurologic memory impairment
- Memory impairment typically is either from a discrete injury point forward or a gradual decline from a past point. Even in neurologic conditions, remote memory is almost always better than recent memory
- Except for the immediate period of trauma or injury, neurologic memory impairment rarely, if ever, is lost only for a discrete point of time

Sensory Storage (Sensory Registration)

The first stage of memory is typically referred to as the sensory storage or sensory registration stage. It refers to the point of time that auditory, visual, gustatory, tactile or olfactory information is initially registered as a conscious phenomenon. This stage of memory is very short in duration, lasting milliseconds to seconds, and decays rapidly if no further attending to/or processing of the stimuli is done. The information in sensory storage must be attended to before being transferred to short-term memory.

Short-Term Memory

Short-term memory is frequently referred to as working memory. The average capacity of short-term memory in humans is typically seven items ±2. This capacity can easily be expanded through superimposing organization such as chunking. For example, the letters in the 4 × 4 array below can be recalled much more easily if organized, thus turning 16 individual items into six items (Fig. 9.1). The array of

Fig. 9.1 Facilitation of memory by chunking

ABCI	AB
AFBI	CI A
NOWS	*FB I*
PCAI	NO W
	SPCA
	I

letters on the left may appear as 16 individual bits of information and difficult to memorize while the array on the right has been altered to facilitate semantic clustering, thus the number of items to be recalled is reduced to six. Without imposing some process such as organizing or rehearsal, information in short-term memory is quickly forgotten.

Long-Term Memory

Long-term memory refers to information which is relatively permanent and can be retrieved volitionally. Several processes facilitate the consolidation of information into long-term memory. The simple act of rehearsal facilitates transfer to long-term memory, but many other factors also facilitate consolidation. Material which is associated with emotional experiences (positive or negative) is more easily encoded and facilitates retrieval. The level at which information is processed makes encoding information more efficient. For example, retrieval of a word list is facilitated when individuals are asked if the words describe themselves compared to being asked if the word was a positive or negative characteristic. Elaborating the material to be learned also associates it with previously acquired information and again facilitates transfer to long-term memory. Yet other processes can affect memory consolidation, including state and environmental learning. State-depending learning reflects improved learning and recall when the emotional and physical states of the individual are congruent. Additionally, the saliency of the material to be recalled influences encoding and retrieval. For example, material which is learned in one physical environment is recalled much better in the same environment or a highly similar environment. This phenomenon is appreciated when examining the discrepancy when recalling high school events while at your old high school (i.e., names, events, faces) compared to recall of the same material while at home. Similarly, the state (i.e., physical state such as inebriation or emotional state such as sadness) facilitates recall of information encoded while in such states. However; this should not be confused with equating the learning efficiency produced in non-inebriated states or non-emotional states as these factors in and of themselves interfere with the efficient encoding of information to be recalled.

The graph below demonstrates the stages of memory and processes by which information is transferred from one stage to another and notes some of the factors which impact consolidation of information into long-term memories (Fig. 9.2).

Types of Memory

Many types of memory have been described (for example, see Kolb & Whishaw, 2009; Squire & Zola, 1996, for reviews), but heuristically two predominant types of memory, each having unique associated anatomical and phenomenological

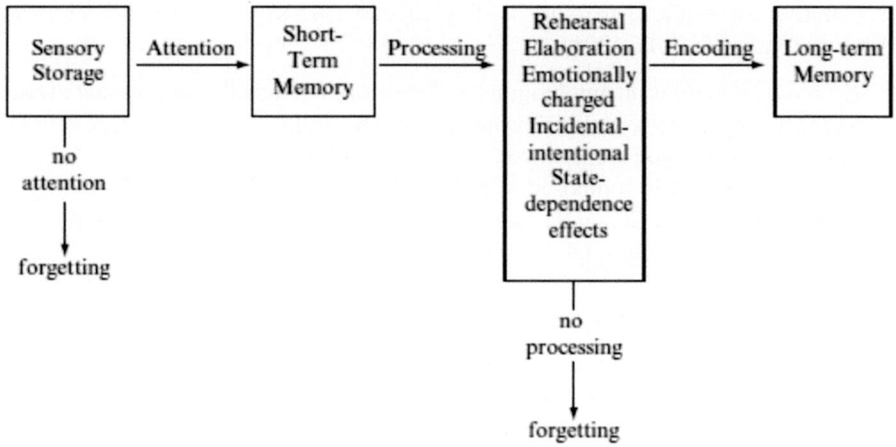

Fig. 9.2 Stages of memory

Table 9.1 Common terms for declarative and nondeclarative memory (adapted from Squire, 1987)

Declarative memory	Nondeclarative memory
Who, what, when, where memory	Classical conditioning
Conscious memory	How memory
Visual memory [a]	Motor memory
Verbal memory [a]	Automatic memory
Explicit memory	Subconscious memory
Autobiographical memory [b]	Perceptual memory
Episodic memory [c]	Habit memory
Semantic memory [c]	Procedural memory
Prospective memory	

[a] Terms describe components of declarative memory often seen in neuropsychological reports
[b] Autobiographical memory is a term to describe components of episodic memory
[c] Episodic and semantic memory are two major divisions of declarative (explicit) memory

characteristics, have remained robust. These memory types are referred to as *Declarative* (or *Explicit*) memory and *Nondeclarative* (or *Implicit*) memory. While these types of memory have been given various names (see Table 9.1) for common terms for Declarative and Nondeclarative memory), the characteristics of each have been well established.

Declarative (Explicit) Memory

Declarative memory refers to those things which we recall including people, names, faces, events, facts, and places, etc. This type of memory is also termed explicit memory, and the two terms (declarative and explicit) are often used interchangeably.

Declarative (or explicit) memory is divided into *episodic memory* and *semantic memory* (Squire & Zola, 1996).

- *Episodic memory* is an autobiographical memory and recalls the personal events and facts which are bound in time and place. This is the memory for what you did yesterday, where you went on your first date or your first car.
- *Semantic memory* is composed of facts and knowledge. This type of memory is not time dependent. Semantic memory is knowing which city is the capital of the USA, the multiplication tables, how many dimes make a dollar or which eight countries border France.

Episodic memory is the active recall of the learning event, while semantic memory recall is retrieval of a fact and does not require one to recall the autobiographical event when the material was learned. Semantic memory is unable to determine a particular place and time the information was learned. The unique aspects of this remembered material is the conscious effort involved in the learning and retrieval process. This is the conscious material that can be recalled which is unique to the experiences of the individual.

Declarative memory is frequently divided into categories, such as verbal–visual, intentional–incidental, recent–remote, etc. Declarative memory is the type of memory which we most commonly refer to when discussing memory in a clinical setting. Episodic memory is also frequently disrupted by injury or diseases such as anoxia, traumatic brain injury and Alzheimer's. The anatomical disassociation will be outlined later in this chapter.

Nondeclarative (Implicit) Memory

Nondeclarative memory refers to memory for skills and procedures which are learned and recalled. Evidence for such a memory system is found by the efficiency and skill gains which accumulate for even complex activities. The origins of the learning process are often lost such as learning to speak or riding a bicycle, but the transfer of learning must occur for such behaviors to be demonstrated and recalled. Nondeclarative memory includes a number of acquired motor skills, but also includes a great number of very complex behaviors such as playing a musical instrument or driving a car. The adaptation of humans to perform repetitive skills with precision and very little conscious processing is astounding. This memory system is often preserved in injury and disease states.

The next section provides an overview of common terms used to describe memory problems followed by a brief review of neuroanatomical correlates of memory.

Terms of Memory Impairment

The loss of memory is called *amnesia*. Classically, amnesia describes the loss of memory while other neuropsychological functions remain intact. The individual exhibits a profound inability to learn new material, in which declarative memory functions are largely lost. Alternatively, nondeclarative (implicit) memory is often preserved. Individuals may have anterograde amnesia and/or retrograde amnesia.

Anterograde Amnesia

Anterograde amnesia describes the inability to encode new material since the event onset or injury. With pure anterograde amnesia, the individual is able to recall previous events, up to very close to the time of the event leading to anterograde amnesia (see below for common causes of anterograde amnesia).

Retrograde Amnesia

Retrograde amnesia refers to loss of memory for events that occurred prior to the event leading to an amnesia syndrome. The most common is an inability to recall immediate previous information from before the event. Retrograde amnesia is frequently temporally graded, such that memories immediately before the event leading to amnesia are markedly poor while memories farther removed from the event (moving increasingly early in recent experience) may be better recalled.

Typical Patterns of Memory Loss

A typical pattern for amnesia is for anterograde memory loss to predominate while retrograde amnesia is temporally graded by hours, days, weeks, months or rarely years. The extent of retrograde amnesia is often dependent upon the extent of damage. Anterograde amnesia may be temporally limited, that is recovery of normal memory functions after a period of hours, days, weeks or rarely months to years. Alternatively, some conditions can result in a permanent amnestic syndrome involving anterograde amnesia. Cases of predominate retrograde amnesia with preserved anterograde amnesia are very rare, but have been reported. However, the loss of memory is typically not relegated to one aspect of one's life (e.g., remembering starting a new job and meeting new friends, but forgetting you got married or had children during this time frame).

Neuropsychological assessment includes assessment of various components of (mostly) declarative memory, but some aspects may also assess nondeclarative memory function. Common terms to describe domains of memory that may be impaired within a neuropsychological evaluation include: recent memory, remote memory, long-term memory, short-term (immediate) memory, working memory and semantic memory. An overview of what these terms measure is provided below.

Memory Terms: A Brief Review

Delayed recall (recall of a previously exposed material after some period of delay, typically less than 1 hour).

Delayed recognition (refers to recognition of stimuli previously presented).

Learning over trials (*LOT*) describes successive performance of immediate recall of material presented over successive trials.

Recent memory is a term to describe memory for events that occurred within the past few days; however, there is disagreement as to the demarcation of recent and remote memory.

Remote memory describes memory for events that occurred before the present. Traditionally, this term may be used to describe the memory of events or experiences of an individual in the distant past; however, as noted above, the demarcation regarding how far in the past is a matter of debate.

Long-term memory in neuropsychological reports refers to memory scores obtained after a delay of usually 30–40 minutes. Performance after a 30-minute delay is highly correlated with memory function after days to weeks, although some temporal forgetting or decay does occur.

Short-term memory describes memory scores obtained following a short period after an exposure to the to be recalled material. Typically seconds to minutes after exposure.

Immediate memory refers to recall of material immediately after presentation. Material to be learned must exceed attention span. The material to be learned may be either verbal or visual (nonverbal).

Working memory is a term to describe immediately processed information before it is sent to short-term memory.

Encoding refers to the process of learning material.

Consolidation refers to the process of transferring information from immediate (short-term memory) to long-term memory.

Retrieval refers to the process of retrieving information from long-term memory; that is, conscious recollection.

Primacy effect refers to the observation of recalling the first part of to-be learned material. May reflect learning the first initial items in word list or the first part of a verbal story or the first series of pictures or presented figures in a series of to-be learned material.

Recency effect refers to the enhanced recall of the last part (most recent) of to-be learned items. The recency effect is easily observed in learning a list of words or a short story with the recall of the last part of a list of words (the last set of words, commonly the last 3–5 words presented in a list of words) or the details of a story that was presented last.

Verbal semantic memory (also termed *verbal contextual memory*) describes memory for short stories that are typically auditorily administered (read out loud). There are typically immediate and delayed recall trials.

List learning refers to immediate and delayed recall for rote memorization of a word list. The word list may have words that are part of several semantic clusters (e.g., furniture, animals, things you can do at a beach, etc.), or the list may have words unrelated to each other.

Visual memory (also termed *nonverbal memory*) describes memory for nonverbal material developed to avoid being easily verbally encoded such as faces, geometric figures or spatial locations. Visual memory typically includes immediate memory and delayed recall of nonverbal material.

Neuropsychological Assessment of Memory Problems

Evaluation of memory processes must include assessment of (1) learning, (2) immediate memory, (3) delayed memory and (4) recognition formats. Evaluating the difference between immediate memory trials and delayed memory provides an index of the efficiency of consolidation (or retention). Including recognition format after delayed recall allows for assessment of retrieval deficits accounting for poor memory. Relatively preserved recognition (true hits without false positives) in the presence of deficient spontaneous recall implicates faulty retrieval processes with intact encoding.

Memory Deficits/Complaints: A Behavioral Guide

While the performance of individuals suspected of memory loss can reflect numerous patterns of performance, several common patterns of memory deficits are listed below, along with some possible hypotheses that may account for these observations.

1. Very poor encoding, delayed recall and recognition: Patient's learning is deficient with a flat learning curve. No gain in memory with repeated presentation of the to-be learned material. Frequent perseverations and/or intrusions. Immediate memory and delayed recall are deficient, and recognition cues do not improve recall (false positive hits and some false negative hits). This is common in diseases which impair encoding and consolidation such as bilateral frontal lobe lesions affecting orbitofrontal and medial frontal structures, medial diencephalic

lesions or bilateral mesial temporal damage found in patients with severe traumatic brain injuries or severe Alzheimer's disease.

2. Poor encoding, severe delayed recall impairment and mildly impaired recognition: Patient's immediate learning is deficient, but some learning may be present (learning curve not flat). Immediate memory is mildly impaired. Delayed memory is markedly deficient. Recognition is impaired although better than recall. This pattern is highly suggestive of deficits in consolidation and rapid forgetting and is classically observed in initial stages of dementia of the Alzheimer's type and bilateral mesial temporal dysfunction.
3. Normal encoding, poor recall and good recognition: Patient's initial learning is normal or nearly normal. Delayed memory is deficient. Recognition is normal. This pattern is highly suggestive of deficits in retrieval and is classically observed in early dementias.
4. Variable encoding, variable recall and good recognition: Patient's learning is variable across trials and may be mildly impaired overall. Immediate memory is variable. Perseverative responses and intrusions may occur. Delayed memory recall is variable and often similar to immediate recall score (no forgetting). Recognition is improved with cues, but patient may exhibit confabulation and/or make high number of false positive errors from any material previously presented to him/her (i.e., interference). Memory of semantically organized information (e.g., stories that make sense) better recalled than word lists of unrelated material. Reflects inefficient encoding with intact consolidation. Common in dementias affecting frontal lobes or etiologies affecting attentions such as traumatic brain injuries.
5. Normal encoding, normal recall and impaired recognition: Patient's learning is normal or nearly normal learning with normal or nearly normal delayed memory recall, but marked and disproportionately deficient recognition. This pattern is irregular and may reflect inattention and/or variable motivation. Non-neurological memory impairment.
6. Material-specific encoding discrepancy, material-specific recall discrepancy and material-specific recognition discrepancy: Patient exhibits learning that is normal or nearly normal for one type of material but deficient for another type of material (e.g., verbal memory is impaired while recall of visual, "nonverbal" learning is normal or nearly normal). Consolidation and retrieval "lateralized." Commonly found in lateralized neurological lesions such as focal epilepsy and/or focal strokes resulting in unilateral mesial temporal lobe or, less often, thalamic or frontal lobe lesion.
7. Poor initial encoding with appropriate improvement across repeated trials, variable recall and normal recognition: Patient's learning slow and/or variable (patient may recall more and then less material with repeated learning trials). Immediate recall mildly impaired. Patient frequently says "I don't know." Delayed recall is variable or mildly impaired and may not differ substantially from immediate delayed memory. Recognition memory is normal. No false positive errors, but false negative error bias may occur (i.e., "I don't know"). This pattern can be seen among individuals with severe depression or anxiety.

Learning Curve Patterns

Below, we provide a brief review of some common patterns to learning. This is particularly true for tests of verbal memory using a word list that is presented multiple times. Normal recall patterns in a word list-learning test include improved recall for both the first words and last words in a list. Recall of words in the first third of the list is called the Primacy Effect while recall of the words in the last third of a list is referred to as the Recency Effect. Normal performance in a list-learning test is to recall a greater percentage from the Primacy and Recency regions of a list on initial trials with gradual inclusion or recall of the middle third of the list on subsequent repeated recall trials. While deviations from this pattern can be produced by the patient deciding to apply different strategies, deviation from this pattern can indicate important information regarding memory processes. Retention of only the primacy or recency region with little improvement across repeated trials is typically indicative of a primary amnestic disorder. Inclusion of words from both the primacy and recency regions with additional improvement across trials from words in the middle region is a normal memory pattern. Recall of words randomly from all regions (an absence of Primacy or Recency effects) is typically associated with secondary factors that affect learning efficiency such as frontal lobe deficits or attentional deficits or may indicate poor motivation or effort.

As can be seen above, a systematic evaluation of memory processes can help to reveal the mechanisms responsible for observed deficits in memory complaints and can be crucial in the differential diagnosis of syndromes associated with amnesia.

Anatomy of Memory

Multiple brain regions are involved in the functioning or process of memory. We previously noted the prerequisite skills of arousal, sensory, motor or perceptual integrity and attentional capacity which are necessary components for efficient encoding of information or transfer of stimuli from one stage of memory to another (for declarative memory functions). Assuming that these prerequisite functions are intact, areas that are involved in memory include the medial temporal lobes, entorhinal cortex, hippocampus and amygdala, cingulate cortex, basal forebrain and diencephalic structures (see Fig. 9.3 and Chap. 3). Classically, there are two well-described circuits underlying memory functions: Papez circuit and the amygdaloid circuit.

The Papez circuit is involved in forming new autobiographical memories and declarative (explicit) memories in general. Figure 9.3 illustrates the basic projection path of the Papez circuit, which makes a functional loop. Input from multimodal association cortex of the brain (frontal, parietal, occipital and temporal lobes) flows to perirhinal and parahippocampal cortices and is relayed to the entorhinal cortex. The entorhinal cortex is the primary input (and an important output)

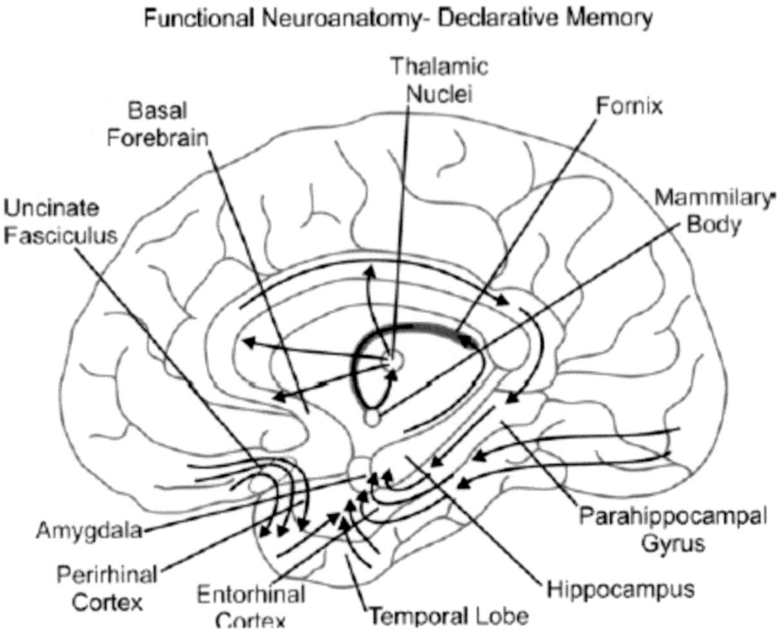

Fig. 9.3 Neuroanatomy of memory figure

pathway of the hippocampal formation, with projections to the dentate gyrus and hippocampus. Projections from hippocampus structures from the subiculum form the fornix which projects to the mammillary bodies. Output fibers from the mammillary bodies (the mammillothalamic tract) go to the anterior thalamic nuclei, then project to the cingulate gyrus. The cingulate gyrus projects back to parahippocampal gyrus and entorhinal cortex via the cingulum (or cingulate bundle) completing the loop.

The amygdaloid circuit includes the amygdala, thalamic nuclei (mediodorsal or pulvinar), orbitofrontal cortex, olfactory piriform cortex, insula (gustatory and somatosensory information), hypothalamus, limbic striatum and nucleus basalis of Meynert. Another important output pathway of the hippocampus and dentate gyrus is the projections from the subiculum back to the entorhinal cortex where projections to parahippocampal association cortex and other multimodal association cortex of the frontal, parietal, occipital and temporal areas occur. Figure 9.3 illustrates potential input pathways from frontal (uncinate and anterior cingulate), parietal, occipital and temporal cortex. The uncinate fasciculus connects the amygdala with the orbital frontal and cingulate cortices.

The diencephalic structures implicated in memory include thalamic nuclei (anterior, dorsomedial, laterodorsal, pulvinar and other intralaminar), fornix and mammillary bodies (hypothalamus). The cerebellum has also demonstrated roles in memory, particularly for nondeclarative memory functions. These neuroanatomic structures have connections to and from temporal and frontal areas such that damage to diencephalic structures can profoundly affect memory (see Chap. 3).

Temporal Lobe and Memory

While many other brain structures have been implicated in the formation of memories, no other brain structure has demonstrated the importance in memory function compared to the temporal lobes. Specifically, the anterior temporal cortex and underlying structures of the hippocampus, parahippocampal gyrus and entorhinal cortex are critically involved in the formation of new memories. This relationship has been repeatedly demonstrated using animals and patient populations (i.e., epilepsy, tumor patients and accident victims). Critical cortical areas in the temporal lobe include the entorhinal cortex which resides in the anterior, medial and inferior aspect of the temporal lobe. The temporal lobe has many afferent and efferent projections to somatosensory cortex (i.e., sight, hearing, tactile, etc.). The hippocampus and its subsections (entorhinal cortex) are the primary areas implicated in amnestic disorders such as Alzheimer's disease or anoxia. The amygdala lies in the anterior aspect of the hippocampus. The amygdala plays a significant role in the impact of emotion on memory encoding as well as retrieval.

Diencephalon and Memory

In addition to the prominent role of the temporal lobes and underlying structures in the formation of memories, several diencephalic (medial subcortical) structures play significant roles in memory formation. The predominant structures in the diencephalon are the thalamus and hypothalamus. The supporting evidence for involvement of these structures in memory comes from the study of patients with discrete lesions in these areas which produce profound amnesic conditions. The debate continues as to the extent and permanence of damage necessary in the anterior nucleus of the thalamus, the mediodorsal (MD) nuclei of the thalamus and mammillary bodies to produce such amnestic conditions. Recent research suggest it is the degeneration of the anterior nucleus of the thalamus that is necessary and sufficient for onset of the amnestic syndrome seen in Korsakoff's syndrome.

Frontal Lobes and Basal Forebrain and Memory

The role of the frontal lobes and basal forebrain in the formation of memories is extended from the finding of memory impairment in dementia and stroke patients that involve the frontal lobes and/or parts of the basal forebrain. Frontal lobe areas affecting memory can include the orbitolateral (ventral) frontal lobe, medial frontal, and some memory dysfunction associated with dorsolateral frontal lobe damage (see Chaps. 3 and 11). The basal forebrain describes the septal nuclei, nucleus basalis of Meynert, substantia innominata and the amygdala. In conditions such as anterior communicating artery aneurysm ruptures or Alzheimer's disease, extensive damage to acetylcholine-producing regions such as nucleus accumbens and septal nucleus that then project to basal forebrain are damaged and can produce profound indirect effects on memory. The issue of whether it is damage specifically to these areas or the secondary loss of acetylcholine production in these areas that is the primary reason for the amnestic effect remains to be settled (see Kandel, 2007, for review).

Laterality and Memory

Evidence for the lateralized effect of memory comes primarily from studies of accident victims and neurosurgery patients (most specifically, unilateral temporal lobectomy). Evaluation of these individuals' memory functioning indicates a significant, although far from perfect, lateralizing effect where memory for stories, words and numbers is most commonly disrupted by left temporal lobe damage and memory for figures, faces and tunes is more frequently impaired in those with right temporal lobe damage. A note of caution is in order, as the lateralized effect of memory material is not definitively dissociative. The process by which the active learner attempts to organize or encode the stimuli to be learned impacts which side of the brain is involved and thus potentially affects the outcome. There is also an interactive effect of the age at which a lesion is acquired and the length of time since the injury that can produce either a re-organizational effect or a compensatory effect which obscures lateralizing signs in memory.

In addition to material-specific memory differences (verbal versus visual or nonverbal memory between the left and right hemispheres noted above), other hemispheric differences have been identified (see Kandel, 2007; Lezak et al., 2004; Tulving et al., 1994, for reviews). Sometimes termed *Hemispheric Encoding and Retrieval Asymmetry* (HERA; see Tulving et al., 1994), studies suggest the left prefrontal cortex is more involved during encoding of episodic and semantic memory material and less involved during retrieval. The right prefrontal cortex (and insula and parietal cortices) are thought to be more involved in retrieval of episodic memories. Finally, retrieval of semantic memory material appears to preferentially involve the dominant (left) inferolateral prefrontal and temporal lobe, while the right hemisphere may be more involved in episodic (autobiographical) memory retrieval.

Storage and Retrieval in Memory

While the role of the temporal lobe and associated subcortical structures is demonstrated in the formation or encoding of memories, the role of structures in the retrieval process is less clear. While it is likely that cortical areas play a more significant role in recall of declarative memory, these areas are likely to be widely dispersed and interactive. Theories of how memories are stored involve associative networks that are formed between the sensory, emotional, behavioral and cognitive elements that represent those particular declarative stimuli (i.e., word, face, event, etc.). The strength of a memory would be associated with the relative strength of each of these component influences. For example, the recall of a person's name might be facilitated if it were presented in multiple sensory modalities, with emotional content, with behavioral cues and cognitive processing or elaboration. Such a process can be achieved by introducing yourself, asking the patient to repeat your name, notice some distinguishing characteristic, asking about an emotional association and then asking questions requiring some cognitive association or processing. An example is given in Table 9.2 that might be used in an interview or bedside evaluation of a patient. The cues can be given as necessary to assess the level of cueing needed to retrieve information if the patient does not recall your name spontaneously when asked.

Once memories are encoded, they are typically retained with a decaying degree of accuracy over time. Even highly encoded memories which maximize encoding facilitators such as those mentioned above demonstrate decay over time without repeated refreshing of the same or highly similar information. The reconstructive nature of many memories does allow people typically to be more confident in the completeness and accuracy of their perceived recall.

Nondeclarative memory is typically better preserved than declarative memory across both aging and injury. The motor and repetitive nature of nondeclarative memory is a distinct system that is less affected by temporal lobe and medial temporal structures. While the debate regarding the area of short-term storage of nondeclarative memory rages on, the presumed area of storage for long-term declarative memory is likely to reside in the cerebellum, basal ganglia, pre-motor and parietal-temporal-occipital association center of the angular and supramarginal gyri. These areas have been shown to be involved in apraxias such as grooming, dressing or feeding oneself. The dissociation of declarative and nondeclarative memory systems can be seen clearly to go beyond simple or repetitive motor tasks in the performance of severely amnestic patients in playing novel music, playing bridge or other skilled games. While typically preserved long after the impairment of declarative memory, even nondeclarative memory fails in late stages of degenerative disorders or severe brain injuries.

Table 9.2 Facilitation of learning in interview or bedside evaluation

	Interviewer behavior	Facilitating process
a.	My name is Dr. Herman Jones.	Auditory presentation
b.	Repeat my name.	Cognitive/auditory repetition
c.	I'm the only doctor you know with a bald head and pug nose.	Associating visual characteristics
d.	How many other Hermans do you know?	Cognitive elaboration
e.	Am I the most handsome Herman you know?	Cognitive/emotional elaboration
f.	Feel my handsome face.	Behavioral/motor elaboration
g.	Now remember my name.	Intentional encoding

Assessment of Memory

The assessment of memory is necessary in many clinical settings from acute assessment to precise laboratory assessment in stable populations. This need for memory assessment in such varied settings requires flexibility in assessment approach and subsequently involves a trade off between the brevity of assessment and the reliability of the results. Brief assessment in acute populations should be reviewed as a snapshot of a moving target which is likely related to the ultimate outcome, but should be viewed with appropriate reservations. This assessment is the least standardized but may yield important information about current impairment. While the lack of stability across assessment in acute populations may give concern to more psychometrically oriented neuropsychologists, its value should not be ignored. Intermediate memory assessment involves more structured and standardized assessment of memory, but continues to make a compromise on the brevity–precision continuum. Lastly, laboratory or standardized assessment yields the most reliable assessment of memory, but does take considerable time and resources to collect the data necessary for such an assessment.

Assessment of memory across stages of illness or trauma must include both immediate recall and spontaneous delayed recall in addition to assessing recall with cues and recognition. Assessing these aspects of memory yields much information about the memory process across encoding and retrieval and can also produce beneficial patient management and safety information. Assessment across all stages also typically includes the use of verbal and nonverbal information. Verbal information is further subdivided into semantic and word list material.

Brief Bedside (Acute) Assessment of Memory

An initial assessment of memory can be done in an interview format as part of an extended mental status examination. This type of assessment relies on environmental factors and is intended to gather information about current memory functioning. Specific accident and/or illness factors are likely to be large influential considerations and statements about functioning garnered from this type of assessment must include the possibility of rapid change. Such an assessment is easily conducted in a nonthreatening manner and can yield very useful information that assists in establishing a baseline, indicating the need for ongoing or future assessment and providing information about the current level of independence or supervision necessary. Table 9.3 lists methods for acute assessment. These items should be recalled with nearly complete accuracy. This assessment yields information about remote and recent memory as well as memory across visual, semantic and verbal domains. While it is not appropriate to assign quantitative levels of performance to such an examination, useful information is gathered about current functioning which serves a baseline function, indicates the need for future assessment, and is helpful in managing patients or providing the degree of supervision necessary to meet their needs.

Table 9.3 Acute/interview assessment of memory

	Item	Example	Area assessed	Record response/ accuracy
1.	Self-introduction	I'm Dr. Herman Jones	Auditory registration	
	• Ask them to repeat.		• Repetition	
	• Give multiple cues.	• My name sounds like ________. • I look like _______. • Touch my pretty face. • How many pretty Hermans do you know?	• Cued recall	
	• Tell them you will ask them your name later.		• Intentional recall	
2.	Ask why they are here.	• What happened? • Last memory prior… • First memory after…	• Remote memory/orientation • Retrograde amnesia • Anterograde amnesia	
	• Provide info if necessary	• You are here because… • You have been here…		
3.	Ask about family	• Who lives with you? • Describe your family. • Who lives in the area, where, when?	• Autobiographical information • Personal facts • Remote memory	
4.	Contemporary information	• How about the Middle East? • What can be done about terrorists, etc.?	• Recent memory • Intentional semantic memory	
	• Tell them you will ask about this topic later.	• What issues are politicians focused on?		
5.	Intervening conversation	• What is your doctor's name? • Is he/she your regular doctor? • What medications do you take? • What do you do to stay healthy?	• Recent memory	
6.	Close your eyes and tell me		• Incidental visual memory	
	a. Items patient is wearing	• Item, color, description		
	b. What you (the interviewer) are wearing	• Shirt or another prominent item		
	c. Where items are in room	• Furniture, door, window, TV		

(continued)

Table 9.3 (continued)

	Item	Example	Area assessed	Record response/ accuracy
7.	Show them three items and ask patient to remember them.	• Cup, paper clip, coins, pen	• Immediate intentional visual memory	
	• Tell patient you will ask again later.			
8.	Ask them to recall your name.	• I'm Dr. ___________.	• Intentional verbal recall	
		• Provide previous cues as necessary.	• Cued facilitation	
9.	Ask patient to recall items previously shown.	• Coins, paper clip, pen	• Intentional visual recall	
		• Provide cues if necessary • Office supply • In my pocket		
10.	Ask patient to recall topic previously discussed.	• Babies, politics, terrorism • Recall accident facts	• Intentional verbal semantic recall	

Intermediate/Bedside Assessment of Memory

Several methods can be used to briefly assess memory functioning in a systematic and structured manner. These methods focus on list-learning tasks, semantic memory tasks and visual memory tasks. The following three-component memory assessment task is offered for an expedient assessment of memory with guidelines provided for interpretation. Caution should be used when applying such interpretation, as many factors influence memory performance and should be considered. This type of assessment of current memory function is not intended to substitute for a more thorough assessment of memory, but rather is offered to assess memory in acute or medical office settings and determine if referral for further assessment is indicated. The guidelines for levels of impairment are also offered for clinical purposes and recognition that these guidelines for levels of performance are not rigid and are certainly affected by age and educational factors. With these cautions in mind, the following Ten-minute Intermediate Memory Evaluation (TIME) is described in Table 9.4. The word list consists of five unrelated words which are presented three times while patients are told which words they forgot in the immediate recall phase. They are reminded that they will be asked to recall these words later. Their immediate spontaneous recall across the three trials is recorded. A semantic message which contains five elements is then related and immediate recall is requested. The message is repeated twice, and the subject is told that they will be asked to recall the story in verbatim detail later. Subsequently, the subject is shown a drawing with five elements and requested to look at the drawing and remember the elements as precisely as possible. The drawing is exposed for 10 seconds and then removed from sight. This is succeeded with spontaneous free recall of the five words and a recall of the story. Cued recall and recognition recall of the words and story are attempted following spontaneous recall trials. Then the spontaneous recall of the figure is requested, followed by recognition of the figure from among five designs. Table 9.5 offers qualitative evaluation descriptors of performance on the TIME. Again, caution should be used when interpreting performance and these descriptors are offered as guidelines and should not be considered an adequate replacement for a thorough memory assessment in a stable neurologic population.

Several screening batteries which incorporate a memory component are available and can often be used in both inpatient and outpatient populations. These measures have the added benefit of briefly assessing other areas of functioning in addition to memory such as attention, language and visuospatial skills. These measures usually take 30 min to 1 hour to administer. Examples of such measures incorporating memory assessment that may be used for bedside assessment include *Dementia Rating Scale—2nd Ed.* (DRS-2, Mattis, 2001), Repeatable Battery for the Assessment of Neuropsychological Status (RBANS, Randolph, 1998) and Cognistat (Kiernan et al., 1995) among others (see Lezak et al., 2004 for review).

Table 9.4 Ten-minute intermediate memory evaluation (TIME)

List Learning	Learning Trials						
	Trial 1	Trial 2	Trial 3	Recall	Cue	Recognition	
Horse	______	______	______	______	Animal ______	Cow ______	Car ______
Bus	______	______	______	______	Transportation ______	Bug ______	Horse ______
Fly	______	______	______	______	Insect ______	Bus ______	Nurse ______
Nurse	______	______	______	______	Occupation ______	Doctor ______	Stove ______
Phone	______	______	______	______	Appliance ______	Phone ______	Fly ______

	Learning trials :_______/15					
	Trial 1	Trial 2	Recall	Cue	Recognition (read pair and circle response)	
Angela called home to say she was *tied up at work* and would *be late*.						
Angela	______	______	______	Who called ______	Maria	Angela
called home	______	______	______	Called where ______	Home	Work
tied up	______	______	______	Why ______	Sick	Tied up
at work	______	______	______	Where ______	School	Work
late	______	______	______	When ______	Late	Absent

Items	Recall		Recognition
Circle	______	Correct______	
Chimney	______	Incorrect______	
Door	______		
Window	______		
Horizontal dissection line	______		

Recall item	Recognition items
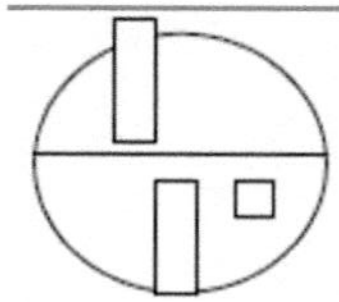	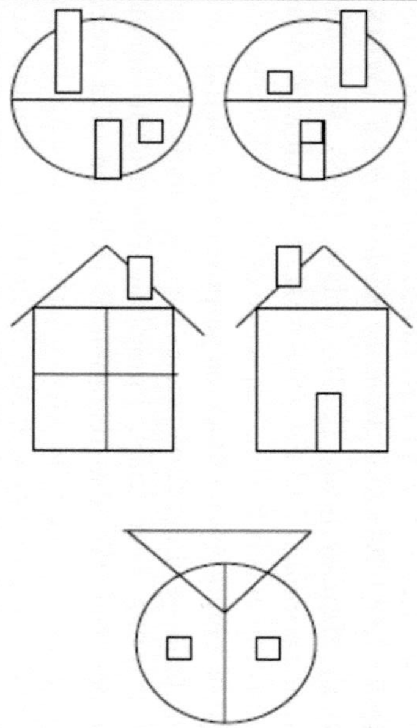

Table 9.5 Qualitative assessment of 10-min intermediate memory evaluation (TIME)

	≤60				>60			
	Normal	Mild	Moderate	Severe	Normal	Mild	Moderate	Severe
List recall								
Total of three trials	12–15	6–9	3–5	<3	9–15	6–8	3–5	<3
Delayed recall	4–5	2–3	1	0	3–5	2–3	1	0
Recognition	9–10	8	7–8	5	8–10	7–8	6	5
Message recall								
Total of two trials	8–10	7–8	5–6	<5	7–10	6–7	4–5	<4
Delayed recall	4–5	3	2	<2	3–5	2	1	0
Recognition	9–10	8	6–7	5	8–10	7–8	6	5
Figure recall								
Recall	4–5	3	2	1	3–5	2	1	0
Recognition	5	4	3	2	5	4	3	2

Comprehensive/Outpatient Laboratory Assessment of Memory

There are a vast array of neuropsychology memory tests, ranging from stand-alone memory tests [e.g., Rey Auditory Verbal Learning Test (AVLT or RAVLT, Rey, 1964), *California Verbal Learning Test—2nd Ed.* (CVLT-2, Delis et al., 2000) and *Hopkins Verbal Learning Test*—Revised (HVLT-R, Benedict et al., 1998) to comprehensive memory batteries (e.g., *Wechsler Memory Scale—4th Ed.* (WMS-IV, Wechsler, 2008); *Children's Memory Scale* (CMS, Cohen, 1998), *Wide Range Assessment of Memory and Learning, 2nd Ed.* (WRAML-2, Sheslow & Adams, 2004)]. A review of these instruments is beyond the scope of this book. Selection of the appropriate measure(s) of memory will reflect the purpose of the referral, patient variables and expertise and training of the clinician. As specified above, we strongly advocate assessment of learning over trials, immediate (short-term) memory, delayed memory and recognition. We also recommend inclusion of a measure allowing for assessment of proactive and retroactive interference effects. Typically, neuropsychological assessment of memory will also include more than one verbal memory test and more than one nonverbal (visual) memory test. Neuropsychological assessment protocols have been established or recommended for several different disease entities [e.g., Consortium to Establish a Registry for Alzheimer's Disease (CERAD, Rosen et al., 1984; Morris et al., 1989) and schizophrenia)], and work is currently underway to identify a series of tests that may be used across a variety of research fields supported by the National Institute of Health. Recommendations are also provided in this volume for various neurological diseases and syndromes.

References

Benedict, R. H. B., Schretlaen, D., Groninger, L., & Brandt, J. (1998). Hopkins verbal learning test—Revised: Normative data and analysis of inter-form and test-retest reliability. *The Clinical Neuropsychologist, 12*, 43–55.
Cohen, M. (1998). *Children's memory scale*. Psychological Corporation.
Delis, D. C., Kramer, J. H., Kaplan, E., & Ober, B. A. (2000). *California verbal learning test (CVLT-II)* (2nd ed.). Pearson.
Kandel, E. (2007). *In search of memory: The emergence of a new science*. W. W. Horton.
Kiernan, R. J., Mueller, J., & Langston, J. W. (1995). *Cognistat (neurobehavioral cognitive status examination)*. Psychological Assessment Resources.
Kolb, B., & Whishaw, I. (2009). *Fundamentals of human neuropsychology* (6th ed.). W. H. Freeman.
Lezak, M. D., Howieson, D. B., & Loring, D. W. (2004). *Neuropsychological assessment* (4th ed.). Oxford University Press.
Mattis, S. (2001). *Dementia rating scale* (2nd ed.). Psychological Assessment Resources.
Morris, J. C., Heyman, A., Mohs, R. C., et al. (1989). The consortium to establish a registry for Alzheimer's disease (CERAD). Part 1. Clinical and neuropsychological assessment of Alzheimer's disease. *Neurology, 39*, 1159–1165.
Randolph, C. (1998). *Repeatable battery for the assessment of neuropsychological status*. The Psychological Corporation.
Rey, A. (1964). *L'examen clinique en psychologie*. Presses Universitaires de France.
Rosen, W. G., Mohs, R. C., & Davis, K. L. (1984). A new rating scale for Alzhiemer's disease. *The American Journal of Psychiatry, 141*, 1356–1364.
Sheslow, D., & Adams, W. (2004). *Wide range assessment of memory and learning (WRAML-2)* (2nd ed.). Multi-Health Systems.
Squire, L., & Zola, S. M. (1996). Structure and function of declarative and nondeclarative memory systems. *Proceedings of the National Academy of Sciences of the United States of America, 93*, 13515–13522.
Squire, L. R. (1987). *Memory and brain*. Oxford Press.
Tulving, E., Kapur, S., Craik, F. I., Moscovitch, M., & Houle, S. (1994). Hemispheric encoding/retrieval asymmetry in episodic memory: Positron emission tomography findings. *Proceedings of the National Academy of Sciences of the United States of America, 91*, 2016–2020.
Wechsler, D. (2008). *Wechsler memory scale (WMS-IV)* (4th ed.). Pearson.

Further Reading

Mesulam, M. (2000). *Principals of behavioral and cognitive neurology* (2nd ed.). Oxford University Press.
Squire, L., & Schacter, D. (2003). *Neuropsychology of memory* (3rd ed.). Guilford.

Chapter 10
Deficits in Visuospatial/Visuoconstructional Skills and Motor Praxis

James G. Scott and Michael R. Schoenberg

Visuospatial and visuoperceptual skills play a significant role in every day functioning; however, they are typically automatic. We process information visually and make identifications and analyze complex visual stimuli and are largely unaware of the visuoperceptual process involved or complexities of the stimuli that were analyzed. As an example, assume that you have purchased a new car and now suddenly that make and model seems to be everywhere. You suddenly notice the different colors in which the car comes, the different trim packages and optional equipment (i.e., roof racks, spoiler, etc.). Soon you find yourself distinguishing among similar year models based on detail changes such as tail light configuration or color-matching door hardware. You can also identify this car from multiple angles (front, side, rear, corner, etc.) These complex stimuli are typically automatically perceived, poorly verbally labeled, yet precisely and accurately analyzed and identified. The centers in the brain that process such information are ever vigilant to visual and visuospatial stimuli and organized to simultaneously and sequentially take that information and transform it into usable, salient information or associated knowledge. All this occurs in a split second and typically below our level of awareness. While this process can certainly be consciously controlled, typically in novel learning or acquisition stages, our nature is to use repetition, familiarity or repeated recurrence to allow for more automatic processing and save the conscious and effortful processing capacities for the novel or necessary tasks at hand.

J. G. Scott (✉)
Department of Psychiatry and Behavioral Sciences, University of Oklahoma, Health Sciences Center College of Medicine, Oklahoma City, OK, USA
e-mail: jim-scott@ouhsc.edu

M. R. Schoenberg
Departments of Psychiatry and Neurosciences, Neurology, and Neurosurgery, University of South Florida College of Medicine, Tampa, FL, USA
e-mail: mschoenb@usf.edu

M. R. Schoenberg, J. G. Scott (eds.), *The Little Black Book of Neuropsychology*,
https://doi.org/10.1007/978-3-032-07777-6_10

If this process is impaired, many types of deficits occur, from failure to process basic elements in the visual stimuli (i.e., color, lines, orientation) to more complex and integrative features such as object identification, faces or familiar scenes. These deficits can include phenomena such as *visual neglect* and *hemi-inattention* or more dramatic *visual agnosias* or *prosopagnosia*. This impairment may include what is referred to as disconnection syndromes in which centers of basic visual sensory functions are dissociated or disconnected from association cortex areas that allow for synthesis or analysis necessary to recognize the sensory stimuli as a specific object.

Key Points and Chapter Summary

- Visuospatial and visuoconstructional deficits are much more likely with right-sided parietal lobe damage especially to the angular gyrus and supramarginal gyrus.
- Much of visuospatial and visuoconstructional processing occurs automatically and may not be evident to the patient or family.
- Praxis deficits can occur in many motor functions including feeding, dressing, tool use, drawing and complex skills such as mechanical skill or musical skill.
- Hemi-inattention or neglect is:
  - Hemi-inattention involves only one modality. Hemi-neglect involves more than one sensory modality.
  - Most frequently associated with right parietal lobe damage but can occur with left parietal lobe damage.
  - Is often severe acutely and may involve neglect in vision, hearing and tactile sensation.
  - Hemi-neglect or hemi-inattention does demonstrate a tendency decrease over time (usually a few months)
  - In the case of hemi-neglect, resolution usually remits across tactile modalities first, auditory modalities second and vision last.

Anatomy of Visual and Visuospatial Processing

Visual and visuospatial processing involves many areas of the cortex as well as subcortical areas depending on the functional aspect of visual processing that is to occur. The occipital lobe contains the primary visual cortex and performs many basic visual functions. The right hemispace or visual field is generally processed by the left occipital lobe while the left visual field is processed by the right visual cortex. In relation to the calcarine fissure (see Fig. 10.1), the processing of information from the perceivable visual field is most easily understood as upside down and anteriorally to posteriorally backward. Thus, the upper half of the visual field is

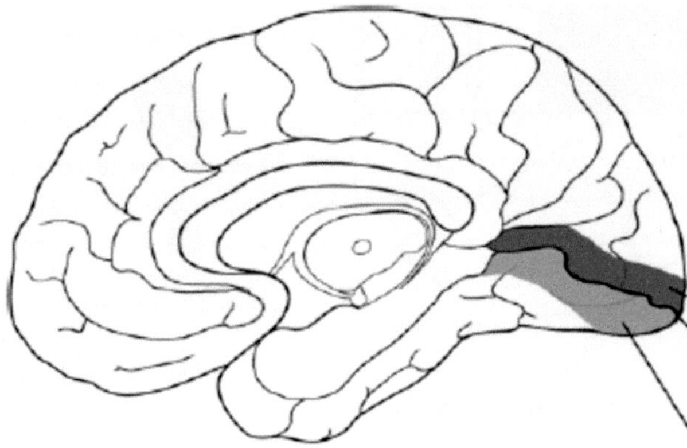

Fig. 10.1 Medial picture of brain illustrating primary visual cortex above/below calcarine fissure

processed by the gyri below the calcarine fissure while the lower half of the visual field is processed by the gyri superior to the calcarine fissure. Similarly, stimuli in the center of the visual field are processed by the cortex in the posterior visual cortex while stimuli from the periphery of the visual field are processed by cortex of the anterior occipital lobe medially to the calcarine fissure.

Key Points: Organization of Retinocortical map for Primary Visual Cortex

- Upside down and backward
  - Upper halves of visual fields are processed by the gyri below the calcarine fissure.
  - Lower halves of the visual fields are processed by the gyri above the calcarine fissure.
  - Visual information from the center is processed by primary visual cortex closest to the occipital pole (posterior visual cortex).
  - Visual information from peripheral vision is processed by occipital lobe closest to the calcarine fissure and anterior to the occipital pole.

In processing visual stimuli, information that provides stimulation to the retinas is transferred via the optic nerve, primarily either to the primary visual cortex or lateral geniculate body. Both these areas have similar topographic organizational representations (i.e., upside down and backward) throughout the visual system. In addition, some visual information is projected to the superior colliculus which is instrumental in visual orientation to movement within the visual field. Figure 10.2 depicts the visual system and process of visual sensation from perception of stimuli to transfer to the visual cortex.

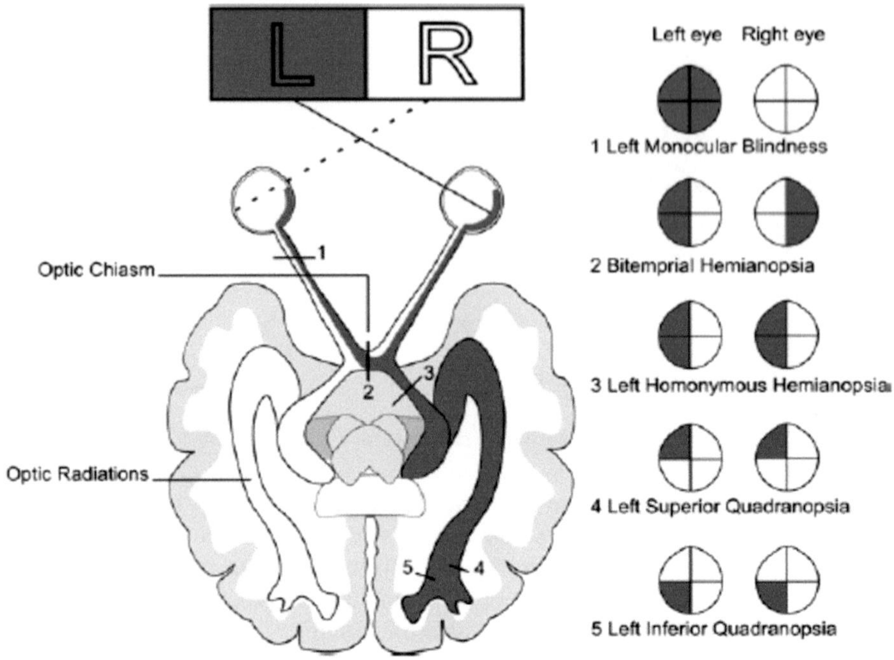

Fig. 10.2 Illustration of optic pathways from retina to primary visual cortex

As visual stimuli are processed, their basic elements are first discerned by the primary visual cortex (area V1) which includes the calcarine fissure and is called striate cortex because of distinct stripes in the gray matter associated with perception of color, shape and motion. Secondary visual cortex refines these perceptions and integrates these basic elements into wholes, allowing association cortex to definitively identify the viewed objects or determining and guiding movement. For example, the stimuli of one straight line and two curved lines are initially processed by the primary visual cortex. This information is further processed with the portion of the three elements being noted and recognized as a familiar unitary stimulus. This is subsequently processed further by tertiary cortex and recognized as an upper case "B." While this is certainly a simplified example of the processing of the elements of a letter "B," the process of recognition of more complicated stimuli such as a face or landscape occurs much the same way. However, in the case of faces, there is a specialized area of the brain to recognize and process faces termed the fusiform face area (FFA) which lies in the fusiform gyrus of the occipitotemporal area. While termed the FFA, this area appears important for specialized visual object discrimination, such as for discriminating between birds and cars (Gauthier et al., 2000).

Visual Processing "Streams"

The visual processing system is traditionally divided into two general systems in humans: (1) a system for processing where stimuli are in space, the so-called where system (or Dorsal stream); and (2) a system for processing what a visual percept is, the so-called what system (or Ventral stream) (Fig. 10.3). The "Where" system begins in the occipital lobe involving the primary visual cortex (area V1) to V2 and V3 projecting to the middle temporal area (MT) and runs dorsally and superiorly to the medial superior area and parietal lobes. Alternatively, the "What" system also begins in primary visual cortex (V1), but with somewhat different pathways that project to V2 and V3 to V4 which then runs ventrally and inferiorly to the posterior and inferior temporal lobes (including the fusiform gyrus). A third system, termed the superior temporal sulcus (STS) system, has been identified, and likely involves complex visuoconstructional and movement processing, running laterally from the primary occipital cortex (area V1) laterally along the superior temporal sulcus and includes regions of the superior temporal gyrus as well.

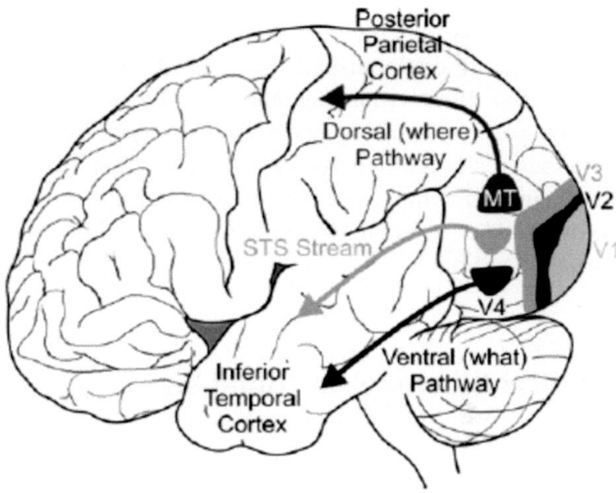

Fig. 10.3 Illustration of dorsal and ventral visual processing "streams" in human brain

Key Points: Visual Processing "Streams"

- "What" stream (visual processing pathway that recognizes objects) = Ventral pathway
- "Where" stream (visual processing where things are in space) = Dorsal pathway
- "Specialized movement" stream (visual analysis of movement of body parts and biological objects) = STS pathway

Visual and Visuospatial Deficits

Visual loss occurs with destruction or impairment of any point in the pathway from the retinas to the primary visual cortex. Lesions occurring before the optic chiasm result in monocular blindness (blindness in one eye). Lesions producing damage to the medial optic chiasm produces a bi-temporal hemianopsia resulting from the disruption of fibers from the medial retinas, which must cross at the optic chiasm. Post-chiasmic lesions produce contralateral visual field loss and are referred to as a homonymous hemianopsia. Lesions in the posterior geniculo striate radiations would produce a contralateral upper quadrant anopsia if in the inferior geniculo striate or a lower quadrant anopsia if in the superior geniculo striate. Figure 10.2 shows the lesion locations and visual deficits associated with each.

Visuoperceptual Distortions

A variety of visuoperceptual distortions have been identified. The visuoperceptual distortions are distinguished from visual agnosias in patients are able to identify objects, but their visual perception is altered in some fashion. Complaints may include perception of objects as too close (pelopsia), too far away (telopsia), larger than they really are (macropsia) or smaller than they really are (micropsia). A syndrome involving the distortion of visual perception and time has been described, the so-called *Alice in Wonderland* (or *Todd's*) syndrome (see Table 10.1 for summary of visual distortions).

Cortical Blindness or "Blind Sight"

Cortical blindness (blind sight) is a rare condition occurring with damage to the primary visual cortex. Traditionally, this term is referred to bilateral occipital lobe damage, but is also present with unilateral occipital lobe destruction, which has been reported with vascular disease or traumatic brain injury. Individuals have no conscious awareness of vision in the damaged visual field(s), and will report being blind. However, these individuals are able to appreciate location or movement, without knowing the content. Individuals have been able to point to where a light was located in their "blind" visual field(s) and able to perceive orientation of lines without conscious perception. While a person with cortical blindness is unable to identify a face in their visual field, patients were able to "guess" the emotional expressions. Lastly, there is some processing of movement, but this perception is outside the clear awareness of patients.

Table 10.1 Visuoperceptual deficits

Term	Description
Achromatopsia	Inability to distinguish colors
Alice in Wonderland (Todd's) syndrome	Alteration in the perception of time, generally for brief time periods. Perceptual alterations include macropsia, metamorphopsia, micropsia, teleopsia and pelopsia (collectively referred to as dysmetropsia). Objects may be perceived as too small (or far away) and/or too large (close). Associated with migraine headache, brain tumor, Epstein–Barr infection and use of psychoactive drugs. The syndrome has also been reported in association with epilepsy and ICP.
Anton's syndrome	Denial of cortical blindness
Balint's syndrome	Rare syndrome composing three classic features: (1) optic ataxia (unable to guide movements using visual information), (2) ocular apraxia (inability to voluntarily move eyes) and (3) visual spatial inattention (features of simultanagnosia). Bilateral parieto-occipital damage.
Cortical blindness (blind sight)	Blindness resulting from destruction of primary visual cortex. Patients unable to identify or perceive colors, lines, shapes or objects. Often associated with Anton's syndrome. Phenomena of "blind sight" occur if patient with cortical blindness able to make better than chance identification of visual stimuli that are not consciously perceived. Blind sight thought to be possible due to intact parietal cortex and preserved visual pathway from superior colliculus.
Dysmetropsia	Term used to describe macropsia, micropsia, pelopsia and teleopsia. Associated with retinopathy (swelling of the cornea), but also reported with migraine headache, brain tumors, lesions of the occipital cortex, Epstein–Barr infection, epilepsy, psychoactive drug use and psychiatric illnesses. Reported to occur at times in some otherwise healthy children and adolescents.
Figure-ground discrimination	Ability to distinguish overlapping objects. Impaired in simultanagnosia.
Macropsia (also known as megalopsia)	Visual distortion in which objects appear much bigger than the objects really are. Objects may also be perceived as closer than they really are (pelopsia), and objects may appear to move in toward the person. Perception may be like looking through a telescope.
Micropsia	Visual distortion in which objects appear much smaller than they really are. Objects are too small and may be associated with teleopsia (perceived as being far off in the distance). The effect may be like looking through the wrong end of a telescope. Some have described objects as also appearing to "move away from them towards the distance." strictly speaking, micropsia describes disruption of perception of size—not distance (teleopsia).
Metamorphopsia	Visual distortion in which shapes and colors are distorted. Straight lines appear to bend.
Pelopsia	Visual distortion in which objects appear much closer (nearer) than the objects actually are.
Teleopsia	Visual distortion in which objects appear farther away than the objects actually are. Has been found in patients with parieto-temporal lesions as well, but most often associated with migraine headache.

(continued)

Table 10.1 (continued)

Term	Description
Ocular dysmetria	Deficit in the motor (ocular) movements of the eye, in which saccades are overshot or undershot. When trying to fixate on an object, the eye will appear to shake back and forth as the eye tries to adjust for over- and under-shooting the object in saccadic movements.
Visuo-integration	Ability to mentally rotate or synthesize objects parts into whole
Visuospatial orientation	Ability to judge orientation of objects in space

Balint's Syndrome

First described in 1909 by Reszo Balint, but coined in 1954 by Hecaen and Ajuriaguerra, this is a disorder of visual perception and attention characteristically associated with three features: (1) *optic ataxia*, (2) *ocular apraxia* and (3) a visual spatial inattention thought to reflect a *simultanagnosia*. *Optic ataxia* is the inability to coordinate visual guided reach for objects in space. The individual is unable to use his/her eyes to guide hand (or feet) movements to desired targets in space. *Ocular apraxia* is the inability to voluntarily shift eye gaze despite intact cranial nerves and functional ocular muscles. It should not be confused with ocular dysmetria (see Table 10.1). Individuals will exhibit a seemingly psychic stare and not be able to voluntarily "look away." Voluntary eye movements can occur if the patient closes his/her eyes. A visual spatial inattention occurs with the patient only being able to appreciate one aspect of a percept at a time. It has been described as almost a "tunnel" vision focusing on one percept. Minimizing the object for perception does not result in the whole image being seen, but a focus on the smaller detail aspects of the scene appreciated, and classically described as simultanagnosia, although some argue the features of the visual inattention of Balint's syndrome differ (subtly) from simultanagnosias. Balint's syndrome has traditionally been associated with bilateral occipitoparietal lesions, and often damage the white matter underlying the angular gyrus for the dorsal "where" stream (e.g., Kolb & Whishaw, 2009). Table 10.1 summarizes common visuoperceptual deficits.

Key Points: Balint's Syndrome

- Optic ataxia = Loss of eye–hand coordination
- Occular apraxia = Loss of voluntary ability to shift gaze
- Simultanagnosia = Cannot see anything but one aspect of an object at a time

Visual Agnosia

Agnosias develop when the meaning is striped from a percept, and there are problems associated with the cortical processing of stimuli which are *not* related to or explained by deficits in the sensory organ. Assuming the mechanisms of visual sensory perception are intact, patients may manifest several deficits in visual processing of stimuli. These deficits can be as basic as the perception of angular lines or as complex as an inability to synthesize or rotate visual images to make a recognizable object.

Deficits in visual processing can involve any aspect of the stimuli including color, texture and spatial orientation and integration.

Achromatopsia is an inability to distinguish among colors, typically in a range of color spectrum (i.e., blue-green, purple-red) and may be traumatically induced or congenital. Deficits may also be seen in inability to judge the spatial orientation of objects or lines in space. The type of visuospatial deficit typically involves deficits in distinguishing line orientation or curved and straight lines or the inability to separate figure and ground overlapping elements in a scene. Table 10.2 lists common visual agnosias.

Several visual agnosias have been delineated, which are associated with various parietal-occipital association cortices. While lesions to the occipital cortex tend to produce deficits in basic perceptual characteristics (i.e., color perception, orientation of stimuli), lesions to parieto-occipital cortex produces deficits in more complicated integrative and synthesizing visual functions. These deficits are included in visual object agnosia, of which two types have been identified, differentiated by clinical features and lesion locations.

Visual object agnosia is an inability to recognize (know) visually presented objects. This must not reflect a deficit in naming, so not only can the patient not name an object, but cannot demonstrate its use or point to the object when it is named by the examiner. Further, it is not a deficit of lack of familiarity or knowledge per se, with the patient being able to name and/or demonstrate use of objects when presented in other sensory domains (auditory, tactile, etc.). Often, real objects can be better perceived (known) than line drawings. The agnosia of visual objects will vary, such that some classes of objects are better known, while other classes of objects are not known (i.e., animals worse than trees or tools). Visual agnosias are further divided into Apperceptive and Associate subtypes.

1. *Apperceptive visual agnosia* is characterized by the inability to demonstrate accurate percept of objects. Patients are unable to draw the object on command, copy the object on paper or match similar classes of objects together. The patient is unable to name the object and cannot sort groups appropriately (types of birds, four-legged mammals, etc.).
2. *Associative visual agnosia* is a deficit in perceiving an object with intact abilities to draw and match visual objects. It can be distinguished from the apperceptive type by the ability of the patient to draw or match similar visual objects together, yet still be unable to name or demonstrate the use of the objects.

Table 10.2 Visual agnosias

Term	Description	Lesion location
Apperceptive agnosia	Inability to perceive visual objects. Involves all visual objects. Patients unable to draw, copy or match (or sort) similar objects. Visual acuity is intact, and able to identify shades, colors and light and dark lines.	Bilateral temporo-occipital-parietal. Often presents as recovery from cortical blindness
Associative agnosia	InaInability to recognize visual objects. A visual percept "stripped of its meaning." Objects seen are not known and cannot be named or use demonstrated. However, objects can be drawn, copied and matched (to a like visual object). Dollar bills can be matched together. May be associated with achromatopsia.	Bilateral posterior mesial temporo-occipital cortex (and underlying white matter).
Auto prosopagnosia	Inability to identify one's own face	
Dorsal simultanagnosia	Unable to appreciate more than one feature of an object or scene at a time. Restriction in perceiving objects more pronounced than in ventral simultanagnosia. Individuals may bump into objects in their environment if several are placed close together (e.g., a couch and a coffee table).	Bilateral parieto-occipital
Prosopagnosia	Cl Classically, the inability to identify familiar faces. However, deficit is the inability to identify specific members of a class. Generic recognition of objects (pen, person, cat) is intact, but patient unable to identify specific members within a class (distinguish types of pens or distinguish pet cat from stray, etc.).	Bilateral temporo-occiptial area, particularly the mesial and inferior lingual and/or parahippocampal gyri (or underlying white matter).
Simultaneous agnosia (simultanagnosia)	Inability to perceive multiple aspects of a single object or multiple aspects of a scene	Bilateral parieto-occipital lesions or left inferior temporo-occipital.
Ventral simultanagnosia	Inability to appreciate multiple aspects of a scene. When trying to read, may read a word, but unable to read a sentence. Less complete restriction in visual perception than dorsal simultanagnosia.	Left inferior temporo-occipital

Key Points: Visual Agnosia

Inability to appreciate the meaning of a visual percept that is not due to loss of visual field or visual acuity or lack of familiarity with object/item. Can demonstrate appropriate use of object if presented in another sensory modality (auditory, touch, etc.).

Simultaneous visual agnosia (*simultanagnosia*) is impairment in the ability to appreciate the multiple aspects of a single object or the relationship of multiple objects in a scene. The patient is unable to appreciate the totality of an object (e.g., picture of an elephant) but can identify discrete features of the object (e.g., eyes, tail, trunk, ears, etc.). Individuals with simultanagnosia are unable to read, as they can appreciate each letter but cannot see the words the letters spell out. Two types of simultanagnosia have been identified, dorsal and ventral types.

1. *Dorsal simultanagnosia* describes individuals unable to appreciate more than one feature of an object or scene at a time. Dorsal simultanagnosia is associated with bilateral occipitoparietal lesions.
2. *Ventral simultanagnosia* is less "complete" with patients being able to identify some multiple features of an object or a scene, but unable to appreciate the entire scene. As an example, a patient with a ventral simultanagnosia may be able to identify two discrete people in a scene, but is unable to describe the scene as two people playing Frisbee. The patient may be able to read short words, but will have more difficulty with longer words and reading a printed sentence along a page. Ventral simultanagnosia has been reported with unilateral (left) inferior occipitoparietal (or is occipitotemporal) lobe lesion.

Prosopagnosia is a deficit in recognizing familiar faces. Patients can describe discrete aspects of a face, nose, mouth, eyes, but cannot recognize the face. Prosopagnosia is not limited to human faces; it has been reported for recognizing animals (e.g., pets). Both apperceptive and associative forms have been described, based on ability to match faces to categories (known and unknown faces). Individuals with the associative form of prosopagnosia can sort familiar faces from unfamiliar faces, but remain unable to name or point to familiar faces if the familiar face is named.

Apraxia

Apraxia refers to an inability to perform previously learned, sequential motor movements. Apraxia should not be confused with ataxia (see Chap. 3, this volume), which is the loss of ability to coordinate motor movements. This loss of ability to perform motor movements cannot be attributable to sensory or simple central or peripheral motor impairment or general condition such as dementia. While many classification schemas of apraxias have been proposed, the most pragmatic involve discrimination among ideational and ideomotor limb apraxias, and constructional apraxia. Ideational and ideomotor apraxias may involve any number of functions such as buccofacial movement, feeding, grooming, dressing or tool usage. The discriminating characteristic between ideomotor and ideational apraxias is the inability of patients with ideomotor apraxia to pantomime motor skills either to imitation or command (demonstrate use of a hammer and nail, hair brush, scissors, etc.) and the failure of ideational apraxia patients to perform sequenced movements in complex motor behaviors despite often retaining the individual components of such behaviors (e.g., demonstrating how to write a letter, fold it, put it in an envelope, address it and put a stamp on it).

Ideomotor apraxia patients have the greatest difficulty in performing tasks to command, but often improve when asked to imitate hand movements, and typically improve further when asked to perform behaviors with actual objects. This is most frequently assessed by asking patients to demonstrate a tool's use by command such as: show me how you would use a hammer, saw or screwdriver. Individuals with ideomotor apraxia often use their hand as the tool rather than demonstrating a proper hand grip and subsequent hammer use movements. Similarly, these patients often have difficulty with daily tool use such as eating utensils, grooming tools (comb, toothbrush) or writing implements. Lesions are typically associated with left hemisphere in right-handed persons. These lesions typically involve the posterior parietal lobe and or the corpus callosum connecting the right and left parietal areas.

In contrast, ideational apraxia involves the failure of sequential movements that make up a purposeful behavior while the constitutional parts remain intact. Patients with ideational apraxia often appear to get lost in the steps involved in a task. For example, the steps in brushing your teeth might include grabbing your toothbrush, holding it in one hand, getting toothpaste, unscrewing the top, squeezing the toothpaste onto the brush, wetting the brush, screwing the top back on the toothpaste and then brushing, followed by rinsing your mouth and then rinsing your toothbrush. Individuals with ideational apraxia often fail at some point in the multi-step sequence. Ideational apraxias are often associated with lesion in the frontal lobes.

Constructional apraxia refers to a loss of ability to draw or make three-dimensional designs despite intact perceptional skills. Individuals with this type of deficit have difficulty with visuospatial relationships and often produce drawings or three-dimensional designs that have correct elements, but in which the elements do not correspond appropriately to each other (see Fig. 10.5 for an example). Individuals with right parietal lesions are most likely to manifest this type of apraxia. It should be noted that this type of apraxia can also be conceptualized as a visuo-agnosia. Table 10.3 lists the above noted apraxia and their associated lesion location and deficit.

Table 10.3 Apraxias

Type	Deficit	Lesion location
Ideomotor limb apraxia	Cannot perform motor movements to command. Difficulty exists with performance to imitation and with actual object	Left posterior parietal lobe or corpus callosum connecting right and left posterior parietal regions
Ideational limb apraxia	Deficits in performing sequenced motor movements to complete a complex behavior, often despite preserved ability to perform individual components.	Typically frontal lobe lesions in supplemental motor cortex. Lesions are more severe with left frontal lesions, but occur with damage to either side.
Constructional apraxia	Inability to copy a drawing or construct a three-dimensional design from a model.	Lesions are typically in the right parietal lobe.

Assessment of Visuospatial (Visual Spatial) Functioning

Prior to assessing visuospatial skills, deficits in sensory functioning need to be ruled out as potential causes for abnormalities. These include assessment of visual acuity as well as occulo-motor movements and visual field deficits. As mentioned in previous chapters, occulo-motor deficits can be attributed to cranial nerve deficits in nerves III, IV or VI (see Chap. 4 for examination of cranial nerves). Visual acuity should be assessed by asking patients about their use of corrective lenses and their last optometrist/ophthalmologist examination, as well as performing a crude bedside examination using a Schnelling Chart. Visual fields should be tested laterally as well as in vertical quadrants as it is possible that a patient may have a quadrant anopsis if lesions are restricted either to the area above the calcarine fissure (produces a lower contralateral quadrant anopsia) or below the calcarine fissure (produces an upper contralateral quadrant anopsia). Oculomotor (ocular motor) movements can also be affected by frontal lobe lesions to the frontal eye fields and usually result in poor voluntary eye control in tasks requiring visual search and sustained gaze. To test, have the patient voluntarily look to the left, right, up and down.

Key Points: Right Versus Left Constructional Apraxias

- Left hemisphere (parietal lesions):
  - Drawings maintain gestalt but lack detail.
  - Organization of spatial features appears piecemeal, but generally in appropriate area.
  - Block designs maintain general organization (2 × 2) but spatial detail (block) often rotated.
  - Right sensory extinction, can be present Gerstmann's syndrome.
- Right hemisphere (parietal lesions):
  - Left visual inattention may be present.
  - Features of left side of drawing/figure omitted.
  - Gestalt of figure often not maintained. Details may be present, but poorly organized.
  - Block designs "strung out" and basic organization (2 × 2) not maintained.
  - Left sensory extinction can be present.

Assessment and Interpretation of Visuoconstructional Functions

Traditionally, qualitative differences in visuoconstructional skills have been identified between patients with left hemisphere versus right hemisphere damage. The differences are thought to reflect the differences between hemisphere functions. For example, the left hemisphere is associated with analyzing visual information into details, while the right hemisphere is associated with appreciating the overall gestalt of the visual percept. Damage to the left hemisphere impairs ability to form detailed percepts, and the constructional drawings tend to be overly simplistic, poorly organized and often lack attention to detail while maintaining the overall gestalt of the object. Performance on block design tests tends to reflect maintaining the gestalt but rotating a detail. Alternatively, patients with right hemisphere, particularly right parietal damage, tend to demonstrate constructional deficits in which the whole gestalt is lost and the drawing will be typified by poor spatial arrangement of many details in which the spatial gestalt may not be maintained. In addition, a visual inattention (or hemi-neglect) may be present such that features in the left hemi-field will be missing or incomplete. Right parietal damage results in block design performance in which the gestalt is not maintained, and the drawing may be "strung" out (such that a 2 × 2 format is not used). The detailed feature of various angles or spatial arrangements may be preserved but the gestalt is lost.

Bedside Assessment of Visuospatial (Visuoconstructional) Skills

Screening assessment of visuospatial skills can be done in interview at the bedside and give an indication of whether more formal, standardized assessment is necessary. Assuming that sensory deficits have been ruled out by assessing visual acuity, bedside assessment of visuospatial skills should progress from simple to more integrated skills. These skills should include assessment of perception, scanning, inattention/neglect, visual recognition, facial recognition, visual form discrimination, construction (drawing) and visual synthesis skills.

Figure 10.4 is an assessment sheet with procedures and examples of ways to assess these skills. It includes a brief assessment of perception of line orientation and form discrimination (Fig. 10.4 number 1) as well as basic color perception (number 2). Number 3 assesses visual scanning and cancellation. Number 4 is an example of a line bisection task in which the patient is instructed to draw a vertical line bisecting the horizontal lines on a page. The patient's performance is evaluated based on any systematic distortion of line bisection either right or left of center. Form recognition can be screened with number 5, while Fig. 10.4 number 6 assesses constructional ability and is useful in evaluating perceptual skills as well as organizational and synthesis skills. Patients need to integrate many elements into the reproduction of more complex drawing.

Assessment of perception at its basic level involves the ability of patients to appropriately perceive angles of straight and curved lines. Patients can be given a sheet with both curved and straight lines and be asked to match or point to the lines that are most similar. Patients should also be asked to name the color of objects in the environment across blue-green and red-purple spectrums to assure correct color perception.

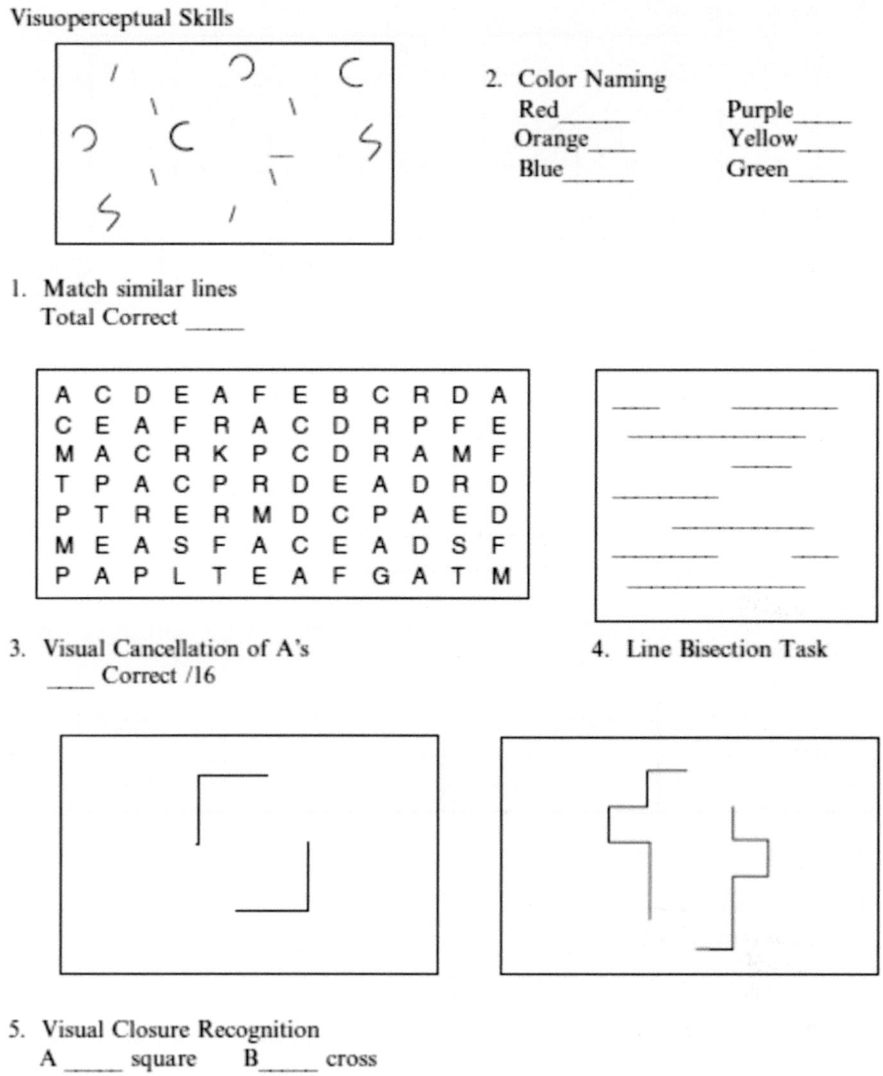

Fig. 10.4 Stimuli for assessing visuoperceptual, visuoconstructional and praxis functioning

Scanning and assessment of neglect should involve the use of both behavioral assessment and tasks which require cancellation. Behaviorally, patients can be simultaneously shown a different number of fingers on each hand of the examiner and asked to report the total number of fingers they were shown. With the patient's gaze focused centrally (i.e., look at my nose), alternately flash multiple (2–3) fingers with one hand and one finger with the other hand to each visual hemi-field and quadrant field. The patient should respond with the total number of fingers shown

Visuoconstructional skills

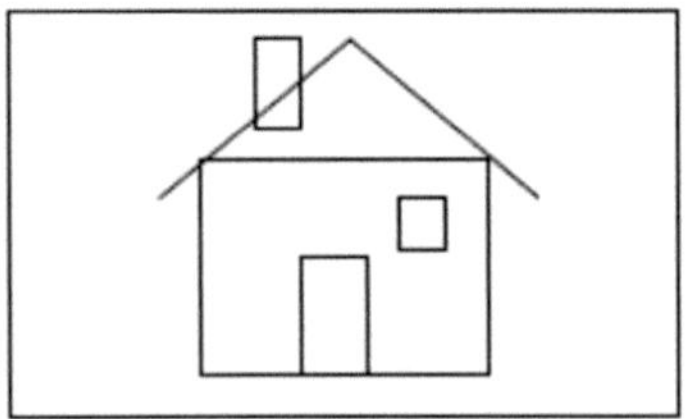

House

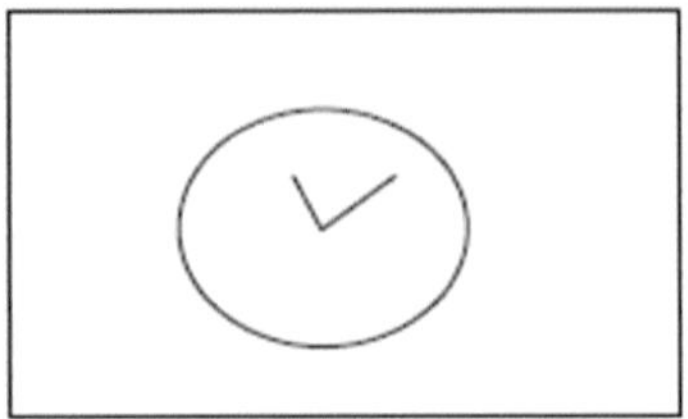

Clock

6. Figure Copying

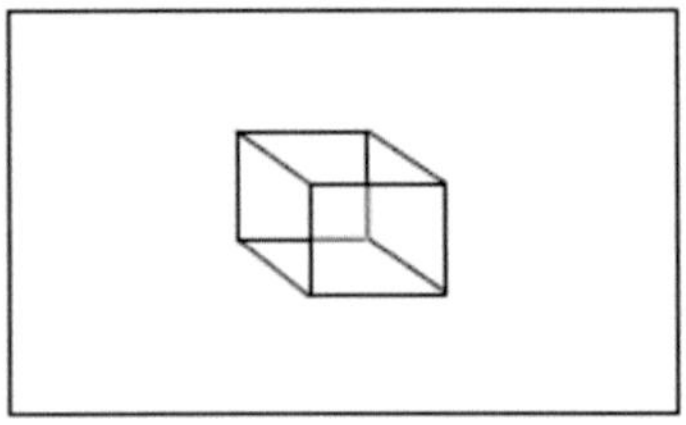

7. Drawing Cube and/or Clock (placing hands at 10 past 11).

Praxis skills

8. Ideomotor apraxia

Show me how to use a

	Command	Imitation	With object
Hammer			
Key			
Screwdriver			

9. Ideational Apraxia. Show me how to

	command	Imitation
Brush your teeth		
Strike a match and blow it out		

Fig. 10.4 (continued)

indicating appropriate perception in all tested visual fields. To confirm a request, fingers from both hands can be presented in the same visual field and should assure perceptual skills in a unilateral visual field. If neglect is present, similar further presentation can be done in the upper and lower visual field quadrants (both unilaterally and bilaterally) to discern a quadrant inattention or neglect. Visual scanning can be readily assessed by drawing letters at various orientations on a page in a random array. The patient is asked to cross off all of a specific letter and the examiner notes any items that are omitted and the side or quadrant in which these items are omitted. Similarly, patients can be shown horizontal lines in a random array on a sheet of paper and asked to draw a vertical line that bisects each horizontal line as close to the middle as possible. Patients should not distort or bias their responses consistently to the left or right.

Visual recognition and facial perception can be assessed quickly by asking patients to recognize and name objects and individuals in that environment. The examiner can carry pictures of common objects or famous people with them and ask for identifications to be made. Common objects may include phones, watches, cups, pens/pencils or books/magazines. Faces can include family members or well-known cultural figures, although identification of cultural figures varies considerably among individuals depending on age, gender and exposure to presented cultural icons.

Visual form recognition, drawing and visual synthesis skills can be assessed by showing patients common objects which have been drawn as separate parts and asking them to tell what that object would be if the parts were mentally rotated and assembled into a single object. Common objects may include cross or addition sign, square or circle. In addition, patients should be asked to copy and draw objects which require appropriate relational elements both in size, shape and elements within the object. For example, patients can be asked to copy a simple house and their copying should include a roof, chimney, walls, window and door in correct proportion and relation to each other. The patient can also be asked to draw an analog clock and put all the numbers in their correct positions. To assess further their ability to plan, they can be asked to place hands on the clock to represent a specific time. It is common for patients to be asked to set the hands so that the clock reads 11:10. Evaluation of patient's performance can be judged not only on the correct position of the numbers, but the patient's understanding of the need to draw hands pointing at 11 and 2 in representing 11:10. The patient's ability to draw complex designs can be assessed by asking them to copy a three-dimensional drawing of a cube. Patients should be able to copy such a design if shown an example.

Laboratory (Outpatient) Neuropsychological Assessments

More thorough assessment of visual spatial and visual constructional tasks can (and should in many cases) be routinely completed. Common measures of visuoconstructional skills are the Wechsler Scales Block Design subtest and/or drawing a complex geometric figure such as the Rey–Osterrieth Complex figure, the Taylor complex figure or the Medical College of Georgia Complex Figures (see Lezak et al., 2004, for review). Figure 10.5 demonstrates a normal drawing of the Rey–Osterrieth Complex Figure along with drawings from patients with a left parietal lesion and a right parietal lesion, respectively. Note the patient with the left parietal lesion ability to preserve the overall design gestalt (the general features or shape is maintained), but the approach is simplistic and piecemeal approach to the task which has resulted in poor integration of sections and lack of details. Alternatively, the patient with the right parietal lesion exhibited left visual inattention (truncated left half of the figure) as well as an inability to synthesize and integrate the elements

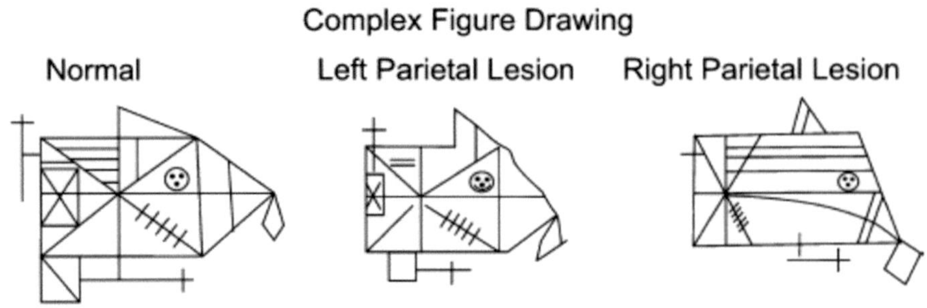

Fig. 10.5 Example of (**a**) normal drawing of Rey–Osterrieth Complex Figure, and then copy by (**b**) a patient with left parietal lesion and by (**c**) a patient with a right parietal lesion

of the drawing suggesting perceptual deficits. These examples provide examples of post-acute left and right hemispheric constructional apraxic features. Namely, left hemisphere damage tends to result in maintained gestalt but simplistic designs, while patients with right hemisphere lesions tend to exhibit deficits in maintaining the gestalt of the figure (details without coherent organization).

References

Gauthier, I., Skudlarski, P., Gore, J. C., & Anderson, A. W. (2000). Expertise for cars and birds recruits brain areas involved in face recognition. *Nature Neuroscience, 3*(2), 191–197.

Kolb, B., & Whishaw, I. (2009). *Fundamentals of human neuropsychology* (5th ed.). W.H. Freeman.

Lezak, M., Howieson, D., & Loring, D. (2004). *Neuropsychological assessment* (4th ed.). Oxford University Press.

Further Reading

Benton, A. L., Hannay, H. J., & Varney, N. R. (1975). Visual perception of line direction in patients with unilateral brain disease. *Neurology, 25*, 907–910. Reprinted in L. Costa & O. Spreen (Eds.) (1985). *Studies in neuropsychology*. Selected papers of Author Benton. New York: Oxford University Press.

Faustenau, P. S. (1996). Development and preliminary standardization of the "extended complex figure test" (ECFT). *Journal of Clinical and Experimental Neuropsychology, 18*, 63–76.

Heilman, K., & Valenstein, E. (2003). *Clinical neuropsychology*. Oxford University Press.

Hooper, H. E. (1983). *Hooper visual organization test manual*. Western Psychological Services.

Hubley, A. M., & Tremlay, D. (2002). Comparability of total score performance on the Rey-Osterrieth complex figure and a modified Taylor complex figure. *Journal of Clinical and Experimental Neuropsychology, 24*, 370–382.

Loring, D. W., & Meador, K. J. (2003). The medical college of Georgia (MCG) complex figures: Four forms for follow-up. In J. Knight & E. Kaplan (Eds.), *Rey-Osterrieth handbook*. Odessa.

Taylor, L. B. (1979). Psychological assessment of neurosurgical patients. In T. Rasmussen & R. Marino (Eds.), *Functional neurosurgery*. Raven.

Chapter 11
Frontal Lobe/Executive Functioning

James G. Scott and Michael R. Schoenberg

Key Points and Chapter Summary

- Frontal lobes include a large area of the cortex and are involved directly or indirectly in most brain functions involving cognition, behavioral and motor skills
- Frontal lobe damage can have profound effects on attention, memory, language, problem-solving/reasoning and general comportment (personality/social behaviors, etc.)
- Frontal lobe damage can be grouped into three syndromes determined by anatomical regions involved and associated with characteristic cognitive, behavioral and/or mood symptoms: (1) Dorsolateral, (2) Orbitofrontal and (3) Medial frontal syndromes
- Behavioral and personality changes are often the most profound change seen in frontal lobe injuries and are not well measured by standardized tests
- Cognition may be minimally impaired on standardized tests administered in controlled environments that minimize distraction and maximize motivation, particularly on tests which emphasize previously acquired knowledge

J. G. Scott (✉)
Department of Psychiatry and Behavioral Sciences, University of Oklahoma, Health Sciences Center College of Medicine, Oklahoma City, OK, USA
e-mail: jim-scott@ouhsc.edu

M. R. Schoenberg
Departments of Psychiatry and Neurosciences, Neurology, and Neurosurgery, University of South Florida College of Medicine, Tampa, FL, USA
e-mail: jim-scott@ouhsc.edu

M. R. Schoenberg, J. G. Scott (eds.), *The Little Black Book of Neuropsychology*,
https://doi.org/10.1007/978-3-032-07777-6_11

Anatomy of the Frontal Lobes

The frontal lobes represent the cerebral cortex anterior of the central sulcus and account for 1/3 of the entire human neocortex and represent more than a third of the cortical surface. The frontal lobe has been described in multitude of systems and areas, but we will review the frontal lobes in terms of basic functional organizations. The frontal lobes can be divided into three broad categories: (1) primary motor cortex, (2) premotor and supplementary motor cortex and (3) prefrontal cortex (see Figs. 11.1, 11.2 and 11.3). The prefrontal cortex is often subdivided into three functional domains, although some authors report two prefrontal functional domains. The three traditional prefrontal domains are: (a) dorsolateral prefrontal, (b) orbitofrontal (inferior or ventral frontal lobe) and (c) the medial frontal/anterior cingulate. The prefrontal cortex derived its name because this area of the frontal lobe received inputs (afferent fibers) from the dorsomedial nucleus of the thalamus. The prefrontal cortex also has extensive afferent and efferent connections to the temporal, parietal and occipital lobes as well as reverberating (input and output) fibers to subcortical regions, including the basal ganglia, thalamus, hypothalamus and tegmentum. The prefrontal projects to, but does not receive input from, the basal ganglia. Combined, the frontal lobe has classically been divided into six functional subdivisions (considering Broca's area, a separate subdivision of the premotor/

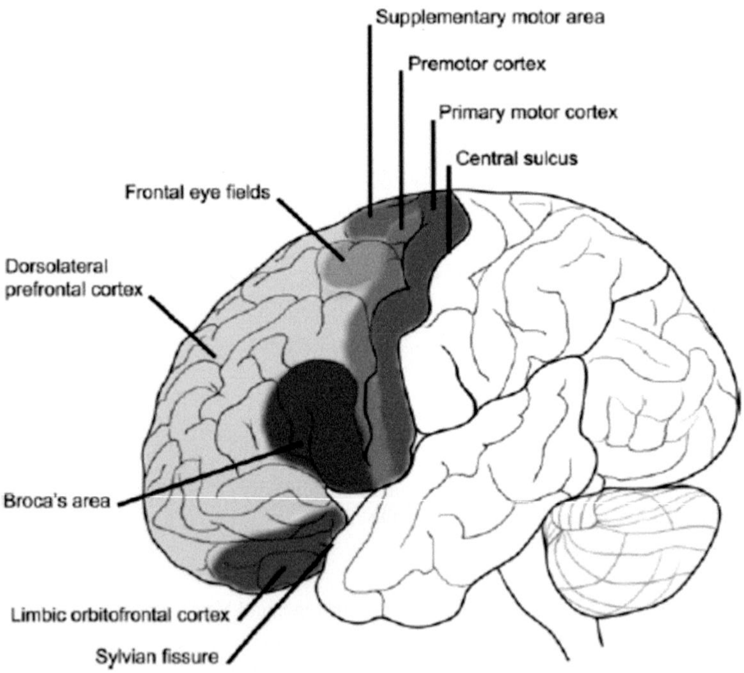

Fig. 11.1 Lateral view of the frontal lobe including primary motor, premotor, visual eye field, Broca's areas (Brodmann's area 44) and prefrontal region

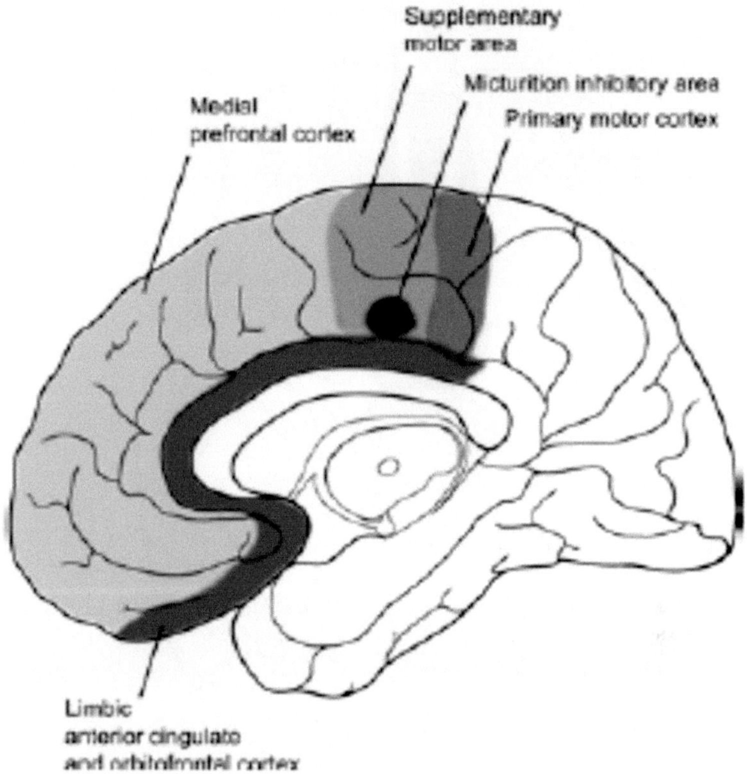

Fig. 11.2 Mesial view of the frontal lobe including primary motor, supplementary motor, micturition center and prefrontal cortex/anterior cingulate

supplementary area like the Frontal Eye Fields would yield seven subdivisions) (see Mesulam, 2000; Salloway et al., 2001, for reviews):

Below, we will briefly review the functional neuroanatomy of each subdivision, and how lesions of the frontal lobes may present symptomatically within each functional area, and conclude with an overview of neuropsychological assessment for frontal lobe functions.

Primary Motor Cortex

The primary motor cortex is the most posterior aspect of the frontal lobes (pre-central gyrus) and contains a motor "homunuclus" representing a somatotopic representation of motor function for the contralateral body that is upside down (e.g., head toward the temporal lobe while the trunk is near the superior convexity and the legs are represented within the medial aspect of the pre-central gyrus lying

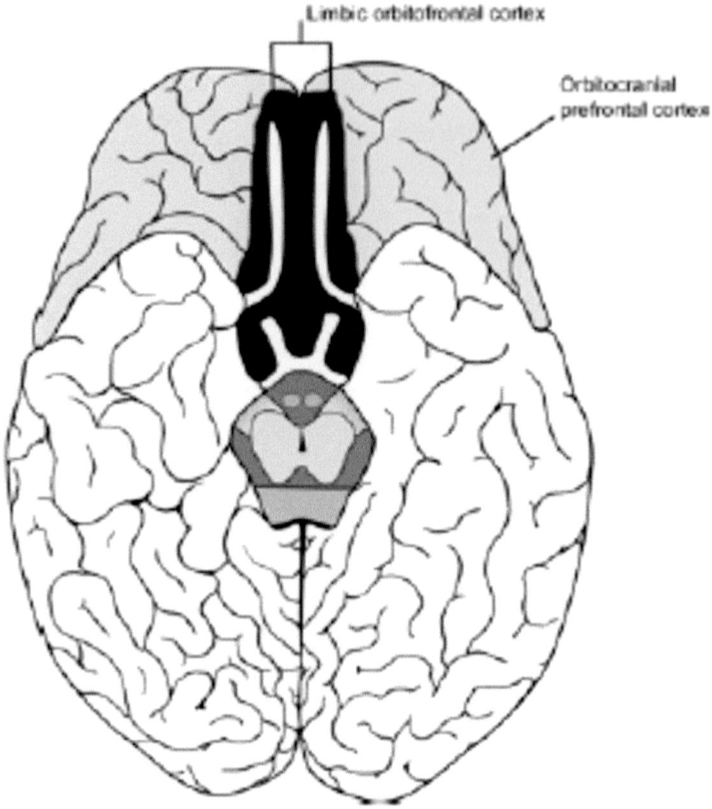

Fig. 11.3 Orbitofrontal (inferior frontal) view of the frontal lobe

within the interhemispheric fissure) (see Figs. 11.1, 11.2, 11.4, 11.5 and 11.6). The primary motor cortex is frequently termed the “motor strip” and is Brodmann’s area 6. The primary motor cortex has efferent projections to the spinal cord and cranial nerve nuclei as well as the basal ganglia and red nuclei, forming part of the corticospinal or corticobulbar tracts, respectively. The initiation of the corticospinal and corticobulbar tracts is the premotor cortex (see below and Chap. 3). The primary motor cortex receives input from the premotor/supplementary motor cortex areas.

Lesions involving the primary motor cortex will result in contralateral motor weakness. Initially, the motor weakness may present as a flaccid hemiplegia (complete lack of motor strength), but strength will often recover to some extent, particularly if premotor and supplementary motor areas are preserved. Larger lesions may resolve into a spastic hemiparesis and smaller lesions may resolve into incoordination and mild hemiparesis which can be difficult to identify without careful examination.

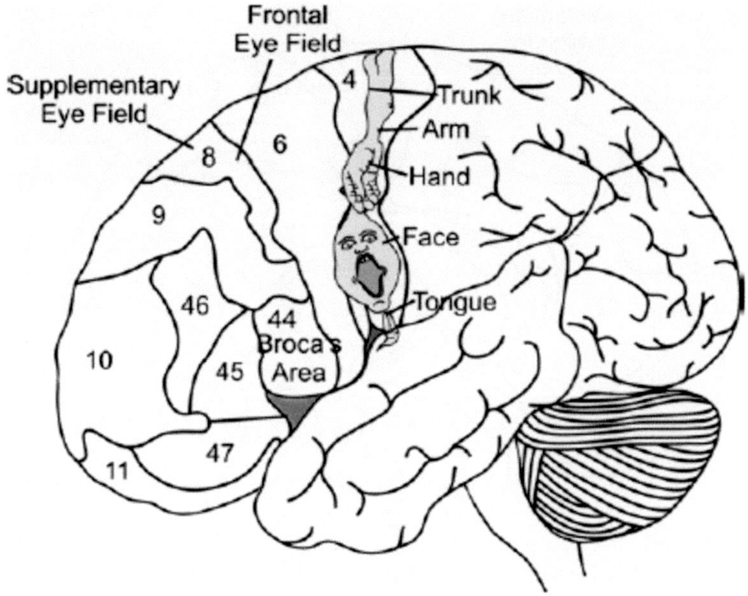

Fig. 11.4 Left dorsolateral prefrontal cortex including Brodmann's areas of dorsolateral cortex

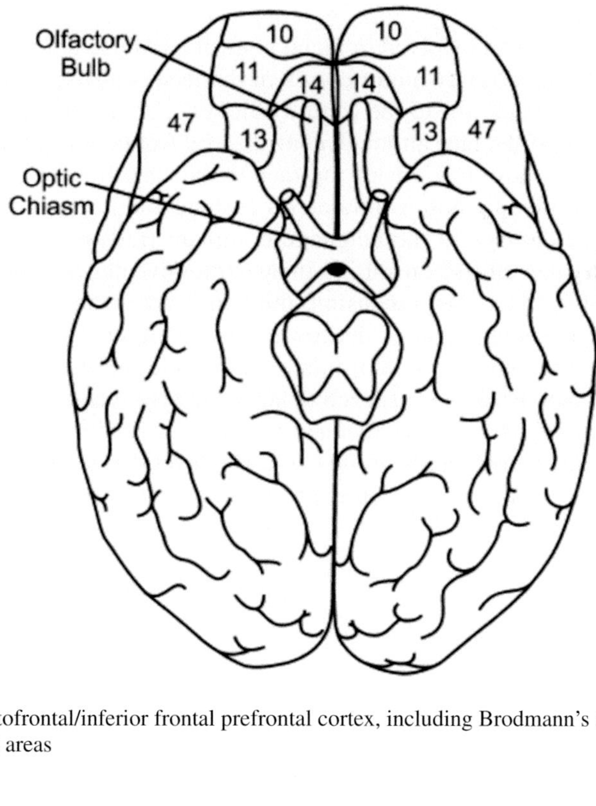

Fig. 11.5 Orbitofrontal/inferior frontal prefrontal cortex, including Brodmann's areas making up orbitofrontal areas

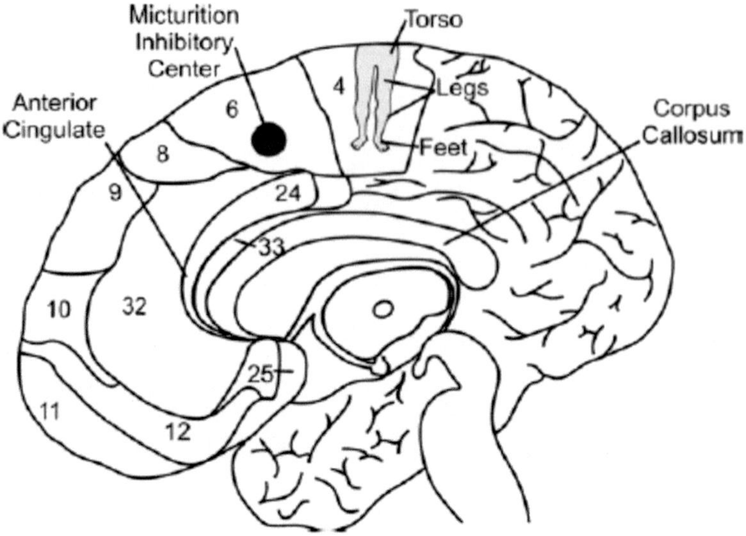

Fig. 11.6 Mesial frontal/anterior cingulate cortex including Brodmann's areas of the mesial frontal/anterior cingulate

Primary Facial Motor Cortex

The primary motor area involved in facial control has some unique aspects summarized below. The primary motor cortex of the face is just superior to the perisylvian fissure and anterior to the central sulcus. Each hemisphere controls the contralateral half of the face although contralateral frontal lobe injury may cause paresis of only the lower 2/3rds of the face (recall that the facial region above the eyes is controlled by both contralateral cortical and ipsilateral cranial nerve function). Focal damage to the language dominant (left) primary motor facial area is typically described as resulting in an expressive deficit (impaired expressive language but intact comprehension) thought to reflect an *oral apraxia*, along with contralateral hemiplegia of the lower face (Kolb & Whishaw, 2009). The oral apraxia is the inability to coordinate the muscle movements necessary for speech production. Expressive speech deficits can also include agraphia (inability to write), thought to reflect damage to the closely situated supplementary area for fine motor movements of the hand. However, focal lesions can result in an initial global aphasia (impaired expressive and receptive speech) (Salloway et al., 2001).

Key Points: Divisions of the Frontal Lobe
- Primary motor
- Premotor/supplementary motor
- Frontal eye fields
- Broca's area
- Prefrontal
- Dorsolateral
- Orbitofrontal
- Medial frontal/anterior cingulate

Premotor and Supplemental Motor

The premotor and supplemental motor cortex areas are involved in fine motor movements and sequenced motor movement such as writing or fastening buttons. The premotor and supplementary motor cortices lie just anterior to the primary motor cortex and include Brodmann's areas 6 and 8. While many areas of the brain are involved in producing smooth, coordinated motor movements (i.e., the cerebellum and basal ganglia; see Chap. 3 for more details), the unique aspect of the premotor/supplemental motor frontal cortex appears critical in two ways: (1) involved in acquiring novel motor skills which have not become overlearned, and (2) sequencing necessary motor movements in complex sequential motor tasks. The premotor/supplementary area has projections directly to the cortico spinal and corticobulbar tracts, but *primarily* has connections to and from the basal ganglia. There are also projections to the primary motor cortex and thalamus. In addition to basal ganglia and thalamus, premotor and supplementary motor cortices receive input (afferent tracts) from the parietal and dorsolateral cortex. Thus, premotor and supplementary motor areas are able to execute complex motor actions and continually adjust and fine tune motor activity. Perhaps a simplistic example is the motor movement necessary for learning to ride a bicycle. Initially, it takes much more conscious effort to focus on the motor movements necessary for balance, propulsion and steering. This motor movement is not initially automatic, and the sequence of balance, pedal and steer is difficult to master and initially requires substantial prefrontal resources. With experience, these motor and sequencing aspects evolve into an automatic sequence of motor skills resulting in a complex behavior. As this occurs, the premotor cortex is less involved and other areas of the brain (cerebellum, parietal cortex) are more involved.

Lesions to the premotor and supplementary motor areas 6 (not involving the frontal eye fields, area 8) typically will result in motor apraxias of the contralateral body/limb, and not hemiparesis. Individuals will also have difficulty synthesizing sensory information into complex motor movements, and complex motor sequencing will be incoordinated and may appear "choppy" or clumsy. However, simple motor movements remain fluid (not ataxic).

Key Points: Primary Motor Cortex

- Mediates contralateral motor movement
- Receives inputs from cerebellum, basal ganglia and supplemental motor cortex
- Projections form part of corticospinal and corticobulbar tracts
- Lesions produce contralateral motor weakness (hemiplegia or hemiparesis)
- Facial primary motor cortex is unique
  - Dominant hemisphere lesions cause expressive language features (oral apraxia) with long-standing residual deficits in: generative verbal fluency, phonemic awareness and spelling.

Broca's Area (Brodmann's Area 44 and 45)

Language production is also a function of the frontal lobes. For most individuals, the left lateral premotor area of the frontal lobe (i.e., Broca's area, Brodmann's area 44 and 45, see Chap. 3) controls expressive language. Lesions in this area can produce expressive aphasias or more subtle language impairment such as decreased verbal fluency and writing (see also Chaps. 8 and 13) or word-finding deficits (dysnomia). The right (nondominant) frontal lobe is less concerned with the actual production of speech, but rather contributes to expressive language *prosody* (see also Chaps. 8 and 13). Prosody refers to the vocal amplitude, tone and inflection that communicate nonsemantic meaning in vocal expressions such as emotion, questioning, confidence, lethargy, etc.

Lesions to Broca's area in the dominant hemisphere will result in loss of expressive speech. Depending upon the extent of damage, repetition may also be disrupted. Lesions to the nondominant hemisphere result in difficulties with expressive prosody (expressive aprosody, see Chaps. 8 and 13 for details). Briefly, speech may sound monotone to others. Several different patterns of aphasia have been identified and extensively studied. These are reviewed in detail in Chap. 13, see also Chap. 8.

Key Points: Pre-Motor and Supplementary Cortex

- Anterior to primary motor cortex
- Beginning of the corticospinal and corticobulbar tracts
- Involved in production of complex movements and motor programming
- Connections with basal ganglia, parietal cortex, primary motor cortex, thalamus and dorsolateral prefrontal cortex
- Lesions result in apraxias and discoordinated movement
- Broca's area, the expressive language center, in dominant hemisphere
- Frontal eye fields involved in volitional eye movements and visual attention

Frontal Eye Fields

The premotor cortex also includes a region referred to as the frontal eye fields, which are involved in voluntary eye movements and fixation of gaze important for novel visually guided activities and visual attention. The frontal eye fields direct visual focus to central elements in an environment that allows us to successfully execute sequences of behaviors. The frontal eye fields (Brodmann's areas 8 and 8A) are anterior to the primary motor cortex. This area of supplementary motor cortex has afferent and efferent tracts to regions of the brain important for controlling eye movements, including the posterior parietal regions and the superior colliculus. As a simplistic act of dressing illustrates, one must first search out articles of clothing, locate each in space, plan motor movement to get each article, manipulate each article prior to putting it on and then successfully execute dressing, including fastening, buttoning and zipping. While many of these behaviors can become automatic through overlearning and repetition, the frontal eye fields must direct vision to each aspect for a successful behavior to be completed. Contrast this simple example with the visual demands in extracting or debulking a tumor located in the frontal lobe of a patient and you quickly become aware of the demands placed on the frontal eye fields every day.

Prefrontal Cortex (Dorsolateral, Orbitofrontal and Medial Frontal/Cingulate Gyrus)

The dorsolateral, orbitofrontal (inferior or ventral frontal lobe) and medial frontal/cingulate gyrus (anterior portion) areas compose the prefrontal cortex. The prefrontal cortex comprised Brodmann's areas 8, 9, 10, 44, 45, 46 and 47 on the lateral side, Brodmann's areas 10, 11, 12, 13, 14 and part of 45 on the ventral (inferior) side and Brodmann's areas 8, 9, 10, 11, 13 and 32 on the mesial (medial) side (see Figs. 11.4, 11.5 and 11.6, respectively). These areas have been subdivided into various regions, most commonly; the dorsolateral, orbitofrontal (inferior or ventral frontal lobe) and medial frontal/cingulate gyrus (anterior portion) areas. Another classification scheme involves the anterior prefrontal, medial prefrontal and ventrolateral prefrontal regions. The roles and demarcations of these frontal lobe areas are less definitively agreed upon and more difficult to describe. Part of this difficulty arises from these functions being impaired or affected to differing degrees by injury to the frontal lobe cortex. These functions are often collectively referred to as "executive functions" and pertain to high level or complex aspects of cognitive, behavioral and emotional aspects of human behavior. These functions are necessarily complex and dependent on integration with many regions of the brain. The proceeding description will necessarily be general and intended to give examples of the frontal lobe influences on these cognitive, behavioral and emotional aspects of frontal lobe functions. Table 11.1 summarizes the role of the frontal lobes.

Table 11.1 Frontal lobe and executive functions

Domain	Region	Deficit
Motor	Left motor strip	Right gross, fine and coordination motor deficits
	Right motor strip	Left gross, fine and coordination deficits
	Left premotor	Poor contralateral sequencing and novel motor acquisition skills
	Right premotor	Poor contralateral sequencing and novel motor acquisition skills
	Frontal eye field	Contralateral voluntary eye movement/coordination
Cognitive	Diffuse frontal	Attentional deficits in sustained and voluntary alternation of attentional focus. Secondary effects on learning and retrieval
	Posterior left frontal	Expressive language, naming, word finding, fluency
	Anterior left frontal	Verbal reasoning, verbal problem-solving, sequencing, reduced generative verbal fluency
	Posterior right frontal	Expressive prosody
	Anterior right frontal	Visuospatial reasoning, visual problem-solving, sequencing
Behavior/emotional	Orbital frontal	Disinhibition, poor social skills, impulsivity, hyperactivity, emotional overreactivity
	Dorsolateral frontal	Impaired problem-solving, concrete, environmental dependency (stimulus bound behaviors), perseveration, poor sequencing, lack of self-monitoring for errors and self-correction. Impaired memory with reduced working memory, poor memory for temporal sequence of events, poor retrieval strategies with intact recognition
	Medial frontal	Apathy, akinetic, mutism, leg weakness contralateral to lesion (may be bilateral). Abulia, apathy, socially disengaged, indifference, lack of initiation, emotionally underreactive with intermittent dysregulation

Symptoms of Frontal Lobe Dysfunction: The "Frontal Lobe" Patient

It is not uncommon for a health care provider to mention "oh, that individual is pretty frontal" or "that individual has a frontal lobe syndrome." But what does that mean, and how is that determined? We will begin the behavioral syndrome review of frontal lobe disease with an overview of more generalized or diffuse prefrontal dysfunction and then turn to a description of selected "Frontal Lobe Syndromes." Table 11.1 summarizes the predominant roles of the frontal lobes and associated deficits.

Prefrontal Cortices (General/Diffuse Symptoms)

Many cognitive functions are mediated either directly or indirectly by the frontal lobes (dorsal lateral, medial and orbital cortex) (see Kolb & Whishaw, 2009; Lezak et al., 2004; Mesulam, 2000; Salloway et al., 2001, for reviews). An overriding function involves many voluntary aspects of attention. Specifically, the ability to attend to relevant aspects of our environment and inhibit being distracted by incidental environmental stimuli is an important cognitive function of the frontal lobes. Failure of this function often has devastating results for individuals and usually manifests as *tangentiality* or *circumloquaciousness* in language or distractibility in performing other tasks. The extent of the influence that voluntary attentional control can produce on other observed or measured skills should not be underestimated. In fact, voluntary attentional control is a prerequisite skill in everything from speaking to cooking and dressing. This function is frequently tested in terms of simple attention, sustained attention and voluntary rapid alternation of attention.

Environmental dependency (and *utilization behaviors*) can often be observed in patients with frontal lobe damage. Patients with environmental dependency respond in the usual way to a stimulus regardless of the appropriateness of the environmental situation. Environmentally bound behaviors can be initiated by an object, persons or situations. They may also be initiated by their own poorly inhibited thought processes. For example, patients may respond sexually to personnel who look at them and smile or respond angrily to personnel who make a request of them. Similarly, environmental cues such as the counter at a nursing station may solicit a patient to order auto parts because of its similarity to an auto parts store. Despite instruction not to shake an examiner's hand, this behavior can be elicited (hand shaking) by offering to shake the patient's hand. An internal trigger, such as a need to urinate, can elicit a patient to urinate in inappropriate social settings. *Utilization behaviors* are a subtype of environmental dependency, and reflect the spontaneous use of an object without apparent need or desire. Examples of utilization behaviors can often be easily initiated by having a hairbrush, toothbrush, pen/pencil, comb or cup/glass within reach of a patient with frontal lobe damage. Patients with utilization behaviors will, despite directions to not touch the items, reach out for the object(s) and begin using the object(s). For example, a patient may begin brushing his/her teeth without toothpaste or a sink or begin brushing his/her hair. Patients may "drink" from an empty cup or begin writing on a desk with a pen/pencil. These patients often demonstrate remorse for inappropriate behavior or verbal recognition of inappropriate behavior when their behavior is confronted, but will be unable to inhibit the behavior if the environmental trigger presents again.

Autonoetic awareness (Tulving, 2002) is a term to describe self-awareness which has been defined as the autobiographical temporal continuum which is able to affect behavior through one's past personal experiences and goals. Patients with prefrontal damage in general, but particularly those with orbitofrontal damage, frequently exhibit deficits in autonoetic awareness (self-awareness) such that they have difficulty with self-regulation of behavior. Patients are unable to reference behaviors to past experiences or goals.

Memory functioning can be adversely affected by lesions of the prefrontal cortex. These are reviewed within each frontal lobe functional domain below. However, a hemispheric difference in memory functions involving frontal lobe regions has been identified and termed *Hemispheric Encoding and Retrieval Asymmetry* (HERA; see Tulving et al., 1994). This model posits the left prefrontal cortex is more involved during encoding of episodic and semantic memory material and less involved during retrieval. The right prefrontal cortex (and insula and parietal cortices) is thought to be more involved in retrieval of episodic memory material.

Paratonia (*Gegenhalten)* may be found with bilateral frontal lobe damage. Paratonia is presentation of increasing muscle tone to oppose efforts to passively move the limb by someone else. This can often be misinterpreted as purposeful noncompliance. Paratonia (gegenhalten) is load- and velocity-dependent resistance, and is outside the control of the patient. While it may be found following bilateral diffuse frontal lobe lesions, it can also be present following bilateral basal temporal lobe damage and more diffuse brain damage, including dementias and encephalopathies.

Several *neuropsychiatric syndromes* are associated with frontal lobe damage. *Personality changes* are commonly reported, particularly with orbitofrontal damage but also with dorsolateral or medial frontal damage (see below). Orbitofrontal personality changes are frequently described as overactive/manic, uncaring, narcissistic and pleasure seeking. Commonly, these individuals are described as disinhibited and impulsive. Emotionally, patients generally have poor emotional regulation, but have a tendency to be overly reactive, in which their emotional response to a situation is often much greater than what might be anticipated or warranted. Individuals with orbitofrontal damage have also been labeled as *pseudopsychopathic* because of their personality changes noted above and apparent disregard for the feelings of others. Patients with dorsolateral or medial frontal damage may be perceived as indecisive, lazy, unmotivated, apathetic or passive. Some may be incorrectly described as "depressed." Indeed, the dorsolateral syndrome has been referred to as *pseudodepressive* or *apathetic* due to their appearance of indifference and abulia. Emotionally, patients with dorsolateral damage tend to exhibit a propensity toward emotional underreactivity with variability or fluctuations when they do become emotionally engaged. Frequently, these individuals will exhibit emotional dysregulation that fluctuates from indifference to overreaction. Patients with mesial frontal damage also exhibit indifference, but exhibit more akinetic qualities, in which these patients may just sit motionless for hours and be potentially mute. These individuals have been incorrectly diagnosed as having catatonic schizophrenia. Other neuropsychiatric syndromes associated with frontal lobe damage include *reduplicative paramnesia* and *Capgras syndrome*. Reduplicative paramnesia is the delusion that a place or an object (clothes, furniture, house, food, etc.) has been exactly duplicated. Capgrass syndrome is the "imposter" delusion, such that the patient believes a person (or persons) has (have) been duplicated, and the person claiming to be the person is an imposter.

Finally, several frontal lobe reflexes (or release signs) normally present in infants are considered pathological in adult patients. While typically not present in adults, some of the reflexes may be present and the presence of one should be interpreted as pathognomic of frontal lobe dysfunction. If frontal release signs are present, there likely is frontal lobe dysfunction. The frontal release signs include: Glabellar, Grasp, Palmomental, Root, Snout and Suck reflexes which are briefly described:

- *Glabellar reflex*. Failure to extinguish eye blink response to gentle tapping to the glabellar muscle in the center of the forehead right above the nose.
- *Grasp reflex*. Perhaps the most helpful frontal release sign, as it is fairly specific of frontal lobe injury and has localizing value to the contralateral supplementary motor area located in the medial frontal lobe. The grasp reflex occurs when the hand grasps onto an object (or examiner's finger). It is elicited by stroking the inside palm in a distal motion toward the base of the fingers. One may also stroke the proximal surface of the fingers (toward the palm). The grasp can be quite strong, allowing the person's torso to be lifted up from a lying position. Release may be voluntary or in some cases, takes considerable effort to release.
- *Palmomental reflex*. Ipsilateral contraction of the muscle of the chin (mentalis muscle) occurring to an unpleasant stimulus of the thenar eminence (body of the palm just proximal to the thumb). The ipsilateral corner of the mouth may also contract. The stimulus eliciting the reflex is started at the lower wrist and up the base of the thumb. The stimulus can be a tongue depressor or the handle of a reflex hammer.
- *Root reflex*. The turning of the patient's head ipsilateral to the side of the cheek that is lightly stroked. It is associated with the suck reflex in its adaptability for infants to breast feed.
- *Snout reflex*. The puckering of the lips to make a "snout" when the top lip is gently tapped (percussed). Typically, the Snout reflex can be elicited by gently tapping on the center of the upper lip when the lips are closed with your finger.
- *Suck reflex*. Sucking movements of the lips when the lips are generally stroked or touched. The sucking movement can be elicited by stroking the upper or lower corners of the mouth.

Key Points: Frontal Lobe Reflexes

- Frontal lobe reflexes are normal in very young children and are suppressed through development
- Frontal lobe reflexes are often seen in acute injuries or in severely impaired patients, but may not be seen in sub-acute populations or less severely impaired patients who continue to have cognitive, behavioral or motoric frontal lobe symptoms

Following a brief review of symptoms reflecting more generalized or diffuse dysfunction, we will review the traditional three prefrontal syndromes: (1) dorsolateral, (2) orbitofrontal and (3) medial frontal. Another viewpoint that specifies two frontal lobe syndromes: (a) *syndrome of frontal abulia* and (b) *syndrome of frontal disinhibition* (e.g., Mesulam, 2000) will be reviewed as well. The syndrome of frontal abulia has been associated with the dorsolateral frontal lobe syndrome while the syndrome of frontal disinhibition collapses the orbitofrontal and medial frontal syndromes together, as features of both are often observed in a patient (Mesulam, 2000).

Key Points: Frontal Lobe Syndromes

- Dorsolateral damage = Dysexecutive syndrome also pseudodepressed syndrome
  - Poor problem-solving, abulia/amotivational, perseverative, stimulus bound
- Orbitofrontal (inferior/ventral frontal) = Disinhibited/pseudopsychopathic syndrome
  - Disinhibited, emotional lability, impulsivity, lack of social graces, personality changes, poor smell discrimination
- Medial frontal/cingulate gyrus = Akinetic/apathetic syndrome
  - Akinetic, amotivation, mute (if bilateral), leg weakness, urinary incontinence

Frontal Lobe Syndromes: Traditional Three (3) Syndrome Model

The three traditional frontal lobe regions have neuroanatomical connections to discrete areas of shared basal ganglia and thalamic nuclei structures. Each of the three systems have segregated tracts, but operate in parallel and have multiple areas where input and output of each region is directed to other parts of the prefrontal cortex and brain. The three systems are thought to process distinct cognitive and emotional information incorporating multiple sensory and motor information from other brain regions.

Dorsolateral Prefrontal (Dysexecutive or Frontal Convexity) Syndrome

Patients often appear distractible, apathetic and "depressed," but also have difficulty reasoning, problem-solving, shifting attention and maintaining a behavior for completion of a task (impersistence). Patients may exhibit environmental dependency and memory problems. The memory problems (detailed below) often reflect difficulty remembering the temporal sequence of when events occurred (as opposed to forgetting something occurred altogether). Learning rate is often slow, and the patient may not remember some things due to reduced working memory/attention but also reduced retrieval. Depending upon extent of lesion, motor weakness of the upper extremity contralateral to the lesion may be present.

Sequencing, problem-solving and reasoning are impaired. The patient can have considerable difficulty with three-step motor sequencing along with sequencing figures or shapes (see Appendix). Problem-solving and reasoning are concrete, but tend to be worse with divergent reasoning (reasoning that requires many possible solutions or answers) than convergent reasoning (drawing similarities or solutions from two or more things). For example, patients would have problems listing the uses for a brick. Besides the obvious use for construction, other uses might include a door stop, stepping stones, hammer, a paper weight, an exercise tool, etc. While many frontal lobe patients have difficulty with divergent reasoning, fewer problems may be found on the convergent reasoning tasks on many intelligence tests. Patients with dorsolateral damage have difficulty solving problems that require sequential steps for problem resolution. Failure reflects difficulty selecting the series of appropriate steps to reach a problem resolution. Their responses in such situations are often simplistic and fail to appreciate the complexities involved in the situation. For example, a patient discovering his/her refrigerator has quit working may recognize the need to have it repaired, but will not spontaneously appreciate the need to use, relocate or otherwise dispose of the contents. The patient will, however, answer correctly when prompted about the contents.

Insight and judgment are often poor. Individuals typically do not appreciate the depth or extent of their cognitive compromises. While patients are able to appreciate or recognize direct failure, they have a diminished capacity to appreciate the degree or extent of their deficits and anticipate the impact it is likely to have on their future performance despite previous failure. This often leads to an astonishing repetition of attempts and failures that are resistant to making appropriate adjustments to future attempts. They may exhibit perseveration or difficulty switching sets when they become engaged. Alternatively, persistence in completing a task (particularly one they are not interested in for themselves) can be reduced, especially when distracters are present in the environment. As an example, a patient spouse may say the patient will start a task if asked, but will get easily distracted and will not finish the task unless repeated requests and redirection to complete the task are given. Patients often exhibit environmental dependency. Verbal output is often reduced, and phrase length is typically shorter.

Memory can be worsened due to the disruption of several systems involved in learning and memory. First, working memory may be reduced and the patient more distractible. Working memory reflects two general processes, the maintenance of information in an attentional "store" and, the ability to manipulate this "online" material. Second, strategies for active learning and efficient encoding and retrieval may be disrupted. Third, memory for facts or events may be out of temporal sequence. Memory encoding of unrelated material is often poor, exhibiting a reduced learning curve. Spontaneous recall is often impaired, particularly for material not semantically (contextually) organized. Alternatively, encoding of material provided to the patient already semantically (contextually) organized that makes sense to the patient can improve encoding and retrieval. Recognition cues often improve recall. However, the temporal organization of memory is frequently disrupted. Thus, patients may remember something happening a month ago as occurring yesterday. While the recall of events and situations may be perfectly reasonable, review of the patient's medical chart and/or report from a reliable collateral informant (spouse, adult child, friend, etc.) will quickly identify the poor temporal organization of memory.

Patients frequently appear to be emotionally blunted, apathetic and abulic (hence the term "pseudodepressed"). However, when emotionally aroused, patients often exhibit difficulty regulating emotional expression, appearing to both over-and underreact to various situations. Patients will not be as behaviorally disinhibited as patients with orbitofrontal syndrome; they demonstrate attentional and initiation deficits that are no less impairing.

This presentation may reflect the dorsolateral (dysexecutive or frontal convexity) syndrome. Because of prominent deficits in problem-solving, reasoning and switching sets, this is known as the dysexecutive syndrome. It has also been termed the pseudodepressed syndrome due to patients often exhibiting apathy and abulia.

Anatomy: The dorsolateral cortex is anterior to the premotor and supplementary cortices and is also termed the frontal convexities, and includes Brodmann's areas 9 and 46 (see Fig. 11.4). Some also include the lateral aspects of Brodmann's area 10 (the anterior prefrontal or frontopolar region). This area of the cortex predominately has reciprocal projections from the posterior parietal and superior temporal sulcus. The dorsolateral prefrontal area also projects to the basal ganglia, thalamus, cingulate gyrus and superior colliculus. The dorsolateral frontal region projects to the dorsolateral caudate nucleus which projects to the lateral and medial globus pallidus, which projects to the dorsomedial and ventral anterior thalamic nuclei and back to the prefrontal cortex. Note the dorsolateral cortex does not receive inputs from the striatum directly, but rather projections from the thalamus. The dorsolateral prefrontal areas are involved in complex human cognitive and behavioral functions for making decisions, problem-solving, sequencing and organizing behaviors. It is also associated with some attention and memory functions.

Causes of damage to the dorsolateral cortex are often the result of blunt trauma, occlusion of the anterior branch of the middle cerebral artery (or hemorrhage of ACA or MCA affecting the frontal convexities), and some neurodegenerative diseases (frontotemporal dementias). Frontal lobe tumors may also affect this area.

Key Points: Dorsolateral Frontal Lobe Damage = Dysexecutive syndrome

- Poor problem-solving (concrete and rigid)
- Poor organizational strategies
- Impaired set-shifting, perseveration and impersistence
- Memory may be disrupted
  - Reduced working memory, encoding/retrieval strategies and temporal organization (order). Retrieval improved with recognition cues.
- Apathy and psychomotor slowing. Poor motivation/abulia
- Decreased emotional range. May appear uncaring or emotionally unresponsive
- Contralateral upper extremity weakness

Orbitofrontal (Disinhibited/Pseudopsychopathy) Syndrome

Patients with lesions differentially affecting the orbitofrontal (the inferior or ventral surface of the frontal lobe) region will appear disorganized, behaviorally disinhibited, impulsive and overactive and often display emotional dysregulation. These individuals often demonstrate impulsivity and poor inhibition of behavior including inappropriate sexual behavior, inability to inhibit verbal outbursts and socially improper behavior. These individuals appear to have little empathy for others and will say and do things which may (at worst) appear as purposeful efforts to hurt the feelings of others and (at best) appear uncaring. Patients may start new (or re-initiate) bad habits or addictive behaviors (e.g., start smoking, drinking, gambling) and may break social rules and norms to attain desired reinforcers. Research has found basic functional distinctions between the lateral and medial orbitofrontal areas. Lateral orbitofrontal regions are associated with the evaluation of punishment which leads to changes in behavior. Medial orbitofrontal regions are associated with the evaluation of reinforcers (primary or secondary) including the learning and memory for the reward value of reinforcers. In addition, a posterior and anterior distinction has also been made, such that the anterior orbitofrontal area is more involved in evaluation of more complex (secondary) reinforcers (such as money, social recognition, etc.) whereas the posterior orbitofrontal regions are more associated with primary reinforcers (e.g., gustatory).

Patients with orbitofrontal damage often exhibit poor judgment, and their behaviors are often governed by seeking reinforcers (often to extremes) and faulty reasoning initiated by environmental cues such as an object, person or situation. These patients often demonstrate remorse for inappropriate behavior or verbal recognition of inappropriate behavior when their behavior is confronted. They tend to be hyperverbal and have difficulty with sustained attention. These individuals have little insight into how their behavior may affect others.

Memory functions are *not* consistently disrupted with lesions restricted to the orbitofrontal area. However, memory is often disrupted *if* damage includes the basal forebrain structures/septum, such that patients exhibit a classically described dense amnesia (Irle et al., 1992; Zola-Morgan & Squire, 1993). Thus, damage restricted to the orbitofrontal region does *not* produce traditional memory impairment, which occurs when basal forebrain/septal structures are involved (Irle et al., 1992; Zola-Morgan & Squire, 1993). The amnesia occurring with septal damage includes both antegrade and a temporally graded retrograde amnesia (see Chap. 9). Encoding is reduced due to poor attention. Learning rate is often deficient with a flat learning curve. Episodic memory is generally impaired, but recall of various events may appear (incorrectly) to be quite vivid reflecting confabulation. This confabulation does not appear to be a purposeful attempt to deceive, and is outside the person's awareness. That is, the examiner should not believe he/she has been purposely deceived by a patient with basal forebrain/septal damage.

Patients with lesions restricted to the orbitofrontal regions may perform normally on most traditional neuropsychological tests. Frequently, behavioral observation and report from reliable informants can provide needed information. However, patients do exhibit more risk-taking behaviors are less likely to adjust their behavior to feedback and perform poorly on tasks of behavioral disinhibition/emotional regulation (e.g., Frontal Systems Behavior Scale; FrSBe, Grace & Malloy, 2001) and modulation of reward-related behaviors (i.e., Iowa Gambling test; Bechara et al., 2000).

The orbitofrontal area (and superior temporal sulcus) is important when individuals make judgments about others' personality characteristics based on their physical characteristics (Winston et al., 2002). Patients with ventral medial (orbitofrontal) lesions (right more than left) have difficulty appreciating deception (Stuss et al., 2001; Rowe et al., 2001).

Emotionally, patients with orbitofrontal dysfunction may exhibit difficulty regulating emotional expression when emotionally aroused and appear to overreact emotionally at various times. Individuals may present with a "hollow" jocularity termed *Witzelsucht*. This presents as an inappropriate humor and/or laughing, often with the patient making inappropriate jokes about self or others. Another common feature of the orbitofrontal syndrome is *anosmia* (or, more correctly, lack of smell discrimination). Because patients often exhibit disinhibition, impulsivity, hyperactivity, lack of insight or empathy for others, emotional lability and distractibility, predominant damage to the orbitofrontal cortex has been called the disinhibited or pseudopsychopathic syndrome.

Anatomy: The orbitofrontal lobe (i.e., the entire ventral or inferior surface of the frontal lobes) incorporates Brodmann's areas 10, 11, 12, 13 and 14, and has been further subdivided into several specific functional regions termed the lateral and medial orbitofrontal areas (see Fig. 11.5). The orbitofrontal area is very complex and has connections with areas throughout the brain including all sensory modalities as well as limbic structures. The main connections are from the temporal lobe (superior temporal cortex, inferior temporal cortex and amygdala) as well as parietal lobe (somatosensory cortex), insula (gustatory cortex) and pyriform (olfactory) cortex. There are also connections to the medial temporal lobe structures, cingulate gyrus, thalamus (medial dorsal and intralaminar nuclei) and hypothalamus. Projections of the orbitofrontal area to the hypothalamus and amygdala allow this area to influence the autonomic nervous system. The orbitofrontal area is implicated in a vast array of cognitive, emotional and somatosensory functions, such as behavioral inhibition, emotional regulation, social cognition, memory and smell discrimination (Frith & Frith, 2003; Lezak et al., 2004; Mesulam, 2000; Siegal & Varley, 2002). Social cognition is an important aspect of behavior, allowing one to interact in complex social networks. An important aspect to social cognition is the ability to appreciate or attribute the mental perspectives to other people, termed *Theory of Mind* (ToM) (Frith & Frith, 2003; Siegal & Varley, 2002; Stuss et al., 2001). Neuroanatomic organization for ToM has been purported to involve amygdala, temporo-parietal junction, orbitofrontal and medial frontal regions. While theory of mind (appreciate mental perspectives of others) was thought to be particularly mediated by medial frontal function (e.g., Frith & Frith, 2003; Siegal & Varley, 2002), other data argue the medial frontal lobes are not involved (Bird et al., 2004). We include social cognition and appreciation of others' mental function here, rather than medial frontal lobe (below), because some recent data do not support the involvement of the medial frontal lobe.

Lesions to the orbitofrontal area is often *not* limited to one focal area, but rather the typical causes of damage to the orbitofrontal area tend to result in diffuse damage to the inferior and ventral frontal lobe areas. The subcortical basal forebrain as well as the medial frontal lobe areas can also be affected. Thus, patients may also present with features of the medial frontal (akinetic-apathetic) syndrome detailed below. Damage is often caused by acceleration-deceleration closed head traumatic brain injuries (which often also affect the anterior temporal lobes as well), neurodegenerative diseases (frontotemporal dementias), brain tumor and/or hemorrhagic stroke of an aneurysm of the ACoA (anterior communicating artery) or an ACA (anterior cerebral artery).

Key Points: Orbitofrontal (Inferior/Ventral) Frontal Lobe Damage = Disinhibited or Psycheduopsychopathic Syndrome

- Disinhibited
  - Hyperactive, intrusive, pressured behavior
- Poor impulse control
  - Loss of social insight, poor situational awareness
- Distractible
  - Focus on single thing and unable to selectively guide attention away from competing stimuli
- Emotional lability/emotional dysregulation
  - Septal/basal forebrain damage can result in amnesia with confabulation

Medial Frontal (Akinetic/Apathetic) Syndrome

Patient symptoms of medial frontal lobe damage often include akinesia, lethargy, not spontaneously initiating behavior, and can appear indifferent to painful stimuli. Memory can be severely disrupted, with a dense antegrade amnesia. Bilateral lesions can result in an akinetic and mute state. Unilateral lesions often result in an incomplete akinetic state, with the patient regaining some self-initiated behaviors. Left medial frontal lesions affecting the anterior cingulate can present with features of a transcortical motor aphasia. Patients with medial frontal lesions often lack insight or awareness and frequently are described as having decreased arousal in general. These patients will often not initiate behavior or speech themselves. In some cases, these patients will be observed to remain in postures likely to be extremely uncomfortable for prolonged periods without complaint or attempt to change positions. Urinary and bowel incontinence can be present, and patients exhibit little concern about the incontinence, making little effort to clean themselves unless given prompt(s).

Memory functions can be severely disrupted (e.g., Bird et al., 2004), reflecting damage to septal region/basal forebrain structures sometimes affected by more extensive orbitofrontal lesions. Memory impairment associated with medial frontal (akinetic-apathetic) syndrome is an amnesia with antegrade as well as a temporally graded retrograde amnesia (see Chap. 8). Encoding is poor and the patient often exhibits a flat learning curve. Episodic memory is generally impaired. Some semantic and nondeclarative memory may be intact. Confabulation is frequently present. Like confabulation associated with more extensive orbitofrontal damage, confabulation is not purposeful and lacks intent to purposefully deceive the examiner.

Patients with mesial frontal/anterior cingulated damage often demonstrate restricted emotional responses and appear disengaged from their environment. Individuals may exhibit little (no) interest in family or friends, exhibiting indifference and apparent lack of concern. Generally, patients will appear dull and unmotivated, but may respond if requested to perform specific behaviors. Patients may exhibit lower extremity weakness contralateral to the side of the lesion (bilateral leg weakness if damage was bilateral). If the corpus callosum is damaged, the patient may also exhibit the so-called alien hand syndrome if the dominant hemisphere is affected. The left extremities may not be under the volitional control of the patient, and the left hand may reach for objects and/or explore the immediate environment outside the apparent control of the patient.

Anatomy: The medial frontal cortex includes the cortex between the two frontal hemispheres, anterior to the primary motor strip, which includes the anterior portion of the cingulate gyrus and includes Brodmann's areas 24, 25 and 32 (see Fig. 11.6). This area of the cortex has connections with the temporal cortices, particularly the amygdala (anterior cingulate) and hippocampus (more posterior cingulated) along with the hypothalamus. Reciprocal connections are with lateral prefrontal cortex (Brodmann's areas 8, 9, 10 and 46), orbitofrontal cortex (Brodmann's area 47), parahippocampal gyrus, amygdala, insula and claustrum. Afferent projects are from entorhinal and perirhinal cortex and hippocampus, thalamus and tegmentum. Projections are also to substantia nigraars compacta, subthalamic nucleus, hypothalamus, globus pallidus and thalamus. This area of the brain is implicated in attention, behavioral inhibition, initiation and motivation, motor function (lower extremities), social cognition, including theory of mind, memory, mood and autonomic (visceral) systems (e.g., Frith & Frith, 2003; Lezak et al., 2004; Mesulam, 2000: Siegal & Varley, 2002; Stuss et al., 2001).

Key Points: Medial Frontal Lobe Damage = Akinetic/Apathetic Syndrome

- Akinetic and apathetic
- Little initiation of movement or speech
- Lack of interest and indifference
- Emotional blunting
- Memory can be impaired (amnesia with confabulation)
- Incontinence (bladder and sometimes bowel)
- Leg weakness

Prefrontal Syndromes: Two Syndromic Model

Below, we briefly review a two syndromic model of prefrontal syndromes: (1) syndrome of frontal abulia and (2) syndrome of frontal disinhibition (e.g., Mesulam, 2000).

(a) *Syndrome of Frontal Abulia*. This syndrome description is the same for that of the dorsolateral frontal lobe syndrome. Generally, patients exhibit poor problem-solving, concrete reasoning, stimulus bound behaviors, lack of creativity, reduced (or no) initiative, apathy and emotional blunting. Patients have difficulty planning and sequencing activities and exhibit deficits in strategic decision-making in light of anticipated consequences for making various decisions.

(b) *Syndrome of Frontal Disinhibition*. This syndrome description reflects the fact that frontal lobe damage to the orbitofrontal area often also involves some aspects of the medial frontal lobe and basal forebrain, resulting in a general pattern of behavioral disinhibition, behavioral impulsivity, lack of judgment, reduced insight and foresight and inability to delay gratification. Like orbitofrontal syndrome patients, the syndrome of frontal disinhibition may also include increased energy level and emotional reactivity. The individual's sleep–wake cycle can be disrupted, and they may not exhibit remorse for their behavior.

Bedside Assessment of Frontal Lobe Functions

General Assessment Issues

Frontal lobe damage can produce a range of deficits from subtle to grossly overt. The complexity of the frontal lobe involvement in many tasks both directly and indirectly means that their effect cannot only run the gamut from noticeable only to those who knew the patient well, to obvious to everyone in the environment but can also include functions which have an impact on other cognitive areas. For example, impairment in frontal lobes can produce simple, sustained and complex voluntary attention deficits which in turn have a discernable impact on seemingly unrelated tasks as object naming, copying a geometric figure or holding a conversation without becoming tangential or circumloquacious.

Assessment of frontal lobe functioning begins with good history taking and includes queries of both the patient and someone else who knows them well such as a parent, spouse, relative or friend. The content of this interview should include an assessment of changes in the cognitive, behavioral and emotional functioning noted previously in this chapter. This discussion should inquire directly about change in these areas as there is considerable naturally occurring variability in behavior, cognition and emotional expressiveness across individuals. Table 11.2 outlines areas of inquiring for frontal lobe assessment. It is important to gain collateral information on these functions, as patient awareness of the existence or extent of the change in these areas of functioning is frequently diminished. If changes are noted, it is often helpful to try to establish an estimate of how much change has occurred and the frequency with which it occurs. It may be informative to ask both patients and collateral informants to give an estimate of current performance using 100% as a baseline and estimating the current level of functioning relative to that baseline. When using this table, we ask patients and a caregiver to rate how much change (percent) has occurred in the areas noted in Table 11.2, and this is written down in the column "Frequency/Duration/Severity." This may also highlight the discrepancy between the patient's perception of change and the perceptions of others who know them well.

In addition to a history of change, many of the functions of frontal lobe deficits can be assessed bedside or informally in the outpatient clinic. While these techniques can yield important information, these functions can also be more precisely measured through formal, standardized, psychometrically evaluated means. The informal assessment of frontal lobe functions can often lead to the decision for referral or further formal assessment of frontal lobe functions identified or suspected to be impaired in the brief examination. Table 11.3 gives some examples of areas of assessment and assessment items.

Table 11.2 Interview assessment of frontal lobe changes

Area	Change	Frequency/ duration/severity[a]
Activity/energy	Hypoactive	
	Hyperactive	
Initiation	Hypo initiative (Abulic)	
	Disinhibited	
Social function	Decreased social skill	
	Social imperturbability	
	Social avoidance	
	Social disinhibition	
Emotional responsiveness	Overreactive	
	Underreactive	
	Rapidly variable	
Attention	Poor sustained attention	
	Difficulty switching attention	
	Perseveration	
Language	Disorganized	
	Unresponsive to questions asked	
	Lapses from attentional difficulty	
Memory	Increased variability/inconsistency	
	Poor detail recall	
	Difficulty with temporal order in recall	
Reasoning/ sequencing	Difficulty sequencing tasks such as cooking, repair or other frequent activities	
	Concrete understanding, inability to see from others perspective	
	Knows conceptually, but cannot problem-solve the solution, step or steps to resolve novel problem	

[a]Column can be used as part of a working guide to note (write down) extent of change in domains listed. We have used percentile change, ranging from no change (around zero%) to total change (10%) in that function/behavior. In some situations, it may be appropriate to not ask percent change, but rather a qualitative description, such as "no, small, medium or large" change in function has occurred

Motor and Sequencing Skills

Patients with frontal lobe damage often have difficulty with fine motor skills and sequencing motor skills. They may exhibit difficulty both with tasks requiring sustained rapid motor responses and sequenced, novel motor skills. Patients may also have difficulty with simple sequencing tasks, exhibiting perseveration. Patients can be asked to rapidly tap their thumb and index finger. They should be instructed to perform this after being shown the examiner performing the task. Observations should be made regarding their ability to sustain their fine motor speed for 15 s to ensure that there is no gross slowing or increasing rigidity as indicated by

Table 11.3 Verbal reasoning and cognitive flexibility assessment

Object pairs	Similarities	Differences
Dog–wolf	Canine	Domesticated–wild
	Social	Geographically widespread–restricted
	Physical characteristics (legs, fur)	Size variable–typically large
	Carnivores	Seeks human contact–avoids human contact
	Mammals	
	Multiple pups	
Shark–whale	Live in water	Size
	Alive (breath oxygen)	Fish–mammal
	Swim	Bones–cartilage
	Widespread	Lungs–gills
	Similar physical characteristics (i.e., fins, skin, organs, teeth)	Horizontal swimming motion–vertical swimming motion
House of representatives–senate	Part of congress	Population proportioned–two per state
	Legislative branch	2-year term–6-year term
	Elected	
	Represent constituencies	Many more representatives–100 senators
	Work at capital	Rules and procedures differ
	Pass bills	

Cognitive flexibility problems	Potential solutions
Refrigerator dysfunction	Check power supply
	Secure alternate food storage
	Call repairman
	Check breaker box/circuit breaker
	Inspect power cord, electrical outlet
	Check with neighbors about power supply
Pet behavior change	Check food supply
	Check for injuries
	Check temperature
	Recall past routine (diet, interactions, elimination)
	Inspect physically
	Call vet
	Call knowledgeable friend
	Offer desired object (treat, toy)
Object use alternatives	*Alternative uses*

(continued)

Table 11.3 (continued)

Cognitive flexibility problems	Potential solutions
Coat hanger	Hang clothes
	Probe
	Fastener
	Toothpick
	Guide wire
	Skewer
	TV antenna
	Open car door lock
	Holder, extender
	Sculpting
	Form for object (i.e., lampshade)
	Made into tongs or a rod for reaching/grabbing objects
	Scraping tool
Brick	Building material
	Water saver device for commode tank
	Message delivery system
	Door stop
	Paper weight
	Hammer
	Stepping stone
	Landscaping
	Art object
	Motor vehicle chock
	Speed bumps
	Self-defense

progressively smaller taps. A second task is to ask them to perform a novel three-step sequenced task (Luria's manual sequencing task) after being shown through modeling. In this case, the examiner places his hand on a table first making a fist, then with palm flat (slap), then on the side (i.e., Karate chop). Figure 11.7 illustrates these movements. The patient is asked to mimic this "fist–palm–side" sequenced movement. After success or failure with one hand, the other hand should be tested. While it is not unusual for some patients (especially elderly) to require repeated modeling to acquire the appropriate sequence, if more than two trials are necessary, a sequencing deficit should be suspected. The patient should be able to complete three complete motor sequences without error.

Rapid motor sequencing can be assessed by asking patients to rapidly alternate hands from palm up to palm down. The examiner asks the patient to observe him (the examiner) doing the task and then requests that the patient mimic the task. The examiner places both hands down on a surface (typically a table or top of legs if seated) and then alternatingly lifts and rotates each hand to be palm up and then palm down.

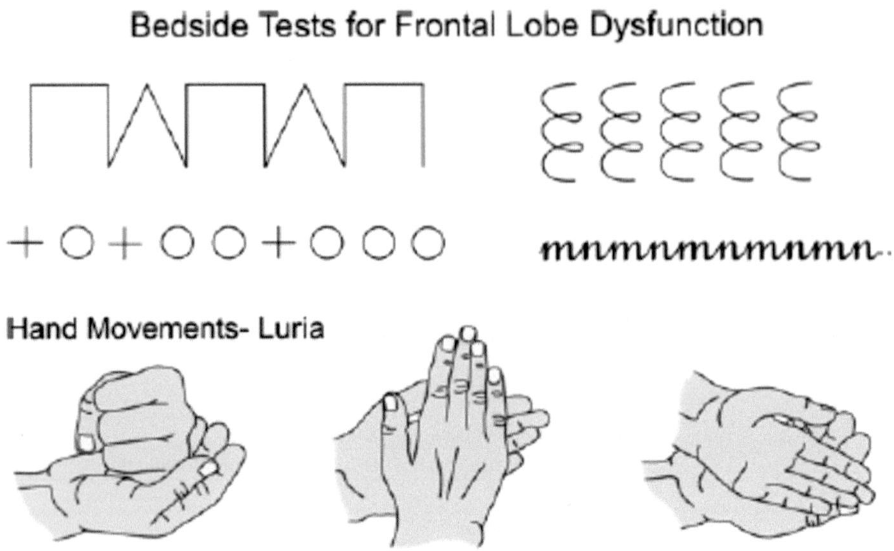

Fig. 11.7 Luria's figures and sequencing tasks. Figures from left to right include ramparts, repeating loops, alternating +'s with increasing O's and alternating cursive M's and N's

Each hand is rotated palm up and palm down and then the alternate hand is rotated. The alternate rotating is then increased in speed and should be sustained in rapid succession for 10–15 s. Patients should be expected to master the sequence of movements rapidly (one or two modeling trials) and be able to sustain the sequence for the duration of the task. If patients have difficulty, the examiner may try to teach the task by adding the verbal label, "all the way over, all the way back," to their demonstration to gauge if verbal cueing or prompting assists in acquiring or maintaining the task performance. If labeling the examiner's modeling of the behavior is unsuccessful, the examiner can take the patient's hands and rotate them and verbalize, "all the way over, all the way back," to see if kinetic cueing is effective in allowing them to master the task. In general, patients are expected to be able to rapidly master the task after being shown a demonstration. Failure to be able to perform rapid alternation or sustain rapid alternations over a 10- to 15-s timeframe should be considered an abnormal performance and reason for further psychometric investigation.

Key Points: Bedside Assessment

- Assess sustained attention with and without distraction
- Assess impulse control by conflicting verbal and behavioral gesture (i.e., say "Don't shake my hand" while simultaneously extending the hand)
- Assess perseveration by using repeating drawings such as loops or Ramparts
- Assess sequencing by asking patient to repeat three-step sequence or rapidly alternate hand movements

Perseveration and deficits in set-shifting may also be identified in having patients complete an alternating sequence such as ramparts (see Fig. 11.7) running half-way across the page. Frontal lobe patients often fail to alternate between rectangle and triangle (often with the patient perseverating making linked triangles or linked rectangles only). Similarly, an alternating pattern of cursive "m"s and "n"s can be used to elicit perseveration in frontal lobe patients (see Fig. 11.7). The patient is asked to complete the pattern, beginning where the examiner stopped. The task is evaluated based on the patient's ability to appropriately alternate and not repeat "m" or "n." A final task is for the examiner to draw (outside of the examinee's vision) a series of large figures with 3 loops each. The patient is asked to complete making the looped figures until reaching the end of the page. Failure reflects having more or less than exactly three loops making up each of the figures. It is not unusual for patients with frontal lobe damage to make the figures with successively more loops (see Fig. 11.7).

Assessing Attention Multiple aspects of attention can be impaired in frontal lobe patients (see also Chap. 6). They may have difficulty with simply attending to relevant stimuli in their environment without distraction, sustaining attention over time or in tasks which require them to switch voluntary attention rapidly. Simple attention can be evaluated by asking them to watch your finger as you move it slowly back and forth horizontally. They should be informed to keep their head still and track the examiner's finger with their eyes. This should be sustained for 15 s. The examiner can then add distraction to the task by prompting a discussion or purposefully diverting their gaze away from the patient. If the patient fails to maintain their voluntary gaze on the examiner's finger under either circumstance, the instructions can be repeated that the examiner wants them to maintain attention on the moving finger no matter what distractions are present. Patients with frontal lobe damage will often demonstrate difficulty with persistent voluntary attention and either lose attention to the task or have difficulty sustaining attention when confronted with verbal or visual competing stimuli in their environment.

Assessing Impulsivity/Disinhibition The ability to initiate or inhibit a behavior is integrally linked to frontal lobe integrity. Patients with frontal lobe injuries often demonstrate changes in their ability to spontaneously initiate appropriate behavior or inhibit the enacting of overlearned or high frequency behavior. These deficits are most frequently observed early in the course of traumatic or acute injuries and progressively worsen in degenerative diseases involving the frontal lobes. These behaviors can be tested in examination of the patient in several ways. Perhaps the easiest way is to use contradictory verbal commands and physical gesture. In such a circumstance, the examiner would tell the patient not to take an object or shake a hand that is offered. This is typically done by offering an object to the patient such as a pen, cup or paper while simultaneously telling them, "Don't take this." A patient who spontaneously takes the object should be asked to repeat what the instructions were and then given a second trial. Failure on a second trial would indicate difficulty with inhibiting the behavior. A second task which emphasizes a subtler disinhibition is referred to as the *go–no-go* task. In this task, the examiner first instructs the patient to hold up one finger when the examiner holds up one finger and hold up two fingers when the examiner holds up two fingers (checking for cooperation and sufficient motor/sensory function). Complete a minimum of two trials in random order of holding up one and then two fingers. Once this is mastered, the examiner then instructs patients to hold up two fingers when the examiner holds up one finger, and to display one finger when the examiner displays two fingers. The examiner displays alternating one and two fingers increasingly rapidly. The patient is evaluated on accuracy of their responses, the consistency of accuracy (i.e., can they maintain response set), how quickly they respond (should be decreasing delay as task is learned) and their spontaneous recognition and correction of errors. Once their responses have stabilized with several correct responses, the examiner randomly alternates holding up one or two fingers and assesses the patient's ability to respond correctly. This sequence of trials should include at least one series in which the same number of fingers is held up repeatedly to allow a habitual response to be established from the patient, at which point the number of fingers displayed by the examiner is switched and the patient's ability to suppress what had become an overlearned response can be gauged. To establish this overlearned response, four to five trials with display of the same number of fingers by the examiner are typically required. Patients are typically expected to make some errors early in learning this task, but quick mastery is expected. Rapid recognition and correction of errors is expected.

Abstract Reasoning Both verbal and nonverbal abstract reasoning can be impaired by frontal lobe injury. These patients tend to have greatest difficulty with divergent abstract reasoning tasks compared to relatively intact convergent reasoning. The conceptual difference between the two being the increased demand in divergent reasoning tasks to escape a single, sometimes concrete (right/wrong) answer of convergent reasoning and attempt to enact creative, multi-solution divergent solutions to a stated problem. Verbally, patients can be asked to list the similarities of a set of things and then be asked to list their differences. Both the similarities and differences should demonstrate an understanding of multiple ways the two are similar and different. The examiner can prompt for the other ways the objects are similar or different but should not provide answers. Examples that can be used may include a dog and a wolf, a shark and a whale, a house of representatives and a senate, a house and a hotel (see Table 11.3). The patient should be able to give 2–3 ways each pair is similar and different and be evaluated based on the quantity of responses, organization of responses and the quality of the explanation they can make for their answers. Again, frontal lobe patients would be expected to have difficulty with switching from similarities to differences and providing adequate number of responses and/or organization of responses. Patients can also be asked to state what they might do in a situation such as their refrigerator quits working or they notice that their pet's behavior changes. Responses should include recognition that these may have multiple causes and that they can be systematically ruled out but may ultimately require seeking additional help (see Table 11.3).

Key Points: Disrupted Functions Associated with Frontal Lobe

- Divergent reasoning more impaired than convergent reasoning
  - For example, test is to "tell me as many uses of a soda pop bottle"
- Poor inhibition
  - Impulsive. Unable to perform "go–no-go" task.
- Set-shifting and perseveration
  - Unable to sequence simple squares and triangles on a page or put three, and only three loops in a series of three looped "3"-shaped figures on a page

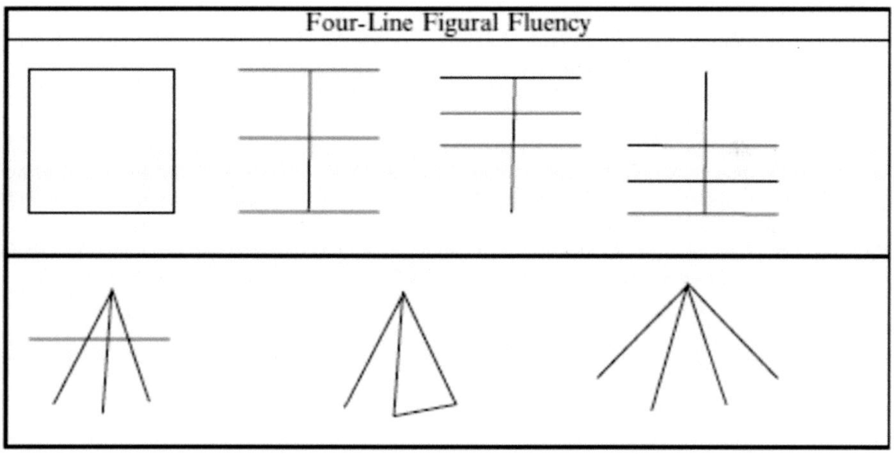

Fig. 11.8 Examples of solutions to a figural fluency task making at least six unique designs with four lines that touch

Visual divergent reasoning can be assessed either by asking the patient to creatively list as many uses for a common object such as a coat hanger, knife or brick or asked to draw as many shapes/designs using four straight lines of similar length that touch as possible. In the first task, the patient should be able to generate at least 3–4 nontraditional uses for each object. Responses are not judged for the quality of the object as a substitute for another purpose or object, but rather for the presence of divergent abstraction and creativity. For example, a brick might be used as a paper weight, a door stop, a water-saving (displacement device) device in a commode tank or an exercise device, etc. (see Table 11.3). In the latter task, patients could draw a sequence, two Xs, a series of crosses or a series of triangles with intersecting lines. Again, the quality of the designs should not be judged, but rather the diversity and number. Patients should be able to spontaneously draw 4–6 designs in less than a minute. Failures can be inquired as to what they found difficult about the task. Possible solution sets for a bedside figure fluency task is presented in Fig. 11.8.

References

Bechara, A., Tranel, D., & Damasio, H. (2000). Characterization of the decision-making deficit of patients with ventromedial prefrontal cortex lesions. *Brain, 123*, 2189–2202.

Bird, C. M., Castelli, F., Malik, O., Frith, U., & Husain, M. (2004). The impact of extensive medial frontal lobe damage on "theory of mind" and cognition. *Brain, 127*, 914–928.

Frith, U., & Frith, C. D. (2003). Development and neurophysiology of mentalizing. *Philosophical Transactions of the Royal Society of London. Series B, Biological Sciences, 358*, 459–473.

Grace, J., & Malloy, P. F. (2001). *Frontal systems behavior scale (FrSBe): Professional manual.* Psychological Assessment Resources.

Kolb, B., & Whishaw, I. (2009). *Fundamentals of human neuropsychology* (6th ed.). W.H. Freeman.

Lezak, M. D., Howieson, D. B., & Loring, D. W. (2004). *Neuropsychological assessment* (4th ed.). Oxford University Press.

Mesulam, M. (2000). *Principals of behavioral and cognitive neurology* (2nd ed.). Oxford University Press.

Rowe, A. D., Bullock, P. R., Polkey, C. E., & Morris, R. G. (2001). "Theory of mind" impairments and their relationship to executive functioning following frontal lobe excisions. *Brain, 124*, 600–616.

Salloway, S. P., Malloy, P. F., & Duffy, J. D. (2001). *The frontal lobes and neuropsychiatric illness.* American Psychiatric Publishing, Inc..

Stuss, D. T., Gallup, G. G., Jr., & Alexander, M. P. (2001). The frontal lobes are necessary for "theory of mind". *Brain, 124*, 279–286.

Tulving, E. (2002). Episodic memory: From mind to brain. *Annual Review of Psychology, 53*, 1–25.

Tulving, E., Kapur, S., Craik, F. I., Moscovitch, M., & Houle, S. (1994). Hemispheric encoding/retrieval asymmetry in episodic memory: Positron emission tomography findings. *Proceedings of the National Academy of Sciences of the United States of America, 91*, 2016–2020.

Winston, J. S., Strange, B. A., O'Doherty, J., & Dolan, R. J. (2002). Automatic and intentional brain responses during evaluation of trustworthiness of faces. *Nature Neuroscience, 5*, 277–283.

Chapter 12
Affect, Emotions and Mood

James G. Scott and Michael R. Schoenberg

> **Key Points and Chapter Summary**
> - Emotional disorders can be a direct or a secondary effect of neurologic disease
> - Diagnostic and Statistical Manual, fifth edition Text Revised (DSM-5-TR) and International Classification of Disease, tenth edition (ICD-10) are used to classify emotional disorders
> - Many neurologic disorders produce symptoms which resemble psychiatric conditions
> - It is critical to differentiate behavioral changes associated with neurologic disease from those associated with psychiatric disease because both the appropriate treatment and the prognosis may be different

While this Table 12.1 is not exhaustive, it covers the major categories which are the primary in DSM 5-TR. In neuropsychology and neurology, the most common diagnoses are often in the categories as major or minor neurocognitive disorders with accompanying etiology. Alternatively, many neuropsychologists and non-psychiatrist physicians use the International Classification of Disease, tenth edition

J. G. Scott
Department of Psychiatry and Behavioral Sciences, University of Oklahoma, Health Sciences Center College of Medicine, Oklahoma City, OK, USA
e-mail: jim-scott@ouhsc.edu

M. R. Schoenberg
Departments of Psychiatry and Neurosciences, Neurology, and Neurosurgery, University of South Florida College of Medicine, Tampa, FL, USA
e-mail: Mschoenb@health.usf.edu

M. R. Schoenberg, J. G. Scott (eds.), *The Little Black Book of Neuropsychology*,
https://doi.org/10.1007/978-3-032-07777-6_12

Table 12.1 Primary diagnostic categories for DSM-5-TR

Category	Description
Neurodevelopmental disorders	Intellectual developmental disorders. Communication disorders, autism spectrum disorder, attention deficit/hyperactivity disorder, specific learning disorders and motor disorders
Bipolar and related disorders Depressive disorders	Includes bipolar I and bipolar II disorder Includes major depressive disorder, premenstrual dysphoric disorder, persistent depressive disorder and depressive disorder due to medical condition
Anxiety disorders Obsessive-compulsive and related disorders	Includes generalized anxiety disorder, separation anxiety disorder, specific phobias, panic disorder, agoraphobia and anxiety due to a medical condition Includes obsessive-compulsive disorder, body dysmorphic disorder, hoarding disorder, excoriation disorder and OCD related to a medical condition
Substance-related disorders	Includes mental disorders that are related to intoxication, dependence or withdrawal of psychoactive substances such as alcohol, amphetamine, opioid or anxiolytics
Trauma and stressor related disorder	Includes a range of disorders marked by stress including PTSD, reactive attachment disorder, acute stress disorder, prolonged grief
Dissociative disorders	Includes disorders like dissociative identity disorder, dissociative amnesia
Somatic symptom and related disorders	Includes disorders which are marked by an excessive concern of physical dysfunction such as somatic symptom disorder (specify symptom), illness anxiety disorder, functional neurologic symptom disorder (specify symptoms) and factitious disorder (self or other imposed).
Feeding and eating disorders	Includes disorders in which the primary symptoms are feeding related. These include pica, rumination disorder, anorexia, bulimia, binge eating disorder, etc.
Sexual dysfunctions	Includes disorders of sexual arousal, sexual desire, sexual pain disorders, orgasmic disorders and sexual disorders associated with medical conditions
Sleep–wake disorders Gender dysphoria Disruptive, impulse-control and conduct disorders	Includes insomnia, hypersomnia, narcolepsy and apneic disorders Includes gender dysphoria in children and adolescents Includes oppositional defiant disorder, intermittence explosive disorder, conduct disorder and other behavior disorders
Major or mild neurocognitive disorders	Includes disorders of cognition due to neurologic etiologies such as Alzheimer's, Lewy body disease, etc. (specify condition)
Personality disorders	Includes disorders associated with personality grouped into three clusters (i.e., paranoid personality disorder, narcissistic personality disorder, personality disorder due to a medical condition, etc.)

(ICD-10) to diagnose patients. This classification schema often has diagnoses which are more appropriate for patients with neurologic diseases for which emotional disorders are a direct result or secondary diagnosis.

Mood/Emotions and Neurologic Illness

Increased rates of psychiatric symptoms/emotional problems are associated with many acute or chronic medical illness (see Hales & Yudofsky, 2008; Lezak et al., 2004). This reflects at least two different, and often interacting, etiologies: (1) affective symptoms related to neurophysiologic changes in the CNS due to neurological disease or dysfunction and (2) the impact on emotional functioning resulting from psychosocial stressors. This biopsychosocial model is the predominate theoretical framework for understanding psychiatric symptoms/emotional problems at this time. Within this model, the psychosocial component reflects the process of adjustment to the changes produced with illness, frequently results in increased stress and elicits coping strategies which are not always adaptive to the patient within his/her environment and disease state. In examining the impact of an illness on mood, behavior and emotions, two factors are paramount. The first is an estimation of change in mood, behavior or emotions from premorbid functioning. The second issue involves examining the areas of the brain which are involved and analyzing the current and future anticipated changes in behavior and emotions.

The issue of change is critical in evaluating the impact of illness on emotional and behavioral functioning. It is important to get an accurate and reliable history of past emotional functioning from which to judge change in current emotional or behavioral functioning. This is crucial in differentiating a re-emergence or exacerbation of a preexisting condition from a new manifestation of emotional symptoms or behaviors. While this may seem trivial at first glance, it is critical for determining the etiology for the psychiatric symptom/emotional problems as well as predicting the course and outcome of emotional and behavioral deficits associated with neurological dysfunction. As an example, the onset of visual hallucinations following a head injury of an adult patient is more likely to trigger a variety of questions and laboratory tests designed to assess for seizures or structural lesions than would be the onset of visual hallucinations in an elderly patient with a history of schizophrenia. The predictive value of obtaining a history is highlighted by consistent data establishing that individuals with extensive histories of recurrent emotional and behavioral deficits are both at much greater risk for subsequent development of such symptoms post injury or illness as well as at increased risk for poorer outcomes from treatment interventions than are individuals with no prior psychiatric history. Indeed, individuals with no psychiatric history are at lower risk for developing emotional and behavioral abnormalities following onset of neurological dysfunction or disease and have better remission rates with treatment.

In addition to obtaining a history of previously diagnosed emotional or behavioral disorders, it is important to obtain a reliable description of personality characteristics as these may be exacerbated to pathological levels following an injury or illness. These characteristics include past anger management, frustration tolerance, assertiveness–passivity, social interactions, suspiciousness, stubbornness, dependency, etc. An assessment of these characteristics will give indications of possible areas of concern in the development of current and future symptoms. It is also important to gain an understanding of the typical pre-injury coping skills/mechanisms of the individual, as

Table 12.2 Emotional history and coping skills history checklist

Emotional history	History	Current	Change
Depression			
Anxiety			
Bipolar disorder			
Post-traumatic stress disorder			
Somatoform disorder			
Development delays			
Attention deficit disorder			
Substance abuse/dependency			
Schizophrenia/psychosis			
Factitious disorder			
Impulse control disorder			
Avoidance			
Hypo/hyper somnolence			
Eating (over/under)			
Substance use/abuse (including tobacco, alcohol and prescriptions)			
Obsessive behavior			
Compulsive behavior			
Agitation/irritability			
Aggression (verbal/physical)			
Suspiciousness/distrust			
Overcontrolling			
Sexual behavior(hyper/hypo)			
Hyperactivity			
Emotional dysregulation (hyper/hypo)			
Inappropriate humor			
Hypervigilance/excessive worry			
Physical symptoms (headache, nausea, diarrhea, fatigue)			

these may be exacerbated following an injury and become a source of needed intervention or treatment. Table 12.2 provides a partial list of emotional and behavioral symptoms and coping skills/mechanisms history to be explored with the patient and a reliable collateral informant. These characteristics should be explored both in regard to the past and also as they pertain to any post-injury changes.

The second issue regarding assessment of patients' emotional and behavioral symptoms is dependent on the type and location of an injury. Both acute and chronic neurologic injuries/illnesses can produce emotional/behavioral changes in patients. Particularly, injuries to the frontal lobes and those affecting the cortico-bulbar tracts bilaterally produce striking emotional and behavioral changes.

Injuries to the orbital-frontal region which involves the inferior medial and anterior frontal lobes produce behavioral changes, which have been termed the orbital-frontal personality syndrome (see Chap. 11 for elaboration). The emotional and behavioral symptoms involved include disinhibition, impulsivity, emotional volatility and socially inappropriate behavior. These individuals are often seen as disregarding the feelings or rights of others and are helpless in stopping or avoiding what they often readily verbalize as inappropriate behavior. This syndrome can be caused by anything that affects the orbital-frontal region, but is most frequently associated with traumatic brain injuries or ruptures of aneurysms involving the anterior communicating artery.

In addition, behavioral syndromes associated with dysfunction of the dorsolateral frontal cortex often result in producing decreased emotional responsiveness, poor awareness of deficits and decreased motivation or spontaneous behavior. These individuals are referred to as having a dorsolateral frontal lobe syndrome (also termed dysexecutive syndrome; see Chap. 11, this volume) and are often described as abulic, dull, emotionally unresponsive and appearing depressed. While these individuals are generally emotionally unresponsive, they are often capable of exaggerated emotional responses when they become emotionally stimulated and display difficulty in regulating or redirecting their emotional response. These changes can be seen with any etiology affecting the lateral and superior frontal convexities, but are most frequently associated with occlusive strokes involving the anterior branch of the middle cerebral artery or traumatic brain injuries. Interestingly, these behavioral/emotional syndromes often do not result in much change in cognitive functioning to the casual observer. Cognitive deficits are most frequently found in sustained attention, alternating attention, processing speed and novel reasoning and problem-solving tasks requiring convergent or divergent reasoning. They do not often exhibit frank deficits in intelligence, language, visuo-spatial processing or memory when attentional variability effects are considered.

A rare but interesting emotional phenomenon is pseudobulbar affect or affective incontinence (see also Chap. 11). This arises when there are bilateral lesions involving the cortico-bulbar tracts and results in the patient displaying an affective response (i.e., crying or laughter) but having no or minimal associated emotional feeling. These individuals often display inappropriate or grossly exaggerated emotional affective behaviors such as hysterical laughter or uncontrollable crying, but upon inquiry report no subjective appreciation of happiness or sadness. While this phenomenon is rarely seen in post-acute populations, there are several documented cases of persistent syndrome symptoms for years after injury. The phenomenon is rare and occurs most frequently in individuals with a history of neurologic injury to one cortico-bulbar tract and who then suffer an acute injury that involves the contralateral cortico-bulbar tract. Exaggerated negative dysphoria (crying) is seen much more frequently than euphoria (laughter). Again, this phenomenon is rare and typically remits or greatly improves in a few months following the injury. This is seen most frequently in individuals with a history of previous CVAs, transient ischemic attacks or multiple sclerosis, but can occur from any etiology affecting the bilateral cortico-bulbar tracts. Differentiation from depression or psychosis can often be made by both distracting the patient on to a neutral topic (What color are my shoes?) and asking them about the appreciation of the internal emotion when they have such an exaggerated/disproportional emotional display.

Finally, injuries to the right hemisphere can produce deficits in expressive and receptive prosody, which can have profound effects on emotional functioning. These individuals lack their previous social skill in understanding or communicating emotional states through the use of vocal tone and inflection or in readily grasping the subtle emotional variability in others' tone or inflection. The resulting behavioral and emotional changes are that these individuals are perceived as socially unskilled, concrete, emotionally unavailable and uncaring. While considerable variability exists among persons in social skill and emotional perception, these individuals represent changes from a previous level of emotional/social skill functioning which is obvious to others who previously knew them. It is, however, often associated or attributed to volitional behavior or negative personality characteristics and subsequently results in social and interpersonal difficulties and stresses. Table 12.3 summarizes the anatomical associations of behavioral and emotional changes.

Below, we review some of the delusional misidentification syndromes. These are often associated with neurological disease, but may be associated with severe psychiatric syndromes as well (i.e., schizophrenia, bipolar disorder, etc.). The delusional misidentification syndromes include: Capgras, Fregoli's, reduplicative paramnesia and subjective doubles syndrome.

Capgras Syndrome: Delusional belief that a person (friend, spouse or family member) has been replaced by an imposter. This imposter appears physically exactly like the person and has the ability to provide memory for previous details about the person he/she is impersonating. Capgras syndrome can also extend to the delusional belief that objects have been replaced by an duplicate, but not the original object (e.g., belief one's shoes have been replaced by duplicates). As an example, a patient may believe his/her clothes or shoes have been replaced by imposter garments, which look just like the patient's clothes and shoes, but are not theirs. Capgras syndrome is associated with schizophrenia as a psychiatric illness, but also found among patients with dementia or brain injury. Patients with Capgras syndrome are able to identify faces (and do not have prosopagnosia); these individuals may have disruption of the autonomic processing aspect of facial recognition processing, such that viewing familiar faces (e.g., family members) does not result in an emotional autonomic response. Capgras syndrome has been reported among patients with dysfunction of the bifrontal lobes and/or diffuse nondominant hemisphere lesions.

Fregoli Syndrome (Delusion): Belief that the same person known to the patient is able to disguise or change him/herself into other people the patient meets. While the people thought to be the same person may not look, sound or behave at all alike, the patient is convinced that physiologically it is the same person who is able to disguise themselves "very well." The person able to disguise him/herself as other people the patient meets is usually identified as a persecutor of the patient. This

Table 12.3 Emotional and behavioral symptoms associated with frontal lobe lesions

Lesion location	Behavioral/emotional symptoms
Orbital-medial-frontal lobe syndrome	Disinhibition, poor social control, emotional dysregulation, impulsivity, inappropriate social or sexual behavior, utilization behavior, distractibility
Dorsal-lateral-frontal lobe syndrome	Abulia, apathy, emotional restriction, emotional dysregulation when emotionally aroused, unmotivated, disregard for hygiene, decreased awareness of deficits, lack of spontaneity, decreased initiative

syndrome is associated with schizophrenia as well as with damage to the right frontal or left temporoparietal areas.

Reduplicative Paramnesia: Delusion that a place or location has been duplicated one more time. The place or location is either "relocated" or duplicated, but both must exist simultaneously. Reduplicative paramnesia can present with a patient believing that his/her home is not his/hers, but recognizes that the other house appears to be identical in detail, but is not the person's real place. Bensen et al. (1976) reported three cases, one of which believed there to be two identical hospitals, one of which was in his hometown. The syndrome has been reported to be often associated with bifrontal lesions, often with more diffuse right hemisphere damage. It is generally thought the disorder reflects a combination of impaired attention, memory and visuoperceptual functions (Forstl et al. 1991).

Subjective Doubles Syndrome: Belief the patient has been duplicated, and the duplicate person is able to act independently of the patient. There may be more than one duplicate of the person, and the duplicates may have different characteristics or mannerisms. Reported for patients with neurological injury and psychiatric diseases (schizophrenia). Neurological injuries associated with subjective doubles syndrome tend to involve right hemisphere damage as well as frontal lesions. It can be comorbid with Capgras syndrome. Subjective doubles syndrome is not the belief that exact duplicates of the person exist, such that the duplicates are the same physiologically and psychologically/behaviorally. This delusion is also termed clonal pluralization of the self.

Visual Hallucinations

Visual hallucinations are more likely neurological than psychiatric, and the type of hallucination and associated phenomena can help identify etiology/neuroanatomical location. Individuals with visual hallucinations produced from neurologic disease often retain awareness that the experiences do not represent reality, often a distinguishing factor from schizophrenia. Simple shapes/figures reflect more posterior cortical involvement (occipital primary association cortex) while complex patterns more occipital-parietal. Hallucinations that occur for brief periods of time (e.g., <90 seconds), and are associated with loss of time, other associated somatosensory phenomena, motor dysfunction or falling, are more likely to be associated with seizure activity. Visual hallucinations developing in older patients suggest encephalopathy, medication effects (e.g., excessive dopamine agonist) or neurodegenerative disorders (e.g., Lewy body dementia).

Psychotic symptoms associated with depression are more typically auditory than visual and are often mood congruent (i.e., auditory perceptions are critical or negative in nature) and may be persistent, well formed and integrated into other delusional belief systems. In bipolar illness (previously called manic-depression), psychotic symptoms are associated primarily with the manic phase and are often dissociable from neurologic etiologies by history (occurring recurrently, with onset at an early age and no history of neurologic trauma or medical illness) as well as their mood congruent nature and lack of insight as to the irrationality of the experience.

Auditory Hallucinations

Auditory hallucinations may be neurologic or psychiatric. Quality of hallucination can provide clues as to likely etiology, but not always. Poorly formed auditory hallucinations (e.g., buzzing, ringing, etc.) are more likely related to neurologic or peripheral nerve problems (e.g., simple partial seizure, tinnitus, etc.). Running auditory commentary of an individual's actions or thoughts for extended periods of time (>several minutes) that is well articulated is more likely to be associated with psychiatric disease (e.g., schizophrenia). Auditory hallucinations of a repeated word/phrase may be neurologic or psychiatric. Auditory hallucinations of repeated words/phrases associated with other somatosensory phenomena, loss of awareness or falls more likely represent neurological etiologies (i.e., seizure) than are auditory hallucinations of repeated words/phrases in isolation.

Olfactory and Gustatory Hallucinations

Olfactory and gustatory hallucinations more likely neurological and occur very infrequently in psychiatric populations. They are most frequently associated with CNS tumors or Epilepsy (Table 12.4).

Somatosensory Hallucinations

The perception of numbness, tingling, pain, bugs moving about the skin or movement/twitching may be either neurological or psychiatric. Determination of the origins is often very challenging. One helpful guide is the extent to which the somatosensory hallucination follows known dermatomes and/or myotomes (see Chap. 3).

Table 12.4 Differentiation of psychiatric and neurologic causes of emotional and behavioral symptoms

Emotion/behavior	Potential neurologic cause	Differentiation from psychiatric condition	Potential psychiatric cause	Differentiation from neurologic cause
Pseudobulbar affect/ affective incontinence (uncontrollable crying or laughter)	Bilateral disruption of the cortico-bulbar tracts	No associated affect appreciated by patient (they do not feel happy or sad); redirection to neutral topic stops affective expression	Bipolar disorder; predominately manic	Confirm history of cyclical affective disorder of patient or family: No structural lesion identified on imaging or history of stroke, trauma or degenerative disorder
Impulsivity/disinhibition	Frontal lobe disruption, particularly orbito-frontal	Significant change in social appropriateness following a neurologic injury or in the course of a degenerative disorder; minimal hyperactivity/sleep disturbance	Bipolar disorder: Predominately manic	History of bipolar disorder, associated insomnia, irritability, pressured speech, hyperactivity
Abulia/lack of initiation, motivation	Frontal lobe disruption, particularly dorso-lateral disruption; degenerative disorders in late stages	Little or no dysphoria associated with reduction in behavior; can frequently perform activities if directed and given structure	Major depressive disorder	Sadness, hopeless, helplessness associated with lack of motivation; recognizes need for behavior, but expresses no desire to perform(i.e., taking out trash)
Visual hallucinations	Temporal-parietal association cortices; often associated with Lewy body disorder or trauma to temporal-parietal area in nondominant hemisphere (typically right); disruption may be transient as in seizures or transient ischemic attacks	No history of hallucinations before age 30, no excessive dopaminergic medications; insight into the factual nature of the hallucinations is often preserved	Schizophrenia; bipolar disorder manic phase; depression with psychotic features	Visual hallucinations are rare in psychiatric disorders; when present they are usually associated with acute exacerbations of long-standing psychiatric conditions; usually mood congruent and insight into the factual nature of the hallucinations is usually lost

(continued)

Table 12.4 (continued)

Emotion/behavior	Potential neurologic cause	Differentiation from psychiatric condition	Potential psychiatric cause	Differentiation from neurologic cause
Auditory hallucinations	Temporal lobe lesions and transient disruption (e.g., seizures)	Hallucinations are often sounds rather than intelligible voices; often are not mood congruent; are often transient rather than persistent	Schizophrenia, bipolar disorder in manic phase, major depressive disorder with psychotic features	Much more frequent than visual hallucinations, often mood congruent, often repetitive with command or negative content, associated with no physical trauma, but may be associated with stress or emotional trauma, history is often positive for previous occurrence of auditory hallucinations
Olfactory hallucinations	Frontal lobe seizures, less frequently frontal traumatic brain injury	Smells are typically unusual (i.e., metallic, acidic) and insight is often preserved as to the fact of the hallucination as not real	Schizophrenia	Rare, insight into the nonfactual nature of the olfactory sensation is often lost; may be incorporated into mood congruent delusion
Expressive aprosody	Lesions of the anterior dorsal right cortex (nondominant)	Retained awareness of what emotion should be expressed, but unable to modulate vocalizations to impart emotional meaning (i.e., cannot say "I'm going to the store" in contrasting happy, sad and angry tones)	Major depression	Prosody is usually retained, but patient may come across as monotone due to sadness and despair

Emotion/behavior	Potential neurologic cause	Differentiation from psychiatric condition	Potential psychiatric cause	Differentiation from neurologic cause
Receptive aprosody	Lesions of the posterior right cortex (nondominant); can be associated with nonverbal learning disabilities and high-level autistic spectrum disorders (i.e., Asperger's disorder)	Often retained awareness of emotions which should be understood, but failure to appropriately interpret and comprehend vocal tone and inflections which communicate emotional tone in language, patients are often surprised when others become frustrated after miscommunication, they often do not grasp sarcasm, innuendo or detect frustration in others that lead to social awkwardness or rejection/avoidance	Major depression; schizophrenia, bipolar disorder	Not typically a major component of these disorders, but may appear as emotional nonresponsiveness/nonreciprocity. Differentiated from neurologic causes often by history and lack of relative change over time
Affective dis-modulation	Frontal lobe lesions; may be nonlocalizing and if so is typically associated with the severity of overall cognitive dysfunction or acuity of trauma (i.e., TBI)	Dysregulation occurs in the presence of environmental stimuli and is often disproportional to the evoking event (i.e., patient is over stimulated and reacts with hyperactivity/agitation and cannot self-regulate back to stasis); when affective arousal is diminished, hypo arousal is often observed	Schizophrenia, bipolar	Arousal is often contextually driven in a desire to get something from the environment or avoid aversive stimuli in the environment, it is often precipitated by the demands of others in the environment and dissipates appropriately when the demand is reduced/removed
Perseveration	Frontal lobe or severe degenerative disorder	Perseveration is typically on some activity in the environment. Behavior is often non-seneschal and not mood congruent	Schizophrenia	Perseveration is often mood congruent and associated with self-stimulation

(continued)

Table 12.4 (continued)

Emotion/behavior	Potential neurologic cause	Differentiation from psychiatric condition	Potential psychiatric cause	Differentiation from neurologic cause
Paranoia/suspiciousness	Nonlocalizing, associated with severity of impairment	Often is exacerbation of pre-existing non-pathological tendencies. Exacerbated by changes in patient that they do not have awareness of and attribute to the motives or behaviors of others (i.e., someone is stealing things they have misplaced, spouse is accused of infidelity because they do not know where they are at all times)	Schizophrenia	Often mood congruent and associated with a fixed pattern of delusions of persecution, grandiosity or espionage. History is often associated with previous occurrences of paranoia/ suspiciousness
Anxiety	Nonlocalizing, but may have preponderance for occurrence in right hemisphere lesions (nondominant)	Anxiety is associated with severity of compromise in cognition and often exacerbated by changes in environment or deviations from routine, often no identifiable attribution is made by the patient	Anxiety disorders	Anxiety is usually associated with a feared or dreaded stimuli. Attributions are made to impending disaster or worries about possible negative outcomes

References

Bensen, A. L., Gardner, H., & Meadows, J. C. (1976). Reduplicative paramnesia. *Neurology, 26*, 147–151.

Forstl, H., Almeida, O. P., Owen, A. M., Burns, A., & Howard, R. (1991). Psychiatric, neurological and medical aspects of misidentification syndromes: A review of 260 cases. *Psychological Medicine, 21*, 905–910.

Hales, R. E., & Yudofsky, S. C. (2008). *Textbook of neuropsychiatry and behavioral neurosciences* (5th ed.). American Psychiatric Press.

Lezak, M. D., Howieson, D. B., & Loring, D. W. (2004). *Neuropsychological assessment* (4th ed.). Oxford University Press.

Chapter 13
Aphasia Syndromes

Michael R. Schoenberg and James G. Scott

Key Points: Left Hemisphere Dominance for Language
- Right handed—90–95%
- Left handed—60–70%

The clinical features of each aphasia syndrome are reviewed below along with neuroanatomical correlates. For rapid review, please see Tables 13.1 and 13.2 and Appendix. For more detailed discussion, please see Heilman and Valenstein (2003), Kolb and Whishaw (2008), Goodglass et al. (2001), Lezak et al. (2004), Mesulam (2000) and/or Victor and Ropper (2001) for reviews.

Clinical Classification of Aphasias

Nonfluent Aphasias

As a group, these aphasic syndromes share a common speech deficit in which verbal output is nonfluent. Speech output may be nonexistent or be slow and effortful.

M. R. Schoenberg
Departments of Psychiatry and Neurosciences, Neurology, and Neurosurgery, University of South Florida College of Medicine, Tampa, FL, USA
e-mail: mschoenb@health.usf.edu

J. G. Scott (✉)
Department of Psychiatry and Behavioral Sciences, University of Oklahoma, Health Sciences Center College of Medicine, Oklahoma City, OK, USA
e-mail: jim-scott@ouhsc.ed

M. R. Schoenberg, J. G. Scott (eds.), *The Little Black Book of Neuropsychology*, https://doi.org/10.1007/978-3-032-07777-6_13

Table 13.1 Common aphasic syndromes

Aphasia syndrome	Expressive speech	Auditory comprehension	Repeat	Naming	Reading
Global	↓↓↓	↓↓↓	↓↓↓	↓↓↓	↓↓↓
Broca's	↓↓↓	↓/Normal	↓↓↓	↓↓/↓↓↓	↓/Normal
Trans motor	↓↓/↓↓↓	↓/Normal	Normal	↓/↓↓	Normal
Wernicke's	Fluent ↓↓↓	↓↓↓	↓↓↓	↓↓/↓↓↓	↓↓↓
Trans sensory	Fluent ↓↓↓	↓↓↓	Normal	↓↓↓	↓↓↓
Mixed trans	↓↓↓	↓↓↓	Normal	↓↓↓	↓↓↓
Conduction	Fluent ↓/↓↓	Normal	↓↓↓	↓/↓↓	Normal
Anomic	↓/Normal	Normal	Normal	↓↓↓	Normal
Aphemia/pure word mutism	Mute only can write	Normal	Normal	Mute. Able to write	Normal
Alexia w/o agraphia (and pure word blindness)	Normal[a]	Normal	Normal	Normal	↓↓↓

Note: Trans motor = Transcortical motor aphasia; Trans sensory = transcortical sensory aphasia; Mixed trans = mixed transcortical aphasia; ↓ = minimal impairment; ↓↓ moderate impairment; ↓↓↓ = severe impairment

[a] Unable to read aloud

Key Points and Chapter Summary

- Most individuals (>90%) are left hemisphere dominant for language
  - Inferior frontal lobe associated with expressive speech (including writing)
  - Superior temporo-parietal cortex associated with receptive language (including reading)
- The right hemisphere plays a significant role in prosodic aspects of language
  - Non-dominant frontal lobe associated with expressive prosody
  - Non-dominant temporo-parietal lobe associated with receptive prosody
- Nonfluent aphasia syndromes have slow, effortful, halting speech that is difficult to understand
- Fluent aphasia syndromes have speech that is fluent and effortless, but is difficult to understand due to lack of real words to convey meaning
- Distinguish aphasia from psychosis, schizophrenia, other psychiatric illness or delirium.
  - Aphasia: Shorter sentences, paraphasias more common and frequent dysnomia. Aphasias often have associated neurologic (motor/sensory) deficits.
  - Psychosis/schizophrenia: "Word salad" is marked by long, tangential responses to questions. Neologisms common while paraphasias rare. Rarely associated with extralanguage focal neurologic symptoms

Table 13.2 Types of aprosodies and associated deficits

Aprosodia syndrome	Anatomical location	Prosodic expression	Prosodic comprehension	Prosodic repetition	Gestural expressive	Gestural comprehend
Global	Right frontal, temporal and parietal	↓↓↓	↓↓↓	↓↓↓	↓↓↓	↓↓↓
Motor	Right lateral frontal, superior anterior temporal	↓↓↓	Normal	↓↓↓	↓↓/↓↓↓	↓/Normal
Trans motor	Right lateral frontal	↓↓	↓/Normal	Normal	↓↓	Normal
Sensory/receptive	Right posterior/inferior temporal lobe	Normal	↓↓↓	↓↓↓	Normal	↓↓↓
Trans sensory	Right inferior temporal/parietal	Normal	↓↓↓	Normal	Normal	↓↓↓
Mixed trans	Right frontal and parietal	↓↓↓	↓↓↓	Normal	↓↓↓	↓↓↓
Conduction	Right superior temporal and inferior frontal lobes	Normal	Normal	↓↓↓	↓/Normal	Normal
Agesureic	Variable right hemisphere	Normal	Normal	Normal	Normal	↓↓↓

Note: See Ross (1997, 2000) for reviews and more details

Global Aphasia

Key Points: Global Aphasia

- Nonfluent aphasia with impaired comprehension and repetition.

Fluency: Patient may be entirely mute or have slow halting speech frequently only with incoherent grunts, single syllables or single words (often neologisms) or short perseverative phrases (e.g., "I, I, I," or "doy, doy, doy" or "I go, I go, I go"). Patients may be able to utter single words or short phrases having an emotional context due to the spontaneous circumvention of typical voluntary language centers under emotional distress. Prosody and inflection may convey some apparent meaning to words, particularly anger or excitement.

Comprehension: Impaired. Comprehension of single words is often impaired, and markedly so for even simple sentences. Reading is similarly impaired. However, patients may follow gestural cues (i.e., hand gestures, facial cues, etc.) quite well. Some ability to comprehend prosodic cues such as vocal tone, volume and inflection is often retained.

Repetition: Impaired.

Naming: Impaired.

Writing: Impaired.

Frequent comorbid conditions: Right hemiparesis involving lower part of face and both upper and lower extremities, right visual field defect, right hemianesthesia, Gerstmann's syndrome, visual agnosias, apraxias (including oral apraxia) and memory impairments.

Neuroanatomical correlates: Large lesions affecting both anterior and posterior areas of the left hemisphere regions involving both Broca's and Wernicke's areas.

Prognosis: Typically, evolve to Broca's (expressive) aphasia, with an improvement in comprehension (Fig. 13.1).

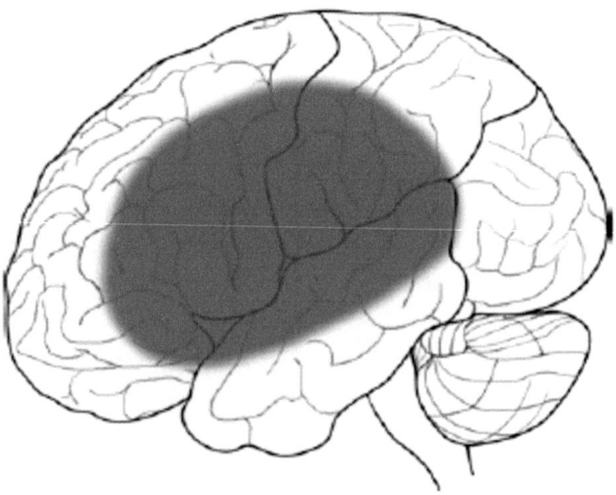

Fig. 13.1 Illustration of left hemisphere damage resulting in a global aphasia syndrome

Mixed Transcortical Aphasia

Key Points: Mixed Transcortical Aphasia

- Nonfluent aphasia with impaired comprehension, but intact repetition.

Fluency: Patient present with slow halting speech. Like global aphasia, speech may include only incoherent grunts, single syllables, or single words (often neologisms) or short perseverative phrases (e.g., "I, I, I," or "doy, doy, dog" or "I go, I go, I go"). Like global aphasia, patients may be able to utter single words or short phrases having an emotional context (e.g., profanity) when under emotional distress. Prosody and inflection may convey some apparent meaning to words, particularly anger or excitement.

Comprehension: Impaired. Like global aphasia, comprehension of single words and phrases is impaired. Reading is similarly impaired. Similarly, individuals may be able to respond appropriately to (nonverbal) gestures or facial expressions. Ability to comprehend prosodic cues such as vocal tone, volume and inflection can be intact.

Repetition: Intact. Single words and complete sentences can be repeated accurately. No comprehension of repeated words or phrases is apparent. Echolalia is common.

Naming: Impaired.

Writing: Impaired.

Frequent comorbid conditions: Right hemiparesis involving lower face and both extremities, right visual field defect, right hemianesthesia, Gerstmann's syndrome, visual agnosias, apraxias and memory impairments.

Neuroanatomical correlates: Isolation of the perisylvian fissure area by diffuse dominant hemisphere lesion. Lesion is large, affecting both anterior and posterior areas of the left hemisphere regions, sparing the arcuate fasciculus. Common etiology is an ischemic-based stroke.

Prognosis: Variable. Patients with vascular etiology may evolve to Broca's (expressive) aphasia or, in some cases, an anomic aphasia (Fig. 13.2).

Broca's Aphasia

Key Points: Broca's (Expressive) Aphasia

- Nonfluent aphasia with intact comprehension, but impaired repetition.

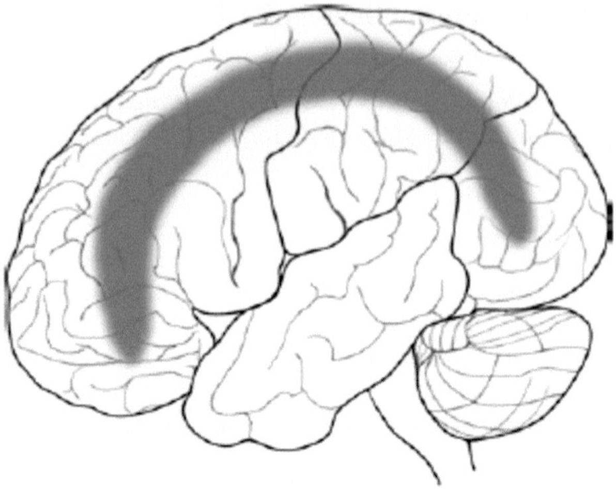

Fig. 13.2 Example of lesion resulting in mixed transcortical aphasia syndrome

Fluency: Impaired. A range of nonfluent speech may be present, from almost complete lack of coherent speech as in global aphasia with single words and neologisms to slow halting speech with few content words and few verbs or adjectives. Verbal utterances are typically limited to less than four–five words in length (e.g., "I go, I go, I go" or "wife…down…hall."). Like global aphasia and mixed transcortical aphasia, patients can frequently utter words and phrases associated with an emotional context (e.g., profanity and obscenities), particularly when under emotional distress. In addition, patients can frequently exhibit much more fluent speech when asked to utter overlearned words (e.g., "no" or "hi") or sing familiar songs (e.g., "Happy Birthday" song). Prosody and inflection of words are typically impaired.

Comprehension: Intact. Comprehension of single words and short phrases is intact. Reading comprehension is also intact. Comprehension of more grammatically complex phrases, particularly syntactically-dependent sentences (e.g., "the cat was eaten by the mouse."), is often impaired. Ability to comprehend prosodic cues such as vocal tone, volume and inflection is intact.

Repetition: Impaired.

Naming: Impaired.

Writing: Impaired, effortful and very slow.

Frequent comorbid conditions: Right hemiparesis of lower part of face (and tongue) and upper extremity, apraxias (oral apraxia can be present), and verbal memory can be impaired (Risse et al., 1984).

Neuroanatomical correlates: Lesion of dominant anterior hemisphere. May include left frontal and temporal lobes, including insula and white matter below these cortical areas. Less extensive lesions involving area anterior to central sulcus result in less severe (more transient) problems with, and better recovery of, language fluency. Posterior perisylvian fissure structures are preserved. Most typical etiology is infarct of superior division of middle superior artery (MCA).

Prognosis: Variable. Patients with vascular etiology frequently improve to an anomic aphasia with mild reduced fluency (Fig. 13.3).

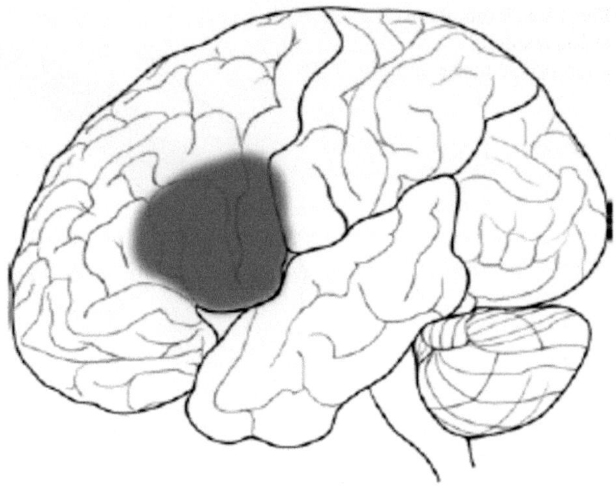

Fig. 13.3 Example of lesion resulting in Broca's aphasia

Transcortical Motor Aphasia

Key Points: Transcortical Motor Aphasia
- Nonfluent aphasia with intact comprehension and repetition.

Fluency: Impaired, but less so than in Broca's or global aphasia. However, patients tend to be quite abulic, offering little speech spontaneously. A range of nonfluent speech may be present, varying from few single words and neologisms to slow halting speech consisting of mostly nouns and few verbs/adjectives, but devoid of conjunctions and prepositions. Verbal utterances are typically limited to less than four–five words in length (e.g., "I go, I go, I go" or "wife…down…hall."). Like the other nonfluent aphasias, patients can frequently utter words and phrases associated with an emotional context (e.g., profanity and obscenities), particularly when under emotional distress. Prosody and inflection of words are limited.

Comprehension: Intact. Comprehension of single words and short phrases is intact. Reading comprehension is also intact. Like Broca's aphasia, comprehension of syntactically-dependent phrases (e.g., "the cat was eaten by the mouse.") and multi-step instructions may be impaired. Ability to comprehend prosodic cues such as vocal tone, volume and inflection is intact.

Repetition: Intact, commonly for even long or complex sentences.

Naming: Impaired.

Writing: Impaired, effortful and very slow.

Frequent comorbid conditions: Depending upon location of lesion, can include either right upper extremity weakness (left frontal dorsolateral lesions) or right lower extremity weakness (medial frontal lesions). Apraxias and memory impairments may be present. Other executive dysfunction, perseveration and behavioral apathy may be present.

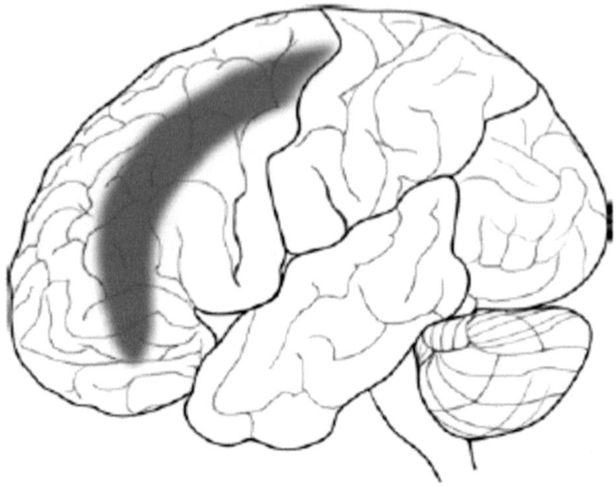

Fig. 13.4 Example of lesion resulting transcortical motor aphasia

Neuroanatomical correlates: Lesion of dominant frontal lobe. Lesions may reflect dorsolateral damage anterior or superior to Broca's area. Lesion can involve mesial left frontal area associated with the anterior cingulated and supplementary motor area. Posterior perisylvian fissure structures are preserved. Alternatively, lesion can reflect damage of the dominant hemisphere basal ganglia or thalamus. Common etiology is infarct of left anterior cerebral artery (ACA) or anterior segment of the superior division of the middle superior artery (MCA).

Prognosis: Variable. Patients with vascular etiology can evolve to an anomic aphasia or symptoms may nearly resolve (Fig. 13.4).

Fluent Aphasias

Key Points: Wernicke's (Receptive) Aphasia
- Fluent aphasia with impaired comprehension and repetition.

As a group, these aphasic syndromes all reflect intact verbal fluency. That is speech output is rapid and effortless. Speech content may be unintelligible, repetition impaired or comprehension poor, but verbal utterances are effortless and fluent.

Wernicke's Aphasia

Fluency: Speech is fluent, but often unintelligible. While speech output is effortless, rapid, and "sentence" length is normal, speech content is unintelligible due to paraphasias (phonemic and semantic) as well as frequent neologisms. Speech content is empty as there are few nouns or verbs, and mostly conjunctions and prepositions. Circumlocution is common, with the speaker frequently substituting "it or thing" for content words (e.g., "the thing whiffle sup it as tbe no…no be surk whe."). Speech can be rapid, particularly if the speaker is excited, which is sometimes referred to logorrhea or press of speech.

Comprehension: Impaired. Comprehension of single words and short phrases is often impaired, and patients have difficulty answering simple yes/no questions or following one-step commands. Reading comprehension is also impaired. Patients appear unaware speech is unintelligible. Ability to comprehend prosodic cues such as vocal tone, volume and inflection is often intact.

Repetition: Impaired. Patients may have difficulty repeating single words (often due to paraphasias), and clear impairment for short and longer sentences.

Naming: Impaired, with frequent paraphasias.

Writing: As with spoken speech, writing is often fluent with letters being identifiable, but the content of writing is unintelligible due to paraphasias and neologisms.

Frequent comorbid conditions: Frequently can present with *no* other obvious neurological signs. Anosognosia of speech deficits is common. Right homonymous visual field deficit, Gerstmann's syndrome, visuoconstructional apraxia and/or memory impairments may be present depending on the extent of lesion and time since onset of disease.

Neuroanatomical correlates: Lesion of dominant inferior persylvian fissure (superior temporal lobe) and often extending superiorly to the parietal region affecting the supramarginal gyrus. Anterior perisylvian fissure structures are preserved. Common etiology is infarct of left inferior division of the middle cerebral artery (MCA).

Prognosis: Variable. Patients with vascular etiology will often exhibit improvement of comprehension, and can evolve to a transcortical sensory aphasia or sometimes conduction aphasia. Very good resolution would result in anomic aphasia (Fig. 13.5).

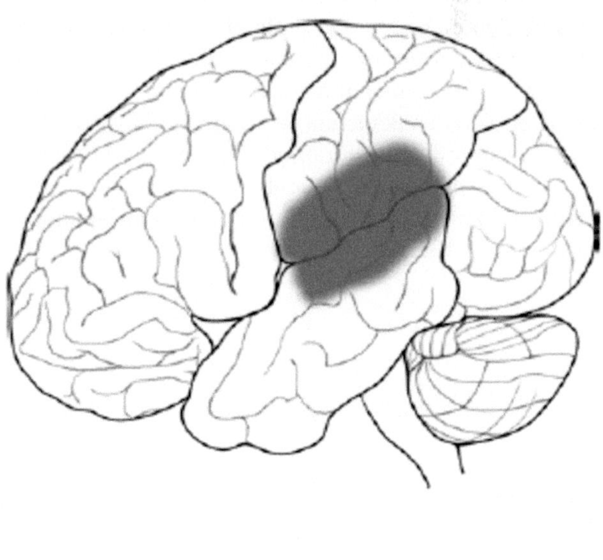

Fig. 13.5 Example of lesion resulting in Wernicke's aphasia

Transcortical Sensory Aphasia

Key Points: Transcortical Sensory Aphasia

- Fluent aphasia with impaired comprehension, but intact repetition.

Fluency: Like Wernicke's aphasia, speech fluency is rapid and effortless, and speech content remains quite unintelligible due to paraphasias (phonemic and semantic) and neologisms. Speech content may be less devoid of nouns and verbs than Wernicke's aphasia. Circumlocution is common.

Comprehension: Impaired, but to less extreme than in classic Wernicke's aphasia. Comprehension of single words may be intact, and able to answer simple yes/no questions. However, comprehension of short phrases is often impaired, and patients are unable to follow two- or three-step instructions or understand syntactically-dependent phrases are impaired. Reading comprehension is similarly impaired. Like Wernicke's aphasia, patients are often unaware their speech is unintelligible, and ability to comprehend prosodic cues such as vocal tone, volume and inflection can be preserved.

Repetition: Intact. Patients are often able to repeat surprisingly complex sentences.

Naming: Impaired, with frequent paraphasias.

Writing: As with spoken speech, writing is often fluent with letters being identifiable, but the content of writing is similarly unintelligible due to paraphasias and neologisms.

Frequent comorbid conditions: Often right visual field loss. Right hemianesthesia is possible. Constructional apraxia may also be present.

Neuroanatomical correlates: Lesion of dominant temporoparietal-occipital area, or less often, the parieto-occipital area. The cerebral tissue affected is posterior (and often mesial) to Wernicke's area. Structures anterior to Wernicke's area are preserved. Common etiology is infarction of watershed zone between the inferior MCA territory and posterior cerebral artery (PCA) territory. Another common lesion is damage to the dominant hemisphere basal ganglia or thalamus. Neurodegenerative diseases, such as dementia of Alzheimer's type, can be associated with language impairment reflecting a transcortical sensory aphasia.

Prognosis: Variable. Patients with vascular etiology will often exhibit improvement of comprehension, and improve to an anomic aphasia or sometimes nearly resolve (Fig. 13.6).

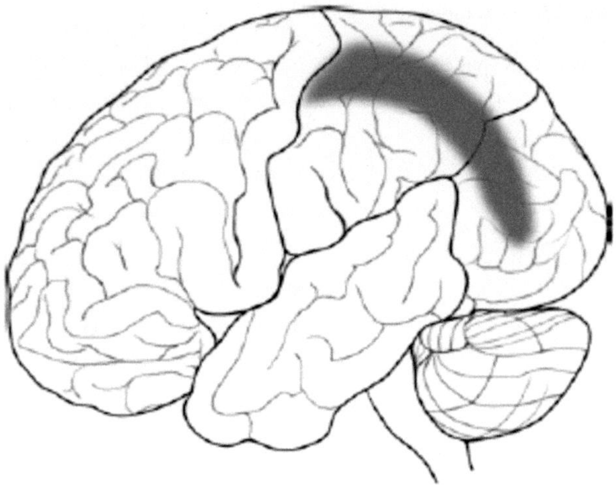

Fig. 13.6 Example of lesion resulting in transcortical sensory aphasia

Conduction Aphasia

Key Points: Conduction Aphasia

- Fluent aphasia. Comprehension intact. Repetition impaired.

Fluency: Speech is generally fluent and rapid, but can be difficult to understand due to frequent phonemic paraphasias and pauses due to naming/word-finding errors (dysnomia). While speech content is reduced by paraphasias and confrontation naming errors, speech is more meaningful and intelligible than produced with Wernicke's or transcortical sensory aphasias. Paraphasias are principally phonemic, and patients often engage in self-correction with increasingly close articulation of the desired word. Classically, some text books describe speech content as WNL/intact.

Comprehension: Grossly intact for conversational speech. Mild impairments may be evident with grammatically complex sentences (particularly syntactically-dependent phrases) and/or multi-step directions. Reading comprehension is grossly intact. Writing impaired with poor spelling (paraphasias). Prosodic cues such as vocal tone, volume and inflection are intact.

Repetition: Markedly impaired in light of preserved comprehension and somewhat fluent speech (frequent paraphasias). Patients are unable to repeat even simple phrases and often have difficulty with single words (e.g., "Massachusetts").

Naming: Impaired, with frequent phonemic paraphasias.

Writing: As with spoken speech, writing is fluent but can be difficult to understand due to misspelling (paraphasic errors).

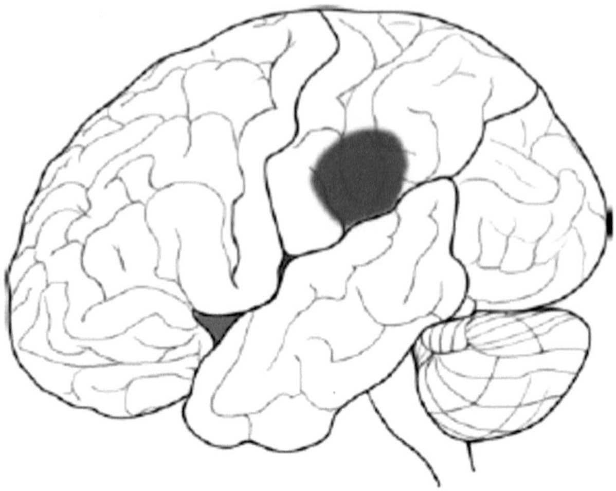

Fig. 13.7 Example of lesion resulting in conduction aphasia

Frequent comorbid conditions: Right hemianesthesia and apraxias are not uncommon. Some right facial weakness can be present. Acalculia can also be present. Right hemiparesis is rare.

Neuroanatomical correlates: Lesion of dominant temporo-parietal area, particularly the supramarginal gyrus and underlying white matter such that the arcuate fasciculus is damaged. Wernicke's area and anterior structures are preserved. Common etiology is infarction of a limb of the inferior MCA territory.

Prognosis: Variable. Patients can recover and evolve to an anomic aphasia or almost completely resolve. Static lesions (head injury) will often result in retained deficit (Fig. 13.7).

Anomic Aphasia

Key Points: Anomic Aphasia

- Expressive speech, comprehension and repetition intact. Naming impaired.

Fluency: Intact, with speech content that is meaningful. While speech output is generally rapid and effortless, speech rate is interrupted by occasional pauses for apparent word-finding problems. Circumlocution is present.

Comprehension: Intact. Comprehension of short and even complex sentences is often intact. Mild difficulty may be evident in complex multi-step directions and/or syntactically-dependent phrases. Reading comprehension is similarly intact.

Repetition: Intact, frequently even for complex sentences.

Naming: Impaired, with frequent circumlocution and/or paraphasias.

Writing: As with spoken speech, writing is fluent and content is intact. Some pauses in writing occur as with speech, suggesting word-finding difficulties.

Frequent comorbid conditions: Varies. Because anomic aphasia can present with a variety of neurological conditions (see below), may be associated with a variety of neurological and neuropsychological deficits. If limited to acute anomic aphasia, can be associated with Gerstmann's syndrome. Limb apraxia and acalculia can be present.

Neuroanatomical correlates: Except in the case of acute, isolated anomic aphasia, there is little localizing value. In acute isolated onset of anomic aphasia, lesion is often dominant (left) hemisphere outside the perisylvian language area in the inferior temporal area or angular gyrus of the parietal lobe area. Anomic aphasia is frequently identified in a variety of neurodegenerative conditions (e.g., dementia of Alzheimer's type), traumatic brain injuries and conditions resulting in intracranial pressure (neoplasms, intraventricular hemorrhages, etc.). In addition, patients with anterior temporal lobectomy often present with an anomic aphasia. A semantic category organization has been proposed with famous faces/people more localized to anterior temporal tip, animals more localized to inferior temporal region, and tools more localized to left posterior lateral region (e.g., Damasio et al., 1996).

Prognosis: Variable. Anomic aphasia is the end phase of recovery from a broad range of mild to moderate aphasia syndromes, and remain quite static in these cases. Recovery from acute, isolated anomic aphasia from localized ischemic event can be nearly complete. Recovery from other etiologies, such as head injury and/or degenerative disorders may not occur, and in fact evolve to other aphasia syndromes (Fig. 13.8 and Table 13.1).

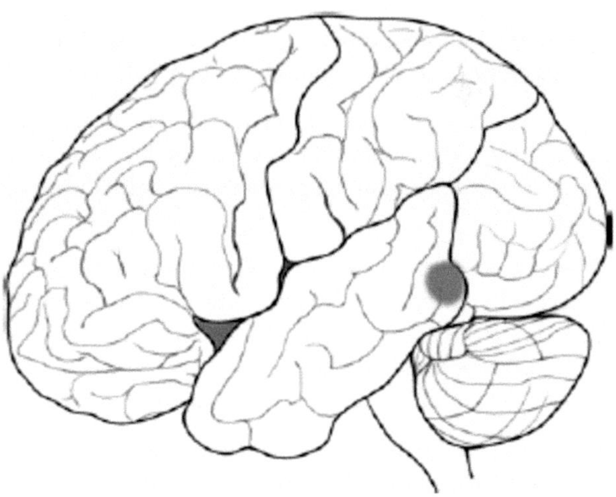

Fig. 13.8 Example of lesion resulting in anomic aphasia

Alexia, Agraphia and Aphemia

Key Points: Alexia, Agraphia and Aphemia

- Alexia is the inability to read not due to simple sensory (letter agnosia) or motor deficits (ocular apraxia).
- Agraphia is the inability to write not due to simple sensory or motor deficits.
- Aphemia refers to inability to speak not due to language deficit and is secondary to severe apraxia of musculature of mouth, larynx and tongue needed for normal speech utterances. Distinguished from aphasia in that patients' ability to read and write is completely intact.

Alexia and *Agraphia* are frequently observed concurrently with aphasia syndromes identified above, and follow the pattern of deficits in comprehension (for alexia) or fluency (for writing) of the aphasia syndromes. However, both alexia and agraphia may be observed independently (and together) and should be individually assessed.

Alexia without agraphia is a classic syndrome in which a patient is able to write fluently with normal content, but who is unable to read, even their own writing. Other language functions, including fluency, comprehension, repetition and naming are entirely intact.

Frequent comorbid conditions: Right homonymous hemianopia and anomias, particularly color anomia.

Neuroanatomical correlates: Alexia without agraphia is a classic disconnection syndrome, reflecting a lesion of the dominant (left) occipital lobe that involves the white matter of the posterior corpus callosum. This type of lesion may occur following an ischemic event of the posterior cerebral artery (PCA).

Prognosis: Variable. Recovery from acute ischemic event can be nearly complete. Recovery from other etiologies, such as head injury, may not occur.

Alexia with agraphia reflects the inability to write or read, with other language functions preserved such that fluency, comprehension, repetition and naming are intact. When alexia with agraphia predominate, mild dysnomia and/or paraphasias may be present.

Frequent comorbid conditions: Components of Gerstmann's syndrome (agraphia, acalculia, finger agnosia and right–left disorientation) are sometimes present.

Neuroanatomical correlates: Discrete lesion of the dominant (left) angular gyrus in the inferior parietal lobe.

Prognosis: Variable. Recovery from acute ischemic event can be full.

Agraphia without aphasia reflects the inability to write in the absence of other language impairments, and is infrequently observed.

Frequent comorbid conditions: Components of Gerstmann's syndrome (agraphia, acalculia, finger agnosia and right–left disorientation) are sometimes present.
Neuroanatomical correlates: Relatively small lesion of the dominant (left) angular gyrus in the inferior parietal lobe.
Prognosis: Variable. Recovery from acute ischemic event can be full.

Aphemia is an acquired inability to articulate speech, such that speech output is slow and very effortful. At its most severe, patients can present as being entirely mute. In milder forms, aphemia may sound as if the speaker was attempting to speak in an unusual accent. In all cases, writing is completely preserved as are the other language functions of comprehension, repetition and naming.

Frequent comorbid conditions: None, on occasion paraphasias and mild dysnomia.
Neuroanatomical correlates: Discrete lesion of the dominant (left) frontal lobe affecting Broca's area.
Prognosis: Variable. Recovery from acute ischemic event can be full.
NOTE: when speech articulation problems are present since birth (e.g., developmental problem), the above speech disturbance is labeled *verbal apraxia* rather than aphemia

Cortical Deafness, Nonverbal Auditory Agnosia and Verbal Auditory Agnosia (Pure Word Deafness)

Key Points: Cortical Deafness, Nonverbal Auditory Agnosia and Verbal Auditory Agnosia

- Cortical deafness—Inability to respond to sounds (verbal auditory sounds or nonverbal sounds) not due to simple sensory impairment.
- Nonverbal auditory agnosia—Inability to identify nonverbal sounds, but can accurately identify verbal sounds accurately (understand speech) not due to simple sensory impairment.
- Verbal auditory agnosia (pure word deafness)—Inability to identify verbal sounds (speech sounds) but is able to identify nonverbal sounds and can read and write normally.

Cortical deafness is a rare, but classic acquired, syndrome in which a patient is unable to respond to either spoken language (verbal sounds) or nonverbal sounds (buzzer, dog bark, etc.). Despite being unable to "hear" sounds, patients can respond to written and gestural instructions. Repetition for writing is intact. Other language functions, including fluency and naming are entirely intact. Distinguish cortical deafness from cortical auditory disorder (both auditory agnosias) by the presence of patient complaining of deafness in the former. Acoustic reflexes are preserved, and patients will orient to sudden loud sounds.

Frequent comorbid conditions: Varies with extent of lesion. Acoustic errors in sound recognition. Paraphasias possible.

Neuroanatomical correlates: Bilateral lesions of Heschl's gyrus (primary auditory cortex). Also bilateral damage to white matter immediately ventral and lateral to the posterior portion of the putamen disrupting projections from medial geniculate bodies.

Prognosis: Variable. Some recovery frequent, but depends upon etiology and extent of lesions. Resolution to amusia, generalized auditory agnosia and/or pure word deafness frequent.

Nonverbal auditory agnosia is the acquired inability to respond to nonverbal sounds (e.g., buzzer, dog bark) in light of preserved ability to respond accurately to speech sounds. Other language skills are entirely preserved.

Frequent premorbid conditions: Amusia.

Neuroanatomical correlates: Lesion of the nondominant (right) hemisphere of Heschl's gyrus and/or subcortical ascending auditory fibers from medial geniculate body.

Prognosis: Good. Typically recovers after several days to weeks.

Verbal auditory agnosia (*pure word deafness*) reflects the acquired inability to understand spoken speech (verbal sounds) with intact ability to respond to nonverbal sounds. Other language functions, including fluency, comprehension (to written language), repetition (read material) and naming are entirely intact.

Frequent comorbid conditions: Paraphasias are sometimes present.

Neuroanatomical correlates: Discrete lesion of the dominant (left) Heschl's gyrus (primary auditory cortex) that also involves the underlying white matter thereby preventing input of the contralateral primary auditory area to left hemisphere language areas.

Prognosis: Good. Symptoms typically resolve over days to weeks.

Aprosodies

The right hemisphere also plays a significant role in language and communication (Heilman and Valenstein, 2003; Lezak et al., 2004). Impairment of the right hemisphere often leads to a group of impairments collectively referred to as Aprosodies (see Ross, 1997, 2000 for review). Prosody refers to the ability to express and interpret vocal tone, inflection and other nonlanguage auditory cues and extract meaning that facilitates communication. The quality of an increased tone at the end of the sentence, "Here he comes," relates that it was a question rather than an affirmative statement. Similar auditory cues are used in detecting sarcasm, irony, innuendo and many other aspects of communication.

Prosodic functions are similarly represented as expressive and receptive language functions in the left hemisphere, with expressive prosody functions being associated with right anterior location and receptive prosody effects being associated with right posterior regions (Ross, 1997, 2000). The effect of prosody deficits in communication can be profound, leading to literal, inefficient communication, which has a significant impact on communication of emotional information. Individuals with expressive aprosody are often viewed by others as dull, emotionless and lacking compassion and empathy. Their verbal output is frequently monotone, flat and lacking the tone and inflection that correlates to the appropriate emotional state. When asked directly, they are often able to verbalize the presence of emotional states that they are not able to communicate in their verbal tone and inflection. Similarly, individuals with receptive aprosodies are often viewed as emotionally unavailable, lacking insight into others' emotional states or uncaring. They often miss verbal cues that would communicate the emotional states of others. This in turn leads to a decrease in appropriate emotional responsiveness and a generally literal interpretation of what is verbally said with little impact for the way it was verbalized or the context in which it occurred. Table 13.2 lists the major Aprosodies and their anatomical correlates.

Assessment

Please see Chap. 8 for a review of assessment of language disorders. Below, we provide an overview of a practical neuropsychological assessment of language disorders. There are many standardized assessment measures commercially available (see Lezak et al., 2004; Strauss et al., 2006, for reviews), and we discuss only some of the many currently available. However, our discussion below does *not* suggest a preference for one measure over another, but rather our familiarity with the measures discussed below. It is important to remember that neuropsychological (and neurological) syndromes are *not* an all or nothing phenomena. That is, a syndrome can be present in a range of severity, from subtle to severe. For example, a patient presenting with slow effortful speech consisting of short sentences (e.g., "I ...go.... home, I.....need....out."), who can repeat short sentences and has intact comprehension, but has difficulty repeating more complex sentences, would be considered to have Broca's aphasia in a mild to moderate form. Table 13.3 lists psychometric measures we commonly use in neuropsychological evaluations in the assessment of language functions.

Assess for Fluency

This assessment is not simply administering a verbal fluency test, e.g., Controlled Oral Word Association Test (COWAT; Benton et al., 1989; Spreen & Strauss, 1998) or confrontation naming tests (see Lezak et al., 2004, for review). Rather, the assessment must assess if the patient's speech output is effortless, articulate (well articulated),

Table 13.3 Commonly used psychometric based tests of language

Language domain	Test	Author
Expressive	Boston diagnostic Aphasia exam (BDAE)	Kaplan et al. (2001)
	Multilingual Aphasia exam (MAE)	Benton et al. (1989)
	Controlled Oral word association test (COWAT)	Benton et al. (1994)
	Neuropsychological Assessment battery (NAB)	Stern and White (2003)
	Semantic verbal fluency test (e.g., animals)	For review, see Straus et al. (2006)
	Woodcock-Johnson psychoeducational battery—third Ed. (WJ-III)	Woodcock et al. (2001)
	Western Aphasia battery (WAB)	Kertesz (1982)
• Writing/ spelling	BDAE	
	NAB	
	Peabody individual achievement test—Revised (PIAT-R)	Markwardt (1989, 1998).
	WAB	
	Wechsler individual achievement test-second Ed. (WIAT-II)	Wechsler (2001)
	WJ-III	Wilkinson and Robertson (2006)
	Wide range achievement test-fourth Ed. (WRAT-IV)	
Receptive	BDAE	
	MAE	
	NAB	
	WAB	
	Token test (part of WAB)	
	WJ-III	
• Reading comprehension	BDAE	
	NAB	
	PIAT-R	
	WJ-III	
	WRAT-IV	
• Oral reading	Grey Oral Reading test–fourth Ed. (GORT-4)	Wiederholt and Bryant (2001)
	WJ-III	
Repetition	BDAE	
	MAE	
	NAB	
	WAB	
Naming	Boston naming test (part of BDAE)	Goodglass et al. (2000)
	Columbia auditory naming test	Hamberger and Seidel (2003)
	MAE	
	NAB	
	WAB	

Note: The particular assessment instruments identified in this table are for convenience only, and authors have no preference for those listed or other measures which might also be available and not identified

rapid and understandable (intelligible). As reviewed above, several aphasia syndromes present with rapid, effortless speech that is not understandable. You will want to be able to assess what is the longest sentence the patient can speak accurately; typically, normal sentence length for native US English speakers is six–eight words. Are there word-finding problems (dysnomia)? Are there paraphasias? Semantic paraphasias include speaking (or writing) an incorrect word that is semantically related to the target word (i.e., “him” for “her” or “banana” for “apple”). Phonemic paraphasia involves speaking a word with an error in a letter sound (e.g., “carmel” for “camel” or “fump” for “dump”). Does the patient engage in circumlocution? Circumlocution can involve thematic circumlocution and provide a description of the term by general synonyms (e.g., “I want a …..thing, you know, the thing you use in your hand to say thank you with, you have one there [points to pen].”) or much more vague (empty) circumlocution (e.g., “the two for…no…big damn…no…there is a one there….one…two..three..”).

Assess for Comprehension

Comprehension is most easily assessed during the initial conversation. However, a careful step-by-step assessment will assure adequate evaluation of this domain. One might begin by asking open-ended questions (e.g., “What brought you in today?” or “Why are you here?”). Assessment should include asking the patient to respond to increasingly complex instructions/requests. The clinician may need to bring assistive devices (e.g., yes/no card or writing pad to assure other impairments will not limit evaluation of language comprehension). Comprehension can be assessed with single-step (point to the ceiling), two-step (point to the door and then the ceiling) and three-step (point to the door and then the floor, but first point to the ceiling) instructions. Comprehension can also follow with increasingly complex sentences. For example, a simple comprehension task can be asking a patient to state “what got hit?” given the following sentence: “the man hit the ball.”; then “the man was hit by the ball.” and finally more difficult still, with a passive negative statement “the man was not hit by the ball.” Subtle comprehension deficits can also be ascertained by inquiring with serious sounding prosodic questions such as “Is my hair on fire?”, followed with more difficult questions such as “Do kangaroos drive cars?” and “Do two pounds of candy weigh less than two pounds of rocks?”

Assess for Repetition

Have the patient begin by repeating simple sentences (The dog is big) to more complex sentences (The little man and the big dog ran around the tree). Finally, ask the patient to repeat grammatically dependent sentences (The cat was eaten by the mouse) and grammatically incorrect sentences (This pink circle heavier than red box).

Assess for Naming

Assess patients' ability to name visual objects by pointing (what do you call this ____?) as well as auditory descriptions (what do we call a four legged animal that barks and is often a household pet?).

Assess for Reading and Writing

Have the patient write a sentence and have the patient read a sentence silently to his/herself and do what it says (e.g., "raise a hand above your head" or "stick out your tongue.") You may also assess for reading out loud, as often with nonfluent aphasias, reading comprehension will be intact while oral reading is impaired. One might have the patient read a sentence (s)he writes as well as a unique sentence (s)he has not had previous exposure to.

Have the most familiarity and clinical experience, but should not be construed to indicate the tests in Table 13.3 are superior to other measures of language functioning.

Ethnic, Age, Diversity and Psychiatric Considerations

The astute clinician will appreciate the need to be sensitive to, and appreciate the potential for ethnic, age and sociocultural impacts on the assessment of language. While a detailed analysis of these issues is beyond the scope of this text, we highlight some ethical and practical considerations below.

Cultural Considerations

First, and foremost, it is essential that assessment of language occur in the patient's primary language. If this is not possible due to some limiting factor, the clinician must weigh the relative merits of completing an evaluation that will underestimate language abilities and potentially result in an incorrect diagnosis or determination for the extent of language impairment. Clinical neuropsychologists are sensitive to cultural and ethnicity variables that may adversely affect the reliability and validity of assessment (see American Psychological Association, 2002). It may be that the assessment of language functions occurs in the patient's second or third language that was acquired later in life and/or not as frequently used. Considerable work has identified that supplementary language areas can develop and/or the fluency or comprehension of the patient in the second or third language may have been reduced at baseline, thereby potentially leading the assessor to believe more language impairment exists than is actually present.

In addition to cultural/ethnicity variables of evaluating or treating an individual not having the same language as the assessor, one must also consider cultural factors with respect to the potential for differences in language dialects and customs for introducing the assessment and assessment procedures.

Pediatric Considerations

The assessment of language functions is particularly difficult in children to differentiate the presence of an acquired language deficit versus a developmental language problem, such as dyslexia or as a component of another neurodevelopmental process such as Autism or Asperger's disorder. It is essential to obtain a detailed history for the presence of developmental language problems prior to the onset of known or suspected neurological injury. In the case of early childhood trauma before onset of language functions, intra-hemispheric and/or inter-hemispheric language re-organization has been well documented (e.g., Kolb & Whishaw, 2008).

Geriatric Considerations

Geriatric assessment of language disorders may, at first blush, appear more clear-cut than in children or adults, but poses unique challenges. In particular, the assessment of language in older adults can be complicated by comorbid medical disorders that can adversely affect a patient's mental status, such as encephalopathies, sepsis, infections (e.g., acute urinary tract infection), cardiovascular insufficiency, pulmonary insufficiency, adverse effects from multiple medications, etc. The examiner should also not forget the potential impact of cultural differences in the doctor–patient relationship, in which the elderly may not wish to respond (functional mutism) during an assessment with a younger clinician.

Psychiatric Considerations

Distinguishing aphasia from psychosis, schizophrenia, other psychiatric illness or delirium may not seem important or difficult, but in clinical settings can be more difficult than is often readily appreciated. Perhaps this is the reason why articles and chapters reviewing the symptoms and signs of aphasia often do not include a discussion on differentiating psychiatric disorders from aphasias. It may also be the reason for some unfortunate patients with aphasia being diagnosed (and treated for) psychiatric disorders. We believe this is an important skill to develop and to provide an overview for distinguishing aphasia syndromes from psychiatric disorders.

Patients with schizophrenia, psychosis and thought disorders, bipolar disorders, primary mood disorders and delirium can present with a variety of speech problems, including speech that is fluent but unintelligible. Patients with primary psychiatric disorders presenting with fluent but unintelligible speech may be mistaken for the language problems associated with a fluent aphasia (e.g., Wernicke's, transcortical sensory or conduction aphasias). Similarly, patients with primary psychiatric disorder (or delirium) can also present with mutism or sparse verbal output that can be mistaken for the symptoms of a nonfluent aphasia (e.g., Broca's aphasia or, more often, transcortical motor or anomic aphasia).

Patients with aphasic syndromes can be misdiagnosed with a primary psychiatric disorder and not having a Wernicke's, conduction and transcortical sensory aphasia may be misdiagnosed as having a psychiatric disorder, due to the appearance of bizarre speech output.

Patients with Broca's and transcortical motor, and mixed transcortical, are at risk of being mislabeled as having a primary psychiatric disorder. However, patients with an aphasia often present with symptoms of apathy and tearfulness.

Aphasia: Shorter sentences, paraphasias more common and frequent dysnomia. Aphasias often have associated neurologic (motor/sensory) deficits.

Patients with Broca's aphasia often present with tearfulness that is greater than observed for patients with more posterior dominant hemisphere lesions that result in fluent aphasias. Their affective expressions are exaggerated, reflecting damage to the frontal lobe (see Chaps. 3 and 11 for further review).

Psychosis/schizophrenia "word salad" is marked by long, tangential responses to questions. Neologisms common while paraphasias rare. Rarely associated with focal neurologic symptoms.

References

American Psychological Association. (2002). Ethical principles of psychologists and code of conduct. *American Psychologist, 57*, 1060–1073.

Benton, A. L., Hamsher, K., & de, S. (1989). *Multilingual aphasia examination*. AJA Associates.

Benton, A. L., De Hamsher, S. K., & Sivan, A. B. (1994). *Multilingual aplasia examination* (3rd ed.). AJA Associates.

Damasio, H., Grabowski, T. J., Tranel, D., Hichwa, R. D., & Damasio, A. R. (1996). A neural basis for lexical retrieval. *Nature, 380*, 499–505.

Kaplan, E., Goodglass, H., & Weintraub, S. (2001). *The Boston naming test*. Lippincott Williams & Wilkins.

Goodglass, H., Kaplan, E., & Barresi, B. (2000). *The Boston diagnostic aphasia examination (BDAE-3)* (3rd ed.). Lippincott Williams & Wilkins.

Goodglass, H., Kaplan, E., & Barresi, B. (2001). *The assessment of aphasia and related disorders* (3rd ed.). Pro-Ed.

Hamberger, M., & Seidel, W. T. (2003). Auditory and visual naming tests: normative and patient data for accuracy, response time and tip-of-the-tongue. *Journal of the International Neuropsychological Society, 9*, 479–489.

Heilman, K. M., & Valenstein, E. (2003). *Clinical neuropsychology* (4th ed.). Oxford University Press.

Kertexz, A. (1982). *Western aphasia battery*. The Psychological Corporation.

Kolb, B., & Whishaw, I. Q. (2008). *Fundamentals of human neuropsychology* (6th ed.). Worth Publishing Company.

Lezak, M. D., Howieson, D. B., & Loring, D. W. (2004). *Neuropsychological assessment* (4th ed.). Oxford University Press.

Markwardt, F. C., Jr. (1989, 1998). The Peabody individual achievement test-revised. : NCS Pearson, Inc.

Mesulam, M. M. (2000). *Principles of behavioral and cognitive neurology* (2nd ed.). Oxford University Press.

Risse, G. L., Rubens, A. B., & Jordan, L. S. (1984). Disturbances in long-term memory in aphasic patients: A comparison of anterior and posterior lesions. *Brain, 107*, 605–617.

Ross, E. D. (1997). The aprosodies. In T. E. Feinberg & M. J. Farah (Eds.), *Behavioral neurology and neuropsychology* (pp. 699–717). McGraw-Hill.

Ross, E. D. (2000). Affective prosody and the aprosodias. In M. M. Mesulam (Ed.), *Principles of behavioral and cognitive neurology* (2nd ed., pp. 316–331). Oxford University Press.

Spreen, O., & Strauss, E. (1998). *A compendium of neuropsychological tests: Administration, norms, and commentary* (2nd ed.). Oxford University Press.

Stern, R. A., & White, T. (2003). *Neuropsychological assessment battery (NAB)*. Psychological Assessment Resources.

Strauss, E., Sherman, E. M. S., & Spreen, O. (2006). *A compendium of neuropsychological tests: administration, norms, and commentary* (3rd ed.). Oxford University Press.

Victor, M., & Ropper, A. H. (2001). *Adams and Victor's principals of neurology* (7th ed.). McGraw-Hill.

Wechsler, D. (2001). *Wechsler individual achievement test—2nd Ed (WIAT-II)*. The Psychological Corporation.

Wiederholt, J. L., & Bryant, B. R. (2001). *Gray oral reading test-fourth edition (GORT-4)*. Pro-Ed.

Wilkinson, G. S., & Robertson, G. J. (2006). *Wide range achievement test-fourth edition*. Psychological Assessment Resources.

Woodcock, R. W., McGrew, K. W., & Mather, N. (2001). *Woodcock-Johnson III*. Riverside Publishing.

Chapter 14
Cerebrovascular Disease and Stroke

Michelle A. Babicz-Boston, Erin K. Bailey, and Joel E. Kamper

Introduction to Cerebrovascular Disease and Stroke

Stroke is broadly defined by a clinical presentation of acute-onset neurological deficit due to cerebrovascular disease. The underlying mechanisms, however, are heterogenous and span a vast array of pathologies, each with distinctive clinical presentations, prognoses and strategies for management. While strokes can occur across the lifespan, incidence increases with age as accumulation of chronic health conditions raises the risk of stroke. For this reason, strokes are also more common in underserved populations where health disparities and socioeconomic factors may limit access to care and exacerbate disease burden. Below, we review the risk factors for cerebrovascular disease, the basic anatomy of cerebral vasculature, classification of strokes and clinical features. We also provide a summary of specific cerebrovascular syndromes associated with different types of strokes and the cognitive presentation of various focal lesions (Fig. 14.1).

M. A. Babicz-Boston · J. E. Kamper
Mental Health Behavioral Science Service, James A. Haley Veteran's Hospital, Tampa, FL, USA

E. K. Bailey (✉)
Mental Health Behavioral Science Service, James A. Haley Veteran's Hospital, Tampa, FL, USA

Department of Psychiatry, University of South Florida, Tampa, FL, USA
e-mail: erin.bailey@va.gov

M. R. Schoenberg, J. G. Scott (eds.), *The Little Black Book of Neuropsychology*,
https://doi.org/10.1007/978-3-032-07777-6_14

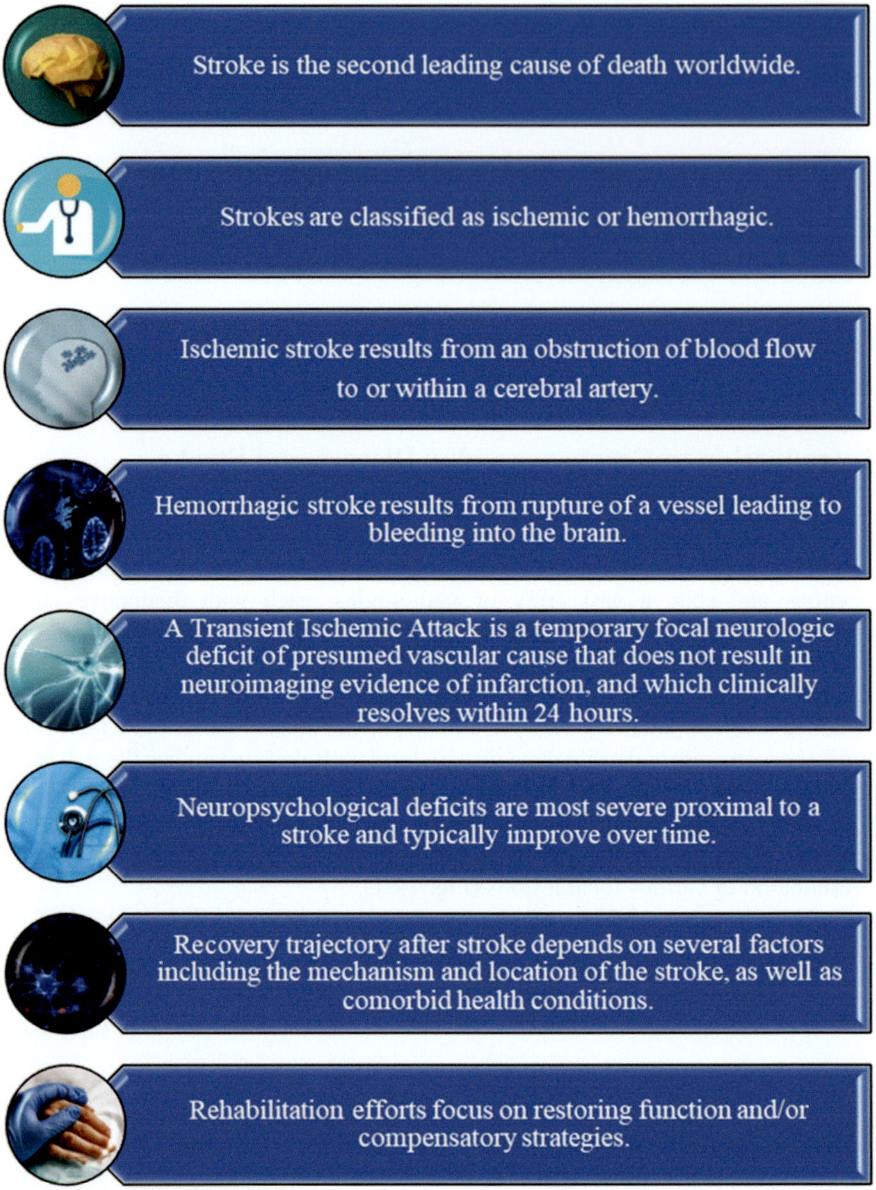

Fig. 14.1 Chapter summary

Overview of Stroke

Stroke is one of the most well-known syndromes affecting the brain. The classic presentation of abrupt onset focal neurologic deficit is well-known to health professionals. Public education campaigns designed to improve recognition and reporting of stroke warning signs and symptoms have traditionally focused on the most common clinical presentations as seen in Fig. 14.2 below.

However, patients may also present with subtle symptoms that are nonspecific, insidious and less expected (e.g., headache, loss of consciousness, etc.). Atypical presentation of stroke may also include little to no change in cognitive status. Similarly, changes in emotion or affect are not as readily recognized as symptoms of stroke. Further, seizures can be seen in about 8–9% of all ischemic strokes and 10–11% of all hemorrhagic strokes, which may complicate the clinical picture (Bladin et al., 2000).

Epidemiology and Risk Factors

Stroke is the second leading cause of death and is one of the most common causes of long-term disability worldwide (Feigin et al., 2022). Mortality from stroke has risen in recent years, especially in lower-income countries. In the United States,

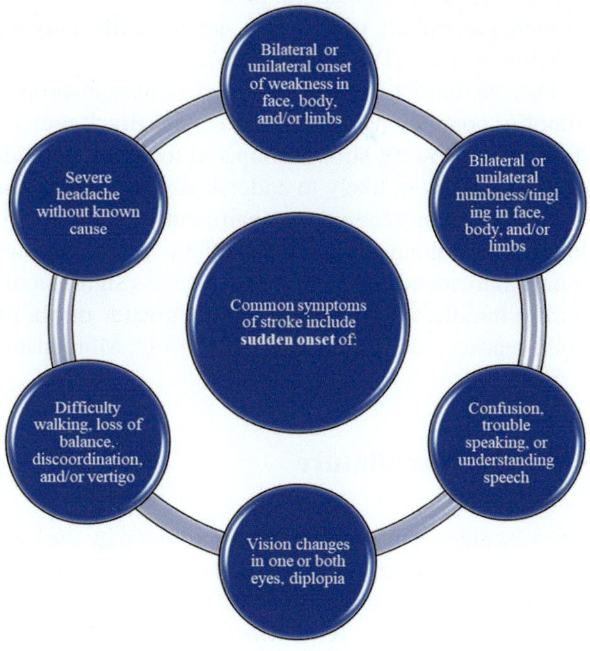

Fig. 14.2 Common symptoms of stroke (National Stroke Association, 2007)

data collected from 2017 to 2020 show a 3.3% prevalence of stroke among those aged 18+. However, this is expected to rise to 3.9% in the next 30 years—representing an increase of 20.5% when compared to stroke prevalence in 2012 (Tsao et al., 2023). Each year, approximately 800,000 individuals in the USA experience an initial (~75%) or recurrent (~25%) stroke.

Numerous health conditions have been identified as risk factors for stroke, including hypertension, hypercholesterolemia, diabetes, tobacco use and atrial fibrillation. While hypertension remains the most common cause of an initial stroke event, diabetes is most associated with stroke recurrence. Psychosocial risk factors include unemployment, extended working hours and adverse working conditions, while having a strong social network has been identified as a protective factor. Rates of stroke recurrence are reduced with improved adherence to secondary stroke prevention guidelines and statin-based therapies.

Latino/a and Black individuals have higher prevalence of stroke due to the disproportional impact of social, environmental and health factors which increase overall population risk. Minority individuals may be less likely to seek care (Gonzalez et al., 2021), may be seen as less compliant with treatment by their providers (Kaplan et al., 2004) and have lower health literacy (Osborn et al., 2009). Minority populations also have increased risk of vascular disease and other conditions which predispose stroke (Gardener, et al., 2020). For example, in the United States, Black adults are nearly twice as likely to die from cardiovascular compared to white adults. High blood pressure, obesity, tobacco use and diabetes are also more prevalent in certain racial/ethnic minority groups in the USA, particularly Black Americans (Kurian & Cardarelli, 2007). Women also have a higher lifetime risk of stroke compared to men. Given these demographic differences, Black women, particularly over age 60, are at significantly higher risk of stroke compared to White women (Tsao et al., 2023).

Disease burden following stroke is also disproportionally represented among minority populations. Both Latino/a and Black individuals report greater cognitive disability following stroke compared to White individuals. Black individuals, specifically, are more likely to endorse stroke-related functional disability at one year and report chronic cognitive impairment within 5 years of having a stroke. Disparities in disease burden across racial/ethnic minorities are compounded by temporal trends in incidence rates. Minorities have a significantly higher prevalence of stroke during middle age, which results in greater disability during prime earning and child-rearing years (Broderick et al., 1998; Morgenstern et al., 2013).

Cerebral Vasculature

The vascular supply to the brain is provided by the internal carotid arteries (anterior circulation) and the vertebral-basilar arteries (posterior circulation) (Fig. 14.3 and Image 14.1). Venous blood is returned to the heart via a complementary network of anterior and posterior veins which generally empty into the jugular vein.

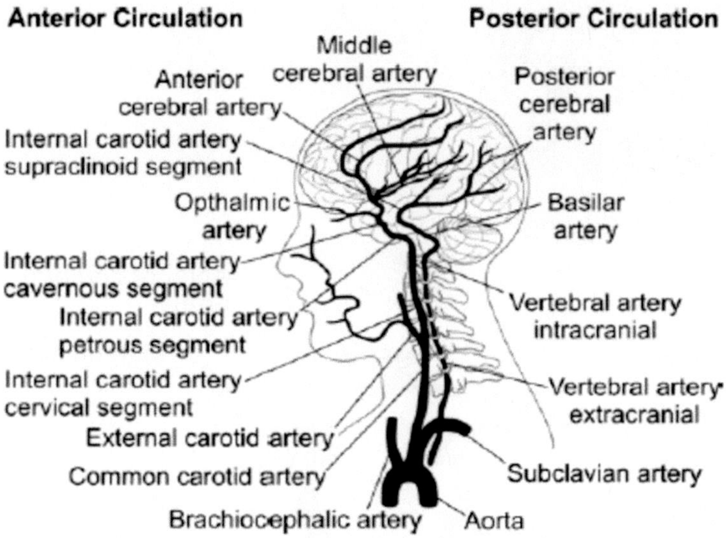

Fig. 14.3 Vasculature of head and brain

Image 14.1 Magnetic resonance angiogram (MRA) showing the common carotid and vertebral arteries

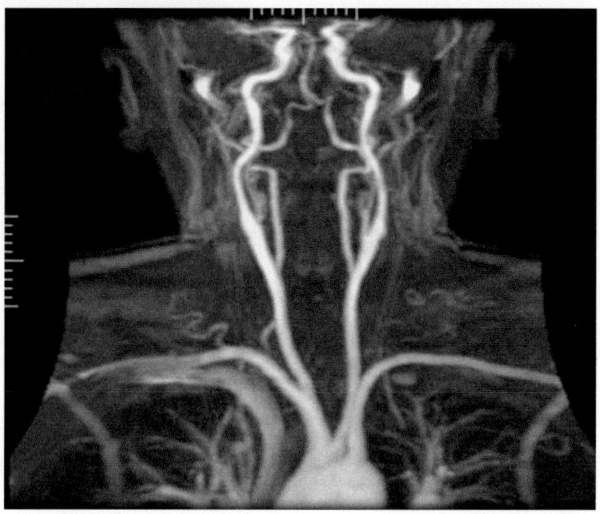

Circle of Willis

The anterior and posterior cerebral circulation systems converge in the Circle of Willis (see Fig. 14.4). The anterior segment of the Circle of Willis includes the Anterior Communicating artery (AComm/ACoA) which allows flow between the right and left Anterior Cerebral Arteries (ACAs). The ACAs form another aspect of the circle as they connect to the Internal Carotid Artery (ICA). The Internal Carotid

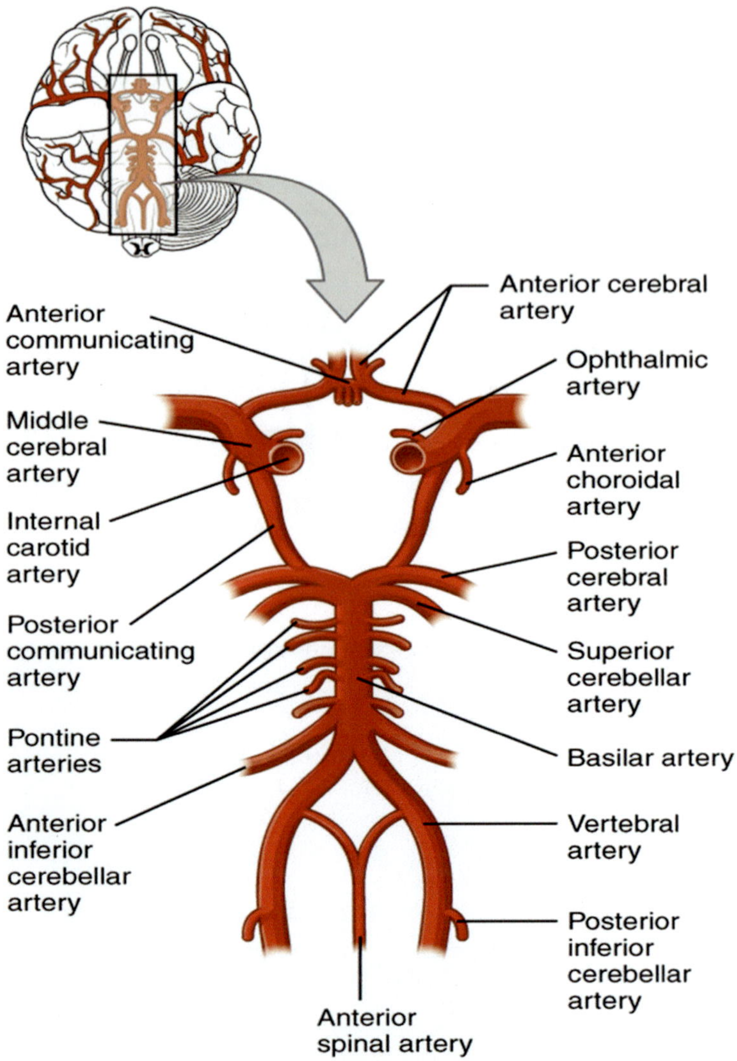

Fig. 14.4 Circle of Willis along with vertebral and internal carotid arteries

arteries are connected to the posterior circulations via Posterior Communicating arteries (PComms/PCoAs). The two PCAs branch off from the top of the Basilar artery. While a complete Circle of Willis is present in about 25% of normal adults, collateral flow is almost always present to varying degrees.

Anterior Circulation

The Common Carotid arteries typically arise from the Aorta (in some individuals, the Common Carotid arteries originate from the brachiocephalic arteries) and extend up to the neck, where they branch into the *External Carotid* and *Internal Carotid* arteries. The External Carotid arteries provide perfusion to the face, scalp and meninges. The Internal Carotid arteries extend nearly vertical until making a quick turn as they enter the dura at the base of the brain. The Internal Carotids then enter the cavernous sinus (referred to as the Carotid Siphon or cavernous segment) and extend through subarachnoid space to the Circle of Willis, where they branch into the Ophthalmic artery, Posterior Communicating artery (PComm/PCoA), Anterior Choroidal artery, Anterior Cerebral artery (ACA) and the Middle Cerebral artery (MCA) (Figs. 14.4 and 14.5).

To remember the arteries originating from the internal carotid artery, remember the acronym OPAAM (Fig. 14.6).

Ophthalmic Artery:

- Provides circulation to the optic nerve and retina.

Posterior Communicating Artery (PComm or PCoA):

- Forms connections between the anterior and posterior circulation systems.

Anterior Choroidal Artery:

- Provides circulation to subcortical areas including part of the lenticular nucleus (i.e., globus pallidus and putamen), thalamus and the posterior limb of the internal capsule.

Anterior Cerebral Artery (ACA):

- Perfuses the anterior medial areas of the brain (area between the interhemispheric fissures dividing the two hemispheres of the brain), including the entire mesial frontal lobes, cingulate gyrus, corpus callosum, fornix (anterior segment) and may extend posteriorly to the mesial area of the parietal lobes. It also perfuses

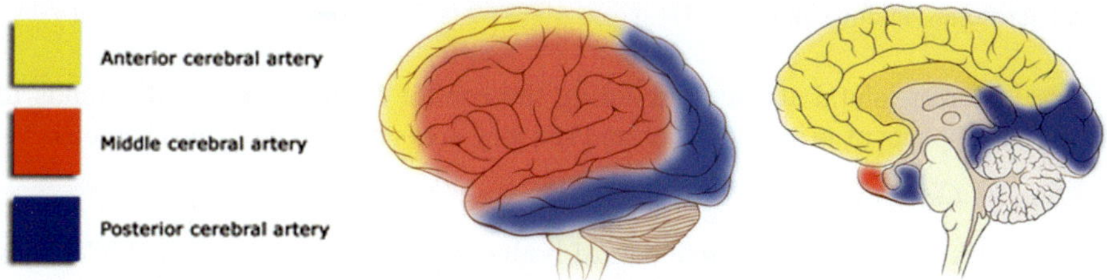

Fig. 14.5 Sagittal planes showing main cerebral arterial vascular territories. From Radiopaedia by Frank Galliard. (https://radiopaedia.org/cases/vascular-territories-of-the-lateral-cerebral-cortex-illustration)

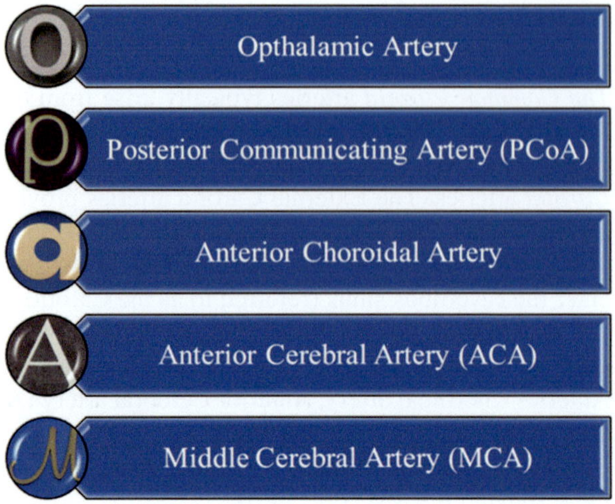

Fig. 14.6 OPAAM Acronym

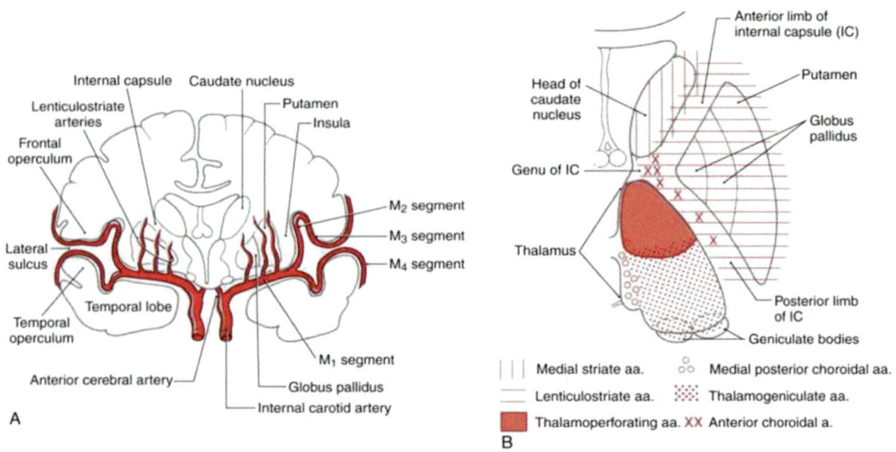

Fig. 14.7 Vascular perfusion of basal ganglia and internal capsule structures in coronal (**a**) and axial (**b**) planes. (**a**) From Neupsykey. (https://neupsykey.com/the-basal-nuclei/). (**b**) From Wikimedia Commons by Frank Gilliard (https://commons.wikimedia.org/wiki/File:Cerebral_vascular_territories_midline.jpg)

the anterior lateral surface, including the orbital frontal lobes, and extends to dorsal aspects of primary motor and sensory areas around the central sulcus.

Middle Cerebral Artery (MCA)

- Provides circulation to a large part of both cerebral hemispheres. The MCA runs horizontally along the base of the brain and, before entering the Sylvian fissure, gives rise to a series of small perforating arteries, the *Lenticulostriate arteries* (See Fig. 14.7), which enter the brain through the anterior perforated substance providing blood to a large area of the basal ganglia and internal capsule. Once the MCA reaches the insula, it branches into superior and inferior divisions.

- The **superior** division of the MCA provides circulation above the Sylvian fissure, including the lateral frontal and most of the lateral parietal lobes.
- The **inferior** division provides blood to the lateral temporal lobe and a posterior portion of the parietal lobes.

Posterior Circulation

As shown in Fig. 14.8, the posterior circulation includes the bilateral vertebral arteries, the basilar artery and its branches. The vertebral arteries arise from the Subclavian arteries and are encased by the foramina transversaria of the cervical vertebrae to enter the skull via the foramen magnum. The vertebral arteries ascend along the ventral surface of the medulla, eventually joining together to form the *Basilar artery* near the pontomedullary junction. Along this course, the vertebral arteries give rise to bilateral *Anterior Spinal arteries* and *Posterior Inferior Cerebellar arteries* (PICA). Arising along with the *Basilar artery* are the two *Anterior Inferior Cerebellar arteries* (AICAs). The Basilar artery then runs

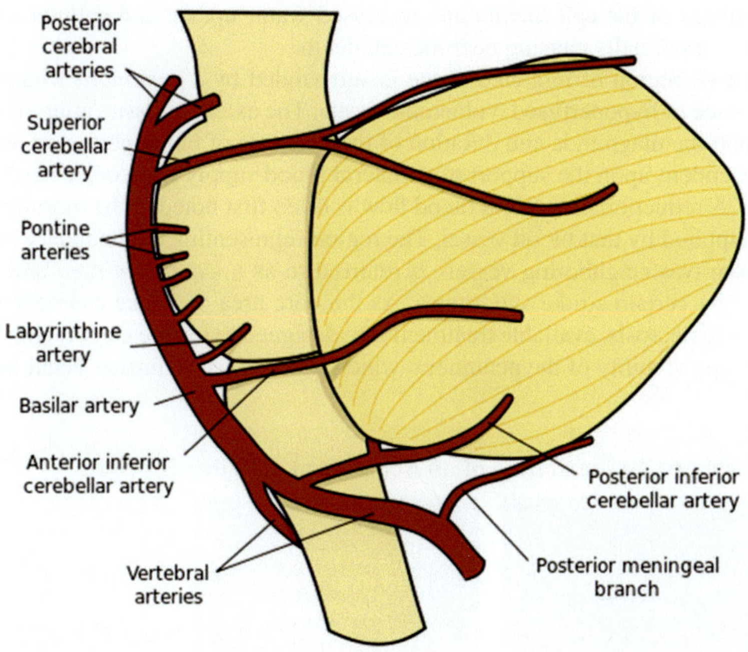

Fig. 14.8 Cerebellar arteries. From Wikimedia Commons (https://commons.wikimedia.org/wiki/File:Cerebellum_arteries_en.svg)

along the ventral surface of the pons and midbrain with branches that form the bilateral *Superior Cerebellar arteries* (SCAs) and, at the distal end, terminates by dividing into the two *Posterior Cerebral arteries* (PCAs). *Posterior Cerebral arteries* perfuse the mesial and inferior temporal lobes (including the hippocampus) as well as the occipital lobes (both inferior, mesial and lateral areas of the occipital lobes).

Ischemic Pathophysiology and Cerebrovascular Disease

Ischemia

A disruption of arterial flow results in rapid dysfunction of the underlying brain tissue due to two processes: (1) loss of oxygen and glucose necessary for cell processes and (2) various alterations to cellular metabolism leading to loss of cell integrity. Several changes occur acutely with ischemia: venous blood darkens with decreased oxygen saturation, blood becomes thicker (more viscous), the area of ischemic tissue pales and arteries narrow. At a molecular level, the normal cellular processes are disrupted (e.g., Krebs cycle) with ATP depletion, increased intracellular calcium and extracellular potassium. Cells release the excitatory neurotransmitters glutamate and aspartate, leading to an influx of sodium and calcium leading to disruption of the cell membrane, increased water update and cellular swelling (edema)—eventually causing necrotic cell death.

The core region of infarcted tissue is surrounded by a *penumbra* which represents a zone of hypoperfused, vulnerable tissue. The extent of tissue injury is dependent upon the magnitude and duration of the decrease of blood perfusion, which is also dependent upon the support of collateral blood supply from other neighboring arteries. A reduction in cerebral blood flow is often first noted in the most distal territory supplied by that blood vessel. The region representing the boundary of blood flow from two neighboring vessels is referred to as a *watershed area* and can be affected by certain stroke syndromes. As the core area of stroke can very rapidly progress to necrosis, available treatments are designed to restore cerebral blood flow and salvage viability of the penumbra, which is discussed in further detail below.

Key Points: In the Setting of an Acute Stroke, "Time is Brain"

- Irreversible neuronal damage can occur rapidly
- Early intervention can lead to improved outcomes

White Matter Disease (Leukoaraiosis)

White matter disease is a common finding on neuroimaging and can reflect a pathologic clinical syndrome. While clinical lore suggests that 1–2 white matter foci after age 40 are "normal," the disease burden can vary greatly depending on a patient's chronic health conditions (the so-called cerebrovascular risk factors), as discussed below. White matter disease is often described by a host of names, including "small vessel disease," "leukoaraiosis," "microvascular disease," "microvascular ischemia," "periventricular white matter changes," and "chronic white matter disease." As suggested by many of these terms, white matter disease is typically relegated to periventricular and subcortical areas, as well as occasionally the pons. White matter disease can be thought of as the diffuse end of the pathological spectrum that encompasses other forms of ischemia (Iadecola et al., 2009).

Brain ischemia is the result of lipohyalinosis and microatheromas in cerebral vessels. Lipohyalinosis refers to decreased vessel elasticity and hardening which leads to a thickened vessel wall. This in turn reduces the lumen of the vessel, which limits the amount of blood and oxygen that can pass through. Microatheroma is the result of atherosclerosis, or arterial plaquing. Flow of blood and oxygen is reduced as plaque accumulates, causing vessels to narrow. Eventually, unstable plaques may break apart, leading to microatheromas that clog downstream arteries. These pathologies are not unique to white matter disease and can also represent the underlying mechanism of larger vessel strokes.

It should also be noted that periventricular white matter is only marginally perfused, with less redundancy than cortical areas which makes it more vulnerable to ischemic injury (Jellinger, 2013). Similarly, the small lenticulostriate arteries that perfuse subcortical white matter tracts are uniquely susceptible to pathological changes both due to their small diameter—even when healthy,—as well as the right angle they take when branching off the MCA. Finally, these arteries are uniquely vulnerable to capillary loss and an increase in microvascular tortuosity with aging (Iadecola et al., 2009). This may explain why some degree of white matter disease burden is commonly seen in healthy, asymptomatic older adults.

In addition to aging, there are several chronic health conditions that can lead to a higher vascular disease burden. Uncontrolled diabetes and hypertension are the two most salient risk factors (Faraco & Iadecola, 2013). Diabetes increases inflammation and can directly affect blood vessels, leading to an increase in atherosclerosis. Untreated hypertension, in contrast, promotes lipohyalinosis, as described above. Untreated sleep apnea also reflects a potent risk factor, albeit one that may be partially reversible with treatment. White matter changes are best appreciated on T2 FLAIR (Fluid Attenuated Inversion Recovery), which nulls the water signal and allows for periventricular pathology to be easily seen (Image 14.2).

When white matter ischemic disease causes clinical symptoms detectable on neuropsychological evaluation, a patient may experience a classic subcortical pattern, involving poor processing speed, psychomotor slowing, reduced attention (basic attention may be preserved) and executive dysfunction. Subcortical executive dysfunction usually involves poor learning and retrieval (with preserved

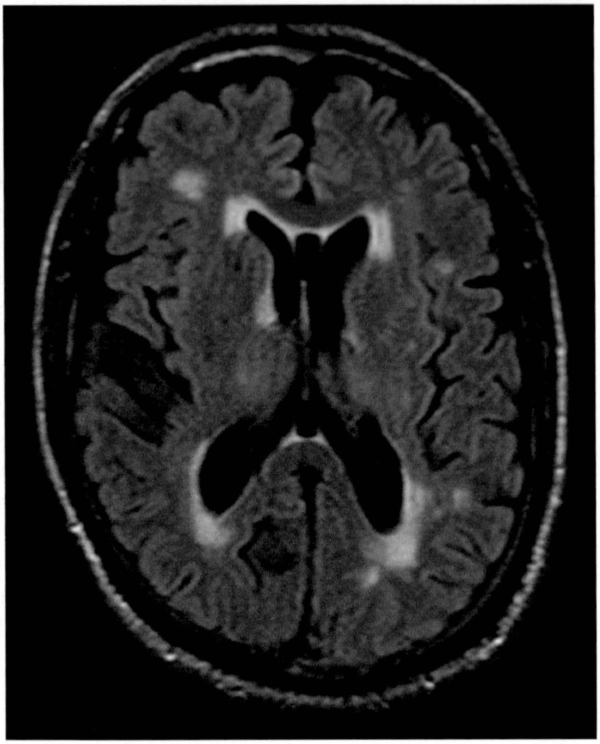

Image 14.2 Magnetic resonance imaging (MRI) demonstrating periventricular and subcortical T2-weighted hyperintensities consistent with small-vessel ischemic disease

recognition) on memory tasks, poor set switching/complex attention, impaired working memory and poor verbal fluency (typically phonemic). "Hard" frontal lobe signs such as perseverations, stimulus-bound behaviors and disinhibition are less often seen but if present are typically of a dorsolateral prefrontal nature. Such patients are typically diagnosed with Vascular Cognitive Impairment (VCI). This term encompasses both mild cognitive disorder and vascular dementia (VaD), the latter of which is diagnosed when the lesion burden begins to interfere with independence in daily functioning. Vascular dementia due to diffuse white matter disease was previously termed "Binswanger's Disease" which was more related to atherosclerosis and did not account for the totality of vascular risk factors (Hachinski et al., 2006).

CADASIL/CARASIL: The differential diagnosis of vascular dementia with multifocal white matter changes includes amyloid angiopathy (described later in the chapter) and *Cerebral Autosomal Dominant Arteriopathy with Subcortical Infarcts and Leukoencephalopathy* (CADASIL). A similar autosomal recessive type (CARASIL) can also be seen, though is extremely rare. CADASIL results from mutations on the notch 3 gene on chromosome 19. As the MRI changes precede the clinical manifestations, neuroimaging should be considered when progressive cognitive decline is associated with a personal and family history of migraine headaches, seizures, TIAs and stroke, and particularly when affecting young individuals (Image 14.3).

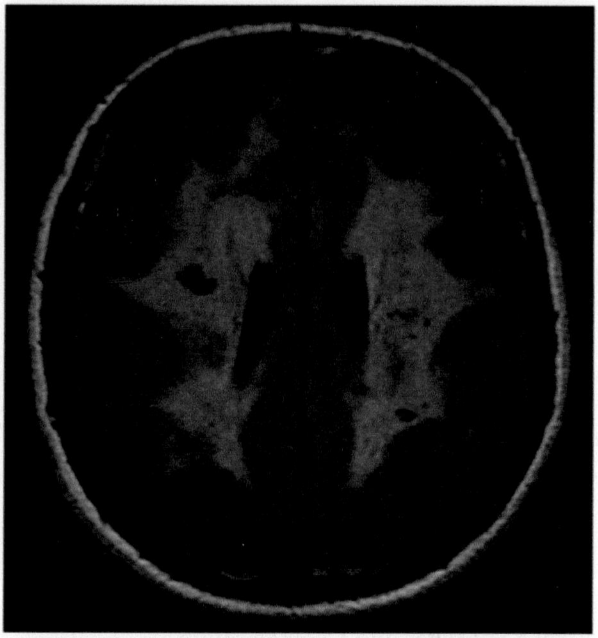

Image 14.3 Profound white matter changes on MRI associated with cavitary changes in a patient with CADASIL

Transient Ischemic Attacks

Transient ischemic attacks (TIAs) are classically defined as a sudden, painless, focal neurologic deficit of presumed vascular origin, in which symptoms resolve in <24 hours. However, the majority of TIAs resolve much more quickly, often in less than 1 hour. Previously, a lack of neuroimaging findings or symptom resolution <24 hours was included in categorization of TIAs. However, diffusion-weighted magnetic resonance imaging (DWI MRI) has led to revision of this definition, as acute lesions/infarctions have been identified in ~13% of individuals with TIA (Tsao et al., 2023). The sensitivity of detecting cerebral injury on neuroimaging varies with the neuroimaging modality used (CT vs. T2-weighted MRI vs. DWI-MRI) and the duration of the symptoms in question, such that no specific time interval is known to accurately distinguish between a TIA and an ischemic stroke. Neuroimaging evidence of a recent cerebral infarction is detected in 15–20% of morphological Head CT scans and 50–71% of diffusion-weighted MRI (DWI) scans with symptoms persisting >6 hours but <24 hours (see Image 14.4).

The presumed mechanism of TIA is a transient occlusion of a cerebral vessel compromised by stenosis, or from an embolus which undergoes spontaneous recanalization. TIAs are important warning symptoms of impending ischemic stroke and are considered a medical emergency warranting urgent medical attention. Within 3 months of a TIA, 8–10% of patients suffer a stroke with half of these occurring within the subsequent 48 hours (e.g., Johnston et al., 2000; Rothwell et al., 2005). The symptom features of TIA follow functional neuroanatomic association of the cerebral vasculature.

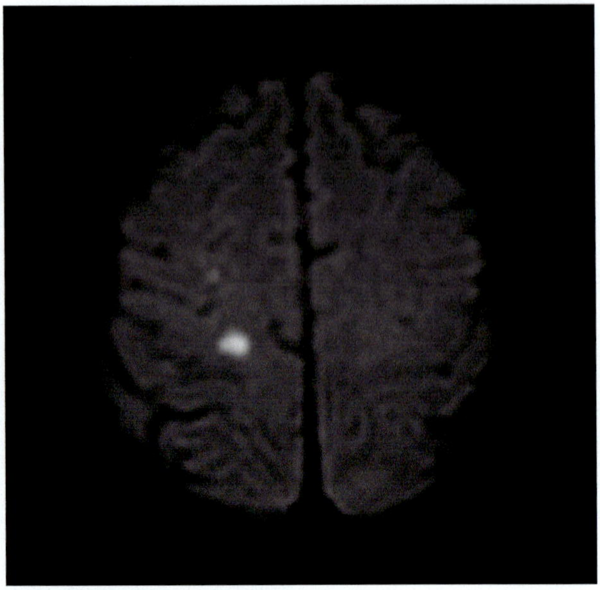

Image 14.4 Diffusion-weighted MRI demonstrating a small infarct in the right parietal lobe (Shaded gray area; recall that on neuroimaging coronal and horizontal images are presented as if the patient is looking at you and thus right and left are reversed) in a patient with 6 hours of left arm paresthesias consistent with embolism to the right middle cerebral artery

Stroke Subtypes and Categorization

Strokes are categorized by pathophysiology (see Fig. 14.9). The major categorization of stroke is whether it is *Ischemic* or *Hemorrhagic*.

Key Points: Stroke Categorization

Ischemic Stroke

- obstruction in blood flow to brain
- ~85% of all strokes

Hemorrhagic Stroke

- bleeding into the brain
- ~15% of all strokes

Ischemic stroke (IS) or *cerebral infarction* occurs when an arterial flow to the brain is obstructed and accounts for ~85% of all strokes. *Hemorrhagic stroke* occurs when an artery or vein ruptures causing intracranial bleeding and accounts for ~15% of all strokes. There are multiple subtypes of ischemic and hemorrhagic strokes, which we review below.

1. Ischemic strokes & Transient ischemic attacks (TIAs)	Large artery atherosclerosis	
	Lacunar or small vessel arteriosclerosis	
	Cardioembolism	
	Crypotogenic	
	Other Known Cause	Cervicocephalic dissection
		Coagulopathy
		Non-atherosclerotic arteriopathy (e.g., CADASIL)
		Metabolic disorders (e.g., MELAS)
		Migraine
		Vasculitis
		Drug abuse
2. Hemorrhagic Strokes	Intracerebral Hemorrhage	Hypertension
		Amyloid angiopathy
		Arteriovenous Malformation (AVM)
		Hematologic disorder
		Hemorrhagic transformation of recent cerebral infarct
		Hemorrhage into tumor
	Subarachnoid Hemorrhage	Saccular aneurysm
		Arteriovenous malformation
		Hematologic disorder
		Mycotic (infectious) aneurysm
3. Cerebral Venous Thrombosis	Dural sinus thrombosis	
	Cortical venous thrombosis	

Fig. 14.9 Stroke subtypes

Ischemic Stroke

Classification

Ischemic strokes (*infarctions*) can be classified in many ways including: by clinical severity, by pathophysiologic process leading to the vascular occlusion, or by presumed underlying mechanism. The latter is the most clinically useful, as the underlying mechanism will determine the optimum treatment plan for prevention of further vascular events. Most vessels become occluded through a process of thrombosis, embolism or both. Thrombotic strokes occur when a vessel is occluded from clot formation at the site of a ruptured atherosclerotic plaque. Embolic strokes refer to a vascular occlusion from material (or *embolus*) originating from a tertiary source, such as a distal artery or the heart. The embolus is typically comprised of fibrin, coagulated blood and/or plaque; but may be some other material (e.g., tumor cells, air, etc.).

The TOAST classification scheme is clinically useful and is often used in practice. Developed for prospective use in the Trial of Org 10,172 in Acute Stroke Treatment (TOAST; Adams et al., 1993), it has limitations when used retrospectively, and employs the clinical presentation, results of neuroimaging studies and laboratory tests to determine an underlying mechanism with varying levels of certainty (definite, probable and possible). The TOAST scheme classifies ischemic stroke into five subtypes: (1) large-artery atherosclerosis, (2) cardioembolism, (3) small-vessel occlusion, (4) stroke of other determined etiology and (5) stroke of undetermined etiology (cryptogenic).

Another commonly used measure is the National Institutes of Health Stroke Scale (NIHSS). This instrument is used to quantify the impairment caused by a stroke and to help predict and plan for rehabilitation and post-acute care needs. It consists of 11 items, assessing level of consciousness, visual gaze/fields, motor functions, sensory functions, language and visual neglect/inattention. Items are on an objective, 0–4-point scale similar to the GCS. NIHSS is meant to be used both for baseline assessment and as a repeated measure to gauge post-stroke recovery.

Large-artery atherosclerosis involving the extracranial or intracranial vessels accounts for about 20% of ischemic strokes. Cardioembolism, which includes the heart and proximal sources of embolism, accounts for 15–20% of ischemic strokes. Lacunar infarcts, resulting from atherosclerotic occlusion of small perforating arteries from hypertension and diabetes, results in characteristic clinical syndromes and accounts for another 20–25% of ischemic strokes. Thus, forms of atherosclerotic disease and cardioembolism account for about two-thirds of all ischemic strokes. Rarer causes including cervicocephalic dissection, nonatherosclerotic arteriopathies, coagulopathies, metabolic disorders, migraine, vasculitis and drug abuse account for about 5% of ischemic strokes. The cause of the remaining 30% of ischemic strokes have been classified as cryptogenic, indicating the cause has not been established, either because an adequate diagnostic evaluation was not performed, an underlying condition was not documented at the time of the evaluation or multiple potential causes were demonstrated. These proportions of the various subtypes vary by the age group under study, with young adults having a higher percentage of "other" causes.

Expected Clinical Presentations

The signs and symptoms of cerebral ischemia and infarction are determined by both the location and the extent of brain tissue injured. Focal neurologic and/or neuropsychologic deficits develop abruptly and are typically painless without depressed consciousness and evolve over the course of seconds to hours. Stroke progression can occur in 10–20% of patients, usually in the setting of a thrombotic occlusion of a vessel with declining blood flow or repeated embolism. The neurologic and neuropsychologic deficits associated with stroke are linked to the areas of the brain perfused by the vessel(s) involved (Figs. 14.10, 14.11, 14.12 and 14.13).

Malignant Stroke Syndromes

A small percentage (<10%) of ischemic strokes are associated with large amounts of edema that is severe enough to cause midline shift and herniation and are termed “Malignant Stroke” (Liebeskind et al., 2019). These infarcts are typically the result of embolic or thrombotic etiologies (i.e., less likely atherosclerotic) and can affect any vessel, though they are most common in the MCA distribution. Unlike a typical infarct, which clinically improves over time assuming no secondary events, malignant strokes often lead to progressive and rapid deterioration within the first several days post-stroke (up to a week in some studies; Hacke et al., 1996). In such cases, the volume of edema can mimic a tumor or other space-occupying lesion, leading to depressed consciousness, pupillary and other cranial nerve signs and worsened motor responses (Wijdicks et al., 2014). Due to swelling and the risk of brainstem herniation, craniectomy and other emergent neurosurgical interventions may be needed.

Cerebral Artery Syndromes

MCA Distribution Stroke

Typical physical deficits include contralateral motor weakness, particularly for tasks requiring fine manual dexterity, contralateral sensory deficits and hemispace neglect or inattention evidenced by extinction to bilateral simultaneous stimulation. Motor weakness is classically worse for upper extremities (vs. lower, which is more common with ACA lesions). While sources differ to some degree, most providers consider neglect and inattention as two ends of a single severity spectrum (with inattention being less severe). Hemispace inattention or neglect is typically due to parietal lesions and is much more common in right hemisphere strokes (producing left hemi-inattention) due to the right hemisphere’s unique role in processing and maintaining attention. Neuropsychologically, hemispace attention or neglect can be understood to be a type of sensory anosognosia. Acutely, stroke often produce hemispace neglect to more than one sensory modality, and may include tactile, auditory and visual stimuli. However, this usually resolves to single-modality, hemi-inattention over days to months, with residual symptoms most often seen in visual perception. Hemi-inattention may be subtle, such that the deficit is detectable only with formal testing procedures. Assessment of language, attention/concentration, memory (verbal and nonverbal), visuoconstructional/visuoperceptual and executive functions along with personality and mood should be incorporated.

Key Points: MCA Strokes

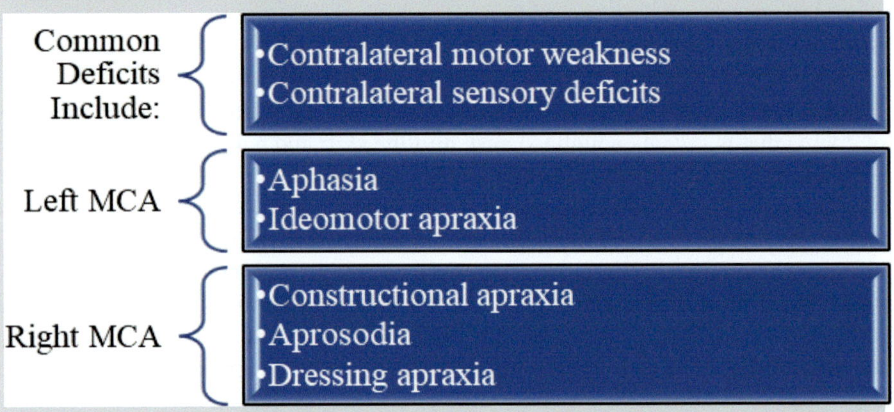

Left MCA: Neuropsychological deficits often include language deficits (aphasia), visuoconstructional deficits and executive dysfunction. Symptoms of Gerstmann's syndrome (finger agnosia, acalculia, agraphia and right-left confusion due to angular gyrus lesions) can be seen acutely but tend to quickly resolve in all but the most significant strokes. Visuoconstructional deficits often reflect drawings that maintain the gestalt (general form) of the figure or design but lack detail. Memory impairments can be present, particularly in large "stem" left MCA infarcts. Verbal memory impairment is likely, while nonverbal (visual) memory may remain relatively intact. As mesial temporal areas are typically perfused by the PCA, memory impairment may present with relatively preserved consolidation. Acutely, aphasias are common, which differ in type based on the severity and location of the stroke. Other language deficits may include poor verbal fluency (phonemic and/or semantic; Benton & Hamsher, 1989; Spreen & Strauss, 1998), confrontation naming (e.g., deficits on visual or auditory naming tasks; Kaplan et al., 2001; Stern & White, 2003), repetition, comprehension (e.g., Token Test; Boller & Vignolo, 1966), reading or writing. Several aphasia assessment batteries are helpful in characterizing the type and severity of language deficits.

These can include:

- Boston Diagnostic Aphasia Battery (BDAE; Goodglass et al., 2000)
- Multilingual Aphasia Examination (MAE; Benton & Hamsher, 1989)
- Neuropsychological Assessment Battery (NAB; Stern & White, 2003)
- Western Aphasia Battery (WAB; Kertesz, 1982)

A "stem" MCA infarct will result in more neuropsychological deficits, reflecting dysfunction of both frontal as well as temporal and parietal cortices. A superior segment MCA infarct will typically not result in sensory deficits or comprehension language problems. An inferior segment MCA infarct will typically present with greater comprehension language and sensory deficits. Ideomotor and/or ideational apraxia is common.

Right MCA: Neuropsychological deficits often involve visuospatial deficits, executive dysfunction, impaired visual/nonverbal memory and left hemineglect or hemi-inattention. As mentioned above, hemispace inattention or neglect is much more common with right MCA stroke (vs. left). Although less common with right hemisphere insult, deficits may also be seen in language pragmatics. Receptive aprosody can be seen in "stem" or right inferior MCA strokes, while expressive aprosody is typically associated with "stem" or right superior MCA stroke.

Visuospatial impairments are a hallmark of Right MCA stroke. Given the more anterior nature of territory perfused by the MCA, symptoms usually do not include frank hemianopsia or other visuoperceptual deficits, except in cases of visual neglect as described above, or when the thalamus or optic radiations are affected. More common are deficits in visuospatial reasoning and construction. Visuospatial reasoning deficits can include difficulty manipulating or relating visual stimuli, or difficulty integrating visuospatial information. Visuoconstructional deficits refer to difficulty outputting visuospatial information in an organized or cogent manner, which often presents with preserved perceptual abilities (e.g., patients can identify that their drawings or figures are incorrectly done but cannot fix or describe their errors). These impairments are mediated by frontoparietal areas and can also include frank executive dysfunction, which classically presents as loss of gestalt with relatively preserved representation of details. Dressing apraxia is also common.

Bilateral MCA: While less common, bilateral MCA infarcts from something like an embolic stroke can lead to a combination of the above symptoms and deficits. Bilateral hemiparesis (worse in the upper extremities) is common. As bilateral MCA lesions likely occur with strokes that are also more severe, hemisensory loss and more profound sensorimotor impairments (e.g., *plegia* rather than *paresis*) are also common. In addition, as these strokes are more likely to be more severe, global aphasia and other more severe language deficits can be seen.

ACA Distribution Stroke

Isolated ACA territory infarcts are less frequent than MCA strokes and are only uncommonly embolic in nature due to the circuitous pathway from ICA to ACA. When they occur, isolated ACA strokes more commonly result from occlusion due to intracranial atherosclerosis or from vasospasm after rupture of an ACoA aneurysm. Unilateral ACA strokes are associated with contralateral hemiparesis, which is worse in lower extremities, with sensory deficits (in a similar distribution of relative severity) and a variety of behavioral deficits. Abulia and emotional apathy are common and, when severe, can manifest as akinetic mutism. Impairment of fronto-striatal circuits can result in deficits in divided and focused attention as well as memory deficits. Delirium and agitation may alternate with apathy and mutism. Neuropsychological Assessment of ACA stroke should include assessment of executive functions and attention/working memory, verbal and nonverbal (visual) memory, language, visuoconstructional and visual spatial, personality/behavior and motor functions.

Key Points: ACA Strokes

Common Deficits Include:
- Contralateral weakness of feet/legs with falls
- Urinary incontinence
- Apathy and abulia
- Lack of spontaneous speech (mute with damage to both medial frontal lobes)
- Executive dysfunction

Left ACA
- Expressive language deficits

Right ACA
- Expressive aprosodies

ACoA aneurysm rupture
- amnesia/memory impairment, mutism, apathy, executive dysfunction

Left ACA: Neuropsychological deficits commonly include executive dysfunction and expressive language deficits. Executive dysfunction can be more pronounced with dominant hemisphere lesions, and involve poor verbal reasoning, motor impersistence and abulia. Patients may also present with features of a transcortical motor aphasia, and psychometric evaluation of phonemic verbal fluency may reveal deficits.

Right ACA: Neuropsychological deficits may present with executive dysfunction. Rather than language deficits, persons may reflect poor social insight and judgment. Impersistence, and abulia or apathy may also be present.

Bilateral ACA: The most common cause for damage to parenchyma of both ACA artery distributions is the result of a ruptured ACoA aneurysm. Deficits can be due to the aneurysm rupture itself or subsequent surgical repair, with 54% of patients experiencing surgery-related deficits (Bendel et al., 2009). Neuropsychological deficits can involve mutism, memory impairments, behavioral apathy, lack of initiation, bilateral weakness (legs greater than arms) and cortical sensory loss involving feet/legs. Memory may be affected to varying severity, with the patient exhibiting retrieval deficits and inefficient consolidation; primary consolidation deficits should not be anticipated with ACA strokes. Short-delay recall may be worse than long-delay recall. Patients tend not to organize material for consolidation, and semantic clustering is often reduced (Lezak et al., 2004). Learning curve is flat or nearly flat and retrieval errors are common, with frequent false positive errors. False positive errors are often of semantically related distracters. Recognition memory is often impaired due to failure of release of proactive interference (improved memory for stimuli that differs from previously presented material), resulting in patients making false positive and false negative errors. Patients may also demonstrate impairment in prospective memory, the ability to "remember to remember" (Lezak et al., 2004).

Neuropsychological assessment may present with deficits on measures of complex and divided attention. Commonly used tests to measure these types of deficits include:

- Trail-Making Tests A & B (TMT; AITB, 1944)
- Paced Auditory Serial Addition Test (PASAT; Gronwald, 1977)
- Wechsler Memory Scale-fourth Ed. (WMS-IV, 2009)
- Rey Complex Figure Test and Recognition Trial (RCFT; Meyers & Meyers, 1995),
- Rey Auditory Verbal Learning Test (RVLT; Rey, 1941, 1964)
- Wide Range Assessment of Memory and Learning, 2nd Ed. (WRAML-2, Sheslow & Adams, 2003),

Varying expressive language deficits are often present, with the more severe cases exhibiting mutism. Executive function deficits reflect poor initiation, apathy and reduced performance on Stroop tasks (Lezak et al., 2004). Behavioral and mood changes can be predominant.

PCA Distribution Strokes

PCA strokes often involve visual sensory or other visuoperceptual dysfunction. Classically this presents as contralateral homonymous hemianopsia (or quadrantanopsia), particularly if primary visual areas in the posterior occipital lobe are involved. Other neuropsychological deficits commonly include other perceptual or visual integration deficits that may cause downstream visuoconstructional deficits, color agnosia, apperceptive agnosia and memory loss. As mesial temporal areas are perfused by the PCA, true consolidation memory deficits can occur, characterized by poor recall with impaired recognition (encoding and learning are variably affected). Specific syndromes that can be seen with PCA stroke include alexia without agraphia, visual agnosia, abnormalities of color perception and depth perception and prosopagnosia. Balint's syndrome, a rare and poorly understood symptom triad, can occur and consists of simultagnosia, optic ataxia and oculomotor apraxia.

Key Points: PCA Strokes

Common Deficits Include:

- Contralateral deficit in hands/arms (light touch, vibration, position)
- Contralateral visual field cut
- Visuoconstructional/visuospatial deficits
- Possible memory deficits

Left PCA

- Associative agnosia
- Ideomotor apraxia
- Symptoms of Gerstmann's syndrome
- Loss of detail in visuoconstruction
- Verbal memory loss

Right PCA

- Visuoconstructional/visuospatial deficits
- Hemineglect or inattention
- Receptive aprosodies
- Visual/non-verbal memory loss

Left PCA: Memory loss (verbal greater than nonverbal/visual), alexia without agraphia, visuoperceptual and visual integration deficits. Right hemibody sensory loss may be present.

Right PCA: Memory loss (nonverbal/visual), visuoperceptual and visual integration deficits and agnosia. Left hemibody sensory loss may be present. Performance on block design tests can reflect problems with object assembly, such as broken configurations or rotation errors. Left hemineglect/inattention and/or other visuoperceptual deficits can be seen and can be elicited on visuospatial tasks such as:

- Line Bisection tests (Schenkenberg et al., 1980)
- Bell's cancellation test (Gauthier et al., 1989)
- Hooper Visual Organization test (HVOT; Hooper, 1983)
- Rey–Osterrieth Complex Figure Test (RCFT; Meyers & Meyers, 1995)
- Test of Face Recognition (Benton et al., 1994)
- Wechsler Intelligence Scales Block Design tests (Wechsler, 2001)
- Sensory-Perceptual exams, such as double simultaneous stimulation in various sensory modalities

Bilateral PCA: Visual hallucinations of simple shapes or well-formed experiences, sometimes associated with other sensory experiences, can occur and may be more noticeable during the evenings and nighttime and may be a source of significant distress. These are often termed "release hallucinations" and are related to reduced sensory input. Visual loss is typically recognized by the patient when the lesion is confined to the occipital lobe, and if complete is termed "cortical blindness." However, if parietal or temporal areas are also involved, patients may exhibit Anton's syndrome, or a denial of true visual deficits.

Neuropsychological evaluation of PCA stroke should include assessment of motor and sensory functions, language, verbal and nonverbal (visual) memory, visuoconstructional and visual spatial, executive and attention/working memory abilities, as well as personality/behavior. Common behavioral deficits include irritability, distractibility and agitation. Psychosis may also occur and, and when associated with visual hallucinations, can be misdiagnosed as delirium or incorrectly managed as a primary psychiatric disorder.

LEFT SIDE	RIGHT SIDE
Left Internal Carotid Artery (ICA)  • "Silent" (having no symptoms) in 30-40% of cases due to collateral flow from other sources	Right Interior Carotid Artery (ICA)  • "Silent" (having no symptoms) in 30-40% of cases
"Incomplete Left ICA" (watershed infarct) Symptoms • Mixed transcortical aphasia or transcortical motor aphasia is most common; transcortical sensory aphasia also possible • Right motor and sensory impairment of the truck, hips, and proximal extremities • Symptoms of Gerstmann's syndrome • Agnosia • Memory deficits "Complete Left ICA" Symptoms • Right hemiparesis of contralateral body including lower face (primary and supplementary cortex) • Right hemianesthesia including pain, temperature, light touch, position, and vibration sense (primary sensory cortex) • Global or nonfluent aphasia • Symptoms of Gerstmann's syndrome • Ideomotor apraxia, ideational apraxia, constructional apraxia (left frontal and parietal cortex) • Acute ipsilateral monocular blindness (damage to optic nerve) and right homonymous hemianopsia, which tends to resolve (optic radiations) • Impaired problem-solving, sequencing, grasp/root/suck reflexes (dorsolateral frontal lobe circuitry disruption) • Memory deficits (verbal worse than visual/nonverbal memory)	"Incomplete Right ICA" (watershed infarct) Symptoms • Expressive aprosody • Left motor and sensory impairment of the trunk, hips, and proximal extremities • Anosognosia, left neglect, ideational apraxia, constructional apraxia (right frontal and parietal cortex) • Memory deficits (visual/nonverbal worse than verbal memory) "Complete Right ICA" Symptoms • Left hemiparesis of contralateral body including lower face (primary and supplementary cortex) • Left hemianesthesia, including pain, temperature, light touch, position, and vibration sense (primary sensory cortex) • Receptive and expressive aprosody • Constructional apraxia (likely severe) • Acute ipsilateral monocular blindness (prechiasmic damage to the optic nerve) and left homonymous hemianopsia (optic radiations) that tend to resolve • Impaired problem-solving, sequencing, grasp/root/suck reflexes (dorsolateral frontal lobe circuitry disruption) • Memory deficits (impaired visual/nonverbal memory)

Fig. 14.10 Cerebral artery syndromes

LEFT SIDE	RIGHT SIDE
Left Anterior Cerebral Artery (ACA) 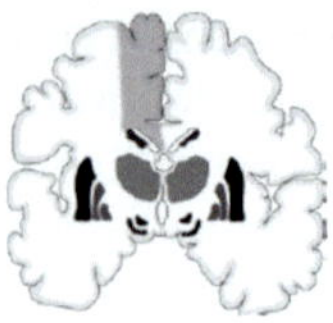 • Right leg motor and sensory loss (primary motor and sensory cortex, supplementary motor cortex) • Akinesia, mutism, abulia, apathy (disruption of medial frontal lobe circuitry) • Transcortical motor aphasia, with complete mutism in rare cases • Impaired executive aspects of memory (poor retrieval)	Right Anterior Cerebral Artery (ACA) 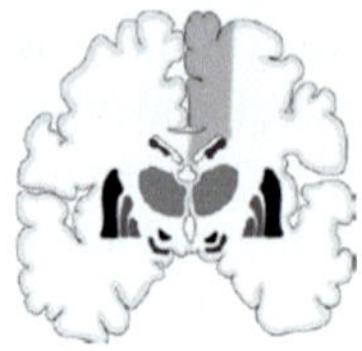 • Left leg sensory and motor loss; left arm weakness can occur in large infarcts • Frontal lobe behaviors (apathy, stimulus bound behaviors, jocularity, hypomania)
Left Middle Cerebral Artery (MCA) Left MCA Stem	Right Middle Cerebral Artery (MCA) Right MCA Stem
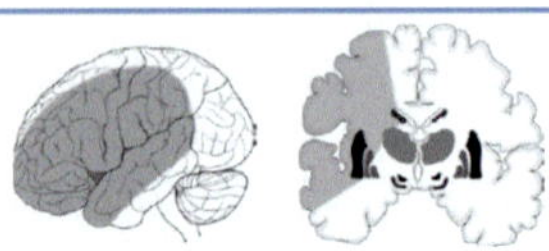 • Right hemiparesis and right hemianesthesia (motor and sensory primary cortex, secondary motor cortex) • Right homonymous hemianopsia, left gaze preference (lesion of left frontal eye field which drives eyes to the right, leading to left gaze) • Global aphasia (assuming dominant left hemisphere for language) • Motor apraxia and visuoconstructional deficits • Acalculia and memory deficits • Depression	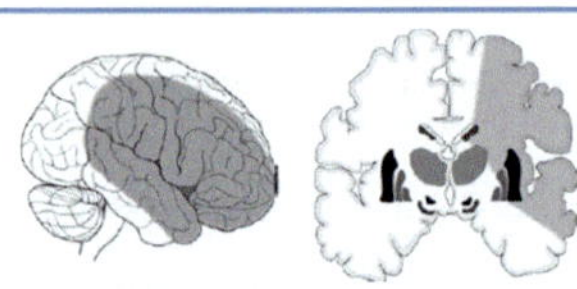 • Left hemiparesis and left hemianesthesia • Possible left homonymous hemianopsia, with right gaze preference (lesion of right frontal eye field that drives eyes to the left, leading to right gaze) • Profound hemi-neglect initially and may resolve to hemi-inattention • Intact speech (assuming left hemisphere dominance for language) • Visuoconstructional deficits are prominent • Motor apraxia • Memory deficits • Anosognosia • Mood changes with initial symptoms of hypomania and jocularity, but affective flattening may occur Aprosody

Fig. 14.10 (continued)

LEFT SIDE	RIGHT SIDE
Left MCA Deep Territory	Right MCA Deep Territory
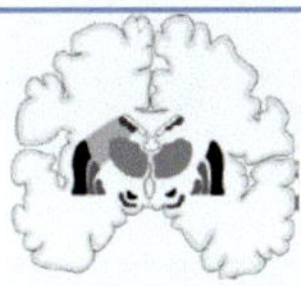 • Pure right side motor hemiparesis • Mild aphasia with large infarcts • Movement deficits (with left basal ganglia involvement) • Depression	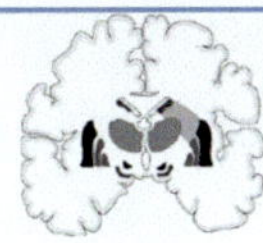 • Pure left motor hemiparesis • Left hemineglect (with large infarcts) • Visuoconstructional deficits
Left MCA Inferior Division	Right MCA Inferior Division
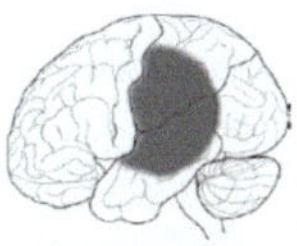 • Fluent aphasia syndrome (i.e., Wernicke's or transcortical sensory) • Right face and arm sensory loss (primary sensory cortex) • Right visual field defect (particularly inferior quadrantanopia) • Possible mild right face and hand motor loss • Symptoms of Gerstmann's syndrome • Visuoconstructional/visuospatial deficits • Depression	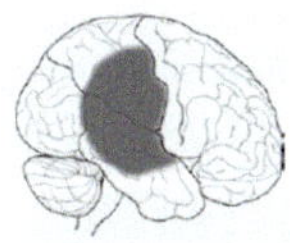 • Left face and arm sensory loss (primary sensory cortex) • Left visual field defect (particularly inferior quadrantanopia) • Possible mild left face and hand motor weakness • Left hemineglect that may gradually resolve to a left hemi-inattention; initially, the left hemineglect can be pronounced and limit the ability to evaluate for left visual field defects or any left motor weakness • Visuoconstructional/visuospatial deficits • Hypomania or affective flattening • Receptive aprosody
Left MCA Superior Division	Right MCA Superior Division
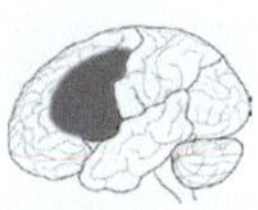 • Right face and arm motor loss (primary and secondary motor cortex) • Possible face and arm sensory loss • Intact motor and sensory function of legs • Nonfluent aphasia • Depression	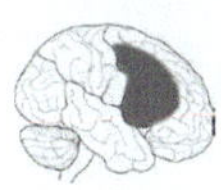 • Left face and arm motor weakness (primary and secondary motor cortex) • Possible face and arm sensory loss • Intact motor and sensory function of legs • Expressive aprosody • Impaired problem-solving, sequencing, grasp/root/suck reflexes (dorsolateral frontal lobe circuitry disruption) • Hypomania and a hollow jocularity

Fig. 14.10 (continued)

LEFT SIDE	RIGHT SIDE

Left Posterior Cerebral Artery (PCA)

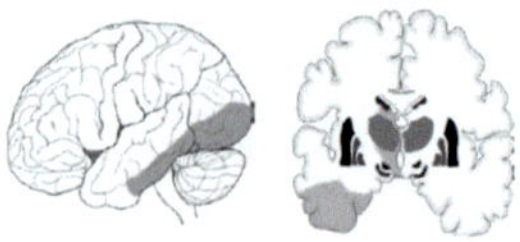

- Right visual field defect will be present, commonly right homonymous hemianopsia
- Visual agnosia
- Alexia without agraphia
- Motor and sensory loss of the hand and face (with damage to the thalamus and internal capsule)
- Verbal memory loss
- Depression

Right Posterior Cerebral Artery (PCA)

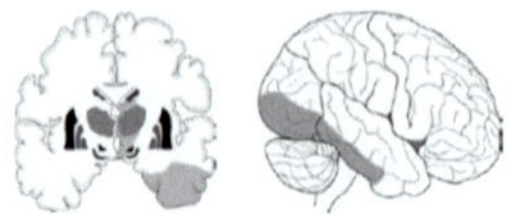

- Left visual field defect will be present, commonly left homonymous hemianopsia
- Visual agnosia
- Receptive aprosody
- Motor and sensory loss of the hand and face with damage to the thalamus and internal capsule
- Nonverbal memory loss
- Depression or anxiety

Left ACA-MCA Borderzone/Watershed Infarct

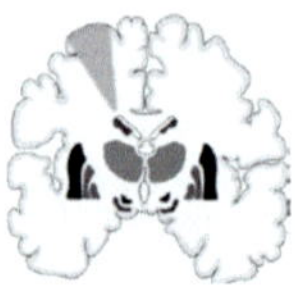

- Transcortical motor aphasia
- Right motor and sensory impairment of the truck, hips, and proximal extremities

Right ACA-MCA Borderzone/Watershed Infarct

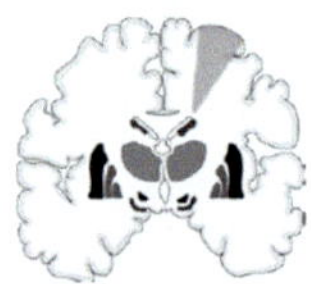

- Left motor and sensory impairment of the truck, hips, and proximal extremities
- Visuoconstructional deficits

LEFT SIDE	RIGHT SIDE

Left MCA-PCA Borderzone/Watershed Infarct

- Transcortical sensory aphasia
- Possible Gerstmann's syndrome
- Agnosia
- Memory deficits (verbal worse than visual/nonverbal memory)

Right MCA-PCA Borderzone/Watershed Infarct

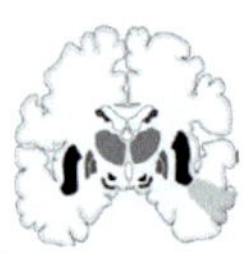

- Visuoconstructional and visuoperceptual deficits
- Visual agnosia
- Memory deficits are possible (worse nonverbal/visual memory than verbal memory)

Fig. 14.10 (continued)

Subcortical Strokes

Due to the predictable anatomy of the small perforating vessels, occlusion of one of these arteries can result in recognizable "lacunar syndromes." The most common are the pure motor hemiparesis, ataxic hemiparesis and pure sensory syndromes. For most patients, neuropsychological deficits are minimal or absent with a few, notable exceptions. Strokes involving the caudate nucleus have prominent behavioral abnormalities of a frontal-lobe nature. Thalamic strokes, particularly the dominant, mesial nuclei, can cause confabulation, anterograde amnesia and behavioral disruptions (as this is part of the Papez circuit). Pseudobulbar affect, or affective incongruency, can be seen with bilateral lesions or some brainstem lesions.

Key Points: Classic Syndromes of Subcortical Strokes

Lacunar syndromes

- Pure motor hemiparesis
- Pure sensory syndrome
- Ataxic hemiparesis
- Dysarthria
- Clumsy hand syndrome
- Sensorimotor syndrome Contralateral visual field cut

Thalamic syndromes

- Pure sensory or sensorimotor syndrome OR
- Neuropsychological impairments
- Memory loss
- Aphasia (dominant hemisphere)
- Hemineglect (nondominant hemisphere)
- Apathy

Syndrome	**Clinical Features**	**Localization**
Pure Sensory Stroke	• Contralateral hemisensory loss • Absence of cortical signs or motor deficits	Ventral posterolateral (VPL) nucleus of the thalamus
Pure Sensorimotor Stroke	• Contralateral hemisensory loss and hemiparesis • Absence of cortical signs	Posterolateral thalamus and posterior limb of the internal capsule
Pure Motor Hemiparesis	• Contralateral complete hemiparesis • Most common lacunar syndrome • Absence of cortical signs and sensory deficits	Posterior limb of internal capsule
Dysarthria-Clumsy Hand Syndrome	• Contralateral facial weakness, dysarthria, and dysphagia • Mild paresis and 'clumsiness' of contralateral hand • No sensory deficits or cortical signs	Genu of internal capsule or basilar part of the pons
Ataxia Hemiparesis	• Unilateral weakness and pyramidal signs • Ipsilateral cerebellar-like ataxia • No sensory deficits or cortical signs	Posterior limb of the internal capsule, basilar part of the pons, or corona radiata

Fig. 14.11 Lacunar syndromes

Lacunar infarcts: Lacunes are small subcortical infarcts (generally considered to be <1.5 cm in diameter) of small deep penetrating arteries. Classically, Fisher (1982) described five lacunar syndromes: pure motor hemiparesis, pure sensory stroke, sensorimotor stroke, ataxic hemiparesis and clumsy-hand dysarthria. Other lacunar syndromes have been described (see Fig. 14.11), but some lacunar infarcts may be asymptomatic. We discuss the lacunar syndromes of the thalamus in a subsection below, as these present with greater neuropsychological deficits.

Thalamic infarcts: Various thalamic syndromes have been described (Fig. 14.12). Perhaps the best known are the pure sensory and the pure sensorimotor strokes, resulting from occlusion of each arterial territory of the thalamus. Neuropsychological deficits can be pronounced in some thalamic syndromes (e.g., tuberothalamic artery) while entirely absent in others (e.g., inferolateral artery). Thalamic pain, a central pain disorder, can result from occlusion of the inferolateral (thalamogeniculate) artery and is contralateral to the lesion (Bogousslavsky et al., 1988; Graff-Radford et al., 1985). Thalamic pain, if present, is usually associated with hemisensory loss, mild hemiparesis, choreoathetotic movements and sometimes a mild hemiataxia and astereognosis. Outcome from occlusion to interolateral artery tends to be good. Alternatively, outcome from occlusion of the tuberothalamic or paramedian arteries tends to be poor, often with persistent neuropsychological deficits.

Key Points: Thalamic Pain (Dejerine–Roussy Syndrome)

Thalamic pain (Dejerine-Roussy syndrome)

- Central pain disorder
- Severe buring contralateral to lesion
- Only touch patient on ipsilateral side
- Cutaneous hypersensitivity limits rehabilitation and functional abilities
- Pain non-responsive to opioids or other analgesics, variably responsive to tricyclic antidepressants or anticonvulsants (carbamazepine)

Brainstem Syndromes: Medulla, Pons and Midbrain

The clinical presentation of vertebral artery ischemia varies considerably, largely dependent upon the vascular development of the individual and where the occlusion occurs. The anatomy of the vertebral arteries can be quite diverse, with almost 10% of individuals having only one functional vertebral artery supplying the basilar artery. In addition, the posterior inferior cerebellar artery (PICA), while traditionally depicted to arise from the vertebral artery, can often arise from the basilar artery along with the anteroinferior cerebellar artery. These anatomic variations provide a host of variable clinical presentations typically taking on the form of various brain stem or lacunar syndromes (described above). However, if a person has two patent

Thalamic artery	Clinical features	Localization
Inferolateral (thalamogeniculate) artery	Contralateral hemisensory loss (light touch, position sense, vibratory sense, temperature, and pain), hemiataxia, and possible thalamic pain syndrome. Hemiparesis (usually mild) and loss of taste may also occur. No neuropsychological deficits. Two common subtypes: 1. Pure sensory stroke 2. Pure sensorimotor stroke	Ventral posterior (VPL) Ventral posterior medial (VPM) Ventral lateral (VL) Motor involvement affects corticospinal and corticobulbar pathways of internal capsule.
Paramedian arteries	Commonly includes a triad of deficits: 1. Impairment of declarative memory (anterograde amnesia). Deficit in memory tends to be retrieval deficits and inefficient consolidation. Bilateral lesion anterograde amnesia Unilateral less memory impairment Confabulation may be present. 2. Behavioral apathy with somnolence Unilateral lesion less persistent apathy. Possible akinetic mutism (with bilateral lesion or dominant hemisphere lesion) 3. Vertical gaze palsy Upward gaze more impaired than downward gaze. 4. Confabulation may be present	Intralaminar nuclei and Mediodorsal (MD) thalamic nuclei
Posterior choroidal artery	Contralateral homonymous quadrantanopia Larger lesion results in hemianopsia.	Lateral geniculate nuclei
Tuberothalamic artery	Primarily neuropsychological deficits that are typically persistent and limit return to previous level of function. Most common deficits are: Memory loss (e.g., anterograde amnesia). Impaired declarative (explicit) memory (autobiographical memory poor from time of lesion, and reduced ability to remember new facts). Dominant hemisphere lesions cause more impairment in verbal memory Nondominant hemisphere lesions cause greater impairment in "nonverbal" (visuospatial) memory. Aphasia (dominant hemisphere lesions) Executive dysfunction (e.g., disinhibition, apathy, lethargy, and abulia). Dominant (left) hemisphere infarct deficits: Aphasia symptoms including hypophonia, paraphasias, reduced spontaneous speech with short sentences, and some comprehension deficits. Repetition is intact. Verbal memory can be particularly affected. Impaired encoding and consolidation. Nondominant (right) hemisphere infarct deficits: Nonverbal (visuospatial) memory may be more impaired than verbal memory. Hemi-neglect and visuoconstructional and visual spatial deficits. Bilateral infarcts present with pronounced apathy, lethargy, and dense anterograde amnesia. Other neurologic deficits: Contralateral facial paresis in which facial movement more impaired for facial movements to emotions (e.g., reduced involuntary smile to joke) than voluntary movement (e.g., request to show teeth) may be present.	Anterior thalamus Anterior nucleus of thalamus Midline thalamic nuclei group

Fig. 14.12 Thalamic vascular syndromes

and functional vertebral arteries, the occlusion of one vertebral artery may not result in any clinical deficits.

Basilar artery syndromes include the midbrain syndromes, paramedian thalamic and subthalamic syndromes (i.e., complete basilar and "top-of-the-basilar" syndromes as well as AICA and SCA syndromes). As the diameters of the vertebral arteries are often smaller than the Basilar artery, an embolus may not lodge until it reaches the top of the Basilar artery where it bifurcates into the smaller PCAs. In this setting, many perforator vessels are affected, and the presentation is clearly more severe than one of the lacunar syndromes. Occlusion of the entire basilar artery (typically involving the lower third of the artery) is generally thrombotic from build-up of atherosclerotic plaque, causing the so-called *complete basilar syndrome*. When perfusion is insufficient to spare the reticular activating system, a rare, but devastating syndrome termed "locked-in" can occur. Figure 14.13 provides the signs and symptoms, neuroanatomical localization and syndrome name of common brain stem and midbrain vascular syndromes. While brainstem syndromes are not associated with higher-level neuropsychological deficits, patients with a *"Top of the Basilar" syndrome* often exhibit memory impairment. In general, patients suffering brain stem or midbrain infarcts tend to exhibit persistent sensorimotor deficits with poor quality of life.

Deficits often involve motor and sensory deficits as well as dysarthria, dysphagia and/or ataxia. While neuropsychological functions are generally entirely intact, motor deficits can often be disabling. In addition, speech articulation and intelligibility may be severely impacted by dysarthria, limiting the patient's ability to communicate via spoken language. Abilities to write (assuming dominant hand motor paresis is not present) and/or comprehension is entirely intact. Dysphagia (difficulty swallowing) may also be present and can be life-threatening. Patients with brain stem strokes are routinely evaluated for swallowing problems.

Key Points: Brain Stem and Midbrain Infarcts

Brainstem and Midbrain strokes

- "Crossed signs"
- Contralateral hemiparesis and/or hemianesthesia
- Ipsilateral facial/body weakness
- Possible ataxia of body
- Dysarthric speech (brainstem infarcts)
- Gaze palsies (brainstem and midbrain infarcts)

Treatment of Ischemic Stroke or Infarction

The treatment of acute ischemic stroke has advanced considerably over the years (see Fig. 14.16 at the end of this chapter) with the introduction of tissue plasminogen activators (tPA) and other revascularization therapies. tPA is an endogenous protein that breaks down blood clots, but is also manufactured and used for thrombolysis, which can quickly restore blood flow following ischemia. Treatment with tPA is not without risk, with hemorrhagic conversion being the primary morbidity of treatment in about 3% of patients. The benefit of tPA is highly dependent on time; when tPA is given within 3 hours of ischemic stroke symptom onset, 33% substantially improve and do not exhibit appreciable neurologic deficits 3 months or 12 months later (Kwiatkowski et al., 1999). However, when administered 3–4.5 hours of ischemic stroke symptom onset, meaningful improvements are only seen in 16% of patients.

Ischemic Stroke Recrudescence

Post-Stroke Recrudescence (PSR) refers to transient worsening of focal stroke-related neurologic deficits and can occur as many as 4 years following the original infarct (Topcuoglu et al., 2017). Symptoms typically follow the pattern seen with the initial infarct or involve worsening of post-stroke residual deficits, albeit in a less severe and time-limited manner. PSR is often co-occurring with toxic-metabolic insults and can be thought of as a specialized type of delirium. While the exact pathophysiological pathway is not fully clear, it is reasonable to assume that apparent focal symptoms are a result of general CNS depression as can be seen in

Syndrome	**Clinical features**	**Localization**
"Top-of-the-Basilar" syndrome	• Alteration of consciousness • Amnestic memory • Hallucinations (poorly formed) • Involuntary movements • Visual abnormalities • Altered pupillary response • Supranuclear paresis or vertical gaze • Ptosis • Eyelid retraction	Distal basil artery impacted by embolus, resulting in bilateral ischemia of upper brainstem structures and of the posterior cerebral artery territories
Benedikt Syndrome	• Ipsilateral oculomotor nerve palsy • Contralateral hemiparesis • Contralateral cerebellar ataxia and/or Holmes tremor and/or choreoathetosis	Midbrain tegmentum, ipsilateral red nucleus, CN III, cerebral peduncle
Weber's syndrome	• Ipsilateral CNIII palsy • Contralateral hemiparesis	Ventral midbrain, CN III, Cerebral peduncle.
Locked-In syndrome	• Paralysis of voluntary muscles of limbs and torso • Mutism • Bulbar palsy • Difficulty with voluntary breathing, apnea, ataxia, hyperpnea • Dizziness • Vertigo • Spared functions: retention of consciousness, language comprehension, orientation, hearing, vertical eye movement and blinking ability	Lesion affecting the ventral pons and midbrain

Fig. 14.13 Syndromes of midbrain and brain stem

Foville's syndrome	Classic presentation has the following symptoms arising from injury to different parts of the pons • Horizontal gaze palsy due to ipsilateral CN VI nucleus injury • Facial weakness or paralysis due to CN VII nerve damage in the ipsilateral pontine region • Hemiparesis or hemiplegia contralateral to the side of the pontine injury due to corticocospinal tract damage above the inferior medullary decussation	Pons, presentation varies by pontine injury location
Medial superior pontine syndrome	**Contralateral:** • Paralysis of face, arm, and leg • Some instances of affected touch, vibration and position **Ipsilateral**: • Cerebellar ataxia • Internuclear ophthalmoplegia (inability to perform conjugate lateral gaze)	Paramedian branches of the upper basilar artery
Lateral superior pontine syndrome (SCA syndrome)	**Contralateral:** • Impaired sense of pain and temperature on face, limbs, and trunk • Possible impairment of touch, vibration, and position (leg more impaired than arm) **Ipsilateral:** • Cerebellar ataxia, falling to side of the lesion • Vestibular dysfunction (dizziness, nausea, vomiting, horizontal nystagmus) • Paresis of conjugate gaze or pontine contralateral gaze seen in Horner's syndrome	Occlusion of spinal cerebellar artery (SCA)

Fig. 14.13 (continued)

Medial midpontine syndrome	**Contralateral:** • Paralysis of face, arm, and leg • Variable loss of touch and proprioception **Ipsilateral:** • Cerebellar ataxia	Occlusion of paramedian branch of basilar artery
Lateral midpontine syndrome	**Contralateral:** • Impaired pain and temperature senation on limbs and trunk **Ipsilateral:** • Cerebellar ataxi • CN V palsy (paresis of mastication muscles, positive jaw jerk reflex) • CN V sensory deficit (anesthesia of side of face)	Occlusion of short circumferential artery
Lateral inferior pontine [Anterior inferior cerebellar artery (AICA)] syndrome	**Contralateral:** • Impaired pain, thermal sensation **Ipsilateral:** • Vertigo, nausea, vomiting, horizontal nystagmus • Oscillopsia • CN VII palsy • Paralysis of conjugate gaze to the affected side • Deafness, tinnitus • Ataxia • Impaired facial sensation	Occlusion of AICA artery
Medial inferior pontine (Pontine "wrong-way eyes") syndrome	**Contralateral:** • Hemiparesis (face, arm, leg) • Hemianasthesia (light touch and proprioception) of arm and leg **Ipsilateral:** • Horizontal gaze palsy (Eyes look away from lesion and toward side of hemiparesis) • Diplopia on lateral gaze • Cerebellar ataxia	Occlusion of paramedian branch of basilar artery
Medial medullary syndrome	**Contralateral:**	Stroke affecting the medial medulla caused by

Fig. 14.13 (continued)

	• Paralysis of upper and lower limbs • Possible decrease in proprioception, vibration, and/or fine touch **Ipsilateral:** • Deviation of the tongue to the ipsilateral side of the lesion	atherothrombotic occlusion of paramedian branches of the anterior spinal artery, vertebral artery, or basilar artery
Wallenberg's syndrome (Lateral medullary syndrome)	**Contralateral:** • Impaired sensation of pain and temperature in the arm and leg • No or only minimal weakness of contralateral side **Ipsilateral:** • Vertigo with nystagmus, nausea, vomiting, intractable hiccups • Dysphonia, dysarthria, dysphagia with ipsilateral loss of the gag reflex • Ataxia with tendency to fall to ipsilateral side • Pain and numbness with impaired facial sensation • Impaired taste sensation	Lesion to lateral medulla

Fig. 14.13 (continued)

delirium, which preferentially brings underlying post-stroke deficits to the forefront. In other words, the general neurologic effects of delirium, while diffuse, may interact with post-stroke vulnerabilities to give the illusion of new-onset neurologic symptoms. Topcuoglu et al. (2017) proposed preliminary diagnostic criteria, as seen in Fig. 14.14.

Hemorrhagic Stroke

Hemorrhagic Strokes Classification

Hemorrhagic strokes are typically nontraumatic in origin, and result from the rupture of a vessel, leading to bleeding within the brain. Hemorrhages may be *intracerebral* (*intraparenchymal*), *subarachnoid* or *intraventricular*, alone or in combination, and account for ~15% of all strokes. Intracranial hemorrhages in the subdural space (subdural hemorrhage) or epidural space (epidural hemorrhage) are typically due to trauma and are often excluded in the definition of stroke. Trauma may also result in intracerebral, subarachnoid and/or intraventricular hemorrhage. *Intracerebral* or *intraparenchymal hemorrhage* (ICH) refers to bleeding within the

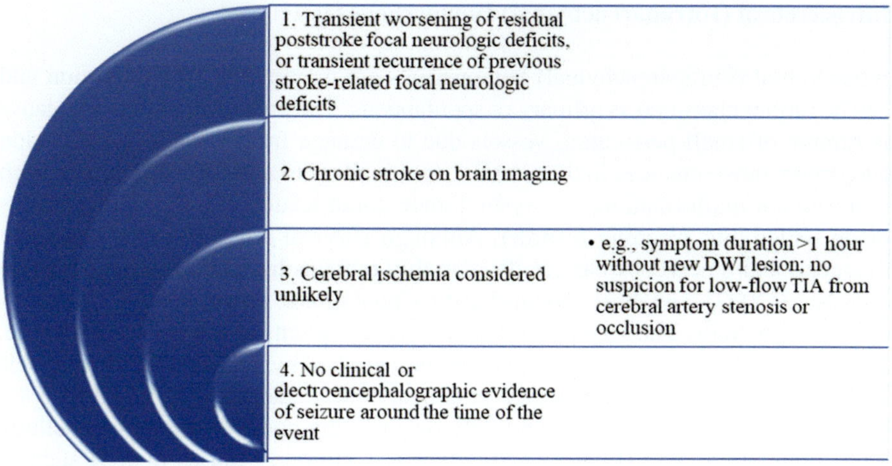

Fig. 14.14 Post-stroke recrudescence

brain tissue and accounts for ~10–12% of all strokes (and about 2/3 of all hemorrhagic strokes). *Subarachnoid hemorrhage* (SAH) involves bleeding within the subarachnoid space and accounts for about ~3–5% of all strokes (1/3 of all hemorrhagic strokes). Hemorrhagic stroke subtypes carry the highest mortality rates: 35–52% of patients die within the first 30 days (Carhuapoma & Hanley, 2002). Below, we provide a more detailed discussion of hemorrhagic stroke classification and associated comorbidities.

Key Points: Hemorrhagic Stroke Classification

- Intracerebral hemorrhage (~10–12%)
- Subarachnoid hemorrhage (~3–5%)
- Intraventricular hemorrhage (<~3%)

The clinical presentation of hemorrhagic strokes depends on pressure within the bleeding vessel, anatomic location, vessel and hemorrhage size, extent of any mass effect and occurrence of secondary comorbid processes (edema, vasospasm, rebleeding, etc.). Symptoms may be focal (in the case of some ICH syndromes), generalized (in the case of some SAH) or a combination of both. Prominent complaints of headache and altered consciousness (progressive obtundation) are typical features of hemorrhagic strokes which help distinguish them from ischemic strokes in the absence of neuroimaging. The common clinical features of hemorrhagic strokes are reviewed below.

Intracerebral (Intraparenchymal) Hemorrhage (ICH)

Intracerebral (intraparenchymal) hemorrhages are nontraumatic by definition and can be further classified as primary or spontaneous. The presumed underlying cause is rupture of small perforating vessels due to damage from chronic hypertension and degenerative changes in the arteries, or secondary to a precipitating cause such as a vascular malformation, aneurysm, tumor, complication of anticoagulant drugs or an underlying bleeding disorder. Although survival has improved with early diagnosis and emergency care, early mortality remains high at 30–40% (Sturgeon & Folsom, 2007), and most patients have residual motor, sensory and/or neuropsychological deficits. The location of the hemorrhage points to the underlying cause. Hypertensive hemorrhages occur in locations supplied by small perforating vessels with 50% involving the deep nuclei (putamen, 35%; thalamus, 10%; caudate, 5%), 30% in the lobar white matter, and 20% occur in the posterior fossa (cerebellum, 15%; brain stem, 5%) (Image 14.5). Other less common causes of ICH such as arteriovenous malformations (AVMs), amyloid angiopathy and Moyamoya disease are described below. ICH can also result from the transformation of infarcts that are initially ischemic, either due to iatrogenic effects (e.g., tPA) or vessel rupture from blockage.

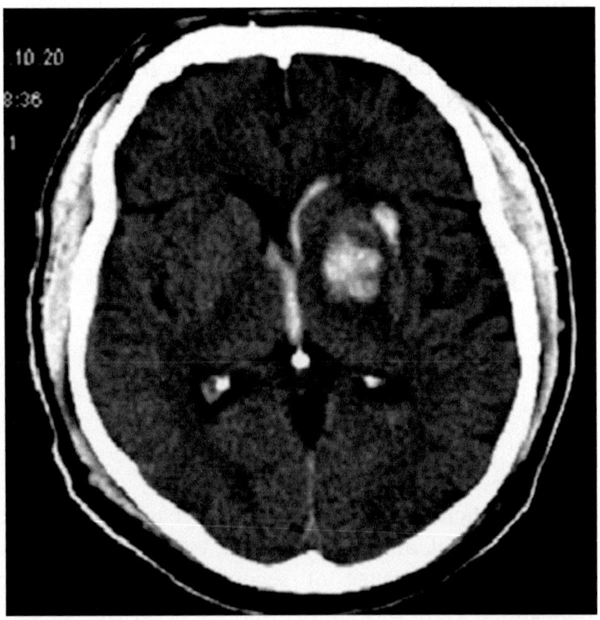

Image 14.5 CT brain scan without contrast of a left basal ganglia intracerebral hemorrhage with extension into the intraventricular space in a patient with chronic hypertension

Amyloid Angiopathy

Cerebral Amyloid angiopathy (CAA) is the most common cause of ICH in older adults, particularly when hypertension is not a factor. Cerebral amyloid angiopathy is the degeneration of vessel walls from amyloid deposits, leading to multiple, recurrent hemorrhages, and is associated with progressive cognitive decline. As beta amyloid is the type of pathology usually associated with CAA, there is a high degree of overlap in prevalence between CAA and Alzheimer's disease. The location of these hemorrhages is typically in the parieto-occipital or temporo-parietal lobar white matter or gray-white junctions—areas not typically affected by white matter ischemia or hypertensive hemorrhages. While they can occasionally be large, CAA typically involves multiple small microhemorrhages which can be difficult to detect on CT or structural MRI. See Diagnosis and Management below for further details on this topic.

Arteriovenous Malformation (AVM)

Arteriovenous Malformations (AVMs) are congenital abnormalities in which a network of blood vessels forms an abnormal communication of arterial and venous blood. This tangle of blood vessels may be very small, such as a few millimeters, or a much larger network of vessels that requires increased cardiac output. The AVM is composed of an arterial vessel that branches, often many times, and directly connects to the venous system without intervening capillary beds. The blood vessels comprising the AVM are abnormal and have thin walls. Arteriovenous malformations can be in any region of the brain but are typically intraparenchymal. Although thought to be present since before birth, onset of clinical symptoms typically occurs between the ages of 10 and 30 years old, although clinical symptoms may not appear until one's 50 s or even later.

AVMs can cause neurologic symptoms regardless of hemorrhagic conversion. In non-ruptured AVMs, headache has been reported as the only symptom in 20% of patients while seizure was reported as the presenting symptom in 17–40% of patients (Hofmeister et al., 2000). Neurologic deficits that are progressive have been reported for large unruptured AVMs that either compress neighboring brain regions and/or through a phenomenon called "intracerebral steal" in which large amounts of blood are shunted away from neighboring regions due to the large vascular volume enabled by such AVMs. AVM rupture (hemorrhage) is the first clinical symptom in about half of patients with AVMs (42–50%). Generally, the hemorrhage is not large and most patients (about 90%) survive the initial bleed. The hemorrhage of an AVM may be limited to a small area of the parenchyma or may involve hemorrhage into the ventricles (intraventricular), arachnoid (SAH) or dura (SDH). The incidence of hemorrhage for untreated AVMs is estimated to be 2–4% annually, with a mortality rate of 1–2% per year.

Moyamoya Disease

Moyamoya disease is an uncommon but important cause of both ischemic and hemorrhagic stroke. Named after the Japanese word for "puffy, or hazy like smoke," it is characterized by progressive stenosis of larger intracranial arteries followed by the development of smaller collateral vessels. This tangle of collateral vessels appears to have a smoky appearance on imaging. Moyamoya disease is much more common in east Asian populations, which strongly implicates a genetic underpinning. While not fully clear, the genetic risk may be characterized as autosomal dominant with incomplete penetrance (Mineharu et al., 2006). However, it has also been secondarily associated with a host of autoimmune, vascular, hematologic, metabolic and genetic disorders, suggesting a potentially more complex etiology (e.g., a diathesis-stress model). The common pathogenic pathway involves vessel wall thickening, classically in the circle of Willis, accompanied by angiogenesis leading to a dense and fragile network of smaller, dilated collateral vessels. Clinical presentation typically includes TIA, ischemic stroke and/or hemorrhage. Bleeds may occur intracerebrally or intraventricularly depending on the individuals' vasculature. Seizures may be the first clinical symptom, but less common and typically secondary to ischemia. Moyamoya is diagnosed with neuroimaging, ideally angiography. Treatment may include antiplatelet therapy (contraindicated in those with hemorrhage), surgical treatment to restore blood flow and supportive care for clinical symptoms. While intervention may aid in mitigation of acute symptoms, Moyamoya is progressive. Studies document a 17% chance of recurrence of hemorrhage in patients with Moyamoya following their initial event (Kim et al., 2017). Risk of recurrence is elevated following intraventricular strokes, in particular.

ICH Symptoms

In general, ICH presents as an acute, focal neurological deficit (e.g., hemiplegia), but as the hematoma expands, deficits progress with headache, emesis and altered consciousness. Seizures have been reported in about 10% of all ICH within the first few days of the stroke, with rates ranging from 4% to 17%. Seizures are more common in lobar hemorrhages than hemorrhages involving deep white matter or the brain stem. Onset of seizures after months or even years of an ICH is less common (Bladin et al., 2000). Extension of the hemorrhage to ventricles or arachnoid space increases risk of developing hydrocephalus within days to weeks of the hemorrhage. High stress has not been consistently identified as an independent risk factor of ICH—with 90% of cases occurring during times of low stress. However, ICH is more likely to occur during wakefulness than while sleeping (Caplan, 1993).

Massive hemorrhages can present with abrupt onset of loss of consciousness and unsteady breathing, dilated and fixed pupils, and within several hours, death. This is often due to mass effect caused by blood volume, which can lead to brainstem herniation. However, the clinical presentation and course of ICH vary as a function of the size of hemorrhage, location and comorbid conditions. Symptoms worsen over minutes to at most several hours to days, followed by a period of gradually resolving symptoms over weeks to 2–3 months. This reflects the physiological processes of the brain and body with edema and subsequent breakdown of blood products in the parenchyma. While clinical lore has historically held that ICH and other hemorrhagic strokes have better functional recovery, studies indicate that the two pathologies have similar rates of post-stroke impairment and outcome (Perna & Temple, 2015).

Lobar Hemorrhage

The signs and symptoms of lobar hemorrhages vary substantially based on where the ICH occurs, but often include abrupt headache, drowsiness and nausea with emesis. Occipital hemorrhages tend to result in contralateral homonymous hemianopsia and pain around the ipsilateral eye. Temporal lobe hemorrhages can produce a variety of symptoms including Wernicke's aphasia (dominant hemisphere lesions), memory impairment, ipsilateral ear pain and visual agnosia. Frontal lobe hemorrhages can cause contralateral hemiparesis, Broca's (nonfluent) aphasia (if in the dominant hemisphere), motor apraxia, dysexecutive (dorsolateral) syndrome and frontal headache. Parietal lobe hemorrhages symptoms include anterior temporal region headache, contralateral hemianesthesia, aphasia (particularly conduction aphasia), symptoms of Gerstmann's syndrome (acalculia, dysgraphia, finger agnosia and right/left confusion) and constructional apraxia. Lobal hemorrhages are much more likely to result from CAA or trauma (vs. hypertension or other intrinsic causes of vessel rupture).

Basal Ganglia Hemorrhage

Hemorrhage involving the basal ganglia is the most common place of primary ICH. The hemorrhage often extends into the internal capsule. The typical clinical course is abrupt onset of headache followed over the course of several minutes (<30 minutes) of progressive deterioration with onset of facial paresis followed by hemiplegia contralateral to the side of the hemorrhage, homonymous hemianopsia (contralateral to side of lesion), slurred speech (nondominant hemisphere ICH) which can include aphasia (dominant hemisphere ICH), deviation of eyes toward the side of the lesion (pupils may remain normal), followed over the course of less than an hour by confusion and obtundation. However, massive hemorrhages may present simply with abrupt onset of coma with hemiplegia contralateral to side of hemorrhage. Respirations become shallow, and as the brain stem becomes compressed, eyes become fixed and dilated, and decerebrate posturing occurs. Smaller hemorrhages confined to the putamen tend to produce either more motor or sensory deficits depending on if the lesion is more anterior or posterior. Anterior putamen hemorrhages are associated with contralateral hemiparesis, Broca's aphasia (dominant hemisphere lesions only), abulia and motor impersistence. Small hemorrhages restricted to the posterior putamen results in mild and more hemianesthesia, loss of visual pursuit to the contralateral hemispace, hemianopia, Wernicke's aphasia (dominant hemisphere lesions only) or anosognosia (dominant or nondominant hemisphere lesions). Extension of these lesions to the lateral ventricle often results in change of mental status (drowsiness and stupor or agitation and confusion).

Thalamic Hemorrhage

Symptoms vary depending upon the size of the hemorrhage, but the most common features are contralateral hemisensory loss, Wernicke's (fluent) aphasia (dominant hemisphere ICH) or contralateral neglect and anosognosia (nondominant hemisphere ICH) and, frequently, various gaze and ocular abnormalities including vertical and lateral gaze palsies, pseudo-abducens palsies in which the eyes are deviated slightly inward and down, and asymmetrical skew deviation with the eye contralateral to the lesion being lower than the eye ipsilateral to the lesion. Ipsilateral Horner's syndrome and/or nystagmus may be present. Contralateral hemiparesis may also be present, but less pronounced than sensory deficits and due to impingement of the hemorrhage on the internal capsule. Homonymous hemianopsia may be seen initially, though tends to remit after several days. Larger lesions can result in compression of the third ventricle which may result in hydrocephalus of the lateral ventricles, necessitating placement of a shunt. Extension of the hemorrhage to the third ventricle has been reported to result in less neurologic comorbidity, but frequently does result in hydrocephalus that requires surgical treatment.

Pontine Hemorrhage

The clinical manifestation of pontine ICH tends to result in coma within minutes. Quadriplegia is often present due to disruption of both corticospinal and corticobulbar tracts. Decerebrate rigidity and small (the so-called pinpoint) pupils that are reactive to light frequently develop within minutes of the ICH. Lateral eye movements are absent. Mortality is common with pontine hemorrhages, with most (60 + %) dying within the first few hours due to brainstem herniation and disruption of critical physiologic brainstem functions. Brainstem herniation, due to pontine hemorrhage or other causes of increased intracranial pressure, can produce *Duret Hemorrhages*, which are small areas of bleeding in the midbrain or pons that can extend into the cerebellum, and often appear as small, rounded hemorrhage near the midline (Parizel et al., 2002). Duret Hemorrhages are often associated with depressed consciousness and are an ominous sign, typically leading to death.

Small hemorrhages are less likely to result in coma or death. If the hemorrhage is small, symptoms include pinpoint pupils, lateral gaze palsies, hemianesthesia, quadriparesis, but retained consciousness. Recovery has been reported to be "functionally good" for a small number of patients with pontine ICH and retained consciousness.

Cerebellar Hemorrhage

Common clinical signs include nausea and emesis, severe occipital headache; and truncal ataxia preventing the patient from walking, standing and in some cases even sitting upright. Depending upon the size of the hemorrhage, symptom onset may be minutes up to several hours. While consciousness is generally retained early in the symptom course, untreated ICH can lead to compression of the brain stem causing rapid onset of coma, decerebrate posturing and death within minutes. Ipsilateral conjugate lateral gaze palsy, ipsilateral sixth nerve palsy or eye deviation to the contralateral side and "pinpoint" pupils that are reactive to light may be present. Other cerebellar signs, including dysarthria, dysphagia, limb ataxia or nystagmus are less common. Vertical eye movements are retained. Sudden onset of these symptoms progressing over minutes should be considered a neurological emergency unless proven otherwise.

Subarachnoid Hemorrhage (SAH)/Epidural Hematoma/ Subdural Hematoma

Most subarachnoid hemorrhages (SAH) are due to the rupture of intracranial aneurysms that commonly develop at bifurcations and branch points within the Circle of Willis at the base of the brain (see Images 14.6, 14.7 and 14.8). There are three types of aneurysms: (1) saccular (or berry), (2) fusiform and (3) dissecting. Most aneurysms are saccular (berry) aneurysms, which originate from a congenital weakness within the artery which enlarges to form a sac- or balloon-like structure protruding from the side of a vessel or in location of vessel branching. In the elderly, atherosclerosis can lead to a fusiform enlargement (aneurysm) of intracranial vessels which are also classified as aneurysms. These rarely rupture but rather cause ischemic strokes by occluding thrombosis or act like an expanding mass and impinge on surrounding brain tissue. The third type of aneurysm is a dissecting aneurysm which is formed when the lumen of the vessel wall is torn, allowing blood to track between the layers of tissue making up the vessel wall; these have a variable prognosis.

The risk of rupture for incidental or asymptomatic saccular aneurysm is 1–2% per year. Factors that increase this risk include aneurysm size, multiplicity, location and the patient's age. Although aneurysms of any size may rupture, many are between 5 and 10 mm in size. Most saccular aneurysms are idiopathic, but 15%

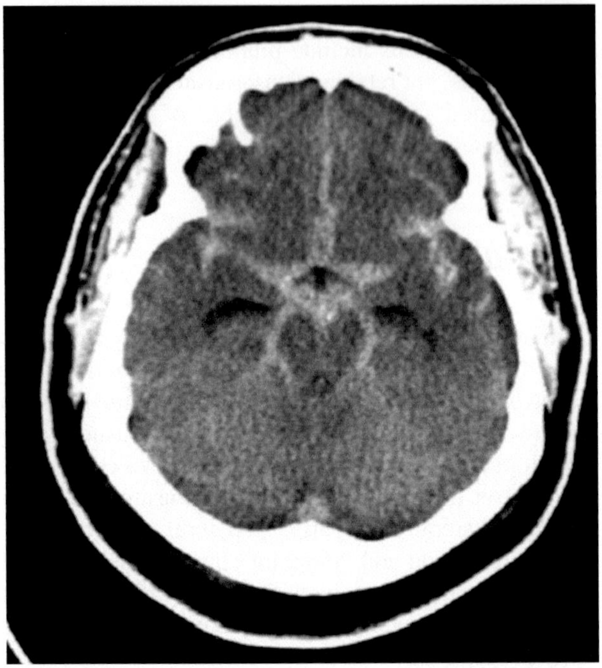

Image 14.6 CT brain scan without contrast demonstrating hyperdense material within the Sylvian fissure characteristic for an aneurysmal subarachnoid hemorrhage

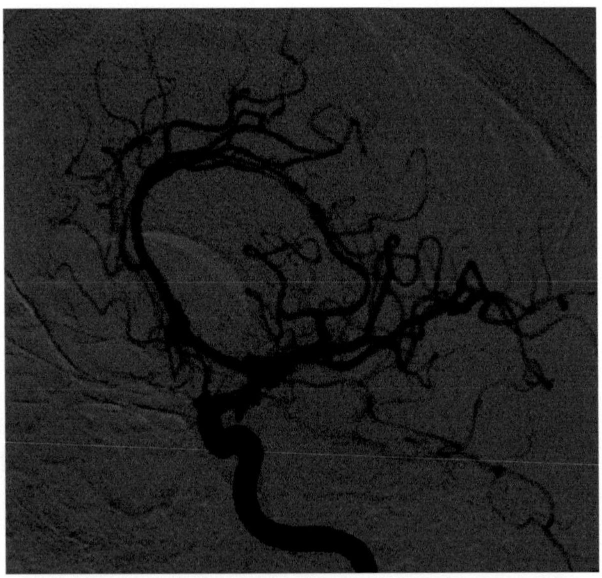

Image 14.7 Cerebral angiogram of internal carotid artery demonstrating ACA and MCA distributions and berry aneurysm at the anterior communicating artery

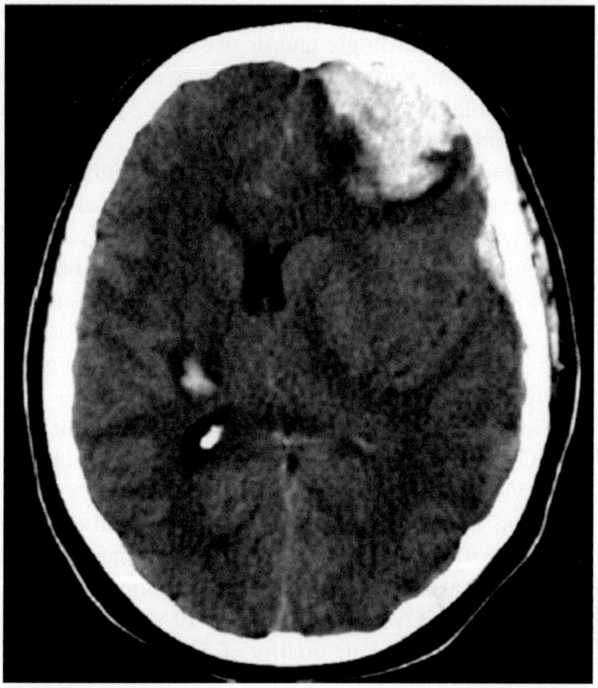

Image 14.8 CT brain scan without contrast depicts a hemorrhage within a region of infarction located at the cortical surface characteristic for rupture of a mycotic aneurysm

are inherited and are associated with other vascular disorders such as polycystic kidney disease, coarctation (narrowing) of the aorta, Ehlers–Danlos syndrome, neurofibromatosis, fibromuscular dysplasia and arteriovenous malformations (AVMs).

Mortality rates are highest for SAH as the acute rupture of blood under arterial pressure produces an abrupt rise in intracranial pressure preventing cerebral blood flow. As of 2009, 10–20% of patients with SAH die prior to reaching the hospital, and 26–46% of surviving patients die within 6 months of the original SAH. The overall mortality rate for SAH has ranged from 32% to 67%. Neurological complications of SAH include rebleeding, vasospasm and hydrocephalus.

Rebleeding is the re-occurrence of blood hemorrhaging after an initial bleed through a ruptured aneurysm and has led to mortality in up to 78% of patients. Rebleeding occurs in up to 50% of patients who are not surgically treated. Of these, about 20% of cases rebleed within 2 weeks of the original hemorrhage, and more than 30% rebleed within the first month. The incidence of rebleeding 6 months after the original SAH is about 2.2% per year in the first 10 years and then 0.9% per year in the following 10 years.

Vasospasm refers to the contraction of the intracerebral artery walls, resulting in lower flow and higher arterial pressure. Vasospasm may be diffuse; however, it occurs most often in arteries proximal to the subarachnoid blood and is correlated with blood products in the subarachnoid space. Vasospasm typically occurs

2–12 days after the initial hemorrhage and will present with a clinical presentation of worsening neurologic and/or neuropsychologic deficits. Up to 50% of patients with vasospasm will suffer an ischemic stroke. The presentation is typically fluctuating neurologic and/or neuropsychologic symptoms associated with vascular territory (territories) of the artery(s).

Hydrocephalus occurs in 15–60% of patients with SAH. Hydrocephalus presents acutely (within 3 days of SAH) in about 20% of patients but may occur at any time (often within 4 weeks) after the hemorrhage. Hydrocephalus in these cases is due to blockage of CSF pathways. Clinical presentation is onset of confusion, cognitive deterioration (dementia), ataxic gait and incontinence. Treatment of acute or subacute hydrocephalus is typically ventriculostomy or lumbar puncture. The Hunt and Hess scale (Hunt & Hess, 1968) is often used to grade the severity of SAH and is provided in Fig. 14.15.

Clinical outcome can be predicted by the Hunt and Hess clinical scale. Patients with Grade I, II and III SAH tend to have better outcomes than patients with Grade IV or V SAH. With appropriate treatment, 30% of patients with Grades I–III make good functional and neurologic outcomes, but even for survivors of lesser severity SAH, the effects of increased intracranial pressure and the delayed cerebral injury from vasospasm-induced cerebral infarction can result in significant long-term cognitive deficits. Overall, about 66% of survivors of SAH and aneurysm clipping never return to the same quality of life.

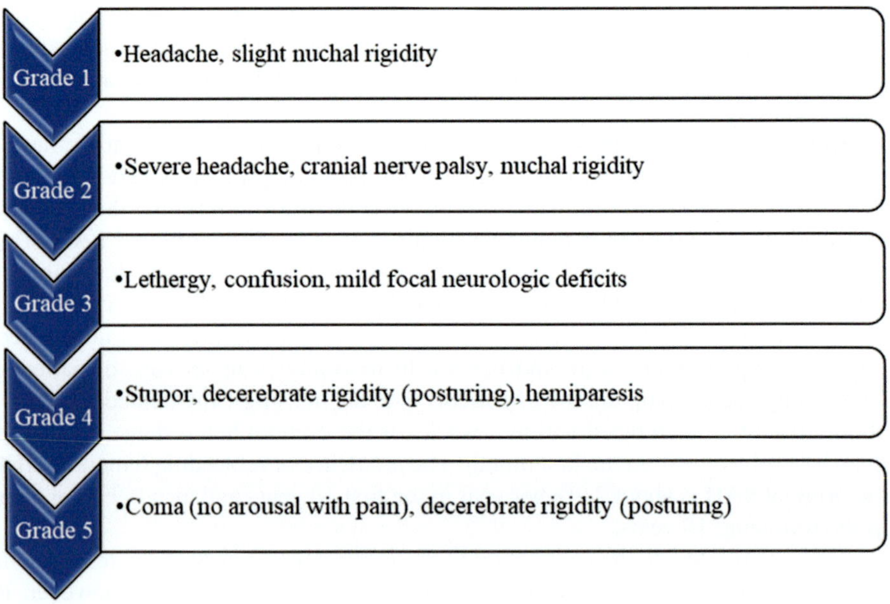

Fig. 14.15 Hunt and Hess Clinical Scale for SAH Severity

SAH Symptoms

The clinical presentation of subarachnoid hemorrhage has typically been described as one of the three patterns: (1) sudden severe generalized headache with vomiting, (2) sudden severe generalized headache with vomiting and loss of consciousness or (3) rapid onset of unconsciousness with no other complaints before the patient collapses to the ground (patient will suddenly topple to the floor). The most common is onset of sudden severe headache and initially retained consciousness. Because bleeding is predominantly around the brain, there are usually no early focal neurological findings. Most (90–95%) of saccular aneurysms arise from the Circle of Willis, with the four most common areas being: (1) anterior communicating artery (ACoA), (2) origin of the PComm from the internal carotid artery, (3) first large bifurcation of the MCA and (4) arising from the bifurcation of the internal carotid artery to form the MCA and ACA.

Key Points: Top Areas for Saccular Aneurysms at Branch Points Within Basal Brain Arteries

Internal carotid (anterior) vascular system	Vertebral-Basilar (posterior) vascular system
•85–95% of all cerebral aneurysms	•5–15% of all cerebral aneurysms
•Anterior cerebral artery and Anterior communicating artery (ACA and ACoA) ~30–35%	•Basilar artery bifurcation (top of the basilar) ~5%
•Terminal Internal Carotid Artery and Posterior communicating artery (tICA and PCoA) ~30–35%	•Remaining posterior circulation arteries ~5%

The clinical syndrome of SAH shares many similarities with ICH in the acute phase. The common clinical picture is an abrupt onset severe headache followed by reduced arousal level, and sometimes coma. Sudden loss of consciousness occurs in about 20% of patients. Nuchal rigidity, seizures, papilledema and/or retinal hemorrhage are common. Seizure as first presenting symptom occurred in 6–18% of patients with SAH (Pinto et al., 1996). Localizing features may not be present for one or more days, but cranial nerve palsies, particularly CN III, IV and VI, are common. Lateralizing features such as headache that primarily involves one hemisphere, monocular pain or unilateral retinal hemorrhage may occur.

While not common, localizing features may be present. These could include:

- Paresis of one or both legs and/or presentation of retained consciousness with mutism and/or akinesia is suggestive of an ACoA aneurysm hemorrhage.

- A third nerve palsy can be indicative of a PComm aneurysm, but CN IV and VI palsies are often due to increased intracranial pressure.
- Immediate hemiparesis and/or global aphasia is suggestive of an aneurysm of the first major bifurcation of the MCA.
- Unilateral blindness with retained consciousness is suggestive of an aneurysm of the ophthalmic artery or the branching of the ICA.

Outcome from SAH is difficult to predict as subsequent sequalae can adversely affect outcome. This may include rebleeding, ischemic stroke due to vasospasm and/or hydrocephalus. In general, individuals with SAH that cannot be identified using angiography have a much better prognosis than patients in which the aneurysm is identifiable. Mortality and increased likelihood of poor outcome occurs with ventricular and/or intraparenchymal extension. Patients with extensions have increased likelihood of coma and development of hydrocephalus.

AComm (ACoA)

Rupture of an ACoA aneurysm between the ACA arteries may result in damage to large or small area of the brain, but typically most affects the inferior and mesial frontal lobes. Damage to the brain parenchyma can occur by a variety of causes, including blood products, ischemia due to decreased arterial blood volume and/or subsequent vasospasm, increased intracranial pressure and effects from craniotomy and/or infection. Damage may also affect the mesial thalamus and cingulate gyrus. Large, unruptured aneurysms can also place pressure on the optic chiasm, leading to bitemporal hemianopsia.

Up to 60% of patients who survive AComm aneurysms present with disabling neuropsychological deficits. Deficits frequently involve attention/concentration, executive skills, memory and language functions as well as personality and mood changes related to bilateral frontal lobe dysfunction. Pseudobulbar affect may be present. Attention deficits typically include reduced sustained attention and increased distractibility. Executive impairments are common, and patients can present with a variety of cognitive and personality changes associated with mesial and/or orbitofrontal lobe syndromes including decreased initiation, behavioral apathy, reduced verbal output (mutism) or, alternatively, behavioral disinhibition, agitation, increased energy level, reduced personal hygiene and difficulty learning from trial and error. Memory can be markedly impaired, particularly if basal forebrain areas are damaged. Memory impairment is of declarative (explicit) memory, and the patient can be densely amnestic. Confabulation is frequently found, and mood symptoms can include paranoia, delusions and obsessive-compulsive behaviors.

Improvement in neuropsychological function after AcoA aneurysm rupture does occur, but most patients will exhibit residual impairments. Return to work and/or independence following ACoA aneurysm is typically poor. Of patients working full-time prior to AComm aneurysm rupture, about 50% do not return to the same level of work due to the long-term cognitive deficits frequently associated with ACoA aneurysms.

Intraventricular Hemorrhage

Intraventricular hemorrhage (IVH) can occur in isolation but is more commonly seen as a complication of subarachnoid hemorrhage or intracerebral hemorrhage and has similar etiologies. In addition to the above-mentioned complications, IVH often results in hydrocephalus requiring ventricular drainage.

Hemorrhagic Stroke Diagnosis and Management

Acute hemorrhagic products are best appreciated on CT, which is convenient given the broader availability and shorter exam time of CT—critical in emergency situations. Fresh blood appears *hyperdense*, and thus bright white, on non-contrast CT, and will slowly become less apparent as it resolves (see Images 14.6 and 14.8 above). *Hypodense* or isodense areas within the hemorrhage, appearing as darker areas within the bright blood volume, is called the *swirl sign* and is indicative of an active bleed. Acute and subacute hemorrhage often leads to midline shift or other types of mass effect due to the Monro–Kellie doctrine. This principle, which also applies to malignant ischemia from edema or any other space-occupying pathology, states that the skull is a fixed volume with the sum of brain, CSF and intracranial blood volumes being constant. Thus, any increase in one of these (e.g., active hemorrhage leading to greater intracranial blood) leads to a decrease in one (or both) of the others. As brain tissue (and CSF) has nowhere to go it becomes compressed and pushed out of the way. In severe cases, this leads to brain herniation through the foramen magnum, which is typically fatal. For this reason, cases of brain displacement or increases in intracranial pressure may be treated with craniotomy (burr hole to allow for evacuation of blood and release of pressure) or craniectomy (temporary removal of a skull flap to reduce permanent brain damage from compression).

In time, blood products are reabsorbed, which rebalances this ratio. However, due to the privileged vascular nature of the brain (protected by the BBB) and post-mitotic nature of most neurons, hemorrhages tend to leave behind a type of iron called *hemosiderin*, which can be detected years or even decades later. Prior history of CNS hemorrhage, either due to trauma, vessel rupture or CAA, can be detected via Susceptibility-Weighted Imaging (SWI) and other gradient echo techniques, which are exquisitely sensitive to this iron deposition.

Differences Between Ischemic and Hemorrhagic Strokes

The extent of neurological and/or neuropsychological deficits typically differs between ischemic and hemorrhagic strokes. As noted above, deficits resulting from ischemic strokes follow cerebral vascular neuroanatomic territory, while ICH can result in more diffuse dysfunction involving areas of several different cerebral vascular territories. Moreover, the ischemic process results in direct damage to brain parenchyma, while hemorrhagic strokes primarily cause damage from tissue displacement which can result in a greater range of possible damage, including broader, more distal damage at the severe end of the scale. Deficits resulting from ischemic stroke will also vary depending upon the completeness of occlusion, duration of the occlusion and the availability of anastomotic blood supply during the ischemic period (e.g., TIA versus completed stroke), while hemorrhagic stroke outcomes are due to the pressure of the ruptured vessel (greater pressure means more bleeding), duration of the blood and neuroanatomic location. Seizures are more common following hemorrhagic stroke than ischemic stroke. Finally, secondary hemorrhage following ischemic stroke is an important consideration; while such bleeds are usually not as severe as a primary hemorrhagic stroke, they will typically complicate the course of recovery.

Neurological and functional outcome from hemorrhagic strokes varies more widely than ischemic strokes. While ischemic damage tends to result in damage to brain parenchyma itself within the vascular distribution territory, hemorrhagic strokes can damage brain tissue outside of the cerebral vascular distribution (e.g., intracerebral hemorrhages with intraventricular extension and/or due to herniation of tissue and subsequent ischemia). Alternatively, other hemorrhagic strokes (e.g., subdural) may not damage the brain itself, with the accumulating blood producing a space-occupying lesion occupying a space and subsequently displacing brain parenchyma, but with no long-term damage once the blood products are removed. The research on functional prognosis in ischemic vs. hemorrhagic stroke is varied. Although some studies suggest better functional recovery in the latter, this is not universally supported (Perna & Temple, 2015) and may rather be a function of mediating factors (Salvadori et al., 2020). For example, patients with hemorrhagic stroke tend to be younger (Kelly et al., 2003) and possibly less likely to have chronic health disorders which predispose to ischemic disease or other pre-existing vulnerabilities that may impact recovery.

In summary, strokes are classified according to pathophysiology being either ischemic or hemorrhagic. While the hallmark clinical features of a stroke are the sudden onset of neurologic and/or neuropsychologic symptoms, the specific symptoms are determined by the location of the lesion and pathophysiology. As the arterial vascular supply is rather uniform and disease states tend to affect certain regions of the vasculature with regularity, the result is a series of recognizable patterns of neurologic deficit representing specific stroke subtypes. The pattern of signs and symptoms will not only reflect the specific vessel(s) affected but will also suggest the underlying mechanism.

Clinical Evaluation and Syndromes

Neuropsychological Evaluation

Neuropsychological evaluation can help identify extent of cognitive and emotional sequelae following stroke, help refine functional prognosis and guide care planning. Treatment of stroke will likely include acute management of symptoms, rehabilitation and pharmaceutical intervention for medical risk factors (e.g., hypertension, hyperlipidemia, diabetes, etc.). Rehabilitation after stroke commonly includes speech and language therapy, cognitive therapy, physical therapy, occupational therapy and vocational therapy. Patients may also be prescribed medications, such as anticonvulsants (for seizure prophylaxis), anticoagulants for ischemic stroke and antidepressants, anxiolytics and antipsychotics for concomitant mood and behavioral disorders.

Deficits in neuropsychological function will depend upon the size and location of the lesion, time elapsed since the stroke, as well as the patient's age and comorbid conditions. Once a deficit is appreciated (e.g., hemineglect, hemiparesis or aphasia syndrome), accommodation of the patient's recognized deficit to evaluate for other potential neuropsychological deficits is recommended. For example, in assessment of a subacute right MCA infarct, it is unnecessary to continue to administer tests in a patient's left visual field after a left hemineglect has been identified. Thus, stimuli to assess other neuropsychological domains should be presented in the preserved visual hemispace.

Assuming no secondary complicating factors, most functional recovery will occur over the first few (3–6) months. Additional, but less pronounced, recovery can occur over the next 6–12 months. Improved functioning after 12 months is largely a function of compensation and adaptation to deficits rather than biological recovery, although younger patients may evidence some biological recovery of function years since injury (Victor & Ropper, 2001). Although there is marked variability in the type and severity of sequalae from cortical and subcortical strokes, damage to cortical structures and supratentorial white matter tends to be more amenable to rehabilitation compared to deep pathways within the brain stem This is, in part, due to basal and life-supporting function of brain stem structures, making stokes in these areas more life-threatening and more likely to cause profound physical impairments, while sparing cortical areas. Cortical strokes in contrast produce the greatest risk for cognitive functioning deficits.

Neuropsychological assessment may be completed any time following a stroke. Common referral questions include requests to document the nature of the deficit, help develop rehabilitation interventions and/or placement decisions, assess for progression of neuropsychological functional recovery and/or identify the development of complicating conditions (e.g., cerebral edema, hemorrhagic conversion, etc.). In acute patients, post-stroke assessment is likely to be limited to brief bedside cognitive exam. In post-acute settings, more comprehensive neuropsychological evaluation can characterize any residual deficits and provide recommendations for functional recovery, including return to work or school (Victor & Ropper, 2001; Lezak et al., 2004). Additionally, neuropsychological evaluation can also assist in determining the patient's competence to manage their personal affairs, make medical/legal/financial decisions, and/or capacity, and accommodations for the ability, to return to employment. In these cases, more detailed psychometric evaluation of the patient's neuropsychological functioning is often completed. Neuropsychological evaluation in patients suspected of multi-infarct and vascular dementia may be reassessed in clinically indicated intervals to assess for change in neuropsychological function with treatment.

Key Points: Identifying Cognitive Strengths Just as Important as Identifying Deficits

Do	Do Not
Attempt to identify strengths and weakness. Accommodation and adaptation of neuropsychological tests is often necessary in acute and sub-acute stroke assessments. For example, presenting visual memory material in the right hemispace will better allow for assessment of visual memory function.	Repeatedly request that a patient attempt tasks where failure is likely (e.g., repeated motor testing of a patient with hemi-paresis).

Emotional Regulation/Personality Changes

Emotional and personality changes frequently occur following stroke—either as new-onset emotional and/or personality disorder or as an exacerbation of a premorbid psychiatric disorder. The most common symptoms are depression and anxiety. Generally, patients with left hemisphere strokes initially present with symptoms of depression while patients with right hemisphere strokes are typically described as emotionally flat and indifferent to their motor and cognitive deficits. A meta-analysis found 52% of patients with stroke reported symptoms of clinical depression. Hemispheric differences have been extensively studied and a review is provided below.

Right Hemisphere

The most common affect change with right hemisphere strokes is indifference and affective flattening. Right hemisphere damage often results in reduced capacity to appreciate emotional or social cues (both nonverbal and verbal). Patients can have little insight into the interpersonal significance of certain facial expressions, body postures and hand gestures. As the right hemisphere is often involved in appreciating and expressing speech prosody, these patients may struggle discern emotional or social salience by changes in the speech prosody of others (receptive aprosody). Patients may also have flat and monotone speech which may be misinterpreted as dysphoric or depressed to a casual observer. While speech prosody and intonation are blunted, speech is of often of normal rate and well-articulated.

Speech content may be about past events, which have little relevance to the listener, or may be repeated explanations for the patient's inability to do certain things. As an example, patients may demonstrate a repeated inaccurate understanding of their reason for hospitalization or utilize basic speech to avoid cognitively burdening activities, such as repeatedly saying "I'm too tired" when offered physical or occupational therapy. Finally, it is not uncommon for patients with right hemisphere dysfunction to present with paranoia and perseveration. Patients with right hemisphere lesions can also develop increasing symptoms of depression and anxiety months and even years following the stroke, especially if the stroke occurred in more posterior regions (Robinson & Starkstein, 2002).

Left Hemisphere

Ischemic damage to the left hemisphere, particularly the caudate and left frontal lobe, is associated with tearful/anxious affect and/or symptoms of depression. Rates of depression vary, but at least 50% of patients endorse depressive symptoms following left hemisphere strokes (Lezak et al., 2004). Depressive symptoms may present in acute settings but resolve over time. However, patients with residual depression tend to exhibit the greatest reduction in social activities years after stroke (Lezak et al., 2004).

Frontal and Subcortical

Frontal lobe damage caused by stroke can present with marked emotional and personality changes. Anterior Communicating Artery (ACoA) aneurysm patients may present with marked personality changes, particularly behavioral flattening, apathy and abulia. Because orbital frontal damage may also occur, patients may also present with behavioral disinhibition, irritability, lack of concern for others and reduced personal hygiene. Damage to the cortico-striato-thalamic-cortico circuitry often presents with symptoms of perseveration and compulsions, resulting in a clinical presentation similar to obsessive-compulsive disorder.

Damage to corticobulbar pathways can release motor control of facial expressions from cortical control (pseudobulbar affective expression). Patients may have restricted spontaneous emotions yet experience sudden laughter or crying without an apparent emotional trigger. The extent of facial weakness does not correlate well with the presence of facial or bulbar motor weakness. The far more common pseudobulbar behavior is the appearance of crying. Asking the patient if they feel sad/despondent or if they want to cry can be very instructive in disentangling the potential presence of pseudobulbar affect from reactive responses to having a neurologic disease. The same line of question for apparent "forced" (pseudobulbar) laughing, asking the patient laughing if they feel a sense of mirth (happiness/funny) is instructive in these cases. Pseudobulbar affect can be very troubling to family members and friends, as the initiation of crying or laughing behaviors can be incongruent with the social setting. Knowing these behaviors are out of the patient's control and due to neurologic disease can be reassuring to the patient and his/her family. Outbursts of pseudobulbar affect can be redirected by directly asking the patient a neutral question such as "what color are your shoes" thus breaking the cycle of affective expression.

Key Points: Changes in Personality and Affect Following Stroke

Left hemisphere

- Catastrophic reactions
- Depression and affective lability are common
- Tearfulness

Right hemisphere

- Affective flattening and indifference
- Monotone speech
- Difficulty appreciating nonverbal cues in social settings

Mesial and Orbital Frontal: Involvement of mesial frontal or orbitofrontal areas often exhibits pronounced behavioral changes, including amotivation, apathy/abulia (akinetic) and/or agitation. Orbitofrontal involvement may result in behavioral changes of decreased inhibition, lack of regard for others and changes in sleep and libido. Pseudobulbar affect is associated with damage to the bulbar pathways. Pseudobulbar crying is most often but laughing also occurs.

Acute and Subacute Stroke Management

Stroke is a medical emergency. While a detailed review of the acute treatment of stroke is beyond the scope of this chapter, Fig. 14.16 provides an overview of stroke interventions. The acute treatment of ischemic stroke focuses on restoring blood flow, preventing reperfusion hemorrhage and determining the cause to guide future preventive therapies. The acute treatment of hemorrhagic stroke focuses on controlling the bleeding and limiting the effects of increased intracranial pressure. Some patients may require surgical therapy to evacuate the clot, clip an aneurysm or remove an AVM. Nonsurgical, endovascular techniques of aneurysm coiling, and

Treatment	**Mechanism of Action**	**Treatment Indications**
Tissue plasminogen activators (tPA)	• Metabolizes plasminogen to plasmin enzyme which hydrolyzes clotting proteins • Treatment window is generally within 3 hours of symptom onset or within 6 hours with direct arterial injection	• Useful for thrombotic and thrombo-embolic (ischemic) strokes • Increases risk for hemorrhagic conversion
Anticoagulant Medication	• Increased prothrombin time (TT) and/or partial TT clotting time	• Useful for thrombotic stroke or occlusion due to carotid artery dissection • Contraindicated in patients with endocarditis
Antiplatelet Medication	• Effective in reducing the risk of stroke and myocardial infarction	• Preventative, does not reverse stroke
Surgical Revascularization	• Carotid endarterectomy for symptomatic or severe accessible carotid stenosis • Surgery recommended within 2 weeks of a mild to moderate infarct to reduce risk of recurrent stroke	• Surgical benefit is greater for symptomatic severe internal carotid stenoses (>70%) than moderate (50-69%) or asymptomatic (>60%) stenoses
Other Surgical Treatments	• Recanalization of vessel by angioplasty stenting and/or balloon angioplasty • Common surgical targets are internal carotid artery, common carotid artery, or subclavian arteries	• Carotid angioplasty and stenting is recommended over endarterectomy for surgically inaccessible lesions and other anatomic high-risk conditions • Less evidence for effectiveness for vertebral or basilar artery stenosis
Treatment of edema (typically in hours to days poststroke, can be fatal due to mass effect and brain herniation)	• Use of hyperventilation and osmotic diuretic agents can provide temporary reduction in intracranial pressure but may aggravate lateral tissue shifts causing worse herniation • Surgical treatment with hemicraniectomy can be lifesaving to these patients	• Symptoms associated with edema include worsening mental status hours to days after a stroke, ipsilateral CNIII nerve palsy and bilateral lower extremity spasticity and Babinski signs

Fig. 14.16 Medical interventions for acute stroke

AVM obliteration may spare a craniotomy for some patients. In all stroke patients, preventing medical complications such as pneumonia, sepsis and deep venous thrombosis is important, as are maintaining adequate nutrition and restoring mobility. Once patients are medically stable to be discharged from the hospital, the longer-term therapies of rehabilitation take center stage.

Neuropsychological Assessment and Rehabilitation

The goal of rehabilitation is to improve a patient's ability to process and interpret information allowing the individual to function better in all aspects of life (adapted from NIH position statement for rehabilitation in TBI, 1999). Rehabilitation involves a step-like process in which gross (large-scale) behaviors/abilities must be present (or developed) before fine motor or specialty behaviors can occur. Recovery of motor function occurs first in proximal muscles prior to distal motor skills. Cognitive rehabilitation utilizes the same pattern, such that basic attention and sensory-perceptual functions must be retained (or developed) before higher-level memory strategies or problem-solving can be acquired. Rehabilitation may be short-term or longer-term programs targeting specific motor, sensory, cognitive and/or behavioral/psychiatric functioning.

Key Points: Primary Purposes of Stroke Rehabilitation

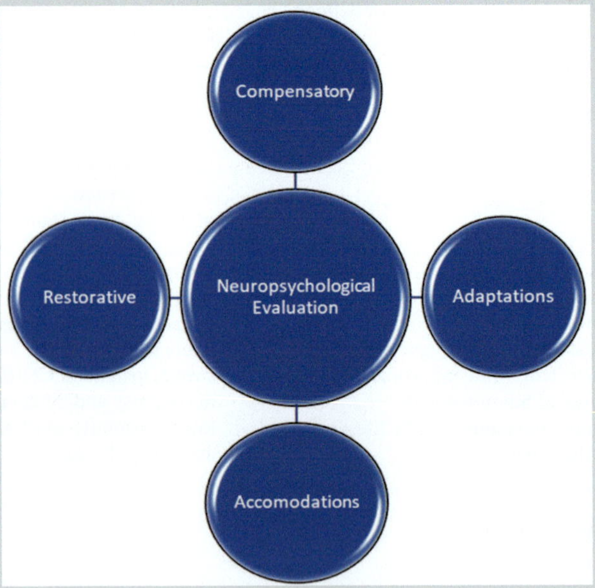

The two primary processes of rehabilitation are *restorative* and *compensatory*. Restorative therapy is designed to enhance a cognitive (or other) function to pre-injury levels or maximal residual function. Restorative therapy typically occurs in the acute phase of rehabilitation and seeks to capitalize on the concurrence of post-stroke neural repair. Ideally, restorative rehabilitation allows a patient's functioning to return to (or approximate) premorbid levels of mastery. For example, speech therapy may initiate a restorative treatment program to reacquire expressive language function.

The second general process of rehabilitation is compensatory therapies. Rather than a goal to restore function, compensatory therapies focus on adapting the patient's function to a deficit (cognitive, motor, behavioral). Compensatory strategies may utilize adaptations and/or accommodations to identified deficits. These often include teaching patients to complete a task differently or modifying the environment to allow the patient to complete a task within the parameters of their current ability.

There are three principal types of accommodations: (1) procedure accommodations, (2) physical accommodations to environment and (3) utilization of assistive devices. Procedure accommodations are often easily implemented by developing sequenced set of steps to complete a more complex task (minimizing attention and memory demands). Physical accommodations adapt an environment (bedroom, kitchen or work site) to allow a patient to complete tasks inclusive of the individual's identified neuropsychological deficits.

Compensatory methods often utilize assistive technologies and/or physical adaptations to accommodate deficits. For example, cognitive compensatory strategies that can facilitate increased independence in a patient with memory deficits include the use of a personal tablet or smart phone to keep a memory notebook or schedule reminders for appointments. Similarly, the advent of Artificial Intelligence (A.I.) and other applications designed specifically for stroke patients has allowed for more tailored rehabilitation training and nuanced analytics to improve management of chronic symptoms. As technology continues to develop, opportunities for more sophisticated compensatory intervention can result in greater functional recovery following stroke than in previous decades.

Neuropsychological Evaluation The role of neuropsychology within rehabilitation of stroke is a complex issue, and assessment of neuropsychological function in recovery from brain attack can play an important role in patient's return to independence. The neuropsychological evaluation provides an objective assessment of specific cognitive deficits and strengths as well as which behaviors and/or emotional functioning are present or disrupted. Comprehensive stroke programs offering several types of therapies (such as those listed below) will utilize a patient's neuropsychological strengths to help develop accommodation techniques for deficits. Without detailed neuropsychological assessment, many cognitive rehabilitation procedures cannot be undertaken, and individuals can be provided unnecessary treatment. Serial neuropsychological assessment also enables monitoring of restorative rehabilitation programming over time.

Speech/Language Therapy Neuropsychological assessment plays an important role in speech/language therapy. Assessment will identify cognitive strengths and weaknesses which are employed by the speech/language therapist to develop a treatment plan.

Physical Therapy Strengthening exercises are essential in recovering from motor deficits to resume safe ambulation and activities of daily living as well as addressing the deconditioning associated with bedrest.

Occupational Therapy Functional exercises are essential in recovering from perceptual and motor deficits to resume activities of daily living including functional activities and fine motor tasks. Driving specialists can also offer specialized assessments geared to determine the safety to resume independent driving.

Vocational Therapy Results of the patient's neurological examination, rehabilitation assessment and neuropsychological testing are used by the vocational counselor to advise the patient on suitability to return to the prior employment, ability to retrain for alternate employment and types of alternate employment that would be possible given the residual deficits.

Post-Stroke Depression and Mental Health Treatment

Post-stroke depression is common, with an estimated prevalence of 18–33% among stroke survivors. Stroke survivors with post-stroke depression are at elevated risk for worse stroke recovery outcomes compared to those without post-stroke depression. There are several risk factors for post-stroke depression which can be conceptualized into pre-stroke, stroke-related and post-stroke risk factors (Medeiros et al., 2020). Pre-stroke risk factors for post-stroke depression include female gender, personal history of mental illness, particularly depression, and family history of mental illness. Stroke-related risk factors for post-stroke depression include large and multiple strokes, strokes in anterior/frontal areas of the brain and strokes in the basal ganglia. Post-stroke risk factors for post-stroke depression include the timeframe of the first-year post-stroke, higher level of disability, lower level of independence, diffuse white matter damage and social isolation. Persons with these risk factors should be carefully monitored and evaluated, if indicated, for post-stroke depression by a mental health professional.

Screening

While there remains no "gold standard" instrument to measure depression in the post-stroke population, several instruments have been validated for this purpose, including the clinician-administered 21-item Hamilton Depression Rating Scale

(HAM-D), the self-reported 20-item Center of Epidemiological Studies—Depression Scale (CES-D) and the self-report nine-item Patient Health Questionnaire (PHQ-9; Meader et al., 2014). There is concern that screenings completed in acute settings immediately after the stroke may be suboptimal given high prevalence of transient mood changes, adjustment reactions, poor sleep/fatigue and confusion that may be present during this period. As such, screening for post-stroke depression is generally recommended in the inpatient rehabilitation and outpatient clinics. Should a patient screen positive for depression in these settings, a comprehensive clinical evaluation is indicated to differentiate post-stroke depression from other disorders with a similar presentation (e.g., adjustment disorder, demoralization), assess severity and safety risk and examine co-occurring psychiatric disorders (e.g., anxiety disorder, substance use disorders).

Pharmacological Treatment

Evidence from RCTs and meta-analyses largely support the efficacy of pharmacological treatment for post-stroke depression. The most recommended antidepressants are SSRIs (e.g., paroxetine, escitalopram). However, there were no significant differences in effectiveness between SSRIs, SNRIs or tricyclics. Tricyclics are generally considered a second line of therapy given contraindications and anticholinergic burden. Of note, SSRIs have been associated with higher stroke risk in the older adult population (Starkstein & Hayhow, 2019).

Psychotherapy Treatment

While pharmacological treatment is considered a first line therapy for treatment of post-stroke depression, there is also evidence for the efficacy of psychotherapy treatment either alone or in combination with an antidepressant. A 2019 meta-analysis suggested some positive effects for cognitive behavioral therapy on depressive symptoms in post-stroke depression, anxiety, functional deficits and neurological recovery though it was noted that there was a high degree of heterogeneity and low quality across many of the studies (Wang et al., 2018). Additional emerging non-pharmacological interventions for post-stroke depression include ecosystem focused therapy (EFT), psychosocial interventions and neuromodulation (repetitive transcranial magnetic stimulation, rTMS).

Factors that Can Impact Recovery

Post-stroke recovery is a complex and dynamic process determined by the interplay of a multitude of factors. In addition to pre-existing medical conditions, these can include sociodemographic characteristics, access to rehabilitative interventions, genetic vulnerability and social support (See Fig. 14.17).

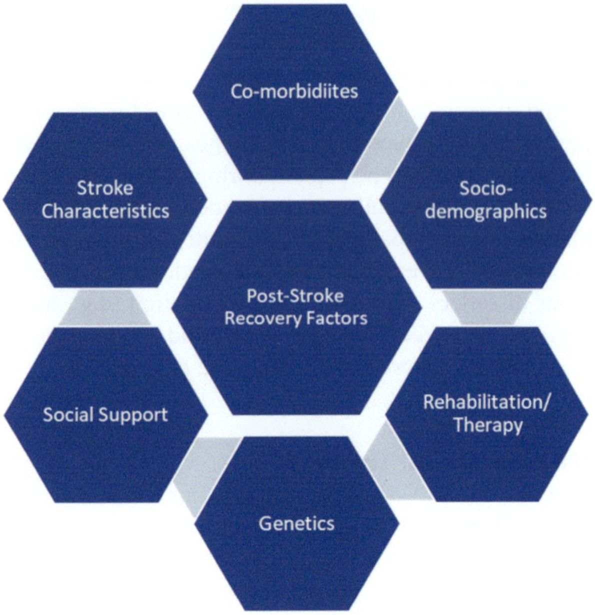

Fig. 14.17 Factors that impact stroke recovery

Stroke Characteristics

Within the two major subtypes of stroke, patients who suffer a hemorrhagic stroke tend to have greater acute functional impairment but then generally have a faster and more pronounced recovery trajectory than those with an ischemic stroke of comparable severity. Generally, those with mild acute deficits have a more positive prognosis than those with more severe initial deficits. Further, persons who experience more severe strokes impacting larger areas of brain tissue typically have poorer long-term recovery outcomes, as there remains less residual neuronal reservoir that can engage in functional recovery.

Comorbidities

Cerebrovascular risk factors that increase risk for stroke are also commonly implicated in suboptimal post-stroke recovery. These include tobacco use, diabetes, hypertension, congestive heart failure, atrial fibrillation and history of a previous stroke. Recent studies have demonstrated that sleep apnea and disorders of sleep–wake disturbances (e.g., hypersomnia, insomnia, restless leg syndrome) increase the risk for stroke and can negatively affect short- and long-term stroke recovery and outcomes (Hermann & Bassetti, 2016). Persons with dementia are also at higher risk for poor post-stroke recovery, possibly due to poor cognitive reserve and decreased ability to fully engage in rehabilitation therapies (Withall et al., 2009).

Sociodemographics

There are several sociodemographic factors that can influence post-stoke recovery. Older age has been consistently shown to be a significant prognostic indicator for poorer stroke recovery, with nearly half of older adults experiencing mild-to-severe disability post-stroke (GBD, 2020). There are also sex differences that contribute to stroke recovery. Women with stroke have generally poorer functional outcomes, increased depression and lower quality of life outcomes following a stroke compared to men. These sex differences may be due to discrepancies in quality of acute care, prevalence of premorbid health conditions and longer life expectancy for women (Reeves et al., 2008). Lower socioeconomic status has also been associated with poorer functioning and biopsychosocial health, as well as increased depressive symptoms following a stroke, particularly for moderate-to-severe strokes (Stulberg et al., 2021).

Research has also identified racial and ethnic disparities at several key points along the continuum of stroke care which can significantly impact functional outcomes. A recent systematic review found that Black, Hispanic and Asian persons reported lower utilization of emergency services, increased time between stroke symptom onset and presentation to the ED, lower rates of tPA administration and reduced likelihood of being transferred to endovascular-capable centers or another acute care facility compared to White persons (Ikeme et al., 2022). Potential barriers to access to stroke care among these racial and ethnic groups included geographic distance from the hospital, systemic racism in healthcare, disparities in medical insurance and health literacy. Proposed interventions to reduce racial and ethnic disparities in stroke care and recovery include mobile stroke unit models of care, increased use of licensed interpreters and implicit bias training for medical providers (Denny et al., 2024).

Rehabilitation/Therapy

There is strong evidence for the efficacy of multidisciplinary rehabilitation services on reducing mortality rates and the likelihood of institutional care and long-term disability, as well as enhancing recovery, and increasing independent in ADLs (Winstein et al., 2016). It has been consistently demonstrated that the timing of rehabilitation services plays an important role in recovery such that there is a higher likelihood for improved functional outcomes the sooner a patient with a stroke begins inpatient rehabilitation (Horn et al., 2005).

Genetics

There is preliminary research suggesting that genetic variation may influence the degree of functional outcome following a stroke (Lindgren, 2014). For example, a variation of a SNP (Val66Met) in the brain-derived neurotropic factor (BDNF) has been shown to be related to improved stroke recovery, while APOE E4 has been related to poorer stroke outcomes. Other genes that have been related to functional outcomes following a stroke include IGF1, COX-2 and GPIIIa. An international stroke genetics consortium recently outlined recommendations for future study of the genetics of stroke outcome and recovery, including the use of harmonized and well-accepted phenotyping instruments across studies and comprehensive evaluation of stroke recovery functional domains (Lindgren et al., 2022).

Social Support

Research has consistently demonstrated that good social support is associated with improved stroke outcomes. Strong social support is beneficial across several areas of recovery including increased likelihood of discharge to home from a rehabilitation facility (Chevalley et al., 2022), lower rates of post-stroke depression (Bi & Wang, 2022) and increased home and community participation (Erler et al., 2019).

References

Adams, H. P., Bendixen, B. H., Kappelle, L. J., Biller, J., Love, B. B., Gordon, D. L., & Marsh, E. E. (1993). Classification of subtype of acute ischemic stroke. Definitions for use in a multicenter clinical trial. TOAST. Trial of Org 10172 in acute stroke treatment. *Stroke, 24*, 35–41.

AITB. (1944). *Army individual test battery, manual of directions and scoring*. War Department, Adjutant General's Office.

Bendel, P., Koivisto, T., Niskanen, E., Kononen, M., Aikia, M., Hanninen, T., Koskenkorva, P., & Vanninen, R. (2009). Brain atrophy and neuropsychological outcome after treatment of ruptured anterior cerebral artery aneurysms: A voxel-based morphometric study. *Neuroradiology, 51*(11), 711–722. ISSN 0028-3940.

Benton, A. L., & de Hamsher, K. S. (1989). *Multilingual aphasia examination*. AJA Associates.

Benton, A. L., Sivan, A. B., Hamsher, K. D. S., Varney, N. R., & Spreen, O. (1994). *Contributions to neuropsychological assessment. A clinical manual* (2nd ed.). Oxford University Press.

Bi, H., & Wang, M. (2022). Role of social support in poststroke depression: A meta-analysis. *Frontiers in Psychiatry, 13*, 924277.

Bladin, C. F., Alexandrov, A. V., Bellavance, A., Bornstein, N., Chambers, B., Cote, R., Lebrun, L., Pirisi, A., & Norris, J. W. (2000). Seizures after stroke: A prospective multicenter study. *Archives of Neurology, 57*, 1617–1622.

Bogousslavsky, J., Regli, F., & Uske, A. (1988). Thalamic infarcts: Clinical syndromes, etiology, and prognosis. *Neurology, 38*, 837–848.

Boller, F., & Vignolo, L. A. (1966). Latent sensory aphasia in hemisphere-damaged patients: An experimental study with the token test. *Brain, 89*, 815–831.

Broderick, J., Brott, T., Kothari, R., Miller, R., Khoury, J., Pancioli, A., et al. (1998). The greater Cincinnati/Northern Kentucky Stroke Study: Preliminary first-ever and total incidence rates of stroke among blacks. *Stroke, 29*(2), 415–421.

Caplan, L. R. (1993). *Stroke: A clinical approach*. Butterworth-Heinemann.

Carhuapoma, J. R., & Hanley, D. F. (2002). Intracerebral haemorrhage. In A. K. Asbury, G. M. McKhann, W. I. McDonald, P. J. Goadsby, & J. C. McArthur (Eds.), *Diseases of the nervous system: Clinical neuroscience and therapeutic principles* (3rd ed.). Cambridge University Press.

Chevalley, O., Truijen, S., Saeys, W., & Opsommer, E. (2022). Socio-environmental predictive factors for discharge destination after inpatient rehabilitation in patients with stroke: A systematic review and meta-analysis. *Disability and Rehabilitation, 44*(18), 4974–4985.

Denny, M. C., Rosendale, N., Gonzales, N. R., Leslie-Mazwi, T. M., & Middleton, S. (2024). Addressing disparities in acute stroke management and prognosis. *Journal of the American Heart Association, 13*(7), e031313.

Erler, K. S., Sullivan, V., McKinnon, S., & Inzana, R. (2019). Social support as a predictor of community participation after stroke. *Frontiers in Neurology, 10*, 480090.

Faraco, G., & Iadecola, C. (2013). Hypertension: A harbinger of stroke and dementia. *Hypertension, 62*(5), 810–817.

Feigin, V. L., Brainin, M., Norrving, B., Martins, S., Sacco, R. L., Hacke, W., Fisher, M., Pandian, J., & Lindsay, P. (2022). World stroke organization (WSO): Global stroke fact sheet 2022. *International Journal of Stroke, 17*(1), 18–29.

Fisher, C. M. (1982). Lacunar strokes and infarcts: A review. *Neurology, 32*, 871–876.

Gardener, H., Sacco, R. L., Rundek, T., Battistella, V., Cheung, Y. K., & Elkind, M. S. (2020). Race and ethnic disparities in stroke incidence in the Northern Manhattan Study. *Stroke, 51*(4), 1064–1069.

Gauthier, L., Dehaut, F., & Joanette, Y. (1989). The Bells Test: A quantitative and qualitative test for visual neglect. *International Journal of Clinical Neuropsychology, 11*, 49–54.

GBD 2016 Neurology Collaborators. (2020). Global, regional, and national burden of neurological disorders, 1990-2016: A systematic analysis for the global burden of disease study 2016. *The Lancet Neurology, 18*, 459–480.

Gonzalez, D., Skopec, L., McDaniel, M., & Kenney, G. M. (2021). *Perceptions of discrimination and unfair judgment while seeking health care*. Urban Institute.

Goodglass, H., Kaplan, E., & Barresi, B. (2000). *The Boston diagnostic aphasia examination (BDAE-3)* (3rd ed.). Lippincott Williams & Wilkins.

Graff-Radford, N. R., Damasio, H., Yamada, T., Eslinger, P. J., & Damasio, A. R. (1985). Nonhaemorrhagic thalamic infarction. *Brain, 108*, 485–516.

Gronwald, D. M. A. (1977). Paced auditory serial addition task: A measure of recovery from concussion. *Perceptual and Motor Skills, 44*, 367–373.

Hachinski, V., Iadecola, C., Petersen, R. C., Breteler, M. M., Nyenhuis, D. L., Black, S. E., Powers, W. J., DeCarli, C., Merino, J. G., Kalaria, R. N., Vinters, H. V., Holtzman, D. M., Rosenberg, G. A., Wallin, A., Dichgans, M., Marler, J. R., & Leblanc, G. G. (2006). National Institute of Neurological Disorders and Stroke–Canadian Stroke Network vascular cognitive impairment harmonization standards. *Stroke, 37*(9), 2220–2241.

Hacke, W., Schwab, S., Horn, M., Spranger, M., De Georgia, M., & von Kummer, R. (1996). 'Malignant' middle cerebral artery territory infarction: Clinical course and prognostic signs. *Archives of Neurology, 53*(4), 309–315.

Hermann, D. M., & Bassetti, C. L. (2016). Role of sleep-disordered breathing and sleep-wake disturbances for stroke and stroke recovery. *Neurology, 87*(13), 1407–1416.

Hofmeister, C., Stapf, C., Hartmann, A., Sciacca, R. R., Mansmann, U., terBrugge, K., Lasjaunias, P., Mast, H., & Meisel, J. (2000). Demographic, morphological, and clinical characteristics of 1289 patients with brain arteriovenous malformations. *Stroke, 31*, 1307–1310.

Hooper, H. E. (1983). *Hooper visual organization test manual*. Western Psychological Services.

Horn, S. D., DeJong, G., Smout, R. J., Gassaway, J., James, R., & Conroy, B. (2005). Stroke rehabilitation patients, practice, and outcomes: Is earlier and more aggressive therapy better? *Archives of Physical Medicine and Rehabilitation, 86*(12), 101–114.

Hunt, W. E., & Hess, R. M. (1968). Surgical risk as related to time of intervention in the repair of intracranial aneurysms. *Journal of Neurosurgery, 28*, 14–20.

Iadecola, C., Park, L., & Capone, C. (2009). Threats to the mind: Aging, amyloid, and hypertension. *Stroke, 40*, S40–S44.

Ikeme, S., Kottenmeier, E., Uzochukwu, G., & Brinjikji, W. (2022). Evidence-based disparities in stroke care metrics and outcomes in the United States: A systematic review. *Stroke, 53*(3), 670–679.

Jellinger, K. A. (2013). Pathology and pathogenesis of vascular cognitive impairment—A critical update. *Frontiers in Aging Neuroscience, 5*(17), 1–19.

Johnston, S. C., Gress, D. R., Browner, W. S., & Sidney, S. (2000). Short-term prognosis after emergency department diagnosis of TAI. *JAMA, 284*, 2901–2906.

Kaplan, E., Goodglass, H., & Weintraub, S. (2001). *The Boston naming test*. Lippincott Williams & Wilkins.

Kaplan, R. C., Bhalodkar, N. C., Brown, E. J., Jr., White, J., & Brown, D. L. (2004). Race, ethnicity, and sociocultural characteristics predict noncompliance with lipid-lowering medications. *Preventive Medicine, 39*(6), 1249–1255.

Kelly, P. J., Furie, K. L., Shafqat, S., Rallis, N., Chang, Y., & Stein, J. (2003). Functional recovery following rehabilitation after hemorrhagic and ischemic stroke. *Archives of Physical Medicine and Rehabilitation, 84*(7), 968–972.

Kertesz, A. (1982). *Western aphasia battery*. Psychological Corporation.

Kim, K. M., Kim, J. E., Cho, W. S., Kang, H. S., Son, Y. J., Han, M. H., & Oh, C. W. (2017). Natural history and risk factor of recurrent hemorrhage in hemorrhagic adult Moyamoya disease. *Neurosurgery, 81*(2), 289–296.

Kurian, A. K., & Cardarelli, K. M. (2007). Racial and ethnic differences in cardiovascular disease risk factors. *Ethnicity & Disease, 17*(1), 143–152.

Kwiatkowski, T. G., Libman, R. B., Frankel, M., Tilley, B. C., Morgenstern, L. B., Lu, M., Borderick, J. P., Lewandoski, C., Marler, J. R., Levine, S. R., & Brott, T. (1999). Effects of tissue plasminogen activator for acute ischemic stroke at one year. *The New England Journal of Medicine, 340*, 1781.

Lezak, M. D., Howieson, D. B., & Loring, D. W. (2004). *Neuropsychological assessment* (4th ed.). Oxford University Press.

Liebeskind, D. S., Jüttler, E., Shapovalov, Y., Yegin, A., Landen, J., & Jauch, E. C. (2019). Cerebral edema associated with large hemispheric infarction: Implications for diagnosis and treatment. *Stroke, 50*(9), 2619–2625.

Lindgren, A. (2014). Stroke genetics: A review and update. *Journal of Stroke, 16*(3), 114–123.

Lindgren, A. G., Braun, R. G., Majersik, J. J., Clatworthy, P., Mainali, S., Derdeyn, C. P., Maguire, J., Jern, C., Rosand, J., Cole, J. W., Lee, J., Khatri, P., Nyquist, P., Debette, S., Wei, L. K., Rundek, T., Leifer, D., Thijs, V., Lemmens, R., Heitsch, L., et al. (2022). International stroke genetics consortium recommendations for studies of genetics of stroke outcome and recovery. *International Journal of Stroke, 17*(3), 260–268.

Meader, N., Moe-Byrne, T., Llewellyn, A., & Mitchell, A. J. (2014). Screening for poststroke major depression: A meta-analysis of diagnostic validity studies. *Journal of Neurology, Neurosurgery & Psychiatry, 85*(2), 198–206.

Medeiros, G. C., Roy, D., Kontos, N., & Beach, S. R. (2020). Post-stroke depression: A 2020 updated review. *General Hospital Psychiatry, 66*, 70–80.

Meyers, J. E., & Meyers, K. R. (1995). *Rey complex figure test and recognition trial: Professional manual*. Psychological Assessment Resources.

Mineharu, Y., Takenaka, K., Yamakawa, H., Inoue, K., Ikeda, H., Kikuta, K. I., Takagi, Y., Nozaki, K., Hashimoto, N., & Koizumi, A. (2006). Inheritance pattern of familial Moyamoya disease: Autosomal dominant mode and genomic imprinting. *Journal of Neurology, Neurosurgery, and Psychiatry, 77*(9), 1025–1029.

Morgenstern, L. B., Smith, M. A., Sánchez, B. N., Brown, D. L., Zahuranec, D. B., Garcia, N., et al. (2013). Persistent ischemic stroke disparities despite declining incidence in Mexican Americans. *Annals of Neurology, 74*(6), 778–785.

National Stroke Association. (2007). *Stroke symptoms*. Retrieved March 4, 2007, from http://www.stroke.org/site/PageServer?pagename=SYMP

Osborn, C. Y., Cavanaugh, K., Wallston, K. A., White, R. O., & Rothman, R. L. (2009). Diabetes numeracy: An overlooked factor in understanding racial disparities in glycemic control. *Diabetes Care, 32*(9), 1614–1619.

Parizel, P. M., Makkat, S., Jorens, P. G., Ozsarlak, O., Cras, P., Van Goethem, J. W., van den Hauwe, L., Verlooy, J., & De Schepper, A. M. (2002). Brainstem hemorrhage in descending transtentorial herniation (Duret hemorrhage). *Intensive Care Medicine, 28*(1), 85–88.

Perna, R., & Temple, J. (2015). Rehabilitation outcomes: Ischemic versus hemorrhagic strokes. *Behavioural Neurology, 2015*, 891651.

Pinto, A. N., Canhao, P., & Ferro, J. M. (1996). Seizures at the onset of subarachnoid haemorrhage. *Journal of Neurology, 243*, 161–164.

Reeves, M. J., Bushnell, C. D., Howard, G., Gargano, J. W., Duncan, P. W., Lynch, G., Khatiwoda, A., & Lisabeth, L. (2008). Sex differences in stroke: Epidemiology, clinical presentation, medical care, and outcomes. *The Lancet Neurology, 7*(10), 915–926.

Rey, A. (1941). L'examen psychologique dans les cas d'encephalopathie traumatique. *Archives de Psychologie, 28*, 286–340.

Rey, A. (1964). *L'examen clinique en psychologie*. Presses Universitaires de France.

Robinson, R. G., & Starkstein, S. E. (2002). Neuropsychiatric aspects of cerebrovascular disorders. In S. C. Yudofsky & R. E. Hales (Eds.), *Textbook of neuropsychiatry and clinical neurosciences* (2nd ed.). American Psychiatric Press.

Rothwell, P. M., Giles, M. F., Flossmann, E., Lovelock, C. E., Redgrave, J. N. E., Warlow, C. P., & Mehta, Z. (2005). A simple score (ABCD) to identify individuals at high early risk of stroke after transient ischemic attack. *Lancet, 366*, 29–36.

Salvadori, E., Papi, G., Insalata, G., Rinnoci, V., Donnini, I., Martini, M., Falsini, C., Hakiki, B., Romoli, A., Barbato, C., Polcaro, P., Casamorata, F., Macchi, C., Cecchi, F., & Poggesi, A. (2020). Comparison between ischemic and hemorrhagic strokes in functional outcome at discharge from an intensive rehabilitation hospital. *Diagnostics, 11*(1), 38.

Schenkenberg, T., Bradford, D. C., & Ajax, E. T. (1980). Line bisection and unilateral visual neglect in patients with neurologic impairment. *Neurology, 30*, 509–517.

Sheslow, D., & Adams, W. (2003). *Wide range assessment of memory and learning second edition administration and technical manual*. Psychological Assessment Resources.

Spreen, O., & Strauss, E. (1998). *A compendium of neuropsychological tests: Administration, norms, and commentary* (2nd ed.). Oxford University Press.

Starkstein, S. E., & Hayhow, B. D. (2019). Treatment of post-stroke depression. *Current Treatment Options in Neurology, 21*, 1–10.

Stern, R. A., & White, T. (2003). *Neuropsychological assessment battery*. Psychological Assessment Resources.

Stulberg, E. L., Twardzik, E., Kim, S., Hsu, C. W., Xu, Y., Clarke, P., Morgenstern, L. B., & Lisabeth, L. D. (2021). Association of neighborhood socioeconomic status with outcomes in patients surviving stroke. *Neurology, 96*(21), e2599–e2610.

Sturgeon, J. D., & Folsom, A. R. (2007). Trends in hospitalization rate, hospital case fatality, and mortality rate of stroke by subtype in Minneapolis-St. Paul, 1980–2002. *Neuroepidemiology, 28*, 39–45.

Topcuoglu, M. A., Saka, E., Silverman, S. B., Schwamm, L. H., & Singhal, A. B. (2017). Recrudescence of deficits after stroke: Clinical and imaging phenotype, triggers, and risk factors. *JAMA Neurology, 74*(9), 1048–1055.

Tsao, C. W., Aday, A. W., Almarzooq, Z. I., Anderson, C. A., Arora, P., Avery, C. L., Baker-Smith, C. M., Beaton, A. Z., Boehme, A. K., Buxton, A. E., Commodore-Mensah, Y., Elkind, M. S. V., Evenson, K. R., Eze-Nliam, C., Fugar, S., Generoso, G., Heard, D. G., Hiremath, S., Ho, J. E., Kalani, R., et al. (2023). Heart disease and stroke statistics—2023 update: A report from the American Heart Association. *Circulation, 147*(8), e93–e621.

Victor, M., & Ropper, A. H. (2001). *Adam's and Victor's principals of neurology* (7th ed.). McGraw-Hill.

Wang, S. B., Wang, Y. Y., Zhang, Q. E., Wu, S. L., Ng, C. H., Ungvari, G. S., Chen, L., Wang, C. X., Jia, F. J., & Xiang, Y. T. (2018). Cognitive behavioral therapy for post-stroke depression: A meta-analysis. *Journal of Affective Disorders, 235*, 589–596.

Wechsler, D. (2001). *Wechsler adult intelligence scale-3rd edition (WAIS-III)*. The Psychological Corporation.

Wechsler, R. (2009). *Wechsler Memory Scale--Fourth Edition (WMS-IV)*. PsycTESTS Database Record.

Wijdicks, E. F., Sheth, K. N., Carter, B. S., Greer, D. M., Kasner, S. E., Kimberly, W. T., Schwab, S., Smith, E. E., Tamargo, R. J., & Wintermark, M. (2014). Recommendations for the management of cerebral and cerebellar infarction with swelling: A statement for healthcare professionals from the American Heart Association/American Stroke Association. *Stroke, 45*(4), 1222–1238.

Winstein, C. J., Stein, J., Arena, R., Bates, B., Cherney, L. R., Cramer, S. C., Deruyter, F., Eng, J. J., Fisher, B., Harvey, R. L., Lang, C. E., Mackay-Lyons, M., Ottenbacher, K. J., Pugh, S., Reeves, M. J., Richards, R. G., Stiers, W., & Zorowitz, R. D. (2016). Guidelines for adult stroke rehabilitation and recovery: A guideline for healthcare professionals from the American Heart Association/American Stroke Association. *Stroke, 47*(6), e98–e169.

Withall, A., Brodaty, H., Altendorf, A., & Sachdev, P. S. (2009). Who does well after a stroke? The Sydney stroke study. *Aging & Mental Health, 13*(5), 693–698.

Chapter 15
Dementias and Mild Cognitive Impairment in Adults

Joseph J. Boscarino, Julia E. Maietta, Michael R. Schoenberg, and Kevin Duff

Chapter Summary

- Normal aging is characterized by slight decrements in speed of processing, memory and other cognitive abilities. Mild cognitive impairment is characterized by isolated impairments, usually in memory. Dementia, however, is characterized by severe impairments in two or more cognitive domains, as well as functional decline.
- The most common types of dementia are: Alzheimer's disease, vascular dementia, frontotemporal dementia and dementia with Lewy bodies.
- A detailed history of symptom onset and the course of its progression can be very valuable in the differential diagnosis of dementia.

(continued)

J. J. Boscarino (✉)
Departments of Psychiatry and Neurosciences, Neurology, and Neurosurgery, University of South Florida College of Medicine, Tampa, FL, USA
e-mail: JosephJ.Boscarino@va.gov

J. E. Maietta
Department of Physical Medicine and Rehabilitation, Harvard Medical School, Boston, MA, USA

Department of Physical Medicine and Rehabilitation, Spaulding Rehabilitation, Boston, MA, USA

Mass General for Children Sports Concussion Program, Boston, MA, USA

M. R. Schoenberg
Mass General for Children Sports Concussion Program, Boston, MA, USA

K. Duff
Department of Neurology, Oregon Health Sciences University, Portland, OR, USA

M. R. Schoenberg, J. G. Scott (eds.), *The Little Black Book of Neuropsychology*,
https://doi.org/10.1007/978-3-032-07777-6_15

(continued)

- Evidence-based neuropsychology can assist in the differential diagnosis of dementia through the identification of distinct cognitive and behavioral presentations.
- Neuropsychological batteries should be tailored to the suspected type of dementia, as well as the severity of the cognitive impairments. Broad coverage of cognitive domains is necessary to accurately evaluate the presence of dementia and its etiology.

Overview

Dementia does not describe a specific disease entity, but rather describes a clinical syndrome characterized by a loss of previously acquired cognitive functions that adversely affects an individual's ability to complete day-to-day activities. The decline in cognitive functioning is greater than what occurs during the normal aging process. This chapter will review prominent definitions of dementia and a number of the etiologies of this syndrome. The prodromal phase between dementia and normal aging, Mild Cognitive Impairment (MCI), is reviewed later in this chapter. Readers interested in a more detailed review of dementia syndromes and conditions presenting as dementia are referred to Dickerson and Atri (2014) or Miller and Boeve (2016).

Diagnostic Criteria and Definitions

There are several different sets of diagnostic criteria for dementia. Some are more clinically based, whereas others are pathologically based and primarily applied in research settings. Given notable differences between different types of dementia (e.g., Alzheimer's disease vs. vascular dementia), specific diagnostic criteria have also been developed to define other clinical states that cause dementia. Below we review proposed diagnostic guidelines for the more common forms of dementia (see Dickerson and Atri (2014) or Miller and Boeve (2016) for additional dementia diagnostic criteria).

Diagnostic and Statistical Manual—fifth Edition, text revision (DSM-5-TR; (American Psychiatric Association, 2022)) is a set of primarily clinical diagnostic criteria that define dementia, and then provide options to classify the cause of the dementia. Broadly, dementia is diagnosed using the Major Neurocognitive Disorder diagnosis within the DSM-5-TR, which requires evidence of deficits in one or more cognitive domains including complex attention, executive function, learning and memory, language, perceptual-motor functioning or social cognitive abilities. These cognitive deficits must represent a decline from a previously higher level of functioning, and must be severe enough to interfere with work, school, activities of daily living or other social activities. Mild Neurocognitive Disorder, which is essentially akin to MCI, requires the same evidence of deficits in at least one of the aforementioned cognitive domains but preserved higher level instrumental activities of daily living (paying bills, driving, etc.). Either neurocognitive disorder diagnosis is excluded if the symptoms directly stem from a mental health disorder or occur exclusively during an episode of encephalopathy (delirium). Within the DSM-5-TR, there are several different etiological possibilities, some of which require additional conditions to be met for diagnosis. For example, the diagnosis of Major Vascular Neurocognitive Disorder also requires sufficient levels of cerebrovascular disease as evidenced by history, physical examination and/or neuroimaging. The different subtypes of Major Neurocognitive Disorder within the DSM-5-TR are listed in Table 15.1.

Alzheimer's Disease

The National Institute on Aging—Alzheimer's Association (NIA-AA, (McKhann et al., 2011)) published an update to the prior 1984 diagnostic criteria (McKhann et al., 1984) for Alzheimer's disease (AD). This revised AD criteria sought to characterize preclinical and mild cognitive impairment stages of AD in addition to dementia, incorporate biomarker evidence and describe atypical AD syndromes. These criteria again make the important distinction between **probable** and **possible** AD, with the presence of AD pathophysiological process (i.e., supportive biomarkers) increasing the likelihood of diagnosis. Within these criteria, **definitive** AD can only occur with histopathological confirmation (e.g., post-mortem autopsy). While the probable AD from the 1984 NINCDS-ADRDA criteria is interchangeable with the 2011 NIA-AA probable AD guidelines, the same is not invariably true with the possible AD criteria between 1984 and 2011. In addition to the core criteria for the

Table 15.1 DSM-5-TR subtypes of major neurocognitive disorder

Major neurocognitive disorder due to Alzheimer's Disease
Major frontotemporal neurocognitive disorder
Major neurocognitive disorder with Lewy bodies
Major vascular neurocognitive disorder
Major neurocognitive disorder due to traumatic brain injury
Substance/medication-induced major neurocognitive disorder
Major neurocognitive disorder due to HIV infection
Major neurocognitive disorder due to prion Disease
Major neurocognitive disorder due to Parkinson's Disease
Major neurocognitive disorder due to Huntington's Disease
Major neurocognitive disorder due to another medical condition
Major neurocognitive disorder due to multiple Etiologies
Unspecified neurocognitive disorder

prototypical amnestic presentation of AD, other research criteria have been published for atypical syndromes, including the visuospatial variant by Crutch et al. (2017) and others (see below for greater detail on Posterior Cortical Atrophy or PCA) and the behavioral variant (bvAD) (Ossenkoppele et al., 2022).

Probable AD Dementia Core Clinical Criteria (McKhann et al., 2011).

A diagnosis of Probable AD dementia can be made when the patient

1. Meets criteria for all-cause dementia (functional decline due to deficits in ≥2 cognitive domains), and has the following characteristics:
    a. Insidious onset: Symptoms have a gradual onset over months to years, not sudden over hours or days
    b. Clear-cut history of worsening of cognition by report or observation and
    c. The initial and most prominent cognitive deficits are evident on history and examination in one of the following categories:
        i. Amnestic presentation: It is the most common syndromic presentation of AD dementia. The deficits should include impairment in learning and recall of recently learned information. There should also be evidence of cognitive dysfunction in at least one other cognitive domain, as defined earlier in the text.
        ii. Non-amnestic presentations:
            1. Language presentation: The most prominent deficits are in word-finding, but deficits in other cognitive domains should be present.
            2. Visuospatial presentation: The most prominent deficits are in spatial cognition, including object agnosia, impaired face recognition, simultanagnosia and alexia. Deficits in other cognitive domains should be present.
            3. Executive dysfunction: The most prominent deficits are impaired reasoning, judgment and problem-solving. Deficits in other cognitive domains should be present.
    d. The diagnosis of probable AD dementia should not be applied when there is evidence of (a) substantial concomitant cerebrovascular disease, defined by a history of a stroke temporally related to the onset or worsening of cognitive impairment; or the presence of multiple or extensive infarcts or severe white matter hyperintensity burden; or (b) core features of Dementia with Lewy bodies other than dementia itself; or (c) prominent features of behavioral variant frontotemporal dementia; or (d) prominent features of semantic variant primary progressive aphasia or nonfluent/agrammatic variant primary progressive aphasia; or (e) evidence for another concurrent, active neurological disease, or a non-neurological medical comorbidity or use of medication that could have a substantial effect on cognition.

Possible AD Dementia Core Clinical Criteria (McKhann et al., 2011)

1. Atypical course meets the core clinical criteria in terms of the nature of the cognitive deficits for AD dementia, but either has
   a. A sudden onset of cognitive impairment or
   b. Demonstrates insufficient historical detail or objective cognitive documentation of progressive decline or
2. Etiologically mixed presentation meets all core clinical criteria for AD dementia but has evidence of
   a. Concomitant cerebrovascular disease, defined by a history of stroke temporally related to the onset or worsening of cognitive impairment; or the presence of multiple or extensive infarcts or severe white matter hyperintensity burden or
   b. Features of Dementia with Lewy bodies other than the dementia itself
   c. Evidence for another neurological disease or a non-neurological medical comorbidity or medication use that could have a substantial effect on cognition

Vascular Cognitive Impairment (VCI)

The 1993 criteria published by the National Institute of Neurological Disorders and Stroke—Association Internationale pour la Recherche et l'Enseignement en Neurosciences (NINDS-AIREN) (Román et al., 1993) remain widely used to define "pure" vascular dementia (VaD) for research purposes likely owing to their high specificity. More recently, the term vascular cognitive impairment (VCI) was incorporated in a consensus statement by the American Heart Association (AHA) and American Stroke Association (ASA) (Gorelick et al., 2011) to enhance the sensitivity of criteria toward the broader continuum of cerebrovascular-related cognitive deficits beyond the level of dementia requiring functional impairment. These 2011 criteria by Gorelick and colleagues included subtypes of vascular mild cognitive impairment (VaMCI) to VaD and conferred levels of diagnostic confidence of possible and probable for both MCI and dementia, with cognitive deficits required in at least two domains. Building off of Gorelick et al.'s (2011) consensus criteria, the Vascular Impairment of Cognition Classification Consensus Study (VICCCS) guidelines were published in 2016 and updated after Delphi consensus with the publication of the second version of the VICCCS (Skrobot et al., 2018), as listed below, with probable and possible again indicating the magnitude of supportive evidence.

VICCCS Definitions and Diagnosis of VCI (Skrobot et al., 2018)

Clinical evaluation and neuropsychological protocols as provided in the National Institute of Neurological Disorders– Canadian Stroke Network guidelines are supported. Core domains for assessment should include executive function, attention and memory, as well as language and visuospatial function.

Mild VCI: Impairment in at least one cognitive domain and mild to no impairment in instrumental activities of daily living (IADLs)/activities of daily living (ADLs), respectively (independent of the motor/sensory sequelae of the vascular event).

Major VCI (VaD): Clinically significant deficits of sufficient severity in at least one cognitive domain (deficits may be present in multiple domains) and severe disruption to IADLs/ADLs (independent of the motor/sensory sequelae of the vascular event).

Subtypes of major VCI (VaD):

1. Post-stroke dementia: A patient described as having PSD may or may not have presented evidence of mild cognitive impairment before stroke. The patient will exhibit immediate and/or delayed cognitive decline that begins within 6 months after a stroke and that does not reverse. PSD can result from several different vascular causes and changes in the brain. It encompasses dementia that develops within 6 months of stroke in patients with multiple cortical-subcortical infarcts and strategic infarcts; patients with subcortical ischemic vascular dementia; and those with various forms of neurodegenerative pathology, including Alzheimer's disease (AD). The temporal relationship between the cognitive decline and the stroke differentiates PSD from other forms of major VCI (VaD).
2. Mixed dementias: A standalone umbrella subgroup termed "mixed dementias" includes phenotypes representing each combination between vascular and neurodegenerative disease, that is, VCI-AD, VCI–dementia with Lewy bodies and so forth. It is recommended that a patient is referred to as having "VCI-AD," for example, according to the clinically probable phenotypes, rather than the less-specific "mixed dementia." Where discrimination is possible, the order of terms should reflect the probable relative contribution of the underlying pathology, that is, AD-VCI or VCI-AD.
3. Subcortical ischemic vascular dementia: Small-vessel disease is the main vascular cause of subcortical ischemic vascular dementia. Lacunar infarcts and ischemic white matter lesions are the main type of brain lesions, which are located predominantly subcortically. This diagnosis incorporates the overlapping clinical entities of Binswanger's disease and the lacunar state.
4. Multi-infarct dementia: Multi-infarct dementia is used to indicate the presence of multiple large cortical infarcts and their likely contribution to the dementia.

Frontotemporal Dementia

Behavioral Variant Frontotemporal Dementia

In 2011, the International Behavioral Variant FTD (bvFTD) Criteria Consortium published the latest update to the consensus criteria (Rascovsky et al., 2011) for the diagnosis of bvFTD due to concerns about prior criteria's inadequate sensitivity to initial disease progression and stringently high number of inclusion and exclusion criteria.. The 2011 criteria demonstrated higher sensitivity at earlier disease stages than prior guidelines (Neary et al., 1998) by requiring fewer symptoms in more condensed syndrome clusters, but at the expense of variable specificity for bvFTD diagnosis based on symptom criteria alone. Notwithstanding, the addition of neuroimaging evidence increased level of certainty and thus specificity of the 2011 criteria. The extent of diagnostic certainty for bvFTD is indicated by the highest level of criteria met across the following: (1) possible, (2) probable and (3) definite.

bvFTD diagnostic criteria (Rascovsky et al., 2011):

I. Possible bvFTD

- Patient must display progressive behavioral and/or cognitive decline evidenced by observation or collateral history
- At least three of the following symptoms (A–F) must be consistently or repeatedly occurring to meet criteria. Early* refers to symptoms that must have been present within three years of initial onset

A. Early* behavioral disinhibition [one of the following symptoms (A.1–A.3) must be present]:

   A.1. Socially inappropriate behavior
   A.2. Loss of manners or decorum
   A.3. Impulsive, rash or careless actions

B. Early apathy or inertia [one of the following symptoms (B.1–B.2) must be present]:

   B.1. Apathy
   B.2. Inertia

C. Early loss of sympathy or empathy [one of the following symptoms (C.1–C.2) must be present]:

   C.1. Diminished response to other people's needs and feelings
   C.2. Diminished social interest, interrelatedness or personal warmth

D. Early perseverative, stereotyped or compulsive/ritualistic behavior [one of the following symptoms (D.1–D.3) must be present]:

   D.1. Simple repetitive movements
   D.2. Complex, compulsive or ritualistic behaviors
   D.3. Stereotypy of speech

E. Hyperorality and dietary changes [one of the following symptoms (E.1–E.3) must be present]:

   E.1. Altered food preferences
   E.2. Binge eating, increased consumption of alcohol or cigarettes
   E.3. Oral exploration or consumption of inedible objects

F. Neuropsychological profile: Executive functioning deficits with relative sparing of memory and visuospatial functions [all of the following symptoms (F.1–F.3) must be present]:

F.1. Deficits in executive tasks
F.2. Relative sparing of episodic memory
F.3. Relative sparing of visuospatial skills

II. Probable bvFTD

All of the following symptoms (A–C) must be present to meet criteria.

A. Meets criteria for possible bvFTD
B. Exhibits significant functional decline (by caregiver report or as evidenced by Clinical Dementia Rating Scale or Functional Activities Questionnaire scores)
C. Neuroimaging results consistent with bvFTD [Either C.1 or C.2 must be present]:

C.1. Frontal and/or anterior temporal atrophy on MRI or CT
C.2. Frontal and/or anterior temporal hypoperfusion or hypometabolism on PET or SPECT

III. Definite bvFTD

Criterion A and either criterion B or C must be present to meet criteria.

A. Meets criteria for possible or probable bvFTD
B. Histopathological evidence of FTLD on biopsy or at post-mortem
C. Presence of a known pathogenic mutation

IV. Exclusionary criteria for bvFTD

Criteria A and B must be answered negatively for any bvFTD diagnosis. Criterion C can be positive for possible bvFTD but must be negative for probable bvFTD.

A. Pattern of deficits is better accounted for by other medical condition
B. Behavioral disturbance is better accounted for by a psychiatric diagnosis
C. Biomarker evidence of other neurodegenerative disease

Primary Progressive Aphasia (PPA)

In 2011, a consensus group reviewed of 12 cases of PPA and published diagnostic guidelines (Gorno-Tempini et al., 2011) in which 80% of the above cases reliably agreed to fit one of the following subtypes: nonfluent/agrammatic variant PPA (nfvPPA), semantic variant PPA (svPPA) or logopenic variant PPA (lvPPA).

Inclusion Criteria (all three required to be present) (Mesulam, 2001)

- Most prominent clinical feature is difficulty with language
- These deficits are the principal cause of impaired daily living activities
- Aphasia should be the most prominent deficit at symptom onset and for the initial phases of the disease

Exclusion Criteria (all four required to be absent) (Mesulam, 2001)

- Pattern of deficits is better accounted for by other nondegenerative nervous system or medical disorders
- Cognitive disturbance is better accounted for by a psychiatric diagnosis
- Prominent initial episodic memory, visual memory and visuoperceptual impairments
- Prominent, initial behavioral disturbance

Criteria for nonfluent/agrammatic variant PPA (nfvPPA) (Gorno-Tempini et al., 2011).

At least **one** of the following core features:

- Agrammatism in language production
- Effortful, halting speech with inconsistent speech sound errors and distortions (apraxia of speech)

At least **two** of the following other features:

- Impaired comprehension of syntactically complex sentences
- Spared single-word comprehension
- Spared object knowledge

Criteria for semantic variant PPA (svPPA) (Gorno-Tempini et al., 2011).

Both of the following core features:

- Impaired confrontation naming
- Impaired single-word comprehension

At least **three** of the following other features:

- Impaired object knowledge, particularly for low-frequency or low-familiarity items
- Surface dyslexia or dysgraphia
- Spared repetition
- Spared speech production (grammar and motor speech)

Criteria for logopenic variant PPA (lvPPA) (Gorno-Tempini et al., 2011).

Both of the following core features:

- Impaired single-word retrieval in spontaneous speech and naming
- Impaired repetition of sentences and phrases

At least **three** of the following other features:

- Speech (phonologic) errors in spontaneous speech and naming
- Spared single-word comprehension and object knowledge
- Spared motor speech
- Absence of frank agrammatism

Dementia with Lewy Bodies

McKeith et al. (2017) provide the fourth consensus guidelines for clinical diagnostic criteria of dementia with Lewy Bodies (DLB). In order to be eligible for a diagnosis of DLB, one must have dementia (i.e., progressive cognitive decline with associated functional impairment) The consensus criteria further includes *core* clinical feature (below) and *supportive* clinical features associated with DLB, as well as indicative and supportive biomarkers that support a diagnosis of DLB. A diagnosis of **probable** DLB has two possible constellations of features and either (1) requires at least two core clinical features (with or without indicative biomarkers), or (2) requires only one core clinical feature with one or more indicative biomarker. **Possible** DLB similarly can be present if either (1) one core clinical feature is present with no indicative biomarker evidence, or (2) one or more indicative biomarkers is present without any core clinical features. Confirmation of clinical diagnosis of DLB requires pathological study.

1. The essential feature of DLB is a progressive decline of cognitive function that is sufficient to interfere with the individual's social or occupational functioning. Cognitive deficits are often present on tests of attention, executive functioning and visuospatial abilities in early stages with memory impairment presenting as the disease progresses.
2. Core clinical features supporting a diagnosis of DLB include all of the following. Notably, the first three symptoms may be present early in the disease course and can persist throughout disease progression.

    a. Fluctuating levels of cognition with pronounced variations in arousal level/attention
    b. Visual hallucinations that are typically well-formed and recurring
    c. REM sleep behavior disorder (which can onset prior to cognitive impairment)
    d. One or more spontaneous parkinsonian motor features (i.e., bradykinesia, resting tremor, rigidity)

3. Supportive clinical features that support a diagnosis of DLB include all of the following. These features, although not diagnostically specific to DLB, are often present early in the disease course. In combination they can be suggestive of DLB in an individual with dementia (see above for criteria of probable versus possible DLB).

    a. Sensitivity to neuroleptic medications
    b. Postural instability
    c. Repeated falls
    d. Transient episodes of unresponsiveness or syncope
    e. Severe autonomic dysfunction (e.g., constipation, orthostatic hypotension, urinary incontinence)
    f. Hypersomnia
    g. Hyposmia

h. Hallucinations in other modalities (e.g., auditory, tactile)
i. Systematized delusions
j. Apathy
k. Anxiety
l. Depression

4. Indicative Biomarkers that Support a Diagnosis of DLB Include

a. Reduced dopamine transporter uptake in the basal ganglia as illustrated on SPECT or PET imaging
b. Abnormal iodine-MIBG myocardial scintigraphy (i.e., low uptake)
c. Sleep study confirmation of REM sleep without atonia via polysomnography

5. Supportive Biomarkers that Support a Diagnosis of DLB Include

a. Preservation of mesial temporal lobe on neuroimaging (i.e., CT or MRI)
b. Reduced occipital activity with or without additional cingulate island sign on FDG-PET imaging as well as global low uptake on SPECT/PET imaging
c. Prominent posterior slow waves with fluctuations in the pre-alpha/theta range on EEG

6. DLB is less likely if there is evidence of another physical or neurologic condition that is able to account for the clinical symptom presentation (e.g., cerebrovascular disease); however, comorbid physical/neurologic conditions do not rule out a DLB diagnosis. Additionally, if parkinsonism is the only core clinical feature present and these symptoms do not present until the severe dementia stage, then DLB is less likely.

Recent evaluation of diagnostic criteria suggests that visual hallucinations and parkinsonism are common in DLB, occurring in up to 80% and 85% of patients, respectively. Additionally, REM sleep behavior disorder is now included in core clinical features due to its prevalence in autopsy-confirmed DLB (76% compared to only 4% in non-DLB patients). The co-occurrence of neuropsychological deficits within 12 months of extrapyramidal (parkinsonian) motor deficits has shown particularly reliable diagnostic utility.

HIV-Associated Neurocognitive Disorders

Although initially described as AIDS dementia complex (Navia et al., 1986), the diagnostic criteria associated with cognitive impairment secondary to HIV and AIDS have evolved over the years. The earliest was HIV-dementia complex (Navia et al., 1986). In 1991, the American Academy of Neurology proposed the HIV-Associated Dementia (HAD) and HIV-associated minor cognitive-motor disorder (MCMD) (Janssen et al., 1991). Most recently, Antinori et al. (2007) proposed a three subtype diagnostic model for HIV-associated neurocognitive disorders

(HAND) summarized below. All diagnoses below require confirmation of HIV infection, and objective neurocognitive testing can be used to empirically support the level of impairment.

- *HIV-associated dementia (HAD)*: Acquired neurocognitive deficits lasting at least one month in which either; (a) scores on neuropsychological tests in at least two neurocognitive domains (e.g., attention/working memory, information processing speed, executive functions, learning/memory, language/speech, visuoperceptual/visuospatial and/or motor skills) that are moderately to severely impaired (e.g., less than or equal to 2 standard deviations below demographically appropriate normative mean), or (b) scores of one neurocognitive domain are more severely impaired (< 2.5 standard deviations below the mean) *and* at least one other neurocognitive domain is at least mildly impaired (i.e., ≤ 1 standard deviations below the mean). At least one of the impaired ability domains must be primarily cognitive.
  - The neurocognitive deficits are severe enough to cause major functional impairment in work or school or activities of daily living, and these neurocognitive and functional impairments may *not* be accounted for by confounding conditions (e.g., opportunistic CNS infections, systemic illness, medication effects and/or substance abuse).
- *HIV-associated mild neurocognitive disorder (MND)*: Acquired neurocognitive deficits lasting at least one month in which; (a) scores on neuropsychological tests in at least two neurocognitive domains that are mildly impaired (i.e., 1 or more standard deviations below the mean). These deficits are severe enough to cause mild functional impairments in work or school or activities of daily living and these impairments are not better accounted for by comorbid conditions.
- *HIV-asymptomatic neurocognitive impairment (ANI)*: Acquired neurocognitive deficits lasting at least one month in which scores on neuropsychological tests in at least two neurocognitive domains that are mildly impaired (i.e., 1 or more standard deviations below the mean). However, the neurocognitive deficits do *not* cause any demonstrated or reported functional impairments.
  - In cases in which standardized neuropsychological assessment is not available, substitution with other assessment (e.g., MMSE or HIV Dementia Scale) can be used. In this case, attempt should be made to approximate criteria above (e.g., MND diagnosis requires mental status exam score to fall at least 1 standard deviations below demographically appropriate normative mean involving at least 2 neurocognitive domains and there is a mild functional deficit).

Before turning to etiologies for the dementias, it is noteworthy to point out some of the operational definitions for diagnosing dementia are more specific than others. For example, HAD specifies the number of standard deviations that cognitive test scores must fall below normative data to be considered impaired, whereas others are more general (e.g., "deficits in executive tasks" in bvFTD). Also noteworthy to add is that the aforementioned criteria endorsed by various consensus panels do not always completely match other diagnostic criteria from other sources. For instance, the DSM-5 TR which only requires one domain of cognitive impairment to diagnose major neurocognitive disorder (dementia), whereas the NIA-AA definition of all-cause dementia mandates deficits in two cognitive domains at minimum. Some diagnostic criteria are more cognitive-focused (e.g., AD), whereas others are more behaviorally focused (e.g., FTD). Many of these criteria sets allow for varying levels of certainty of the diagnosis (e.g., probable vs. possible), but neuropsychological dysfunction is present in all dementias, and neuropsychological assessment assists in differential diagnosis and prognosis of dementia (Dickerson & Atri, 2014; Miller & Boeve, 2016; Petersen et al., 1999, p. 199, 2001, 2018; Bondi et al., 2014; Belleville et al., 2017; Ducharme et al., 2020; Duff et al., 2011; Pedersen et al., 2013; Kral, 1962; Gutierrez et al., 1993; Morris & Cummings, 2005; Petersen, 2004; Manly et al., 2008; DeCarli et al., 2004; Duff et al., 2007; Jack et al., 1999, 2000; Tuokko et al., 2003; Chamberlain & Sahakian, 2006; Rosenstein, 1998; Wright & Persad, 2007; Fleisher et al., 2007; Dubois et al., 2005; Carnahan et al., 2006; Peters, 1989). The definitions of dementia have been revised as new research refines our understanding of the dementias and aging. Future changes will undoubtedly occur.

Prevalence of Dementia

Dementia rates increase steadily with age (Launer et al., 1999; Livingston et al., 2020). Cognitive impairment of this severity is rare in young and middle aged adults (e.g., 0.5%). Prevalence at age 60 is thought to be about 1%. This steadily increases as individuals get older, with the prevalence at age 65 being 5–8%, the prevalence at age 74 is 15–20%, and the prevalence at age 85 years and older is 30–50%.

Etiologies of Dementia

Factors that can cause the syndrome of dementia can be divided into multiple classes. Some conditions are primarily degenerative and will slowly progress over time. At its broadest definition, dementia is anything resulting in a loss of previously acquired skill in multiple cognitive domains, which is of sufficient severity to interfere with everyday functioning. This potentially includes nearly every chronic disease. For this chapter, however, we will more narrowly focus on primary central nervous system (CNS) diseases that have a neurodegenerative course for which the loss of cognitive/neuropsychological function is a primary disease characteristic. Some of these degenerative conditions have hallmark neuropathological signs that differentiate them from other conditions (e.g., beta-amyloid and phosphorylated tau inclusions in AD), while others are a secondary result of multiple illnesses that have a primary CNS deterioration (e.g., hypertension, diabetes and hypercholesterolemia in VCI/VaD). Dementias can be caused by a variety of medical (e.g., cerebrovascular, metabolic, infectious, systemic) and psychiatric illnesses (e.g., substance abuse). Table 15.2 summarizes some of the etiologies for dementias. The table is not exhaustive, but includes both common and rare causes of dementia, and includes illnesses that can result in cognitive decline (dementia) in children and/or younger adults. For a review of conditions leading to cognitive decline in childhood through young adulthood, the readers may review Chap. 27, this volume.

Clinical Descriptions of Common Dementia Conditions

A brief clinical description of common diseases presenting with dementia is presented below. These descriptions are summaries of multiple empirical studies, which can form a basis for evidence-based neuropsychology practice, and some

Table 15.2 Etiologies of dementia

Degenerative dementias	Cerebrovascular disease
Alzheimer's disease	Subdural hematoma
Dementia with Lewy bodies	Small-vessel disease
Frontotemporal dementia	Binswanger's disease
Huntington's disease	Multi-infarct dementia
Parkinson's disease	CADASIL
Corticobasal syndrome	Infections
Progressive supranuclear palsy	Syphilis
Multisystem atrophies	Chronic meningitis
Metabolic and deficiency conditions	Progressive multifocal leukoencephalopathy
Cushing syndrome	HIV infection/AIDS
Hepatic encephalopathy	Lyme disease
Hypothyroidism	Prion diseases
Porphyria	Creutzfeldt-Jakob disease
Wilson's disease	Variant Creutzfeldt-Jakob disease
Vitamin deficiencies (B12, thiamine, folate)	Kuru
Hypoglycemia	Demyelinating disorders
Kidney disease (renal failure, dialysis)	Multiple sclerosis
Head injury	Acute disseminated encephalomyelitis
Toxins and drugs	Systemic disorders
Heavy metals	Systemic lupus erythematosus
Carbon monoxide	Sarcoidosis
Alcohol (Wernicke–Korsakoff syndrome)	Neoplasms
Illegal drugs and prescription medications (e.g., anticholinergic)	Normal pressure hydrocephalus
Psychiatric syndromes	Epilepsy
Depression	

relevant references are cited below each diagnostic condition. Readers are also encouraged to review Table 15.3, which provides a brief description of the historical, behavioral, neuropsychological and psychological presentation of these conditions.

Alzheimer's disease (AD)

Prevalence: AD is the most prevalent of dementia syndromes, accounting for about 35% of all cases of dementia. Another 15% of dementias include mixed pathologies of both AD and VaD. Therefore, 50% of all dementia are either pure or "mixed" AD.

Risk factors: Older age, female gender (but this might be an artifact of longevity differences in gender), lower levels of education, family history of dementia (especially with onset before age 65), homozygous for the apolipoprotein e4 allele (APOE e4), Down's syndrome, history of head injury, history of psychiatric illness and history of alcohol abuse.

Onset: The majority of cases of AD develop after age 65 (i.e., late onset AD). The number of cases significantly increases across the seventh, eighth and ninth decades of life (2%, 6%, 50 + %, respectively). A minority of AD cases develop before age 65 (i.e., early-onset AD), and these cases often demonstrate a stronger genetic etiology (familial) mostly commonly associated with presenilin (PSEN) and amyloid precursor protein (APP) pathogenic mutations. However, a rare genetic mutation (APOE3 Christchurch) has been suggested to be protective and delayed onset of cognitive decline despite amyloid burden in a case report of a Colombian patient with an autosomal dominant mutation.

Course: Late onset AD tends to have a slow and insidious course, lasting 10+ years. Early onset has a more rapid progression with greater likelihood of atypical variants of AD (e.g., visuospatial and dysexecutive/behavioral subtypes). All types of AD are progressive, without remission.

Behavioral Symptoms/Clinical Presentation: Early in the course of AD, subtle personality changes (e.g., less energy, socially withdrawn, greater dependence on others, indifference) may be evident; however, this may be a product of early cognitive changes. Symptoms of depression may be present, but affect often is dependent upon environmental stimuli (e.g., visiting grandchildren improves mood). Patients often will minimize cognitive problems, and may confabulate to cover memory deficits. As the disease progresses, agitation, confusion, wandering, apathy, decreased sleep and appetite and emotional blunting become more common. Delusions and hallucinations can also occur later in AD, but can also occur earlier in atypical variants such as behavioral variant of AD. The foregoing variant of AD is generally also younger-onset (≤65 years old). Research guidelines were published for behavioral variant AD, which require a minimum of 2 of the 5 diagnostic criteria of bvFTD provided by Rascovsky et al. (2011). However, no formal consensus criteria exist at present.

Table 15.3 Clinical presentation of dementia syndromes

Cognitive domain	AD	FTD	DLB	VaD	PD-D	PSP	CBS	MSA	PCA	Depression
Behavioral observation	Early–Deny memory impairment, may appear depressed Late—Irritable, paranoid, anosognosia Sundowning may be present.	Early—Personality changes. Poor initiation, disinhibition, reflexive and stereotyped use of objects, poor mood modulation, poor judgment.	Early—Fluctuation in mental status common. Mental status orientation fluctuates. Not sundowning. Visual hallucinations. Late—Pronounced mental status variation. Distractible. Psychiatric symptoms. Psychosis. Sensitivity to dopamine antagonists.	Apathy common, symptoms of depression, incontinence, psychomotor retardation. Neurologic signs (e.g., Babinski, spasticity, abnormal reflexes). Gait instability, rigidity.	Early—Slowed processing speed. Autonomic dysfunction not prominent. Apathy and/or depression symptoms common. Late—Similar to DLD, BUT hallucinations not prominent and/or related to medication dosing. Depression common.	Early—Vertical gaze palsy. Dysphagia. Upward gaze is first affected, but also reduced in normal aging. Downward gaze palsy more specific. Parkinsonism. Gait change with open eyed stare. Depression common.	Early—Apraxia (alien hand sign present about 40%). Asymmetric parkinsonian features (bradykinesia, rigidity and tremor). Tremor is course, also present with posture, and does not respond to levodopa. Gait abnormality.	Early—Autonomic symptoms (orthostatic hypotension, erectile dysfunction, constipation) spasticity. Limited to no levodopa response.	Early—Visual complaint. Anxiety common, particularly in visually overwhelming environments. Late—Functional blindness.	Complain of cognitive problems, particularly forgetfulness. Progression of problems often rapid.
General cognitive	Early—Verbal IQ WNL. Nonverbal IQ mildly impaired. Processing speed WNL. Late—IQ declines with slowed processing speed.	Early—Verbal IQ WNL. Nonverbal IQ mildly impaired. Late—IQ declines.	Early—Vocabulary remains intact. Gross decline in attention. Verbal IQ WNL. Nonverbal IQ mildly impaired.	Early—May not be affected. Some deficit possible. Processing speed often impaired.	Early—Verbal IQ WNL. Nonverbal IQ mildly reduced due to poor motor speed and processing speed. Late—Vocabulary often preserved.	Early—Generally considered WNL. Late—Impaired.	Early—Verbal IQ WNL. Nonverbal IQ may be reduced due to motor impairments. Late—General deficits.	Early—Verbal IQ WNL. Nonverbal IQ may be slightly reduced in MSA-P, less so in MSA-C.	Early—Generally WNL. Late—Performance can be impacted by visuospatial dysfunction.	Early—IQ WNL. Psychomotor retardation common.

Attention	Simple attention (e.g., digit span forward, trails A) WNL. Complex attention (e.g., letter #, trails B) impaired.	Simple attention generally intact (e.g., digit span forward, trails A). Complex attention impaired (trails B, digit symbol, arithmetic).	Early gross impairment. Working memory is particularly affected. Digit span, trails A, etc., impaired. Poor ability to maintain vigilance.	Often impaired. Simple and complex attention impaired (Digit Span & Arithmetic, trails A & B, vigilance often impaired).	Often impaired. Simple attention generally preserved (e.g., digit span). Complex attention (trails B, digit symbol) impaired.	Varied. Simple attention intact (e.g., digit span). Complex attention (trails B, digit symbol) impaired.	Early—Mild to moderate deficits. Simple attention WNL. Complex attention impaired Visual inattention may be present. Late—Moderate to severe deficits	Varied. Mild to moderate deficits in complex/divided attention common. Processing speed deficits common. Simple attention intact.	Early—Often spared. Late—Often impacted by visuospatial dysfunction	Attention often variable. Some scores may be WNL other scores impaired. Depressed score less well than healthy controls but perform better than patients with dementia.
Learning/memory	Early—Impaired encoding and retention (learning over trials, short and long-delay free recall & recognition). Retention <50%. High false + rate on recognition. Implicit memory intact. Remote memories (e.g., early adulthood) intact. Late—Immediate and delayed memory markedly impaired. Remote memories impaired. Semantic memory impaired.	Early—Severe impairment in immediate free recall (CVLT or RAVLT). May not show much decline from immediate to delay recall.	Early—Memory deficits may not be severe. Learning reduced due to poor encoding strategies. Visual memory may be more impaired than verbal memory. Memory more impaired than in similar staged patient with PD. Late—Impairment in immediate and delayed memory. Recognition cues do not improve recall.	Memory impairment may be severe. Poor consolidation (e.g., semantic clustering CVLT, logical memory). Short and delayed free recall impaired. Recognition is often WNL.	Early—Generally preserved, but learning may be slowed. Late—Impairment in efficiency of encoding. Recognition improves recall and is WNL.	Early—Generally preserved. Late—Impairment common. Reflects reduced encoding. Recognition improves recall and is often WNL.	Early—Mild to moderate impairment. Tend to reflect frontal/ subcortical memory impairments (recognition cues improves recall)	Early—Mild frontal-subcortical memory deficits, more so in MSA-C than MSA-P.	Relatively spared with nonverbal memory impacted by visuospatial difficulties rather than memory dysfunction.	Mixed. Immediate and delayed recall may be impaired. Patient often say "don't know." good cued recall and recognition.

(continued)

Table 15.3 (continued)

Cognitive domain	AD	FTD	DLB	VaD	PD-D	PSP	CBS	MSA	PCA	Depression
Language	Early—Mild impairment in verbal fluency (semantic more impaired than phonemic). Confrontation naming mild impaired. Vocabulary not impaired. Late—Impaired fluency (semantic and phonemic), naming, comprehension, reading.	Early—Varied. Deficits in verbal fluency (phonemic more impaired than semantic). Confrontation naming impaired. Stereotyped output and/or reduced output common. Comprehension may be decreased (e.g., token test).	Early—Varied. Deficits in semantic verbal fluency and confrontation naming. Hypophonia and micrographia may be present. Late—Worsening symptoms as above.	Early—Mixed, depending upon lesions. Dysarthria may be present. Impaired verbal fluency (phonemic may be more impaired than semantic fluency), expressive aphasia with large lesions, may have impaired confrontation naming. Comprehension can be impaired.	Early—Impaired with dysarthria, hypophonia and micrographia. Verbal fluency (phonemic and semantic) can be impaired. Confrontation naming impaired later in disease. Repetition and comprehension preserved.	Early—slowed responses to questions fluency impaired (phonemic worse than semantic)	Early—Often WNL. Phonemic fluency may be impaired. Late—Fluency impaired (phonemic and semantic)	Early—Verbal fluency deficits most common. Dysarthria common. Confrontation naming generally intact.	Early—Generally spared. Visual perception may impact reading and writing skills (i.e., dysgraphia). Late—Reading and writing severely affected by visuospatial dysfunction.	Early—Expressive and receptive language intact, often with cues. Verbal fluency, naming, comprehension, reading WNL (often improved with general encouragement).
Visuoperceptual/ visuoconstructional	Early—May be impaired. Late—Impaired. Visuoperceptual and visuoconstructional deficits worsen as disease progresses.	Poor block design, planning in copy (drawing). Early—Simple figures drawn correctly. Late—Generally impaired.	Early—Often markedly impaired visuoperceptual skills and constructional apraxia. Late—Severe impairment	Early—Mixed. Can be mild to moderate impaired. Not all patients impaired. Late—Moderate to severe impairment common	Early—Impaired. Dysfunction beyond difficulty due to motor deficits.	Early—Mild to moderate impairment	Early—Mild to moderate impairment	MSA-P may have worse visuospatial/ constructional deficits than MSA-C.	Early—Prominent visuospatial impairment. Simultanagnosia is common. Late—Visuospatial impairment effects performance on other domains (e.g., naming).	Mixed, but visuoperceptual and visuoconstructional skills WNL.

Executive functions	Early—Mild impairments present. Poor problem-solving, sequencing, abstract reasoning. Late—Moderate to severe deficits. Utilization behaviors.	Severe perseveration. Utilization behaviors present. Poor reasoning, judgment, insight, sequencing. Cognitive inflexibility.	Early—Moderate to severe dysfunction can be present. Reduced problem-solving, sequencing, abstract reasoning. Late—Severe impairment common.	Early—Mild to moderate. Can be severe. Decreased problem-solving, reasoning, initiation and increase in perseverations.	Early—Mild to moderate impairment (less than PSP) reduced mental flexibility. Late—General impairment. Apathy, poor sequencing, abstract reasoning.	Early—Prominent impairment. "Applause" sign (pts. unable to clap hands just 3 times). Impaired initiation/ perseveration.	Early—Mild to moderate. Late—Moderate.	Mild to moderate impairment. Greater deficits in perseveration, initiation and response inhibition. MSA-C have greater deficits on EF tests with attentional component than MSA-P.	Early—Relatively spared. Late—Can be impacted by visuospatial dysfunction.	Can be reduced, but often WNL. Set-shifting (trails B) slightly reduced or WNL. Perseveration, utilization behaviors not present.
Sensory/motor	Early—Generally WNL. Olfaction may be impaired very early in AD. Late—Dyspraxia common.	Poor motor programming (Luria alternating movements). Grasp, root and snout reflexes may be present.	Parkinsonian motor dysfunction may be present, with onset typically occurring within 12 months of cognitive decline. Autonomic symptoms also common.	Mixed. Motor deficits common (i.e., paresis, poor fine motor skills). Sensory loss (i.e., extinction) often present. Deep tendon reflexes may be abnormal. Clonus possible.	Parkinsonian motor impairment presents before dementia. Dementia last. Akinesia and dyskinesias common. "On-off" motor fluctuations.	Falls and gait problems. Falls are typically backward parkinsonian features.	Asymmetric motor/sensory deficits.	Ataxia, dysdiadochokinesia present in MSA-C. Parkinsonism more prominent in MSA-P. Autonomic symptoms most prominent, may cause patient to be in wheelchair early or bed-ridden.	Aspects of Balint's syndrome (i.e., oculomotor apraxia, optic ataxia) & Gerstmann's syndrome (left-right disorientation, dyscalculia, dysgraphia, finger agnosia) common.	Mixed, but grossly WNL. Deficits, if any, are inconsistent. Motor programming WNL. Deep tendon reflexes WNL.
History	Slow insidious onset, family history common, gradual decline. No neurological signs.	Early—Insidious onset (compared to AD). Mean age of onset = 54 years-old. Progression more rapid than AD. Personality changes prominent.	Slow insidious onset. Early—Mental status fluctuates and visual hallucinations. Gait abnormalities/ akinesia, tremor may occur within 12 months of cognitive problems. REM sleep behavior disorder common.	Slow onset, may have stepwise progression. Hx of risk factors (i.e., stroke, diabetes, hyperlipidemia, hypertension). Other neurological signs (e.g., sensory extinction)	Dementia presents after movement disorder. Autonomic dysfunction not primary. Family history.	Slow insidious onset. Falls often present first, followed by neuropsychological deficits and psychological problems (anxiety and depression).	Early—Asymmetric onset of motor deficits. Parkinsonian features (akinetic and rigid) followed by cognitive deterioration (often years after motor deficits).	Slow insidious onset. May be more rapid motor/autonomic in MSA-C, while MSA-P may display greater neuropsychological decline.	Insidious onset with early frequent visits to optometry/ ophthalmology and previous attempts to correct visual acuity (e.g., eye surgery).	Hx of depression, symptoms associated with increase stress. 2–26% of elderly depressed. Symptoms may decrease with enjoyable activities.

(continued)

Table 15.3 (continued)

Cognitive domain	AD	FTD	DLB	VaD	PD-D	PSP	CBS	MSA	PCA	Depression
Task engagement	Early—Generally good. Late—Variable.	May be variable—Often dependent on examiner cues.	Early—Generally good. Late—May be reduced due to variable mental status.	Generally good until late in disease.	Generally good	Generally good	Generally good	Generally good	Generally good	Inconsistent performances may be present (e.g., digit forward worse than digit backward).
Cardinal features	Social withdrawal, poor memory with rapid forgetting, dysnomia, constructional apraxia.	Onset typically in 50 s. personality changes early with "frontal" signs. PPA—language deficits	Variable mental status, parkinsonian motor symptoms (tremor not predominant), visual hallucinations, REM sleep behavior disorder.	Motor/sensory abnormalities, poor attention, recognition cues improve recall. Apraxias common.	Slowed processing speed, attention deficits, constructional apraxia, learning slow, but retention can be normal. Parkinsonian motor features.	Vertical gaze palsy, falling backward, "applause sign." frontal/subcortical cognitive deficits	Ideomotor apraxia, asymmetric parkinsonian rigidity and bradykinesia, alien hand sign, later dementia	Prominent dysautonomia and either parkinsonism or cerebellar dysfunction. Frontal/ subcortical deficits common but generally not severe.	Early visual complaints. Prominent visuospatial dysfunction, simultanagnosia and features of Balint's and/or Gerstmann's syndrome.	Complains of memory problems, good description of perceived difficulties, withdrawn, speech fluent and articulate. No apraxias.

Neuropsychological symptoms: Memory impairment, dysnomia and temporal disorientation are some of the earliest cognitive symptoms in AD. Memory loss reflects deficits in consolidation and recall with rapid forgetting of new information (e.g., retention rate < 50%). The learning curve is impaired. Immediate memory may be less impaired than delayed recall, but is still below peers. Recognition memory is impaired, with frequent false positive or false negative errors. Other process scores have shown promise, including the association between reduced practice effects on serial testing and increased likelihood of amyloid burden. Attenuated primacy effects on verbal memory tasks have also more frequently found in individuals with a family history of AD prior to onset of MCI. Confrontation naming is generally impaired, and markedly so as the disease progresses. Verbal fluency is often impaired, and semantic fluency may be worse than letter fluency. Temporal disorientation (e.g., confusion on date, month and day of the week) is more common than geographic disorientation (e.g., city, state). Constructional apraxia is common. Simple attention is intact until late in the disease. As AD progresses, global cognitive impairment is observed, with agnosia, apraxia and aphasia defining the syndrome. Motor function is often preserved late into the disease, but eventually becomes impaired. Initial diagnostic guidelines were proposed for dysexecutive variant of AD (Townley et al., 2020), which mandate a progressive deficit in at least one aspect of executive functioning in the absence of behavioral variant clinical features, but no consensus criteria are available for this variant to date.

Neuropathology: Amyloid plaques and neurofibrillary tau tangles are the two most common markers of AD in the brain. These neuropathological conditions begin in the medial temporal lobes (entorhinal cortex, hippocampi), spread to the parietal and frontal cortices and eventually consume most of the neocortex; however, growing evidence has supported that tau deposition may start in the brainstem (locus coeruleus) prior to cortical deposition. Antemortem evidence of AD neuropathological changes may be more informative in early-onset cases given the increased prevalence of amyloid in cognitively intact older adults. These cellular changes lead to gross morphological changes in the brain, with MRI studies showing cortical atrophy that is more prominent in temporal and parietal areas. Enlargement of ventricles is an effect of this global cerebral atrophy.

Selected references: (Dickerson & Atri, 2014; Miller & Boeve, 2016; Kim et al., 2005; Launer et al., 1999; Livingston et al., 2020; McKhann et al., 2011; Sperling et al., 2011; Albert et al., 2011; Bondi et al., 2017; Townley et al., 2020; Ossenkoppele et al., 2015b; Salmon & Filoteo, 2007; Yaari & Corey-Bloom, 2007; Arboleda-Velasquez et al., 2019).

Key Points: Alzheimer's Disease Dementia

- Memory impairment (poor consolidation and recognition)
  - Learning curve flat, quickly lose information, false positive errors on recognition testing
- Dysnomia (poor confrontation naming)
- Temporal disorientation
- Social withdrawal common
- Symptoms of depression can occur, but tend to vary with environment

Posterior Cortical Atrophy (PCA)

Prevalence: Relatively rare presentation (atypical AD). Between 5 and 15% of AD pathology-confirmed cases. Population prevalence is unclear.

Risk factors: APOE e4 may contribute some risk but less than the conferred risk in typical AD. Further genetic studies pending. Emerging evidence suggests there may also be a higher risk of PCA in those with nonverbal/arithmetic learning disorders.

Onset: Early-onset condition, typically starting between 50 and 65 years old. Average onset is approximately 59 years of age. 83% have onset before age 65 but older onsets have been reported.

Course: Early symptoms are somewhat ambiguous with vague complaints of visual problems and frequent visits with optometrists and ophthalmologists. Possible unsuccessful surgical or other attempts to correct visual acuity may be present in the clinical history. Visuospatial worsening is insidious and gradual but often progresses to include difficulty reading and difficulty visually navigating environments that occurs within the first few years. Most patients are functionally blind by later disease stages. Distinct variants have been proposed for further research including early prominent visuospatial dysfunction, and features of Balint's/Gerstmann's syndrome (biparietal, dorsal variant), early impairment in visual identification (occipitotemporal, ventral variant) and early disturbance of basic visual processing (primary visual, caudal, variant).

Behavioral Symptoms/Clinical Presentation: Anxiety is common at initial presentation. Anxiety may occur due to difficulty perceiving visual stimuli (e.g., riding escalators, crossing busy streets, finding items on a cluttered desk). Personality changes and other neuropsychiatric symptoms are relatively uncommon. Limb apraxia, dressing apraxia, environmental agnosia, alexia and homonymous visual field deficits also occur.

Neuropsychological Symptoms: Prominent visuospatial dysfunction with relatively spared memory, language and executive functions, especially early on in the disease course. Simultanagnosia is common with complex and simple figure copy demonstrating a detail-focused approach (i.e., loss of gestalt for the image). Constructional dyspraxia is also common. Visual perception difficulties may impact naming performance and picture description performance (e.g., Boston Cookie Theft). Other aspects of Balint's syndrome (i.e., oculomotor apraxia and optic ataxia) as well as features of Gerstmann's syndrome (i.e., left-right disorientation, dyscalculia, dysgraphia and finger agnosia) also occur. Writing samples are notable for distortion of the shapes of letters due to visuospatial dysfunction.

Neuropathology: Most commonly AD pathology. Volume loss on MRI is most prominent in posterior regions (e.g., parietal and occipital lobes). Hippocampal volumes are relatively preserved. As mentioned previously, proposed criteria for specific variants may be related to distinct neuroanatomical correlates. Further research is necessary.

Selected references: Diagnostic criteria can be found in Best et al. (2023), Crutch et al. (2017), Rusconi (2018), Schott and Crutch (2019).

Key Points: Posterior Cortical Atrophy (PCA)

- Rare atypical AD presentation with early onset (50–65 years) and slow progression
- Atrophy in posterior regions
- Prominent visuospatial dysfunction with relatively spared memory, language and executive functions.
- Features of Balint's syndrome (i.e., simultanagnosia, oculomotor apraxia, optic ataxia) and Gerstmann's syndrome (i.e., left-right disorientation, dyscalculia, dysgraphia and finger agnosia) are common

Limbic-Predominant Age-Related TDP-43 Encephalopathy (LATE)

LATE was recognized and codified in 2019 as a distinct neurodegenerative disease characterized by neuropathological inclusions of transactivation response DNA-binding protein 43 (TDP-43). LATE occurs in the "oldest old" (e.g., 80+ years old) with a similar cognitive syndrome to that of Alzheimer's disease; however, LATE is pathologically distinct from AD and other TDP-43 proteinopathies, such as frontotemporal degeneration (Duong & Wolk, 2022; Nelson et al., 2019).

Prevalence: Autopsy studies suggest LATE occurs in 20 to 40% of older adults over 80 years old. LATE is more common than other TDP-43 proteinopathies (e.g.,100-fold increased prevalence compared to FTD).

Risk factors: Females are at increased risk due to living longer than males. Age is another risk factor, especially after 85 years old. There is mixed evidence regarding APOE e4 genetic risk.

Onset: Occurs in the "oldest old" (i.e., greater than 80 years of age) and is likely to manifest as episodic memory impairment.

Course: The clinical syndrome of pure-LATE (i.e., LATE without comorbid neuropathology) is slowly progressing compared to AD. Comorbid LATE and AD neuropathology is faster progressing than both pure-LATE and AD alone.

Behavioral Symptoms/Clinical Presentation: Apathy, disinhibition and personality change are common in those with comorbid LATE and AD when LATE is the predominant pathology. Depressed mood is more common in LATE at the MCI stage. At later disease stages, disorientation may be slightly more common in LATE. Hallucinations in the advanced disease stage are less common. Frontal behaviors (e.g., disinhibition and apathy) are much less pronounced than in FTD. Motor deficits as an initial symptom are very uncommon, even in those with comorbid Lewy Body pathology.

Neuropsychological symptoms: Pure-LATE is a slowly progressing, prominent and isolated amnestic syndrome that is slower to encompass other cognitive domains compared to AD alone or comorbid AD and LATE. Episodic memory impairment is present with or without additional impairment in semantic fluency and working memory domains. As with AD, global decline in all cognitive domains is found in advanced LATE disease stages.

Neuropathology: One of the first distinct neuropathological features of LATE that distinguished it from AD was severe hippocampal sclerosis (i.e., neuronal loss and gliosis); however, hippocampal sclerosis is not specific to LATE and can be seen in other neurodegenerative conditions. MRI studies suggest more severe, asymmetric hippocampal atrophy to be indicative of LATE. Progression begins in the amygdalae (Stage 1), advances to hippocampi (Stage 2), and finally to the middle frontal gyrus (Stage 3). Stage 2 begins onset of noticeable cognitive impairment. Often comorbid with other pathologies but with unique contributions to cognitive impairment above and beyond other neuropathological contributions.

Selected references: (Duong & Wolk, 2022; Gauthreaux et al., 2022; Nelson et al., 2019).

Key Points: Limbic-Predominant Age-Related TDP-43 Encephalopathy (LATE)

- Recently identified as a distinct neurodegenerative disease
- TDP-43 proteinopathy that occurs in the "oldest old" (onset after 85 years of age)
- Frequently comorbid with other pathologies (including AD)
- Amnestic syndrome similar to that seen in AD but typically sparing other cognitive domains until very advanced stages
- Much more slowly progressive than AD
  - Comorbid AD+LATE progresses faster than either pathology alone
- Behavioral features of apathy, disinhibition and depression may be more common in LATE than in AD

Vascular Cognitive Impairment (VCI)/Vascular Dementia (VaD)

Prevalence: Excluding "mixed" AD, VaD is the second or third most common cause of dementia. Approximately 10% of dementia cases are due to pure VaD, and another 15–38% are attributable to some combination of VaD and AD.

Risk factors: History of stroke, atherosclerosis, arteriolosclerosis, hypertension, diabetes, hypercholesterolemia, smoking cigarettes, obesity, male gender and older age.

Onset: As individuals age, their risk for strokes and other vascular problems increase, and so does their risk for VaD. Onset of VaD typically occurs between 60 and 75 years of age. Cerebral autosomal dominant arteriopathy with subcortical infarcts and leukoencephalopathy (CADASIL) is a rare genetic cause of earlier onset VCI (ages 30–50) that leads to thickening of small blood vessels due to granular osmiophilic material aggregation.

Course: The course of VaD is quite variable due to the many different sizes and locations of ischemic events within the brain. Many cases progress in a "stepwise" manner, with periods of stability followed by rapid deterioration due to additional strokes. However, this "stepwise" course can be hard to identify and may appear more continuously progressive. Other cases can progress slowly and gradually.

Behavioral Symptoms/Clinical Presentation: The clinical presentation of VaD can also vary widely, depending on the site of the stroke and penumbra. Neurological signs and symptoms can be minimal or severe (e.g., gait and balance problems, plantar flexor response, increased deep tendon reflexes, spasticity, rigidity, visual field deficits, clonus, etc.). Vascular parkinsonism primarily affects the lower extremities bilaterally. Symptoms of depression and anxiety are common. Apathy and social withdrawal are also common. Disinhibition can occur. Urinary incontinence may be present. Migraines, mood disorders and recurrent strokes/TIAs are frequently seen in CADASIL with a family history but limited to no vascular risk factors.

Neuropsychological Symptoms: Psychomotor slowing, impaired attention/concentration and visuoperceptual/constructional deficits could all be present. Memory is likely impaired on both immediate and delayed free recall tasks. This memory deficit, however, tends to reflect poor retrieval, as recognition cues improve memory scores. Language deficits can lead to aphasia syndromes depending upon lesion location. As additional strokes occur, more global cognitive and motor impairments will be observed. Deep white matter disease is associated with a predominantly frontal-subcortical profile, while occlusion of larger arteries often yields more diffuse/multifocal deficits.

Neuropathology: The neuroanatomical damage in VaD varies depending upon vascular etiology. Multi-infarct dementia typically reflects multiple small lesions throughout the gray and white matter of the cerebral cortex. Binswanger's disease or subcortical cerebrovascular disease reflects multiple small lesions throughout the white matter of the cerebral hemispheres, predominately affecting the internal capsule and periventricular/deep white matter. Strategic vascular dementias can reflect focal lesions of the anterior thalamus or mediodorsal thalamus, or angular gyrus typically of the dominant hemisphere. Atherosclerosis tends to impact larger arterial supplies. Arteriolosclerosis is more likely to underlie lacunes/small vessel disease of narrower arterioles in deep white matter tracts. Cerebral amyloid angiopathy (CAA) is an aggregation of amyloid-beta in the cortical vessels and carries a greater risk of hemorrhage. In general, the lesion volume is not the best predictor of the severity of cognitive impairment, as strategic small infarcts in the thalamus can result in dense amnestic syndromes not usually observed until extensive microvascular disease is present. CADASIL white matter lesions are diffuse but predominate earlier in the external capsule and temporal poles, and the NOTCH3 genetic mutation is present in the vast majority of cases.

Selected references: (Dickerson & Atri, 2014; Miller & Boeve, 2016; Gorelick et al., 2011; Park et al., 2014; Román et al., 1993; Skrobot et al., 2018; Di Donato et al., 2017).

Key Points: Vascular Cognitive Impairment/Dementias
- Neurologic signs (plantar flexors, unilateral motor and/or sensory deficits)
- Course may be stepwise (multi-infarct) or gradual progression (small vessel disease)
- Early deficits in processing speed, attention, executive functions, visuoconstructional skills
- Recognition memory may be relatively intact early in course of disease
- Poor verbal fluency (phonemic may be more impaired than semantic)
- Psychomotor deficits

Dementia with Lewy Bodies (DLB)

Prevalence: After AD, DLB is the second most prevalent of the neurodegenerative diseases, accounting for approximately 8%–23% of all diagnosed dementias.

Risk factors: Older age and other causes of dementia (e.g., patients with AD and Parkinson's disease [PD] often have Lewy bodies). Several genetic risk factors (e.g., APOE e4, Presenilin 1 and 2) appear to modulate risk of developing DLB, but no disease-specific genes. More common in men than in women.

Onset: DLB usually develops earlier than AD and VaD, with onsets typically between 50 and 70 years of age.

Course: The course of DLB is slow and insidious, and it is often mistaken for other types of dementia (e.g., AD or PD) before correct diagnosis. Generally, the course is more rapid than AD, with a 5–7-year course from diagnosis. Prodromal patterns may include: mild cognitive impairment onset, delirium-onset or psychiatric-onset. Factors associated with worse outcomes include older age, as well as prominent fluctuations and/or hallucinations at onset.

Behavioral Symptoms/Clinical Presentation: Dementia is an essential component of DLB with four possible core clinical features including fluctuating cognition/consciousness, recurrent visual hallucinations, REM sleep behavior disorder and parkinsonism. The first three features often present early on in the disease course and may be persistent throughout the course. Supportive clinical features can include sensitivity to neuroleptic medication, postural instability, repeated falls, transient episodes of unresponsiveness or syncope, severe autonomic dysfunction, hypersomnia, hyposmia, hallucinations in other sensory modalities (e.g., tactile), systematized delusions, apathy, anxiety and depression. As previously mentioned, research criteria have been proposed suggesting three possible prodromal patterns including (1) a cognitive predominant prodrome characterized by visuospatial and attention/executive dysfunction without substantial functional impairment, (2) a delirium-onset prodrome characterized by prominent fluctuations and (3) a psychiatric-onset prodrome characterized by prominent early visual hallucinations and/or delusions often resulting in misdiagnosis of DLB as a primary psychiatric disorder. Marked fluctuation in mental status/orientation and/or prominent hallucinations and delusions gives early DLB a variable appearance which can lead to initial misdiagnosis. Patient families often remark on this variability, particularly when fluctuations are present, when they describe the deficits demonstrated by patients with DLB. As the disease progresses, disability increases with worsening cognition, hallucinations and delusions and Parkinsonism. Treatments aimed at reducing hallucinations (e.g., neuroleptics) can actually worsen motor functioning in these patients. Unlike PD with dementia, DLB often presents with neuropsychological deficits and parkinsonism co-occurring within 12-months or neuropsychological deficits prior to other symptoms (but within 12 months of other symptoms), while dementia associated with PD develops after several years of Parkinsonism.

Neuropsychological Symptoms: Frequently the most marked neuropsychological deficits involve attention/executive, particularly working memory, and visuoperceptual/visuoconstructional functions. Unlike AD, early in the course of DLB, memory (particularly delayed free recall) is not markedly affected, with memory often being mildly impaired due to poor encoding strategies. Recognition cues do not improve recall. Nonverbal (visual) memory may be more impaired than verbal memory, perhaps reflecting marked impairment in visuoperceptual/visuoconstructional skills. Early in disease, language functions may not be markedly affected, although deficits in verbal fluency (phonemic and semantic) and naming develop. Executive functions are often moderately to severely impaired. Disorientation to time and place is likely to occur as mental status fluctuates over hours to days. Later in the course of DLB, global cognitive impairment is notable, although mental status will continue to wax and wane. At the MCI stages, deficits in visuoconstruction, attention and executive functions tend to differentiate progression to DLB versus other neurodegenerative disorders, such as AD.

Neuropathology: Gross pathology of the brain in patients with DLB might be absent (or quite minimal). It is the accumulation of Lewy bodies, alpha-synuclein protein, in the nuclei of neurons that differentiates this condition from other causes of dementia. Although Lewy bodies are present in PD and also in AD, it is their widespread (i.e., diffuse) distribution that separates DLB from these other conditions.

Selected references: (McKeith et al., 2017, 2020; Prasad et al., 2023).

Key Points: Dementia with Lewy Bodies (DLB)

- Onset of dementia within 12 months of parkinsonian motor deficits
  - (i.e., Co-occurrence of cognitive deficits and parkinsonian motor deficits)
- Fluctuating mental status/cognitive functioning over hours or days
- Visual hallucinations (well-formed)
- REM sleep behavior disorder
- Early deficits in attention, executive and visuoperceptual/constructional skills
  - Memory often not severely impaired early

Frontotemporal Dementia (FTD)

FTD is an umbrella term used to describe several clinical syndromes of dementia all sharing a pathology of frontotemporal lobar degeneration. There are several relatively distinct clinical presentations of FTD that are broadly comprised of three subtypes. The FTDs include (1) *behavioral variant FTD* (bvFTD), (2) the language variants otherwise known as *primary progressive aphasia (PPA) and (3) the motor variants of FTD*. Initially, primary progressive aphasia (PPA) was traditionally divided into two clinical subtypes, namely *nonfluent/agrammatic variant of primary progressive aphasia (nfvPPA),semantic variant of primary progressive aphasia (svPPA); however,* the most recent consensus guidelines (Gorno-Tempini et al., 2011) added a third clinical subtype termed *logopenic variant of primary progressive aphasia (lvPPA). The motor variants of FTD include corticobasal degeneration (CBD), progressive supranuclear palsy (PSP) and amyotrophic lateral sclerosis (ALS)/motor neuron disease (MND).*

Prevalence: Representing the fourth most common form of dementia are FTDs, accounting for 5–9% of cases. Among persons under 65 years old, FTDs are the second most common type of dementia. bvFTD is the most common subtype of FTD, comprising about 50% of cases.

Risk factors: Family history of dementia and older age (25% of cases display initial onset older than age 65). Preexisting autoimmune disorders are more prevalent in FTD (svPPA). Majority of cases are not hereditary, but advances in genetics have identified autosomal dominant inheritance in 20–30% of cases. Various abnormalities of the tau protein gene on chromosome 17q21–22 have been identified. Other genetic mutations associated with FTD include chromosome 9 open reading frame 72 (c9orf72), microtubule associated protein tau (MAPT), progranulin (GRN) and fused in sarcoma (FUS). In patients with PPA, a growing body of research has suggested verbal learning disorders such as dyslexia may be a risk factor for these language-predominant dementias.

Onset: Developing earlier than most other common dementias, onset of FTDs is typically between 50 and 60 years of age (mean age of onset is 59). There are reports of FTDs onset in early 20 s.

Course: Gradually developing symptoms is the most common course in this type of dementia. However, once diagnosed, progression can be more rapid than AD, often evolving over 5–7 years. Select cases have been reported to demonstrate an initial decline that presents similarly to bvFTD followed by a stable course with no supportive neuroimaging features, termed the phenocopy syndrome of bvFTD. As FTDs progress, some patients present with parkinsonian features.

Behavioral Symptoms/Clinical Presentation: The clinical variants of FTD are typically described as having relatively distinct clinical presentations, but overlap in symptoms is often present.

1. *Behavioral variant (bvFTD)* often presents with personality changes reflecting apathy, social withdrawal, loss of social awareness, decreased personal hygiene, affective flattening and apathy. As such, it is not uncommon for bvFTD to be initially misdiagnosed as a late-onset mood disorder. The behavioral disturbance might also reflect social disinhibition, impulsivity, impersistence and perseveration. Language deficits (poor confrontation naming, reduced verbal fluency) are common. Other frequent frontal symptoms include utilization behaviors, perseveration and stimulus bound behaviors. Echolalia, echopraxia and mutism may present in rare, and/or severe cases. Hoarding of unusual items and change in libido (increase or decrease) can occur. FTD reflecting greater pathology of the right hemisphere has been reported to present with flat affect, socially aloof, and aprosodic speech. Research criteria have been proposed for right temporal variant frontotemporal dementia (rtvFTD), characterized by behavioral changes due to social semantic loss including associative prosopagnosia, obsessive/compulsive behaviors, interpersonal coldness and disinhibition. Greater left hemisphere (dominant hemisphere) involvement results in greater language impairment. As the disease progresses, more marked personality changes will occur, including emotional incontinence, stereotyped behaviors and agitation or marked apathy and indifference. Frontal release signs (positive snout, grasp and palmomental responses and/or glabellar sign) and/or oculomotor abnormalities may be present. Gait abnormalities with parkinsonian features are present in some cases, and can be pronounced in a minority of cases. These FTD with more prominent parkinsonian features may represent a unique subset type of FTDs that includes cortical-basal ganglionic degeneration (CBGD) and some cases of PSP.
2. *Primary progressive aphasias (PPA)* (e.g., logopenic variant (lvPPA), nonfluent agrammatic variant [nfvPPA] and semantic variant [svPPA]) collectively present with reductions in speech/language (see below) and/or verbal comprehension with social withdrawal and depression not uncommon. Traditionally, these disorders are not associated with changes in personality or behaviors (other than social withdrawal and may also develop symptoms of anxiety and depression

thought to be associated with loss of ability to speak). nfvPPA presents with speech articulation errors (dysarthria/speech apraxia is common) and reduced verbal output, the latter of which may be misperceived as depression or apathy. Some patients with nfvPPA develop motor features of CBGD and/or PSP such as oculomotor abnormalities and/or parkinsonian features. Semantic and logopenic variants do not present with motor speech deficits. No oculomotor abnormalities have been found in patients with svPPA, but these patients are more likely to engage in ritualistic preoccupations (e.g., clock watching), hoarding and obsessive somatic complaints.

3. *FTD motor variants*, as described above, tend to overlap greatly with other behavioral and language phenotypes. Apathy is common in CBS and PSP. CBS and PSP will be discussed in greater depth below in their respective sections and Chap. 19. FTD-MND is commonly associated with initial onset psychotic symptoms (hallucinations, delusions), which is more uncommon on the whole in FTD, and ALS motor features (fasciculations, upper and lower motor neuron symptoms). c9orf72 mutations are associated with psychotic symptoms and FTD-MND.

Neuropsychological Symptoms

1. *bvFTD* (also formerly referred to as Pick's disease) tends to present first with changes in personality and social behaviors as above-described; thus, initial neuropsychological evaluation may be normal. A burgeoning body of research has indicated deficits in social cognition may present as one of the early signs of bvFTD on evaluation. Cognitive deficits of executive dysfunction reflected in impaired mental flexibility, distractibility, poor verbal fluency and deficient problem-solving (e.g., concrete verbal reasoning, poor design/verbal fluency and limited insight) often will follow personality changes. In contrast to patients with AD, patients with bvFTD exhibit greater executive impairment than memory impairment. Memory may be surprisingly intact, particularly in the first 2 years of the disease. However, memory impairments may become more apparent later in the course of the disease, particularly in difficulty accurately recalling the temporal sequence of events, proactive interference and retrieval deficits. In addition, memory deficits may present due to comorbidities resulting from sequelae of their behavioral symptoms (e.g., hyperorality-related alcohol misuse). Language deficits (e.g., impaired confrontation naming, decreased letter verbal fluency, slower word reading and color naming) are present (see also PPAs below). Stimulus bound and utilization behaviors may be present, particularly in later stages of the disease. *Gegenhalten* or *paratonia* (involuntary resistance to efforts to passively move limbs) and *witzelsucht* (hallow and inappropriate humor/jokes) may be exhibited. Generally visuospatial skills, orientation and arithmetic skills remain intact early on.
2. *Primary Progressive Aphasia*

a. *Nonfluent/Agrammatic variant (nfvPPA)* presents with a largely circumscribed progressive decline in speech (and writing). Speech is nonfluent and effortful, and gradually presents with increasing phonological and grammatical errors. Comprehension of words and objects remains intact (as opposed to semantic and logopenic types below), but understanding syntactically complex sentences (e.g., the cat was eaten by the mouse) is characteristically impaired. Speech articulation is disturbed (i.e., dysarthria/speech apraxia), although some research has advocated for a separate primary progressive apraxia of speech syndrome (primary progressive apraxia of speech, see Duffy et al., 2021 for review). Repetition is relatively spared but may appear impaired due to articulation deficits. Other cognitive domains remain largely unaffected for several years.
b. *Semantic* variant (svPPA) is associated with loss of semantic knowledge, resulting in severe deficits in confrontation naming, poor verbal comprehension due to disrupted knowledge of word meanings (typically pronounced for low-frequency things), surface alexia/agraphia and visual associative agnosia (due to loss of knowledge of visual material). Category fluency is often disproportionately impaired relative to letter fluency. Conversational speech remains quite fluent and is not dysarthric. While semantic memory is poor, performance on tests of episodic memory (e.g., word lists, stories, figures) is often spared, at least in the early stages.
c. *Logopenic variant (lvPPA)* presents with dysnomia, phonemic paraphasias, telegraphic speech with pauses for word-retrieval, auditory working memory deficits and impaired repetition for sentences. However, single-word repetition and comprehension are intact. Aspects of a Gerstmann syndrome or mild visuospatial/constructional deficits may present when disease progression leads to involvement of the left angular gyrus. Unlike svPPA, semantic knowledge of words and objects is intact. Memory, early in the disease, is intact.

Neuropathology: Given the multiple variants of FTD, there are various neuropathological etiologies. However, all are characterized by degeneration of some aspect of the frontal and/or temporal lobes. Degeneration tends to be asymmetric to match the clinical presentation.

1. *bvFTD:* Presents with atrophy, gliosis and neuronal loss of frontal cortex. Predominant degeneration of frontal lobes with involvement of anterior temporal lobe cortices is typical. Four anatomic subtypes of bvFTD have been proposed with differing clinical syndromes: (1) frontal and (2) frontotemporal atrophy of the salience network (frontoinsular and anterior cingulate cortex), (3) semantic appraisal network atrophy (anterior temporal and subgenual cingulate) and (4) subcortical atrophy. There are three classes of neuropathology that predominantly comprise bvFTD cases, namely TDP-43 (50%), tauopathies (40%) and fused in sarcoma (FUS) (5–10%).

a. *Pick's disease* (but not all bvFTD) is a neuoropathological subtype typified by 3-repeat (3R) tau inclusions, swollen (ballooned) neurons (Pick cells) and Pick bodies (i.e., argentophilic neuronal inclusions) in the frontotemporal regions of the cortex. Characteristic Kluver–Bucy symptoms are thought to reflect degeneration of the amygdala.
b. 4-repeat (4R) tauopathies include PSP and CBD and are typified by tufted astrocytes and astrocytic plaques.
c. TDP-43 pathologies have four different subtypes (A-D) and are defined by their intra-nuclear and cytoplasmic deposition.
d. FUS is frequently associated with prominent volume loss of the caudate nucleus.

2. *Nonfluent/Agrammatic variant* is commonly associated with greater degeneration of the left posterior inferior frontal cortex, anterior insular and basal ganglia. Many cases of nfvPPA are tauopathies, and do not have AD pathology.
3. *Semantic variant* is often associated with polar and inferolateral temporal cortex atrophy (left greater than right). Many cases of svPPA are positive for TDP-43 type C, most of which case were previously characterized as FTLD-ubiquitin (FTLD-U) until TDP-43 was discovered.
4. *Logopenic variant* has been reported with consistent reduction in metabolism of the posterior aspect of the left superior and middle temporal gyri and left parietal inferior lobule. Most cases of logopenic type PPA were found to have AD pathology.
5. *FTD-MND/ALS* has a strong clinicopathological correlation with TDP-43 (Type B > A). Diffuse atrophy may be present and prominent in sensorimotor cortices. T2 FLAIR Hyperintensity may be found the corticospinal tract. "Motor band sign" (iron accumulation in primary motor cortex) on SWI/GRE may also be present in around 50% of cases.

Selected references: (Ducharme et al., 2020; Gorno-Tempini et al., 2011; Neary et al., 1998; Rascovsky et al., 2011; Ulugut Erkoyun et al., 2020; DeJesus-Hernandez et al., 2011; Woolley & Rush, 2017; Ranasinghe et al., 2016; Perry et al., 2017; Duffy et al., 2021; Marshall et al., 2018).

Key Points: Frontotemporal Dementia

- Early onset of personality changes and executive dysfunction
- Deficits in language (confrontation naming and verbal fluency)
- Memory and visuoperceptual skills are relatively intact in early stages

Primary Progressive Aphasia characterized by

- Effortful speech (confrontation naming, verbal fluency and/or comprehension)
- Mild arithmetic problems, attention deficits, ideomotor apraxia, and perseveration can be present with speech deficits during first two years, but this presentation cannot be the primary presentation

- Memory and visuoperceptual skills intact and no apathy, disinhibition or motor deficits in the first 2 years of illness

Subtypes of PPA traditionally include:

- Nonfluent/Agrammatic variant—Primary disruption in speech fluency/apraxia
- Semantic variant—Primary disruption in semantic knowledge
- Logopenic variant—primarily repetition and naming deficits

Huntington's Disease (HD)

Prevalence: HD is a rare autosomal dominant neurodegenerative disorder that leads to motor dysfunction, psychiatric symptoms and cognitive impairments. Not all patients with HD develop dementia, and HD probably accounts for 1–2% of dementias.

Risk factors: Earlier development of HD and greater genetic loading (i.e., longer CAG repeat lengths on the huntingtin [*HTT*] gene).

Onset: Although HD typically develops between the ages of 40 and 50 years old, juvenile cases can occur before the age of 20, as well as late-onset cases up to ages 70–80 years old.

Course: Dementia slowly develops in individuals with HD.

Behavioral Symptoms/Clinical Presentation: Recent research suggests that behavioral and motor symptoms may develop at least 10–15 years before the diagnosis of HD. Depression and obsessive-compulsive traits are some of the earliest psychiatric symptoms. Chorea and dystonia are the most common early motor signs, while parkinsonism tends to occur later on in adult-onset patients. As HD progresses, the motor and psychiatric symptoms worsen to include choreiform movements, personality changes, delusions and hallucinations. Rate of completed suicide in HD is 7–10 times higher than the general population and remains higher than in other neurodegenerative diseases.

Neuropsychological symptoms: Early cognitive changes in HD include psychomotor slowing, executive dysfunction and decreased working memory. Deficits in reading emotional expressions may precede all other impairments. Retrieval deficits probably explain most of the early "memory changes" in HD. Some of the cognitive declines might be an artifact of the loss of voluntary motor control. As with most other progressive dementias, the cognitive impairments in HD worsen across time, becoming more global and more profound. Rate of MCI has been estimated to be around 40% in prodromal HD. Three MCI subtypes have been preliminarily proposed, namely executive predominant, representational-predominant (impaired language and memory) and mixed executive-representational (Julayanont et al., 2020).

Neuropathology: The subcortical striatum (caudate and putamen) is primarily affected in HD. However, extra-striatal changes have also been reported, and might better correlate with the different clinical presentations of HD.

Selected references: (Dickerson & Atri, 2014; Miller & Boeve, 2016; Paoli et al., 2017; Paulsen et al., 2008; Snowden, 2017; Wetzel et al., 2011).

Key Points: Huntington's Disease (HD)

- Early onset of psychiatric changes may occur
- Movement disorder (voluntary and involuntary disturbances)
- Subcortical cognitive impairments can occur early in HD, with frank dementia occurring later

Parkinson's Disease with Dementia (PD-D)

Prevalence: Like with HD, Parkinson's disease (PD) is a neurodegenerative disease with motor, psychiatric and cognitive dysfunction. Not all patients with PD will develop dementia (~30%), although rates ranging from 2–93% have been reported. PD-D probably accounts for 2% of all dementias.

Risk factors: Risk for dementia (and cognitive dysfunction in general) is higher for individuals with onset of PD after age 60. Other risk factors include long-term pesticide exposure and male sex.

Onset: Typically between 60 and 70 years of age.

Course: Insidious onset, slowly progressing over years. Cognitive deterioration is more rapid for patients with onset of PD later in life, particularly for those after age 70. Incidence of dementia in patients with onset of PD before age 45 is 10% of those with onset of PD after age 60.

Behavioral Symptoms/Clinical Presentation: Motor symptoms include resting tremor (typically), rigidity, bradykinesia/akinesia and postural instability (See Chap. 19, this volume). Patients with PD are likely to suffer from apathy, depression, anxiety and sleep problems. Later in PD, marked gait impairment, dyskinesias and urinary incontinence can develop. Falls can be a debilitating consequence of the motor dysfunction. Sleep problems, such as REM sleep disorder, and depression may worsen. Visual hallucinations and impulse control disorders may develop, but are associated with doses of dopamine agonists. Patients often exhibit increasing "on-off" fluctuations, and derive less time with good motor control, and more quickly fluctuate between akinesia to dyskinesias.

Neuropsychological symptoms: PD-MCI criteria have been published with levels of certainty from 1 (abbreviated screeners) to 2 (comprehensive testing). Impairments are common in processing speed (bradyphrenia), attention/concentration, executive functions and visuospatial and visuoconstructional abilities. Retrieval deficits likely explain early memory performances (e.g., poor immediate and delayed recall, but generally intact recognition). Language problems include hypophonia and micrographia. Confrontation naming and verbal fluency (usually worse letter than semantic) are often impaired in PD-D, with naming deficits typically occurring later on. Patients with PD with greater impairment in digit span backward, memory (reduced list learning and recognition memory) and more perseverative errors on the Wisconsin Card Sorting Test were at greater risk for developing dementia at one year follow-up (Woods & Tröster, 2003). Patients with gait/postural-predominant PD may also be more likely to progress to dementia faster than tremor-predominant PD (Kelly et al., 2015). Some evidence suggests action verbal fluency may be sensitive for fronto-striatal dysfunction affected in PD, while others have contested this is more indicative of broader executive dysfunction.

Neuropathology: Gross neuropathology associated with PD-D is in the substantia nigra, with depigmentation, neuronal loss and Lewy bodies. Additionally, the characteristic brain changes of AD (plaques, tangles, hippocampal atrophy) are also seen in PD-D.

Selected references: (Beatty et al., 2003; Biundo et al., 2016; Getz & Levin, 2017; Litvan et al., 2012; Pedersen et al., 2013; Postuma et al., 2015).

Key Points: Parkinson's Disease with Dementia (PD-D)

- Parkinsonian motor deficits precede dementia by at least one year
- Bradyphrenia
- Micrographia, hypophonia and masked facies (i.e., reduced facial expressions) are common
- Early executive function deficits with reduced flexibility, set-shifting
- Recognition memory is intact (cueing improves recall)
- Visuoconstructional/visuoperceptual impaired
- Apathy is not depression. Motor slowing may appear affective, but is neurological
- Visual hallucinations not prominent and associated with dopamine agonist medication.

Progressive Supranuclear Palsy (PSP)

Prevalence: Although PSP might be the third most common cause of parkinsonism (behind PD and DLB), it is quite rare as a cause of dementia, representing 1–2% of dementias.

Risk factors: Male gender, parkinsonism, older age and lower education.

Onset: Typically between 40 and 70 years of age, with a mean age of onset of 63 years.

Course: Progressive decline. Rates of decline vary by phenotype, but mortality was reported with a median disease duration of 9.7 years; however, disease course has ranged from 2 to 15+ years. PSP-Parkinsonism is associated with the relatively longest course, whereas PSP-Richardson subtype (prototypical presentation) confers the shortest course.

Behavioral Symptoms/Clinical Presentation: The 1996 diagnostic criteria were extremely specific but inadequately sensitive for PSP. Revised 2017 criteria by Hoglinger and colleagues addressed this issue by providing eight subtypes based on presenting symptoms, with varying levels of confidence applicable to different settings (definite, probable, possible and suggestive). Diagnostic likelihood is based on a broader spectrum across four symptom domains: oculomotor dysfunction, postural instability, cognitive dysfunction and akinesia. Classically in PSP-Richardson syndrome, prominent changes in gait with frequent falls, parkinsonism (bradykinesia, rigidity) without prominent resting tremor, early dysphagia and vertical gaze palsy are early clinical manifestations. Downward gaze palsy is more diagnostically useful, since upward gaze is normally reduced in healthy older adults, while horizontal gaze palsy often occurs later. Blink rate is slowed, and patients may appear to stare ("Mona Lisa gaze"). Eyelid movements can be impaired, and development of involuntary closing of eyes (blepharospasm) or inability to open eyelids may occur. The upper eyelids are often retracted, and the unblinking, wide-eyed stare with raised eyebrows gives rise to a characteristic facial expression of surprise ("astonished facies"). Pseudobulbar palsy, apathy and social withdrawal are also frequently present. As the disease progresses, these clinical manifestations worsen (e.g., inability to walk, more restricted gaze, urinary incontinence, more severe personality changes). PSP-corticobasal and cerebellar-predominant syndromes have also been described.

Neuropsychological symptoms: Psychomotor slowing (bradyphrenia) predominates. Impaired executive function and complex attention are common, but may not be pronounced early. Mild memory impairment is common with interference present. Speech is often dysarthric and hypophonic. Confrontation naming is often mildly impaired, and letter fluency deficits frequently occur (≤ -1.5 SDs using age-/education-adjusted norms). Visuoperceptual function may be nearly normal early in disease. With no time limits, patient responses can be remarkably accurate. PSP-Speech Language (nfvPPA or progressive speech apraxia presentation) and PSP-frontal syndromes have also been added by the 2017 criteria.

Neuropathology: Atrophy along with neurofibrillary tangles, and gliosis occur in the basal ganglia (globus pallidus, subthalamic nucleus, substantia nigra) and superior colliculus, substantia innominata and pretectal area. PSP is generally considered a 4Rtau protein disorder. Functional neuroimaging studies often demonstrate hypometabolism of fronto-subcortical regions, and PET labeling of dopamine has shown marked deficiency. Structural neuroimaging may demonstrate atrophy of the midbrain (when pronounced called the Hummingbird sign) in PSP-Richardson syndrome.

Selected references: (Dickerson & Atri, 2014; Dubois et al., 2005; Gerstenecker, 2017; Gerstenecker et al., 2013; Hoglinger et al., 2017; Miller & Boeve, 2016).

Key Points: Progressive Supranuclear Palsy (PSP)

- Early onset of supranuclear palsy (impaired vertical gaze, particularly downward gaze)
- Frequent falls (often backward)
- Parkinsonism (predominant axial rigidity)
- Bradyphrenia is pronounced. "Subcortical" dementia pattern with prominent executive dysfunction.
- No visual hallucinations.

Corticobasal Syndrome (CBS)

Prevalence: Less than 1% of dementias.

Risk factors: Parkinsonism (onset is typically asymmetric and unresponsive to levodopa), positive family history and older age.

Onset: Late 50 s–70 years of age is typical.

Course: Slowly progressive over 8+ years.

Behavioral Symptoms/Clinical Presentation: In 2013, Armstrong et al. revised diagnostic criteria were published, which also sought to improve the sensitivity of prior clinical guidelines. These included possible and probable levels of certainty based on number of symptoms present, as well as provided four subtypes that expanded the clinical spectrum. Early symptoms include: lateralized motor impairments (e.g., asymmetric rigidity or myoclonus) and bradykinesia. Tremor is typically present during action (postural) and may reduce or resolve at rest. Gait becomes ataxic and has a "shuffling" appearance. Symptoms of depression may be severe, although apathy and disinhibition may also present in a concurrent bvFTD-like syndrome, but other neuropsychiatric symptoms are less common. Asymmetric cortical sensory loss (graphesthesia, astereognosis and visual extinction) may be present. A PSP syndrome may be caused by CBD pathology.

Neuropsychological symptoms: Prominent limb or oral apraxia is often present. Alien limb (limb is "foreign" and moves seemingly on its own) is a hallmark, but present in only about 40% of cases. Dementia with particular deficits in executive function, complex attention and verbal fluency is found. Early in the disease, memory is not markedly affected, and can be near normal, although atypical AD pathology in CBS may underlie memory deficits if present. Recognition cues improve recall, reflecting a "subcortical" memory retrieval problem. A frontal behavioral-spatial syndrome has been proposed with visuospatial impairment, executive deficits or behavioral changes. A nfvPPA syndrome may also occur.

Neuropathology: Asymmetrical profiles are often identified on neuroimaging (structural and functional), especially in the frontoparietal regions. In addition to cortical loss, the substantia nigra is severely affected with intraneuronal inclusions. Inclusions tend to be 4R tau positive, but studies have indicated 15–54% of CBS cases are positive for AD neuropathology.

Selected references: (Armstrong et al., 2013; Dickerson & Atri, 2014; Gerstenecker, 2017; Miller & Boeve, 2016; Polsinelli & Apostolova, 2022).

Key Points: Corticobasal Syndrome (CBS)

- Prominent asymmetric motor deficits including parkinsonism (rigidity, bradykinesia), and limb dystonia
- Myoclonus and tremor (at action and rest) may be present
- Ideomotor and ideational apraxia (e.g., alien hand sign)
- Oculomotor function is often normal (as opposed to PSP)
- Dementia with early subcortical pattern (executive dysfunction)

Multisystem Atrophy (MSA)

Prevalence: MSA is a term to describe three previously identified causes of dementia (striatonigral disease, Shy-Drager syndrome and olivopontocerebellar atrophy) sharing parkinsonian features that are not typically significantly improved with levodopa, although 12–65% of cases may show an initial, short-lived response. MSA is now delimited by predominant symptoms into 1 of 2 subtypes: MSA-cerebellar type (MSA-C) and MSA-Parkinsonian type (MSA-P), with 2022 updated criteria recently published by Wenning et al. The presentation includes components of parkinsonian movement disorders along with other neurologic, autonomic, cognitive and affective features.

Risk factors: Little is known about risk factors. SCNA is a genetic risk factor for MSA and is related to alpha-synuclein regulation. Evidence has been mixed on alcohol misuse as a risk factor of MSA but it may be related to earlier onset of ataxia.

Onset: Typically between 50 and 60 years of age.

Course: Progression occurs over 8–10 years.

Behavioral Symptoms/Clinical Presentation: Patients present with different features of parkinsonism. Both MSA subtypes often present as having prominent signs of autonomic failure (postural hypotension, erectile dysfunction, anhidrosis, etc.). MSA-C (formerly olivopontocerebellar atrophy) presents as having predominant cerebellar dysfunction reflecting ataxia. MSA-P (formerly striatonigral degeneration) presents as predominant symmetric parkinsonism (symmetric rigidity, bradykinesia, tremor, etc.) and is difficult to distinguish from PD. As opposed to PD, patients with MSA present with greater and earlier postural hypotension, erectile dysfunction, urinary and bowel incontinence, anhidrosis, constipation and muscle rigidity. Little information is available on the behavioral/psychiatric manifestations of MSA, but preliminary research has suggested that that depression, anxiety and apathy may be quite common. Disinhibition, hallucinations and agitation occur less frequently. MSA-C tends to show the "wheelchair sign" and earlier debilitating physical symptoms. However, this is not always the case and in fact, MSA prognosis appears to be best predicted by earlier onset and worse severity of autonomic symptoms.

Later on, progressive autonomic, cerebellar failure, fluctuating blood pressure, headaches, dysphagia, irregular heartbeat and problems in breathing are more likely to occur.

Neuropsychological symptoms: MSA-P tends to exhibit a worse neuropsychological prognosis than MSA-C on the whole. Early cognitive impairments are often overshadowed by neurological and medical concerns (e.g., patients often quickly become wheelchair bound and suffer from autonomic failure). However, deficits in aspects of memory and attention/executive functions have been reported. Memory deficits are generally in slowed learning with reduced scores on immediate memory tasks while delayed memory scores may be normal or nearly normal. However, consistent with other "subcortical" dementia processes, patients with MSA often exhibit retrieval problems with intact recognition. Visuoconstructional deficits are also frequently present.

Neuropathology: "Hot-cross bun sign" is commonly found in MSA-C, and to a lesser extent, MSA-P, which is defined as a pontocerebellar cross-like T2 hyperintensity on MRI reflecting gliosis. Atrophy is often present in the putamen, cerebellum and pons. MSA is characterized pathologically by alpha-synuclein positive glial inclusions, most often in the putamen and basal ganglia. Skin biopsy for alpha-synuclein is now available to evaluate for MSA in vivo biomarkers. Concomitant Lewy bodies may also be present.

Selected references: (Dickerson & Atri, 2014; Gerstenecker, 2017; Kawai et al., 2008; Miller & Boeve, 2016; Stankovic et al., 2014; Wenning et al., 2022).

Key Points: Multisystem Atrophy (MSA)

- Parkinsonism features
- Autonomic dysfunction (greater than PD or CBS or PSP)
- Negligible response to dopamine agonists

Two distinct MSA variants:

1. MSA-C (olivopontocerebellar atrophy) is characterized by prominent cerebellar dysfunction
2. MSA-P (striatonigral disease) characterized by predominant symmetric parkinsonism

HIV-Associated Neurocognitive Disorders (HAND)

Prevalence: Recent meta-analysis estimated the overall worldwide rate of HIV-related dementia has substantially declined to around 5% owing to earlier use of highly active antiretroviral therapy (HAART), but milder HAND prevalence has remained relatively unchanged (42.6%). In the USA, prevalence in asymptomatic HIV patients is lower (<1%) and much higher for patients with advanced AIDS (10–20%). However, neurological involvement of HIV infection (HIV-associated neurocognitive disorders) is present in up to 65% of adults with HIV and the majority of children with HIV. Prevalence rates in low SES populations and countries without HAART are much higher, with research estimating 14.9% of sub-Saharan HIV patients met criteria for HIV dementia and another 27.6% had some neuropsychological impairments. Incidence rate in the USA for 19–49 year-olds is about 0.7%.

Risk factors: HIV infection, increasing age, substance misuse, lower education, HIV genes (DNA) present in CNS, lower CD4 counts and/or higher CSF HIV viral load and co-occurring Hepatitis C infection. Women with HIV may be at greater risk of neurocognitive disorder than men with HIV even when controlling for virus-related factor such as CD4 levels.

Onset: Variable. Can affect individuals of any age with HIV infection.

Course: Onset and progression vary, but generally thought to be slow with a long period (e.g., 2–20 years) of relative asymptomatic problems followed by increasing physical and neurocognitive morbidity as HIV infection evolves with AIDS, eventually leads to mortality. However, up to 44% of cases of asymptomatic HIV infection present with neurocognitive symptoms (10–30% is generally accepted). Course is usually progressive, but reduction in symptoms with antiretroviral therapy and protease inhibitors in un- or under-treated patients has been reported. Three subtypes identified among spectrum of extent of deficits (1) HIV-associated dementia, (2) HIV-associated mild neurocognitive disorder and (3) HIV-asymptomatic neurocognitive impairment (see above for diagnostic criteria).

Behavioral Symptoms/Clinical Presentation: Motor dysfunction often involves limb incoordination, weakness, corticospinal tract signs (hyperreflexia). Significant apathy and social withdrawal are common. Alternatively, onset of disinhibition, poor judgment, irritability and emotional lability may also occur.

Neuropsychological symptoms: Early impairments can be mild and typically involve attention/executive dysfunction, deficient verbal fluency and word-finding problems, reduced memory and/or psychomotor slowing (bradyphrenia). Deficits in fine manual speed and/or dexterity are common. Deficits in visuoperceptual/visuospatial functions develop along with worsening memory impairments. Memory deficits initially reflect inefficient encoding and poor retrieval (recognition cues improve recall), but worsen as disease progresses. As the dementia progresses, increasing global cognitive deterioration is present with onset of seizures, prominent motor deficits, mutism, incontinence and, eventually, coma.

1. In addition, the HIV related cognitive disorders, there are often complications associated with HIV infection that can lead to transitory or permanent neuropsychological deficits including: brain abscess (bacterial or fungal), cerebral toxoplasmosis, primary CNS lymphoma, progressive multifocal leukoencephalopathy, meningitis, encephalitis, meningoencephalitis, meningovasculitis, transverse myelitis and vasculitis. Finally, about 4% of patients with HIV suffer a stroke (ischemic or hemorrhagic).

Neuropathology: The HIV virus enters the CNS and is found throughout the brain, particularly involving frontal and subcortical white and gray matter. Cerebral atrophy with prominent lesions of subcortical white matter and subcortical gray matter structures (e.g., basal ganglia and thalamus).

Selected references: (Dickerson & Atri, 2014; Miller & Boeve, 2016; Antinori et al., 2007; Chan & Brew, 2014; Janssen et al., 1991; Saylor et al., 2016; Wang et al., 2020; HNRC Group et al., 2008).

Key Points: HIV Associated Neurocognitive Disorders (HAND)

- HIV has direct and indirect effects on both CNS and PNS
- Neurocognitive deficits present in up to 65% of people with HIV, but neurological involvement may be very mild (i.e., HIV-asymptomatic neurocognitive impairment)
- HIV dementia is rare in asymptomatic individuals with HIV
- Early neuropsychological deficits include:
  - Processing speed/psychomotor speed (bradyphrenia), attention/executive, verbal fluency, confrontation naming, visuoperceptual/visuoconstructional skills.
  - Memory deficits typically mild early in disease (inefficient encoding and retrieval)
  - Basic language functions remain intact early in disease

Aging and Cognitive Impairment

Extensive empirical evidence indicates that some cognitive processes normally decline with age, while others remain more stable across the lifespan (for reviews, see (Baltes & Mayer, 2001; Harada et al., 2013; Salthouse, 2009)). However, the identification of the transition from "normal aging" to a pathological process requiring treatment is an area of active research and debate. Numerous terms and diagnostic criterion have been proposed to distinguish normal aging from abnormal, including; (1) age-associated memory impairment (AAMI (Crook et al., 1986)), (2) aging-associated cognitive decline (Levy, 1994), (3) benign senescent forgetfulness (Kral, 1962), (4) cognitive impairment no dementia (CIND) (Graham et al., 1997), (5) mild cognitive disorder (Christensen et al., 1995), (6) mild cognitive impairment (MCI) (Petersen et al., 1999, 2018), (7) mild neurocognitive disorder (American Psychiatric Association, 2022; Gutierrez et al., 1993), (8) questionable dementia (Morris & Cummings, 2005), (9) subjective cognitive decline (Jessen et al., 2014) and (10) mild behavioral impairment (Ismail et al., 2016). Moreover, researchers have proposed preclinical AD stages to capture the subtle changes occurring even before MCI, which include stage 1 with only amyloid deposition, stage 2 typified by subsequent neurodegeneration and stage 3 characterized by the addition of subtle cognitive problems on more difficult tasks (Sperling et al., 2011). Further complicating the division between normal and abnormal aging processes is the variability in neuropathological and neuropsychological functions between and within samples. Prognostically, research studies have demonstrated that individuals whom have suffered prior neurologic injuries or diseases are at increased risk for developing subsequent cognitive decline, which may contribute to the picture of dementia. For example, an individual whom suffered a moderate to severe head injury or ischemic stroke in middle adulthood is at increased risk for developing a dementia in older age. Although this information cannot yet be used on individual patient level to predict risk for dementia, this is a growing area of development in making the neuropsychology of dementia more evidence based. Below we review MCI and MBI, which are commonly used concepts to describe the area between normal aging changes in cognition/behavior and dementia.

Mild Behavioral Impairment (MBI)

Provisional criteria for mild behavioral impairment (MBI) have been published by the International Society to Advance Alzheimer's Research and Treatment (ISTAART), Neuropsychiatric Symptoms Professional Interest Area (Ismail et al., 2016) to encapsulate the pathological changes in behavior that may precede both cognitive decline and dementia. Prior MBI criteria were published in an attempt to capture prodromal bvFTD manifestations (see Taragano et al., 2009), but the broader expansion of the criteria was indicated given the overlap between neuropsychiatric symptoms and other dementia syndromes. Longitudinal research has indicated the presence of neuropsychiatric symptoms is a stronger risk factor for MCI than either APOE4 status or mesial temporal lobe volume loss (Geda et al., 2014). Patients with MCI and neurobehavioral symptoms have also been associated with higher rates of dementia conversion (25% per year when MCI+MBI). However, the frequency of remission and impact of treatment on disease trajectory in those with MBI remain to be seen. MBI is also thought to be different than psychogenic-related cognitive decline or "pseudodementia," which is generally thought to be reversible and includes psychiatric symptoms that occur for shorter periods than 6 months and spontaneously remit or likely extend back further than age 50 or older. Ultimately, MBI is a burgeoning concept that will undoubtedly continue to evolve over time with additional research.

ISTAART MBI provisional criteria (Ismail et al., 2016):

1. Changes in behavior or personality observed by patient, informant or clinician, starting later in life (age $\geq$ 50 years) and persisting at least intermittently for 6 months. These represent clear change from the person's usual behavior or personality as evidenced by at least one of the following:

    a. Decreased motivation (e.g., apathy, aspontaneity, indifference)
    b. Affective dysregulation (e.g., anxiety, dysphoria, changeability, euphoria, irritability)

   c. Impulse dyscontrol (e.g., agitation, disinhibition, gambling, obsessiveness, behavioral perseveration, stimulus bound)
   d. Social inappropriateness (e.g., lack of empathy, loss of insight, loss of social graces or tact, rigidity, exaggeration of previous personality traits)
   e. Abnormal perception or thought content (e.g., delusions, hallucinations)

2. Behaviors are of sufficient severity to produce at least minimal impairment in at least one of the following areas:

   a. Interpersonal relationships
   b. Other aspects of social functioning
   c. Ability to perform in the workplace

The patient should generally maintain his/her independence of function in daily life, with minimal aids or assistance.

3. Although comorbid conditions may be present, the behavioral or personality changes are not attributable to another current psychiatric disorder (e.g., generalized anxiety disorder, major depression, manic or psychotic disorders), traumatic or general medical causes or the physiological effects of a substance or medication.
4. The patient does not meet criteria for a dementia syndrome (e.g., Alzheimer's disease, frontotemporal dementia, dementia with Lewy bodies, vascular dementia, other dementia). MCI can be concurrently diagnosed with MBI.

Key Points: Mild Behavioral Impairment (MBI)
Provisional Diagnostic Criteria:

- Persistent (6+ months), late-onset (age ≥ 50yo) behavioral or mood symptoms that preclude primary psychiatric disorders
- Adversely impact social, occupational or interpersonal functioning but still independent in IADLs
- May co-occur with MCI
- Correlated with faster cognitive decline and increased risk of dementia
- No delineated subtypes

Conversion:

- MBI + MCI ➡ Dementia 25% per year

Mild Cognitive Impairment (MCI)

Petersen et al. (1999) first proposed the term MCI to describe a select group of individuals from the Mayo Older Adult Normative Studies whom demonstrated cognitive decline, but did not meet diagnostic criteria for dementia. The initial criteria by the Mayo group for MCI were:

- Memory complaint
- Abnormal memory for age
- Normal general cognitive function
- Normal activities of daily living
- Not demented

Subsequently, these criteria have been modified based on new findings (e.g., collateral information on subjective memory complaint is useful, memory deficit should be relative to age- and education-corrected normative data, some declines in other cognitive abilities are expected, mild deficits in activities of daily living might be present), but the concept has endured (Petersen, 2004). Much like the criteria for HIV-related cognitive dysfunction, the criteria for MCI have traditionally provided objective benchmarks (e.g., cognitive functioning falling 1.5 standard deviations below expectations) that allow for the diagnosis of this condition. However, even this widely cited demarcation point for MCI may be less clear-cut than typically employed in neuropsychology. For example, Petersen et al. (2001) noted that the MCI group's mean performance on memory testing was 1.5 standard deviations below their peers, which means that nearly half of the group had scores above that "cutoff." Indeed, Jak et al. (2009) found that a more comprehensive and neuropsychologically informed criteria for MCI (e.g., two scores within a cognitive domain falling at least 1 standard deviation below normative data) led to more reliable diagnoses of MCI, were more likely to be biomarker-positive and were more likely to progress over time (Bondi et al., 2014).

MCI has also evolved from a singular condition to several different subtypes, including single domain impairment (either memory or non-memory) and multiple domain impairments (with or without memory impairment) (Petersen et al., 2001). Single domain memory impaired MCI (i.e., only memory score(s) ≤ -1.5 SD) is termed amnestic MCI (aMCI). Single domain not memory impaired (i.e., other neuropsychological domain test score(s) ≤ -1.5 SD) is termed non-amnestic MCI. Multiple domain MCI involving memory plus at least one other neuropsychological domain is termed multiple domain aMCI. It has been theorized that each subtype of MCI could progress to its own dementia outcome. For example, the amnestic, single-domain subtype of MCI is likely to progress to AD, whereas the single, non-memory domain subtype (e.g., executive dysfunction) might reflect a prodromal stage of FTD. Multiple domain MCI (e.g., deficits in memory and processing speed) might be indicative of eventual VaD. Although this theoretical framework has clear appeal and some studies have found support for the expected progression patterns (Luis et al., 2004), other studies have less consistently found that different clinical subtypes of MCI were associated with unique disease etiologies (Manly et al., 2008). Nevertheless, the identification of MCI, and increasingly the different MCI subtypes, has clear implications for initiating and evaluating treatments for neurodegenerative diseases, particularly in AD.

Although the Petersen et al. (1999) definition of MCI has been most widely referenced, a second view of MCI comes from Morris et al. at Washington University whom argue MCI is not a separate disease entity, but rather individuals with MCI are in a very early or mild, but definite, stage of AD (Morris et al., 2001; Morris & Cummings, 2005). This is supported by the long-term prognosis of dementia diagnosis in many patients diagnosed with MCI (Storandt et al., 2002), as well as neuropathological findings that most patients with MCI have the hallmark signs of AD. Importantly, these are not mutually exclusive views of MCI, which is largely viewed as a prodrome of dementia. In keeping with this broader view, many etiology-specific subtypes of MCI have been proposed for earlier detection of neurodegenerative diseases across clinical spectrum (Albert et al., 2011; Barker et al., 2022; Litvan et al., 2012; McKeith et al., 2020).

Given the range of diagnostic criteria that have been proposed, MCI prevalence rates have varied with estimates of 10.5% for amnestic MCI and 16.2% for both non-amnestic and amnestic MCI in those age 65 and older (Petersen et al., 2018). Regardless of the definition of MCI, it has attracted attention because of its practical and prognostic value. Whereas community-dwelling elders develop dementia at 1–2% per year, individuals with amnestic MCI developed dementia at 12–15% per year (Petersen et al., 1999). Although other studies have varied the definition of MCI and obtained different rates of progression, all indicate an increased risk of developing dementia in this "at-risk" sample. Other negative outcomes associated with MCI include: mortality, institutionalization, disability and psychiatric symptoms.

Although MCI progresses to dementia at a higher-than-normal rate, not everyone with MCI will progress. Even over 6 years, 20–30% of the original Mayo sample of MCI participants did not develop dementia (Petersen et al., 1999), with similar rates reported for other studies. Notwithstanding, those who reverted back from MCI to normal cognition had a 6-times higher risk of developing dementia than those who were never diagnosed with MCI in the first place (Roberts et al., 2014). The search for variables to predict conversion from MCI to dementia is an active area of research, and neuropsychology is contributing to this evidence-based prognostic investigation. Demographically, increasing age and lower education have been linked to progression to dementia. Clinically, collateral reports of memory problems were more suggestive of dementia conversion. An important neuropsychological risk factor for converting to dementia from MCI is the presence of more severe memory deficits (DeCarli et al., 2004; Griffith et al., 2006) and/or executive dysfunction. Individuals with non-amnestic MCI are at less risk of converting to dementia than are patients with amnestic MCI. An absence of expected practice effects has also been linked to continued cognitive decline (Duff et al., 2007), biomarker positivity (Duff et al., 2017, 2018) and treatment response (Duff et al., 2011) in MCI. Structural imaging has focused on medial temporal lobe volumes as indicators of potential progression. For example, Jack et al. (1999) found baseline hippocampal volumes on MRI were related to rates of progression from MCI to dementia. Similarly, rates of hippocampal volume change with sequential neuroimaging have shown utility in predicting progression to dementia (Jack et al., 2000). Structures outside the medial temporal lobe have also demonstrated significant changes in patients with MCI, but fewer of these structures have been linked with predicting conversion to dementia. Functional imaging (e.g., PET, fMRI) has been utilized, and patients who cognitively declined across three years had 18% lower resting metabolism in the entorhinal cortex compared to non-decliners (de Leon et al., 2001). Lastly, several biomarkers have been identified as potentially useful to identify disease progression, including APOE e4, increased cerebrospinal fluid levels of total tau protein and phosphorylated tau protein, and decreased levels of amyloid-beta (Aβ) 40 and 42. However, no demographic, clinical, neuropsychological, imaging or biomarker is a "gold standard" for identifying which patients will progress to dementia and whom will not. It is likely a combinations of markers (e.g., baseline hippocampal volume, executive dysfunction, inflamation markers and/or APOE e4) will best predict progression.

Key Points: Mild Cognitive Impairment (MCI)
Diagnosis:

- Complaints of cognitive impairment
- Objective deficit in neuropsychological function (i.e., 1.5 or more standard deviations below age- and education-matched normative data)
- Not demented and generally intact daily functioning

Subtypes:

- Amnestic MCI = Memory score
- Non-amnestic MCI = One non-memory domain score
- Multi-domain MCI = Two (or more) domain scores

Conversion:

- MCI ➡ Dementia 10–15% per year

Cognitive Decline in Childhood or Young Adulthood

Cognitive decline in childhood and young adulthood is rare, and difficult to identify. During childhood, any deterioration in cognitive and motor skills from a neurodegenerative condition or disease is affected by neurodevelopmental processes, making it difficult to ascertain the onset of cognitive and/or motor skill decline. In young adulthood, cognitive decline may occur with psychiatric symptoms, medication use/abuse and/or illicit drug use/abuse. However, the importance of identifying the presence of conditions which present with cognitive deterioration in childhood and early adulthood is essential. Table 15.4 lists some diseases resulting in cognitive deterioration in childhood that may not have other predominant neurological or medical

Table 15.4 Disorders presenting in childhood or adolescence which have early predominant cognitive deterioration and/or personality/behavioral changes as primary feature without other neurological symptoms

Adrenoleukodystrophy
Adult GM2 Gangliosidosis
Gaucher disease (juvenile and adult form)
Hallervorden–Spatz disease
Kuf's disease (late-onset NCL)
Lafora-body myoclonic episode
Metachromatic leukodystrophy
Mucolipidosis I

symptoms. Other causes having other neurologic manifestations include Rett's disorder in females as a childhood onset neurodegenerative disorder. In addition, various disorders affecting metabolic functions [e.g., Tay–Sachs disease, Niemann–Pick disease, Batten/Kuf's disease, phenylketonurias (PKU), Wilson's disease, etc.) frequently are associated with cognitive deterioration. Sickle cell disease and CADISIL also cause neuropsychological decline due to cerebrovascular disease (e.g., ischemic stroke). Other etiologies for onset of dementia in childhood through early adulthood can include infection [e.g., AIDS infection or acute disseminated encephalomyelitis (ADEM)], dysfunction of cerebrospinal fluid (hydrocephalus or pseudotumor cerebri), lack of nutrition/metabolic (B12 deficiency) or disorder of endocrine/thyroid functions (Hashimoto's encephalopathy) or those associated with epilepsy encephalopathies (e.g., Landau–Kleffner syndrome). Please see Chap. 28 this volume for overview (see also (Duff et al., 2007; Griffith et al., 2006) for reviews).

Medication, Metabolic and Psychiatric Considerations for Cognitive Complaints

A vast array of conditions can cause cognitive deterioration. This chapter reviewed features and etiologies of the more common neurological diseases giving rise to dementia. However, numerous other causes must be considered, and include infections [e.g., acute disseminated encephalomyelitis (ADEM)], strategic lesions resulting in cognitive impairment (e.g., anterior thalami infarct), medical disorders, medications, illicit drugs and alcohol abuse, psychiatric diseases and poor testing effort/task engagement (with such poor effort patient can appear "demented"). Delirium or encephalopathy is a common disorder encountered in the elderly, with prevalence rates ranging from 10 to 56% exhibited among elderly patients in hospitals. Etiology of encephalopathy or delirium can vary substantially (see Chap. 15 this volume), but is often related to infections (urinary tract infection), metabolic disturbances, medications, drugs/alcohol abuse/dependence or combinations of above. The evaluation for encephalopathy and delirium is reviewed in Chaps. 5 and 15, but in general onset of cognitive and behavioral abnormalities is relatively rapid (but may remain chronic for months or even years without treatment) that classically ebb and flow during the day and/or night. Typically, level of arousal varies with poor orientation along with fluctuating energy level (i.e., manic-like agitation to lethargic). Attention is often impaired and hallucinations (visual and/or tactile) are common. Medications with anticholinergic qualities, such as tricyclics, antihistamines, antiemetics, some cough suppressants, analgesics etc., can adversely affect cognitive function. A relative rating system for anticholinergic effects has been developed (Carnahan et al., 2006) and rates medications from a low of 0 for no known effects to 3 for medications that are markedly anticholinergic (see Table 15.5). A mnemonic for symptoms associated with anticholinergic toxicity is: "Hot as a Hades, blind as a bat, dry as a bone, red as a beet, and mad as a hatter." (Peters, 1989) for the hyperthermia, mydriasis, anhidrosis, vasodilation and psychosis that are commonly observed. In addition to medications, various substances and drugs can result in dementia. Alcohol remains a common cause of cognitive impairment, although debate continues whether the dementia related to alcohol abuse/dependence (Wernicke's or Korsakoff's syndrome) may be related to other conditions associated with alcohol abuse/dependence, such as hepatic encephalopathy, cerebrovascular disease, head injuries and nutritional problems. Psychiatric disease is often found in the elderly, and patients with depression and/or anxiety may complain of, and perform poorly on, neuropsychological tests. In addition to patients with major depressive disorders, individuals with bipolar disease, schizophrenia,

Key Points: Conditions that Can Present as "Pseudodementias"

- Infections (ADEM, urinary tract, etc.)
- Strategic lesions (vascular, infectious, space occupying)
- Traumatic head injury
- Medical disorders
- Metabolic dysfunction
- Toxins
- Medications (anticholinergics)
- Illicit drugs, alcohol abuse/dependence
- Psychiatric diseases

Key Points: Anticholinergic Toxicity

- Hot as a Hades, Blind as a bat, Dry as a bone, Red as a beet and Mad as a hatter

  - Hot = Patient has a fever (hyperthermia)
  - Blind = "Blown" or dilated pupils (mydriasis)
  - Dry = Skin dry and no perspiration (anhydrosis)
  - Red = Patient will appear flush (vasodilation)
  - Mad = Patient exhibits delirium (confusion/agitation/psychosis)

Table 15.5 Common medications with anticholinergic effects

Medication/class/use	Common examples
Narcotics	Morphine
	Hydrocodone
	Fentanyl
Benzodiazepines	Lorazepam
	Clonazepam
	Diazepam
Anti-depressants	
	Tricyclics (e.g., amitriptyline, imipramine, etc.)
	Selective serotonin reuptake inhibitors (e.g., paroxetine, sertraline, etc.)—*Less effect than tricyclics*
Antihistamines	
	Clemastine (Dayhist)
	Diphenhydramine (Benadryl)
	Promethazine (Phenergan)
	Hydroxyzine
Cough and cold suppressants	
	Dextromethorphan/pseudoephedrine
Skeletal muscle relaxants	
	Cyclobenzaprine (Flexeril)
Antispasmodics	
	Atropine
	Oxybutynin (Ditropan)
	Ranitidine (Zantac)
	Cimetidine (Tagamet)
Antidiarrheals	
	Diphenoxylate
Anti-parkinsonian (some)	
	Trihexyphenidyl
	Benztropine
	Artane
Travel sickness medications	
	Meclizine
	Scopolamine
Anticonvulsants (some)	
	Oxcarbazepine
	Carbamazepine
	Valproic acid
Sleep aids	
	Diphenhydramine

schizoaffective and other mood disorders may perform poorly on neuropsychological tests. Participants with depression tend to perform poorly on neuropsychological tests and often respond to questions with "I don't know" or "I give up" or "I can't." These patients may appear to be easily frustrated and tearful. Neuropsychological test performances vary across and within neuropsychological domains, and it is not uncommon for patients with depression to provide accurate examples to illustrate their memory problems. Spontaneous memory is poor, but cueing often improves recall, with nay saying response set (answering "no" to questions regardless of content). We provide an overview of the presentation of pseudodementia due to depression below. The neuropsychological features of severe and persistent mental illness are reviewed in Chap. 11. Finally, the possibility of somatoform, conversion and malingering must also be considered in some cases. The potential for malingering is increased when there is clear secondary gain to being diagnosed with a dementia (e.g., in the case of criminal or civil litigation or applying for disability). Consideration to the above factors for etiology of a dementia has important implications for treatment and prognosis, as treatment can reverse cognitive deficits.

Depressive Cognitive Disorders (Formerly Known as "Pseudodementia")

Prevalence: Depression and other psychiatric conditions account for about 4% of patients presenting with dementia symptoms. These are among the most common form of "reversible" conditions presenting as a dementia.

Risk factors: Prior depressive episodes with cognitive impairment, older age, lower education.

Onset: Can occur at any age, but chances of onset increases with age. Patients may be especially precise when describing onset.

Course: Slowly develops and progresses over months, with waxing and waning of depressive and cognitive symptoms. Although cognitive impairments due to depression can significantly improve with the treatment of depression, some cases will progress to a "true" dementia.

Behavioral Symptoms/Clinical Presentation: Symptoms of depression will often appear early, including: depressed mood, anhedonia, social withdrawal, sleep and appetite disturbances and irritability. Individuals commonly complain of "memory problems," which, on further examination, tend to reflect difficulties focusing and sustaining attention. Importantly, patients often provide accurate recent and remote histories, with discrete examples of their "memory problems." Fear of dementia is often present. During evaluation, patients often defer to family members to answer questions, "give-up" quickly on tasks and give many "I don't know" responses to questions. As mood worsens or improves, cognitive complaints can worsen or improve, respectively. No official diagnostic criteria exist.

Neuropsychological symptoms: Psychomotor slowing associated with depression often leads to impairments on measures requiring speed, effort, and attention. Symptom validity testing is often below criteria. Learning and memory scores often fall below expectations, while recognition memory is often normal or nearly normal (e.g., more "hits" than on delayed recall, although false negative errors can occur). Conversational speech is often fluent and articulate. Confrontation naming often normal or nearly normal. Fluency scores can be normal or impaired. Executive and visuoperceptual/visuoconstructional scores vary, but functions are grossly intact. Variable and inconsistent performances are usually present.

Neuropathology: Minimal (or no) gross pathological changes. Age-appropriate related changes, such as mild cerebral atrophy and/or minimal periventricular white matter changes may be present.

Selected references: (Chamberlain & Sahakian, 2006; Kang et al., 2014; Rosenstein, 1998; Wright & Persad, 2007).

Key Points: Depressive Cognitive Disorders (Formerly "Pseudodementia")

- Flat affect (tearfulness and affective feelings as opposed to apathy)
- Frequent "I don't know" responses to questions
- Conversational speech is typically fluid (and often articulate)
- Memory improves with recognition formats
- Tend to perform poorly on symptom validity testing
- History can be detailed and accurate with recent and remote events
- Evaluate for potential of medication (anticholinergic) effects on cognition

Biomarkers

The National Institute of Health (NIH) defines a biomarker as "a characteristic that is objectively measured and evaluated as an indicator of normal biological processes, pathogenic processes or pharmacological responses to therapeutic intervention" (Biomarkers Definitions Working Group, 2001). It is worth noting, as others have raised in the past (Pasternak & Smith, 2019), that neuropsychological tests warrant consideration as a dementia biomarker given that these standardized measures meet the NIH biomarker criteria, despite their lack of inclusion in Jack et al.'s (2018) NIA-AA definition of AD. In this vein, neuropsychological test scores reliably correlate with neuropathological burden and neuroimaging abnormalities, are used to help determine clinical severity and often define clinical trial success and treatment response. Even in preclinical or prodromal stages of neurodegenerative diseases prior to significant cognitive deficits, the early neuropathological manifestation has been associated with the absence of practice effects, process scores and more subtle decline that may only manifest across serial neuropsychological testing (Chelune & Duff, 2019).

In addition to neuropsychological tests, there are many biomarkers related to neuropathologies that are used for further investigation, the majority of which exist primarily for the detection of AD. Based on the most recent biological classification guidelines (Jack et al., 2018), AD biomarkers are organized as: amyloid-beta, tau, and neurodegeneration (ATN), which can be seen in Table 15.6. However, comorbid biomarkers have been shown to be the norm rather than the exception, thus further obfuscating clinicopathological relationships (Rabinovici et al., 2017). These biomarkers may be obtained by a variety of means, including blood plasma, functional/structural neuroimaging, skin biopsy and cerebrospinal fluid (CSF) analysis. Other biometrics such as digital monitoring and genetic testing for mutations (e.g., APOE4, presenilin) may also be used as part of the work-up, although these have yet to become standard in clinical care.

An ongoing topic of debate mired in controversy remains whether AD should be defined exclusively by its neuropathology (Dubois et al., 2021; Jack et al., 2018). Importantly, it is not currently possible to definitively predict whether all patients with amyloid deposition but intact cognition will develop dementia and present with a prototypical amnestic profile. Further compounding this relationship is the high frequency of multiple co-occurring neuropathologies, which can only be directly assessed at post-mortem autopsy when the culmination of neuropathological aggregation has occurred over the lifespan (Rabinovici et al., 2017). As such, it is important to keep in mind that many of the above-mentioned in vivo biomarkers have not been fully validated for universal clinical use across all settings. In addition, biomarker cutoffs may range from liberal to conservative values depending on the particular setting and level of confidence required. The following section will provide a brief overview on dementia biomarkers that providers may encounter, as well as important caveats regarding their diagnostic accuracy across patient populations.

Table 15.6 AD Neuropathology NIA-AA Research Classification System (Jack et al., 2018)

Profile	Biomarker category	Risk of cognitive decline
A+T+N− A+T+N+	AD neuropathological changes	1
A+T−N+	Alzheimer's and comorbid non-AD neuropathological changes	2
A+T−N−	Alzheimer's neuropathological changes	3
A−T−N−	Normal/negative for AD pathologic changes	4
A−T+N+ A−T−N+ A−T+N−	Non-AD neuropathological changes	Unknown

Note: Adapted from Jack et al. (2018). A = amyloid-beta, T = tau, N = neurodegeneration. 1 = highest risk of decline, 4 = lowest risk of decline. The above biomarker categories should be taken into consideration with clinical presentation and cognitive functioning. In other words, any one of these profiles could be seen with a patient with normal cognition, MCI or dementia. The associated disease severity is positively correlated with risk of future progression. As can be seen, only individuals with at least A+T+ biomarkers are labeled as having AD pathologic changes, while those with only A+ are labeled as Alzheimer's pathologic changes given the higher risk of clinical progression in A+T+ subjects

CSF/Blood Plasma Analysis

CSF analysis was the first antemortem method approved by the FDA for clinical use to evaluate for both beta-amyloid and tau pathologies. In AD, positive CSF analyses typically yield low levels of beta-amyloid 42 and high levels of phosphorylated tau ([p-tau] for review of clinical recommendations, see (Simonsen et al., 2017)). Increased total tau is associated with overall neurodegeneration (Olsson et al., 2016). The above CSF biomarkers have demonstrated sensitivity and specificity between 85 and 95% for MCI to dementia stages of AD (Höglund et al., 2015). Noteworthy is that these markers do not correspond one-to-one with neuropathology deposition and instead are thought to be related to the CSF waste removal of these proteinopathies (Blennow & Zetterberg, 2018; Strozyk et al., 2003). Indeed, amyloid PET scans have been found to exhibit higher specificity for AD but commensurate overall accuracy compared to CSF biomarkers (Mattsson et al., 2014). While these biomarkers have been especially sensitive to AD in patients with concordant symptoms, studies have yielded inconsistent predictive validity across the general population and poor ability for CSF to accurately differentiate underlying clinical phenotype (Frisoni et al., 2017). Although not approved for routine clinical use, blood plasma has also recently emerged as a potentially earlier marker of amyloid and p-tau, with p-tau 181 and p-tau 217 demonstrating the highest sensitivity for AD to date (Thijssen et al., 2021). Another more recent development has been the discovery of non-specific pathologies indicative of a neurological disease process but not suggestive of any particular etiology, namely neurofilament light chain (NfL) and glial fibrillary acidic protein (GFAP) (Benedet et al., 2021; Rohrer et al., 2016). While neither are available for clinical investigation, both markers hold promise for improved earlier detection of neuropathological changes in vivo, especially in differentiating neurobehavioral changes from psychiatric disorders.

Neuroimaging

The presence, location and degree of atrophy due to neurodegeneration are typically ascertained from structural neuroimaging, namely MRI and/or Computed Tomography (CT) of the brain. While MRI confers overall improved spatial resolution and better visualization of cerebrovascular disease (CVD), CT is less expensive, less time-consuming and less restrictive (Bermingham, 2014). Although patterns of atrophy and white matter changes can be supportive of certain etiologies, these structural changes are not pathognomonic of dementia and in fact have been associated with normal aging, albeit to a lesser extent (Peters, 2006). Alternatively, individual factors such as higher educational and occupational attainment can confer greater cognitive reserve that staves off decline despite neuropathological insults (Stern, 2012). Equally important is that the absence of atrophy does not definitively rule out a neurodegenerative disease since volume loss is a gradual, downstream process following neuropathological deposition (Raji & Benzinger, 2022). Images are usually interpreted by qualitative visual scanning or volumetric measurement (e.g., NeuroQuant) (Brewer, 2009). Structural neuroimaging is typically the first biomarker collected after clinical exam owing to its relatively lower cost, timely acquisition and utility to rule out other etiologies. However, a Cochrane review (Lombardi et al., 2020) cautioned that relying on neuroimaging alone was an inadequate means of diagnosing AD dementia, with 27% false positive and 29% false negative errors.

Nuclear imaging is another clinical tool commonly utilized for further evaluation of incipient neurodegeneration. Fluorodeoxyglucose-Positron Emission Tomography (FDG-PET) assesses the uptake of glucose across the brain, in which decreased metabolism is thought to be a reflect a precursor state of synapse dysfunction prior to brain atrophy. Akin to structural imaging, specific regional patterns of hypometabolism can support certain dementia etiologies, but FDG-PET may be more sensitive to earlier stages of neurodegenerative diseases. Despite this, one Cochrane review (Smailagic et al., 2015) of the extant literature did not find sufficient evidence to endorse the routine clinical use of FDG-PET due to heterogenous accuracy and lack of systematic interpretation across centers. In addition, research has revealed that patients with mental health disorders may also display hypometabolism (Vijverberg et al., 2016), thus leading to higher false positive rates and limiting this biomarker's clinical utility. Other burgeoning areas of neuroimaging include amyloid and tau PET, only the former of which is approved for limited clinical use. Limitations of amyloid and tau PET currently include their relatively exorbitant costs, infrequent availability outside of specialty memory disorder clinics and lack of sensitivity to earliest neuropathology deposition (e.g., amyloid positivity typically refers to moderate stage aggregation) (Ossenkoppele et al., 2015a). Positive amyloid scans may be found in individuals 20–30 years prior to dementia onset, while tau has been found to more closely relate to cognitive symptoms (Jansen et al., 2015). Guidelines surrounding clinical utilization of amyloid imaging have been published (Johnson et al., 2013).

Treatment

The mainstay of neurodegenerative disease treatment remains symptomatic at present with no cure available. For AD, acetylcholinesterase inhibitors (e.g., donepezil, galantamine, rivastigmine) have been thought to attenuate memory loss for 6–12 months (temporarily "turning the clock back 6–12 months") due to suspected deficiencies in the neurotransmitter associated with learning/memory, acetylcholine (Budson & Solomon, 2016; Marucci et al., 2021). Later adjunctive pharmacotherapy with memantine (NMDA-antagonist) modulates glutamate activity to treat symptoms of moderate to severe AD dementia (Kishi et al., 2017). The above medications have been trialed in other forms of dementia, but are not necessarily indicated or approved for these uses. Nonpharmacological interventions have the strongest evidence base in neurodegenerative disease treatment, as illustrated by the FINGER study that found addressing modifiable lifestyle factors including healthy diet (Mediterranean diet), regular moderate cardiovascular exercise, high-quality sleep and adequate socialization confers the greatest positive impact on cognitive presentation and rate of progression (Barnes & Yaffe, 2011; Kivipelto et al., 2013; Ngandu et al., 2015; Rosenberg et al., 2018). However, these lifestyle changes may be more helpful in preventing or slowing dementia, rather than arresting it. Although pharmacological treatments in dementia focus on the cognitive symptoms, these patients also present with possible psychiatric disturbances, which can be amenable to medical intervention (Cummings et al., 2019; Madhusoodanan & Ting, 2014; Masopust et al., 2018). Respite care, caregiver support and behavioral management (see (Smith & Bondi, 2013) for a comprehensive review of nonpharmacological interventions) are also important facets of treatment that should be considered prior to initiating pharmacological treatment of behavioral symptoms of dementia (Kales et al., 2015). Cognitive rehabilitation has yielded some research support for its utility in treating MCI and dementia, which is generally augmented when combined as part of a multi-pronged healthy lifestyle approach, with typically small effect sizes albeit still clinically significant (Bahar-Fuchs et al., 2013; Sitzer et al., 2006; Smith et al., 2009). Additional treatment avenues of movement disorders are detailed further in Chap. 19 of this book.

Recent clinical trials have shed light on possible disease-modifying treatments for AD. In particular, two anti-amyloid intravenous infusions (aducanumab and lecanemab) were recently approved by the FDA due to their empirical support demonstrating removal of beta-amyloid and attenuated cognitive decline in randomized double-blind, controlled trials (Sevigny et al., 2016; van Dyck et al., 2023). Aducanumab showed a dose-dependent reduction in cognitive decline relative to placebo by about 22% on a clinician rating scale (CDR Sum of Boxes score) (Beshir et al., 2022), while lecanemab was found to slow decline 27% on the same rating scale as well as 26% on cognitive screener and 37% on functional measures (van Dyck et al., 2023). Notwithstanding, caution has been advised due to increased rates of amyloid related imaging abnormalities (ARIA), including cerebral edema and hemosiderin aggregation that can lead to microhemorrhages, but most subjects with ARIA are not symptomatic (Salloway et al., 2022). Empirical evidence supporting amyloid monoclonal antibody treatment has been limited to patients with MCI and mild dementia due to AD thus far. Preliminary evidence suggests positive APOE4 status, initial administration and higher dose of anti-amyloid drug are associated with elevated rates of ARIA (Withington & Turner, 2022). Aducanumab and lecanemab also remain far more costly than other treatment options and increased rates of brain atrophy of unknown clinical significance are associated with these drugs. Other emerging anti-amyloid drugs (e.g., donanemab) have also shown disease-modifying potential for AD (Mintun et al., 2021; Wessels et al., 2023), but also come with elevated risk of hemorrhages and seizures (Salloway et al., 2022), which call for longer study and more diverse clinical samples to validate its safety and results. Even though these disease-modifying agents are not yet standard of care for dementia, they hold promise of a new wave of treatments for these previously intractable conditions.

Evidence-Based Neuropsychology in Dementia

There is a growing literature providing empirical evidence for the unique contribution of neuropsychological assessment in the diagnosis and management of MCI and dementia. Neuropsychological scores can be crucial for making a diagnosis of MCI, for identifying subtypes of MCI (50–58) and for tracking progression across time. Although the importance of the differential diagnosis in MCI continues to be explored, different subtypes of MCI based on different neuropsychological profiles appear to have different rates of progression to dementia (or reversion to "normal" status) (Busse et al., 2006; Chen et al., 2000; DeCarli et al., 2004; Fleisher et al., 2007; Griffith et al., 2006; Luis et al., 2004; Manly et al., 2008; Morris & Cummings, 2005; Petersen et al., 2001; Roberts et al., 2014; Storandt et al., 2002; Tuokko et al., 2003). Neuropsychological deficits in multiple domains (amnestic MCI-multiple domain, non-amnestic MCI-multiple domain) and amnestic MCI-single domain increase the risk of progression to a diagnosis of dementia compared to individuals having MCI in one domain that is not memory (i.e., non-amnestic MCI) (Busse et al., 2006). Additionally, subjects with non-amnestic MCI-multiple domain are more likely to progress to a dementia that is not of the Alzheimer's type than are patients diagnosed with amnestic MCI-single or multiple domain. Specific neuropsychological measures have also been shown to predict future progression to dementia in patients with MCI. For example, in a large study of the progression of MCI to AD, Fleisher et al. (2007) found that the five best predictors of progression included four cognitive tests (Symbol Digit Modalities Test, delayed recall of a list of words, delayed recall of a paragraph and global cognitive score) and one biomarker (APOE 4 status). Using machine learning in a cohort of patients with MCI from the Alzheimer's Disease Neuroimaging Initiative, neuropsychological measures (e.g., total recall on the Rey Auditory Verbal Learning Test, delayed recall of Logical Memory from the Wechsler Memory Scale-Revised and Trail Making Test Part B) significantly contributed to the prediction of progression to dementia (Grassi et al., 2019).

There is extensive empirical support for evidence-based neuropsychology practice in dementia. Indeed, the presence of neuropsychological deficits in older adults increases the risk for development of dementia and even death (Barnes et al., 2009; Busse et al., 2006; Chen et al., 2000; de Leon et al., 2001; DeCarli et al., 2004; Duff et al., 2007; Fleisher et al., 2007; Griffith et al., 2006; Jack et al., 1999, 2000; Luis et al., 2004; Macdonald et al., 2008; Manly et al., 2008; Morris et al., 2001; Storandt et al., 2002; Tuokko et al., 2003). Barnes et al. (2009) developed a Dementia Risk Index and found measures of neuropsychological function were independent predictors for the development of dementia 6 years later above and beyond demographic and other medical variables, including neuroimaging. The Dementia Risk

Index (Barnes et al., 2009) found poor performance on the 3MS (Teng & Chui, 1987) and digit symbol substitution test from the WAIS-R were independent predictive variables for development of dementia 6 years later. Similarly, Chen et al. (2000) found poor performance on delayed recall on a list learning task and Trails B were the best predictors of developing AD 1.5 years later. Development of dementia for patients with PD is also higher for patients exhibiting greater frontal/executive dysfunction (Woods & Tröster, 2003). Finally, neuropsychological data can provide unique data in the differential diagnosis of dementias, including AD, VaD, FTD (including FTD subtypes), DLB, PD-D and dementia with cortical-basal ganglionic degeneration (CBGD) (see (Dickerson & Atri, 2014; Miller & Boeve, 2016) for review, (Diehl et al., 2005; Gerstenecker, 2017; Huey et al., 2009)). For example, Diehl et al. (2005) found performance on the Boston Naming Test and Animal fluency score correctly classified 90.5% of patients as either having AD, semantic dementia or FTD. A correct classification rate between AD and semantic dementia was reported in 96.3% of patients using scores on the Boston Naming Test and MMSE total score (Diehl et al., 2005).

Assessment of Dementia

The diagnosis of dementia requires a thorough evaluation to identify its subtype and/or etiological cause. Many conditions must be ruled out to make even a "probable" diagnosis of dementia. Components of a comprehensive evaluation are listed in Table 15.7.

A neuropsychological evaluation is an important part of a comprehensive assessment for dementia. A clinical interview should inquire if there are problems with cognition, including memory, problem-solving skills and/or language. Evaluation of apraxias and agnosias is recommended. It is particularly helpful to identify the impact of any cognitive dysfunction on day-to-day functioning, since social or occupational impairment is necessary for the diagnosis of dementia in some criteria. The temporal onset and course of symptoms are absolutely essential, including cognitive complaints, mood/personality changes, motor dysfunction and urinary incontinence. The evaluation of symptom onset and progression is often *crucial* in the differential diagnosis of dementia syndromes, as well as distinguishing progressive neurodegenerative diseases from reversible causes of dementia. For example, a several year history of progressive and insidiously worsening memory with no motor impairment is more suggestive of AD than would the occurrence of gait problems, urinary urgency and cognitive problems over several months (much more suggestive of NPH). Family history of, and risk factors for, dementia should also be ascertained. Ideally, information should be obtained from the patient and a reliable collateral source (e.g., spouse, adult child), as patient provided information can be compromised by dementia conditions.

An initial screening of cognitive functioning with a brief measure can be helpful to evaluate what extent of neuropsychological testing is needed. For example, scores

Table 15.7 Components of a dementia evaluation

History and physical exam
Routine laboratory tests
Chest X-ray
Complete blood count
Electrolyte and screening metabolic panel
Thyroid function tests
Syphilis serology
Vitamin B12, folate
Neurological exam
CT or MRI
Psychiatric evaluation
Other tests for atypical presentation
EEG
Lumbar puncture
HIV titer
Lyme titer
Serologic testing for vasculitis
Heavy metal screening
Angiography
PET study
Brain biopsy

of 20 or less on the Mini Mental Status Examination (MMSE) suggest that a brief neuropsychological assessment is all that is possible (or needed), although a sensorimotor and cranial nerve exam can be helpful. However, the converse is not true: perfect scores on screening measures (MMSE = 30/30) does not mean neuropsychological functioning is normal.

Evidence-based neuropsychology practice is guided by extensive literature finding differential diagnosis of dementia and MCI should involve an evaluation of orientation, attention/executive, memory, language and visuoperceptual/visuoconstructional skills. Orientation to person, place, time and circumstances should be assessed. Simple and complex attention should be evaluated, as should visuospatial perception and visuoconstruction, along with praxis. Language assessment should include evaluation of naming, fluency and comprehension. Prosody may be assessed in less impaired individuals. Memory testing should allow to test for learning, immediate free recall and delayed free recall. Furthermore, memory tests that incorporate recognition trials can be valuable in differentiating patients that benefit from cueing compared to those who do not, which can have importance for etiological considerations and rehabilitation potential. Executive functions (e.g., planning, organizing, sequencing, set-shifting, conceptual reasoning, response inhibition) should be assessed. Detailed assessment of all domains may not be necessary, but assessment of each domain has empirical support. We recommend an evaluation of motor function, if only basic motor speed, to better understand any potential difficulties in processing speed and/or identify any lateralizing profiles. A recent expert panel (Ducharme et al., 2020) recommended the inclusion of at least one socioemotional measure when evaluating for bvFTD, such as the social cognition and Emotional Assessment or Ekman 60 Faces Test. Finally, a brief evaluation of psychiatric functioning (e.g., depression, anxiety) is needed.

A vast number of neuropsychological measures may be employed, but the evaluation should be tailored to the extent of suspected neuropsychological impairment and should endeavor to assess the domains identified above. The battery of tests will need to be adapted to the patient skill level and patients with less severe deficits may require more extensive testing to accurately describe the presence and degree of deficit.

Tables 15.8 and 15.9 provide examples of neuropsychological batteries for patients with suspected mild and severe impairments, respectively. Although test selection should be guided by many factors, these are some examples of common measures used in the field for dementia evaluations.

Table 15.8 Examples of tests used in a memory disorders evaluation if mild impairments are suspected and/or rule out pseudodementia due to depression

Clinical interview
North American adult Reading test or Wechsler test of adult Reading or wide range achievement Test-4 word Reading and/or Oklahoma premorbid intellectual Estimate-3
Wechsler adult intelligence scale—Third edition short form (WAIS-IV) or Wechsler adult intelligence scale -fourth Ed. (WAIS-IV; selected subtests for prorated PRI, VCI and PSI) or Wechsler abbreviated scale of intelligence—Second edition (WASI-II)
Wechsler memory scale-fourth edition or California verbal Learning test—Third edition or Rey auditory verbal Learning test or Hopkins verbal Learning test-revised or brief visuospatial memory test-revised
Boston naming test (60-item or 30-item)
Controlled Oral word association test
Semantic verbal fluency test (e.g., animals)
Language screening for repetition, comprehension, writing and reading
Hooper visual organization test and/or Benton line orientation test
Rey–Osterrieth complex figure test
Praxis evaluation
Sensory-perceptual exam/screening
Finger tapping test
Wisconsin card sorting test or Delis–Kaplan executive function scale (selected subtests)
Trail making test parts A & B
Geriatric depression scale (GDS) or Beck depression inventory—Second edition (BDI-II)
Spielberger state-trait anxiety inventory (STAI) or Beck anxiety inventory (BAI)
In very limited cases: Personality assessment inventory (PAI) or Minnesota multiphasic personality Inventory-2 (MMPI-2, short form). Note: If PAI or MMPI-2, GDS/BDI-II nor STAI/BAI administered

Table 15.9 Examples of tests used in a dementia evaluation if mild to moderate or moderate-severe impairments are suspected

Clinical interview
North American adult Reading test or Wechsler test of adult Reading or wide range achievement test-fourth Ed. word Reading and/or Oklahoma premorbid intellectual Estimate-3(MR)
Mini mental status examination or Montreal cognitive assessment (MoCA)[65][a]
Repeatable battery for the assessment of neuropsychological status (RBANS) or Dementia rating scale—Second edition (DRS-2)[b]
Trail making test, parts A & B
Controlled Oral word association test
Semantic verbal fluency test (e.g., animals)
WAIS-IV similarities and matrix reasoning subtests[b]
Luria 3-step motor sequencing
Praxis evaluation
Sensory perception exam/screening
Geriatric depression scale[b]

Note: [a]MMSE or MOCA may not be administered if completed as part of earlier memory screen by physician or nurse; [b]May not be administered in patients exhibiting more severe dementia

Assessment of Cognitive Change in MCI and Dementia

Since neuropsychologists are frequently asked to evaluate change in older adults to inform diagnosis (e.g., progression from MCI to dementia) and effectiveness of interventions (e.g., impact of cholinesterase inhibitors), a better understanding of the methods for evaluating cognitive change in an individual patient is consistent with evidence-based neuropsychological practices. Although there are multiple statistical formulae for quantifying change on neuropsychological scores, the estimated standardized regression-based (SRB) change formula of Maassen et al. (2006) is one that might be most flexibly applied in routine clinical practice. The following describes this approach, and then provides two case examples of its application.

Maassen et al. (2006) demonstrated that an SRB model can be estimated from basic test-retest data that is found in most test manuals and empirical papers (e.g., means and standard deviations of scores at Time 1 and Time 2, test-retest correlations). In the traditional SRB model, a change score is calculated as SRB = $(T_2 - T_2')/SEE$, where T_2 is the observed score at Time 2, T_2' is the predicted score at Time 2 and SEE is the standard error of the estimate. Traditionally, T_2' is calculated as $bT_1 + c$, where b is the beta weight for the Time 1 score and c is the constant. Traditionally, b, c and SEE values all come from the results of a regression model, which requires one to have access to some normative dataset with scores at both Time 1 and Time 2. However, in Maassen's model, the estimated b is calculated by dividing the standard deviation of the control group at Time 2 (S_2) by the standard deviation of the control group at Time 1 (S_1), as in $b = S_2/S_1$. The estimated c is calculated by finding the product of b and the mean of the control group at Time 1 (M_1), and subtracting the value from the mean of the control group at Time 2 (M_2), as in $c = M_2$—(bM_1). The estimated SEE is calculated by: a. find the sum of the S_1 squared and S_2 squared, as in $S_1^2 + S_2^2$; b. find one minus the control group's test-retest correlation (r_{12}), as in $1-r_{12}$; c. multiply $S_1^2 + S_2^2$ and $1 - r_{12}$, as in $(S_1^2 + S_2^2)(1-r_{12})$; and d. take the square root of the resulting product, as in $SEE = \sqrt{((S_1^2 + S_2^2)(1 - r_{12}))}$. Once b, c and SEE are estimated, then they can be applied back to the traditional SRB formulae to derive an estimated T_2' (i.e., $T_2' = bT_1 + c$). Then, the estimated SRB z-score can be calculated by subtracting the T_2' score from T_2, and dividing the result by the estimated SEE (i.e., $SRB = (T_2 - T_2')/SEE$). The resulting z-score can then be compared to a normal distribution, where −1.645 or less traditionally indicates "decline," −1.644 to +1.644 traditionally indicates "no change," and +1.645 or higher traditionally indicates "improvement" between T_1 and T_2. Separate SRBs can be calculated for each score for which a clinician or researcher wants to evaluate change.

The Repeatable Battery for the Assessment of Neuropsychological Status (RBANS; Randolph, 1998) is a widely used cognitive battery with older adults due to its brevity and extent literature related to aging, MCI and dementia. In the manual's update in 2012, test-retest data was provided for a group of largely older adults (mean age = 70.7 years) who were tested twice with the same form of the RBANS across approximately 9 months. Focusing just on the Total Scale score of the RBANS, this normative group's M_1 score was 106.7, S_1 was 13.9, M_2 was 110.6, S_2 was 13.2 and their r_{12} was 0.81. Applying these normative change values to Maassen's formulae, b is 0.95 (i.e., $b = S_2/S_1 = 13.2/13.9 = 0.95$), c is 9.23 (i.e., $c = M_2 - (bM_1) = 110.6 - (0.95*106.7) = 110.6 - 101.37 = 9.23$) and SEE is 8.36 (i.e., $SEE = \sqrt{((S_1^2 + S_2^2)(1 - r_{12}))} = \sqrt{((13.9^2 + 13.2^2)(1 - 0.81))} = \sqrt{((193.21 + 174.24)(0.19))} = \sqrt{((367.45)(0.19))} = \sqrt{(69.82)} = 8.36$). Suppose that there is an elderly patient who was given the RBANS at two time points, and her Total Scale scores were 85 at T_1 and 76 at T_2. Then, her T_2' is 89.98 (i.e., $T_2' = bT_1 + c = (0.95*85) + 9.23 = 80.75 + 9.23 = 89.98$), which is her predicted T_2 score based on her observed T_1 score and the expected change in the normative sample. Finally, her SRB z-score is −1.67 (i.e., $SRB = (T_2 - T_2')/SEE = (76 - 89.98)/8.36 = -13.98/8.36 = -1.67$). Since this z-score falls below the traditional cutoff of −1.645, then it could be concluded that she has declined on the RBANS Total Scale score from her initial visit to her follow-up visit, even though her scores only declined by 9 standard score points. In an additional example, another elderly patient was given the RBANS at two time points, and his Total Scale scores were 85 at T_1 and 100 at T_2. Since b, c and SEE are based on the normative data, those values remain the same for this second patient. His T_2' is also 89.98 (i.e., $T_2' = bT_1 + c = (0.95*85) + 9.23 = 80.75 + 9.23 = 89.98$), since he had the same T_1 score as the first patient. His SRB z-score is 1.20 (i.e., $SRB = (T_2\ T_2')/SEE = (100\ 89.98)/8.36 = 10.02/8.36 = 1.20$). Since this z-score falls between −1.645 and +1.645, then it could be concluded that he has remained stable on the RBANS Total Scale score at his follow-up visit, even though his score increased by 15 standard score points (i.e., a full standard deviation).

This estimated SRB of Maassen et al. (2006) is a "simple" SRB, as it only uses a patient's/participant's T_1 score to predict his/her T_2 score. Since T_1 scores are frequently the best predictors of T_2 scores, the use of such an estimated model may prove valuable in many situations. However, “complex” SRBs can include other variables in the prediction of T_2, including demographic variables (e.g., age, education, sex), clinical variables (g., premorbid intellect, cognitive status) or test setting variables (e.g., retest interval). These additional predictor variables may lead to more sensitive indicators of change. Unfortunately, at this time, there are no methods for estimated complex SRBs, and access to the dataset is required to generate them. Nonetheless, this simple SRB estimated by Maassen and colleagues should be applicable in many clinical and research situations when a quantified amount of cognitive change is needed to inform diagnosis, track progression or evaluate the effects of an intervention. The interested reader can contact the final author of this chapter for a spreadsheet that will do the calculations for the estimated SRB, as well as other change score formulae.

Conclusions

As expected, the field of MCI and dementia has grown exponentially over the past decade with the refinement of diagnostic criteria and advent of new biomarkers. New developments will undoubtedly continue to emerge and move the needle toward earlier diagnosis and improved treatments across the clinical continuum. Over the past ten years, many syndromic definitions have been revised to account for inconsistent clinicopathological relationship and enhance the overall sensitivity of available criteria. While neuropathology has provided important markers of neurodegenerative disease progression and potential therapeutic targets, neuropsychology remains sine qua non in the diagnosis of MCI and dementia and defining response to intervention.

References

Albert, M. S., DeKosky, S. T., Dickson, D., Dubois, B., Feldman, H. H., Fox, N. C., Gamst, A., Holtzman, D. M., Jagust, W. J., Petersen, R. C., Snyder, P. J., Carrillo, M. C., Thies, B., & Phelps, C. H. (2011). The diagnosis of mild cognitive impairment due to Alzheimer’s disease: Recommendations from the National Institute on Aging-Alzheimer’s association workgroups on diagnostic guidelines for Alzheimer’s disease. *Alzheimer’s & Dementia, 7*(3), 270–279. https://doi.org/10.1016/j.jalz.2011.03.008

American Psychiatric Association. (2022). *Diagnostic and statistical manual of mental disorders fifth edition text revision—DSM-5-TR* (Fifth Edition Text Revision). American Psychiatric Association.

Antinori, A., Arendt, G., Becker, J. T., Brew, B. J., Byrd, D. A., Cherner, M., Clifford, D. B., Cinque, P., Epstein, L. G., Goodkin, K., Gisslen, M., Grant, I., Heaton, R. K., Joseph, J., Marder, K., Marra, C. M., McArthur, J. C., Nunn, M., Price, R. W., et al. (2007). Updated research nosology for HIV-associated neurocognitive disorders. *Neurology, 69*(18), 1789–1799. https://doi.org/10.1212/01.WNL.0000287431.88658.8b

Arboleda-Velasquez, J. F., Lopera, F., O'Hare, M., Delgado-Tirado, S., Marino, C., Chmielewska, N., Saez-Torres, K. L., Amarnani, D., Schultz, A. P., Sperling, R. A., Leyton-Cifuentes, D., Chen, K., Baena, A., Aguillon, D., Rios-Romenets, S., Giraldo, M., Guzmán-Vélez, E., Norton, D. J., Pardilla-Delgado, E., et al. (2019). Resistance to autosomal dominant Alzheimer's disease in an APOE3 Christchurch homozygote: A case report. *Nature Medicine, 25*(11), 11. https://doi.org/10.1038/s41591-019-0611-3

Armstrong, M. J., Litvan, I., Lang, A. E., Bak, T. H., Bhatia, K. P., Borroni, B., Boxer, A. L., Dickson, D. W., Grossman, M., Hallett, M., Josephs, K. A., Kertesz, A., Lee, S. E., Miller, B. L., Reich, S. G., Riley, D. E., Tolosa, E., Tröster, A. I., Vidailhet, M., & Weiner, W. J. (2013). Criteria for the diagnosis of corticobasal degeneration. *Neurology, 80*(5), 496–503. https://doi.org/10.1212/WNL.0b013e31827f0fd1

Bahar-Fuchs, A., Clare, L., & Woods, B. (2013). Cognitive training and cognitive rehabilitation for persons with mild to moderate dementia of the Alzheimer's or vascular type: A review. *Alzheimer's Research & Therapy, 5*(4), 35. https://doi.org/10.1186/alzrt189

Baltes, P. B., & Mayer, K. U. (2001). *The Berlin Aging study: Aging from 70 to 100*. Cambridge University Press.

Barker, M. S., Gottesman, R. T., Manoochehri, M., Chapman, S., Appleby, B. S., Brushaber, D., Devick, K. L., Dickerson, B. C., Domoto-Reilly, K., Fields, J. A., Forsberg, L. K., Galasko, D. R., Ghoshal, N., Goldman, J., Graff-Radford, N. R., Grossman, M., Heuer, H. W., Hsiung, G.-Y., Knopman, D. S., et al. (2022). Proposed research criteria for prodromal behavioural variant frontotemporal dementia. *Brain, 145*(3), 1079–1097. https://doi.org/10.1093/brain/awab365

Barnes, D. E., & Yaffe, K. (2011). The projected impact of risk factor reduction on Alzheimer's disease prevalence. *The Lancet Neurology, 10*(9), 819–828. https://doi.org/10.1016/S1474-4422(11)70072-2

Barnes, D. E., Covinsky, K. E., Whitmer, R. A., Kuller, L. H., Lopez, O. L., & Yaffe, K. (2009). Predicting risk of dementia in older adults: The late-life dementia risk index. *Neurology, 73*(3), 173–179. https://doi.org/10.1212/WNL.0b013e3181a81636

Beatty, W. W., Ryder, K. A., Gontkovsky, S. T., Scott, J. G., McSwan, K. L., & Bharucha, K. J. (2003). Analyzing the subcortical dementia syndrome of Parkinson's disease using the RBANS. *Archives of Clinical Neuropsychology: The Official Journal of the National Academy of Neuropsychologists, 18*(5), 509–520.

Belleville, S., Fouquet, C., Hudon, C., Zomahoun, H. T. V., & Croteau, J. (2017). Neuropsychological measures that predict progression from mild cognitive impairment to Alzheimer's type dementia in older adults: A systematic review and meta-analysis. *Neuropsychology Review, 27*(4), 328–353. https://doi.org/10.1007/s11065-017-9361-5

Benedet, A. L., Milà-Alomà, M., Vrillon, A., Ashton, N. J., Pascoal, T. A., Lussier, F., Karikari, T. K., Hourregue, C., Cognat, E., Dumurgier, J., Stevenson, J., Rahmouni, N., Pallen, V., Poltronetti, N. M., Salvadó, G., Shekari, M., Operto, G., Gispert, J. D., Minguillon, C., et al. (2021). Differences between plasma and cerebrospinal fluid glial fibrillary acidic protein levels across the Alzheimer Disease continuum. *JAMA Neurology, 78*(12), 1471–1483. https://doi.org/10.1001/jamaneurol.2021.3671

Bermingham, S. (2014). The appropriate use of neuroimaging in the diagnostic work-up of Dementia. *Ontario Health Technology Assessment Series, 14*(2), 1–67.

Beshir, S. A., Aadithsoorya, A. M., Parveen, A., Goh, S. S. L., Hussain, N., & Menon, V. B. (2022). Aducanumab therapy to treat Alzheimer's Disease: A narrative review. *International Journal of Alzheimer's Disease, 2022*, 9343514. https://doi.org/10.1155/2022/9343514

Best, J., Chapleau, M., & Rabinovici, G. D. (2023). Posterior cortical atrophy: Clinical, neuroimaging, and neuropathological features. *Expert Review of Neurotherapeutics, 23*(3), 227–236. https://doi.org/10.1080/14737175.2023.2190885

Biomarkers Definitions Working Group. (2001). Biomarkers and surrogate endpoints: Preferred definitions and conceptual framework. *Clinical Pharmacology and Therapeutics, 69*(3), 89–95. https://doi.org/10.1067/mcp.2001.113989

Biundo, R., Weis, L., & Antonini, A. (2016). Cognitive decline in Parkinson's disease: The complex picture. *NPJ Parkinson's Disease, 2*(1), 1. https://doi.org/10.1038/npjparkd.2016.18
Blennow, K., & Zetterberg, H. (2018). Biomarkers for Alzheimer's disease: Current status and prospects for the future. *Journal of Internal Medicine, 284*(6), 643–663. https://doi.org/10.1111/joim.12816
Bondi, M. W., Edmonds, E. C., Jak, A. J., Clark, L. R., Delano-Wood, L., McDonald, C. R., Nation, D. A., Libon, D. J., Au, R., Galasko, D., & Salmon, D. P. (2014). Neuropsychological criteria for mild cognitive impairment improves diagnostic precision, biomarker associations, and progression rates. *Journal of Alzheimer's Disease, 42*(1), 275–289. https://doi.org/10.3233/JAD-140276
Bondi, M. W., Edmonds, E. C., & Salmon, D. P. (2017). Alzheimer's disease: Past, present, and future. *Journal of the International Neuropsychological Society: JINS, 23*(9–10), 818–831. https://doi.org/10.1017/S135561771700100X
Brewer, J. B. (2009). Fully-automated volumetric MRI with normative ranges: Translation to clinical practice. *Behavioural Neurology, 21*(1–2), 21–28. https://doi.org/10.3233/BEN-2009-0226
Budson, A. E., & Solomon, P. R. (2016). Chapter 16—Cholinesterase inhibitors. In A. E. Budson & P. R. Solomon (Eds.), *Memory loss, Alzheimer's disease, and dementia* (2nd ed., pp. 160–173). Elsevier. https://doi.org/10.1016/B978-0-323-28661-9.00016-0
Busse, A., Hensel, A., Gühne, U., Angermeyer, M. C., & Riedel-Heller, S. G. (2006). Mild cognitive impairment: Long-term course of four clinical subtypes. *Neurology, 67*(12), 2176–2185. https://doi.org/10.1212/01.wnl.0000249117.23318.e1
Carnahan, R. M., Lund, B. C., Perry, P. J., Pollock, B. G., & Culp, K. R. (2006). The anticholinergic drug scale as a measure of drug-related anticholinergic burden: Associations with serum anticholinergic activity. *Journal of Clinical Pharmacology, 46*(12), 1481–1486. https://doi.org/10.1177/0091270006292126
Chamberlain, S. R., & Sahakian, B. J. (2006). The neuropsychology of mood disorders. *Current Psychiatry Reports, 8*(6), 458–463. https://doi.org/10.1007/s11920-006-0051-x
Chan, P., & Brew, B. J. (2014). HIV associated neurocognitive disorders in the modern antiviral treatment era: Prevalence, characteristics, biomarkers, and effects of treatment. *Current HIV/AIDS Reports, 11*(3), 317–324. https://doi.org/10.1007/s11904-014-0221-0
Chelune, G. J., & Duff, K. (2019). The assessment of change: Serial assessments in dementia evaluations. In *Handbook on the neuropsychology of aging and dementia* (2nd ed., pp. 61–76). Springer Nature Switzerland AG. https://doi.org/10.1007/978-3-319-93497-6_5
Chen, P., Ratcliff, G., Belle, S. H., Cauley, J. A., DeKosky, S. T., & Ganguli, M. (2000). Cognitive tests that best discriminate between presymptomatic AD and those who remain nondemented. *Neurology, 55*(12), 1847–1853. https://doi.org/10.1212/wnl.55.12.1847
Christensen, H., Henderson, A. S., Jorm, A. F., Mackinnon, A. J., Scott, R., & Korten, A. E. (1995). ICD-10 mild cognitive disorder: Epidemiological evidence on its validity. *Psychological Medicine, 25*(1), 105–120. https://doi.org/10.1017/s0033291700028130
Crook, T., Bartus, R. T., Ferris, S. H., Whitehouse, P., Cohen, G. D., & Gershon, S. (1986). Age-associated memory impairment: Proposed diagnostic criteria and measures of clinical change — Report of a national institute of mental health work group. *Developmental Neuropsychology, 2*(4), 261–276. https://doi.org/10.1080/87565648609540348
Crutch, S. J., Schott, J. M., Rabinovici, G. D., Murray, M., Snowden, J. S., van der Flier, W. M., Dickerson, B. C., Vandenberghe, R., Ahmed, S., Bak, T. H., Boeve, B. F., Butler, C., Cappa, S. F., Ceccaldi, M., de Souza, L. C., Dubois, B., Felician, O., Galasko, D., Graff-Radford, J., et al. (2017). Consensus classification of posterior cortical atrophy. *Alzheimer's & Dementia, 13*(8), 870–884. https://doi.org/10.1016/j.jalz.2017.01.014
Cummings, J., Ritter, A., & Rothenberg, K. (2019). Advances in management of neuropsychiatric syndromes in neurodegenerative diseases. *Current Psychiatry Reports, 21*(8), 79. https://doi.org/10.1007/s11920-019-1058-4
de Leon, M. J., Convit, A., Wolf, O. T., Tarshish, C. Y., DeSanti, S., Rusinek, H., Tsui, W., Kandil, E., Scherer, A. J., Roche, A., Imossi, A., Thorn, E., Bobinski, M., Caraos, C., Lesbre, P., Schlyer, D., Poirier, J., Reisberg, B., & Fowler, J. (2001). Prediction of cognitive decline in

normal elderly subjects with 2-[18F]fluoro-2-deoxy-d-glucose/positron-emission tomography (FDG/PET). *Proceedings of the National Academy of Sciences of the United States of America, 98*(19), 10966–10971. https://doi.org/10.1073/pnas.191044198

DeCarli, C., Mungas, D., Harvey, D., Reed, B., Weiner, M., Chui, H., & Jagust, W. (2004). Memory impairment, but not cerebrovascular disease, predicts progression of MCI to dementia. *Neurology, 63*(2), 220–227. https://doi.org/10.1212/01.wnl.0000130531.90205.ef

DeJesus-Hernandez, M., Mackenzie, I. R., Boeve, B. F., Boxer, A. L., Baker, M., Rutherford, N. J., Nicholson, A. M., Finch, N. A., Flynn, H., Adamson, J., Kouri, N., Wojtas, A., Sengdy, P., Hsiung, G.-Y. R., Karydas, A., Seeley, W. W., Josephs, K. A., Coppola, G., Geschwind, D. H., et al. (2011). Expanded GGGGCC Hexanucleotide repeat in noncoding region of C9ORF72 causes chromosome 9p-linked FTD and ALS. *Neuron, 72*(2), 245–256. https://doi.org/10.1016/j.neuron.2011.09.011

Di Donato, I., Bianchi, S., De Stefano, N., Dichgans, M., Dotti, M. T., Duering, M., Jouvent, E., Korczyn, A. D., Lesnik-Oberstein, S. A. J., Malandrini, A., Markus, H. S., Pantoni, L., Penco, S., Rufa, A., Sinanović, O., Stojanov, D., & Federico, A. (2017). Cerebral autosomal dominant arteriopathy with subcortical infarcts and leukoencephalopathy (CADASIL) as a model of small vessel disease: Update on clinical, diagnostic, and management aspects. *BMC Medicine, 15*(1), 41. https://doi.org/10.1186/s12916-017-0778-8

Dickerson, B., & Atri, A. (Eds.). (2014). *Dementia: Comprehensive principles and practices.* Oxford University Press.

Diehl, J., Monsch, A. U., Aebi, C., Wagenpfeil, S., Krapp, S., Grimmer, T., Seeley, W., Förstl, H., & Kurz, A. (2005). Frontotemporal dementia, semantic dementia, and Alzheimer's disease: The contribution of standard neuropsychological tests to differential diagnosis. *Journal of Geriatric Psychiatry and Neurology, 18*(1), 39–44. https://doi.org/10.1177/0891988704272309

Dubois, B., Slachevsky, A., Pillon, B., Beato, R., Villalponda, J. M., & Litvan, I. (2005). "Applause sign" helps to discriminate PSP from FTD and PD. *Neurology, 64*(12), 2132–2133. https://doi.org/10.1212/01.WNL.0000165977.38272.15

Dubois, B., Villain, N., Frisoni, G. B., Rabinovici, G. D., Sabbagh, M., Cappa, S., Bejanin, A., Bombois, S., Epelbaum, S., Teichmann, M., Habert, M.-O., Nordberg, A., Blennow, K., Galasko, D., Stern, Y., Rowe, C. C., Salloway, S., Schneider, L. S., Cummings, J. L., & Feldman, H. H. (2021). Clinical diagnosis of Alzheimer's disease: Recommendations of the international working group. *The Lancet Neurology, 20*(6), 484–496. https://doi.org/10.1016/S1474-4422(21)00066-1

Ducharme, S., Dols, A., Laforce, R., Devenney, E., Kumfor, F., van den Stock, J., Dallaire-Théroux, C., Seelaar, H., Gossink, F., Vijverberg, E., Huey, E., Vandenbulcke, M., Masellis, M., Trieu, C., Onyike, C., Caramelli, P., de Souza, L. C., Santillo, A., Waldö, M. L., et al. (2020). Recommendations to distinguish behavioural variant frontotemporal dementia from psychiatric disorders. *Brain: A Journal of Neurology, 143*(6), 1632–1650. https://doi.org/10.1093/brain/awaa018

Duff, K., Beglinger, L. J., Schultz, S. K., Moser, D. J., McCaffrey, R. J., Haase, R. F., Westervelt, H. J. K., Langbehn, D. R., Paulsen, J. S., & Huntington's Study Group. (2007). Practice effects in the prediction of long-term cognitive outcome in three patient samples: A novel prognostic index. *Archives of Clinical Neuropsychology, 22*(1), 15–24. https://doi.org/10.1016/j.acn.2006.08.013

Duff, K., Lyketsos, C. G., Beglinger, L. J., Chelune, G., Moser, D. J., Arndt, S., Schultz, S. K., Paulsen, J. S., Petersen, R. C., & McCaffrey, R. J. (2011). Practice effects predict cognitive outcome in amnestic mild cognitive impairment. *The American Journal of Geriatric Psychiatry: Official Journal of the American Association for Geriatric Psychiatry, 19*(11), 932–939. https://doi.org/10.1097/JGP.0b013e318209dd3a

Duff, K., Hammers, D. B., Dalley, B. C. A., Suhrie, K. R., Atkinson, T. J., Rasmussen, K. M., Horn, K. P., Beardmore, B. E., Burrell, L. D., Foster, N. L., & Hoffman, J. M. (2017). Short-term practice effects and amyloid deposition: Providing information above and beyond baseline cognition. *The Journal of Prevention of Alzheimer's Disease, 4*(2), 87–92. https://doi.org/10.14283/jpad.2017.9

Duff, K., Anderson, J. S., Mallik, A. K., Suhrie, K. R., Atkinson, T. J., Dalley, B. C. A., Morimoto, S. S., & Hoffman, J. M. (2018). Short-term repeat cognitive testing and its relationship to hippocampal volumes in older adults. *Journal of Clinical Neuroscience: Official Journal of the Neurosurgical Society of Australasia, 57*, 121–125. https://doi.org/10.1016/j.jocn.2018.08.015

Duffy, J. R., Utianski, R. L., & Josephs, K. A. (2021). Primary progressive apraxia of speech: From recognition to diagnosis and care. *Aphasiology, 35*(4), 560–591. https://doi.org/10.1080/02687038.2020.1787732

Duong, M. T., & Wolk, D. A. (2022). Limbic-predominant age-related TDP-43 encephalopathy: LATE-breaking updates in clinicopathologic features and Biomarkers. *Current Neurology and Neuroscience Reports, 22*(11), 689–698. https://doi.org/10.1007/s11910-022-01232-4

Fleisher, A. S., Sowell, B. B., Taylor, C., Gamst, A. C., Petersen, R. C., Thal, L. J., & Alzheimer's Disease Cooperative Study. (2007). Clinical predictors of progression to Alzheimer disease in amnestic mild cognitive impairment. *Neurology, 68*(19), 1588–1595. https://doi.org/10.1212/01.wnl.0000258542.58725.4c

Frisoni, G. B., Boccardi, M., Barkhof, F., Blennow, K., Cappa, S., Chiotis, K., Démonet, J.-F., Garibotto, V., Giannakopoulos, P., Gietl, A., Hansson, O., Herholz, K., Jack, C. R., Nobili, F., Nordberg, A., Snyder, H. M., Ten Kate, M., Varrone, A., Albanese, E., et al. (2017). Strategic roadmap for an early diagnosis of Alzheimer's disease based on biomarkers. *The Lancet Neurology, 16*(8), 661–676. https://doi.org/10.1016/S1474-4422(17)30159-X

Gauthreaux, K. M., Teylan, M. A., Katsumata, Y., Mock, C., Culhane, J. E., Chen, Y.-C., Chan, K. C. G., Fardo, D. W., Dugan, A. J., Cykowski, M. D., Jicha, G. A., Kukull, W. A., & Nelson, P. T. (2022). Limbic-predominant age-related TDP-43 encephalopathy: Medical and pathologic factors associated with comorbid hippocampal sclerosis. *Neurology, 98*(14), e1422–e1433. https://doi.org/10.1212/WNL.0000000000200001

Geda, Y. E., Roberts, R. O., Mielke, M. M., Knopman, D. S., Christianson, T. J. H., Pankratz, V. S., Boeve, B. F., Sochor, O., Tangalos, E. G., Petersen, R. C., & Rocca, W. A. (2014). Baseline neuropsychiatric symptoms and the risk of incident mild cognitive impairment: A population-based study. *The American Journal of Psychiatry, 171*(5), 572–581. https://doi.org/10.1176/appi.ajp.2014.13060821

Gerstenecker, A. (2017). The neuropsychology (broadly conceived) of multiple system atrophy, progressive Supranuclear palsy, and Corticobasal degeneration. *Archives of Clinical Neuropsychology, 32*(7), 861–875. https://doi.org/10.1093/arclin/acx093

Gerstenecker, A., Mast, B., Duff, K., Ferman, T. J., & Litvan, I. (2013). Executive dysfunction is the primary cognitive impairment in progressive Supranuclear palsy. *Archives of Clinical Neuropsychology, 28*(2), 104–113. https://doi.org/10.1093/arclin/acs098

Getz, S. J., & Levin, B. (2017). Cognitive and neuropsychiatric features of early Parkinson's disease. *Archives of Clinical Neuropsychology, 32*(7), 769–785. https://doi.org/10.1093/arclin/acx091

Gorelick, P. B., Scuteri, A., Black, S. E., Decarli, C., Greenberg, S. M., Iadecola, C., Launer, L. J., Laurent, S., Lopez, O. L., Nyenhuis, D., Petersen, R. C., Schneider, J. A., Tzourio, C., Arnett, D. K., Bennett, D. A., Chui, H. C., Higashida, R. T., Lindquist, R., Nilsson, P. M., et al. (2011). Vascular contributions to cognitive impairment and dementia: A statement for healthcare professionals from the American Heart Association/American Stroke Association. *Stroke, 42*(9), 2672–2713. https://doi.org/10.1161/STR.0b013e3182299496

Gorno-Tempini, M. L., Hillis, A. E., Weintraub, S., Kertesz, A., Mendez, M., Cappa, S. F., Ogar, J. M., Rohrer, J. D., Black, S., Boeve, B. F., Manes, F., Dronkers, N. F., Vandenberghe, R., Rascovsky, K., Patterson, K., Miller, B. L., Knopman, D. S., Hodges, J. R., Mesulam, M. M., & Grossman, M. (2011). Classification of primary progressive aphasia and its variants. *Neurology, 76*(11), 1006–1014. https://doi.org/10.1212/WNL.0b013e31821103e6

Graham, J. E., Rockwood, K., Beattie, B. L., Eastwood, R., Gauthier, S., Tuokko, H., & McDowell, I. (1997). Prevalence and severity of cognitive impairment with and without dementia in an elderly population. *The Lancet, 349*(9068), 1793–1796. https://doi.org/10.1016/S0140-6736(97)01007-6

Grassi, M., Rouleaux, N., Caldirola, D., Loewenstein, D., Schruers, K., Perna, G., Dumontier, M., & Alzheimer's Disease Neuroimaging Initiative. (2019). A novel ensemble-based machine learning algorithm to predict the conversion from mild cognitive impairment to Alzheimer's Disease using socio-demographic characteristics, clinical information, and neuropsychological measures. *Frontiers in Neurology, 10*, 756. https://doi.org/10.3389/fneur.2019.00756

Griffith, H. R., Netson, K. L., Harrell, L. E., Zamrini, E. Y., Brockington, J. C., & Marson, D. C. (2006). Amnestic mild cognitive impairment: Diagnostic outcomes and clinical prediction over a two-year time period. *Journal of the International Neuropsychological Society: JINS, 12*(2), 166–175. https://doi.org/10.1017/S1355617706060267

Gutierrez, R., Atkinson, J. H., & Grant, I. (1993). Mild neurocognitive disorder: Needed addition to the nosology of cognitive impairment (organic mental) disorders. *The Journal of Neuropsychiatry and Clinical Neurosciences, 5*(2), 161–177. https://doi.org/10.1176/jnp.5.2.161

Harada, C. N., Natelson Love, M. C., & Triebel, K. (2013). Normal cognitive aging. *Clinics in Geriatric Medicine, 29*(4), 737–752. https://doi.org/10.1016/j.cger.2013.07.002

HNRC Group, Dawes, S., Suarez, P., Casey, C. Y., Cherner, M., Marcotte, T. D., Letendre, S., Grant, I., & Heaton, R. K. (2008). Variable patterns of neuropsychological performance in HIV-1 infection. *Journal of Clinical and Experimental Neuropsychology, 30*(6), 613–626. https://doi.org/10.1080/13803390701565225

Hoglinger, G. U., Respondek, G., Stamelou, M., Kurz, C., Josephs, K. A., Lang, A. E., Mollenhauer, B., Muller, U., Nilsson, C., Whitwell, J. L., Arzberger, T., Englund, E., Gelpi, E., Giese, A., Irwin, D. J., Meissner, W. G., Pantelyat, A., Rajput, A., van Swieten, J. C., et al. (2017). Clinical diagnosis of progressive Supranuclear palsy: The movement disorder society criteria. *Movement Disorders: Official Journal of the Movement Disorder Society, 32*(6), 853–864. https://doi.org/10.1002/mds.26987

Höglund, K., Fourier, A., Perret-Liaudet, A., Zetterberg, H., Blennow, K., & Portelius, E. (2015). Alzheimer's disease—Recent biomarker developments in relation to updated diagnostic criteria. *Clinica Chimica Acta, 449*, 3–8. https://doi.org/10.1016/j.cca.2015.01.041

Huey, E. D., Goveia, E. N., Paviol, S., Pardini, M., Krueger, F., Zamboni, G., Tierney, M. C., Wassermann, E. M., & Grafman, J. (2009). Executive dysfunction in frontotemporal dementia and corticobasal syndrome. *Neurology, 72*(5), 453–459. https://doi.org/10.1212/01.wnl.0000341781.39164.26

Ismail, Z., Smith, E. E., Geda, Y., Sultzer, D., Brodaty, H., Smith, G., Agüera-Ortiz, L., Sweet, R., Miller, D., Lyketsos, C. G., & Area, I. N. S. P. I. (2016). Neuropsychiatric symptoms as early manifestations of emergent dementia: Provisional diagnostic criteria for mild behavioral impairment. *Alzheimer's & Dementia, 12*(2), 195–202. https://doi.org/10.1016/j.jalz.2015.05.017

Jack, C. R., Petersen, R. C., Xu, Y. C., O'Brien, P. C., Smith, G. E., Ivnik, R. J., Boeve, B. F., Waring, S. C., Tangalos, E. G., & Kokmen, E. (1999). Prediction of AD with MRI-based hippocampal volume in mild cognitive impairment. *Neurology, 52*(7), 1397–1403. https://doi.org/10.1212/wnl.52.7.1397

Jack, C. R., Petersen, R. C., Xu, Y., O'Brien, P. C., Smith, G. E., Ivnik, R. J., Boeve, B. F., Tangalos, E. G., & Kokmen, E. (2000). Rates of hippocampal atrophy correlate with change in clinical status in aging and AD. *Neurology, 55*(4), 484–489. https://doi.org/10.1212/wnl.55.4.484

Jack, C. R., Bennett, D. A., Blennow, K., Carrillo, M. C., Dunn, B., Haeberlein, S. B., Holtzman, D. M., Jagust, W., Jessen, F., Karlawish, J., Liu, E., Molinuevo, J. L., Montine, T., Phelps, C., Rankin, K. P., Rowe, C. C., Scheltens, P., Siemers, E., Snyder, H. M., et al. (2018). NIA-AA research framework: Toward a biological definition of Alzheimer's disease. *Alzheimer's & Dementia, 14*(4), 535–562. https://doi.org/10.1016/j.jalz.2018.02.018

Jak, A. J., Bondi, M. W., Delano-Wood, L., Wierenga, C., Corey-Bloom, J., Salmon, D. P., & Delis, D. C. (2009). Quantification of five neuropsychological approaches to defining mild cognitive impairment. *The American Journal of Geriatric Psychiatry: Official Journal of the American Association for Geriatric Psychiatry, 17*(5), 368–375. https://doi.org/10.1097/JGP.0b013e31819431d5

Jansen, W. J., Ossenkoppele, R., Knol, D. L., Tijms, B. M., Scheltens, P., Verhey, F. R. J., Visser, P. J., Amyloid Biomarker Study Group, Aalten, P., Aarsland, D., Alcolea, D., Alexander, M., Almdahl, I. S., Arnold, S. E., Baldeiras, I., Barthel, H., van Berckel, B. N. M., Bibeau, K., Blennow, K., et al. (2015). Prevalence of cerebral amyloid pathology in persons without dementia: A meta-analysis. *JAMA, 313*(19), 1924–1938. https://doi.org/10.1001/jama.2015.4668

Janssen, R. S., Cornblath, D. R., Epstein, L. G., Foa, R. P., et al. (1991). Nomenclature and research case definitions for neurologic manifestations of human immunodeficiency virus-type 1 (HIV-1) infection. Report of a working Group of the American Academy of neurology AIDS task force. *Neurology, 41*, 778–785. https://doi.org/10.1212/WNL.41.6.778

Jessen, F., Amariglio, R. E., van Boxtel, M., Breteler, M., Ceccaldi, M., Chételat, G., Dubois, B., Dufouil, C., Ellis, K. A., van der Flier, W. M., Glodzik, L., van Harten, A. C., de Leon, M. J., McHugh, P., Mielke, M. M., Molinuevo, J. L., Mosconi, L., Osorio, R. S., Perrotin, A., et al. (2014). A conceptual framework for research on subjective cognitive decline in preclinical Alzheimer's disease. *Alzheimer's & Dementia: The Journal of the Alzheimer's Association, 10*(6), 844–852. https://doi.org/10.1016/j.jalz.2014.01.001

Johnson, K. A., Minoshima, S., Bohnen, N. I., Donohoe, K. J., Foster, N. L., Herscovitch, P., Karlawish, J. H., Rowe, C. C., Hedrick, S., Pappas, V., Carrillo, M. C., & Hartley, D. M. (2013). Update on appropriate use criteria for amyloid PET imaging: Dementia experts, mild cognitive impairment, and education. *Journal of Nuclear Medicine, 54*(7), 1011–1013. https://doi.org/10.2967/jnumed.113.127068

Julayanont, P., McFarland, N. R., & Heilman, K. M. (2020). Mild cognitive impairment and dementia in motor manifest Huntington's disease: Classification and prevalence. *Journal of the Neurological Sciences, 408*, 116523. https://doi.org/10.1016/j.jns.2019.116523

Kales, H. C., Gitlin, L. N., & Lyketsos, C. G. (2015). Assessment and management of behavioral and psychological symptoms of dementia. *BMJ, 350*, h369. https://doi.org/10.1136/bmj.h369

Kang, H., Zhao, F., You, L., Giorgetta, C., D, V., Sarkhel, S., & Prakash, R. (2014). Pseudodementia: A neuropsychological review. *Annals of the Indian Academy of Neurology, 17*(2), 147–154. https://doi.org/10.4103/0972-2327.132613

Kawai, Y., Suenaga, M., Takeda, A., Ito, M., Watanabe, H., Tanaka, F., Kato, K., Fukatsu, H., Naganawa, S., Kato, T., Ito, K., & Sobue, G. (2008). Cognitive impairments in multiple system atrophy: MSA-C vs MSA-P. *Neurology, 70*(16 Part 2), 1390–1396. https://doi.org/10.1212/01.wnl.0000310413.04462.6a

Kelly, V. E., Johnson, C. O., McGough, E. L., Shumway-Cook, A., Horak, F. B., Chung, K. A., Espay, A. J., Revilla, F. J., Devoto, J., Wood-Siverio, C., Factor, S. A., Cholerton, B., Edwards, K. L., Peterson, A. L., Quinn, J. F., Montine, T. J., Zabetian, C. P., & Leverenz, J. B. (2015). Association of cognitive domains with postural instability/gait disturbance in Parkinson's disease. *Parkinsonism & Related Disorders, 21*(7), 692–697. https://doi.org/10.1016/j.parkreldis.2015.04.002

Kim, K. Y., Wood, B. E., & Wilson, M. I. (2005). Risk factors for Alzheimer's disease: An overview for clinical practitioners. *The Consultant Pharmacist: The Journal of the American Society of Consultant Pharmacists, 20*(3), 224–230. https://doi.org/10.4140/tcp.n.2005.224

Kishi, T., Matsunaga, S., Oya, K., Nomura, I., Ikuta, T., & Iwata, N. (2017). Memantine for Alzheimer's disease: An updated systematic review and meta-analysis. *Journal of Alzheimer's Disease: JAD, 60*(2), 401–425. https://doi.org/10.3233/JAD-170424

Kivipelto, M., Solomon, A., Ahtiluoto, S., Ngandu, T., Lehtisalo, J., Antikainen, R., Bäckman, L., Hänninen, T., Jula, A., Laatikainen, T., Lindström, J., Mangialasche, F., Nissinen, A., Paajanen, T., Pajala, S., Peltonen, M., Rauramaa, R., Stigsdotter-Neely, A., Strandberg, T., et al. (2013). The Finnish geriatric intervention study to prevent cognitive impairment and disability (FINGER): Study design and progress. *Alzheimer's & Dementia: The Journal of the Alzheimer's Association, 9*(6), 657–665. https://doi.org/10.1016/j.jalz.2012.09.012

Kral, V. A. (1962). Senescent forgetfulness: Benign and malignant. *Canadian Medical Association Journal, 86*(6), 257–260.

Launer, L. J., Andersen, K., Dewey, M. E., Letenneur, L., Ott, A., Amaducci, L. A., Brayne, C., Copeland, J. R., Dartigues, J. F., Kragh-Sorensen, P., Lobo, A., Martinez-Lage, J. M., Stijnen, T., & Hofman, A. (1999). Rates and risk factors for dementia and Alzheimer's disease: Results from EURODEM pooled analyses. EURODEM incidence research group and work groups. European studies of Dementia. *Neurology, 52*(1), 78–84. https://doi.org/10.1212/wnl.52.1.78

Levy, R. (1994). Aging-associated cognitive decline. Working Party of the International Psychogeriatric Association in collaboration with the World Health Organization. *International Psychogeriatrics, 6*(1), 63–68.

Litvan, I., Goldman, J. G., Tröster, A. I., Schmand, B. A., Weintraub, D., Petersen, R. C., Mollenhauer, B., Adler, C. H., Marder, K., Williams-Gray, C. H., Aarsland, D., Kulisevsky, J., Rodriguez-Oroz, M. C., Burn, D. J., Barker, R. A., & Emre, M. (2012). Diagnostic criteria for mild cognitive impairment in Parkinson's Disease: Movement disorder society task force guidelines. *Movement Disorders: Official Journal of the Movement Disorder Society, 27*(3), 349–356. https://doi.org/10.1002/mds.24893

Livingston, G., Huntley, J., Sommerlad, A., Ames, D., Ballard, C., Banerjee, S., Brayne, C., Burns, A., Cohen-Mansfield, J., Cooper, C., Costafreda, S. G., Dias, A., Fox, N., Gitlin, L. N., Howard, R., Kales, H. C., Kivimäki, M., Larson, E. B., Ogunniyi, A., et al. (2020). Dementia prevention, intervention, and care: 2020 report of the lancet commission. *The Lancet, 396*(10248), 413–446. https://doi.org/10.1016/S0140-6736(20)30367-6

Lombardi, G., Crescioli, G., Cavedo, E., Lucenteforte, E., Casazza, G., Bellatorre, A., Lista, C., Costantino, G., Frisoni, G., Virgili, G., & Filippini, G. (2020). Structural magnetic resonance imaging for the early diagnosis of dementia due to Alzheimer's disease in people with mild cognitive impairment. *The Cochrane Database of Systematic Reviews, 2020*(3), CD009628. https://doi.org/10.1002/14651858.CD009628.pub2

Luis, C. A., Barker, W. W., Loewenstein, D. A., Crum, T. A., Rogaeva, E., Kawarai, T., St George-Hyslop, P., & Duara, R. (2004). Conversion to dementia among two groups with cognitive impairment. A preliminary report. *Dementia and Geriatric Cognitive Disorders, 18*(3–4), 307–313. https://doi.org/10.1159/000080124

Maassen, G. H., Bossema, E. R., & Brand, N. (2006). Reliable change assessment with practice effects in sport concussion research: A comment on Hinton-Bayre. *British Journal of Sports Medicine, 40*(10), 829–833. https://doi.org/10.1136/bjsm.2005.023713

Macdonald, S. W. S., Hultsch, D. F., & Dixon, R. A. (2008). Predicting impending death: Inconsistency in speed is a selective and early marker. *Psychology and Aging, 23*(3), 595–607. https://doi.org/10.1037/0882-7974.23.3.595

Madhusoodanan, S., & Ting, M. B. (2014). Pharmacological management of behavioral symptoms associated with dementia. *World Journal of Psychiatry, 4*(4), 72–79. https://doi.org/10.5498/wjp.v4.i4.72

Manly, J. J., Tang, M.-X., Schupf, N., Stern, Y., Vonsattel, J.-P. G., & Mayeux, R. (2008). Frequency and course of mild cognitive impairment in a multiethnic community. *Annals of Neurology, 63*(4), 494–506. https://doi.org/10.1002/ana.21326

Marshall, C. R., Hardy, C. J. D., Volkmer, A., Russell, L. L., Bond, R. L., Fletcher, P. D., Clark, C. N., Mummery, C. J., Schott, J. M., Rossor, M. N., Fox, N. C., Crutch, S. J., Rohrer, J. D., & Warren, J. D. (2018). Primary progressive aphasia: A clinical approach. *Journal of Neurology, 265*(6), 1474–1490. https://doi.org/10.1007/s00415-018-8762-6

Marucci, G., Buccioni, M., Ben, D. D., Lambertucci, C., Volpini, R., & Amenta, F. (2021). Efficacy of acetylcholinesterase inhibitors in Alzheimer's disease. *Neuropharmacology, 190*, 108352. https://doi.org/10.1016/j.neuropharm.2020.108352

Masopust, J., Protopopová, D., Vališ, M., Pavelek, Z., & Klímová, B. (2018). Treatment of behavioral and psychological symptoms of dementias with psychopharmaceuticals: A review. *Neuropsychiatric Disease and Treatment, 14*, 1211–1220. https://doi.org/10.2147/NDT.S163842

Mattsson, N., Insel, P. S., Landau, S., Jagust, W., Donohue, M., Shaw, L. M., Trojanowski, J. Q., Zetterberg, H., Blennow, K., Weiner, M., & Alzheimer's Disease Neuroimaging Initiativea. (2014). Diagnostic accuracy of CSF Ab42 and florbetapir PET for Alzheimer's disease. *Annals of Clinical and Translational Neurology, 1*(8), 534–543. https://doi.org/10.1002/acn3.81

McKeith, I. G., Boeve, B. F., Dickson, D. W., Halliday, G., Taylor, J.-P., Weintraub, D., Aarsland, D., Galvin, J., Attems, J., Ballard, C. G., Bayston, A., Beach, T. G., Blanc, F., Bohnen, N., Bonanni, L., Bras, J., Brundin, P., Burn, D., Chen-Plotkin, A., et al. (2017). Diagnosis and management of dementia with Lewy bodies: Fourth consensus report of the DLB consortium. *Neurology, 89*(1), 88–100. https://doi.org/10.1212/WNL.0000000000004058

McKeith, I. G., Ferman, T. J., Thomas, A. J., Blanc, F., Boeve, B. F., Fujishiro, H., Kantarci, K., Muscio, C., O'Brien, J. T., Postuma, R. B., Aarsland, D., Ballard, C., Bonanni, L., Donaghy, P., Emre, M., Galvin, J. E., Galasko, D., Goldman, J. G., Gomperts, S. N., et al. (2020). Research criteria for the diagnosis of prodromal dementia with Lewy bodies. *Neurology, 94*(17), 743–755. https://doi.org/10.1212/WNL.0000000000009323

McKhann, G., Drachman, D., Folstein, M., Katzman, R., Price, D., & Stadlan, E. M. (1984). Clinical diagnosis of Alzheimer's disease: Report of the NINCDS-ADRDA work group under the auspices of Department of Health and Human Services Task Force on Alzheimer's Disease. *Neurology, 34*(7), 939–944. https://doi.org/10.1212/wnl.34.7.939

McKhann, G. M., Knopman, D. S., Chertkow, H., Hyman, B. T., Jack, C. R., Jr., Kawas, C. H., Klunk, W. E., Koroshetz, W. J., Manly, J. J., Mayeux, R., Mohs, R. C., Morris, J. C., Rossor, M. N., Scheltens, P., Carrillo, M. C., Thies, B., Weintraub, S., & Phelps, C. H. (2011). The diagnosis of dementia due to Alzheimer's disease: Recommendations from the National Institute on Aging-Alzheimer's Association workgroups on diagnostic guidelines for Alzheimer's disease. *Alzheimer's & Dementia, 7*(3), 263–269. https://doi.org/10.1016/j.jalz.2011.03.005

Mesulam, M. M. (2001). Primary progressive aphasia. *Annals of Neurology, 49*(4), 425–432.

Miller, B. L., & Boeve, B. F. (Eds.). (2016). *The behavioral neurology of Dementia* (2nd ed.). Cambridge University Press. https://doi.org/10.1017/9781139924771

Mintun, M. A., Lo, A. C., Duggan Evans, C., Wessels, A. M., Ardayfio, P. A., Andersen, S. W., Shcherbinin, S., Sparks, J., Sims, J. R., Brys, M., Apostolova, L. G., Salloway, S. P., & Skovronsky, D. M. (2021). Donanemab in early Alzheimer's Disease. *The New England Journal of Medicine, 384*(18), 1691–1704. https://doi.org/10.1056/NEJMoa2100708

Morris, J. C., & Cummings, J. (2005). Mild cognitive impairment (MCI) represents early-stage Alzheimer's disease. *Journal of Alzheimer's Disease: JAD, 7*(3), 235–239. https://doi.org/10.3233/jad-2005-7306. discussion 255-262.

Morris, J. C., Storandt, M., Miller, J. P., McKeel, D. W., Price, J. L., Rubin, E. H., & Berg, L. (2001). Mild cognitive impairment represents early-stage Alzheimer disease. *Archives of Neurology, 58*(3), 397–405. https://doi.org/10.1001/archneur.58.3.397

Navia, B. A., Jordan, B. D., & Price, R. W. (1986). The AIDS dementia complex: I. Clinical features. *Annals of Neurology, 19*(6), 517–524. https://doi.org/10.1002/ana.410190602

Neary, D., Snowden, J. S., Gustafson, L., Passant, U., Stuss, D., Black, S., Freedman, M., Kertesz, A., Robert, P. H., Albert, M., Boone, K., Miller, B. L., Cummings, J., & Benson, D. F. (1998). Frontotemporal lobar degeneration: A consensus on clinical diagnostic criteria. *Neurology, 51*(6), 1546–1554. https://doi.org/10.1212/WNL.51.6.1546

Nelson, P. T., Dickson, D. W., Trojanowski, J. Q., Jack, C. R., Boyle, P. A., Arfanakis, K., Rademakers, R., Alafuzoff, I., Attems, J., Brayne, C., Coyle-Gilchrist, I. T. S., Chui, H. C., Fardo, D. W., Flanagan, M. E., Halliday, G., Hokkanen, S. R. K., Hunter, S., Jicha, G. A., Katsumata, Y., et al. (2019). Limbic-predominant age-related TDP-43 encephalopathy (LATE): Consensus working group report. *Brain: A Journal of Neurology, 142*(6), 1503–1527. https://doi.org/10.1093/brain/awz099

Ngandu, T., Lehtisalo, J., Solomon, A., Levälahti, E., Ahtiluoto, S., Antikainen, R., Bäckman, L., Hänninen, T., Jula, A., Laatikainen, T., Lindström, J., Mangialasche, F., Paajanen, T., Pajala, S., Peltonen, M., Rauramaa, R., Stigsdotter-Neely, A., Strandberg, T., Tuomilehto, J., et al. (2015). A 2 year multidomain intervention of diet, exercise, cognitive training, and vascular risk monitoring versus control to prevent cognitive decline in at-risk elderly people (FINGER): A randomised controlled trial. *The Lancet, 385*(9984), 2255–2263. https://doi.org/10.1016/S0140-6736(15)60461-5

Olsson, B., Lautner, R., Andreasson, U., Öhrfelt, A., Portelius, E., Bjerke, M., Hölttä, M., Rosén, C., Olsson, C., Strobel, G., Wu, E., Dakin, K., Petzold, M., Blennow, K., & Zetterberg, H. (2016). CSF and blood biomarkers for the diagnosis of Alzheimer's disease: A systematic review and meta-analysis. *The Lancet Neurology, 15*(7), 673–684. https://doi.org/10.1016/S1474-4422(16)00070-3

Ossenkoppele, R., Jansen, W. J., Rabinovici, G. D., Knol, D. L., van der Flier, W. M., van Berckel, B. N. M., Scheltens, P., Visser, P. J., Amyloid PET Study Group, Verfaillie, S. C. J., Zwan, M. D., Adriaanse, S. M., Lammertsma, A. A., Barkhof, F., Jagust, W. J., Miller, B. L., Rosen, H. J., Landau, S. M., Villemagne, V. L., et al. (2015a). Prevalence of amyloid PET positivity in dementia syndromes: A meta-analysis. *JAMA, 313*(19), 1939–1949. https://doi.org/10.1001/jama.2015.4669

Ossenkoppele, R., Pijnenburg, Y. A. L., Perry, D. C., Cohn-Sheehy, B. I., Scheltens, N. M. E., Vogel, J. W., Kramer, J. H., van der Vlies, A. E., Joie, R. L., Rosen, H. J., van der Flier, W. M., Grinberg, L. T., Rozemuller, A. J., Huang, E. J., van Berckel, B. N. M., Miller, B. L., Barkhof, F., Jagust, W. J., Scheltens, P., et al. (2015b). The behavioural/dysexecutive variant of Alzheimer's disease: Clinical, neuroimaging and pathological features. *Brain, 138*(9), 2732–2749. https://doi.org/10.1093/brain/awv191

Ossenkoppele, R., Singleton, E. H., Groot, C., Dijkstra, A. A., Eikelboom, W. S., Seeley, W. W., Miller, B., Laforce, R. J., Scheltens, P., Papma, J. M., Rabinovici, G. D., & Pijnenburg, Y. A. L. (2022). Research criteria for the behavioral variant of Alzheimer disease. *JAMA Neurology, 79*(1), 48–60. https://doi.org/10.1001/jamaneurol.2021.4417

Paoli, R. A., Botturi, A., Ciammola, A., Silani, V., Prunas, C., Lucchiari, C., Zugno, E., & Caletti, E. (2017). Neuropsychiatric burden in Huntington's Disease. *Brain Sciences, 7*(6), 67. https://doi.org/10.3390/brainsci7060067

Park, J.-H., Seo, S. W., Kim, C., Kim, S. H., Kim, G. H., Kim, S. T., Jeon, S., Lee, J. M., Oh, S. J., Kim, J. S., Choe, Y. S., Lee, K.-H., Shin, J. S., Kim, C. H., Noh, Y., Cho, H., Yoon, C. W., Kim, H. J., Ye, B. S., et al. (2014). Effects of cerebrovascular disease and amyloid beta burden on cognition in subjects with subcortical vascular cognitive impairment. *Neurobiology of Aging, 35*(1), 254–260. https://doi.org/10.1016/j.neurobiolaging.2013.06.026

Pasternak, E., & Smith, G. (2019). Chapter 6—Cognitive and neuropsychological examination of the elderly. In S. T. Dekosky & S. Asthana (Eds.), *Handbook of clinical neurology* (Vol. 167, pp. 89–104). Elsevier. https://doi.org/10.1016/B978-0-12-804766-8.00006-6

Paulsen, J. S., Langbehn, D. R., Stout, J. C., Aylward, E., Ross, C. A., Nance, M., Guttman, M., Johnson, S., MacDonald, M., Beglinger, L. J., Duff, K., Kayson, E., Biglan, K., Shoulson, I., Oakes, D., Hayden, M., & Predict-HD Investigators and Coordinators of the Huntington Study Group. (2008). Detection of Huntington's disease decades before diagnosis: The predict-HD study. *Journal of Neurology, Neurosurgery, and Psychiatry, 79*(8), 874–880. https://doi.org/10.1136/jnnp.2007.128728

Pedersen, K. F., Larsen, J. P., Tysnes, O.-B., & Alves, G. (2013). Prognosis of mild cognitive impairment in early Parkinson disease: The Norwegian ParkWest study. *JAMA Neurology, 70*(5), 580–586. https://doi.org/10.1001/jamaneurol.2013.2110

Perry, D. C., Brown, J. A., Possin, K. L., Datta, S., Trujillo, A., Radke, A., Karydas, A., Kornak, J., Sias, A. C., Rabinovici, G. D., Gorno-Tempini, M. L., Boxer, A. L., De May, M., Rankin, K. P., Sturm, V. E., Lee, S. E., Matthews, B. R., Kao, A. W., Vossel, K. A., et al. (2017). Clinicopathological correlations in behavioural variant frontotemporal dementia. *Brain, 140*(12), 3329–3345. https://doi.org/10.1093/brain/awx254

Peters, N. L. (1989). Snipping the thread of life. Antimuscarinic side effects of medications in the elderly. *Archives of Internal Medicine, 149*(11), 2414–2420.

Peters, R. (2006). Ageing and the brain. *Postgraduate Medical Journal, 82*(964), 84–88. https://doi.org/10.1136/pgmj.2005.036665

Petersen, R. C. (2004). Mild cognitive impairment as a diagnostic entity. *Journal of Internal Medicine, 256*(3), 183–194. https://doi.org/10.1111/j.1365-2796.2004.01388.x

Petersen, R. C., Smith, G. E., Waring, S. C., Ivnik, R. J., Tangalos, E. G., & Kokmen, E. (1999). Mild cognitive impairment: Clinical characterization and outcome. *Archives of Neurology, 56*(3), 303–308. https://doi.org/10.1001/archneur.56.3.303

Petersen, R. C., Doody, R., Kurz, A., Mohs, R. C., Morris, J. C., Rabins, P. V., Ritchie, K., Rossor, M., Thal, L., & Winblad, B. (2001). Current concepts in mild cognitive impairment. *Archives of Neurology, 58*(12), 1985–1992. https://doi.org/10.1001/archneur.58.12.1985

Petersen, R. C., Lopez, O., Armstrong, M. J., Getchius, T. S. D., Ganguli, M., Gloss, D., Gronseth, G. S., Marson, D., Pringsheim, T., Day, G. S., Sager, M., Stevens, J., & Rae-Grant, A. (2018). Practice guideline update summary: Mild cognitive impairment. *Neurology, 90*(3), 126–135. https://doi.org/10.1212/WNL.0000000000004826

Polsinelli, A. J., & Apostolova, L. G. (2022). Atypical Alzheimer Disease variants. *Continuum (Minneapolis, Minn.), 28*(3), 676–701. https://doi.org/10.1212/CON.0000000000001082

Postuma, R. B., Berg, D., Stern, M., Poewe, W., Olanow, C. W., Oertel, W., Obeso, J., Marek, K., Litvan, I., Lang, A. E., Halliday, G., Goetz, C. G., Gasser, T., Dubois, B., Chan, P., Bloem, B. R., Adler, C. H., & Deuschl, G. (2015). MDS clinical diagnostic criteria for Parkinson's disease. *Movement Disorders, 30*(12), 1591–1601. https://doi.org/10.1002/mds.26424

Prasad, S., Katta, M. R., Abhishek, S., Sridhar, R., Valisekka, S. S., Hameed, M., Kaur, J., & Walia, N. (2023). Recent advances in Lewy body dementia: A comprehensive review. *Disease-a-Month: DM, 69*(5), 101441. https://doi.org/10.1016/j.disamonth.2022.101441

Rabinovici, G. D., Carrillo, M. C., Forman, M., DeSanti, S., Miller, D. S., Kozauer, N., Petersen, R. C., Randolph, C., Knopman, D. S., Smith, E. E., Isaac, M., Mattsson, N., Bain, L. J., Hendrix, J. A., & Sims, J. R. (2017). Multiple comorbid neuropathologies in the setting of Alzheimer's disease neuropathology and implications for drug development. *Alzheimer's & Dementia (New York, N. Y.), 3*(1), 83–91. https://doi.org/10.1016/j.trci.2016.09.002

Raji, C. A., & Benzinger, T. L. S. (2022). The value of neuroimaging in dementia diagnosis. *Continuum (Minneapolis, Minn.), 28*(3), 800–821. https://doi.org/10.1212/CON.0000000000001133

Ranasinghe, K. G., Rankin, K. P., Pressman, P. S., Perry, D. C., Lobach, I. V., Seeley, W. W., Coppola, G., Karydas, A. M., Grinberg, L. T., Shany-Ur, T., Lee, S. E., Rabinovici, G. D., Rosen, H. J., Gorno-Tempini, M. L., Boxer, A. L., Miller, Z. A., Chiong, W., DeMay, M., Kramer, J. H., et al. (2016). Distinct subtypes of behavioral-variant frontotemporal dementia based on patterns of network degeneration. *JAMA Neurology, 73*(9), 1078–1088. https://doi.org/10.1001/jamaneurol.2016.2016

Randolph, C. (1998). *Repeatable battery for the assessment of neuropsychological Status: RBANS*. Pearson.

Rascovsky, K., Hodges, J. R., Knopman, D., Mendez, M. F., Kramer, J. H., Neuhaus, J., van Swieten, J. C., Seelaar, H., Dopper, E. G. P., Onyike, C. U., Hillis, A. E., Josephs, K. A., Boeve, B. F., Kertesz, A., Seeley, W. W., Rankin, K. P., Johnson, J. K., Gorno-Tempini, M.-L., Rosen, H., et al. (2011). Sensitivity of revised diagnostic criteria for the behavioural variant of frontotemporal dementia. *Brain: A Journal of Neurology, 134*(Pt 9), 2456–2477. https://doi.org/10.1093/brain/awr179

Roberts, R. O., Knopman, D. S., Mielke, M. M., Cha, R. H., Pankratz, V. S., Christianson, T. J. H., Geda, Y. E., Boeve, B. F., Ivnik, R. J., Tangalos, E. G., Rocca, W. A., & Petersen, R. C. (2014). Higher risk of progression to dementia in mild cognitive impairment cases who revert to normal. *Neurology, 82*(4), 317–325. https://doi.org/10.1212/WNL.0000000000000055

Rohrer, J. D., Woollacott, I. O. C., Dick, K. M., Brotherhood, E., Gordon, E., Fellows, A., Toombs, J., Druyeh, R., Cardoso, M. J., Ourselin, S., Nicholas, J. M., Norgren, N., Mead, S., Andreasson, U., Blennow, K., Schott, J. M., Fox, N. C., Warren, J. D., & Zetterberg, H. (2016). Serum neurofilament light chain protein is a measure of disease intensity in frontotemporal dementia. *Neurology, 87*(13), 1329–1336. https://doi.org/10.1212/WNL.0000000000003154

Román, G. C., Tatemichi, T. K., Erkinjuntti, T., Cummings, J. L., Masdeu, J. C., Garcia, J. H., Amaducci, L., Orgogozo, J.-M., Brun, A., Hofman, A., Moody, D. M., O'Brien, M. D., Yamaguchi, T., Grafman, J., Drayer, B. P., Bennett, D. A., Fisher, M., Ogata, J., Kokmen, E., et al. (1993). Vascular dementia: Diagnostic criteria for research studies: Report of the NINDS-AIREN international workshop. *Neurology, 43*(2), 250–250. https://doi.org/10.1212/WNL.43.2.250

Rosenberg, A., Ngandu, T., Rusanen, M., Antikainen, R., Bäckman, L., Havulinna, S., Hänninen, T., Laatikainen, T., Lehtisalo, J., Levälahti, E., Lindström, J., Paajanen, T., Peltonen, M., Soininen, H., Stigsdotter-Neely, A., Strandberg, T., Tuomilehto, J., Solomon, A., & Kivipelto, M. (2018). Multidomain lifestyle intervention benefits a large elderly population at risk for cognitive decline and dementia regardless of baseline characteristics: The FINGER trial. *Alzheimer's & Dementia: The Journal of the Alzheimer's Association, 14*(3), 263–270. https://doi.org/10.1016/j.jalz.2017.09.006

Rosenstein, L. D. (1998). Differential diagnosis of the major progressive dementias and depression in middle and late adulthood: A summary of the literature of the early 1990s. *Neuropsychology Review, 8*(3), 109–167. https://doi.org/10.1023/a:1025628925796

Rusconi, E. (2018). Gerstmann syndrome: Historic and current perspectives. *Handbook of Clinical Neurology, 151*, 395–411. https://doi.org/10.1016/B978-0-444-63622-5.00020-6

Salloway, S., Chalkias, S., Barkhof, F., Burkett, P., Barakos, J., Purcell, D., Suhy, J., Forrestal, F., Tian, Y., Umans, K., Wang, G., Singhal, P., Budd Haeberlein, S., & Smirnakis, K. (2022). Amyloid-related imaging abnormalities in 2 phase 3 studies evaluating Aducanumab in patients with early Alzheimer Disease. *JAMA Neurology, 79*(1), 13–21. https://doi.org/10.1001/jamaneurol.2021.4161

Salmon, D. P., & Filoteo, J. V. (2007). Neuropsychology of cortical versus subcortical dementia syndromes. *Seminars in Neurology, 27*(1), 7–21. https://doi.org/10.1055/s-2006-956751

Salthouse, T. A. (2009). When does age-related cognitive decline begin? *Neurobiology of Aging, 30*(4), 507–514. https://doi.org/10.1016/j.neurobiolaging.2008.09.023

Saylor, D., Dickens, A. M., Sacktor, N., Haughey, N., Slusher, B., Pletnikov, M., Mankowski, J. L., Brown, A., Volsky, D. J., & McArthur, J. C. (2016). HIV-associated neurocognitive disorder—Pathogenesis and prospects for treatment. *Nature Reviews. Neurology, 12*(4), 234–248. https://doi.org/10.1038/nrneurol.2016.27

Schott, J. M., & Crutch, S. J. (2019). Posterior cortical atrophy. *Continuum (Minneapolis, Minn.), 25*(1), 52–75. https://doi.org/10.1212/CON.0000000000000696

Sevigny, J., Chiao, P., Bussière, T., Weinreb, P. H., Williams, L., Maier, M., Dunstan, R., Salloway, S., Chen, T., Ling, Y., O'Gorman, J., Qian, F., Arastu, M., Li, M., Chollate, S., Brennan, M. S., Quintero-Monzon, O., Scannevin, R. H., Arnold, H. M., et al. (2016). The antibody aducanumab reduces Aβ plaques in Alzheimer's disease. *Nature, 537*(7618), 50–56. https://doi.org/10.1038/nature19323

Simonsen, A. H., Herukka, S.-K., Andreasen, N., Baldeiras, I., Bjerke, M., Blennow, K., Engelborghs, S., Frisoni, G. B., Gabryelewicz, T., Galluzzi, S., Handels, R., Kramberger, M. G., Kulczyńska, A., Molinuevo, J. L., Mroczko, B., Nordberg, A., Oliveira, C. R., Otto, M., Rinne, J. O., et al. (2017). Recommendations for CSF AD biomarkers in the diagnostic evaluation of dementia. *Alzheimer's & Dementia, 13*(3), 274–284. https://doi.org/10.1016/j.jalz.2016.09.008

Sitzer, D. I., Twamley, E. W., & Jeste, D. V. (2006). Cognitive training in Alzheimer's disease: A meta-analysis of the literature. *Acta Psychiatrica Scandinavica, 114*(2), 75–90. https://doi.org/10.1111/j.1600-0447.2006.00789.x

Skrobot, O. A., Black, S. E., Chen, C., DeCarli, C., Erkinjuntti, T., Ford, G. A., Kalaria, R. N., O'Brien, J., Pantoni, L., Pasquier, F., Roman, G. C., Wallin, A., Sachdev, P., Skoog, I., VICCCS group, Ben-Shlomo, Y., Passmore, A. P., Love, S., & Kehoe, P. G. (2018). Progress toward standardized diagnosis of vascular cognitive impairment: Guidelines from the vascular impairment of cognition classification consensus study. *Alzheimer's & Dementia: The Journal of the Alzheimer's Association, 14*(3), 280–292. https://doi.org/10.1016/j.jalz.2017.09.007

Smailagic, N., Vacante, M., Hyde, C., Martin, S., Ukoumunne, O., & Sachpekidis, C. (2015). 18F-FDG PET for the early diagnosis of Alzheimer's disease dementia and other dementias in people with mild cognitive impairment (MCI). *The Cochrane Database of Systematic Reviews, 2015*(1), CD010632. https://doi.org/10.1002/14651858.CD010632.pub2

Smith, G. E., & Bondi, M. W. (2013). *Mild cognitive impairment and dementia: Definitions, diagnosis, and treatment*. Oxford University Press.

Smith, G. E., Housen, P., Yaffe, K., Ruff, R., Kennison, R. F., Mahncke, H. W., & Zelinski, E. M. (2009). A cognitive training program based on principles of brain plasticity: Results from the improvement in memory with plasticity-based adaptive cognitive training (IMPACT) study. *Journal of the American Geriatrics Society, 57*(4), 594–603. https://doi.org/10.1111/j.1532-5415.2008.02167.x

Snowden, J. S. (2017). The neuropsychology of Huntington's Disease. *Archives of Clinical Neuropsychology, 32*(7), 876–887. https://doi.org/10.1093/arclin/acx086

Sperling, R. A., Aisen, P. S., Beckett, L. A., Bennett, D. A., Craft, S., Fagan, A. M., Iwatsubo, T., Jack, C. R., Kaye, J., Montine, T. J., Park, D. C., Reiman, E. M., Rowe, C. C., Siemers, E., Stern, Y., Yaffe, K., Carrillo, M. C., Thies, B., Morrison-Bogorad, M., et al. (2011). Toward defining the preclinical stages of Alzheimer's disease: Recommendations from the National Institute on Aging-Alzheimer's association workgroups on diagnostic guidelines for Alzheimer's disease. *Alzheimer's & Dementia: The Journal of the Alzheimer's Association, 7*(3), 280–292. https://doi.org/10.1016/j.jalz.2011.03.003

Stankovic, I., Krismer, F., Jesic, A., Antonini, A., Benke, T., Brown, R. G., Burn, D. J., Holton, J. L., Kaufmann, H., Kostic, V. S., Ling, H., Meissner, W. G., Poewe, W., Semnic, M., Seppi, K., Takeda, A., Weintraub, D., Wenning, G. K., & Movement Disorders Society MSA (MODIMSA) Study Group. (2014). Cognitive impairment in multiple system atrophy: A position statement by the neuropsychology task force of the MDS multiple system atrophy (MODIMSA) study group. *Movement Disorders: Official Journal of the Movement Disorder Society, 29*(7), 857–867. https://doi.org/10.1002/mds.25880

Stern, Y. (2012). Cognitive reserve in ageing and Alzheimer's disease. *Lancet Neurology, 11*(11), 1006–1012. https://doi.org/10.1016/S1474-4422(12)70191-6

Storandt, M., Grant, E. A., Miller, J. P., & Morris, J. C. (2002). Rates of progression in mild cognitive impairment and early Alzheimer's disease. *Neurology, 59*(7), 1034–1041. https://doi.org/10.1212/wnl.59.7.1034

Strozyk, D., Blennow, K., White, L. R., & Launer, L. J. (2003). CSF Abeta 42 levels correlate with amyloid-neuropathology in a population-based autopsy study. *Neurology, 60*(4), 652–656. https://doi.org/10.1212/01.wnl.0000046581.81650.d0

Taragano, F., Allegri, R., Krupitzki, H., Sarasola, D., Serrano, C., Loñ, L., & Lyketsos, C. (2009). Mild behavioral impairment and risk of dementia. *The Journal of Clinical Psychiatry, 70*(4), 584–592.

Teng, E. L., & Chui, H. C. (1987). The modified mini-mental state (3MS) examination. *The Journal of Clinical Psychiatry, 48*(8), 314–318.

Thijssen, E. H., La Joie, R., Strom, A., Fonseca, C., Iaccarino, L., Wolf, A., Spina, S., Allen, I. E., Cobigo, Y., Heuer, H., VandeVrede, L., Proctor, N. K., Lago, A. L., Baker, S., Sivasankaran, R., Kieloch, A., Kinhikar, A., Yu, L., Valentin, M.-A., et al. (2021). Association of Plasma P-tau217 and P-tau181 with clinical phenotype, neuropathology, and imaging markers in Alzheimer's disease and frontotemporal lobar degeneration: A retrospective diagnostic performance study. *The Lancet Neurology, 20*(9), 739–752. https://doi.org/10.1016/S1474-4422(21)00214-3

Townley, R. A., Graff-Radford, J., Mantyh, W. G., Botha, H., Polsinelli, A. J., Przybelski, S. A., Machulda, M. M., Makhlouf, A. T., Senjem, M. L., Murray, M. E., Reichard, R. R., Savica, R., Boeve, B. F., Drubach, D. A., Josephs, K. A., Knopman, D. S., Lowe, V. J., Jack, C. R., Petersen, R. C., & Jones, D. T. (2020). Progressive dysexecutive syndrome due to Alzheimer's disease: A description of 55 cases and comparison to other phenotypes. *Brain Communications, 2*(1), fcaa068. https://doi.org/10.1093/braincomms/fcaa068

Tuokko, H., Frerichs, R., Graham, J., Rockwood, K., Kristjansson, B., Fisk, J., Bergman, H., Kozma, A., & McDowell, I. (2003). Five-year follow-up of cognitive impairment with no dementia. *Archives of Neurology, 60*(4), 577–582. https://doi.org/10.1001/archneur.60.4.577

Ulugut Erkoyun, H., Groot, C., Heilbron, R., Nelissen, A., van Rossum, J., Jutten, R., Koene, T., van der Flier, W. M., Wattjes, M. P., Scheltens, P., Ossenkoppele, R., Barkhof, F., & Pijnenburg, Y. (2020). A clinical-radiological framework of the right temporal variant of frontotemporal dementia. *Brain: A Journal of Neurology, 143*(9), 2831–2843. https://doi.org/10.1093/brain/awaa225

van Dyck, C. H., Swanson, C. J., Aisen, P., Bateman, R. J., Chen, C., Gee, M., Kanekiyo, M., Li, D., Reyderman, L., Cohen, S., Froelich, L., Katayama, S., Sabbagh, M., Vellas, B., Watson, D., Dhadda, S., Irizarry, M., Kramer, L. D., & Iwatsubo, T. (2023). Lecanemab in early Alzheimer's Disease. *New England Journal of Medicine, 388*(1), 9–21. https://doi.org/10.1056/NEJMoa2212948

Vijverberg, E. G. B., Wattjes, M. P., Dols, A., Krudop, W. A., Möller, C., Peters, A., Kerssens, C. J., Gossink, F., Prins, N. D., Stek, M. L., Scheltens, P., van Berckel, B. N. M., Barkhof, F., & Pijnenburg, Y. A. L. (2016). Diagnostic accuracy of MRI and additional [18F]FDG-PET for behavioral variant frontotemporal Dementia in patients with late onset behavioral changes. *Journal of Alzheimer's Disease, 53*(4), 1287–1297. https://doi.org/10.3233/JAD-160285

Wang, Y., Liu, M., Lu, Q., Farrell, M., Lappin, J. M., Shi, J., Lu, L., & Bao, Y. (2020). Global prevalence and burden of HIV-associated neurocognitive disorder: A meta-analysis. *Neurology, 95*(19), e2610–e2621. https://doi.org/10.1212/WNL.0000000000010752

Wenning, G. K., Stankovic, I., Vignatelli, L., Fanciulli, A., Calandra-Buonaura, G., Seppi, K., Palma, J.-A., Meissner, W. G., Krismer, F., Berg, D., Cortelli, P., Freeman, R., Halliday, G., Höglinger, G., Lang, A., Ling, H., Litvan, I., Low, P., Miki, Y., et al. (2022). The Movement Disorder Society criteria for the diagnosis of multiple system atrophy. *Movement Disorders: Official Journal of the Movement Disorder Society, 37*(6), 1131–1148. https://doi.org/10.1002/mds.29005

Wessels, A. M., Dennehy, E. B., Dowsett, S. A., Dickson, S. P., & Hendrix, S. B. (2023). Meaningful clinical changes in Alzheimer Disease measured with the iADRS and illustrated using the Donanemab TRAILBLAZER-ALZ study findings. *Neurology: Clinical Practice, 13*(2). https://doi.org/10.1212/CPJ.0000000000200127

Wetzel, H. H., Gehl, C. R., Dellefave, L., Schiffman, J. F., Shannon, K. M., & Paulsen, J. S. (2011). Suicidal ideation in Huntington disease: The role of comorbidity. *Psychiatry Research, 188*(3), 372–376. https://doi.org/10.1016/j.psychres.2011.05.006

Withington, C. G., & Turner, R. S. (2022). Amyloid-related imaging abnormalities with anti-amyloid antibodies for the treatment of Dementia due to Alzheimer's Disease. *Frontiers in Neurology, 13*, 862369. https://doi.org/10.3389/fneur.2022.862369

Woods, S. P., & Tröster, A. I. (2003). Prodromal frontal/executive dysfunction predicts incident dementia in Parkinson's disease. *Journal of the International Neuropsychological Society: JINS, 9*(1), 17–24. https://doi.org/10.1017/s1355617703910022

Woolley, S. C., & Rush, B. K. (2017). Considerations for clinical neuropsychological evaluation in amyotrophic lateral sclerosis. *Archives of Clinical Neuropsychology, 32*(7), 906–916. https://doi.org/10.1093/arclin/acx089

Wright, S. L., & Persad, C. (2007). Distinguishing between depression and dementia in older persons: Neuropsychological and neuropathological correlates. *Journal of Geriatric Psychiatry and Neurology, 20*(4), 189–198. https://doi.org/10.1177/0891988707308801

Yaari, R., & Corey-Bloom, J. (2007). Alzheimer's disease. *Seminars in Neurology, 27*(1), 32–41. https://doi.org/10.1055/s-2006-956753

Chapter 16
Episodic Neurologic Symptoms

Priyanka Atit and Selim R. Benbadis

Key Points and Chapter Summary

- Paroxysmal neurologic symptoms are common, and identification relies on a comprehensive history.
- Global symptoms include seizures, syncope, encephalopathy and delirium and are classically present with altered mental status with minimal focal or lateralizing signs.
- Focal symptoms may be negative (aphasia, visual loss, weakness or numbness) or positive (visual auras, paresthesia's, jerks and other abnormal movements). In general, mental status is preserved.
- The physician should be familiar with these symptoms and their related disorders, to derive a focused testing and treatment plan.
- The neuropsychologist who suspects altered mental status should direct the patient to follow up immediately with their physician.

Overview

Paroxysmal neurologic symptoms are common and broad in scope. A comprehensive history is key to obtaining a focused differential diagnosis. History even supersedes neuroimaging and adjunct diagnostic techniques, which cannot adequately replace clinical judgment. Time course is one feature that can be particularly helpful

P. Atit
University of South Florida, Tampa, FL, USA

S. R. Benbadis (✉)
Department of Neurology, University of South Florida College of Medicine and Tampa General Hospital, Tampa, FL, USA
e-mail: sbenbadi@health.usf.edu

M. R. Schoenberg, J. G. Scott (eds.), *The Little Black Book of Neuropsychology*,
https://doi.org/10.1007/978-3-032-07777-6_16

regarding episodic neurologic symptoms. For example, onset and progression of symptoms, duration of episodes (seconds, minutes, hours) and resolution can help differentiate among the disorders described here.

This chapter will cover common causes of episodic neurologic symptoms. Based on the clinical presentation, we will divide syndromes into "global" or "focal."

Global Symptoms

Loss of Consciousness and Convulsions

- **Seizures:**
  - **Generalized tonic-clonic seizures**, also known as "grand mal" seizures, are the most common and dramatic type of seizures. They are stereotyped and consist of onset of rigid muscle tone (tonic phase) followed by rhythmic jerky movements (clonic phase) along with loss of awareness. The entire episode lasts 1–3 minutes. During the tonic phase, patients may bite the lateral aspect of their tongue which is a highly specific identifier for epileptic seizures. Urinary incontinence is also common, but not specific and can be seen in other global events such as syncope. Postictal somnolence may last from minutes to a few hours. Some patients experience a brief prodromal vague sensation such as depression or irritability for a few hours before the event (Benbadis, 2001). Focal onset seizures with secondary generalization may also be associated with other prodromal features such as déjà vu, an abdominal rising sensation, etc.
  - **Other seizure types include** myoclonic (brief, abrupt jerks), tonic (abrupt, generalized tonic stiffening with loss of consciousness) and atonic seizures (abrupt loss of muscle tone). The last two usually occur in severe childhood-onset epilepsies with static encephalopathy (Benbadis, 2001).
- See Chap. 17 in this volume for a detailed review of seizures and epilepsy.
- **Psychogenic Nonepileptic Seizures (PNES) also termed Psychogenic Nonepileptic Attacks (PNEA)** are an important and common misdiagnosis seen with epilepsy. Debate remains over terminology with some epileptologists referencing these events as psychogenic/functional seizures vs psychogenic attacks, with functional seizures currently being the preferred term. However, the word "seizure" can create confusion among patients and contribute to diagnostic uncertainty. Thus, attempts to move away from this nomenclature in favor of others such as PNEA continue to occur (Benbadis, 2010, 2020).

  PNEA should be suspected in patients with a high frequency of episodes that do not improve with medications (particularly with multiple medications) as well as changing semiology. Specific triggers such as stress, strong emotions and pain can be present which are unusual for epileptic seizures. PNEA tends to occur in

the presence of an audience, and occurrence in the physician's office or waiting room is particularly suggestive (Benbadis, 2005). Similarly, PNEA is not common in sleep. Characteristics seen during an event include long duration; gradual onset or termination; pseudo sleep; discontinuous (stop and go), irregular or asynchronous (out of phase) activity; side-to-side head movements; pelvic thrusting; opisthotonic posturing; stuttering; weeping; preserved awareness during bilateral motor activity; and persistent eye closure (Benbadis et al., 1996). Postictal rapid blinking, head shaking, looking around the room and whispering are highly specific and sensitive for PNEA (Gilmour et al). Psychogenic diagnoses, such as irritable bowel syndrome, fibromyalgia, chronic pain or chronic fatigue syndrome, are strong associations (Benbadis, 2005). Similarly, a florid review of systems (especially written lists of symptoms or diagnoses, i.e., hypergraphia) suggests somatization (Benbadis, 2006a). A premorbid psychiatric history should also raise the suspicion of PNEA. PTSD has been found to be the most associated psychiatric disorder, and a history of trauma (physical, sexual or emotional) is frequently reported among patients as well (Gilmour et al., 2021). EEG video monitoring is the "gold standard" for diagnosis of PNEA (Benbadis, 2006b).
  See Chap. 17 for a detailed review of PNEA.
- **Syncope** is commonly known as fainting and has various cardiac vs non-cardiac etiologies. A prodrome (i.e., presyncope) is typically present and includes features such as lightheadedness, nausea, diaphoresis or tunnel vision. Patients may also have chest pain, palpitations or shortness of breath which are more specific for non-neurologic causes of syncope. This prodrome, which typically lasts seconds to minutes, is followed by a loss of consciousness which consists of loss of tone. Brief myoclonic jerks may be seen which can mimic a seizure also known as "convulsive syncope." In contrast to seizures, these jerks occur after loss of consciousness (rather than before), and recovery is rapid (vs a prolonged postictal period). Studies have also shown that less than 10 myoclonic jerks favor syncope vs greater than 20 are more suspicious for epileptic seizures (Leibetseder et al., 2020). Syncopal etiologies frequently have triggers; pain, medical procedures, strong emotions or heat can be seen with vasovagal syncope and position in orthostatic hypotension/syncope. Urinary incontinence is seen with "global" events as described earlier and not a specific sign. Anterior tongue bites may occur, but lateral tongue bites should raise concern for an alternative etiology (seizures) if clinical history can be corroborated.
- **Hypoglycemia** rarely causes complete loss of consciousness. When it does, it resembles syncope and is preceded by florid prodromes of hunger, weakness, tremulousness, malaise and abnormal behaviors. Hypoglycemia typically occurs in reasonably obvious settings (e.g., a diabetic patient on insulin or oral hypoglycemics). If prolonged and severe, hypoglycemia can also cause an epileptic seizure (Cryer, 1999).
- **Narcolepsy** is characterized by frequent attacks of irresistible sleepiness, several times a day. This usually occurs after meals, while sitting in class or in unusual situations such as driving, talking or eating. The individual falls sleep for about

15 minutes, can be awoken easily and feels somewhat refreshed afterward. About 70 percent of patients report cataplexy, which consists of an abrupt loss of tone and is typically triggered by emotions such as laughter (Guilleminault & Gelb, 1995). Other associated features include sleep paralysis and vivid and terrifying hallucinations (hypnagogic hallucinations). Sleep studies usually confirm the diagnosis by demonstrating a short sleep latency of less than 10 minutes and sleep-onset REM appearing within 15 minutes after sleep onset.

- **Nonepileptic myoclonic jerks** arise from subcortical regions and are therefore not visible on EEG. They can be associated with a variety of causes such as toxic or metabolic disorders, or spinal cord lesions. Hiccups and hypnic jerks are examples of normal nonepileptic myoclonus. Hypnic jerks are benign myoclonic jerks that occur when falling asleep. They occur at all ages and can lead to evaluations for seizures, especially when the jerks are unusually violent. They are easily identified on EEG video because they occur in the transition state from wakefulness to stage 1 non-REM sleep and have no EEG correlation associated with the jerks (Montagna et al., 1988).
- **Transient ischemic attacks (TIAs)** are brief, transient episodes of focal neurologic symptoms caused by ischemia. A common misconception is that TIAs cause global cerebral symptoms like loss of consciousness. Instead, symptoms should be focal and localize to an intra-parenchymal vascular territory. For example, TIAs arising from the anterior circulation (carotids) might result in negative symptoms like weakness, aphasia or numbness. Carotid disease may also result in an unusual phenomenon called "limb shaking TIAs" which causes positive symptoms, i.e., rhythmic, jerky movements of a limb. The face should not be involved (Feyissa & Bower, 2022; Nadarajan et al., 2014). Vertebrobasilar insufficiency, on the other hand, results from transient hypoperfusion/ischemia to the posterior circulation, which supplies the reticular activating system, and can cause an impairment in consciousness. However, this typically occurs in association with other brain stem signs such as nausea/vomiting, dysarthria, balance difficulties and double vision.

  See Chap. 14 in this volume for a review of cerebrovascular disease and TIAs.

Key Points: Loss of Consciousness/Loss of Awareness and Convulsions

- Premonitory lightheadedness and rapid recovery of consciousness characterize syncope whereas convulsions and postictal confusion favor seizures.
- Consider PNEA if seizures are frequent and intractable and there is a comorbid psychogenic and psychiatric history.
- Check blood glucose, especially in diabetic patients.
- TIAs typically do not cause loss of consciousness.

Confusion, Mental Status Changes, Abnormal Behaviors

- **States of confusion** (i.e., encephalopathies) manifest with impairments in alertness, attention, orientation and recent memory. These abnormalities fluctuate in severity and tend to be worse at night. Illusions (misinterpretation of reality) are common. Depending on the etiology, confusion might progress to stupor or coma in advanced stages. The common etiologies of encephalopathy can be divided into three categories:
  - Systemic causes include metabolic (uremia, liver disease, anoxia, hyponatremia, hypoglycemia), toxic (alcohol or drug intoxication/withdrawal), nutritional (vitamin B12 and thiamine deficiencies) and infectious (sepsis, pneumonia) etiologies. Asterixis ("flapping tremor") is common if the underlying cause is metabolic or toxic. Typically, there are no lateralizing neurologic signs. Neuroimaging and CSF may show abnormalities in certain disorders such as infection, anoxia or hyponatremia. EEG generally demonstrates diffuse slowing or periodic patterns/triphasic waves which are nonspecific. No clinical finding is pathognomonic of a specific etiology and diagnosis is based on history and laboratory tests. See Table 16.1 for clinical features and laboratory findings that may help orient the clinician to a specific etiology.
  - Structural brain lesions such as tumors, strokes and abscesses can also present with confusion. However, in these instances, the physical examination should demonstrate focal signs (hemiparesis, aphasia, etc.) and brain imaging studies are abnormal.
  - Disorders that cause meningeal irritation such as meningoencephalitis and subarachnoid hemorrhage. Signs of meningeal irritation include headache, fever and nuchal rigidity. Typically, there are no lateralizing neurologic signs, and the CSF is abnormal demonstrating blood (subarachnoid hemorrhage) or pleocytosis (meningitis). Brain imaging may show signs of meningeal involvement.
- **Delirium** is a state of fluctuating confusion marked by significant inattention, altered perception (illusions and hallucinations) and psychomotor overactivity (agitation, tremor, insomnia). Autonomic overactivity is a distinguishing feature and is manifested by tachycardia, profuse sweating, hypertension and hyperthermia. After recovery, patients are typically amnestic to the episode. Delirium and encephalopathy are terms often used interchangeably since the diagnostic and therapeutic approaches are similar. However, as described above, delirium has several distinguishing features and recognizing them may help the clinician narrow the differential diagnosis since this condition is usually due to drug toxicity and withdrawal (most commonly alcohol) or systemic illness.
- It is of critical importance to differentiate between delirium and dementia since the underlying pathologic process and prognosis are different. There are clear features that distinguish the two. Dementia develops slowly, has a chronic course, and is usually not reversible. In contrast, delirium generally develops acutely, has

a fluctuating course (worse at night) and is frequently reversible if the underlying medical cause is treated. Dementia denotes cognitive decline, classically memory, with disturbances of consciousness or perception seen in advanced stages. On the other hand, delirium manifests with prominent deficits in attention and consciousness from onset. Agitation and visual hallucinations are frequently present. A common situation encountered in everyday practice is that of an elderly patient with a presumed pre-existing dementia who presents with delirium. This condition, also known as "beclouded dementia," is usually triggered by an acute illness such as infections, electrolyte abnormalities, surgeries or new medications. The underlying dementia (and onset of this) might not be obvious in an acute state of confusion. Please see Chap. 15, this volume, for a detailed review of dementia and mild cognitive impairment (MCI).

- Review of Table 16.1 illustrates a summary of common sources of encephalopathy and associated clinical features and laboratory findings. An EEG may be helpful to identify potential encephalopathies. For instance, periodic patterns can be seen in severe encephalopathies such as anoxic brain injuries. Triphasic waves are typically seen in liver failure and uremia. Hypoglycemia is readily identified by low blood glucose; a common threshold for levels resulting in encephalopathy is below 30 mg/dl. Wernicke's encephalopathy is caused by a thiamine deficiency which is seen more commonly in alcoholics, and characterized by a triad of confusion, ataxia and abnormal eye movements.

- **Seizures** can also present with abnormal behavior, rather than convulsions with loss of consciousness (Benbadis, 2001). See Chap. 17 in this volume for more information.

Table 16.1 Clinical and laboratory features of common etiologies of encephalopathy

Disorder	Important clinical findings	Important laboratory findings
Liver failure	Asterixis, jaundice, ascites	Elevated blood ammonia, elevated liver enzymes EEG: Triphasic waves
Uremia	Hypertension, dry skin, uriniferous breath, myoclonic jerks, seizures	Elevated BUN and creatinine EEG: Triphasic waves
Anoxia	Rigidity, decerebrate posture Seizures, myoclonus	Hypoxemia EEG: Periodic patterns
Hypoglycemia	Tremor, hunger, sweating, headache, palpitations	Low blood glucose (usually below 30 mg/dl)
Alcohol intoxication	Slurred speech, ataxia, alcohol breath, Hypothermia, hypotension	High alcohol levels
Alcohol withdrawal	Tremors, seizures, delirium	Normal alcohol levels
Wernicke's encephalopathy	Confusion, ataxia and ophthalmoplegia in alcoholics	Low transketolase activity (index of thiamine deficiency)
B12 deficiency	Apathy, emotional instability, paresthesias, loss of vibratory sense, leg weakness, ataxia	Low blood B12 levels, elevated homocysteine and elevated methylmalonic acid

    - **Focal seizures with impaired awareness** commonly originate in the temporal lobe. The episode may start with an aura which the patient is aware of. Common aura descriptions include visceral sensations such as nausea, butterflies, or a rising epigastric sensation (French et al., 1993). This may be accompanied by fear, or fear may exist alone as the second most common aura. Other less common features include olfactory and gustatory hallucinations, alteration of visual perceptions (micropsia, macropsia) and dyscognitive states (déjà vu, jamais vu). As the seizure spreads within a neuronal network, altered awareness follows where individuals may demonstrate associated automatisms (lip smacking, chewing, swallowing or picking on clothes). A postictal state is common and may last for minutes to hours. After the attack, the patient typically has no memory of the events.
    - **Absence seizures** are much briefer and present with blank staring (behavioral arrest) for only a few seconds. They almost always begin in childhood. Adult-onset absence seizures are highly atypical.

- **Transient global amnesia (TGA)** is characterized by profound anterograde amnesia. Patients are awake, alert, aware of their identity, and otherwise cognitively intact but cannot form new memories, and ask repetitive questions. This can last up to several hours and then self-resolve. TGA is considered a monophasic phenomenon. Repeated episodes should alert the clinician to evaluate for alternative etiologies. The cause is not known but stressful events may trigger episodes. Compared to seizures, TGA episodes are longer, and persistent postictal anterograde amnesia is also not typical after seizures (Feyissa & Bower, 2022; Bartsch & Butler, 2013; Quinette et al., 2006).
- **Dissociative fugue** is characterized by the sudden inability to remember pertinent information coupled with leaving home and taking on a different identity. The person is usually not aware that they have assumed a new identity.
- **Panic attacks** are paroxysmal manifestations of anxiety or a panic disorder. Abrupt and intense fear is accompanied by at least four of the following symptoms: palpitations, diaphoresis, tremulousness or shaking, shortness of breath or sensation of choking, chest discomfort, nausea or abdominal discomfort, dizziness, or lightheadedness, derealization or depersonalization, fear of losing control, fear of dying, paresthesia's and chills or hot flashes. The symptoms typically peak within 10 minutes. Panic disorder often coexists with other manifestations of anxiety such as agoraphobia, social phobia and depressive disorders. Panic attacks can be mistaken for seizures since fear is a relatively common (psychic) aura in patients with temporal lobe epilepsy. If the episode evolves into a clear seizure, the diagnosis is easy but can be difficult in the absence of other seizure types (Biraben et al., 2001).
- **Parasomnias** are short-lived paroxysmal behaviors that occur out of sleep. In particular, the non-REM parasomnias (night terrors, sleepwalking and confusional arousals) can superficially resemble seizures since they include complex behaviors and some degree of unresponsiveness and amnesia for the event. The non-REM parasomnias are most common between the ages of 4 and 12 years,

and night terrors are particularly common. They are often familial and may be worsened by stress, sleep deprivation and intercurrent illnesses. Similarly, rhythmic movement disorder is a parasomnia typically seen at transition or stage 1 sleep, which can also resemble partial seizures. One common example is head banging (jactatio capitis). Among REM sleep parasomnias, nightmares rarely present a diagnostic challenge, but REM behavior disorders may with violent and injurious behaviors during REM sleep. The diagnosis of REM behavior disorder is usually easy as it affects older men and the description of acting out a dream is quite typical. However, EEG video may be necessary to make the distinction (provided that the episodes are frequent enough). EEG video will confirm the absence of an EEG seizure and usually shows that the behavior arises from a specific stage of sleep (Iranzo et al., 2005).

Key Points: Confusion and Mental Status Changes

- Encephalopathy presents with confusion, distractibility, memory loss and decreased level of consciousness.
- Encephalopathy can be due to
    - Systemic causes (metabolic, infectious, toxic, etc.)
    - Structural lesions
    - Meningeal irritation
- Delirium presents like encephalopathy but differs with perceptual changes (hallucinations or illusions), psychomotor agitation and autonomic dysfunction.
- Parasomnias are paroxysmal behaviors occurring out of sleep (sleep walking, confusional arousals, night terrors).

Global Weakness

Generalized *fatigue* is not usually a symptom of neurologic disease and is typically related to systemic factors. True *motor (muscular) weakness* (different from global fatigue) can be indicative of a neurologic process. When this is the case, mental status (sensorium, alertness and attention) is normal.

- **Myasthenia Gravis** is an autoimmune disorder of the neuromuscular junction, which typically causes weakness of the ocular, facial, oropharyngeal and limb muscles. Ocular involvement with ptosis (eye lid droop) and diplopia (double vision) typically presents first. These small muscles fire frequently and thus fatigue easily. Other symptoms include dysphagia, dysphonia and dysarthria due to weakness of the facial and bulbar muscles. Proximal limb and neck weakness is present in 20–30 percent of patients. The distinguishing feature is a fluctuation of symptoms, worsening with activity or toward the end of the day. This can be demonstrated on the physical exam by fatigable weakness. Respiratory muscle weakness or failure may also be present in severe cases. Deep tendon reflexes are spared. The diagnosis is supported by the presence of serum antibodies to the neuromuscular junction such as acetylcholine receptors (AcHR), muscle-specific kinase (MuSK) and lipoprotein receptor-related protein 4 (LRP4), as well as neurophysiology studies. EMG/NCV will be normal at rest. With repetitive nerve stimulation, a decremental response can be seen with slow stimulation. SFEMG (single-fiber EMG) is the most sensitive test and can assist with clarification as well.

- **Lambert-Eaton myasthenic syndrome (LEMS)** is also an autoimmune disorder of the neuromuscular junction. Compared to myasthenia, weakness predominantly affects proximal limb muscles with relative sparing of ocular and bulbar muscles. Deep tendon reflexes are typically decreased, but strength and reflexes can be improved by a brief period of contraction (facilitation). Autonomic symptoms, such as dry mouth, are frequently part of the syndrome. The diagnosis is confirmed by the presence of antibodies against presynaptic voltage-gated calcium channels. EMG/NCV baseline motor studies are abnormal, with improvement shown with brief exercise or rapid stimulation. About two-thirds of patients have an associated malignancy, most commonly small cell lung cancer.
- **Periodic paralysis** can present with attacks of acute, severe limb weakness. Primary hyperkalemic periodic paralysis typically presents during childhood with attacks of muscle weakness lasting up to a few hours. Triggers include rest after exercise and potassium-rich foods. Hypokalemic periodic paralysis is more common and typically presents in childhood or adolescence with episodes of acute paralysis during the night or early morning. These attacks can be precipitated by meals rich in carbohydrates and sodium, stress and strenuous exercise. The ocular and bulbar muscles are typically spared. Reflexes are diminished or absent. For both syndromes, strength returns to baseline in between episodes.
- **Metabolic myopathies** are a group of disorders caused by abnormalities in muscle metabolism. It includes disorders of glycogen, lipid or mitochondrial metabolism. Typical symptoms are exercise intolerance, muscle pain, stiffness, cramps, fatigue and sometimes weakness of proximal and distal muscles. Genetic testing and muscle biopsy are used for diagnosis.

Key Points: Generalized Weakness

- Weakness can reflect systemic illness or a symptom of a neurologic process.
- Neuromuscular diseases include:
  - Myasthenia Gravis—predominately weakness of ocular, facial/bulbar, oropharyngeal and limb muscles.
  - Lambert-Eaton myasthenic syndrome—weakness of proximal extremities, with sparing of ocular and facial/bulbar muscles. Diminished reflexes and autonomic dysfunction are also present.

- Metabolic myopathies often include muscle pain, stiffness, cramps, fatigue and weakness of proximal and distal muscles which are triggered by exercise.
- Episodic limb weakness may indicate a periodic paralysis.
- Somatic, conversion, factitious or malingering disorders present with generalized weakness that is variable or inconsistent. Discontinuous resistance during testing of power ("give way weakness") is noted.

Dizziness and Vertigo

- **Benign paroxysmal positional vertigo (BPPV)** consists of brief (less than 1 minute) episodes of vertigo prompted by a change in head position, such as turning over in bed. Vertigo is described as an illusion of movement (usually spinning). Nausea can be present. Typically, BPPV manifests with symptomatic episodes lasting from a few days to several months, interspersed by asymptomatic intervals of several months to years in duration. The diagnosis is confirmed by the Dix-Hallpike maneuver which involves provocation of vertigo by position testing and observation of typical nystagmus (Lanska & Remler, 1997). Treatment involves vestibular therapy with otoconia re-positioning via maneuvers similar to the Dix-Hallpike.
- **Vertebrobasilar TIAs** are caused by transient ischemia in the territory supplied by the vertebrobasilar system, namely, the brain stem and cerebellum. They can present with episodes of vertigo or lightheadedness but are almost always accompanied by other signs of brain stem dysfunction such as diplopia, dysarthria, bifacial numbness, ataxia and weakness or numbness. Rarely, isolated vertigo can be a manifestation of vertebrobasilar insufficiency and should be suspected in patients with cerebrovascular risk factors (Gomez et al., 1996).
- **Basilar migraine** is a form of migraine with prominent brainstem symptoms. Patients are usually young women or children with a family history of migraines. The first symptoms of the attack involve visual phenomena affecting both complete visual fields, such as "flashing lights," scintillating scotomas and sometimes temporary blindness. The visual symptoms are often associated with vertigo, staggering incoordination of the limbs, dysarthria and tingling in the hands and feet. These symptoms last 10–30 minutes and are usually followed by an occipital headache. In some patients, the basilar-type aura may occur without a headache (Kirchmann et al., 2006).
- **Meniere disease and other labyrinthine diseases** are a constellation of labyrinthine diseases. Symptoms include acute, recurring episodes of severe vertigo with nausea and vomiting, as well as mild tinnitus and deafness. Other symptoms include nystagmus beating away from the impaired labyrinthine and falling/swaying while walking which is often ipsilateral to labyrinthine impairment. In

classic Meniere disease, vertigo attacks occur with a rapid onset and last for minutes to 1–2 hours in duration.

- **Presyncope,** as described above, is a constellation of prodromal symptoms preceding a syncopal (i.e., fainting) episode. Patients complain of queasiness and lightheadedness. If the individual has enough time to lie down, loss of consciousness may be prevented. Patients frequently describe these symptoms as "dizziness" which can be confused with vertigo (illusion of movement).
- **Vestibular Neuronitis (Labyrinthitis) also known as acute unilateral peripheral vestibulopathy** classically describes a paroxysmal, often single attack, of vertigo without tinnitus or deafness (as is found in Meniere disease). Typical onset is in early to middle adulthood and may be preceded by an upper respiratory infection. Vertigo onset is over hours to a few days and can last several days in duration. During the period of severe vertigo, extreme nausea is also common. Symptoms subside in days.

Key Points: Dizziness and Vertigo

- Vertigo is NOT dizziness.
  - Vertigo is a sensation of rotation, whirling or spinning (movement) or perception of objects spinning around or moving rhythmically in one direction.
  - Dizziness as a complaint may include vertigo, but may also describe non-moving perception such as lightheadedness, faintness (syncope), blurred vision and unsteadiness.
- Causes of vertigo include:
  - Benign paroxysmal positional vertigo
  - TIAs (involving vertebral or basilar arteries)
  - Migraine (basilar)
  - Meniere disease and labyrinthine diseases
  - Vestibular neuronitis

Focal Symptoms

A focal neurologic deficit typically affects a specific location, such as the unilateral face, arm or leg. When there is cortical involvement, specific functions such as speech, writing or calculation can also be involved as well as vision. Focal neurologic deficits may result from both central and peripheral neurologic disorders, but central is more common. Negative symptoms (loss of movement or sensation, visual field cuts, etc.) or positive symptoms (abnormal movements, tingling or visualization of flashing lights) may result. The type, location and severity of the change can

Table 16.2 Common disorders causing transient *focal* neurologic symptoms

	Clinical features	Time frame	Helpful tests
TIA	Negative symptoms (monocular visual loss, focal sensory loss or weakness)	Onset within a few seconds (<5 s), maximum deficit at onset Duration: minutes to hours	MRI CTA/MRA/US carotids EKG, echocardiogram
Seizure	Positive symptoms (twitching, tingling). Focal symptoms may evolve into GTC seizure	Onset or march in several seconds	EEG MRI
Migraine	Mixed positive and negative symptoms Evolution into clear migraine	Onset or march of symptoms over the course of minutes	None

indicate the area of the brain or nervous system that is affected. The most common disorders causing transient focal neurologic symptoms are outlined in Table 16.2.

Abnormal Movements

- **Focal motor seizures** consist of simple motor movements, typically a single type of clonic or tonic contraction of a muscle or group of muscles. They are usually brief (15 seconds to 2 min) and consciousness is not impaired. These seizures typically arise from motor regions of the frontal lobe. Interictal EEG may show focal epileptiform discharges localized to the affected area. Because the ictal discharge involves only a small area of the brain, ictal scalp EEG is only abnormal about 25% of the time (Devinsky et al., 1989). Please also see Chap. 17 in this volume for a review of seizures and epilepsy.
- **Acute dystonic reactions** are seen in the setting of dopamine receptor blockade such as with antipsychotics (neuroleptics, including atypical ones) and antiemetics. Other drugs can also be involved (e.g., carbamazepine, lithium, trazodone, illicit drugs). Dystonic reactions typically occur within one to four days of medication administration and are characterized by torsion/twisting movements affecting the cranial, pharyngeal and cervical muscles. Oculogyric crisis is a subtype characterized by acute conjugate eye deviation, usually in an upward direction. The typical attack lasts one to two hours, during which the abnormal movement occurs repetitively for seconds to minutes. These dystonic reactions respond very well and rapidly to anticholinergics (trihexyphenidyl, benztropine, diphenhydramine) and levodopa (Dressler & Benecke, 2005).
- **Hemifacial spasm (HFS)** is a chronic progressive disorder that causes painless irregular clonic contractions of muscles within the facial nerve territory. HFS typically affects the periorbital muscles first and then spreads to other ipsilateral facial muscles over a period of months to years. Over time or with exacerbations,

the clonic movements can result in a sustained tonic contraction causing forceful unilateral eyelid closure. HFS can be idiopathic or symptomatic and may resemble a facial clonic seizure, but clear differences make the differentiation easy. By contrast, seizures are paroxysmal (not chronic progressive) and typically affect the perioral muscles due to a large representation on the motor homunculus.

- **Tics** are characterized by involuntary, sudden, purposeless, repetitive, stereotyped, motor movements such as blinking, shoulder shrugging, mouth opening or vocalizations (sniffing, throat clearing, barking). Stereotypy and irresistibility are the main identifying features. The patient will admit to making the movements and feels compelled to do so to relieve perceived tension. Such movements can be suppressed for a short time by an effort of will, but they reappear as soon as the subject's attention is diverted.

Key Points: Focal Abnormal Movements
- Focal motor seizures
- Acute dystonic reactions
- Hemifacial spasm
- Motor tics

Weakness

- **Transient ischemic attacks (TIAs)** are a common cause of focal weakness, especially in older individuals with cerebrovascular risk factors. Unlike the transient focal weakness in migraine which tends to spread from one part of the body to another within several minutes, symptoms in TIA are stroke-like, i.e., maximal acutely and involving all affected parts simultaneously. Seizures do not manifest with ictal weakness. However, some confusion between TIAs and seizures may occur when the seizure is un-witnessed and the patient appears with a focal deficit (e.g., Todd's paralysis described below), especially since both will improve over time (Benbadis, 2007). In these cases, an accurate history of the event is essential to differentiate the two. Most TIA symptoms last 2–15 minutes but may range from seconds to an hour. Episodes lasting more than an hour are more likely to leave permanent neurologic deficits. TIAs may result in a single episode of transient symptoms, but events recurring several times over days, weeks or months also occur. It is important to separate a single transient episode from repeated ones that present with the same symptoms. The latter are more often a warning sign of impending vascular occlusion. See Chap. 14 as well for details of cerebrovascular disease.
- **Todd's paralysis** typically follows a focal motor seizure. There might be transient paralysis of the affected limbs lasting for minutes to a few hours, usually in proportion to the duration of the seizure. Continued focal paralysis beyond this time usually indicates a focal brain lesion (stroke, tumor, etc.) as the cause of the

seizure. A similar phenomenon can occur with seizures involving the language, sensory and visual areas.

- **Migraine auras** can cause transient focal neurologic symptoms. Usually these are positive phenomenon such as visual auras and paresthesias but may include weakness as well. Migraine symptoms tend to evolve in minutes and "march" (spread from one involved part to the other). As the symptoms begin to recede, they are followed by a unilateral throbbing headache. In some patients, the weakness is prolonged and may outlast the headache. This rare condition is known as hemiplegic migraine and has a strong familial trait.
- **Spinal cord or plexus damage/impingement** can cause focal neurologic weakness that rarely may be transient or fluctuating.

Key Points: Focal Weakness/Paralysis

- Transient ischemic attacks (TIAs)—symptoms tend to present acutely and resolve over minutes to an hour.
- Migraine auras/headache—symptoms tend to present over minutes and can spread from one part to the other.
- Todd's paralysis—transient paralysis of the affected face or limb lasting minutes to hours following a seizure.
- Conversion/factitious/malingering disorder—weakness due to psychogenic etiology.

Headaches and Facial Pain

- **Migraine** is characterized by periodic headaches beginning in childhood, adolescence or early adult life. Migraine with aura, termed *classic migraine*, presents with focal neurologic symptoms ("aura"), most often visual (flashing, flickering lights, scintillating scotomas) followed within several minutes by a unilateral, less often bilateral, throbbing headache accompanied by nausea, vomiting and sensitivity to light (photophobia) and sounds (phonophobia). More commonly, migraine headaches appear without preceding neurologic symptoms (migraine without aura) and are termed *common migraine*. Migraine is a ubiquitous familial disorder. About 60–80 percent of classic migraine cases have a family history.
- **Cluster headaches** are characterized by severe, unilateral pain localized in the orbital, supraorbital or temporal area lasting from 15 to 180 minutes. The typical patient is a young adult man. The episodes occur from one every other day to eight per day and nightly occurrence is characteristic. Autonomic symptoms are invariably present on the side of the pain and include rhinorrhea, lacrimation, conjunctival injection, ptosis and myosis. The headache tends to recur regularly

for periods ("clusters") extending over 6–12 weeks followed by pain-free intervals for many months.

- **Paroxysmal hemicrania** is a unilateral headache that resembles cluster headaches in some respects including the short duration of the attacks, the location in the temporo-orbital region and the accompanying autonomic symptoms on the same side of the pain. Unlike cluster headaches, the episodes occur many times a day, are even shorter in duration (2–45 minutes) and recur daily for long periods that could extend to years (Goadsby, 2001). This disorder affects more women than men and responds dramatically to indomethacin.
- **Trigeminal neuralgia** presents with paroxysmal, excruciating pain, described as stabbing or electric-like sensations, localized in the distribution of the trigeminal nerve (usually second or third divisions). The pain is brief (seconds to less than two minutes) and can be triggered by touching the face, brushing the teeth, talking or eating. Physical exams are unremarkable. Most of the cases are idiopathic or due to compression of the nerve by a tortuous blood vessel. On the other hand, the finding of facial sensory loss or an abnormal corneal reflex should raise suspicion for a structural brain lesion such as tumor, basilar artery aneurysm or multiple sclerosis.

Key Points: Headache and Facial Pain

- Cluster headache is characterized by severe unilateral pain localized in the orbital, supraorbital or temporal areas lasting 15 minutes to 3 hours, occurring typically at night, 1–8 times per day for weeks to 3 months, followed by an interval of months with no headache (headaches occur in clusters).
- Migraine is typically a unilateral throbbing headache associated with nausea, phonophobia and photophobia lasting minutes to hours.
  - Common—no aura
  - Classic—headache preceded by aura
- Paroxysmal hemicrania is a unilateral headache like cluster headaches but of shorter duration (2–45 minutes), occurs more frequently per day and occurs for longer periods of time (up to several years with daily headache). Responds well to indomethacin.
- Trigeminal neuralgia is abrupt paroxysmal excruciating pain of stabbing quality that lasts seconds to several minutes and is localized to the trigeminal nerve distribution (typically second and third divisions). Onset can be triggered by touching the face, gums, eating or talking. A blood vessel compressing the nerve may be seen.
- Conversion/Factitious/malingering disorder—headache with psychogenic etiology.

Limb Pain

- **Episodic limb pain** is usually caused by non-neurological conditions such as musculoskeletal disorders. However, the "shooting" character of the pain due to nerve root disease (radiculopathy) can be perceived as episodic or intermittent. Radiculopathies frequently cause paresthesias (numbness or tingling) and the physical examination typically reveals decreased sensation and, if severe, weakness and decreased deep tendon reflexes in the distribution of one or more nerve roots. Painful dystonia (sustained, unnatural posture of a limb due to co-contraction of agonist and antagonist muscles) is not uncommon in patients with Parkinson's disease and occurs frequently at night, particularly when the dopaminergic medications wear off (Grandas & Iranzo, 2004).

Aphasia

- **TIAs** involving the cortical language areas are by far the most common cause of transient aphasia (fluent, non-fluent or both) in which symptoms typically last several minutes. Commonly, language disturbance is accompanied by negative symptoms, such as focal weakness and numbness, but it can present in isolation. In a patient with cardiovascular risk factors, transient aphasia should be considered a TIA until proven otherwise. If symptoms persist after hours to days, a stroke is significantly more likely.
- **Focal seizure** arising from the cortical language areas may give rise to a brief aphasic disturbance (ictal aphasia). In most cases, it is usually followed by other focal or generalized seizure activity but may (rarely) occur in isolation. Episodes should be brief, lasting less than 15 minutes in duration. More commonly, aphasia is a component of a postictal state (postictal aphasia) which typically lasts minutes or a few hours.
- See also Chaps. 8 and 13 for a detailed review of language problems and aphasia syndromes.

Visual Loss

- **Transient monocular blindness or amaurosis fugax** is caused by ischemia of the ophthalmic artery or its branches such as the central retinal artery (CRAO) or branch retinal arteries (BRAO). This may occur from atherosclerotic risk factors or vasculitis such as giant cell arteritis. Transient ocular ischemia is the most common mechanism of transient visual loss (Biousse & Trobe, 2005). Patients usually report negative symptoms such as graying, blurring, darkening, fogging or dimming of vision in the eye. Some patients describe a curtain that descends quickly over the eye. The visual loss is painless and can involve partial or complete visual fields depending on arterial involvement. For example, CRAO occlusions will cause complete vision loss while BRAO occlusions may cause partial vision loss. The most important and common ophthalmoscopic finding in patients with transient monocular blindness is occlusion of the retinal arteries. There should be no optic disk edema.

- **Migraine**. Occasionally patients with migraines have attacks of monocular or binocular visual loss. Descriptors of the visual loss are not different from those used by patients with carotid artery occlusive disease. Most patients have complete loss of vision rather than altitudinal symptoms (Winterkorn & Teman, 1991). Some have aches or discomfort in the eye during attacks. Attacks can be frequent and occur more than once a day. This diagnosis should be considered in patients with a history of migraine after excluding other disorders such as carotid artery disease.
- **Increased intracranial pressure in patients with pseudotumor cerebri**. Patients with pseudotumor cerebri (idiopathic intracranial hypertension) have transient visual obscurations (Merle et al., 1998). These are often monocular but can be binocular. The episodes are usually brief and often precipitated by coughing, straining or other maneuvers that elevate intracranial pressure. Bilateral abducens nerve palsies may be present. Prominent headaches are invariably associated (Digre, 2002).
- **Optic neuritis** typically begins with subacute central vision loss over hours to days (Glaser, 1990). Optic neuritis is typically unilateral but can present as bilateral in certain syndromes such as neuromyelitis optica spectrum disorder (NMOSD) and myelin oligodendrocyte glycoprotein antibody-associated disease (MOGAD). It is associated with pain (90%) in or behind the eye, particularly with eye movement, and the involved pupil reacts poorly to light (afferent pupillary defect). Ophthalmologic exam will show optic nerve edema which is also seen in brain imaging. This disorder most frequently affects young individuals and can be seen in demyelinating disorders such as multiple sclerosis or NMOSD and MOGAD.
- **Giant cell arteritis** is likely the most well-known cause of arteritic anterior ischemic optic neuropathy (AAION). The disorder classically affects patients older than 55 (with a female predominance) and is frequently associated with headaches. Scalp tenderness, jaw claudication and systemic symptoms such as low-grade fever, malaise, weight loss and polymyalgia rheumatica may also occur. AAION and CRAO are the most common etiologies of vision loss in this disorder. Most of these patients have persistent rather than transient monocular visual loss. Elevated ESR, thrombocytopenia, anemia and abnormalities on temporal

artery ultrasound are suggestive for the diagnosis. Diagnosis is confirmed by a temporal artery biopsy.

Key Points: Vision Loss

- Transient monocular blindness (amaurosis faux) is loss of vision in one eye typically presenting as blurring or graying of vision due to transient ocular ischemia.
- Migraine auras/headache is typically described as monocular visual loss and can occur more than once per day.
- Pseudotumor cerebri (increased intracranial pressure) results in transient vision loss that is typically monocular but can be binocular. Vision loss is of short duration (seconds to minutes) and associated with straining (coughing, laughing, sneezing, etc.).
- Optic neuritis is progressive loss of vision over several days and is associated with pain in or behind the affected eye and there is often an afferent pupillary defect (no pupil constriction).
- Conversion/factitious/malingering disorder—vision complaints due to psychogenic etiology.

Sensory Symptoms ("Numbness, Tingling")

The main disorders that cause transient focal weakness, such as TIA, seizures and migraine, can also present with focal sensory symptoms involving a limb, part of the face or the entire hemibody when the disease affects the somatosensory pathways (e.g., the parietal cortex). Focal seizures typically cause "positive" symptoms (e.g., tingling) that spread or "march" over seconds. In contrast, TIAs produce negative symptoms ("dead numbness or sensory loss") involving all affected parts simultaneously. Migraine can produce both negative and positive symptoms, which typically "march" over minutes and are usually followed by a headache. Recurrent attacks of multiple sclerosis can manifest as focal numbness, tingling or pain, but the episodes classically evolve over days or weeks, not seconds or minutes.

Hallucinations

In general hallucinations that are of organic origin tend to be *unformed*, whereas hallucinations of psychiatric origin are *formed* and have a strong "content" (usually paranoid). The main causes of organic hallucinations are seizures and migraines.

- **Migraines** tend to cause visual hallucinations in the aura phase. They are usually unformed (fortification spectra), associated with a scotoma (negative symptom), and evolve or "march" slowly (over minutes). Of course, they are usually followed by a typical headache, but "acephalgic" migraine does exist.

- **Hallucinations caused by seizures** can involve any of the 5 senses are unformed and evolve or "march" over seconds. Their epileptic nature can be impossible to prove or disprove when they occur with no other seizure types, since even ictal EEG is less helpful with focal seizures without impaired awareness. Fortunately, when hallucinations are seizures, they usually will evolve into other (obvious) seizure types.

The most common disorders causing transient focal neurologic signs are illustrated in Table 16.2. Transient ischemic attacks (TIAs) typically produce negative symptoms, such as "dead numbness" and weakness reaching maximal severity within seconds. The presence of carotid or vertebrobasilar artery disease on the MRI or a cardiac source of emboli identified by echocardiogram supports the diagnosis. In contrast, focal seizures cause positive symptoms (twitching, tingling) that spread ("march") from one part of the body to another over a few seconds. The EEG confirms the diagnosis if an epileptic focus is identified.

Many of the transient neurologic symptoms above can be differentiated by a good clinical history alone. However, cell phone videos are a very valuable extension of this history and can help clarify ambiguous events and facilitate a diagnosis. For example, cell phone videos have been used with great accuracy to clarify epileptic vs nonepileptic events (Amin et al., 2021; Benbadis, 2023; Tatum et al., 2020).

References

Amin, U., Primiani, C. T., MacIver, S., Rivera-Cruz, A., Frontera, A. T., Jr., & Benbadis, S. R. (2021 September). Value of smartphone videos for diagnosis of seizures: Everyone owns half an epilepsy monitoring unit. *Epilepsia, 62*(9), e135–e139. https://doi.org/10.1111/epi.17001

Bartsch, T., & Butler, C. (2013, February). Transient amnesic syndromes. *Nature Reviews Neurology, 9*(2), 86–97. https://doi.org/10.1038/nrneurol.2012.264

Benbadis, S. R. (2001). Epileptic seizures and syndromes. *Neurologic Clinics, 19*, 251–270.

Benbadis, S. R. (2005). A spell in the epilepsy clinic and a history of "chronic pain" or "fibromyalgia" independently predict a diagnosis of psychogenic seizures. *Epilepsy & Behavior, 6*(2), 264–265.

Benbadis, S. R. (2006a). Hypergraphia and the diagnosis of psychogenic attacks. *Neurology, 67*(5), 904.

Benbadis, S. R. (2006b). Psychogenic non-epileptic seizures. In E. Wyllie (Ed.), *The treatment of epilepsy: Principles and practice* (4th ed., pp. 623–630). Lippincott Williams & Wilkins.

Benbadis, S. R. (2007). Differential diagnosis of Epilepsy. *Continuum: Lifelong Learning in Neurology, 13*(4), 48–70.

Benbadis, S. R. (2010, July 6). Psychogenic nonepileptic "seizures" or "attacks"? It's not just semantics: Attacks. *Neurology, 75*(1), 84–86. https://doi.org/10.1212/WNL.0b013e3181e6216f

Benbadis, S. R. (2020). Functional seizures? "So I still have seizures, right?". *Epilepsy & Behavior*. https://doi.org/10.1016/j.yebeh.2020.107082

Benbadis, S. R. (2023, February). The best seizure diagnostic tool is not a medical device: Why stand-alone video review needs a current procedural terminology code. *Neurology Clinical Practice, 13*(1), e200117. https://doi.org/10.1212/CPJ.0000000000200117

Benbadis, S. R., Lancman, M. E., King, L. M., & Swanson, S. J. (1996). Preictal pseudosleep: A new finding in psychogenic seizures. *Neurology, 47*(1), 63–67.

Biousse, V., & Trobe, J. D. (2005). Transient monocular visual loss. *American Journal of Ophthalmology, 140*, 717–721.
Biraben, A., Taussig, D., Thomas, P., et al. (2001). Fear as the main feature of epileptic seizures. *Journal of Neurology, Neurosurgery and Psychiatry, 70*(2), 186–191.
Cryer, P. E. (1999). Symptoms of hypoglycemia, thresholds for their occurrence, and hypoglycemia unawareness. *Endocrinology and Metabolism Clinics of North America, 28*(3), 495–500, v–vi.
Devinsky, O., Sato, S., Kufta, C. V., et al. (1989). Electroencephalographic studies of simple partial seizures with subdural electrode recordings. *Neurology, 39*(4), 527–533.
Digre, K. B. (2002). Idiopathic intracranial hypertension headache. *Current Pain and Headache Reports, 6*, 217–225.
Dressler, D., & Benecke, R. (2005). Diagnosis and management of acute movement disorders. *Journal of Neurology, 252*(11), 1299–1306.
Feyissa, A. M., & Bower, J. H. (2022, October 12). Evaluation of the patient with paroxysmal spells mimicking epileptic seizures. *Neurologist*. https://doi.org/10.1097/NRL.0000000000000469
French, J. A., Williamson, P. D., Thadani, V. M., et al. (1993). Characteristics of medial temporal lobe epilepsy: I. Results of history and physical examination. *Annals of Neurology, 34*, 774–780.
Gilmour, G. S., MacIsaac, R., Subotic, A., Wiebe, S., & Josephson, C. B. (2021, August). Diagnostic accuracy of clinical signs and symptoms for psychogenic nonepileptic attacks versus epileptic seizures: A systematic review and meta-analysis. *Epilepsy & Behavior, 121*(Pt A), 108030. https://doi.org/10.1016/j.yebeh.2021.108030
Glaser, J. S. (1990). *Clinical neuro-ophthalmology* (2nd ed.). Lippincott.
Goadsby, P. J. (2001). Cluster and other short-lived headaches. In *American Academy of Neurology, 53rd Annual Meeting, Philadelphia, May 5–11, 2001*.
Gomez, C., Cruz-Flores, S., Malkoff, C., Sauer, M., & Burch, C. (1996). Isolated vertigo as a manifestation of vertebrobasilar ischemia. *Neurology, 47*, 94–97.
Grandas, F., & Iranzo, A. (2004). Nocturnal problems occurring in Parkinson's disease. *Neurology, 63*(8), S8–S11.
Guilleminault, C., & Gelb, M. (1995). Clinical aspects and features of cataplexy. *Adv Neurol, 67*, 65–77.
Iranzo, A., Santamaria, J., Rye, D. B., et al. (2005). Characteristics of idiopathic REM sleep behavior disorder and that associated with MSA and PD. *Neurology, 65*(2), 247–252.
Kirchmann, M., Lykke Thomsen, L., & Olesen, J. (2006). Basilar-type migraine, clinical, epidemiologic, and genetic features. *Neurology, 66*, 880–886.
Lanska, D. J., & Remler, B. (1997). Benign paroxysmal positioning vertigo: Classic descriptions, origins of the provocative positioning technique, and conceptual developments. *Neurology, 48*, 1167–1177.
Leibetseder, A., Eisermann, M., LaFrance, W. C., Jr., Nobili, L., & von Oertzen, T. J. (2020, December 1). How to distinguish seizures from non-epileptic manifestations. *Epileptic Disorders, 22*(6), 716–738. https://doi.org/10.1684/epd.2020.1234
Merle, H., Smadja, D., Ayeboua, L., et al. (1998). Benign intracranial hypertension. Retrospective study of 20 cases. *Journal Francais d'Ophtalmologie, 21*, 42–50.
Montagna, P., Liguori, R., Zucconi, M., et al. (1988). Physiological hypnic myoclonus. *Electroencephalography and Clinical Neurophysiology, 70*(2), 172–176.
Nadarajan, V., Perry, R. J., Johnson, J., & Werring, D. J. (2014, February). Transient ischaemic attacks: Mimics and chameleons. *Practical Neurology, 14*(1), 23–31. https://doi.org/10.1136/practneurol-2013-000782
Quinette, P., Guillery-Girard, B., Dayan, J., et al. (2006). What does transient global amnesia really mean? Review of the literature and thorough study of 142 cases. *Brain, 129*(pt 7), 1640–1658.
Tatum, W. O., Hirsch, L. J., Gelfand, M. A., Acton, E. K., LaFrance, W. C., Jr., Duckrow, R. B., Chen, D. K., Blum, A. S., Hixson, J. D., Drazkowski, J. F., Benbadis, S. R., Cascino, G. D., & OSmartViE Investigators. (2020, May 1). Assessment of the predictive value of outpatient

smartphone videos for diagnosis of epileptic seizures. *JAMA Neurology, 77*(5), 593–600. https://doi.org/10.1001/jamaneurol.2019.4785
Winterkorn, J. M., & Teman, A. J. (1991). Recurrent attacks of amaurosis fugax treated with calcium channel blockers. *Annals of Neurology, 30*, 423–425.

Chapter 17
Epilepsy and Seizures

Michael R. Schoenberg, Mary Ann Werz, Cady Block, Luis Cruz-Saavedra, Angelica Rivera-Cruz, Selim Benbadis, and Daniel L. Drane

Key Points and Chapter Summary

- Epilepsy is a common neurological disorder occurring across the lifespan and often associated with neurocognitive, emotional-behavioral and social-adaptive deficits/comorbidities.
- Neuropsychological deficits are greatest for patients with symptomatic epilepsies and catastrophic epilepsy syndromes, but idiopathic "benign" epilepsies also have been found to produce at least mild neuropsychological deficits—Even in newly diagnosed but untreated epilepsy.
- Controlling seizures (seizure freedom) is strongly related to decreasing cognitive comorbidity
- 30–40% of patients with epilepsy are refractory to current medications
- Neuropsychological data have value in predicting surgical outcome among adults with no currently identifiable lesion on structural neuroimaging and temporal lobe seizure onset

M. R. Schoenberg (✉)
Departments of Psychiatry and Neurosciences, Neurology, and Neurosurgery, University of South Florida College of Medicine, Tampa, FL, USA
e-mail: Mschoenb@health.usf.edu

M. A. Werz
Department of Neurology, University of Iowa Carver School of Medicine, Iowa City, IA, USA
e-mail: mary-werz@uiowa.edu

C. Block
Emory University, Atlanta, GA, USA
e-mail: Cady.Block@mayo.edu

M. R. Schoenberg, J. G. Scott (eds.), *The Little Black Book of Neuropsychology*,
https://doi.org/10.1007/978-3-032-07777-6_17

Overview

Epilepsy represents an important area of clinical neuropsychological practice and research. Historically, clinical neuropsychological studies primarily involved patients with seizures that were not adequately controlled by antiseizure medications (ASMs), termed medically refractory or intractable epilepsy. However, the role of the neuropsychological evaluation and the clinical neuropsychologist has expanded well beyond a narrow focus on patients with medically intractable epilepsy. This chapter provides an overview of the application of neuropsychology, psychology and quality of life to patients with epilepsy (Sect. "Overview"), followed by special sections for the clinical neuropsychologist in the surgery team (Sect. "Neuropsychological (Cognitive and Behavioral) Comorbidity in Epilepsy") and an overview of assessment practices (Sect. "Neuropsychological Assessment Guide").

The provision of neuropsychological services to persons with epilepsy often requires the practitioner to fill a variety of roles, which are most often rooted in evidence-based practices (e.g., Chelune, 2008). In 2020, the International League Against Epilepsy (ILAE; Baxendale et al., 2020) outlined several important functions of neuropsychological assessment in the context of epilepsy, including (a) presurgical assessment; (b) baseline for outcome comparison; (c) contribution to seizure characterization, lateralization and localization; (d) identification of cognitive risks associated with the procedure; (e) feedback and presurgical counseling; and (f) postsurgical assessment. We add further detail to this across six aspects:

1. *Predicting neurocognitive and emotional-behavioral outcomes.* Neuropsychological data have shown to be independent predictors of cognitive outcome following neurological surgery for treatment of medication refractory epilepsy (e.g., (Baxendale & Thompson, 2020; Chelune, 1995; Novais et al., 2022; Rausch, 2006; Seidenberg et al., 1998; Stroup et al., 2003). An emphasis is to identify patients at high risk for meaningful decline (generally regarded

---

L. Cruz-Saavedra
Mayo Clinic, Jacksonville, FL, USA
e-mail: Luis.Cruz-Saavedra@mayo.edu

A. Rivera-Cruz
University of South Florida, College of Medicine, Tampa, FLA, USA
e-mail: Acruz@health.usf.edu

S. Benbadis
Department of Neurology, University of South Florida College of Medicine and Tampa General Hospital, Tampa, FL, USA
e-mail: sbenbadi@health.usf.edu

D. L. Drane
Department of Neurology, School of Medicine, Emory University, Atlanta, GA, USA

Department of Neurology, University Washington School of Medicine, Seattle, WA, USA
e-mail: ddrane@emery.edu

as decline sufficient to result in functional change in social, occupational, academic or self-care). While traditional neuropsychological assessment is the mainstay here, efforts at calculators and nomograms have been underway (e.g., https://riskcalc.org/CognitiveAndMoodAfterEpilepsySurgery) (Busch et al., 2018).

2. *Predicting seizure freedom.* Although limited to select cases, emerging studies have shown neuropsychological data can add unique variance in predicting the likelihood a patient will be seizure free after surgical treatment (e.g., Helmstaedter & Kockelmann, 2006; Keary et al., 2007; Potter et al., 2009; Sawrie et al., 1998; Seidenberg et al., 1998). Often the additive predictive value is demonstrated for individuals with normal neuroimaging (i.e., nonlesional) or incongruent ictal and interictal EEG findings, and generally has not included multiple non-invasive studies in addition to neuropsychological data (e.g., MEG/MSI, fMRI, PET, SISCOM studies). Some studies have not found unique variance for neuropsychological evaluation as a seizure outcome predictor (Baxendale & Thompson, 2020), but the issues involved are complicated and in need of further study.
3. *Assessing postsurgical cognitive and behavioral function.* Postsurgical neuropsychological evaluation can help guide postsurgical planning of (a) medical treatment and rehabilitation, and (b) educational/vocational pursuits, and can (c) assist in determining competency, and/or (d) assist in making placement decisions (e.g., Drane, 2015; Fastenau et al., 2004; Hermann et al., 2008)
4. *Confirming lateralization and/or localization of the epileptogenic zone and the presence of brain dysfunction.* Within surgical contexts, neuropsychological data can be quite useful for confirming seizure onset zones, but dysfunction is often broader due to a variety of issues related to seizure spread and sensitivity to broader medical, psychiatric and neurological comorbidities. Due to these latter factors, neuropsychological testing can be less effective than other presurgical studies predicting specific regions of dysfunction, although support for lateralizing value is increasing (Helmstaedter, 2004; Hennessy et al., 2001; Keary et al., 2007; Potter et al., 2009; Rausch, 2006; Sawrie et al., 1998). Neuropsychological data have proven somewhat useful for evaluating the functional adequacy of medial temporal lobes and other cerebral areas (e.g., Chelune, 1995; Hermann & Loring, 2008; Seidenberg et al., 1998; Stroup et al., 2003), although there is room for significant improvement in this area.
5. *Providing a baseline assessment of cognitive function.* Neuropsychological baseline data may be used, along with other variables, to identify children and adults at increased risk for the development of neuropsychological, cognitive, academic and psychiatric problems from time of first recognized seizure (Byars et al., 2008; Fastenau et al., 2009). Neuropsychological data provide an objective method to monitor for changes in patients' cognitive and behavioral functioning over time (i.e., longitudinal assessment of cognitive function for patients with focal or generalized epilepsies) and assist in formulating interventions to offset potential for further neuropsychological and academic deficits (Fastenau et al., 2009; Helmstaedter et al., 2003; Hermann et al., 2008).
6. *Assessing the effects of ASMs on neurocognitive and emotional-behavioral function.* Neuropsychological testing has been very useful over the years for measur-

ing potential side effects of ASMs (e.g., Aldenkamp et al., 2003; Drane & Meador, 2002; Kluger & Meador, 2008) (see Table 17.8).

7. *Identifing and formulating treatment plans for patients with psychogenic nonepileptic seizures* (also termed psychogenic nonepileptic attacks or functional seizures) (See Chap. 18, this volume).

The clinical care of epilepsy has reflected an area of medicine having a strong multidisciplinary model, particularly with respect to neuropsychology. Neurological surgery is often successful at eliminating seizures in carefully selected patients (see Sect. "Neuropsychological (Cognitive and Behavioral) Comorbidity in Epilepsy"; e.g., Ojemann & Valiante, 2006); however, resection of brain tissue presents with a variety of risks extending beyond more traditional surgical morbidity (i.e., hemorrhage, infection) and mortality (i.e., death) such as postsurgical neurological (e.g., somatosensory loss or hemiparesis), cognitive and/or psychiatric morbidity (e.g., Baxendale et al., 2013; Helmstaedter et al., 1998; Macrodimitris et al., 2011; Ojemann & Valiante, 2006). The cognitive risks to neurological surgery were highlighted by the report of Scoville and Milner (1957) of patient "H.M.," who underwent bilateral temporal lobectomy in 1953 for the treatment of refractory epilepsy that resulted in a profound amnestic syndrome. Thus, the clinician and patient must balance the potential of being seizure free following surgical treatment against the possible neurological, neurocognitive, emotional-behavioral and social-adaptive risks to the patient's outcome (Ojemann & Jung, 2006). The presurgical neuropsychological evaluation continues to provide important data to inform this clinical decision-making process (e.g., Hermann et al., 2007; Stroup et al., 2003). From a research standpoint, data from patients who underwent elective neurological surgery have helped to formulate our current understanding of the functional neuroanatomy of memory and language (e.g., Drane et al., 2015; Drane & Pedersen, 2019; Hermann et al., 1999; Lezak et al., 2004; Ojemann et al., 1989; Saling, 2009). Indeed, the understanding of human neuropsychology owes a profound debt to patients who have provided data over the many years.

This chapter is meant as a targeted review of the neuropsychological aspects of epilepsy and its treatment. However, we will also endeavor to provide a review of the diagnosis of epilepsy, seizure classification, seizure semiology and the prevalence and incidence of seizures and epilepsy. Because neuropsychologists are integral members of epilepsy centers, it is important for the neuropsychologist to be aware of factors affecting the treatment and variables affecting surgical outcome, both in terms of neuropsychological outcome and in terms of seizure freedom. We then summarize the treatment of seizures and components of a presurgical evaluation for medication-refractory (intractable) epilepsy. Finally, we summarize decades of research attempting to delineate risk factors for postsurgical neuropsychological impairment following neurological surgery for the treatment of medically refractory epilepsy. Table 17.1 lists some common terms in epilepsy and epilepsy treatment.

Table 17.1 Diagnostic tools in epilepsy

Study	Description	Purpose
Neurological exam	Cursory mental status exam along with cranial nerve, motor, coordination and sensory exams	Lateralize and/or localize neurologic dysfunction
EEG interictal	Regional slowing, sharp waves, spikes and polyspikes	Support a diagnosis of epilepsy and help determine epilepsy syndrome
Ictal video EEG	Provides seizure semiology and EEG changes during a seizure	Diagnose epilepsy and determine epilepsy syndrome
MRI	High-resolution imaging. Studies at epilepsy centers include specific high-resolution imaging sequences with increased sensitivity	Identify lesions that are associated with epilepsy such as tumors, vascular malformations and cortical malformations
Interictal PET	Measures regional blood flow and glucose metabolism in the brain	These are often decreased at the seizure focus consistent with impaired brain function. The area of hypometabolism (dysfunction) is usually larger than the seizure focus, and may be bilateral. The area of hypometabolism can decrease (improved regional blood flow) after successful epilepsy surgery
Ictal SPECT	Short half-life radioligands serving as indirect measures of neuronal activity based on regional blood flow changes in the brain	Blood flow markedly increases during a seizure. The radioligand must be injected immediately at seizure onset to identify the seizure onset zone and not seizure propagation pathways
Wada	Amobarbital, methohexital or ethosuximide is injected into an internal carotid artery resulting in a short duration of brain anesthesia to areas of the brain affected (usually the middle cerebral, anterior cerebral and, less often, posterior cerebral artery areas). During the period of anesthesia (often measured by EEG) and typically lasting 3–5 minutes with amobarbital, language and memory function are evaluated. The patient is asked to follow commands, repeat and name words/pictures. Memory is assessed after drug effects have worn off with recall and recognition of words and/or objects previously presented	Lateralize specific language functions (i.e., comprehension, repetition, naming, fluency, reading) to a hemisphere as well as lateralize memory function generally considered to measure the functional adequacy of each hemisphere to support language and memory function

(continued)

Table 17.1 (continued)

Study	Description	Purpose
MEG/MSI	Record magnetic fields produced by currents from cortical neurons. Sharp waves corresponding to those seen on surface EEG can be identified. During magnetic source imaging (MSI), functional mapping of language, motor and sensory cortex is done	Localize interictal activity from the seizure focus. MEG can detect sharp waves from deep cortical sulci that may not be detectable by surface EEG. MSI may provide alternative to Wada test and fMRI to identify functional areas of cognitive functions (language and memory)
fMRI	Measures cerebral blood flow, known as BOLD MRI sequences. Areas of brain involved in performing tasks theorized to have increased blood flow	Functional mapping of eloquent cortex (i.e., cortex involved in activities such as language and hand movements). Has also been applied to memory function

Note: EEG, electroencephalogram; *fMRI*, functional magnetic resonance imaging; *MEG*, magnetoelectroencephalogram; *MRI*, magnetic resonance imaging; *MSI*, magnetic source imaging that is a combination of MEG and MRI; *PET*, position emission tomography; *SPECT*, single-photon emission computed tomography

Making a Diagnosis

Seizures are paroxysmal (abrupt) events due to abnormal hypersynchronous discharge of neurons associated with behavioral change (Falco-Walter et al., 2018; Porter, 1993). Seizures may be provoked due to a variety of conditions or unprovoked (Benbadis, 2009; Krumholz et al., 2015). Anyone can have a seizure that is provoked. Common etiology for a provoked seizure includes (a) hyponatremia or low sodium in the blood, (b) hypoglycemia or low blood sugar, (c) injury to the brain parenchyma such as a stroke, open head injury or central nervous system infection, (d) sudden cessation of drinking alcohol in a person physically addicted to alcohol and (e) overdose of some medications and/or illicit drugs.

Epilepsy is traditionally defined as the occurrence of more than one unprovoked seizure (i.e., a seizure not provoked by an illness or brain injury) (Falco-Walter et al., 2018; Fisher et al., 2014). However, diagnosing epilepsy is a complicated process and involves both identifying the *type* of seizure (generalized or focal) and the presumed etiology of the epilepsy (or epilepsy syndrome). Epilepsy syndromes include seizures with similar semiology and epidemiologic characteristics. For example, juvenile myoclonic epilepsy is genetic in etiology and includes absence, myoclonic and generalized tonic-clonic seizures often upon awakening that typically has an onset in adolescence (Janz & Durner, 1995). A classification scheme for epilepsy has been evolving over the years, but the most commonly used is the ILAE (Epilepsy, 1989) and includes approximately 30 distinct syndromes (see Appendix 1). This classification system continues to be revised over time, with an initial revision published in 2017 (see Appendix 2). In summary, remember that patients with epilepsy have seizures, but not all patients who have had a seizure meet diagnostic criteria for epilepsy.

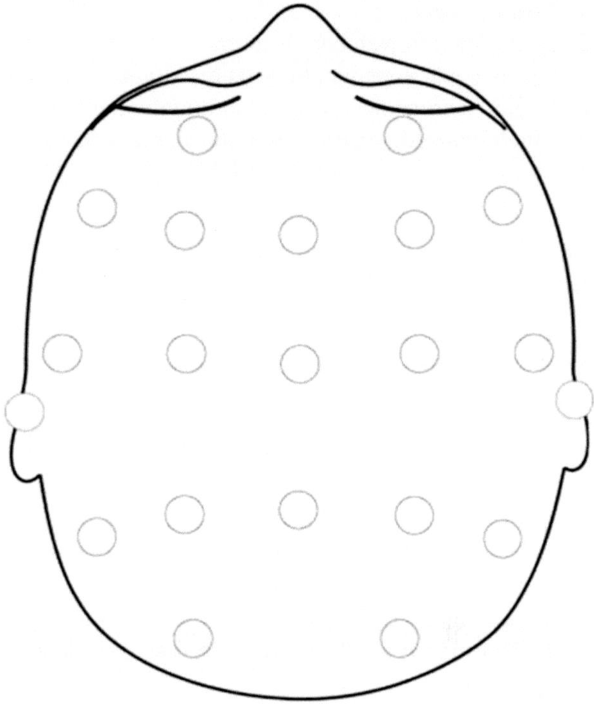

Fig. 17.1 EEG electrode placement of 10–10 standard

Diagnosing seizures is ideally made by measuring the neuronal activity of the brain by placement of electrodes on the scalp, termed an electroencephalogram (EEG), as well as semiology. Electrode placement has been standardized. Figure 17.1 displays the placement of EEG electrodes with the older 10–20 placement, and Fig. 17.2 displays the current 10–10 electrode placement (Society, 1986). The semiology of a seizure reflects the evaluation of the behavioral features associated with the period immediately before a seizure (pre-ictal period), during a seizure (ictus or ictal period) and immediately following a seizure (postictal period). The time between seizures is termed the interictal period. Seizure semiology (i.e., clinical expression of a seizure) varies depending upon the localization of seizure onset, duration, and propagation pathways of discharging neurons. These are reviewed in detail below (see also Tables 17.6 and 17.7).

Seizures must be distinguished from other conditions that can mimic features of a seizure. Common conditions that may present with symptoms suggestive of a seizure include:

1. Cardiac conditions
   a. Structural (i.e., hypertrophic cardiomyopathy, aortic stenosis)
   b. Rhythm (i.e., sick sinus syndrome, ventricular tachycardia)
2. Migraine headache
3. Metabolic conditions (hypoglycemia, hyponatremia, etc.)

4. Parasomnias
5. Paroxysmal movement disorders
6. Psychogenic nonepileptic seizures/attacks (pnes/pnea/fs)
7. Reflex neurogenic syncope (autonomic neuropathy, vasovagal, post-exertional, cough induced, micturition induced, medication related, etc.)
8. Transient ischemic attack(s)/stroke

Incidence/Prevalence

Seizures/epilepsy is the third most common neurological disorder after headache and dementia (see Table 17.2) and is one of the top five largest contributors to neurological disability (Collaborators, 2024). This burden is further compounded by health inequities; nearly 80% of the 50 million people living with seizures/epilepsy reside in lower- and middle-income countries, with respective treatment gaps of 75% and 50% (World Health Organization, 2019). In fact, the World Health Organization (WHO) recently developed a global action plan to address epilepsy diagnosis and care (see https://iris.who.int/handle/10665/371495).

In general, the prevalence of epilepsy is thought to be about 1% (Helmers et al., 2015; Thurman et al., 2016). The lifetime prevalence rate of epilepsy is thought to

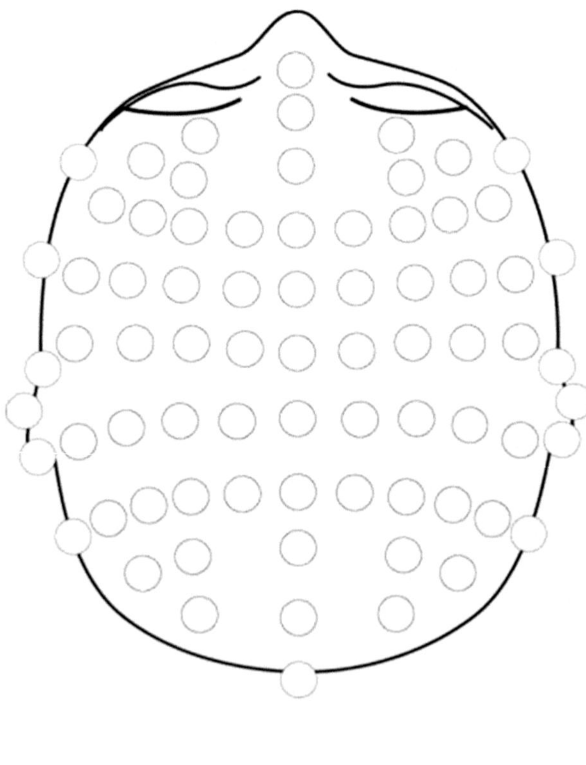

Fig. 17.2 EEG electrode placement of 10–20 standard

Table 17.2 Prevalence of seizures and epilepsy

Prevalence	Seizures	Epilepsy
Lifetime	9–10%	3%
Point	0.6%	1%

be about 3%. The lifetime prevalence rate of seizures is about 9–10%. The annual incidence rate of seizures is 44–88:100,000. It is thought about 300,000 people in the USA have a seizure each year. The incidence rate for seizures is highest for individuals under the age of 2 years and older than 65 years, with common precipitating factors including fever, traumatic brain injury, cerebrovascular disease/insult, infection and metabolic insults. Epilepsy incidence is higher in lower- and middle-income countries (139:100,000 vs 48.9:100,000, respectively), and in lower socioeconomic classes in higher-income countries—especially persons of color (Beghi & Hesdorffer, 2014; Fiest et al., 2017; Kaiboriboon et al., 2013).

Injury or infection to the brain increases the risk for developing seizures and epilepsy. A seizure due to injury is termed posttraumatic seizure (PTS), and experiencing two or more seizures after a head injury is termed posttraumatic epilepsy (PTE). The terminology and definition of PTS and PTE represent another area where terminology and definitions continue to be refined. At present, a seizure is now considered provoked if occurring within 7 days of the traumatic brain injury (TBI), while seizures after the first 7 days are defined as unprovoked. Another differential is for "early" and "late" seizures. Early seizures are those occurring after 24 hours of TBI but within 7 days of TBI. Late seizures are defined as onset of seizures 7 days after injury. The risk of posttraumatic seizures and epilepsy is lowest for closed head injuries and highest for penetrating head injuries. Seizure risk also varies by injury severity, such that individuals with mild closed head brain injury have a risk of seizure that is less than one percent (0.7%), increasing to 1.2% for moderate TBI, and 10% with severe TBI. The risk of PTE is highest for penetrating injuries, and is generally considered to be about 53%. The risk of having an unprovoked seizure *after* a first unprovoked seizure is about 86%. Most posttraumatic epilepsy develops within the first year of injury, but posttraumatic seizures may develop years after the injury. Table 17.3 summarizes prevalence for TBI. Risk factors for developing PTE are depressed skull fracture, brain contusion, intracranial hemorrhage, longer coma duration, lower Glasgow Coma Scale score and older age at time of TBI.

Seizure Classification

The classification of epilepsies allows clinicians to provide a diagnosis, and inform patients and their families about factors that play a key role in the disease, such as seizure triggers, risks of comorbidities, treatment considerations and overall prognosis. It provides researchers with tools to further investigate the pathophysiology behind the disease, and work on the development of new therapeutic modalities. The ILAE updated the classification of seizure types and epilepsies in 2017 (Fisher

Table 17.3 Prevalence of posttraumatic epilepsy

Head injury type	Injury subtype	Epilepsy prevalence
Closed	Normal imaging (mild TBI)	0.7–1%
	Normal imaging (moderate to severe TBI)	1.2–5%
	Abnormal imaging	10–25%
	Overall prevalence	0.7–7.3%
Open	Korean and Vietnam veterans	53%
	Overall	35–80%

et al., 2017a, 2017b; Scheffer et al., 2017). These were revisions from the latest seizure type classification system published in 1981, and the latest epilepsy classification system published in 1989. This new ILAE classification system is centered on three diagnostic stages: seizure type, epilepsy type and epilepsy syndrome.

These revisions were necessary for several reasons: some seizure types can have both a focal and generalized onset, some seizures are unclassifiable, new seizure types needed to be included and some terminologies needed clarification. Some of the main changes are as follows: (1) The term "partial" is changed to "focal." (2) Some seizures can be classified as unknown onset. (3) The terms "simple partial," "complex partial" and "secondary generalized" were eliminated, and are now termed "focal aware," "focal unaware" and "focal to bilateral tonic-clonic seizures," respectively. (4) New focal seizure types are described, including automatisms, cognitive, hyperkinetic and sensory. (5) Some seizure types could have a focal or a generalized onset, including epileptic spasms, myoclonic, atonic, tonic and clonic seizures. (6) New generalized seizure types were added, including epileptic spasms, myoclonic-tonic-clonic, myoclonic-atonic, myoclonic absence and absence with eyelid myoclonia. (7) The term convulsion is eliminated, as this is ambiguous, and could represent tonic, clonic, tonic-clonic or myoclonic seizures (Fisher et al., 2017a) (Table 17.4).

The first objective in seizure type classification is to determine whether the seizure is of focal onset, generalized onset or unknown onset. Focal seizures can be subclassified as aware versus impaired awareness, and motor versus nonmotor onset. A special category of focal to bilateral tonic-clonic seizure was added to this subgroup due to its unique seizure type, but it is more reflective of a seizure propagation pattern rather than a seizure type. Generalized seizures can be subclassified as motor versus nonmotor onset, and impaired awareness is not used as a classifier since the vast majority of these patients have impaired awareness. At times, there is not enough clinical, electrodiagnostic or imaging evidence to support a focal or generalized onset seizure, during which a classification of an unknown onset seizure can be made. Unknown onset seizures can be subclassified into motor, nonmotor and unclassified seizure types. Once these initial classifications and subclassifications have been made, these can sometimes be further described, with the ultimate goal of delineating the epileptogenic network involved (Fisher et al., 2017a, 2017b); see Tables 17.5 and 17.6 and Fig. 17.3).

Focal seizures: These can be classified based on whether awareness is impaired or retained, and/or whether it is of motor or nonmotor onset. Often, it is difficult to

Table 17.4 Old versus updated seizure classification and primary types

Focal—Old		**Focal—Updated**
Simple-partial (aura) seizure	→	Focal aware seizure
Complex partial (dialeptic seizure)	→	Focal impaired awareness seizure
With secondary generalization	→	Focal to bilateral tonic-clonic seizure
Generalized—Old		**Generalized—Updated**
Petit-mal seizure	→	Generalized absence seizure
Grand mal	→	Generalized tonic-clonic seizure
Other—Old		**Other—Updated**
Drop attack seizure	→	Focal or generalized atonic seizure
Tonic seizure	→	Focal or generalized tonic seizure
Myoclonic seizure	→	Focal or generalized myoclonic seizure

Note: New classification system cited from Scheffer, I. E., Berkovic, S., Capovilla, G., Connolly, M. B., French, J., Guilhoto, L., … & Zuberi, S. M. (2017). ILAE classification of the epilepsies: Position paper of the ILAE Commission for Classification and Terminology. Epilepsia, 58(4), 512–521. New system also includes an etiologic specifier from one of the following: structural, genetic, infectious, metabolic, immune and unknown. Table does not include a new group of combined generalized and focal epilepsy, as these patients have both generalized and focal seizures. For a more complete listing of all old versus new nomenclature, please see: https://onlinelibrary.wiley.com/doi/full/10.1111/epi.13671

Table 17.5 Summary of seizure localization based on behavioral presentation

Lobe	Location	Behavioral presentation
Frontal	General features	Often brief and occur at night, which can lead to a parasomnia misdiagnosis. Predominantly behavioral presentation involving vocalizations (e.g., screaming, swearing, laughing) and movements (e.g., head turning to one side, gaze to one side, kicking or pedaling of the legs, pelvic thrusting)
	Dorsolateral	Forced head and eye deviation (termed version) is common. Seizures are typically tonic, but may also be clonic. Disruption of speech common for dominant hemisphere seizures
	Opercular	Swallowing, salivation, speech arrest and facial clonic activity
	Orbitofrontal, cingulate, mesial frontal	Motor agitation, emotional feelings and complex gestural automatisms. Movements can be bizarre and include bicycle pedaling and pelvic thrusting but preserved awareness, and there can be little postictal confusion. Vigorous movements combined with emotional expression can lead to a misdiagnosis of functional origin. Clues that argue for epilepsy include stereotypy and brief duration
	Supplementary motor area	Asymmetric tonic posturing of bilateral limbs, monotonous vocalization and variably preserved consciousness
	Precentral gyrus	Focal motor seizures that can evolve to sequential areas of motor strip (Jacksonian march)
	Insular cortex	Rising epigastric sensation, nausea, autonomic changes such as changes in heart rate or piloerection. Gustatory (taste) hallucinations may also be associated with insular cortex seizures
	Language-dominant perisylvian fissure	Periictal aphasia

(continued)

Table 17.5 (continued)

Lobe	Location	Behavioral presentation
Temporal	General features	A wide-eyed stare with behavioral arrest, and possible oro-alimentary automatisms or manual autisms (hand washing, picking at clothes)
	Mesial	Rising epigastric sensation, fear, deja vu, jamais vu and dreamy states. Olfactory (smell) hallucinations related to anterior mesial (amygdala) involvement. Rising epigastric sensation associated with insular cortex and superior bank of sylvian fissure
	Lateral	Posterior lateral temporal onset can present as visual hallucinations. These hallucinations are generally well formed and include people and/or objects. Some lateral temporal seizures can also present with auditory hallucinations. Poorly formed sounds (buzzing) reflect involvement of Heschl's gyrus. If sounds are lateralizable, the onset is generally contralateral to where the sound is heard
	Anterior/amygdala	Sense of fear or panic is common. Olfactory (smell) hallucinations are classically associated with amygdala/uncinate cortex seizures. Smells are usually unpleasant, e.g., (burning rubber)
Parietal	General features	Somatosensory (tingling or burning) and/or sense of movement. Seizures may propagate frontally or temporally, producing semiology that leads to false localization
	Dominant side	Loss of language functions can occur, frequently with features of receptive and/or conductive aphasia
	Nondominant side	Loss of orientation, metamorphopsia (visual phenomena), neglect and/or asomatognosia (lack of awareness of body)
	Anterior	Somatosensory phenomena that may be positive (i.e., tingling, electrical "shock" feeling, sensation that body parts are being moved and/or pain) or negative (i.e., loss of sensation, such as numbness, feeling body parts are missing or neglect). Loss of muscle tone is also possible
	Posterior	Immobility, alteration of vision perception (metamorphopsia) and/or complex visual hallucination are common. Can experience the perception that objects are closer or farther away, or other complex visual distortions. Visual hallucinations involve well-formed objects and/or people/animals, and are typically of short duration and/or are the same images. Rarely associated with auditory hallucinations at onset
	Inferior	Disorientation and vertigo may be present. Involvement of superior bank of the Sylvian fissure (and/or insular cortex—See mesial temporal lobe) associated with abdominal sensations, including sensation of rising epigastric sensation
Occipital	General features	Positive visual phenomena (i.e., hallucinations of elementary visual phenomena that are typically not well-formed and include perception of colors, shapes and/or lights) as well as negative visual phenomena (i.e., loss of vision, scotomas, hemianopsia or general graying/blacking out of vision/amaurosis). The visual phenomena tend to be contralateral to the side of seizure. Postictal phenomena can last for hours. Other features include eye movements that may be either tonic or clonic, sensation of eye movements, nystagmus or eye blinking
Other	Hypothalamus	Hypothalamic hamartomas commonly entail gelastic seizures (i.e., laughing without feeling of mirth). Otherwise may present similar to temporal lobe seizures

Table 17.6 Lateralizing and localizing seizure signs

Sign	Lateralization/Localization
Receptive or expressive aphasia, postictal aphasia	Dominant hemisphere, typically on the left
Auditory phenomena that are not well-formed (i.e., buzzing, humming or other nondescript hearing changes)	Heschl's gyrus and primary auditory association cortex
Unilateral automatisms such as picking at clothes and other nonpurposeful extremity movements	Ipsilateral to the extremity
Unilateral dystonic arm posturing	Contralateral to the extremity
Eye/head version, especially immediately preceding secondary generalization	Contralateral to the direction of version
"Figure four sign" (i.e., as secondary generalization develops, one arm becomes extended while the other is abducted and flexed at elbow, with both arms together having the appearance of the number four)	Contralateral to the extended arm
Lip smacking/chewing movements	Insular cortex
Postictal nose-wiping	Ipsilateral to the hand used to wipe the nose
Ictal speech	Nondominant hemisphere, typically on the right
Pre-ictal sensation of urinary urgency	Nondominant hemisphere
Visual phenomena (not well-formed) sometimes in the visual hemifield	Contralateral occipital cortex
Visual phenomena (well-formed) that include objects, people and animals	Contralateral occipitotemporal lobe
Ictal vomiting	Nondominant hemisphere, typically on the right

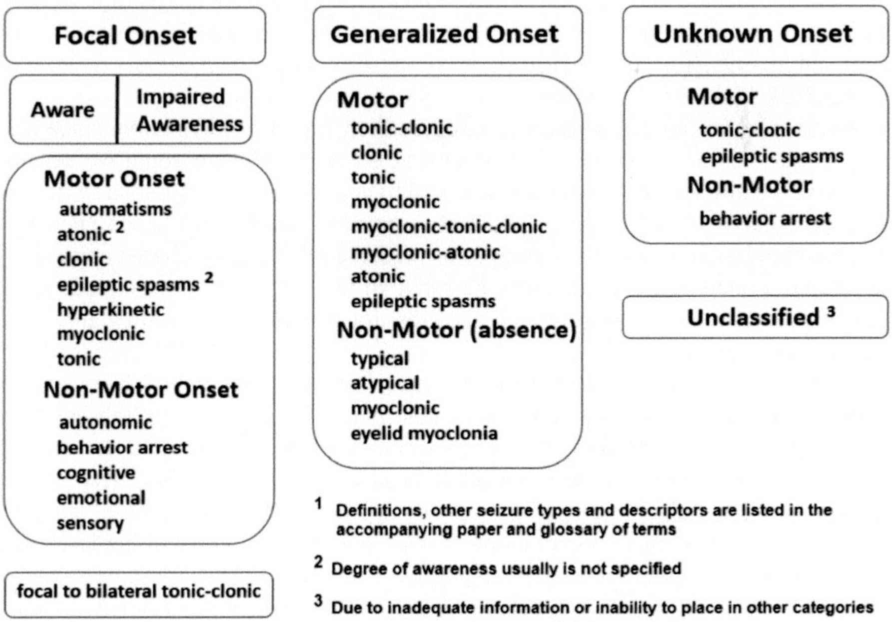

Fig. 17.3 ILAE 2017 classification system (Fisher et al., 2017b)

discern whether awareness was impaired or not, and whether there are motor manifestations involved. In these cases, you can classify the seizure based on awareness alone, motor or nonmotor manifestations alone or both. For example, all of these seizure type classifications are valid: focal aware seizure, focal aware motor seizure, focal impaired awareness nonmotor seizure or focal impaired awareness seizure. Furthermore, focal seizures can be described based on the initial manifested symptoms (seizure semiology). The ILAE has developed a glossary of seizure semiology, including the different terms and their significance in seizure onset localization (Beniczky et al., 2022).

Focal seizures can manifest in a wide variety of ways, including both subjective symptoms that the patient might experience and objective symptoms that the patient or a witness might observe. Some postictal signs and symptoms can have localizing value as well, so these also need to be described. Clinical manifestations can be cognitive, emotional or affective, motor (elementary vs complex), autonomic and sensory. Examples of cognitive phenomena include aphasia, amnesia, déjà vu or jamais vu, attention impairment, dissociation, illusions, among others. Examples of emotional or affective phenomena include anger, anxiety, crying, laughing, fear, paranoia, pleasure or agitation. Motor phenomena can be elementary, such as atonic, dystonic, epileptic nystagmus, epileptic spasms, versive, myoclonic, clonic, tonic, tonic-clonic and myoclonic-atonic. Motor phenomena can also be complex, including hyperkinetic behavior (pedaling, pelvic thrusting, walking or running) and automatisms (manual or orofacial stereotyped and nonpurposeful movements, vocalizations, grasping, perseveration). Examples of autonomic phenomena include cardiovascular symptoms (bradycardia, tachycardia, asystole), cutaneous (piloerection, flushing, sweating), gastrointestinal (hypersalivation, spitting, vomiting, epigastric sensation), pupillary and respiratory manifestations. Examples of sensory phenomena include auditory, gustatory, olfactory, somatosensory (painful vs nonpainful), vestibular and visual. Postictally, there can be hemiparesis, aphasia, blindness, autonomic signs, psychiatric signs and nose-wiping, among others (Beniczky et al., 2022; Fisher et al., 2017b).

Focal seizures must be classified based on their initial manifestation, since it is common to see an evolution of symptoms (e.g., a focal aware cognitive seizure based on the initial symptoms, later followed by automatisms with impaired awareness). It is useful to add the propagation of symptoms; however, the seizure needs to be classified based on the initial symptoms presented. Descriptors based on semiology can be added for a more detailed narrative of the event (examples include focal sensory seizures, focal aware clonic seizures, focal autonomic seizures and focal hyperkinetic seizures).

Generalized seizures: Generalized seizures involve both cerebral hemispheres from onset. They are further subclassified as motor versus nonmotor (absence). It is important to note that the patients can often experience nonspecific feelings of an impending seizure or a brief period of head or limb version, but these do not invalidate a generalized onset (Fisher et al., 2017a, 2017b). Motor onset seizures can be classified as tonic-clonic, clonic, tonic, myoclonic, myoclonic-tonic-clonic, myoclonic-atonic, atonic or epileptic spasms. Nonmotor (absence) seizures can be classified as typical, atypical, myoclonic absence and absence with eyelid myoclonia.

Description of Some Important Semiology Terms (Beniczky et al., 2022; Fisher et al., 2017a, 2017b):

1. Tonic: limb stiffening or elevation, not followed by clonic activity. A sustained posture, either in flexion or extension, can be seen.
2. Myoclonic: sudden, brief, irregular jerks.
3. Clonic: regular and repetitive jerks
4. Atonic: sudden loss or decrease in muscle tone, which can involve the head, trunk, jaw and limbs.
5. Tonic-clonic: tonic phase followed by a clonic phase
6. Epileptic spasms: sudden flexion, extension or mixed extension-flexion predominantly involving proximal head, limbs and trunk muscles.
7. Myoclonic-atonic (or myoclonic-astatic): myoclonic jerk followed by atonia.
8. Automatisms: irrepressible, repetitive motor activity that resembles a voluntary behavior. Examples include nonpurposeful writing or eating movements, lip pursing, chewing, licking, swallowing, body rocking, kicking, fist clenching, grasping, tapping, finger snapping and exploratory movements, among many others including genital automatisms such as grabbing or scratching the genital region or copulatory movements.
9. Versive: forced and sustained movement of the eyes, head, trunk or whole body to one side.
10. Absence: sudden cessation of activity and awareness. It may be difficult to differentiate from focal impaired awareness seizures, and EEG may be required to distinguish these.
11. Myoclonic absence: absence seizure with rhythmic three-per-second myoclonic movements, leading to progressive ratcheting arm elevation.
12. Absence with eyelid myoclonia: absence seizure with myoclonic jerks of the eyelids and upward elevation of the eyes.

The objective is to be able to classify the epilepsy type and epilepsy syndromes in as descriptive a manner as possible, with the goal of identifying the epileptogenic network involved (Beniczky et al., 2022). Sometimes, clinical manifestations and initial noninvasive workup such as scalp EEG and brain MRI are not sufficient to localize this network, and the seizure semiology can play a key role in determining the most appropriate further diagnostic workup, including both invasive and noninvasive diagnostic procedures. In recent years, stereo-electroencephalography (SEEG), which involves the implantation of electrodes into the brain to more invasively determine seizure onset, has been gradually usurping the role of grids and strips in the United States given the increasing use of minimally invasive surgical techniques (Drane et al., 2021a). SEEG electrode placement is guided by semiology, and stimulation procedures can be used in an effort to simulate the patient's typical seizure. Semiological patterns may also contribute to decisions regarding therapeutic options (Table 17.7).

Table 17.7 Presumed etiologies for epilepsy

Name	Etiology
Structural	Seizures are due to a lesion or other abnormal findings are denoted by neuroimaging, although the underlying cause may either be acquired (i.e., as in stroke, anoxic/hypoxic injury and traumatic brain injury) or genetic (i.e., inherited or *de novo* mutations)
Genetic	Seizures are due to a known (or suspected/presumed) disease-causing genetic condition. This typically entails heritable conditions, typically autosomal dominant, although it is also possible that there is an underlying *de novo* mutation. Involved genes can be specific to epilepsy or related to neurodevelopment more generally. These typically begin in childhood or adolescence, and are often generalized in nature (Myers & Meffort, 2015). Examples include channelopathies (e.g., Dravet syndrome, Ohtahara syndrome, juvenile myoclonic epilepsy), progressive myoclonic epilepsies (e.g., Unverricht disease, Lafora disease), malformations of cortical development (e.g., hamartomas, lissencephaly, heterotopias) or tumors with a strong genetic component (e.g., dysembryoplastic neuroepithelial tumor, hypothalamic hamartoma). Focal epilepsies are possible, however, including familial mesial temporal lobe epilepsy (FMTLE, chromosome 4q13.2-q21.3) and autosomal dominant nocturnal frontal lobe epilepsy (LGI1 gene, 10q24 locus), among others. Seizures may also be associated with conditions such as Down's syndrome, Angelman's syndrome, tuberous sclerosis and neurofibromatosis. Also includes epileptic encephalopathies (noted below)
Infectious	Seizures are due to a known (or suspected/presumed) central nervous system infection impacting the brain, causing prolonged proinflammatory signaling and leading to blood–brain barrier dysfunction/damage, neuronal death and persisting neuronal hyperexcitability. This is the most common cause of epilepsy worldwide, primarily owing to higher prevalence in lower- and middle-income countries (Vezzani et al., 2016). Examples are diverse and include things like human immunodeficiency virus, meningitis, encephalitis, neurocysticercosis, cerebral malaria and TORCH infections
Metabolic	Seizures due to a known (or suspected/presumed) metabolic derangement involving disruption to energy production within the brain. These are typically genetic/congenital but can be due to a *de novo* mutation, and are classified by the defective molecule or mechanism. Small-molecule disorders include amino acidopathies, acidemias, demyelinating conditions like Canavan disease, defective GABA metabolism and mitochondrial disorders. Large-molecule disorders include disruption of lysosomal storage, peroxisomal disorders and leukodystrophies. There are also some acquired conditions like cerebral folate deficiency or other vitamin-dependent conditions (e.g., pyridoxine)
Immune	Seizures due to a known (or suspected/presumed) abnormality in the body's normal immune response, impacting brain structure and/or function. Common features include focal onset, facial-brachial dystonic seizures, reduced responsiveness to ASMs and abnormalities such as paranoia or hallucinations. Examples of autoimmune epilepsies include anti-NMDA-receptor encephalitis, GAD65 antibody-related epilepsy, limbic encephalitis (LG1-CASPR2 and others)
Unknown	Seizure due to an unknown (or as-yet unidentified) cause

(continued)

Table 17.7 (continued)

Name	Etiology
Special epilepsy categories	
Epilepsy encephalopathies	Reflects syndromes in which the epileptic abnormalities may contribute to progressive neurologic and/or neuropsychological dysfunction (e.g., Dravet syndrome, Landau-Kleffner syndrome, Lennox-Gastaut syndrome, west syndrome and more)
Reflex epilepsies	Epilepsies associated with specific sensory stimuli (e.g., idiopathic photosensitive occipital lobe epilepsy, primary reading epilepsy, startle epilepsy and more)
Progressive myoclonus epilepsies	Refers to a series of rare epilepsy syndromes all having myoclonic seizures as part of the disease presentation. Includes severe myoclonic epilepsy of infancy (Dravet syndrome), Lafora disease, mitochondrial encephalopathies and more

Epilepsy Etiology and Syndromes

Epilepsy is classified according to presumed etiologies and epileptic syndromes. According to the most recent ILAE update (Fisher et al., 2017b), the etiological groups are (a) structural, (b) genetic, (c) infectious, (d) metabolic (e) immune and (f) unknown.

Epilepsy due to a structural etiology refers to abnormalities visible on neuroimaging that are likely the cause of the patient's seizures. Structural etiologies can be acquired (stroke, trauma) or genetic (malformations of cortical development). Genetic epilepsy refers to seizures secondary to a known or presumed genetic mutation (e.g., SCN1A mutation causing Dravet Syndrome). Patients with epilepsy due to an infectious etiology have seizures as a direct result from a known infection (e.g., toxoplasmosis) or post-infectious (viral encephalitis). Of note, an infectious etiology refers to a patient with epilepsy, rather than a patient with acute symptomatic seizures occurring in the setting of acute infection (meningitis or encephalitis). Metabolic epilepsy results from a known or presumed metabolic disorder in which seizures are a core symptom of the disorder (e.g., pyridoxine dependent seizures). Epilepsy of immune etiology is considered where there is evidence of autoimmune-mediated brain inflammation (e.g., anti-NMDA receptor encephalitis). Finally, epilepsy of unknown etiology refers to patients with epilepsy for whom the cause is not known (Fig. 17.4).

In general, the classification system identifies epilepsies according to localization, semiology and understood etiology. Some selected syndromes are included below, but the focus for the rest of the chapter will be on focal seizures.

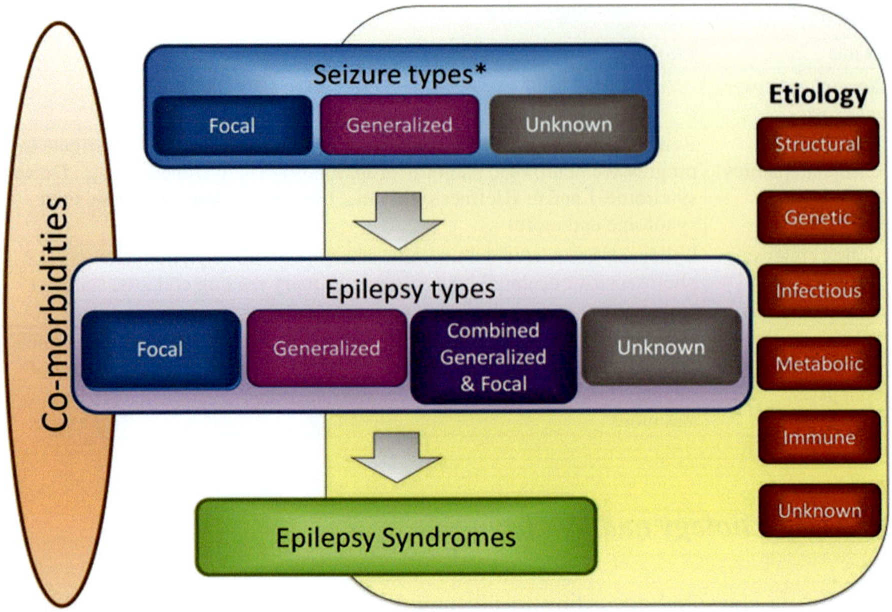

Fig. 17.4 ILAE 2017 classification system. From Scheffer et al. (2017)

Selected Epilepsy Syndromes

Syndromes with childhood onset can be divided into three groups (Specchio et al., 2022): (1) self-limited focal epilepsies, (2) generalized epilepsies and (3) developmental and/or epileptic encephalopathies. Each of these syndromes is characterized by specific seizure types, a characteristic EEG presentation and age of onset and specific diagnostic findings (e.g., MRI, genetics). Nearly one-third of all childhood epilepsies are thought to be represented by these syndromes (Wirrell et al., 2011), although all available data are retrospective in nature only.

According to the latest ILAE update on Epilepsy Syndromes, the term "idiopathic" is now recommended only for use with the four syndromes termed the idiopathic generalized epilepsies: childhood absence epilepsy, juvenile absence epilepsy, juvenile myoclonic epilepsy and generalized tonic seizures alone. The ILAE has now proposed dropping the term "benign" as it has become clear that there are often cognitive and behavioral issues associated with these syndromes when carefully examined (Scheffer et al., 2017). The term "self-limited" has also been recommended to reflect that these conditions have age-dependent onset and remission (Specchio et al., 2022).

Self-limited Syndromes

Self-limited epilepsy with centrotemporal spikes: Self-limited epilepsy with centrotemporal spikes (ECTS), at the time of writing the first edition of this chapter, was known as benign childhood epilepsy with centrotemporal spikes (BECTS) (Specchio et al., 2022). However, as already noted and more fully addressed below, it has become clear that such patients can have neurocognitive issues which are not benign (Garcia-Ramos et al., 2016). This syndrome is also referred to as "benign" rolandic epilepsy. ECTS typically presents between the ages of 3 and 13. It is common, accounting for about 25% of all epilepsies in children. The EEG interictally shows very high amplitude sharp waves with a field centrotemporally, involving the precentral and postcentral gyri of the perisylvian region (see Chap. 3 for neuroanatomic reference). Seizures predominately occur during sleep or shortly after awakening. The epileptiform discharges markedly increase in frequency during non-REM sleep. Seizures out of sleep are focal aware with onset in the centrotemporal region and spread to adjacent areas and may secondarily generalize. Seizures onset may shift from one hemisphere to the other. Rarely, atypical EEG patterns may present, including continuous spike-and-wave during slow sleep or focal motor facial status epilepticus. Seizure frequency is generally low, although significant variation occurs (about 10% may have only one recognized seizure while about 20% can have multiple seizures in a 24-hour period). Ictal features classically present with motor, sensory and autonomic symptoms (hypersalivation), generally involving one side of the mouth, face and throat. Patients may present with drooling, guttural noises, involuntary clonic retraction of one side of the face, tonic contraction of mouth and/or tongue, numbness and/or tingling of hemi-face, lips, and/or gums, and speech arrest. Sensory and/or motor activity of the hand, trunk, and/or leg as well as abdominal pain has been reported. This syndrome as well as *benign partial epilepsy of childhood with occipital paroxysms* is a dominantly inherited condition with normal MRI despite the "focal" EEG findings. Prognosis is generally considered excellent, and ECTS is considered an age-related syndrome, in which almost all patients exhibit seizure remission (so-called growing out of seizures) by adulthood, often by the age of 16 (Vannest et al., 2015). Treatment may not require medication, and the initiation of ASMs is typically not made until the patient has a second unprovoked seizure. Because seizures almost always disappear by adulthood, medical treatment beyond this point is not needed.

Neuropsychological morbidity as noted was traditionally not associated with ECTS. Over the last decade, however, it has become clear that it is not uncommon for such patients to experience mild cognitive issues, which can effect function in an academic and social setting. For example, compared to healthy controls, child-aged patients have exhibited significantly lower scores on tests of general cognitive function (IQ), attention, memory (short- and long-term), language (e.g., letter fluency, comprehension), visuoperceptual/visuospatial skills and behavioral problems (e.g., impulsivity, mood lability) (e.g., Elger et al., 2004; Kavros et al., 2008). More recent reviews have highlighted that executive dysfunction (particularly inhibitory control and cognitive flexibility) (Lima et al., 2017; Neri et al., 2012; Nicolai et al., 2006), attention problems and speech production issues are often present across this cohort of patients (Zanaboni et al., 2021). Academic problems requiring accommodations are not uncommon, which can involve a variety of learning disabilities. In general, neuropsychologic deficits have been more related to the frequency of EEG abnormalities than the number of clinical seizures. A few studies have found that volumetric structural brain changes were related to performance. There is a growing appreciation that disturbance of sleep may contribute to the presence of deficits (Nicolai et al., 2006). Neuropsychological function of adolescents and young adults with remission of ECTS has generally not differed from healthy controls.

Key Points: Self-Limited Epilepsy with Centrotemporal Spikes (Aka Rolandic Epilepsy)

- Onset typically 3–13 years of age
- Seizures arise from centrotemporal region (often switching sides)
- Seizures commonly occur during sleep or when waking up
- Considered an age-limited epilepsy syndrome (seizures often remit by 16-years-old)
- Neuropsychological Deficits: Generally mild in childhood, and primarily include speech production, executive function (inhibitory control and cognitive flexibility) and attention. However, deficits are also seen in language (letter fluency, comprehension) and visuospatial function, and there is often an elevation in behavioral problems. Deficits often contribute to academic problems/learning disabilities, and some of these issues persist after seizures resolve.
- Sleep disturbance may contribute to comorbid cognitive and academic issues.

Idiopathic (Generalized) Syndromes

Idiopathic Generalized Epilepsies (IGE): IGEs are a group of epilepsies that are genetically determined, having no structural or anatomic cause, and seizures are the only manifestation of the condition (see Benbadis, 2005). They usually, but not always, begin early in life from childhood to early adulthood; often, they are not diagnosed correctly for several years. Neurologic examination is normal, intelligence is normal, imaging studies are normal, and EEG is normal other than for the epileptiform abnormalities (i.e., there is no abnormal slow activity or evidence for diffuse encephalopathy). Thus, IGE are best viewed as a spectrum of conditions, and many of them may indeed represent a single entity with slightly different clinical phenotypes, and there are good reasons to study them as a group.

Seizure types that occur in IGE include a combination of generalized motor, absence and myoclonic seizures (Benbadis, 2005; Koren et al., 2024).

- Typical focal aware seizures are clinically characterized by a brief (5–15 s) impairment of consciousness with abrupt onset and termination and the classic monomorphic 3 Hz spike-wave complexes (ictally and interictally).
- Myoclonic seizures consist of brief sporadic jerks, usually appendicular and symmetrical, associated electrically with generalized epileptiform discharges typically polyspikes. Patients sometimes report them as an electric shock sensation.
- Generalized motor seizures are the most common type of seizures. Generalized seizures in the IGE are by definition primary generalized motor seizures. They are typically characterized by a tonic phase that is gradually interrupted by quiescence, thus giving rise to the clonic phase with rhythmic spikes and spike-wave complexes decreasing in frequency. Often primary generalized motor seizures begin with clonic or myoclonic jerks before the tonic phase and thus are clonic-tonic-clonic rather than tonic-clonic.

The EEG findings of IGE are characteristic and consist of generalized epileptiform discharges with normal background activity (i.e., no abnormally slow background and no superimposed slow activity). Epileptiform discharges can take the form of spikes, sharp waves, spike-wave complexes and polyspikes. Spike-wave complexes can be viewed as the EEG correlates of absence seizures, and polyspikes as the EEG correlate of myoclonic seizures.

There is a growing awareness that cognitive dysfunction occurs in the IGE conditions when carefully studied (Loughman et al., 2014). Limitations in studies over the years have included small sample sizes, lack of control for comorbidities, an absence of control groups, assessment measures that do not thoroughly cover potential areas of dysfunction, and issues with recruitment setting. Therefore, thorough cognitive profiles for the IGE conditions are still being developed, as is the longitudinal outcome pattern. IGE patients appear to perform worse than healthy controls across most cognitive domains with the exception of visuoperceptual and spatial processing. On the basis of a meta-analysis, Loughman and colleagues felt the largest reductions were observed in cognitive processing speed (large effect size), intelligence and working memory (medium to large effect sizes) and long-term memory (small to medium effect sizes).

For patients with clear IGE, broad-spectrum ASMs are the drug of choice. Commonly used broad-spectrum ASMs include valproic acid, lamotrigine, topiramate and perampanel, among others (Elosua-Bayes et al., 2024). Importantly, some ASMs are ill-advised in IGE (such as phenytoin and carbamazepine) since these can worsen generalized onset seizures (e.g., focal unaware seizures).

Classic IGE Syndromes

Childhood Absence Epilepsy: Childhood absence epilepsy (CAE) is common, accounting for 18% of all childhood epilepsies (Hirsch et al., 2022). The seizures reflect the classic 3 Hz spike and wave complexes (range = 2.5 to 4 Hz) on EEG that are often induced by hyperventilation. Clinically, these seizures often present as a brief (few seconds) "blank" stare, although longer seizures up to 20–30 seconds in duration can be associated with automatisms such as blinking or mouth movements (Sadleir et al., 2006). There is loss of awareness, and children have no memory of events during a seizure. There are no postictal sensory, motor or cognitive changes. Onset typically occurs between the ages of 4 and 8 (peak period is six to seven years old), and this condition is more common in girls (60%–75% of cases) (Ma et al., 2011). Children can have dozens or hundreds of seizures per day. These seizures need to be distinguished from Attention Deficit Hyperactivity Disorder (ADHD) and focal onset seizures, as certain ASMs may be of no benefit or even worsen absence seizures. A helpful clinical distinction between absence seizures and focal seizures is the lack of postictal manifestations after absence seizures. Prognosis is generally considered quite good (but see below for vocational and psychosocial function in adulthood), with about 80% responding to medication treatment. Complete remission rates are highly variable, but the majority of patients with typical CAE remit in late teens to early adulthood. Those patients with generalized tonic-clonic seizures are at increased risk for persistent seizures. First-line ASMs include ethosuximide and valproic acid as well as lamotrigine and topiramate. Alternatively, carbamazepine and oxcarbazepine exacerbate absence seizures, and gabapentin is ineffective at reducing absence seizures. Exacerbation of absence (and myoclonic) seizures has also been reported for some patients treated with tiagabine and vigabatrin.

Neuropsychological dysfunction has traditionally not been associated with CAE, save for higher rates of diagnosed learning disorders and ADHD (Caplan et al., 2008; Shinnar et al., 2017; Wirrell et al., 1997). Indeed, as a group, children with CAE have demonstrated overall IQ scores that are slightly above average. However, Fastenau et al. (2009) found that children with CAE exhibited, as a group, significant deficits in attention/executive/constructional, language and learning/memory domains when compared to healthy siblings within 6 months of the first seizure being recognized. Deficits in children with idiopathic generalized seizures included attention/executive/constructional, language and learning/memory deficits. There were no significant deficits in measures of academic achievement. Similarly, other work has found mild neuropsychological deficits among children with CAE in attention, memory (visual/nonverbal) and visuospatial functions. Deficits in language function (verbal fluency, naming, comprehension) and verbal memory are less consistently found, but both language and verbal memory deficits have been reported (e.g., Henkin et al., 2005; Pavone et al., 2001). Psychiatric diagnoses (e.g., ADHD, depression, anxiety disorders) have been reported for over half of patients with CAE (Gruenbaum et al., 2021; Hirsch et al., 2022). Duration of seizures, seizure frequency and ASM treatment were associated with more neuropsychological and psychological problems. While prognosis is generally considered good, long-term outcome studies found patients with CAE at risk for lower vocational attainment, poor social adjustment and increased rates of psychiatric diagnoses in adulthood compared to healthy peers or to patients with juvenile rheumatoid arthritis (e.g., Wirrell et al., 1997).

Key Points: Childhood Focal Aware Seizures
- Onset typically 4–8 years of age
- Seizures have characteristic generalized 3 Hz spike and wave complexes
- Seizures with brief (several seconds) staring spells with loss of awareness
- May remit in adulthood, but some patients continue to seizures into adulthood.
- Neuropsychological Deficits: Traditionally considered mild to none, but growing data suggest mild deficits in attention/executive, delayed and immediate memory (visual/nonverbal), visuospatial and increased rates of learning disorders, ADHD, depression and anxiety disorders. With seizure remission, deficits do not persist into adulthood. However, patients with absence seizures in adulthood exhibit neuropsychological deficits.

Juvenile myoclonic epilepsy (JME): Juvenile myoclonic epilepsy onset is usually in adolescence, although occasionally diagnosis is not made until after the fourth decade. JME is considered an inherited epileptic syndrome, with six abnormal genes mapped to chromosomes 6 and 15. JME has a complex and heterogenous genetic background. The mode of inheritance remains uncertain (Marini et al., 2004). A relatively common epilepsy syndrome, JME accounts for about 3–12% of all epilepsies (higher rates reported from hospital records, lower rates from population studies). Affected individuals usually have three types of seizures: myoclonus, generalized tonic clonic and absence. Myoclonic seizures (jerks) with preserved consciousness are a cardinal feature of JME, and the only seizure type for about 17% of patients with JME. The myoclonic jerks are generally bilateral and involve the shoulders and/or arms, although involvement of the lower extremities, head or trunk has been reported. Lateralized myoclonus does occur. The majority (about 80%) of patients with JME will present with generalized tonic-clonic seizures in addition to myoclonic seizures. While absence seizures are less often found in patients with JME (about 28% of patients), when present, absence seizures are typically the first clinical manifestation of JME. Classically, the seizures are markedly exacerbated by sleep deprivation and occur shortly after awakening. The EEG shows more irregular 3–7 Hz generalized discharges. Brain imaging is normal in patients with JME, although neuropathologic studies have reported microscopic abnormalities (increased partially dystopic neurons, indistinct boundary between lamina 1 and 2 of the cerebral cortex and irregular columnar arrangement of some cortical neurons termed microdysgenesis). Prognosis is generally considered good, although JME is considered a lifelong condition. Treatment with ASMs (e.g., levetiracetam, lamotrigine, topiramate, zonisamide, valproic acid) is often efficacious in controlling seizures. Vagus nerve stimulation (VNS) implantation has been offered to select patients with medication-refractory JME. Surgical resection is *not* indicated for JME.

Cognitive function in patients with JME has traditionally been viewed as unaffected, and IQ is often in the average ranges. However, more detailed neuropsychological studies have demonstrated patients with JME can exhibit mild deficits in processing speed, attention/working memory, language (confrontation naming and verbal fluency), memory (verbal immediate and verbal and visual delayed), visuospatial and executive functions (i.e., abstract reasoning, mental flexibility, behavioral inhibition) when compared to matched healthy peers. Patients with JME have more pronounced deficits in executive function than matched patients diagnosed with temporal lobe epilepsy (see below for neuropsychological deficits of temporal lobe epilepsy). An association between neuropsychological deficits and duration of epilepsy has been observed, although this trend disappears for patients with more education (12 years or more), particularly those with college education.

Key Points: Juvenile Myoclonic Epilepsy (JME)

- Onset typically in adolescence, but diagnosis delayed past fourth decade reported.
- Triad of seizure types: myoclonus, generalized motor and focal aware
- Myoclonus with preserved awareness is the cardinal feature of JME
- Seizures exacerbated by sleep deprivation and 20–30% with photic stimulation.
- Neuropsychological Deficits: Generally mild, but deficits in processing speed, attention/working memory, language (verbal fluency, naming), memory (verbal immediate and delayed), visuospatial and executive functions reported. Most consistent deficits are in executive function, which can be more pronounced than patients with temporal lobe epilepsy. Deficits typically <u>not</u> present in adulthood.

Developmental and Epileptic Encephalopathies (Previously Generalized, Symptomatic Epilepsies)

The term developmental and epileptic encephalopathy (DEE) is used when both developmental impairment and epileptic activity have an impact on the cognitive and behavioral state of the affected person (Raga et al., 2021). Most patients with DEE have a genetic variant, but other common etiologies are structural (e.g., hemimegalencephaly), metabolic (e.g., GLUT1 deficiency) and immune disorders (e.g., Rasmussen syndrome). Usually, DEE presents during early infantile or childhood periods. In this group of patients, uncontrolled seizures contribute to severe cognitive and behavioral impairments which can worsen over time (Fisher et al., 2017b). Early recognition of DEE has important implications for counseling, treatment and prognosis. Confirming the underlying etiology is extremely important to explore targeted treatment options such as surgery (e.g., TSC), dietary interventions and choice of ASM.

West's syndrome. West's syndrome accounts for about two percent of all epilepsies, but 25% of epilepsies in the first year of life. Associated with a high mortality rate (5–31%), it is a classic epilepsy syndrome presenting with a characteristic triad of infantile spasms, developmental stagnation or regression and interictal EEG pattern that is distinctively "chaotic" (called hypsarrhythmia). Most recently, the term Infantile Epileptic Spasms Syndrome (IESS) has been proposed to encompass both West Syndrome and infants presenting with epileptic spasms who do not fulfill all the criteria for West syndrome (Zuberi et al., 2022). The age of onset is between 3 and 12 months, with a range of 1–24 months.

The EEG consists of high voltage multifocal spikes, sharp waves and slow waves in a random distribution usually presenting between the ages of 6–18 months. Diagnosis can be made if two of the three characteristic features are present. "Infantile spasms" has been used to describe the seizure type, and the term infantile spasm has also been used to describe the epilepsy syndrome.

Treatment is usually a course of adrenocorticotropic hormone (ACTH) or prednisone (Hrachovy et al., 1983; Song et al., 2017; Wilmshurst et al., 2015). Second-line medication includes several ASMs. However, there is no one treatment that yields satisfactory control, and in some cases, patients with identified focal lesions can obtain reduction in seizures from surgical treatment (Gettings et al., 2023; Macdonald-Laurs et al., 2024; Mosely et al., 2012). Prognosis is generally poor, with a variety of neurologic, neuropsychological, academic and psychiatric problems (Lagae et al., 2010). Psychomotor slowing, autistic features, and up to 70% of patients will present with moderate to severe intellectual disability (Yoshitomi et al., 2021). Patients with West's syndrome can develop other types of seizures, and 18–50% develop Lennox-Gastaut syndrome (Bhanudeep et al., 2021).

Key Points: West's Syndrome (Aka Infantile Spasms)

- Onset typically between 6 and 18 months of age.
- Clinical triad of infantile spasms, developmental arrest and hypsarrhythmia EEG pattern
- Intellectual disability, autistic features and behavioral problems common.

Lennox-Gastaut syndrome. Lennox-Gastaut syndrome (LGS) is a severe developmental epileptic encephalopathy (DEE). It accounts for 0.5–4% of all epilepsies, but accounts for about 10% of epilepsy in children with onset of seizures before five years of age. It is a classic epilepsy syndrome that often follows West's syndrome with a mean age of onset around 27 months of age, with the majority presenting by six years of age. This severe epilepsy syndrome is difficult to medically control, and is characterized by a mix of seizure types (Gastaut et al., 1966; Markand, 2003). Seizure types include atonic (drop attacks), atypical focal aware seizures and tonic seizures that occur frequently throughout the day. The interictal EEG has a classic generalized 1.5–2.5 Hz slow spike and wave discharge pattern in childhood. The classical triad of characteristics includes multiple seizure types (as mentioned above), slow spike-and-wave pattern on EEG and intellectual disability.

In adulthood, EEG abnormalities show multifocal independent epileptic discharges. About 75% of patients with LGS have symptomatic epilepsy (identifiable underlying pathologies) including encephalitis/meningitis, brain malformations (cortical dysplasias), tuberous sclerosis, hypoxic/ischemic injuries, other brain lesions (particularly located in the frontal lobe) and/or birth/early infant trauma. Prognosis is considered poor (but is somewhat variable), and patients typically manifest developmental delays, psychomotor slowing, intellectual disability and behavioral problems including autistic features (Oguni et al., 1996). Several ASMs have been approved for the treatment of seizures associated with LGS, including lamotrigine, topiramate, rufinamide and clobazam (Montouris et al., 2020). Most recently, cannabidiol and fenfluramine have also shown to be effective.

Other treatment options include corpus callosotomy which can be helpful in minimizing drop attacks (atonic seizures) (Maehara & Shimizu, 2001), ketogenic diet and vagus nerve stimulation which is considered as a palliative option (Majoie et al., 2001).

Key Points: Lennox-Gastaut Syndrome

- Onset typically between 26 and 28 months of age (most by the age of 6 years).
- Triad of seizure types: Atonic, atypical absence and tonic seizures.
- Interictal EEG has classic 1.5–2.5 Hz slow spike and wave discharges
- Intellectual disability, autistic features, and behavioral problems common.

Landau-Kleffner syndrome. Also called acquired epileptic aphasia, it is a rare (less than 1% of epilepsies), but unique, epilepsy syndrome associated with acquired aphasia (receptive and expressive speech) and epileptic discharges of the temporoparietal regions beginning in the first decade of life (Landau & Kleffner, 1957; Robinson et al., 2001). Symptoms present after a period of normal motor and language development. Seizure onset is associated with the onset of language problems, but deterioration in language can precede the presentation of seizures. Inattention to auditory stimuli and receptive language dysfunction are often the first symptoms of language dysfunction (although initial loss of expressive speech has been reported). In addition to an acquired aphasia, children will often present with a myriad of other psychomotor and behavioral problems and may appear on the autistic spectrum. Prognosis is variable, and some patients do experience an improvement in aphasic symptoms while others do not. Patients with younger age of onset (5 years and younger) tend to exhibit less improvement in language than older patients (6 years old and older). Resolution of language deficits are not strongly associated with resolution of EEG abnormalities, which may decrease with age. Neurological surgery, multiple subpial transection of the epileptic cortex (eloquent language cortex), has shown to improve language function in up to 79% of patients who had been unable to speak for a minimum of 2 years.

Key Points: Landau-Kleffner Syndrome (Aka Acquired Epileptic Aphasia)

- Onset typically between 3 and 10 years of age (occurs after a period of normal language development).
- Seizures: Clinical seizures may not be present, but epileptic abnormalities on EEG in temporoparietal area required.
- Language decline may proceed presentation of seizures.
- Recovery of language function strongly related to the age of onset:
    - Less than 6 years of age have worse outcome than older patients

Focal Epilepsies

These are epilepsies with focal onset of seizures, and may be amenable to resection of the epileptogenic zone (minimal area of brain tissue needed to be removed for seizure freedom) (see (Devinsky et al., 2018; Scheffer et al., 2017). These include temporal lobe epilepsies, but also other neocortical epilepsies (frontal, parietal and occipital) as well as Rasmussen syndrome, hemiconvulsion-hemiplegia syndrome and migrating partial seizures of early infancy. Etiology may be dysplastic tissue, mesial temporal sclerosis (MTS), tumor, hemorrhage, other focal abnormality or idiopathic. Focal epilepsies can present with a focal aware seizure (aura) and/or other semiology (behavioral presentation of the seizure, including aura and postictal phenomena) that provide clues as to localization or hemisphere lateralization of seizure onset (see Tables 17.5 and 17.6).

Temporal Lobe Epilepsy (TLE). TLE is the most common type of epilepsy, thought to affect 25% of children and 50% of adults with epilepsy (Riney et al., 2022). Seventy to 85% of patients diagnosed with focal seizures will end up having their onset zone determined to be of TL origin. Patients with MTS, which is neuronal loss and gliotic scarring of the hippocampal formation, are typically medication refractory. Individuals with TLE are often ideal candidates for surgical treatment to achieve seizure control (see Sect. "Neuropsychological (Cognitive and Behavioral)

Comorbidity in Epilepsy") (Wiebe et al., 2001). In general, about 60–80% of carefully selected patients undergoing anterior temporal lobectomy are seizure free at one year, although significant variability exists, particularly with nonlesional cases, and with proportions of seizure freedom declining with less invasive neurosurgical approaches (Donos et al., 2018; Gross et al., 2018).

Temporal lobe seizures typically involve an aura (Gupta et al., 1983). Although variable, classically, the aura of TLE typically involves wide-eyed stare followed by oro-alimentary automatisms (lip smacking, swallowing and chewing) and/or automatisms of the upper extremities (pill rolling or picking movements of the hands) (Santana et al., 2010). Auras typical of medial temporal onset include rising epigastric sensation, fear, deja vu, jamais vu and dreamy states (Bartolomei et al., 2004; French et al., 1993), with a network that may include broader limbic interconnections, such as the insular cortex (Van Buren, 1963). Auditory and complex visual auras suggest lateral temporal neocortical onset. Patients with lateral TLE more often report unformed auditory hallucinations (e.g., buzzing or ringing) or sound distortion (e.g., perceive sounds are farther away or differ in pitch or tone). The auditory hallucination may also be a formed sound (e.g., voices of others and/or songs). Elementary auras are usually related to Heschl's gyrus, while more complex auditory auras are typically related to deep posterior areas within the Sylvian fissure (Penfield & Perot, 1963). Complex visual hallucinations typically involve the occipito-temporo-parietal (OTP) junction (Gloor, 1990). Other lateralizing features include unilateral automatisms, unilateral dystonic posturing and postictal paraphasias (Chee et al., 1993; Kanemoto & Janz, 1989). Patients with lateral TLE less often exhibit characteristic automatisms (e.g., oro-alimentary) and contralateral dystonia than do patients with medial TL onset (Gil-Nagel & Risinger, 1997). Lateral TL seizures have wider spread patterns and also a tendency for secondary generalization. Another TLE variant that has been described is temporo-polar seizures (Kahane et al., 2002). Due to connections with the inferior and basal frontal lobe, seizures arising from the temporal pole can manifest as a "frontal-like" semiology (Wang et al., 2008).

Neuropsychological impairment is frequently identified among patients with TLE, and may include deficits in general cognitive ability (IQ), academic achievement, language (i.e., naming and verbal fluency), learning and memory, attention/executive, motor skills, socio-emotional function, and visuospatial/constructional skills (see Sect. "Neuropsychological (Cognitive and Behavioral) Comorbidity in Epilepsy" for more detail) (Drane, 2015; Hermann et al., 1997). More recent research suggests that certain tests have greater localizing value (e.g., recognition of famous persons, aspects of visual naming, rapid long-term forgetting) (Busch et al., 2018; Drane et al., 2009b, 2013; Griffith et al., 2009).

Risk Factors for TLE. Patients suffering from a complicated febrile seizure (characterized by long duration or focal features) are at greater risk (5–20 times) for the development of TLE than patients having no history of complicated febrile seizure (Tarkka et al., 2003). However, individuals with a history of uncomplicated febrile seizure do *not* have an increased risk of TLE compared to the general population.

Among patients with identified TLE and hippocampal sclerosis, 40–60% have a history of a childhood complicated febrile seizure.

Pathology Associated with TLE. At one time, about 70% of TLE patients exhibited evidence of hippocampal sclerosis (Falconer et al., 1955). However, the proportion of patients with MTS has dropped significantly over the last 20 years and is now seemingly less than 50% of patients with TLE presenting for surgical evaluation. A variety of reasons for this decline have been put forward. Other pathologies associated with TLE include developmental misgrowth of cortical structures (cortical dysgenesis, cortical malformation), benign growths such as DNET (dysembryoplastic neuroepithelial tumor) or gangliogliomas, malignant tumors or vascular malformations (Babb & Brown, 1987). Some patients have MTS plus an additional pathology (dual pathology) (Cendes et al., 1995).

Key Points: Temporal Lobe Epilepsy (TLE)

Term for epilepsy with seizures arising from temporal lobe. TLE is divided into two types:

1. Medial temporal lobe seizure onset (MTLE) (account for ~70% of patients)
2. Lateral temporal lobe seizure onset

Features of MTLE

1. Seizures Present with an Aura (Focal Unaware Seizure before Losing Awareness)
   a. Most frequent auras associated with MTLE are:
      i. Rising epigastric sensation
      ii. Fear
      iii. Déjà vu
      iv. Piloerection (goose pimples)
      v. Memory flashbacks
      vi. Olfactory hallucinations (uncinate fits)
      vii. Dreamy states

Features of Lateral TLE.

1. Presentation similar to MTLE, but auras can differ:
   a. Auditory hallucinations—unformed (e.g., buzzing, muffled sound or ringing)
   b. Visual hallucinations (unformed figures, objects, rarely faces)

TLE often refractory to medication—about 33 percent medication refractory in 2009.

Seizure freedom in about 70% of selected patients after temporal lobectomy.

Frontal Lobe Epilepsy. Frontal lobe epilepsy (FLE) is the second most prevalent type of focal epilepsy after TLE (Bonini & McGonigal, 2020). Of those patients with FLE, most patients have seizure onset involving the dorsolateral prefrontal cortex (Lee & Worrell, 2012). Positive surgical outcome is around 50%, although great variability exists across studies. Seizure-free rates are highest for those individuals with a lesion demonstrated by MRI. Seizure-free rates at 1 year for individuals with a demonstrable lesion are about 70%.

Typical features of seizures in FLE are seizures of a relative short duration that may occur in clusters which result in no clear loss of awareness (Bonini et al., 2014; Cetin et al., 2021). Interictal EEG can be normal or demonstrate unilateral or bilateral abnormalities that can include the temporal leads. Compared to seizures from the TL, frontal lobe seizures are often briefer, and involve more motor activity. The behavioral features of FLE vary widely depending on the localization of onset and propagation (Williamson et al., 1985), and some have behavioral features that may be misidentified as nonepileptic events (i.e., pelvic thrusting and wild random limb movements) (Savqi et al., 1992). The more common seizure types in FLE are summarized below:

a. <u>Dorsolateral</u>: Several more typical presentations are described below (Bonini & McGonigal, 2020; Bonini et al., 2014):

   1. *Focal motor seizures.* Seizures begin with unilateral clonic motor jerks corresponding to the region of the motor strip (precentral gyrus) with epileptic discharges. The seizure may spread to sequential areas of the motor strip resulting in clonic motor activity as dictated by the motor functional organization of the precentral gyrus (Jacksonian March). Consciousness (awareness) is maintained unless the seizure propagates outside of the motor (and supplementary motor) areas of the frontal lobe.
   2. *Supplementary motor area (anterior to the primary motor strip) seizures*: Semiology is sudden asymmetric tonic posturing of both limbs, forced head and eye deviation (termed version) away from the seizure focus, monotonous vocalization (or speech arrest) and variably preserved consciousness.
   3. *Frontal lobe seizures with impaired awareness.* Seizures present behaviorally as sudden onset of vigorous bilateral motor automatisms of extremities that can appear as nonpurposeful movements or organized purposeful activity (e.g., swimming like arm motions, bicycling, laughing and shouting). Termed "hypermotor seizures," these are classically associated with frontal lobe epilepsy. Hypermotor seizures can exhibit aggressive or sexually related behaviors. Most patients (50–90%) have an aura of tightness or tingling of body parts, a vague psychic feeling, or fear. Awareness is lost during these seizures, and the patient is amnestic for the event. These seizures can arise from the frontopolar, opercular-insular, cingulate gyrus (anterior portion) and orbitofrontal areas (see also below).
   4. *Frontal lobe absence seizures (behavioral arrest).* These seizures, which frequently occur in clusters, involve a sudden arrest in motor/speech activity that lasts several seconds in duration. Awareness is lost during the ictal period, but there is no postictal confusion. Subtle automatisms may be present with fron-

tal lobe absence seizures. Can be associated with medial frontal or orbitofrontal seizure onset.

5. Aphasic seizures. Seizures with speech arrest.

b. Opercular: Seizures behaviorally characterized by swallowing, salivation, speech arrest and sometimes clonic activity of the face.
c. Orbitofrontal, cingulate and medial frontal: Semiology can include motor agitation, emotional feelings and complex gestural automatisms, which are also associated with frontal focal seizures (above and Table 17.6). The behavioral/neurologic features of seizures involving these regions can be bizarre and include "bicycle pedaling" and pelvic thrusting. Consciousness can be retained and there may be little postictal confusion. The vigorous movements along with the emotional content can lead to a misdiagnosis of psychogenic origin [see Chap. 17 for coverage of psychogenic nonepileptic seizures (aka psychogenic nonepileptic attacks or functional seizures)]. Clues that argue for epilepsy include the stereotypy and brief duration.

As supramodal associative areas in the human frontal lobe are highly connected to distant cortico-cortical efferent pathways, which involve multiple brain regions and can be multidirectional, seizure spread originating in the frontal lobe can be rapid and widespread (Bonini & McGonigal, 2020). This contributes to the diagnostic complexity, as it leads to a wider range of semiological symptoms and makes EEG analysis more difficult. This is further complicated by the spatial extent of the frontal lobe, which represents 35–40% of total cortical volume in the human brain (Semendeferi et al., 2002), and has a great deal of deeper cortex that can be difficult to assess from standard scalp electrode recordings.

Neuropsychological deficits in FLE have been highly variable, ranging from deficits in attention to gross deficits in attention/executive functions (e.g., planning, initiation, maintaining or altering behavior and/or anticipating outcomes), language (particularly generative verbal fluency), metamemory and self-monitoring and motor functions (Baldo et al., 2001; Drane et al., 2006; Farrant et al., 2005; Giovagnoli et al., 2011; Lhermitte, 1983; McDonald et al., 2001, 2005a, 2005b; Milner, 1964; Risse, 2006; Shallice, 2001; Stuss et al., 2001a, 2001b; Tucha et al., 1999). Less researched than patients with TLE, patients with FLE can exhibit diffuse as well as focal deficits (Risse, 2006) (see Sect. "Neuropsychological (Cognitive and Behavioral) Comorbidity in Epilepsy", this chapter for more details).

Key Points: Frontal Lobe Epilepsy (FLE)

Term for epilepsy with seizures arising from the frontal lobes. Patients with FLE often have short seizures, which can present in a myriad of ways, and the behavioral features can easily be ascribed to PNES/functional seizures (i.e., pelvic thrusting).

Seizure freedom is less known, but varies from 30 to 100% of selected patients after frontal resections. Best seizure free rates among patients with lesional findings on MRI (tumor, focal dysgenesis, etc.).

Parietal Lobe Epilepsy (PLE). Parietal lobe epilepsy is rare, accounting for 5% or less of the epilepsies (Salanova et al., 1995). The semiologic manifestations of PLE are widely varied, and its diagnosis can be challenging since it can mimic seizures arising from other cortices (Blume et al., 1991). This is because the parietal lobe has broad connectivity to other nearby structures (Yeo et al., 2014). The symptoms resulting from parietal lobe seizures will be determined by the location of the epileptogenic zone, and the nearby structures involved by the ictal spread (Nascimento et al., 2020).

Seizures arising from the primary sensory cortex can manifest as contralateral sensory changes such as tingling, numbness or pain. If it spreads to the nearby motor cortex, common motor manifestations such as focal clonic, tonic, head or eye deviation can be seen. When the parietal association cortex is involved, disturbances of body images can be seen. These can include macro- or microsomatognosia (perceiving a body part as being enlarged or shrunken, respectively). Visual illusions can also occur, and examples of these include the illusion of seeing a stationary object moving, or objects appearing smaller or larger than they are. If the dominant temporoparietal region is involved, language impairment can occur. In general, the superior parietal lobe is involved in sensory processing, motor learning, spatial perception, attention, visuomotor transformations and aspects of memory (Nobre et al., 2003). Superior parietal stimulation can result in astereognosis, optic ataxia, optic apraxia and object orientation agnosia (Iacoboni & Zaidel, 2004). Furthermore, if the ictal spread involves the temporal lobe, it can manifest as typical temporal lobe auras or automotor seizures (Chowdhury et al., 2021; Nascimento et al., 2020). Surgical interventions involving the posterior cortical epilepsies are much less common than TL and FL surgeries, and therefore research in parietal lobe surgeries remains lacking (Zhang et al., 2022).

Key Points: Parietal Lobe Epilepsy (PLE)
Term for epilepsy with seizures arising from the parietal lobes. Patients with PLE can have seizures that mimic seizures arising from the frontal, occipital or temporal lobe.

Early reports suggest 55–88% of selected patients are seizure free after resections. Best seizure free rates among patients with lesional findings on MRI (tumor, focal dysgenesis, etc.).

Occipital Lobe Epilepsy. Occipital lobe epilepsy is uncommon (Salanova et al., 1992). Seizures originating from the occipital lobe tend to manifest most commonly with visual phenomena, such as visual hallucinations, ictal blindness, hemianopsia and visual illusions (Maillard et al., 2022). Seizures involving the primary visual cortex tend to cause elementary visual auras such as flashing lights or colors with or without movement, stars, wheels and circular or triangular figures (Lee et al., 2005; Salanova et al., 1992). All these might vary in number and size as the seizure progresses. If the visual association cortex is involved, complex visual hallucinations such as autoscopy (perceiving visual images of one's self) and macro- or micropsia (seeing objects as larger or small than they are, respectively) can occur (Maillard et al., 2004). Less commonly, if the parieto-occipital junction region is involved, occipital lobe seizures can manifest with nonvisual phenomena, particularly oculomotor manifestations. These can include contralateral tonic eye deviation, oculoclonic eye movements or nystagmus and repetitive blinking or eye fluttering.

Similar to parietal lobe seizures, occipital lobe seizures commonly spread to extraoccipital regions such as the frontal, parietal or temporal lobes (Williamson et al., 1992). Impairment of awareness is common. Depending on the ictal spread, other semiology features such as elementary motor (e.g., clonic, tonic) or complex motor (e.g., automatisms) phenomena and emotional (e.g., fear, laughter), sensory, autonomic or cognitive (e.g., aphasia, neglect) symptoms can be seen. Postictally, symptoms such as aphasia or hemianopsia can occur (Chowdhury et al., 2021; Nascimento et al., 2020).

Key Points: Occipital Lobe Epilepsy (OLE)
Term for epilepsy with seizures arising from the occipital lobes. The most common clinical onset is visual aura (about 60%). Visual aura may be simple or complex, and may be positive (shape, animal, face, etc.) or negative (blind spot).

Seizure freedom for selected patients is not well established, and varies from 45 to 85%, with about 60–65% being generally accepted. Patients with developmental lesions (e.g., cortical dysplasia) are less likely to be seizure free (45%) than patients with tumors (e.g., gliomas) (85%).

Neurologic/neuropsychological risks generally include visual-field defects and visuoperceptual deficits.

Treatment of Seizures

It is important to note that not all seizure presentations require pharmacological treatment. If after a first seizure, a neurologic evaluation, EEG and MRI are normal, ASMs are not prescribed and a diagnosis of epilepsy is not made as most will not go on to have a second seizure. As noted previously, as many as 10% of the general population will have a seizure, but only 10% of this population will develop subsequent seizures necessary for the diagnosis of epilepsy (Fisher et al., 2017b; Krumholz et al., 2015). For our purposes, we will focus on patients diagnosed with epilepsy. Front-line treatment is drug therapy with ASMs (Kanner & Bicchi, 2022). Additional therapies for those patients having seizures despite medications include (a) diet (Nordli, 2002), (b) destructive surgery [including surgical resection (Engel et al., 2003; Silbergeld & Ojemann, 1993), laser interstitial thermal therapy (LITT) (Sperling et al., 2020; Willie et al., 2014), radiofrequency (RF) ablation (Catenoix et al., 2018; Shields et al., 2023), gamma knife (Regis et al., 1999) and focused ultrasound (Krishna et al., 2023)] and c) implantation of medical devices including the vagus nerve stimulator (VNS) (Medscape, 2017; Sackeim et al., 2001), the responsive neurostimulator (RNS) (Sun & Morrell, 2014) and the deep brain stimulator (DBS) (Boon et al., 2007; Vetkas et al., 2022).

Medication Treatment

Initiation of ASMs is the front-line treatment for patients with epilepsy (Brodie & Kwan, 2002). Only four front-line ASMs were available prior to 1995. Currently, over two dozen are available, and more are in development. Some ASMs are "broad spectrum" and treat both partial and generalized epilepsies. Others are "narrow spectrum" and may not treat focal epilepsies (i.e., ethosuximide) or may worsen myoclonic epilepsies (i.e., gabapentin). The recently developed ASMs have not significantly increased the percent of patients who are seizure free, but do offer different side effect profiles, which are often less pronounced than the older ASMs (See Table 17.8) (Chen et al., 2020). Side effects can be either positive or negative. For example, topiramate may help with weight loss but can have an adverse effect on cognition in some individuals (Ojemann et al., 2001). Most investigators have found 60–70% of patients with epilepsy are successfully treated with ASMs (Kwan & Brodie, 2000). Alternatively, 30–40% of patients with epilepsy continue to have seizures despite medications.

After failing more than three ASMs, the likelihood of achieving seizure control with another ASM trial is around 3% (Kwan & Brodie, 2000). Typically, individuals

Table 17.8 Cognitive and behavioral/mood effects of antiseizure medications (ASMs)

Medication	Behavior/mood effects	Cognitive effects
Carbamazepine	↓	↓↕
Clonazepam	↓↓↓	↓↓↓
Gabapentin	↓	↓
Lamotrigine	↑[a]	↕[b]↑
Levetiracetam	↓	[b] ↓
Lacosamide	[b]↓	[b]↓ (dizziness ↓↓)
Oxcarbazepine	↓	↓↕
Phenytoin	↓	↓↓↓
Phenobarbital	↓↓↓	↓↓↓
Pregabalin	↓	[b]↓ (dizziness ↓↓)
Sodium valproate	↓↑[a]	↓
Tiagabine	↓	[b]↕
Topiramate	↓↑[a]	↓↓↓[c]
Zonisamide	[b]↓	[b]↓↓↓

Note: ↓ = negative impact; ↕ = no meaningful impact; ↑ = positive impact; [a]Reports of positive impact on mood and/or mood stabilization; [b]Limited or inconsistent data; [c]Some participants exhibit more deficits than others in a dose-dependent fashion

failing two to three adequate ASM trials are labeled as medication refractory (intractable) and considered for surgical intervention (Camfield & Camfield, 1996; Perry & Duchowny, 2013). Those who are not surgical candidates can be treated with other therapies (see below).

Diet and Behavioral Therapies (Ketogenic and Other Diets)

Dietary changes to initiate ketosis represent a first-line treatment for epilepsies associated with deficiency in glucose transporter protein and pyruvate dehydrogenase. The ketogenic diet has also demonstrated efficacy for patients with Lennox-Gastaut syndrome (Nordli, 2002). Efficacy for treating symptomatic (or probably symptomatic) epilepsies with complex-partial (focal) seizures is unknown. Ketosis occurs when the brain shifts from primary glucose metabolism to ketone body metabolism due to a diet that is high in fats and low carbohydrates and protein. The fat to carbohydrate and protein ratio is ideally 4:1. While often effective, it is often difficult to maintain this diet over long periods of time and there is a potential long-term health risk from the high lipid diet.

Other therapies for medication-refractory epilepsy can include behavioral treatment and hormone treatment. Neither intervention has good support and will not be discussed here.

Refractory Epilepsies

The majority of patients with medication-refractory epilepsy have focal seizures of a symptomatic (or probably symptomatic) origin. Patients with focal epilepsy involving the temporal lobes, particularly those with mesial temporal sclerosis (MTS), are typically intractable to medication. Patients with intractable epilepsy are at risk (one per 200 patient years) for death secondary to a seizure, termed sudden unexplained death in epilepsy or SUDEP (Tomson et al., 2008). In addition, patients with refractory epilepsies are at risk for progressive neuropsychological deficits (Hermann et al., 2003), psychiatric dysfunction (Hermann et al., 2000), poor academic achievement (Austin et al., 1998), reduced occupational success and lower quality of life (Poochikian-Sarkissian et al., 2007). Alternatively, a landmark randomized study (Wiebe et al., 2001) confirmed the efficacy of seizure surgery for the treatment of refractory temporal lobe epilepsy with ~60% becoming seizure free with temporal lobectomy, but only ~8% becoming seizure free with continued medication management. While temporal lobectomy carries an approximate 5–10% risk of complications such as death, stroke or infection, the only death in the clinical trial occurred in the medically managed group. Seizure-free rates for selected patients with temporal lobe epilepsies vary, but a rate of 60–80% after one year is generally accepted following anterior temporal lobectomy (ATL) (Cohen-Gadol et al., 2006; de Tisi et al., 2011), and patients presenting with MTS are typically ideal candidates for surgical treatment to achieve seizure control (seizure-free rates after one year above 90% reported). Thus, seizure control after surgical treatment may decrease the risk of seizure-related complications, including death, and can improve quality of life and independence.

Key Points: Refractory Epilepsy
30–40% of patients with epilepsy are currently refractory to medication.

The majority of refractory epilepsies have focal seizures that arise from the temporal lobe.

Seizure freedom with surgical resection in about 70% of patients versus about 3% with ongoing medication, making surgery a highly effective treatment for refractory epilepsy.

The purpose of elective neurosurgical treatment is complete resolution of seizures. However, the determination of "seizure freedom" has varied in the literature, with some experts considering lack of "debilitating" seizures as a good outcome, while other experts argue the term "seizure free" should equate to having no seizures of any kind. Several classification schemes have been developed, with perhaps the most common being that by Engel et al. (1993) (see Table 17.9). We now summarize the surgical and nonsurgical treatments for refractory epilepsies.

Surgical Treatments

Surgical interventions for medication-refractory epilepsy currently include (1) surgical resection of brain parenchyma thought to be necessary for the cessation of seizures (the epileptogenic zone), (2) stereotactic laser ablation or (3) radiofrequency ablation of the epileptogenic zone, (4) hemispherectomy, (5) corpus callosotomy, (6) multiple subpial resection, (7) implantation of vagus nerve stimulator

Table 17.9 Engel et al.'s (1993) classification scale for outcome from surgery for treatment of epilepsy

Engel class	Emotional-behavioral
Ia	Seizure free without auras
Ib	No disabling seizures (e.g., complex partial), but patient may have simple-partial seizures (auras)
II	Rare (several per year) disabling (complex-partial or seizures that secondarily generalize) seizures
III	Greater than 50% reduction in frequency of disabling seizures
IV	Less than 50% reduction in frequency of disabling seizures

Note: Adapted from Engel et al. (1993)

(VNS), (8) implantation of a deep brain stimulator (DBS), (9) implantation of responsive neurostimulator (RNS), (10) stereotaxic gamma-knife radiation and (11) focused ultrasound.

(1) Anterior temporal lobectomy (ATL): This is a surgical resection in which the anterior temporal lobe is resected en bloc. There are multiple ATL procedures, and resections vary from 3 to 8 cm measured from the anterior tip of the temporal lobe. Left (language-dominant) temporal resections often include the anterior 3–5 cm of the temporal lobe, while right (nondominant) temporal resections typically involve the anterior 4–8 cm. The extent of resection has traditionally been determined in one of two ways: One approach tailors the extent of the resection to the patient's pathophysiological findings obtained either extraoperatively or intraoperatively (Ojemann & Valiante, 2006; Silbergeld & Ojemann, 1993). Extraoperative techniques to tailor a resection include placing subdural grid, strip or depth electrodes in the region of the suspected epileptogenic zone and typically obtaining ictal onset data. Intraoperatively, surgeons typically rely on interictal epileptic activity to determine the extent of resection. With the tailored approaches, functional mapping is often used to determine eloquent cortex (e.g., language and motor) (Ojemann et al., 1989). The second approach bases the extent of the temporal resection on anatomical standards (Falconer et al., 1955; Spencer et al., 1984). Resections typically include most of the medial and lateral temporal structures, while much of the superior temporal gyrus is retained in the dominant hemisphere.

a. Selective amygdalohippocampectomy (SAH): In an effort to minimize cognitive/psychological postsurgical deficits associated with standard temporal lobectomy, anatomically standardized open resection operations resecting primarily the medial temporal lobe structures have been developed (Wieser & Yasargil, 1982). These procedures are typically referred to as selective amygdalohippocampectomy (Neimeyer, 1958). There are three more commonly employed routes used to access the medial temporal structures.

   These include (i) transcortical—this involves going through the superior temporal gyrus, (ii) subtemporal—this involves retracting the basal-temporal cortex temporarily to allow access to the medial temporal lobe structures and (iii) trans-sylvian—this involves going through the sulcus between the middle and superior temporal gyri (Olivier, 2000; Shimizu et al., 1989). There are also differences in opinion regarding the extent of resection of medial temporal structures (Feindel & Rasmussen, 1991), although most contemporary series of patients include a resection of some or all of the hippocampal formation. The selective amygdalohippocampectomies have not proven as effective as the ATL at controlling seizures (although the reduction in efficacy is mild) (Hu et al., 2013; Olivier, 2000), but those approaches that have been studied have not proven particularly efficacious at preserving cognition either (Bartha et al., 2004; Kuang et al., 2014). The least studied approach seems to be the subtemporal, and this requires additional research (Burchiel & Christiano, 2006). When the epileptic focus involves eloquent cortex [e.g., primary motor or sensory cortex, Wernicke's or Broca's area(s)], resection can be combined with multiple subpial transections (see below) (Morrell et al., 1989; Wyler, 2006). The latter technique utilizes small cuts perpendicular to the cortical surface, which is intended to disrupt horizontal connections needed for seizure spread, but allows the columnar processing necessary for normal cognitive functioning.

(2) Stereotactic laser ablation (SLA): Since the last version of this book, a novel, minimally invasive surgical approach emerged that involves using a small optical fiber to perform laser interstitial thermal therapy (LITT) (Sperling et al., 2020; Willie et al., 2014). Stereotactic laser amygdalohippocampotomy (SLAH) is a term used when the target is the amygdalohippocampal complex with negligible disturbance to anterior, basal or lateral TL structures (Gross et al., 2016). An FDA trial was recently completed, which resulted in the approval of SLAH as an epilepsy treatment (Sperling et al., 2020), and for which initial data are starting to be released (Gross et al., 2024). LITT of broader brain regions has also been established (Drane, 2018; Hawasli et al., 2014a, 2014b), and this surgical technique has also been used with cavernous malformations (McCracken et al., 2016; Willie et al., 2019), focal cortical dysplasias (Lewis et al., 2015), nodular heterotopias (Esquenazi et al., 2014) and a variety of tumors (e.g., DNETS, high-grade gliomas) (Gupta et al., 2020; Hawasli et al., 2014a, 2014b; Jethwa et al., 2012; Mohammadi et al., 2014). Cognitive outcomes appear to be better in SLAH as compared to ATL/SAH approaches (see Chap. 14 this volume) (Drane, 2018; Drane et al., 2015, 2021c; Gross et al., 2018), although much more research is required. While language function can be completely spared with SLAH (Drane et al., 2015; Drane & Pedersen, 2019), decline can occur in memory, although it is typically less severe and occurs less frequently (Donos et al., 2018; Drane et al., 2021c; Jermakowicz et al., 2017). Deficits can occur using LITT if the tissue to be resected is functional even if the extent of ablation is small (Drane, 2018).

(3) Radiofrequency ablation (RFA): The RFA procedure is a minimally invasive epilepsy surgery technique that uses a stereotactic thermocoagulation probe containing a thermistor or thermocouple for temperature-guided ablations (Shamim et al., 2021; Shields et al., 2023). This can be completed using implanted depth electrodes as used in stereo-electroencephalography (SEEG), which allows the creation of a very focal lesion directly from the same electrode contacts used diagnostically to record seizure activity and to deliver electrical current for cognitive stimulation mapping. RFA is much less likely to create seizure freedom than either ATL or SLAH/LITT (Catenoix et al., 2018; Moles et al., 2018), but it is widely available, can be completed from already implanted electrodes and can be performed by precise functional mapping (Drane et al., 2021a). Additionally, RFA sometimes leads to improved seizure control, and appears to be more successful for small, targeted lesions, such as heterotopias (Cossu et al., 2018; Shamim et al., 2021), and offers a surgical option when standard resections are considered too great a risk to neighboring eloquent cortex.

(4) Hemispherectomy: The removal of all (or most) of an entire hemisphere (Krynauw, 1950; McKenzie, 1938; Rasmussen, 1983). There are two common procedures of hemispherectomy: anatomical hemispherectomy and functional hemispherectomy. The latter procedure attempts to avoid complications (e.g., chronic subdural fluid collection, obstructive hydrocephalus), by simply functionally disconnecting the dysfunctional cerebral hemisphere from the healthy hemisphere (Delalande et al., 2007; Schramm et al., 1995; Villemure & Daniel, 2006). Success rates are similar between the two procedures, yet following up a failed hemispherectomy with an anatomical hemispherectomy can lead to seizure freedom in another one-third of these patients. This procedure is generally limited to those patients with functional hemiparesis and severe seizures (e.g., Rasmussen's encephalitis or Sturge-Weber syndrome). While seemingly dramatic, these procedures can offer patients a favorable outcome from a typically crippling epilepsy syndrome, and up to 75% of patients can have a good outcome, defined as no additional significant deterioration of function beyond the neurological and neuropsychological deficits present at the time of surgery. Surgical complications do occur, and may include motor, sensory, cognitive and psychological deficits (Karagianni et al., 2023). One complication that can occur early or later in life is hydrocephalus. This occurs in less than 5% of patients undergoing functional hemispherectomy, while a slightly higher risk of this complication is observed in hemispherectomy. Overall, studies have suggested that neurological complications are generally low. A worsening of pre-existing or de novo hemiparesis sometimes occurs, with studies showing a range from 5 to 20% (Gowda et al., 2010; Karagianni et al., 2023; Schusse et al., 2018). Of note, most patients have been reported to remain ambulatory even when this complication occurs. There have been some reports of temporary mutism (Liang et al., 2013; Schusse et al., 2018), and there have also been reports of postoperative visual-field deficits, with some studies showing greater than 70% of patients experiencing such changes (Meer et al., 2021). Neurocognitive outcome remains poorly studied, which is a gap that needs to be rectified over time. Nevertheless, on a positive note, there have been several published case series that have demonstrated improved postsurgical learning abilities (Iwasaki et al., 2021; Ramantani et al., 2013).

(5) Corpus callosotomy: This is a procedure in which the corpus callosum is transected in order to minimize the spread of seizures from one hemisphere to another. Typically, this procedure is limited to patients with unknown seizure focus or multiple seizure foci with debilitating seizures that are frequently atonic and/or tonic in nature (e.g., "drop attacks"), which can result in injury. Outcome is variable, but the outcome of the procedure is not to decrease seizure frequency per se, but rather to alter the "spread" of the seizures to spare one hemisphere and hopefully limit the behavioral effect of seizures (i.e., preventing drop attacks) (Bower et al., 2013; Kasasbeh et al., 2014). Following callosotomy, various disconnection syndromes are present initially, particularly when stimuli are presented to one hemisphere alone (Jea et al., 2008; Mamelak et al., 1993). Classic neuropsychologic syndromes of agnosias,

apraxias (e.g., alien hand phenomena), alexia and agraphia have been reported. The severity of disconnection syndrome generally decreases over a period of months such that the deficit is often not appreciable in everyday activities.

(6) Multiple subpial transection: A surgical procedure in which horizontal axonal fiber tracts in the brain are transected while preserving the vertical oriented axonal fiber tracts (Morrell et al., 1989). The surgery is currently offered to patients with seizure focus in eloquent cortex (i.e., cortex with vital functions such as motor, sensory or language functions and is increasingly employed with memory functions) (Wyler, 2006). This procedure arose from observations that seizures typically propagate along horizontal axonal fiber tracts while cortical functions (motor, language) typically propagate along vertical axonal fiber tracts. Surgical transection limits the spread of seizures. Preliminary studies of multiple subpial resection found benefit of greater than 95% seizure reduction in 71% of patients with generalized seizures, 62% of patients with complex-partial seizures and 62% of patients with simple-partial seizures (Spencer et al., 2002). However, data are limited at this time, and concerns remain regarding the long-term outcome for seizure freedom with this procedure.

(7) Vagus nerve stimulator implantation: Vagus nerve stimulation (VNS) is the chronic stimulation of the left vagal nerve by implantation of an electrode attached to the left vagus nerve and a programmable signal generator placed subdermally under the clavicle (Gonzalez et al., 2020; Koo, 2001; Penry & Dean, 1990). Vagus nerve stimulation is approved by the US Food and Drug Administration (FDA) as adjunctive treatment of adult and adolescent patients with refractory complex-partial seizures (Medscape, 2017). In general, VNS is thought to benefit about 33% of patients with a 50% or greater reduction in the frequency and severity of seizures. The other 67% of patients obtained no significant benefit. Studies have shown about 10% of patients can become seizure free (Gonzalez et al., 2019). Studies have shown that the benefits of VNS increase after one year of treatment (Handforth et al., 1998). VNS treatment is typically reserved for patients who are not surgical candidates and/or have had unsuccessful surgical resection procedures. Benefits of VNS have also been observed among a limited number of patients with auras (simple-partial seizures) of relatively long duration (Morris et al., 2013). These patients can sometimes turn on the VNS during their auras, which reportedly can lead to the avoidance of the seizure progressing to a complex-partial or secondarily generalized tonic-clonic event. The mechanism underlying the benefit of VNS remains unknown, but is thought to reflect alteration of the vagus nerve afferents to the brainstem. This is thought to alter the reticular activating, autonomic and limbic systems, including the noradrenergic neurotransmitter system. Common adverse effects of VNS include cough, dyspnea, voice alteration (hoarseness), paresthesias and throat pain (Ben-Menachem, 2001). Less common adverse effects include left vocal cord paralysis and left lower facial nerve (CN VII) paralysis. There is evidence VNS has a positive effect on depression (Rush et al., 2005; Sackeim et al., 2001), and VNS was approved

several years ago for the treatment of patients with refractory major depressive disorder (Austelle et al., 2022).

(8) Deep brain stimulator (DBS) implantation: Deep brain stimulator (DBS) implantation has revolutionized the treatment of movement disorders (see Chap. 19, this volume), and has become a solid, FDA-approved treatment option for the care of medication-refractory epilepsy as well (Fisher et al., 2010). DBS surgery involves the implantation of very thin electrodes to apply chronic electrical stimulation to brain structures, commonly the thalamus, basal ganglia or cingulate gyrus. The two most commonly targeted and researched areas have been the anterior nucleus of the thalamus (ANT DBS) and the centromedian nucleus of the thalamus (CN DBS), although other targets are currently being explored (Vetkas et al., 2022). Selection of potential targets generally follows one of three theoretical models (Zangiabadi et al., 2019): (1) direct stimulation of the epileptogenic zone for the purpose of creating an inhibitory effect, thought to result from alterations in tissue excitability and neuronal synchronization (targets have included the hippocampus, amygdala or focal cortical regions), (2) stimulation of deep subcortical structures to interrupt epileptic networks (most common to date; targets include the thalamus, basal ganglia and cerebellum) and (3) stimulation of deep fiber bundles, particularly those connected to critical structures in a presumed seizure network for the purpose of altering the threshold of seizure induction (targets include the fornix or corpus callosum).

There are two DBS systems: an "open-loop" system and a "closed-loop" system. The open-loop system maintains a static electrical stimulation parameter based on external programming. The "closed-loop" system allows for the monitoring and alteration of the electrical stimulation settings by the function of the brain by an implanted recorder and dynamic computer system. Both methods are currently being investigated as adjunctive therapy for refractory epilepsy. Clinical trials continue to determine ideal brain targets and stimulation parameters. Adverse effects of DBS can include infection, hemorrhage, and depending upon stimulation location, aphasia, dysarthria, weakness and cognitive and mood/behavioral effects.

Several studies have reported promising results of long-term high-frequency DBS in reducing, and in some cases, eliminating medical refractory epilepsy (Fisher et al., 2010; Kerrigan et al., 2004). Boon et al. (2007) reported outcome of a prospective open label trial of DBS of mesial temporal structures for 10 carefully selected patients (Boon et al., 2007). Following at least one year of DBS, 1 patient was seizure free and an additional six patients exhibited a greater than 50% reduction in seizures. An additional two patients had a 30–49% reduction in seizures. Only one patient (10%) failed to respond to DBS. Results of a prospective, randomized, double-blind clinical trial of DBS targeting the anterior thalamus in refractory epilepsy known as the Stimulation of the Anterior Nucleus of the Thalamus in Epilepsy (SANTE) were presented several years ago (Fisher, 2008). At the end of the blinded phase of the study (4 months post-op), 37% of patients receiving DBS exhibited a significant reduction in the median frequency of seizures compared to 14.5% of patients receiving no stimulation. Through the open label period (13 months after DBS surgery), the entire sample (both those in the experimental and control arms) exhibited a 40% reduction in seizure frequency. These results are promising for individuals who have refractory epilepsy and are not candidates for other neurosurgical treatments.

DBS appears to be fairly well tolerated from a neuropsychological standpoint to the extent that it has been examined, although varied results have been observed that can be both positive and negative. Fisher et al. (2010) reported no significant effect of ANT DBS in an early, large clinical study. Similarly, the SANTE trial followed ANT DBS patients for 10 years and did not report any negative results at the group level (Salanova et al., 2021). One small study reported improvement in verbal memory and verbal fluency one year after treatment (Oh et al., 2012). A small, randomized-controlled trial of 18 patients with TLE demonstrated significant improvement on 2 of 22 measures at one year outcome (e.g., measures of attention and motor speed) (Heminghyt et al., 2022). In contrast, a small case series reported negative effects on visual memory and mental flexibility in ANT DBS patients (Osorio et al., 2007). Likewise, another recent study reported some degree of impairment in 13 subjects followed over approximately 4 years (Olaciregui Dague et al., 2023). With regard to memory, they found that a few patients declined over time and a few improved. Many of these studies are limited by small sample sizes, limited test coverage and lack of stimulation parameter detail. It is likely that results will prove differential over time based on stimulation targets, stimulation parameters (e.g., frequency and timing of stimulation), and individual patient characteristics once more fully studied.

(9) Responsive neurostimulator (RNS) implantation: Responsive neurostimulation

(RNS) provides responsive cortical stimulation via a programmable neurostimulator connected to 1 or 2 recording and stimulating depth or subdural cortical strip leads (Morrell and RNS System in Epilepsy Study Group, 2011). The leads are surgically placed in the brain according to the seizure focus. The neurostimulator continually senses electrocorticographic activity and is programmed by the physician to detect abnormal activity and then provide stimulation, hence the term responsive neurostimulation. The RNS system is the first responsive (closed-loop) focal cortical stimulator. The physician adjusts detection and stimulation parameters for each patient to optimize control of seizures. It allows the physician to objectively assess treatment response, quantify seizure burden and identify circadian patterns among others (Morrell, 2019; Quigg, 2016).

The RNS system was approved by the US Food and Drug Administration in 2013 for individuals 18 years of age or older with drug-resistant focal epilepsy. Several studies have demonstrated the efficacy and safety of RNS as an adjunctive treatment for medically intractable focal epilepsy. In 2011, Morell et al. conducted a multicenter, double-blind randomized controlled trial of 191 patients with medically refractory focal epilepsy (Morrell and RNS System in Epilepsy Study Group, 2011). Seizures were significantly reduced in the treatment compared to the sham group (−37.09% vs −17.3%, respectively). They also showed that there was no deterioration in mood or neuropsychological function. Other studies have shown similar findings, although there have also been reports that mood and cognitive issues can be created by electrodes placed in the wrong location (e.g., seizure onset zone was not adequately targeted) or when stimulation is occurring too frequently . The procedure appears to be a durable treatment, as based on one recent study prospectively evaluating the safety and efficacy of RNS over 9 years (Morrell & Study, 2020). The median percent reduction in seizure frequency was 75% ($p < 0.0001$) and 35% had a ≥ 90% reduction in seizure frequency. They also showed that epilepsy-targeted and cognitive domains of QOLIE-89 remained significantly improved ($p < 0.05$). Other studies showed that electrocorticography data can be used to determine surgical candidacy. In a study conducted by Morell et al. (Morrell, 2020), electrocorticography data from 157 patients treated with RNS with bilateral medial temporal leads due to presumed bitemporal epilepsy were analyzed. Sixteen percent subsequently had unilateral temporal lobe resection informed by RNS data. The findings suggest that RNS data can provide information about lateralization of seizures and can identify additional patients who may benefit from epilepsy surgery. Taken altogether, RNS is a safe and effective treatment for patients with drug-resistant focal epilepsy, particularly those at high risk for cognitive decline with a more destructive procedure, multifocal epilepsy, or those with a less certain onset zone.

(10) Stereotaxic gamma-knife radiation treatment: Gamma-knife radiation treatment uses focused radiation in several beams to target an area of tissue. Each beam alone does not result in brain damage, but the focused concentration of where all the beams converge results in radiation doses sufficient to cause cell death in a preplanned discrete area. This procedure is particularly well suited to the treatment of brain tumors that would otherwise be inoperable. Gamma-knife radiation has also been applied to vascular malformations with favorable outcomes. Stereotaxic gamma-knife radiation has been applied to patients with TLE (Regis et al., 1999). A multicenter trial reported seizure freedom rates at 36 months post-gamma-knife radiosurgery of 76% in a high-dose group (receiving 24 Gy) and 59% in the low-dose group (receiving 20 Gy), which approached the seizure freedom rates of standard ATL without the potential surgical risks of infection (Barbaro et al., 2009). The benefits of seizure reduction related to gamma-knife radiation are not immediately appreciated, with the average time to seizure freedom reported to be about 12 months after the procedure (Bartolomei et al., 2008). Interestingly, patients often experience an increase in simple-partial seizures at the onset of seizure reduction (Regis et al., 1999). This coincides with the onset of structural neuroimaging changes 9–12 months after surgery. A long-term (6–10 years) seizure freedom rate (Engle I) is reported to be ~60% (Bartolomei et al., 2008). Neuropsychological outcome from gamma-knife surgery may be better than

standard temporal lobectomy, with pilot data finding that a significant decline in verbal memory occurred in 15% of subjects, while 12% of participants exhibited a significant improvement (Barbaro et al., 2009). Another study found a significant decline in verbal memory among 100% of patients ($n = 3$), while no decline in visual memory, IQ or language/speech measures was evident (McDonald et al., 2004).

Presurgical Evaluation

Once a patient has failed to respond to adequate medication trials, surgical evaluation should proceed. The presurgical evaluation will typically include a comprehensive neurological evaluation that includes a detailed history, high-quality MRI and video-EEG study (Velis et al., 2007). Neuropsychological evaluation is often ordered (Rausch, 2006). Other procedures often include the Wada test and/or other functional neuroimaging studies such as functional MRI (fMRI), SPECT and/or PET studies (Van Passchen et al., 2007). SPECT studies, particularly an ictal SPECT, can be helpful in localizing the seizure focus. PET studies can also prove useful in identifying areas of dysfunction not presenting on structural MRI studies. Often the hypometabolic region is larger than the area generating seizures, even involving the contralateral lobe, which may improve after successful seizure surgery. Finally, MEG and MSI are increasingly used in epilepsy centers to identify interictal activity suggesting the seizure focus (Kharkar & Knowlton, 2015; Pataraia et al., 2005). MSI is used to localize brain functions including language and memory (Knowlton et al., 2009; Tovar-Spinoza et al., 2008). Based on these studies, surgical candidacy is determined, and treatment options provided to the patient. We now provide a brief review of the neuropsychological aspects of the presurgical evaluation and then turn our attention to the neuropsychological aspects of epilepsy more generally.

Pre-surgical Neuropsychological Evaluation: Basic Concepts

In most comprehensive epilepsy centers providing surgery (Level IV centers), clinical neuropsychologists are considered core members of the treatment team (Baxendale et al., 2019; Jones-Gotman et al., 2010). Neuropsychologists most often conduct pre-surgical neuropsychological evaluations. These are useful for a number of reasons, including for (a) characterizing a patient's cognitive profile and whether it matches the expected archetypal pattern as well as converges with other studies with regard to confirmation of seizure lateralization/localization; (b) assisting to establish a pre-surgical baseline and stratify risk for postsurgical cognitive decline or emotional-behavioral dysfunction; and (c) providing comparison data against any postsurgical evaluation to monitor for potential treatment consequences. While evaluation batteries are quite heterogenous around the globe and in the United

States (Berl et al., 2017; Brissart et al., 2019; Djordjevic & Jones-Gotman, 2011; Helmstaedter et al., 2020; Vogt et al., 2017), many seasoned epilepsy neuropsychologists usually include recommended measures from the US National Institute of Neurological Disorders and Stroke (NINDS) Common Data Elements in their test batteries ((Loring et al., 2011); https://www.commondataelements.ninds.nih.gov/epilepsy). The tests included in the Common Data Elements reflect only a small core that allows for a common metric of tests to be used across research and clinical studies.

One role of the clinical neuropsychologist is to provide consultation to the team and the patient with respect to the possible cognitive and psychological risks of undergoing elective neurosurgical treatment. In addition to the pre-surgical neuropsychological evaluation, neuropsychologists also often conduct other ancillary tests such as the Wada evaluation (Loring, 1990; Wada & Rasmussen, 1960) and various neuroimaging techniques (e.g., structural and functional MRI (Binder et al., 2008a; Kaestner et al., 2020, 2024; McDonald et al., 2008; Sabsevitz et al., 2003)), and intra- or extraoperative cortical stimulation mapping of language and other cognitive functions may also be used (Drane et al., 2021a). The clinical neuropsychologist should also be aware of the medical aspects of epilepsy which can affect the patient's neuropsychological outcome, as well as the potential impact of ASMs and other medications. Equally important is providing information about the patient's neuropsychological risks to NOT having surgery (see Sect. "Neuropsychological (Cognitive and Behavioral) Comorbidity in Epilepsy" below).

Neuropsychologists may also be involved in treatment, and evaluations can help to identify patients who may benefit from pre- or postsurgical rehabilitative intervention(s) such as HOBSCOTCH (Caller et al., 2016); https://www.dartmouth-hitchcock.org/hobscotch-institute) or other programs addressing cognitive or psychosocial needs (Baxendale et al., 2020; Dilorio et al., 2011; Fraser et al., 2015; Mittan, 2009) (Shegog et al., 2013). This includes engaging in interventions designed to reduce the frequency and the effects of functional seizures (see Chap. 18) as well as the ReACT and e-PROGRAM models (Carlson & Nicholson Perry, 2017; Fobian & Szaflarski, 2021; Higson et al., 2023; Stager et al., 2021, 2023).

Neuropsychological (Cognitive and Behavioral) Comorbidity in Epilepsy

Although a medically recognized phenomenon throughout much of human history, epilepsy (particularly idiopathic epilepsies) was not generally thought to affect cognitive and emotional-behavioral functions until the twentieth century. In the early 1900s, a comparison of healthy adults against cognitively "normal" persons with epilepsy and those with "marked dementia" was published (Smith, 1905). Nowadays, epilepsy has been reconceptualized as a network disorder (Holmes, 2015), and studies have demonstrated cognitive, emotional-behavioral and social-adaptive perturbations as early as onset of the first seizure or time of diagnosis (Austin et al., 2001;

Fastenau et al., 2009; Hermann et al., 2006b; Hutchinson et al., 2010; Jones et al., 2007; Pugh et al., 2024a). There is a growing body of research on accelerated brain aging in persons with epilepsy (Breuer et al., 2016, 2019; Hwang et al., 2020; Kaestner et al., 2021), as well as how this may be further compounded by type, number and/or duration of effect of ASMs and other comorbidities (Brodie et al., 2009; Italiano & Perucca, 2013). Consequently, there is increasing concern about the longer-term potential cognitive, emotional-behavioral and social/adaptive functioning of persons with epilepsy (including those successfully managed with medication and/or the so-called benign epilepsies (Garcia-Ramos et al., 2016; Hermann et al., 2008; Lima et al., 2017; Sillanpaa et al., 1998; Vannest et al., 2015; Verotti et al., 2014).

In terms of cognitive functioning, studies of general epilepsy suggest a prevalence of cognitive impairment in the 30–50% range for adults (Kwan & Brodie, 2001) and 40–50% in children (or higher as in severe epilepsies such as Lennox-Gasteau or West syndrome (Camfield & Camfield, 2007)). Rates of impairment are as high as 70% in the case of TLE, one of the most common presentations in adults (Bell et al., 2011). In the past 10–15 years, studies have emerged that delineate cognitive phenotypes of various epilepsies in both adults and children (Abarrategui et al., 2018; Arrotta et al., 2022; Caciagli et al., 2023; Cano-Lopez et al., 2024; Dabbs et al., 2009; Elverman et al., 2019; Giovagnoli et al., 2020; Hermann et al., 2007; Reyes et al., 2019, 2023; Schraegle et al., 2022; Shah et al., 2024; Valente et al., 2016), and whether there are implications for postsurgical outcomes (Baxendale & Thompson, 2020) or associations with specific emotional-behavioral disturbances (Bingaman et al., 2023; Catalan-Aguilar et al., 2023; Hermann et al., 2021). Nevertheless, while a positive development, many of these studies are significantly hindered by limitations in test batteries used to categorize function. For example, many of these papers had few tests in major domains of function, which will result in skewed and incomplete phenotypes.

Functionally, persons with epilepsy have consistently reported higher unemployment, less occupational success and lower educational achievement than healthy peers in the general population (for a review, see Hermann et al., 2008). Socially, children with epilepsy exhibit reduced social competence and continue to experience interpersonal difficulties into adulthood (Camfield & Camfield, 2007; Russ et al., 2012). Adults with epilepsy are less likely to marry and to have children than are healthy peers in the general population (Hermann et al., 2008), and those persons experiencing deficits in social cognition are at particular risk for poor social inclusion (Steiger & Jokeit, 2017).

The etiology for the increased risk of neuropsychological (cognitive and emotional-behavioral) dysfunction is multifactorial. Variables implicated in the neuropsychological dysfunction among persons with epilepsy include (a) underlying pathology giving rise to seizures (Lin et al., 2012), (b) the epileptic electroneurophysiological dysfunction—particularly frequency and severity of seizures (Elger et al., 2004; Wang et al., 2011), (c) ASMs (Drane & Meador, 2002; Kanner & Bicchi, 2022), (d) medical complications (multiple episodes of status epilepticus, falls resulting in head injuries, etc.) (Cooper et al., 2009; Dodrill & Wilensky, 1990;

Fontaine et al., 2020; Gramstad et al., 2021; Wasterlain et al., 1993) and (e) other factors (e.g., psychosocial variables, neurodevelopmental and aging effects; see Fig. 17.5) (Dodrill, 1986b; Fastenau et al., 2004; Sarkis et al., 2018; Shackleton et al., 2003).

Review of this figure highlights the interactive, non-independent interrelationships of these factors on neuropsychological function, the epilepsy syndrome/underlying pathology and psychosocial functioning. First, neurodevelopmental forces can have both positive and negative effects on neuropsychological function. For example, seizures from the language-dominant hemisphere are known to result in inter- and/or intra-hemispheric reorganization of neuropsychological functions, allowing for normal or near-normal neuropsychological functioning (Duchowny et al., 1996; Liegeois et al., 2004; Muller et al., 1999; Satz et al., 1994), and early bilingualism has been shown to confer enhanced cognitive reserve over the lifespan (Reyes et al., 2018; Royer & Bernhardt, 2023; Stasenko et al., 2022, 2023). However, aging processes of the brain negatively affect persons with epilepsy whereby those with refractory epilepsy appear to be at higher risk for accelerated brain aging and/or development of dementia than the general population—perhaps in part owing to shared pathological mechanisms (Breuer et al., 2016; Huang et al., 2022; Sen et al., 2018; Subota et al., 2021). Next, ASM type and monotherapy/polytherapy status have increasingly been recognized as having adverse

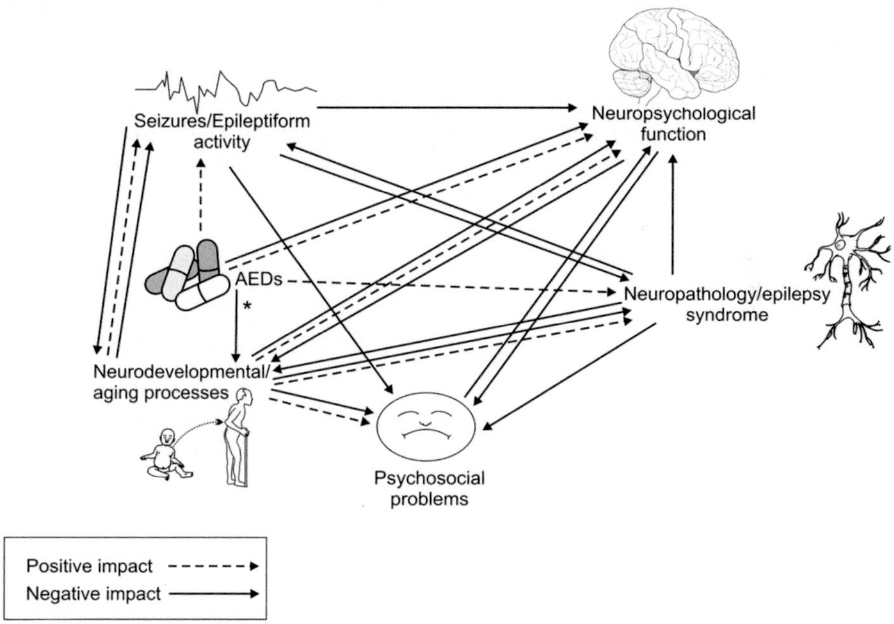

Fig. 17.5 Non-independent variables interacting to affect neuropsychological function for patients with epilepsy. Note: Adapted from Baker and Taylor (2008). *Adverse effect shown only for neurodevelopmental processes and is limited some medications and not all individuals exposed have demonstrated adverse effect

neuropsychological effects on the patient, although the magnitude of adverse cognitive effect is generally considered to be small (Aldenkamp et al., 2003; Loring et al., 2007; Mermi Dibek et al., 2024). Data do indicate that some ASMs can adversely affect neurodevelopmental processes—in particular older-generation ASMs (e.g., benzodiazepines, sodium valproate, topiramate; Honybun et al., 2024; Meador et al., 2009; Olney et al., 2002). The potential for a negative impact on neurodevelopmental processes in a child with seizure onset not previously exposed remains to be determined. Clearly, the relative contributions of these variables to neuropsychological dysfunction vary. For example, the effect of underlying neuropathology and seizures in some idiopathic epilepsies is reduced given the lack of structural lesion and often well-controlled seizures, thus leaving the factors largely affecting neuropsychological function to be the epilepsy syndrome itself, the effects of ASMs, and potentially, medical complications (Elger et al., 2004; Grivas et al., 2006).

In the remainder of this section, we review what is known about the neuropsychological functioning of persons with epilepsy, including emerging data suggesting aspects of behavioral and cognitive function are compromised in at least some individuals at seizure onset (Fastenau et al., 2009; Pugh et al., 2024a; Witt & Helmstaedter, 2012) or even before first recognized seizure (Jones et al., 2007). Further, some persons with epilepsy experience a progressive decline in cognitive functioning over time due to increased burden posed by mechanisms such as structural changes in gray and white matter, hippocampal sclerosis, neurotoxicity, neuroinflammation and psychiatric comorbidities (Helmstaedter et al., 2003; Ngadimon et al., 2024; Reimers et al., 2022; Seidenberg et al., 2007)—although recent data suggest that resective surgery may prevent progressive cortical thinning in persons with TLE (Federico & Wiebe, 2020; Galovic et al., 2020). We also summarize cognitive differences between the generalized epilepsies and patients with focal seizures, and then review the effects of surgical intervention on cognition.

Cognitive and Behavioral Dysfunction Before Seizure Onset?

There is recent evidence that argues cognitive and emotional-behavioral problems are present prior to the first recognized seizure in at least some individuals (Austin et al., 2001; Hermann et al., 2008; Jones et al., 2007). For example, Jones et al. (2007) found approximately one-quarter of children diagnosed with new-onset epilepsy exhibited academic problems prior to first recognized seizure (Jones et al., 2007). Additionally, nearly half of children with new-onset epilepsy exhibited psychiatric and behavioral problems prior to first recognized seizure than age-matched peers (primarily depressive disorders, anxiety disorders and ADHD). Taken together, these data suggest some epilepsy syndromes manifest with cognitive and psychiatric dysfunction prior to seizure onset.

Cognitive Status at Seizure Onset

In patients with symptomatic epilepsy, the etiology of seizure onset (i.e., brain tumor, cortical dysgenesis, head trauma, encephalitis, developmental disorder) typically produces brain dysfunction independent of the epilepsy syndrome. However, epidemiological studies have found children and adults with new-onset epilepsy, including those with unknown etiology, exhibit some deficits in cognitive functioning, higher rates of academic problems and increased rates of psychiatric syndromes (Austin et al., 2002; Davies et al., 2003; Elger et al., 2004; Fastenau et al., 2009; Hermann et al., 2012; Noeker et al., 2005; Rutter et al., 1970; Taylor et al., 2011).

Children. Neuropsychological deficits in attention/executive, memory, processing speed and visuoconstructional/visuospatial skills along with psychiatric disorders have been observed in children at seizure onset, and approximately 50% of children with new-onset epilepsy also exhibit academic difficulties (Jackson et al., 2013). Children with focal (localized) epilepsies tend to exhibit the least neuropsychological deficits, with some studies observing no neuropsychological deficits (Fastenau et al., 2009). Patients with symptomatic focal and generalized epilepsies tend to exhibit neuropsychological deficits. While academic problems have previously been reported among children with first onset epilepsy, Fastenau et al. (2009) did not find deficits in academic achievement in a well-controlled study of children with a variety of epilepsy syndromes (Fastenau et al., 2009). Indeed, the authors argued that neuropsychological evaluation in children with one or more identified risk factors for cognitive deficits may provide an avenue to arrest or reduce the adverse effects of epilepsy and neuropsychological deficits on academic development. The risk factors for neuropsychological dysfunction in children with a first recognized seizure were (1) multiple unprovoked seizures [odds ratio (OR) = 1.97], (2) use of ASMs [OR = 2.27], (3) unknown etiology of seizures [OR = 2.15] and (4) epileptiform discharges on the EEG at first recognized seizure [OR = 1.90]. The presence of all 4 risk factors increased the risk of neuropsychological deficits within 6 months of first recognized seizures to 3 times that of their healthy siblings. The adverse effect of seizures (electroneurophysiological dysfunction) on neuropsychological function is clear for both children and adults, and in children can serve as a biomarker for deficits in processing speed and other neuropsychological functions. Interestingly, research has found that children with first recognized seizure do not consistently exhibit MRI structural abnormalities (Fastenau et al., 2009; Hermann et al., 2008).

Adults. Neuropsychological deficits in memory, attention/executive, reaction time and visuomotor tasks have been observed in at least some patients at the time of first recognized seizure, as are emotional-behavioral concerns such as depression, anxiety and fatigue (Cronin et al., 2023; Pugh et al., 2024a, 2024b; Vu et al., 2018)—even in drug-naïve patients. For example, impairments were observed in attention and executive functioning (49.4%) and memory (47.8%) domains in one study of 247 untreated persons with newly diagnosed epilepsy—with another quarter of the sample reporting subjective cognitive concerns (Witt & Helmstaedter, 2012). In another study comparing 32 persons with new-onset epilepsy and 30 healthy matched controls from the community, cognitive dysfunction was observed in similar domains and one-third of the sample were also considered high risk for major depression and anxiety disorders (Pugh et al., 2024a).

Taken together, greater neuropsychological and emotional-behavioral problems are observed among persons with epilepsy around the time of first recognized seizure, arguing against the possibility that neuropsychological deficits merely reflect a progression of disease based on the adverse effects of recurrent seizures and/or ASMs. However, decades of research with patients having medication-refractory epilepsy have established greater neuropsychological dysfunction with earlier age of onset and longer duration of seizures (Elger et al., 2004; Strauss et al., 1995), as well evidence for accelerated brain aging (Breuer et al., 2016, 2019), raising the clear possibility that at least some epilepsy syndromes are a progressive disease.

Epilepsy as a Potentially Progressive Disorder

There has been interest for many years in determining whether epilepsy syndromes contribute to declines in physiological and neuropsychological status over time. While the majority of these studies have used a cross-sectional design, a few longitudinal studies have reported data more recently. Nevertheless, definitive studies are yet to be performed that adequately control for the large number of factors present in patients with epilepsy that may contribute to change over time. The following summary should be interpreted with these caveats in mind.

Longitudinal data ultimately provide actuarial data for change in cognitive, behavioral and brain neurophysiology over time among persons with epilepsy (Helmstaedter et al., 2003; Hermann et al., 2008; Seidenberg et al., 2007), with particularly poor prognosis noted for persons with lower baseline intellectual capacity, longer epilepsy duration and older chronic age (Hermann et al., 2006a). Further, Seidenberg et al. (2007) argued for including a healthy control group in order to recognize change in neurocognitive functioning (Seidenberg et al., 2007). Longitudinal studies without control groups failed to recognize decline, as this can be obscured by practice effects related to repeat testing (e.g., Helmstaedter et al., 2003; Holmes et al., 1998). More specifically, persons with epilepsy often fail to show normal improvements in scores with repeat testing (practice effects) exhibited by healthy controls (e.g., Seidenberg et al., 2007; Thompson & Duncan, 2005). While evidence for frank deterioration in neuropsychological function over time has varied, more robust findings for decline in memory are evident (Hermann et al., 2006a; Seidenberg et al., 2007).

In general, duration of epilepsy, age of seizure onset, seizure frequency and history of status epilepticus play a role in the occurrence of progressive cognitive decline (Breuer et al., 2016; Dodrill, 1986a; Jokeit & Ebner, 1999, 2002; Jokeit & Schacher, 2004; Oyegbile et al., 2004), although not all studies have found this relationship (Holmes et al., 1998). It has been suggested the effect of epilepsy duration on cognitive decline may also reflect the effects of chronic ASM use and recurring interictal epileptiform activity (Thompson & Duncan, 2005). Nevertheless, research with children and adults with first onset seizure and naive to ASMs has demonstrated that neuropsychological dysfunction was already present, showing that neuropsychological dysfunction is not due solely to ASM use (Fastenau et al., 2009). Some studies have also suggested that experiencing two or more different seizure types correlates with poorer outcome over time (Dodrill, 1984); multiple seizure types may be seen in epilepsies with more severe clinical courses such as Lennox-Gastaut or Dravet syndrome, and this has been associated with cognitive impairment, pharmacoresistance and poorer overall prognosis (Camfield & Camfield, 2008; Scheffer et al., 2017). Seidenberg et al. (2007) suggested a three- to four-year follow-up period is sufficient to detect change over time, but argued that changes in cognition may be more apparent with longer test–retest time intervals (Seidenberg et al., 2007).

Cognitive deterioration across epilepsy syndrome types is quite variable, although certain syndromes are more associated with greater cognitive dysfunction (e.g., TLE) than others (benign epilepsy syndromes). For example, patients with TLE are generally considered to be at high risk for cognitive morbidity, with data suggesting at least 20–25% experience a progressive decline in cognitive function over time, defined as 3–7 years (Hermann et al., 2008; Seidenberg et al., 2007) with the rates increased to 40–60% in persons having undergone ATL of the language-dominant hemisphere (Bell et al., 2011). Moreover, patients with Lennox-Gastaut and Landau-Kleffner syndromes often exhibit catastrophic cognitive impairments, including intellectual developmental deficits in the former and acquired global aphasia in the latter. In contrast, patients with JME more frequently possess normal intellectual abilities and have preserved and neuropsychological impairment often does not arise until adulthood (Raatikainen et al., 2020).

Neuroimaging studies have also found structural and functional brain abnormalities which support the hypothesis that uncontrolled (medication-refractory) epilepsy is a progressive disease. Most of these studies have been conducted in patients with TLE, and patients often exhibit significant abnormalities that extend outside of the epileptogenic temporal lobe (Hermann et al., 2003). In fact, TLE patients have exhibited alterations in (1) total cerebral tissue, (2) white matter volumes, (3) neocortical thickness, (4) parietal and frontal lobes and (5) thalamic volumes and metabolism as compared to normal controls (Bernasconi et al., 2003, 2004, 2005, 2019; Caciagli et al., 2017; Ding et al., 2014; Hermann et al., 2003; Keller & Roberts, 2008). Tract- and connectome-based approaches implicate both extratemporal and temporo-limbic white matter disruptions (Concha et al., 2009, 2012; Tavakol et al., 2019; Vaughan et al., 2017). While some data suggest extratemporal atrophy may represent early cerebral damage (Chiang et al., 2015), there is increasing evidence that such abnormalities are progressive in nature and likely due to structural brain changes associated with ongoing seizure activity (e.g., deafferentation of white matter following chronic seizure occurrence) (Sone et al., 2024). Studies using diffusion tensor imaging (DTI), for example, have shown that fronto-temporal white matter integrity is disrupted by seizure activity in TLE patients in the hemisphere ipsilateral to seizure onset (Riley et al., 2010). Broader white matter dysfunction has been shown to reduce the likelihood of seizure freedom following surgical intervention (Bonilha et al., 2015; Gleichgerrcht et al., 2020; Taylor et al., 2018). Similarly, studies have demonstrated prefrontal metabolic abnormalities among patients with TLE using both PET (Jokeit et al., 1997) and magnetic resonance spectroscopy (MRS: (Bernasconi et al., 2019)). These metabolic abnormalities can normalize following treatment resulting in seizure freedom (Cendes et al., 1997). The forces affecting the extent and progression of impairment appears to reflect a combination of noxious and beneficial factors impinging upon the brain [e.g., underlying disease pathology, duration and type of seizures, chronic ASM exposure, seizure freedom, psychosocial variables, neurodevelopmental/aging forces].

Neuropsychological Profiles

Below we summarize the neuropsychological findings for patients with both generalized epilepsy syndromes and focal epilepsies.

Generalized Epilepsy Syndromes

Broadly speaking, generalized seizures are more likely to impair cognitive functions than focal seizures, particularly for patients with multiple episodes of status epilepticus (Dodrill, 1986a; Jokeit & Schacher, 2004); however, even without status epilepticus multiple generalized seizures can be just as detrimental to cognition—with one study suggesting that 10 or more generalized seizures may be comparable to one episode of status (Power et al., 2017). While there are a number of different primary generalized epilepsy syndromes, the onset of seizures in all of these syndromes is defined as involving electrical discharges that appear simultaneous throughout the brain on scalp EEG. In actuality, there has historically been debate over whether seizures originate in the thalamus or the cortex, but more recent research has helped to elucidate the thalamocortical network's role in seizure generalization (Holmes et al., 2004; Slaght et al., 2002; Wills et al., 2021). It is also known that frontal lobe structures play a significant role in generalized epilepsies (Pavone & Niedermeyer, 2000). Accordingly, patients with generalized epilepsies have exhibited impairment in functions associated with the frontal lobes (executive functions), such as mental flexibility, working memory and task shifting. Concordantly, MRI morphometry has revealed frontal lobe abnormalities in patients with primary generalized epilepsy (Savic et al., 1998).

Neurocognitive Profiles in Focal Epilepsy and the Effects of Surgical Intervention

There is a vast literature examining the cognitive and emotional/psychiatric functioning in patients with focal epilepsy, particularly for TLE (Tani & Adawi, 2024). This emphasis reflects TLE being the most common focal epilepsy syndrome, and the predominant subset of patients referred to epilepsy surgery programs. The surgical evaluation process has allowed extensive data to be collected across electroneurophysiological, neuroanatomical (gross to molecular level), neurophysiological, neurological, neuropsychological, psychiatric, psychological, quality of life and a variety of psychosocial/cultural variables. The goal for the collection and analysis of data has been to establish seizure focus and propagation as well as predict surgical outcome [i.e., cognitive sequelae, psychiatric sequelae, seizure freedom (see Engel surgery outcome scale at https://seizure.mgh.harvard.edu/engel-surgical-outcome-scale)] to improve quality of life and reduce morbidity/mortality.

Neuropsychological outcome is increasingly considered an important marker of successful seizure surgery outcome (Hermann & Loring, 2008; Lineweaver et al., 2006), and several variables have consistently proven to reduce risk for cognitive morbidity following epilepsy surgery including longer duration of seizures, MTS, impaired presurgical memory scores and Wada failure ipsilateral to the side of seizure onset, among others (for a brief review, see Drane, 2015). Some research suggests that invasive monitoring used as part of the presurgical workup may confer additional risk to patients' cognitive outcomes; however, Busch et al. (2015) showed that while there were score declines in aspects of cognition, pre/postsurgical reliable change analyses indicated that they were not clinically meaningful (Busch et al., 2015). Detailed below, prototypical neuropsychological profiles that have lateralizing/localizing value (e.g., language deficits, material-specific memory deficits in TLE) have been identified. In this section, we will also discuss other schemas for conceptualizing or predicting the deficits associated with TLE that go beyond the prototypical models. We also summarize the more limited research on the various extratemporal epilepsies. Finally, the major findings related to predicting surgical outcome are detailed for patients with TLE.

Findings in Temporal Lobe Epilepsy

Preoperative: For many years, the prototypical pattern of deficit in presurgical TLE patients has been described as a material-specific pattern of memory dysfunction (Milner, 1958). The lateralization of dysfunction has been used to predict side of seizure onset (see predicting side of seizure below). In particular, greater auditory/verbal memory deficits are often observed in patients in language-dominant TLE, while visual/nonverbal memory deficits have been more associated with nondominant TLE (Blakemore & Falconer, 1967; Jones-Gotman, 1986; Loring et al., 1988;

McDonald et al., 2001; Milner, 1968; Pillon et al., 1999; Wilde et al., 2001). This finding has also been bolstered by neuroimaging studies that have found that auditory/verbal and nonverbal/visual stimuli can preferentially activate the left or right MTL, respectively (Golby et al., 2001; Powell et al., 2005). Of note, however, fMRI results have proven inconsistent, and it can be difficult to reliably activate the hippocampus. Additionally, the "textbook" neuropsychological profile for TLE has not been found consistently (Barr et al., 1997; Pigott & Milner, 1993; Wilde et al., 2001). Indeed, visual/nonverbal memory deficits associated with nondominant hemisphere dysfunction have been particularly difficult to establish, and the lateralizing effect may actually be contingent in part on stimulus type and testing format; one recent study showed that faces demonstrated greater lateralizing effect than did designs, and for recall versus recognition paradigms (Bentvelzen et al., 2022). Overall, material-specific memory dysfunction can be observed in presurgical TLE patients, although broader patterns of impairment are frequently observed. In part, this reflects that neuropsychological deficits may be sensitive to more than just the epileptogenic zone. That is, patterns of dysfunction may reflect seizure spread, effects of ASMs and other broader conditions. Beyond memory dysfunction, individuals with TLE frequently exhibit a range of other deficits, including impaired expressive language (particularly visual or auditory naming and verbal fluency) (Drane et al., 2008; Drane & Pedersen, 2019; Hamberger & Tamny, 1999; Martin et al., 1990), attention/executive functions (Bocquillon et al., 2008; Culhand-Shelburne et al., 2002; Hermann & Seidenberg, 1995; Yang et al., 2024), and, less commonly, visuospatial/constructional abilities (Tallarita et al., 2023). Finally, it is not uncommon for patients with TLE to exhibit reduced overall IQ (Novais et al., 2022) as well as limitations in academic achievement (Craggs et al., 1997; Helmstaedter et al., 2003). For example, Fig. 17.6 graphs the average performance of adult patients with TLE (n = 36) who underwent presurgical evaluation at the University of South Florida Epilepsy Center (Fig. 17.6). Our data are similar to other presurgical findings.

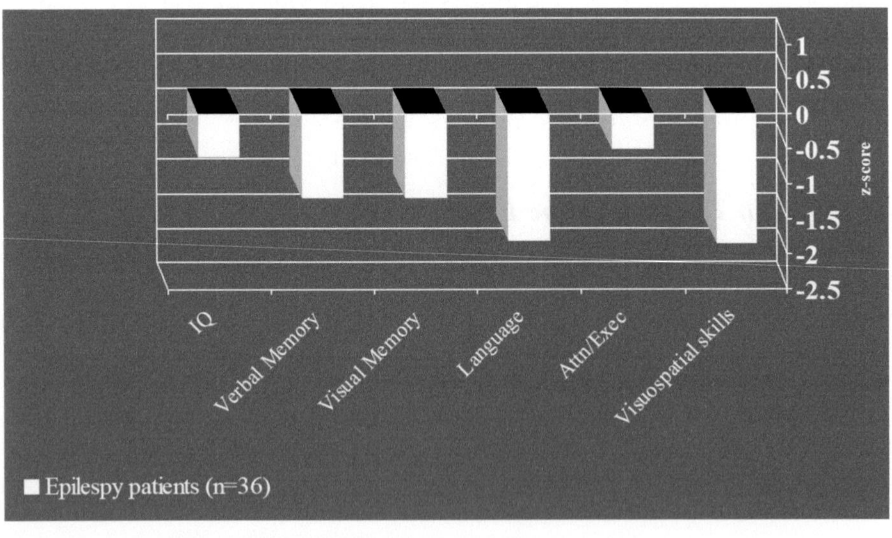

Fig. 17.6 Presurgical neuropsychological deficits for adults with temporal lobe epilepsy

Language Deficits and Seizure Lateralization

Seizure lateralization has been predicted by naming deficits (Busch et al., 2005, 2009). Busch et al. (2005) developed a regression equation using the Boston Naming Test (BNT) to aid in preoperative seizure localization and demonstrated its diagnostic utility, with cross-validation in a subsequent follow-up study. Hamberger and colleagues have also introduced an auditory naming task that has demonstrated some value in predicting preoperative seizure lateralization (i.e., Columbia Auditory Naming Test; (Hamberger & Seidel, 2003; Hamberger & Tamny, 1999); however, these data are limited and more studies in this area are needed. Extensive research finds that patients with TLE, particularly those with dominant seizure onset, are more likely to experience deficits in naming ability (e.g., confrontation naming, naming to description) than healthy controls and patients with extratemporal seizure onset (e.g., Hamberger & Tamny, 1999; Mayeux et al., 1980). Left TLE groups tend to perform worse than right TLE groups on visual confrontation naming tasks (Drane et al., 2008; Hamberger et al., 2010; Hermann et al., 1988, 1991; Langfit & Rausch, 1996), although the right TLE groups often perform worse than healthy controls (Langfit & Rausch, 1996).

The confrontation naming deficits among patients with TLE can be extensive. Patients with left (dominant) TLE are impaired at naming famous faces (Drane et al., 2008, 2013; Glosser et al., 2003; Seidenberg et al., 2002), and at least two of these studies suggested these deficits may be worse following ATL resection. Findings have recently been extended to include other visually complex item categories (e.g., famous landmarks, nonunique animals) even when performance is normal on a standard naming test (i.e., BNT) (Drane et al., 2008, 2009a). The broader naming deficits in TLE are supported by functional imaging that highlight a critical role for the anterior temporal lobes in naming certain object categories (Damasio et al., 1996) although there is also evidence supporting involvement of basal-temporal language regions (Kaestner et al., 2022; Luders et al., 1986, 1991; Maillard et al., 2022; Palmini et al., 2004) and perhaps even the insula (Ardila et al., 2014; Cargnelutti et al., 2024).

Deficits in verbal fluency (i.e., generating items from categories and/or letter fluency) are commonly found among patients with TLE (Tailby et al., 2017; Troster et al., 1995). However, preoperative deficits in semantic fluency (category fluency) have not shown consistent value in seizure lateralization, since impaired scores are observed for patients with either dominant or nondominant temporal lobe epilepsy (Bartha et al., 2004, 2005; Joanette & Goulet, 1986; Martin et al., 1990) or localization as deficits may be observed in temporal and frontal lobe epilepsies (Drane et al., 2006; Metternich et al., 2014). Semantic fluency requires both an executive component mediated by frontal lobe regions (i.e., organization/retrieval from semantic memory stores as well as initiation of action and self-monitoring (Sylvester & Shimamura, 2002) and a semantic memory component thought to be mediated by the temporal lobes (Martin & Fedio, 1983). Patients with frontal lobe seizure onset can be distinguished preoperatively from patients with TLE using a semantic fluency paradigm that contrasts cued and uncued performance (Drane et al., 2006). Similarly, performance on letter fluency tasks can be impaired preoperatively due to both frontal lobe and temporal lobe dysfunction (Helmstaedter et al., 1996; Martin et al., 2000). Thus, simply having a poor score on a semantic or phonemic verbal fluency task may not be of much localizing or lateralizing value in and of themselves, but may be helpful for localizing (temporal vs frontal) if the component parts of the tests are examined.

Visuospatial and visuoperceptual deficits are also commonly found among patients with TLE. These deficits may be more pronounced in patients with nondominant (right) TLE, but the lateralizing aspect of visuoconstructional deficits is not consistent, with both left and right TLE patients performing poorly (see Lezak et al., 2004). Research in this area implicates volumetric reductions in parietal lobe regions in persons with TLE (Fonseca et al., 2023), although the medial and anterior temporal lobes have also been noted to be critical for perceptual and recognition functions (Avidan et al., 2005; Behrmann et al., 2016; Drane et al., 2013; Lee et al., 2012; Rudebeck et al., 2013; Thomas et al., 2009). That said, there is a body of research showing normal spatial performance relative to healthy controls or other epilepsy lobar types (Grant et al., 2008; Santangelo et al., 2017; Tallarita et al., 2023), although it must again be cautioned that more research is required to overcome limitations of testing.

Adults and children with TLE may demonstrate deficits in executive functioning tasks. The "nociferous cortex hypothesis" of Wilder Penfield is sometimes invoked to explain this phenomenon (Penfield & Jasper, 1954), in which epilepsy disrupts wider neural networks; later studies by Hermann and Seidenberg (1995) and Martin et al. (2000) have supported this (Hermann & Seidenberg, 1995; Martin et al., 2000). Functional neuroimaging data have demonstrated patients with TLE often show hypometabolism of the frontal lobes that correlates with executive dysfunction (Jokeit et al., 1997; Takaya et al., 2006), as well as functional disruption to the executive control network (Oyegbile et al., 2018; Ren et al., 2020)—even in those with first episode, treatment-naive TLE (Gao et al., 2021).

With the exception of interest in visual memory functioning, less work has been focused on the nondominant TL in the context of epilepsy. While current visual memory test scores and memory complaints are not strongly associated, most neuropsychological studies do not adequately assess function of the right (nondominant) temporal lobe (see Chap. 3 of this volume). For example, route learning/way finding is rarely clinically assessed, yet several experimental studies suggest performance on these tasks is compromised by right anterior TL damage (Spiers et al., 2001). Similarly, patients with right (nondominant) TLE often exhibit object recognition deficits, and deficits in identifying famous faces and some animals have been found among patients following right anterior temporal lobectomy (Drane et al., 2008, 2009b, 2013; Seidenberg et al., 2002). Clinically, patients with these deficits have greater difficulty recognizing familiar individuals. There is also documented difficulty with emotional recognition (Drane et al., 2021b; Meletti et al., 2014)—although newer research suggests that this effect may be stronger for specific emotions (i.e., fear and disgust) and varied as a function of emotional intensity (Nineuil et al., 2023). Both of these contribute to compromised social functioning (Meletti et al., 2014).

The material-specific pattern of memory dysfunction model may be affected by other task parameters and disease-related variables. For example, material-specific findings may be easier to detect when examining both learning and recall patterns rather than only examining one trial learning (Jones-Gotman et al., 1997). Further, material-specific findings may be altered by the side of seizure onset (Vannest et al., 2008; Weber et al., 2007), and both temporal lobes may eventually be affected by a chronic duration of unilateral TLE (Cheung et al., 2006). It is also possible that material discrepancies are of relatively low prevalence but *when* observed may be considered highly specific (see Castro et al., 2013). Future studies will no doubt help to shape our understanding of language and memory in new and thought-provoking ways [e.g., the LuM model (Roger et al., 2022); new ways of conceptualizing memory mechanisms (Neisser et al., in press)], especially as it pertains to persons with epilepsy (e.g., cognitive phenotypes; Reyes et al., 2019). Ultimately, while this portion of the chapter highlights considerable variability in the presurgical neuropsychological presentation of patients with epilepsy, patients experience *better* seizure control and *better* functional outcome when the prototypical neurocognitive profiles line up with other diagnostic findings (e.g., EEG, MRI; Holmes et al., 2003; Lineweaver et al., 2006). We now turn to postoperative neuropsychological findings.

Postoperative findings. While it is increasingly appreciated that meaningful postoperative neuropsychological deficits should mark a clear adverse comorbidity to neurosurgical treatment to be avoided, patients can exhibit postoperative declines in neurological and neuropsychological function. A common neurologic deficit of a standard ATL is a visual-field defect due to resection of some optic radiations of Meyers loop resulting in a superior quadrantanopia. One advantage of the minimally invasive surgical procedures, such as SLAH, has been a reduction in postsurgical visual defects (Donos et al., 2020; Voets et al., 2019) as well as other physical adverse events of open resection (Gross et al., 2024; Sperling et al., 2020). Decline in memory, particularly among patients having dominant (left) ATL, can occur (e.g., Baxendale et al., 2013; Bentvelzen et al., 2022; Brown et al., 2010; Chelune et al., 1993; Helmstaedter & Kurthen, 2001; Helmstaedter et al., 2002; Kaestner et al., 2024; Lineweaver et al., 2006; LoGalbo et al., 2005; Ojemann & Dodrill, 1985; Voets et al., 2009). Indeed, 10–60% of patients having had an ATL will exhibit a decline in memory (Baxendale et al., 2013; Lineweaver et al., 2004, 2006; Ojemann & Dodrill, 1985; Sawrie et al., 1998) that is greater than expected for practice and error effects (e.g., reliable change). Ten years post-ATL, the risk for decline is relatively higher for those with lower baseline functioning and presurgical focal memory impairment (Fleury et al., 2024). Risk for decline is relatively lower in more selective procedures (i.e., stereotactic laser amygdalohippocampotomy, e.g., Drane, 2018; Drane et al., 2019); nomograms and other methods have also been developed in an attempt to predict level of postsurgical decline in memory (Busch et al., 2021; Stroup et al., 2003). While the rate of decline in memory may seem excessive, keep in mind that 20–25% of patients with medication-refractory epilepsy have exhibited declines in memory over a period of several years, and that there is also a risk for death due to SUDEP in medication-refractory epilepsy. Nevertheless, there are also likely greater deficits occurring in all patients due to the limitations of our current neuropsychological measures (Bilder & Reise, 2019; Loring et al., 2022; Neisser et al., in press).

Language/naming decline after ATL is also generally common. Patients having dominant TL resections may exhibit significant declines in naming (~40–50%) (Bell et al., 2003; Busch et al., 2016; Drane et al., 2008, 2015; Hageboutros et al., in press; Hermann et al., 1999; Sawrie et al., 2000), while those undergoing non-dominant TL resection typically do not unless language lateralization is atypical (Saykin et al., 1995). Hamberger and colleagues provided a useful auditory naming to description task (Hamberger & Seidel, 2003; Hamberger & Tamny, 1999), although initial claims about hippocampal damage being responsible for visual naming deficits while sparing auditory naming have not been borne out over time (Hamberger et al., 2007; Hamberger et al., 2010). More specifically, minimally invasive surgeries, ablating only the amygdalohippocampal complex (AHC), have almost never resulted in any confrontation naming deficits of any type (Curry et al., 2012; Donos et al., 2018; Drane et al., 2008, 2015; Hageboutros et al., in press), while such deficits have arisen from lesions to the basal-temporal language area, ventral visual white matter stream, lateral TL regions and temporal pole instead (Drane & Pedersen, 2019; Snyder et al., 2023). Additionally, Drane and colleagues recently demonstrated that patients undergoing a highly selective, posterior cerebral artery (PCA) Wada procedure virtually never experienced any language dysfunction, again suggesting that the AHC is not contributing to language processing in any meaningful, detectable manner (Drane et al., 2024a). Finally, sequential surgeries in the same individuals demonstrate that destruction of the AHC did not lead to any naming deficits while eventual destruction of the broader TL did cause naming problems in the same individuals (Raghu et al., in press).

Standard anterior TL resection typically does *not* lead to declines in basic language function (comprehension, repetition and expression) (Drane & Pedersen, 2019; Saykin et al., 1995). While classic aphasia is not present following ATL, decline in semantic (category) fluency following dominant ATL resection does occur. While a decline in semantic verbal fluency following nondominant TL resection can occur (Martin et al., 1990), more pronounced adverse effects on semantic verbal fluency generally occur for patients with dominant ATLs (Jokeit et al., 1998). Postoperative decline is typically *not* observed following TL procedures on letter fluency tasks. Rather, patients who are seizure free can exhibit a postoperative improvement in performance. The improved performance is thought to reflect the presurgical widespread disruption of neural networks by epilepsy (see nociferous cortex hypothesis above) (Helmstaedter et al., 1998).

Improved neuropsychological function following ATL has been reported for patients who are seizure free; conversely, progressive postsurgical declines are associated with poorer seizure control (Baxendale et al., 2012). In addition to seizure reduction, reduced medication burden has been associated with the higher likelihood of improvement (Helmstaedter et al., 2018). However, damage to functional tissue leads to cognitive decline no matter what the seizure outcome is. Patients who underwent a nondominant (right) TL procedure can exhibit an improvement in verbal memory postoperatively (e.g., Martin et al., 1998). A similar finding was demonstrated by Salvato et al. (2016); interestingly, this study also demonstrated that while persons with left TLE did experience memory decline in the immediate post-surgical period, repeat assessment after five years did reveal some improvement (Salvato et al., 2016). As noted elsewhere, much broader assessment of complex mental functions is required to truly evaluate change in the short or long term following surgery, as is an evaluation of functional outcome. Drane and colleagues recently demonstrated that functional decline was much more likely to occur as they move from focal ablations to standard ATL procedures in the same individuals (Raghu et al., in press).

Frontal Lobe Epilepsy

Research examining the neuropsychological functioning of patients with frontal lobe epilepsy (FLE) remains less expansive than for TLE (for a review see Verche et al., 2018). Patients with FLE (children and adults) often exhibit deficits in attention/executive functions (working memory, response inhibition, complex problem solving, verbal generative fluency, design fluency) and motor functions (psychomotor speed, coordination, motor sequencing and bimanual hand movements) when compared to controls and patients with TLE (Cocoran & Upton, 1993; Culhand-Shelburne et al., 2002; Hernandez et al., 2002; Oyegbile et al., 2018; Upton & Thompson, 1996). Generative fluency, both verbal and design, is often impaired among patients with FLE (Drane et al., 2006; Metternich et al., 2014; Moguilner et al., 2021). Deficits in semantic and letter verbal fluency can occur. Action (verb) fluency is also decreased in FLE patients (Drane et al., 2006; Moguilner et al., 2021). Design fluency can be impaired in FLE patients relative to other epilepsy patients or healthy controls, with some studies suggesting lateralization to the nondominant hemisphere (Jones-Gotman & Milner, 1977), but not consistently (McDonald et al., 2005a, 2005b). Other areas of impairment include (a) cost estimation (Upton, 1996), (b) reasoning (Upton & Thompson, 1999), (c) determining temporal order (McAndrews & Milner, 1991), (d) action comprehension (Moguilner et al., 2021) and (e) social cognition/theory of mind (e.g., humor appreciation, recognition of facial emotion, perception of eye gaze expression, mentalization; Farrant et al., 2005). The latter may in part relate to altered deactivation of the default mode network in persons with FLE, which subserves a range of processes including self-awareness, mind-wandering and social cognition (Ziaei et al., 2023). Helmstaedter (2001) also reported patients with FLE had more behavioral problems than patients with TLE and healthy controls; alternatively, persons with FLE demonstrated fewer behavioral problems than persons with frontal lobe structural lesions (Helmstaedter, 2001).

Memory deficits also exist in persons with FLE (Phillips et al., 2024), but are typically milder than in TLE and more commonly entail encoding and retrieval inefficiencies (Centeno et al., 2010). Patients with FLE exhibit greater deficits in the release of proactive interference, such that earlier memory interferes with learning new information (Pigott & Milner, 1993). Patients with FLE also have difficulty recalling the temporal order of when events/information occurred/learned (Milner et al., 1985). With regard to underlying functional neuroanatomy, persons with FLE tend to recruit more widely distributed brain regions to support memory—with compensatory involvement of the contralateral frontal lobe (Centeno et al., 2012).

Cognitive phenotypes in persons with FLE have been identified. Using the criteria developed as part of the International Classification of Cognitive Disorders in Epilepsy (IC-Code; McDonald et al., 2023; Norman et al., 2021), a 2022 study of 106 persons with FLE found that 36% met the criteria for the domain-specific phenotype (i.e., impairment in two or more domains—most commonly language, followed by attention, executive dysfunction and processing speed with learning being the least impacted domain), 25% for the generalized phenotype (i.e., impairment in at least four domains), 20% for the tri-domain phenotype (i.e., impairment in three domains) and 19% for the intact/no impairment phenotype (Arrotta et al., 2022). The generalized and tri-domain phenotypes in particular appeared to have greater spread of epileptogenicity compared to other subtypes, suggesting more widespread seizure involvement is related to a greater risk for cognitive impairment.

In summary, patients with FLE present with a variety of deficits involving motor functioning, executive control processes, attention, speed of processing, aspects of memory and possible behavioral abnormalities. While overlap in neuropsychological deficits exists between patients with TLE and FLE, there also appear to be some distinct neuropsychological differences between patients with FLE and TLE, which may yet be useful for confirming the region of seizure onset (i.e., differences in reasons for memory deficits, complex motor programming, etc.). Postoperative decline in motor and neuropsychological functions can occur in children, adolescents and adults having undergone frontal lobe surgery (Helmstaedter et al., 1996); however, some studies also report areas of cognitive stability postsurgery (Ferguson et al., 2021; Nitta et al., 2021).

Posterior Cortical Epilepsy

Posterior cortical epilepsies (PCEs) is a term to describe patients with seizures arising from the parietal, occipital or occipital border of the temporal lobes (Dalmagro et al., 2005). Recognized syndromes include some of the benign childhood epilepsies, epilepsies due to mitochondrial encephalomyopathy with stroke-like episodes (MELAS), cortical developmental malformations and other acquired traumatic or neoplastic insults. PCEs are rare relative to FLE and TLE, with parietal lobe epilepsy (PLE) representing only 5–6% of persons with focal epilepsies while occipital lobe epilepsy (OLE) represents another 5–8% (Traianou et al., 2019). Referrals for surgical evaluation to epilepsy centers are also rare (accounting for less than 10% of surgical patients) but do respond favorably to surgical treatment for carefully selected patients (Binder et al., 2008b).

Neuropsychological studies of PCE are emerging (Luerding et al., 2004). Defects in visual processing are common, and vary from visual-field cuts to deficits in facial processing, color perception, object localization, object recognition (including letters/words) and other visuospatial/visuoconstructional skills (Kiper et al., 2002; Santangelo et al., 2017). Deficits in sensory discrimination, arithmetic and language functioning (spelling, reading, etc.) have also been reported. Patients with seizure onset involving the mesial occipital lobe exhibited more visual-field defects (e.g., 40 to 50%) than patients with lateral occipital lobe seizure onset (e.g., 0 to 18%). Patients with seizure onset involving the parietal lobes tend to exhibit deficits in visuoperceptual/visuospatial and/or visuoconstructional deficits (Siegel & Williamson, 2000). Children with occipital lobe seizure onset exhibited academic problems, psychiatric disorders (i.e., primarily depression) and visuospatial deficits (including problems with face processing) (Chilosi et al., 2006).

Postoperative data are generally lacking, but surgical resections risk visual-field defects (42% of occipital lobe epilepsy experienced new or increased field cuts). Following resections for PCE, an index of nonverbal general cognitive function (WAIS-R Performance IQ) mildly declined, while Verbal IQ remained stable and some performances on measures of executive functions improved. In one pre/post-study of 28 adults having undergone posterior cortical resection, recovery of visuoperceptual functioning appeared to lag behind verbal functioning (Luerding et al., 2004). A similar pattern was observed in a smaller but longer-term study of five children having undergone parieto-occipital resection, but added specific deficits in object recognition, visual attention and praxis (Lippe et al., 2010). Deficits may be broader than just spatial/perceptual functions, however; a recent review of 33 studies indicated that surgery involving the precuneus was associated with deficits in aspects of language, memory and information processing (Gates et al., 2024). One final note relates to research into cognitive phenotypes in epilepsy; at present, studies in this area have unfortunately largely omitted the visuospatial domain as few participants received such a measure, however, future research may have more to reveal here.

Factors that May Obscure Neuropsychological Profiles in Presurgical Epilepsy Patients

A variety of factors can obscure neuropsychological deficits attributable to the underlying epilepsy syndrome/pathology. These variables reflect effects from treatment (effect of ASMs), comorbid medical and psychiatric conditions, acute ictal/interictal epileptiform activity, test selection, emotional/mood, effort and/or unrelated disease variables (sleep deficits) (see Fig. 17.5). As potential sources of error, these variables can obfuscate dysfunction due to underlying disease and/or effect from seizures, and lead to increased error in studying neuropsychological functioning of patients with epilepsy.

As noted earlier, many ASMs can have both positive and negative effects on neuropsychological function (Drane & Meador, 2002; Loring et al., 2012). While ASMs might improve function by reducing or eliminating seizures, as ASMs lower neuronal excitability, this can lead to cognitive deficits. For example, topiramate may adversely affect attention, verbal fluency and processing speed, which is entirely separate from the effects of the underlying neuropathology (Kockelmann et al., 2003). The effects of ASMs can be quite pronounced in some individuals, thereby confounding the ability to identify any lateralizing or localizing neuropsychological deficits. Adverse effects from medication could also lead to underestimating the patient's level of cognitive function. Historically, older-generation ASMs, higher dosages of ASMs and polytherapy were thought to be associated with worse cognitive functioning (Eddy et al., 2011). As noted by Witt et al. (2020), adverse cognitive effects are dependent on the choice of ASM, but also its combination with other medications as well as its individual and cumulative drug burden (Witt et al., 2020); in fact, findings of one recent study suggest that the number of ASMs is *more* impactful for cognitive functioning than ASM generation (Quon et al., 2020). Regardless, good working knowledge of the neuropsychological impact of ASMs is critical to neuropsychological test interpretation and psychosocial assessment, as the number of ASMs has also been shown to moderate the relationship between cognition and subjective quality of life (Catalan-Aguilar et al., 2023). In general, we do *not* advocate a patient withdrawing ASMs prior to a neuropsychological evaluation, as this increases the risk of seizures and related medical morbidity/mortality. Discontinuation of ASMs should only be done with supervision of the patient's treating physician.

Medical and psychiatric conditions comorbid with epilepsy can also introduce measurement error into neuropsychological assessment (Lezak et al., 2004). Seizures may develop following a head injury or be the presenting symptom of brain tumor(s), stroke or encephalitis. The primary disease or injury contributes uniquely to the patient's pattern of dysfunction, and there may be multifocal dysfunction related to brain tumor(s) as well as the cerebral dysfunction of epilepsy. For example, patients with focal TL seizure onset resulting from posttraumatic epilepsy may exhibit significant executive dysfunction due to the head trauma. Psychiatric comorbidities, particularly depression and anxiety symptoms, are higher for patients with epilepsy than the general public (Blumer et al., 1995; Manchanda, 2002), and performance on neuropsychological tests can be adversely affected by depression and anxiety as well as negatively impact subjective quality of life (Kanner et al., 2020; Lezak et al., 2004).

Finally, there is growing awareness that acute ictal or interictal epileptiform discharges can alter neuropsychological functioning (Drane et al., 2016; Faught et al., 2018; Holmes, 2013, 2014; Holmes & Lenck-Santini, 2006; Kleen et al., 2013) and consequently that EEG capture concurrent with neuropsychological assessment can aid test interpretation (Karakis et al., 2020). While the effects of epileptiform activity can accentuate lateralized dysfunction in the case of focal seizure onset (Privitera & Kim, 2010); however, it can also obscure this pattern when there is secondary generalization or non-focal interictal discharges (Aarts et al., 1984; Aldenkamp & Arends, 2004; Binnie, 2003; Kasteleijn-Nolst Trenite & Vermeiren, 2005).

Problems with features of test design and selection can also muddle the interpretation of neurocognitive data. For example, it is frequently argued that neuropsychological tests are not particularly sensitive to nondominant medial temporal functions, thought to reflect "visual" memory functions (Barr, 1997). For example, the Family Pictures subtest of the Wechsler Memory Scale—third edition (Wechsler, 1997) contributes to the Visual Memory index from this battery, yet variance of the test loads on a verbal factor (Dulay et al., 2002). Thus, patients who have had a dominant (left) TL resection can exhibit a decline on Family Pictures, as well as the Visual Memory index to which it contributes (Chapin et al., 2009). More recent studies with the WMS fourth edition have shown that memory tasks inherent to this test do not add much incremental predictive utility for lateralization purposes beyond the Rey Auditory Verbal Learning Test (Bauman et al., 2019; Soble et al., 2014). Scoring paradigms for the Rey-Osterrieth Complex Figure Test also did not correlate well with right TLE patients before *or* after surgery and in at least two instances were more strongly associated with left TLE patients (Kneebone et al., 2007; McConley et al., 2008) purportedly due to its susceptibility to verbalization strategies. Thus far, it has been extremely difficult to develop a visual memory test that does not allow for verbal processing/mediation of information. Similarly, more complex list learning tasks place greater demands on executive systems than do less complex contextual memory tasks (e.g., story recall) (Tremont et al., 2000), and list learning can be impaired due to lesions in many brain regions (Umeda et al., 2006). There are some promising potential applications of measures such as the Austin Maze Test (Hocking et al., 2013) and RUCHE-M (Zimmermann et al., 2024) and others, as well as newer modalities for test development and delivery such as virtual and augmented reality (Drane et al., 2024b; Okada et al., 2024; Parsons & McMahan, 2017). There is also evidence suggesting that there may be some differential contribution based on stimulus type and task type (Bentvelzen et al., 2022) and that stimulus repetition and familiarity are more likely to engage the parietal memory network (Gilmore et al., 2015); these beg the question of whether our nonverbal memory test paradigms must be reconceptualized rather than discarded.

Overall, prototypical neuropsychological profiles can be identified in some cases of epilepsy, but has not been identified in others. There are many potentially confounding factors that can make it challenging to obtain an accurate baseline measure of neuropsychological function in patients with epilepsy. We believe it is increasingly possible to recognize and control for variables that can potentially adversely affect neuropsychological function. In this manner, one may be able to better assess neuropsychological deficits and predict surgical outcome.

Predicting Seizure Freedom, Side of Seizure Onset and Cognitive Outcome Following Epilepsy Surgery

Predicting Seizure Freedom from Epilepsy Surgery

Seizure-Free Rates

With selected patients with TLE, up to 80% of patients have been reported to be seizure free at one year, but vary from as little as 30% to as much as 80% depending on the study, its patient selection, surgical target/location (i.e., temporal versus extratemporal) and surgical approach, positive structural MRI findings and outcome classification system (Gracia et al., 2019; Ojemann & Jung, 2006). It is generally accepted that one-year seizure-free rates for patients with TLE undergoing an ATL are around 70% (Kuang et al., 2014). Long-term longitudinal data report 10-year seizure-free rates ranging from 37 to 80%. Overall, patients with MTS as the sole pathology tend to experience the highest likelihood of seizure freedom at one year (70% or higher), and are most likely to remain seizure free at 10 or more years after surgery; however, it should be noted that many patients are not "cured" of their epilepsy and remain on ASMs—although one may argue that epilepsy surgery transformed an intractable patient to one that is responsive to ASMs (Andermann et al., 1993). While complete seizure freedom is the goal, it is worth mentioning that there is still a sizeable reduction in seizure frequency for patients who continue to experience seizures after undergoing resection. In one recent study from India, Jayalakshmi et al. (2023) showed a mean reduction of 76.2% in those who continued to experience seizures postoperatively—and that more than 90% still experienced a seizure-free period of at least one year (Jayalakshmi et al., 2023). Complete seizure freedom also may not present immediately after resection (in fact, nearly half of Jayalaksmi et al.'s sample of persons who were ultimately seizure free were unable to achieve this immediately but did over time), which is an interesting finding given that many studies in this area only report one- to two-year postsurgical outcomes. Of note, however, the overall trend for seizure outcome is some degree of decrease in initial rates of seizure freedom over time.

Variables Predicting Seizure Remission

Factors that predict seizure remission have been an area of aggressive research. Recent data suggest neurological and demographic variables provide the best predictors of becoming seizure free (unilateral EEG abnormalities, single pathology of MTS, duration of seizures, age of seizure onset; for a review see Drane, 2015). Neuropsychological variables may be of significant value to lateralizing seizure onset or may contribute to the prediction of seizure outcome in some cases (e.g., Helmstaedter & Kockelmann, 2006; Hennessy et al., 2001; Keary et al., 2007; LoGalbo et al., 2005; Potter et al., 2009; Sawrie et al., 1998; Seidenberg et al.,

1998). Several studies are combining other imaging and electrophysiologic methods with neuropsychological predictors. For example, researchers at the University of South Florida demonstrated that patients with stronger functional connectivity of brain regions that were negatively correlated with the epileptogenic zone exhibited higher baseline memory function and were more likely to be seizure free after surgery (Neal et al., 2021). Dickey and colleagues recently published a seizure outcome prediction scale specifically for SLAH, which demonstrates that certain patients with MTS (usually considered the best open resection candidates) may have a low chance of seizure freedom when certain diagnostic findings are present (Dickey et al., 2024). Outside of potential gains, however, it is also important for the neuropsychologist to provide input to the epilepsy surgery program regarding the potential neuropsychological risks with surgery. It can be the case that a patient may present with neurological findings supportive of having a good seizure-free outcome, but the risk of pronounced neuropsychological deficits could outweigh the potential benefits of becoming seizure free (Hermann & Loring, 2008). This is especially critical in our current era of having multiple options for neurosurgical care of varying degrees of invasiveness. Variables found to be predictive of seizure freedom are presented below. A more detailed review of evidence-based neuropsychology for predicting neuropsychological outcome follows.

Importance of brain pathology in predicting seizure freedom. The brain pathology underlying epilepsy can be the best predictor of seizure freedom. Meta-analysis found that patients with either TLE or extratemporal epilepsy who exhibited a lesion by MRI or histopathology were 2.5 times (95% CI 2.1, 3.0, $p < 0.001$) more likely to be seizure free than patients without a lesion (Téllez-Zenteno et al., 2010). Patients with TLE were 2.7 times more likely to be seizure free when they had a lesion, while those with extratemporal lobe epilepsy with a lesion were 2.9 times more likely to be seizure free.

MTS is the most common pathology found in patients with TLE. MTS is defined as gliosis and loss of neurons within the hippocampal formation (Blumcke et al., 2007). Hippocampal sclerosis is associated with loss of neuron density in the CA1, hillar regions and CA3 of the hippocampus. The CA2 area is often spared. MRI findings of MTS include decreased volume associated with increased fluid attenuated inversion recovery (FLAIR) and T2 signal of the hippocampus. MTS is the sole pathology in many adult-onset cases. While this proportion was once as high as 65% of adult patients with TLE, it has been falling over recent decades, for which reasons are still being determined. Isolated MTS is associated with an especially good surgical outcome, with more than 80% of patients remaining seizure free at one year, and 72% seizure free at 10 years (Cohen-Gadol et al., 2006) (see Table 17.10).

When the MRI is negative in TLE, pathology after en bloc resection often shows "microscopic" abnormalities deviating from the normal cortical structure. A panel of neurologists and neuropathologists in 2004 described and categorized these abnormalities (Palmini et al., 2004), which include architectural abnormalities of laminar or columnar organization or dysmorphic neurons. Surgical outcome for temporal lobectomies with pathology showing dysplasia has ranged from 60 to 70%

free of disabling seizures (Engel class I) with a mean follow-up duration of 2.8 to 4.4 years. Seizure-free outcome is less positive than that for isolated MTS presumably because the microdysgenesis is more diffuse and less circumscribed than MTS.

Neurological and Demographic Variables Predicting Seizure Remission

The most important variables predicting seizure freedom include results from EEG, structural MRI, age at time of surgery and duration of epilepsy. A summary of the effects of these variables on seizure remission is below.

1. Unilateral interictal EEG with seizure focus restricted to unilateral hemisphere
2. Presence of exclusively ipsilateral temporal interictal epileptiform discharges
3. Presence of structural abnormalities, including focal cortical dysgenesis, cyst or mesial temporal sclerosis (MTS)

4. Younger patients are more likely to be seizure free.
   a. Younger patients (x < 30 years of age) at the time of surgery are more likely to be seizure free.
      i. 94 ± 5% were seizure free at 2 years
      ii. 89 ± 6% were seizure free at 3 years
      iii. 78 ± 8% were seizure free at 5 years
      iv. 66 ± 10% were seizure free at 10 years
   b. Middle-aged patients (30–59) recently found to have comparable likelihood of being seizure free (Grivas et al., 2006).
5. Shorter duration of preoperative epilepsy increases the likelihood that the patient will be seizure free (less likely to relapse) (see Table 17.11)

Risk Factors for Surgery Failure (Continued Uncontrolled Seizures)

1. Presence of bilateral EEG abnormalities
2. Presence of secondarily generalized tonic-clonic seizures with TLE
3. No structural pathology with high-resolution MRI (imaging negative)
4. Contralateral memory function intact on Wada test (TLE only)

Table 17.10 Percentage of patients who are seizure free after anterior temporal lobectomy (ATL) based on presence of a structural abnormality

Years post-ATL	Structural abnormality	No structural abnormality
2	89 ± 5%	77 ± 18%
3	83 ± 6%	64 ± 20%
5	72 ± 7%	58 ± 21%
10	56 ± 9%	40 ± 2%

Table 17.11 Percentage of patients who are seizure free after anterior temporal lobectomy (ATL) based on duration of epilepsy

Years post-ATL	≥20 years of epilepsy	>20 years of epilepsy
2	92 ± 5%	82 ± 10%
3	86 ± 7%	77 ± 10%
5	80 ± 8%	60 ± 12%
10	69 ± 10%	37 ± 15%

Neuropsychological variables predicting seizure remission: Evidence-based neuropsychology: In general, neuropsychological data are not helpful in predicting seizure outcome. One recent meta-analysis did indicate that presence of a severe learning disability was a predictor of poor prognosis (Alim-Marvasti et al., 2022), although this is more likely to be identified on the basis of historical interview or records review rather than a presurgical neuropsychological evaluation. However, some studies have shown neuropsychological data incrementally improve prediction of seizure freedom (Hennessy et al., 2001; Potter et al., 2009; Sawrie et al., 1998). Hennessy et al. (2001) found that impaired verbal memory was associated with a higher likelihood of seizure freedom for patients having undergone a left ATL. Potter et al. (2009) observed that an index of language function that included confrontation naming along with nonverbal memory added unique variance to predicting seizure freedom beyond that provided by demographic variables (side of surgery, age of epilepsy onset) and MRI findings of hippocampal sclerosis. Overall, the multivariate prediction model provided accurate classification of 93% of the patients who were seizure free versus not.

Predicting Side of Seizure Onset

In general, electroneurophysiological and structural neuroimaging are the most powerful predictors of side of seizure onset zone. Ictal EEG remains the gold standard for assessing the side of seizure onset, although there is some differential benefit in surface versus depth electrodes; the former has been noted to be preferred when the suspected epileptogenic zone is located in the cortex such as in perirolandic and interhemispheric regions, whereas the latter is considered more advantageous in zones that are deeper or multifocal (Wu et al., 2024). Structural MRI is also of high predictive utility, and the advent of higher-field MRI has been shown to enhance diagnostic sensitivity, with 7 T showing gains from 8% to 67% (pooled average of 31%) over conventional MRI (van Lanen et al., 2021). There are still many cases that do not appear to demonstrate structural brain changes, with a much greater proportion of cases with normal neuroimaging results being seen in epilepsy surgical settings. PET, SISCOM and MEG/MSI studies are also increasingly being employed in an effort to identify the epileptogenic and/or seizure onset zone, particularly in these cases where seizure onset cannot be readily lateralized and/or localized.

Neuropsychological Variables Predicting Side of Seizure Onset: Evidence-Based Neuropsychology

While neuropsychological deficits have long been associated with side of surgery, only more recently has the incremental variance of neuropsychological data to determining side of surgery (side of seizure onset) been explored. Neuropsychological data do provide significant prediction to lateralizing side of seizure onset (e.g., Busch et al., 2005; Drane et al., 2008; Hamberger et al., 2010; Helmstaedter & Kockelmann, 2006; Jones-Gotman et al., 1993; Keary et al., 2007; Kim et al., 2004; Kneebone et al., 1997; Rausch & Babb, 1993; Sass et al., 1992; Seidenberg et al., 1998). Indeed, Sawrie et al. (2001) found WMS Logical Memory scores to significantly improve prediction of seizure lateralization among patients with bilateral hippocampal atrophy (Sawrie et al., 2001). While memory scores are generally found to be predictive of side of seizure onset, other neuropsychological measures of language [visual confrontation naming (BNT) and WRAT-III word reading] and executive functions (Wisconsin Card Sorting Test) have also shown predictive value. Keary et al. (2007) found that a multivariate model provided the correct lateralization of seizure onset in 69% of mixed left and right TLE cases (Keary et al., 2007). It should also be noted that Wada test results also have predictive value (and may be more predictive) to lateralize side of seizure onset in children and adults (Lee et al., 2002; Perrine et al., 1995).

Predicting Memory Impairment Following Epilepsy Surgery: Evidence-Based Neuropsychology

Defining postsurgical outcome as a marker of surgical success (Hermann & Loring, 2008), much attention has been focused on predicting the relative risk of decline for patients with TLE and represents an area of evidence-based neuropsychology. A constellation of variables has consistently shown to be predictive of neuropsychological outcome (see below). Among these, particularly strong predictors are the neuropsychological presurgical test scores, which provide unique variance to predicting memory outcome, and form a cornerstone for evidence-based neuropsychology practice and research (e.g., Baxendale et al., 2006; Chelune, 1995; Chelune & Najm, 2000; Helmstaedter, 2004; Hermann & Loring, 2008; Lineweaver et al., 2006). As an example, Chelune and Najm (2000) report a relative risk for a postsurgical memory deficit that is 4.9 times greater for individuals with memory scores above 90 (mean 100 and standard deviation 15) compared to those with memory scores below 90. A more recent study using a longer-term follow-up interval demonstrated that a combination of lower baseline verbal and performance ability with focal memory impairment predicted poorer memory outcomes in persons having undergone ATL (Fleury et al., 2024). Busch et al.' (2021) nomograms have clinical utility in predicting memory decline for ATL but may not apply to other neurosurgical procedures. There is not yet sufficient evidence for other procedures such as MEG, fMRI and Wada (Höller et al., 2020). Cognitive phenotypes studies have also begun exploring this area, but to date have shown better prediction for nonverbal memory than verbal memory or language outcomes (Baxendale & Thompson, 2020).

Hippocampal Adequacy Versus Hippocampal Functional Reserve

Chelune (1995) detailed two perspectives for predicting postsurgical cognitive outcome from epilepsy surgery. One hypothesis was the *functional reserve of the contralateral hippocampus* predicted postsurgical memory outcome (functional reserve hypothesis). The second hypothesis, known as the *functional adequacy* model, predicted the functional adequacy of the ipsilateral hippocampus tissue resected would determine the risk for material-specific memory decline.

The *functional reserve* hypothesis was based primarily on studies documenting severe amnestic disorders of patients with bilateral mesial temporal lobe dysfunction and, in several cases, bilateral temporal lobe resection (Scoville & Milner, 1957). Additional support was provided by data from Wada testing, as patients with poor memory when the contralateral (e.g., remaining) temporal lobe was tested (injecting the ipsilateral side) exhibited more memory deficits postsurgically. However, the presence of a functionally intact contralateral hippocampal structure has not predicted material-specific memory impairment following unilateral ATL.

The *functional adequacy* model has been supported by data that the functional adequacy of the ipsilateral hippocampus (memory functioning of the temporal lobe structures to be resected) better predicts material-specific memory declines after ATL. From this model, it is predicted that individuals with left (dominant) TLE with intact memory function are likely to experience a more pronounced decline in verbal memory than patients with left TLE whose left hippocampal memory functioning is impaired (Witt et al., 2015). This has generally been supported, particularly the observation that patients with high presurgical memory functioning are at greater risk for significant declines in memory (both verbal and visual) than those patients with low-to-poor presurgical memory functioning.

Cognitive and Socio-Emotional Outcome from Epilepsy Surgery

The treatments of epilepsy, both surgical and nonsurgical, can both improve and impair neuropsychological function. The goal of surgery is to better manage seizures, with the ultimate goal of rendering the patient seizure free, while either not affecting or perhaps improving neurocognitive function. The latter can occur if epileptiform activity can be curtailed or stopped, as this diminishes the effect of aberrant electrical activity on the brain, but also can lead to the discontinuation of psychopharmacological management of seizures, and potential progressive effects of either. Any intervention that disrupts the integrity of functional neural networks has the potential to harm the patient. A large focus of neuropsychology in the setting of epilepsy surgery should be able to calculate/delineate the risk–benefit matrix of potential treatments.

In the case of surgery for TLE, there are certainly risks to learning and memory, language functions (when operating on the language-dominant cerebral hemisphere), object and face recognition deficits and socio-emotional processing deficits, among other things. It has been reported that 10–60% of TLE patients undergoing ATL experience a significant decline (defined by change in scores that is statistically significant in group studies) in memory. When controlling for practice effects and error, 18–50% of patients exhibited declines on at least one memory test (Baxendale et al., 2006; Lineweaver et al., 2006; Martin et al., 1998). Individuals with MTS and lower presurgical memory scores are significantly less likely to exhibit a decline in memory than individuals with average or better memory scores (at least on these same measures). Fewer patients with nondominant (right) TLE who undergo a right ATL will exhibit a significant decline in visual memory (or verbal memory) and some may have an improvement in verbal memory test scores (Martin et al., 1998). Following right ATL, patients may exhibit poor performance on visual memory tests but normally on verbal delayed memory tasks, while the other portion may perform poorly on both verbal and visual memory tests. Other changes with right ATL may also include reductions in an individual's ability to appreciate the nonverbal cues to interpersonal interactions (e.g., facial emotion recognition), associated with right amygdala function, with recognition of fearful expressions in particular being reduced following right ATL in persons with epilepsy beginning before the age of six (McClelland et al., 2006). Long-term neuropsychological outcome data suggest individuals undergoing left temporal lobectomy may exhibit continuing declines in verbal memory for up to 2 years after surgery (Alpherts et al., 2006). Individuals having a right ATL had an overall increase in verbal memory scores at 6 months after surgery, but these gains were lost at 2 years after surgery. Relatively little memory change has been observed in memory from 2 years to 6 years after surgery. The best predictors of postoperative memory scores 6 years after surgery were side of seizure (left TLE had lower scores than right TLE), preoperative verbal memory scores (higher scores more predictive of decline) and age at surgery (older patients at increased risk for memory decline).

With the rise of minimally invasive procedures, it is clear that cognitive deficits can be reduced or eliminated but this also decreases the chance of complete seizure freedom to some degree. It is more important than ever to definitively determine the epileptiform zone in order to minimize potential neuropsychological harm. Studies have been completed that demonstrate that deficits in visual naming and object or face recognition that are common with open resection procedures can be avoided by restricting the TL destructive zone to the AHC (Donos et al., 2018; Drane et al., 2015; Hageboutros et al., in press; Ono et al., 2020). Similarly, learning and memory deficits seem to be less frequent and less severe when surgical destruction zones are kept smaller, although they can result from the destruction of a single hippocampus (Donos et al., 2018; Drane et al., 2021c; Gross et al., 2018; Jermakowicz et al., 2017; Ono et al., 2020; Waseem et al., 2015). We have also noted that small destructive lesions created with laser ablation techniques or RF ablation can result in cognitive deficits if the tissue destroyed is critical to a functioning neural network (Drane, 2018; Shields et al., 2023).

Neuromodulation approaches round out the minimally invasive options for surgical intervention (RNS, VNS, DBS) (Boon et al., 2007; Morrell & Study, 2020; Sun & Morrell, 2014). While less likely to produce curative results, they tend to result in stable cognitive performances with some caveats (Loring et al., 2015). It is possible that stimulation of functional regions or during suboptimal diurnal periods (e.g., REM sleep stages) could be detrimental to cognition at least transiently (Jarvenpaa et al., 2018), and some groups have raised the possibility of electrode placement resulting in structural damage of importance, although the latter hypotheses remain very controversial. Ultrasonic therapies are also being explored for the treatment of epilepsy, but in general have not yet reached a point where cognitive outcomes are reported. There was a recent phase 1, open-label trial of focused ultrasound ablation of anterior thalamic nucleus in two patients, and this did result in significant seizure reduction although it also resulted in short-term declines in aspects of language and memory (Krishna et al., 2023).

Evidence-Based Neuropsychology: Summary of Variables Important in Predicting Postsurgical Neuropsychological Outcome

1. <u>Presence of Hippocampal/Mesial Temporal Lobe Sclerosis</u>
   Memory decline. In general, the risk for material-specific memory decline (in particular verbal memory) *decreases* in patients with hippocampal sclerosis, in particular those (Sass et al., 1990) undergoing ATL although the same effect is not observed in those undergoing more selective procedures.

   - *Language/naming decline.* The risk of significant dysnomia following surgery is decreased when MTS is present in those having undergone ATL (although it may occur), with minimal to no impact in those having undergone more selective procedures.

2. <u>Presurgical neuropsychological immediate and delayed memory scores</u>
   In general, the better (more intact) a patient's neuropsychological memory is prior to surgery, the greater the persons' risk will be for memory decline. This is particularly true for left TLE patients with verbal memory functioning that is average or better when compared to peers, while in those with low average or lower memory scores being much less likely to experience declines of over 10 points. Material-specific memory decline with right ATL is less consistent, but most experts agree decline in visual memory tasks is likely among patients with average or better visual memory test scores that undergo a right ATL, particularly if there is no right hippocampal sclerosis or other structural lesion.

   (a) <u>Presurgical Wada results</u> (Chelune, 1995)
   Evidence-based practice for the Wada test has become increasingly complex, and its relative incremental validity over neuroimaging and neuropsychological data continues to be debated. Memory decline is less likely among patients in which memory recall is impaired when the contralateral

temporal lobe is injected (testing of the ipsilateral temporal lobe), but memory is intact when the temporal lobe to be resected is injected (testing the contralateral temporal lobe function) (Naugle et al., 1993)

(b) Presurgical IQ

Patients with higher cognitive functioning (better cognitive "reserve") typically have a better outcome from surgery overall. Patients presenting with impaired memory scores, but IQ scores in the average ranges, are at less risk for substantial declines in memory than those patients with memory scores being in the average ranges.

3. Duration of Epilepsy

   Patients with a longer duration of epilepsy are at less risk for postsurgical cognitive decline (but likely have poorer neuropsychological function prior to surgery).

4. Age at Onset of Seizures

   Patients with early age of onset epilepsy are at decreased risk for significant decline in confrontation naming following left ATL, although decline will still occur in a subset of patients.

5. Type of surgery

   (a) Postsurgical memory decline (decrease in verbal memory test scores) may be less with more focused resections (amygdalohippocampectomies) as compared to standard ATL, although this is disputed. Minimally invasive procedures, SLAH or RF ablation, tend to be less impactful on memory. Change in language functioning (e.g., scores on confrontation naming and verbal fluency tasks) is more likely to occur when lateral TL regions, temporal pole, fusiform gyrus or basal TL regions are included in surgical resections/ablations.
   (b) The extent of superior temporal gyrus resection correlated with a decline in BNT scores among patients undergoing left ATL. Most patients undergoing left ATL will exhibit a decline in BNT scores; however, 24% of one series did not exhibit a significant decline.
   (c) More selective procedures (e.g., subSLAH, SLAH) tend to result in less memory decline, and in some aspects of cognition no decline or even improvement (e.g., naming). Neurostimulation paradigms such as DBS and RNS may also yield stable to improved cognition.

Impact of the Wada (Intracarotid Amobarbital/Methohexital) Procedure for Predicting Outcome

The Wada test is, arguably, the gold standard for evaluating the lateralized functional neuroanatomical organization of language and memory (Baxendale, 2009). Predicting neuropsychological outcome from the Wada test remains an important variable for neuropsychologists to consider (Loring et al., 2009). Some comprehensive epilepsy centers have replaced the Wada test with fMRI and/or MEG; however, predicting neuropsychological outcome from these procedures remains less well understood than Wada's test, and research suggests data obtained from the Wada test are, to some extent, independent from that of fMRI or MEG. This may well be related to the behavioral effect of the procedure. The Wada test assesses behavior with inactivation, while fMRI and MSI assess behavior with activation (Loring et al., 2004). Predicting outcome from Wada's test will be discussed in terms of language dominance and side of anticipated surgery (See Table 17.12 for summary). The prediction estimates below assume a valid Wada test (good behavioral response to anesthesia with contralateral hemiparesis, hemi-anesthesia, angiogram demonstrating normal cerebral vasculature, adequate patient cooperation and the examiner administered the Wada test correctly. If EEG is used, EEG should demonstrate adequate ipsilateral hemisphere slowing during the administration of the to-be remembered items).

Language Dominant to Ipsilateral Side of Surgery

Memory adequate with ipsilateral injection but poor for contralateral injection. This test result is favorable. Decreased risk of memory decline following surgical resection.

Memory adequate with ipsilateral and contralateral injection. This test result is somewhat favorable, but there is considerable risk for verbal memory decline. Extent of risk largely dependent upon neuropsychological verbal memory test scores (average or better scores at high risk) and structural MRI. Some risk also for "visual" memory decline.

Memory poor with ipsilateral injection and adequate with contralateral injection. This test result is a "failure." High risk for memory decline. See "Wrong-way" Wada section below.

Table 17.12 Relative risk for decline in memory and language functions after anterior temporal lobectomy (ATL) as a function of Wada performance

Injection side (performance)	Ipsilateral language	Contralateral language	Bilateral language
IAP memory			
Ipsilateral (+)/contralateral (+)	↓↓	↓↓	↓↓
Ipsilateral (+)/contralateral (−)	↓	↓	↓
Ipsilateral (−)/contralateral (+)	↓↓↓↓	↓↓↓	↓↓↓
Ipsilateral (−)/contralateral (−)	↓↓↓	↓↓↓	↓↓↓
IAP language			
Language loss	↓↓↓	↓	↓↓

Note: IAP = intracarotid amobarbital procedure (Wada). Ipsilateral (+) = memory adequate with ipsilateral injection; Contralateral (+) = memory adequate with contralateral injection; Ipsilateral (−) = memory poor with ipsilateral injection; Contralateral (−) = memory poor with contralateral injection

Memory poor with ipsilateral injection and contralateral injection. This test result is a "failure." Traditionally, relative risk has been weighed against preoperative neuropsychological memory test scores. Poor memory preoperatively has been thought to reduce the relative risk of pronounced memory decline following surgical resection. Nevertheless, personal experience from one of our authors (Drane) has been that our standard memory measures do not adequately assess the full extent of memory (e.g., consolidation processes, integration of multimodal information, effects of attention/emotional factors in memory encoding, autobiographical), and if the patient remains functional in various life areas significant memory compromise can yet occur. The relative potential benefit of seizure freedom and outcome must be balanced upon the functional level of the patient. Among patients with poor memory on neuropsychological functioning, but functioning independently, surgical resection could worsen the amnestic syndrome, decreasing the patient's functional independence.

Language Dominant to Contralateral Side of Surgery

Memory adequate with ipsilateral injection but poor for contralateral injection. This test result is favorable. Decreases risk of memory decline following surgical resection.

Memory adequate with ipsilateral and contralateral injection. This test result is also somewhat favorable, but there is risk for memory ("visual" and verbal) decline. Extent of risk largely dependent upon neuropsychological memory test scores (average or better scores at higher risk) and structural MRI.

Memory poor with ipsilateral injection and adequate with contralateral injection. This test result is a "failure." High risk for memory decline. See "Wrong-way" Wada section below.

Memory poor with ipsilateral injection and contralateral injection. See bilateral memory test failure above.

The "wrong-way"/"Reversed" Wada test. This describes a test result in which the ipsilateral injection to the side of the proposed surgical resection (testing the contralateral hemisphere language and memory function) results in poor memory functioning. Alternatively, injection of the contralateral hemisphere to the proposed resection (testing ipsilateral hemisphere language and memory function) results in adequate memory. Traditionally, this test finding (so-called "failing" the Wada test) is generally considered to pose considerable neuropsychological risk to the patient with an amnestic syndrome following surgery being the worst-case outcome (Loring et al., 2004). While decades of research establish patients with "wrong-way" Wada test results are at increased risk for memory decline, data suggest the risk of memory decline may be similar to those patients without structural pathology (Lezak et al., 2004). The astute reader will recall that patients without structural pathology are at increased risk for memory decline. Thus, while having a "wrong-way" Wada test result does not absolutely preclude surgical treatment, the risk of memory decline is greater. Indeed, patients with average or near-average preoperative neuropsychological memory scores will almost certainly exhibit a meaningful decline in memory following a standard ATL.

Key Points: Avoiding the "Double Loser" (Not Seizure Free and Memory/Language Loss)

- Presence of lesion (e.g., mesial temporal sclerosis) ipsilateral to seizure focus
- Unilateral EEG abnormalities
- Presurgical lateralizing neuropsychological data in which memory impaired for ipsilateral temporal lobe (e.g., patient with left TLE exhibiting poor verbal memory, but good visual memory)
  - Presurgical memory scores above 90 are at 4.9 times greater risk for memory deficit postoperatively than patients with memory scores <90.
- Longer duration of epilepsy
- Higher presurgical general cognitive ability (IQ)
- Asymmetric functional neuroimaging findings (PET hypometabolism ipsilateral to seizure focus)
- Asymmetric Wada test results with ipsilateral injection memory good while contralateral injection memory impaired
- Presence of confrontation naming deficits prior to surgery

Psychiatric Status and Quality of Life in Epilepsy

Review of Fig. 17.3 highlights the inter-related effect of psychosocial factors in epilepsy. Patients with epilepsy (both adults and children) are diagnosed with psychiatric disorders at a greater frequency than in the general population (Gaitatzis et al., 2004), and report a poor quality of life than healthy peers (Jacoby & Baker, 2008). Treatment of epilepsy, including epilepsy surgery, can have a positive impact on mood and adjustment. In addition to understanding that certain psychiatric diseases commonly occur in patients with epilepsy, it is also important to recognize some patients also experience acute psychiatric symptoms that are ictal, periictal or interictal manifestations of their seizures, many of which may not fit the standard diagnostic rubrics of the Diagnostic and Statistical Manuel of Mental Disorders-5 (DSM-5). It appears psychiatric symptomatology (depression and/or anxiety symptoms) has been found *before* the onset of epilepsy (Austin et al., 2001), and there has been a growing debate about whether each disease may uniquely contribute to the development of the other in some cases. Neuropsychologists need to recognize behavioral deficits and psychiatric issues when they occur, both to identify and address these problems and to consider their concomitant impact upon neuropsychologic status. Thus, the neuropsychological evaluation of patients with epilepsy should include an assessment of emotional/psychiatric functioning as well as quality of life. It should be noted that a neuropsychological evaluation is not equivalent to a psychiatric evaluation, and the patient with epilepsy will benefit from both.

Common psychiatric disorders occurring in epilepsy include mood disorders (major depressive disorders, bipolar disorder symptoms), anxiety disorders, psychosis, personality disorders and substance abuse (Hermann et al., 2000; LaFrance et al., 2008). A variety of factors can contribute to psychiatric or behavioral disturbance in ES patients, including the ictal seizure discharge, the peri- or postictal state, CNS pathology, effects of ASMs, adverse psychosocial consequences of having epilepsy (reactive) and cognitive and temperamental (personality) attributes. Prevalence estimates of psychiatric disturbance in epilepsy tend to range from 20 to 50%, with higher estimates arising in specialty clinics and lower estimates coming from community-based samples. Similar prevalence rates have been observed in children and adults (Davies et al., 2003; Rutter et al., 1970). Studies examining prevalence rates of psychiatric comorbidity in epilepsy have been limited by a lack of large community-based surveys (Manchanda, 2002), and a frequent failure to employ reliable standardized measures of psychopathology (Swinkels et al., 2005). However, study methodology and measures have improved over the past decade, particularly for symptoms of depression.

Depression in Epilepsy

The association between epilepsy and depression has been recognized for recorded medical history. Hippocrates noted in about 400 B.C., "Melancholics ordinarily become epileptics, and epileptics melancholics: What determines the preference is the direction the malady takes; if it bears upon the body, epilepsy, if upon the intelligence, melancholy (Lewis, 1934)."

Prevalence rates of depression in epilepsy range from 10 to 60% among patients with recurrent seizures and 3 to 9% in patients with controlled epilepsy (Ettinger et al., 2004; Fuller-Thomson & Brennenstuhl, 2009; Gilliam & Kanner, 2002; Kanner & Palac, 2000). Variability across studies has been attributed to genuine differences across samples (e.g., Canadian vs USA), methods of sampling and statistical analysis and differences in assessment instruments. Increased risk of depression among patients with epilepsy is associated with female gender, minority status, older age, being unmarried, unemployment, lower levels of education and lower socioeconomic status (Ettinger et al., 2004; Fuller-Thomson & Brennenstuhl, 2009; Jacoby et al., 1996; Mensah et al., 2006). However, epilepsy is a powerful risk factor for depression. For example, researchers found epilepsy resulted in increased odds of depression by 43% after adjusting for demographic factors (Fuller-Thomson & Brennenstuhl, 2009). Patients with epilepsy also experience higher rates of suicidal ideation and suicidal behavior than the general population. The lifetime prevalence rate of suicide and suicide attempts is between 5 and 14.3% in people with epilepsy, which is 6–25 times higher than in the general population (Robertson, 1997). Despite the increased risk for depression and suicide in epilepsy, mood disorders in this population often go unrecognized and/or untreated by practitioners. For example,

Fuller-Thomson and Brennenstuh found nearly 40% of patients with depression had not received mental health treatment, suggesting that better screening for psychiatric conditions is needed in this population. The reasons for not recognizing depression in this population appear to be multifactorial and include (1) patients may minimize their psychiatric symptoms for fear of being further stigmatized, (2) clinical manifestations of certain types of depressive disorders in epilepsy differ from depressive disorders in patients without epilepsy and (3) clinicians frequently fail to inquire about psychiatric symptoms (Gilliam & Kanner, 2002; Hermann et al., 2000). Both patients and clinicians can minimize symptoms of depression because they consider depression to be a "normal adaptation process" to having epilepsy (Kanner & Palac, 2000). The concern that antidepressant drugs may lower the seizure threshold has also resulted in reluctance among some clinicians to use psychotropic medications to treat patients with epilepsy (Gilliam & Kanner, 2002).

Although there is general agreement that prevalence rates of psychiatric comorbidity are higher among patients with epilepsy than the general population, the relationship between seizure type, seizure focus and psychiatric status remains uncertain. Depression is more common among patients with TLE, as these groups have been shown to have lifetime prevalence rates for major depression of up to 50% (Gaitatzis et al., 2004). Patients with multiple seizure types also appear to experience greater emotional maladjustment than those without (Dodrill, 1984; Hermann et al., 1982). Comorbid depression in epilepsy has been associated with a greater likelihood of adverse events to ASMs, more frequent medical visits and higher costs of medical care related to seizures rather than psychiatric treatment (Cramer et al., 2004). Depression is also associated with a poor outcome following ATL to control seizures (Anhoury et al., 2000; Kanner et al., 2009).

Intriguing findings involve evidence that depression often antedates seizure onset and that epilepsy and depression may be bidirectional in terms of causality. For example, behavioral abnormalities have been observed more than six months prior to seizure onset in children with new onset seizures as compared to sibling controls (Austin et al., 2001; Dunn et al., 2002). Jones et al. (2007) demonstrated that approximately 45% of children with new onset seizures exhibited a DSM disorder that predated their seizure onset. Academic problems were thought to precede initial seizure onset in children (Berg et al., 2005), but this was not confirmed in a large prospective study of first onset seizure (Fastenau et al., 2009). Taken together, these data argue an underlying neurobiological influence (that is not appreciated in current structural neuroimaging technologies) apart from seizures and ASM treatment leading to both seizures and psychopathology (Hermann et al., 2006b).

Treatment of Depression in Epilepsy. There are limited data regarding the efficacy of standard treatment interventions (pharmacological or psychotherapeutic) for depression in patients with epilepsy (Kanner, 2008; LaFrance et al., 2008). However, patients with epilepsy respond favorably to pharmacological treatment, and some data suggest antidepressant medication may have some anticonvulsant properties at therapeutic doses, although most data are derived from animal models (Kanner, 2016). The effectiveness of psychological treatment at reducing depressive symptoms has also been demonstrated for patients with epilepsy. Gilliam (1990) reported that patients involved in psychotherapy not only showed significant improvement in rating scales of depression and anxiety, but also showed a decline in seizure frequency. Research also suggests the presence of a psychiatric disorder increases the risk for seizures (lowers the seizure threshold), while antidepressant medications may potentially reduce the risk for seizures among patients with epilepsy (Cardamone et al., 2013).

Key Points: Depression in Epilepsy

- 10–60% of patients with active epilepsy meet criteria for depressive disorder
- 3–9% of patients with controlled epilepsy meet criteria for depressive disorder
- Risk of suicide 6 to 25 times the general population
- Treatment of depressive symptoms undertreated/under-recognized
- Treatment for depressive symptoms is efficacious
- Depressive symptoms can antedate seizure onset

Anxiety in Epilepsy

Anxiety disorders are the second most common psychiatric disorder among patients with epilepsy, with prevalence rates reported to vary from 10 to 50% (see Kwon et al., 2024; Mensah et al., 2007). Rates of anxiety in community-based samples are generally lower, ranging from 14 to 25%. Hospital-based studies report the prevalence of anxiety disorders ranges from 25 to 50%, and studies among patients who are candidates for epilepsy surgery due to refractory TLE report prevalence rates of 10 to 31%. Anxiety symptoms are frequently comorbid with symptoms of depression, and there is an increased association of anxiety symptoms with female gender, unemployment, perceived side effects of ASMs and chronic illness, as well as lower educational attainment. Anxiety symptoms were not strongly associated with epilepsy variables, including side of seizures or if seizures were focal or generalized (e.g., Mensah et al., 2007).

Treatment of anxiety disorders in epilepsy. Like the treatment of depression, psychopharmacological and psychological treatment has demonstrated some success, although both are less well researched than treatment for depression in epilepsy (Mula, 2013; Ribot et al., 2017).

Key Points: Anxiety in Epilepsy

- 10–50% of patients with active epilepsy meet criteria for anxiety disorder
- Anxiety symptoms/disorders often comorbid with depressive symptoms/disorders
- Treatment of depressive symptoms undertreated/under-recognized.
- Anxiety symptoms not associated with side of seizure
- Treatment for anxiety symptoms is efficacious

Broader Psychopathology in Epilepsy

We have chosen to focus on depression and anxiety in epilepsy, as they appear to be the most commonly occurring psychiatric comorbidities. Nevertheless, substance abuse, personality disorders and psychosis also occur with significant frequency in this population.

Role of Neuropsychology in Managing the Psychiatric Aspects of Epilepsy. Clinical neuropsychologists represent a core group of clinicians that can obtain objective data on the presence of psychiatric disorders in patients, which is necessary to track disease prevalence and to recognize the need for intervention. Neuropsychological evaluations frequently include a psychometric-based instrument of mood/psychiatric functioning, and many epilepsy centers also include a measure of quality of life. Measure of mood is useful for monitoring levels of distress, tracking change over time and picking up on critical issues in need of intervention (e.g., active suicidal ideation). Personality profiles can also provide greater insight into the presence of disease and the underlying personality traits that may contribute to their development and recalcitrance. Measures of mood do not typically allow for making psychiatric diagnoses and do not provide any information with regard to lifetime prevalence rates. Kanner and colleagues have demonstrated that knowledge of psychiatric syndrome and personal and familial psychiatric history can be of benefit in predicting adverse responses to ASMs, and in determining the optimal treatment regimen for patients with such comorbid conditions (Kanner, 2009; Kanner et al., 2003).

Quality of Life and Psychosocial Consequences

Patients with epilepsy experience higher rates of unemployment, have lower income, have lower education and remain unmarried at rates that exceed the general population (Kobau et al., 2006; Strine et al., 2005). The worst functioning tends to be observed in patients with active epilepsy, and those with comorbid psychiatric conditions. A review found quality of life is lower for patients with epilepsy than the general population and lower than among patients with other chronic medical conditions (e.g., asthma) (Jacoby & Baker, 2008; Jacoby et al., 1996, 2009). Factors that have particular salience in affecting quality of life include epilepsy/medical (seizure frequency, side effects of ASMs) and psychosocial (psychiatric symptoms of anxiety/depression, psychological resilience, family/social stigma and discrimination) variables. A particularly powerful effect on QOL is from perceived seizure frequency followed by perceived adverse effects of ASMs. Non-epilepsy variables (psychosocial) appear to have less impact, but several variables, including family/parent variables, can significantly impact children with epilepsy. In general, psychosocial variables negatively affecting QOL include presence of psychiatric disorders and/or perception of stigma. Interestingly, an aspect of cognitive function, the so-called cognitive reserve phenomena, finds that individuals with higher educational and/or occupational attainment and/or increased involvement in tasks that involved cognitive activity appear to moderate QOL by modifying cognitive morbidity in epilepsy. In general, patients with higher cognitive reserve report better QOL than those individuals with less cognitive reserve/activities.

In general, patients experiencing one or few seizures and then are seizure free report an initial acute dip in QOL after the seizure(s), and then gradually return to normal (or near normal) QOL one to two years after the seizure (last seizure) as compared to healthy peers without a seizure. For patients with active epilepsy (defined as having had a seizure in the last 12 months), QOL is lower than for individuals with one or several unprovoked seizures, and no additional seizures. There is a clear relationship between frequency of seizures (particularly the patients' *perceived* seizure frequency), with seizures occurring monthly or more had the lowest quality of life, while QOL was better (but not normal) for individuals having a seizure once a year. For those individuals with active epilepsy, treatment variables have a large impact. In general, individuals having successful surgery (Engle Class Ia or 1b) after 1 or 2 years have better QOL than individuals with continued epilepsy. Quality of life can profoundly improve for patients who are seizure free shortly after successful surgery, and the majority of patients' QOL was normal (or near normal) compared to healthy peers without epilepsy 2–3 years after being seizure free. For patients not having successful surgery, QOL is generally poor, and may decline beyond baseline presurgical levels. Decline in QOL from presurgical baseline is particularly likely for patients with ongoing seizures and experiencing a neuropsychological decline (memory loss) after surgical treatment. Modifiable variables that can improve QOL include reducing seizure frequency, reducing ASMs, promoting cognitive activity/reserve, reducing psychopathology (eliminate or minimize anxiety and/or depression symptoms) and trying to reduce negative social/cultural variables of stigma and discrimination (Jacoby & Baker, 2008).

Key Points: Quality of Life in Epilepsy

- Epilepsy associated with lower quality of life.
- Patients are less likely to be employed, have less education, have less income and are more likely to be single.
- Quality of life related to epilepsy/medical and psychosocial variables.
  - Epilepsy/Medical—most important predictors of quality of life
    - Perceived seizure frequency (lower QOL with more frequent seizures)
    - Perceived adverse effects from AEDs
    - Perceived cognitive problems due to epilepsy and/or AEDs
    - Limitations in independence due to seizures/not driving/unemployment
  - Psychosocial variables decreasing QOL
    - Psychiatric comorbidity
    - Presence of social stigma of epilepsy

- QOL improves to near-normal levels with seizure freedom
  - Surgical patients' QOL increased to near healthy peers within 2–3 years of being seizure free
- Variables improving QOL
  - Reducing seizure frequency
  - Reducing AEDs
  - Promote cognitive reserve/activity
  - Decrease psychiatric symptomatology
  - Reduce family/social/cultural stigma/discrimination of epilepsy

Taxonomic description of neuropsychological function in epilepsy. A new approach to studying the neuropsychologic aspects of epilepsy has been to assess if distinct patient groups could be empirically derived based on similarities and differences in presurgical neuropsychological function (Hermann et al., 2007). Among patients with TLE, three distinct cognitive phenotype patient groups emerged: (1) minimally impaired, (2) predominately memory impaired and (3) memory, executive and speed impaired. The minimally impaired group accounted for 47% of the total sample. This group did not differ from healthy controls in regard to IQ or perception. While scores on measures of immediate and delayed memory, confrontation naming, executive control processes (e.g., generative fluency) and psychomotor speed were significantly below the mean of healthy control group, the difference in scores was no more than one (1) standard deviation (SD). Thus, these lower scores are probably not clinically meaningful. Structural neuroimaging found the minimally impaired group exhibited hippocampal volume atrophy, but no other significant differences from the control group. The predominately memory impaired group included about 27% of the TLE sample. As a group, immediate and delayed memory scores were more than 2 SDs below the mean of the healthy control group, and also displayed mild deficits in all remaining cognitive domains (IQ, perception, language, executive and psychomotor speed). This patient cluster exhibited greater structural brain abnormalities, with more atrophy of the hippocampus along with significantly less total cerebral brain volume and CSF volume. The memory, executive and speed impaired group included about 29% of the TLE patients. As a group, this patient taxonomy exhibited the greatest neuropsychological impairment, scoring 2 or more SDs below controls on measures of IQ, immediate and delayed memory, language, executive and psychomotor speed. In contrast to primarily memory impaired group, the most pronounced deficits were in executive and psychomotor speed. The third cluster tended to be the oldest sample, to have the longest duration of epilepsy, took the most antiepileptic medications and showed the greatest volumetric brain abnormalities. Volumetric brain abnormalities included marked hippocampal atrophy and significant changes in total cerebral tissue, reduced gray and white matter and greater CSF volume. This group also exhibited the worst cognitive course of the three samples. A more recent 2019 study by Reyes and colleagues identified four phenotypes based on patterns of performance across language and memory measures, including a language and memory impaired phenotype (representing nearly one-quarter of the sample, and overall performing the poorest upon neuropsychological assessment suggesting more pervasive dysfunction), isolated memory or language impairment phenotypes (together representing nearly one-half of the sample) and a no impairment phenotype. Using diffusion tensor imaging, language and memory impaired as well as isolated memory impairment phenotypes demonstrated significant microstructural superficial and deep white matter changes within tracts implicated in language and memory—at both regional and global network levels. Despite relatively intact global network structure, the isolated language impairment phenotype nonetheless showed abnormal perisylvian white matter network structure. Altogether, this study suggests underlying neurobiological differences in white matter structure and connectivity contributing to unique cognitive phenotypes above and beyond known clinical characteristics. There have since been a number of additional studies in this area examining phenotypes in both children and adults (Arrotta et al., 2022; Baxendale & Thompson, 2020; Bingaman et al., 2023; Caciagli et al., 2023; Cano-Lopez et al., 2024; Catalan-Aguilar et al., 2023; Giovagnoli et al., 2020; Hermann et al., 2021; Reyes et al., 2019, 2023; Schraegle et al., 2022; Shah et al., 2024).

Neuropsychological Assessment Guide

Neuropsychological evaluations for patients with epilepsy are generally broad and we believe should incorporate sensory and motor testing along with symptom validity tests (SVTs) and performance validity tests (PVTs) (see Table 17.13 for a recommended neuropsychological assessment battery).

Review of medical records: This is absolutely crucial for a proper neuropsychological evaluation (Helmstaedter & Witt, 2017). Important records for review include EEG report identifying the suspected seizure focus and/or seizure types. Often, a report of the MRI study of the brain will identify any structural abnormalities, particularly involving the temporal lobe. The presence of MTS greatly aids in predicting neuropsychological outcome. Report for language dominance based on either or combination of Wada (intracarotid amobarbital) test, fMRI and/or MEG/MSI is helpful to predict memory and language outcome. Knowledge of age of seizure onset and duration of epilepsy can be helpful. Review of the medication regimen is recommended to identify ASMs or other medications that may negatively affect neuropsychological function (see Table 17.8).

Clinical interview: Carefully listen for dysnomias, paraphasias or slurring. Also, carefully watch for abnormal eye movements or episodes in which the patient appears to briefly pause while talking or "space off." These brief episodes when you think the patient may be thinking may actually reflect a seizure. Ask the patient if (s)he has experienced a loss of time or if they recall what they were thinking about.

Table 17.13 Summary of basic neuropsychological assessment battery

Neuropsychological domain	Recommended measures
General cognitive ability	Wechsler intelligence scales
Attention and executive	Wechsler intelligence scales, attention subtests (i.e., digit span, digit symbol, letter-number sequencing) Trail making test Wisconsin card sorting test Figural fluency test (D-KEFS or ruff)
Psychomotor speed and reaction time	Reaction time test Finger tapping test Grooved pegboard test
Speech and language	Boston naming test Columbia auditory naming test Controlled Oral word association test (COWAT) Semantic verbal fluency *If patient is a child, add achievement screening of:* Word knowledge, receptive vocabulary, sentence reading, spelling, arithmetic skills.
Learning and memory	Rey auditory verbal Learning test (RAVLT) Wechsler memory scales
Visuoperceptual and visuoconstructional	Rey-Osterrieth complex figure test (or Taylor figure) Wechsler Block design
Emotional/mood and Quality of life	Beck depression inventory–second edition Beck anxiety inventory QOLIE−10 or QOLIE-31
Task engagement	At least one performance validity test
Sensory and perceptual	Light touch (hand and face) Visual fields Apraxia screen Auditory extinction to finger rub

Note: *QOLIE*, Quality of Life Inventory-Epilepsy

You might also carefully evaluate the patient's orientation. Look also for facial asymmetries (Tinuper et al., 1992), which can occur among patients with epilepsy.

Sensory-perceptual examination: The clinical neuropsychologist can evaluate for gross visual-field cuts, tactile sensory function (extinction task), simple audition functions and apraxias (Manzone et al., 2024). We recommend evaluating for hemi-inattention to visual, auditory and tactile sensation. Inattention can be rapidly assessed by using a brief bedside bilateral simultaneous stimulation test. One may also assess for finger agnosia, astereognosis, right/left orientation and apraxia. Cranial nerve exam and evaluation of deep tendon reflexes may also assist the neuropsychologist complete the evaluation.

Motor examination: Evaluation of grip strength and manual dexterity of both upper extremities is recommended.

Neuropsychological psychometric instruments: The selection of instruments should (a) have demonstrated validity (evidence-based) and (b) assist the neuropsychologist to make some statement about the relative risk for neuropsychological impairment following surgery. Ideally, this will include a statement about the type and extent of neuropsychological and psychological impairments that may occur from the proposed surgical procedure (e.g., right anterior temporal lobectomy). Secondarily, the neuropsychologist may assist with confirming the lateralization or localization of the seizure focus, keeping in mind that this information will be misleading in some patients and assumes normal functional neuroanatomic organization (i.e., left hemisphere dominant for language). While the selection of specific assessment instruments can certainly differ (e.g., assessing verbal memory), the assessment should assess domains likely to be adversely affected by the epilepsy syndrome and/or proposed neurological surgery procedure. The neuropsychological measures specified below are guides, and as new tests are developed, neuropsychologists should evaluate the evidence-based research of older and newer instruments, and how new tests may better serve the needs of the patient (Loring & Bauer, 2010). Neuropsychologists interested in performing evaluations on persons with epilepsy should be familiar with the adult and pediatric measures recommended as part of the Common Data Elements from the National Institute of Neurological Disorders and Stroke (NINDS; https://www.commondataelements.ninds.nih.gov/epilepsy).

General Cognitive

The assessment of general cognitive functioning can be helpful in epilepsy surgery evaluations, but differences in Verbal IQ and Performance (nonverbal) IQ should *not* be used to discriminate left TLE from right TLE. Using a General Ability Index can help ascertain overall cognitive functioning, and this is relevant as borderline-to-impaired general cognitive functioning prior to elective surgery could raise concerns about poorer general outcome over the short term as well as place the patient at increased risk for decline in neuropsychological function over the long term (perhaps reflecting magnified age-related changes). Poor general cognitive functioning may also raise questions about the patient's ability to cope with psychosocial stressors, independently manage medications and understand the benefits and potential risks of elective neurological surgery. Patients with early onset of refractory epilepsy, long duration of epilepsy and history of multiple episodes of generalized tonic-clonic status epilepticus typically exhibit significantly worse IQ scores than patients with shorter duration of seizures, later onset of seizures and no history of generalized tonic-clonic status epilepticus.

Recommended measures: Wechsler Intelligence Scales have an extensive literature (Wechsler, 2009). Abbreviated administration or short-form versions are often used. The processing speed and working memory indices can be useful for examining the effects of medications, acute seizures and other transient, acute factors.

Academic achievement measures: Including a measure of academic functioning can be helpful, and is often important in academic placement issues for children and adolescents. For children, we recommend a screening of word reading, reading comprehension, spelling and arithmetic skills. In adults, an assessment of reading ability can be useful in TLE cases, while arithmetic may be more important in extra-temporal resections (i.e., parietal).

Recommended measures: Wide Range Achievement Test–fifth Edition (WRAT-5) (Wilkinson & Robertson, 2017), Peabody Individual Achievement Test–Revised (PIAT-R) (Markwardt, 1998), Woodcock-Johnson Tests of Achievement–fourth Edition (Schrank et al., 2014).

Attention/Concentration and "Executive Functions"

We recommend an evaluation of simple, focused and divided attention.

Recommended measures (Attention): Commonly used measures include digit span forward and backward as well as letter-number sequencing and coding subtests of the Wechsler Intelligence Scales (Wechsler, 2009), Trail Making Test (either parts A/B or from the Delis-Kaplan Executive Function System battery) (Delis et al., 2001; Reitan, 1992), Symbol Digit Modalities Test (SDMT) (Smith, 1973) and others. A measure of reaction time is often helpful as well.

"Executive functions" refers to a range of complex cognitive and behavioral adaptive functions often associated with frontal lobe function, but also involve other brain regions (see Chap. 10, this volume for details).

Recommended measures (executive functions): Commonly included measures include the Wisconsin Card Sorting Test (Grant & Berg, 2014), Category Test of the Halstead-Reitan battery (Reitan & Wolfson, 1985), Figural fluency task (e.g., DKEFS Figural Fluency, Ruff Figural Fluency Test) (Delis et al., 2001), verbal fluency (Controlled Oral Word Association Test, animal fluency test or the fluency subtest from the Delis-Kaplan Executive Function System battery) (Benton & Hamsher, 1989), Stroop Color-Word Test (Golden version or from the Delis-Kaplan Executive Function System battery), competing programs/serial motor programming tasks, Go/No-Go tasks. Other tests include the Iowa Gambling task and Frontal Assessment Battery. In addition, assessment for motor impersistence, motor weakness and personality changes including apathy, social disinhibition and/or irritability is suggested. The latter may be best captured by questionnaires such as the Frontal Systems Behavior Scale (FrSBe), Behavioral Rating Inventory of Executive Function (BRIEF) (Gioia et al., 2000) or Dysexecutive Questionnaire–Revised (DEX-R).

Language and speech: Psychometric evaluation of naming and generative fluency is critical in the evaluation of epilepsy surgery patients. These domains are frequently impaired among patients with epilepsy, and can also be negatively impacted by neurological surgery. Reading and spelling functions may also be assessed, and can also be impacted by some surgical interventions. Interictally, patients with epilepsy rarely exhibit gross aphasia symptoms, but aphasic symptoms postictally can predict seizure laterality and seizure outcome (Privetera et al., 1991).

Recommended measures: Boston Naming Test, Columbia Auditory Naming Test or verbal fluency tests (as noted above). Assessment of reading and spelling may include the PIAT-R, WRAT-4 or W-J-IV (as noted above). Measures of vocabulary, both receptive and expressive, can be helpful in the assessment of children with epilepsy (Peabody Picture Vocabulary Test– fourth Edition and Vocabulary subtest of the WAIS-IV or WISC-IV).

Learning/memory: Neuropsychological assessment of declarative memory functions has predictive value of postsurgical memory outcome. Moreover, in cases in which structural neuroimaging fails to identify a lesion, assessment of memory has been shown to be predictive of surgical outcome and side of seizure onset (e.g., Hennessy et al., 2001; Sawrie et al., 1998, 2001). Deficient short-term spontaneous recall of verbal material (paragraphs, list of words and word-pairs), with normal verbal intellectual functioning, is indicative of focal language-dominant (left) mesial temporal lobe dysfunction. Poor recall of verbal material, particularly list learning tasks, as well as word-pairs or short paragraphs is consistently associated with mesial temporal sclerosis and histopathological evidence of CA1 and CA3 hippocampal gliosis. The predictive value of "visual" memory tests on outcome is not consistent. While nondominant (right) hemisphere seizure onset can present with specific deficits in recall of complex geometric shapes and human faces, patients with right TLE can also exhibit deficits in verbal and nonverbal (visual) memory. It is thought the major shortcoming of current "visual" memory tasks is the stimuli can be verbally encoded.

Recommended measures: Verbal memory tests include the Rey Auditory Verbal Learning Test (RAVLT) or California Verbal Learning Test (CVLT) (Rey, 1941; Schmidt, 1996). The RAVLT has more predictive value identifying left TLE than the CVLT (Loring et al., 2008). As of 2010, we are unaware of any visual memory measure that consistently discriminates patients with right TLE from left TLE. Visual memory tasks we recommend include the Rey-Osterrieth Complex Figure (Gagnon et al., 2003) (or Taylor Complex figure) or the Visual Reproduction subtest of the Wechsler Memory Scales-IV (Wechsler, 2009). Other commonly used "visual" memory tests [Benton Brief Visual Retention Test, Hospital Facial Memory Test, Medical College Georgia Complex Figure (MCG-CF) test] (Loring & Meador, 2003; Steck, 2005) have also not consistently distinguished right TLE from left TLE.

Visuoperceptual/Visuoconstructional skills: Deficits are common, but scores on measures of visuoconstructional tests have *not* consistently discriminated patients with left TLE from right TLE. Although rarely present, visual inattention has clear indications for the lateralization of brain dysfunction (see Lezak et al., 2004).

Recommended measures: Frequently used measures of visuoconstructional and visuoperceptual function include the Rey-Osterrieth Complex Figure (or Taylor complex figure test) and the Block Design subtest of the Wechsler Intelligence scales. The Benton Tests [e.g., Judgment of Line Orientation, Facial Recognition Test (FRT)] are also widely used (Benton et al., 1994). Patients with TLE have exhibited postoperative decline on the FRT in one study. The Visual Object Space Perception Battery (Warrington & James, 1991) may hold promise to improve lateralization, and includes four subtests that load on a perceptual factor and four that load on a spatial processing factor (Rapport et al., 1998). Bedside assessments of visuoconstructional skills can also be used in lower functioning patients such as drawing a clock face, cube or the Halstead-Reitan aphasia screening instrument.

Psychological/Emotional Functioning

Evaluation for symptoms of depression and anxiety is important in evaluating patients with refractory epilepsy given the high comorbidity of psychiatric symptoms in this population. It should be recognized patients may present with symptoms of anxiety and depression secondary to the neurophysiological dysfunction associated with the epilepsy syndrome. There is currently no conclusive data regarding hemispheric laterality for symptoms of depression or anxiety symptoms. Furthermore, the so-called temporal lobe personality associated with interpersonal "stickiness" and religiosity is *not* consistent among patients with TLE. A rare but disabling psychiatric feature associated with TLE is psychosis. Psychosis can result from postictal psychosis or may appear as part of a rare schizophrenic like presentation. Even more rare is the onset of psychosis following ATL. In addition, the patient's expectations for surgery outcome and ways to cope with both good and poor surgical outcome need to be assessed. A component of this should include an evaluation to the extent that there the individual exhibits somatic pre-occupation and/or a history of psychogenic nonepileptic seizures (PNES, or pseudoseizure) and/or panic attacks. The presence of PNES along with refractory epilepsy would *not*, in our view, prohibit a patient from undergoing surgical treatment for refractory epilepsy, but the presence of PNES should alert the team to an increased risk for poor surgical outcome from a psychiatric and quality of life standpoint. Lastly, assessment of the patient's social support network is recommended.

Recommended measures: Screening for symptoms of depression and anxiety can include the Beck Depression Inventory—second Edition (BDI – 2), the Beck Anxiety Inventory (BAI) (Beck et al., 1996, 1988) and the Spielberger State-Trait Anxiety Inventory (STAI) (Spielberger et al., 1983). More detailed assessment may include the Minnesota Multiphasic Personality Inventory—second Edition (MMPI–2) or the Personality Assessment Inventory (PAI) (Butcher et al., 1989, 2001; Morey, 1991; Thompson et al., 2010).

Quality of life: Assessment of quality of life with epilepsy can be obtained from the Quality of Life in Epilepsy Inventories (QOLIE) (Meador, 1993) of which there are long and short versions, including the QOLIE–10, –31 and –89 item versions (Connell et al., 1996; Cramer et al., 1996; Vickrey et al., 1993).

Analysis of Change in Neuropsychology Test Scores

Repeat neuropsychological evaluations are common in epilepsy, with the goal being to evaluate for change in neuropsychological function following surgical or medical interventions. In addition to monitoring for change following surgical intervention, increasing attention is being given to monitoring for the cognitive effects of ASMs. Another common referral is to evaluate for change in cognitive functioning for individuals with refractory epilepsy to monitor their progress. Traditional approaches have included evaluation of change in neuropsychology test scores by change in raw scores and some in standard scores. Beginning in the 1990s, two much more sophisticated measures of change were developed: (1) the Reliable Change Indices (RCIs) and (2) standard regression-based (SRB) change score norms (Hermann et al., 1996; Sawrie et al., 1996). The statistical approaches vary, but a common theme is to statistically control for test–retest effects and measurement error. Measurement of change is typically based on well-selected clinical samples of patients who are typically medically managed to determine the extent of change (if any) that might occur with the disease and medical treatment alone. Once change over time due to progression of disease has been determined, comparison to change associated with a new treatment (surgery, etc.) allows clinicians to empirically answer if a change from time one to time two is greater than what might have occurred due to disease and measurement error. However, the change is based on a clinical population, in this case, patients with epilepsy, so using particular RCI values to other patient populations or healthy controls should not be done.

We provide RCI and SRB change scores below (see Tables 17.14, 17.15, 17.16 and 17.17). These tables summarize available RCI and/or SRB data we were aware of as of 12/2009. While RCI/SRB are available for some commonly used measures in epilepsy, by no means are there plentiful data at this time. One might attempt to develop RCI at the 80 and 90 percent confidence intervals for neuropsychological measures using the test manual using the following algorithm: $Sdiff = (SEM1^2 + SEM2^2)^{1/2}$. However, keep in mind this is the least accurate measures of reliable change, as it is based on healthy controls.

Summary

Epilepsy is a disease associated with more than one unprovoked seizure, and is a common neurological disorder. In general, the prognosis for most epilepsies is good. Neuropsychological deficits are observed in focal epilepsies as well as some idiopathic generalized epilepsies. Moreover, neuropsychological studies of the "benign epilepsy" syndromes, which have identified subtle deficits in some cases, have begun to change our understanding of epilepsy and seizures themselves.

Neuropsychologists are integral members of the epilepsy surgical team, and neuropsychological data provide important data for the diagnosis and management of

Table 17.14 Reliable change of common neuropsychological tests for adult epilepsy patients after anterior temporal lobectomy (ATL)

Neuropsychological domains and tests	Practice correct	80% RCI CI	90% RCI CI	Metric	Source
Intellectual functioning					
WAIS-III	–	–	–	–	Martin et al. (2002)
Full scale IQ	+1	≤ −5, ≥ +7	≤ −6, ≥ +8	Standard score	
Verbal IQ	0	≤ −6, ≥ +6	≤ −8, ≥ +8	Standard score	
Performance IQ	+3	≤ −5, ≥ +11	≤ −7, ≥ +13	Standard score	
Verbal comprehension index	+1	≤ −5, ≥ +7	≤ −7, ≥ +9	Standard score	
Perceptual organization index	+3	≤ −5, ≥ +11	≤ −8, ≥ +14	Standard score	
Working memory index	−2	≤ −15, ≥ +9	≤ −17, ≥ +13	Standard score	
WAIS-R	–	–	–	–	Hermann et al. (1996)
Full scale IQ	+1	≤−4, ≥ + 8	≤−6, ≥ + 10	Standard score	
Verbal IQ	+3	≤−4, ≥ + 6	≤−5, ≥ + 7	Standard score	
Performance IQ	+2	≤−4, ≥ + 8	≤−6, ≥ + 10	Standard score	
Information	0	≤−3, ≥ + 3	≤−4, ≥ + 4	Scaled score	
Digit span	0	≤−3, ≥ + 3	≤−4, ≥ + 4	Scaled score	
Vocabulary	0	≤−2, ≥ + 2	≤−3, ≥ + 3	Scaled score	
Arithmetic	0	≤−3, ≥ + 3	≤−4, ≥ + 4	Scaled score	
Comprehension	0	≤−3, ≥ + 3	≤−4, ≥ + 4	Scaled score	
Similarities	0	≤−4, ≥ + 4	≤−5, ≥ + 5	Scaled score	
Picture completion	+1	≤−3, ≥ + 5	≤−4, ≥ + 6	Scaled score	
Picture arrangement	0	≤−4, ≥ + 4	≤−5, ≥ + 5	Scaled score	
Block design	0	≤−3, ≥ + 3	≤−3, ≥ + 3	Scaled score	
Object assembly	0	≤−3, ≥ + 3	≤4, ≥ + 4	Scaled score	

(continued)

Table 17.14 (continued)

Neuropsychological domains and tests	Practice correct	80% RCI CI	90% RCI CI	Metric	Source
Digit symbol	0	≤−3, ≥ + 3	≤−3, ≥ + 3	Scaled score	
Academic achievement					
WRAT-R	–	–	–	–	Hermann et al. (1996)
Reading	+2	≤−5, ≥ + 9	≤−7, ≥ + 11	Standard score	
Spelling	+2	≤−5, ≥ + 9	≤−6, ≥ + 10	Standard score	
Arithmetic	+1	≤−7, ≥ + 9	≤−9, ≥ + 11	Standard score	
Processing speed					
ABPIMB	–	–	–	–	Baxendale and Thompson (2005)[a]
Information processing A total	–	<−11.3, > + 11.3	<−14.7, > + 14.7	–	
Information processing A speed	–	<−8.7, > + 8.7	<−11.3, > + 11.3	–	
Information processing B total	–	<−8.4, > + 8.4	<−10.8, > + 10.8	–	
Information processing B speed	–	<−8.0, > + 8.0	<−10.3, > + 10.3	–	
Trail making test-part A	-2	≤−17, ≥ + 13	≤−21, ≥ + 17	Raw (seconds)	Hermann et al. (1996)
Attention and executive					
WCST	–	–	–	–	Hermann et al. (1996)
Categories	0	≤−3, ≥ + 3	≤−4, ≥ + 4	Raw	
Preservative responses	−1	≤−18, ≥ + 16	≤−21, ≥ + 21	Raw	
Trail making test-part B	+3	≤−47, ≥ + 53	≤−61, ≥ + 67	Raw (seconds)	Hermann et al. (1996)
Speech and language					
MAE	–	–	–	–	Hermann et al. (1996)
Visual naming	0	≤ −7, ≥ +7	≤ −8, ≥ +8	Raw score	
Sentence repetition	0	≤ −4, ≥ +4	≤ −4, ≥ +4	Raw score	
Oral fluency	-1	≤ −12, ≥ +10	≤ −14, ≥ +12	Raw score	

(continued)

Table 17.14 (continued)

Neuropsychological domains and tests	Practice correct	80% RCI CI	90% RCI CI	Metric	Source
Oral spelling	0	≤ −3, ≥ +3	≤ −4, ≥ +4	Raw score	
Token test	0	≤ −4, ≥ +4	≤ −5, ≥ +5	Raw score	
Aural comprehension	0	≤ −2, ≥ +2	≤ −2, ≥ +2	Raw score	
Reading comprehension	0	≤ −2, ≥ +2	≤ −2, ≥ +2	Raw score	
Learning and memory					
AMIPB	–	–	–	–	Baxendale and Thompson (2005)[a]
Story recall-immediate	–	<−10, > + 10	<−12.9, > + 12.9	–	
Story recall-delayed	–	<−9.4, > + 9.4	<−12.1, > + 12.1	–	
List Learning total 1–5	–	<−9.6, > + 9.6	<−12.4, > + 12.4	–	
List Learning delay	–	<−2.9, > + 2.9	<−3.8, > + 3.8	–	
List B	–	<−3.0, > + 3.0	<−3.9, > + 3.9	–	
Figure immediate recall	–	<−17.5, > + 17.5	<−22.5, > + 22.5	–	
Figure delayed recall	–	<−24.9, > + 24.9	<−32.0, > + 32.0	–	
Design Learning total 1–5	–	<−10.0, > + 10.0	<−12.8, > + 12.8	–	
Design Learning delay	–	<−3.9, > + 3.9	<−5.1, > + 5.1	–	
WMS-III	–	–	–	–	Martin et al. (2002)
Auditory immediate index	+1	≤ −11, ≥ +13	≤ −14, ≥ +16	Standard score	
Visual immediate index	+3	≤ −11, ≥ +17	≤ −15, ≥ +21	Standard score	
General immediate memory	+2	≤ −9, ≥ +13	≤ −12, ≥ +16	Standard score	
Auditory delayed index	−2	≤ −15, ≥ +11	≤ −19, ≥ +15	Standard score	
Visual delayed index	+5	≤ −9, ≥ +19	≤ −13, ≥ +23	Standard score	
Auditory Recog. Delayed index	−1	≤ −18, ≥ +16	≤ −22, ≥ +20	Standard score	

(continued)

Table 17.14 (continued)

Neuropsychological domains and tests	Practice correct	80% RCI CI	90% RCI CI	Metric	Source
General memory index	+1	≤ −13, ≥ +15	≤ −16, ≥ +18	Standard score	
Working memory index	-2	≤ −18, ≥ +14	≤ −22, ≥ +18	Standard score	
Logical memory I	0	≤ −3, ≥ +3	≤ −3, ≥ +3	Scaled score	
Logical memory II	0	≤ −3, ≥ +3	≤ −4, ≥ +4	Scaled score	
Faces I	+1	≤ −2, ≥ +4	≤ −3, ≥ +5	Scaled score	
Faces II	+1	≤ −2, ≥ +4	≤ −3, ≥ +5	Scaled score	
Verbal paired associates I	0	≤ −3, ≥ +3	≤ −3, ≥ +3	Scaled score	
Verbal paired associates II	0	≤ −3, ≥ +3	≤ −4, ≥ +4	Scaled score	
Family pictures I	0	≤ −3, ≥ +3	≤ −3, ≥ +3	Scaled score	
Family pictures II	0	≤ −3, ≥ +3	≤ −4, ≥ +4	Scaled score	
Letter/number sequencing	0	≤ −3, ≥ +3	≤ −4, ≥ +4	Scaled score	
Spatial span	+1	≤ −3, ≥ +5	≤ −4, ≥ +6	Scaled score	
WMS	–	–	–	–	Hermann et al. (1996)
Logical memory I	+2	≤ −4, ≥ +8	≤ −5, ≥ +9	Raw score	
Logical memory II	+1	≤ −5, ≥ +7	≤ −7, ≥ +9	Raw score	
Logical memory % retention	+2	≤ −30, ≥ +32	≤ −39, ≥ +43	Raw score	
Associate learning-easy	0	≤ −3, ≥ +3	≤ −4, ≥ +4	Raw score	
Associate learning-hard	+1	≤ −3, ≥ +5	≤ −4, ≥ +6	Raw score	
Visual reproduction I	+1	≤ −3, ≥ +5	≤ −3, ≥ +5	Raw score	
Visual reproduction II	+1	≤ −3, ≥ +5	≤ −4, ≥ +6	Raw score	
Visual reproduction % retention	−1	≤ −29, ≥ +27	≤ −37, ≥ +35	Raw score	
CVLT	–	–	–	–	Hermann et al. (1996)

(continued)

Table 17.14 (continued)

Neuropsychological domains and tests	Practice correct	80% RCI CI	90% RCI CI	Metric	Source
Total words	+2	≤ −8, ≥ +12	≤ −11, ≥ +15	Raw score	
Trial 1	+1	≤ −3, ≥ +5	≤ −3, ≥ +5	Raw score	
Trial 2	+1	≤ −3, ≥ +5	≤ −4, ≥ +6	Raw score	
Trial 3	+1	≤ −4, ≥ +4	≤ −4, ≥ +4	Raw score	
Trial 4	0	≤ −4, ≥ +6	≤ −5, ≥ +7	Raw score	
Trial 5	+1	≤ −3, ≥ +5	≤ −3, ≥ +5	Raw score	
Short-delay free recall	+1	≤ −6, ≥ +8	≤ −8, ≥ +10	Raw score	
Long-delay free recall	+2	≤ −2, ≥ +6	≤ −3, ≥ +7	Raw score	
Discriminability	+3	≤ −13, ≥ +19	≤ −17, ≥ +23	Raw score	
False positives	-1	≤ −7, ≥ +5	≤ −8, ≥ +6	Raw score	
Recognition hits	+1	≤ −3, ≥ +5	≤ −4, ≥ +6	Raw score	
Visuoperceptual and Visuoconstructional					
Form discrimination test	0	≤ −5, ≥ +5	≤ −6, ≥ +6	Raw score	Hermann et al. (1996)
Hooper Organization test	+1	≤ −2, ≥ +4	≤ −3, ≥ +5	Raw score	
Line orientation test	+2	≤ −2, ≥ +6	≤ −3, ≥ +7	Raw score	
Facial recognition test	0	≤ −5, ≥ +5	≤ −6, ≥ +6	Raw score	

Note: *AMIPB*, Adult Memory and Information Processing Battery; *CI*, confidence interval; *CVLT*, California Verbal Learning Test; *IQ*, Intelligence Quotient; *MAE*, Multilingual Aphasia Examination; *RCI*, reliable change index; *WAIS-III/R*, Wechsler Adult Intelligence Test-third Edition/Revised; *WMS-III*, Wechsler Memory Scales-third Edition/Revised; *WTAR-R*, Wide Range Achievement Test-Revised; *WCST*, Wisconsin Card Sorting Test. [a]RCI data from personal communication. Assistance with Table by Eric Rinehardt, PhD, Department of Psychiatry and Behavioral Sciences, University of South Florida College of Medicine. [b]AK Coughlan & SE Hollows. Adult memory and information processing battery. UK, Leeds: St. James Hospital; 1985

Table 17.15 Summary of proportion (%) of adults with epilepsy exhibiting change on selected neuropsychological measures after anterior temporal lobectomy (ATL)

Neuropsychological domains and tests	% Declined	% Stable	% Improved
CVLT	–	–	–
Long delay Free recall-dominant ATL	46	54	0
Long delay Free recall-nondominant ATL	11	89	0
WMS-R	–	–	–
Logical memory II-dominant ATL	37	60	3
Logical memory II-nondominant ATL	11	82	7

Note: From Stroup et al. (2003). RCI's were used to assess change. CVLT = California Verbal Learning Test; WMS-R = Wechsler Memory Scales-Revised

Table 17.16 Reliable change of common neuropsychological tests for pediatric epilepsy patients after anterior temporal lobectomy (ATL)

Neuropsychological domains and tests	Practice correct	90% RCI CI	Metric
WISC-III	–	–	–
Full scale IQ	7.72	≤ –0, ≥ +16	Standard score
Verbal IQ	2.32	≤ –6, ≥ +11	Standard score
Performance IQ	12.35	≤ 1, ≥ +23	Standard score
Verbal comprehension index	2.26	≤ –7, ≥ +12	Standard score
Perceptual organization index	10.99	≤ 0, ≥ +2	Standard score
Freedom from distractibility index	2.96	≤ –10, ≥ +16	Standard score
Processing speed index	9.09	≤ –5, ≥ +23	Standard score
Information	0.47	≤ –3, ≥ +4	Scaled score
Similarities	0.81	≤ –3, ≥ +4	Scaled score
Arithmetic	0.31	≤ –3, ≥ +4	Scaled score
Vocabulary	0.14	≤ –3, ≥ +3	Scaled score
Comprehension	0.26	≤ –4, ≥ +4	Scaled score
Digit span	0.74	≤ –2, ≥ +4	Scaled score
Picture completion	1.78	≤ –2, ≥ +6	Scaled score
Coding	1.97	≤ –2, ≥ +6	Scaled score
Picture arrangement	2.96	≤ –1, ≥ +7	Scaled score
Block design	1.04	≤ –2, ≥ +4	Scaled score
Object assembly	1.57	≤ –3, ≥ +6	Scaled score
Symbol search	1.53	≤ –2, ≥ +3	Scaled score
CMS	–	–	–
Visual immediate index	11.06	≤ –7, ≥ +29	Standard score
Visual delayed index	8.50	≤ –9, ≥ +26	Standard score
Verbal immediate index	12.13	≤ –1, ≥ +26	Standard score
Verbal delayed index	11.35	≤ –4, ≥ +26	Standard score
General memory index	16.42	≤ 5, ≥ +27	Standard score
Attention/Concentration index	3.95	≤ –9, ≥ +17	Standard score
Learning index	9.43	≤ –5, ≥ +24	Standard score
Auditory delayed recognition	3.88	≤ –12, ≥ +20	Scaled score

(continued)

Table 17.16 (continued)

Neuropsychological domains and tests	Practice correct	90% RCI CI	Metric
Dot learning	0.75	≤ −3, ≥ +5	Scaled score
Dot Total	0.98	≤ −3, ≥ +5	Scaled score
Dot Short delay	0.78	≤ −4, ≥ +6	Scaled score
Dot long delay	0.56	≤ −3, ≥ +5	Scaled score
Stories immediate	1.68	≤ −2, ≥ +6	Scaled score
Stories delayed	1.97	≤ −2, ≥ +6	Scaled score
Stories delayed recognition	1.11	≤ −3, ≥ +5	Scaled score
Faces immediate	2.60	≤ −2, ≥ +7	Scaled score
Faces delayed	2.25	≤ −2, ≥ +6	Scaled score
Word pair learning	2.07	≤ −1, ≥ +5	Scaled score
Word pair total	2.32	≤ −1, ≥ +5	Scaled score
Word pair immediate	0.87	≤ −3, ≥ +5	Scaled score
Word pair long delay	1.78	≤ −2, ≥ +5	Scaled score
Word pair delayed recognition	0.17	≤ −4, ≥ +4	Scaled score
Numbers	0.73	≤ −3, ≥ +4	Scaled score
Sequences	0.53	≤ −3, ≥ +4	Scaled score
Family pictures immediate	1.23	≤ −4, ≥ +6	Scaled score
Family pictures delayed	1.39	≤ −3, ≥ +6	Scaled score
Word list learning	1.72	≤ −2, ≥ +5	Scaled score
Word list delayed	1.33	≤ −3, ≥ +6	Scaled score
Word list delayed recognition	0.68	≤ −3, ≥ +4	Scaled score

Note: CMS = Children's Memory Scale; WISC-III = Wechsler Intelligence Scale for Children-3rd Edition. Data obtained from personal communication with Haut et al. (2006). Assistance with Table by Eric Rinehardt, PhD, Department of Psychiatry and Behavioral Sciences, University of South Florida College of Medicine

Table 17.17 Summary of proportion (%) of pediatric patients with epilepsy exhibiting change on selected neuropsychological measures with and without surgery

	Surgical (n = 30)			Nonsurgical (n = 21)		
Neuropsychological domains and tests	% Declined	% Stable	% Improved	% Declined	% Stable	% Improved
Intelligence						
WISC-III & WAIS-III	–	–	–	–	–	–
Verbal comprehension index	10.3	86.3	3.4	15.8	84.2	0.0
Perceptual organization index	6.9	89.7	3.4	5.3	84.2	10.5
Freedom from distractibility index	21.4	75.0	3.6	15.8	78.9	5.3
Processing speed index	7.1	85.8	7.1	10.5	84.2	5.3
Academic achievement						
WRAT	–	–	–	–	–	–
Reading decoding	3.4	96.6	0.0	0.0	100	0.0

(continued)

Table 17.17 (continued)

Neuropsychological domains and tests	Surgical (n = 30) % Declined	% Stable	% Improved	Nonsurgical (n = 21) % Declined	% Stable	% Improved
Reading comprehension	23.1	73.1	3.8	5.3	84.2	10.5
Spelling	6.9	93.1	0.0	10.0	85.0	5.0
Arithmetic	20.7	69.0	10.3	5.0	90.0	5.0
Visual sustained attention[a]						
Vigilance	–	–	–	–	–	–
Correct	42.3	26.9	30.8	21.1	36.8	42.1
Errors of commission	34.6	50.0	15.4	10.5	42.1	47.4
Distractibility	–	–	–	–	–	–
Correct	30.4	34.8	34.8	14.3	42.8	42.9
Errors of commission	17.4	34.8	47.8	0.0	35.7	64.3
Learning and memory						
CMS & DNMS	–	–	–	–	–	–
Recall of story	34.5	44.8	20.7	33.3	47.7	19.0
CAVLT-2	–	–	–	–	–	–
Recall of word list	39.3	50.0	10.7	15.0	75.0	10.0
ROCFT, CMS, & DNMS						
Recall of geometric design	29.6	51.9	18.5	18.8	49.9	31.3
Recognition of faces	12.0	52.0	36.0	10.5	73.7	15.8

Note: *CAVLT-2*, Children's Auditory Verbal Learning Test-2nd Edition; *CMS*, Children's Memory Scale; *DNMS*, Denman Neuropsychology Memory Scale; *ROCFT*, Rey-Osterrieth Complex Figure Test; *WAIS-III*, Wechsler Adult Intelligence Test-3rd Edition; *WISC-III*, Wechsler Intelligence Scale for Children-3rd Edition; *WRAT*, Wide Range Achievement Test. [a]Vigilance and distractibility tasks from Gordon Diagnostic System. From ML Smith et al. (2004). Mean age is 13. Data reflects various seizure foci and severity pre surgery. Change reflects ≥ or ≤ 1 SD one year post surgery. Assistance with Table by Eric Rinehardt, PhD, Department of Psychiatry and Behavioral Sciences, University of South Florida College of Medicine

patients with epilepsy. Within the frame of neuropsychological science and practice, epilepsy provides data for guiding an evidence-based neuropsychology practice. Neuropsychological data have clear implications for predicting postsurgical memory and language outcome following anterior temporal lobectomy for medication-refractory epilepsy. Moreover, there is data establishing that neuropsychological data are helpful in predicting the side of seizure onset (lateralized dysfunction in focal epilepsy), and there are limited contexts in which neuropsychological data can assist in predicting seizure outcome (seizure freedom). These limited settings tend to involve cases in which there is no clear lesion or for which EEG findings for lateralization are mixed. However, these data are preliminary, and largely do not integrate other noninvasive neuroimaging techniques that have recently been developed (e.g., MEG/MSI, functional neuroimaging or PET studies), although Potter et al. (2009) did find limited support for neuropsychological variables in a multivariate model including MRI data. However, another recent study combining multiple noninvasive studies (MRI, SISCOM) to predict seizure outcome did not find neuropsychological data added to the prediction of seizure freedom (Bell et al., 2009).

Neuropsychological study is providing a longitudinal perspective for epilepsy, in which the presence of neuropsychological dysfunction appears to be present at the time of first recognized seizure (Fastenau et al., 2009), and this data is not consistently associated with structural brain changes. Moreover, data are developing that establish neuropsychological dysfunction may be progressive over time and when present at first onset seizure appears to increase the risk for further cognitive and academic deficits. The long-term course of epilepsy remains to be detailed, but initial data suggest neuropsychological function may be quite stable for years (up to 10 years) for some patients, but appears to decline in 20–25% of patients. The long-term impact of seizure surgery on cognitive dysfunction remains to be delineated, but initial deficits may resolve at one or two years after surgery, although initial data for long-term follow-up in older patients suggest there may be a decline, particularly in verbal memory and left temporal resections.

The impact of epilepsy on neuropsychological function and quality of life is beginning to emerge. While a detailed review of QOL was beyond the scope of this chapter, the literature clearly indicates epilepsy/medical variables of perceived seizure frequency and adverse effects of ASMs have a negative effect on QOL, and treatment resulting in seizure freedom improves quality of life. In addition to these epilepsy-related variables, reducing psychiatric symptoms of anxiety and/or depression, increasing cognitive activity and improving resilience variables of the patient along with reducing negative stigma and discrimination of epilepsy can improve QOL. The role of the neuropsychologist can not only provide consultation for assessing, monitoring over time and predicting cognitive outcome, but can also improve patients QOL.

Appendices

Appendix 1. International Classification of Epilepsies, Epileptic Syndromes and Related Seizure Disorders

I. Localization-related (focal, partial, local)

   A. Idiopathic (primary)

      1. Benign childhood epilepsy with centrotemporal spikes (benign rolandic epilepsy)
      2. Childhood epilepsy with occipital paroxysms.
      3. Primary reading epilepsy

B. Symptomatic (secondary)

1. Temporal lobe epilepsies
2. Frontal lobe epilepsies
3. Parietal lobe epilepsies
4. Occipital lobe epilepsies
5. Chronic progressive epilepsia partialis continua of childhood (Kojewnikoff's syndrome)
6. Syndromes characterized by seizures with specific modes of precipitation (e.g., reflex epilepsies and startle epilepsies).

C. Probably symptomatic (formally cryptogenic), defined by:

1. Seizure type
2. Clinical features
3. Etiology
4. Anatomical localization

II. Generalized

A. Primary idiopathic, in order of age of onset

1. Benign neonatal familial convulsions
2. Benign neonatal convulsions
3. Benign myoclonic epilepsy in infancy
4. Childhood absence epilepsy (pyknolepsy)
5. Juvenile absence epilepsy
6. Juvenile myoclonic epilepsy (of Janz)
7. Epilepsy with generalized tonic-clonic convulsions on awakening
8. Other generalized idiopathic epilepsies
9. Epilepsies with seizure precipitated by specific modes of activation

B. Probably symptomatic (formally cryptogenic), in order of age of onset

1. West's syndrome
2. Lennox-Gastaut syndrome
3. Epilepsy with myoclonic-astatic seizures
4. Epilepsy with myoclonic absences

C. Symptomatic (secondary)

1. Nonspecific etiology

(a) Early myoclonic encephalopathy
(b) Early infantile epileptic encephalopathy with suppression bursts
(c) Other symptomatic generalized epilepsies

2. Specific syndromes

(a) Neurological diseases with seizures as a prominent feature

III. Epilepsies undetermined whether focal or generalized

A. With both focal and generalized seizures

1. Neonatal seizures
2. Severe myoclonic epilepsy of infancy
3. Epilepsy with continuous spike waves during slow-wave sleep
4. Acquired epileptic aphasia (Landau-Kleffner syndrome)
5. Other undetermined epilepsies

IV. Special syndromes

A. Situation-related seizures

1. Febrile convulsions
2. Isolated seizures or isolated status epilepticus
3. Seizures occurring only with acute metabolic or toxic events due to factors such as alcohol, drugs, eclampsia and nonketotic hyperglycemia

Appendix 2. Example of Newly Proposed Classification of Epilepsy Syndromes (2001)

I. Localization-related (focal, partial, local)

A. Idiopathic (primary) epilepsies of infancy and childhood

1. Benign infantile seizures
2. Benign childhood epilepsy with centrotemporal spikes (benign rolandic epilepsy)
3. Childhood epilepsy with occipital paroxysms

B. Familial (autosomal dominant)

1. Benign familial neonatal seizures
2. Benign familial infantile seizures
3. Autosomal dominant nocturnal frontal lobe epilepsy
4. Familial temporal lobe epilepsy
5. Familial focal epilepsy with variable foci

C. Symptomatic (or probably symptomatic) epilepsies

1. Limbic epilepsies

(a) Mesial temporal lobe epilepsy with hippocampal sclerosis
(b) Mesial temporal lobe epilepsy defined by specific etiologies
(c) Other types defined by location and etiology

2. Neocortical epilepsies
    (a) Rasmussen syndrome
    (b) Hemiconvulsion-hemiplegia syndrome
    (c) Other types defined by location and etiology (frontal, parietal and occipital lobe epilepsies)
3. Migrating partial seizures of early infancy

II. Generalized

A. Idiopathic, in order of age of onset
1. Benign myoclonic epilepsy in infancy
2. Epilepsy with myoclonic-astatic seizures
3. Childhood absence epilepsy (pyknolepsy)
4. Epilepsy with myoclonic absences
5. Idiopathic generalized epilepsies with variable phenotypes
    (a) Juvenile absence epilepsy
    (b) Juvenile myoclonic epilepsy (of Janz)
    (c) Epilepsy with generalized tonic-clonic seizures only
6. Other generalized idiopathic epilepsies

B. Familial
7. Benign neonatal familial convulsions

III. Epileptic encephalopathies (epileptiform abnormalities may contribute to progressive dysfunction)

A. Early myoclonic encephalopathy
B. Ohtahara syndrome
C. West's syndrome
D. Dravet syndrome (also known as severe myoclonic epilepsy in infancy)
E. Myoclonic status in nonprogressive encephalopathies
F. Lennox-Gastaut syndrome
G. Landau-Kleffner syndrome (acquired epileptic aphasia)
H. Epilepsy with continuous spike-waves during slow-wave sleep

IV. Reflex epilepsies

A. Idiopathic photosensitive occipital lobe epilepsy
B. Other visual sensitive epilepsy
C. Primary reading epilepsy
D. Startle epilepsy

V. Progressive myoclonus epilepsies

A. Various specific diseases

VI. Seizures not necessarily requiring a diagnosis of epilepsy

A. Benign neonatal seizures
B. Febrile seizures
C. Reflex seizures
D. Alcohol or other drug induced seizures
E. Immediate and early posttraumatic seizures
F. Single seizures or isolated clusters of seizures
G. Rarely repeated seizures (oligoepilepsy)

References

Aarts, J. H., Binnie, C. D., Smit, M., & Wilkins, A. J. (1984). Selective cognitive impairment during focal and generalized epileptiform EEG activity. *Brain, 107*(1), 239–308.

Abarrategui, B., Parejo-Carbonell, B., Garcia, M. E. G., Capua, D. D., & Garcia-Morales, I. (2018). The cognitive phenotype of idiopathic generalized epilepsy. *Epilepsy & Behavior, 89*, 99–104.

Aldenkamp, A. P., & Arends, J. (2004). The relative influence of elileptic EEG discharges, short nonconvulsive seizures, and type of epilepsy on cognitive function. *Epilepsia, 45*(1), 54–63.

Aldenkamp, A. P., De Krom, M., & Reijs, R. (2003). Newer antiepileptic drugs and cognitive issues. *Epilepsia, 44*(Suppl 4), 21–29.

Andermann, F., Bourgeois, B., Leppik, I. E., Ojemann, L., & Sherwin, A. L. (1993). Postoperative pharmacotherapy and discontinuation of antiepileptic drugs. In J. J. Engel (Ed.), *Surgical treatment of the epilepsies* (2nd ed., pp. 679–684). Raven Press.

Anhoury, S., Brown, R. J., Krishnamoorthy, E. S., & Trimble, M. R. (2000). Psychiatric outcome after temporal lobectomy: A predictive study. *Epilepsia, 41*, 1608–1615.

Arrotta, K., Reyes, A., Kaestner, E., McDonald, C. R., Hermann, B. P., Barr, W. B., Sarmey, N., Sundar, S., Kondylis, E., Najm, I., Bingaman, W., & Busch, R. M. (2022). Cognitive phenotypes in frontal lobe epilepsy. *Epilepsia, 63*(7), 1671–1681.

Austelle, C. W., O'Leary, G. H., Thompson, S., Manett, A. J., Short, B., & Badran, B. W. (2022). A comprehensive review of vagus nerve stimulation for depression. *Neuromodulation, 25*(1), 309–315.

Austin, J. K., Huberty, T. J., Huster, G. A., & Dunn, D. W. (1998). Academic achievement in children with epilepsy or asthma. *Developmental Medicine and Child Neurology, 40*(4), 248–255.

Austin, J. K., Harezlak, J., Dunn, D. W., Huster, G. A., Rose, D. F., & Ambrosius, W. T. (2001). Behavior problems in children before first recognized seizures. *Pediatrics, 107*(1), 115–122.

Austin, J. K., Dunn, D. W., Caffrey, H. M., Perkins, S. M., Harezlak, J., & Rose, D. F. (2002). Recurrent seizures and behavior problems in children iwth first recognized seizures: A prospective study. *Epilepsia, 43*(12), 1564–1573.

Avidan, G., Hasson, U., Malach, R., & Behrmann, M. (2005). Detailed exploration of face-related processing in congential prosopagnosia: 2. Functional neuroimaging findings. *Journal of Cognitive Neuroscience, 17*, 1150–1167.

Babb, T. L., & Brown, W. J. (1987). Pathological findings in epilepsy. In J. J. Engel (Ed.), *Surgical treatment of the epilepsies* (pp. 511–540). Raven Press.

Baldo, J. V., Shimamura, A. P., Delis, D. C., Kramer, J., & Kaplan, E. (2001). Verbal and design fluency in patients with frontal lobe lesions. *Journal of the International Neuropsychological Society, 7*(5), 586–596.

Barr, W. B. (1997). Examining the right temporal lobe's role in nonverbal memory. *Brain and Cognition, 35*, 26–41.

Barr, W. B., Chelune, G. J., Hermann, B. P., Loring, D. W., Perrine, K., Strauss, E., Trenerry, M. R., & Westerveld, M. (1997). The use of figural reproduction tests as measures of nonverbal memory in epilepsy surgery candidates. *Journal of the International Neuropsychological Society, 3*, 435–443.

Bartha, L., Trinka, E., Ortler, M., Donnemiller, E., Felber, S., Bauer, G., & Benke, T. (2004). Linguistic deficits following left selective amygdalohippocampectomy: A prospective study. *Epilepsy and Behavior, 5*(3), 348–357.

Bartha, L., Benke, T., Bauer, G., & Trinka, E. (2005). Interictal language functions in temporal lobe epilepsy. *Journal of Neurology Neurosurgery and Psychiatry, 76*, 808–814.

Bartolomei, F., Barbeau, E., Gavaret, M., Guye, M., McGonigal, A., Régis, J., & Chauvel, P. (2004). Cortical stimulation study of the role of rhinal cortex in déjà vu and reminiscence of memories. *Neurology, 63*, 858–864.

Bauman, K., Devinsky, O., & Liu, A. A. (2019). Temporal lobe surgery and memory: Lessons, risks, and opportunities. *Epilepsy & Behavior, 101*, 106596.

Baxendale, S. (2009). The Wada test. *Current Opinion in Neurology, 22*(2), 185–189.

Baxendale, S., & Thompson, P. (2020). The association of cognitive phenotypes with postoperative outcomes after epilepsy surgery in patients with temporal lobe epilepsy. *Epilepsy and Behavior, 112*, 107386.

Baxendale, S., Thompson, P., Harkness, W., & Duncan, J. (2006). Predicting memory decline following epilepsy surgery: A multivariate approach. *Epilepsia, 47*(11), 1887–1894.

Baxendale, S., Thompson, P. J., & Duncan, J. S. (2012). Neuropsychological function in patients who have had epilepsy surgery: A long-term follow-up. *Epilepsy and Behavior, 23*(1), 24–29.

Baxendale, S., Thompson, P. J., & Sander, J. W. (2013). Neuropsychological outcomes in epilepsy surgery patients with unilateral hippocampal sclerosis and good preoperative memory function. *Epilepsia, 54*(9), 131–134.

Baxendale, S., Wilson, S. J., Baker, G. A., Barr, W., Helmstaedter, C., Hermann, B. P., Langfitt, J., Reuner, G., Rzezak, P., Samson, S., & Smith, M. L. (2019). Indications and expectations for neuropsychological assessment in epilepsy surgery in children and adults: Exxecutive summary of the report of the ILAE neuropsychology task Force diagnostic methods commission: 2017-2021. *Epilepsia, 60*(9), 1794–1796.

Baxendale, S. A., Wilson, S. J., Baker, G. A., Barr, W., Helmstaedter, C., Hermann, B. P., Langfitt, J., Reuner, G., Rzezak, P., Samson, S., & Smith, M. L. (2020). Ten things every neurologist needs to know abbout neuropsychological assessments and interventions inn people with epilepsy. *European Journal of Neurology, 27*(2), 215–220.

Beck, A. T., Epstein, N., Brown, G., & Steer, R. A. (1988). An inventory for measuring clinical anxiety: Psychometric properties. *Journal of Consulting and Clinical Psychology, 56*, 893–897.

Beck, A. T., Steer, R. A., & Brown, G. K. (1996). *Manual for the Beck depression inventory - II*. The Psychological Corporation.

Beghi, E., & Hesdorffer, D. (2014). Prevalence of epilepsy - An unknown quantity. *Epilepsia, 55*(7), 963–967.

Behrmann, M., Lee, A. C., Geskin, J. Z., Graham, K. S., & Barense, M. D. (2016). Temporal lobe contribution to perceptual function: A tale of three patient groups. *Neuropsychologia, 90*, 33–45.

Bell, B. D., Seidenberg, M., Hermann, B. P., & Doubille, K. (2003). Visual and auditory naming in patients with left or bilateral temporal lobe epilepsy. *Epilepsy Research, 55*, 29–37.

Bell, B., Lin, J. J., Seidenberg, M., & Hermann, B. (2011). The neurobiology of cognitive disorders in temporal lobe epilepsy. *Nature Reviews Neurology, 7*(3), 154–164.

Benbadis, S. R. (2005). Practical management issues for idiopathic generalized epilepsies. Idiopathic generalized epilepsies: A review and modern approach. *Epilepsia, 46*, 125–132.

Benbadis, S. (2009). The differential diagnosis of epilepsy: A critical review. *Epilepsy & Behavior, 15*, 15–21.

Beniczky, S., Tatum, W. O., Blumenfeld, H., Stefan, H., Mani, J., Maillard, L., Fahoum, F., Vinayan, K. P., Mayor, L. C., Vlachou, M., Seeck, M., Ryvlin, P., & Kahane, P. (2022). Seizure semiology: ILAE glossary of terms and their significance. *Epileptic Disorders, 24*(3), 447–495.

Ben-Menachem, E. (2001). Vagus nerve stimulation, side effects, and long-term safety. *Journal of Clinical Neurophysiology, 18*(5), 415–418.

Benton, A. L., & Hamsher, K. (1989). *Multilingual aphasia examination*. AJA Associates.

Benton, A. L., Sivan, A. B., Hamsher, K. D., Varney, N. R., & Spreen, O. (1994). *Contributions to neuropsychological assessment: A clinical manual* (2nd ed.). Oxford University Press.

Bentvelzen, A. C., Kessels, R. P. C., Badcock, N. A., & Savage, G. (2022). The impact of right temporal lobe Epilepsy on nonverbal memory: Meta-regression of stimulus- and task-related moderators. *Neuropsychology Review, 32*(3), 537–557.

Berg, A. T., Smith, S. N., & Frobish, D. (2005). Special education needs of children with newly diagnosed epilepsy. *Developmental Medicine and Child Neurology, 47*, 749–753.

Berl, M. M., Smith, M. L., Bulteau, C., & the Task Froce for Pediatric Epilepsy Surgery for the ILAE Commissionns of Pediatrics, S. T. (2017). ILAE survey of neuropsychology practice in pediatric epilepsy surgery evaluation. *Epileptic Disorders, 19*(2), 166–177.

Bernasconi, A., Bernasconi, N., Natsume, J., Antel, S. B., Andermann, F., & Arnold, D. L. (2003). Magnetic resonance spectroscopy and imaging fo the thalamus in idiopathic generlalized epilepsy. *Brain, 126*, 2247–2254.

Bernasconi, N., Duchesne, S., Janke, A., Lerch, J., Collins, D. L., & Bernasconi, A. (2004). Whole-brain voxel-based statistical analysis of gray matter and white matter in temporal lobe epilepsy. *NeuroImage, 23*, 717–723.

Bernasconi, N., Natsume, J., & Bernasconi, A. (2005). Progression in temporal lobe epilepsy: Differential atrophy in mesial temporal structures. *Neurology, 65*(2), 223–228.

Bernasconi, A., Cendes, F., Theodore, W. H., Gill, R. S., Koepp, M. J., Hogan, R. E., Jackson, G. D., Federico, P., Labate, A., Vaudano, A. E., Blumcke, I., Ryvlin, P., & Bernasconi, N. (2019). Recommendations for the use of structural mangetic resonance imaging in the care of patients with epilepsy: A consensus report from the international league against Epilepsy neuroimaging task Force. *Epilepsia, 60*(6), 1054–1068.

Bhanudeep, S., Madaan, P., Sankhyan, N., Saini, L., Malhi, P., Suthar, R., Saini, A. G., Ahuja, C. K., Vyas, S., Singh, P., Kaur, A., Singh, G., Sharma, R., Negi, S., Jayashree, M., Attri, S. V., Singhi, P., & Sahu, J. K. (2021). Long-term epilepsy control, motor function, cognition, sleep and quality of life in chlldren with West syndrome. *Epilepsy Research, 173*, 106629.

Bilder, R. M., & Reise, S. P. (2019). Neuropsychological tests of the future: How do we get there from here? *The Clinical Neuropsychologist, 33*(2), 220–245.

Binder, J. R., Sabsevitz, D. S., Swanson, S. J., Swanson, S. J., Hammeke, T. A., Raghavan, M., & Mueller, W. M. (2008a). Use of preoperative functional MRI to predict verbal memory decline after temporal lobe epilepsy surgery. *Epilepsia, 49*(8), 1377–1394.

Binder, D. K., Von Lehe, M., Kral, T., Bien, C. G., Urbach, H., Schramm, J., & Clusmann, H. (2008b). Surgical treatment of occipital lobe epilepsy. *Journal of Neurosurgery, 109*(1), 57–69.

Bingaman, N., Ferguson, L., Thompson, N. C., Reyes, A., McDonald, C. R., Hermann, B. P., Arrotta, K., & Busch, R. M. (2023). The relationship between mood and anxiety and cognitive phenotypes in adults with pharmacoresistant temporal lobe epilepsy. *Epilepsia, 64*(12), 3331–3341.

Binnie, C. D. (2003, December). Cognitive impairment during epileptiform discharges: Is it ever justifiable to treat the EEG? *The Lancet Neurology, 2*(12), 725–730. http://www.sciencedirect.com/science/article/B6X3F-4B1SKNM-K/2/1769525fb0a48fb9d42d6cb882a542c0

Blakemore, C. B., & Falconer, M. A. (1967). Long-term effects of anterior temporal lobectomy on certain cognitive functions. *Journal of Neurology, Neurosurgery, and Psychiatry, 30*, 364–367.

Blumcke, I., Pauli, E., Clusmann, H., Schramm, J., Becker, A., Elger, C., Merschhemke, M., Meencke, H. J., Lehmann, T., von Deimling, A., Scheiwe, C., Zentner, J., Volk, B., Romstock, J., Stefan, H., & Hildebrandt, M. (2007). A new clinico-pathological classification system for mesial temporal sclerosis. *Acta Neuropathologica, 113*, 235–244.

Blume, W. T., Whiting, S. E., & Girvin, J. P. (1991). Epilepsy surgery in the posterior cortex. *Annals of Neurology, 29*, 638–645.

Blumer, D., Montouris, G., & Hermann, B. (1995). Psychiatric morbidity in seizure patients on a neurodiagnostic monitoring unit. *The Journal of Neuropsychiatry and Clinical Neurosciences, 7*, 445–456.

Bocquillon, P., Dujardin, K., Betrouni, N., Phalempin, V., Houdayer, E., Bourriez, J. L., Derambure, P., & Szurhaj, W. (2008). Attention impairment in temporal lobe epilepsy: A neurophysiological approach via analysis of the P300 wave. *Human Brain Mapping, 30*(7), 2267–2277.

Bonilha, L., Jensen, J. H., Baker, N., Breedlove, J., Nesland, T., Lin, J. J., Drane, D. L., Saindane, A. M., binder, J. R., & Kuzniecky, R. (2015). The brain connectome as a personalized biomarker of seizure outcomes after temporal lobectomy. *Neurology, 84*(18), 1845–1853.

Bonini, F., & McGonigal, A. (2020). Frontal lobe epilepsy. In S. Schuele (Ed.), *A practical approach to stereo EEG* (pp. 136–156). Springer.

Bonini, F., McGonigal, A., Trébuchon, A., Gavaret, M., Bartolomei, F., Giusiano, B., & Chauvel, P. (2014). Frontal lobe seizures: From clinical semiology to localization. *Epilepsia, 55*, 264–277.

Boon, P., Vonck, K., De Herdt, V., Van Dycke, A., Goethais, M., Goossens, L., Van Zandijicke, M., De Smedt, T., Dewaele, I., Achten, R., Wadman, W., Dewaele, F., Caemaert, J., & Van Roost, D. (2007). Deep brain stimulation in patients with refractory temporal lobe epilepsy. *Epilepsia, 48*(8), 1551–1560.

Bower, R. S., Wirrell, E., Nwojo, M., Wetjen, N. M., Marsh, W. R., & Meyer, F. B. (2013). Seizure outcomes after corpus callosotomy for drop attacks. *Neurosurgery, 73*(6), 993–1000.

Breuer, L. E. M., Boon, P., Bergmans, J. W. M., Mess, W. H., Besseling, R. M. H., de Louw, A., Tijhuis, A. G., Zinger, S., Bernas, A., Klooster, D. C. W., & Aldenkamp, A. P. (2016). Cognitive deterioration in adult epilepsy: Does accelerated cognitive ageing exist? *Neuroscience and Biobehavioral Reviews, 64*, 1–11.

Breuer, L. E. M., Bernas, A., Boon, P., Besseling, R. M. H., Carrette, E. C. B., de Louw, A., & Aldenkamp, A. (2019). Accelerated cognitive ageing in epilepsy: A neuropsychological evaluation of cognitive deterioration. *Archives of Clinical Neuropsychology, 34*(3), 301–309.

Brissart, H., Planton, M., Bilger, M., Bulteau, C., Forhoffer, N., Guinet, V., Hennion, S., Kleitz, C., Laguitton, V., Mirabel, H., Mosca, C., Pecheux, N., Pradier, S., Samson, S., E., T., Voltzenlogel, V., Denos, M., & Boutin, M. (2019). French neuropsychological procedure consensus in epilepsy surgery. *Epilepsy & Behavior, 100*, 106522.

Brodie, M. J., & Kwan, P. (2002). Staged apporach to epilepsy management. *Neurology, 58*(Suppl. 5), S2–S8.

Brodie, M. J., Elder, A. T., & Kwan, P. (2009). Epilepsy in later life. *The Lancet Neurology, 8*(11), 1019–1030.

Brown, F. C., Tuttle, E., Westerveld, M., Ferraro, F. R., Chmielowiec, T., Vandemore, M., Gibson-Beverly, G., Bemus, L., Roth, R. M., Blumenfeld, H., Spencer, D. D., & Spencer, S. S. (2010). Visual memory in patients after anterior right temporal lobectomy and adult normative data for the Brown location test. *Epilepsy and Behavior, 17*, 215–220.

Burchiel, K. J., & Christiano, J. A. (2006). Review of selective amygdalophippocampectomy techniques. In J. W. Miller & D. L. Silbergeld (Eds.), *Epilepsy surgery: Principles and controversies* (pp. 451–463). Taylor & Francis.

Busch, R. M., Frazier, T. W., Haggerty, K. A., & Kubu, C. S. (2005). Utility of the Boston naming test in predicting ultimate side of surgery in patients with medically intractable temporal lobe epilepsy. *Epilepsia, 46*(11), 1773–1779.

Busch, R. M., Frazier, T. W., Lampietro, M. C., Chapin, J. S., & Kubu, C. S. (2009). Clinical utility of the Boston naming test in predicting ultimate side of surgery in patients with medically intracctable temporal lobe epilepsy: A double cross-validation study. *Epilepsia, 50*(5), 1270–1273.

Busch, R. M., Love, T. E., Jehi, L. E., Ferguson, L., Yardi, R., Najm, I., Bingaman, W., & Gonzalez-Martinez, J. (2015). Effect of invasive EEG monitoring on cognitive outcome after left temporal lobe epilepsy surgery. *Neurology, 85*(17), 1475–1481.

Busch, R. M., Floden, D. P., Prayson, B., Chapin, J. S., Kim, K. H., Ferguson, L., Bingaman, W., & Najm, I. M. (2016). Estimating risk of word-finding problems in adults undergoing epilepsy surgery. *Neurology, 87*, 2363–2369.

Busch, R. M., Hogue, O., Kattan, M. W., Hamberger, M. J., Drane, D. L., Hermann, B., Kim, M., Ferguson, L., Bingaman, W., Gonzalez-Martinez, J., Najm, I., & Jehi, L. (2018). Nomograms to predict naming decline after temporal lobe surgeryt in adults with epilepsy. *Neurology, 91*, e2144–e2152.

Busch, R. M., Hogue, O., Miller, M., Ferguson, L., McAndrews, M. P., Hamberger, M., Kim, M., McDonald, C. R., Reyes, A., Drane, D. L., Hermann, B. P., Bingaman, W., Najm, I. M., Kattan, M. W., & Jehi, L. (2021). Nomograms to predict verbal memory decline after temporal lobe resection in adults with Epilepsy. *Neurology, 97*(3), e263–e274.

Butcher, J., Dahlstrom, W., Graham, J., Tellegen, A., & Kaemmer, B. (1989). *MMPI-2 manual for administration and scoring*. University of Minnesota Press.

Butcher, J. N., Graham, J. R., Ben-Porath, Y. S., Tellegen, A., Dahlstrom, W. G., & Kaemmer, B. (2001). *MMPI-2: Manual for administration and scoring* (Revised edn). University of Minnesota Press.

Byars, A. W., Byars, K. C., Johnson, C. S., DeGrauw, T. J., Fastenau, P. S., Perkins, S., Austin, J. K., & Dunn, D. W. (2008). The relationship between sleep problems and neuropsychological functioning inn children with first recognized seizures. *Epilepsy & Behavior, 13*(4), 607–613.

Caciagli, L., Bernasconi, A., Wiebe, S., Koepp, M. J., Bernasconi, N., & Bernhardt, B. C. (2017). A meta-analysis on progressive atrophy in intractable temporal lobe epilepsy: Time is brain? *Neurology, 89*(5), 506–516.

Caciagli, L., Ratcliffe, C., Xiao, F., van Graan, L. A., Trimmel, K., Vollmar, C., Centeno, M., Duncan, J. S., Thompson, P. J., Baxendale, S., Koepp, M. J., & Wandschneider, B. (2023). Cognitive phenotype of juvenile absence epilepsy: An investigation of patients and unaffected siblings. *Epilepsia, 64*(10), 2792–2805.

Caller, T. A., Ferguson, R. J., Roth, R. M., Secore, K. L., Alexandre, F. P., Zhao, W., Tosteson, T. D., Henegan, P. L., Briney, K., & Jobst, B. C. (2016). A cognitive behavioral intervention (HOBSCOTCH) improves quality of life and attention in epilepsy. *Epilepsy & Behavior, 57*, 111–117.

Camfield, P. R., & Camfield, C. S. (1996). Antiepileptic drug therapy: When is epilepsy truly intractable? *Epilepsia, 37*, S60–S65.

Camfield, C. S., & Camfield, P. R. (2007). Long-term social outcomes for children with epilepsy. *Epilepsia, 48*, 3–5.

Camfield, C., & Camfield, P. (2008). Twenty years after childhood-onset symptomatic generalized epilepsy the social outcome is usually dependency or death: A population-based study. *Developmental Medicine and Child Neurology, 50*(11), 859–863.

Cano-Lopez, I., Catalan-Aguilar, J., Lozano-Garcia, A., Hidalgo, V., Hampel, K. G., Tormos-Pons, P., Salvador, A., Villanueva, V., & Gonzalez-Bono, E. (2024). Cognitive phenotypes in patients with drug-resistant temporal lobe epilepsy: Relationships with cortisol and affectivity. *The Clinical Neuropsychologist*, 1–24.

Caplan, R., Siddarth, P., Stahl, L., Lanphhier, E., Vona, P., Gurbani, S., Koh, S., Sankar, R., & Shields, W. D. (2008). Childhood absence epilepsy: Behavioral, cognitive, and linguistic comorbidities. *Epilepsia, 49*(11), 1836–1846.

Cardamone, L., Salzberg, M. R., O'Brien, T. J., & Jones, N. C. (2013). Antidepressant therapy in epilepsy: Can treating the comorbidities affect the underlying disorder? *British Journal of Pharmacology, 168*(7), 1531–1554.

Carlson, P., & Nicholson Perry, K. (2017). Psychological interventions for psychogenic nonepileptic seizures: A meta-analysis. *Seizure, 45*, 142–150.

Castro, L. H., Silva, L. C. A. M., Adda, C. C., Banaskiwitz, N. H. C., Xavier, A. B., Jorge, C. L., Valerio, R. M., & Nitrini, R. (2013). Low prevalence but high specificity of material-specific memory impairment in epilepsy associated with hippocampal sclerosis. *Epilepsia, 54*(10), 1735–1742.

Catalan-Aguilar, J., Gonzalez-Bono, E., Lozano-Garcia, A., Tormos-Pons, P., Hampel, K., Villanueva, V., & Cano-Lopez, I. (2023). Stress phenotypes in epilepsy: Impact on cognitive functioning and quality of life. *Frontiers in Psychology, 14*, 259150131.

Catenoix, J., Bbourdillon, P., Guenot, M., & Isnard, J. (2018). The combination of stereo-EEG and radiofrequency ablationn. *Epilepsy Research, 142*, 117–120.

Cendes, F., Cook, M. J., Watson, C., Andermann, F., Fish, D. R., Shorvon, S. D., Bergin, P., Free, S., Dubeau, F., & Arnold, D. L. (1995). Frequency and characteristics of dual pathology in patients with lesional epilepsy. *Neurology, 45*, 2058–2064.

Cendes, F., Andermann, F., Dubeau, F., Matthews, P. M., & Arnold, D. L. (1997). Normalization of neuronal metabolic dysfunction after surgery for temporal lobe epilepsy: Evidence from proton MR spectroscopic imaging. *Neurology, 49*, 1525–1533.

Centeno, M., Thompson, P. J., Koepp, M. J., Helmstaedter, C., & Duncan, J. S. (2010). Memory in frontal lobe epilepsy. *Epilepsy Research, 91*, 123–132.

Centeno, M., Vollmar, C. O., Muircheartaigh, J., Stretton, J., Bonelli, S. B., Symms, M. R., Barker, G. J., Kumari, V., Thompson, P. J., Duncan, J. S., Richardson, M. P., & Koepp, M. J. (2012). Memory in frontal lobe epilepsy: An fMRI study. *Epilepsia, 53*(10), 1756–1764.

Cetin, E., Sirin, N. G., Elmali, A. D., Baykan, B., & Bebek, N. (2021). Different faces of frontal lobe epilepsy: The clinical, electrophysiologic, and imaging experience of a tertiary center. *Clinical Neurology and Neurosurgery, 203*, 106532.

Chapin, J. S., busch, R. M., Naugle, R. I., & Najm, I. M. (2009). The family pictures subtest of the WMS-III: Relationship to verbal and visual memory following temporal lobectomy for intractable epilepsy. *Journal of Clinical and Experimental Neuropsychology, 31*(4), 498–504.

Chee, M. W., Kotagal, P., Van Ness, P. C., Gragg, L., Murphy, D., & Luders, H. O. (1993). Lateralizing signs in intractable partial epilepsy: Blinded multiple-observer analysis. *Neurology, 43*, 2519–2525.

Chelune, G. J. (1995). Hippocampal adequacy versus functional reserve: Predicting memory functions following temporal lobectomy. *Archives of Clinical Neuropsychology, 10*(5), 413–432.

Chelune, G. J. (2008). Evidence-based research and practice in clinical neuropsychology. *The Clinical Neuropsychologist, 24*, 454–467.

Chelune, G. J., & Najm, I. M. (2000). Risk factors associated with postsurgical decrements in memory. In H. O. Luders & Y. Comair (Eds.), *Epilepsy surgery* (pp. 497–504). Lippincott-Raven.

Chelune, G. J., Naugle, R. I., Luders, H., Sedlak, J., & Awad, I. A. (1993). Individual change after epilepsy surgery: Practice effects and base-rate information. *Neuropsychology, 7*(1), 41–52.

Chen, Z., Brodie, M. J., & Kwan, P. (2020). What has been the impact of new drug treatments on epilepsy? *Current Opinion in Neurology, 33*(2), 185–190.

Cheung, M. C., Chan, A. S., Chan, Y. L., Lam, J. M., & Lam, W. (2006). Effects of illness duration on memory processing of patients iwth temporal lobe epilepsy. *Epilepsia, 47*(8), 1320–1328.

Chiang, S., Levin, H. S., Wilde, E., & Haneef, Z. (2015). Whhite matter structural connectivity changes correlate with epilepsy duration in temporal lobe epilepsy. *Epilepsy Research, 120*, 37–46.

Chilosi, A. M., Brovedani, P., Moscatelli, M., Bonanni, P., & Guerrini, R. (2006). Neuropsychological findings in idiopathic occiptial lobe epilepsies. *Epilepsia, 47*(Suppl. 2), 76–78.

Chowdhury, F. A., Silva, R., Whatley, B., & Walker, M. (2021). Localisation in focal epilepsy: A practical guide. *Practical Neurology, 21*, 481–491.

Cocoran, R., & Upton, D. (1993). A role for the hippocampus in card sorting? *Cortex, 29*, 293–304.

Cohen-Gadol, A. A., Wilhelmi, B. G., Collignon, F., White, J. B., Britton, J. W., Cambier, D. M., Christianson, T. J., Marsh, W. R., Meyer, F. B., & Cascino, G. D. (2006). Long-term outcome of epilepsy surgery among 399 patients with nonlesional seizure foci including mesial temporal lobe sclerosis. *Journal of Neurosurgery, 104*(4), 513–524.

Collaborators, G. N. S. D. (2024). Global, regional, and national burden of disorders affecting the nervous system, 1990-2021: A systematic analysis for the global burden of disease study 2021. *The Lancet Neurology, 23*(4), 344–381.

Concha, L., Beaulieu, C., Collins, D. L., & Gross, D. W. (2009). White-matter diffusion abnormalities in temporal-lobe epilepsy with and without mesial temporal sclerosis. *Journal of Neurology, Neurosurgery and Psychiatry, 80*, 312–319.

Concha, L., Kim, H., Bernasconi, A., Bernhardt, B. C., & Bernasconi, N. (2012). Spatial patterns of water diffusion along white matter tracts in temporal lobe epilepsy. *Neurology, 79*(5), 455–462.

Connell, B. E., Harver, A., Tebbutt, D., & Wilner, A. N. (1996). Assessment of quality of life by QOLI and QOLIE-89 yields differential effects in patients with intractable epilepsy versus Pseudoseizures. *Archives of Clinical Neuropsychology, 11*(5), 377–378. http://www.sciencedirect.com/science/article/B6VDJ-3VW8K93-4N/2/a89aba120b3a713ec1e531d7a5a5d730

Cooper, A. D., Britton, J. W., & Rabinstein, A. A. (2009). Functional and cognitive outcome in prolonged refractory status epilepticus. *Archives of Neurology, 66*, 1505–1509.

Cossu, M., Mirandola, L., & Tassi, L. (2018). RF-ablation in periventricular heterotopia-related epilepsy. *Epilepsy Research, 142*, 121–125.

Craggs, J. C., Stanford, L. D., & Thornton, A. E. (1997). Neuropsychological functioning and seizure focus: Relationship to academic achievement in children with Epilepsy. *Archives of Clinical Neuropsychology, 12*(4), 303. http://www.sciencedirect.com/science/article/B6VDJ-3SWY8JS-4S/2/ca05535aa628a41432e048c906a314c6

Cramer, J. A., Perrine, K., Devinsky, O., & Meador, K. (1996). A brief questionnaire to screen for quality of life in epilepsy: The QOLIE-10. *Epilepsia, 37*(6), 577–582.

Cramer, J. A., Blum, D., Fanning, K., Reed, M., & Group, T. E. I. P. (2004). The impact of comrbid depression on health resource utilization in a community sample of people with epilepsy. *Epilepsy & Behavior, 5*, 337–342.

Cronin, W., Kwan, P., & Foster, E. (2023). Anxiety and depressive symptoms in adults with new-onset seizures: A scoping review. *Epilepsia Open, 8*(3), 758–772.

Culhand-Shelburne, K., Chapieski, L., Hiscock, M., & Glaze, D. (2002). Executive functions in children with frontal and temporal lobe epilepsy. *Journal of the International Neuropsychological Society, 8*, 623–632.

Curry, D. J., Gowda, A., McNichols, R. J., & Wilfong, A. A. (2012). MR-guided stereotactic laser ablation of epileptogenic foci in children. *Epilepsy and Behavior, 24*(4), 408–414.

Dabbs, K., Jones, J., Seidenberg, M., & Hermann, B. (2009). Neuroanatomical correlates of cognitive phenotypes in temporal lobe epilepsy. *Epilepsy and Behavior, 15*(4), 445–451.

Dalmagro, C. L., Bianchin, M. M., Velasco, T. R., Alexandre, J. V., Walz, R., Terra-Bustamonte, V. C., Inuzuka, L. M., Wichert-Ana, L., Araujo, J. D., Serafini, L. N., Carlotti, J. C. G., Assirati, J. J. A., Machado, H. R., Santos, A. C., & Sakamoto, A. C. (2005). Clinical features of patients with posterior cortical epilepsies and predictors of surgical outcome. *Epilepsia, 46*(9), 1442–1449.

Damasio, H., Grabowski, T. J., Tranel, D., Hichwa, R. D., & Damasio, A. (1996). A neural basis for lexical retrieval. *Nature, 380*, 499–505.

Davies, S., Heyman, I., & Goodman, R. (2003). A population survey of mental health problems in children with epilepsy. *Development Medicine & Child Neurology, 45*(5), 292–295.

de Tisi, J., Bell, G. S., Peacock, J. L., McEvoy, A. W., Harkness, W. F. J., Sander, J. W., & Duncan, J. S. (2011). The long-term outcome of adult epilepsy surgery, patterns of seizure remission, and relapse: A cohort study. *Lancet, 378*, 1388–1395.

Delalande, O., Bulteau, C., Dellatolas, G., Fohhlen, M., Jalin, C., Buret, V., Viguier, D., Dorfmuller, G., & Jambaque, I. (2007). Vertical parasagittal hemispherotomy: Surgical procedures and clinical long-term outcomes in a population of 83 children. *Neurosurgery, 60*(2 Suppl 1), ONS19–ONS32.

Delis, D. C., Kaplan, E., & Kramer, J. H. (2001). *Delis-Kaplan executive function system: Examiner's manual*. The Psychological Corporation.

Devinsky, O., Vezzani, A., O'Brien, T. J., Jette, N., Scheffer, I. E., de Curtis, M., & Perucca, P. (2018). Epilepsy. *Nature Reviews Disease Primers, 4*, 18024.

Dickey, A. S., Bullinger, K. L., Grogan, D., Asmar, M. M., Alwaki, A., Kheder, A., Shivamurthy, V. K. N., Faraj, R. R., Greven, A., Willie, J. T., Drane, D. L., & Gross, R. E. (2024). An ordinal clinical score predicts seizure freedom after minimally invasive epilepsy surgery. *Annals of Clinical and Translational Neurology, 11*(9), 2327–2336.

Dilorio, C., Bamps, Y., Walker, E. R., & Escoffery, C. (2011). Results of a research study evaluating WebEase, an online epilepsy self-management program. *Epilepsy & Behavior, 22*(3), 469–474.

Ding, K., Gong, Y., Gupta, P., Frol, A., McColl, R., Agostini, M., Modur, P., Van Ness, P., & Diaz-Arrastia, R. (2014). Regional atrophy in temporal lobe epilepsy: Correlations with cognitive impairment. *Journal of Neurological Disorders and Stroke, 2*(3), 1053–1060.

Djordjevic, J., & Jones-Gotman, M. (2011). Inquiry on assessments across epilepsy centers in different countries. In C. Helmstaedter, B. Hermann, M. Lassonde, P. Kahane, & A. Arzimanoglou (Eds.), *Neuropsychhology in the care of people with epilepsy*. John Libbey Eurotext.

Dodrill, C. (1984). Number of seizure types in relation to emotional and psychosocial adjusment in epilepsy. In R. J. Porter et al. (Eds.), *Advances in Epileptology: XVth Epilepsy international symposium* (pp. 541–544). Raven Press.

Dodrill, C. (1986a). Correlates of generalized Tonic-Clonic seizures with Intelectual, neuropsychological, emotional, and social function in patients with Epilepsy. *Epilepsia, 27*(4), 399–411.

Dodrill, C. (1986b). Psychosocial consequences of epilepsy. In S. B. Filskov & T. J. Poll (Eds.), *Handbook of clinical neuropsychology* (pp. 338–363). Wiley.

Dodrill, C. B., & Wilensky, A. J. (1990). Intellectual impairment as an outcome of status epilepticus. *Neurology, 40*, 23–27.

Donos, C., Breier, J., Friedman, E., Rollo, P., Johnson, J., Moss, L., Thompson, M. T., Hope, O., Slater, J., & Tandon, N. (2018). Laser ablation for mesial temporal lobe epilepsy: Surgical and cognitive outcomes with and without mesial temporal sclerosis. *Epilepsia, 59*(7), 1421–1432.

Donos, C., Rollo, P., Tombridge, K., Johnson, J. A., & Tandon, N. (2020). Visual field deficits following laser ablation of the hippocampus. *Neurology, 94*(12), e1303–e1313.

Drane, D. L. (2015). Neuropsychological evaluation of the epilepsy surgical candidate. In W. B. Barr & C. Morrison (Eds.), *Handbook on the neuropsychology or epilepsy* (pp. 87–121). Springer.

Drane, D. L. (2018). MRI-guided stereotactic laser ablation for epilepsy surgery: Promising preliminary results for cognitive outcome. *Epilepsy Research, 142*, 170–175.

Drane, D. L., & Meador, K. J. (Eds.). (2002). *Cognitive toxicity of antiepileptic drugs*. Butterworth-Heinemann.

Drane, D. L., & Pedersen, N. P. (2019). Knowledge of language function and underlying neural networks gained from complex partial seizures and epilepsy surgery. *Brain and Language, 189*, 20–33.

Drane, D. L., Lee, G. P., Cech, H., Huthwaite, J. S., Ojemann, G. A., Ojemann, J. G., Loring, D. W., & Meador, K. J. (2006). Structured cueing on a semantic fluency task differentiates patients with temporal versus frontal lobe seizure onset. *Epilepsy & Behavior, 9*(2), 339–344.

Drane, D. L., Ojemann, G. A., Aylward, E., Ojemann, J. G., Johnson, L. C., Silbergeld, D. L., Miller, J. W., & Tranel, D. (2008). Category-specific naming and recognition deficits in temporal lobe epilepsy. *Neuropsychologia, 46*(5), 1242–1255.

Drane, D. L., Ojemann, J. G., Aylward, E., Phatak, V., Hebb, A., Tranel, D., Miller, J. W., & Ojemann, G. A. (2009a). Category-related naming and recognition deficits in epilepsy surgery patients reflect disconnection syndromes. *Epilepsia, 50*(Suppl. 11), 281.

Drane, D. L., Ojemann, G. A., Ojemann, J. G., Aylward, E. A., Silbergeld, D. L., Miller, J. W., & Tranel, D. (2009b). Category-specific recognition and naming deficits following resection of a right anterior temporal lobe tumor in a patient with atypical language lateralization. *Cortex, 45*(5), 630–640.

Drane, D. L., Ojemann, J. G., Phatak, V., Loring, D. W., Gross, R. E., Hebb, A. O., Silbergeld, D. L., Miller, J. W., Voets, N. L., Saindane, A. M., Barsalou, L., Meador, K. J., Ojemann, G. A.,

& Tranel, D. (2013). Famous face identification in temporal lobe epilepsy: Support for a multimodal integration model of semantic memory. *Cortex, 49*, 1648–1667.

Drane, D. L., Loring, D. W., Voets, N. L., Price, M., Ojemann, J. G., Willie, J. T., Saindane, A. M., Phatak, V., Ivanisevic, M., Millis, S., Helmers, S. L., Miller, J. W., & Gross, R. E. (2015). Better object recognition and naming outcome with MRI-guided stereotactic laser amygdalohippocampotomy for temporal lobe epilepsy. *Epilepsia, 56*, 101–113.

Drane, D. L., Ojemann, J. G., Kim, M., Gross, R. E., Miller, J. W., Faught, R. E., Jr., & Loring, D. W. (2016). Interictal epileptiform discharge effects on neuropsychological assessment and epilepsy surgical planning. *Epilepsy & Behavior, 56*, 131–138.

Drane, D. L., Willie, J. T., Pedersen, N. P., Hewitt, K. C., Qiu, D., Gleichgerrcht, E., Bonilha, L., Voets, N. L., Millis, S., Staikova, E., Loring, D. W., Meador, K. J., & Gross, R. E. (2019). *Functional outcome is superior following stereotactic laser amygdalohippocampotomy than after open resection for epilepsy management*. American Epilepsy Society.

Drane, D. L., Pedersen, N. P., Savsevitz, D., Block, D., Dickey, A., Alwaki, A., & Kheder, A. (2021a). Cognitive and emotional mapping with stereoelectroencephalography (SEEG). *Frontiers in Neuroscience, 12*, 627981.

Drane, D. L., Valentin, E., Shade, T., Pedersen, N. P., Hewitt, K. C., Wickham, S., Millis, S., James, G. A., Block, C., Staikova, E., Price, M., Loring, D. W., van Rooij, S. J. H., Hamann, S., Willie, J. T., & Gross, R. E. (2021b). *Declines in socio-emotional functioning occur in a subset of patients with medial temporal lobe epilepsy following surgical intervention*. American Epilepsy Society, Virtual 2021 Annual Meeting.

Drane, D. L., Willie, J. T., Pedersen, N. P., Qiu, D., Voets, N. L., Millis, S. R., Soares, B. P., Saindane, A. M., Hu, R., Kim, M. S., Hewitt, K. C., Hakimian, S., Grabowski, T., Ojemann, J. G., Loring, D. W., Meador, K. J., Faught, E., Jr., Miller, J. W., & Gross, R. E. (2021c). Superior verbal memory outcome after stereotactic laser amygdalohippocampotomy. *Frontiers in Neurology, 12*, 779495. https://doi.org/10.3389/fneur.2021.779495

Drane, D. L., Acerbo, E., Rogers, A., Pedersen, N. P., Williamson, A., Stern, M. A., Dickey, A. S., Howard, B. M., Bearden, D. J., Okada, N. S., Staikova, E., Gutekunst, C. A., Alwaki, A., Gershon, T., Jirsa, V., Gross, R. E., Loring, D. W., Kheder, A., & Willie, J. T. (2024a). Selective posterior cererbral artery Wada better predicts good memory and naming outcomes following selective stereotactic thermal ablation for medial temporal lobe epilepsy than internal carotid artery Wada. *medRxiv*. https://doi.org/10.1101/2024.03.24.24304488

Drane, D. L., Okada, N., Rajeh, Y., Paek, E., Adams, K., & Wall, E. (2024b). Novel methods of assessing memory with technology: Addressing the need for new theory and measures in the setting of minimally invasive epilepsy surgery. *Annual Review of Cybertherapy and Telemedicine, 22*, 183–187.

Duchowny, M., Jayakar, P., Harvey, A. S., Resnick, T., Alvarez, L., Dean, P., & Levin, B. (1996). Language cortex representation: Effects of developmental versus acquired pathology. *Annals of Neurology, 40*, 31–38.

Dulay, M. F., K., S. B., M., T. S., Fargo, J. D., Privitera, M., & Yeh, H. S. (2002). What does the family picture subtest of the Wechsler memory scale-III measure? Insight gained from patients evaluated for epilepsy surgery. *The Clinical Neuropsychologist, 16*(4), 452–462.

Dunn, D. W., Harezlak, J., Ambrosius, W. T., Austin, J. K., & Hale, B. (2002). Teacher assessment of behaviour in children with new-onset seizures. *Seizure, 11*, 169–175.

Eddy, C. E., Rickards, H. E., & Cavanna, A. E. (2011). The cognitive impact of antiepileptic drugs. *Therapeutic Advances in Neurological Disorders, 4*(6), 385–407.

Elger, C., Helmstaedter, C., & Kurthen, M. (2004). Chronic epilepsy and cognition. *The Lancet Neurology, 3*(11), 663–672.

Elosua-Bayes, I., Abraira, L., Fonseca, E., Lallana, S., Campos-Fernandez, D., Lopez-Maza, S., Quintana, M., Santamarina, E., Salas-Puig, J., & Toledo, M. (2024). Trends in antiseizure medication prescription in idiopathic generalized epilepsy over the last 20 years. *Epilepsy & Behavior, 163*, 110158.

Elverman, K. H., Resch, Z. J., Quasney, E. E., Sabsevitz, D. S., Binder, J. R., & Swanson, S. J. (2019). Temporal lobe epilepsy is associated with distinct cognitive phenotypes. *Epilepsy and Behavior, 96*, 61–68.

Engel, J. J., Van Ness, P. C., Rasmussen, T. B., & Ojemann, L. M. (1993). Ouctome with respect to epileptic seizures. In J. J. Engel (Ed.), *Surgical treatment of the epilepsies* (pp. 609–621). Raven Press.

Engel, J. J., Wiebe, S., French, J., Sperling, M., Williamson, P., Spencer, D., Gummit, R., Zahn, C., Westbrook, E., & Enos, B. (2003). Practice parameter: Temporal lobe and localized neocortical resections for epilepsy. *Neurology, 60*, 538–547.

Epilepsy, I. L. A. (1989). Proposal for revised classification of epilepsies and epileptic syndromes: Commission on classification and terminology of the international league against Epilepsy. *Epilepsia, 30*(4), 389–399.

Esquenazi, Y., Kalamangalam, G. P., Slater, J. D., Knowlton, R. C., Friedman, E., Morris, S.-A., Shetty, A., Gowda, A., & Tandon, N. (2014). Stereotactic laser ablation of epileptogenic periventricular nodular heterotopia. *Epilepsy Research, 108*(3), 547–554.

Ettinger, A., Reed, M., & Cramer, J. (2004). Depression and comorbidity in community-based patients with epilepsy or asthma. *Neurology, 63*(6), 1008–1014.

Falconer, M. A., Meyer, A., Hill, D., Mitchell, W., & Pond, D. A. (1955). Treatment of temporal-lobe epilepsy by temporal lobectomy; A survey of findings and results. *The Lancet, 268*, 827–835.

Falco-Walter, J. J., Scheffer, I. E., & Fisher, R. S. (2018). The new definition and classification of seizures and epilepsy. *Epilepsy Research, 139*, 73–79.

Farrant, A., Morris, R. G., Russell, T., Elwes, R., Akanuma, N., Alarcon, G., & Koutroumanidis, M. (2005). Social cogntion in frontal lobe epilepsy. *Epilepsy & Behavior, 7*(3), 506–516.

Fastenau, P. S., Shen, J., Dunn, D. W., Perkins, S. M., Hermann, B. P., & Austin, J. K. (2004). Neuropsychological predictors of academic underachievement in pediatric epilepsy: Moderating roles of demographic, seizure, and psychosocial variables. *Epilepsia, 45*(10), 1261–1272.

Fastenau, P. S., Johnson, C. S., Perkins, S. M., Byars, A. W., deGrauw, T. J., Austin, J. K., & Dunn, D. W. (2009). Neuropsychological status at seizure onset in children: Risk factors for early cognitive deficits. *Neurology, 73*(7), 526–534.

Faught, E., Karakis, I., & Drane, D. L. (2018). The impact of interictal discharges on performance. *Current Neurology and Neuroscience Reports, 18*(12), 88.

Federico, P., & Wiebe, S. (2020). Is bad brain worse than no brain? Salvaging the cerebral cortex in epilepsy. *Brain, 143*(11), 3172–3175.

Feindel, W., & Rasmussen, T. (1991). Temporal lobectomy with amygdalectomy and minimal hippocampal resection: Review of 100 cases. *Canadian Journal of Neurological Science, 18*, 603–605.

Ferguson, L., Miller, M., Whiting, A., Haut, J., Klaas, P., Bingaman, W., Lachhwani, D., Lineweaver, T. T., Floden, D., & Busch, R. M. (2021). Cognitive outcomes following frontal lobe resection for treatment of epilepsy in children and adolescents. *Epilepsy and Behavior, 124*, 108265.

Fiest, K. M., Sauro, K. M., Wiebe, S., Patten, S. B., Kwon, C.-S., Dykeman, J., Pringsheim, T., Lorenzetti, D. L., & Jette, N. (2017). Prevalence and incidence of epilepsy: A systematic review and meta-analysis of international studies. *Neurology, 88*(3), 296–303.

Fisher, R., Salanova, V., Witt, T., Worth, R., Henry, T., Gross, R., Oommen, K., Osorio, I., Nazzaro, J., Labar, D., Kaplitt, M., Sperling, M., Sandok, E., Neal, J., Handforth, A., Stern, J., DeSalles, A., Chung, S., Shetter, A., Bergen, D., Bakay, R. A., Henderson, J., French, J., Baltuch, G., Rosenfeld, W., Youkilis, A., Marks, W., Garcia, P. A., Barbaro, N., Fountain, N., Bazil, C., Goodman, R., McKhann, G., Babu, K. K., Papavassiliou, S., Epstein, C., Pollard, J., Tonder, L., Grebin, J., Coffey, R., Graves, N., & Group, S. S. (2010). Electrical stimulation of the anterior nucleus of thalamus for treatment of refractory epilepsy. *Epilepsia, 51*(5), 899–908.

Fisher, R. S., Acevedo, C., Arzimanoglou, A., Bogacz, A., Cross, J. H., Elger, C. E., Engel, J., Jr., Forsgren, L., French, J. A., Glynn, M., Hesdorffer, D. C., Lee, B. J., Mathern, G. W., Moshe,

S. L., Perucca, E., Scheffer, I. E., Tomson, T., Watanabe, M., & Wiebe, S. (2014). ILAE official report: A practical clinical definition of epilepsy. *Epilepsia, 55*(4), 475–482.
Fisher, R. S., Cross, J. H., D'Souza, C., French, J. A., Haut, S. R., Higurashi, N., Hirsch, E., Hansen, F. E., Lagae, L., Moshe, S. L., Peltola, J., Roulet Perez, E., Scheffer, I. E., Schulze-Bonhage, A., Somerville, E., Sperling, M., Yacubian, E. M., & Zuberi, S. M. (2017a). Instruction manual for the ILAE 2017 operational classification nof seiure types. *Epilepsia, 58*(4), 531–542.
Fisher, R. S., Cross, J. H., French, J. A., Higurashi, N., Hirsch, E., Jansen, F. E., Lagae, L., Moshe, S. I., Peltola, J., Roulet Perez, E., Scheffer, I. E., & Zuberi, S. M. (2017b). Operational classification of seizure types by the international league against Epilepsy: Position paper of the ILAE Commission for Classification and Terminology. *Epilepsia, 58*(4), 522–530.
Fleury, M. N., Binding, L. P., Taylor, P., Xiao, F., Giampiccolo, D., Caciagli, L., Buck, S., Winston, G. P., Thompson, P. J., Baxendale, S., Koepp, M. J., Duncan, J. S., & Sidhu, M. K. (2024). Predictors of long-term memory and network connectivity 10 years after anterior temporal lobe resection. *Epilepsia, 65*(9), 2641–2661.
Fobian, A. D., & Szaflarski, J. P. (2021). Identifying and evaluating novel treatment targets for the development of evidence-based interventions for functional neurological disorder. *Epilepsy and Behavior, 16*, 100479.
Fonseca, E., Sarria-Estrada, S., Pareto, D., Turon, M., Quintana, M., Santamarina, E., Abraira, L., Tortajada, C., Rovira, À., & Toledo, M. (2023). Relationship between visuoperceptual functions and parietal structural abnormalities in temporal lobe epilepsy. *Brain Imaging and Behavior, 17*, 35–43.
Fontaine, C., Jacq, G., Perier, F., Holleville, M., & Legriel, S. (2020). The role of secondary brain insults in status epilepticus: A systemtic review. *Journal of Clinical Medicine, 9*(8), 2521.
Fraser, R. T., Johnson, E. K., Lashley, S., Barber, J., Chaytor, N., Miller, J. W., Ciechanowski, P., Temkin, N., & Caylor, L. (2015). PACES in epilepsy: Results of a self-management randomized controlled trial. *Epilepsia, 56*(8), 1264–1274.
French, J. A., Williamson, P. D., Thadani, V. M., Darcey, T. M., Mattson, R. H., Spencer, S. S., & Spencer, D. D. (1993). Characteristics of medial temporal lobe epilepsy: I. Results of history and physical examination. *Annals of Neurology, 34*, 774–780.
Fuller-Thomson, E., & Brennenstuhl, S. (2009). The association between depression and epilepsy in a nationally representative sample. *Epilepsia, 50*(5), 1051–1058.
Gagnon, M.-A., Nesrine-Mertens, V. B., & Messier, C. (2003). Comparing the Rey and Taylor complex figures: A test-retest study in young and older adults. *Journal of Clinical and Experimental Neuropsychology, 25*(6), 878–890.
Gaitatzis, A., Trimble, M. R., & Sander, J. W. (2004). The psychiatric comorbidity of epilepsy. *Acta Neurologica Scandinavica, 110*, 207–220.
Galovic, M., de Tisi, J., McEvoy, A. W., Miserocchi, A., Vos, S. B., Borzi, G., Rosillo, J. C., Vuong, K. A., Nachev, P., Duncan, J. S., & Koepp, M. J. (2020). Resective surgery prevents progressive cortical thinning in temporal lobe epilepsy. *Brain, 143*(11), 3262–3272.
Garcia-Ramos, C., Jackson, D. C., Lin, J. J., Dabbs, K., Jones, J., Hsu, D. A., Stafstrom, C. E., Zawadzki, L., Seidenberg, M., Prabhakaran, V., & Hermann, B. P. (2016). Cognition and brain development in chlldren with benign epilepsy with centrotemporal spikes (BECTS). *Epilepsia, 56*(10), 1615–1622.
Gastaut, H., Roger, J., Soulayrol, R., Tassinari, C. A., Regis, H., Dravet, C., Bernard, R., Pinsard, N., & Saint-Jean, M. (1966). Childhood epileptic encephalopathy of children with diffuse slow spike-waves (otherwise known as "petit mal variant") or Lennox syndrome. *Epilepsia, 7*, 139–179.
Gates, S., 2nd, Hackman, D. E., Agarwal, N., Zhang, W., Barnard, P., & White, J. R. (2024). Postoperative neurologic outcome in patients undergoing resective surgery for parietal lobe epilepsy: A systematic review. *Neurology, 102*(12), e209322.
Gettings, J. V., Shafi, S., Boyd, J., Snead, O. C., Rutka, J., Drake, J., McCoy, B., Jain, P., Whitney, R., & Go, C. (2023). The epilepsy surgery experience in children with infantile epileptic spasms syndrome at a tertiary care center in Canada. *Journal of Child Neurology, 38*(3–4), 113–120.

Gilliam, R. A. (1990). Refractory epilepsy:An evaluation of psychological methods in outpatient management. *Epilepsia, 31*, 427–432.

Gilliam, F., & Kanner, A. M. (2002, October). Treatment of depressive disorders in epilepsy patients. *Epilepsy & Behavior, 3*(5, Supplement 1), 2–9. http://www.sciencedirect.com/science/article/B6WDT-473VWN8-5/2/488cf74b59952e6cc2c8662579df1edb

Gilmore, A. W., Nelson, S. M., & McDermott, K. B. (2015). A parietal memory network revealed by multiple MRI methods. *Trends in Cognitive Sciences, 19*(9), 534–543.

Gil-Nagel, A., & Risinger, M. W. (1997). Ictal semiology in hippocampal versus extrahippocampal temporal lobe epilepsy. *Brain, 120*, 183–192.

Gioia, G. A., Isquith, P. K., Guy, S. C., & Lutz, K. L. (2000). *Behavior rating inventory of executive function professional manual*. Psychological Assessment Resources.

Giovagnoli, A. R., Franceschetti, S., Reati, F., Parente, A., Maccagnano, C., Villani, F., & Spreafico, R. (2011). Theory of mind in frontal and temporal lobe epilepsy: Cognitive and neural aspects. *Epilepsia, 52*(11), 1995–2002.

Giovagnoli, A., Tallarita, G., Parente, A., Pastori, C., & de Curtis, M. (2020). The understanding of mental states and the cognitive phenotype of frontal lobe epilepsy. *Epilepsia, 61*, 747–757.

Gleichgerrcht, E., Keller, S. S., Drane, D. L., Munsell, B. C., Davis, K. A., Kaestner, E., Weber, B., Krantz, S., Vandergrift, W. A., Edwards, J. C., McDonald, C. R., Kuzniecky, R., & Bonilha, L. (2020). Temporal lobe epilepsy surgical outcomes can be inferred based on structural connectome hubs: A machine learning study. *Annals of Neurology, 88*(5), 970–983. https://doi.org/10.1002/ana.25888

Gloor, P. (1990). Experiential phenomena of temporal lobe epilepsy: Facts and hypotheses. *Brain, 13*, 1673–1694.

Glosser, G., Salvucci, A. E., & Chiaravalloti, N. D. (2003). Naming and recognizing famous faces in temporal lobe epilepsy. *Neurology, 61*, 81–86.

Golby, A. J., Poldrack, R. A., Brewer, J. B., Spencer, D., Desmond, J. E., Aron, A. P., & Gabrieli, J. D. (2001). Material-specific lateralization in the mesial temporal lobe and prefrontal crotex during memory encoding. *Brain, 124*, 1841–1854.

Gonzalez, H. F. J., Yengo-Kahn, A., & Englot, D. J. (2019). Vagus nerve stimulation for the treatment of epilepsy. *Neurosurgery Clinics of North America, 30*(2), 219–230.

Gonzalez, H. F. J., Yengo-Kahn, A., & Englot, D. J. (2020). Vagus nerve stimulation for the treatment of epilepsy. *Neurosurgical Clinics of North America, 30*(2), 219–230.

Gowda, A., Salazar, F., Bingaman, W. E., Kotagal, P., Lachhwani, D. L., Gupta, A., Davis, S., Niezgoda, J., & Wyllie, E. (2010). Surgery for catastrophic epilepsy in infants 6 months of age and younger. *Journal of Neurosurgery, Pediatrics, 5*(6), 603–607.

Gracia, C. G., Chagin, K., Kattan, M. W., Ji, X., Kattan, M. G., Crotty, L., Najm, I., Gonzalez-Martinez, J., Bingaman, W., & Jehi, L. (2019). Predicting seizure freedom after epilepsy surgery, a challenge in clinical practice. *Epilepsy & Behavior, 95*, 124–130.

Gramstad, A., Power, K. N., & Engelsen, B. A. (2021). Neuropsychological performance 1 yaar after status epilepticus in adults. *Archives of Clinical Neuropsychology, 36*(3), 329–338.

Grant, D. A., & Berg, E. A. (2014). *Wisconsin card sorting test*. APA Psychnet.

Grant, A. C., Donnelly, K. M., Chubb, C., Barr, W. B., Kuzniecky, R., & Devinsky, O. (2008). Temporal lobe epilepsy does not impair visual perception. *Epilepsia, 49*(4), 710–713.

Griffith, H. R., Pyzalski, R., O'Leary, D., Magnotta, V., Rutecki, P., Sheth, R., Bell, B., Dow, C., Wendt, G., Seidenberg, M., & Hermann, B. (2009). Neuroanatomical correlates of rapid forgetting in temporal lobe epilepsy. *Epilepsy and Behavior, 15*(4), 445–451.

Grivas, A., Schramm, J., Kral, R., von Lehe, M., Helmstaedter, C., Elger, C. E., & Clusmann, H. (2006). Surgical treatment for refractory temporal lobe epilepsy in the elderly: Seizure outcome and neuropsychological sequels compared with a younger cohort. *Epilepsia, 47*(8), 1364–1372.

Gross, R. E., Willie, J. T., & Drane, D. L. (2016). The role of stereotactic laser amygdalohippocampotomy in mesial temporal lobe epilepsy. *Neurosurgery Clinics of North America, 27*(1), 37–50.

Gross, R. E., Stern, M. A., Willie, J. T., Fasano, R. E., Saindane, A. M., Soares, B. P., Pedersen, N. P., & Drane, D. L. (2018). One-year outcomes following stereotactic lase amygdalohippocampotomy for the treatmnt of mesial temporal lobe epilepsy: 5-year experience in 58 patients. *Annals of Neurology, 83*, 575–587.

Gross, R. E., Drane, D. L., McKhann, G. M., Salanova, V., Van Gompel, J., Jagid, J., Cabaniss, B., Tandon, N., Knowlton, R., Wallace, K., Gracia, A., Sharan, A. D., Giftakis, J., Sperling, M. R., & Group, o. B. O. T. M. S. S. (2024). Stereotactic laser ablation for mesial temporal lobe epilepsy (SLATE) study: A prospective, single-arm, multicenter study.

Gruenbaum, B. F., Sandhu, M. R. S., Bertasi, R. A. O., Bertasi, T. G. O., Schonwald, A., Kurup, A., Gruenbaum, S. E., Freedman, I. G., Funaro, M. C., Blumenfeld, H., & Sanacora, G. (2021). Absence seizures and their relationship to depression and anxiety: Evidence for bidirectionality. *Epilepsia, 62*(5), 1041–1056.

Gupta, A. K., Jeavons, P. M., Hughes, R. C., & Covanis, A. (1983). Aura in temporal lobe epilepsy: Clinical and electroencephalographic correlation. *Journal of Neurology, Neurosurgery, and Psychiatry, 46*(12), 1079–1083.

Gupta, K., Cabaniss, B., Kheder, A., Gedela, S., Koch, P., Hewitt, K. C., Alwaki, A., Rich, C., Ramesha, S., Hu, R., Drane, D. L., Gross, R. E., & Willie, J. T. (2020). Stereotactic MRI-guided laser interstitial thermal therapy for extratemporal lobe epilepsy. *Epilepsia, 61*(8), 1723–1734.

Hageboutros, K., Hewitt, K. C., Lee, G. P., Bansal, A., Block, C., Pedersen, N. P., Willie, J. T., Loring, D. W., Schoenberg, M. R., Smith, K. A., Giller, C. A., Gross, R. E., & Drane, D. L. (in press). Comparison of minimally invasive to standard temporal lobectomy approaches to epilepsy surgery: Seizure relief and language outcomes. *Epilepsy & Behavior.*

Hamberger, M. J., & Seidel, W. T. (2003). Auditory and visual naming tests: Normative and patient data for accuracy, response time, and tip-of-the-tongue. *Journal of the International Neuropsychological Society, 9*(3), 479–489.

Hamberger, M. J., & Tamny, T. R. (1999). Auditory naming and temporal lobe epilepsy. *Epilepsy Research, 35*, 229–243.

Hamberger, M. J., McClelland, S., McKhann, G. M., Williams, A. C., & Goodman, R. R. (2007). Distribution of auditory and visual naming sites in nonlesional temporal lobe epilepsy patients and patients with space-occupying temporal lobe lesions. *Epilepsia, 48*(3), 531–538.

Hamberger, M. J., Seidel, W. T., McKhann, G. M., & Goodman, R. R. (2010). Hippocampal removal affects visual but not auditory naming. *Neurology, 74*(19), 1488–1493.

Handforth, A., DeGiorgio, C. M., Schachter, S. C., Uthman, B. M., Naritoku, D. K., Tecoma, E. S., Henry, T. R., Collins, S. D., Vaughn, B. V., Gilmartin, R. C., Labar, D. R., Morris, G. L., 3rd, Salinsky, M. C., Osorio, I., Ristanovic, R. K., Labiner, D. M., Jones, J. C., Murphy, J. V., Ney, G. C., & Wheless, J. W. (1998). Vagus nerve stimulation therapy for partial-onset seizures: A randomized active-control trial. *Neurology, 51*(1), 48–55.

Hawasli, A. H., Bandt, S. K., Hogan, R. E., Werner, N., & Leuthardt, E. C. (2014a). Laser ablation as treatment strategy for medically refractory dominant insular epilepsy: Therapeutic and functional considerations. *Stereotactic and Functional Neurosurgery, 92*, 397–404.

Hawasli, A. H., Kim, A. H., Dunn, G. P., Tran, D. D., & Leuthardt, E. C. (2014b). Stereotactic laser ablation of high-grade gliomas. *Neurosurgical Focus, 37*(6), E1.

Helmers, S. L., Thhurman, D. J., Durgin, T. L., Pai, A. K., & Faught, E. (2015). Descriptive epidemiology of epilepsy in the U.S. population: A different approach. *Epilepsia, 56*, 942–948.

Helmstaedter, C. (2001). Behavioral aspects of frontal lobe epilepsy. *Epilepsy & Behavior, 2*, 384–395.

Helmstaedter, C. (2004, February). Neuropsychological aspects of epilepsy surgery. *Epilepsy & Behavior, 5*(Supplement 1), 45–55. http://www.sciencedirect.com/science/article/B6WDT-4B7N6PK-1/2/d12dbc9bf156c6b4cecad75533f28410

Helmstaedter, C., & Kockelmann, E. (2006). Cognitive outcomes in patients with chronic temporal lobe epilepsy. *Epilepsia, 47*, 96–98.

Helmstaedter, C., & Kurthen, M. (2001). Memory and epilepsy: Characteristics, course, and influence of drugs and surgery. *Current Opinion in Neurology, 14*, 211–216.

Helmstaedter, C., & Witt, J. A. (2017). How neuropsychology can improve the care of individual patients with epilepsy. Looking back and into the future. *Seizure, 44*, 113–120.
Helmstaedter, C., Kemper, B., & Elger, C. E. (1996). Neuropsychological aspects of frontal lobe epilepsy. *Neuropsychologia, 34*(5), 399–406.
Helmstaedter, C., Gleissner, U., Zentner, J., & Elger, C. E. (1998). Neuropsychological consequences of epilepsy surgery in frontal lobe epilepsy. *Neuropsychologia, 36*, 681–689.
Helmstaedter, C., Reuber, M., & Elger, C. C. E. (2002). Interaction of cognitive aging and memory deficits related to epilepsy surgery. *Annals of Neurology, 52*, 89–94.
Helmstaedter, C., Kurthen, M., Lux, S., Reuber, M., & Elger, C. E. (2003). Chronic epilepsy and cognition: A longitudinal study in temporal lobe epilepsy. *Annals of Neurology, 54*(4), 425–432. https://doi.org/10.1002/ana.10692
Helmstaedter, C., Elger, C. E., & Vogt, V. L. (2018). Cognitive outcomes more than 5 years after temporal lobe epilepsy surgery: Remarkable functional recovery when seizures are controlled. *Seizure, 62*, 116–123.
Helmstaedter, C., Sadat-Hossieny, Z., Kanner, A. M., & Meador, K. J. (2020). Cognitive disorders in epilepsy II: Clinical targets, indications and selection of test instruments. *Seizure, 83*, 223–231.
Heminghyt, E., Herrman, H., Skogan, A. H., Konglund, A., Egge, A., Lossius, M., Dietrichs, E., & Taubøll, E. (2022). Cognitive change after DBS in refractory epilepsy: A randomized-controlled trial. *Acta Neurologica Scandinavica, 145*(1), 111–118.
Hennessy, M. J., Elwes, R. D., Honavar, M., Rabe-Hesketh, S., Binnie, C. D., & Polkey, C. E. (2001). Predictors of outcome and pathological considerations in the surgical treatment of intractable epilepsy associated with temporal lobe lesions. *Journal of Neurology, Neurosurgery, and Psychiatry, 70*(4), 450–458.
Hermann, B. P., & Loring, D. W. (2008). Improving neuropsychological outcomes of epilepsy surgery. *Epilepsy and Behavior, 13*(1), 5–6.
Hermann, B., & Seidenberg, M. (1995). Executive system dysfunction in temporal lobe epilepsy: Effects of nociferous cortex versus hippocampal pathology. *Journal of Clinical and Experimental Neuropsychology, 17*, 809–819.
Hermann, B. P., Dikmen, S. S., & Wilensky, A. J. (1982). Increased psychopathology associated with multiple seizure types: Fact or articfact? *Epilepsia, 23*, 587–596.
Hermann, B. P., Wyler, A. R., Steenman, H., & Richey, E. T. (1988). The interrelationship between language function and verbal learning/memory performance in patients with complex partial seizures. *Cortex, 24*(2), 245–253.
Hermann, B. P., Wyler, A. R., & Somes, G. (1991). Language function following anterior temporal lobectomy: Frequency and correlates. *Neurosurgery, 35*, 52–57.
Hermann, B. P., Seidenberg, M., Schoenfeld, J., Peterson, J., Leveroni, C., & Wyler, A. R. (1996). Empirical techniques for determining the reliability, magnitude, and pattern of neuropsychological change after epilepsy surgery. *Epilepsia, 37*(10), 942–950.
Hermann, B. P., Seidenberg, M., Schoenfeld, J., & Davies, K. (1997). Neuropsychological characteristics of the syndrome of mesial temporal lobe epilepsy. *Archives of Neurology, 54*, 369–376.
Hermann, B., Davies, K., Foley, K., & Bell, B. (1999). Visual confrontation naming outcome after standard left anterior temporal lobectomy with sparing versus resection of the superior temporal gyrus: A randomized prospective clinical trial. *Epilepsia, 40*(8), 1070–1076.
Hermann, B., Seidenberg, M., & Bell, B. (2000). Psychiatric comorbidity in chronic epilepsy: Indentification, consequences, and treatment of major depression. *Epilepsia, 41*(Suppl 2), S31–S41.
Hermann, B., Seidenberg, M., Bell, B., Rutecki, P., Sheth, R. D., Wendt, G., O'Leary, D., & Magnotta, V. (2003). Extratemporal quantitative MR volumetrics and neuropsychological status in temporal lobe epilepsy. *Journal of the International Neuropsychological Society, 9*(3), 353–362.
Hermann, B. P., Seidenberg, M., Dow, C., Jones, J., Rutecki, P., Bhattacharya, A., & Bell, B. (2006a). Cognitive prognosis in chronic temporal lobe epilepsy. *Annals of Neurology, 60*(1), 80–87.

Hermann, B., Jones, J., Sheth, R., Dow, C., Koehn, M., & Seidenberg, M. (2006b). Children with new-onset epilepsy: Neuropsychological status and and brain structure. *Brain, 129*, 2609–2619.

Hermann, B., Seidenberg, M., Lee, E. J., Chan, F., & Rutecki, P. (2007). Cognitive phenotypes in temporal lobe epilepsy. *Journal of the International Neuropsychological Society, 13*, 12–20.

Hermann, B., Seidenberg, M., & Jones, J. (2008). The neurobehavioral comorbidities of epilepsy: Can a natural history be developed? *The Lancet Neurology, 7*(2), 151–160.

Hermann, B. P., Jones, J. E., Jackson, D. C., & Seidenberg, M. (2012). Starting at the beginning: The neuropsychological status of children with new-onset epilepsies. *Epileptic Disorders, 14*(1), 12–21.

Hermann, B. P., Struck, A. F., Dabbs, K., Seidenberg, M., & Jones, J. E. (2021). Behavioral phenotypes of temporal lobe epilepsy. *Epilepsia Open, 6*(2), 369–380.

Hernandez, M. T., Sauerwein, H. C., Jambaque, I., De Guise, E., Lussier, F., Lortie, A., Dulac, O., & Lassonde, M. (2002). Deficits in executive function and motor coordination in children with frontal lobe epilepsy. *Neuropsychologia, 40*(4), 384–400.

Higson, L., Hipgrave, W., O'Brien, T. J., Rayner, G., Alpitsis, R., Kanaan, R. A., & Winton-Brown, T. (2023). Improving the treatment of functional seizures through a public specialist outpatient clinic. *Epilepsy & Behavior, 144*, 109259.

Hirsch, E., French, J. E. S. I., Bogacz, A., Alsaadi, T., Sperling, M. R., Abdulla, F., Zuberi, S. M., Trinka, E., Specchio, N., Somerville, E., Samia, P., Riney, K., Nabbout, R., Jain, S., Wilmshurst, J. O. M., Auvin, S., Wiebe, S., Perucca, E., Moshe, S. L., Tinuper, P., & Wirrell, E. C. (2022). ILAE definition of thhe idiopathic generalized epilepsy syndromes: Position statement by the ILAE task force on nosology and definitions. *Epilepsia, 63*(6), 1475–1499.

Hocking, J., Thomas, H. J., Dzafic, I., Williams, R. J., Reutens, D. C., & Spooner, D. M. (2013). Disentangling the cognitive components supporting Austin maze performance in left versus right temporal lobe epilepsy. *Epilepsy & Behavior, 29*(3), 485–491.

Höller, Y., Butz, K. H. G., Thomschewski, A. C., Schmid, E. V., Hofer, C. D., Uhl, A., Bathke, A. C., Staffen, W., Nardone, R., Schwimmbeck, F., Leitinger, M., Kuchukhidze, G., Derner, M., Fell, J., & Trinka, E. (2020). Prediction of cognitive decline in temporal lobe Epilepsy and mild cognitive impairment by EEG, MRI, and neuropsychology. *Computational Intelligence and Neuroscience, 2020*, 8915961.

Holmes, G. L. (2013). EEG abnormalities as a biomarker for cognitive comorbidities in pharmacoresistant epilepsy. *Epilepsia, 54*(Suppl. 52), 60–62.

Holmes, G. L. (2014). What is more harmful, seizures or epileptic EEG abnormalities? Is there any clinical data? *Epileptic Disorders, 16*(Suppl. 1), 12–22.

Holmes, G. L. (2015). Cognitive impairment in epilepsy: The role of network abnormalities. *Epileptic Disorders, 17*(2), 101–116.

Holmes, G. L., & Lenck-Santini, P. P. (2006). Role of interictal epileptiform abnormalities in cognitive impairment. *Epilepsy and Behavior, 8*(3), 504–515.

Holmes, M. D., Dodrill, C. B., Wilkus, R. J., Ojemann, L. M., & Ojemann, G. A. (1998). Is partial epilepsy progressive? Ten-year follow-up of EEG and neuropsychological changes in adults with partial seizures. *Epilepsia, 39*(11), 1189–1193.

Holmes, M. D., Miles, A. N., Dodrill, C. B., Ojemann, G. A., & Wilensky, A. J. (2003). Identifying potential surgical candidates in patients with evidence of bitemporal epilepsy. *Epilepsia, 44*(8), 1075–1079.

Holmes, M. D., Brown, M., & Tucker, D. M. (2004). Are "generalized" seizures truly generalized? Evidence of localized mesial frontal and frontopolar discharges in absence. *Epilepsia, 45*(12), 1568–1579.

Honybun, E., Cockle, E., Malpas, C. B., O'BBrien, T. J., Vajda, F. J., Perucca, P., & Rayner, G. (2024). Neurodevelopmental and functional outcomes following in utero exposure to antiseizure medication. *Neurology, 102*(8), e209175.

Hrachovy, R. A., Frost, J. D., Jr., Kellaway, P., & Zion, T. E. (1983). Double-blind study of ACTH vs prednisone therapy in infantile spasms. *Journal of Pediatrics, 103*, 641–645.

Hu, W. H., Zhang, C., Zhang, K., Meng, F. G., Chen, N., & Zhang, J. G. (2013). Selective amygdalohippocampectomy versus anterior temporal lobectomy in the management of mesial temporal lobe epilepsy: A meta-analysis of comparative studies. *Journal of Neurosurgery, 119*(5), 1087–1357.

Huang, L., Fu, C., Li, J., & Peng, S. (2022). Late-onset epilepsy and the risk of dementia: A systematic review and meta-analysis. *Aging Clinical and Experimental Research, 34*(8), 1771–1779.

Hutchinson, E., Pulsipher, D., Dabbs, K., Myers y Gutierrez, A., Sheth, R., Jones, J., Seidenberg, M., Meyerand, E., & Hermann, B. (2010). Children with new-onset epilepsy exhibit diffusion abnormalities in cerebral white matter in the absence of volumetric differences. *Epilepsy Research, 88*, 208–214.

Hwang, G., Hermann, B., Nair, V. A., Conant, L. L., Dabbs, K., Mathis, J., Cook, C. J., Rivera-Bonet, C. N., Mohanty, R., Zhao, G., Almane, D. N., Nencka, A., Felton, E., Struck, A. F., Birn, R., Maganti, R., Humphries, C. J., Raghavan, M., DeYoe, E. A., Bendlin, B. B., Prabhakaran, V., Binder, J. R., & Meyerand, M. E. (2020). Brain aging in temporal lobe epilepsy: Chhronological, structural and functional. *Neuroimaging Clinics of North America, 25*, 102183.

Iacoboni, M., & Zaidel, E. (2004). Interhemispheric visual-motor integration in humas: The role of the superior parietal cortex. *Neuropsychologia, 42*(4), 419–425.

Italiano, D., & Perucca, E. (2013). Clinical pharmacokinetics of new-generation antiepileptic drugs at the extremes of age: An update. *Clinical Pharmacokinetics, 52*(8), 627–645.

Iwasaki, M., Iijima, K., Kawashima, T., Tachimori, H., Takayama, Y., Kimura, Y., Kaneko, Y., Ikegaya, N., Sumitomo, N., Saito, T., Nakagawa, E., Takahashi, A., Sugai, K., & Otsuki, T. (2021). Epilepsy surgery in children under 3 years of age: Surgical and developmental outcomes. *Journal of Neurosurgery. Pediatrics, 28*(4), 395–403.

Jackson, D. C., Dabbs, K., Walker, N. M., Jones, J. E., Hsu, D. A., Stafstrom, C. E., Seidenberg, M., & Hermann, B. P. (2013). The neuropsychological and academic subbstrate of new/recent-onset epilepsies. *Journal of Pediatrics, 162*(5), 1047–1053.

Jacoby, A., & Baker, G. A. (2008). Quality-of-life trajectories in epilepsy: A review of the literature. *Epilepsy and Behavior, 12*(4), 557–571.

Jacoby, A., Baker, G. A., Steen, N., Potts, P., & Chadwick, D. W. (1996). The clinical course of epilepsy and its psychosocial correlates: findings from a U.K. Community study. *Epilepsia, 32*(2), 148–161.

Jacoby, A., Snape, D., & Baker, G. A. (2009). Determinants of quality of life in people with epilepsy. *Neurologic Clinics, 27*(4), 843–863.

Janz, D., & Durner, M. (1995). Juvenile myoclonic epilepsy. In J. Engel & T. A. Pedley (Eds.), *Epilepsy: A comprehensive textbook* (pp. 2389–2400). Lippincott-Raven Publishers.

Jarvenpaa, S., Peltola, J., Raineslo, S., Leinonen, E., Lehtimaki, K., & Jarventausta, K. (2018). Reversible psychiatric adverse effects related to deep brain stimulation of the anterior thalamus in patients with refractory epilepsy. *Epilepsy & Behavior, 88*, 373–379.

Jayalakshmi, S., Vasireddy, S., Sireesha, J., Vooturi, S., Patil, A., Sirisha, S., Vadapalli, R., Chandrasekhar, Y. B. V. K., & Panigrahi, M. (2023). Long-term seizure freedom, resolution of epilepsy and perceived life changes in drug resistant temporal lobe epilepsy with hippocampal sclerosis: Comparison of surgical versus medical management. *Neurosurgery, 92*(6), 1249–1258.

Jea, A., Vachhrajani, S., Widjaja, E., Nilsson, D., Raybaud, C., Shroff, M., & Rutka, J. T. (2008). Corpus callosotomy in children and the disconnection syndromes: A review. *Child's Nervous System, 24*(6), 685–692.

Jermakowicz, W. J., Kanner, A. M., Sur, S., Bermudez, C., D'Haese, P. F., Kolcun, J. P. G., Cajigas, I., Li, R., Millan, C., Ribot, R., Serrano, E. A., Velez, N., Lowe, M. R., Rey, G. J., & Jagid, J. R. (2017). Laser thermal ablation for mesiotemporal epilepsy: Analysis of ablation volumes and trajectories. *Epilepsia, 58*(5), 801–810.

Jethwa, P. R., Barrese, J. C., Gowda, A., Shetty, A., & Danish, S. F. (2012). Magnetic resonance thermometry-guided laser-induced thermal therapy for intracranial neoplasms: Initial experience. *Neurosurgery, 71*(1 Suppl Operative), 133–145.

Joanette, Y., & Goulet, P. (1986). Criterion-specific reduction of verbal fluency in right brain-damaged right-handers. *Neuropsychologia, 24*, 875–879.

Jokeit, H., & Ebner, A. (1999). Long term effects of refractory temporal lobe epilepsy on cognitive abilities: A cross sectional study. *Journal of Neurology, Neurosurgery, and Psychiatry, 67*, 44–50.

Jokeit, H., & Ebner, A. (2002). Effects of chronic epilepsy on intellectual functions. *Progress in Brain Research, 135*, 455–463.

Jokeit, H., & Schacher, M. (2004, February). Neuropsychological aspects of type of epilepsy and etiological factors in adults. *Epilepsy & Behavior, 5*(Supplement 1), 14–20. http://www.sciencedirect.com/science/article/B6WDT-4B721P5-2/2/4cf9701a3367fa9c3768196d5c09ea1a

Jokeit, H., Seitz, R., Markowitsch, H., Neumann, N., Witte, O., & Ebner, A. (1997). Prefrontal asymmetric interictal glucose hypometabolism and cognitive impairment in patients with temporal lobe epilepsy. *Brain, 120*, 2283–2294.

Jokeit, H., Heger, R., Ebner, A., & Markowitsch, H. J. (1998). Hemispheric asymetries in category-specific word retrieval. *Neuroreport, 9*, 2371–2373.

Jones, J. E., Watson, R., Sheth, R., Caplan, R., Koehn, M., Seidenberg, M., & Hermann, B. (2007). Psychiatric comorbidity in children with new onset epilepsy. *Developmental Medicine and Child Neurology, 49*(7), 493–497.

Jones-Gotman, M. (1986). Right hippocampal excision impairs learning and recall of a list of abstract designs. *Neuropsychologia, 24*, 659–670.

Jones-Gotman, M., & Milner, B. (1977). Design fluency: The invention of nonsense drawings after focal cortical lesions. *Neuropsychologia, 15*, 653–674.

Jones-Gotman, M., Smith, M. L., & Zatorre, R. J. (1993). Neuropsychological testing for localizing and lateralizing the epileptogenic region. In J. J. Engel (Ed.), *Surgical treatment of the epilepsies* (2nd ed.). Raven Press.

Jones-Gotman, M., Zatorre, R. J., Olivier, A., Andermann, F., Cendes, F., Staunton, H., McMackin, D., Jones-Gotman, M., Dubeau, F., Gotman, J., Lukban, A., Dean, G., Evans, A., Lisbona, R., Siegel, A. M., & Wieser, H. G. (1997). Learning and retention of words and designs following excision from medial or lateral temporal-lobe structures. *Neuropsychologia, 35*, 963–973.

Jones-Gotman, M., Smith, M. L., Risse, G. L., Westerveld, M., Swanson, S. J., Giovagnoli, A. R., Lee, T., Mader-Joaquim, M. J., & Piazzini, A. (2010). The contribution of neuropsychology to diagnostic assessment in epilepsy. *Epilepsy and Behavior, 18*, 3–12.

Kaestner, E., Balachandra, A., Bahrami, N., Reyes, A., Lalani, S., Macari, A. C., Voets, N. L., Drane, D. L., Paul, B. M., Bonilha, L., & McDonald, C. R. (2020). The white matter connectome as an individualized biomarker of language impairment in TLE. *NeuroImage: Clinical, 25*, 102125. https://doi.org/10.1016/j.nicl.2019.102125

Kaestner, E., Reyes, A., Chen, A., Rao, J., Macari, A. C., Choi, J. Y., Qiu, D., Hewitt, K., Wang, Z. I., Drane, D. L., Hermann, B., Busch, R. M., Punia, V., & McDonald, C. R. (2021). Atrophy and cognitive profiles in older adults with temporal lobe epilepsy are similar to mild cognitive impairment. *Brain, 144*(1), 236–250.

Kaestner, E., Stasenko, A., ben-Haim, S., Shih, J., Paul, B. M., & McDonald, C. R. (2022). The importance of basal-temporal white matter to pre- and post-surgical naming ability in temporal lobe epilepsy. *NeuroImage: Clinical, 34*, 102963.

Kaestner, E., Stasenko, A., Schadler, A., Roth, R., Hewitt, K., Reyes, A., Qiu, D., Bonilha, L., Voets, N., Hu, R., Willie, J., Pedersen, N., Shih, J., Ben-Haim, S., Gross, R., Drane, D., & McDonald, C. R. (2024). Impact of white matter networks on risk for memory decline following resection versus ablation in temporal lobe epilepsy. *Journal of Neurology, Neurosurgery and Psychiatry, 95*(7), 663–670.

Kahane, P., Chabardès, S., Minotti, L., Hoffmann, D., Benabid, A. L., & Munari, C. (2002). The role of the temporal pole in the genesis of temporal lobe seizures. *Epileptic Disorders, 4*, S51–S58.

Kaiboriboon, K., Bakaki, P. M., Lhatoo, S. D., & Koroukian, S. (2013). Incidence and prevalence of treated epilepsy among poor health and low-income Americans. *Neurology, 80*(21), 1942–1949.

Kanemoto, K., & Janz, D. (1989). The temporal sequence of aura-sensations in patients with complex focal seizures with particular attention to ictal aphasia. *Journal of Neurology, Neurosurgery and Psychiatry, 52*, 52–56.

Kanner, A. M. (2008). Mood disorder and epilepsy: A neurobiologic perspective of their relationship. *Dialogues in Clinical Neuroscience, 10*(1), 39–45.

Kanner, A. M. (2009). Can antiepileptic drugs unmask a susceptibility to psychiatric disorders? *Nature Clinical Practice Neurology, 5*, 132–133.

Kanner, A. M. (2016). Most antidepressant drugs are safe for patients with epilepsy at therapeutic doses: A review of the evidence. *Epilepsy and Behavior, 61*, 282–286.

Kanner, A. M., & Bicchi, M. M. (2022). Antiseizure medications for adults with epilepsy: A review. *Journal of the American Medical Association, 327*(13), 1269–1281.

Kanner, A. M., & Palac, S. (2000, February). Depression in Epilepsy: A common but often unrecognized comorbid malady. *Epilepsy & Behavior, 1*(1), 37–51. http://www.sciencedirect.com/science/article/B6WDT-45F549C-20/2/400a33d30a653f6116c06b3ecbcfb2d6

Kanner, A. M., Wuu, J., Faught, E., Tatum, W. O., 4th, Fix, A., French, J. A., & Investigators, T. P. (2003). A past psychiatric history may be a risk factor for topiramate-related psychiatric and cognitive adverse events. *Epilepsy & Behavior, 4*(5), 548–552.

Kanner, A. M., Byrne, R. W., Chicharro, A. V., Wuu, J., & Frey, M. (2009). Is a lifetime psychiatric history predictive of a worse postsurgical seizure outcome following a temporal lobectomy? *Neurology, 72*, 793–799.

Kanner, A. M., Helmstaedter, C., Sadat-Hossieny, Z., & Meador, K. (2020). Cognitive disorders in epilepsy I: Clinical experience, real-world evidence and recommendations. *Seizure, 83*, 216–222.

Karagianni, M. D., Brotis, A. G., Tasiou, A., Delev, D., von Lehe, M., Schijns, O. E. M. G., & Fountas, K. N. (2023). Hemispherotomy revised: A complication overview and a systematic review meta-analysis. *Brain and Spine, 3*, 101766.

Karakis, I., Lynam, C., Taraschenko, O., Staikova, E., & Drane, D. L. (2020). Concurrent EEG monitoring helps interpret neuropsychological testing results in patients with epilepsy. *Epilepsy & Behavior, 111*, 207275.

Kasasbeh, A. S., Smyth, M. D., Steger-May, K., Jalilian, L., Bertrand, M., & Limbrick, D. D. (2014). Outcomes after anterior or complete corpus callosotomy in children. *Neurosurgery, 74*(1), 17–28.

Kasteleijn-Nolst Trenite, D. G., & Vermeiren, R. (2005). The impact of subclinical epileptiform discharges on complex tasks and cognition: Relevance for aircrew and air traffic controllers. *Epilepsy and Behavior, 6*, 31–34.

Kavros, P. M., Clarke, T., Strug, L. J., Halperin, J. M., Dorta, N. J., & Pal, D. K. (2008). Attention impairment in rolandic epilepsy: Systematic review. *Epilepsia, 49*(9), 1570–1580.

Keary, T. A., Frazier, T. W., Busch, R. M., Kubu, C. S., & Lampietro, M. (2007). Multivariate neuropsychological predictionn of seizure lateralization in temporal epilepsy surgical cases. *Epilepsia, 48*(8), 1438–1446.

Keller, S. S., & Roberts, N. (2008). Voxel-based morphometry of temporal lobe epilepsy: An introduction and review of the literature. *Epilepsia, 49*(5), 741–757.

Kerrigan, J. F., Litt, B., Fisher, R. S., Cranstoun, S., French, J. A., Blum, D. E., Dichter, M., Shetter, A., Baltuch, G., Jaggi, J., Krone, S., Brodie, M. J., Rise, M., & Graves, N. (2004). Electrical stimulation of the anterior nucleus of the thalamus for the treatment of intractable epilepsy. *Epilepsia, 45*(4), 346–354.

Kharkar, S., & Knowlton, R. (2015). Magnetoencephalography in the presurgical evaluation of epilepsy. *Epilepsy and Behavior, 46*, 19–26.

Kim, H., Yi, S., Son, E. I., & Kim, J. (2004). Lateralization of epileptic foci by neuropsychological testing in mesial temporal lobe epilepsy. *Neuropsychology, 18*(1), 141–151.

Kiper, D. C., Zesiger, P., Maeder, P., Deonna, T., & Innocenti, G. M. (2002). Vision after early-onset lesions of the occipital cortex: I. Neuropsychological and psychophysical studies. *Neural Plasticity, 9*(1), 1–25.

Kleen, J. K., Scott, R. C., Holmes, G. L., Roberts, D. W., Rundle, M. M., Testorf, M., Lenck-Santini, P. P., & Jobst, B. C. (2013). Hippocampal interictal epileptiform activity disrupts cognition in humans. *Neurology, 81*(1), 18–24.

Kluger, B. M., & Meador, K. J. (2008). Teratogenicity of antiepileptic medications. *Seminars in Neurology, 28*(3), 328–335.

Kneebone, A. C., Chelune, G. J., & Luders, H. O. (1997). Individual patient prediction of seizure lateralization in temporal lobe epilepsy: A comparison between neuropsychological memory measures and the Intracarotid Amobarbital procedure. *Journal of the International Neuropsychological Society, 3*, 159–168.

Kneebone, A. C., Lee, G. P., Wade, L. T., & Loring, D. W. (2007). Rey complex figure: Figural and spatial memory before and after temporal lobectomy for intractable epilepsy. *Journal of the International Neuropsychological Society, 13*(4), 664–671.

Knowlton, R. C., Razdan, S. N., Limdi, N., Elgavish, R. A., Killen, J., Blount, J., Burneo, J. G., Ver Hoef, L., Paige, L., Faught, E., Kankirawatana, P., Bartolucci, A., Riley, K., & Kuzniecky, R. (2009). Effect of epilepsy magnetic source imaging on intracranial electrode placement. *Annals of Neurology, 65*(6), 716–723.

Kobau, R., Gilliam, F., & Thurman, D. J. (2006). Prevalence of self-reported epilepsy or seizure disorder and its association with self-reported depression and anxiety: Results from the 2004 HealthStyles survey. *Epilepsia, 45*, 1915–1921.

Kockelmann, E., Elger, C. E., & Helmstaedter, C. (2003). Significant improvement in frontal lobe associated neuropsychological functions after withdrawal of topiramate in epilepsy patients. *Epilepsy Research, 54*, 171–178.

Koo, B. (2001). EEG changes with vagus nerve stimulation. *Journal of Clinical Neurophysiology, 18*(5), 434–441.

Koren, J., Lang, C., Gritsch, G., Mayer, L., Hartmann, M., Hafner, S., Kluge, T., & Baumgartner, C. (2024). Idiopathic generalized epilepsies in the epilepsy monitoring unit: Systematic quantification of focal EEG and semiological signs. *Clinical Neurophysiology, 162*, 82–90.

Krishna, V., Mindel, J., Sammartino, F., Block, C., Dwivedi, A. K., Van Gompel, J. J., Fountain, N., & Fisher, R. (2023). A phase 1 open-label trial evaluating focused ultrasound unilateral anterior thalamotomy for focal onset epilepsy. *Epilepsia, 64*(4), 831–842.

Krumholz, A., Wiebe, S., Gronseth, G. S., Gloss, D. S., Sanchez, A. M., Kabir, A. A., Liferidge, A. T., Martello, J. P., Kanner, A. M., Shinnnar, S., Hopp, J. L., & French, J. A. (2015). Evidence-based guideline: Management of an unprovoked first seizure in adults: Report of the guideline development subcommittee of the American Academy of Neurology and the American Epilepsy Society. *Neurology, 84*(16), 1705–1713.

Krynauw, R. A. (1950). Infantile hemiplegia treated by removing one cerebral hemisphere. *Journal of Neurology, Neurosurgery, and Psychiatry, 13*(4), 243–267.

Kuang, Y., Yang, T., Gu, J., Kong, B., & Cheng, L. (2014). Comparison of therapeutic effects between selective amygdalohippocampectomy and anterior temporal lobectomy for the treatment of temporal lobe epilepsy: A meta-analysis. *British Journal of Neurosurgery, 28*(3), 374–377.

Kwan, P., & Brodie, M. J. (2000). Epilepsy after the first drug fails: Substitution or add-on. *Seizure, 9*(7), 464–468.

Kwan, P., & Brodie, M. J. (2001). Neuropsychological effects of epilepsy and antiepileptic drugs. *Lancet, 357*, 216–222.

Kwon, C. S., Rafati, A., Ottman, R., Christensen, J., Kanner, A. M., Jetté, N., & Newton, C. R. (2024). Psychiatric comorbidities in persons with epilepsy compared with persons without epilepsy: A systematic review and meta-analysis. *JAMA Neurology, 2024*, e243976.

LaFrance, W. C., Jr., Kanner, A. M., & Hermann, B. (2008). Psychiatric comorbidities in epilepsy. *International Review of Neurobiology, 83*, 347–383.

Lagae, L., Verhelst, H., Ceulemans, B., De Meirleir, L., Nassogne, M. C., de Borchgrave, V., D'Hooghe, M., Foulon, M., & Van Bogaert, P. (2010). Treament and long term outcome in west syndrome: The clinical reality. A multicentre follow up study. *Seizure, 19*, 1590164.

Landau, W. M., & Kleffner, F. R. (1957). Syndrome of acquired aphasia with convulsive disorder in children. *Neurology, 7*, 523–530.

Langfit, J. T., & Rausch, R. (1996). Word-finding deficits persist after left anterotemporal lobectomy. *Archives of Neurology, 53*(1), 72–76.

Lee, R. W., & Worrell, G. A. (2012). Dorsolateral frontal lobe epilepsy. *Journal of Clinical Neurophysiology, 29*(5), 379–384.

Lee, G. P., Park, Y. D., Westerveld, M., Hempel, A., & Loring, D. W. (2002). Effect of Wada methodology in predicting lateralized memory impairment in pediatric epilepsy surgery candidates. *Epilepsy and Behavior, 3*(5), 439–447.

Lee, S. K., Lee, S. Y., Kim, D. W., Lee, D. S., & Chung, C. K. (2005). Occipital lobe Epilepsy: Clinical characteristics, surgical outcome, and role of diagnostic modalities. *Epilepsia, 46*, 688–695.

Lee, A. C. H., Yeung, L. K., & Barense, M. D. (2012). The hippocampus and visual perception. *Frontiers in Human Neuroscience, 6*, 91.

Lewis, A. J. (1934). Melancholia: A historical review. *Journal of Mental Science, 80*, 1–42.

Lewis, E. C., Well, A. G., Duchowny, M., Bhatia, S., Ragheb, J., & Miller, I. (2015). MR-guided laser interstitial thermal therapy for pediatric drug-resistant lesional epilepsy. *Epilepsia, 56*(10), 1590–1598.

Lezak, M. D., Howieson, D. B., & Loring, D. W. (2004). *Neuropsychological assessment* (4th ed.). Oxford University Press.

Lhermitte, F. (1983). "Utilization behavior" and its relation to lesions of the frontal lobes. *Brain, 106*, 237–255.

Liang, S., Zhang, G., Li, Y., Ding, C., Yu, T., Wang, X., Zhang, Z., Jiang, H., Zhang, S., & He, S. (2013). Hemispherectomy in adult patients with severe unilateral epilepsy and hemiplegia. *Epilepsy Research, 106*, 257–263.

Liegeois, F., Connelly, A., Cross, J. H., Boyd, S. G., Gadian, D. G., Vargha-Khadem, F., & Baldeweg, T. (2004). Language reorganization in children with early-onset lesions of the left hemisphere: An fMRI study. *Brain, 127*, 1229–1236.

Lima, E. M., Rzezak, P., Guimaraes, C. A., Montenegro, M. A., Guerreiro, M. M., & Valennte, K. D. (2017). The executive profile of children with benign epilepsy of childhood with centrotemporal spikes and temporal lobe epilepsy. *Epilepsy & Behavior, 72*, 173–177.

Lin, J. J., Mula, M., & Hermann, B. P. (2012). Uncovering the neurobehavioral comorbidities of epilepsy over the lifespan. *Lancet, 380*, 1180–1192.

Lineweaver, T. T., Naugle, R. I., Cafaro, A. M., Bingaman, W., & Luders, H. O. (2004). Patients' perceptions of memory functioning before and after surgical intervention to treat medically refractory epilepsy. *Epilepsia, 45*(12), 1604–1612.

Lineweaver, T. T., Morris, H. H., Naugle, R. I., Najm, I. M., Diehl, B., & Bingaman, W. (2006). Evaluating the contributions of state-of-the-art assessment techniques to predicting memory outcome after unilateral anterior temporal lobectomy. *Epilepsia, 47*(11), 1895–1903.

Lippe, S., Bulteau, C., Dorfmuller, G., Audren, F., Delalande, O., & Jambaque, I. (2010). Cognitive outcome of parietooccipital resection in children with epilepsy. *Epilepsia, 51*(10), 2047–2057.

LoGalbo, A., Sawrie, S., Roth, D. L., Kuzniecky, R., Knowlton, R., Faught, E., & Martin, R. (2005, May). Verbal memory outcome in patients with normal preoperative verbal memory and left mesial temporal sclerosis. *Epilepsy & Behavior, 6*(3), 337–341. http://www.sciencedirect.com/science/article/B6WDT-4FG897C-1/2/bbcd7fc1e78f73be9ddacbc7c1214f18

Loring, D. W. (1990). Wada testing. In *Continuing Education Program of the European Conference of the International Neuropsychological Society.*

Loring, D. W., & Bauer, R. M. (2010). Testing the limits: Cautions and concerns regarding the new Wechsler IQ and memory scales. *Neurology, 74*(8), 685–690.

Loring, D. W., & Meador, K. J. (2003). The medical College of Georgia (MCG) complex figures: Four forms for follow-up. In J. A. Knight & E. Kaplan (Eds.), *The handbook of Rey-Osterrieth complex figure: Clinical and research applications* (pp. 313–321). Psychological Assessment Resources.

Loring, D. W., Lee, G. P., Martin, R. C., & Meador, K. J. (1988). Material-specific learning in patients with partial complex seizures of temporal lobe origin: Convergent validation of memory constructs. *Journal of Epilepsy, 1*, 53–59.

Loring, D. W., Meador, K. J., Lee, G. P., & Smith, J. R. (2004, April). Structural versus functional prediction of memory change following anterior temporal lobectomy. *Epilepsy & Behavior, 5*(2), 264–268. http://www.sciencedirect.com/science/article/B6WDT-4BMTF1K-1/2/78bd71 3be3e81e123aa0fc185551e3f2

Loring, D. W., Marino, S., & Meador, K. J. (2007). Neuropsychological and behavioral effects of antiepilepsy drugs. *Neuropsychology Review, 17*(4), 431–425.

Loring, D. W., Strauss, E., Hermann, B. P., Barr, W. B., Perrine, K., Trenerry, M. R., Chelune, G., Westerveld, M., Lee, G. P., Meador, J. K., & Bowden, S. C. (2008). Differential neuropsychological test sensitivity to left temporal lobe epilepsy. *Journal of the International Neuropsychological Society, 14*(3), 394–400.

Loring, D. L., Bowden, S. C., Lee, G. P., & Meador, K. J. (2009). Diagnostic utility of Wada memory assymetries: Sensitivity, specificity, and likelihood ratio characterization. *Neuropsychology, 23*, 687–693.

Loring, D., Lowenstein, D. H., Barbaro, N. M., Fureman, B. E., Odenkirchen, J., Jacobs, M. P., Austin, J. K., Dlugos, D. J., French, J. A., Gaillard, W. D., Hermann, B. P., Hesdorffer, D. C., Roper, S. N., Van Cott, A. C., Grinnon, S., & Stout, A. (2011). Common data elements in epilepsy research: Development and implementation of the NINDS Epilepsy CDE project. *Epilepsia, 52*(6), 1186–1191.

Loring, D. W., Marino, S. E., Parfitt, D., Finney, G. R., & Meador, K. J. (2012). Acute lorazepam effects on neurocognitive performance. *Epilepsy and Behavior, 25*(3), 329–333.

Loring, D. W., Kapur, R., Meador, K. J., & Morrell, M. J. (2015). Differential neuropsychological outcomes following targeted responsive neurostimulation for partial-onset epilepsy. *Epilepsia, 56*(11), 1836–1844.

Loring, D. W., Bauer, R. M., Cavanagh, L., Drane, D. L., Enriquez, K. D., Reise, S. P., Shih, K., Umfleet, L. G., Wahlstrom, D., Whelan, F., Widaman, K. F., Bilder, R. M., & Group, N. S. (2022). Rationale and design of the National Neuropsychology Network. *Journal of the International Neuropsychological Society, 28*(1), 1–11. https://doi.org/10.1017/S1355617721000199

Loughman, A., Bowden, S. C., & D'Souza, C. (2014). Cognitive functioning in idiopathic generalised epilepsies: A systematic review and meta-analysis. *Neuroscience and Biobehavioral Reviews, 43*, 20–34.

Luders, H., Lesser, R. P., Hahn, J. F., Dinner, D. S., Morris, H., Resor, S., & Harrison, M. (1986). Basal temporal language area demonstrated by electrical stimulation. *Neurology, 36*(4), 505–510.

Luders, J., Lesser, R. P., Hahn, J., Dinner, D. S., Morris, H. H., Wyllie, E., & Godoy, J. (1991). Basal temporal language area. *Brain, 114*, 743–754.

Luerding, R., Boesebeck, F., & Ebner, A. (2004). Cogntive changes after epilepsy surgery in the posterior cortex. *Journal of Neurology, Neurosurgery, and Psychiatry, 75*, 583–587.

Ma, X., Zhang, Y., Yang, Z., Liu, X., Sun, H., Qin, J., Wu, X., & Liang, J. (2011). Childhood asence epilepsy: Electroclinical features and diagnostic criteria. *Brain and Development, 33*(2), 114–119.

Macdonald-Laurs, E., Dzau, W., Warren, A. E. L., Coleman, M., Mignone, C., Stephenson, S. E. M., & Howell, K. B. (2024). Identification and treatment of surgically-remediable causes of infantile epileptic spasms syndrome. *Expert Review of Neurotherapeutics, 24*(7), 661–680.

Macrodimitris, S., Sherman, E. M., Forde, S., Tellez-Zenteno, J. F., Metcalfe, A., Hernadez-Ronquillo, L., Wiebe, S., & Jette, N. (2011). Psychiatric outcomes of epilepsy surgery: A systematic review. *Epilepsia, 52*(5), 880–890.

Maehara, T., & Shimizu, H. (2001). Surgical outcome of corpus callosotomy in patients with drop attacks. *Epilepsia, 42*, 67–71.

Maillard, L., Vignal, J. P., Anxionnat, R., Taillandier, L., & Vespignani, H. (2004). Semiologic value of ictal Autoscopy. *Epilepsia, 45*, 391–394.

Maillard, L., Ferrand, M., Aron, O., Cheval, M., Tyvaert, L., Jonas, J., & Vignal, J. P. (2022). Visual phenomena and anatomo-electro-clinical correlations in occipital lobe seizures. *Revue Neurologique, 178*(7), 644–648.

Majoie, H. J., Berfelo, M. W., Aldenkamp, A. P., Evers, S. M., Kessels, A. G., & Renier, W. O. (2001). Vagus nerve stimulation in children with therapy-resistant epilepsy diagnosed as Lennox-Gastaut syndrome: Clinical results, neuropsychological effects, and cost-effectiveness. *Journal of Clinical Neurophysiology, 18*, 419–428.

Mamelak, A. N., Barbaro, N. M., Walker, J. A., & Laxer, K. D. (1993). Corpus callosotomy: A quantitative study of the extent of resection, seizure control, and neuropsychological outcome. *Journal of Neurosurgery, 79*(5), 688–695.

Manchanda, R. (2002). Psychiatric disorders in epilepsy: Clinical aspects. *Epilepsy and Behavior, 3*, 39–45.

Manzone, D. M., Nava, E., & Bolognini, N. (2024). Methods for the assessment of multisensory processing: Behavioral and neuropsychological approaches. In M. Valeriani & M. de Tommaso (Eds.), *Psychophysiological methods*. Springer Nature.

Marini, C., Scheffer, I. E., Crossland, K. M., Grinton, B. E., Phillips, F. L., McMahon, J. M., Turner, S. J., Dean, J. T., Kivity, S., Mazarib, A., Neufeld, M. Y., Korczyn, A. D., Harkin, L. A., Dibbens, L. M., Wallace, R. H., Mulley, J. C., & Berkovic, S. F. (2004). Genetic architecture of ideopathic generalized epilepsy: Clinical genetic analysis of 55 multiplex families. *Epilepsia, 45*(5), 467–478.

Markand, O. N. (2003). Lennox-Gastaut syndrome (childhood epileptic encephalopathy). *Journal of Clinical Neurophysiology, 20*, 426–441.

Markwardt, F. C. (1998). *Peabody individual achievement test-revised*. American Guidance Service.

Martin, A., & Fedio, P. (1983). Word production and comprehension in Alzheimer's disease: The breakdown of semantic knowledge. *Brain and Language, 19*, 124–141.

Martin, R. C., Loring, D. W., Meador, K. J., & Lee, G. P. (1990). The effects of lateralized temporal lobe dysfunction on formal and semantic word fluency. *Neuropsychologia, 28*, 823–829.

Martin, R. C., Sawrie, S. M., Roth, D. L., Gilliam, F. G., Faught, E., Morawetz, R. B., & Kuzniecky, R. (1998). Individual memory change after anterior temporal lobectomy: A base rate analysis using regression-based outcome methodology. *Epilepsia, 39*(10), 1075–1082.

Martin, R. C., Sawrie, S. M., Edwards, R., Roth, D. L., Faught, E., Kuzniecky, R. I., Morawetz, R. B., & Gilliam, F. G. (2000). Investigation of executive function change following anterior temporal lobectomy: Selective normalization of verbal fluency. *Neuropsychology, 14*(2), 501–508.

Mayeux, R., Brandt, J., Rosen, J., & Benson, D. F. (1980). Interictal memory and language imparment in temporal lobe epliepsy. *Neurology, 30*, 120–125.

McAndrews, M. P., & Milner, B. (1991). The frontal cortex and memory for temporal order. *Neuropsychologia, 29*(9), 849–859.

McClelland, S., 3rd, Garcia, R. E., Peraza, D. M., Shih, T. T., Hirsch, L. J., Hirsch, J., & Goodman, R. R. (2006). Facial emotion recognition after curative nondominant temporal lobectomy in patients with mesial temporal sclerosis. *Epilepsia, 47*(8).

McConley, R., Martin, R., Palmer, C. A., Kuzniecky, R., Knowlton, R., & Faught, E. (2008). Rey Osterrieth complex figure test spatial and figural scoring: Relations to seizure focus and hippocampal pathology in patients with temporal lobe epilepsy. *Epilepsy and Behavior, 13*, 174–177.

McCracken, D. J., Willier, J. T., Fernald, B., Saindane, A. M., Drane, D. L., Barrow, D. L., & Gross, R. E. (2016). Magnetic thermometry-guided stereotactic laser ablation of cavernous malformations in drug resistant epilepsy: Imaging and clinical results. *Operative Neurosurgery, 12*(1), 39–48.

McDonald, C. R., Bauer, R. M., Grande, L., Gilmore, R., & Roper, S. (2001). The role of the frontal lobes in memory: Evidence from unilateral frontal resections for relief of intractable epilepsy. *Archives of Clinical Neuropsychology, 16*, 571–585.

McDonald, C. R., Delis, D. C., Norman, M. A., Tecoma, E. S., & Iragui, V. J. (2005a). Discriminating patients with frontal-lobe epilepsy and temporal-lobe epilepsy: Utility of a multilevel design fluency test. *Neuropsychology, 19*(6), 806–813.

McDonald, C. R., Delis, D. C., Norman, M. A., Wetter, S. R., Tecoma, E. S., & Iragui, V. J. (2005b). Response inhibition and set shifting in patients with frontal lobe epilepsy or temporal lobe epilepsy. *Epilepsy and Behavior, 7*, 438–446.

McDonald, C. R., Ahmadi, M. E., Hagler, D. J., Tecoma, E. S., Iragui, V. J., Gharapetian, L., Dale, A. M., & Halgren, E. (2008). Diffusion tensor imaging correlates of memory and language impairments in temporal lobe epilepsy. *Neurology, 71*(23), 1869–1876.

McKenzie, K. G. (1938). The present status of a patient who had the right cerebral hemisphere removed. *Journal of the American Medical Association, 111*, 168–183.

Meador, K. J. (1993). Research use of the new quality-of-life in Epilepsy inventory. *Epilepsia, 34*(suppl 4), S34–S38.

Meador, K. J., Baker, G. A., Browning, N., Clayton-Smith, J., Combs-Cantrell, D. T., Cohen, M. J., Kalayjian, L. A., Kanner, A., Liporace, J. D., Pennell, P. B., Privitera, M., Loring, D. W., & NEAD Study Group. (2009). Cognitive function at 3 years of age after fetal exposure to antiepileptic drugs. *New England Journal of Medicine, 360*, 1597–1605.

Medscape. (2017, June 30). *FDA okays VNS therapy for epilepsy in children as young as 4 years.*

Meer, E. A., Chen, M. E., Jones, M., Mathern, G. W., & Pineles, S. L. (2021). Long-term patient-reported outcomes of visual field defects and compensatory mechanisms in patients after cerebral hemispherectomy. *Journal of the North American Neuro-Ophthalmology Society, 41*(2), 147–153.

Meletti, S., Cantalupo, G., Santoro, F., Benuzzi, F., Marliani, A. F., Tassinari, C. A., & Roubboli, G. (2014). Temporal lobe epilepsy and emotion recognition without amygdala: A case study of Urbach-Wiethe disease and review of the literature. *Epileptic Disorders: International Epilepsy Journal with Vidotape, 16*(4), 518–527.

Mensah, S. A., Beavis, J. M., Thapar, A. K., & Kerr, M. (2006). The presence and clinical implications of depression in a community population of adults with epilepsy. *Epilepsy and Behavior, 8*, 213–219.

Mensah, S. A., Beavis, J. M., Thapar, A. K., & Kerr, M. P. (2007). A community study of the presence of anxiety disorder in people with epilepsy. *Epilepsy and Behavior, 11*(1), 118–124.

Mermi Dibek, D., Erasian Boz, H., Oztura, I., & Baklan, B. (2024). Investigation of the effect of antiseizure medications on cognition in patients with epilepsy. *Clinical EEG and Neuroscience, 55*(6), 643–650.

Metternich, B., Buschmann, F., Wagner, K., Schulze-Bonhage, A., & Kriston, L. (2014). Verbal fluency in focal epilepsy: A systematic review and meta-analysis. *Neuropsychology Review, 24*, 200–218.

Milner, B. (1958). Psychological deficits produced by temporal lobe excision. *Research Publications - Association for Research in Nervous and Mental Disease, 36*, 244–257.

Milner, B. (1968, September). Visual recognition and recall after right temporal-lobe excision in man. *Neuropsychologia, 6*(3), 191–209. http://www.sciencedirect.com/science/article/B6T0D-45RD8SB-20/2/920ce1c103ea7555351d2d6aaa7932f1

Milner, B., Petrides, M., & Smith, M. L. (1985). Frontal lobes and the temporal organization of memory. *Human Neurobiology, 4*, 137–142.

Mittan, R. J. (2009). Psychosocial treatment programs in epilepsy: A review. *Epilepsy and Behavior, 16*(3), 371–380.

Moguilner, S., Birba, A., Fino, D., Isoardi, R., Huetagoyena, C., Otoya, R., Tirapu, V., Cremaschi, F., Sedeño, L., Ibáñez, A., & García, A. M. (2021). Structural and functional motor-network disruptions predict selective action-concept deficits: Evidence from frontal lobe epilepsy. *Cortex, 144*, 43–55.

Mohammadi, A. M., Hawasli, A. H., Rodriguez, A., Schroeder, J. L., Laxton, A. W., Elson, P., Tatter, S. B., Barnett, G. H., & Leuthardt, E. C. (2014). The role of laser interstitial thermal therapy in enhancing progression-free survival of difficult-to-access high-grade gliomas: A multicenter study. *Cancer Medicine, 3*(4), 971–979.

Moles, A., Guenot, M., Rheims, S., Berthiller, J., Catenoix, H., & Montavont, A. (2018). SEEG-guided radiofrequency coagulation (SEEG-guided RF-TC) versus anterior temporal lobectomy (ATL) in temporal lobe epilepsy. *Journal of Neurosurgery, 265*(9), 1998–2004.

Montouris, G., Aoumatar, S., Burdette, D., Kothare, S., Kuzniecky, R., Rosenfeld, W., & Chung, S. (2020). Expert opinion: Proposed diagnostic and treatment algorithms for Lennox-Gastaut syndrome in adult patients. *Epilepsy & Behavior, 110*, 107146.

Morey, L. C. (1991). *The personality assessment inventory: Professional manual.* Psychological Assessment Resources.

Morrell, M. J. (2019). Brain-responsive neurostimulation for epilepsy (RNS system). *Epilepsy Research, 153*, 68–70.

Morrell, M. J. (2020). Mesial temporal resectionn following long-term ambulatory inntracranial EEG monitoring with a direct brain-responsive neurostimulation system. *Epilepsia, 61*(3), 408–420.

Morrell, M. J., & RNS System in Epilepsy Study Group. (2011). Responsive cortical stimulation for the treatment of medically intractable partial epilepsy. *Neurology, 77*(13), 1295–1304.

Morrell, M. J., & Study, R. S. L. (2020). Nine-year prospective efficacy and safety of brain-responsive neurostimulation for focal epilepsy. *Neurology, 95*(9), e1244–e1256.

Morrell, F., Whisler, W. W., & Bleck, T. P. (1989). Multiple subpial transection: A new approach to the surgical treatment of focal epilepsy. *Journal of Neurosurgery, 70*, 231–239.

Morris, G. L., 3rd, Gloss, D., Buchhalter, J., Mack, K. J., Nickels, K. C., & Harden, C. (2013). Evidence-based guideline update: Vagus nerve stimulation for the treatment of epilepsy: Report of the guideline development Subcommittee of the American Academy of neurology. *Neurology, 81*(16), 1453–1459.

Mosely, B. D., Nickels, K., & Wirrell, E. C. (2012). Surgical outcomes for intractable epilepsy in children with epileptic seizures. *Journal of Clinical Neurology, 27*(6), 713–720.

Mula, M. (2013). Treatment of anxiety disorders in epilepsy: An evidence-based approach. *Epilepsia, 54*, 13–18.

Muller, R. A., Behen, M. E., Rothermel, R. D., Muzik, O., Chakraborty, P. K., & Chugani, H. T. (1999). Brain organization for language in children, adolescents, and adults with left hemisphere lesion: A pet study. *Progress in Neuro-Psychopharmacology and Biological Psychiatry, 23*(4), 657–668.

Nascimento, F. A., Culler, G., Schuele, S. U., & Gavvala, J. R. (2020). Posterior cortex epilepsy. In S. Schuele (Ed.), *A practical approach to stereo EEG* (pp. 136–156). Springer.

Naugle, R. I., Chelune, G. J., Cheek, R., Luders, H., & Awad, I. A. (1993). Detection of changes in material-specific memory following temporal lobectomy using the Wechsler memory scale-revised. *Archives of Clinical Neuropsychology, 8*(5), 381–395.

Neal, E. G., Schoenberg, M. R., Maciver, S., Bezchlibnyk, Y. B., & Vale, F. L. (2021). Seizure freedom after epilepsy surgery and higher baseline ccgnition may be associated with a negatively correlated epilepsy network in temporal lobe epilepsy. *Frontiers in Neuroscience, 14*, 629667.

Neimeyer, P. (1958). The transventricular Amygdalohippocampectomy in temporal lobe epilepsy. In M. Baldwin & P. Bailey (Eds.), *Temporal lobe epilepsy* (pp. 461–482). CC Thomas.

Neisser, J., Abreu, G., Drane, D. L., Pedersen, N. P., Parsons, T. D., McNeely-White, K. L., & Cleary, A. M. (in press). Opening a conceptual space for metamemory experience. *New Ideas in Psychology*.

Neri, M. L., Guimaraes, C. A., Oliveira, E. P., Duran, M. H., Medeiros, L. L., Montenegro, M. A., Boscariol, M., & Guerreiro, M. M. (2012). Neuropsychological assessment of children with rolandic epilepsy: Executive functions. *Epilepsy and Behavior, 24*(4), 403–407.

Ngadimon, I. W., Mohan, D., Shaikh, M. F., Khoo, C. S., Tan, H. J., Xhamhuri, N. S., Cheong, W. L., Aledo-Serrano, A., Yong, L. L., Lee, Y. M., Fadzil, F., & Thanabalan, J. (2024). Incidence and predictors of posttraumatic epilepsy and cognitive impairment in patients with traumatic brain injury: A retrospective cohort study in Malaysia. *Epilepsia, 65*(7), 1962–1974.

Nicolai, J., Aldenkamp, A. P., Arends, J., Weber, J. W., & Vles, J. S. H. (2006). Cognitive and behavioral effects of nocturnal epileptiform discharges in children with benign childhood epilepsy with centrotemporal spikes. *Epilepsy and Behavior, 8*, 56–70.

Nineuil, C., Houot, M., Dellacherie, D., Méré, M., Denos, M., Dupont, S., & Samson, S. (2023). Revisiting emotion recognition in different types of temporal lobe epilepsy: The influence of facial expression intensity. *Epilepsy and Behavior, 142*, 109191.

Nitta, N., Usui, N., Kondo, A., Tottori, T., Terada, K., Kasai, Y., Takahashi, Y., Nozaki, K., & Inoue, Y. (2021). Neuropsychological outcomes after frontal lobectomy to treat intractable epilepsy. *Epilepsy & Behavior, 123*, 108240.

Nobre, A. C., Coull, J. T., Walsh, V., & Frith, C. D. (2003). Brain activations during visual search: Contributions of search efficiency versus feature binding. *NeuroImage, 18*(1), 91–103.

Noeker, M., Haverkamp-Krois, A., & Haverkamp, F. (2005). Development of mental health dysfunction in childhood epilepsy. *Brain Development, 27*(1), 5–16.

Nordli, D. (2002). The ketogenic diet. Uses and abuses. *Neuropsychology Review, 58*(12 Suppl 7), S21–S24.

Novais, F., Andrea, M., Andrade, G., Loureiro, S., Pimentel, J., & Pestana, L. C. (2022). Intelligence quotient (IQ) as a predictor of epilepsy surgery outcome. *Epilepsy & Behavior, 132*, 108708.

Oguni, H., Hayashi, K., & Osawa, M. (1996). Long-term prognosis of Lennox-Gastaut syndrome. *Epilepsia, 37*(Suppl. 3), 44–47.

Oh, Y. S., Kim, H. J., Lee, K. J., Kim, Y. I., Lim, S. C., & Shon, Y. M. (2012). Cognitive improvement after long-term electrical stimulation of bilateral anterior thalamic nucleus in refractory epilepsy patients. *Seizure, 21*(3), 183–187.

Ojemann, G. A., & Dodrill, C. B. (1985). Verbal memory deficits after left temporal lobectomy for epilepsy: Mechanism and intraoperative prediction. *Journal of Neurosurgery, 62*, 101–107.

Ojemann, L. M., & Jung, M. E. (2006). Outcomes of temporal lobe epilepsy surgery. In J. W. Miller & D. L. Silbergeld (Eds.), *Epilepsy surgery: Principle and controversies* (pp. 661–689). Taylor & Francis.

Ojemann, G. A., & Valiante, T. (2006). Resective surgery for temporal lobe epilepsy. In J. W. Miller & D. L. Silbergeld (Eds.), *Epilepsy surgery: Principles and controversy* (pp. 403–413). Taylor and Francis.

Ojemann, G., Ojemann, J., Lettich, E., & Berger, M. (1989). Cortical language localization in left, dominant hemisphere. An electrical stimulation mapping investigation in 117 patients. *Journal of Neurosurgery, 71*(3), 316–326.

Ojemann, L. M., Ojemann, G. A., Dodrill, C. B., Crawford, C. A., Holmes, M. D., & Dudley, D. L. (2001). Language disturbances as side effects of topiramate and zonisamide therapy. *Epilepsy and Behavior, 2*, 579–584.

Okada, N. S., McNeely-White, K. L., Cleary, A. M., Carlaw, B. N., Drane, D. L., Parsons, T. D., McMahan, T., Neisser, J., & Pedersen, N. P. (2024). A virtual reality paradigm with dynamic scene stimuli for use in memory research. *Behavior Research Methods, 56*(8), 6440–6463.

Olaciregui Dague, K., Witt, J. A., von Wrede, R., Helmstaedter, C., & Surges, R. (2023). DBS of the ANT for refractory epilepsy: A single center experience of seizure reduction, side effects and neuropsychological outcomes. *Frontiers in Neurology, 14*, 1106511.

Olivier, A. (2000). Transcortical selective amygdalohippocampectomy in temporal lobe epilepsy. *Canadian Journal of Neurological Science, 27*, S68–S76. discussion S92.

Olney, J. W., Wozniak, D. F., Jevtovic-Todorovic, V., Farber, N. B., Bittigau, P., & Ikonomidou, C. (2002). Drug-induced apoptotic neurodegeneration in the developing brain. *Brain Pathology, 12*(4), 488–498.

Ono, K. E., Bearden, D. J., Adams, E., Doescher, J., Koh, S., Eksioglu, Y., Gross, R. E., & Drane, D. L. (2020). Cognitive and behavioral outcome of stereotactic laser amygdalohippocampotomy in a pediatric setting. *Epilepsy & Behavior Reports, 14*, 100370.

Osorio, I., Overman, J., Giftakis, J., & Wilkinson, S. B. (2007). High frequency thalamic stimulation for inoperable mesial temporal epilepsy. *Epilepsia, 48*(8), 1561–1571.

Oyegbile, T. O., Dow, C., Jones, J., Bell, B., Rutecki, P., Sheth, R., Seidenberg, M., & Hermann, B. P. (2004). The nature and course of neuropsychological morbidity in chronic temporal lobe epilepsy. *Neurology, 62*(10), 1736–1742.

Oyegbile, T. O., VanMeter, J. W., Motamedi, G., Zecavati, N., Santos, C., Chun, C. L. E., Gaillard, W. D., & Hermann, B. (2018). Executive dysfunction is associated with an altered executive control network in pediatric temporal lobe epilepsy. *Epilepsy and Behavior, 86*, 145–152.

Palmini, A., Najm, I., Avanzini, G., Babb, T., Guerrini, R., Foldvary-Schaefer, N., Jackson, G., Lüders, H. O., Prayson, R., Spreafico, R., & Vinters, H. V. (2004). Terminology and classification of the cortical dysplasias. *Neurology, 62*(6 Suppl. 3), S2–S8.

Parsons, T. D., & McMahan, T. (2017). An initial validation of the virtual environment grocery store. *Journal of Neuroscience Methods, 291*, 13–19. https://doi.org/10.1016/j.neurometh.2017.07.027

Pataraia, E., Lindinger, G., Deecke, L., Mayer, D., & Baumgartner, C. (2005). Combined MEG/EEG analysis of the interictal spike complex in mesial temporal lobe epilepsy. *NeuroImage, 24*(3), 607–614.

Pavone, A., & Niedermeyer, E. (2000). Absence seizures and the frontal lobe. *Clinical EEG (electroencephalography), 31*(3), 153–156.

Penfield, W., & Jasper, H. H. (1954). *Epilepsy and the functional anatomy of the human brain*. Little, Brown.

Penfield, W., & Perot, P. (1963). The brain's record of auditory and visual experience: A final summary and discussion. *Brain, 86*, 595–696.

Penry, J. K., & Dean, J. C. (1990). Prevention of intractale partial seizures by intermittent vagal stimulation in humans: Preliminnary results. *Epilepsia, 31*, S40–S43.

Perrine, K., Westerveld, M., Sass, K. J., Devinsky, O., Dogali, M., Spencer, D. D., Luciano, D. J., & Nelson, P. K. (1995). Wada memory disparities predict seizure laterality and postoperative seizure control. *Epilepsia, 36*(9), 851–856.

Perry, M. S., & Duchowny, M. (2013). Surgical versus medical treatment for refractory epilepsy: Outcomes beyond seizure control. *Epilepsia, 54*(12), 2060–2070.

Phillips, K. H. T., Patterson, K., Butler, C. R., Woodberry, E., Ralph, M. A. L., & Cope, T. E. (2024). Does epilepsy differentially affect different types of memory? *Seizure, 121*, 217–225.

Pigott, S., & Milner, B. (1993, January). Memory for different aspects of complex visual scenes after unilateral temporal- or frontal-lobe resection. *Neuropsychologia, 31*(1), 1–15. http://www.sciencedirect.com/science/article/B6T0D-45Y0NBH-89/2/7c32dcefd3dae57f0233074937c31004

Pillon, B., Bazin, B., Deweer, B., Ehrlé, N., Baulac, M., & Dubois, B. (1999). Specificity of memory deficits after right or left temporal lobectomy. *Cortex, 35*(4), 561–571.

Poochikian-Sarkissian, S., Wennberg, R. A., Sidani, S., & Devins, G. M. (2007). Quality of life in epilepsy. *Canadian Journal of Neuroscience and Nursing, 29*(1), 20–25.

Porter, R. F. (1993). Classification of epileptic seizures and epileptic syndromes. In A. R. J. Laidlaw & D. Chadwick (Eds.), *A textbook of Epilepsy* (4th ed., pp. 1–22). Churchill Livingstone.

Potter, J. L., Schefft, B. K., Beebe, D. W., Howe, S. R., Yeh, H. S., & Privatera, M. D. (2009). Presurgical neuropsychological testing predicts cognitive and seizure outcomes after anterior temporal lobectomy. *Epilepsy & Behavior, 16*, 246–253.

Powell, H. W., Koepp, M. J., Symms, M. R., Boulby, P. A., Salak-Haddadi, A., Thompson, P. J., Duncan, J. S., & Richardson, M. P. (2005). Material-specific lateralization of memory encoding in the medial temporal lobe: Blocked versus event-related design. *Neuroimage, 27*, 231–239.

Power, K. N., Gramstad, A., Gilhus, N. E., Hufthammer, K. O., & Engelsen, B. A. (2017). Cognitive function after status epilepticus versus after multiple generalized tonic-clonic seizures. *Epilepsy Research, 140*, 39–45.

Privitera, M., & Kim, K. K. (2010). Postictal language function. *Epilepsy and Behavior, 19*(2), 140–145.

Pugh, R., Vaughan, D. N., Jackson, G. D., Ponsford, J., & Tailby, C. (2024a). Cognitive and psychological dysfunction is present after a first seizure, prior to epilepsy diagnosis and tretament at a first seizure clinic. *Epilepsia Open, 9*(2), 717–726.

Pugh, R., Vaughan, D. N., Jackson, G. D., Ponsford, J., & Tailby, C. (2024b). Memory compromise at extended delays in people withnew-onset epilepsy. *Epilepsia Open, 9*(5), 1621–2005.
Quigg, M. (2016). Circadian and ultradian patterns of epileptiform discharges differ by seizure-onset location during long-term ambulatory intracranial monitoring. *Epilepsia, 57*(9), 1495–1502.
Quon, R. J., Mazanec, M. T., Schmidt, S. S., Andrew, A. S., Roth, R. M., MacKenzie, T. A., Sajatovic, M., Spruill, T., & Jobst, B. C. (2020). Antiepileptic drug effects on subjective and objective cognition. *Epilepsy and Behavior, 104*, 106906.
Raatikainen, M., Kälviäinen, R., Jutila, L., & Äikiä, M. (2020). Cognitive functioning in new-onset juvenile myoclonic epilepsy. *Epilepsy and Behavior, 106*, 107015.
Raga, S., Specchio, N., Rheims, S., & Wilmshurst, J. M. (2021). Developmental and epileptic encephalopathies: Recognition and approahces to care. *Epileptic Disorders, 23*(1), 40–52.
Raghu, A. L. B., Lau, J., Stern, M. A., Faraj, R. R., Isbaine, F., Grogan, D., Bullinger, K., Roth, R. W., Dickey, A. S., Wllie, J. T., Drane, D. L., & Gross, R. E. (in press). The surgical learning curve for successful stereotactic laser amygdalohippocampotomy and surgical strategies to rescue failures: A single-Centre cohort study. *Epilepsia*.
Ramantani, G., Kadish, N. E., Brandt, A., Strobl, K., Stathi, A., Wiegand, G., Schubert-Bast, S., Mayer, H., Wagner, N., Korinthenberg, R., Stephani, U., van Velthoven, V., Zentner, J., Schulze-Bonhage, A., & Bast, A. (2013). Siezure control and developmental trajectories after hemispherotomy for refractory epilepsy in childhood and adolescence. *Epilepsia, 54*(6), 1046–1055.
Rapport, L. J., Millis, S. R., & Bonello, P. J. (1998). Validation of the Warrington theory of visual processing and the visual object and space perception battery. *Journal of Clinical and Experimental Neuropsychology, 20*, 211–220.
Rasmussen, H. (1983). Hemispherectomy for seizures revisited. *The Canadian Journal of Neurological Sciences, 10*(2), 71–78.
Rausch, R. (2006). Integrative neuropsychology in the preoperative workup of the epilepsy surgery patient. In J. W. Miller & D. L. Silbergeld (Eds.), *Epilepsy surgery: Principles and controversies* (pp. 183–199). Taylor & Francis.
Rausch, R., & Babb, T. L. (1993). Hippocampal neuron loss and memory scores before and after temporal lobe surgery for epilepsy. *Archives of Neurology, 50*(8), 812–817.
Regis, J., Bartolomei, F., Rey, M., Genton, P., Dravet, C., Semah, F., Gastaut, J. L., & Chauvel, P. (1999). Gamma knife surgery for mesial temporal lobe epilepsy. *Epilepsia, 40*, 1551–1556.
Reimers, A., Helmstaedter, C., Elger, C. E., Pitsch, J., Hamed, M., Becker, A. J., & Witt, J. A. (2022). Neuropathological insights into unexpected cognitive decline in epilepsy. *Annals of Neurology, 93*(3), 536–550.
Reitan, R. M., & Wolfson, D. (1985). *The Halstead-Reitan neuropsychological test battery: Theory and interpretation*. Neuropsychology Press.
Ren, Y., Pan, L., Du, X., Hou, Y., Li, X., & Song, Y. (2020). Functional brain network mechanism of executive control dysfunction in temporal lobe epilepsy. *BMC Neurology, 20*(1), 137.
Rey, A. (1941). L'examen psychologique dans les cas d'encephalopathie traumatique. *Archives of Psychologie, 28*, 21.
Reyes, A., Paul, B. M., Marshall, A., Chang, Y.-H., Bahrami, N., Kansal, L., Iragui, V. J., Tecoma, E. S., Gollan, T. H., & McDonald, C. R. (2018). Does bilingualism increase brain or cognitive reserve in patients with temporal lobe epilepsy? *Epilepsia, 59*, 1037–1047.
Reyes, A., Kaestner, E., Bahrami, N., Balachandra, A., Hegde, M., Paul, B. M., Hermann, B., & McDonald, C. R. (2019). Cognitive phenotypes in temporal lobe epilepsy are associated with distinct patterns of white matter network abnormalities. *Neurology, 92*(17), e1957–e1968.
Reyes, A., Schneider, A. L. C., Kucharska-Newton, A. M., Gottesman, R. F., Johnson, E. L., & McDonald, C. R. (2023). Cognitive phenotypes in late-onset epilepsy: Results from the atherosclerosis risk in communities study. *Frontiers in Neurology, 14*, 1230368.
Ribot, R., Ouyang, B., & Kanner, A. M. (2017). The impact of antidepressants on seizure frequency and depressive and anxiety disorders of patients with epilepsy: Is it worth investigating? *Epilepsy and Behavior, 70*, 5–9.

Riley, J. D., Franklin, D. L., Choi, V., Kim, R. C., Binder, D. K., Cramer, S. C., & Lin, J. J. (2010). Altered white matter integrity in temporal lobe epilepsy: Association with cognitive and clinical profiles. *Epilepsia, 51*(4), 536–545.

Riney, K., Bogacz, A., Somerville, E., Hirsch, E., Nabbbout, R., Scheffer, I. E., Zuberi, S. M., Alsaadi, T., Jain, S., French, J., Specchio, N., Trinka, E., Wiebe, S., Auvin, S., Caral-Lim, L., Naidoo, A., Perucca, E., Moshe, S. L., Wirrell, E. C., & Tinuper, P. (2022). International league against Epilepsy classification and definition of epilepsy syndromes with onset at a variable age: Position statement by the ILAE task Force of Nosoly and definitions. *Epilepsia, 63*(6), 1443–1474.

Risse, G. L. (2006). Cognitive outcomes in patients with frontal lobe epilepsy. *Epilepsia, 2*, 87–89.

Robertson, M. M. (1997). Suicide, parasuicide, and epilepsy. In J. Engel & T. A. Pedley (Eds.), *Epilepsy: A comprehensive textbook* (pp. 2141–2151). Lippicott-Raven.

Robinson, R. O., Baird, G., Robinson, G., & Simonoff, E. (2001). Landau-Kleffner syndrome: Course and correlates with outcome. *Developmental Medicine and Child Neurology, 43*(4), 243–247.

Roger, E., Banjac, S., Thiebaut de Schotten, M., & Baciu, M. (2022). Missing links: The functional unification of language and memory (L∪M). *Neuroscience and Biobehavioral Reviews, 133*, 104489.

Royer, J., & Bernhardt, B. (2023). Bilingualism, epilepsy, and connectome resilience. *Neurology, 100*(18), 847–848.

Ruan, Y., Chen, L., She, D., Chung, Y., Ge, L., & Han, L. (2022). Ketogenic diet for epilepsy: An overview of systematic review and meta-analysis. *European Journal of Clinical Nutrition, 78*(9), 1234–1244.

Rudebeck, S. R., Filippini, N., & Lee, A. C. (2013). Can complex visual discrimination deficits in amnesia be attributed to the medial temporal lobe? An investigation into the effects of medial temporal lobe damage on brain connectivity. *Hippocampus, 23*(1), 7–13.

Rush, A. J., Marangell, L. B., Sackeim, H. A., George, M. S., Brannan, S. K., Davis, S. M., Howland, R., Kling, M. A., Rittberg, B. R., Burke, W. J., Rapaport, M. H., Zajecka, J., Nierenberg, A. A., Husain, M. M., Ginsberg, D., & Cooke, R. G. (2005). Vagus nerve stimulation for treatment-resistant depression: A randomized, controlled acute phase trial. *Biological Psychiatry, 58*(5), 347–354.

Russ, S. A., Larson, K., & Halfon, N. (2012). A national profile of childhood epilepsy and seizure disorder. *Pediatrics, 129*, 256–264.

Rutter, M., Graham, P., & Yule, W. (1970). *A neuropsychiatric study in childhood. Clinics in developmental medicine Nos. 35/36*. S.I.M.P./William Heineman Medical Books.

Sabsevitz, D. S., Swanson, S. J., Hammeke, T. A., Spanaki, M. V., Possing, E. T., Morris, G. L., 3rd, Mueller, W. M., & Binder, J. R. (2003). Use of preoperative functional neuroimaging to predict language deficits from epilepsy surgery. *Neurology, 60*(11), 1788–1792.

Sackeim, H. A., Rush, A. J., George, M. S., Marangell, L. B., Husain, M. D., Nahas, Z., Johnson, C. R., Seidman, S., Giller, C., Haines, S., Simpson, R. K., & Goodman, R. R. (2001). Vagus nerve stimulation (VNS) for treatment-resistant depression: Efficacy, side effects, and predictors of outcome. *Neuropsychopharmacology, 25*, 713–728.

Sadleir, L. G., Farrell, K., Smith, S., Connolly, M. B., & Scheffer, I. E. (2006). Electroclinical features of absence seizures in childhood absence epilepsy. *Neurology, 67*(3), 413–418.

Salanova, V., Andermann, F., Olivier, A., Rasmussen, T., & Quesney, L. F. (1992). Occipital lobe epilepsy: Electroclinical manifestations, electrocorticography, cortical stimulation and outcome in 42 patients treated between 1930 and 1991. Surgery of occipital lobe epilepsy. *Brain, 115*, 1655–1680.

Salanova, V., Andermann, F., Rasmussen, T., Olivier, A., & Quesney, L. F. (1995). Parietal lobe epilepsy: Clinical manifestations and outcomes in 82 patients treated surgically between 1929 and 1988. *Brain, 118*, 607–627.

Salanova, V., Sperling, M. R., Gross, R. E., Irwin, C. P., Vollhaber, J. A., Giftakis, J. E., Fisher, R. S., & SANTE Study Group. (2021). The SANTÉ study at 10 years of follow-up: Effectiveness, safety, and sudden unexpected death in epilepsy. *Epilepsia, 62*(6), 1306–1317.

Saling, M. M. (2009). Verbal memory in mesial temporal lobe epilepsy: Beyond material specificity. *Brain, 132*, 570–582.

Salvato, G., Scarpa, P., Francione, S., Mai, R., Tassi, L., Scarano, E., Lo Russo, G., & Bottini, G. (2016). Declarative long-term memory and the mesial temporal lobe: Insights from a 5-year postsurgery follow-up study on refractory temporal lobe epilepsy. *Epilepsy and Behavior, 64*, 102–109.

Santana, M. T. C. G., Jackowski, A. P., da Silva, H. H., Caboclo, L. O. S. F., Centeno, R. S., Bressan, R. A., Carrete, H. J., & Yacubian, E. M. T. (2010). Auras and clinical features in temporal lobe epilepsy: A new approach on the basis of voxel-based morphometry. *Epilepsy Research, 89*(2–3), 327–338.

Santangelo, G., Trojano, L., Vitale, C., Improta, I., Alineri, I., Meo, R., & Bilo, L. (2017). Cognitive dysfunctions in occipital lobe epilepsy compared to temporal lobe epilepsy. *Journal of Neuropsychology, 11*(2), 277–290.

Sarkis, R. A., McGinnis, S., Rushia, S. N., Park, S., Ansari, E. E., & Willment, K. C. (2018). Growing older with drug-resistant epilepsy: Cognitive and psychosocial outcomes. *Journal of Neurology, 265*(5), 1059–1064.

Sass, K. J., Spencer, D. D., Kim, J. H., Westerveld, M., Novelly, R. A., & Lencz, T. (1990). Verbal memory impairment correlates with hippocampal pyramidal cell density. *Neurology, 40*(11), 1694–1697.

Sass, K. J., Sass, A., Westerveld, M., Lencz, T., Novelly, R. A., Kim, J. H., & Spencer, D. D. (1992). Specificity in the correlation of verbal memory and hippocampal neuron loss: Dissociation of memory, language, and verbal intellectual ability. *Journal of Clinical and Experimental Neuropsychology, 14*(5), 662–672.

Satz, P., Strauss, E., Hunter, M., & Wada, J. (1994). Re-examination of the crowding hypothesis: Effects of age of onset. *Neuropsychology, 8*(2), 255–262.

Savic, I., Seitz, R. J., & Pauli, S. (1998). Brain distortions in patients with primarily generalized tonic-clonic seizures. *Epilepsia, 39*(4), 364–370.

Savqi, S., Katz, A., Marks, D. A., & Spencer, S. S. (1992). Frontal lobe partial seizures and psychogenic seizures: Comparison of clinical and ictal characteristics. *Neurology, 42*(7), 1274–1277.

Sawrie, S. M., Chelune, G. J., Naugles, R. I., & Luders, H. O. (1996). Empirical methods for assessing meaningful neuropsychological change following epilepsy surgery. *Journal of the International Neuropsychological Society, 2*(6), 556–564.

Sawrie, S. M., Martin, R. C., Gilliam, F. G., Roth, D. L., Faught, E., & Kuzniecky, R. (1998). Contribution of neuropsychological data to the prediction of temporal lobe epilepsy surgery outcome. *Epilepsia, 39*(3), 319–325.

Sawrie, S. M., Martin, R. C., Gilliam, F. G., Faught, E., Maton, B., Hugg, J. W., Bush, N., Sinclair, K., & Kuzniecky, R. (2000). Visual confrontation naming and hippocampal function: A neural network study using quantitative 1H magnetic resonance spectroscopy. *Brain, 123*, 770–780.

Sawrie, S. M., Martin, R. C., Gilliam, F., Knowlton, R., Faught, E., & Kuzniecky, R. (2001). Verbal retention lateralizes patients with unilateral temporal lobe epilepsy and bilateral hippocampal atrophy. *Epilepsia, 42*(5), 651–659.

Saykin, A. J., Stafiniak, P., Robinson, L. J., Flannery, K. A., Gur, R. C., O'Connor, M. J., & Sperling, M. R. (1995). Language before and after temporal lobectomy: Specificity of acute changes and relation to early risk factors. *Epilepsia, 33*(11), 1071–1077.

Scheffer, I. E., Berkovic, S., Capovilla, G., Connolly, M. B., French, J., Guilhoto, L., Hirsch, E., Jain, S., Mathern, G. W., Moshe, S. L., Nordil, D. R., Perucca, E., Tomson, T., Wiebe, S., Zhang, Y. H., & Zuberi, S. M. (2017). ILAE classification of the epilepsies: Position paper of the ILAE Commissionn for classification and terminology. *Epilepsia, 58*(4), 512–521.

Schmidt, M. (1996). *Rey auditory verbal learning test: A handbook*. Western Psychological Association.

Schraegle, W. A., Nussbaum, N. L., DeLeon, R. C., & Titus, J. B. (2022). Neuropsychological phenotypes in pediatric temporal lobe epilepsy. *Journal of the International Neuropsychological Society, 28*, 916–925.

Schramm, J., Behrens, E., & Entzian, W. (1995). Hemispherical deafferentation: An alternative to functional hemispherectomy. *Neurosurgery, 36*(3), 509–516.
Schrank, F. A., Mather, N., & McGrew, K. S. (2014). *Woodcock-Johnson IV tests of achievement.* Riverside.
Schusse, C. M., Smith, K., & Drees, C. (2018). Outcomes after hemispherectomy in adult patients with intractable epilepsy: Institutional experience and systematic review of the literature. *Journal of Neurosurgery, 128*(3), 853–861.
Scoville, W. B., & Milner, B. (1957). Loss of recent memory after bilateral hippocampal lesions. *Journal of Neuropsychiatry and Clinical Neurosciences, 12*(1), 103–113.
Seidenberg, M., Hermann, B., Wyler, A. R., Davies, K., Dohan, F. C., & Leveroni, C. (1998). Neuropsychological outcome following anterior temporal lobectomy in patients with and without the syndrome of mesial temporal lobe epilepsy. *Neuropsychology, 12*(2), 303–316.
Seidenberg, M., Griffith, R., Sabsevitz, D., Moran, M., Haltiner, A., Bell, B., Swanson, S., Hammeke, T., & Hermann, B. (2002). Recognition and identification of famous faces in patients with unilateral temporal lobe epilepsy. *Neuropsychologia, 40*(4), 446–456. http://www.sciencedirect.com/science/article/B6T0D-448BDT6-T/2/08876cfc2b9646b1c2d9274600c5055d
Seidenberg, M., Pulsipher, D. T., & Hermann, B. (2007). Cognitive progression in epilepsy. *Neuropsychology Review, 17*(4), 445–454.
Semendeferi, K., Lu, A., Schenker, N., & Damasio, H. (2002). Humans and great apes share a large frontal cortex. *Nature Neuroscience, 5*, 272–276.
Sen, A., Capelli, V., & Husain, M. (2018). Cognition and dementia in older patients with epilepsy. *Brain, 141*(6), 1592–1608.
Shackleton, D. P., Trenite, D. G. A. K.-N., de Crain, A. J. M., Vanderbroucke, J. P., & Westendorp, R. G. J. (2003). Living with epilepsy. Long-term prognosis and psychosocial outcomes. *Neurology, 61*, 64–70.
Shah, U., Rajeshree, S., Sahu, A., Kalika, M., Ravat, S., Reyes, A., Stasenko, A., Busch, R. M., Hermann, B. P., McDonald, C. R., & ILAE IC-CoDE Task Force. (2024). Cross-cultural application of the international classification of cognitive disorders in epilepsy cognitive phenotypes in people with temporal lobe epilepsy in India. *Epilepsia, 65*(8), 2386–2396.
Shallice, T. (2001). 'Theory of mind' and the prefrontal cortex. *Brain, 124*(Pt 3), 247–248.
Shamim, D., Cheng, J., Pearson, C., & Landazuri, P. (2021). Network radiofrequency ablation for drug resistant epilepsy. *Epilepsy & Behavior Reports, 16*, 100471.
Shegog, R., Bamps, Y. A., Patel, A., Kakacek, J., Escoffery, C., Johnson, E. K., & Ilozumba, U. O. (2013). Managing epilepsy well: Emerging e-tools for epilepsy self-management. *Epilepsy and Behavior, 29*(1), 133–140.
Shields, J., Greven, A. C. M., Shivamurthy, V. K. N., Matthews, R. E., McMahon, T., Laxpati, N. G., Alwaki, A., Drane, D. L., Isbaine, F., Willie, J. T., Bullinger, K., & Gross, R. E. (2023). SEEG-guided radiofrequency ablation of the epileptogenic zone as a treatment and predictor of future success of further surgical intervention. *Epilepsia, 64*(8), 2081–2093.
Shimizu, H., Suzuki, I., & Ishijima, B. (1989). Zygomatic approach for resection of mesial temporal epileptic focus. *Neurosurgery, 25*, 798–801.
Shinnar, R. C., Shinnar, S., Cnaan, A., Clark, P., Dlugos, D. J., Hirtz, D. G., Hu, F., Liu, C., Masur, D., Weiss, E. F., Glauser, T. A., & Childhood Absence Epilepsy Study Group. (2017). Pretreatment behavior and subsequent medication effects in childhood asence epilepsy. *Neurology, 89*(16), 1698–1706.
Siegel, A. M., & Williamson, P. D. (2000). Parietal lobe epilepsy. *Advances In Neurology, 84*, 189–199.
Silbergeld, D. L., & Ojemann, J. G. (1993). The tailored temporal lobectomy. *Neurosurgical Clinics of North America, 4*(2), 273–281.
Sillanpaa, M., Jalava, M., Kaleva, O., & Shinnar, S. (1998). Long-term prognosis of seizures with onset in childhood. *The New England Journal of Medicine, 338*(24), 1715–1722.

Slaght, S. J., Leresche, N., Deniau, J. M., Crunelli, V., & Charpier, S. (2002). Activity of thalamic reticular neurons during spontaneous genetically determined spike and wave discharges. *Journal of Neuroscience, 22*(6), 2323–2334.

Smith, W. G. (1905). A comparison of some mental and physical tests in their application to epileptic and to normal subjects. *British Journal of Psychology, 2*, 240–260.

Smith, A. (1973). Symbol digit modalities test. Western Psychological Services.

Snyder, K. M., Forseth, K. J., Donos, C., Fischer-Baum, S., Breier, J., & Tandon, N. (2023). The critical role of the ventral temporal lobe in naming. *Epilepsia, 54*(5), 1200–1213.

Soble, J. R., Eichstaedt, K. E., Waseem, H., Mattingly, M. L., Benbadis, S. R., Bozorg, A. M., Vale, F. L., & Schoenberg, M. R. (2014). Clinical utility of the Wechsler Memory Scale--Fourth Edition (WMS-IV) in predicting laterality of temporal lobe epilepsy among surgical candidates. *Epilepsy & Behavior, 41*, 232–237.

Society, A. E. (1986). Guidelines in EEG, 1-7 (revised 1985). *Journal of Clinical Neurophysiology, 3*, 131–168.

Sone, D., Sato, N., Shigemoto, Y., Behheshti, I., Kimura, Y., & Matsuda, H. (2024). Estimated disease progression trajectory of white matter disruption in unilateral temporal lobe epilepsy: A data-driven machine learning approach. *Brain Sciences, 14*(10), 992.

Song, J. M., Hahn, J., Kim, S. E., & Chang, M. J. (2017). Efficacy for treatment of infantile spasms: A systematic review. *Clinical Neuropharmacology, 40*(2), 63–84.

Specchio, N., Wirrell, E. C., Scheffer, I. E., Nabbout, R., Riney, K., Samia, P., Guerreiro, M., Gwer, S., Zuberi, S. M., Wilmshurst, J. M., Yozawitz, E., Pressler, R., Hirsch, E., Wiebe, S., Cross, H. J., Perucca, E., Moshe, S. L., Tinuper, P., & Auvin, S. (2022). International league against Epilepsy classification and definition of epilepsy syndromes with onnset in childhood: Position paper by the ILAE task Force on nosology and definitions. *Epilepsia, 63*(6), 1398–1442.

Spencer, D. D., Spencer, S. S., Mattson, R. H., Williamson, P., & Novelly, R. A. (1984). Access to the posterior medial temporal loe structures in thhe surgical treatment of temporal lobe epilepsy. *Neurosurgery, 15*(5), 667–671.

Spencer, S. S., Schramm, J., Wyler, A., O'Connor, M., Orbach, D., Krauss, G., Sperling, M., Devinsky, O., Elger, C., Lesser, R., Mulligan, L., & Westerveld, M. (2002). Multiple subpial transection for intractable parital epilepsy: An international meta-analysis. *Epilepsia, 43*, 141–145.

Sperling, M. R., Gross, R. E., Alvarez, G. E., McKhann, G. M., Salanova, V., & Gilmore, J. (2020). Stereotactic laser ablation for mesial temporal lobe epilepsy: A prospective, multicenter, single-arm study. *Epilepsia, 61*(6), 1183–1189.

Spielberger, C. D., Gorsuch, R. L., Lushene, R., Vagg, P. R., & Jacobs, G. A. (1983). *Manual for the state-trait anxiety inventory*. Consulting Psychologists Press.

Spiers, H. J., Burgess, N., Maguire, E. A., Baxendale, S. A., Hartley, T., Thompson, P. J., & O'Keefe, J. (2001). Unilateral temporal lobectomy patients show lateralized topographical and episodic memory deficits in a virtual town. *Brain, 124*, 2476–2489.

Stager, L., Szaflarski, J. P., & Fobian, A. D. (2021). One-year follow-up of treatment outcomes and patient opinions of retraining and control therapy (ReACT) for pediatric functional seizures. *Epilepsy & Behavior Reports, 16*, 100503.

Stager, L. M., Mueller, C., Morriss, S., Szaflarski, J., & Fobian, A. D. (2023). Sense of control, selective attention, cognitive inhibition, and psychosocial outcomes after retraining and control therapy (ReACT) in pediatric functional seizures. *Epilepsy & Behavior, 142*, 109143.

Stasenko, A., Schadler, A., Kaestner, E., Reyes, A., Diaz-Santos, M., Polczynska, M., & McDonald, C. R. (2022). Can bilingualism increase neuroplasticity of language networks in epilepsy? *Epilepsy Research, 182*, 106893.

Stasenko, A., Kaestner, E., Arienzo, D., Schadler, A., Reyes, A., Shih, J. J., Helm, J. L., Potczynska, M., & McDonald, C. R. (2023). Bilingualism and structural network organization in temporal lobe epilepsy. *Neurology, 100*(18), e1887–e1889.

Steck, P. H. (2005). A revision of A. L. Benton's visual retention test (BVRT) in two parallel forms. *Archives Of Clinical Neuropsychology, 20*(3), 409–416.

Steiger, B. K., & Jokeit, H. (2017). Why epilepsy challenges social life. *Seizure, 44*, 194–198.

Strauss, E., Hunter, M., & Wada, J. (1995). Risk factors for cognitive impairment in epilepsy. *Neuropsychology, 9*(4), 457–463.

Strine, T. W., Kobau, R., Chapman, D. P., Thurman, J., Price, P., & Balluz, L. S. (2005). Psychological distress, comorbidities, and health behaviors among U. S. Adults with seizures: Results from the 2002 National Health Interview Survey. *Epilepsia, 46*(7), 1133–1139.

Stroup, E. S., Langfit, J. T., Berg, M., McDermott, M., Pilcher, W., & Como, P. (2003). Predicting verbal memory decline following anterior temporal lobectomy. *Neurology, 60*, 1266–1273.

Stuss, D. T., Floden, D., Alexander, M. P., Levine, B., & Katz, D. (2001a). Stroop performance in focal lesion patients: Dissociation of processes and frontal lobe lesion location. *Neuropsychologia, 39*, 771–786.

Stuss, D. T., Bisschop, S. M., Alexander, M. P., Levine, B., Katz, D., & Izukawa, D. (2001b). The trail making test: A study in focal lesion patients. *Psychological Assessment, 13*(2), 230–239.

Subota, A., Jette, N., Josephson, C. B., McMillan, J., Keezer, M. R., Gonzalez-Izquierdo, A., & Holroyd-Leduc, J. (2021). Risk factors for dementia development, frailty, and mortality in older adults with epilepsy - A population-based analysis. *Epilepsy and Behavior, 120*, 108006.

Sun, F. T., & Morrell, M. J. (2014). The RNS system: Responsive cortical stimulation for the treatment of refractory partial epilepsy. *Expert Review of Medical Devices, 11*(6), 563–572.

Swinkels, W. A. M., Kuyk, J., van Dyck, R., & Spinhoven, P. (2005). Psychiatric comorbidity in epilepsy. *Epilepsy & Behavior, 7*(1), 37–50.

Sylvester, C.-Y. C., & Shimamura, A. P. (2002). Evidence for intact semantic representations in patients with frontal lobe lesions. *Neuropsychology, 16*(2), 197–207.

Tailby, C., Kowalczyk, M. A., & Jackson, G. D. (2017). Cognitive impairment in epilepsy: The role of reduced network flexibility. *Annals of Clinical and Translational Neurology, 5*(1), 29–40.

Takaya, S., Hanakawa, T., Hashikawa, K., Ikeda, A., Sawamoto, N., Nagamine, T., Ishizu, K., & Fukuyama, H. (2006). Prefrontal hypofunction in patients with mesial temporal lobe epilepsy. *Neurology, 67*(9), 1674–1676.

Tallarita, G. M., Parente, A., & Giovagnoli, A. R. (2023). The visuospatial pattern of temporal lobe epilepsy. *Epilepsy & Behavior, 140*, 109086.

Tani, A., & Adawi, N. (2024). Cognitive disorders, depression and anxiety in temporal lobe epilepsy: An overview. *Journal of Biosciences and Medicines, 12*, 77–93.

Tarkka, R., Paakko, E., Pyhtinene, J., Uhari, M., & Rantala, H. (2003). Febrile seizures and mesial temporal sclerosis: No association in a long-term follow-up study. *Neurology, 60*, 215–218.

Tavakol, S., Royer, J., Lowe, A. J., Bonilha, L., Tracy, J. I., Jackson, G. D., Duncan, J. S., Bernasconi, A., Bernasconi, N., & Bernhardt, B. C. (2019). Neuroimaging and connectomics of drug-resistant epilepsy at multiple scales: From focal lesions to macroscale networks. *Epilepsia, 60*(4), 593–604.

Taylor, J., Jacoby, A., baker, G. A., Marson, A. G., Ring, A., & Whitehead, M. (2011). Factors predictive of resilience and vulnerability in new-onset epilepsy. *Epilepsia, 52*(3), 610–618.

Taylor, P. N., Sinha, N., Wang, Y., Vos, S. B., de Tisi, J., Miserocchi, A., McEvoy, A. W., Winston, G. P., & Duncan, J. S. (2018). The impact of epilepsy surgery on the structural connectome and its relation to outcome. *Neuroimage: Clinical, 18*, 202–214.

Téllez-Zenteno, J. F., Hernández Ronquillo, L., Moien-Afshari, F., & Wiebe, S. (2010). Surgical outcomes in lesional and non-lesional epilepsy: A systematic review and meta-analysis. *Epilepsy Research, 89*, 310–318.

Thomas, C., Avidan, G., Humphreys, K., Jung, K., Gao, F., & Behrmann, M. (2009). Reduced structural connectivity in ventral visual cortex in congenital prosopagnosia. *Nature Neuroscience, 12*, 29–31.

Thompson, P. J., & Duncan, J. S. (2005). Cognitive decline in severe intractable epilepsy. *Epilepsia, 46*(11), 1780–1787.

Thompson, A. W., Hantke, N., Phatak, V., & Chaytor, N. (2010). The personality assessment inventory as a tool for diagnosing psychogenic nonepileptic seizures. *Epilepsia, 51*, 161–164.

Thurman, D. J., Kobau, R., Luo, Y. H., Helmers, S. L., & Zack, M. M. (2016). Health-care access among adults with epilepsy: The U.S. National Health Interview Survey, 2010-2013. *Epilepsy & Behavior, 55*, 184–188.

Tinuper, P., Plazzi, G., Provini, F., Cerullo, A., Leonardi, M., Agati, R., Righini, A., & Montagna, P. (1992). Facial asymmetry in partial epilepsies. *Epilepsia, 33*(6), 1097–1100.

Tomson, T., Nashef, L., & Ryvlin, P. (2008). Sudden unexpected death in epilepsy: Current knowledge and future directions. *Lancet Neurology, 7*(11), 1021–1031.

Tovar-Spinoza, Z. S., Ochi, A., Rutka, J. T., Go, C., & Otsubo, H. (2008). The role of magnetoencephalography in epilepsy surgery. *Neurosurgical Focus, 25*(3), 1–6.

Traianou, A., Patrikelis, P., Kosmidis, M. H., Kimiskidis, V. K., & Gatzonis, S. (2019). The neuropsychological profile of parietal and occipital lobe epilepsy. *Epilepsy and Behavior, 94*, 137–143.

Tremont, G., Halpert, S., Javorsky, D. J., & Stern, R. A. (2000). Differential impact of executive dysfunction on verbal list learning and story recall. *The Clinical Neuropsychologist, 14*(3), 295–302.

Troster, A. I., Warmflash, V., Osorio, I., Paolo, A. M., Alexander, L. J., & Barr, W. B. (1995, May). The roles of semantic networks and search efficiency in verbal fluency performance in intractable temporal lobe epilepsy. *Epilepsy Research, 21*(1), 19–26. http://www.sciencedirect.com/science/article/B6T34-3YCM2V6-N/2/f07cfdf935f067c5a8c828470883dba8

Tucha, O., Smely, C., & Lange, K. W. (1999). Verbal and figural fluency in patients with mass lesions of the left or right frontal lobes. *Journal of Clinical and Experimental Neuropsychology, 21*(2), 229–236.

Umeda, S., Nagumo, Y., & Kato, M. (2006). Dissociative contributions of medial temporal and frontal regions to prospective remembering. *Review of Neuroscience, 17*, 267–278.

Upton, D., & Thompson, P. J. (1996). General neuropsychological characteristics of frontal lobe epilepsy. *Epilepsy Research, 23*, 169–177.

Upton, D., & Thompson, P. J. (1999). Twenty questions task and frontal lobe dysfunction. *Archives of Clinical Neuropsychology, 14*(2), 203–216.

Valente, K. D., Rzezak, P., Moschetta, S. P., de Vincentiis, S., Coan, A. C., & Guerreiro, C. A. (2016). Delineating behavioral and cognitive phenotypes in juvenile myoclonic epilepsy: Are we missing the forest for the trees? *Epilepsy & Behavior, 54*, 95–99.

Van Buren, J. M. (1963). The abdominal aura: A study of abdominal sensations occurring in epilepsy and produced by depth stimulation. *Electroencephalography and Clinical Neurophysiology, 15*, 1–19.

van Lanen, R. H. G. J., Colon, A. J., Wiggins, C. J., Hoeberigs, M. C., Hoogland, G., Roebroeck, A., Ivanov, D., Poser, B. A., Rouhl, R. P. W., Hofman, P. A. M., Jansen, J. F. A., Backes, W., Rijkers, K., & Schijns, O. E. M. G. (2021). Ultra-high field magnetic resonance imaging in human epilepsy: A systematic review. *Neuroimage: Clinical, 30*, 102602.

Van Passchen, W., Dupont, P., Sunaert, S., Goffin, K., & Van Laere, K. (2007). The use of SPECT and PET in routine clinical practice in epilepsy. *Current Opinion in Neurology, 20*(2), 194–202.

Vannest, J., Szaflarski, J. P., Privitera, M. D., Schefft, B. K., & Holland, S. K. (2008). Medical temporal fMRI activation reflects memory lateralization and memory performance in patients with epilepsy. *Epilepsy & Behavior, 12*(3), 410–418.

Vannest, J., Tenney, J. R., Gelineau-Morel, R., Maloney, T., & Glauser, T. A. (2015). Cognitive and behavioral outcomes in benign childhood epilepsy with centrotemporal spikes. *Epilepsy & Behavior, 45*, 85–91.

Vaughan, D. N., Raffelt, D., Curwood, E., Tasi, M. H., Tournier, J. D., Connelly, A., & Jackson, G. D. (2017). Tract-specific atrophy in focal epilepsy: Disease, genetics, or seizures? *Annals Of Neurology, 81*(2), 240–250.

Velis, D., Plouin, P., Gotman, J., da Silva, F. L., & Neurophysiology, I. D. S. O. (2007). Recommendations regarding the requirements and applications for long-term recordings in epilepsy. *Epilepsia, 48*(2), 379–384.

Verche, E., San Luis, C., & Hernández, S. (2018). Neuropsychology of frontal lobe epilepsy in children and adults: Systematic review and meta-analysis. *Epilepsy & Behavior, 88*, 15–20.

Verotti, A., Filippi, M., Matricardi, S., Agostinelli, M. F., & Gobbi, G. (2014). Memory impairment in benign Epilepsy with centrotemporal spike (BECTS): A growing suspicion. *Brain and Cognition, 84*(1), 123–131.

Vetkas, A., Fomenko, A., Germann, J., Sarica, C., Lorio-MOrin, C., Samuel, N., Yamamoto, K., Milano, V., Cheyuo, C., Zemmar, A., Elias, G., Boutet, A., Loh, A., Santyr, B., Gwun, D., Tasserie, J., Kalia, S. K., & Lozano, A. M. (2022). Deep brain stimulation targets in epilepsy: Systematic review and metaanalysis of anterior and centromedian thalamic nnuclei and hippocampus. *Epilepsia, 63*(3), 513–524.

Vickrey, B., Perrine, K., Hays, R., Hermann, B. P., Cramer, J. A., Meador, K. J., & Devinsky, O. (1993). *Quality of life in epilepsy QOLIE-31 (version 1.0): Scoring manual and patient inventory*. RAND.

Villemure, J. G., & Daniel, R. T. (2006). Peri-insular hemisphherotomy in paediatric epilepsy. *Childs Nerovus System, 22*, 967–981.

Voets, N. L., Adcock, J. E., Stacey, R., Hart, Y., Carpenter, K., Matthews, P. M., & Beckmann, C. F. (2009). Functional and structural changes in memory network associated with left temporal lobe epilepsy. *Human Brain Mapping, 30*(12), 4070–4081.

Voets, N. L., Alvarez, I., Qiu, D., Leatherday, C., Willie, J. T., Sotiropoulos, S., Gleichgerrcht, E., Bonilha, L., Pedersen, N. P., Kadom, N., Saindane, A. M., Gross, R. E., & Drane, D. L. (2019). Mechanisms and risk factors contributing to visual field deficits following stereotactic laser amygdalohippocampotomy. *Stereotactic and Functional Neurosurgery, 97*, 255–265.

Vogt, V. L., Aikia, M., del Barrio, A., Boon, P., Borbely, C., Bran, E., Braun, K., Carette, E., Clark, M., Cross, J. H., Dimova, P., Fabo, D., Foroglou, N., Francione, S., Gersamia, A., Gil-Nagel, A., Guekht, A., Harrison, S., Hecimovic, H., Heminghyt, E., Hirsch, E., Javurkova, A., Kalviainen, R., Kavan, N., Kelemen, A., Kimiskidis, V. K., Kirschner, M., Kleitz, C., Kobulashvili, T., Kosmidis, M. H., Kurtish, S. Y., Lesourd, M., Ljunggren, S., Lossius, M. I., Malmgren, K., Mamenisklene, R., Martin-Sanfilippo, P., Marusic, P., Miatton, M., Ozkara, C., Hanoglu, L., Keskinkilic, C., Yeni, N., Aysal, F., Uzan, M., Ozyurt, E., Karaagac, N., Pelle, F., Rubbboli, G., Rudebeck, S., Ryvlin, P., van Schooneveld, M., Schmid, E., Schmidt, P. M., Seeck, M., Steinhoff, B. J., Shavel-Hessop, S., Tarta-Arsene, O., Trinka, E., Viggedal, G., Wending, A. S., Witt, J. A., Helmstaedter, C., & E-PILEPSY consortium. (2017). Current standards of neuropsychological assessment in epilepsy surgery centers across Europe. *Epilepsia, 58*(3), 345–355.

Vu, L. C., Piccenna, L., Kwan, P., & O'Brien, T. J. (2018). New-onset epilepsy in the elderly. *British Journal of Clinical Pharmacology, 84*(10), 2208–2217.

Wada, J., & Rasmussen, T. (1960). Intracarotid injection of sodium amytal for the lateralization of cerebral speech dominance: Experimental and clinical observations. *Journal of Neurosurgery, 17*, 266–282.

Wang, L., Mathews, G. C., Whetsell, W. O., & Abou-Khalil, B. (2008). Hypermotor seizures in patients with temporal pole lesions. *Epilepsy Research, 82*(1), 93–98.

Wang, W. H., Liou, H. H., Chen, C. C., Chiu, M. J., Chen, T. F., Cheng, T. W., & Hua, M. S. (2011). Neuropsychological performance and seizure-related risk factors in patients with temporal lobe epilepsy: A retrospective cross-sectional study. *Epilepsy and Behavior, 22*(4), 728–734.

Warrington, E. K., & James, M. (1991). *Visual object and space perception battery*. Thames Valley Company.

Waseem, H., Osborn, K. E., Schoenberg, M. R., Kelley, V., Bozong, A. M., Cabello, D., Benbadis, S. R., & Vale, F. L. (2015). Laser ablation therapy: An alternative treatment for medically resistant mesial temporal lobe epilepsy after age 50. *Epilepsy & Behavior, 51*, 152–157.

Wasterlain, C. G., Fujikawa, D. G., Penix, L., & Sankar, R. (1993). Pathophysiological mechanisms of brain damage from status epilepticus. *Epilepsia, 34*, S37–S53.

Weber, B., Fliessbach, K., Lange, N., Kugler, F., & Elger, C. E. (2007). Material-specific memory processing is related to language dominance. *NeuroImage, 37*, 611–617.

Wechsler, D. (1997). *Wechsler memory scale* (3rd ed.). The Psychological Corporation.
Wechsler, D. (2009). *Wechsler memory scale - 4th edition (WMS-IV) technical and interpretive manual*. Pearson.
Wiebe, S., Blume, W. T., Girvin, J. P., & Eliasziw, M. (2001). Effectiveness and efficiency of surgery for temporal lobe Epilepsy group. A randomized, controlled trial of surgery for temporal-lobe epilepsy. *New England Journal of Medicine, 345*(5), 311–318.
Wieser, H. G., & Yasargil, M. G. (1982). Selective amygdalohippocampectomy as a surgical treatment of mesiobasal limbic epilepsy. *Surgical Neurology, 17*, 445–457.
Wilde, N., Strauss, E., Chelune, G. J., Loring, D. W., Martin, R. C., Hermann, B. P., Sherman, E. M. S., & Hunter, M. (2001). WMS-III performance in patients with temporal lobe epilepsy: Group difference and individual classification. *Journal of the International Neuropsychological Society, 7*, 881–891.
Wilkinson, G. S., & Robertson, G. J. (2017). *Wide range achiement test professional manual* (5th ed.). Pearson.
Williamson, P., Spencer, D. D., Spencer, S. S., Novelly, R. A., & Mattson, R. H. (1985). Complex partial seizures of frontal lobe origin. *Annals of Neurology, 18*, 497–504.
Williamson, P., Thadani, V., Darcey, T., Spencer, D., Spencer, S., & Mattson, R. (1992). Occipital lobe epilepsy: Clinical characteristics, seizure spread patterns, and results of surgery. *Annals of Neurology, 31*(1), 3–13.
Willie, J. T., Laxpati, N. G., Drane, D. L., Gowda, A., Appin, C., Hao, C., Helmers, S. L., Saindane, A., Nour, S. G., & Gross, R. E. (2014). Real-time magnetic resonance-guided stereotactic laser amygdalohippocampotomy (SLAH) for mesial temporal lobe epilepsy. *Neurosurgery, 74*(6), 569–585.
Willie, J. T., Malcolm, J. G., Stern, M. A., Lowder, L. O., Neill, S. G., Cabaniss, B. T., Drane, D. L., & Gross, R. E. (2019). Stereotactic laser ablation is a safe and effective treatment for epileptogenic cerebral cavernous malformations. *Epilepsia, 60*(2), 220–232.
Wills, K. E., Gonzalez, H. F. J., Johnson, G. W., Haas, K. F., Morgan, V. L., Narasimhan, S., & Englot, D. J. (2021). People with mesial temporal lobe epilepsy have altered thalamo-occipital brain networks. *Epilepsy and Behavior, 115*, 107645.
Wilmshurst, J. M., Gaillard, W. D., Vinayan, K. P., Tsuchida, T. N., Plouin, P., Van Bogaert, P., Carrizosa, J., Elia, M., Craiu, D., Jovic, N. J., Nordli, D., Hirtz, D., Wong, V., Glauser, T., Mizrahi, E. M., & Cross, J. H. (2015). Summary of recommendations for the management of infantile seizures: Task froce report for thhe ILAE Commission of Pediatrics. *Epilepsia, 56*(8), 1185–1197.
Wirrell, E. C., Camfield, C. S., & Camfield, P. R. (1997). Long-term psychosocial outcome in typical absence epilepsy. Sometimes a wolf in sheeps' clothing. *Archives of Pediatric and Adolescent Medicine, 151*(2), 152–158.
Wirrell, E. C., Grossardt, B. R., Wong-Kisiel, L. C. L., & Nickels, K. C. (2011). Incidence and classification of new-onset epilepsy and epilepsy syndromes in children in Olmsted County, Minnesota from 1980 to 2004: A population-based study. *Epilepsy Research, 95*, 110–118.
Witt, J. A., & Helmstaedter, C. (2012). Should cognition be screened in new-onset epilepsies? A study in 247 untreated patients. *Neurology, 259*, 1727–1731.
Witt, J. A., Coras, R., Schramm, J., Becker, A. J., Elger, C. E., Blümcke, I., & Helmstaedter, C. (2015). Relevance of hippocampal integrity for memory outcome after surgical treatment of mesial temporal lobe epilepsy. *Journal of Neurology, 262*(10), 2214–2224.
Witt, J. A., Nass, R. D., Baumgartner, T., von Wrede, R., Elger, C. E., Surges, R., & Helmstaedter, C. (2020). Does the accumulated antiepileptic drug load in chronic epilepsy reflect disease severity? *Epilepsia, 61*(12), 2685–2695.
World Health Organization. (2019). *Epilepsy: A public health imperative: Summary*. World Health Organization. https://iris.who.int/hanndle/10665/325440
Wu, S., Issa, N. P., Rose, S. L., Haider, H. A., Nordli, D. R. J., Towle, V. L., Warnke, P. C., & Tao, J. K. (2024). Depth versus surface: A critical review of subdural and depth electrodes in intracranial electroencephalographic studies. *Epilepsia, 65*(7), 1868–1878.

Wyler, A. R. (2006). Multiple subpial transections: A review and arguments for use. In J. W. Miller & D. L. Silbergeld (Eds.), *Epilepsy surgery: Principles and controversies* (pp. 524–529). Taylor & Francis.

Yang, H., Wei, X., Huang, K., Wu, Z., Zhang, Q., Wen, S., Wang, Q., & Feng, L. (2024). Features of attention network impairment in patients with temporal lobe epilepsy: Evidence from eye-tracking and electroencephalogram. *Epilepsy and Behavior, 157*, 109887.

Yeo, B. T., Krienen, F. M., Chee, M. W., & Buckner, R. L. (2014). Estimations of segregation ad overlap of functional connectivity networks in the human cerebral cortex. *Neuroimage, 88*, 212–227.

Yoshitomi, S., Hamano, S. I., Hayashi, M., Sakuma, H., Hirose, S., Ishii, A., Imai, K., Jin, K., Kada, A., Kakita, A., Kato, M., Kawai, K., Kawakami, T., Kobayashi, K., Matsuishi, T., Matsuo, T., Nabatame, S., Okamoto, N., Ito, S., Okumura, A., Saito, A., Shiraishi, H., Shirozu, H., Saito, T., Sugano, H., Takahashi, Y., Yamamoto, H., Fukuyama, T., Kuki, I., & Inoue, Y. (2021). Current medico-psycho-social conditions of patients with West syndrome in Japan. *Epileptic Disorders, 23*(4), 579–589.

Zanaboni, M. P., Varesio, C., Pasca, L., Foti, A., Totaro, M., Celario, M., Provenzi, L., & De Giorgis, V. (2021). Systematic review of executive functions in children with self-limited epilepsy with centrotemporal spikes. *Epilepsy and Behavior, 123*, 108254.

Zangiabadi, N., Ladino, L. D., Sina, F., Orozco-Hernández, J. P., Carter, A., & Téllez-Zenteno, J. F. (2019). Deep brain stimulation and drug-resistant Epilepsy: A review of the literature. *Frontiers in Neurology, 10*, 601.

Zhang, D., Cui, X., Zheng, J., Zhang, S., Wang, M., Lu, W., Sang, L., & Li, W. (2022). A retrospective study of parietal lobe epilepsy: Functional anatomy annd surgical treatment. *Alternative Therapies in Health and Medicine, 28*(6), 138–143.

Ziaei, M., Arnold, C., Thompson, K., & Reutens, D. C. (2023). Social cognition in temporal and frontal lobe Epilepsy: Systematic review, meta-analysis, and clinical recommendations. *Journal of the International Neuropsychological Society, 29*(2), 205–229.

Zimmermann, N., Pontes, M., da Silva Fontana, R., D'Andrea Meira, I., Fonseca, R., & Delaere, F. J. (2024). The modified Ruche visuospatial learning test (RUCHE-M) for the assessment of visuospatial episodic memory in patients with temporal lobe epilepsy: Preliminary evidence for the investigation of memory binding. *Applied Neuropsychology, 31*(4), 412–427.

Zuberi, S. M., Wirrell, E., Yozawitz, E., Wilmshurst, J. M., Specchio, N., Riney, K., Pressler, R., Auvin, S., Samia, P., Hirsch, E., Galicchio, S., Triki, C., Snead, O. C., Wiebe, S., Cross, J. H., Tinuper, P., Scheffer, I. E., Perucaa, E., Moshe, S. L., N'aout, R., & Kaoua, B. (2022). ILAE classification and definition of epilepsy syndromes with onset in neonates and infants: Position statement by the ILAE task Force on nosology and definitions. *Epilepsia, 63*(6), 1349–1397.

Chapter 18
Neuropsychology of Psychogenic Nonepileptic Seizures

Daniel L. Drane, Erica Coady, David J. Williamson, Michele Price, John W. Miller, and Selim Benbadis

Key Points and Chapter Summary

- Video EEG is the gold standard for diagnosing psychogenic nonepileptic seizures (PNES); however, neuropsychological assessment can provide data helpful for diagnosis and planning treatment by assessing emotional and cognitive functioning and assisting in treatment planning and implementation.
- Contrary to clinical lore, epileptic seizures and PNES co-occur relatively infrequently (less than 15% of the time).
- There is no single psychological profile associated with PNES, and some of these patients are at higher risk for poor psychological and social adjustment.
- Psychogenic status epilepticus and reported histories of abuse are particularly poor prognostic signs.
- Performance validity testing can provide valuable guidance when drawing conclusions about the presence and severity of neuropsychological impairment, particularly in the absence of obvious neurodevelopmental delay or an objectively documented seizure or epileptiform discharges within the 24 hours preceding testing.
- An integrated treatment team with clear communication between neurology and mental health professionals is most likely to achieve success, and significant progress has been made in describing the types of medical and psychological treatments most likely to be beneficial.

D. L. Drane (✉)
Departments of Neurology and Pediatrics, Emory University School of Medicine, Atlanta, GA, USA

Department of Neurology, University of Washington School of Medicine, Seattle, WA, USA
e-mail: ddrane@emery.edu

M. R. Schoenberg, J. G. Scott (eds.), *The Little Black Book of Neuropsychology*,
https://doi.org/10.1007/978-3-032-07777-6_18

Overview

Nonepileptic seizures (NES) are operationally defined as episodes of involuntary movement, altered responsiveness or subjective experience that resemble epileptic seizures (ES), but are not accompanied by the abnormal electrical discharges in the brain characteristic of a seizure (Lesser, 1996; Reuber & Elger, 2003). When these episodes are caused by psychological processes, they have been termed psychogenic nonepileptic seizures (PNES), though this terminology has and continues to shift over time (see terminology discussion below).

Obtaining a better understanding of PNES and their clinical features is important for several reasons. Foremost, this diagnosis is typically associated with genuine suffering that in many cases can be alleviated. One recent study demonstrated that mortality rates for patients with PNES are similar to those of patients with epilepsy, with both significantly elevated compared to healthy individuals (Nightscales et al., 2020). In younger individuals with PNES in particular, there was a significantly increased risk of suicide. Improved diagnosis of PNES events is critical to developing appropriate treatments for this disorder. Some clinicians have suggested that 75–95% of patient with PNES show improvement in their condition if an accurate diagnosis can be established, with 19–52% of these patients seeing their PNES events resolve, at least in the short term (Ettinger, Devinsky, et al., 1999; Ettinger, Dhoon, et al., 1999; Hall-Patch et al., 2009; Walczak et al., 1995). The likelihood of improvement seems particularly good for those patients whose PNES began relatively recently, who have good social support and who have few comorbid psychiatric diagnoses (Kanner et al., 1999; Lempert & Schmidt, 1990; Massot-Tarrus et al., 2021).

PNES are costly as well. Considerable medical resources are directed to patients with PNES in the forms of emergency department visits, hospitalizations, physician visits, unnecessary diagnostic testing and pharmaceutical treatment. The lifetime cost of treating undiagnosed PNES may be equivalent to that of epilepsy, estimated

E. Coady
MINCEP Epilepsy Care, Minneapolis, MN, USA

D. J. Williamson
Ortho-McNeil Janssen Scientific Affairs, LLC, Mobile, AL, USA

M. Price
Department of Neurology, Emory University School of Medicine, Atlanta, GA, USA

J. W. Miller
Department of Neurology, University of Washington School of Medicine, Seattle, WA, USA

S. Benbadis
Department of Neurology, University of South Florida, Tampa, FL, USA

to be $231,432 per patient in 1995 (Begley et al., 2000). In fact, a more recent study from Denmark indicated that the cost of PNES exceeds that of epilepsy if both the direct and indirect costs of these disorders are considered, and estimated that the yearly cost of PNES was over 30 thousand pounds (Jennum et al., 2019).

Finally, another benefit of understanding patients with PNES is the unique perspective they provide in the development, diagnosis and treatment of medically unexplained symptom presentations [more recently termed functional neurological disorder (FND) for those symptoms constellations with neurobehavioral manifestations]. Within neuropsychology, such presentations are often seen in the context of litigation or other forms of compensation seeking. This is far less often the case in patients with PNES. Furthermore, there exists a "gold standard" diagnostic technology for PNES that simply does not exist for other such disorders. Thus, we are able to gain insight and understanding into the cause and course of PNES unobscured by confounds related to compensation-seeking or ambiguous diagnoses.

This chapter provides an overview of PNES, including diagnosis, semiology, prevalence, etiology, neuropsychological features, associated psychopathology and treatment. We encourage healthcare providers to approach these patients with care and respect. While PNES poses many challenges, neuropsychology is uniquely suited to help patients, their families and their healthcare providers.

Definition and Diagnosis

Terminology. Epilepsy has always been with us, appearing in Egyptian hieroglyphics earlier than 700 BC (Fisch & Olejniczak, 2001). Descriptions of psychogenic events also date back several centuries, with reports that Hippocrates and Aretaeus distinguished between epileptic and "hysterical" seizures (Gates & Erdahl, 1993; Massey, 1982). Since that time, descriptions of psychogenic based spells have been commonplace, and much effort has been made to distinguish PNES from epilepsy. For example, during the late 1800s, Gowers wrote about "hysteroid seizures," Charcot described "epileptiform hysteria" (Krumholz, 1999) and Freud described hysterical seizures (Freud, 1966). The term *pseudoseizure*, reportedly first coined by Liske and Forster (Liske & Forster, 1964), had been one of the more frequently used terms for PNES. The term PNES came to replace pseudoseizures, since the term *pseudo* is often accompanied by negative connotations, and PNES is both more specific and less pejorative.

Over the past 15 years, some have used labels for these events that dropped the word "seizure" in order to prevent diagnostic and etiological confusion on the part of both patients and healthcare providers, replacing it with attack, spell or episode (Brigo et al., 2015; Lowenberger et al., 2020). The use of the term *seizure* for all of these spells regardless of etiology (i.e., epileptic seizure vs. psychogenic nonepileptic seizure/attack vs. nonepileptic seizure of other physiological origin) has led to diagnostic confusion and is often misunderstood by patients and healthcare providers alike (Benbadis, 2020; Sethi, 2013). Patients will often go away from a feedback session still thinking they have some form of epileptic seizure. Similarly, healthcare providers with less direct experience with epilepsy are often reluctant to discontinue antiseizure medications (ASMs) due to their persisting concern that psychogenic "seizures" represent epilepsy. Due to such confusion, some clinicians refer to these events as "nonepileptic episodes" or functional seizures in discussions with patients (Asadi-Pooya et al., 2020; Benbadis, 2020; Bratanov et al., 2023). Most recently, the term functional seizures (FS) or dissociative seizures has been more generally accepted, although there is still no total consensus (Asadi-Pooya et al., 2020; Asadi-Pooya, Brigo, et al., 2023). This terminology fits into the functional neurological disorder (FND) nomenclature that has developed for all conditions considered to reflect psychogenic or conversion disorder processes, and for which there is now an international society bearing this name (Stone, 2016). We have chosen to continue to use the term PNES throughout this chapter, although we may see the term FS replace PNES over the next decade.

Diagnosis. While the gold standard for the diagnosis of PNES is continuous long-term video EEG (vEEG) that captures the patient's typical spell, clinicians and researchers still disagree over the behavioral component needed to diagnose an event as PNES, as well as the criteria used to rule out seizure activity (e.g., some clinicians will capture a PNES event during monitoring, yet assume the patient also had epilepsy based on self-report alone). These are important issues, as the mean time from onset to diagnosis of PNES is 7–8 years (Abubakr et al., 2003; ALKhaldi et al., 2024; Reuber et al., 2002; Spierer & Herskovitz, 2024), the exposure of patients to ASMs is not inconsequential (see Chap. 16, this volume for a review of ASMs' side effects), and diagnosing PNES in a timely manner can reduce healthcare costs, as well as improve prognosis and management of symptoms (Kamil et al., 2019).

Video EEG monitoring involves obtaining continuous EEG data synchronized with video recording of the patient's behavior for a span of 1–7 days in the hospital. There are numerous specialty epilepsy centers throughout the world that perform vEEG monitoring, and more centers are being established (Lado et al., 2024). ASMs are typically discontinued during monitoring, or the doses are reduced to increase the chance a patient will experience a clinical event in this controlled environment. If certain activities or stimuli are associated with eliciting a patient's typical event, an effort is sometimes made to recreate these conditions (e.g., exercise, sleep deprivation, photic stimulation).

Guidelines for diagnosing PNES events have been created by groups such as the International League Against Epilepsy (ILAE) (LaFrance Jr. et al., 2013). PNES has been classified in the fifth edition of the Diagnostic and Statistical Manual (DSM-5) as a functional neurological disorder, or conversion disorder, and as a somatic symptom disorder (Asadi-Pooya & Bazrafshan, 2021; Reuber & Brown, 2017). In practice, although tighter diagnostic criteria seem to be applied as the study of PNES matures, one still observes variability in classification practices. The main areas where some disagreement can be observed are how to treat (a) historical reports that sound like seizures (i.e., does one require EEG verification of all events that are diagnosed vs. accepting a historical description) and (b) cases in which the semiology of the seizure is minimal (e.g., subjective feeling) and which may not result in observable electrical changes on a scalp EEG.

Some epilepsy programs, such as the Regional Epilepsy Center at the University of Washington (UW) and others (Martin et al., 2003; Syed et al., 2008), have established conservative diagnostic criteria for PNES, such that events are not classified solely on the basis of subjective report (see Appendix A for the UW diagnostic classification scheme). The UW diagnostic criteria for PNES require (1) a definitive motor component (e.g., shaking or writhing of the torso or limbs, convulsive or rocking movements, head shaking) or (2) a discrete episode of unresponsiveness in the absence of epileptiform activity on EEG or another known physiological cause (e.g., syncope). An *indeterminant* spell, in contrast, is one in which the motor component was restricted to minor motor movements (e.g., myoclonic jerks) in a fully responsive individual, or the spell is evident only by the subjective patient report about his or her internal state (e.g., patient reports feeling "funny" or hot). The absence of epileptiform EEG activity in events of this type does not definitively demonstrate the event was a PNES. Frontal lobe seizures and focal aware seizures, for example, can result in both types of behavioral and subjective phenomena in the absence of epileptiform EEG abnormality on standard scalp monitoring (French, 1995) (see also Chap. 16 this volume). However, other epileptologists may disagree and classify these same events as PNES (Ahmed & Patil, 2024). The diagnostic decision in these less definitive spells should be influenced by the perceived risk of a misclassification error (e.g., potentially discontinuing ASMs in a patient with epilepsy misdiagnosed as having PNES or prescribing ASMs to a patient not having seizures).

Diagnosis of events based purely on patient self-report or even clinical observation of an actual event leaves room for error but still occurs in both clinical and research settings. While there are behavioral features of spells more commonly observed with either PNES or ES events (see Table 18.1 for a list), there are usually exceptions for both types of paroxysmal events. Deacon et al. found epileptologists were accurate at identifying seizures, but tended to over-diagnose PNES as ES when relying on clinical history alone rather than the results of vEEG monitoring in patients with suspected temporal lobe epilepsy (Deacon et al., 2003). One study having a variety of physician and allied health groups to make a diagnosis of epilepsy vs. PNES on the basis of video presentation only showed very wide-ranging accuracy, with epileptologists performing with 87.5% accuracy and emergency room physicians performing at 44.4% (Wasserman & Herskovitz, 2017). This suggests that training and education can improve one's ability to recognize PNES and ES events based on semiology but also highlights that the most experienced providers will continue to struggle with a significant number of cases. While a few behaviors (e.g., ictal stuttering) may be highly specific to PNES, they often do not occur with great frequency, and thus provide good specificity but lack diagnostic sensitivity (Cuthill & Espie, 2005; Hoerth et al., 2008). A few findings have shown promise for distinguishing between PNES and ES (e.g., ictal whispering, alteration in the event characteristics depending on the presence of bystanders), but have not been well studied or replicated (Chabolla & Shih, 2006; Syed et al., 2011). Leibetseder

Table 18.1 Usefulness of behavioral semiology to distinguish between psychogenic nonepileptic seizures (PNES) and epileptic seizures (ES)

Semiology/ Behavior	PNES	ES	Research studies (representative)
Tongue biting	Low frequency/ uncommon (self-report is much higher)	Common	Benbadis et al. (1995), Dufresne et al. (2019), Oliva et al. (2008) and Peguero et al. (1995)
Urinary incontinence	Rare (self-report is much higher)	Common	Oliva et al. (2008) and Peguero et al. (1995)
Weeping	Occasional	Very rare	Bergen and Ristanovic (1993) and Elzawahry et al. (2010)
Ictal stuttering	Uncommon	Absent	Vossler et al. (2004)
Ictal eye closure	Common (eyes closed for longer periods)	Rare (often brief when it occurs)	Chung et al. (2006), LaFrance Jr. et al. (2013) and Syed et al. (2008, 2011)
Ictal "cry"	Uncommon	Frequent (for GTCs only)	Elzawahry et al. (2010)
"Teddy bear sign"	Uncommon	Rare	Burneo et al. (2003)
Pelvic thrusting	Low frequency Rare in children	Uncommon (but occurs in frontal lobe seizures)	Devinsky et al. (1996), Geyer et al. (2000) and Szabo et al. (2012)
Self-injury	Low frequency to common	Common	Peguero et al. (1995)
Post-ictal drowsiness or confusion	Uncommon	Frequent	Ettinger, Devinsky, et al. (1999) and Syed et al. (2011)
Post-ictal whispering or partial motor responses to commands	High frequency (single study)	Absent	Chabolla and Shih (2006)
Long spell duration	Common	Rare	Devinsky et al. (1996), Saygi et al. (1992) and Seneviratne et al. (2017)
Situational onset	Common	Rare	Cragar et al. (2002)
Purposeful movements	Occasional	Very rare	Cragar et al. (2002)
Self-reported sleep events	Low frequency	Common	Duncan et al. (2004)
Sleep event during vEEG	Uncommon	Common	Bazil and Walczak (1997))
Abrupt onset	Low frequency	Common	Syed et al. (2011)
Preserved awareness			Syed et al. (2011)

(continued)

Table 18.1 (continued)

Semiology/ Behavior	PNES	ES	Research studies (representative)
Bystanders can intensify or alleviate	Frequent	Very rare	Syed et al. (2011)
Stereotypic behavior	Common	Common	Herskovitz (2017) and Seneviratne et al. (2010)
Déjà vu experiences	Frequent	Frequent (can be diagnostic for epilepsy if combined with epigastric aura and phenomena such as depersonalization)	Adachi et al. (2010)

Note: *PNES* psychogenic nonepileptic seizures; *ES* epileptic seizures; *vEEG* video EEG monitoring

and colleagues recently published a review article on distinguishing features, and we have included a table pulling from all available articles (Leibetseder et al., 2021).

The use of ambulatory EEG to diagnose PNES events has been greatly enhanced by the availability of cell phone video. Recent publications have demonstrated that the use of these technologies can extend the availability of diagnostic assessment to more individuals, especially those in rural areas lacking easy access to inpatient monitoring at a hospital (Amin et al., 2021; Benbadis, 2023). The goal for all event assessments is to capture a typical episode while obtaining an EEG and video recording for optimal diagnostic value, and these studies are useful only if the typical event is captured and/or clear epileptiform activity is recorded. The absence of evidence does not preclude the presence of either PNES or ES. Inpatient monitoring, when available, allows for a reduction or cessation of ASMs, constant monitoring in a controlled setting and the use of "induction techniques" (Benbadis, 2015; Benbadis et al., 2020). Induction techniques were established primarily for diagnostic and financial reasons to increase the chance of recording the patient's usual event. Induction techniques have included the use of hyperventilation, photic stimulation, saline injection, hypnosis or simple suggestion (Benbadis, 2001). However, a weakness of induction techniques is that the patient's typical spell may not occur (be monitored), and thus not provide an answer regarding PNES versus ES. Indeed, atypical spells occurred in 15% of patients with epilepsy and 8% of patients with PNES when a saline injection induction technique was used (Walczak et al., 1994). For diagnosis, it is imperative to capture the patient's typical event.

It is worth noting that a number of checklists and predictive algorithms have been developed over the last decade which have proved to be particularly useful for planning when seizure events have been difficult to capture. These have included checklists and questionnaires such as the Scale for Suspicion of PNES (SS-PNES) (Baroni et al., 2021), the Anxiety, Abuse, and Somatization Questionnaire (AASQ) (Trainor et al., 2020) and the Psychogenic Nonepileptic Seizure Diagnostic Suspicion Checklist (PNES-DSC) (Sobregrau et al., 2024). Proposed algorithms typically use demographic and disease-related factors to predict classification likelihood. For example, Emory University researchers developed the Differential Diagnosis of Epileptic Seizures vs. Functional Seizure Scale (DDEVSFS), identifying variables that were predictive of the results of diagnostic monitoring of more than 200 patients (Janocko et al., 2021). In the final model, eight predictors were identified as significant in differentiating ES from FS: normal electroencephalogram (−3 points), predisposing factors for FS (−3 points), increased number of comorbidities (−3 points), semiology suggestive of FS (−4 points), increased seizure frequency (−4 points), longer disease duration (+3 points), antiepileptic polypharmacy (+2 points) and compliance with ASMs (+3 points). A score calculator is available online for the DEFVSFS (http://ec2-3-89-59-25.compute-1.amazonaws.com/DDESVSFS/), and the authors can be contacted for updated link information over time (Fig. 18.1).

Key Points

Continuous vEEG of typical episode is the gold standard to diagnosis PNES, although ambulatory EEG bolstered with cell phone video can be an adequate alternative, especially for patients in rural areas.

Neuropsychological assessment, behavioral features of the ictal event, demographic variables and the presence of comorbid psychiatric features can play an adjunctive diagnostic role (particularly helpful when a typical event is not captured during vEEG monitoring).

Inducing PNES may be useful for diagnosis, but the typicality of the observed spell should always be ascertained before drawing diagnostic conclusions.

There are a number of paroxysmal events, some of which have been termed non-epileptic seizure of other physiological origin, which can appear like a seizure or PNES and involve a physiological rather than psychogenic etiology (see Chap. 16 for a review). Briefly, etiologies for paroxysmal spells not due to seizure include cardiovascular disorders, metabolic disturbances and movement disorders. These other paroxysmal events typically make up only a very small proportion of the referrals seen in specialty epilepsy centers.

Prevalence and Incidence

Variability in diagnostic decision rules for PNES events and epileptic seizures used by different medical providers throughout the world has contributed to confusion regarding the *incidence* (the rate of newly identified cases of a given condition over a specified time span), *prevalence* (the proportion of a population with it at a given time) and co-existence of these disorders. In addition, selection biases as well as small study samples have contributed to a wide variation in estimates of prevalence rates of PNES.

The easiest information to obtain regarding rates of PNES occurrence involves the number of patients with PNES identified by long-term vEEG monitoring. Based on all referrals to epilepsy centers, 10–50% of patients receive a diagnosis of PNES

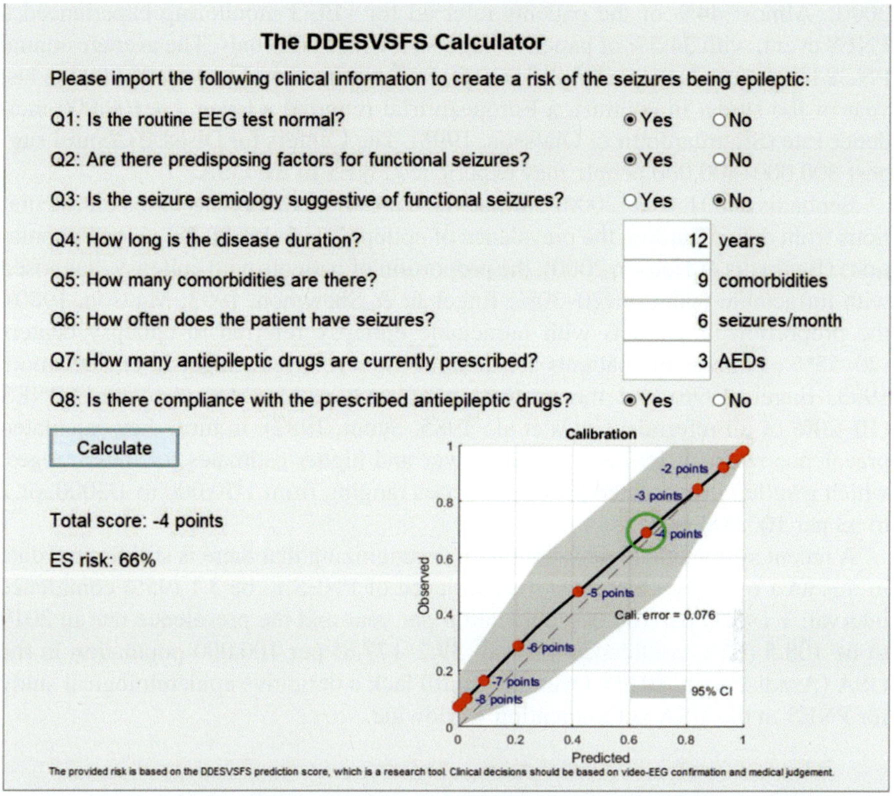

Fig. 18.1 Sample form for the online DDESVSFS Calculator for use in diagnosing PNES

Table 18.2 Prevalence of PNES, epilepsy and a single seizure

	PNES only	Epilepsy	Seizure (single)
Lifetime prevalence	Unknown	3%	9–10%
Point prevalence	0.0002–0.0003%	1%	0.6%
Incidence (per 100,000)	4.6	30	55

Note: *PNES* psychogenic nonepileptic seizures

(with or without comorbid epilepsy). The higher estimates have occurred in more recent years, as rates of 10–20% of patients referred for vEEG are found in reviews from the 1980s and 1990s (Gates et al., 1985; Scoot, 1982). Potential reasons for the variability in the prevalence include differences in referral patterns, different diagnostic criteria used, increased monitoring of patients with paroxysmal events and/or increased rates of this condition (Table 18.2).

Studies of PNES incidence have typically made estimates based on data obtained at specialty epilepsy centers. Szaflarski et al. (2000) estimated the 4-year incidence of PNES for one county in Ohio, USA, based on vEEG monitoring (Szaflarski et al.,

2000). Almost 44% of the patients referred for vEEG monitoring experienced a PNES event, with 34.5% of patients diagnosed with PNES only. The average annual PNES incidence was reported as 3.03/100,000, but increased to 4.6/100,000 the last year of the study. In contrast, a European trial reported a lower 1.4/100,000 incidence rate (Sigurdardottir & Olafsson, 1998). The Centers for Disease Control suggest 300,000–400,000 people may experience PNES in the USA.

Benbadis and Hauser (2000) estimated the prevalence of PNES based on calculations from data regarding the prevalence of epilepsy (0.5–1% of the general population) (Benbadis & Hauser, 2000), the proportion of patients with epilepsy diagnosed with intractable epilepsy (20–30%: Engel Jr. & Shewmon, 1993; Mattson, 1980), the proportion of patients with intractable epilepsy referred to epilepsy centers (20–55% of intractable patients are thought to be referred: Engel Jr. & Shewmon, 1993; Engel, 1996) and the proportion of such patients found to have PNES (10–20% of all referrals: Gates et al., 1985; Scoot, 1982). In turn, they calculated prevalence rates for PNES using the lower and higher estimates for these ranges, which resulted in estimated prevalence rates ranging from 1/50,000 to 1/3000, or 2 to 33 per 100,000 persons.

A recent systematic review, admittedly recognizing that there is still limited data in this area of study, calculated the incidence of PNES to be 3.1 (95% confidence interval: 1.1–5.1) per 100,000 population per year and the prevalence rate in 2019 to be 108.5 (95% confidence interval: 39.2–177.8) per 100,000 population in the USA (Asadi-Pooya, 2023). Overall, we still lack a definitive epidemiological study for PNES in the USA not to mention worldwide.

Key Points: PNES Prevalence Trends and Comorbidity

- As many as 50% of patients presenting to tertiary epilepsy centers in the USA experience PNES.
- 10–34% of patients referred for vEEG diagnosed as having PNES exclusively.
- The prevalence of PNES appears to have increased over the past few decades.

Prevalence of PNES/Epilepsy Co-Occurrence (CO)

Determining the prevalence rate of PNES among individuals diagnosed with epilepsy has proved to be challenging. Prevalence rates vary based on diagnostic criteria and on whether one considers how many patients *with epilepsy* have PNES or how many patients *with PNES* have epilepsy. The latter is probably the more useful statistic, as arguably the more medically dangerous situation is not diagnosing epileptic seizures in someone already diagnosed with PNES. O'Sullivan et al. (2007) (O'Sullivan et al., 2007) reported as many as 50% of patients with PNES will also have comorbid epilepsy; however, studies using more explicit and conservative diagnostic criteria place this figure far lower, typically less than 10% (Benbadis et al., 2001; Lesser et al., 1983; Martin et al., 2003).

Key Points: Prevalence of Epileptic Seizures and PNES
Only 5–10% of patients diagnosed with PNES using vEEG also have seizures when using well-defined diagnostic criteria and vEEG.

Etiology

Despite decades of study, we still do not "know" what causes or maintains PNES. However, a variety of correlates have been identified: demographic variables, medical, social and psychiatric history and psychological test results. There has also been a focus in recent years on predisposing, precipitating, perpetuating and protective factors in both diagnosis and treatment.

Demographic Correlates

The most common demographic presentation of the patient with PNES is the same as that seen with other functional somatic syndromes: females with somatic complaints beginning in young adulthood make up 60–80% of all patients, with the gender disparity less in older adults and the intellectually disabled (Duncan et al., 2011; LaFrance Jr. & Devinsky, 2004; McKenzie et al., 2010; Neumann & Buskila, 2003; Reuber & Elger, 2003; Tojek et al., 2000). With regard to the intellectually disabled, NES events often have a very different behavioral presentation, which often reflects the attempt of the patient to control their environment often with an absence of somatizational/dissociative features. See Table 18.3 for a listing of some of the characteristic studies demonstrating the higher incidence of PNES events among women.

Similarly, data concerning the typical age of onset of PNES are strikingly consistent. PNES events tend to begin in early adulthood, often between 20 and 30 years of age (Reuber & Elger, 2003). There is some suggestion that the age of onset may vary by the phenomenology of PNES, in which PNES associated with epilepsy and developmental delay has an earlier onset while PNES associated with health-related trauma is later in onset (Duncan & Oto, 2008a, 2008b; Reuber, 2008). It is not uncommon for children as young as 5 years old to have PNES events, although it is believed the onset of PNES in middle or older adult age is less common (Kellinghaus et al., 2004). As the onset of PNES moves later into adulthood, the ratio of women to men appears to decrease (Duncan et al., 2006).

Over the past decade, it has also become clear that PNES is more frequently diagnosed in individuals from lower socioeconomic groups (Duncan et al., 2012). Goldstein et al. (2019) demonstrated that more than 50% of patients diagnosed with

Table 18.3 Demographic features that have been commonly associated with PNES events

Demographic feature	Characteristic studies	Findings
Higher incidence of PNES among women	Reuber, Pukrop, Bauer, Derfuss and Elger (2004)	Of 85 patients diagnosed with PNES, 82.3% were female
	Reuber and Elger (2003)	Review article indicating approximately three-quarters of all patients with PNES are female
	Fiszman et al. (2004)	A meta-analysis of 17 studies of patients with PNES taken from neuropsychological literature between 1945 and 2004 found women comprised 64–100% of the samples
Age of onset is most typically during young adult years	Reuber, Pukrop, Mitchell, Bauer and Elger (2003)	Mean age of onset = 20.3 years
	Reuber, Fernandez, Bauer, Helmstaedter et al. (2002)	Mean age of onset = 25.5 years
	Reuber, Fernandez, Bauer, Singhh and Elger (2002)	Mean age of onset = 26.1 years

Note: *PNES* psychogenic nonepileptic seizures

PNES in a large cohort from the United Kingdom lived in the lowest quartile of socioeconomic status, and two-thirds of all subjects were unemployed at the time of receiving the PNES diagnosis (Goldstein et al., 2019).

Key Points: Demographic Characteristics of Patients with PNES

- PNES are more common in women than men.
- PNES often begins between 20 and 30 years.
- PNES and ES are more prevalent among lower socioeconomic groups.

Medical Histories

In addition to its potential relationship with epilepsy, PNES has been reported after brain injury, neurosurgery (Fiszman et al., 2004), and in patients with intellectual disability (Reuber, Qurishi, et al., 2003). Patients with PNES frequently report more neurological injury or disease than patients with epilepsy or the general population (e.g., head trauma, CNS infection, possible birth traumas) (Dodrill & Holmes, 2000; Drake et al., 1993; Wilkus & Dodrill, 1989). However, such histories are typically based upon self-report and may not be valid (Schrag et al., 2004). Additionally, some studies have suggested that the history of mild head trauma can become the focus of possible problems while they appear to be driven more by comorbid psychiatric factors (Salinsky et al., 2018).

Mirroring the tendency demonstrated in other groups with functional somatic syndromes, patients with PNES report higher rates of fibromyalgia, chronic pain syndromes and other medically unexplained illnesses than age-matched controls. Benbadis and colleagues found 75% of patients evaluated in an epilepsy clinic during a 5-year period who had been previously diagnosed with fibromyalgia or a chronic pain syndrome were later diagnosed with PNES (Benbadis, 2005a). Also, 75% of the patients who had a spell while waiting in the lobby or examination room were diagnosed with PNES. Benbadis hypothesized that PNES may be a product of coping with fibromyalgia/chronic pain. However, he also noted that fibromyalgia and chronic pain are broad diagnoses that are often considered psychogenic themselves.

Body mass index (BMI) may also differ in patients with PNES. Patients with PNES tend to have higher BMIs than patients with epilepsy (30.5 vs. 26.1) (Marquez et al., 2004).

Key Points: Medical History of Patients with PNES

- More neurological trauma/dysfunction reported (in addition to epilepsy)
- More common with diagnosis of fibromyalgia, chronic pain, chronic fatigue syndrome, multiple chemical sensitivity, etc.
- Higher body mass index (BMI)

Social Histories

A factor frequently mentioned in discussions of PNES etiology is a history of long-term psychological conflict (LaFrance Jr. & Devinsky, 2004). LaFrance Jr. and Devinsky (2004) describe unresolved conflict as evidenced by chronic use of poor coping techniques. These poor coping techniques are often accompanied by patient reported histories of abuse during childhood, head trauma, psychiatric disturbance and socially reinforced behaviors that mimic epilepsy symptoms. Histories of physical, sexual or emotional abuse are commonly reported. Bowman and Markand found 84% of patients with PNES had a history of abuse, including sexual (67%), physical (67%) and other trauma (74%) (Bowman, 1993, 2001; Markand et al., 2000). Other studies report lower but still substantial rates of abuse that exceed controls (Alper et al., 1993; Duncan & Oto, 2008a; Fiszman et al., 2004; Selkirk et al., 2008). A meta-analysis examining the frequency of traumatic events and post-traumatic stress disorder (PTSD) in PNES populations found 44–100% reported a history of general trauma, whereas 23–77% reported histories of physical and/or sexual abuse (Fiszman et al., 2004). Selkirk and colleagues provide data suggesting patients experiencing PNES within the context of a reported history of abuse tend to have worse social and psychological adjustment than patients with PNES who do not have an abuse history (Selkirk et al., 2008). Thus, abuse history may be relevant in better understanding etiology, but also the relative likelihood of poor adjustment.

LaFrance Jr. and Devinsky (2004) proposed a conceptual model that incorporated the prevalent themes of chronic maladjustment and abuse and divided PNES into two categories: posttraumatic and developmental (LaFrance Jr. & Devinsky, 2004). *Posttraumatic* PNES results from an individual's maladaptive response to chronic contact with traumatic experiences. Patients with posttraumatic PNES have often been exposed to physical, sexual or psychological trauma. *Developmental* PNES, in contrast, is thought to arise from an individual's difficulties in coping with the psychosocial tasks encountered along the developmental spectrum. For example, it is common for PNES to occur in the midst of trauma or social or family conflict (Berkhoff et al., 1998). Psychogenic events are common in patients with personal conflict over anger, expression of anger, dependency, sexuality and extensive patterns of avoiding one's awareness of these frustrations (Abubakr et al., 2003). Patients with a history of poor adjustment after troublesome interactions with others, and those with difficulties in managing anger, may manifest their poor psychosocial adjustment in the form of PNES (Lesser, 2003). Additionally, patients with PNES perceive their families as being less supportive of each other, exhibit less commitment and also place less of an emphasis on ethical values when compared to healthy controls and patients with epilepsy (Szaflarski et al., 2003). In contrast, social support is clearly one of the protective factors that can contribute to a positive treatment outcome.

Key Points: Social History of Patients with PNES

- More likely to have history of abuse (sexual, physical, etc.)—84% of patients
- More common for PNES to occur in times of trauma or family/interpersonal conflict
- More likely with individuals having poor coping skills and/or poor psychosocial adjustment

Psychiatric Comorbidities

In addition to a history of aversive childhood events and poor psychosocial development, patients with PNES tend to report more psychiatric symptoms than the general population as well as patients with epilepsy. Anywhere from 43% to 100% of patients with PNES meet the criteria for a psychiatric disorder (Baslet et al., 2021; Bowman, 2001; Drane et al., 2006; Stroup et al., 2004). This is almost twice the rate reported for patients with epilepsy (Szaflarski et al., 2003), who themselves have a higher rate of psychiatric comorbidities than the general population. Common psychiatric comorbidities in patients with PNES include PTSD, panic disorder with or without agoraphobia and other anxiety disorders, depressive disorders, personality disorders, prior conversion disorders, somatization disorders and dissociative disorders (Bowman, 1993, 2006; Reuber & Elger, 2003; Reuber, House, et al., 2003).

Somatization, conversion and dissociation. PNES are generally considered a type of conversion disorder, which has been classified by the DSM-V as a functional neurological disorder (American Psychiatric Association, 2013). Perhaps the most obvious traits characterizing patients with PNES are higher levels of somatization, suggestibility and dissociation (Bowman, 2006; Goldstein et al., 2000). These processes, by definition, are core components of the disorder. Conversion disorder, a specific type of somatoform disorder, is the current classification for a disorder Sigmund Freud originally termed *hysteria*. The phrase *conversion* extended from the hypothesis that the patient's somatic symptom represented "a symbolic resolution of an unconscious psychological conflict, reducing anxiety and serving to keep the conflict out of awareness" (American Psychiatric Association, 2013). PNES are frequently seen in conversion disorders, with 15% of conversion disordered patients exhibiting PNES events (Devinsky et al., 2001). This relationship works in the other direction as well, as Devinsky et al. (2001) found that 9 out of 79 patients with PNES had other conversion symptoms, such as paralysis and nonanatomic sensory loss.

Goldstein et al. found that patients with PNES scored significantly higher than healthy controls on a measure of dissociative experiences (Goldstein et al., 2000). In this study, patients with PNES specifically used escape–avoidance behaviors and tended to use more emotionally based coping strategies. In contrast, the control group used significantly more problem-focused coping techniques. Thus, escape avoidance and emotion-based coping may be coping mechanisms that increase the risk for the development of PNES.

Posttraumatic stress disorder (PTSD). Given the rates of abuse and trauma described earlier, the prevalence of PTSD in this population comes as no surprise. Fiszman et al. (2004) found higher rates of PTSD in patients with PNES than those seen in the general population (Fiszman et al., 2004), which the Department of Veteran's Affairs estimates to be at approximately 8%. PTSD symptoms are reported in patients with epilepsy as well, however, but in and of themselves are not sufficient to diagnose PNES (Dikel et al., 2003).

Anxiety. Patients with PNES report higher levels of anxiety more generally (Bermeo-Ovalle & Kanner, 2018), some displaying chronic anxiety as a heightened trait (van Merode et al., 2004). Mokleby et al. (2002) found that patients with PNES have significantly higher levels of self-reported anxiety, anger, hostility and depression when compared to healthy controls (Mokleby et al., 2002). This is consistent with the idea that hostility is often manifested as a coping style in individuals with anger and mistrust in others (Lesser, 2003). Patients who have been diagnosed with PNES are at higher risk of specifically having a comorbid anxiety disorder, which can also increase the possibility of developing dissociative symptoms in addition to PNES (Green et al., 2017; Volbers et al., 2022). Abe et al. also found in their study that patients who have PNES had increased anxiety scores on self-report measures (Abe et al., 2020). Finally, one recent study determined that the prevalence of anxiety in PNES patients was significantly higher in females as compared to males (Rocamora et al., 2021).

Depression. Of significant clinical concern is the high rate of depression in patients with PNES, as this conveys a higher risk for suicide. One recent meta-analysis estimated rates of depression in patients with PNES to be approximately 40% (Walsh et al., 2018). Further, it is not unusual for patients with PNES to have a history of parasuicidal behavior. Reuber et al. (2000) noted this was particularly true of patients who have a history of psychogenic status epilepticus (with features resembling epileptic status epilepticus, in that the patient has repeated PNES events without recovery in between) (Reuber et al., 2000). In a case series of five patients who originally presented with postoperative status epilepticus but whose episodes were later diagnosed as psychogenic in origin, nearly two-thirds of the patients had a history of suicide attempts (Reuber et al., 2000).

Eating disorders. Although investigated less frequently, there is some indication that bulimia may also be more frequent among patients presenting with psychogenic status epilepticus (Rechlin et al., 1997). Rechlin and colleagues found that one-third of a PNES sample hospitalized for PNES "status epilepticus" was bulimic. Consistent with Reuber et al. (2000), this PNES group was also characterized by higher than expected rates of personality disorder and suicide attempts.

Personality disorders. Estimates of the prevalence of personality disorder among patients with PNES vary widely, ranging from 30% to 80% (Harden et al., 2009; Lacey et al., 2007). The most carefully diagnosed sample to date (via the Structured Clinical Interview for the DSM-IV, Axis II version or SCID-II) yields one of the highest prevalence rates, though the sample size ($n = 16$) was quite small (Harden et al., 2009). Notably, estimates of personality pathology among patients with epilepsy are also higher than those seen in the general population, ranging from 18% to 75%. Again, the study of Harden and colleagues (with 16 patients with epilepsy as well) yielded the estimate on the high end of this range. There is a clear distinction between the personality pathology seen most commonly in PNES and patients with epilepsy, as patients with epilepsy tend to be avoidant and dependent (cluster C), whereas patients with PNES more frequently demonstrate pathological emotional lability or idiosyncratic perceptions of their social environment (clusters A and B). Common personality disorder diagnoses in the PNES population are borderline, histrionic and antisocial personality disorder. This is relevant clinically, as personality disorder among patients with PNES is associated with intractability and diminished access to appropriate treatment (Harden et al., 2003; Kanner et al., 1999).

Key Points: Psychiatric History of Patients with PNES

- Psychiatric comorbidity is higher in PNES than for patients with epilepsy.
- PNES is a conversion disorder.
- Patients with PNES have high rates of depression and at risk for suicidal gestures.

Psychological Testing and Evidence-Based Psychology Practice

Patients with PNES tend to have distinctive profiles on personality testing, often reflecting aspects of somatization (Cragar et al., 2003; Cragar et al., 2005; Locke et al., 2010; Wagner et al., 2005; Wilkus & Dodrill, 1989). Patients with PNES often show significant clinical elevations on scales 1, 2, 3, 6, 7 and 8 of the MMPI/MMPI-2, with the most common profile configuration being the 1-3/3-1 profile (scale 1: hypochondriasis; scale 3: hysteria) (Cragar et al., 2005). On the MMPI-2-RF, elevations are seen on validity scales Fs and FBS-r, restructured clinical scales RC1 and RC3 and somatic scales MLS, GIC, HPC and NUC (Locke et al., 2010). On the NEO-PI-R, patients with PNES tend to score higher on the neuroticism scale, particularly facets of anxiety, angry hostility and depression, but lower on the extraversion and agreeableness scales, potentially reflecting a facet of modesty (Cragar et al., 2005).

A number of studies have been conducted to determine how well such characteristics distinguish patients with PNES from patients with epilepsy. Wilkus and Dodrill (1989) suggested that PNES should be suspected when one of three MMPI configural patterns is present: (1) scale 1 or 3 exceeds 69 and is one of the two most elevated scales, disregarding scales 5 and 0, (2) scale 1 or 3 exceeds 79 regardless of whether either is a high point or (3) both 1 and 3 exceed 59, and both are at least 10 points higher than scale 2 (Wilkus et al., 1984). These rules have been generalized to the MMPI-2 (Warner et al., 1996). Other configural patterns have been suggested (Derry & Mclachlan, 1996). Dodrill and Holmes (2000) reviewed nine studies examining the sensitivity of the MMPI/MMPI-2 to PNES, and found an overall accuracy of 71% for these configural patterns (Dodrill & Holmes, 2000). An evidence-based neuropsychology/psychology practice finding is that if a patient with seizures of uncertain etiology meets these criteria, they are approximately *five times more likely* to be diagnosed with PNES than with epilepsy (Williamson et al., 2007). Storzbach et al. (2000) developed an algorithm by which diagnostic accuracy can be improved to approximately 80% by also taking duration of spells and results of routine EEGs into account (Schramke et al., 2007; Storzbach et al., 2000) establishing an evidence-based neuropsychology practice when using the MMPI-2.

Approximately 30% of patients with epilepsy produce this same profile on the MMPI/MMPI-2. It has been assumed that such elevations in patients with epilepsy are related to endorsement of symptoms associated with their seizures (e.g., loss of consciousness, lapses in awareness, bizarre sensory experiences). However, patients with epilepsy actually endorse these and other items that directly indicate ictal symptoms only infrequently (Nelson et al., 2004). In addition, the majority of patients with epilepsy (~70%) do not produce significant elevations on scales 1 and 3 despite this apparent overlap of symptoms.

Although the MMPI/MMPI-2 clearly has the most extensive evidence-based support for use with this population, data are available with other scales as well. Wagner et al. (2005) developed an algorithm to discriminate patients with epilepsy from patients with PNES using the Personality Assessment Inventory (PAI) (Wagner et al., 2005). An evidence-based neuropsychology/psychology finding was that

PNES was approximately 15 times more likely when the T-score from the health concerns subscale was less than the T-score from the conversion subscale. However, this rate of accuracy was not replicated by Testa et al. (2011), who found in a sample for 62 patients with PNES, 55 patients with epilepsy and 45 healthy controls that Wagner et al.'s NES indicator was not much better than chance, whereas the conversion subscale displayed 74% sensitivity and 67% specificity (Testa et al., 2011). Given the mixed findings, the optimal approach to use with PAI data remains unresolved, other than to state that no profile pathognomonic of PNES has emerged.

Cragar et al. (2005) have explored personality characteristics of patients with PNES as well, using the NEO-PI-R to supplement the information gained from the MMPI-2. Cluster analysis of the data derived from the two measures combined revealed three distinct clusters of patients with PNES. The first group was characterized as experiencing negative affect, low levels of energy and sociability and clinical symptoms of depression via the MMPI-2 Scale 2. This cluster was termed the "depressed neurotics" and had MMPI-2 elevations on scales 2 and 3. The second group clustered around a profile that was characterized by somatic tendencies when dealing with psychosocial stress factors. This group was called the "somatic defender" and had MMPI-2 elevations on scales 1 and 3, with a lower score on scale 2 (i.e., conversion V pattern). The third group, the "activated neurotic" group, was characterized by negative affect similar to that of the "depressed neurotics" but was more actively, socially engaged, thus exhibiting anxiety as a symptom of distress where elevations were highest on scales 1 and 8.

One recent study has suggested that a combination of scales could provide even greater diagnostic accuracy, although the need for efficiency in practice may make such an approach less practical in the modern age of healthcare (Webber et al., 2021).

Key Points: Evidence-Based Practice for Psychological Assessment of Patients with PNES

- Five times more likely to be diagnosed with PNES than epilepsy if:
  - MMPI-2 Scale 1 or 3 exceeds T-score of 64 and is one of the two most elevated scales

  OR
  - MMPI-2 Scale 1 or 3 exceeds T-score of 74 regardless of whether either is a high point

  OR
  - Both MMPI-2 Scales 1 and 3 exceed T-score of 54, and both are at least 10 points higher than scale 2.

Neuropsychological Testing

In contrast to the psychological and emotional differences consistently found when comparing patients with epilepsy to patients with PNES, such differences are not evident when comparing the performances of the two groups on neuropsychological tests. No focal patterns of cognitive abnormalities have been found among patients with PNES. However, studies have reported that patients with PNES score as poorly as, or often worse than, patients with epilepsy (Dodrill & Holmes, 2000; Drake et al., 1993; Hermann, 2000; Wilkus et al., 1984; Wilkus & Dodrill, 1989), although not consistently (Sackellares et al., 1985). These early findings have continued to be replicated over the years, and are well summarized in a recent meta-analysis of more than 80 research studies exploring cognition in patients with PNES, which again concludes that there are minimal differences between the profiles of patients with either PNES or epilepsy, with both groups performing worse than controls at a group level (Van Patten et al., 2024) (Table 18.4).

The question then becomes "why would a group without significant, objectively verifiable neuropathology (PNES) perform as badly as patients with epilepsy?" There have been three proposed reasons for worse neuropsychological scores in PNES as compared to patients with epilepsy:

1. Patients with PNES have actual neuropathological insults that current neuroimaging technology cannot detect (Dodrill & Holmes, 2000; Drake Jr., 1993; Wilkus et al., 1984; Wilkus & Dodrill, 1989). This hypothesis is based on the

Table 18.4 Summary of representative studies comparing neurocognitive function in patients with PNES to patients with ES

Study reference	Specific findings	Neurocognitive deficits
(Wilkus and Dodrill (1989), Wilkus et al. (1984) and Dodrill and Holmes (2000)	Both groups perform outside of normal limits on approximately half of the measures in the neuropsychological battery for epilepsy	PNES = ES or PNES <= ES
Drake et al. (1993)	Four of 20 individuals with PNES performed in the intellectually disabled range, while an additional 13 exhibited cognitive impairment on the Halstead-Reitan battery	PNES impaired relative to normative data
Hermann (2000)	No difference in neurocognitive performance between small groups of patients with either PNES or ES	PNES = ES
Sackellares et al. (1985)	Patients with PNES performed better than patients with generalized ES or those with co-occurring ES and PNES	ES < PNES
Prigatano and Kirlin (2008)	Patients with ES performed worse than patients with PNES on a few variables (e.g., naming). Memory performance correlated with anxiety levels for the PNES sample only	ES < PNES
Drane et al. (2006)	Both groups perform outside of normal limits on approximately half of the measures in the neuropsychological battery for epilepsy. However, the patients with PNES failed SVT measures at a much higher rate, and this accounted for their decreased performance	ES < PNES

Note: *PNES* psychogenic nonepileptic seizures, *ES* epileptic seizures

finding that patients with PNES frequently report more neurological injury or disease (e.g., head injury, CNS infection) than patients with epilepsy.
2. Patients with PNES perform worse than patients with epilepsy due to intervening variables such as the detrimental effects of medication, pain, physical fatigue and forms of emotional distress that have been variably linked to impaired cognitive performance (e.g., depression, anxiety, posttraumatic stress disorder).
3. Patients with PNES perform worse than patients with epilepsy due to inconsistent task engagement, as evidenced by much higher rates of performance validity test failure in patients with PNES than seen in patients with epilepsy (Drane et al., 2006). Mechanisms for poor task engagement could subsume hypothesis #2, although these researchers have expanded the range of these latent variables to include psychological processes (e.g., dissociative tendencies, and motivation issues).

Research examining the relative merits of these explanations continues. From our perspective, we have noted performance validity test (PVT) failure rate for selected patients with epilepsy who have not had a seizure in the past 24 hours and do not have pronounced neurodevelopmental delay is approximately 8–10%, the same as reported in general medical populations (Green et al., 1999; 2001; Howe & Loring, 2009; Mittenberg et al., 1996; Williamson et al., 2005). In contrast, despite the lack of identifiable seizure activity or lifelong cognitive disability, the PVT failure rate of patients with PNES remains at or above 28%. There is growing evidence-based neuropsychology research that the most likely reason patients with PNES perform poorly on neuropsychological tests is poor task engagement (explanation #3 above), the cause of which is more difficult to ascertain and probably varies between patients and may be multifactorial.

It is important to note what can and cannot be interpreted from PVT failure in this patient group (see also Chaps. 17, 19 and 20, this volume). PVT performance rarely tells one *why* a patient performs in such a manner as to compromise the interpretability of test results. While patients with PNES as a group put forth less effort than patients with epilepsy, malingering (conscious effort to perform poorly) does *not* appear to be a major contributor to the PVT failures seen in the PNES population (Orbach et al., 2003). A number of other factors which could be proposed to negatively impact PVT performance include (1) fatigue, (2) depression or psychiatric symptomatology, (3) pain, (4) the side effects of medications and (5) dissociative tendencies among other possible factors. We know pain and depression do not necessarily lead to poorer PVT performance (Gervais et al., 2001; 2004; Rohling et al., 2002), and there is no evidence that ASMs impair cognitive performance to such an extent as to cause PVT failure. However, careful examination of the impact of specific ASMs on performance in specific PVTs has yet to be reported. Likewise, patients with epilepsy sometimes experience epileptiform discharges that do not manifest themselves in visible behavioral changes but may have effects upon cognition (Aldenkamp & Arends, 2004; Drane, Ojemann, et al., 2016; Ebus et al., 2012; Glennon et al., 2016; Horak et al., 2017; Karakis et al., 2020; Kleen et al., 2013), and there is now some indication that these discharges can contribute to PVT failure as well (Drane, Ojemann, et al., 2016; Henry et al., 2018).

We recently demonstrated that a patient with PNES initially failing PVT measures and performing in a generally impaired range normalized on most tasks following successful psychotherapeutic treatment of her PNES events (Drane et al., 2023). This also involved removing most of the medications with which her PNES events and comorbidities were being treated (including narcotics, ASMs, psychotropics and an opioid). The patient also had comorbidities of PTSD and mood successfully managed and experienced a reduction in dissociative tendencies. Overall, it is difficult to determine the relative contribution of factors to the patient's compromised function, but it does appear that performance can be affected by such variables, and this case highlights that failed PVT does not necessarily suggest that the patient is unmotivated to participate in therapy.

Key Points: Neuropsychological Assessment and PVTs in Patients with PNES

- Patients with PNES often exhibit equivalent or greater neurocognitive dysfunction as patients with ES.
- PVT failure rate of patients with PNES 28% + (8% for patients with epilepsy).
- PVT failure of patients with PNES may reflect invalid performances resulting from psychological factors or other possible variables (e.g., effects of medications, pain).

Counting Elephants: Are There Meaningful PNES Subtypes?

We are all familiar with the story of the four blind children, each of whom excitedly describes to their teacher their respective finds of (1) a rough but warm and pliable tree, (2) a curved bone, (3) a rough and pliable tube-like object and (4) a large, flat leathery pad of some sort, and how surprised these children are when their teacher tell them that they have just described the leg, tusk, trunk and ear of a single animal. Without the presence of an overriding, unifying principle that can bring together the morass of correlates of PNES that have been described, we remain unsure about the extent to which we are playing the part of the blind children or the teacher. A number of groups have attempted to bring some sense of order to the disparate findings for PNES phenomenology, although each group has organized the data from different perspectives (Cragar et al., 2005; Drane et al., 2006; Holmes et al., 2001; Kuyk et al., 2003; LaFrance Jr. & Devinsky, 2004; Selkirk et al., 2008). LaFrance Jr. and Devinsky (2004) proposed posttraumatic vs. developmental PNES. Cragar et al. (2005) divided PNES patients into subtypes based on personality characteristics derived from psychological testing. The Glasgow group has demonstrated subgroup differences if one categorizes according to the presence of developmental delay (Duncan & Oto, 2008b), age of onset (Duncan et al., 2006) or report of sexual abuse (Selkirk et al., 2008). We have viewed these patients from the perspective of performance on PVTs (Drane et al., 2006) or behavioral presentation of the PNES events (Benbadis, 2005a, 2005b). Each of these perspectives provides a starting point for further questions, many of which have yet to be explored (e.g., to what extent do the proposed subtypes predict response to treatment? Are different types of treatment indicated for different subtypes? Does the level of emotional suffering and disability vary according to subtype?). Answers to these questions will provide information critical for treatment planning.

At a broader level, one cannot help but be struck by the similarities between the histories and presentations of patients with PNES and patients with other disorders in which emotional processes are felt to play an important role. Some of these have long been characterized variably as functional somatic syndromes or varying manifestations of somatoform, somatization or conversion disorders. As evident in Table 18.5, these disorders share a number of similarities in the manner and extent to which affected patients differ from the general population. Are these similarities

Table 18.5 Comparison of syndromes with prominent emotional features

	Gender ratio	Age of onset	History of trauma	Association with higher BMI	Educational attainment and SES	Comorbid psychiatric condition
PNES	F > M (3:1)	Most common in young adulthood	Frequent (>70%)	Yes	Higher rates among low education and low SES	Frequent
Fibromyalgia	F > M (7–9:1)	Most common in 40–60 s	Common[a]	Yes	Some evidence of higher rates among low SES	Common
Chronic fatigue syndrome	F > M (4:1)	Most common in 40–50 s	Common to frequent	No (due to diagnostic criteria)[b]	Higher rates among low education and low SES	Frequent
Chronic daily headache	F > M (1.7–2:1)	Most common in 20–30 s	Common	Yes	Higher rates among low education and low SES	Frequent
IBS	F > M (2-3:1)	Most common in young adulthood	Common	Yes	Higher rates among individuals from higher SES	Common

Note: *PNES* psychogenic nonepileptic seizures, *IBS* irritable bowel syndrome, *BMI* body mass index, *F>M* female greater prevalence than male, *SES* socioeconomic status. Ratios represent rough approximations based on available data

[a]Trauma in the fibromyalgia group often appears to include physical injury (e.g., onset following a car accident), whereas the other groups in this table are more likely to report childhood abuse (e.g., physical, sexual, emotional)

[b]High BMI is typically included among exclusionary criteria for CFS, as this condition is believed to be independently associated with fatigue

merely coincidence, or do they speak to a common primary neurological, psychological, metabolic, environmental and genetic contribution to these problems that can bolster our understanding of these disorders and thereby help to alleviate the suffering of those affected? Or, alternatively, do they speak to a common final pathway depicting the manner in which certain individuals react to disparate primary problems? These questions have certainly been taken up by others (Binder & Campbell, 2004; Brown, 2004), but remain critical to understanding the extent to which we are dealing with varying manifestations of the same underlying problem or similar manifestations of fundamentally different problems.

Treatment

When we wrote the last version of this chapter, there had been some preliminary efforts to study possible treatments for PNES, but the extent of these studies was extremely limited, and was primarily represented by some small pioneering efforts by researchers who have been championing this area of need for the last decade (Ataoglu et al., 2003; Brooks et al., 2007; LaFrance et al., 2006, 2008; Lesser, 2003; Reuber et al., 2005; Rusch et al., 2001; Wood et al., 2004).

The first step of any treatment of PNES is helping the patient to understand the nature of the problem. Clear communication between clinician and patient can be challenging under optimal circumstances, but is even more so when the patient may not fully understand the nature of their disorder. Therefore, a basic educational component to treatment is essential, and often sets the stage for alleviating the occurrence of events. Early work in this area suggested that a more standardized approach to diagnostic delivery by practitioners and an empathic approach to the patient result in better outcome (LaFrance et al., 2006; Shen et al., 1990; Thompson et al., 2005, 2009). Providing education around PNES can increase the patient's understanding and acceptance of the diagnosis, and can lead to more positive outcomes (Lanzillotti et al., 2021). Once the diagnosis has been delivered, the patient should be connected with behavioral health providers and co-occurring disorders should be assessed to determine the best course of treatment (Kamil et al., 2019; Lanzillotti et al., 2021). When patients with PNES do not receive treatment, they are more likely to continue experiencing emotional pain, have psychological stress, have unhealthy relationships and may continue to engage in avoidance behaviors (Green et al., 2017).

Potential algorithms to provide this information have been provided and to some extent reviewed in terms of their performance (Shen et al., 1990; Thompson et al., 2005). Our own group demonstrated that providing diagnostic information regarding PNES was insufficient by itself to produce meaningful change in patient outcome (Drane, LaRoche, et al., 2016). Instead, structured feedback coupled with psychiatric consultation significantly reduced PNES events and improved aspects of quality of life. Mood improved as well if the patient was provided with weekly phone follow-up for a brief span of time, which we felt better ensured that they understood the diagnostic information, conveyed that we were committed to assisting them with their issues and increased the chance that they became engaged in some form of ongoing mental health treatment.

It is helpful to include a PNES-specific psychoeducational component into treatment, which can assist with reducing psychopathology related to PNES. Zaroff et al. (2004) created a group psychotherapy program that included a PNES-specific psychoeducational component (Zaroff et al., 2004). In their study, seven participants with PNES completed a group psychotherapy program that consisted of weekly visits lasting 1-hour each, for a period of 10 weeks. The goals of the program were to provide education around PNES and also to explain the roles of depression, anxiety and trauma. The groups consisted of themed discussions, and participants were provided with comprehensive information around the definition of PNES and its precipitating factors. Results from their study showed that three of the group participants had achieved cessation in PNES symptoms at the beginning of treatment, two participants had a decline in seizure frequency and one participant experienced an increase in seizure frequency. The researchers also found that the participants' PTSD and dissociative symptoms decreased, and their quality of life improved as a result of their treatment program (Zaroff et al., 2004).

Treatment guidelines have been proposed in the literature and consist of four phases: delivering the diagnosis, providing psychoeducation around PNES, treatment engagement and creating a longstanding intervention plan (Baslet et al., 2015). The first phase addressed the initial delivery of the diagnosis by a neurologist, followed by ensuring that the patient had an understanding around the diagnosis and that they had an acceptance around the diagnosis (Asadi-Pooya, 2017). The second phase outlined treatment engagement with a mental health provider, where clinical skills can be used to promote acceptance, understanding and behavioral change. The third phase outlines acute treatment and focuses on exploring predisposing, precipitating and perpetuating factors. The last stage of treatment includes more long-term approaches, such as continued psychotherapy, case management and continuation of psychotropic medications to help with co-occurring disorders. The best course of treatment for PNES seems to be psychological interventions, such as cognitive behavioral therapy (CBT), psychoeducation, psychodynamic therapy and mindfulness-based interventions, although much more research is needed to truly evaluate their relative efficacy (Carlson & Nicholson Perry, 2017; Cope et al., 2017; Kamil et al., 2019).

It is encouraging that efforts to develop therapeutic programs are increasing around the world, given that there has been a historical dearth of treatment options for patients with functional disorders. CBT interventions have been the most widely studied treatment for patients living with PNES (Baslet et al., 2020). CBT-based interventions have been found to reduce seizure frequency, decrease co-occurring psychiatric symptoms, improve psychosocial functioning and increase quality of life (Kamil et al., 2019). Currently, there is a recent meta-analysis of treatment studies for PNES, which compares CBT to standard medical treatment in this population, and found "high-quality evidence" supporting the benefits of CBT in treating this condition (Moro et al., 2024). There have still only been a handful of studies that used a randomized control trial (RCT) approach, with only one of these being sufficiently powered (Goldstein et al., 2020). We cover these trials in more detail.

Goldstein et al. (2010) developed a CBT-based treatment using the fear-avoidance model that consisted of 12 sessions that were aimed at addressing the emotional, cognitive and behavioral components of PNES (Goldstein et al., 2010). There were five stages to their treatment protocol, which included commitment to treatment, coping skills, exposure techniques to decrease avoidance symptoms, management of thoughts and feelings around PNES and relapse prevention strategies. Goldstein et al. (2010) conducted an RCT on this CBT-based protocol and compared it to standard medical care (SMC). The results of their study determine that SMC alone was not sufficient for managing PNES events, but instead indicated that CBT in conjunction with SMC significantly decreased seizure frequency. Goldstein et al. (2020) subsequently conducted an RCT called the CODES trial, which utilized a 12-session, CBT approach to treat PNES (Goldstein et al., 2020). The researchers found that SMC alone or combined with CBT did not reduce seizure frequency. They reported that secondary outcomes were clinically relevant when CBT was added to SMC. Their findings suggest that adults with PNES may improve with CBT interventions that are geared toward PNES and that are administered by a trained specialist.

LaFrance et al. (2014) also conducted an RCT to evaluate if CBT-informed psychotherapy was effective in treating patients with PNES (LaFrance et al., 2014). They had four treatment groups of participants with PNES, which consisted of a CBT alone group, a CBT with sertraline group, a sertraline only group or a treatment as usual group. Greater than 50% of those receiving CBT only experienced a reduction in their seizures, decreased levels of depression and anxiety and improved quality of life. Nearly 60% of those receiving CBT and sertraline together experienced decreased seizure frequency and also improved global functioning. Those receiving sertraline only or treatment as usual did not show any improvements in PNES symptoms. These researchers used these findings to support using a manualized psychotherapy approach. The sample sizes used in these studies was very small, making firm conclusions tenuous. More recently, Lopez and LaFrance have highlighted the need for continued psychotherapeutic interventions using a holistic and multidisciplinary approach.

Another CBT-based intervention study was conducted by Cope and colleagues, which involved the creation of a three-session protocol with 90-minute group sessions that were based on psychoeducation (Cope et al., 2017). The goal of these sessions was to increase the patient's understanding of the diagnosis, to connect with others who had PNES, to identify unhelpful thoughts and to learn how to address and cope with their symptoms. In the beginning of their program, 11% of participants were seizure-free, and at the end of treatment, 40% of participants were seizure-free. The researchers also found that their protocol significantly decreased psychological stress and improved levels of understanding around PNES.

While CBT has been shown to be effective in treating PNES, not all patients will have a decrease in PNES symptoms, and other treatment modalities should be considered and further studied (Cope et al., 2017; Gutkin et al., 2020). Myers et al.

(2017) adapted a prolonged exposure (PE) psychotherapy protocol that was aimed at treating comorbid PNES and PTSD (Myers et al., 2017). Sixteen adult participants engaged in 12–15, 90-minute sessions, which included psychoeducation around trauma and teaching coping skills such as deep breathing exercises and grounding techniques, and also provided an exposure component related to the traumatic event. The results of their study showed a decrease in seizure frequency and PTSD symptoms, as well as improved mood. These results were sustained at follow-up and suggest that PE may be beneficial in treating comorbid PNES and PTSD.

Mindfulness-based therapies (MBT) have also been shown to be effective in treating PNES (Baslet et al., 2020). MBT promotes awareness and acceptance of the present moment through adopting a curious and open attitude and encourages taking a non-judgmental stance. Baslet et al. (2020) developed an MBT that was delivered over 12 sessions to 26 patients with PNES. Their program consisted of modules that discussed psychoeducation, mindfulness, stress-management techniques, emotion regulation skills and relapse prevention strategies. The results of their study determined that their MBT reduced PNES symptoms, including seizure frequency and intensity, as well as improved overall quality of life.

Another mindfulness-based intervention with some initial research for treating PNES is Acceptance and Commitment Therapy (ACT) (Barrett-Naylor et al., 2018; Cope et al., 2017). ACT differs from CBT, as it focuses on mindfulness-based techniques, such as acceptance, increasing psychological flexibility and improving quality of life. Unlike other treatment modalities, ACT does not primarily focus on reducing symptoms, but is more geared toward improving the relationships that a patient has with unhelpful thoughts, feelings and body sensations (Cope et al., 2017). The goal of ACT is to help the patient gain acceptance over the distressing experience without having to remove or change it. ACT helps to increase mindfulness, psychological flexibility and acceptance and aims to decrease experiential avoidance (Burrows, 2013). This can be accomplished through taking committed action, and living in accordance with one's values. In ACT cognitive fusion is identified and discussed, and cognitive diffusion strategies are introduced to help create distance between the self and unhelpful thoughts.

ACT has been shown to increase positive outcomes in PNES patients, including reducing symptoms of PNES frequency and intensity, decreasing experiential avoidance and increasing psychological flexibility and acceptance of the present moment (Cope et al., 2017). Barrett-Naylor et al. (2018) conducted a study with ACT to treat PNES and found that it decreased PNES frequency, as well as improved depression and anxiety symptoms (Barrett-Naylor et al., 2018). Patients who went through the ACT treatment program reported having positive changes, including gaining more acceptance around the diagnosis, feeling more confident and experienced decreased avoidance behaviors.

Research has identified several treatment prognostic indicators (Durrant et al., 2011). The duration a patient is diagnosed with having PNES versus seizures or epilepsy is a powerful predictor of treatment outcome (Reuber et al., 2007). Patients with a history of longer duration of incorrect diagnosis tend to have worse outcomes in which there is maintenance of PNES symptoms. In addition, the duration a patient with PNES is treated with ASMs is also a prognostic indicator (Carton et al., 2003). Patients treated with ASMs for longer periods of time demonstrate worse outcomes, maintaining PNES symptoms for longer periods of time. As noted above, the social consequences of PNES are not inconsequential, and more than half of patients having PNES symptoms for more than 10 years in duration remain on disability for income. Because data indicate patients with PNES incorrectly diagnosed and/or treated with ASMs have worse outcomes, Benbadis has argued that the assessment for PNES may not be sufficiently sensitive (Benbadis, 2005b).

PNES in Children and Adolescents

Since the last version of this chapter was written, much more attention has been focused on children with PNES, although research in adults and children with PNES remains in the early stages of development (Kotagal et al., 2002; Lancman et al., 1994; Vincentiis et al., 2006). The few empirical investigations available have suggested a few general trends among pediatric patients with PNES: (a) as patients get younger, the gender ratio moves closer to 1:1, (b) as patients get younger, the rate of the epilepsy co-occurrence increases, and (c) family dysfunction is common, though not necessarily physical, emotional or sexual abuse (Kotagal et al., 2002; Patel et al., 2007; Sawchuk et al., 2020; Vincentiis et al., 2006). Family histories of epilepsy also appear to be more common, and some studies have suggested elevated comorbid psychiatric disorders, including depression in particular (Vincentiis et al., 2006). Nevertheless, other studies have suggested an absence of elevated psychiatric comorbidities and a much lower incidence of unnecessary treatment with ASMs (Plioplys et al., 2014; Reuber, 2008; Sawchuk et al., 2020). Children have been thought to have a better prognosis for recovery (i.e., resolution of PNES symptoms) following diagnosis of PNES than do adults (Madaan et al., 2018; Wyllie et al., 1990, 1999, 2002). However, some recent studies have suggested that prognosis may be less good than once thought (Yong et al., 2023). Unfortunately, there have been no controlled trials for the treatment of PNES in children, with some authors suggesting that until we have established more firmly the rates of comorbid developmental and psychiatric issues (e.g., ADHD, depression, anxiety, PTSD), such trials are premature (LaFrance et al., 2006).

Neuropsychological Assessment Strategies with PNES

In our opinion, an adequate neuropsychological evaluation of patients with PNES has six potential goals, each of which may carry varying weight depending on the need of the evaluation setting. These include:

1. Assist with diagnosis.

2. Determine if cognitive issues exist that need to be addressed as part of the patient's care. This could include ruling out contributions of cogniform disorder and somatization, ruling out transient causes of dysfunction and determining whether any non-transient changes in performance may be related to any number of accompanying factors as discussed in other sections (e.g., medication effects).
3. Determine whether psychiatric comorbidities exist (e.g., anxiety, depression, PTSD, substance use).
4. Assess underlying psychological processing that may be contributing to FND (e.g., dissociative tendencies, depersonalization, locus of control, somatization).
5. Assess socio-emotional processing and potential deficits (e.g., alexithymia, emotional dysregulation).
6. Determine functional capacity (e.g., ability to live alone, manage money, hold down a job), which may also influence and inform the type of treatment/therapy that can be provided.

Toward these goals, neuropsychological evaluation can function to provide a detailed analysis of cognitive performance and functional capacity, attempting to measure "latent" or intervening factors that may distort patient presentation (e.g., effects of medications, patient motivation/effort, recent seizures, pain, psychiatric factors, such as psychosis). Depending upon the need/context of the patient referral this may call for a full assessment or instead a cognitive screen supplemented by a thorough history and a selection of relevant measures of mood/emotional functioning, personality variables and related traits (e.g., resiliency).

We tended to use a more in-depth evaluation in the context of our epilepsy monitoring unit or perhaps in the outpatient evaluation setting, when attempting to contribute to diagnostic decisions and an assessment of treatment needs. In contrast, we have typically gone with a cognitive screening model for referrals to our PNES clinic. We typically like to screen standard areas of broad function to cover most neurocognitive domains (e.g., attention, processing speed, language, declarative memory, motor function, executive function, visual-spatial). This can be augmented by PVTs to assess task engagement/validity and should include tasks sensitive to transient/latent variables (evidence-based practice recommends the use of PVTs for most assessments) (Bush et al., 2005; Larrabee, 2012). For this purpose, in addition to PVTs, we prefer to examine subdomains such as primary attention, speed (including motor, cognitive processing and speech rate), generative fluency and possibly more complex dependent skills. Many researchers failing to use PVT measures have concluded patients with PNES have profound cognitive impairment and are unable to benefit from standard psychotherapeutic interventions. Whenever possible, we prefer to include some form of psychiatric screening (e.g., Mini Neuropsychiatric Inventory) (Sheehan et al., 1998), particularly if no psychiatric evaluation has been performed. As trauma is often a contributory factor or comorbidity of PNES, we usually employ a screen for PTSD and general trauma (e.g., PTSD checklist for DSM-5 [PCL-5], Child Abuse and Trauma Scale) (Sanders & Becker-Lausen, 1995; Weathers et al., 2013). For a screen of current mood and psychiatric state, we will most often use the Beck Scales (e.g., depression, anxiety)(Beck et al., 1988, 1996) or comparable screening tools, and a measure of quality of life, such as one of the Quality of Life in Epilepsy (QOLIE) measures (Devinsky et al., 1995; Vickrey et al., 1993) and/or the SF-36 for general life adjustment (Callahan et al., 2005; Ware et al., 1994). Typically, we find a measure of personality style to be of great benefit for both diagnostic purposes and to explore other tendencies and traits of the patient (evidenced-based practice supports MMPI-2 or PAI) (Butcher et al., 2001; Morey, 1991). Additionally, such measures can aid in determining tendencies toward dissociation, the presence of mood or personality disorders, levels of anger and other factors that might be useful to inform those attempting PNES treatment. It is also useful to explore characteristics of how the patient with PNES interacts with their environment (e.g., measures of locus of control, resiliency, dissociative tendencies, suggestibility) (Bernstein & Putnam, 1986; Goldstein et al., 2000). Finally, measures evaluating socio-emotional processing deficits can be particularly informative to treatment, and are areas that often appear to change with effective treatment (e.g., alexithymia, emotional Stroop, recognizing emotion from voice or facial expression) (Bagby et al., 1994; Baron-Cohen et al., 2001; Fani et al., 2019). Once again, we can overestimate the value of a careful history, as this can help to identify potential risk factors for either PNES (e.g., sexual abuse or trauma, history of fibromyalgia or chronic pain) or epilepsy (e.g., neurological injury or disease) and can be useful for understanding the development and maintenance of PNES (and subsequently for guiding treatment). Many times, as the patient becomes more engaged with the therapist, more material will emerge as the relational trust deepens, so it can be good to reexplore some of these areas as needed.

Table 18.6 includes some suggestions for specific tests that we have found useful as part of neuropsychological assessments with this patient population.

Future Directions for Research, Detection and Treatment of PNES

To make optimal progress in PNES, researchers and clinicians need to carefully define this condition and make the diagnostic classification rules clear. While vEEG represents the gold standard for diagnosis, working toward a consensus definition of the behavioral component of PNES would be helpful. In addition, we may find that combining diagnostic tools allows us to bolster our confidence in decisions where vEEG has failed to capture any typical spells. For example, it is likely the presence of demographic and medical variables (e.g., history of sexual abuse, comorbid fibromyalgia), specific personality profiles and performance on performance validity testing can be combined with EEG data to provide a more accurate decision about "indeterminate" cases than clinical judgment alone. Research should continue developing classification algorithms, assessment of subtypes of patients with PNES and potential etiological factors that may contribute to the onset of PNES. Improving

Table 18.6 Examples of possible neuropsychological tests and measures to use with a PNES population

Mood and personality measures:
Minnesota multiphasic personality inventory (MMPI/MMPI2/MMPI-RF)
Personality assessment inventory (PAI)
Quality of life measures:
Quality of life in epilepsy
Performance validity measures:
Green's word memory test
Embedded PVTs
Neurocognitive measures—General intelligence:
Wechsler adult intelligence scales
Estimates of premorbid function:
Test of premorbid functioning
Language:
Boston naming test
Letter and semantic fluency tests
Attention:
Trail making test
Working memory index from some version of the WAIS
Visuo-perception/visual-spatial:
Visual object and space perception (VOSP) battery
Memory and learning:
Wechsler memory scales (select subtests)
List Learning paradigm (e.g., Rey auditory verbal Learning test)
Executive control processes:
Stroop color-word interference test
Wisconsin card sorting test

Note: *PNES* psychogenic nonepileptic seizures

diagnostic abilities could both cut down on the costs associated with this condition and what is often a lengthy time span between its onset and identification. Understanding the subtypes and their etiologies has the potential to increase sensitivity or specificity for treatment decisions and to lead to strategies to prevent the onset of this condition in potentially vulnerable populations.

Efforts to determine why neuropsychological/psychological test scores can be so variable and often invalid (demonstrate lack of adequate task engagement in testing) among patients with PNES also need to be further explored (e.g., potential effects of comorbid conditions such as chronic pain and its treatment with analgesics or dissociation associated with chronic abuse histories).

Finally, development and evaluation of specific treatment strategies for patients with PNES remains in its early development stage and represents a very important area of outcomes research that has been sorely missing. There is clearly a newfound interest in this large patient population, exhibited both by the US National Institutes of Health and many US national organizations devoting to the care of epilepsy, and this interest bodes well for the future care of individuals suffering from this malady.

One area not covered by this chapter relates to the neurophysiology of PNES/FND, another area that has been explored with functional and structural neuroimaging over the past decade (for a review, see works such as Drane et al., 2020; Perez et al., 2021; Pick et al., 2024). Relatedly, one area where almost no work exists is in the area of genetic exploration of PNES/FND. A recent scoping review cited only three studies, all of which were small exploratory analyses in this area, but suggests that such studies might increase our knowledge of the pathophysiological and neurobiological problems that may underlie this condition (Asadi-Pooya, Hallett, et al., 2023). There will hopefully be an increase of studies exploring neural mechanisms that in some way contribute to the development or continuation of this condition over the next decade.

In conclusion, there is much work yet to be done in enhancing our understanding of PNES/FND and developing appropriate diagnostic and treatment interventions to deal with this debilitating condition. Neuropsychologists are poised to play a pivotal role in this field of study, and in the delivery of clinical services. This can be a rewarding venture, particularly when one is able to contribute to the resolution of these debilitating events, thereby restoring and enhancing the lives of our patients.

Appendix: Diagnostic Nomenclature Used at the University of Washington Regional Epilepsy Center

Epileptic seizures (ES)—Evidence of definite EEG abnormalities during video EEG monitoring. This includes both ictal and interictal epileptiform activity.

Psychogenic nonepileptic seizures (PNES)—Episodes of unresponsiveness or behavioral abnormality in the absence of EEG changes. Subjective episodes (e.g., “funny” feeling) or minor motor movements (e.g., myoclonic jerks) are not felt to be definitive enough to warrant this diagnosis.

Physiological nonepileptic seizures (PhyNES)—Episodes of unresponsiveness or behavioral abnormality in the absence of EEG changes, but due to another specific physiological cause (e.g., movement disorders, sleep disturbance, syncopal episodes).

Indeterminate spells (IS)—Diagnosis given to patients who either have no spells during vEEG monitoring or those that only experience subjective episodes (e.g., patient indicates experiencing a feeling of fear or disgust) or minor motor movements (e.g., myoclonic jerks) in the absence of EEG change.

Co-occurrence (CO)—Both ES and PNES events have been established using the above criteria during a single or across multiple vEEG admissions.

References

Abe, C., Denney, D., Doyle, A., Cullum, M., Adams, J., Perven, G., Dave, H., Dieppa, M., Hays, R., Agostini, M., & King, K. (2020). Comparison of psychiatric comorbidities and impact on quality of life in patients iwth epilepsy or psychogenic nonepileptic spells. *Epilepsy and Behavior, 102*, 106649.

Abubakr, A., Kablinger, A., & Caldito, G. (2003). Psychogenic seizures: Clinical features and psychological analysis. *Epilepsy and Behavior, 4*(3), 241–245.

Adachi, N., Akanuma, N., Ito, M., Adachi, T., Takekawa, Y., Adachi, Y., Matsuura, M., Kanemoto, K., & Kato, M. (2010). Two forms of deja vu experiences in patinets with epilepsy. *Epilepsy and Behavior, 18*(3), 218–222.

Ahmed, A., & Patil, P. S. (2024). Identifying myoclonic epilepsy misdagnosed as psychogenic nonepileptic seizures: Challenges in differential diagnosis. *Cureus, 16*(6), e62653.

Aldenkamp, A. P., & Arends, J. (2004). Effects of epileptiform EEG discharges on cognitive function: Is the concept of "transient cognitive impairment" still valid? *Epilepsy & Behavior, 5*(Supplement 1), 25–34. http://www.sciencedirect.com/science/article/B6WDT-4B7N6PK-4/2/811598cb9462ddd6c6c5ccaa46dcee7e

ALKhaldi, N. A., Paredes-Aragon, E., Kim, D. D., Yu, Y. J., ALKhateeb, M., & Mirsattari, S. M. (2024). Psychogenic non-epileptic seizures with and without epilepsy: Exploring the influence of co-existing psychiatric disorders on clinical characteristics and outcomes. *Epilepsy Research, 199*, 107279.

Alper, K., Devinsky, O., Perrine, K., Vazquez, B., & Luciano, D. (1993). Nonepileptic seizures and childhood seual and physical abuse. *Neurology, 43*(10), 1950–1953.

American Psychiatric Association, D. S. M. T. F.,, American Psychiatric Association. (2013). *Diagnostic and statistical manual of mental disorders: DSM-5* (Vol. Vol. 5, No. 5). American Psychiatric Association.

Amin, U., Primiani, C. T., MacIver, S., Rivera-Cruz, A., Frontera, A. T., Jr., & Benbadis, S. R. (2021). Value of smartphone videos for diagnosis of seizures: Everyone owns half an epilepsy monitoring unit. *Epilepsia, 62*(9), e135–e139.

Asadi-Pooya, A. A. (2017). Psychogenic nonepileptic seizures: A concise review. *Neurological Sciences, 38*, 935–940.

Asadi-Pooya, A. A. (2023). Incidence and prevalence of psychogenic nonepileptic seizures (functional seizures). A systematic review and an analytical study. *International Journal of Neuroscience, 133*(6), 598–603.

Asadi-Pooya, A. A., & Bazrafshan, M. (2021). Employment and disability status in patients with functional (psychogenic nonepileptic) seizures. *Brain and Behavior, 11*, e02016.

Asadi-Pooya, A. A., Brigo, F., Mildon, B., & Nicholson, T. R. (2020). Terminology for psychogenic nonepileptic seizures: Making the case for "functional seizures". *Epilepsy and Behavior, 104*, 106895.

Asadi-Pooya, A. A., Brigo, F., Trinka, E., Lattanzi, S., Kishk, N. A., Karakis, I., Ristic, A., Alsaadi, T., Alkhaldi, M., Turuspekova, S. T., Aljandeel, G., Al-Asmi, A., Contreras, G., Daza-Restrepo, A., Kutlubaev, M. A., Guekht, A., Calle-Lopez, Y., Jusupova, A., San-Juan, D., Khachatryan, S. G., Gigineishvili, D., Mesraoua, B., Dubenko, A., Damabi, N. M., & Consortium, I. R. i. E. I.-E. (2023). A global survey of the attitudes of neurologists and psychiatrists about functional/psychogenic/dissociative/nonepileptic seizures/attacks, in the search of its name. *Epilepsy and Behavior, 145*, 109292.

Asadi-Pooya, A. A., Hallett, M., Mirzaei Damabi, N., & Fazelian Dehkordi, K. (2023). Genetics of functional seizures: A scoping systematic review. *Genes, 14*(8), 1537.

Ataoglu, A., Ozcetin, A., Icmeli, C., & Ozbulot, O. (2003). Paradoxical therapy in conversion reaction. *Journal of Korean Medical Science, 18*(4), 581–584.

Bagby, R. M., Parker, J. D. A., & Taylor, G. J. (1994). The twenty-item Toronto alexithymia scale-I. Item selection and cross-validation of the factor structure. *Journal of Psychosomatic Research, 38*, 23–32.

Baron-Cohen, S., Wheelwright, S., Hill, J., Raste, Y., & Plumb, I. (2001). The "Reading the mind in the eyes" test revised version: A study with normal adults, and adults with Asperger syndrome or high-functioning autism. *The Journal of Child Psychology and Psychiatry and Allied Disciplines, 42*, 241–251.

Baroni, G., Martins, W. A., Rodrigues, J. C., Piccinini, V., Marin, C., de Lara Machado, W., Bandeira, D. R., Paglioli, E., Valente, K. D., & Palmini, A. (2021). A novel scale for suspicion of psychogenic nonepileptic seizures: Development and accuracy. *Seizure, 89*, 65–72.

Barrett-Naylor, R., Gresswell, D. M., & Dawson, D. L. (2018). The effectiveness and acceptability of a guided self-help acceptance and commitment therapy (ACT) intervention for psychogenic nonepileptic seizures. *Epilepsy and Behavior, 88*, 332–340.

Baslet, G., Bajestan, S. N., Aybek, S., Modirrousta, M., Price, J., Cavanna, A., Perez, D. L., Lazarow, S. S., Raynor, G., Voon, V., Ducharme, S., & LaFrance, W. C. J. (2021). Evidence-based practice for the clinical assessment of psychogenic nonepileptic seizures: A report from the American neuropsychiatric association committee on research. *Journal of Neuropsychiatry and Clinical Neuroscience, 33*(1), 27–42.

Baslet, G., Dworetzky, B., Perez, D. L., & Oser, M. (2015). Treatment of psychogenic nonepileptic seizures: Updated review and findings from a mindfulness-based intervention case series. *Clinical EEG Neurosci, 46*(1), 54–64.

Baslet, G., Ehlert, A., Oser, M., & Dworetzky, B. A. (2020). Mindfulness-based therapy for psychogenic nonepileptic seizures. *Epilepsy and Behavior, 103*, 106534.

Bazil, C. W., & Walczak, T. S. (1997). Effects of sleep and sleep stage on epileptic and nonepileptic seizures. *Epilepsia, 38*(1), 56–62.

Beck, A. T., Epstein, N., Brown, G., & Steer, R. A. (1988). An inventory for measuring clinical anxiety: Psychometric properties. *Journal of Consulting and Clinical Psychology, 56*, 893–897.

Beck, A. T., Steer, R. A., & Brown, G. K. (1996). *Manual for the Beck depression inventory – II*. The Psychological Corporation.

Begley, C. E., Famulari, M., Annergers, J. F., Lairson, D. R., Reynolds, T. F., Coan, S., Dubinsky, S., Newmark, M. E., Leibson, C., So, E. L., & Rocca, W. A. (2000). The cost of epilepsy in the United States: An estimate from population-based clinical and survey data. *Epilepsia, 41*(3), 342–351.

Benbadis, S. (2001). Provocative techniques should be used for the diagnosis of psycghogenic nonepileptic seizures. *Archives of Neurology, 58*(12), 2063.

Benbadis, S. (2015). What type of EEG (or EEG-video) does your patient need? *Expert Review of Neurotheraputics, 15*(5), 461–464.

Benbadis, S., Agrawal, V., & Tatum, W. O. (2001). How many patients with psychogenic nonepileptic seizures also have epilepsy? *Neurology, 57*, 915–917.

Benbadis, S., Beniczky, S., Bertram, E., MacIver, S., & Moshe, S. I. (2020). The role of EEG in patients with suspected epilepsy. *Epileptic Disorders, 22*(2), 143–155.

Benbadis, S. R. (2005a). Association between chronic pain or fibromyalgia and psychogenic seizures. *American Journal of Pain Management, 15*(4), 117–119.

Benbadis, S. R. (2005b). The problem of psychogenic symptoms: Is the psychiatric community in denial? *Epilepsy and Behavior, 6*, 9–14.

Benbadis, S. R. (2020). Functional seizures? "So I still have seizures, right?". *Epilepsy and Behavior, 109*, 107082.

Benbadis, S. R. (2023). The best seizure diagnostic tool is not a medical device: Why stand-alone video review needs a current procedural terminology code. *Neurology: Clinical Practice, 13*(1), e200117.

Benbadis, S. R., & Hauser, W. A. (2000). An estimate of the prevalence of psychogenic nonepileptic seizures. *Seizure, 9*, 280–281.

Benbadis, S. R., Wolgamuth, B. R., Goren, H., Rener, S., & Fouad-Tarazi, F. (1995). Value of tonngue biting in the diagnosis of seizures. *Archives of Internal Medicine, 155*(21), 2346–2349.

Bergen, D., & Ristanovic, R. (1993). Weeping as a common element of pseudoseizures. *Archives of Neurology, 50*(10), 1059–1060.

Berkhoff, M., Briellmann, R. S., Radanov, B. P., Donati, F., & Hess, C. W. (1998). Developmental background and outcome in patients with nonepileptric versus epileptic seizures: A congrolled study. *Epilepsia, 39*(5), 463–469.

Bermeo-Ovalle, A., & Kanner, A. M. (2018). Comorbidities in psychogenic nonepileptic seizures. In G. Rowan (Ed.), *Nonepileptic seizures* (pp. 245–256). Cambridge University Press.

Bernstein, E. M., & Putnam, F. W. (1986). Development, reliability and validity of a dissociation scale. *Journal of Nervous and Mental Disease, 174*(12), 727–737.

Binder, L. M., & Campbell, K. A. (2004). Medically unexplained symptoms and neuropsychological assessment. *Journal of Clinical and Experimental Neuropsychology, 26*(3), 369–392.

Bowman, E. S. (1993). Etiology and clinical course of pseudoseizures. Relationship to trauma, depression, and dissociation. *Psychosomatics, 34*, 333–342.

Bowman, E. S. (2001). Psychopathology and outcome in pseudoseizures. In A. B. Ettinger & A. M. Kanner (Eds.), *Psychiatric issues in epilepsy* (pp. 355–377). Lippincott, Williams, and Wilkins.

Bowman, E. S. (2006). Why conversion seizures should be classified as a dissociative disorder. *Psychiatric Clinics of North America, 29*(1), 185–211.

Bratanov, C., Hot, P., & Vercueil, L. (2023). The natural history of terms describing functional (neurological) disorders in the medical literature of the last 60 years. *Journal of Neurology, 270*(4), 2010–2017.

Brigo, F., Igwe, S. C., Ausserer, H., Nardone, R., Tezzon, F., Bongiovanni, L. G., Tinazzi, M., & Trinka, E. (2015). Terminology of psychogenic nonepileptic seizures. *Epilepsia, 56*(3), e21–e25.

Brooks, J. L., Goodfellow, L., Bodde, N. M., Aldenkamp, A., & Baker, G. A. (2007). Nondrug treatments for psychogenic nonepileptic seizures: What's the evidence. *Epilepsy & Behavior, 11*(3), 367–377.

Brown, R. J. (2004). Psychhological mechanisms of medically unexplained symptoms: An integrative conceptual model. *Psychological Bulletin, 130*(5), 793–812.

Burneo, J. G., Martin, R., Powell, T., Greenlee, S., Knowlton, R. C., Faught, R. E., Prasad, A., Mendez, M., & Kuzniecky, R. I. (2003). Teddy bears: An observational finding in patients with non-epileptic events. *Neurology, 61*(5), 714–715.

Burrows, C. J. (2013). Acceptannce and commitment therapy with survivors of adult sexual assault: A case study. *Clinical Case Studies, 12*(3), 246–259.

Bush, S. S., Ruff, R. M., Troster, A. I., Barth, J. T., Koffler, S. P., Pliskin, N. H., Reynolds, C. R., & Silver, C. H. (2005). Symptom validity assessment: Practice issues and medical necessity NAN policy and planning committee. *Archives of Clinical Neuropsychology, 20*, 419–426.

Butcher, J. N., Graham, J. R., Ben-Porath, Y. S., Tellegen, A., Dahlstrom, W. G., & Kaemmer, B. (2001). *MMPI-2: Manual for administration and scoring* (Vol. Rev. ed.). University of Minnesota Press.

Callahan, C. D., Young, P. L., & Barisa, M. T. (2005). Using the SF-36 for longitudinal outcomes measurement in rehabilitation. *Rehabilitation Psychology, 50*(1), 65–70.

Carlson, P., & Nicholson Perry, K. (2017). Psychological interventions for psychogenic nonepileptic seizures: A meta-analysis. *Seizure, 45*, 142–150.

Carton, S., Thompson, P. J., & Duncan, J. S. (2003). Non-epileptic seizures: Patients' understanding and reaction to the diagnosis and impact on outcome. *Seizure, 12*(5), 287–294.

Chabolla, D. R., & Shih, J. J. (2006). Postictal behaviors associated with psychogeic nonepileptic seizures. *Epilepsy and Behavior, 9*(2), 307–311.

Chung, S. S., Gerber, P., & Kirlin, K. A. (2006). Ictal eye closure is a reliable indicator for psychogenic nonepileptic seizures. *Neurology, 66*(11), 1730–1731.

Cope, S. R., Poole, N., & Agrawal, N. (2017). Treating functional non-epileptic attacks – Should we consider acceptance and commitment therapy. *Epilepsy and Behavior, 93*, 197–203.

Cragar, D. E., Berry, D. T., Schmitt, F. A., & Fakhoury, T. A. (2005). Cluster analysis of normal personality traits in patients with psychogenic nonepileptic seizures. *Epilepsy and Behavior, 6*(4), 593–600.

Cragar, D. E., Berry, D. T. R., Fakhoury, T. A., Cibula, J. E., & Schmitt, F. A. (2002). A review of diagnostic techniques in the differential diagnosis of epileptic and nonepileptic seizures. *Neuropsychology Review, 12*(1), 31–64.

Cragar, D. E., Schmitt, F. A., Berry, D. T. R., Cibula, J. E., Dearth, C. M. S., & Fakhoury, T. A. (2003). A comparison of MMPI-2 decision rules in the diagnosis of nonepileptic seizures. *Journal of Clinical and Experimental Neuropsychology, 25*(6), 793–804.

Cuthill, F. M., & Espie, C. A. (2005). Sensitivity and specificity of procedures for the differential diagnosis of epileptic and non-epileptic seizures: A systematic review. *Seizure, 14*(5), 293–303.

Deacon, C., Wiebe, S., Blume, W. T., McLachlan, R. S., Young, G. B., & Matijevic, S. (2003). Seizure identification by clinical description in temporal lobe epilepsy: How accurate are we? *Neurology, 61*(12), 1686–1689.

Derry, P. A., & Mclachlan, R. S. (1996). The MMPI-2 as an adjunct to the diagnosis of pseudoseizures. *Seizure, 5*, 35–40.

Devinsky, O., Mesad, S., & Alper, K. (2001). Nondominant hemisphere lesions and conversion nonepileptic seizures. *Journal of Neuropsychiatry and Clinical Neuroscience, 13*, 367–373.

Devinsky, O., Sanchez-Villaseñor, F., Vazquez, B., Kothari, M., Alper, K., & Luciano, D. (1996). Clinical profile of patients with epileptic and nonepileptic seizures. *Neurology, 46*, 1530–1533.

Devinsky, O., Vickrey, V. G., Cramer, J., Perrine, K., Hermann, B., Meador, K., & Hays, R. D. (1995). Development of the quality of life in epilepsy inventory. *Epilepsia, 36*, 1089–1104.

Dikel, T. N., Fennell, E. B., & Gilmore, R. L. (2003). Posttraumatic stress disorder, dissociation, and sexual abuse histlry in epileptic and nonepileptic seizure patients. *Epilepsy and Behavior, 4*, 644–650.

Dodrill, C. B., & Holmes, M. D. (2000). Psychological and neuropsychological evaluation of the patient with non-epileptic seizures. In J. R. Gates & A. J. Rowan (Eds.), *Non-epileptic seizures* (2nd ed.). Butterworth-Heinemann.

Drake, M. E., Jr. (1993). Conversion hysteria and cominant hemisphere lesions. *Psychosomatics, 34*(6), 524–530.

Drake, M. E., Huber, S. J., Pakalnis, A., & Phillips, B. B. (1993). Neuropsychological and event-related potential correlates of nonepileptic seizures. *The Journal of Neuropsychiatry & Clinical Neuroscience, 5*(1), 102–104.

Drane, D. L., Fani, N., Hallett, M., Khalsa, S. S., Perez, D. L., & Roberts, N. A. (2020). A framework for understanding the pathophysiology of functional neurological disorder. *CNS Spectrums*, 1–7.

Drane, D. L., Hewitt, K. C., Price, M. E., Rush, B., Blackmon, K., Okada, N., Shade, T., Valentin, E., Vinson, J. A., Rosen, P., & Loring, D. W. (2023). Case study of invalid to valid shift in cognitive performance following successful treatment of psychogenic nonepileptic seizure events. *Journal of Clinical and Experimental Neuropsychology, 45*(10), 1024–1038.

Drane, D. L., LaRoche, S. M., Ganesh, G. A., Teagarden, D., & Loring, D. W. (2016). A standardized diagnostic approach and ongoing feedback improves outcome in psychogenic nonepileptic seizures. *Epilepsy and Behavior, 54*, 34–39.

Drane, D. L., Ojemann, J. G., Kim, M., Gross, R. E., Miller, J. W., Faught, R. E., Jr., & Loring, D. W. (2016). Interictal epileptiform discharge effects on neuropsychological assessment and epilepsy surgical planning. *Epilepsy and Behavior, 56*, 131–138.

Drane, D. L., Williamson, D. J., Stroup, E. S., Holmes, M. D., Jung, M., Koerner, E., Chaytor, N., Wilensky, A. J., & Miller, J. W. (2006). Cognitive impairment is not equal in patients with epileptic and psychogenic nonepileptic seizures. *Epilepsia, 47*(11), 1879–1886.

Dufresne, D., Dubovek, K., So, N. K., & Kotagal, P. (2019). Ictal biting injuries in the epilepsy monitoring unit a cohort study of incidence and semiological significance. *Seizure, 66*, 39–41.

Duncan, R., & Oto, M. (2008a). Predictors of antecedent factors in psychogenic nonepileptic attacks: Multivariate analysis. *Neurology, 71*(13), 1000–1005.

Duncan, R., & Oto, M. (2008b). Psychogenic nonepileptic seizures in patients with learning disability: Comparison with patients with no learning disability. *Epilepsy and Behavior, 12*(1), 183–186.

Duncan, R., Oto, M., Martin, E., & Pelosia, A. (2006). Late onset psychogenic nonepileptic attacks. *Neurology, 66*(11), 1644–1647.
Duncan, R., Oto, M., Russell, A., & Conway, P. (2004). Pseudosleep events in patients with psychogenic non-epileptic seizures: Prevalence and associations. *Journal of Neurology, Neurosurgery, and Psychiatry, 75*(7), 1009–1012.
Duncan, R., Oto, M., Wainman-Lefley, J., & Pelosi, A. (2012). Mortality in a cohort of patients with psychogenic non-epileptic seizures. *Journal of Neurology, Neurosurgery and Psychiatry, 83*(7), 761–762.
Duncan, R., Razvi, S., & Mulhern, S. (2011). Newly presenting psychogenic nonepileptic seizures: Incidence, population characteristics, and early outcome from a prospective audit of a first seizure clinic. *Epilepsy and Behavior, 20*(2), 308–311.
Durrant, J., Rickards, H., & Cavanna, A. E. (2011). Prognosis and outcome predictors in psychogenic nonepileptic seizures. *Epilepsy Research Treatment*, 274736.
Ebus, S., Arends, J., Hendriksen, J., van der Horst, E., de la Parra, N., Hendriksen, R., Santegoeds, E., Boon, P., & Aldenkamp, B. (2012). Cognitive effects of interictal epileptiform discharges in children. *European Journal of Paediatric Neurology, 16*(6), 707–715.
Elzawahry, H., Do, C. S., Lin, K., & Benbadis, S. R. (2010). The diagnostic utility of the ictal cry. *Epilepsy and Behavior, 18*(3), 306–307.
Engel, J. J. (1996). Surgery for seizures. *New England Journal of Medicine, 334*, 647–652.
Engel, J., Jr., & Shewmon, D. A. (1993). Overview: Who should be considered a surgical candidate? In J. Engel Jr. (Ed.), *Surgical treatment of epilepsies* (Vol. 2nd, pp. 23–34). Raven Press.
Ettinger, A. B., Devinsky, O., Weisbrot, D. M., Ramakrishna, R. K., & Goyal, A. (1999). A comprehensive profile of clinical, psychiatric, and psychosocial characteristics of patients with psychogenic nonepileptic seizures. *Epilepsia, 40*, 1292–1298.
Ettinger, A. B., Dhoon, A., Weisbrot, D. M., & Devinsky, O. (1999). Predictive factors for outcome of nonepileptic seizures after diagnosis. *Journal of Psychiatric Neuroscience, 11*(4), 458–463.
Fani, N., King, T. Z., Clendinen, C., Hardy, R. A., Surapaneni, S., Blair, J. R., White, S. F., Powers, A., Ely, T. D., Jovanovic, T., Ressler, K. J., & Bradley, B. (2019). Attentional control abnormalities in posttraumatic stress disorder: Functional, behavioral, and structural correlates. *Journal of Affective Disorders, 253*, 343–351.
Fisch, B. J., & Olejniczak, D. W. (2001). Generalized tonic-clonic seizures. In E. Wyllie (Ed.), *The treatment of epilepsy* (pp. 369–393). Lippincott, Williams, and Wilkins.
Fiszman, A., Alves-Leon, S. V., Nunes, R. G., D'Andea, I., & Figueira, I. (2004). Traumatic events and posttraumatic stress disorder in patients with psychogenic nonepileptic seizures: A critical review. *Epilepsy and Behavior, 5*(6), 818–825.
French, J. (1995). Pseudoseizures in the era of video-electroencephalogram monitoring. *Current Opinion in Neurology, 8*(2), 117–120.
Freud, S. (1966). Hysteria. In J. Strachey (Ed.), *The standard edition of the complete psychological works of Sigmund Freud* (Vol. 1, pp. 41–59). Hogarth Press.
Gates, J. R., & Erdahl, P. (1993). Classification of non-epileptic events. In A. J. Rowan & J. R. Gates (Eds.), *Non-epileptic Seizures* (pp. 21–30). Butterworth-Heinemann.
Gates, J. R., Ramani, V., Whalen, S., & Lowenson, R. N. (1985). Ictal characteristics of pseudoseizures. *Archives of Neurology, 42*, 1183–1187.
Gervais, R. O., Rohling, R. L., Green, P., & Ford, W. (2004). A comparison of WMT, CARB, and TOMM failure rates in non-head injury disability claimants. *Archives of Clinical Neuropsychology, 19*, 475–487.
Gervais, R. O., Russell, A. S., Green, P., Allen, L. M., Ferrari, R., & Pieschl, S. D. (2001). Effort testing in patients with fibromyalgia and disability incentives. *Journal of Rheumatology, 28*, 1892–1899.
Geyer, J. D., Payne, T. A., & Drury, I. (2000). The value of pelvic thrusting in the diagnosis of seizures and pseudoseizures. *Neurology, 54*(1), 227–229.
Glennon, J. M., Weiss-Croft, L., Harrison, S., Cross, J. H., Boyd, S. G., & Baldeweg, T. (2016). Interictal epileptiform discharges have an independent association with cognive impairment in children with lesional epilepsy. *Epilepsia, 57*, 1436–1442.

Goldstein, L. H., Chalder, T., Chigwedere, C., Khondoker, M. R., Moriarty, J., Toone, B. K., & Mellers, J. D. (2010). Cognitive-behavioral therapy for psychogenic nonepileptic seizures: A pilot RCT. *Neurology, 74*(24), 1986–1994.

Goldstein, L. H., Drew, C., Mellers, J., Mitchell-O'Malley, S., & Oakley, D. A. (2000). Dissociation, hypnotizability, coping styles and health locus of control: Characteristics of pseudoseizure patients. *Seizure, 9*(5), 314–322.

Goldstein, L. H., Robinson, E. J., Mellers, J. D. C., Stone, J., Carson, A., Reuber, M., Medford, N., McCone, P., Murray, J., Richardson, M. P., Pilecka, I., Eastwood, C., Moore, M., Mosweu, I., Perdue, S., Landau, S., Chalder, T., & CODES study group. (2020). Cognitive behavioural therapy for adults with dissociative seizures (CODES): A pragmatic, multicentre, randomised controlled trial. *Lancet Psychiatry, 7*(6), 491–505.

Goldstein, L. H., Robinson, E. J., Reuber, M., Chalder, T., Callaghan, H., Eastwood, C., Landau, S., McCrone, P., Medford, N., Mellers, J. D. C., Moore, M., Mosweu, I., Murray, J., Perdue, I., Pilecka, I., Richardson, M. P., Carson, A., Stone, J., & Group, C. S. (2019). Demographics of 698 patients with dissociative seizures participating in a UK multi-Centre treatment study. *Epilepsia, 60*(11), 2183–2193.

Green, B., Norman, P., & Reuber, M. (2017). Attachment style, relationship quality, and psychological distress in patients with psychogenic non-epileptic seizures versus epilepsy. *Epilepsy and Behavior, 66*, 120–126.

Green, P., Iverson, G. L., & Allen, L. (1999). Detecting malingering in head injury litigation with the word memory test. *Brain Injury, 13*(10), 813–819.

Green, P., Rohling, M. L., Lees-Haley, P. R., & Allen, L. M. (2001). Effort has a greater effect on test scores than severe brain injury in compensation claimants. *Brain Injury, 15*(12), 1045–1060.

Gutkin, M., McLean, L., Brown, R., & Kanaan, R. A. (2020). Systematic review of psychotherapy for adults with functional neuorlogical disorder. *Journal of Neurology, Neurosurgery, and Psychiatry*, 321926.

Hall-Patch, L., Brown, R., House, A., Howlett, S., Kemp, S., Lawton, G., Mayor, R., Smith, P., Reuber, M., & collaborators, f. t. N. (2009). Acceptability and effectiveness of a strategy for the communication of the diagnosis of psychogenic nonepileptic seizures. *Epilepsia, 51*(1), 70–78.

Harden, C. L., Burgut, F. T., & Kanner, A. M. (2003). The diagnostic significance of video-EEG recordings on pseudoseizure patients differs between neurologists and psychiatrists. *Epilepsia, 44*(3), 453–456.

Harden, C. L., Jovine, L., Burgut, F. T., Carey, B. T., Nikolov, B. G., & Ferrando, S. J. (2009). A comparison of personality disorder characteristics of patients with nonepileptic psychogenic pseudoseizures with those of patients with epilepsy. *Epilepsy and Behavior, 14*(3), 481–483.

Henry, G. K., Heilbronner, R., Suhr, J., Gorbein, J., Wagner, E. B., & Drane, D. L. (2018). Illness perception and beliefs predict cognitive performance validity. *Journal of the International Neuropsychological Society, 7*, 735–745.

Hermann, B. P. (2000). Neuropsychological assessment in the diagnosis of non-epileptic seizures. In J. R. Gates & A. J. Rowan (Eds.), *Non-epileptic seizures*. Butterworth-Heinemann.

Herskovitz, M. (2017). Stereotypy of psychogenic nonepileptic seizures. *Epilepsy and Behavior, 70*, 140–144.

Hoerth, M. T., Wellik, K. E., Demaerschalk, B. M., Drazkowski, J. F., Noe, K. H., Sirvin, J. I., & Wingerchuk, D. M. (2008). Clinical predictors of psychogenic nonepileptic seizures. *The Neurologist, 14*, 266–270.

Holmes, M. D., Dodrill, C. B., Bachtler, S., Wilensky, A. J., Ojemann, L. M., & Miller, J. W. (2001). Evidence that emotional maladjustment is worse in men than in women with psychogenic nonepileptic seizures. *Epilepsy and Behavior, 2*, 568–573.

Horak, P. C., Meisenhelter, S., Song, Y., Testorf, M. E., Kahana, M. J., Viles, W. D., Bujarski, K. A., Connolly, A. C., Robbins, A. A., Sperling, M. R., Sharan, A. D., Worrell, G. A., Miller, L. R., Gross, R. E., Davis, K. A., Roberts, D. W., Lega, B., Sheth, S. A., Zaghloul, K. A., Stein, J. M., Das, S. R., Rizzuto, D. S., & Jobst, B. C. (2017). Interictal epileptiform discharges impair word recall in multiple brain areas. *Epilepsia, 58*(3), 373–380.

Howe, L. L., & Loring, D. W. (2009). Classification accuracy and predictive ability of the medical symptom validity test's dementia profile and general memory impairment profile. *The Clinical Neuropsychologist, 23*(2), 329–342.

Janocko, N. J., Jing, J., Fan, Z., Teagarden, D., Villarreal, H. K., Morton, M. L., Groover, O., Loring, D. W., Drane, D. L., Westover, M. B., & Karakis, I. (2021). DDESVSFS: A simple, rapid and comprehensive screening tool for the differential diagnosis of epileptic seizures VS functional seizures. *Epilepsy Research, 171*, 106563.

Jennum, P., Ibsen, R., & Kiellberg, J. (2019). Welfare consequences for people diagnosed with non-epileptic seizures: A matched nationwide study in Denmark. *Epilepsy and Behavior, 98*, 59–65.

Kamil, S. H., Qureshi, M., & Patel, R. S. (2019). Cognitive behavioral therapy (CBT) in psychogenic non-epileptic seizures (PNES): A case report and literature review. *Behavioral Sciences, 9*(2), 15.

Kanner, A. M., Parra, J., Frey, M., Stebbins, G., Pierre-Louis, S., & Iriarte, J. (1999). Psychiatric and neurologic predictors of psychogenic pseudoseizure outcome. *Neurology, 53*(5), 933–938.

Karakis, I., Lynam, C., Taraschenko, O., Staikova, E., & Drane, D. L. (2020). Concurrent EEG monitoring helps interpret neuropsychological testing results in patients with epilepsy. *Epilepsy and Behavior, 111*, 207275.

Kellinghaus, C., Loddenkemper, T., Dinner, D. S., Lachwani, D., & Luders, H. O. (2004). Non-epileptic seizures of the elderly. *Journal of Neurology, 251*(6), 704–709.

Kleen, J. K., Scott, R. C., Holmes, G. L., Roberts, D. W., Rundle, M. M., Testorf, M., Lenck-Santini, P. P., & Jobst, B. C. (2013). Hippocampal interictal epileptiform activity disrupts cognition in humans. *Neurology, 81*(1), 18–24.

Kotagal, P., Costa, M., Wyllie, E., & Wolgamuth, B. (2002). Paroxysmal nonepileptic events in children and adolescents. *Pediatrics, 110*(4), e46.

Krumholz, A. (1999). Nonepileptic seizures: Diagnosis and management. *Neurology, 53*(5 Suppl. 2), S76–S83.

Kuyk, J., Swinkels, W. A. M., & Spinhoven, P. (2003). Psychopathologies in patients with non-epileptic seizures with and without comorbid epilepsy: How different are they? *Epilepsy and Behavior, 4*(1), 13.

Lacey, C., Cook, M., & Salzberg, M. (2007). The neurologist, psychogenic nonepileptic seizures, and borderline personality disorder. *Epilepsy and Behavior, 11*(4), 492–498.

Lado, F. A., Ahrens, S. M., Riker, E., Richardson, R. M., Gray, J., Small, B., Lewis, S. Z., Schofield, T. J., Clarke, D. F., Hopp, J. L., Lee, R. R., Salpekar, J. A., Arnold, S. T., & Panel, f. t. N. A. o. E. G. f. S. E. C. (2024). Guidelines for specialized epilepsy centers: Executive summary of the report of the National Association of epilepsy centers guideline panel. *Neurology, 102*(4). https://doi.org/10.1212/WNL.0000000000208087

LaFrance, W. C., Jr., Baker, G. A., Duncan, R., Goldstein, L. H., & Reuber, M. (2013). Minimum requirements for the diagnosis of psychogenic nonepileptic seizures: A staged approach: A report from the international league against epilepsy nonepileptic seizure task force. *Epilepsia, 54*(11), 2005–2018.

LaFrance, W. C., Jr., & Devinsky, O. (2004). The treatment of nonepileptic seizures: Historical perspectives and future directions. *Epilepsia, 45*, 15–21.

LaFrance, W. C. J., Alper, K., Babcock, D., Barry, J. J., Benbadis, S., Caplan, R., Gates, J., Jacobs, M., Kanner, A., Martin, R., Rundhaugen, L., Stewart, R., Vert, C., & participants, N. T. W. (2006). Nonepileptic seizures treatment worshop summary. *Epilepsy and Behavior, 8*(3), 451–461.

LaFrance, W. C. J., BBaird, G. L., Barry, J. J., Blum, A. S., Webb, A. F., Keitner, G. I., Machan, J. T., Miller, I., Szaflarski, J. P., & Consortium, N. E. T. T. N.-T. (2014). Multicenter pilot treatment trial for psychogenic nonepileptic serizures: A randomized clinical trial. *JAMA Psychiatry, 71*(9), 997–1005.

LaFrance, W. C. J., Rusch, M. D., & Machan, J. T. (2008). What is "treatment as usual" for non-epileptic seizures? *Epilepsy and Behavior, 12*(3), 388–394.

Lancman, M. E., Asconape, J. J., Graves, S., & Gibson, P. A. (1994). Psychogenic seizures in children: Long-term analysis of 43 cases. *Journal of Child Neurology, 9*(4), 404–407.

Lanzillotti, A. I., Sarudiansky, M., Lombardi, N. R., Korman, G. P., & D Alessio, L. (2021). Updated review on thediagnosis and primary managemenbt of psychogenic nonepileptic seizure disorders. *Neuropsychiatric Disease and Treatment, 17*, 1825–1838.

Larrabee, G. J. (2012). Performance validity and symptom validity in neuropsychological assessment. *Journal of the International Neuropsychological Society, 18*, 625–631.

Leibetseder, A., Eisermann, M., LaFrance, W. C. J., Nobili, L., & von Oertzen, T. J. (2021). How to distinguish seizures from non-epileptic manifestations. *Epileptic Disorders, 22*(6), 716–738.

Lempert, T., & Schmidt, D. (1990). Natural history and outcome of psychogenic seizures: A clinical study in 50 patients. *Journal of Neurology, 237*(1), 35–38.

Lesser, R. P. (1996). Psychogenic seizures. *Neurology, 46*, 1499–1507.

Lesser, R. P. (2003). Treatment and outcome of psychogenic nonepileptic seizures. *Epilepsy Currents, 3*(6), 198–200.

Lesser, R. P., Leuders, H., & Dinner, D. S. (1983). Evidence for epilepsy is rare in patients with psychogenic nonepileptic seizures. *Neurology, 33*, 502–504.

Liske, E., & Forster, F. M. (1964). Pseudoseizures: A problem in the diagnosis and management of epileptic patients. *Neurology, 14*(1), 41–49.

Locke, D. E., Kirlin, K. A., Thomas, M. L., Osborne, D., Hurst, D. F., & Drazkowski, j. F., Sirven, J. I., & Noe, K. H. (2010). The Minnesota multiphasic Pesonality inventory – 2 – Restrctured form in the epilepsy monitoring unit. *Epilepsy and Behavior, 17*, 252–258.

Lowenberger, A., Cope, S. R., Poole, N., & Agrawal, N. (2020). An investigation into the preferred terminology for functional seizures. *Epilepsy and Behavior, 111*, 107183.

Madaan, P., Gulati, S., Chakrabarty, B., Sapra, S., Sagar, R., Mohammad, A., Pandey, R. M., & Tripathi, M. (2018). Clinical spectrum of psychogenic non epileptic seizures in children; an observational study. *Seizure, 59*, 60–66.

Markand, O. N., Salanova, V., Whelihan, E., & Emsley, C. L. (2000). Health-related quality of life outcome in medical refractory epilepsy treated with anterior temporal lobectomy. *Epilepsia, 41*(6), 749–759.

Marquez, A. V., Farias, S. T., Apperson, M., Koopmans, S., Jorgensen, J., Shatzel, A., & Alsaadi, T. M. (2004). Psychogenic nonepileptic seizures are associated with an increased risk of obesity. *Epilepsy and Behavior, 5*(1), 88–93.

Martin, R., Burneo, J. G., Prasad, A., Powell, T., Faught, E., Knowlton, R., Mendez, M., & Kuzniecky, R. (2003). Frequency of epilepsy in patients with psychogenic nonepileptic seizures monitored by video-EEG. *Neurology, 61*(12), 1791–1792.

Massey, W. E. (1982). History of epilepsy and hysteria. In T. Riley & A. Roy (Eds.), *Pseudo-Seizures* (pp. 1–20). Williams and Wilkins.

Massot-Tarrus, A., Joe Yu, Y., Alkhateeb, M., & Mirsattari, S. M. (2021). Predicting outcome of patients with psychogenic nonepileptic seizures after diagnosisin an epilepsy monitoring unit. *Epilepsy and Behavior, 120*, 108004.

Mattson, R. H. (1980). Value of intensive monitoring. In J. A. Wada & J. K. Penry (Eds.), *Advances in Epileptology* (pp. 43–51). Raven Press.

McKenzie, P., Oto, M., Russell, A., Pelosi, A., & Duncan, R. (2010). Early outcomes and predictors in 260 patients with psychogenic nonepileptic attacks. *Neurology, 74*(1), 64–69.

Mittenberg, W., Rotholc, A., Russell, E., & Heilbronner, R. (1996). Identification of malingered head injury on the Halstead-Reitan battery. *Archives of Clinical Neuropsychology, 11*(4), 271–281. http://www.sciencedirect.com/science/article/B6VDJ-3Y2G16K-2/2/9990cbebb9228d0c0aef89ef38b9a980

Mokleby, K., Biomhoff, S., Malt, U. F., Dahlstrom, A., Tauboll, E., & Gjerstad, L. (2002). Psychiatric comorbidity and hostility in patients with psychogenic nonepileptic seizures compared with somatoform disorders and healthy controls. *Epilepsia, 43*(2), 193–198.

Morey, L. C. (1991). *The personality assessment inventory: Professional manual*. Psychological Assessment Resources.

Moro, P., Lattanzi, S., Beier, C. P., Bonaventura, C. D., & Irelli, E. C. (2024). Cognitive behavioral therapy in adults iwth functional seizures: A systematic review and meta-analysis of randomized controlled trials. *Epilepsy and Behavior, 159*, 109981.

Myers, L., Vaidya-Mathur, U., & Lancman, M. (2017). Prolonged exposure therapy for the treatment of patients diagnosed with psychogenic non-epileptic seizures (PNES) and post-traumatic stress disorder (PTSD). *Epilepsy and Behavior, 66*, 86–92.

Nelson, L. D., Mitrushina, M., Satz, P., Sowa, M., Cohen, S., Elder, J. T., Groot, J., Tehrani, P., & Grant, A. C. (2004). Personality testing and epilepsy: Comparison of two MMPI-2 correction procedures. *Epilepsy and Behavior, 5*(6), 911–918.

Neumann, L., & Buskila, D. (2003). Epidemiology of fibromyalgia. *Current Pain and Headache Reports, 7*(5), 362–368.

Nightscales, R., McCartney, L., Auvrez, C., Tao, G., Barnard, S., Malpas, C. B., Perucaa, P., McIntosh, A., Chen, Z., Sivathamboo, S., Ignatiadis, S., Jones, S., Adams, S., Cook, M. J., Kwan, P., Velakoulis, D., D'Souze, W., Berkovic, S. F., & O'Brien, T. J. (2020). Mortality in patients with psychogenic nonepileptic seizures. *Neurology, 95*(6), 3643–3652.

Oliva, M., Pattison, C., Carino, J., Roten, A., Matkovic, Z., & O'rien, T. J. (2008). The diagnostic value of oral lacerations and incontinence duringconvulsive "seizures". *Epilepsia, 49*(6), 962–967.

Orbach, D., Ritaccio, A., & Devinsky, O. (2003). Psychogenic, nonepileptic seizures associated iwth video-EEG-verified sleep. *Epilepsia, 44*(1), 64.

O'Sullivan, S. S., Spillane, J. E., McMahon, E. M., Sweeney, B. J., Galvin, R. J., McNamara, B., & Cassidy, E. M. (2007). Clinical characteristics and outcome of patients diagnosed with psychogenic nonepileptic seizures: A 5-year review. *Epilepsy and Behavior, 11*, 77–84.

Patel, H., Scott, E., Dunn, D., & Garg, B. (2007). Nonepileptic seizures in chilldren. *Epilepsia, 48*(11), 2086–2092.

Peguero, E., Abou-Khalil, B., Fakhoury, T., & Matthews, G. (1995). Self-injury and incontinence in psychogenic seizures. *Epilepsia, 36*, 586–591.

Perez, D. L., Nicholson, T. R., Asadi-Pooya, A. A., Begue, I., Butler, M., Carson, A. J., David, A. S., Deeley, Q., Diez, I., Edwards, M. J., Espay, A. J., Gelauff, J. M., Hallett, M., Horovitz, S. G., Jungilligens, J., Kanaan, R. A. A., Tijssen, M. A. J., Kozlowska, K., Lafaver, K., LaFrance, W. C., Jr., Lidstone, S. C., Marapin, R. S., Maurer, C. W., Modirrousta, M., Reinders, A. A. T. S., Sojka, P., Staab, J. P., Stone, J., Szaflarksi, J., & Aybek, S. (2021). Neuroimaging in functional neurological disorder: State of the field and research agenda. *Neuroimage Clinical, 30*, 102623.

Pick, S., David, A. S., Edwards, M. J., Goldstein, L. H., Hodsoll, J., Millman, L. S. M., Nicholson, T. R., Reinders, A. A. T. S., Stanton, B., Winston, J. S., Mehta, M. A., Chalder, T., & Hotopf, M. (2024). Investigating psychobiological causes and mechanisms in functional seizures and functional motor symptoms: Study protocol. *PLoS One, 19*(6), e0305015.

Plioplys, S., Doss, J., Siddarth, P., Bursch, B., Falcone, T., Forgey, M., Hinman, K., LaFrance, W. C., Jr., Laptook, R., Shaw, R. J., Weisbrot, D. M., Willis, M. D., & Calan, R. (2014). A multisite controlled study of risk factors in pediatric psychogenic nonepileptic seizures. *Epilepsia, 55*(11), 1739–1747.

Prigatano, G. P., & Kirlin, K. A. (2008). Self-appraisal and objective assessment of cognitive and affective functioning in persons with epileptic and nonepileptic seizures. *Epilepsy and Behavior, 14*(2), 387–392.

Rechlin, T., Loew, T. H., & Joraschky, P. (1997). Pseudoseizure "status". *Journal of Psychosomatic Research, 42*(5), 495–498.

Reuber, M. (2008). Psychogenic nonepileptic seizures: Answers and questions. *Epilepsy and Behavior, 12*(4), 622–635.

Reuber, M., & Brown, R. J. (2017). Understanding psychogenic nonepileptic seizures – Phenomenology, semiology and the integrative cognitive model. *Seizure, 44*, 199–205.

Reuber, M., & Elger, C. E. (2003). Psychogenic nonepileptic seizures: Review and update. *Epilepsy and Behavior, 4*, 205–216.

Reuber, M., Enright, S. M., & Goulding, P. J. (2000). Postoperative pseudostatus: Not everything that shakes is epilepsy. *Anaesthesia, 55*(1), 74–78.

Reuber, M., Fernandez, G., Helmstaedter, C., Qurishi, A., & Elger, C. E. (2002). Evidence of brain abnormality in patients with psychogenic nonepileptic seizures. *Epilepsy and Behavior, 3*, 249–254.

Reuber, M., House, A. O., Pukrop, R., Bauer, J., & Elger, C. E. (2003). Somatization, dissociation and general psychopathology in patients with psychogenic non-epileptic seizures. *Epilepsy Research, 57*(2-3), 159–167.

Reuber, M., Howlett, S., & Kemp, S. (2005). Psychologic treatment of patients with nonepileptic seizures. *Expert Review of Neurotherapeutics, 5*(6), 737–752.

Reuber, M., Howlett, S., Khan, A., & Grunewald, R. A. (2007). Non-epileptic seizures and other functional neurological symptoms: Predisposing, precipitating, and perpetuating factors. *Psychosomatics, 48*(3), 230–238.

Reuber, M., Qurishi, A., Bauer, J., Helmstaedter, C., Fernandez, G., Widman, G., & Elger, C. (2003). Are there physical risk factors for psychogenic non-epileptic seizures in patients with epilepsy? *Seizure, 12*(8), 561–567.

Rocamora, R., Chavarria, B., Perez, E., Perez-Enriquez, C., Barguilla, A., Panades-de Oliveira, L., Principe, A., & Zucca, R. (2021). Mood disturbances, anxiety, and impact on quality of life in patients admitted to epilepsy monitoring units. *Frontiers in Neurology, 12*, 761239.

Rohling, M. L., Green, P., Allen, L. M., III, & Iverson, G. L. (2002). Depressive symptoms and neurocognitive test scores in patients passing symptom validity tests. *Archives of Clinical Neuropsychology, 17*(3), 205–222.

Rusch, M. D., Morris, G. L., Allen, L., & Lathrop, L. (2001). Psychological treatment of nonepileptic events. *Epilepsy and Behavior, 2*(3), 277–283.

Sackellares, J., Giordani, B., Berent, S., Seidenberg, M., Dreifuss, F., Vanderzant, C., & al., e. (1985). Patients with pseudoseizures: Intellectual and cognitive performance. *Neurology, 35*, 116–119.

Salinsky, M., Rutecki, P., Parko, K., Goy, E., Storzbach, D., O'Neil, M., Binder, L., & Joos, S. (2018). Psychiatric comorbidity and traumatic brain injury attribution in patients with psychogenic nonepileptic or epileptic seizures: A multicenter study of US veterans. *Epilepsia, 59*(10), 1945–1953.

Sanders, B., & Becker-Lausen, E. (1995). The measurement of psychological maltreatment: Early data on the child abuse and trauma scale. *Child Abuse and Neglect, 19*(3), 315–323.

Sawchuk, T., Asadi-Pooya, A. A., Myers, L., Valente, K. D., Restrepo, A. D., D'Alessio, L., Homayoun, M., Bahrami, Z., Alessi, R., Paytan, A. A., Kochen, S., Taha, F., Lazar, L. M., Pick, S., Nichholson, T. R., & Buchhalter, J. (2020). Clinical characteristics of psychogenic nonepileptic seizures across the lifespan: An international retrospective study. *Epilepsy and Behavior, 102*, 106705.

Saygi, S., Katz, A., Marks, D. A., & Spencer, S. S. (1992). Frontal lobe partial seizures and psychogenic seizures: Comparison of clinical and ictal characteristics. *Neurology, 42*(7), 1274–1277.

Schrag, A., Brown, R. J., & Trimble, M. R. (2004). Reliability of self-reported diagnoses in patients with neurologically unexplained symptoms *journal of neurology. Neurosurgery, and Psychiatry, 75*, 608–611.

Schramke, C. J., Valeri, A., Valeriano, J. P., & Kelly, K. M. (2007). Using the Minnesota multiphasic inventory 2, EEGs, and clinical data to predict nonepileptic events. *Epilepsy and Behavior, 11*(3), 343–346.

Scoot, D. F. (1982). Recognition and diagnostic aspects of non-epileptic seizures. In T. L. Riley & A. Roy (Eds.), *Pseudoseizures* (pp. 21–34). Williams & Wilkins Co.

Selkirk, M., Duncan, R., Oto, M., & Pelosi, A. (2008). Clinical differences between patients with nonepileptic seizures who report antecedent sexual abuse and those who do not. *Epilepsia, 49*(8), 1446–1450.

Seneviratne, U., Minato, E., & Paul, E. (2017). How reliable is ictal durationn to differentiate psychogenic nonepileptic seizures from epileptic seizures? *Epilepsy and Behavior, 66*, 127–131.

Seneviratne, U., Reutens, D., & Souza, D. W. (2010). Stereotypy of psychogenicnonepileptic seizures: Insights from video-EEG monitoring. *Epilepsia, 51*(7), 1159–1168.
Sethi, N. K. (2013). Psychogenic nonepileptic seizure: The name matters. *Journal of the American Medical Association Neurology, 70*(4), 528–529.
Sheehan, D. V., Lecrubier, Y., Sheehan, K. H., Amorim, P., Janavs, J., Weiller, E., Hergueta, T., Baker, R., & Dunbar, G. C. (1998). The mini-international neuropsychiatric interview (M.I.N.I.): The development and validtation of a structured diagnostic psychiatric interview for DSM-IV and ICD-10. *Journal of Clinical Psychiatry, 59*(Suppl 20), 22–33.
Shen, W., Bowman, E. S., & Markand, O. N. (1990). Presenting the diagnoses of pseudoseizure. *Neurology, 40*(5), 756–759.
Sigurdardottir, K. R., & Olafsson, E. (1998). Incidence of psychogenic seizures in adults: A population-based study in Iceland. *Epilepsia, 39*(7), 749–752.
Sobregrau, P., Bailles, E., Radua, J., Carreno, M., Donaire, A., Setoain, X., Bargallo, N., Rumia, J., Sanchez Vives, M. V., & Pintor, L. (2024). Design and validation of a diagnostic suspicion checklist to differentiate epileptic from psychogenic nonepileptic seizures (PNES-DSC). *Journal of Psychosmatic Research, 180*, 111656.
Spierer, R., & Herskovitz, M. (2024). Which psychogenic nonepileptic seizure (PNES) patients are more likely to be treated with anti-seizure medications? *Seizure, 117*, 111–114.
Stone, J. (2016). Functional neurological disorders: The neurological assessment as treatment. *Practical Neurology, 16*(1), 7–17.
Storzbach, D., Binder, L. M., Salinsky, M. C., Campbell, B. R., & Mueller, R. M. (2000). Improved prediction of nonepileptic seizures iwth combined MMPI and EEG measures. *Epilepsia, 41*(3), 332–337.
Stroup, E. S., Drane, D. L., Wilson, K. S., Miller, J. W., Holmes, M. D., & Wilensky, A. J. (2004). Utility of the Perosnality assessment inventory (PAI) in the evaluation of patients on a long-term monitoring unit. *Epilepsia, 45*(Suppl. 7), 239–240.
Syed, T. U., Arozullah, A. M., Suciu, G. P., Toub, J., Kim, H., Dougherty, M. L., Wehner, T., Stojic, A., Syed, I., & Alexopoulos, A. V. (2008). Do observer and self-reports of ictal eye closure predict psychogenic nonepileptic seizures? *Epilepsia, 49*(5), 898–904.
Syed, T. U., LaFrance, W. C. J., Kahriman, E. S., Hasan, S. N., Rajasekaran, V., Gulati, D., Borad, S., Shahid, A., Fernandez-Baca, G., Garcia, N., Pawlowski, M., Loddenkemper, T., Amina, S., & Koubeissi, M. Z. (2011). Can semiology predict psychogenic nonepileptic seizures? A prospective study. *Annals of Neurology, 69*(6), 997–1004.
Szabo, L., Siegler, Z., Zubek, L., Liptai, Z., Korhegyi, I., & BBansagi, B., & Fogarasi, A. (2012). A detialed semiologic analysis of childhood psychogenic nonepileptic seizures. *Epilepsia, 53*(3), 565–570.
Szaflarski, J. P., Ficker, D. M., Cahill, W. T., & Privatera, M. D. (2000). Four-year incidence of psychogenic nonepileptic seizures in adults in Hamilton County, OH. *Neurology, 55*, 1561–1563.
Szaflarski, J. P., Szaflarski, M., Hughes, C., Ficker, D. M., Cahill, W. T., & Privitera, M. (2003). Psychopathology and quality of life: Psychogenic non-epileptic seizure versus epilepsy. *Medical Science Monitor, 9*(4), 113–118.
Testa, S. M., Lesser, R. P., Krauss, G. L., & Bbrandt, J. (2011). Personality assessment inventory among patinets with psychogenic seizures and those with epilepsy. *Epilepsia, 52*(8), e84–e88.
Thompson, N. C., Osorio, I., & Hunter, E. E. (2005). Nonepileptic seizures: Reframing the diagnosis. *Perspective Psyiatric Care, 41*(2), 71–78.
Thompson, R., Isaac, C. L., Rowse, G., Tooth, C. L., & Reuber, M. (2009). What is it like to receive a diagnosis of nonepileptic seizures? *Epilepsy and Behavior, 14*(3), 508–515.
Tojek, T. M., Lumley, M., Barkley, G., Mahr, G., & Thomas, A. (2000). Stress and other psychosocial characteristics of patients with psychogenic nonepileptic seizures. *Psychosomatics: Journal of consultation liaison. Psychiatry, 41*(3), 221.
Trainor, D., Foster, E., Rychkova, M., Lloyd, M., Leong, M., Wang, A. D., Velakoulis, D., O'Brien, T. J., Kwan, P., Loi, S. M., & Malpas, C. B. (2020). Development and validation of a screening questionnaire for psychogenic nonepileptic seizures. *Epilepsy and Behavior, 112*, 107482.

van Merode, T., Twellaar, M., Kotsopoulos, I. A., Kessles, A. G., Merckelbach, H., de Krom, M. C. F. T. M., & Knottnerus, J. A. (2004). Psychological characteristics of patients with newly developed psychogenic seizures. *Journal of Neurology, Neurosurgery and Psychiatry, 75*(8), 1175–1177.

Van Patten, R., Austin, T. A., Cotton, E., Chan, L., Bellone, J. A., Mordecai, K., Altalib, H., Correia, S., Twamley, E. W., Jones, R. N., Sawyer, K., & LafFrance, W. C., Jr. (2024). Cognitive performance in functional seizures compared with epilepsy and healthy controls: A systematic review and meta analysis. *Lancet Psychiatry, 11*(7), 516–525.

Vickrey, B., Perrine, K., Hays, R., Hermann, B. P., Cramer, J. A., Meador, K. J., & Devinsky, O. (1993). *Quality of life in epilepsy QOLIE-31 (version 1.0): Scoring manual and patient inventory*. RAND.

Vincentiis, S., Valente, K. D., Thome-Souza, S., Kuczinsky, E., Fiore, L. A., & Negrao, N. (2006). Risk factors for psychogenic nonepileptic seizures in children and adolescents with epilepsy. *Epilepsy and Behavior, 8*(1), 294–298.

Volbers, B., Walther, K., Kurzbuch, K., Erdmann, L., Gollwitzer, S., DLang, J. D., Onugoren, M. D., Schwarz, M., Schwab, S., & Hamer, H. M. (2022). Psychogenic nonepileptic seizures: Clinical characteristics and outcome. *Brain and Behavior, 12*(5), e2567.

Vossler, D. G., Haltiner, A. M., Schepp, S. K., Friel, P. A., Caylor, L. M., Morgan, J. D., & Doherty, M. J. (2004). Ictal stuttering: A sign suggestive of psychogenic nonepileptic seizures. *Neurology, 63*, 516–519.

Wagner, M. T., Wymer, J. H., Topping, K. B., & Pritchard, P. B. (2005). Use of the personality assessment inventory as an efficacious and cost-effective diagnostic tool for nonepileptic seizures. *Epilepsy and Behavior, 7*(2), 301–304.

Walczak, T. S., Papcostas, S., Williams, D. T., Scheuer, M. L., Lebowitz, N., & Notarfrancesco, A. (1995). Outcome after diagnosis of psychogenic nonepileptic seizures. *Epilepsia, 36*(11), 1131–1137.

Walczak, T. S., Williams, D. T., & Berten, W. (1994). Utility and reliability of placebo infusion in the evaluation of patients with seizures. *Neurology, 44*, 394–399.

Walsh, S., Levita, L., & Reuber, M. (2018). Comorbid depression and associated factors in PNES versus epilepsy: Systematic review and meta-analysis. *Seizure, 60*, 44–56.

Ware, J. E., Kosinski, M., & Keller, S. D. (1994). *SF-36 physical and mental health summary scales: A users' manual*. The Health Institute.

Warner, M., Wilkus, R., Vossler, D., Wyler, A., & Abson-Kraemer, D. (1996). MMPI-2 profiles in differential diagnosis of epilepsy vs. psychogenic seizures. *Epilepsia, 37*, 19.

Wasserman, D., & Herskovitz, M. (2017). Epileptic vs psychogenic nonepileptic seizures: A video-based survey. *Epilepsy and Behavior, 73*, 42–45.

Weathers, F. W., Litz, B. T., Keane, T. M., Palmieri, P. A., Marx, B. P., & Schnurr, P. P. (2013). The PTSD Checklist for DSM-5 (PCL-5). *Scale available from the National Center for PTSD at 222.ptsd.va.gov*.

Webber, T. A., Collins, R. L., Sullivan, K. L., Chen, D. K., & Grabyan, J. M. (2021). Clinical identification of psychogenic nonepileptic events using combinations of psychological tests in a veteran sample. *Epilepsy and Behavior, 115*, 107631.

Wilkus, R. J., & Dodrill, C. B. (1989). Factor affecting the outcome of MMPI and neuropsychological assessments of psychogenic and epileptic seizure patients. *Epilepsia, 30*, 339–347.

Wilkus, R. J., Dodrill, C. B., & Thompson, P. M. (1984). Intensive EEG monitoring and psychological studies of patients with pseudoepileptic seizures. *Epilepsia, 25*(1), 100–107.

Williamson, D. J., Drane, D. L., & Stroup, E. S. (2007). Symptom validity tests in the epilepsy clinic. In K. Boone (Ed.), *Assessment of feigned cognitive impairment*. Guilford.

Williamson, D. J., Drane, D. L., Stroup, E. S., Wilensky, A. J., Holmes, M. D., & Miller, J. W. (2005). Recent seizures may distort the validity of neurocognitive test scores in patients with epilepsy. *Epilepsia, 46*(8), 74.

Wood, B. L., Haque, S., Weinstock, A., & Miller, B. D. (2004). Pediatric stress-related seizures: Conceptualization, evaluation, and treatment of nonepileptic seizures in adolescents. *Current Opinion in Pediatrics, 16*(5), 523–531.

Wyllie, E., Benbadis, S. R., & Kotagal, P. (2002). Psychogenic seizures and other nonepileptic paroxysmal events in children. *Epilepsy and Behavior, 3*, 46–50.

Wyllie, E., Friedman, D., Rothner, A. D., Luders, H., Dinner, D., Morris, H., 3rd, Curse, R., Erenberg, G., & Kotagal, P. (1990). Psychogenic seizures in children and adolescents: Outcome after diagnosis b y ictal video and electroencephalographic recording. *Pediatrics, 85*(4), 480–484.

Wyllie, E., Glazer, J. P., Benbadis, S. R., Kotagal, P., & Wolgamuth, B. (1999). Psychiatric features in children and adolescents with pseudoseizures. *Archives of Pediatric and Adolescent Medicine, 153*(3), 244–248.

Yong, K., Chin, R. F. M., Shetty, J., Hogg, K., Burgess, K., Lindsay, M., McLellan, A., Stone, J., KamathTallur, K., & Group, E. P. F. N. D. S. (2023). Functional neurological disorder in chhildren and young people: Incidence, clinical features, and prognosis. *Developmental Medicine and Child Neurology, 65*(9), 1238–1246.

Zaroff, C. M., Myers, L., Barr, W. B., Luciano, D., & Devinsky, O. (2004). Group psychoeducationn as treatment for psychological nonepileptic seizures. *Epilepsy and Behavior, 5*(4), S87–S92.

Chapter 19
Somatoform/Somatic Symptom Disorders, Conversion Disorder (Functional Neurologic Disorder), Factitious Disorder and Malingering

Kyle Boone

Key Points and Chapter Summary

- Neuropsychologists provide critical information as to (1) whether neurocognitive performance is credible, and if so, the nature and extent of any cognitive dysfunction, and to what cause(s) it can best be attributed, (2) whether report of psychiatric, physical and cognitive/memory complaints is credible and (3) the nature and extent of any psychological conditions and their causes.
- The current diagnostic categories of conversion disorder, factitious disorder and malingering are problematic in that there are no reliable tools to determine "consciousness" of symptom presentation (required for factitious disorder and malingering and used to rule out conversion disorder), with the exception that failure on multiple PVTs arguably documents deliberate feigning of symptoms.

Somatoform and Somatic Symptom Disorders

Definition/Terminology

Broadly, somatoform/somatic symptom disorders are characterized by somatization, a process in which an individual magnifies minor symptoms, channels stress into symptoms, becomes preoccupied and overidentified with symptoms and

K. Boone (✉)
Independent Practice, Torrance, CA, USA

M. R. Schoenberg, J. G. Scott (eds.), *The Little Black Book of Neuropsychology*,
https://doi.org/10.1007/978-3-032-07777-6_19

perceives him or herself as more dysfunctional than is actually the case. However, in the case of conversion disorder, the individual actually creates symptoms lacking a physiological basis. The Diagnostic and Statistical Manual for psychiatry—IV (DSM-IV, 1994) described the following subtypes of somatoform disorder:

- Somatization disorder: Combination of unexplained pain, gastrointestinal, sexual and peudoneurological symptoms which present before the age of 30
- Conversion disorder: Unexplained sensory and/motor symptoms which mimic a neurological or general medical condition
- Pain disorder: Unexplained pain symptoms thought to be causally related to psychological factors
- Hypochondriasis: Chronic fear and/or fixed belief that one has a serious disease despite the absence of confirming medical laboratory findings and which is due to misperception of benign bodily symptoms
- Body dysmorphic disorder: Preoccupation with imagined or inflated defect in physical appearance

The somatoform category also includes diagnoses of undifferentiated somatoform disorder and somatoform disorder not otherwise specified, in which somatoform symptoms do not meet the criteria for any of the other disorders.

More recently, the DSM-V (2013) provided a revised category of somatic symptom and related disorders with the following subtypes:

- Somatic symptom disorder: Symptoms are distressing and/or disruptive to daily life, and the patient has excessive/abnormal thoughts, feelings and behaviors associated with the symptoms.
- Illness anxiety disorder: The individual is preoccupied with having/acquiring an illness; any actual symptoms are not present or mild; there is a high level of anxiety regarding illness; and excessive health-related behaviors are displayed.
- Conversion disorder (functional neurologic symptom disorder): Symptoms involve voluntary motor/sensory function, with an incompatibility between symptoms and actual neurologic or medical conditions.
- Psychological factors affecting other medical conditions: Psychological or behavioral factors adversely impact a medical condition.

The somatic symptom disorder category also includes factitious disorder, which will be discussed below, and other specified somatic symptom and related disorder and unspecified somatic symptom and related disorder, in which full criteria are not met for any of the above listed disorders.

The International Classification of Diseases, tenth edition (World Health Organization, 1992), included four Somatoform disorders: somatization disorder, hypochondriacal disorder, somatoform autonomic dysfunction (involving symptoms in organ systems thought to be under autonomic control, such as cardiovascular, GI, respiratory and urogenital) and persistent somatoform pain disorder. However, conversion disorder was moved to the dissociative disorder category, and divided into dissociative motor disorders, dissociative convulsions and dissociative anesthesia and sensory loss. In the ICD-11 (World Health Organization, 2021), conversion disorder remains in the dissociative disorders category and is now termed "dissociative neurological symptom disorder"; it has numerous subcategories, including "dissociative neurological symptom disorder, with cognitive symptoms" (impaired performance that is internally inconsistent, or not consistent with neurological/medical, neurodevelopmental, neurocognitive or mental/behavioral disorders); separate categories of dissociative amnesia and trance disorder remain. There is no discussion as to whether dissociative neurological symptom disorder symptoms are nonconsciously produced with the exception that they are described as "involuntary." The somatoform category is now collapsed into "bodily distress disorder," reflecting excessive attention and distress related to physical symptoms, and with subcategories of mild, moderate and severe. In addition, a diagnosis of body integrity dysphoria is introduced; in this condition the person has an intense and persistent desire to become physical disabled.

The above diagnostic classification systems were silent regarding the occurrence of nonphysiologic cognitive symptoms in conversion disorder until the ICD-11. However, examination of Freud's original writings on conversion disorder describes reversible amnesia and clouding of consciousness accompanying hysterical attacks and neuralgias (Mace, 1994). Claimed cognitive symptoms have been described in the context of functional motor neurological disorders (Alluri et al., 2020) including nonepileptic seizures (Drane et al., 2021), and in such probable somatoform disorders as toxic mold exposure (McCaffrey & Lynch, 2021), multiple chemical sensitivity (McCaffrey & Lynch, 2021), chronic fatigue syndrome (Suhr & Bryant, 2021), chronic pain/fibromyalgia (Suhr & Bryant, 2021) and in many cases of "long COVID" (Greißel et al., 2024; Kachaner et al., 2022; Selvakumar et al., 2023; Whiteside et al., 2022). Presentations in which patients claim significant cognitive dysfunction but on cognitive exam are found to be cognitively normal can be termed "cognitive hypochondriasis" (Boone, 2009) and functional memory disorder (Metternich et al., 2009). Recently, a category of functional cognitive disorder has been postulated (Kemp et al., 2022), although this seems to be an umbrella term capturing both health anxiety related to nonexistent to minor cognitive dysfunction and frank functional (i.e., conversion disorder-created) cognitive symptoms, and therefore does not appear to add diagnostic clarity.

Prevalence

According to the DSM-V, prevalence of somatic symptom disorder in the general adult population ranges between 4% and 6%. Research using DSM-IV criteria for hypochondriasis and health anxiety (as cited in the DSM-V) has described prevalence rates of 1.3–10%. However, upward of 60% of neurological inpatients and outpatients have been found to report at least one medically unexplained symptom, with 35% meeting the DSM-IV criteria for somatoform disorder (Fink et al., 2005). Estimates of rates of conversion/functional neurological symptom disorder provided by the DSM-V have suggested that the condition is present in 5–15% of neurology clinic patients.

Etiology

Originally, somatoform disorders (especially conversion disorders) were conceptualized within psychoanalytic theory as representing psychological conflict that was "converted" and displaced into dysfunction of a body part or system. More modern theories have viewed somatoform symptoms as being created by psychological distress that is not properly identified as such in nonpsychologically minded individuals; the resulting stress "has to go somewhere" and appears in the form of physical complaints that these patients are more comfortable facing than the underlying emotional pain. Empirical studies point to several factors as contributing to the development of somatization. First, research frequently documents longstanding elevated fears and concerns regarding bodily functions including hypervigilance to physical symptoms and perceptions that one is particularly fragile and vulnerable (Kellner et al., 1987; Rief et al., 1998). Second, social factors play a role, such as problematic early attachment (Waller et al., 2004), sexual abuse (Samelius et al., 2007; Spitzer et al., 2008), family history/modeling of functional symptoms (Taylor & Asmundson, 2004) and lowered levels of social support (Nakao et al., 2005) and psychosocial stressors (Haftgoli et al., 2010), as well as the possibility that somatization is adaptive from an evolutionary perspective in terms of securing resources (Mealy, 1995) and increasing survival odds by visually signaling to predators that one is not a threat (Bracha et al., 2005. Third, research describes co-occurring psychiatric disorders in somatization, including depression (Lieb et al., 2007), anxiety (Grover et al., 2015; Huang et al., 2016) and personality disorders (Binzer et al., 1997), especially borderline (Schmaling & Fales, 2018). However, these variables are generally static/trait characteristics and would not explain acute onset or fluctuating course of somatoform symptoms. In fact, somatoform symptoms likely develop in predisposed individuals when illness is particularly advantageous to the individual (e.g., in allowing one to be excused from stressful work responsibilities, in securing support and attention from others, in providing one with a special identity and unique life role, etc.). In terms of conversion disorder symptoms, they likely originate from a world view, locked in place at a young age, as to what the world is like, how others behave and what one must do to stay safe and survive in that world.

Malingering and Factitious Disorder

Definition/Terminology

According to the DSM-V (p. 726–727), malingering refers to conscious, deliberate feigning of symptoms for an obvious external incentive (i.e., for monetary compensation in the context of a lawsuit or disability benefits, to avoid military duty or criminal responsibility, to obtain drugs, etc.). As such, it is viewed as a volitional act which emerges in relation to external contingencies and is not a static condition.

In contrast, in factitious disorder, the symptom feigning is also thought to be conscious and deliberate, but the goal of the symptom fabrication is obscure and idiosyncratic to the individual, and in the service of securing psychological goals. Common associated characteristics include employment within the healthcare system and particularly maladaptive coping skills (Wang et al., 2005).

Factitious disorder patients appear to crave the notoriety and attention from medical personnel that accompany unusual symptoms, and to derive fulfillment from believing that one has "outsmarted" the typically better-educated physicians (e.g., see Sneddon, 1983).

In both malingering and factitious disorders, symptom feigning can appear in discrete cognitive skills such as memory (verbal and/or visual), processing speed, motor function, visual perceptual/spatial skills, math calculation ability, basic attention, language skills including reading and spelling, executive/problem-solving and remote memory. Alternatively, subjects may feign global cognitive impairment such as that observed in dementia or intellectual disability. The choice of which symptoms to fabricate is driven by beliefs held by the individual as to what cognitive deficits accompany the disorder that is being feigned (i.e., brain injury, toxic exposure, anoxia, stroke, dementia), and is likely based on the type of cognitive symptoms that have been observed in persons with those disorders, and also how the disorders have been depicted on TV and in movies.

Prevalence

Malingering is found in those situations in which there is external incentive to be symptomatic. Mittenberg et al. (2002) reported survey results showing that experienced neuropsychologists estimated that in the presence of motive to feign symptoms (litigating or disability seeking), malingering was present in 41% of mild traumatic brain injury, 39% of fibromyalgia/chronic fatigue, 34% of chronic pain, 30% of neurotoxic exposure, 26% of electrical injury, 16% of depressive disorders, 14% of anxiety conditions, 11% of dissociative disorders, 9% of seizure disorders and 9% of moderate/severe head injury patients. Similarly, Boone et al. (2021) found a consistent rate of approximately 45% noncredible cognitive performance in compensation-seeking mTBI claims.

The base rate for malingered neurocognitive dysfunction in pretrial inpatient criminal defendants referred for neuropsychological evaluation likely ranges from 63% to 73% (Denney & Fazio, 2021). Larrabee et al. (2009) proposed a "magical number" of 40% +/− 10% "representing the average base rate or prevalence of invalid data/probable malingering in settings with external incentive" (p. 843). Thus, malingering of cognitive symptoms is not rare, which has precipitated admonitions within the field of neuropsychology that measures of response bias be routinely administered, particularly in contexts in which there is motive to be symptomatic (Bush et al., 2005; Sweet et al., 2021).

Rates of factitious disorder are less known and according to the DSM-V may be found in 1% of general medical hospital patients referred for psychiatric consultation; no data are available regarding specific prevalence of factitious-related cognitive symptom fabrication.

Etiology

Malingering is a volitional act in the service of a tangible goal, and thus, traditional concepts of "etiology" do not apply. In contrast, the deliberate feigning of symptoms in the absence of such obvious goals as monetary compensation or avoidance of criminal or work responsibility typically only occurs in conjunction with significant psychiatric disturbance, and in particular, borderline personality disorder (Bass & Wade, 2019; Caselli et al., 2018; Goldstein, 1998; Gordon & Sansone, 2013; Lazzari et al., 2023; Lazzari & Rabottini, 2023; Sharma et al., 2021). The goal of such factitious behavior is to adopt the sick role, and while the acts themselves are conscious, the motivations behind the behaviors are considered to be nonconscious (Wang et al., 2005). Some have argued that factitious disorder may resemble an addictive or impulse control disorder whose behaviors patients are unable to stop (Onofrj et al., 2021).

Differential Diagnosis: Can We Distinguish Conversion Disorders Versus Factitious Conditions Versus Malingering, or Is it Time to Reconceptualize These Diagnostic Categories?

Within the DSM-IV, conversion disorder symptoms were judged to be not intentionally produced (i.e., lack "conscious intent") in contrast to malingering and factitious disorder in which symptoms were considered to be deliberately fabricated. However, in the DSM-V, guidance on this issue is murky. For example, it is stated that "*the diagnosis of conversion disorder does not require the judgment that the symptoms are not intentionally produced (i.e., or feigned), as the definite absence of feigning may not be reliably discerned*" (p. 320) "*and because assessment of conscious intention is unreliable*" (p. 321). The authors go on to suggest that "*definite evidence of feigning (e.g., clear evidence that loss of function is present during the examination but not at home) would suggest a diagnosis of factitious disorder if the individual's apparent aim is to assume the sick role or malingering if the aim is to obtain an incentive such as money.*" This would appear to leave open the door that symptoms are not consciously produced or feigned in conversion disorder. The DSM-V-TR (2022) in fact confirms nonconscious generation of symptoms: "*functional neurological symptom disorder describes genuinely experienced symptoms that are not intentionally produced (i.e., not feigned). However, definite evidence of feigning (e.g., marked discrepancy between reported and observed activities of daily living) would suggest malingering if the individual's apparent aim is to obtain an obvious external reward, or factitious disorder in the absence of such reward*" (p. 364). Symptoms "not intentionally produced" appear to refer to nonconscious symptom production, although the use of the term "nonconscious" is side-stepped.

Can clinical neuropsychology provide information relevant as to whether symptoms are deliberately/consciously versus nonconsciously or "not intentionally" created? Within the last three decades in clinical neuropsychology, there has been a paradigm shift in appreciation of the need to assess the credibility of performance on neurocognitive testing through the use of validated "performance validity tests" (PVTs; Sweet et al., 2021). Administration of such tests is mandated to verify that obtained test results are accurate (i.e., that the test taker has performed to true ability), and the use of PVTs is endorsed by 99% of neuropsychologists (Martin, Schroeder, Heinrichs, & Baade, 2015a; Martin, Schroeder, & Odland, 2015b). In the same vein, symptom validity tests (SVTs) are to be relied upon when assessing the veracity of self-report of psychiatric, cognitive and physical symptoms (Sweet et al., 2021).

While sporadic failures of PVTs can be observed in credible test takers (Victor et al., 2009), the empirical literature is nearly uniform in documenting that failure on three or more PVTs is associated with virtually 100% specificity for failure to perform to true ability (i.e., no false positive errors; Chafetz, 2011; Davis & Millis, 2014; Larrabee, 2003, 2008; Meyers & Volbrecht, 2003; Meyers et al., 2014; Sollman et al., 2010; Victor et al., 2009) except in populations with major neurocognitive disorder (e.g., dementia, Bortnik & Dean, 2021; very low intelligence, Smith et al., 2014; Victor & Boone, 2021). Recent revised diagnostic criteria for malingered neurocognitive dysfunction include failure on ≥two out of seven PVTs (Sherman et al., 2020); failure on two or more PVTs is also the most common approach endorsed by neuropsychologists to document performance invalidity when multiple validity measures are administered (Martin, Schroeder, Heinrichs, & Baade, 2015a; Martin, Schroeder, & Odland, 2015b). Failure on increasing numbers of PVTs can be viewed as evidence of deliberate feigning of cognitive dysfunction given that multiple failures on the types of easy tasks that constitute PVTs likely exceed one's ability to self-deceive regarding one's cognitive function (Boone, 2021). In other words, the multiple failures on simple tasks (e.g., involving counting, letter identification, finger tapping, recognition of information just presented) would be in conflict with repeated observations by the test taker as to their actual intact level of cognitive function. When forced choice methods have been adapted to cases of functional blindness (Theodor & Mandelcorn, 1973; in Sackeim et al., 1979), functional hearing loss (Pankratz et al., 1975) and functional sensory loss (Greve et al., 2003), significantly below chance performance has been reported, thereby confirming conscious feigning of dysfunction (i.e., to score significantly below chance requires awareness of correct answers, and deliberate selection of incorrect answers).

Using these conclusions, namely, that credible patients without major neurocognitive disorder rarely fail more than two PVTs, and that increasing numbers of PVT failures, and significantly below chance performance on forced choice measures, signal intentional symptom fabrication, we can apply the findings from PVTs to our understanding as to the unconscious versus conscious underpinnings of nonphysiologic symptoms in conversion disorder. Research suggests that the somatization/hypochondriacal/health anxiety category, in which dysfunction, including cognitive symptoms, is "perceived" but does not actually exist and is not found on cognitive testing, is associated with minimal PVT failures (4% in non-compensation-seeking fibromyalgia, Iverson et al., 2007). However, multiple PVT failures, or single PVT failures that are associated with 100% specificity (e.g., significantly below chance performance), are often observed in conversion disorder. As discussed above, forced choice testing conducted in case reports of nonphysiological blindness, tactile sensory loss and hearing loss has shown significantly below chance performance, thereby confirming deliberate misrepresentation of symptoms. Failure rates above 50% have also been reported in some investigations of forced choice memory tests in PNES patients (e.g., Word Memory Test; Drane et al., 2006). The few investigations employing multiple PVTs in primarily conversion disorder patients have reported relatively low rates of multiple failures (Di Vico et al., 2023; Kemp et al., 2008), but unfortunately the tests and/or cut-offs employed had low sensitivity (e.g., Finger Tapping cut-score = 62, Axelrod et al., 2014; significantly below chance performance required for failure on forced choice tests which occurs <10% in non-credible test takers, Kim et al., 2010), thereby handicapping attempts to document multiple PVT failures.

The above findings would argue that rather than conversion symptoms representing nonconscious symptom fabrication, it is more likely that the individual is engaging in deliberate symptom production. However, what may well remain nonconscious to the individual is why they are feigning symptoms (Boone, 2021; Wang et al., 2005). Conversion disorder symptoms have been reported to occur within the context of significant dysfunction within the family of origin, including abuse and family psychopathology (Fiszman et al., 2004; Griffith et al., 1998; Kaplan et al., 2013; Krawetz et al., 2001), and are accompanied by inability to adequately process and cope with emotional distress/anxiety [as reflected in alexithymia (Demartini et al., 2014; Gulpek et al., 2014; Kaplan et al., 2013) which is related to reduced inner speech and "self-talk" (Girbau, 2007; TenHouten et al., 1988)]. Kozlowska and Williams (2009) conclude that "conversion symptoms are associated with strong emotions or situations that threaten the individual's physical or psychological integrity." Stress becomes channeled into physical symptoms, which are used to control others and protect the individual (including from powerful emotions). The need for the symptoms is so all-consuming that sabotage to the quality of life caused by the symptoms (e.g., using a wheelchair for nonexistent sensory and motor deficits) is viewed as "worth it."

In fact, there is a large literature, summarized elsewhere (Boone, 2021; Boone, in press), providing evidence for conscious creation of symptoms in conversion disorder (e.g., PNES and functional movement disorders), and showing that the symptoms are only present when the individual is focusing attention on them, which arguably precludes a nonconscious basis for the symptoms. Interestingly, functional brain imaging has demonstrated that in patients diagnosed with conversion disorder (Burke et al., 2014; Marshall et al., 1997; Saj et al., 2009; van Beilen et al., 2010), in patients hypnotized to display conversion disorder symptoms (Halligan et al., 2000), in simulators instructed to feign sensory (hearing) loss (McPherson et al., 2012) and in individuals instructed to lie (Kozel, Padgett, & George, 2004; Kozel, Revell, et al., 2004; Langleben et al., 2002; Spence et al., 2004), all show activation of anterior cingulate and/or right orbitofrontal cortex. This is the same area that activates with the Stroop interference task (naming colors of printed words, while stopping oneself from reading the words; Leung et al., 2000; Peterson et al., 2002), and likely reflects the extent of focused attention on a task or behavior.

In this context, conversion disorder symptoms would appear to be better represented by the category of factitious disorder, in which symptoms are deliberately created for idiosyncratic psychological needs. Nicholson et al. (2011) argue that the "neat distinction between malingering, factitious disorder and conversion disorder is relatively new," and that the current system in which each is placed in its own category "was political as much as medical." Evidence suggests that factitious disorder is in fact underdiagnosed, and physicians are more comfortable diagnosing conversion disorder than factitious disorder (Bass & Halligan, 2014). Examination of historical arcs within society and within the mental health field shows that the idea that behaviors can be conducted nonconsciously is falling from favor, while there is a growing appreciation that symptoms/conditions are often deliberately feigned, particularly in secondary gain contexts (Boone, 2021). Conversion disorder, a condition first conceptualized over 100 years ago and historically diagnosed in women, conveniently meshes with views of women in the Victorian age, namely that they were "*fragile, innocent, modest, polite, obedient, chaste, submissive, delicate flower incapable of deciding anything except menu and her evening attire*" (https://byronsmuse.wordpress.com/2013/11/18/women-in-the-victorian-era). A person with such characteristics would not be viewed as able to deliberately feign symptoms. A conversion disorder diagnosis conveniently solves this conundrum of nonphysiological symptoms in a patient judged not capable of deliberately feigning symptoms. It should be appreciated that psychiatric diagnoses very much reflect societal beliefs, as evidenced by homosexuality being considered as a psychiatric disorder until its removal from the DSM in 1973.

The separate categories of factitious disorder and malingering are also problematic, because the two conditions are identical with the exception of impetus, i.e., deliberate feigning of symptoms for external versus internal/psychological goals. Further, just because an external incentive is putatively present does not automatically mean that it is the over-riding driver for symptom fabrication. Research shows that the use of the term malingering is markedly dropping in use by neuropsychologists (e.g., Martin, Schroeder, Heinrichs, & Baade, 2015a; Martin, Schroeder, & Odland, 2015b) in recognition that while evidence for performance invalidity is often incontrovertible, the reason(s) for the deliberate underperformance may not be as definitive. Additionally, factitious disorder and malingering can co-exist, or alternate, in the same patient. While mental health practitioners create distinctions between external and internal goals, it is unlikely that patients do so.

Given this unsatisfactory and confusing diagnostic quagmire, it might be more parsimonious to have an "umbrella term," such as pseudo-symptoms or nonphysiologic symptoms, coded as to:

1. Type of created symptom (psychiatric, cognitive and/or physical) and as determined by PVT and SVT data, and laboratory or other medical findings
2. Context (external motive, psychological goal or both)
3. Developmental level of the behavior and coping skills
   (a) For example, immature/regressed (as is found in conversion/factitious presentations) versus sophisticated/"mature" (as is typically found in malingering)
   (b) Impact of symptoms on quality of life (symptoms only donned for examinations, as is typically found in malingering, versus continuous or semi-continuous symptoms that interfere with the quality of life, as is found in factitious and conversion disorder)
4. Extent to which personality disorder plays a role in symptom manifestation, with more severe and bizarre symptoms accompanied by personality disorder, particularly borderline.

Whether symptom production is "conscious" or "nonconscious" would not be addressed in such a schema, just as whether symptom production is conscious or nonconscious is not pondered in other psychiatric diagnoses, such as hoarding, extreme anorexia, pyromania and other impulse control/addictive-type behaviors, which are associated with marked impact to quality of life.

Data to Be Gathered in the Neuropsychological Exam

Until psychological diagnostic categories evolve to address emerging research on conscious mechanisms in conversion disorder, how does the neuropsychologist navigate differential diagnosis and management of patient care? That is, what information should be obtained that is of use in conceptualizing patients with illness anxiety and conversion/factitious disorder, and in providing treatment?

Step 1: Obtaining a Full History

Neuropsychological testing originally was developed in the 1940s and 1950s to address the need to identify "brain damage" given primitive state of neuroimaging methods at that time. Neuropsychological test results were interpreted as showing evidence for or against the presence of "organicity" (brain damage), and were used to predict in which areas of the brain the damage was likely located. However, over the ensuing decades, and with the development of sophisticated neuroimaging to precisely measure "brain damage," neuropsychological testing has evolved to focus on documenting neurocognitive function. Concurrent with the emerging focus on "function" rather than "brain damage" has been the growing awareness that neuropsychological deficits have many causes, of which frank brain damage is only one. As cataloged elsewhere (Chafetz et al., under submission), numerous non-neurological medical and psychiatric conditions are associated with cognitive abnormalities, including medical illnesses [hypertension, diabetes, microvascular ischemic white matter disease, cardiac abnormalities, sleep apnea, hepatitis, prenatal exposure to substances, birth complications and developmental abnormalities (including learning disability, ADHD)] and psychiatric conditions (bipolar disorder, major depression, childhood maltreatment and substance abuse). Therefore, it is critically important that the neuropsychologist be aware of this literature and obtain information regarding these conditions during the interview with the patient, but also from medical and other records.

In regard to the cause of current psychiatric conditions, it is important to obtain a full personal and family history of psychiatric disorders and current and past major stressors. Given that somatoform conditions typically arise in the context of significant stressors, it is important to understand what these are for any given patient. In this vein, Nicholson et al. (2016) describe a method for documenting severe life events in conversion disorder, including "escape" events (those in which physical symptoms serve to provide escape from stressors); they report that only 9% of conversion disorder patients had no identifiable severe life events, and that "life events of potential aetiological relevance were not identified by routine clinical assessments." This indicates that unearthing of this critical information may require going beyond typical interview questioning to incorporate the use of specialized tools. Additional pertinent information to gather would be evidence for ACEs (adverse childhood experiences, including abuse, neglect), which predispose to reduced coping ability (Shah et al., 2018), alexithymia (Cerqueira & Almeida, 2023) and psychiatric conditions, including somatoform and conversion disorders (Imbierowicz & Egle, 2003; Maaranen et al., 2004; Steffen-Klatt et al., 2019).

Step 2: Assessment of Performance Validity

It is imperative that neuropsychological exams of patients contain numerous performance validity tests (PVTs)—"standalone" (i.e., which have a single purpose to measure performance validity) and "embedded" validity indicators (i.e., those contained within standard neuropsychological tests)—to verify whether the test taker has in fact performed to true ability. Survey data from Martin, Schroeder, Heinrichs and Baade (2015); Martin, Schroeder and Odland (2015) indicate that the average number of PVTs administered in a clinical exam is five, and within a forensic exam is six, and among experts in performance validity testing, an average of six to eight PVTs are administered (Schroeder et al., 2016). As detailed in the 2021 updated "consensus statement on validity assessment" (Sweet et al., 2021), PVTs should be selected to tap various cognitive domains to confirm that adequate performance has been documented across numerous types of cognitive skills.

Failure on two or more performance validity indicators has been found to best discriminate between credible and noncredible populations (Larrabee, 2003; Meyers & Volbrecht, 2003; Victor et al., 2009), and failure on three or more PVTs approaches perfect specificity in that this number of failures is rare in truly symptomatic clinic populations (Victor et al., 2009). However, careful consideration should be given to the possibility of false-positive validity test failures in populations particularly at risk for performing poorly on measures of response bias despite performing to true ability, namely patients with major neurocognitive disorder, including dementia (Bortnik & Dean, 2021) and intellectual disability (Victor & Boone, 2021).

The goal of a neuropsychological evaluation is to document the level of cognitive function. However, if a patient fails numerous performance validity indicators, this objective is no longer attainable (because test scores are not valid), and instead the goal becomes to document performance invalidity. Once incontrovertible documentation of response bias is obtained through multiple PVT failures, the exam may be discontinued.

If performance validity indicators are passed, the neuropsychologist can obtain standard neurocognitive data, and then interpret those findings as to whether cognitive dysfunction is present, in which domains and to what severity. As discussed above, it is important to carefully consider the etiologies of any detected cognitive abnormalities within the context of a full medical and psychiatric history; many times the most likely cause of cognitive abnormalities is not necessarily the patient's self-identified etiology (e.g., claimed residuals from a remote concussion, when the patient has a recent onset of major depression, poorly controlled diabetes, use of pain medications).

Key Points in Use of PVTs

- Employ multiple PVTs to provide greater confidence in conclusions
- Utilize PVTs with good sensitivity when cut-offs are set to high specificity, and use up-to-date cut-offs informed by current research
- Choose a range of PVTs that encompass various cognitive domains (e.g., memory, attention, processing speed, visual spatial skills, motor function)
- Provide results of PVTs in your report but in a manner that does not compromise test security (e.g., do not describe test stimuli or administration format)

Step 3: Assessment of Symptom Validity and Measurement of Psychological Conditions Including Somatoform Orientations

It is critical to administer symptom validity tests (SVTs) and objective personality inventories with scales that measure somatoform as well as other psychiatric tendencies. SVTs refer to measures that assess the veracity of self-reported symptoms.

Several objective personality inventories have scales to check that test takers have reported psychological, physical and cognitive symptoms in a credible manner. For example, the Minnesota Multiphasic Personality Inventory-3 (MMPI-3; Ben-Porath & Tellegen, 2020) Fs, FBS and RBS scales document whether report of physical, cognitive and memory complaints is plausible; extreme elevations on these scales are judged to reflect malingering of emotional symptoms, somatic symptoms and cognitive/memory symptoms, respectively. Likewise, on the Personality Assessment Inventory (PAI; Morey, 1991), a recently developed Cognitive Bias Scale (Gaasedelen et al., 2019) functions in a manner similar to the MMPI-3 RBS scale; elevations on this scale signal that the test taker has responded to the test in a manner comparable to that of individuals who have failed PVTs.

Objective personality tests also contain scales to assess the nature and extent of physical symptom report (e.g., MMPI-3 somatic complaints, malaise, neurological complaints scales; PAI somatic complaints scale). It is important to use such types of tests because results from somatic scales are more accurate than interview data in detecting somatoform orientations (i.e., patients are not likely to endorse presence of somatic preoccupation, magnifying of minor symptoms and seeing oneself as more dysfunctional than is actually the case, on interview).

Objective personality inventories also measure the extent of other psychiatric conditions, such as depression, anxiety, PTSD, impulse control disorders, substance abuse, coping resources and personality disorders while also confirming that psychiatric symptom report is likely accurate, and not overstated or sanitized.

Future evolution in assessment of nonphysiologic and medically unexplained symptom presentations should include quantifying other important aspects of symptom presentation. Patients with conversion/factitious disorders often have regressed and immature coping resources and have not learned to engage in self-talk used to self-soothe and problem-solve, and as a result have difficulty identifying, labeling and processing emotions (alexithymia) and in developing approaches to problem situations that do not sabotage quality of life. Assessment batteries may well shift to include measures to categorize the extent of inner speech (e.g., Siegrist, 1995), level of coping ability (e.g., Bonanno et al., 2011), presence of alexithymia (e.g., Kooiman et al., 2002) and symptom impact on quality of life (Burckhardt & Anderson, 2003). Such information could be used to best target and guide treatment interventions.

Key Points in Measurement of Psychological Conditions and sympatom Validity

- Administer objective, comprehension personality inventories that contain
  - Over-report validity scales to verify accuracy and plausibility of reported psychiatric, physical and cognitive/memory symptoms
  - A wide range of clinical scales to measure the nature and extent of psychological conditions, including somatoform tendencies, depression, anxiety, PTSD, impulsivity, substance abuse and personality disorder

Step 4: Putting the Data Together

Example A
Likely diagnosis: Illness anxiety (no neurocognitive disorder)

- Few PVT failures
- Normal to near-normal scores on neurocognitive testing
- Moderate elevations on SVTs assessing the veracity of report of physical and/or cognitive symptoms, and significant elevations on clinical scales measuring physical and/or cognitive symptom report

This pattern would most likely signal the presence of an illness anxiety-type condition. Concurrent psychiatric conditions, such as anxiety and depression, may also be present. In this context, the exam report would indicate that cognitive function is normal, but that the test taker is catastrophizing minor cognitive glitches and perceiving dysfunction that is not present. Recommendations would include (1) care in describing potential diagnoses to patients so as to not foster iatrogenesis and further preoccupation with symptoms and (2) psychotherapy, such as cognitive behavioral therapy, to explore stressors that may have provoked focus on and use of symptoms to manage or shield oneself from life problems, to help the individual process and label feelings and reactions and to explore alternative methods of coping and problem-solving. To the extent that the individual is also experiencing depression and/or anxiety, treatment would also focus on these conditions.

Example B
Likely diagnosis: Somatic symptom disorder and neurocognitive disorder

- Few PVT failures
- Lowered scores on neuropsychological testing
- Moderate elevations on SVTs assessing the veracity of report of physical and/or cognitive symptoms, and significant elevations on clinical scales measuring physical and/or cognitive symptom report

This description would be the similar to the above, with the exception that it will be important to determine the most likely causes for cognitive dysfunction, which hopefully are treatable, and which may or may not correspond to the patient's perception as to the cause. Patients with actual cognitive disorder do not obtain significant elevations on cognitive symptom over-report scales and clinical cognitive complaints scales (e.g., Gervais et al., 2009; Martin, Schroeder, Heinrichs, & Baade, 2015a; Martin, Schroeder, & Odland, 2015b); thus, when elevations are present on these scales in the setting of documented cognitive deficits, a likely diagnosis is somatic symptom disorder.

Example C
Likely diagnosis: Noncredible symptom presentation

- Multiple PVT failures in the absence of independent evidence of major neurocognitive disorder
- Very high elevations on personality inventory over-report scales

These patterns would be most consistent with deliberate attempts to fabricate or otherwise misrepresent symptoms. The determination should then be made as to the presence of external (e.g., compensation-seeking, test accommodations) and/or internal (e.g., to reduce anxiety, protect oneself from others, to gain visibility and attention) incentives for symptoms. Rather than attempting to determine if feigning is conscious versus nonconscious, a more informative approach would be to assume the presence of conscious symptom fabrication, but, more importantly, to analyze the level of coping ability and, relatedly, the extent of sabotage to quality of life. In this endeavor, assessment for the presence of personality disorder is highly relevant.

Marked reduction in quality of life occurs with symptom creation driven by psychological needs and imperatives; in this context, psychotherapy would be used to explore more effective and less self-sabotaging methods of navigating stressors and problems. However, such patients often consider the collateral impact of symptoms on quality of life as "worth it" if the symptoms satisfy psychological needs. If the patient perceives the psychological gains from symptoms as greater than the cost to quality of life, treatment will not likely be effective. When individuals feign symptoms primarily in the context of external motives, they typically do not maintain their symptoms outside of the evaluation context, and hence, there is no sabotage to the quality of life. In these individuals, coping resources are intact, and often quite analytical and highly goal-directed. Treatment interventions would not likely be indicated or recommended.

References

Alluri, P. R., Solit, J., Leveroni, C. L., Goldberg, K., Vehar, J. V., Pollak, L. E., et al. (2020). Cognitive complaints in motor functional neurological (conversion) disorders: A focused review and clinical perspective. *Cognitive and Behavioral Neurology, 33*(2), 77–89.

American Psychiatric Association. (1994). *Diagnostic and statistical manual of mental disorders* (4th ed.). American Psychiatric Association.

American Psychiatric Association, DSMTF, & American Psychiatric Association. (2013). *Diagnostic and statistical manual of mental disorders: DSM-5* (Vol. 5, No. 5). American Psychiatric Association.

Axelrod, B. N., Meyers, J. E., & Davis, J. J. (2014). Finger tapping test performance as a measure of performance validity. *The Clinical Neuropsychologist, 28*(5), 876–888.

Bass, C., & Halligan, P. (2014). Factitious disorders and malingering: Challenges for clinical assessment and management. *The Lancet, 383*(9926), 1422–1432.

Bass, C., & Wade, D. T. (2019). Malingering and factitious disorder. *Practical Neurology, 19*(2), 96–105.

Ben-Porath, Y. S., & Tellegen, A. (2020). *MMPI-3 manual for administration, scoring, and interpretation*. University of Minnesota Press.

Binzer, M., Andersen, P. M., & Kullgren, G. (1997). Clinical characteristics of patients with motor disability due to conversion disorder: A prospective control group study. *Journal of Neurology, Neurosurgery & Psychiatry, 63*(1), 83–88.

Bonanno, G. A., Pat-Horenczyk, R., & Noll, J. (2011). Coping flexibility and trauma: The perceived ability to cope with trauma (PACT) scale. *Psychological Trauma: Theory, Research, Practice, and Policy, 3*(2), 117.

Boone, K. B. (2009). Fixed belief in cognitive dysfunction despite normal neuropsychological scores: Neurocognitive hypochondriasis? *The Clinical Neuropsychologist, 23*(6), 1016–1036.

Boone, K. B. (2021). Performance validity in somatoform/conversion disorders, factitious disorder, and malingering: Do we need a new diagnostic schema? In K. B. Boone (Ed.), *Assessment of feigned cognitive impairment* (2nd ed.). Guilford Publications.
Boone, K. B., Litvin, P., & Victor, T. L. (2021). Base rates of feigned mild traumatic brain injury. In K. B. Boone (Ed.), *Assessment of feigned cognitive impairment* (2nd ed.). Guilford Publications.
Bortnik, K. E., & Dean, A. C. (2021). Performance validity testing in patients with dementia. In K. B. Boone (Ed.), *Assessment of feigned cognitive impairment* (2nd ed.). Guilford Publications.
Bracha, H. S., Yoshioka, D. T., Masukawa, N. K., & Stockman, D. J. (2005). Evolution of the human fear-circuitry and acute sociogenic pseudoneurological symptoms: The Neolithic balanced-polymorphism hypothesis. *Journal of Affective Disorders, 88*(2), 119–129.
Burckhardt, C. S., & Anderson, K. L. (2003). The quality of life scale (QOLS): Reliability, validity, and utilization. *Health and Quality of Life Outcomes, 1*(1), 1–7.
Burke, M. J., Ghaffar, O., Staines, W. R., Downar, J., & Feinstein, A. (2014). Functional neuroimaging of conversion disorder: The role of ancillary activation. *NeuroImage: Clinical, 6*, 333–339.
Bush, S. S., Ruff, R. M., Troster, A. I., Barth, J. T., Koffler, S. P., Pliskin, N. H., et al. (2005). Symptom validity assessment: Practice issues and medical necessity (NAN Policy and Planning Committee). *Archives of Clinical Neuropsychology, 20*, 419–426.
Caselli, I., Poloni, N., Ceccon, F., Ielmini, M., Merlo, B., & Callegari, C. (2018). A systematic review on factitious disorders: Psychopathology and diagnostic classification. *Neuropsychiatry, 8*(1), 281–292.
Cerqueira, A., & Almeida, T. C. (2023). Adverse childhood experiences: Relationship with empathy and alexithymia. *Journal of Child & Adolescent Trauma, 16*, 1–10.
Chafetz, M. D. (2011). The psychological consultative examination for social security disability. *Psychological Injury and Law, 4*(3–4), 235–244.
Davis, J. J., & Millis, S. R. (2014). Examination of performance validity test failure in relation to number of tests administered. *The Clinical Neuropsychologist, 28*(2), 199–214.
Demartini, B., Petrochilos, P., Ricciardi, L., Price, G., Edwards, M. J., & Joyce, E. (2014). The role of alexithymia in the development of functional motor symptoms (conversion disorder). *Journal of Neurology, Neurosurgery & Psychiatry, 85*(10), 1132–1137.
Denney, R. L., & Fazio, R. L. (2021). Assessment of feigned cognitive impairment in criminal forensic neuropsychological settings. In K. B. Boone (Ed.), *Assessment of feigned cognitive impairment* (2nd ed.). Guilford Publications.
Di Vico, I. A., Stone, J., Mcwhirter, L., Riello, M., Zanolin, M. E., Colombari, M., et al. (2023). Performance validity tests in nonlitigant patients with functional motor disorder. *European Journal of Neurology, 30*(4), 806–812.
Drane, D. L., Williamson, D., Hewitt, K., & Jordan, T. (2021). Performance validity tests in the epilepsy clinic. In K. B. Boone (Ed.), *Assessment of feigned cognitive impairment* (2nd ed.). Guilford Publications.
Drane, D. L., Williamson, D. J., Stroup, E. S., Holmes, M. D., Jung, M., Koerner, E., et al. (2006). Cognitive impairment is not equal in patients with epileptic and psychogenic nonepileptic seizures. *Epilepsia, 47*(11), 1879–1886.
Fink, P., Hansen, M. S., & Søndergaard, L. (2005). Somatoform disorders among first-time referrals to a neurology service. *Psychosomatics, 46*(6), 540–548.
Fiszman, A., Alves-Leon, S. V., Nunes, R. G., Isabella, D. A., & Figueira, I. (2004). Traumatic events and posttraumatic stress disorder in patients with psychogenic nonepileptic seizures: A critical review. *Epilepsy & Behavior, 5*(6), 818–825.
Gaasedelen, O. J., Whiteside, D. M., Altmaier, E., Welch, C., & Basso, M. R. (2019). The construction and the initial validation of the cognitive bias scale for the personality assessment inventory. *The Clinical Neuropsychologist, 33*(8), 1467–1484.
Gervais, R. O., Ben-Porath, Y. S., & Wygant, D. B. (2009). Empirical correlates and interpretation of the MMPI-2-RF cognitive complaints (COG) scale. *The Clinical Neuropsychologist, 23*(6), 996–1015.

Girbau, D. (2007). A neurocognitive approach to the study of private speech. *The Spanish Journal of Psychology, 10*(1), 41–51.

Goldstein, A. B. (1998). Identification and classification of factitious disorders: An analysis of cases reported during a ten year period. *The International Journal of Psychiatry in Medicine, 28*(2), 221–241.

Gordon, D. K., & Sansone, R. A. (2013). A relationship between factitious disorder and borderline personality disorder. *Innovations in Clinical Neuroscience, 10*(11–12), 11.

Greißel, A., Schneider, A., Donnachie, E., Gerlach, R., Tauscher, M., & Hapfelmeier, A. (2024). Impact of pre-existing mental health diagnoses on development of post-COVID and related symptoms: A claims data-based cohort study. *Scientific Reports, 14*(1), 2408.

Greve, K. W., Bianchini, K. J., & Ameduri, C. J. (2003). Use of a forced-choice test of tactile discrimination in the evaluation of functional sensory loss: A report of 3 cases. *Archives of Physical Medicine and Rehabilitation, 84*(8), 1233–1236.

Griffith, J. L., Polles, A., & Griffith, M. E. (1998). Pseudoseizures, families, and unspeakable dilemmas. *Psychosomatics, 39*(2), 144–153.

Grover, S., Aneja, J., Sharma, A., Malhotra, R., Varma, S., Basu, D., & Avasthi, A. (2015). Do the various categories of somatoform disorders differ from each other in symptom profile and psychological correlates. *International Journal of Social Psychiatry, 61*(2), 148–156.

Gulpek, D., Kelemence Kaplan, F., Kesebir, S., & Bora, O. (2014). Alexithymia in patients with conversion disorder. *Nordic Journal of Psychiatry, 68*(5), 300–305.

Haftgoli, N., Favrat, B., Verdon, F., Vaucher, P., Bischoff, T., Burnand, B., & Herzig, L. (2010). Patients presenting with somatic complaints in general practice: Depression, anxiety and somatoform disorders are frequent and associated with psychosocial stressors. *BMC Family Practice, 11*, 1–8.

Halligan, P. W., Athwal, B. S., Oakley, D. A., & Frackowiak, R. S. (2000). Imaging hypnotic paralysis: Implications for conversion hysteria. *The Lancet, 355*, 986–987.

Huang, W. L., Chen, T. T., Chen, I. M., Ma, H. M., Lee, M. T., Liao, S. C., & Gau, S. F. (2016). Depression and anxiety among patients with somatoform disorders, panic disorder, and other depressive/anxiety disorders in Taiwan. *Psychiatry Research, 241*, 165–171.

Imbierowicz, K., & Egle, U. T. (2003). Childhood adversities in patients with fibromyalgia and somatoform pain disorder. *European Journal of Pain, 7*(2), 113–119.

Iverson, G. L., Page, J. L., Koehler, B. E., Shojania, K., & Badii, M. (2007). Test of memory malingering (TOMM) scores are not affected by chronic pain or depression in patients with fibromyalgia. *The Clinical Neuropsychologist, 21*(3), 532–546.

Kachaner, A., Lemogne, C., Dave, J., Ranque, B., de Broucker, T., & Meppiel, E. (2022). Somatic symptom disorder in patients with post-COVID-19 neurological symptoms: A preliminary report from the somatic study (Somatic Symptom Disorder Triggered by COVID-19). *Journal of Neurology, Neurosurgery & Psychiatry, 93*, 327899. https://doi.org/10.1136/jnnp-2021-327899

Kaplan, M. J., Dwivedi, A. K., Privitera, M. D., Isaacs, K., Hughes, C., & Bowman, M. (2013). Comparisons of childhood trauma, alexithymia, and defensive styles in patients with psychogenic non-epileptic seizures vs. epilepsy: Implications for the etiology of conversion disorder. *Journal of Psychosomatic Research, 75*(2), 142–146.

Kellner, R., Abbott, P., Winslow, W. W., & Pathak, D. (1987). Fears, beliefs, and attitudes in DSM-III hypochondriasis. *The Journal of Nervous and Mental Disease, 175*(1), 20–25.

Kemp, S., Coughlan, A. K., Rowbottom, C., Wilkinson, K., Teggart, V., & Baker, G. (2008). The base rate of effort test failure in patients with medically unexplained symptoms. *Journal of Psychosomatic Research, 65*, 319–325.

Kemp, S., Kapur, N., Graham, C. D., & Reuber, M. (2022). Functional cognitive disorder: differential diagnosis of common clinical presentations. *Archives of Clinical Neuropsychology, 37*(6), 1158–1176.

Kim, M. S., Boone, K. B., Victor, T., Marion, S. D., Amano, S., Cottingham, M. E., et al. (2010). The Warrington recognition memory test for words as a measure of response bias: Total score and response time cutoffs developed on "real world" credible and noncredible subjects. *Archives of Clinical Neuropsychology, 25*(1), 60–70.

Kooiman, C. G., Spinhoven, P., & Trijsburg, R. W. (2002). The assessment of alexithymia: A critical review of the literature and a psychometric study of the Toronto Alexithymia Scale-20. *Journal of Psychosomatic Research, 53*(6), 1083–1090.

Kozel, F. A., Padgett, T. M., & George, M. S. (2004). A replication study of the neural correlates of deception. *Behavioral Neuroscience, 118*, 852–856.

Kozel, F. A., Revell, L. J., Lorberbaum, J. P., Shawstri, A., Elhia, J. D., Horner, M. D., et al. (2004). A pilot study of functional magnetic resonance imaging brain correlates of deception in healthy young men. *Journal of Neuropsychiatry and Clinical Neurosciences, 16*, 295–305.

Kozlowska, K., & Williams, L. M. (2009). Self-protective organization in children with conversion and somatoform disorders. *Journal of Psychosomatic Research, 67*(3), 223–233.

Krawetz, P., Fleisher, W., Pillay, N., Staley, D., Arnett, J., & Maher, J. (2001). Family functioning in subjects with pseudoseizures and epilepsy. *The Journal of Nervous and Mental Disease, 189*(1), 38–43.

Langleben, D. D., Schroeder, L., Maldjian, J. A., Gur, R. C., McDonald, S., Ragland, J. D., et al. (2002). Brain activity during simulated deception: An event-related functional magnetic resonance study. *NeuroImage, 15*, 727–732.

Larrabee, G. J. (2003). Detection of malingering using atypical performance patterns on standard neuropsychological tests. *The Clinical Neuropsychologist, 17*, 410–425.

Larrabee, G. J. (2008). Aggregation across multiple indicators improves the detection of malingering: Relationship to likelihood ratios. *The Clinical Neuropsychologist, 22*(4), 666–679.

Larrabee, G. J., Millis, S. R., & Meyers, J. E. (2009). 40 plus or minus 10, a new magical number: Reply to Russell. *The Clinical Neuropsychologist, 23*, 841–849.

Lazzari, C., & Rabottini, M. (2023). Comorbidity between factitious and borderline personality disorder: A narrative analysis. *Psychiatria Danubina, 35*(1), 16–26.

Lazzari, C., Shoka, A., & Rabottini, M. (2023). Factitious disorder comorbid with borderline personality disorder and dysthymia: From medically unexplained physical symptoms to functional neurological disorder. *Rivista di Psichiatria, 58*(5), 205–219.

Leung, H. C., Skudlarski, P., Gatenby, J. C., Peterson, B. S., & Gore, J. C. (2000). An event-related functional MRI study of the Stroop color word interference task. *Cerebral Cortex, 10*(6), 552–560.

Lieb, R., Meinlschmidt, G., & Araya, R. (2007). Epidemiology of the association between somatoform disorders and anxiety and depressive disorders: An update. *Psychosomatic Medicine, 69*, 860–863.

Maaranen, P., Tanskanen, A., Haatainen, K., Koivumaa-Honkanen, H., Hintikka, J., & Viinamäki, H. (2004). Somatoform dissociation and adverse childhood experiences in the general population. *The Journal of Nervous and Mental Disease, 192*(5), 337–342.

Mace, C. J. (1994). Reversible cognitive impairment related to conversion disorder. *Journal of Nervous and Mental Disease, 182*, 186–187.

Marshall, J. C., Halligan, P. W., Fink, G. R., Wade, D. T., & Frackowiak, R. S. (1997). The functional anatomy of a hysterical paralysis. *Cognition, 64*, B1–B8.

Martin, P. K., Schroeder, R. W., Heinrichs, R. J., & Baade, L. E. (2015a). Does true neurocognitive dysfunction contribute to Minnesota multiphasic personality inventory–restructured form cognitive validity scale scores? *Archives of Clinical Neuropsychology, 30*(5), 377–386.

Martin, P. K., Schroeder, R. W., & Odland, A. P. (2015b). Neuropsychologists' validity testing beliefs and practices: A survey of North American professionals. *The Clinical Neuropsychologist, 29*(6), 741–776.

McCaffrey, R. J., & Lynch, J. K. (2021). Toxic mold syndrome and multiple chemical sensitivity: The continued search for a causal link to neuropsychological functioning. In K. B. Boone (Ed.), *Assessment of feigned cognitive impairment: A neuropsychological perspective* (2nd ed.). Guilford Press.

McPherson, B., McMahon, K., Wilson, W., & Copland, D. (2012). I know you can hear me: Neural correlates of feigned hearing loss. *Human Brain Mapping, 33*(8), 1964–1972.

Mealy, L. (1995). The sociobiology of sociopathy: An integrated evolutionary model. *Behavior and Brain Sciences, 18*, 523–599.

Metternich, B., Schmidtke, K., & Hüll, M. (2009). How are memory complaints in functional memory disorder related to measures of affect, metamemory and cognition? *Journal of Psychosomatic Research, 66*(5), 435–444.

Meyers, J. E., Miller, R. M., Thompson, L. M., Scalese, A. M., Allred, B. C., Rupp, Z. W., et al. (2014). Using likelihood ratios to detect invalid performance with performance validity measures. *Archives of Clinical Neuropsychology, 29*(3), 224–235.

Meyers, J. E., & Volbrecht, M. E. (2003). A validation of multiple malingering detection methods in a large clinical sample. *Archives of Clinical Neuropsychology, 18*, 261–276.

Mittenberg, W., Patton, C., Canyock, E. M., & Condit, D. (2002). Bases rates of malingering and symptom exaggeration. *Journal of Clinical and Experimental Neuropsychology, 24*, 1094–1102.

Morey, L. C. (1991). *Personality assessment inventory*. Psychological Assessment Resources.

Nakao, M., Tamiya, N., & Yano, E. (2005). Gender and somatosensory amplification in relation to perceived work stress and social support in Japanese workers. *Women & Health, 42*, 41–54.

Nicholson, T. R., Aybek, S., Craig, T., Harris, T., Wojcik, W., David, A. S., & Kanaan, R. A. (2016). Life events and escape in conversion disorder. *Psychological Medicine, 46*(12), 2617–2626.

Nicholson, T. R., Stone, J., & Kanaan, R. A. (2011). Conversion disorder: a problematic diagnosis. *Journal of Neurology, Neurosurgery & Psychiatry, 82*(11), 1267–1273.

Onofrj, M., Digiovanni, A., Ajdinaj, P., Russo, M., Carrarini, C., Di Giannantonio, M., et al. (2021). The factitious/malingering continuum and its burden on public health costs: A review and experience in an Italian neurology setting. *Neurological Sciences, 42*, 4073–4083.

Pankratz, L., Fausti, S. A., & Peed, S. (1975). A forced-choice technique to evaluate deafness in the hysterical or malingering patient. *Journal of Consulting and Clinical Psychology, 43*(3), 421.

Peterson, B. S., Kane, M. J., Alexander, G. M., Lacadie, C., Skudlarski, P., Leung, H. C., et al. (2002). An event-related functional MRI study comparing interference effects in the Simon and Stroop tasks. *Cognitive Brain Research, 13*(3), 427–440.

Rief, W., Hiller, W., & Margraf, J. (1998). Cognitive aspects of hypochondriasis and the somatization syndrome. *Journal of Abnormal Psychology, 107*, 587–595.

Sackeim, H. A., Nordlie, J. W., & Gur, R. C. (1979). A model of hysterical and hypnotic blindness: Cognition, motivation, and awareness. *Journal of Abnormal Psychology, 88*(5), 474.

Saj, A., Arzy, S., & Vuilleumier, P. (2009). Functional brain imaging in a woman with spatial neglect due to conversion disorder. *JAMA, 302*(23), 2552–2554.

Samelius, L., Wijma, B., Wingren, G., & Wigma, K. (2007). Somatization in abused women. *Journal of Women's Health (Larchmt), 16*, 909–918.

Schmaling, K. B., & Fales, J. L. (2018). The association between borderline personality disorder and somatoform disorders: A systematic review and meta-analysis. *Clinical Psychology: Science and Practice, 25*(2), e12244.

Schroeder, R. W., Martin, P. K., & Odland, A. P. (2016). Expert beliefs and practices regarding neuropsychological validity testing. *The Clinical Neuropsychologist, 30*(4), 515–535.

Selvakumar, J., Havdal, L. B., Drevvatne, M., Brodwall, E. M., Berven, L. L., Stiansen-Sonerud, T., et al. (2023). Prevalence and characteristics associated with post-COVID-19 condition among nonhospitalized adolescents and young adults. *JAMA Network Open, 6*(3), e235763.

Shah, A. N., Beck, A. F., Sucharew, H. J., Litman, S., Pfefferman, C., Haney, J., et al. (2018). Parental adverse childhood experiences and resilience on coping after discharge. *Pediatrics, 141*(4), e20172127.

Sharma, V., Singh Bhandari, S., Singh, V., & Chandra, A. (2021). A case of factitious disorder: Red herring of psychiatry. *Psychiatria Danubina, 33*(br 3), 371–372.

Sherman, E. M., Slick, D. J., & Iverson, G. L. (2020). Multidimensional malingering criteria for neuropsychological assessment: A 20-year update of the malingered neuropsychological dysfunction criteria. *Archives of Clinical Neuropsychology, 35*(6), 735–764.

Siegrist, M. (1995). Inner speech as a cognitive process mediating self-consciousness and inhibiting self-deception. *Psychological Reports, 76*(1), 259–265.

Smith, K., Boone, K., Victor, T., Miora, D., Cottingham, M., Ziegler, E., et al. (2014). Comparison of credible patients of very low intelligence and non-credible patients on neurocognitive performance validity indicators. *The Clinical Neuropsychologist, 28*(6), 1048–1070.

Sneddon, I. B. (1983). Simulated disease: Problems in diagnosis and management. The parkes weber lecture 1982. *Journal of the Royal College of Physicians of London, 17*(3), 199–205.

Sollman, M. J., Ranseen, J. D., & Berry, D. T. (2010). Detection of feigned ADHD in college students. *Psychological Assessment, 22*(2), 325.

Spence, S. A., Hunter, M. D., Farrow, T. F., Green, R. D., Leung, D. H., Hughes, C. J., & Ganesan, V. (2004). A cognitive neurobiological account of deception: Evidence from functional neuroimaging. *Philosophical Transactions of the Royal Society B: Biological Sciences, 359*(1451), 1755.

Spitzer, C., Barnow, S., Gau, K., Freyberger, H. J., & Grabe, H. J. (2008). Childhood maltreatment in patients with somatization disorder. *The Australian and New Zealand Journal of Psychiatry, 42*, 335–341.

Steffen-Klatt, A., Fiess, J., Beckh, J., Schmidt, R., & Rockstroh, B. (2019). The impact of adverse childhood experience on symptom severity in patients with functional neurological symptom disorder (FNSD). *Mental Health & Prevention, 13*, 169–175.

Suhr, J., & Bryant, A. (2021). Noncredible presentations in neuropsychological assessment of pain- and fatigue-related disorders: Clinical and research implications. In K. B. Boone (Ed.), *Assessment of feigned cognitive impairment: A neuropsychological perspective* (2nd ed.). Guilford Press.

Sweet, J. J., Heilbronner, R. L., Morgan, J. E., Larrabee, G. J., Rohling, M. L., Boone, K. B., et al. (2021). American Academy of Clinical Neuropsychology (AACN) 2021 consensus statement on validity assessment: Update of the 2009 AACN consensus conference statement on neuropsychological assessment of effort, response bias, and malingering. *The Clinical Neuropsychologist, 35*(6), 1053–1106.

Taylor, S., & Asmundson, G. J. G. (2004). *Treating health anxiety: A cognitive-behavioral approach*. Guilford Press.

TenHouten, W. D., Walter, D. O., Hoppe, K. D., & Bogen, J. E. (1988). Alexithymia and the split brain: VI. Electroencephalographic correlates of alexithymia. *The Psychiatric Clinics of North America, 11*(3), 317–329.

Theodor, L. H., & Mandelcorn, M. S. (1973). Hysterical blindness: A case report and study using a modern psychophysical technique. *Journal of Abnormal Psychology, 82*(3), 552.

Van Beilen, M., Vogt, B. A., & Leenders, K. L. (2010). Increased activation in cingulate cortex in conversion disorder: What does it mean? *Journal of the Neurological Sciences, 289*(1–2), 155–158.

Victor, T. L., & Boone, K. B. (2021). Identification of feigned intellectual disability. In K. B. Boone (Ed.), *Assessment of feigned cognitive impairment: A neuropsychological perspective* (2nd ed.). Guilford Press.

Victor, T. L., Boone, K. B., Serpa, J. G., Buehler, J., & Ziegler, E. A. (2009). Interpreting the meaning of multiple symptom validity test failure. *The Clinical Neuropsychologist, 23*(2), 297–313.

Waller, E., Scheidt, C. E., & Hartman, A. (2004). Attachment representation and illness behavior in somatoform disorder. *Journal of Nervous and Mental Disease, 192*, 200–209.

Wang, D., Nadiga, D. N., & Jenson, J. J. (2005). Factitious disorders. In *Kaplan & Sadock's comprehensive textbook of psychiatry* (8th ed.). Lippincott, Williams, & Wilkins.

Whiteside, D. M., Naini, S. M., Basso, M. R., Waldron, E. J., Holker, E., Porter, J., et al. (2022). Outcomes in post-acute sequelae of COVID-19 (PASC) at 6 months post-infection part 2: Psychological functioning. *The Clinical Neuropsychologist, 36*(4), 829–847.

World Health Organization. (1992). *The ICD-10 classification of mental and behavioural disorders: Clinical descriptions and diagnostic guidelines* (Vol. 1). World Health Organization.

World Health Organization. (2021). *International statistical classification of diseases and related health problems (ICD)*. https://www.who.int/standards/classifications/classification-of-diseases

Chapter 20
Functional Neurological Disorder: A Primer for Neuropsychologists

Nicholas Kavish and Julia Maietta

Key Points

- Functional neurologic (and cognitive) disorders are real, involuntary syndromes consisting of symptoms affecting motor, sensory and/or cognitive functioning.
- The core feature of any presentation of FND/FCD is internal inconsistency or incompatibility between symptoms and current understanding of neural mechanisms and medical disorders.
- Although trauma and mood disorders may increase the risk for FND, FND can present without an identifiable stressor or other diagnosable psychiatric condition.
- Functional disorders likely result from dysfunction in neural networks that underlie attention, agency, emotional processing, interoception and predictive processing.
- Neurocognitive performance is variable, but weaknesses with attention, working memory and processing speed are most common.

N. Kavish (✉)
Department of Neurological Sciences, University of Nebraska Medical Center, Omaha, NE, USA
e-mail: Nkavish@unmc.edu

J. Maietta
Cornerstone Behavioral Health, Wooster, MA, USA
e-mail: DrMaietta@evalprosolutions.com

M. R. Schoenberg, J. G. Scott (eds.), *The Little Black Book of Neuropsychology*,
https://doi.org/10.1007/978-3-032-07777-6_20

A Brief History of FND

This section will provide an abbreviated overview of the history of FND—for a more thorough review of the history of FND, see Trimble and Reynolds (2016), Goetz (2016) and Kanaan (2016). Presentations which would meet the criteria for diagnosis of what is currently known as functional neurological disorder have long preceded modern medicine. For example, previous authors (see Trimble & Reynolds, 2016) have pointed to the speech disorder of King Mursili II, a Hittite king from 1200 BCE, as a likely functional disorder. Available records indicate the King was caught in a particularly powerful thunderstorm (the Hittites worshiped a Storm God) and experienced a temporary speech disturbance resembling mutism. His symptoms resolved, but he experienced nightmares and even a temporary relapse years later. Presentations such as the King's have previously been known by a variety of terms including hysteria or hysterical neuroses, dissociative disorders, somatoform disorders, conversion disorders, psychogenic disorders and posttraumatic stress disorders. The explanations for these disorders have been equally numerous: affliction by a "roaming ghost," symptoms of a "wandering uterus," evidence of witchcraft or the result of sexual frustration (Trimble & Reynolds, 2016).

Charcot

In the late nineteenth century, FND (then known as hysteria) became increasingly defined as a neurologic diagnosis due largely to the work of Jean-Martin Charcot (Goetz, 2016). Charcot's contributions to neurology, including developing a nosology for neurologic diseases and an anatomo-clinical method for localizing clinical neurological signs (allowing, for example, the identification of amyotrophic lateral sclerosis and differentiation between upper and lower motor neuron diseases), have resulted in many considering him the "father" of modern neurology. Charcot was keenly interested in presentations, including hysteria, for which he was unable to identify an underlying lesion. In his view, the often-intermittent features of functional symptoms suggested a dynamic problem in the same location as he would find a lesion in a patient with more static symptoms. For example, transient paresis would be assumed to result from transient disruption in the regions (e.g., precentral gyrus) in which he had observed post-stroke lesions or tumors in patients with static paresis (Goetz, 2016).

Over time, Charcot began to hypothesize that hysteric diseases were the result of a combination of hereditary vulnerability (he believed all neurologic diseases had a hereditary component) and an environmental trigger, such as stress (e.g., physical injury and/or emotional distress). He consulted for a railroad company and observed a surprising rate of neurologic presentations following seemingly mild physical injuries. He suggested that the initial injury triggers a hereditary vulnerability in the patient and that repetitive thinking about the injurious event could continue to trigger the underlying physiological dysfunction (a so-called functional lesion; Goetz, 2016). Additionally, Charcot observed that "hysterics" were easy to hypnotize and their symptoms could be activated or reduced at the suggestion of the hypnotist; however, his work with hypnosis received fierce criticism. Late in his career, Charcot appeared to question most of his beliefs (hereditary nature of all neurologic disease, that hysteria was caused by a transient lesion, and the importance of susceptibility to hypnosis) about FND, ultimately writing in at least one monograph that "hysteria is for the most part a mental illness."[1]

Freud

In 1885, Sigmund Freud briefly studied neuropathology under Charcot, during which time he witnessed many of Charcot's "hysteric" patients, met with other clinicians interested in hysteria and joined hypnosis sessions. His time with Charcot had a profound impact on Freud's understanding of hysteria (and many other illnesses) and resulted in Freud—then a neurologist—developing a model of hysteria as a psychiatric disorder. This psychiatric model became the dominant view of hysteria for over 50 years—until its rejection by the third edition of the *Diagnostic and Statistical Manual of Mental Disorders* (DSM-III) in 1980. Freud's ideas even retained some popularity into the turn of the twenty-first century (Kanaan, 2016).

The foundation of Freud's model of hysteria was the concepts of repression and conversion. In Freud's view, people with FND repress an unwanted thought (an idea, urge or memory) and push it out of conscious experience. The unwanted thought had an "affective energy" which also must be accommodated. Conversion referred to a process that assisted repression by transforming the affective energy into a physical symptom, relieving the energy and keeping the unwelcome thought out of the conscious realm (Kanaan, 2016). According to Freud, this overall process was initiated intentionally—the patient actively seeks to repress the unwanted thought; however, ultimately the conversion process occurs in the unconscious and the patient becomes an unwitting victim. The condition could thus be treated through catharsis—bringing the unwelcome thought into conscious awareness and confronting it. As his cathartic approach (through hypnosis or simply insisting the patient remember the unwanted thought) was not consistently successful, Freud increasingly elaborated his concept of repression and added complexity to his formulations of the past experiences that ultimately led to the presenting symptom—tracing events further and further back into childhood and sometimes to infancy (Kanaan, 2016).

[1] Notably, Goetz (2016) argues that Charcot's formal publications continued to focus on a neuroanatomic perspective and do not conclusively demonstrate that he ever embraced a psychogenic view of FND.

DSM-III–DSM-5-TR

The 1980 publication of DSM-III represented a seismic shift in American psychiatric nosology. In its third iteration, the authors of the DSM sought to develop nomenclature more consistent with the widely used International Classification of Diseases (ICD) and to increase diagnostic consistency through the development of standard diagnostic criteria. In the case of functional neurologic symptoms, this resulted in a separation of presentations, with syndromes such as functional amnesia or fugue states being classified as dissociative disorders and other functional symptoms, now labeled conversion disorder (previously "conversion reaction" and "hysterical neurosis, conversion type" in earlier iterations of the DSM), being classified within the somatoform disorders category (Levenson & Sharpe, 2016). This separation of dissociative disorders and functional neurologic symptoms was heavily criticized, with critics arguing that functional neurologic symptoms represent or involve a physical form of dissociation similar to the psychologic dissociation of various types of identity disturbance and amnesiac states (Brown, 2016). Indeed, the ICD system classified dissociative disorders and functional neurologic symptoms side by side, and the newest iteration, ICD-11, refers to FND as "dissociative neurological symptom disorder." DSM-5-TR continues to separate dissociative and functional neurologic disorders, but now notes their potential overlap.

Regarding definitions of FND within the DSM over time, the new phenomenological definition of FND ("conversion disorder"; with a parenthetical option to retain the hysterical neurosis label) within DSM-III required a loss of or alteration in physical function which the clinician judged to involve psychological factors in its etiology. DSM-III further required that the symptoms were not voluntary and could not be explained by known neuro-pathophysiology. The publication of DSM-IV in 1994 involved a shift away from etiological assumptions, and the section for conversion disorder dropped the option for inclusion of the hysteria label. The criteria were broadly similar to DSM-III but included a new requirement that the symptom must cause clinically significant impairment or distress. DSM-IV also introduced subtyping of conversion disorder, with subcategories for motor, sensory, seizure or mixed presentations (Levenson & Sharpe, 2016). Published in 2013, the DSM-5 represented incremental change in the definition of conversion disorder (now with FND included as a parenthetical label), with the removal of explicit criteria that feigning be ruled out (as feigning is a differential for all disorders in the DSM), the removal of the required identifiable stressor preceding the symptom and a switch from a focus on exclusion of "organic disease" to including positive evidence of incompatibility with known neuro-pathophysiology (Levenson & Sharpe, 2016). Most recently, the DSM-5 text revision (DSM-5-TR) has flipped the parenthetical label, such that FND is now the first name listed and conversion disorder is retained in parentheses (American Psychiatric Association, 2022). The current diagnostic criteria for FND will be further discussed in subsequent sections.

Epidemiology and Diagnosis

FND is an overarching diagnosis that encompasses several subtypes of symptom clusters. In the FND literature, these subtypes are discussed broadly and include functional seizures (often called psychogenic non-epileptic seizures, PNES), functional movement disorders (i.e., tremor, dystonia, gait/balance, jerks/myoclonus, weakness), functional dizziness (often called persistent postural perceptual dizziness, PPPD) and functional cognitive disorder. The DSM-5-TR also provides additional symptom subtypes (see Table 20.1 specifiers; American Psychiatric Association, 2022). Diagnosis and clinical presentation are specific to the distinct FND subtypes and will be described below.

Table 20.1 DSM-5 and ICD-10 criteria for functional neurologic disorder

	DSM-5-TR	ICD-11
	Functional neurological symptom disorder (conversion disorder)	Dissociative neurological symptom disorder
Description	An additional description section is not included in DSM-5-TR	Dissociative neurological symptom disorder is characterized by the presentation of motor, sensory or cognitive symptoms that imply an involuntary discontinuity in the normal integration of motor, sensory or cognitive functions and are not consistent with a recognized disease of the nervous system, other mental or behavioral disorder or other medical condition. The symptoms do not occur exclusively during another dissociative disorder and are not due to the effects of a substance or medication on the central nervous system, including withdrawal effects, or a sleep-wake disorder
Diagnostic criteria/ essential features	• One or more symptoms of altered voluntary motor or sensory function • Clinical findings provide evidence of incompatibility between the symptom and recognized neurological or medical conditions • The symptom or deficit is not better explained by another medical or mental disorder • The symptom or deficit causes clinically significant distress or impairment in social, occupational or other important areas of functioning or warrants medical evaluation	• Involuntary disruption or discontinuity in the normal integration of motor, sensory or cognitive functions, lasting at least several hours • Clinical findings are not consistent with a recognized disease of the nervous system (e.g., a stroke) or another medical condition (e.g., a head injury). • The symptoms do not occur exclusively during episodes of trance disorder, possession trance disorder, dissociative identity disorder or partial dissociative identity disorder • The symptoms are not due to the effects of a substance or medication on the central nervous system, including withdrawal effects, do not occur exclusively during hypnagogic or hypnopompic states and are not due to a sleep-wake disorder (e.g., sleep-related rhythmic movement disorder, recurrent isolated sleep paralysis) • The symptoms are not better accounted for by another mental disorder (e.g., schizophrenia or other primary psychotic disorder, posttraumatic stress disorder) • The symptoms result in significant impairment in personal, family, social, educational, occupational or other important areas of functioning

(continued)

Table 20.1 (continued)

	DSM-5-TR	ICD-11
	Functional neurological symptom disorder (conversion disorder)	Dissociative neurological symptom disorder
Symptom specifiers	• With abnormal weakness or paralysis • With abnormal movements • With swallowing symptoms • With speech symptoms • With attacks or seizures • With anesthesia or sensory loss • With special sensory symptoms • With mixed symptoms	• With visual disturbance • With auditory disturbance • With vertigo or dizziness • With other sensory disturbance • With non-epileptic seizures • With speech disturbance • With paresis or weakness • With gait disturbance • With movement disturbance • With cognitive symptoms • With other specified symptoms • With unspecified symptoms

Epidemiology & Comorbidity

FND is the second most common referral to general neurology clinics, after headache (Hallett et al., 2022; Stone et al., 2014; Weiss et al., 2021). Indeed, prevalence of FND, in general, is roughly 4–12/ 100,000 per year (1–17/100,000 per year for children) and can represent up to 15% of referrals for general neurology practices (American Psychiatric Association, 2022; Aybek & Perez, 2022; Bennett et al., 2021; Weiss et al., 2021). Functional movement disorders are slightly more common than functional seizure disorders with prevalence estimates of 4–5/100,000 per year for motor FND and 1.5–4.9/100,000 per year for PNES (Aybek & Perez, 2022).

FND has been identified across the lifespan; however, diagnosis tends to peak between the ages of 20 and 40 depending on the subtype (American Psychiatric Association, 2022; Bennett et al., 2021). For most symptom subtypes, there is a much higher rate of females with FND compared to males; however, the preponderance of women decreases slightly in early onset and later onset cases (i.e., generally 2–3:1 female to male ratio; American Psychiatric Association, 2022; Bennett et al., 2021; Hallett et al., 2022; Weiss et al., 2021). There is also evidence, albeit limited, of a higher prevalence of FNDs in sexual and gender minority individuals (Lerario et al., 2023). To date, there is a lack of research on FND in non-majority-white samples and in non-industrialized nations to provide evidence regarding racial or ethnic differences in prevalence; however, there is limited existing data on general somatic conditions suggesting minimal differences across racial/ethnic groups (Carson & Lehn, 2016). Furthermore, although not speaking directly to the question of prevalence, there is substantial data supporting similarity in FND presentations around the world (e.g., very similar seizure semiology from samples across North America, Europe, the Middle East, Africa and Asia; see Edwards et al., 2023).

FND is commonly comorbid with other neurologic disorders (e.g., PNES and epilepsy syndromes), with up to 20% of cases also having separate, diagnosed neurological disorders (Bennett et al., 2021). Other somatic symptom disorders, such as chronic pain syndromes, fibromyalgia and irritable bowel syndromes, are also commonly seen in FND (Hallett et al., 2022; Stone et al., 2014). In some cases, neurological insult or injury is a precipitating factor in the onset of FND symptoms (Hallett et al., 2022). Indeed, criteria for functional dizziness denote a precipitating vestibular injury, PNES is commonly preceded by an epilepsy syndrome, migraines can bring on functional weakness, etc. (Hallett et al., 2022). Other identified risk factors for FND across the lifespan may include genetic predispositions to be less resilient to physiological distress (Hallett et al., 2022).

Although many clinicians frequently associate FND with psychological distress or significant trauma history, these factors are actually present in less than 50% of FND cases (and less than 25% of childhood FND cases), and the presence of a recent stressor is no longer a requirement for diagnosing FND (American Psychiatric Association, 2022; Hallett et al., 2022; Weiss et al., 2021). The DSM-5-TR does provide specifier options to clarify if the diagnosis is associated with or without an identifiable psychological stressor (American Psychiatric Association, 2022). Childhood adversity, however, does increase the risk of developing FND with a 2–4 times increased risk compared to those with no childhood adversity exposure (Hallett et al., 2022). In children, additional risk factors include bullying, dysfunctional family systems and peer pressure (Hallett et al., 2022). While psychiatric conditions can also occur commonly in FND populations, these comorbidities are not unique to FND and, instead, occur within a wide variety of neurological conditions (e.g., depression in Parkinson's disease; Hallett et al., 2022).

Overarching Diagnostic Issues

FND can feel to some like a difficult diagnosis to make, and many are concerned about diagnostic errors, including false-positive and false-negative errors. Readers can be reassured, however, that misdiagnosis of FND is relatively uncommon and does *not* occur more frequently than misdiagnosis of other neurological and psychiatric disorders (Aybek & Perez, 2022; Bennett et al., 2021; Hallett et al., 2022). This is likely due, in part, to the diagnostic criteria's focus on *positive* FND symptoms that are incompatible with known neurologic disease, exclusion of neurological disorder (i.e., not better explained by another medical or mental condition) and thorough evaluation with signs that are both sensitive and specific to FND (which will be discussed more in depth below). It is important to be aware that FND symptoms are not "unexplained" but, rather, are a distinct neuropathophysiological phenomenon with specific diagnostic signs and symptoms. As such, the diagnostic evaluations' focus is on exam findings that are inconsistent and/or incongruous with known neurologic disease. Importantly, diagnosis of FND should *not* be made in the presence of "bizarre" symptoms alone, as some rare neurologic conditions can present with such symptoms (e.g., frontal lobe seizures with intact awareness and bicycle-like motor movements; Bennett et al., 2021; Hallett et al., 2022). Consultation with neurology, to ensure that neurologic conditions have been thoroughly evaluated and ruled out, is an important aspect of diagnosing FND (Weiss et al., 2021). Neuropsychologists should feel empowered to suggest FND as a possible differential in cases in which full neurology workup has not been completed yet, as early identification and diagnosis of FND can result in better prognosis (Weiss et al., 2021).

Diagnosis by FND Subtype

Overarching DSM-5-TR diagnostic criteria for FND are provided in Table 20.1. Table 20.2 provides examples of positive diagnostic signs for different FND subtypes. This table should not be considered exhaustive, and interested readers are referred to the table note for more detailed information on each positive sign.

Further Diagnostic Framework Changes on the Horizon?

As illustrated in earlier sections on the history of functional symptoms, views on FND have evolved significantly over time, with varying influences from psychiatry and neurology and changes in nomenclature and operationalization. Concerns remain regarding stigma among both clinicians and the public that functional symptoms are "less real" than so-called organic symptoms (raising risk for iatrogenic harm), potential for confusion of the meaning of functional in FND versus in the field of functional medicine and how to bridge the gap between FND and other conditions (e.g., fibromyalgia, postconcussion syndrome) which are increasingly thought to have overlapping etiological and maintenance mechanisms with FND symptoms (Maggio et al., 2023).

Maggio et al. (2023) recently proposed a brain–mind–body interface disorders framework, which may serve to address concerns about the meaning of "functional" and encompass traditional FNDs along with overlapping somatic disorders. This proposed category includes "conditions with physical symptoms where there is likely a therapeutic benefit to factor in psychological processes (e.g., biased attention, fear avoidance, somatic hypervigilance, illness beliefs, alexithymia, catastrophizing, impaired self-agency, and dissociation) as core to the development or maintenance of symptoms" (Maggio et al., 2023). They argue that their framework removes the reliance on dualistic functional versus organic classification and approaches various conditions as existing on a spectrum regarding the degree to which a brain–mind–body interface component plays a central role and is a suitable target for intervention. We expand below upon the growing evidence regarding the pathophysiology that underlies functional symptoms, which Maggio and colleagues have drawn upon to support their proposed framework.

Table 20.2 Examples of positive signs that help "rule in" FND

Subtype	Symptom	Clinical features	Positive finding
Functional movement disorder	Tremor	Most frequent functional movement disorder [a]; tremor may increase or move to another body part when the tremor-affected limb is immobilized [b]; do not consider increases during stress or absence during sleep as positive signs [b]	Variability in frequency; entrainment; "whack-a-mole" [c]
	Dystonia	Second most common functional movement disorder [a]; abnormal posture is fixed vs. other dystonia which is mobile; pain is common; overlap is common with complex regional pain syndrome [b]; functional hemifacial spasm is a common stroke mimic [b]	Resistance to movement; abnormal posturing (e.g., flexion of digits 3–5 sparing pincer function in functional fixed hand dystonia); lack of spasms in sleep (in functional hemifacial spasm) [c]
	Gait/balance problems	Patients may be able to walk in everyday life but not during physical exam [d]; severity of gait disorder may be inconsistent with functional limitations; inconsistency with automatic movements (e.g., undressing for physical exam)	Dragging monoplegic gait; chair test[e]; falls toward support [e]; improvement of gait with cognitive or physical dual task distraction [d]
	Jerks/myoclonus	Abrupt onset often preceded by physical event; rapid progression; variable course with some experiencing fluctuations in symptoms; axial jerks are most likely to be functional; tend to decrease with distraction and increase with attention [c]	Variability, entrainment, variability in stimulus sensitivity [c]
	Tics	Sudden onset, complex vocal and motor tics; common in adolescence; no family history of tics; [f]; lack of premonitory urge; inability to suppress tic; more common in females; poor response to medication [e,f]; recently, presentation of tic patterns seen on social media has been common [f]	Significant variability of symptoms (compared to stereotyped tics); symptoms begin in extremities before traveling to face and neck; severe "attacks" that last minutes to several hours with abrupt onset and ending [f]; inability to suppress temporarily; more severe in the presence of others [f]
	Limb weakness or general motor weakness/ dysfunction	Commonly unilateral; sudden onset (common stroke mimic)[b]; voluntary movement impaired while automatic movement preserved; often feel like the limb is a foreign body; flexors and extensors equally affected [b]	Hoover's sign; drift without pronation; give-way weakness/collapse [e,b]

(continued)

Table 20.2 (continued)

Subtype	Symptom	Clinical features	Positive finding
Functional dizziness		Symptom severity may wax and wane [a]; may be exacerbated by upright posture, movement, moving visual stimuli or complex visual environments [a]; triggered by events that cause vertigo, dizziness, etc.; may represent up to 20% of patients with vestibular symptoms and up to 40% in dedicated dizziness specialty clinics [a]; neuroticism and hypervigilance to bodily sensations could be predisposing features; secondary functional gait disorder may develop	Dissociation between objective balance testing and subjective balance; situational or social events as triggers of dizziness; fear of falls with no fall history; chronic dizziness after transportation in vehicles [g]
Functional seizures		Up to 20% have a comorbid epilepsy syndrome [b]; commonly longer in duration, fluctuating in course, and include memory of the event; post-ictal confusion suggests an epileptic seizure; urinary incontinence and physical injury are poor distinguishers between epileptic seizures and functional seizures [b]; high frequency of seizures is common; 1/3 can appear syncopal and refer to cardiology services rather than neurology [b]	Active resistance to eye opening; flutter or blinking on eyelash rub; change in semiology in response to others during the event; side-to-side head or body movements [b]; ictal crying, stuttering, whispering, hyperventilation [e]; asynchronous limb movements; ictal eye closure [h]
Functional cognitive disorder		Up to 24% of memory clinic referrals may meet the criteria for functional cognitive disorder [b]; cognitive testing patterns of performance are not specific to this disorder; memory perfectionism may be a feature in some cases [i]	Dense retrograde amnesia without a temporal gradient; dense anterograde amnesia that resets daily; detail-rich narratives with great recall of numerous cognitive lapses; delayed onset (e.g., days to weeks later) and worsening over time (in the subsequent month) of cognitive complaints after concussion; attending appointment alone; bringing a written list of symptoms [j]

Note. [a] (See Hallett et al., 2022). [b](See Bennett et al., 2021). [c](See Dreissen et al., 2016; Gilmour et al., 2022). [d](See Nonnekes et al., 2020). [e](See Aybek & Perez, 2022; Daum et al., 2014). [f](See Demartini et al., 2015; Malaty et al., 2022). [g](See Brandt et al., 2015). [h](See Syed et al., 2011; Wardrope et al., 2020). [i](See Larner, 2021; Picon et al., 2022, 2023). [j](See Cabreira et al., 2023; Silverberg & Rush, 2023)

Etiology/Pathophysiology

Functional neurological disorder encompasses a highly heterogenous population of presentations, and the combination of factors that underlie any particular case is undoubtedly equally varied. Nevertheless, as research on FND has progressed, helpful biopsychosocial models and pathophysiological frameworks have been developed in attempts to further our understanding of both how and why FND occurs. With the revival of academic interest in FND, there has been a significant increase in the number of studies attempting to understand FND at the neurobiological level, using a variety of functional neuroimaging techniques (e.g., fMRI), connectivity-based approaches and even transcranial magnetic stimulation (TMS). To date, the research has been limited by typically small sample sizes, lack of controls for comorbidities and medication effects, few longitudinal studies and a lack of preregistration. Yet, relatively consistent themes have emerged to implicate alterations in constructs such as emotion processing, attention, interoception, agency and predictive processing (Drane et al., 2021).

A Disorder of Emotional Processing

Emotional processing alterations appear to be an integral aspect of FND. Stressful life events (e.g., physical illness or interpersonal difficulties) are known risk factors for FND, and people with FND frequently endorse anxiety, depression, emotion dysregulation and/or alexithymia (difficulty recognizing, expressing or describing their own emotions; Pick et al., 2019). Evidence from behavioral, psychophysiological and task-based neuroimaging studies supports impairments in social-emotional cognition, with the strongest evidence supporting an attentional bias toward emotional faces in those with FND. Furthermore, research has demonstrated increased amygdala sensitivity, reduced habituation and reduced modulation of the amygdala by the prefrontal cortex in those with FND, which may explain observations of increased sensitivity and responsivity to negative emotions, reduced fear extinction and dissociative responses (Drane et al., 2021; Lanius et al., 2010; Pick et al., 2019).

Functional neuroimaging research has also uncovered alterations, in this case increases, in connectivity between key emotional processing circuitry (e.g., salience network and limbic/paralimbic networks) and aspects of motor circuitry and the pain matrix, which may explain some of the more perplexing features commonly seen in FND (Aybek et al., 2015; Baizabal-Carvallo et al., 2019; Denk et al., 2014; Diez et al., 2019). For example, some FND patients report their symptoms worsen with stress (likely due to increased connectivity between limbic and motor areas; Voon et al., 2010), whereas others may experience alexithymia and deny negative affect while showing signs of autonomic arousal—with evidence suggesting that differences in connectivity of the anterior insula affect self-awareness, including for emotional states (Craig, 2009). Similarly, overlap between circuitry of the pain matrix and the salience network—which consists primarily of the anterior insula and dorsal anterior cingulate cortex (dACC) and is heavily involved in self-awareness and integration of sensory, emotional and cognitive information—may explain high rates of pain complaints in people with FND and high rates of comorbid FND in chronic pain clinic samples (Gazzola et al., 2012; Mason et al., 2023; Stone, Burton, & Carson, 2020; Stone, Warlow, et al., 2020).

A Disorder of Attention

Another construct frequently altered in those with FND is attention (Drane et al., 2021). Clinical observations suggest perseveration on symptoms/affected body parts, which is further supported by research, such as the finding of increased visual focus on the trembling limb in functional versus "organic" tremor (van Poppelen et al., 2011). Furthermore, the symptoms often improve or remit with distraction (e.g., in functional movement disorders), with symptom distractibility being a positive sign toward diagnosis of FND (Perez et al., 2021). On neuropsychological measures, studies have found that people with FND evidence reduced sustained and selective attention (de Vroege et al., 2021; Kozlowska et al., 2015; O'Brien et al., 2015). Understanding of attentional abnormalities in those with FND at the neural level remains in its infancy, but there is growing evidence that people with FND tend to have greater fronto-parietal activation. It increasingly appears that the rigid fixation on symptoms and affected body parts with difficulty shifting attention to unaffected areas may result from similar changes in circuitry (e.g., posterior parietal cortex, ACC) seen in neglect syndromes (Perez et al., 2012; Perez et al., 2015).

A Disorder of Interoception

Interoception refers to our sense of our body's physiological condition (Craig, 2002), generated by bidirectional flow of information between the brain and body, which creates an internal representation of the body. It is through these networks of internal bodily signals that our nervous system monitors and predicts our bodily state in order to guide the initiation of processes to promote homeostasis. Reduced interoceptive awareness or accuracy has been documented across multiple paradigms (e.g., dyspnea, Bogaerts et al., 2010; heartbeat perception, Ricciardi et al., 2016; Schaefer et al., 2012) in individuals with functional symptoms. In Brown and Reuber's (2016) integrative theory of psychogenic non-epileptic (i.e., functional) seizures, and subsequently extended to all FND types in Fobian and Elliott's (2019) integrated etiological summary model, attentional biases and symptom monitoring can combine with interoceptive inaccuracies to activate an individual's seizure, or more broadly, health scaffold—a cognitive representation of symptoms created by a person's unique beliefs/expectations, experiences, sociocultural context and personal knowledge. Activation of the health scaffold results in the manifestation of the functional symptoms, which can be conditioned and/or reinforced over time, producing a functional disorder.

A Disorder of Prediction/Predictive Processing

In the previous section, we discussed how interoception serves to enable our brains to sense our internal states. Historically, the dominant view of neural perception posited a hierarchical model with feedforward loops in which the brain receives real-time sensory signals and translates or interprets them, to create our perceptions. In other words, our sensory pathways consist of feature detectors which create a representation of the outside world before a separate part of the brain decides how to interpret and respond to such signals (Keller & Mrsic-Flogel, 2018). Input initially goes to very simple feature detectors, such as neurons that detect dots, and then proceeds through ever more specialized and complex feature detectors (e.g., lines, angles and eventually faces; Walsh et al., 2020). This view has been invaluable for understanding cortical functioning, yet it could not account for how we distinguish between externally received sensory input (e.g., visual information entering through the eyes) and self-generated sensory feedback (e.g., the optokinetic reflex which moves our eyes in order to stabilize the image on our retinas). A solution to this problem is for the brain to cancel out the self-generated feedback by creating a simulation of sensory input based on expectations of the effects of the motor command (e.g., the optokinetic reflex) and past sensory experiences—which may then be compared to external sensory input. There are a number of variations of this concept (e.g., Bayesian inference, Körding & Wolpert, 2004), which can be grouped under the umbrella of predictive processing theories (Clark, 2015; Keller & Mrsic-Flogel, 2018).

In the predictive processing framework, the brain constructs generative models to "understand" the causes of sensory experiences. Predictions of the generative models are generated by one set of neurons and communicated to other neurons tasked with comparing the predictions to external sensory input to identify any errors (i.e., prediction errors). The predictions are transmitted along a processing pipeline, with congruent information (i.e., perceptual information that matches the prediction) being suppressed, so that only the prediction errors are carried onward to higher levels of processing. The brain then uses the errors to update its predictions in its generative models for a given perceptual experience until it generates a prediction that best fits external sensory input and minimizes error (Walsh et al., 2020). Furthermore, in one extension of this framework, a higher-order part of the model engages in metacognitive evaluation of perceptual contents in the generative model, which produces awareness states.

There are a number of examples that can illustrate how errors in the brain's predictive processing system can result in inaccurate sensory experiences. In some cases, lesions may disrupt connections between a modality-specific region and metacognitive processing regions, preventing appropriate updating and resulting in lack of awareness of a deficit (e.g., anosognosia for visual loss or motor dysfunction; see Kletenik et al., 2023). Alternatively, with a more distal injury, there may be awareness of the deficit; however, the brain may still overemphasize its predictions and down-weights or disregards afferent signals (or the lack thereof). For example, the majority of individuals who have lost a limb will at least temporarily experience phantom limb syndrome. Similarly, many people who experience a sudden onset of deafness will present with tinnitus. In some individuals with FND, the opposite appears to occur, where instead of the brain failing to update the loss of sensory input, it might instead mistakenly predict sensory loss or muscle weakness and fail to update when contradictory signals are received. This hypothesis is supported by findings that individuals with functional movement disorders demonstrate a sensory information processing deficit in an experimental task relative to healthy controls. Thus, returning to Fobian and Elliott's (2019) integrated etiological summary model, it may be the case that prior experiences (i.e., illness, injury or other factors that comprise the health scaffold) of those with FND inform the brain's expectations and predictions and override the sensory input they are receiving.

A Disorder of Agency

Agency refers to our experience of volition—you consciously will your arm to raise to wave to a friend and you experience that movement occurring. There are a number of components to volitional movement. The decision to move likely begins in the frontal, predominantly mesial frontal, lobes of the brain. As the decision to move enters conscious awareness and is traveling through the primary and secondary motor cortices and preceding through a variety of motor networks and ultimately down the spinal cord and into the peripheral nervous system to activate the muscles of the arm, feedforward signals are activating the predictive portion of the predictive processing system. The arm moves and afferent (i.e., feedback) signals are sent from somatosensory neurons in the arm (visual neurons in the eyes and so forth) back to the brain. The brain matches the afferent signals to its predictions, and we experience a sense of causation—we used our agency to produce the arm movement (Drane et al., 2021).

In the past couple decades, significant advances have been made in our understanding of how the brain integrates different types of afferent information with our own internal cognitions to construct our reality in a coherent manner. For example, Sepulcre and colleagues used a network neuroscience method called stepwise functional connectivity analysis to identify a large-scale multimodal integration network, mapping how the neural architecture transitions from the primary perceptual cortices to modality-specific association areas and onward to multimodal and increasingly complex regions before ultimately transitioning to regions integrating multimodal sensory information with higher-order cognitive functions. Their work highlighted critical areas in which much multimodal integration appears to occur, including the right temporoparietal junction (TPJ), a region frequently implicated in neglect syndromes (Kletenik et al., 2023).

Patients with functional movement disorders with a hyperkinetic component (e.g., tremor), and those with functional seizures with a large motor component, experience a lack of agency. That is, their movements occur outside of conscious volition. In contrast to individuals with conditions such as Parkinson's disease, the functional movement symptoms of people with FND occur in the context of a seemingly normally functioning motor system. Additionally, those with FND do not generally have sensory abnormalities that are likely to produce incorrect afferent feedback signals (Drane et al., 2021). Instead, many people with FND appear to have differences in key multimodal integration areas such as hypoactivity in the right TPJ (Voon et al., 2010).

Etiology

The sections on pathophysiology above discuss aspects of the growing understanding of the mechanisms that underlie FND, yet they fail to explain why FND develops. Although several etiological models exist (e.g., Fobian & Elliott, 2019), a complete biopsychosocial understanding of FND remains elusive, and there are undoubtedly a variety of pathways that can lead to FND (equifinality), just as it is likely that the same etiological factors can manifest with different functional symptoms (multifinality). Nevertheless, most models appear to assume that some combination of internal and external predisposing factors (e.g., internal: predisposition toward anxiety; external: past illness experiences) paired with misinterpretations and hypervigilance toward physical symptoms—with factors related to disrupted agency, interoception, attention, prediction and emotional processing (see above)—serves to maintain the symptoms over time.

Considerations for the Neuropsychologist

Performance Validity Testing in FND

Despite widespread consensus regarding the importance of including performance validity testing (PVT) in neuropsychological evaluations (see Sweet et al., 2021), the interpretation of PVT failures in patients with FND has been questioned due to the frequency of such failures (see McWhirter et al., 2020a; failure rates in some FND samples were as high as 25%) and the involuntary aspect of functional symptoms (see Edwards et al., 2023). Although the methodology of McWhirter and colleague's review has been questioned, subsequent meta-analysis similarly found a high PVT failure rate (33%) in the only FND subgroup included (i.e., functional seizures/PNES; see Roor et al., 2023). However, the proposed reasons for PVT failure in those with FND suggested by McWhirter et al. (2020a)—distraction by physical symptoms, excessive effort to perform a task paradoxically resulting in poorer performance and/or dissociation—do not have significant empirical support. Silverberg and Rush (2023) argue there is a lack of direct evidence for dissociation fully explaining performance on PVTs, there is experimental evidence that induced pain and distraction through the use of cognitively demanding tasks does not affect PVT failure rates, and PVTs present the patient with a novel situation (wholly different from the paradoxical difficulty due to excessive effort sometimes seen with overlearned tasks in athletes with the "yips"). McWhirter's fourth explanation for PVT failure in some patients with FND—cogniphobia or fear that cognitive effort will result in headache or other symptoms—while certainly plausible would still represent suboptimal task engagement, which PVTs are designed to capture (Silverberg & Rush, 2023).

PVT failure in FND, as with other conditions, is not necessarily due to malingering. For example, prior research has found that an external financial incentive was not associated with PVT failure in individuals with PNES (Williamson et al., 2012). Similarly, there is evidence that the presence of external incentive to perform poorly is not strongly associated with either unexpected symptoms or PVT failure in those with a recent concussion (Picon et al., 2021). Nevertheless, failure of multiple valid PVTs raises concern for suboptimal effort. There is rarely certainty regarding the cause of PVT failure in most clinical contexts, but failure of validated PVTs requires that neuropsychological test data be considered invalid and unable to accurately capture the patient's true cognitive abilities (Sweet et al., 2021). This does not negate the presence of a functional disorder, including functional cognitive symptoms—just as a patient may have cognitive impairment from a stroke in addition to poor test engagement—but rather indicates that there is something beyond FND (e.g., low effort to perform well) which is biasing the test data.

Functional Cognitive Disorder

Although not currently included in the DSM as a subtype of FND, there is growing literature on presentations that include predominant or exclusive cognitive symptoms (see Cabreira et al., 2023; Silverberg & Rush, 2023), and ICD-11 includes cognitive symptoms as a potential presentation (i.e., "with cognitive symptoms"). As this literature has developed, diagnostic criteria for what has been labeled

Table 20.3 Diagnostic criteria for functional cognitive disorder

1. One or more symptoms of impaired cognitive function
2. Clinical evidence of internal inconsistency
3. The symptoms or deficit are not better explained by another medical or psychiatric disorder
4. The symptoms or deficit cause clinically significant distress or impairment in social, occupational or other important areas of function, or warrant medical evaluation

"functional cognitive disorder" (FCD) have been proposed (see Table 20.3; Ball et al., 2020; McWhirter et al., 2020b).

The core feature of functional cognitive symptoms is the rule in/positive evidence of internal inconsistency. Importantly, internally inconsistent in the context of functional cognitive symptoms does not refer to variability in task performance across an evaluation (e.g., waxing and waning attention and working memory scores as can sometimes be seen in patients with multiple sclerosis), nor does it refer to fluctuations in cognition (e.g., as seen in Lewy body dementia). Rather, internal inconsistencies may include the ability to drive oneself to the appointment unaccompanied, yet describe severe and disabling memory impairment (e.g., "can't remember anything"), or the ability to successfully hold a high-level job with no significant errors while describing significant and severe attentional impairments. Furthermore, Silverberg and Rush (2023) caution that the neuropsychologist must consider other potentially misleading inconsistencies that do not provide evidence of functional cognitive symptoms. Examples include subjective complaints preceding identifiable declines on objective testing in the prodromal phase of neurodegenerative disease, subjective complaints associated with a medical condition such as migraine which is episodic and may not be present at the time of evaluation, and functional impairment in a real-world setting not reflected by poor test performance because of less-than-ideal ecological validity.

In FCD, the inconsistency might be seen in patient report of serious memory dysfunction that conflicts with collateral report of normal memory functioning. Alternatively, the clinician may observe an incompatibility between the severity of reported memory deficit and the patient's ability to provide a detailed description of many different memory lapses over the preceding months. Indeed, individuals diagnosed with FCD are more likely to present to their evaluation alone (even if instructed to bring a collateral), answer questions independently and seek less assistance from an accompanying person if present, and provide lengthy detailed listings of cognitive symptoms and examples of lapses, so much so that the account provides evidence of intact recall and working memory (Cabreira et al., 2023). Additional supportive (but not independently specific) signs include abrupt onset of symptoms after a major life event or a very lengthy history of symptoms without progression, poor immediate recall and recognition memory performances on testing with normal delayed recall, very strong patient confidence that there is a neurocognitive problem and an emphasis on the need for treatment, bringing an organized written list of symptoms and self-referral for evaluation (Cabreira et al., 2023). Sleep disturbance, mood symptoms and comorbid FND or other functional somatic syndromes (e.g., fibromyalgia) are also common (Silverberg & Rush, 2023).

Cognitive lapses, such as briefly forgetting passwords or forgetting a close acquaintance's name, are frequently reported in people with FCD. It is questionable, however, if such lapses occur more frequently in patients with functional symptoms (e.g., Rioux et al., 2022). Given that such lapses are commonly reported by healthy young adults without cognitive concerns (McWhirter, King, et al., 2022), it may instead be that patients with functional symptoms simply pay more attention to or over-interpret lapses when they occur.

Clinicians should also be aware that functional cognitive symptoms can be present with comorbid (traditional) neurologic conditions. Just as patients with EEG-confirmed epilepsy can experience EEG-confirmed functional seizures and persons with Parkinson's disease can experience functional motor symptoms, individuals with neurocognitive impairment can present with a functional overlay. Identification of functional overlay remains challenging, and more research is warranted to help guide clinical assessment.

A final point worth considering regarding FCD is whether there are unique etiological or maintenance features associated with FCD relative to other functional presentations. Two such mechanisms have been hypothesized in the recent literature: memory perfectionism and reduced metacognition. Memory perfectionism refers to placing an emphasis on the importance of memory and experiencing significant distress whenever an individual has a memory lapse (see Teodoro et al., 2018). Metacognition refers to self-monitoring of cognitive performance and the accuracy with which an individual is able to perceive that they made a correct versus incorrect response (e.g., Larner, 2021). Thus far, there is greater evidence in support of a role for memory perfectionism in FCD (e.g., Picon et al., 2022), though there is at least some evidence for a role of reduced global (i.e., poorer ability to evaluate long-run or overall performance) rather than local (i.e., evaluation of item-to-item or immediate performance) metacognition (see Bhome et al., 2022).

Cognitive Performance in FND

The literature on neuropsychological profiles of patients with FND is highly heterogeneous, likely due to a combination of variability in the FND population being studied (e.g., functional movement disorders versus functional seizures), variability in the neuropsychological tests administered, and use of prevalence of low scores versus between-group differences using control groups. For example, de Vroege et al. (2021) defined a deficit as a score <20th percentile using published norms and identified high rates of low scores across cognitive domains, whereas Pick et al. (2023) compared the mean performance of a sample of those with FND to a sample of healthy controls using one-tailed t-tests and reported no significant differences. One recent review of the literature found the most consistent evidence for lower scores on tests of attention, working memory and processing speed (Teodoro et al., 2018). There also appears to be relatively strong evidence of attentional biases and social cognitive weaknesses, including an attentional bias toward threatening stimuli and weaker affect recognition (Teodoro et al., 2018).

Discussing the Diagnosis with Patients

Depending on the severity and chronicity of functional neurologic symptoms, patients may need extensive psychoeducation regarding the diagnosis and possible treatment mechanisms available. A focus on positive clinical FND signs may be beneficial to help patients gain insight (Stone, Burton, & Carson, 2020; Stone, Warlow, et al., 2020; Weiss et al., 2021). Indeed, psychoeducation itself has been shown to demonstrate improvement for many patients (Hall-Patch et al., 2010; Weiss et al., 2021). Patients with FND experience genuine symptoms and are not feigning or malingering. Therefore, avoidance of a "there is no problem" approach is suggested. Instead, discussing the differential diagnoses and why each potential diagnosis was excluded may be beneficial. Discussing and explaining the positive signs of their specific presentation of FND is also recommended (Weiss et al., 2021). Not explicitly doing so can leave patients and families with a feeling that the provider has not tested the "right thing" to diagnose them properly. Again, approximately half of all FND patients do not have a precipitating psychological event or stressor, so a focus on psychological etiologies is not recommended. If there is a clear psychological trigger or comorbidity, then identifying this connection with the patient may help to guide treatment planning (Weiss et al., 2021). Some practitioners may employ the "there is a software not a hardware problem" analogy with patients to prime them for treatment recommendations of "retraining the brain" (Stone, Burton, & Carson, 2020; Stone, Warlow, et al., 2020). Another commonly utilized analogy is explaining the cognitive association between a particular food and nausea after a bout of food poisoning or the stomach flu and how functional symptoms may have developed the same way (e.g., functional dizziness after vestibular injury; Weiss et al., 2021). Overall, multidisciplinary explanation of the diagnosis may be helpful for patients (e.g., having the neurologist review their neurologic examination and explain incongruity with known neurologic disease patterns; having physical therapy demonstrate the possibility of normal movement; Weiss et al., 2021). Reassurance of a good recovery and potential for improvement is also an important feature of explaining the diagnosis to patients.

Interventions for FND

As both cognitive and emotional factors play a role in maintaining FNDs, there has been a focus on behavioral treatment of the condition. Cognitive behavioral therapy, for example, focuses on challenging maladaptive cognitive patterns, illness-related behaviors and fear avoidance (Gutkin et al., 2021). Cognitive behavioral therapy (CBT) has shown promise in several subtypes of FND (Gilmour et al., 2020; Gutkin et al., 2021). Indeed, CBT has been shown to demonstrate moderate improvements in well-being, functioning and reduction of functional seizure frequency in those with PNES (Gilmour et al., 2020; Gutkin et al., 2021). In patients with PNES, anti-epileptic medication is only indicated for those with a comorbid epilepsy syndrome (Gilmour et al., 2020). Treatment for functional movement disorders may be more individualized based on the wide heterogeneity among the different subtypes. In general, however, physical therapy tends to have the most robust evidence for functional motor symptoms (Gilmour et al., 2020). The goal of physical therapy for functional movement disorders is to disconnect the patient's illness beliefs from functional movement patterns, use distraction to resolve symptoms and demonstrate that normal motor abilities are possible by retraining movements (Gilmour et al., 2020). Although there has been a paucity of evidence for the treatment of functional cognitive disorder, individual and group CBT shows promise as an effective treatment, with a focus on normalizing memory lapses and treating health anxiety (Gilmour et al., 2020). For functional dizziness, there is evidence for vestibular physical therapy as well as emerging evidence for selective serotonin reuptake inhibitors and selective norepinephrine reuptake inhibitors (Gilmour et al., 2020).

Conclusion

Functional neurologic disorder (and functional cognitive disorder) refers to real, involuntary symptoms which are inconsistent or incompatible with known neurologic mechanisms or medical disorders. Despite historical views of FND which attributed symptoms to purely psychiatric cause (e.g., conversion of emotional distress into physical symptoms), an identifiable stressor or underlying mental health condition is not an inherent feature of FNDs. Although a thorough evaluation and exclusion of plausible alternative etiologies is important, the diagnosis of FND should be driven primarily by the identification of positive signs and evidence of internal inconsistency, evidence of which varies by FND subtype. Accurate diagnosis and communication to patients (with an emphasis on positive signs) of the diagnosis of FND are critical. The neuropsychologist is well-suited—through our training in neuroscience and clinical psychology, longer appointment times, use of cognitive tests with reference norms and use of performance validity testing—to contribute to the evaluation and care of individuals with FND, through ruling out malingering, identifying focal weaknesses that may suggest a different or comorbid presentation, identifying strengths and weaknesses that may be informative to the patient and referral source and delivery of empathic feedback based on a biopsychosocial conceptualization of the patient. Moving forward, neuropsychologists may further contribute through engagement in research that continues to investigate the validity and sensitivity/specificity of positive signs, as well as evaluation of potential interventions.

References

American Psychiatric Association. (2022). *Diagnostic and statistical manual of mental disorders.* (5th ed., Text Revision). American Psychiatric Association.

Aybek, S., Nicholson, T. R., O'Daly, O., Zelaya, F., Kanaan, R. A., & David, A. S. (2015). Emotion-motion interactions in conversion disorder: An FMRI study. *PLoS One, 10*(4), e0123273.

Aybek, S., & Perez, D. L. (2022). Diagnosis and management of functional neurological disorder. *BMJ, 376*, o64. https://doi.org/10.1136/bmj.o64

Baizabal-Carvallo, J. F., Hallett, M., & Jankovic, J. (2019). Pathogenesis and pathophysiology of functional (psychogenic) movement disorders. *Neurobiology of Disease, 127*, 32–44.

Ball, H. A., McWhirter, L., Ballard, C., Bhome, R., Blackburn, D. J., Edwards, M. J., Fleming, S. M., Fox, N. C., Howard, R., Huntley, J., Isaacs, J. D., Larner, A. J., Nicholson, T. R., Pennington, C. M., Poole, N., Price, G., Price, J. P., Reuber, M., Ritchie, C., et al. (2020). Functional cognitive disorder: Dementia's blind spot. *Brain: A Journal of Neurology, 143*(10), 2895–2903. https://doi.org/10.1093/brain/awaa224

Bennett, K., Diamond, C., Hoeritzauer, I., Gardiner, P., McWhirter, L., Carson, A., & Stone, J. (2021). A practical review of functional neurological disorder (FND) for the general physician. *Clinical Medicine, 21*(1), 28–36. https://doi.org/10.7861/clinmed.2020-0987

Bhome, R., McWilliams, A., Price, G., Poole, N. A., Howard, R. J., Fleming, S. M., & Huntley, J. D. (2022). Metacognition in functional cognitive disorder. *Brain Communications, 4*(2), fcac041.

Bogaerts, K., Van Eylen, L., Li, W., Bresseleers, J., Van Diest, I., De Peuter, S., et al. (2010). Distorted symptom perception in patients with medically unexplained symptoms. *Journal of Abnormal Psychology, 119*(1), 226.

Brandt, T., Huppert, D., Strupp, M., & Dieterich, M. (2015). Functional dizziness: Diagnostic keys and differential diagnosis. *Journal of Neurology, 262*(8), 1977–1980.

Brown, R. J. (2016). Dissociation and functional neurologic disorders. In M. Hallett, J. Stone, & A. Carson (Eds.), *Handbook of clinical neurology* (Vol. 139, pp. 85–94).

Brown, R. J., & Reuber, M. (2016). Towards an integrative theory of psychogenic non-epileptic seizures (PNES). *Clinical Psychology Review, 47*, 55–70.

Cabreira, V., Frostholm, L., McWhirter, L., Stone, J., & Carson, A. (2023). Clinical signs in functional cognitive disorders: A systematic review and diagnostic meta-analysis. *Journal of Psychosomatic Research*, 111447.

Carson, A., & Lehn, A. (2016). Epidemiology. In M. Hallett, J. Stone, & A. Carson (Eds.), *Handbook of clinical neurology* (Vol. 139, pp. 47–60).

Clark, A. (2015). *Surfing uncertainty: Prediction, action, and the embodied mind.* Oxford University Press.

Craig, A. D. (2002). How do you feel? Interoception: The sense of the physiological condition of the body. *Nature Reviews Neuroscience, 3*(8), 655–666.

Craig, A. D. (2009). How do you feel—now? The anterior insula and human awareness. *Nature Reviews Neuroscience, 10*(1), 59–70.

Daum, C., Hubschmid, M., & Aybek, S. (2014). The value of 'positive' clinical signs for weakness, sensory and gait disorders in conversion disorder: A systematic and narrative review. *Journal of Neurology, Neurosurgery & Psychiatry, 85*(2), 180–190.

de Vroege, L., Koppenol, I., Kop, W. J., Riem, M. M., & van der Feltz-Cornelis, C. M. (2021). Neurocognitive functioning in patients with conversion disorder/functional neurological disorder. *Journal of Neuropsychology, 15*(1), 69–87.

Demartini, B., Ricciardi, L., Parees, I., Ganos, C., Bhatia, K. P., & Edwards, M. J. (2015). A positive diagnosis of functional (psychogenic) tics. *European Journal of Neurology, 22*(3), 527–e36. https://doi.org/10.1111/ene.12609

Denk, F., McMahon, S. B., & Tracey, I. (2014). Pain vulnerability: A neurobiological perspective. *Nature Neuroscience, 17*(2), 192–200.

Diez, I., Ortiz-Terán, L., Williams, B., Jalilianhasanpour, R., Ospina, J. P., Dickerson, B. C., et al. (2019). Corticolimbic fast-tracking: Enhanced multimodal integration in functional neurological disorder. *Journal of Neurology, Neurosurgery & Psychiatry, 90*(8), 929–938.

Drane, D. L., Fani, N., Hallett, M., Khalsa, S. S., Perez, D. L., & Roberts, N. A. (2021). A framework for understanding the pathophysiology of functional neurological disorder. *CNS Spectrums, 26*(6), 555–561.

Dreissen, Y. E. M., Cath, D. C., & Tijssen, M. A. J. (2016). Functional jerks, tics, and paroxysmal movement disorders. In M. Hallett, J. Stone, & A. Carson (Eds.), *Handbook of clinical neurology* (Vol. 139, pp. 247–258). Elsevier. https://doi.org/10.1016/B978-0-12-801772-2.00021-7

Edwards, M. J., Yogarajah, M., & Stone, J. (2023). Why functional neurological disorder is not feigning or malingering. *Nature Reviews Neurology, 19*(4), 246–256.

Fobian, A. D., & Elliott, L. (2019). A review of functional neurological symptom disorder etiology and the integrated etiological summary model. *Journal of Psychiatry and Neuroscience, 44*(1), 8–18.

Gazzola, D. M., Carlson, C., Rugino, A., Hirsch, S., Starner, K., & Devinsky, O. (2012). Psychogenic nonepileptic seizures and chronic pain: A retrospective case-controlled study. *Epilepsy & Behavior, 25*(4), 662–665.

Gilmour, G. S., Lidstone, S. C., & Lang, A. E. (2022). The diagnosis of functional movement disorder. *Practical Neurology*, 40–53.

Gilmour, G. S., Nielsen, G., Teodoro, T., Yogarajah, M., Coebergh, J. A., Dilley, M. D., Martino, D., & Edwards, M. J. (2020). Management of functional neurological disorder. *Journal of Neurology, 267*(7), 2164–2172. https://doi.org/10.1007/s00415-020-09772-w

Goetz, C. G. (2016). Charcot, hysteria, and simulated disorders. In M. Hallett, J. Stone, & A. Carson (Eds.), *Handbook of clinical neurology* (Vol. 139, pp. 11–23).

Gutkin, M., McLean, L., Brown, R., & Kanaan, R. A. (2021). Systematic review of psychotherapy for adults with functional neurological disorder. *Journal of Neurology, Neurosurgery & Psychiatry, 92*(1), 36–44. https://doi.org/10.1136/jnnp-2019-321926

Hallett, M., Aybek, S., Dworetzky, B. A., McWhirter, L., Staab, J. P., & Stone, J. (2022). Functional neurological disorder: New subtypes and shared mechanisms. *The Lancet Neurology, 21*(6), 537–550. https://doi.org/10.1016/S1474-4422(21)00422-1

Hall-Patch, L., Brown, R., House, A., Howlett, S., Kemp, S., Lawton, G., Mayor, R., Smith, P., Reuber, M., & NEST collaborators. (2010). Acceptability and effectiveness of a strategy for the communication of the diagnosis of psychogenic nonepileptic seizures. *Epilepsia, 51*(1), 70–78. https://doi.org/10.1111/j.1528-1167.2009.02099.x

Kanaan, R. A. A. (2016). Freud's hysteria and its legacy. In M. Hallett, J. Stone, & A. Carson (Eds.), *Handbook of clinical neurology* (Vol. 139, pp. 37–44).

Keller, G. B., & Mrsic-Flogel, T. D. (2018). Predictive processing: A canonical cortical computation. *Neuron, 100*(2), 424–435.

Kletenik, I., Gaudet, K., Prasad, S., Cohen, A. L., & Fox, M. D. (2023). Network localization of awareness in visual and motor anosognosia. *Annals of Neurology*. https://doi.org/10.1002/ana.26709

Körding, K. P., & Wolpert, D. M. (2004). Bayesian integration in sensorimotor learning. *Nature, 427*(6971), 244–247.

Kozlowska, K., Palmer, D. M., Brown, K. J., Scher, S., Chudleigh, C., Davies, F., & Williams, L. M. (2015). Conversion disorder in children and adolescents: A disorder of cognitive control. *Journal of Neuropsychology, 9*(1), 87–108.

Lanius, R. A., Vermetten, E., Loewenstein, R. J., Brand, B., Schmahl, C., Bremner, J. D., & Spiegel, D. (2010). Emotion modulation in PTSD: Clinical and neurobiological evidence for a dissociative subtype. *American Journal of Psychiatry, 167*(6), 640–647.

Larner, A. J. (2021). Functional cognitive disorders (FCD): How is metacognition involved? *Brain Sciences, 11*(8), 8. https://doi.org/10.3390/brainsci11081082

Lerario, M. P., Rosendale, N., Waugh, J. L., Turban, J., & Maschi, T. (2023). Functional neurological disorder among sexual and gender minority people. *Neurologic Clinics, 41*(4), 759–781.

Levenson, J. L., & Sharpe, M. (2016). The classification of conversion disorder (functional neurologic symptom disorder) in ICD and DSM. In M. Hallett, J. Stone, & A. Carson (Eds.), *Handbook of clinical neurology* (Vol. 139, pp. 189–192).

Maggio, J., Adams, C., & Perez, D. L. (2023). Creating a "brain-mind-body interface disorders" diagnostic category across specialties. *The Journal of Neuropsychiatry and Clinical Neurosciences*. https://doi.org/10.1176/appi.neuropsych.20230071

Malaty, I. A., Anderson, S., Bennett, S. M., Budman, C. L., Coffey, B. J., Coffman, K. A., Greenberg, E., McGuire, J. F., Müller-Vahl, K. R., Okun, M. S., Quezada, J., Robichaux-Viehoever, A., & Black, K. J. (2022). Diagnosis and management of functional tic-like phenomena. *Journal of Clinical Medicine, 11*(21), 21. https://doi.org/10.3390/jcm11216470

Mason, I., Renée, J., Marples, I., McWhirter, L., Carson, A., Stone, J., & Hoeritzauer, I. (2023). Functional neurological disorder is common in patients attending chronic pain clinics. *European Journal of Neurology*.

McWhirter, L., King, L., McClure, E., Ritchie, C., Stone, J., & Carson, A. (2022). The frequency and framing of cognitive lapses in healthy adults. *CNS Spectrums, 27*(3), 331–338.

McWhirter, L., Ritchie, C. W., Stone, J., & Carson, A. (2020a). Performance validity test failure in clinical populations—A systematic review. *Journal of Neurology, Neurosurgery & Psychiatry, 91*(9), 945–952.

McWhirter, L., Ritchie, C., Stone, J., & Carson, A. (2020b). Functional cognitive disorders: A systematic review. *The Lancet Psychiatry, 7*(2), 191–207.

Nonnekes, J., **Růžička**, E., Serranová, T., Reich, S. G., Bloem, B. R., & Hallett, M. (2020). Functional gait disorders: A sign-based approach. *Neurology, 94*(24), 1093–1099. https://doi.org/10.1212/WNL.0000000000009649

O'Brien, F. M., Fortune, G. M., Dicker, P., O'Hanlon, E., Cassidy, E., Delanty, N., et al. (2015). Psychiatric and neuropsychological profiles of people with psychogenic nonepileptic seizures. *Epilepsy & Behavior, 43*, 39–45.

Perez, D. L., Aybek, S., Popkirov, S., Kozlowska, K., Stephen, C. D., Anderson, J., et al. (2021). A review and expert opinion on the neuropsychiatric assessment of motor functional neurological disorders. *The Journal of Neuropsychiatry and Clinical Neurosciences, 33*(1), 14–26.

Perez, D. L., Barsky, A. J., Daffner, K., & Silbersweig, D. A. (2012). Motor and somatosensory conversion disorder: A functional unawareness syndrome? *The Journal of Neuropsychiatry and Clinical Neurosciences, 24*(2), 141–151.

Perez, D. L., Dworetzky, B. A., Dickerson, B. C., Leung, L., Cohn, R., Baslet, G., & Silbersweig, D. A. (2015). An integrative neurocircuit perspective on psychogenic nonepileptic seizures and functional movement disorders: Neural functional unawareness. *Clinical EEG and Neuroscience, 46*(1), 4–15.

Pick, S., Goldstein, L. H., Perez, D. L., & Nicholson, T. R. (2019). Emotional processing in functional neurological disorder: A review, biopsychosocial model and research agenda. *Journal of Neurology, Neurosurgery & Psychiatry, 90*(6), 704–711.

Pick, S., Millman, L. M., Sun, Y., Short, E., Stanton, B., Winston, J., et al. (2023). Objective and subjective neurocognitive functioning in functional motor symptoms and functional seizures: Preliminary findings. *Journal of Clinical and Experimental Neuropsychology*.

Picon, E. L., Perez, D. L., Burke, M. J., Debert, C. T., Iverson, G. L., Panenka, W. J., & Silverberg, N. D. (2021). Unexpected symptoms after concussion: Potential links to functional neurological and somatic symptom disorders. *Journal of Psychosomatic Research, 151*, 110661.

Picon, E. L., Todorova, E. V., Palombo, D. J., Perez, D. L., Howard, A. K., & Silverberg, N. D. (2022). Memory perfectionism is associated with persistent memory complaints after concussion. *Archives of Clinical Neuropsychology, 37*(6), 1177–1184. https://doi.org/10.1093/arclin/acac021

Picon, E. L., Wardell, V., Palombo, D. J., Todd, R. M., Aziz, B., Bedi, S., & Silverberg, N. D. (2023). Factors perpetuating functional cognitive symptoms after mild traumatic brain injury. *Journal of Clinical and Experimental Neuropsychology, 0*(0), 1–15. https://doi.org/10.1080/13803395.2023.2247601

Ricciardi, L., Demartini, B., Crucianelli, L., Krahé, C., Edwards, M. J., & Fotopoulou, A. (2016). Interoceptive awareness in patients with functional neurological symptoms. *Biological Psychology, 113*, 68–74.

Rioux, M., Wardell, V., Palombo, D. J., Picon, E. L., Le, M. L., & Silverberg, N. D. (2022). Memory for forgetting in adults with persistent symptoms following concussion. *Journal of Clinical and Experimental Neuropsychology, 44*(1), 19–30.

Roor, J. J., Peters, M. J., Dandachi-FitzGerald, B., & Ponds, R. W. (2023). Performance validity test failure in the clinical population: A systematic review and meta-analysis of prevalence rates. *Neuropsychology Review*, 1–21.

Schaefer, M., Egloff, B., & Witthöft, M. (2012). Is interoceptive awareness really altered in somatoform disorders? Testing competing theories with two paradigms of heartbeat perception. *Journal of Abnormal Psychology, 121*(3), 719.

Silverberg, N. D., & Rush, B. K. (2023). Neuropsychological evaluation of functional cognitive disorder: A narrative review. *The Clinical Neuropsychologist*. https://doi.org/10.1080/13854046.2023.2228527

Stone, J., Burton, C., & Carson, A. (2020). Recognising and explaining functional neurological disorder. *BMJ, 371*, m3745. https://doi.org/10.1136/bmj.m3745

Stone, J., Hallett, M., Carson, A., Bergen, D., & Shakir, R. (2014). Functional disorders in the neurology section of ICD-11. *Neurology, 83*(24), 2299–2301. https://doi.org/10.1212/WNL.0000000000001063

Stone, J., Warlow, C., Deary, I., & Sharpe, M. (2020). Predisposing risk factors for functional limb weakness: A case-control study. *The Journal of Neuropsychiatry and Clinical Neurosciences, 32*(1), 50–57.

Sweet, J. J., Heilbronner, R. L., Morgan, J. E., Larrabee, G. J., Rohling, M. L., Boone, K. B., et al. (2021). American Academy of Clinical Neuropsychology (AACN) 2021 consensus statement on validity assessment: Update of the 2009 AACN consensus conference statement on neuropsychological assessment of effort, response bias, and malingering. *The Clinical Neuropsychologist, 35*(6), 1053–1106.

Syed, T. U., LaFrance, W. C., Jr., Kahriman, E. S., Hasan, S. N., Rajasekaran, V., Gulati, D., et al. (2011). Can semiology predict psychogenic nonepileptic seizures? A prospective study. *Annals of Neurology, 69*(6), 997–1004.

Teodoro, T., Edwards, M. J., & Isaacs, J. D. (2018). A unifying theory for cognitive abnormalities in functional neurological disorders, fibromyalgia and chronic fatigue syndrome: Systematic review. *Journal of Neurology, Neurosurgery & Psychiatry, 89*(12), 1308–1319.

Trimble, M., & Reynolds, E. H. (2016). A brief history of hysteria: From the ancient to the modern. *Handbook of Clinical Neurology, 139*, 3–10.

van Poppelen, D., Saifee, T. A., Schwingenschuh, P., Katschnig, P., Bhatia, K. P., Tijssen, M. A., & Edwards, M. J. (2011). Attention to self in psychogenic tremor. *Movement Disorders, 26*(14), 2575–2576.

Voon, V., Brezing, C., Gallea, C., Ameli, R., Roelofs, K., LaFrance, W. C., Jr., & Hallett, M. (2010). Emotional stimuli and motor conversion disorder. *Brain, 133*(5), 1526–1536.

Walsh, K. S., McGovern, D. P., Clark, A., & O'Connell, R. G. (2020). Evaluating the neurophysiological evidence for predictive processing as a model of perception. *Annals of the New York Academy of Sciences, 1464*(1), 242–268.

Wardrope, A., Wong, S., McLaughlan, J., Wolfe, M., Oto, M., & Reuber, M. (2020). Peri-ictal responsiveness to the social environment is greater in psychogenic nonepileptic than epileptic seizures. *Epilepsia, 61*(4), 758–765.

Weiss, K. E., Steinman, K. J., Kodish, I., Sim, L., Yurs, S., Steggall, C., & Fobian, A. D. (2021). Functional neurological symptom disorder in children and adolescents within medical settings. *Journal of Clinical Psychology in Medical Settings, 28*(1), 90–101. https://doi.org/10.1007/s10880-020-09736-2

Williamson, D. J., Holsman, M., Chaytor, N., Miller, J. W., & Drane, D. L. (2012). Abuse, not financial incentive, predicts non-credible cognitive performance in patients with psychogenic non-epileptic seizures. *The Clinical Neuropsychologist, 26*(4), 588–598.

Chapter 21
Parkinson's Disease and Other Movement Disorders

Steven A. Gunzler, Michael R. Schoenberg, David E. Riley, Benjamin L. Walter, Jennifer A. Sweet, and Robert J. Maciunas

Common Movement Disorders: Neurological and Neuropsychological Features

Parkinsonism

Parkinsonism is a syndrome comprising four cardinal clinical features: resting tremor, rigidity, akinesia (including bradykinesia) and postural instability. The rest tremor is typically a slow tremor that occurs mainly when the involved body part is inactive. Rigidity is increased muscle tone, causing a stiffness of the trunk and limbs. "Akinesia" describes a reduction in size, speed and quantity of movement, while "bradykinesia" means slowness of movement. Postural instability is an inability to maintain oneself in a stable or balanced position and is a risk factor for falls.

S. A. Gunzler · B. L. Walter
Department of Neurology, The Neurological Institute, University Hospitals Case Medical Center and Case Western Reserve University School of Medicine, Cleveland, OH, USA

M. R. Schoenberg (✉)
Departments of Psychiatry and Behavioral Sciences, Neurology, and Neurosurgery, University of South Florida College of Medicine, Tampa, FL, USA
e-mail: Mschoenb@health.usf.edu

D. E. Riley
Department of Neurology, The Neurological Institute, University Hospitals Case, Cleveland, OH, USA

Medical Center and Case Western Reserve, Unviersity School of Medicine, Cleveland, OH, USA

J. A. Sweet · R. J. Maciunas
Department of Neurological Surgery, The Neurological Institute, University Hospitals Cleveland Medical Center and Case Western Reserve University School of Medicine, Cleveland, OH, USA

M. R. Schoenberg, J. G. Scott (eds.), *The Little Black Book of Neuropsychology*, https://doi.org/10.1007/978-3-032-07777-6_21

A common definition used in clinical trials is that two of these four components must be present to establish a diagnosis of parkinsonism (Mitchell & Rockwood, 2001).

Key Points: Parkinson's disease symptoms = TRAP
- Tremor, Rigidity, Akinesia/Bradykinesia and Postural instability.

There are many diseases and syndromes that have parkinsonism as a prominent symptom complex. Some of these diagnoses are listed in Table 21.1. The spectrum of neuropsychological symptoms is largely determined by the specific disorder causing parkinsonism. As discussed below, early detection of cognitive deficits can be a clue to the proper diagnosis.

Neuroanatomy and Parkinsonism

The neuropathology of PD and movement disorders is typically associated with dysfunction involving the basal ganglia and/or cerebellum. The basal ganglia are a complex of interconnected deep gray matter brain nuclei, illustrated in Fig. 21.1, which receive input from a variety of regions of the cerebral cortex, and send output back to the cortex (via the *thalamus*) and *brainstem*. The basal ganglia are traditionally associated with the initiation and control of motor movements (eye and body), but are involved in a variety of cognitive and affective processing as well.

The basal ganglia comprise the *caudate nucleus,* the *putamen,* the *globus pallidus,* the *subthalamic nucleus (STN)* and substantia nigra. The *nucleus accumbens* and *intralaminar nuclei of the thalamus* are also often included in the basal ganglia. The putamen and globus pallidus are anatomically juxtaposed and together referred to as the *lentiform nucleus*. However, the putamen is embryologically and functionally united with the caudate nucleus in a complex known as the *striatum*. The globus pallidus is divided into the *globus pallidus interna (GPi)* and the *globus pallidus externa (GPe)*. The substantia nigra is divided into the *substantia nigra pars compacta (SNc)* and *substantia nigra pars reticulata (SNr).*

Table 21.1 Common etiologies for parkinsonism

Disorders that can cause parkinsonism	
Cortical-basal ganglionic degeneration	Pantothenate kinase-associated neurodegeneration
Creutzfeld-Jakob disease	Parkinson's disease
Drug-induced parkinsonism	Progressive supranuclear palsy
Hereditary forms of parkinsonism	Psychogenic parkinsonism
Huntington's disease	Vascular parkinsonism
Multiple system atrophy	Wilson's disease

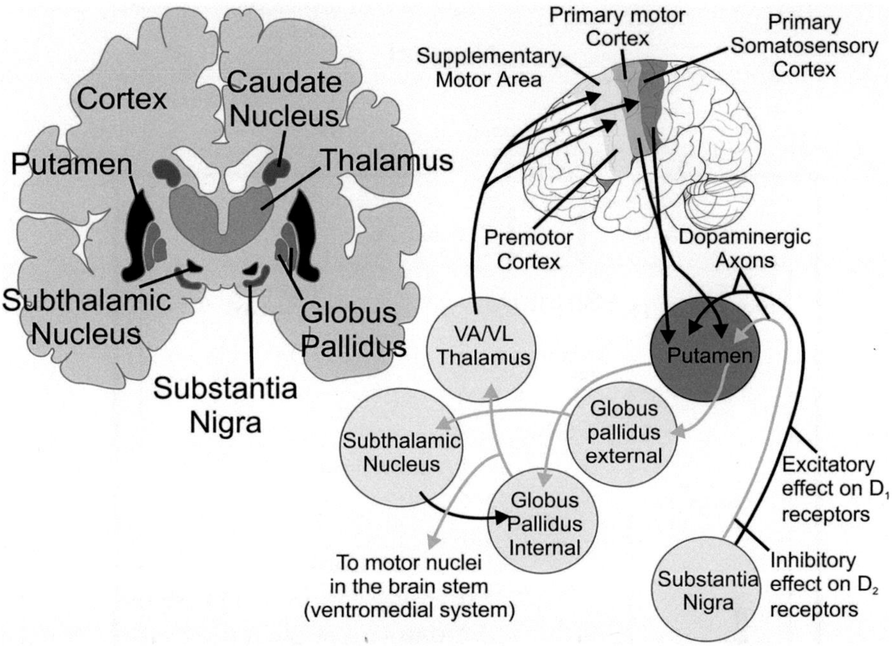

Fig. 21.1 Anatomy (coronal section) of basal ganglia

Input, Output and Intrinsic Connections of the Basal Ganglia

The main inputs to the basal ganglia are projections from the frontal lobes (motor and associative/cognitive) and limbic system (affective/cognitive) to the striatum (caudate ad putamen) and the nucleus accumbens (ventral striatum). The inputs are generally excitatory and glutamatergic. The SNc, a midbrain structure pigmented black to the naked eye, also provides input to the striatum via dopaminergic projections. Output from the basal ganglia is primarily through the GPi and the SNr. Limbic outputs occur from SNr and ventral palladium.

Direct and Indirect Pathways

Classically, processing through the basal ganglia had been described in terms of a *direct pathway* and *indirect pathway* (see Fig. 21.2). While this dichotomy provides an easily understandable framework for understanding the function of the basal ganglia, recent data have demonstrated this framework is, at best, incomplete and, at worst, wrong. However, because of its intrinsic value in providing a basic framework for understanding the basal ganglia, we provide an overview of the direct and indirect pathways below and diagrammed with Fig. 21.2.

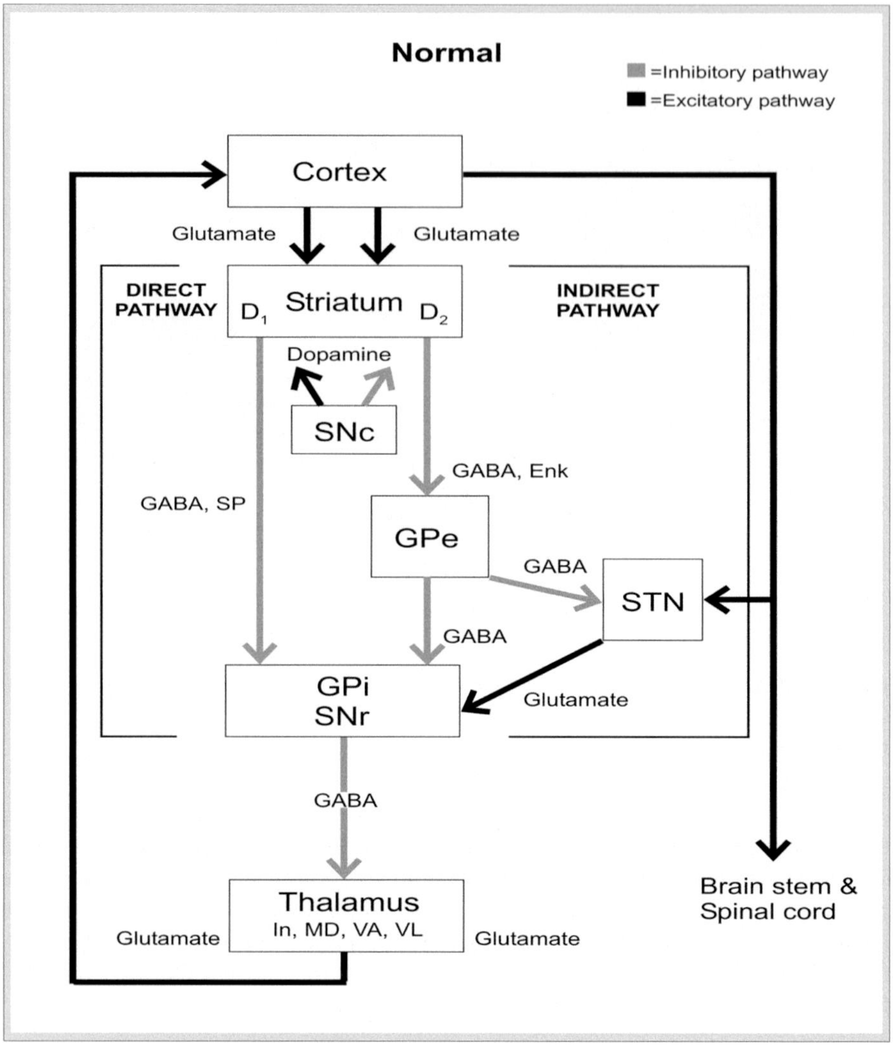

Fig. 21.2 Figure of the basal ganglia circuitry function in healthy individual

The *direct pathway* consists of inhibitory neurons from the striatum to the GPi and SNr, which in turn inhibit the cortex via thalamic nuclei (VA and VL as well as medial dorsal).The *indirect pathway* consists of striatal neurons projecting to GPe using GABA, which is inhibitory. Then, inhibitory pathways from GPe project to the STN using GABA, and the STN projects to GPi and SNr using glutamate. GPi and SNr then have inhibitory (GABA) projections to thalamic nuclei (VL and VA), which send excitatory glutamatergic projections to the cortex.

The SNc projections to the striatum involve dopamine and are *excitatory* toward the direct pathway, but *inhibitory* toward the indirect pathway. Thus, the dopaminergic neurons from the SNc *generally activate the direct pathway* and *inhibit the indirect pathway*. The net effect of the direct pathway is excitation of the cerebral cortex, whereas the net effect of the indirect pathway is cortical inhibition. In PD, the loss of dopaminergic neurons in the SNc favors the indirect pathway, causing a net inhibition of cortex and hence motor inactivity, a hypokenetic movement disorder (see Fig. 21.3).

Key Points: Basal Ganglia's two major functional neuroanatomic systems
- *Indirect* pathway *Inhibits* action of the cortex.
- *Direct* pathway *Excites* the cerebral cortex.

Data from Deep Brain Stimulation (DBS) and high-frequency stimulation as well as pathological studies have demonstrated much more complex interactions among the previously described direct and indirect pathways, cerebral cortex and brainstem nuclei. These more complex interactions account for the limited ability of the traditional direct and indirect models to explain or predict outcome from DBS and/or lesioning treatments of various movement disorders (see below). Another model for understanding the basal ganglia reflects a series of major parallel pathways coursing through the basal ganglia, as described below.

Major Pathways of the Basal Ganglia

The basal ganglia are functionally and structurally connected to the cortex and thalamus by five (5) parallel circuits that are anatomically and functionally segregated, but have projections to shared brain regions to provide for feedback from other circuits. The five circuits are (1) *motor*, (2) *oculomotor*, (3) *dorsolateral frontal*, (4) *lateral orbitofrontal* and (5) *medial frontal/anterior cingulate*. Each circuit shares common neuroanatomical structures (e.g., basal ganglia, frontal cortex, thalamus) and neurotransmitters (e.g., dopamine, GABA, glutamate), but utilize unique neuroanatomic pathways within each anatomic structure, which are maintained throughout the circuit (e.g., the orbital frontal area has projections to the ventral palladium, while the supplementary motor and primary motor pathways of the frontal lobe project to the lateral caudate and putamen).

Motor pathway is associated with general motor control. The basal ganglia influence function of the lateral motor pathways (corticospinal tracts) and the medial motor systems (reticulospinal and tectospinal tracts), enabling smooth, regulated motor control. Major input is from the cortex via the putamen. Major output is through the GPi and SNr to the VL and VA thalamic nuclei, and subsequently to the sensory and motor cortex.

Oculomotor pathway is involved in the control of eye movements. Major input is from the frontal eye fields and posterior parietal cortices via the caudate nucleus. Output is via GPi and SNr to the VA thalamic nuclei and then to frontal and supplementary eye fields.

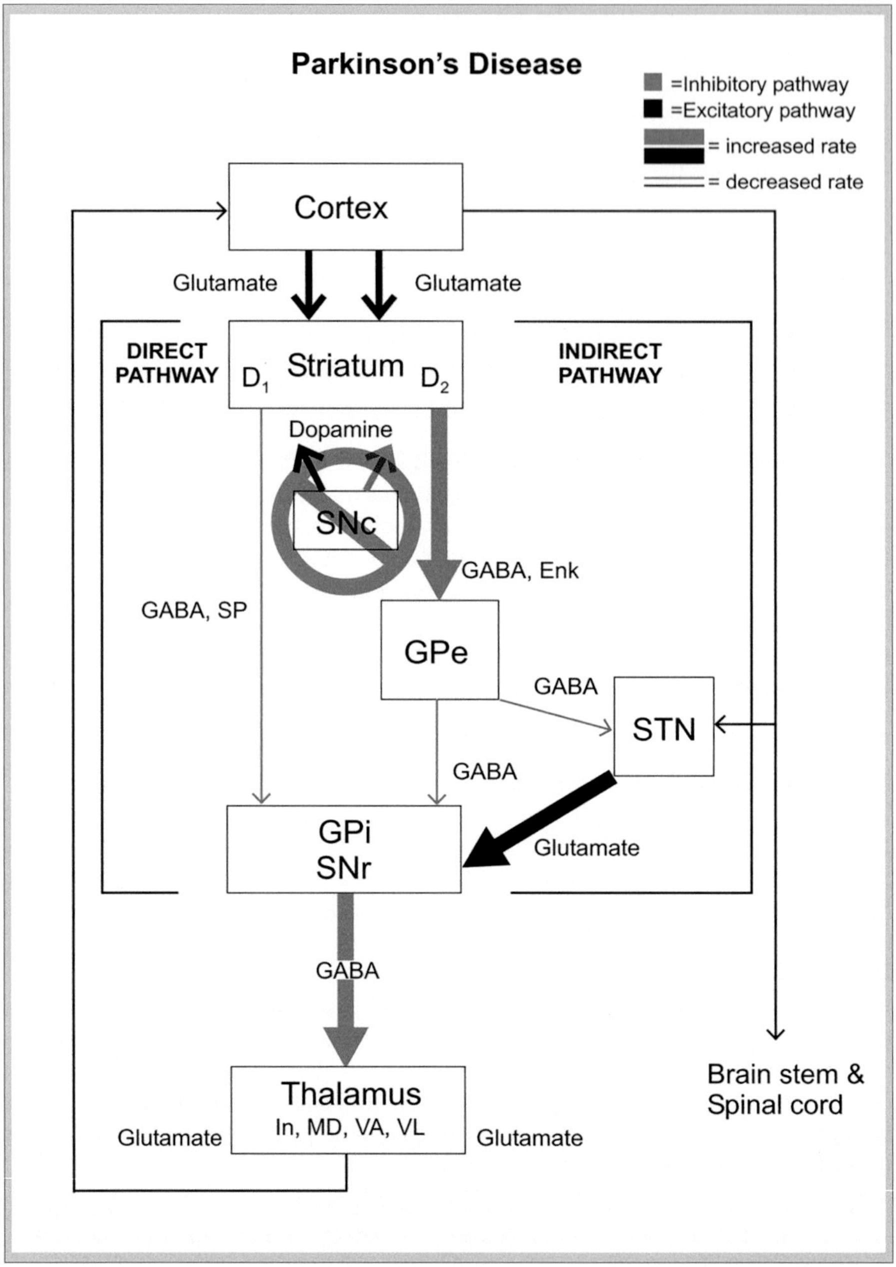

Fig. 21.3 Figure of the basal ganglia circuitry function in a patient with Parkinson's disease

Dorsolateral frontal pathway is associated with cognitive executive functions such as organization, mental flexibility and problem-solving. Damage leads to impaired problem-solving, perseveration, stimulus-bound behaviors and poor mental flexibility. Major input is from the cortex via the dorsolateral caudate. Major output is to the dorsolateral GPi and then the cortex via the intralaminar thalamic nuclei (VA and MD).

Lateral orbitofrontal pathway is involved in processing the affective value of reinforcers (stimuli such as money, taste of food, social benefits) and planning behavior in response to reinforcement or punishment. Damage can lead to behavioral disinhibition (such as public swearing, telling off-color jokes, hypersexuality, excessive gambling and increased alcohol/drug use) and environmental dependency. Input is from the cortex to the ventral GPi/nucleus accumbens. Major output is to ventral GPe (ventral palladium) to cortex via intralaminar thalamic nuclei (VA and MD).

Medial frontal/anterior cingulate pathway is associated with motivation, emotional regulation and memory functions. An individual's appreciation of the mental state of others has been associated with medial frontal functions. Damage can lead to akinetic states, antereograde amnesia and lack of motivation and behavioral apathy. Major inputs are projections from limbic structures (hippocampus, amygdala) to ventral striatum/nucleus accumbens. Major output is ventral GPe (ventral palladium) to cortex via intralaminar thalamic nuclei (MD).

In summary, one can think the motor pathway is involved in motor control, the oculomotor pathway is involved in eye movements, and the dorsolateral, orbitofrontal and medial frontal/anterior cingulate pathways are involved in cognition and emotions.

Parkinson's Disease

Parkinson's disease (PD) is the most common subtype of parkinsonism, with a prevalence of about 100–200 patients per 100,000 population (Marras & Tanner, 2004). The prevalence of PD increases with age, with a peak age of onset around 60 years. Persons who develop symptoms before 40 years of age are often said to have *young-onset PD.*

Diagnostic Criteria

PD is defined pathologically by the loss of dopaminergic cells within the *substantia nigra* projecting to the *striatum* and by the presence in surviving nigral neurons of intracellular inclusion bodies called *Lewy bodies.* Lewy bodies are round eosinophilic cytoplasmic inclusions that have a peripheral halo. In PD, Lewy bodies are found in the substantia nigra, locus coeruleus, dorsal vagal nucleus, nucleus basalis of Meynert, hypothalamus and autonomic ganglia. However, due to the lack of premortem diagnostic tests, PD remains a clinical diagnosis based on history and physical examination findings. It is thought the motor features of PD present after about 50–70% of dopaminergic neurons in the substantia nigra are lost.

To diagnose PD clinically, parkinsonism must be present (see Table 21.2 for signs and symptoms of PD). Most often, symptoms start unilaterally (usually in an arm). With time, symptoms will begin to affect the other side of the body, but the side manifesting symptoms first often remains more severely affected. Soft voice (hypophonia), lack of facial expression (masked facies), small handwriting (micrographia) and paucity and slowness of voluntary movement (akinesia or bradykinesia) are classic manifestations of PD. Tremor is not present in a minority of patients with PD (Gelb et al., 1999). In PD, postural instability is usually a late development, generally only after a decade or more. In making a diagnosis of PD, it is important to look for so-called atypical features that might indicate an alternative diagnosis. Some of these features, and diagnoses that they may suggest, are listed in Table 21.3. Dopamine transporter (DaT) SPECT scan can be useful in cases of diagnostic uncertainty to make a diagnosis of neurodegenerative parkinsonism such as PD (as opposed to medication-induced parkinsonism or essential tremor, for instance) in select cases. Additionally, research is underway studying the role of CSF biomarkers in early diagnosis of PD (e.g., Schrag et al., 2017).

Table 21.2 Parkinson's disease cardinal symptoms and classic signs

Cardinal symptoms	Classic signs
Tremor (resting, 4–6 Hz)	Hypophonia (quiet soft voice)
Rigidity (cogwheel or lead pipe)	Masked facies (reduced facial expression)
Akinesia/bradykinesia (slow movement)	Micrographia (small handwriting)
Postural instability	Shuffling gait (small steps and arms do not swing when walking)
	Stooped posture (with no arm swing)

Table 21.3 Features suggestive of an atypical parkinsonism

Atypical features on history or examination	Disease or syndrome that is suggested by the atypical feature
Acute onset	Vascular or drug-induced parkinsonism
Ataxia	MSA
Chorea, dementia and family history	HD
Early or prominent dementia	Vascular parkinsonism, HD, DLBD
Disproportionate gait disturbance	Vascular parkinsonism
Dystonia and liver disease	Wilson's disease
Early falls	PSP or MSA
History of neuroleptic medication	Drug-induced parkinsonism
Prominent orthostasis or dysautonomia	MSA
Unilateral apraxia, reflex myoclonus	CBGD
Vertical eye movement abnormality	PSP

Note: CBGD = cortical-basal ganglionic degeneration; DLBD = diffuse Lewy body disease; HD = Huntington's Disease; MSA = multiple system atrophy; PSP = progressive supranuclear palsy

PD causes nonmotor features in addition to the classical motor manifestations described above. Foremost among these are cognitive deficits, depression, autonomic disturbances and sleep disturbances. Nonmotor manifestations of PD reflect nervous system pathology outside the substantia nigra.

The severity of PD can be quantified in several ways. The *Modified Hoehn and Yahr Scale* rates only the severity of motor manifestations (parkinsonism). The *Unified Parkinson's Disease Rating Scale (UPDRS)*, on the other hand, assesses nonmotor as well as motor symptoms (Fahn & Elton, 1987). It includes questions about cognition and mood, activities of daily living and complications of therapy, and lists numerous motor items to be scored by the examiner. The *Schwab & England Scale* asks patients to evaluate their independence and ability to perform activities of daily living on a spectrum from 0% (helpless) to 100% (normal).

Generally, PD is slowly but relentlessly progressive, with considerable patient-to-patient variability. Patients with young-onset PD tend to exhibit a slower progression of PD symptoms, but are more prone to develop levodopa-induced dyskinesias than are late-onset patients, who exhibit more rapid progression of PD symptoms. Neuropsychological variables may predict not only the progression of PD motor symptoms, but especially progression of cognitive deficits in PD, and neuropsychological deficits in particular, compared to SPECT (cerebral blood flow) data (Dujardin et al., 2004).

Neuropsychological Symptoms

Neuropsychological deficits are found in a majority of non-demented PD patients, and the prevalence of neuropsychological deficits increases with disease duration (Caballol et al., 2007). Neuropsychological decline can occur early in the course of the disease, particularly for individuals with PD onset later in life, but is not pronounced. REM sleep behavioral disorder and loss of sense of smell may be predictors of cognitive decline in PD (Chahine et al., 2016; Fullard et al., 2016). Vascular risk factors may also be associated with cognitive decline in PD (Pilotto et al., 2016). Non-amnestic mild cognitive impairment (MCI) occurs more commonly than amnestic MCI (Kalbe et al., 2016) in PD. Dementia, if it occurs, generally does not present until later in the course of PD. Neuropsychological deficits in PD are well described and include bradykinesia/bradyphrenia (slowed psychomotor speed/information processing speed) and impairments in visuoperceptual/visuoconstructional, attention/executive, memory, and language functions. Visuospatial and visuoconstructional problems often present early in the course of PD and can be quite pronounced. Memory deficits are not predominant early in the disease, although reduced retrieval and efficiency in encoding are consistently found. Thus, spontaneous recall is often impaired, but recognition memory is normal or near normal. Language problems include hypophonia and micrographia. Verbal fluency and confrontation naming are not typically impaired early in the course, but become impaired later in the disease.

Key Points: Neuropsychological deficits in PD
- Bradykinesia/bradyphrenia
- Attention/executive deficits
- Visuoperceptual/visuoconstructional deficits
- Language (hypophonia, micrographia)
- Memory (poor retrieval, intact recognition)
- Depression and anxiety symptoms (80–90%)

Depression and anxiety are common in PD, and many patients (up to 90%) with PD meet diagnostic criteria for a mood disorder; in one study about 40% of patients met criteria for depression, of whom 21% met criteria for major depression and 19% met criteria for dysthymia (Nuti et al., 2004). Additionally, 40% of patients with PD met diagnostic criteria for generalized anxiety disorder (11%) or panic disorder (30%). Pathological studies demonstrated that mood disorder symptoms were associated with the neuropathologic changes that occur in PD, rather than simply a response to chronic illness (Levy et al., 1998; Nuti et al., 2004; Wolters & Braak, 2006). Symptoms of depression may be related to "off" periods of levodopa motor response, and may improve with administration of levodopa. Apathy is common among patients with PD, and is not necessarily secondary to depression (Levy et al., 1998). Apathy in PD may, however, be exacerbated by symptoms of depression, including sadness, social isolation and hopelessness. Apathy can be very troubling to patients' families and is often not adequately addressed by medical treatment. Apathy may be mistaken for "laziness," but is associated with neuropsychological dysfunction in initiating activities.

Parkinson's disease dementia (PD-D) has been well described (see Chap. 14, this volume). The lifetime incidence of overt dementia in PD is controversial, but is typically thought to be about 2–30% (Caballol et al., 2007; Emre et al., 2007), although up to 70% of patients with diagnosed Parkinson's disease developed dementia after 10 years of motor symptoms (McKeith & Mosimann, 2004). The risk of developing dementia over a 1-year period is greater for patients exhibiting more deficits in attention/executive (digit span backward, Wisconsin Card Sorting Test perseverative errors) and memory (poor list learning and recognition), which support evidenced-based neuropsychology practice (Woods & Troster, 2003). Additionally, mild cognitive impairment (MCI) in PD patients was a risk factor for the development of dementia at 5 years, even when MCI transiently improved (Pedersen et al., 2017). Confounders that can affect cognition include mood disorder, hypersomnolence, white matter ischemic change (Malek et al., 2016), obstructive sleep apnea (Mery et al., 2017), and even orthostatic hypotension (Centi et al., 2017).

The clinical, neuropsychological, radiological and pathological manifestations of dementia in PD are similar to those of dementia with Lewy bodies (DLB) (see Chap. 14), with the exception of earlier onset of dementia in DLB.

Diffuse Lewy Body Disease/Dementia with Lewy Bodies

Diffuse Lewy body disease, also known as dementia with Lewy bodies (DLB), often presents with dementia and parkinsonian symptoms including stiffness, bradykinesia, shuffling gait and resting tremor (see Chap. 18). Other core features include fluctuating mental status (waxing and waning of mental status such that patients appear confused, disoriented, lethargic or drowsy and staring off into space), visual hallucinations and REM sleep behavioral disorder (McKeith et al., 2017). Sensitivity to antipsychotic medication and dysautonomia are common as well. The name reflects the pathology, with a diffuse distribution of Lewy bodies in predictable locations in the brain (McKeith et al., 1996).

Differential diagnosis between DLB, PD and Alzheimer's disease can be challenging, particularly for patients with an onset of PD in older age. The clinical history is often key to differential diagnosis. While patients with PD may develop dementia, it is often late into the course of the disease. Patients with DLB develop dementia within the first year of having parkinsonian motor symptoms (see also Chap. 18: Dementias, this volume). Indeed, patients with DLB often present first with neuropsychological deficits, and then develop parkinsonism. There is an evidence-based neuropsychological practice in differential diagnosis between DLB and Alzheimer's disease, particularly early in the course of the disease (Calderon et al., 2001). Patients with DLB exhibit greater deficits in attention/working memory and visuoperceptual functions compared to Alzheimer's disease. Visual hallucinations and onset of REM sleep behavioral disorder (RBD) are also common early symptoms. Unlike Parkinson's disease, patients with DLB can have visual hallucinations prior to starting dopaminergic medications, and the patient can have prominent RBD. Patients with DLB are often sensitive to neuroleptic medications (i.e., haloperidol) with marked exacerbation of their PD motor symptoms. They also may not show as much benefit from levodopa, which may cause an increase in hallucinations. However, it should be noted that, of all drugs used to treat PD motor symptoms, levodopa is the least likely to provoke hallucinations and cognitive deficits.

Neuropsychological Symptoms

The neuropsychological deficits in DLB have been increasingly well delineated [e.g., (Collerton et al., 2003; McKeith & Mosimann, 2004), with marked deficits in attention/executive and visuoperceptual/visuoconstructional functions. Impairments in memory are typically mild early in the course of the disease and worsen over time. Memory deficits are due to inefficient encoding. Language deficits are not pronounced early in DLB, but impaired fluency and confrontation naming do develop. Phonemic and semantic verbal fluency may be impaired (see also Chap. 18). Mood symptoms of DLB can be pronounced early in the course of the disease, with hallucinations and delusions.

"Parkinson's Plus" Syndromes

"Parkinson's plus" is a blanket term encompassing diseases other than PD that are associated with parkinsonism. The more common "Parkinson's plus" diseases and associated clinical features are described below. These diseases tend to be more rapidly progressive than PD and often lead to earlier disability. Patients tend to respond less briskly to medications like levodopa than patients with PD.

Corticobasal Degeneration (CBD, a.k.a. Cortical-Basal Ganglionic Degeneration)

The classical syndrome of CBD is strikingly asymmetric in its parkinsonism, even more so than that of PD. Clinical diagnosis requires a combination of symptoms and signs indicating involvement of both cerebral cortex and basal ganglia. The cardinal cerebral cortical features are apraxia, cortical sensory deficits and the "*alien limb phenomenon/alien hand sign*." The principal basal ganglia findings are akinesia, rigidity and dystonia. Additional clinical features may include action and focal reflex myoclonus, corticospinal tract signs, impaired ocular and eyelid motility, dysarthria and dementia (see below and Chap. 18, this volume). These various phenomena may render the more involved hand functionally useless to the patient, due to a combination of dystonia, apraxia, akinesia and myoclonus (Riley et al., 1990). Aphasia may occur. In a case series of 15 patients in combination with 13 previously reported CBD cases, our group found a 43% incidence of dementia and a 21% incidence of aphasia (Riley et al., 1990). Depression is also common (Massman et al., 1996). MRI studies have found perirolandic frontal atrophy that is asymmetric. CBD is a tauopathy and clinical features have been associated with a frontotemporal dementia (Mathuranath et al., 2000).

Neuropsychological Symptoms

Apraxia appears clinically to be a more prominent feature of CBD than neuropsychological deficits, although dementia is a common manifestation later in the disease course (Grimes et al., 1999). Neuropsychological deficits of CBD are commonly highly lateralized and may be described as exhibiting early deficits in attention and executive function, bradyphrenia (slowed information processing speed) and language. Memory may not be adversely affected, and if affected, may present in a lateralized pattern with memory impairments that are generally mild and spontaneous recall worse than recognition memory (see Chap. 18, this volume for more details) (Grafman et al., 1995). Cognitive dysfunction in CBD patients differed from mild AD dementia in that memory was not impaired in the CBD patients, whereas attention, processing speed, mental control and verbal fluency were impaired (Massman et al., 1996). Nonfluent expressive aphasia is common in CBD, and has been listed as one of five core presenting syndromes ("phenotypes") in revised diagnostic criteria for CBD (Armstrong et al., 2013).

Multiple System Atrophy (MSA)

Once thought to be separate diseases, *olivopontocerebellar atrophy (OPCA)*, *Shy-Drager syndrome* and *striatonigral degeneration (SND)* are but different variations of MSA. Patients can present with primarily parkinsonian (striatonigral degeneration), autonomic (Shy-Drager syndrome) or cerebellar (OPCA) manifestations of MSA. MSA progresses much more quickly than PD. The cerebellar features are slow in onset and progression. Autonomic features include bowel, bladder and sexual dysfunction, as well as orthostatic hypotension (a drop in blood pressure with sitting up or standing up). Orthostatic hypotension is sometimes treated with medications that raise blood pressure.

Neuropsychological Symptoms

Neuropsychological deficits of MSA are commonly described as mild and can reflect deficits in attention/executive, slowed information processing speed, visuoperceptual/visuoconstructional skills, verbal fluency (semantic and phonemic) and memory functions (Boeve, 2007; Bürk et al., 2006). Overall, mild cognitive impairment is common in MSA, while dementia is rare (Fiorenzato et al., 2017). There is considerable variability, as patients with MSA-cerebellar (MSA-C, formerly OPCA) tend not to exhibit neuropsychological deficits beyond visuoperceptual/visuoconstructional deficits (Jacobson & Truax, 1991), while patients with MSA-parkinsonism (MSA-P, formerly SND) tend to have more extensive neuropsychological deficits. A comparison between patients with MSA-P and MSA-C found patients with MSA-P exhibited more pronounced neuropsychological deficits, particularly on measures of verbal fluency and executive functions, but also visuoperceptual/visuoconstructional skills (Kawai et al., 2008).

Progressive Supranuclear Palsy (PSP)

PSP is a syndrome characterized by predominantly axial parkinsonism, eye movement abnormalities (particularly affecting vertical eye movements), slurred speech (dysarthria), trouble swallowing (dysphagia) and a prominent gait disorder (gait apraxia and rigidity) with postural instability and early falls. PSP must be differentiated from vascular disease within the brainstem, which can cause similar symptoms (Winikates & Jankovic, 1994). The vertical gaze palsy of PSP will affect both upward and downward gaze, although deficient downward gaze is more diagnostically useful than upward gaze, since upward gaze can diminish with normal aging. As PSP progresses, horizontal gaze palsy develops. Other clinical features of PSP include a facial expression resembling a wide-eyed stare of surprise. Tremor is not common or predominant. Multiple subtypes of PSP have been proposed. Then most common is the Richardson subtype, distinguished by early-onset supranuclear gaze palsy, postural instability and neuropsychological deficits. The second type, termed PSP-parkinsonism, has features more consistent with PD, and patients exhibit some clinical response to levodopa. MRI studies have found atrophy of the midbrain and pons, particularly the upper midbrain.

Neuropsychological Symptoms

Neuropsychological deficits of PSP are commonly described as mild to moderate deficits in attention/executive, slowed information processing speed and memory (spontaneous recall worse than recognition memory) functions (see Chap. 18, this volume for more details) (Grafman et al., 1995). Dementia typically does not occur in most patients, and we have been struck how relatively preserved the cognitive function can be in some advanced PSP patients, while these patients present with a severe non-treatment responsive parkinsonism inclusive of progressive paralysis of eye movements. When dementia does develop, the early and predominant executive dysfunction, slowed information processing speed and movement disorder differentiate PSP-associated dementia from other dementias (Grafman et al., 1995). Visuospatial and executive deficits in PSP correlated with recurrent falls (Kim et al., 2014). Patients with PSP often exhibit the "applause sign," the inability to clap hands only three times in rapid succession (patients clap more than 3 times); in one study this discriminated PSP from FTD with 81.2 hit rate and distinguished PSP from PD (Dubois et al., 2005). However, follow-up study found the applause sign can also be found in patients with CBD and MSA (Wu et al., 2008). Depression and behavioral changes (although not psychosis) are commonly associated with later stages of PSP (Chiu & Psych, 1995; Rampello et al., 2005). A pseudobulbar syndrome (emotional expression without associated internalized feeling, i.e., crying with no associated sadness) may also occur (Rampello et al., 2005).

Drug-Induced Parkinsonism

Neuroleptic medications can cause parkinsonism, usually after a period of weeks to months of exposure. These psychiatric medications are used mostly to treat psychosis, such as in schizophrenic patients. The older "*typical*" neuroleptics (which include haloperidol, fluphenazine and pimozide) are most likely to cause parkinsonism. "*Atypical*" neuroleptics (such as risperidone, olanzapine and aripiprazole) also cause parkinsonism, though less often (Selfani et al., 2017). Of these, quetiapine and clozapine are the least likely antipsychotic medications to exacerbate or cause parkinsonism (Kurlan et al., 2007). Hence, they have been the antipsychotic medications of choice for patients with PD. These have been supplanted by the serotonin 5-HT2A receptor inverse agonist pimavanserin, because the efficacy of quetiapine for psychosis or agitation in PD is poor, while clozapine requires frequent blood tests (Kurlan et al., 2007). The treatment of choice for drug-induced parkinsonism (DIP) is discontinuing the responsible medication or switching to one that is less likely to cause parkinsonism. Finally, it should be noted that *antidopaminergic antiemetic medications* (e.g., prochlorperazine, promethazine and metoclopramide) can be as potent in causing drug-induced parkinsonism as neuroleptics.

Neuropsychology Symptoms
Neuropsychological testing may be confounded by the underlying psychopathology that was the indication for the antipsychotic medication in the first place. Apraxia is absent with DIP (Leiguarda et al., 1997). Depending upon underlying etiology for psychosis, patients may present with a variety of neuropsychological dysfunction.

Vascular Parkinsonism

Vascular parkinsonism is a usually symmetric parkinsonism caused by either strokes or more often so-called white matter ischemic disease (WMD). WMD is accumulation of many very small confluent strokes, giving the MRI FLAIR sequence the appearance of diffuse increased signal. Vascular parkinsonism is usually manifest by a gait disorder with prominent freezing, leading to the nickname "lower-body parkinsonism." The features of vascular parkinsonism are similar to those of PD. Like PD, the patient may have a slow and shuffling gait and take many small steps to turn around (called en bloc turns). In addition, patients with vascular disease often present with bradykinesia/bradyphrenia (slowed psychomotor speed and processing speed) and postural instability. Typically, the upper extremities are less affected by parkinsonism features. Tremor is rare, and it is more likely to be postural than resting tremor. Importantly, in vascular parkinsonism, parkinsonism is associated with other features of cerebrovascular disease, including dementia (see below), and focal neurological signs may be present. Most patients will have comorbid hypertension, diabetes or both. History of previous strokes or TIAs is also not uncommon. Patients with vascular parkinsonism may also have intact sense of smell, which is frequently impaired among patients with PD.

Neuropsychology Symptoms
Multi-infarct dementia is a common accompaniment of vascular parkinsonism, including deficits in attention/executive, memory, language and visuoperceptual/visuoconstructional functions (see Chaps. 13 and 14 this volume for more details of cerebrovascular disease-based impairments) (Román, 2003). Briefly, neuropsychological deficits tend to reflect greater impairments in attention/executive, visuoperceptual/visuoconstructional and language functions. Memory may not be initially impaired, but is often impaired in later stages of disease (Román, 2003). The treatment of vascular dementia consists of addressing cerebrovascular risk factors (blood pressure, cholesterol, diabetes, etc.) and symptom treatment when available.

Other Movement Disorders

Essential Tremor

Essential tremor (ET) is the most common cause of tremor, and results in an *action and postural tremor*, as opposed to the resting tremor that is seen in PD (see Chap. 2 for a description of tremor types). Tremor most often affects the arms, but also can affect the head and larynx (voice). The 8–12 Hz tremor typically begins gradually, and often adversely affects daily activities such as writing, eating and other fine motor tasks. In addition to tremor, patients often exhibit deficits with tandem gait and balance along with nonmotor deficits in neuropsychological function and psychiatric/psychological functioning (see below). Prevalence ranges from 4.0 to 5.6% among people older than 40 years old, and 9% among individuals aged older than 60 years of age. Pathophysiology has not been firmly established, but cerebellar dysfunction is clearly involved. Frontal lobe dysfunction is also suspected. Neuroimaging (i.e., SPECT, fMRI, PET) studies have identified cerebellar dysfunction, and SPECT studies have found bilateral frontal hypometabolism.

Neuropsychological Symptoms

Neuropsychological deficits have not traditionally been associated with ET; however, patients with ET often exhibit mild neuropsychological deficits in attention/executive (i.e., complex auditory and visual attention, behavioral inhibition, set-shifting), immediate memory (short-term recall for a word list) and language (i.e., phonemic verbal fluency and confrontation naming) (Benito-León et al., 2006). Deficits in visuoperceptual functions have been found, but not consistently. Visuoconstructional skills (taking into account tremor) are generally unaffected. Furthermore, a larger proportion of patients with ET have been found to meet diagnostic criteria for dementia (25%) than a comparable age-matched sample (9.2%), suggesting ET increases the risk of dementia (Louis, 2009). The pattern of neuropsychological deficits generally reflects cortico-striatal-thalamic-cerebellar dysfunction. When compared to patients with PD without dementia, patients with ET and no dementia exhibited greater impairment in verbal fluency and working memory tasks (Lombardi et al., 2001), while patients with PD exhibited greater impairment in visuospatial/visuoconstructional skills. Finally, patients with ET frequently report symptoms of depression and/or anxiety (Benito-León et al., 2006). Symptoms of depression were present before the onset of tremor, suggesting psychiatric/psychological symptoms may be associated with the ET disease process rather than a psychiatric response to tremor (Louis, 2009).

Key Points: Neuropsychological deficits in ET
- Attention/executive deficits (mild),
- Language (phonemic verbal fluency, confrontation naming, dystonic speech (vocal tremor quality))
- Memory (generally WNL, mild deficit in immediate recall for list learning tests)
  - Neuropsychological deficits can become more pronounced, with higher rates of dementia found for patients with ET
- Depression and anxiety symptoms typically present

Dystonia

Dystonia is characterized by sustained muscle contractions, usually resulting in abnormal postures. Dystonia can cause coarse clonic (jerky) as well as tonic (sustained) movements, and can even be paroxysmal (intermittently present) in rare cases. Dystonia is classified as *focal*, *multifocal, segmental* or *generalized*, depending on the affected body region(s). For example, torticollis (or cervical dystonia) is a focal dystonia characterized by abnormal muscle contractions in the neck, causing a forced turning of the head. Other dystonias can involve the face, limbs or trunk. Dystonia is also subclassified into *primary* (occurring as a spontaneous or genetic condition) or *secondary* (caused by an identifiable general medical condition or injury) categories.

Neuropsychology Symptoms

Neuropsychological studies in dystonic patients have generally been normal, although executive function can be impaired (Jahanshahi & Torkamani, 2017). Semantic word fluency deficits were found in a sample of patients with primary dystonia (Jahanshahi et al., 2003). Problems with the set-shifting were found in another study that aimed to recruit only patients with primary dystonia, but may have included patients with secondary dystonia (Scott et al., 2003).

Tourette Syndrome

Tourette syndrome (TS) is characterized by motor and sonic tics, which are stereotyped movements and/or sounds that can sometimes be quite complex. Diagnosis of TS requires at least two motor tics and at least one sonic tic (also referred to as a phonic or vocal tic) over a 1-year period before the age of 18 years (American Psychiatric Association, 2000; Watkins et al., 2005). The tics generally start at 5–7 years of age, peak in late childhood and decline in frequency and severity in adolescence and early adulthood, although TS may persist, or rarely worsen, in adulthood. Comorbid attention deficit-hyperactivity disorder (ADHD) is reported in 21–90% of patients with TS, while obsessive-compulsive disorder (OCD) or obsessive-compulsive behaviors have been reported in 11–80% of patients with TS.

Neuropsychological Symptoms

Neuropsychological deficits associated with TS traditionally were characterized as impairments in fine motor coordination, visuoperceptual/visuoconstructional, attention/executive (particularly behavioral disinhibition), memory and verbal fluency (Watkins et al., 2005). However, early studies of TS included individuals with comorbid ADHD and/or OCD, and more recent studies with patients having no comorbid ADHD or OCD show less neuropsychological dysfunction.

Patients with uncomplicated TS generally demonstrate mild deficits in fine motor coordination, visuoperceptual/visuoconstructional skills, and less consistently, executive function deficits (Como, 2001, Crawford et al., 2005). In one recent study (Crawford et al., 2005), patients with uncomplicated TS scored worse on two measures of inhibition, the Flanker task (Eriksen & Eriksen, 1974) and Haylings Test (Burgess & Shallice, 1997), but otherwise performed normally on a variety of tests associated with frontal lobe function (e.g., Stroop Color-Word test and Wisconsin Card Sorting test).

Key Points: Tourette's Syndrome

- 2 motor and at least one phonic (vocal) tic by 18 years
- Neuropsychological deficits in:
  - Fine motor coordination
  - Visuoperceptual/visuoconstructional skills
  - Executive dysfunction (types of inhibition)
- Neuropsychological deficits likely worse if comorbid ADHD and/or OCD

Huntington's Disease

Huntington's disease (HD) is an autosomal dominant cytosine-adenine-guanine (CAG) trinucleotide repeat disorder that leads to excessive production of the huntingtin protein. While the cardinal features of HD are chorea (a series of brief, randomly occurring twitching movements), dementia and psychiatric symptoms, other features of HD include eye movement abnormalities, dystonia, parkinsonism and gait disturbances.

Neuropsychology Symptoms

Dementia and psychiatric symptomatology are prominent and often early findings in HD (see Chap. 18 this volume for details). The age of onset is often in 30 s or 40 s, but earlier and later onset have been reported. Briefly, prominent deficits are typically seen in attention/executive, psychomotor speed, memory and visuoconstructional functions (Ward et al., 2006). There is an elevated rate of depression among HD patients, with a high suicide rate. Personality and mood changes can be the first symptom of HD. For example, Leori et al. reported 81% of patients with HD met criteria for a personality disorder and/or a mood disorder. The most common symptoms reported were of mood lability, apathy, disinhibition and paranoia. A total of 42.8% of patients with HD met diagnostic criteria for a mood disorder.

Ataxia

Ataxia is a descriptive term for a specific type of motor coordination deficit in the face of preserved motor strength. Ataxia presents with a characteristic incoordination of the arms and/or legs and the gait tends to be wide-based (see Chap. 2, this volume). Speech can be slurred with variable intonation, volume and cadence ("scanning dysarthria"). Ataxia, like parkinsonism, is a clinical presentation that has many different causes, including medications such as anticonvulsants, alcohol abuse and MSA, as discussed above.

Genetic ataxia syndromes are subdivided into *autosomal dominant (AD)* and *autosomal recessive (AR)* etiologies. Autosomal dominant ataxia disorders most commonly consist of the spinocerebellar ataxias (SCAs), which also cause a host of other neurological symptoms. Like HD, most SCAs are CAG repeat disorders, and genetic tests for some SCAs are commercially available. A common autosomal recessive ataxia is Friedreich's ataxia, which is due to GAA repeat on chromosome 9q, and accounts for almost half of all cases of autosomal recessive hereditary progressive ataxia. Onset of Friedreich's ataxia is from age 2 or 3 to about age 25 years, although some patients with onset later in life have been reported. However, most patients develop symptoms before the age of 10. The initial symptom is progressive ataxia of the legs with gait ataxia, with subsequent involvement of the upper extremities and dysarthria. There is no specific treatment for the genetic causes of ataxia (with the exception of ataxia with vitamin E deficiency), aside from physical therapy.

Neuropsychology Symptoms

Neuropsychological deficits have been associated with SCAs, including dementia and prominent mood disorders, but have not been reported among patients with Friedreich's ataxia (Bürk et al., 2003, Evidente et al., 2000, McMurtray et al., 2006). Patients with SCAs 1–3, the most common SCA mutations, often exhibit deficits in memory and executive functions (particularly in SCA 1 patients), but no visuoperceptual deficits (Bürk et al., 2003). Rate of cognitive decline is variable and is dependent upon the SCA subtype (Moriarty et al., 2016). Depressive symptoms were present in 60% of SCA 3 patients (McMurtray et al., 2006), and another study found 67.7% of a mixed patient sample inclusive of patients with degenerative cerebellar disorders (MSA, sporadic spinocerebellar atrophy and SCA variants). Dementia can also occur in DRPLA and some other SCAs, and psychosis can occur in DRPLA (Evidente et al., 2000).

Myoclonus

Myoclonus is a rapid jerking movement. Some forms of myoclonus are within normal physiologic experience, such as hiccups (myoclonus of the diaphragm) and hypnic jerks (single generalized myoclonic jerks when falling asleep). However, excessive myoclonus may indicate a neurological or toxic-metabolic disorder that requires treatment. For instance, myoclonus can occur in some epilepsy syndromes, many different genetic diseases, and as a side effect of some medications. Most commonly, myoclonus is caused by a general medical condition such as liver failure or kidney failure.

Neuropsychological Symptoms

Neuropsychological function is typically completely normal. However, if myoclonus occurs in the setting of delirium, diffuse neuropsychological impairments are observed, including altered sensorium. Creutzfeld-Jakob disease causes rapidly progressive cognitive decline in addition to myoclonus. The most common symptomatic treatment for myoclonus is clonazepam, but several other medications can be used.

Stiff-Person Syndrome

Stiff-person (also called stiff-man) syndrome presents in adulthood with intermittent uncontrolled proximal and axial muscle contractions that are present only during wakefulness. The muscle contractions may be precipitated by a variety of stimuli, including movement, noise or application of heat or cold to the patient. The cramps are often extremely painful. Stiff-person syndrome is thought to be an autoimmune disorder. It is treated long term with diazepam, clonazepam or other muscle relaxants.

Neuropsychology Symptoms

Aside from anticipatory anxiety (precipitated by the unpredictability of their episodes of stiffness), patients have not demonstrated neuropsychological deficits (Ameli et al., 2005).

Medical and Surgical Treatment of the Movement Disorders

In this section, we will outline the medical and surgical treatments for the movement disorders. In general, the goal of treatment is to eliminate symptoms and return the patient to their previous functional level. For many patients a return to their former functional status is possible, at least for some time. However, the treatment of most movement disorders either medically or surgically does not allow for complete resolution of symptoms. The medication-based therapies are reviewed first, followed by surgical therapies.

Medication Effects and Neurological and Neuropsychological Side Effects

Parkinson's Disease

Treatment of PD is symptomatic and based generally upon correction of dopamine deficiency caused by loss of dopaminergic neurons in the substantia nigra. Patients eventually require medical treatment, and levodopa (administered as carbidopa/levodopa) is the most effective PD treatment. As the disease progresses, patients develop a variety of increasingly troublesome symptoms. Patients may develop fluctuation between periods of unmedicated *"off" state* (in which they are at or near their worst motor function) and the medicated *"on" state* (in which they are at or near their best motor function). Dyskinesia is a choreoathetotic movement that can occur as a side effect of levodopa. Psychosis, such as visual hallucinations and paranoia, can also occur as a side effect of dopaminergic medications in PD. During "off" states, patients may exhibit akinesia (including freezing), tremor and dystonias as well as paresthesias, tachycardia and shortness of breath.

The COMT inhibitors entacapone (Comtan) and tolcapone (Tasmar) can lengthen the duration of levodopa effect, and can therefore augment the side effects of levodopa. Extended-release levodopa (Rytary or Sinemet CR) can also lengthen the duration of levodopa response. Other PD medications include the dopamine agonists: pramipexole (Mirapex), ropinirole (Requip), the rotigotine patch (Neupro) and apomorphine (Apokyn) injections. Selegiline (Eldepryl) and rasagiline (Azilect) are MAO-B inhibitors that can be helpful either in early PD or as adjunct therapy for later stages of PD. Amantadine is used in mild PD and to treat dyskinesia. Anticholinergic medications, such as benztropine and trihexyphenidyl, are especially useful in treating resting tremor. However, anticholinergics should be avoided in elderly or demented patients, since they are the worst offenders among antiparkinsonian drugs in causing sedation, cognitive impairment and psychiatric changes.

Diffuse Lewy Body Disease/Dementia with Lewy Bodies

Levodopa is less effective and less well tolerated by patients with DLB compared to patients with PD. It has a tendency to cause or worsen hallucinations and confusion. However, levodopa is the least likely to provoke hallucinations and cognitive deficits of all drugs used to treat PD motor symptoms. Anticholinergics and dopamine agonists are best avoided in DLB. Rivastigmine can be used to treat dementia in patients with parkinsonism. Neuroleptic medications, which treat hallucinations or delusions by blocking dopamine receptors, are not always well tolerated by patients with DLB due to aggravation of concomitant PD symptoms (Weintraub & Hurtig, 2007).

The “Parkinson’s Plus” Syndromes

Compared to patients with PD, patients with Parkinson’s plus diseases benefit much less from levodopa. In MSA, levodopa and especially dopamine agonists may cause more adverse effects, including exacerbation of symptoms of orthostatic hypotension (OH). Symptoms of OH can be treated with medication, and ataxia can be addressed with physical therapy. Patients with PSP or CBGD typically show little if any response to medication.

Essential Tremor

The most effective medications for treating symptoms of essential tremor are primidone and propranolol. Topiramate, gabapentin, methazolamide, mirtazapine and clonazepam can also be used. Most of these medications are sedating, and primidone and propranolol are poorly tolerated in some elderly patients.

Dystonia

The first line of therapy for focal and segmental dystonias is botulinum toxin, which is injected directly into affected muscles. Other common medications used to treat dystonias include anticholinergic and muscle relaxant medications.

Tourette's Syndrome

Treatment of TS is symptomatic. A variety of medications can be used to treat tics, including alpha-2 adrenergic agonist medications (clonidine and guanfacine) and neuroleptic medications. Depression and OCD are often treated with antidepressant medication. ADHD may be treated with a stimulant medication, which has the potential to exacerbate tics, although clinical studies indicate stimulants are well tolerated by TS patients. Deep brain stimulation (DBS) surgery has been studied in the treatment of Tourette's syndrome, and further study is underway (52–54).

Huntington's Disease

HD chorea is treated if it is bothersome to the patient. Generally, chorea is first treated using an atypical neuroleptic medication, but typical neuroleptics may be used, particularly to treat more severe chorea. Tetrabenazine and deutetrabenazine can be useful in treating chorea, and may have fewer long-term side effects than neuroleptic medications, although they do have the potential to worsen depression. Unfortunately, treatment of chorea often does not result in improved quality of life, because of dementia, persistent parkinsonism and other symptoms of HD. Neuroleptics can cause lethargy or can exacerbate parkinsonism. Behavioral and psychiatric symptoms of HD may respond to treatment with antidepressant or neuroleptic medication.

Common Side Effects of Medications to Treat Movement Disorders
Table 21.4 lists common medications involved in the treatment of movement disorders and frequent physical and cognitive side effects. An important risk of neuroleptic use is neuroleptic malignant syndrome, which is a life-threatening condition associated with muscle rigidity and elevated temperature (hyperthermia), along with confusion and agitation progressing to somnolence and coma.

Surgical Treatment: Neurological and Neuropsychological Effects

Patients being considered for neurosurgical treatment of movement disorder typically undergo a comprehensive pre-surgical evaluation to maximize the likelihood of a positive response to the surgical procedure and minimize risks to neurological, neuropsychological and psychiatric comorbidity. A detailed review of the preoperative evaluation is beyond the scope of this chapter; however, general guidelines for surgical selection are provided below, along with a more detailed review of neuropsychological variables in evaluating surgical candidacy.

Table 21.4 Medications and medication side effects commonly used to treat movement disorders

Medication Class	Medication	Physical side-effects	Neuropsychological side-effects
Alpha-2 adrenergic agonists	clonidine, guanifesin, etc.	Cardiac rhythm changes Dizziness Dry mouth/eyes Orthostatic hypotension	Sedation / somnolence Depression Vivid dreams
Anti-viral	Amantadine	Edema (particularly legs) Dizziness Insomnia Dyscoordination GI symptoms (nausea, vomiting, diarrhea, constipation) Headache Weakness	Confusion Depression Drowsiness Hallucinations Slurred speech Note: Improved neuropsychological function (i.e., nootropic qualities), including delay in dementia onset reported for patients with PD and Huntington's disease
Anticholinergic medications	trihexyphenidyl, benztropine, procyclidine, biperiden, ethopropazine, diphenhydramine, orphenadrine	Constipation Dry mouth Narrow angle glaucoma Urinary retention.	Confusion visual hallucinations impaired memory
Anticonvulsant / Antiepileptics	Gabapentine, primidone, lamotrigine, levetiracetam, oxcarbazepine, topiramate, etc.	ataxia Decreased appetite fatigue Drowsiness / somnolence / Sedation GI symptoms (emesis and nausea) Headache Vision changes (diplopia, nystagmus)	mood changes (depression, irritability, emotional lability) Cognitive deficits (generally mild): • attention/concentration • processing speed • memory • language Note: Some newer AEDs (lamotrigine, leviteracetam, neurontin, etc.) have little adverse cognitive effects. Note: Topiramate and Zonisimide have greater cognitive deficits in some patients, particularly on verbal fluency, memory, and processing speed, but adverse effects are reduced with lower doses and slower titration.

(continued)

Table 21.4 (continued)

Neurotoxin	Botulinum toxin	Few side-effects of focal IM injected dosing	No cognitive adverse effects
COMT* inhibitors	Entacapone, tolcapone	GI problems (e.g., nausea, vomiting, constipation, diarrhea) Headache hyperkinetic movements (e.g., dyskinesias) Hypotension Sedation (generally mild) Sleep disorders Tolcapone can result in increased liver tansaminase enzyme levels and fulfilmant hepatitis Neuroleptic malignant syndrome has been reported	Hallucinations (related to L-Dopa medication) Mild positive effects on working memory/short term memory reported.
Dopamine agonists	bromocriptine, pergolide, pramipexole, ropinirole, etc.	GI symptoms (constipation, diarrhea, nausea) hyperkinetic movement disorders (dyskinesias, choreiform movements, hemibalismus) insomnia postural hypotension Somnolence (including rapid and unpredictable onset of extreme tiredness and somnolence at inappropriate times, which has resulted in car accidents	Confusion Hallucinations (often visual) Impulse control behavior problems (compulsive gambling, shopping, and/or sexual behaviors) has been reported (estimated prevalence 0.5 to about 7%). Risk of impulse control problems with medication is more likely among individuals with a history of impulse control problems prior to onset of PD. Delusions (frequently paranoid).
	L-Dopa (Levodopa)	Acute effects: nausea dizziness insomnia cardiac irregularities orthostatic hypotension anorexia emesis Late effects (particularly with increased L-Dopa dosages): Hyperkinetic movements (dyskinesias, choreiform movements, hemibalismus)	Acute effects: anxiety Confusion Depression and/or anxiety Late effects: Hallucinations (visual) Delusions Increased psychomotor speed May improve performance on complex executive function measures among patients with severe PD. Improved subjective alertness [35, 36]. Improved mood [35]

(continued)

Table 21.4 (continued)

Neuroleptics	Clozapine, Olanzapine, Risperidone, Quetiapine, etc.	Cardiac rhythm changes (arrhythmias, tachycardia) Dry skin/eyes Hyperthermia or hypothermia Urinary retention Movement disorders (parkinsonism, akathesias, dystonia, dyskinesias, tardive dyskinesia) Orthostatic hypotension Seizures Sedation	Acute: Reduced vigilance/attention (younger patients) Improved orientation and memory (some older patients). Late: Increased rate of cognitive decline for patients with dementia
Antihypertensives/Beta blockers	Propranolol	Dizziness Fatigue Weakness Weight gain (some older beta-blockers) Insomnia	Depression Mild memory impairment for individuals with dementia

Note: * COMT = catechol-O-methyl transferase is an enzyme that degrades catecholamine neurotransmitters (e.g., dopamine, epinephrine, norepinephrine)

General Surgical Candidacy Inclusion/Exclusion Criteria

There have been no universally agreed-upon selection criteria for choosing candidates for surgical procedures to treat movement disorders. Generally, surgical candidacy is dependent upon the type of movement disorder, proposed surgical target and particular patient characteristics. However, some general inclusion and exclusion criteria are provided below.

Surgical Inclusion/Exclusion Criteria

The general criteria below reflect our opinion based upon review of the literature and experiences.

- Patients must have no pronounced dementia, as determined in their neuropsychological evaluation.
- Motor symptoms can become medication refractory and result in significant disability. Motor deficits may reflect either impairment due to the disease itself or undesired but unavoidable side effects from medication given to treat the disease, which are debilitating and/or can adversely affect the patient's quality of life. Certain motor symptoms are more likely to benefit from surgical intervention, and thus the right constellation of motor symptoms, no longer responding well to medical intervention, should be present.
- Mood disorder, if present, is not predominant and is being treated.

Pre-surgical Neuropsychological Evaluation

Neuropsychological evaluation can be a crucial component in assessing a patient's candidacy for surgical treatment. Neuropsychological data can be helpful in reducing postoperative risks to cognitive function (Smeding et al., 2009, but see also Kalbe et al., 2009). While the particular emphasis of pre-surgical neuropsychological evaluations will vary depending upon the type of movement disorder, patient characteristics and proposed surgical procedure, a triad of general objectives should generally be considered:

1. Rule out presence of dementia. Assessment should quantify the extent and severity of neuropsychological impairment.
   - Psychological function should also be assessed, including psychosis, manic behaviors and history of suicidal ideation.
2. Assist in evaluating a patient's decision-making capacity and appreciation of the risks/benefits of surgical treatment.
   - Assist in determining patient's ability to cooperate in post-surgical follow-up.
3. Establish a baseline for future comparison of neuropsychological domains more likely to be affected by surgical treatment, including attention/executive function, verbal fluency (semantic and phonemic) and verbal memory. Other frequent domains assessed include general cognitive and visuoperceptual/visuoconstructional skills.

Key Points: Pre-surgical Neuropsychological Evaluation
- Rule out prominent dementia and quantify cognitive strengths/weakness
- Assess psychologic risk factors (hypomania, suicidal ideation/attempts)
- May assist to assess patient's decision-making capacity
- Determine the extent to which the patient can cooperate in post-surgical follow-up.
- At a minimum, assess attention/executive, verbal memory, verbal fluency (semantic and phonemic) and mood (anxiety, depression)

Postoperative neuropsychological evaluations can assist in the care of the patient with a movement disorder to identify if, and to what extent, the patient's cognitive function changes over time, develop rehabilitation programming and determine risks to completing activities of daily living.

Details regarding particular surgical procedures are reviewed below, beginning with ablation procedures for selected movement disorders followed by a review of deep brain stimulation (DBS). The discussion below includes disease-specific information, including neuropsychological aspects of surgery and selection criteria.

Ablation Techniques

Neurological surgery for the treatment of movement disorders predates the pharmacological approach to these diseases, including Parkinson's disease, essential tremor, dystonia, tardive dyskinesia and Tourette's syndrome. Open surgical procedures to treat movement disorders began in the late nineteenth century with corticalectomies in the premotor area to cure choreoathetosis. Stereotactic technique, or "the touching of tissue with respect to a specific three-dimensional coordinate reference system," was first developed by Horsley and Clark in 1903 (Horsley & Clarke, 1908). Spiegel et al. (1947) stereotactically targeted the pallidum to treat a variety of movement disorders in the 1940s (Spiegel et al., 1947). The surgical procedures involved a variety of ablation methods to destroy brain tissue using heat, freezing, compression or neurotoxins. The benefits of neurological surgery are often most appreciated contralateral to the side of surgery, reflecting the decussation (crossing) of motor and sensory pathways in the human CNS (see Chap. 3, this volume).

Interest in surgical treatment for PD decreased with the introduction of levodopa in 1961. However, by the 1970s, the effects of chronic dopaminergic treatment and progression of the disease became evident (reviewed above), and a renewed interest in movement disorder surgery began anew. The first resurgence began with ventral intermediate nucleus of the thalamus (VIM) thalamotomies for asymmetrical tremor and posteroventrolateral pallidotomies ablating the globus pallidus interna (GPi) for the side effects of chronic levodopa treatment.

Deep Brain Stimulation (DBS) surgery in which an electrode was permanently implanted at targeted sites allowing for application of continuous electrical stimulation was introduced in the 1980s by Alim Benabid and colleagues (e.g., Benabid et al., 1987; Benabid et al., 1998]. DBS surgery has become the preferred surgical treatment for movement disorders because it (a) provides a nondestructive and potentially reversible technique, (b) the range of stimulation can be adjusted easily and safely postoperatively to maximize patient response and (c) the rate of neurological complications is lower for DBS than ablative procedures. Despite the popularity of DBS, some selected patients are still offered ablative surgical treatments. Lesion techniques most often involved radiofrequency heating of tissue with thermocouple probes, stereotactic radiosurgery with devices such as Gamma Knife Radiosurgery and focused ultrasound.

Ablation Surgical Candidacy Inclusion/Exclusion Criteria

Ablation surgeries, as with DBS, can be offered to patients with movement disorders who are refractory to medical management. While most patients tend to proceed with DBS rather than ablative procedures, patients who are best suited for ablation include the following: (1) those who are felt to be poor surgical candidates due to medical reasons and/or extremely advanced age; (2) patients whose access to postoperative follow-up for DBS programming is limited, e.g., those who live abroad in countries without DBS technologies, those who live in rural areas, and/or those who cannot reliably get transportation to and from the medical centers post-operatively; (3) individuals with a predominantly unilateral presentation of motor symptoms; and (4) patients who refuse DBS. In these rare cases, selection criteria are similar to those mentioned above for DBS.

Surgical Inclusion/Exclusion Criteria

- Patients must demonstrate motor symptoms that would benefit from surgical intervention and are refractory to medical management.
  - Motor symptoms are medication refractory and result in significant disability and reduced quality of life.
- Patients should have no pronounced dementia.
- Mood disorder, if present, is not predominant, and if present, is being treated.
- Patients who refuse DBS surgery.
  - Surgical candidate should demonstrate decision-making capacity and awareness he/she is not a candidate for DBS and/or reasons for refusing DBS treatment.
- Patients who are poor surgical candidates due to medical conditions and/or advanced age.
- Patients who have limited access to postoperative follow-up, precluding them from DBS postoperative programming.
  - Live abroad in a country without regular access to DBS technologies.
  - Live in a rural location and/or have difficulty obtaining transportation to medical centers.

Parkinson's Disease

Surgical treatment of PD has a long history, and the interested reader is referred to Tarsy et al. (2003) for a review. This history includes ablative surgeries, which are less frequently performed today. Except in circumstances where either the patient is unwilling or unable to undergo DBS implantation procedures, ablative surgeries are not considered to be treatment options. These surgeries have included pallidotomies and thalamotomies, ablating either targeted areas of the globus pallidus (e.g., GPi) or thalamus (e.g., VIM). These surgeries have largely fallen out of favor as treatments of choice because of their side effects, introduction of DBS and some data finding reduced effectiveness over time. Table 21.5 lists the side effects from these surgeries and long-term complications from these surgeries.

Parkinsonian symptoms that are most responsive to surgical intervention include motor symptoms. Most notably, these symptoms are akinesia, rigidity and tremor of the extremities (upper limbs greater than lower limbs). Poor gait due to balance and/or instability is notoriously more difficult to treat. Finally, dyskinesias due to the side effects of dopaminergic agents, as well as medication-induced on–off motor fluctuations in general, may all be improved with surgery.

Table 21.5 Surgical benefit and adverse effects of pallidotomy and thalamotomy

Ablation procedure	Benefits	Adverse Effects
Palidotomy (i.e., GPi)		
Parkinson's disease	Tremor Bradykinesia Drug induced dyskinesias "On -Off" dystonias "On - Off" Motor fluctuations	Perioperative mortality (death) in 0.4 – 1 % of patients Contralateral hemiparesis (1-6%) Seizures (< 1.3 %) Aphasia Ataxia Apraxia Abulia Paresethesias (1-2 %) usually involving lips and/or finger tips Dysarthria (up to 20% of patients) Dysphagia
Thalamotomy (i.e., VIM)		
Parkinson's disease	Tremor (reduction of 45-92 % from pre-surgical baseline) Rigidity (reduction of 41-92 % from pre-surgical baseline) Ten year outcome of bilateral thalamotomy found sustained benefit of reduced tremor by 33-73% and rigidity by 22-74% compared to pre-surgical baseline (Kelly et al., 2080).	Bilateral thalamotomy • Dysarthria (worsened in up to 33% of patients) • Dysphagia • Aphasia • Apraxia • Abulia • Ataxia • Seizures (< 1.3 %) • Contralateral hemiparesis (1-26%) • Paresthesias (1-3 %) usually involving lips and/or finger tips • Perioperative mortality (death) in 0.4 – 6 % of patients
Essential Tremor	Tremor (reduction of 75-95 % from pre-surgical baseline)	Same as thalamotomy for Parkinson's disease.

Pallidotomy

Pallidotomy (generally targeting GPi) has been a surgical treatment for patients with PD since the 1950s (Tarsy et al., 2003, for a review). Initial ablation techniques targeted the anterodorsal paladium, which resulted in reduction of tremor and rigidity. However, both rigidity and tremor recurred in up to 25% of patients in some surgical series. Laitinen et al. (1992) resuscitated interest in the posteroventral lateral GPi as a surgical target for PD, with beneficial effects upon abnormal involuntary movements with marked reduction of contralateral tremor, rigidity and akinesia. Dystonia, postural instability, dysarthria and drug-induced dyskinesias also improved, but benefit to balance and gait was temporary.

Surgical Inclusion/Exclusion Criteria

Pallidotomy is rarely offered to patients today. Palidotomy may be a surgical option in special cases when DBS is judged to be a poor option.

- Patients must obtain clear reduction of PD motor symptoms from dopamine agonists (e.g., levodopa).
- Refuse or otherwise be a poor candidate for DBS.
- No pronounced dementia.
- Motor symptoms of PD are medication refractory and result in significant disability. Motor deficits may reflect either significant PD motor deficits that are no longer responsive to medication and/or significant medication-induced motor complications (e.g., fluctuations, dyskinesias, dystonias).
- Depression/anxiety is not predominant, and if present, is being treated.

Thalamotomy

Thalamotomy was found to result in a lower rate of recurrence of rigidity and tremor (11%) compared to anterodorsal pallidotomy. While thalamotomy has demonstrated benefit, bilateral thalamotomy has been associated with an increased incidence of adverse neurological and neuropsychological effects (see Table 21.5). Thus, thalamotomy is rarely offered to patients, particularly as bilateral thalamotomy is associated with higher incidences of complications involving speech (worsening of dysarthria or aphasia) and/or dysphagia, as well as possible worsening of postural instability. Thalamotomy is rarely, if ever, offered and unilateral thalamotomy may be offered in very unusual circumstances to patients who are unwilling or unable to undergo DBS surgery.

Surgical Inclusion/Exclusion Criteria

- Thalamotomy may be offered to patients with PD manifesting as tremor predominant. The tremor must be refractory to medication.

- Patients should obtain benefit from dopamine agonists (e.g., levodopa) in reduction of tremor, although cases of dopamine agonist-resistant tremor responding to thalamotomy do occur.
- No pronounced dementia.
- Resting tremor is of sufficient severity to markedly disable a patient's quality of life.
- Depression/anxiety is not the predominant disability, and if present, is being treated.

The "Parkinson's Plus" Syndromes

Although patients suffering from Parkinson's plus syndromes can demonstrate improved motor function from neurosurgical interventions, the associated signs and symptoms of Parkinson's plus syndromes (e.g., dementia, autonomic dysfunction, psychiatric disease) do not respond favorably to neurosurgical intervention. Because any benefits from reducing motor dysfunction are overshadowed by their unchanged or even worsened cognitive deficits, surgery is rarely offered in this context.

Essential Tremor

Thalamotomy has been a target for treating the cardinal feature of essential tremor since the 1950s, and between the 1950s and 1970s a number of stereotactic neurosurgeons treating tremor came out in favor of targeting the VIM nucleus of the thalamus over the VL nucleus (see Tarsy et al., 2003, for a review). Deep Brain Stimulation has largely replaced thalamotomy, but unilateral thalamotomy remains a surgical option among very select patients who cannot or choose not to undergo DBS surgery.

Surgical Inclusion/Exclusion Criteria

- Patients should have failed to achieve complete relief of tremor with primidone or propranolol.
- Not a candidate for DBS surgery.
- No pronounced dementia.
- Essential tremor is medication refractory (lack of adequate response to medication and/or onset of intolerable side effects (sedation)) AND symptoms adversely affect the patient's quality of life.
- Mood disorder, if present, is being treated.

Deep Brain Stimulation (DBS) Surgery and Chronic High-Frequency Stimulation

Deep Brain Stimulation (DBS) surgery has become a mainstay in ameliorating medication-refractory symptoms of Parkinson's disease (PD), essential tremor (ET) and generalized and focal dystonia (Grimes et al., 1999; Mathuranath et al., 2000; Weaver et al., 2009). Surgical targets for DBS in the basal ganglia include the globus pallidus interna (GPi), subthalamic nuclei (STN) and the ventral intermediate nucleus (VIM) of the thalamus (16–17). Chronic high-frequency electrical stimulation of basal ganglia nuclei has been found to decrease the primary motor manifestations of PD, ET and generalized dystonia. DBS to reduce the motor and sonic tics in Tourette's syndrome has shown variable benefit (Servello et al., 2016).

Rather than reviewing DBS treatment individually for each movement disorder, a general description of DBS and the resulting motor benefit as well as neurological, neuropsychological and psychiatric side effects will be reviewed below. This will be followed by unique comments or findings for DBS in a particular movement disorder.

The DBS Surgical Procedure

Surgery may involve unilateral or bilateral electrode placement, either in staged procedures weeks or months apart, or increasingly commonly, on the same day. At the onset of the surgical procedure for DBS, the patient undergoes application of a stereotactic headframe or a frameless stereotaxic system. The patient then undergoes volumetric stereotactic imaging. Imaging data are transferred electronically to a computer workstation with stereotactic treatment planning software in the surgical theater and are fused with preoperative MRI and/or other preoperative imaging. The surgeon defines coordinate reference points, using a combination of both direct and indirect targeting when possible. The trajectory to the target avoids, whenever possible, traversing any cerebral vasculature, sulci or the ventricular ependyma. These targets and trajectories are translated into geometric parameters relating the stereotactic frame or frameless system and MRI image to the target, and the lead is passed through the substance of the brain to the desired point. Targeting is precise with tolerances of 1–3 microns. Following implantation of the electrodes, the implantable programmable generator (IPG) is typically placed in the subcutaneous space of the infraclavicular region, above the pectoral muscle.

During the surgery, the patient is positioned supine upon the operating table, with the base-ring of the stereotactic headframe or head-holder secured to the operating table. After setting the frame-arc or frameless system to the predetermined coordinates, the frontal incisions are made behind the hairline, and a small opening in the bone is drilled. If microelectrode recording (MER) is performed, one or more microelectrodes are passed along the proposed surgical trajectory to the target (some centers use macroelectrode targeting only). Single-cell recording makes apparent neuronal cellular electrical activity that enables the surgical team to identify specific deep gray nuclei and the surrounding white matter tracts for precise placement of the DBS electrode. The DBS electrode contains four sequential 1.4 mm leads at its tip, and the spacing between leads is either 1.5 mm or 0.5 mm apart depending upon the electrode model. Intraoperative stimulation can evaluate untoward effects and confirm benefit to motor function, particularly for tremor.

Placement of the implantable program generator(s) (IPG), either unilaterally or bilaterally, can be done on the same day as the electrode, or at a later date 1–4 weeks after the DBS electrodes are placed. Programming of the DBS system begins in the outpatient setting following implantation of the IGP(s). Optimization can take several programming sessions.

DBS surgery has shown minimal adverse effects, but do include the following:

- Perioperative mortality (death) in 0.4–1% of patients
- Intracranial bleeding (2.0–2.5%)
- Contralateral hemiparesis (1–6%)
- Seizures (< 1.3%)
- Aphasia
- Ataxia
- Apraxia
- Abulia
- Paresthesias (1–2%) usually involving lips and/or finger tips
- Dysarthria (up to 20% of patients)
- Dysphagia

Mechanism of Action for DBS and Chronic High-Frequency Stimulation

Acute Surgical Effect

Evidence suggests there is a microlesioning effect lasting several days in the DBS surgical procedure. This microlesioning effect is suggested by the brief (hours to days) resolution of PD or ET motor symptoms without the DBS electrodes being attached to a power source.

Chronic High-Frequency Electrical Stimulation

The physiological mechanisms accounting for the clinical benefits observed with chronic high-frequency stimulation remain to be fully understood. The therapeutic effects of DBS generally appear to be similar to that obtained from lesioning, and thus, high-frequency stimulation is thought to result in functional inhibition of the targeted brain area. Spread of electrical current with DBS decreases as the square of the distance from the active electrode contact, but is generally thought

Table 21.6 Deep Brain Stimulation basic settings* for chronic high-frequency stimulation

	Amplitude (v)	**Pulse Width (μs)** microseconds	**Pulse Frequency (Hz)**
Parkinson's disease			
STN DBS^	2.0 – 3.0	60 – 90	130 - 185
GPi DBS	2.0 – 4.0	60 – 90	130 - 185
Essential Tremor			
VIM DBS	2.0 - 7.0	100 - 300	80-140
Dystonia			
GPi DBS	2.2 – 7.0	200 - 400	90 - 190

Note: *Optimal stimulation parameters for DBS have not been established. The values above reflect general settings, but stimulation parameters can vary widely from individual to individual; ^ Patients with more severe PD and gait disturbances have benefited from higher amplitude and lower frequency (e.g., 60 Hz) compared to younger patients

to reflect a spherical electrical field with a radius of about 3 mm. The mechanism by which the functional inhibition action results remains unknown, but the predominant possibilities include (1) depolarization block, (2) so-called neural jamming or (3) the activation of inhibitory afferents (Benabid et al., 2002). The mechanism underlying the functional inhibition action appears to require a threshold level of voltage, in which a minimum of about 1 volt is required, and increased voltage to about 3.0 volts can increase response. However, beyond this level of stimulation, no further benefit is found, with increasing unpleasant side effects. With voltage fixed, increasing pulse width reduced tremor and decreased rigidity. With adequate volts, beginning about 50 Hz, increasing frequency (pulse rate) to 190 Hz has been found to decrease tremor and bradykinesia. Data have established differential effect of voltage (amplitude) and frequency (pulse rate) on neuronal circuitry and motor function. In VIM DBS, higher voltage was found to result in a linear increase in cerebral blood flow to thalamic areas in close proximity to the microelectrode while simultaneously increasing blood flow in a nonlinear fashion of neuroanatomically linked cortical areas beyond the area receiving DBS. Alternatively, increasing electrical frequency had a nonlinear effect on cortical blood flow around the microelectrode, while a more linear change in cerebral blood flow occurred in anatomically linked areas outside the immediate DBS stimulation area. Despite advances, understanding of physiological mechanisms remains unknown, and the variability in stimulation parameters among individuals with similarly staged movement disorders with similar targets of DBS stimulation is thought to reflect a variety of factors including individual variability in anatomy, disease pathology and variations in surgical targeting. Table 21.6 provides a summary of general stimulation parameters for DBS for selected movement disorders and surgical targets.

Parkinson's Disease

DBS of the STN and GPi in PD has been demonstrated to be superior over best medical care at reducing the cardinal motor symptoms of PD and improving quality of life (Fraix et al., 2006; Weaver et al., 2009). While STN and GPi are the most common targets, thalamic DBS was the original surgical target in patients with tremor-predominant PD. The STN has increasingly become a popular surgical target, as STN DBS allows for reductions in levodopa equivalent dose not observed with GPi DBS. It may provide longer motor benefit, but has been associated with more reports of adverse mood and cognitive effects (e.g., Contarino et al., 2007). The reduction in levodopa equivalent dose varies, but a reduction of about 50% is common at 12 months post-op compared to pre-surgical dosages. The reduction of medication is thought to account for the sometimes greater reduction in drug-induced dyskinesias reported for STN DBS compared to GPi DBS over the long term. STN DBS has demonstrated to be economically superior to medication-only treatment over the long term (estimated time for economic benefit was 2.2 years of DBS versus medication), in part due to reduced medication costs (Fraix et al., 2006). Some reports suggest GPi DBS may lose benefit for several cardinal features of PD after 5 years of chronic stimulation, including bradykinesia, postural instability and in some cases tremor (Volkmann et al., 2004). Alternatively, GPi DBS has less reported adverse mood effects than reported for STN DBS, although many more published studies are available for STN DBS, and this may be a sampling bias (e.g., Okun et al., 2009).

In an effort to answer many of these questions regarding the optimal surgical DBS target for PD, the Congress of Neurological Surgeons recently completed a systematic review and evidence-based guidelines on the selection of STN versus GPi for a DBS target. After an extensive literature review of all articles published between 1966 and 2017, the following questions were answered with Class I evidence: Bilateral STN DBS is as effective or more effective than bilateral GPi DBS for the treatment of motor symptoms of PD. Bilateral STN DBS is more effective in the reduction of dopaminergic medications. Bilateral STN DBS is as effective as bilateral GPi DBS in treating medication-induced dyskinesias and in improving quality of life. Bilateral STN DNS is associated with a greater neurocognitive decline on specific domains and a greater or equal risk of mood disturbance than bilateral GPi DBS. Yet, regardless of the target, DBS has demonstrated a frontline treatment for appropriately selected patients with PD (Weaver et al., 2009).

Key Points: Dopamine Equivalent Dose
100 mg standard levodopa = 140 mg sustained-release levodopa = 100 ml liquid levodopa = 10 mg bromocriptine = 1 mg pergolide = 5 mg ropinirole = 1 mg pramipexole = 10 mg selegiline.

Neurological (Primary) Outcome of DBS for PD

There is clear evidence-based support for DBS in the treatment of PD. The clinical effect of GPi DBS and STN DBS can be appreciated within seconds to minutes of placement of the DBS leads in the surgical theater. The initial benefit observed immediately following DBS surgery (thought to reflect a microlesioning effect) decreases after several days, and does not return until electrical stimulation is applied. The clinical effect of DBS on motor function is lost within seconds to minutes of stimulator deactivation, but is nearly always regained within seconds to minutes of reinitiating stimulation. Below, we detail the PD symptoms responsive to GPi and STN DBS within the first year of surgery. Dysarthria, if present, can also be improved with STN DBS. In general, drug-induced dyskinesias, tremor, rigidity and akinesia are affected more by DBS than is postural instability. Rates of improvement for postural instability vary widely, but improvement tends to be small.

Key Points: PD symptoms responsive to GPi DBS

- Tremor (20–60% reduction)
- Rigidity (20–60% reduction)
- Akinesia (20–60% reduction)
- Postural instability (20–40% improvement)
- "On–off" motor fluctuations
- "On–off" dystonias
- Drug-induced dyskinesias (47–89% reduction)

Key Points: PD symptoms responsive to STN DBS

- Tremor (40–81% reduction)
- Rigidity (40–63% reduction)
- Akinesia (40–52% reduction)
- Postural instability (27–50% improvement)
- "On–off" motor fluctuations
- "On–off" dystonias
- Drug-induced dyskinesias (41–94% reduction)

A commonly used metric to quantify motor benefit of DBS in PD is improvement in UPDRS motor scores. Studies have generally found sustained motor benefit from STN DBS with UPDRS motor scores in the on-DBS and off-medication condition improved by 44–71% after 6 months, 56% after 12 months, 47–51% after 2 years and 26–49% after 5 years compared with preoperative *off*-medication scores (e.g., Hamani et al., 2005). Similar results have generally been found for GPi DBS, at least for the first 3 years such that the *on*-DBS and *off*-medication condition improved by 56% after 12 months and 43% after 3 years, but only 24% after 5 years compared to preoperative *off*-medication scores (Volkmann et al., 2004). In a prospective comparison study, Okun et al. (2009) reported no difference between STN DBS (29.9% reduction) and GPi DBS (26.6% reduction) in UPDRS motor scores at 7 months post-op. However, subtest analysis found the STN DBS group exhibited significantly better rigidity scores compared to the GPi DBS group.

Figures 21.4 and 21.5 illustrate current thought regarding DBS effects on the frontostriatal circuit in PD following GPi DBS and STN DBS, respectively. GPi DBS is thought to result in a re-regulation of action by the GPi in PD. STN DBS in PD is thought to lead to re-regulation of action of the STN on the GPe/SNr.

Surgical Inclusion/Exclusion Criteria

Identification of patients with PD who are good DBS surgical candidates remains a challenging and difficult determination. At present, there are no universally agreed-upon exclusion criteria, but general selection criteria commonly proposed include:

- Patients must have obtained clear benefit from dopamine agonists (e.g., levodopa) in reduction of PD motor symptoms (minimum of 30% benefit from "off" state is sometimes used).
- No pronounced dementia, particularly dementia with fluctuation in mental status (fluctuating orientation and/or arousal) and/or presence of severe cognitive deficits. Presence of "mild to moderate" cognitive impairment is *not* a contraindication (e.g., Okun et al., 2004).
- Patients must not have a history of moderate to severe traumatic brain injury or comorbid neurodegenerative neurological disease.
- Motor symptoms of PD are medication refractory. This may reflect either significant PD motor deficits that are no longer responsive to medication and/or significant medication-induced motor deficits (e.g., fluctuations, dyskinesias, dystonias).
  - Motor symptoms include tremor of the upper extremities, akinesia, rigidity and dyskinesias.
  - Motor symptoms that respond less well to surgery include gait unsteadiness/balance difficulty, dysarthria, hypophonia, swallowing difficulty and other similar midline-type symptoms.
- Symptoms result in significant disability.
- Mood symptoms, if present, are not predominante, and if present, are being treated.

The following criteria below are less agreed upon and reflect efforts to reduce neuropsychological or psychiatric adverse outcomes:

- Any medical condition(s) that lead(s) to unacceptable surgical risk that outweighs benefits of surgery may be a contraindication. With aging into the 80 s–90 s, the surgical risk and risk of cognitive deficits often rise, although age alone is not an absolute contraindication to surgery.

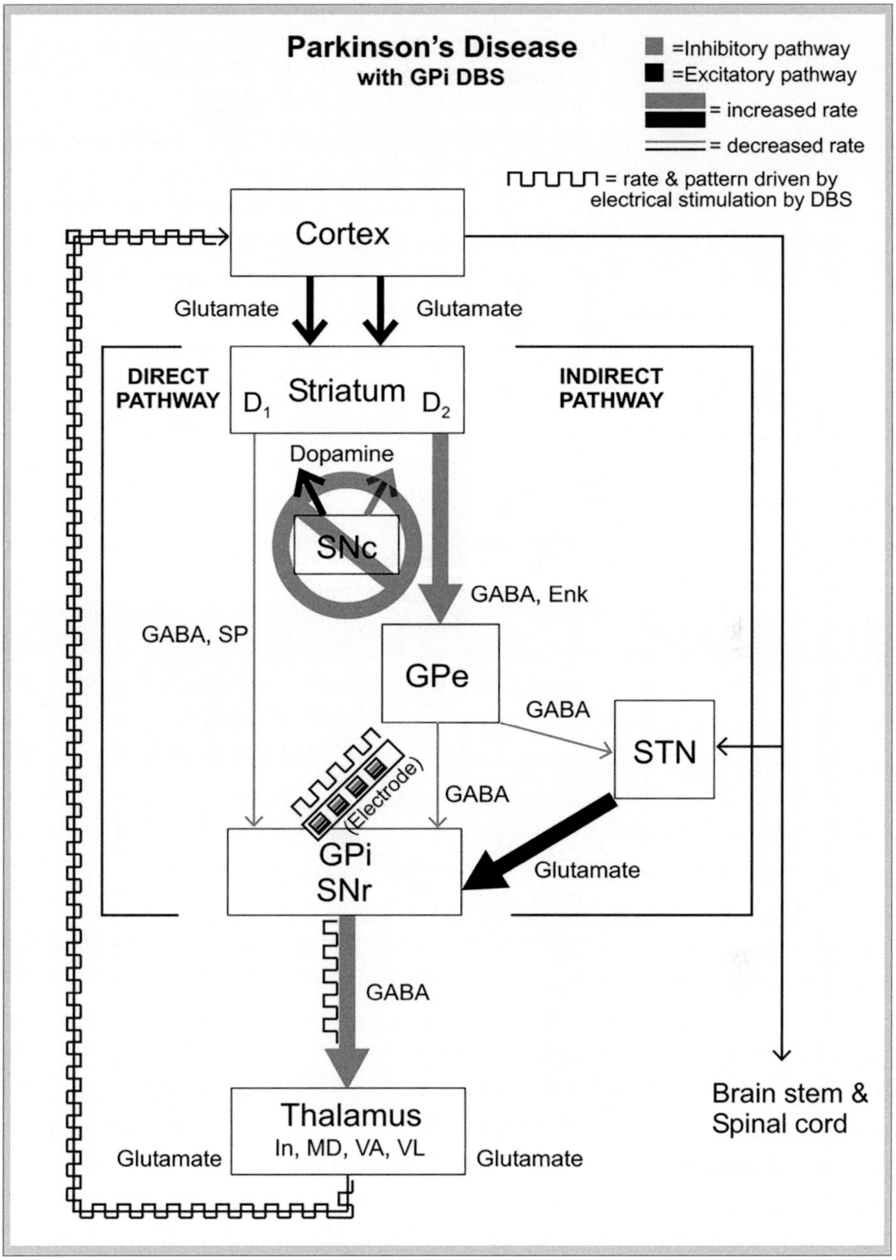

Fig. 21.4 Basal ganglia circuitry function in Parkinson's disease with GPi DBS

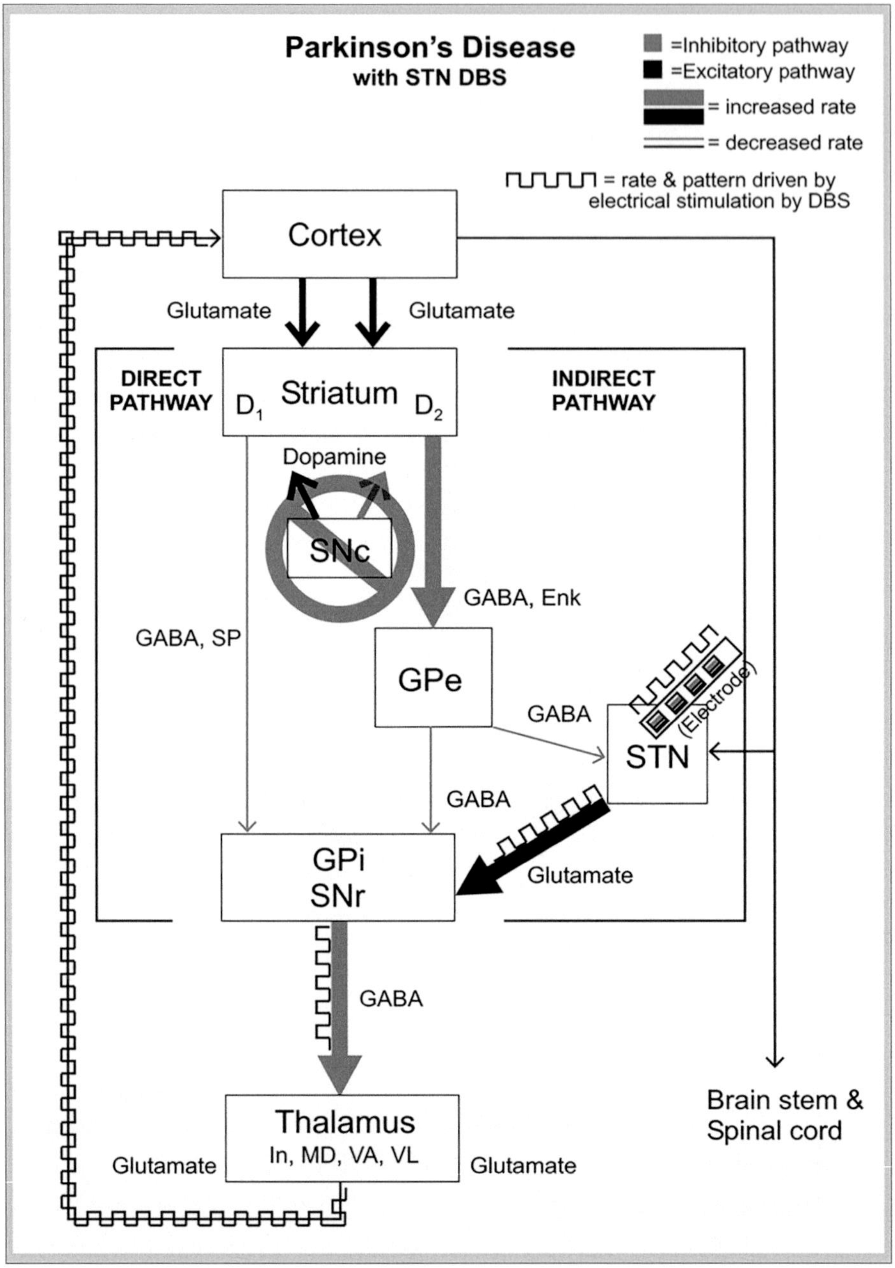

Fig. 21.5 Basal ganglia circuitry function in Parkinson's disease with STN DBS

- Patients with severe mood disorder and/or history of suicidal attempts.
- Patients with significant premorbid history of gambling, risk-taking behaviors/ impulsivity and/or hypersexuality.
- Patients with significant language deficits (marked dysarthria or severely impaired verbal fluency likely at increased risk for worse outcome)

The following may not preclude DBS surgery at some point, but may preclude surgery until the condition is corrected/treated:

- Uncontrolled hypertension or other serious systematic disease
- Current systemic infection (e.g., UTI, pneumonia, etc.)
- Unwilling or unable to cooperate in post-surgical follow-up care, including attending DBS programming
- Abnormal blood clotting that cannot be corrected

The selection process remains a largely qualitative one, and through 2009 there remains considerable variability in how the general patient selection criteria above are applied across surgical centers. However, a screening questionnaire, the Florida Surgical Questionnaire for PD or FLASQ-PD (Okun et al., 2004), has been proposed as a means of providing a more quantitative approach in patient selection. The FLASQ-PD assesses surgical candidacy across 5 domains: (1) the extent to which patients' symptoms meet criteria for the diagnosis of "probable" idiopathic PD; (2) potential contraindications to PD surgery ("red flags"); (3) general patient characteristics; (4) favorable/unfavorable characteristics; and (5) medication trials (response to medications). Higher scores reflect better surgical candidacy, ranging from the best surgical candidate score of 34 with 0 "red flags" to the worst surgical candidate score of 0 and 8 "red flags." A cut-off score of around 25 has been proposed for a good surgical candidate (and/or having any "red flags"), but there remains little validation of this measure. The "red flags" reviewed by Okun et al. (2004) include many of the general contraindications above (no pronounced dementia, no severe psychosis, motor symptoms are responsive to levodopa, patients are disabled by PD) but also include some additional contraindications including:

1. Snout, grasp, root or suck reflexes, or Myerson's sign being present
2. Presence of pronounced autonomic dysfunction within the first 1–2 years of onset of parkinsonian motor symptoms (not due to medications or previously chronic medical problem)
3. Ideomotor apraxia/alien hand sign being present
4. Supranuclear gaze palsy
5. History of wide-based gait early in the course of PD symptom presentation

The surgical inclusion/exclusion variables reviewed above reflect data and clinical experience in maximizing response to DBS while minimizing morbidity and mortality (e.g., Okun et al., 2004; Weaver et al., 2009). However, predicting individual neuropsychological or psychiatric outcome from DBS for PD remains very challenging (e.g., Kalbe et al., 2009; Smeding et al., 2009).

Neuropsychological Outcome Following STN or GPi DBS in PD

Attention must be given to the post-acute cognitive and emotional effects of DBS surgery and chronic high-frequency electrical stimulation. Postoperative neuropsychological outcome from DBS surgery and chronic high-frequency stimulation for PD has varied (see Weaver et al., 2009), but is generally regarded as cognitively "safe" (e.g., Weaver et al., 2009). While some authors have observed postoperative declines in attention/executive, memory and verbal fluency, other studies fail to show declines and some patients exhibit improvement (Jahanshahi et al., 2000). The pronounced variability in neuropsychological function continues to pose problems for predicting individual outcome, with some individuals exhibiting considerable decline in cognitive functioning, while others with similarly staged PD disease may exhibit little if any significant deterioration in cognitive functioning (e.g., Kalbe et al., 2009).

The most consistent neuropsychological change in group studies has been a significant decline in generative verbal fluency, with a meta-analysis of STN DBS reporting a moderate effect for semantic verbal fluency (Cohen's $d = 0.73$) and phonemic verbal fluency (Cohen's $d = 0.51$). A prospective randomized clinical trial found only a significant decline in phonemic verbal fluency and the Brief Visuospatial Memory Test delayed recall 6 months after STN DBS (Weaver et al., 2009). The decline in measures of verbal memory and attention/executive measures has been inconsistent, and overall effect size changes are generally small (Cohen's $d < 0.09$), but medium in some studies. Effect size reflects a standardized measure of the strength of association between variables or the magnitude of change in a variable over time. Cohen's d values between 0 and 0.3 are considered small, and generally meaningless. Values ranging from above 0.3–0.7 are considered medium. Effect sizes of 0.8 and greater reflect a large effect size, and are considered of particular importance. Table 21.7 summarizes effect size changes in neuropsychological functioning for patients undergoing STN DBS for PD. However, because a particularly challenging aspect of evaluating the effect of DBS on Parkinson's disease is the neurodegenerative process of PD on neuropsychological function, Table 21.8 provides the effect size change in neuropsychological measures among patients with PD who did not have surgery, and were treated only with medication. For example, review of Table 21.7 reveals the effect size (Cohen's d) change in verbal fluency for patients undergoing STN DBS ranges from 0.17 (small effect) to 1.02 (large effect), while review of Table 21.8 identifies verbal fluency performance change over time among patients with PD *not* undergoing surgery (reflecting medication controls) ranged from 0.05 to 0.17 (small effect size).

The relative significance of any change in function must also be considered in terms of duration in which follow-up was completed (i.e., post-op at 3 months, 12 months, 2 years or 5 years) and framed by the neurodegenerative course of

Table 21.7 Effect size change in scores for common neuropsychological measures following bilateral STN DBS for patients with Parkinson's disease

Test or Neuropsychological Domain	Effect size	Source
Attention and Concentration		
Wechsler Memory Scale - Revised		MK York et al., 2007^
Digit Span (Total)	0.21†	
Attention and Concentration*	0.02	TD. Parsons et al., 2006
Executive Functions		
Wisconsin Card Sorting Test (WCST)		CI Higginson et al., 2009
Categories (/6)	0.14†	
Perseverative Errors	0.16†	
Failure to maintain set	0.00	
Trail Making Test-B	0.32†	MK York et al., 2007^
Executive Functions*	0.08†	TD. Parsons et al., 2006
Wisconsin Card Sorting Test (WCST)		A. Funkiewiez et al., 2004 [1 yr/3 yrs]^
Categories (/6)	[0.08/0.07] †	
Total Errors (/128)	[0.04/0.02†]	
Perseverative Errors	[0.08/n/a] †	
Failure to maintain set	[0.12/0.12] †	
Psychomotor Speed		
Trail Making Test-A	0.30†	MK York et al., 2007^
Stroop Word Reading	0.43	
Psychomotor Speed*	0.22	TD. Parsons et al., 2006
Memory		
California Verbal Learning Test		CI Higginson et al., 2009
Learning Trails 1-5	0.46†	
Long Delay Free Recall	0.17†	
Recognition Discriminability	0.30†	
Rey Auditory Verbal Learning Test (RAVLT)		MF. Contarino et al., 2007 [1 yr/5 yrs]^
Total for Trials 1-5 (/75)	[0.06/0.22]	
Short delayed recall (/15)		
Long delayed recall (/15)	[0.14/0.41]	
Rey Auditory Verbal Learning Test (RAVLT)		MK York et al., 2007^
Total for Trials 1-5 (/75)	0.28†	
Delayed Recall	0.44†	
Brief Visual Memory Test		
Total Learning	0.10	
Delayed Recall	0.00	
Verbal Functions/Memory*	0.21†	TD. Parsons et al., 2006
Grober & Buschke Test**		A. Funkiewiez et al., 2004 [1 yr/3 yrs]^
Free recall	[0.03/0.12] †	
Total recall	[0.08/0.09†]	
Delayed free recall	[0.29/0.14] †	
Delayed total recall	[0.00/0.19] †	
Recognition	[0.11/0.20] †	

(continued)

Table 21.7 (continued)

Language		
Verbal Fluency (semantic, category)	0.50†	CI Higginson et al., 2009
Verbal Fluency (phonemic, letter)	0.35†	
Boston Naming Test	0.07†	
Verbal Fluency*	0.64†	TD. Parsons et al., 2006
Verbal Fluency (semantic, category)	0.73†	
Verbal Fluency (phonemic, letter)	0.51†	
Verbal Fluency (phonemic, letter)	[0.51/1.02] †	MF. Contarino et al., 2007 [1 yr/5 yrs]^
Verbal Fluency (semantic, category)	[0.48/0.44] †	A. Funkiewiez et al., 2004 [1 yr/3 yrs]^
Verbal Fluency (phonemic, letter)	[0.17/0.23] †	
Cognitive Screening		
RBANS Index Scores		Schoenberg et al., 2008
Total Score	0.18	
Immediate Memory	0.32	
Visuospatial/Constructional	0.32	
Language	0.11	
Attention	0.05	
Delayed Memory	0.23	
RBANS Subtest Scores		
List Learning	0.22	
Story Memory	0.23	
Figure Copy	0.17	
Line Orientation	0.20	
Picture Naming	0.42†	
Semantic Fluency	0.49†	
Digit Span	0.19†	
Coding	0.04†	
List Delayed Recall	0.14	
Story Dealyed Recall	0.45	
Delayed Figure Recall	0.49	
Mattis Dementia Rating Scale		A. Funkiewiez et al., 2004 [1 yr/3 yrs]^
Attention (/37)	[0.10/0.27] †	
Initiation/Perseveration (/37)	[0.34/0.33] †	
Construction (/6)	[0.50/0.35] †	
Conceptualization (/39)	[0.05/0.15] †	
Memory (/25)	[0.15/0.09] †	
Total (/144)	[0.15/0.26] †	
Mood/Depression		
Beck Depression Inventory	0.34††	MK York et al., 2007^
Beck Depression Inventory	[0.54/0.36] ††	A. Funkiewiez et al., 2004 [1 yr/3 yrs]^

Note: ^ Calculated Cohen's *d* based on mean and SD provided in report
* Based on TD Parsons' meta-analysis
** From H. Grober & H. Buschke. Genuine memory deficits in dementia. Developmental Neuropsychology, 1987; 3: 13–36
† Indicates cognitive deterioration following STN DBS
†† Improved mood following STN DBS
RBANS = Repeatable Battery of the Assessment of Neuropsychological Status

Parkinson's disease. Several studies have found initial cognitive declines at 3-months postoperative follow-up (e.g., verbal memory) that resolve and return to baseline levels at the 12-month postoperative follow-up. Initially, it was thought STN DBS could be neuroprotective with slowing or reversal of the neurodegeneration process in PD. However, long-term follow-up studies have not found evidence of neuroprotection from DBS, with 5-year follow-up studies observing a decline in cognitive function over time (e.g., Contarino et al., 2007; Krack et al., 2003), thought to be reflective of natural course of PD. Finally, PET changes reflecting continued neurodegeneration were observed among a group of patients following STN DBS (Hilker et al., 2005).

Estimating Outcome at an Individual Level

Risk factors for both acute and chronic cognitive decline and behavioral problems have been difficult to identify. However, data suggest patients who are older, exhibit more cognitive or emotional problems and/or have smaller hippocampal volumes at baseline (pre-surgical assessment) are at greater risk for neuropsychologic morbidity. Age has shown to be a risk factor for cognitive morbidity and increased risk of surgical adverse events (Derost et al., 2007; Ory-Magne et al., 2007). However, older patients can obtain similar motor benefit (Derost et al., 2007), and there is not a consistent relationship between age and cognitive morbidity (Ory-Magne et al., 2007). Evidence-based neuropsychology practice findings suggest the presence of dementia prior to DBS is generally associated with poor cognitive outcome and reduced quality of life. Smeling et al. found advancing age, pre-surgical impaired attention and poor response to L-Dopa challenge at baseline to be significant predictors of cognitive outcome and quality of life 12 months after STN DBS. Alternatively, Kalbe et al. (2009) did not find neuropsychological function nor PET metabolism to be predictive of cognitive or metabolic outcome at 6-month post-op. While all patients demonstrated a decline in right anterior cingulate metabolism following STN DBS, this did not correlate with cognitive outcome. Expectedly, postoperative PET metabolism did correlate with cognitive performance such that decreased metabolism of the left frontal lobe and dorsal cingulum correlated with decreased verbal fluency and verbal memory. Another potential marker for individual risk is hippocampal volume, and one study found smaller preoperative hippocampal volume increased the risk of developing dementia an average of 25 months following STN DBS (Aybek et al., 2009). However there was such overlap in hippocampal volumes between individuals who progressed to dementia after STN DBS and those that did not that no cut-off hippocampal volume could be identified. While individual outcome remains difficult to predict, some general statements can be made regarding reducing cognitive morbidity of DBS and chronic high-frequency stimulation in PD.

Table 21.8 Effect size change over time on common neuropsychological measures for patients with Parkinson's disease only treated with medication (no surgery)

Test or Neuropsychological Domain	Effect size	Source
Attention and Concentration		
Wechsler Memory Scale - Revised		D. Muslimovic et al., 2009*
Digit Span Forward	0.03	
Digit Span Backward	0.07	
Wechsler Memory Scale - Revised		A. Troster et al., 2007^
Digit Span Forward	0.21†	
Digit Span Backward	0.15†	
Attention and Processing Speed**	0.01	D. Muslimovic et al., 2007
Processing Speed		
Trail Making Test-A	0.82†	D. Muslimovic et al., 2009*
Stroop Test (Word Reading)	0.39†	
Stroop Test (Color Naming)	0.29†	
Executive Functions		
Trail Making Test-B	0.43†	D. Muslimovic et al., 2009*
Stroop Test (Interference)	0.17	
Wisconsin Card Sorting Test		A. Troster et al., 2007^
Categories (/6)	0.20†	
Number of Trials (/128)	0.00	
Perseverative Errors	0.09†	
Failure to maintain set	0.34	
Mental Flexibility/Reasoning**	0.10†	D. Muslimovic et al., 2007
Verbal Memory		
Rey Auditory Verbal Learning Test		D. Muslimovic et al., 2009*
Total for Trials 1-5 (/75)	0.21†	
Delayed recall (/15)	0.23†	
Delayed recognition	0.34†	
Wechsler Memory Scale - III		D. Muslimovic et al., 2009*
Faces Immediate	0.40	
Faces Delayed	0.07	

(continued)

Table 21.8 (continued)

California Verbal Learning Test		A. Troster et al., 2007^
Total Trials 1-5 (/80)	0.14	
List B (/16)	0.04†	
Short-Delay free recall (/16)	0.13	
Short-Delay cued recall (/16)	0.18	
Long-Delay free recall (/16)	0.08	
Long-Delay cued recall (/16)	0.15	
Long-Delay discriminability (%)	0.15	
Wechsler Memory Scale - Revised		A. Troster et al., 2007^
Logical Memory I (/50)	0.12†	
Logical Memory II (/50)	0.07	
Memory**	0.29†	D. Muslimovic et al., 2007
Language		
Boston Naming Test (/60)	0.24†	D. Muslimovic et al., 2009*
Verbal Fluency (semantic, category) Animals	0.09	
Verbal Fluency (semantic, category) Supermarket	0.09	
Verbal Fluency (phonemic, letter) COWAT	0.17†	
Verbal Fluency (semantic, category)	0.16†	A. Troster et al., 2007^
Verbal Fluency (phonemic, letter)	0.06	
Verbal Fluency**	0.05†	D. Muslimovic et al., 2007
Boston Naming Test (/60)	0.31†	A. Troster et al. 2007^
Visuospatial Construction		
Visuoconstructive Skills**	0.32†	D. Muslimovic et al., 2007

(continued)

Table 21.8 (continued)

Cognitive Screening		
Mattis Dementia Rating Scale		A. Troster et al., 2007^
Attention (/37)	0.30†	
Initiation/Perseveration (/37)	0.11	
Construction (/6)	0.50†	
Conceptualization (/39)	0.06†	
Memory (/25)	0.32†	
Total (/144)	0.19†	
Global Cognitive Ability**	0.40†	D. Muslimovic et al., 2007
Mood/Depression		
Beck Depression Inventory (/63)	0.37	A. Troster et al., 2007^

Note: * Newly diagnosed with PD; Retest period was 3 years; calculated Cohen's *d* based on mean and SD provided in report
^ Retest period was 17 months
** Based on D. Muslimovic's meta-analysis
† Decline over time

General Risk Factors for Increased Cognitive Morbidity Following DBS in PD

1. Dementia

   - Pronounced deficits in attention/executive function have support as a risk factor for poor cognitive outcome.

2. Neuropsychological deficits due to other neurological insult (e.g., history of head injury, herpes encephalitis, etc.).
3. History of hallucinations unrelated to dopamine agonist treatment for PD (e.g., comorbid severe psychiatric disorder).

   - The presence of marked history of gambling, risk-taking behaviors, marked behavioral disinhibition and/or history of active suicidal ideation and/or suicidal attempt(s) are likely risk factors for an increased risk of adverse psychiatric comorbidity.

Variables with emerging support as risk factors for cognitive morbidity are:

1. Increased age (age > 70)
2. Smaller hippocampal volumes

The determination of dementia in a patient with severe PD is very challenging, and the establishment of a cut-off in neuropsychological impairment to determine surgical candidacy can be one of the most challenging aspects of a pre-surgical work-up. It is common for individuals with severe PD to present with neuropsychological deficits in attention/executive, memory, language and visuoconstructional/visuoperceptual functions (e.g., Lezak et al., 2004). It is also common for these individuals to present with marked limitations in their ability to complete activities of daily living. However, careful clinical evaluation is needed to assess whether poor performances on neuropsychological measures and/or ability to complete activities of daily living is secondary to bradyphrenia and the motor disability associated with PD or dementia. In our practice, we tend to be quite liberal (not excluding patients who present with some neuropsychological deficits) in the determination of surgical candidacy. We recommend a patient not undergo DBS only for cases in which neuropsychological functioning has been severely compromised, typically reflected by impairment across at least two cognitive domains by scores that fall two or more SD below demographically matched peers. It is also important to evaluate patients' performance on tasks involving a motor component during "on" periods, as scores on many neuropsychological tests can be adversely affected by slowed psychomotor speed.

While group statistics (effect size) provide general guidance about risk to groups, they are less helpful in predicting outcome in a particular patient who is a candidate for DBS. Much more predictive of individual outcome is evaluation of a proportion of a sample exhibiting a decline in function not due to measurement error and/or disease process itself (reliable change) and/or relative risk ratios identifying particular risk factors predicting worse (or better) outcome.

Evaluation of the proportion of a study sample that exhibits a decline in function exceeding a specified threshold provides information to delineate the relative magnitude of the sample exhibiting a decline. As an example, similar effect sizes may be reported, but for one domain, 100% of patients exhibited a small decline, while another 40% of the sample exhibited a large decline. Table 21.9 provides the proportion of patients with PD who exhibited a change postoperatively following STN DBS on selected neuropsychological measures. As an example, 18% of patients declined on phonemic verbal fluency, 82% did not change and no patient exhibited an improvement at 1-year post-op. At 5 years post-op, 54% of patients exhibited a decline in phonemic verbal fluency while 46% of patients' score did not change. More variability in outcome was reported for verbal memory using the Rey Auditory Verbal Memory Test (RAVLT) delayed recall, in which 27% of patients declined, 46% did not change and 27% exhibited improved performance 1 year after surgery (Contarino et al., 2007). Table 21.10 provides the proportion of patients with PD not having surgery (medication only) exhibiting change in performance over time on selected neuropsychological measures. Review of Table 21.10 semantic verbal fluency shows that performance did not decline over time, 97% remained stable and 3% demonstrated improvement. However, the determination of what threshold a score must change in order to be meaningful has varied in the literature, with some

Table 21.9 Proportion (%) of patients with Parkinson's disease treated with STN DBS exhibiting reliable change^ on selected neuropsychological measures

Test or Neuropsychological Domain	Decline	Stable	Improve	Source
Attention and Concentration				
Wechsler Memory Scale - Revised				MF. Contarino et al., 2007 [1 yr/5 yrs]^
Digit Span Forward	[18/36]	[82/46]	[0/18]	
Digit Span Backward	[0/27]	[73/55]	[27/18]	
Wechsler Memory Scale - Revised				MK York et al., 2007^
Digit Span (Total)	50	31.8	18.2	
Corsi's Block Span				MF. Contarino et al., 2007 [1 yr/5 yrs]^
Forward	[9/27]	[73/55]	[18/18]	
Backward	[9/18]	[82/82]	[9/0]	
Executive Functions				
Wisconsin Card Sorting Test (WCST)				CI Higginson et al., 2009
Categories (/6)	5.3	89.5	5.3	
Perseverative Errors	0	89.5	10.5	
Failure to maintain set	5.3	89.5	5.3	
Trail Making Test-B	57.1	19.0	23.8	MK York et al., 2007^
Modified WCST (Jahanshahi et al., 2000)				MF. Contarino et al., 2007 [1 yr/5 yrs]^
Categories (/6)	[11/22]	[89/67]	[0/11]	
Total Errors (/48)	[22/22]	[45/78]	[33/0]	
Perseverative Errors (/48)	[22/11]	[78/89]	[0/0]	
Wisconsin Card Sorting Test				A. Funkiewiez et al., 2004^^
Categories (/6)	14.9	76.1	9.0	
Total Errors (/128)	9.0	77.6	13.4	
Frontal Score (Benbadis et al.)	21.7	68.2	10.1	
Psychomotor Speed				
Trail Making Test-A	22.7	40.9	36.4	MK York et al., 2007^
Stroop Word Reading	21.1	73.7	5.3	

(continued)

Table 21.9 (continued)

Verbal Memory				
California Verbal Learning Test				CI Higginson et al., 2009
Learning Trails 1-5	15.8	84.2	0	
Long Delay Free Recall	15.8	84.2	0	
Recognition Discriminability	5.3	94.7	0	
Rey Auditory Verbal Learning Test				MF. Contarino et al., 2007 [1 yr/5 yrs]^
Total Trials 1-5 (/75)	[18/18]^	[64/73]^	[18/9]^	
List B (/15)	n/a	n/a	n/a	
Short-Delay free recall (/15)	n/a	n/a	n/a	
Long-Delay free recall (/15)	[27/36]^	[46/55]^	[27/9]^	
Rey Auditory Verbal Learning Test (RAVLT)				MK York et al., 2007^
Total for Trials 1-5 (/75)	30.4	52.2	17.4	
Immediate Recall	26.1	65.2	8.7	
Delayed Recall	13.0	87.0	0.0	
Brief Visual Memory Test				
Total Learning	13.6	68.2	18.2	
Delayed Recall	22.7	63.6	13.6	
Language				
Verbal fluency (semantic, category)	5.6	88.8	5.6	CI Higginson et al., 2009
Verbal Fluency (phonemic, letter)	22.2	72.2	5.6	
Boston Naming Test	0	100	0	
Verbal Fluency (phonemic, letter)	[18/54]	[82/46]	[0/0]	MF. Contarino et al., 2007 [1 yr/5 yrs]^
Verbal Fluency (semantic, category)	33.3	63.8	2.9	A. Funkiewiez et al., 2004^^
Verbal Fluency (phonemic, letter)	16.0	79.7	4.3	
Cognitive Screening				
Mattis Dementia Rating Scale				A. Funkiewiez et al., 2004^^
Attention (/37)	16.7	75.7	7.6	
Initiation/Perseveration (/37)	19.7	71.2	9.1	
Total (/144)	7.6	90.9	1.5	

Note: ^ Change reflects change > +/−1 SD
^^ Change reflects change > +/−1 SD over 3 years post-surgery

Table 21.10 Proportion (%) of patients with Parkinson's disease treated with levodopa and/or dopamine agonists exhibiting reliable change from pre-surgery to post-surgery on selected neuropsychological measures

Test or Neuropsychological Domain	Decline	Stable	Improve
Attention and Concentration			
Wechsler Memory Scale - Revised			
Digit Span Forward	1.6	95.1	3.3
Digit Span Backward	3.3	95.1	1.6
Executive Functioning			
Wisconsin Card Sorting Test (WCST)			
Categories (/6)	7.4	88.9	3.7
Total Errors (/128)	7.4	83.3	9.3
Perseverative Errors	3.7	92.6	3.7
Failure to maintain set	3.7	92.6	3.7
Verbal Memory			
California Verbal Learning Test			
Total Trials 1-5 (/80)	1.6	91.8	6.6
List B (/16)	6.6	90.2	3.3
Short-Delay free recall (/16)	8.2	85.2	6.6
Short-Delay cued recall (/16)	4.9	83.6	11.5
Long-Delay free recall (/16)	8.2	86.9	4.9
Long-Delay cued recall (/16)	1.6	93.4	4.9
Long-Delay discriminability (%)	3.3	93.4	3.3
Wechsler Memory Scale - Revised			
Logical Memory I (/50)	5.1	88.1	6.8
Logical Memory II (/50)	5.1	93.2	1.7
Language			
Verbal fluency (semantic, category)	0.0	96.6	3.4
Verbal Fluency (phonemic, letter)	3.4	89.8	6.8
Boston Naming Test	3.2	96.8	0.0
Cognitive Screening			
Mattis Dementia Rating Scale			
Attention (/37)	3.2	93.5	3.2
Initiation/Perseveration (/37)	3.2	90.3	6.5
Construction (/6)	6.5	93.5	0.0
Conceptualization (/39)	6.5	87.1	6.5
Memory (/25)	6.5	91.9	1.6
Total (/144)	3.2	95.2	1.6
Mood/Depression			
Beck Depression Inventory	7.6	88.7	3.4

Note: From Troster et al. (2007); $N = 62$ older adults with PD; Change reflects RCI methodology determined by base rates; Test–retest about 17 month interval

authors reporting change beyond one standard deviation, while others have begun to utilize reliable change indices (RCIs; Jacobson & Truax, 1991; Temkin et al., 1999).

Reliable Change and Measurement of Change with DBS

The application of Reliable Change Indices (RCIs; Jacobson & Truax, 1991; Temkin et al., 1999) has aided in the identification of meaningful change in neuropsychological functioning over time. Reliable Change Indices are developed from individuals with the population of interest (e.g., Parkinson's disease) who receive conservative medical management. The change in neuropsychological function over time would reflect the course of known or suspected neurodegenerative disease had no intervention been provided. Thus, comparison to a medication management group better allows for identifying change due to surgical intervention itself, rather than the effects of neurodegenerative disease. While limited at this point, RCIs have become available for several commonly used neuropsychological measures for patients with PD (Troster et al., 2007) and are summarized in Table 21.11. The RCI values are derived from a test–retest period of about 17 months. For example, a patient's score on the verbal fluency test must decline by more than 7 raw score points (or increase by more than 5 points) to reflect a change in performance that is not likely due to chance, measurement errors and/or variables related to Parkinson's disease itself.

To account for the apparent variability in outcome from DBS for PD, several variables have been proposed that include disease variables, methodological limitations of reported studies and several moderator variables. A disease variable that likely accounts for some intra-individual variability in outcome is the inter-individual variability in the neuropathological dysfunction associated with PD (Jahanshahi et al., 2003). Methodological problems of published data include small sample sizes, poor experimental power, variable patient inclusion/exclusion criteria and lack of appropriate control groups. Finally, authors have explored the potential effect of several variables as moderators of cognitive (and motor) outcome of DBS surgery that include patient age, presence of dementia, reductions in dopaminergic medication after surgery and stimulation parameters. A recent meta-analysis did not find a significant effect for moderator variables, including stimulation parameters on neuropsychological outcome. However, Francel et al. and Schoenberg et al. reported significant correlations between STN DBS stimulation parameters and neuropsychological measures. We believe data are too limited and study variability too great to rule out the differential impact of moderator variables on neuropsychological function. Clearly, changes in DBS stimulation parameters have a marked effect on motor function, and it seems unlikely neuropsychological function cannot be differentially affected by variation in stimulation parameters as well.

Table 21.11 Reliable Change Indices (RCIs) of common neuropsychological measures for patients with Parkinson's disease treated with medication

Test or Neuropsychological Domain	90% RCI
Attention and Concentration	
Wechsler Memory Scale - Revised	
Digit Span Forward	≤ -3.2, ≥ 2.2
Digit Span Backward	≤ -3.9, ≥ 3.3
Executive Functions	
Wisconsin Card Sorting Test	
Categories (/6)	≤ -3.3, ≥ 2.4
Number of Trials (/128)	≤ -46.0, ≥ 45.5
Perseverative Errors	≤ -24.8, ≥ 21.8
Failure to maintain set	≤ -2.5, ≥ 3.1
Verbal Memory	
California Verbal Learning Test	
Total Trials 1-5 (/80)	≤ -10.0, ≥ 13.7
List B (/16)	≤ -2.9, ≥ 2.7
Short-Delay free recall (/16)	≤ 4.0, ≥ 4.9
Short-Delay cued recall (/16)	≤ -2.8, ≥ 4.0
Long-Delay free recall (/16)	≤ -2.9, ≥ 3.5
Long-Delay cued recall (/16)	≤ - 3.1, ≥ 4.1
Long-Delay discriminability (%)	≤ -9.9, ≥ 3.0
Wechsler Memory Scale - Revised	
Logical Memory I (/50)	≤ -9.2, ≥ 7.4
Logical Memory II (/50)	≤ -9.3, ≥ 10.3
Language	
Verbal Fluency (semantic, category)	≤ -7.3, ≥ 5.7
Verbal Fluency (phonemic, letter)	≤ -12.7, ≥ 11.1
Boston Naming Test (/60)	≤ -15.4, ≥ 10.5
Cognitive Screening	
Mattis Dementia Rating Scale	
Attention (/37)	≤ -8.4, ≥ 6.4
Initiation/Perseveration (/37)	≤ -5.2, ≥ 6.1
Construction (/6)	≤ -2.0, ≥ 1.1
Conceptualization (/39)	≤ -7.5, ≥ 7.0
Memory (/25)	≤ -6.3, ≥ 4.2
Total (/144)	≤ -19.8, ≥ 15.2
Mood/Depression	
Beck Depression Inventory (/63)	≤ -6.5, ≥ 10.7

Note: From Troster et al. (2007); N = 62 older adults with PD; Test-retest about 17 month interval

Neuropsychological Assessment

Neuropsychological assessment of patients with PD is complicated by several factors. First, most patients with PD who are candidates for surgical treatment will be older adults who present with various comorbid medical conditions which can affect neuropsychological functions. Second, many advanced PD patients will suffer from unpredictable fluctuations in motor function that range from pronounced akinesia and prominent (and painful) dystonias to nearly continuous and uncomfortable dyskinesias. Tremor may also markedly vary during the evaluation. Thus, the duration available to complete the neuropsychological evaluation is often time limited, with administration of tasks having a strong motor component limited to periods when the patient's motor functioning is at his/her best. Finally, patients may also exhibit a host of related PD symptoms (see Sect. 1), including autonomic problems and psychiatric complications of medication (e.g., visual hallucinations) and/or comorbid depression and/or anxiety. Suicidal ideation is not uncommon. Patients (and their family members) may have high expectations for the treatment benefit from DBS surgery, which can far exceed actual benefit derived. Risk of suicide should be evaluated, particularly if benefit from DBS does not meet the patient's expectations. The presence of medication-induced pathological gambling, hypersexuality and other impulse-control disorders must be assessed, and may increase the risk of post-surgical hypomanic symptoms.

Recommended Neuropsychological Evaluation

In addition to providing pre-surgical screening for dementia and psychological complications as well as assessment for a patient's understanding of the relative benefits/risks of surgery, the neuropsychological assessment provides a baseline measure of the patient's pre-surgical functioning against which postoperative evaluations may be compared. Ideally, neuropsychological assessment will quantify general cognitive function (i.e., intellectual function), attention/executive, language (naming, semantic verbal fluency, phonemic verbal fluency), memory, visuoperceptual/visuoconstructional ability and mood (see Table 21.12). A typical neuropsychological evaluation may total 2–4 h, inclusive of clinical interview and test administration. Assessment of general cognitive ability is often abbreviated or a general index of cognitive functioning used [e.g., Dementia Rating Scale-2 (DRS-2; Jurica et al., 2002) total score].

Post-surgical follow-ups can be an important component of medical care for patients who have undergone DBS surgery, with a common practice being 3-month postoperative evaluations followed by a 1-year follow-up evaluation. The follow-up time frames noted above are guidelines, and adjustment of the post-surgical follow-up evaluation is often made for patients who require post-surgical rehabilitation and/or experience postoperative complications. Post-surgical neuropsychological battery should ideally use the same tests (alternate forms when available), but not all tests (e.g., estimating premorbid intellectual function) need to be repeated.

Table 21.12 A neuropsychological battery for patients with PD who are candidates for DBS

Neuropsychological Test/Task	Domain(s) assessed
North American Adult Reading Test (NAART) and/or Oklahoma Premorbid Intelligence Estimate – 3 (OPIE-3) and/or Wide Range Achievement Test – 4th Ed. (WRAT-4) Reading subtest	Premorbid General Cognitive Function
Repeatable Battery for the Assessment of Neuropsychological Status (RBANS; Randolph, 1998). OR Dementia Rating Scale – 2nd Edition (DRS-2; Jurica, Leitten, & Mattis, 2002).	General neuropsychological function (includes screen of attention, memory, language, visuoperceptual/visuoconstructional)
Trail Making Test, parts A and B (Reitan, 1958)	Attention/Executive
Stroop Color-Word Test (Golden, 1978) or for more impaired patients: Go, No-Go task (Luria, 1943)	Attention/Executive
In higher functioning patients, Wisconsin Card Sorting Test-64 (WCST-64, Kongs et al., 2000) or California Card Sorting Test (Delis et al., 1992)	Attention/Executive
Boston Naming Test (Goodglass & Kaplan, 2001)	Language
Verbal Fluency [Controlled Oral Word Association Test (phonemic fluency; Benton & Hamsher, 1989; Spreen & Strauss, 1998) and Category fluency]	Language
Repetition of simple and complex sentence.	Language
Comprehension (simple command, complex command)	Language
Read and Write (e.g., write sentence and read it)	Language
Sensory exam (see chapter 4)	Sensory
Evaluation for Ideomotor Apraxia (See Chapter 4)	Motor/Motor Planning
Halstead Reitan Finger Tapping Test	Motor
Beck Depression Inventory – 2nd Edition (or Geriatric Depression Scale)	Mood/Psychological
Speilberger State-Trait Anxiety Inventory (or Beck Anxiety Inventory)	Mood/Psychological
SVT's or imbedded measures of task engagement	Task engagement and motivation

Key Points: Overview of DBS for Parkinson's disease

- Effective at reducing cardinal symptoms of PD
- Cognitively safe for carefully selected patients
- Psychiatric complications rare, but possible
- Neuropsychologic Evaluation:
  - Rule-out prominent dementia
  - Assess for psychologic risk factors
  - May assist to assess patient's decision making/cooperate in follow-up
  - Minimal: attention/executive, verbal memory, verbal fluency and mood

Essential Tremor

DBS for the treatment of ET has generally targeted the ventral intermediate (VIM) nucleus of the thalamus. VIM DBS has been found to be remarkably effective treatment for reducing debilitating essential tremor in the contralateral limb.

VIM DBS may be unilateral or bilateral for selected patients. The average age of patients undergoing VIM DBS for the treatment of ET is in the 50 s, but patients aged from the 30 s to the 90 s have undergone surgery. Like DBS for PD, the surgical benefit of VIM DBS for the treatment of ET occurs within minutes of when the DBS is activated following IPG placement. The microlesion effect is reduced tremor contralateral to the electrode placement occurring immediately postoperatively, which gradually decreases, resulting in return of severe tremor.

The surgical complication rate for VIM DBS is generally similar to that for GPi or STN DBS. It is more common for patients with ET to have unilateral DBS as compared to patients with PD, because bilateral STN implantation is required in PD in order to obtain the benefit of postoperative medication reduction with its concomitant reduction in medication-induced side effects. Whether DBS for ET is bilateral or unilateral depends on the degree of asymmetry of the disease and the patient's resultant functional disability.

ET Symptoms Responsive to VIM DBS

- Action or essential tremor of contralateral limbs.
- Tremor involving the axial muscles (jaw and head) may also be ameliorated, although this is typically less significantly achieved as a benefit.

Surgical Inclusion/Exclusion Criteria

While either VIM may be a surgical site, unilateral VIM DBS is much more common than bilateral VIM DBS. Surgical inclusion criteria are as follows:

- No pronounced dementia.
- Patients should have failed to achieve satisfactory reduction of tremor from primidone and/or propranolol. This may reflect either significant unilateral tremor that prevents completion of activities of daily living and/or bilateral involvement (one side will be more affected than the other in true ET). Response to medication may still occur, but require doses that produce intolerable side effects (e.g., sedation).
- Mood disorder, if present, is not predominant, and if present, is being treated.

Neuropsychological Assessment

See general neuropsychological battery recommended in Table 21.12.

Neuropsychological Outcome Following DBS in ET

Neuropsychological outcome from DBS for ET is generally considered good. Postoperative neuropsychological outcomes from VIM DBS surgery and chronic high-frequency stimulation for ET have limited data. Troster et al. found changes in neuropsychological function for VIM DBS to treat ET were small, with marked reduction in tremor. Like DBS for PD, the most consistent findings have been declines in semantic and phonemic verbal fluency and verbal memory. Table 21.13 provides effect size change for patients with ET having undergone unilateral VIM DBS. As expected, motor function with the dominant hand (target for unilateral VIM DBS) exhibits a large effect size improvement (i.e., $d = 1.30$ for Grooved Pegboard), while measures of neuropsychologic function generally exhibited a small change (either improvement or decline), although changes in phonemic verbal fluency varied from medium to large effect size decrease to small effect (i.e., $d = 0.77–.20$). Through 2009, we are unaware of any published RCI values for patients with ET.

Estimating Outcome at an Individual Level

Risk factors for both acute and chronic cognitive decline and behavioral problems have been difficult to identify. However, data suggest patients with ET who are older and have more cognitive or emotional problems at baseline (pre-surgical assessment) are at greater risk. While age had been considered a risk factor for cognitive morbidity, individuals as old as 90 have benefited from VIM DBS. While individual outcome remains difficult to predict, some general statements can be made regarding reducing cognitive morbidity with VIM DBS for patients with ET.

General Risk Factors for Increased Cognitive Morbidity Following DBS in ET:

1. Presence of dementia
2. Neuropsychological deficits due to other neurological insult (e.g., history of head injury, encephalitis, etc.)
3. Presence of psychosis unrelated to medication

Key Points: Overview of DBS for Essential Tremor:

- Effective at reducing tremor
- Cognitively safe for carefully selected patients
- Complications generally rare, but possible
- Neuropsychologic Evaluation:
  - Rule-out prominent dementia
  - Assess for psychologic risk factors (psychosis not related to meds)
  - May assist to assess patient's decision making/cooperate in follow-up
  - Minimal: attention/executive, verbal memory, verbal fluency and mood

Table 21.13 Summary of effect size change on common neuropsychological measures for patients with essential tremor following unilateral thalamic DBS

Test or Neuropsychological Domain	Effect size	Source
Attention and Concentration		
Wechsler Memory Scale - Revised		JA. Fields et al., 2003 [3 mo/12 mo]^
Digit Span Forward	[0.14/0.16]	
Digit Span Backward	[0.20†/0.03]	
Wechsler Memory Scale - Revised		A. Troster et al., 1999 ^^
Digit Span Forward	<0.23	
Digit Span Backward	0.29†	
Visual Span Forward	<0.23	
Visual Span Backward	0.61	
Executive Functions		
Wisconsin Card Sorting Test		JA. Fields et al., 2003 [3 mo/12 mo]^
Categories (/6)	[0.07†/0.11]	
Trials to first category (/128)	[0.02/0.11]	
Perseverative Errors	[0.11/0.06]	
Failure to maintain set	[0.32†/0.11]	
Wisconsin Card Sorting Test		A. Troster et al., 1999^^
Categories (/6)	<0.23	
Trials to first category (/128)	0.28	
Perseverative Responses	0.28	
Perseverative Errors	0.28	
Stroop Neuropsychological Screening		
Color-Word Condition	<0.23†	
Psychomotor Speed		
Grooved Pegboard		JA. Fields et al., 2003 [3 mo/12 mo]^
Dominant Hand	[0.9/0.68]	
Non-dominant Hand	[0.06/0.01]	
Grooved Pegboard		A. Troster et al., 1999^^
Dominant Hand	1.30	
Non-dominant Hand	<0.23	
Verbal Memory		
California Verbal Learning Test		JA. Fields et al., 2003 [3 mo/12 mo]^
Total Trials 1-5 (/80)	[0.06/0.46]	
Short-Delay free recall (/16)	[0.18/0.38]	
Long-Delay free recall (/16)	[0.27/.039]	
Recognition hits	[0.66/0.71]	
Wechsler Memory Scale - Revised		

(continued)

Table 21.13 (continued)

Logical Memory I (/50)	[0.13/0.28]	
Logical Memory II (/50)	[0.39/0.54]	
California Verbal Learning Test		A. Troster et al., 1999^^
Immediate recall	<0.23†	
Short-Delay free recall (/16)	0.30	
Long-Delay free recall (/16)	0.46	
Recognition hits	0.57	
Recognition discriminability %	<0.23†	
Wechsler Memory Scale - Revised		
Figural Memory	<0.23	
Logical Memory I (/50)	0.30	
Logical Memory II (/50)	0.69	
Language		
Verbal Fluency (semantic, category)	[0.04/0.05] †	JA. Fields et al., 2003 [3 mo/12 mo]^
Verbal Fluency (phonemic, letter)	[0.20/0.20] †	
Boston Naming Test (/60)	[0.03†/0.28]	
Verbal Fluency (semantic, category)	<0.23†	A. Troster et al., 1999^^
Verbal Fluency (phonemic, letter)	0.77†	
Boston Naming Test (/60)	<0.23†	
Cognitive Screening		
Mattis Dementia Rating Scale		JA. Fields et al., 2003 [3 mo/12 mo]^
Attention (/37)	[0.21†/0.07]	
Initiation/Perseveration (/37)	[0.31/0.30]	
Construction (/6)	[0.72/0.7]	
Conceptualization (/39)	[0.10†/0.26]	
Memory (/25)	[0.28/0.14]	
Mattis Dementia Rating Scale		A. Troster et al., 1999^^
Attention (/37)	<0.23	
Initiation/Perseveration (/37)	0.25	
Construction (/6)	0.91	
Conceptualization (/39)	<0.23†	
Memory (/25)	0.41	
Total (/144)	0.43	

Note: ^ Calculated Cohen's *d* based on mean and SD provided in report
^^ Calculated Cohen's *d* based on t-score provided in report
† Indicates cognitive deterioration following unilateral thalamic DBS

Dystonia

DBS has been shown to be effective in treating both generalized dystonia and focal dystonia, particularly cervical dystonia. Both STN and GPi have been targeted. GPi DBS is effective for medication-refractory focal and segmental dystonia affecting the cranial and cervical regions. STN DBS has also been reported to be effective for treating generalized and cervical dystonia. However, some patients with GPi DBS exhibited subtle motor disturbances in previously non-dystonic body regions (i.e., arms and legs), which has not been observed for patients with STN DBS used for cranial and cervical dystonia. Greatest benefit is observed contralateral to the side of DBS, although some ipsilateral benefit is observed for both GPi DBS and STN DBS. In addition to patients with primary (idiopathic) dystonias obtaining benefit from DBS, patients with secondary (i.e., traumatic or medication-induced) dystonias may also gain benefit from GPi DBS.

Surgical benefit of GPi DBS for dystonia is typically slow, with reduction in muscle dystonia not observed until months of chronic high-frequency DBS. Unlike DBS for PD or ET, DBS for dystonia often will not result in an immediate therapeutic benefit upon activation of the DBS system. The surgical complication rate in treating dystonia is similar to that for ET (see above).

Dystonic Symptoms Responsive to GPi DBS Include

- Muscle dystonias of contralateral limbs are more affected by unilateral GPi stimulation, although significant ipsilateral effects are also noted.
- Dystonia involving the axial muscles (jaw, head or back) may also be ameliorated, although to a lesser extent.
- Pain due to dystonic posturing (reduced pain).
- Secondary tremor.

Surgical Inclusion/Exclusion Criteria

DBS of the GPi or STN can be offered to patients under a humanitarian device exemption as of 2009. General surgical inclusion criteria are as follows:

- Patients may have obtained some benefit from botulinum toxin.
- No pronounced dementia. However, patients after moderate to severe traumatic brain injury with structural damage to basal ganglia structures have benefited from GPi DBS
- Dystonia is medication refractory. Response to medication may still occur, but require doses that produce intolerable side effects.
- Mood disorder, if present, is not predominant, and if present, is being treated.

Neuropsychological Assessment

See Table 21.12.

Neuropsychological Outcome Following GPi DBS in Dystonia

Neuropsychological outcome from DBS for cervical dystonia is generally similar to that reported for GPi DBS in PD; however, there is less likely to be pronounced neurodegenerative neuropsychological deficits in idiopathic dystonia. Postoperative neuropsychological outcome from DBS surgery and chronic high-frequency stimulation for dystonia have limited data (Halbig et al., 2005; Vidailhet et al., 2007). Initial studies suggest neuropsychological outcome is similar to DBS procedures in general, with no marked decline in general cognitive function. However, significant declines (greater than 2 SD) have been reported for verbal fluency (phonemic and semantic) and, less often, memory scores. Table 21.14 provides effect size change following bilateral GPi DBS for patients with dystonia. Outcome has varied markedly, from overall small decline (Cohen's $d = 0.29$) to moderate-sized improvement (Cohen's $d = 0.64$) in semantic verbal fluency has been reported.

Estimating Outcome at an Individual Level

There are very limited data for neuropsychological outcome of DBS for dystonia. At this time, risk factors for neuropsychological decline are based on data derived from other patient populations in which DBS has been applied, particularly essential tremor and Parkinson's disease. Thus, patients with dystonia who are older and have more cognitive or emotional problems at baseline (pre-surgical assessment) are at greater risk (e.g., Vidailhet et al., 2007). While individual outcome remains difficult to predict, some general statements can be made regarding reducing cognitive morbidity with DBS.

General Risk factors for Increased Cognitive Morbidity Following DBS in Dystonia:

1. Pronounced dementia. However, several case reports worldwide have reported patients after moderate to severe traumatic brain injuries and later secondary dystonia have reported good benefit from GPi DBS without significant cognitive morbidity.
2. Psychosis unrelated to medications.

Key Points: Overview of DBS for Dystonia:

- Effective treating generalized and focal dystonias
  - Symptom relief may not be evident for months after DBS.
- Cognitively safe for carefully selected patients.
- Complications generally rare, but possible.
- Neuropsychologic Evaluation:
  - Document cognitive function.

    Patients with traumatic brain injury have shown benefit.
  - Asses for psychologic risk factors (suicide/homicide ideation, psychosis not related to meds)
  - May assist to assess patient's decision making/cooperate in follow-up
  - Minimal: attention/executive, memory, verbal fluency and mood

Table 21.14 Summary of effect size change in common neuropsychological measures for patients with dystonia following bilateral pallidal (GPi) DBS

Test or Neuropsychological Domain	Effect size	Source
Attention and Concentration		
Wechsler Memory Scale - Revised		D. Gruber et al., 2009^+
Digit Span Forward	0.08†	
Digit Span Backward	0.09†	
Wechsler Memory Scale - Revised		TD. Halbig et al., 2005^
Digit Span Forward	0.06	
Digit Span Backward	0.00	
Executive Functions		
Wisconsin Card Sorting Test		M. Vidailhet et al., 2007 [1 yr/3 yrs]^
Categories (/6)	[0.35/0.83]	
Perseverative Errors	[0.17/0.72†]	
Failure to Maintain Set	[0.44/0.97]	
Total Errors	[0.38/1.19]	
Wisconsin Card Sorting Test		B. Pillon et al., 2006^
Categories (/6)	0.35	
Perseverative Errors	0.17	
Failure to Maintain Set	0.44	
Total Errors	0.38	
Trail Making Test-B	0.00	
Stroop Neuropsychological Screening		TD. Halbig et al., 2005^
Color-Word Condition	0.22†	
Trail Making Test-B	0.44	
Processing Speed		
Trail Making Test-A	0.28	B. Pillon et al., 2006^
Trail Making Test-A	0.59	TD. Halbig et al., 2005^
Verbal Memory		
Rey Auditory Verbal Learning Test		D. Gruber et al., 2009^+
Total for Trials 1-5 (/75)	0.46	
List B (/15)	0.85†	
Delayed recall (/15)	0.14	
Delayed recognition	0.26†	
Grober & Buschke Test		M. Vidailhet et al., 2007 [1 yr/3 yrs]^
Free recall	[0.34/0.47]	
Total recall	[0.53/0.59]	
Recognition	[0.41/0.41]	
Delayed free recall	[0.00/0.25]	
Delayed total recall	[0.40/0.46]	
Grober & Buschke Test*		B. Pillon et al., 2006^

(continued)

Table 21.14 (continued)

Free recall	0.34	
Total recall	0.53	
Recognition	0.42	
Delayed free recall	0.00	
Delayed total recall	0.41	
Rey Auditory Verbal Learning Test		TD. Halbig et al., 2005^
Total for Trials 1-5 (/75)	0.22	
List B (/15)	0.34	
Delayed recall (/15)	0.23	
Delayed recognition	0.19†	
Language		
Verbal Fluency (semantic, category)	0.64	D. Gruber et al., 2009^+
Verbal Fluency (phonemic, letter)	0.57	
Verbal Fluency (semantic, category)	[0.29†/0.02]	M. Vidailhet et al., 2007 [1 yr/3 yrs]^
Verbal Fluency (phonemic, letter)	[0.24†/0.10]	
Verbal Fluency (semantic, category)	0.29†	B. Pillon et al., 2006^
Verbal Fluency (phonemic, letter)	0.24†	
Verbal Fluency (semantic, category)	0.20	TD. Halbig et al., 2005^
Verbal Fluency (phonemic, letter)	0.04	
Cognitive Screening		
Mattis Dementia Rating Scale		D. Gruber et al., 2009^+
Attention (/37)	0.00	
Initiation/Perseveration (/37)	0.31	
Construction (/6)	0.00	
Conceptualization (/39)	0.40	
Memory (/25)	0.03	
Total (/144)	0.03†	
Mini Mental Status Exam	0.20	B. Pillon et al., 2006^
Mattis Dementia Rating Scale		TD. Halbig et al., 2005^
Attention (/37)	0.31	
Initiation/Perseveration (/37)	0.45†	
Construction (/6)	0.00	
Conceptualization (/39)	0.22†	
Memory (/25)	0.46	
Total (/144)	0.52	
Mood/Depression		
Montgomery-Asberg Depression Scale	1.33††	D. Gruber et al., 2009^+
Beck Depression Inventory	[0.41/0.48] ††	M. Vidailhet et al., 2007 [1 yr/3 yrs]^
Beck Depression Inventory	0.41††	B. Pillon et al., 2006^
Beck Depression Inventory	0.42††	TD. Halbig et al., 2005^

Note: ^ Calculated Cohen's *d* based on mean and SD provided in report
† Indicates cognitive deterioration following bilateral GPi DBS
†† Improved mood following STN DBS
*From H. Grober & H. Buschke. Genuine memory deficits in dementia. Developmental Neuropsychology, 1987; 3: 13–36
+ Study based on tardive dystonia rather than generalized dystonia

References

Ameli, R., Snow, J., Rakocevic, G., et al. (2005). A neuropsychological assessment of phobias in patients with stiff person syndrome. *Neurology, 64*, 1961–1963.

American Psychiatric Association (Ed.). (2000). *Diagnostic and statistical manual of mental disorders, DSM-IV-TR* (4th ed.). American Psychiatric Association.

Armstrong, M. J., Litvan, I., Lang, A. E., et al. (2013). Criteria for the diagnosis of corticobasal degeneration. *Neurology, 80*(5), 496–503.

Aybek, S., Lazeyras, F., Gronchi-Perrin, A., Burkhard, P. R., Villemure, J. G., & Vingerhoets, J. G. (2009). Hippocampal atrophy predicts conversion to dementia after STN-DBS in Parkinson's disease. *Parkinsonism and Related Disorders, 15*, 521–524.

Benabid, A. L., Benazzouz, A., Hoffmann, D., Limousin, P., Krack, P., & Pollack, P. (1998). Long-term electrical inhibition of deep brain targets in movement disorders. *Movement Disorders, 13*(suppl. 3), 119–125.

Benabid, A. L., Benazzouz, A., & Pollack, P. (2002). Mechanisms of deep brain stimulation. *Movement Disorders, 17*(suppl 3), S73–S74.

Benabid, A. L., Pollak, P., Louveau, A., Henry, S., & de Rougemont, J. (1987). Combined (thalamotomy and stimulation) stereotactic surgery of the VIM thalamic nucleus for bilateral Parkinson disease. *Applied Neurophysiology, 50*(1–6), 344–346.

Benito-León, J., Louis, E. D., Bermejo-Pareja, F., et al. (2006). Population-based case-control study of cognitive function in essential tremor. *Neurology, 66*, 69–74.

Boeve, B. F. (2007). Parkinson-related dementias. *Neurologic Clinics, 25*, 761–781.

Burgess, P. W., & Shallice, T. (1997). *The Hayling and Brixton tests: Manual*. Thames Valley Test Company.

Bürk, K., Daum, I., & Rüb, U. (2006). Cognitive function in multiple system atrophy of the cerebellar type. *Movement Disorders, 21*(6), 772–776.

Bürk, K., Globas, C., Bosch, S., et al. (2003). Cognitive deficits in spinocerebellar ataxia type 1, 2, and 3. *Journal of Neurology, 250*, 207–211.

Caballol, N., Martí, M. J., & Tolosa, E. (2007). Cognitive dysfunction and dementia in Parkinson disease. *Movement Disorders, 22*(S17), S358–S366.

Calderon, J., Perry, R. J., Erzinclioglu, S. W., Berrios, G. E., Dening, T. R., & Hodges, J. R. (2001). Perception, attention, and working memory are disproportionately impaired in dementia with lewy bodies compared with Alzheimer's disease. *Journal of Neurology, Neurosurgery, and Psychiatry, 70*, 157–164.

Centi, J., Freeman, R., Gibbons, C. H., Neargarder, S., Canova, A. O., & Cronin-Golomb, A. (2017). Effects of orthostatic hypotension on cognition in Parkinson disease. *Neurology, 88*, 17–24.

Chahine, L. M., Xie, S. X., Simuni, T., et al. (2016). Longitudinal changes in cognition in early Parkinson's disease patients with REM sleep behavior disorder. *Parkinsonism & Related Disorders, 27*, 102–106.

Chiu, H. F. K., & Psych, M. R. C. (1995). Psychiatric aspects of progressive supranuclear palsy. *General Hospital Psychiatry, 17*, 135–143.

Collerton, D., Burn, D., McKeith, I., & O'Brien, J. (2003). Systematic review and meta-analysis show that dementia with lewy bodies is a visual-perceptual and attentional-executive dementia. *Dementia and Geriatric Cognitive Disorders, 16*, 229–237.

Como, P. G. (2001). Neuropsychological function in Tourette syndrome. *Advances in Neurology, 85*, 103–111.

Contarino, M. F., Daniele, A., Sibilia, A. H., Romito, L. M. A., Bentivoglio, A. R., Gainotti, G., & G, & Albanese A. (2007). Cognitive outcome 5 years after bilateral chronic stimulation of subthalamic nucleus in patients with Parkinson's disease. *Journal of Neurology, Neurosurgery, and Psychiatry, 78*, 248–252.

Crawford, S., Channon, S., & Robertson, M. M. (2005). Tourette's syndrome: Performance on tests of behavioural inhibition, working memory, and gambling. *Journal of Child Psychology and Psychiatry, 46*, 1327–1336.

Derost, P. P., Ouchchane, L., Morand, D., et al. (2007). Is DBS-STN appropriate to treat severe Parkinson disease in an elderly population? *Neurology, 68*, 1345–1355.

Dubois, B., Slachevsky, A., Pillon, B., Beato, R., Villalponda, J. M., & Litvan, I. (2005). "Applause sign" helps to discriminate PSP from FTD and PD. *Neurology, 64*, 2132–2133.

Dujardin, K., Defbvre, L., Duhamel, A., Lecouffe, P., Rogelet, P., Steinling, M., & Destee, A. (2004). Cognitive and SPECT characteristics predict progression of Parkinson's disease in newly diagnosed patients. *Journal of Neurology, 251*, 1432–1459.

Emre, M., Aarsland, D., Brown, R., et al. (2007). Clinical diagnostic criteria for dementia associated with Parkinson's disease. *Movement Disorders, 22*(12), 1689–1707.

Eriksen, B. A., & Eriksen, C. W. (1974). Effects of noise letters upon the identification of a target letter in a nonsearch task. *Perception & Psychophysics, 16*, 143–149.

Evidente, V. G. H., Gwinn-Hardy, K. A., Caviness, J. N., et al. (2000). Hereditary ataxias. *Mayo Clinic Proceedings, 75*, 475–490.

Fahn, S., & Elton, R. L. (1987). Members of the UPDRS Development Committee: Unified Parkinson's disease rating scale. In S. Fahn, C. D. Marsden, D. B. Calne, & M. Goldstein (Eds.), *Recent developments in Parkinson's disease* (Vol. 2, pp. 153–163). Macmillan Health Care Information.

Fiorenzato, E., Antonini, A., Wenning, G., & Biundo, R. (2017). Cognitive impairment in multiple system atrophy. *Movement Disorders, 32*, 1338. https://doi.org/10.1002/mds.27085

Fraix, V., Houeto, J. L., Lagrange, C., Le Pen, C., Krystkowiak, P., Guehl, D., Ardouin, C., Welter, M. L., Maurel, F., Defebvre, L., Rougier, A., Benabid, A. L., Mesnage, V., Ligier, M., Blond, S., Burbaud, P., Bioulac, B., Destee, A., Cornu, P., Pollak, P., & on behalf of the SPARK Study Group. (2006). Clinical and economic results of bilateral subthalamic nucleus stimulation in Parkinson's disease. *Journal of Neurology, Neurosurgery, and Psychiatry, 77*, 443–449.

Fullard, M. E., Tran, B., Xie, S. X., et al. (2016). Olfactory impairment predicts cognitive decline in early Parkinson's disease. *Parkinsonism & Related Disorders, 25*, 45–51.

Gelb, D. J., Oliver, E., & Gilman, S. (1999). Diagnostic criteria for Parkinson disease. *Archives of Neurology, 56*, 33–39.

Grafman, J., Litvan, I., & Stark, M. (1995). Neuropsychological features of progressive supranuclear palsy. *Brain and Cognition, 28*, 311–320.

Grimes, A., Lang, A. E., & Bergeron, C. B. (1999). Dementia as the most common presentation of cortical-basal ganglionic degeneration. *Neurology, 53*, 1969.

Halbig, T. D., Gruber, D., Kopp, U. A., Schneider, G. H., Trottenberg, T., & Kupsch, A. (2005). Pallidal stimulation in dystonia: Effects on cognition, mood, and quality of life. *Journal of Neurology, Neurosurgery, and Psychiatry, 76*, 1713–1716.

Hamani, C., Richter, E., Schwalb, J. M., & Lozano, A. M. (2005). Bilateral subthalamic nucleus stimulation for Parkinson's disease: A systematic review of the clinical literature. *Neurosurgery, 56*, 1313–1321.

Hilker, R., Portman, A., Voges, J., Stall, M., Burghaus, L., van Laar, T., Koulousakis, A., Maguire, R., Pruim, J., de Jong, B. M., Herholz, K., Sturm, V., Heiss, W., & Leenders, K. (2005). Disease progression continues in patients with advanced Parkinson's disease and effective subthalamic nucleus stimulation. *Journal of Neurology, Neurosurgery, and Psychiatry, 76*, 1217–1221.

Horsley, V., & Clarke, R. H. (1908). The structure and function of the cerebellum examined by a new method. *Brain, 31*, 45–124.

Jacobson, N. S., & Truax, P. (1991). Clinical significance: A statistical approach to defining meaningful change in psychotherapy research. *Journal of Consulting and Clinical Psychology, 59*, 12–19.

Jahanshahi, M., Ardouin, C. M., Brown, R. G., et al. (2000). The impact of deep brain stimulation on executive function in Parkinson's disease. *Brain, 123*, 1142–1145.

Jahanshahi, M., Rowe, J., & Fuller, R. (2003). Cognitive executive function in dystonia. *Movement Disorders, 18*, 1470–1481.

Jahanshahi, M., & Torkamani, M. (2017). The cognitive features of idiopathic and DYT1 dystonia. *Movement Disorders, 32*, 1348.

Jurica, P. J., Leitten, C. L., & Mattis, S. (2002). *Dementia Rating Scale-2 (DRS-2). Professional manual*. Psychological Assessment Resources.
Kalbe, E., Rehberg, S. P., Heber, I., Kronenbuerger, M., et al. (2016). Subtypes of mild cognitive impairment in patients with Parkinson's disease: Evidence from the LANDSCAPE study. *Journal of Neurology, Neurosurgery, and Psychiatry, 87*, 1099–1105.
Kalbe, E., Voges, J., Weber, T., Haarer, M., Baudrexel, S., Klein, J. C., Kessler, J., Sturm, V., Heiss, W. D., & Hilker, R. (2009). Frontal FDG-PET activity correlates with cognitive outcome after SNT-DBS in Parkinson's disease. *Neurology, 72*, 42–49.
Kawai, Y., Suenaga, M., Takeda, A., Ito, M., Watanabe, H., Tanaka, F., Kato, K., Fukatsu, H., Naganawa, S., Kato, T., Ito, K., & Sobue, G. (2008). Cognitive impairments in multiple system atrophy: MSA-C vs. MSA-P. *Neurology, 70*, 1390–1396.
Kim, S. L., Lee, M. J., & Lee, M. S. (2014). Cognitive dysfunction associated with falls in progressive supranuclear palsy. *Gait & Posture, 40*, 605–609.
Krack, P., Batir, A., Blercom, N. V., Chabardes, S., Fraix, V., Ardouin, C., Koudsie, A., Limousin, P. D., Benazzouz, A., LeBas, J. F., Benabid, A. L., & Pollak, P. (2003). Five-year follow-up of bilateral stimulation of the subthalamic nucleus in advanced Parkinson's disease. *New England Journal of Medicine, 349*, 1925–1934.
Kurlan, R., Cummings, J., Raman, R., et al. (2007). Quetiapine for agitation or psychosis in patients with dementia and parkinsonism. *Neurology, 68*, 1356–1363.
Laitinen, L. V., Bergenheim, A. T., & Hariz, M. I. (1992). Leksell's posteroventral pallidotomy in the treatment of Parkinson's disease. *Journal of Neurosurgery, 77*, 487–488.
Leiguarda, R. C., Pramstaller, P. P., Merello, M., et al. (1997). Apraxia in Parkinson's disease, progressive supranuclear palsy, multiple system atrophy and neuroleptic-induced parkinsonism. *Brain, 120*, 75–90.
Levy, M. L., Cummings, J. L., Fairbanks, L. A., et al. (1998). Apathy is not depression. *Journal of Neuropsychiatry Clinical Neurosciences, 10*, 314–319.
Lezak, M. D., Howieson, D. B., & Loring, D. W. (2004). *Neuropsychological assessment* (4th ed.). Oxford University Press.
Lombardi, W. J., Woolston, D. J., Roberts, J. W., & Gross, R. E. (2001). Cognitive deficits in patients with essential tremor. *Neurology, 57*, 785–790.
Louis, E. D. (2009). Essential tremor as a neuropsychiatric disorder. *Journal of Neurological Sciences*. https://doi.org/10.1016/j.jns.2009.08.029
Malek, N., Lawton, M. A., Swallow, D. M., Grosset, K. A., Marrinan, S. L., Bajaj, N., Barker, R. A., Burn, D. J., Hardy, J., Morris, H. R., Williams, N. M., Wood, N., Ben-Shlomo, Y., & Grosset, D. G. (2016). PRoBaND Clinical Consortium. *Movement Disorders, 31*, 1518–1526.
Marras, C., & Tanner, C. M. (2004). Epidemiology of Parkinson's disease. In R. L. Watts & W. C. Koller (Eds.), *Movement disorders: Neurologic principles & practice* (2nd ed., pp. 177–195). McGraw-Hill.
Massman, P. J., Kreiter, K. T., Jankovic, J., et al. (1996). Neuropsychological functioning in cortical-basal ganglionic degeneration: Differentiation from Alzheimer's disease. *Neurology, 46*(3), 720–726.
Mathuranath, P. S., Xuereb, J. H., Bak, T., et al. (2000 Mar). Corticobasal ganglionic degeneration and/or frontotemporal dementia? A report of two overlap cases and review of literature. *Journal of Neurology, Neurosurgery, and Psychiatry, 68*(3), 304–312.
McKeith, I. G., Boeve, B. F., Dickson, D. W., et al. (2017). Diagnosis and management of dementia with Lewy bodies. *Neurology, 89*, 88–100.
McKeith, I. G., Galasko, D., Kosaka, K., et al. (1996). Consensus guidelines for the clinical and pathologic diagnosis of dementia with Lewy bodies (DLB): Report of the consortium on DLB international workshop. *Neurology, 47*, 1113–1124.
McKeith, I. G., & Mosimann, U. P. (2004). Dementia with Lewy bodies and Parkinson's disease. *Parkinsonism & Related Disorders, 10*(Suppl 1), S15–S18.

McMurtray, A. M., Clark, D. G., Flood, M. K., et al. (2006). Depressive and memory symptoms as presenting features of spinocerebellar ataxia. *The Journal of Neuropsychiatry and Clinical Neurosciences, 18*, 420–422.
Mery, V. P., Gros, P., Lafontaine, A. L., Robinson, A., Benedetti, A., Kimoff, R. J., & Kaminska, M. (2017). Reduced cognitive function in patients with Parkinson disease and obstructive sleep apnea. *Neurology, 88*, 1120–1128.
Mitchell, S. L., & Rockwood, K. (2001). Defining Parkinsonism in the Canadian study of health and aging. *International Psychogeriatrics, 13*(S1), 107–113.
Moriarty, A., Cook, A., Hunt, H., et al. (2016). A longitudinal investigation into cognition and disease progression in spinocerebellar ataxia types 1, 2, 3, 6, and 7. *Orphanet Journal of Rare Diseases, 11*, 82.
Nuti, A., Ceravolo, R., Piccinni, A., Dell'Agnello, G., Bellini, G., Gambaccini, G., Rossi, C., Logi, C., Dell'Osso, L., & Bonuccelli, U. (2004). Psychiatric comorbidity in a population of Parkinson's disease patients. *European Journal of Neurology, 11*, 315–320.
Okun, M. S., Fernandez, H. H., Pedraza, O., Misra, M., Lyons, K. E., Pahwa, R., Tarsy, D., Scollins, L., Corapi, K., Friehs, G. M., Grace, J., Romrell, J., & Foote, K. D. (2004). Development and initial validation of a screening tool for Parkinson disease surgical candidates. *Neurology, 63*, 161–163.
Okun, M. S., Fernandez, H. H., Wu, S. S., Kirsch-Darrow, L., Bowers, D., Bova, F., Suelter, M., Jacobson, C. E., Wang, X., Gordon, C. W., Zeilman, P., Romrell, J., Martin, P., Ward, H., Rodriguez, R. L., & Foote, K. D. (2009). Cognition and mood in Parkinson's disease in subthalamic nucleus versus globus pallidus interna deep brain stimulation: The COMPARE trial. *Annals of Neurology, 65*, 586–595.
Ory-Magne, F., Brefel-Courbon, C., Simonetta-Moreau, M., et al. (2007). Does ageing influence deep brain stimulation outcomes in Parkinson's disease? *Movement Disorders, 22*, 1457–1463.
Pedersen, K. F., Larsen, J. P., Tysnes, O. B., & Alves, G. (2017). Natural course of mild cognitive impairment in Parkinson disease: A 5-year population-based study. *Neurology, 88*, 767–774.
Pilotto, A., Turrone, R., Liepelt-Scarfone, I., et al. (2016). Vascular risk factors and cognition in Parkinson's disease. *Journal of Alzheimer's Disease, 51*, 563–570.
Rampello, L., Buttà, V., Raffaele, R., et al. (2005). Progressive supranuclear palsy: A systematic review. *Neurobiology of Disease, 20*(2), 179–186.
Riley, D. E., Lang, A. E., Lewis, A., et al. (1990). Cortical-basal ganglionic degeneration. *Neurology, 40*, 1203–1212.
Román, G. C. (2003). Vascular dementia: Distinguishing characteristics, treatment, and prevention. *Journal of the American Geriatrics Society, 51*(5 Suppl Dementia), S296–S304.
Schrag, A., Siddiqui, U. F., Anastasiou, Z., Weintraub, D., & Schott, J. M. (2017). Clinical variables and biomarkers in prediction of cognitive impairment in patients with newly diagnosed Parkinson's disease: A cohort study. *Lancet Neurology, 16*, 66–75.
Scott, R. B., Gregory, R., Wilson, J., et al. (2003). Executive cognitive deficits in primary dystonia. *Movement Disorders, 18*, 539–550.
Selfani, K., Soland, V. L., Chouinard, S., & Huot, P. (2017). Movement disorders induced by the "atypical" antipsychotic aripiprazole. *The Neurologist, 22*, 24–28.
Servello, D., Zekaj, E., Saleh, C., Zanaboni Dina, C., & Porta, M. (2016 Jun). Sixteen years of deep brain stimulation in Tourette's Syndrome: A critical review. *Journal of Neurosurgical Sciences, 60*(2), 218–229.
Smeding, H. M. M., Speelman, J. D., Huizenga, H. M., Schuurman, P. R., & Schmand, B. (2009). Predictors of cognitive and psychosocial outcome after STN DBS in Parkinson disease. *Journal of Neurology, Neurosurgery, and Psychiatry*. https://doi.org/10.1136/jnnp.2007.140012
Spiegel, E. A., Wycis, H. T., Marks, M., et al. (1947). Stereotaxic apparatus for operations on the human brain. *Science, 106*, 349–350.
Tarsy, D., Vitek, J. L., & Lozano, A. M. (2003). *Surgical treatment of Parkinson's disease and other related movement disorders (current clinical neurology)*. Humana Press Inc.

Temkin, N. R., Heaton, R. K., Grant, I., & Dikmen, S. S. (1999). Detecting significant change in neuropsychological test performance: A comparison of four models. *Journal of the International Neuropsychological Society, 5*, 357–369.

Troster, A. I., Woods, S. P., & Morgan, E. E. (2007). Assessing cognitive change in Parkinson's disease: Development of practice effect-corrected reliable change indices. *Archives of Clinical Neuropsychology, 22*, 711–718.

Vidailhet, M., Vercueil, L., Houeto, J. L., Krystkowiak, P., Lagrange, C., Yelnik, J., et al. (2007). Bilateral, pallidal, deep-brain stimulation in primary generalised dystonia: A prospective 3 year follow-up study. *Lancet Neurology, 6*, 223–229.

Volkmann, J., Allert, N., Voges, J., Sturm, V., Schnitzler, A., & Freund, H. J. (2004). Long-term results of bilateral pallidal stimulation in Parkinson's disease. *Annals of Neurology, 55*, 871–875.

Ward, J., Sheppard, J.-M., Shpritz, B., et al. (2006). A four-year prospective study of cognitive functioning in Huntington's disease. *Journal of the International Neuropsychological Society, 12*, 445–454.

Watkins, L. H., Sahakian, B. J., Robertson, M. M., et al. (2005). Executive function in Tourette's syndrome and obsessive-compulsive disorder. *Psychological Medicine, 35*, 571–582.

Weaver, F. M., Follett, K., Stern, M., Hur, K., Harris, C., Marks, W. J., Jr., Rothlind, J., Sagher, O., Reda, D., Moy, C. S., Pahwa, R., Burchiel, K., Hogarth, P., Lai, E. C., Duda, J. E., Holloway, K., Samii, A., Horn, S., Bornstein, J., Soner, G., Heemskerk, J., Huan, G. D., & for the CSP 468 Study Group. (2009). Bilateral deep brain stimulation vs best medical therapy for patients with advanced Parkinson's disease. *JAMA, 301*, 63–73.

Weintraub, D., & Hurtig, H. I. (2007). Presentation and management of psychosis in Parkinson's disease and dementia with Lewy bodies. *The American Journal of Psychiatry, 164*(10), 1491–1498.

Winikates, J., & Jankovic, J. (1994). Vascular progressive supranuclear palsy. *Journal of Neural Transmission. Supplementa, 42*, 189–201.

Wolters, E. C., & Braak, H. (2006). Parkinson's disease: Premotor clinico-pathological correlations. *Journal of Neural Transmission. Supplementum, 70*, 309–319.

Woods, S. P., & Troster, A. I. (2003). Prodromal frontal/executive dysfunction predicts incident dementia in Parkinson's disease. *Journal of the International Neuropsychological Society, 9*, 17–24.

Wu, L. J., Sitburana, O., Davidson, A., & Jankovic, J. (2008). Applause sign in Parkinsonian disorders and Huntington's disease. *Movement Disorders, 15*, 2307–2311.

Chapter 22
Multiple Sclerosis

Juliette Galindo and Christopher T. Copeland

> **Key Points and Chapter Summary**
> - MS often presents acutely with sensory, motor, cognitive, constitutional and mood disturbances. Fatigue is the most common patient complaint.
> - MS pathology most often involves demyelination of long white matter tracks, but can involve inflammation, demyelination and degeneration, which can present throughout in the central nervous system.
> - The course of MS can vary considerably between individuals but most often begins with reversible, episodic symptoms early in the course of the disease and eventually becomes gradually progressive over time.
> - Slow processing speed is the most common cognitive deficit in MS. Deficits in episodic memory, executive functioning, visuospatial skills and language skills may also occur. Cognitive deficits are further exacerbated by fatigue, pain and mood disturbances.
> - Neuropsychological testing is useful for identifying cognitive deficits, informing prognosis, assessing capacity, tracking change over time and for making pre- and post-treatment comparisons.
> - Management of cognitive symptoms with medication, rehabilitation and accommodation are promising, but more research is needed.

J. Galindo (✉)
Department of Psychiatry and Behavioral Sciences, University of Oklahoma, Health Sciences Center College of Medicine, Oklahoma City, OK, USA
e-mail: juliette-galindo@ouhsc.edu

C. T. Copeland
Department of Psychiatry & Behavioral Sciences, College of Medicine, The University of Oklahoma Health Sciences Center, Oklahoma City, OK, USA

M. R. Schoenberg, J. G. Scott (eds.), *The Little Black Book of Neuropsychology*,
https://doi.org/10.1007/978-3-032-07777-6_22

Neuropathology

MS pathology is characterized by focal gray matter lesions and white matter lesions of the central nervous system (CNS) and diffuse neurodegeneration of the entire brain (Lassmann, 2018). Pathological axes of MS (Pitt et al., 2022) are:

- Inflammation
- Demyelination
- Gliosis
- Neuronal axonal damage
- Neuron loss
- Remyelination

In MS, peripheral inflammatory immune cells (T-cells, B-lymphocytes and monocytes) are activated in the lymphatic system, invade the CNS through a compromised blood–brain barrier (BBB) in the subarachnoid space and damage neuronal axonal sheaths (*myelin*), myelin-producing cells (*oligodendrocytes*) and neuronal axons. Over time, immune cell infiltration becomes more diffuse, and axonal injury and atrophy of white matter and gray matter become more widespread.

This entire process by which peripheral immune cells are activated, invade the BBB and damage the CNS is undefined and somehow involves a genetic susceptibility to environmental triggers and events (Zéphir, 2018). A viral or bacterial infection or a specific sequence of inflammatory, BBB-weakening and antibody-disturbing events following an infection may explain MS pathogenesis (van Noort et al., 2023). The Epstein–Barr virus (Soldan & Lieberman, 2023), spirochetal bacteria, chlamydophila pneumoniae and Varicella zoster (Joy & Johnston, 2001) have been identified as possible activating pathogens.

Focal white matter demyelinated lesions develop along deep medullary veins perpendicular to the lateral ventricles and in juxtacortical regions of the brain, the cerebellum and the spinal cord (Futatsuya et al., 2016; Geraldes et al., 2018). Gray matter demyelinated lesions are found in the neocortex (Haider et al., 2014; Kutzelnigg et al., 2005), hippocampus (Geurts et al., 2007), basal ganglia, thalamus (Gilmore, Donaldson, et al., 2009; Vercellino et al., 2009), cerebellum (Gilmore, DeLuca, et al., 2009; Kutzelnigg et al., 2007) and spinal cord (Gilmore, DeLuca, et al., 2009; Gilmore, Geurts, et al., 2009). Active tissue injury from demyelination is associated with activation of astrocytes. Inactive lesions are the result of gliotic scarring. *Dawson fingers* are the radiologic sign of fused and expanded perivenous demyelinating lesions with demyelinating plaques into surrounding, normal appearing white matter (Dawson, 1916). The sequence of volume loss in different areas of the CNS may be relatively uniform across MS phenotypes. Early atrophy in relapse-onset MS occurs in the posterior cingulate cortex, followed by atrophy of the precuneus, middle cingulate cortex, thalamus, brainstem, cerebellum and caudate and putamen regions (Eshaghi et al., 2018).

Epidemiology

Age

MS onset is usually between 20 and 40 years of age, although onset may occur in early childhood and in older age (McGinley et al., 2021; Prosperini et al., 2022). MS is more prevalent (Koch-Henriksen & Sorensen, 2011), begins about 5 years earlier, is less disabling and is less cognitively impairing in women than in men (Beatty & Aupperle 2002; Olek, 2005; Reipert 2004). Some studies suggest younger age of adult-onset MS is a positive prognostic factor (Trojano et al., 1995). When accounting for current age, however, others have found that current age informs prognosis while age at onset does not (Liguori et al., 2000). Age of onset may be more important for late-onset MS (onset after age 50).

Approximately 10%, 50% and 90% of Relapsing-Remitting Multiple Sclerosis (RRMS) cases convert from RRMS to Secondary-Progressive Multiple Sclerosis (SPMS) at 10, 20 and 30 years, respectively, after symptom onset (Barzegar et al., 2021; i.e., respectively, around ages 40, 50 and 60 based on the average age of RRMS onset at age 30).

Current age, and not age of MS onset, may be the most important risk factor for conversion from RRMS to SPMS for most people (Liguori et al., 2000). Late-onset MS (after age 50) progression is more rapid than other phenotypes (Polliack et al., 2001).

Onset age is influenced by genetics. Onset age tends to "cluster" among siblings with MS (Bulman et al., 1991; Doolittle et al., 1990).

Race and Ethnicity

MS is most prevalent in White people of Northern European heritage. The prevalence of the disease ranges between 2 and 150 per 100,000 depending on the country or specific population (Rosati, 2001).

Among all people with adult-onset MS, 77% are White, about 10% are Black and about 7% are Hispanic (Hittle et al., 2023). The lifetime risk of adult-onset MS is 1 in 400 among White people (Compston & Coles, 2002).

Geography

MS is generally more prevalent at greater degrees of northern and southern latitude than in temperate zones near the equator (Kurtzke, 2000). Climate, diet, geomagnetism, toxins, sunlight exposure and infectious exposure have all been offered as possible reasons for regional differences in MS incidence and prevalence (Koch-Henriksen & Sorensen, 2011).

Sex

MS is more prevalent by a factor of nearly 3–1 (Hittle et al., 2023), begins about 5 years earlier and is typically less severe in women than in men. Pregnancies mitigate relapses and delays MS progression for unclear reasons that implicate an important role for estrogen (D'hooghe et al., 2010).

Dominant Hand

There is a modest increase in risk of MS among left- versus right-handed women, suggesting prenatal exposure to sex hormones that influence hand preference may also play a role in MS risk (Gardener et al., 2009).

Family History

Concordance rates of MS are approximately 30% and 4% for monozygotic and dizygotic twins, respectively. First-degree relatives of MS patients have a 2–5% risk of developing the disease, compared to the average risk in the general population of 0.1% (Vollmer, 1999).

Clinical Features

Phenotypes

MS phenotype labels describe clinical presentation and course.

- *Radiologically Isolated Syndrome* (RIS): Positive, typically incidental radiological finding without clinical symptoms.
- *Clinically Isolated Syndrome* (CIS): The first clinical presentation of symptoms that may be due to MS but without dissemination in time.
- *Relapsing-remitting MS* (RRMS): The first stage of MS for most people. Well-defined relapses, without progression between relapses. Common relapse triggers include warm weather, infections and emotional distress.

- *Secondary-progressive MS* (SPMS): Usually the second stage of MS progression. Acute worsening without remission. About 80% of people with RRMS eventually convert to SPMS, and the annual conversion rate is approximately 2–3% (Lublin et al., 1996).
- *Primary progressive MS* (PPMS): Progressive, without acute exacerbation or remission of symptoms. Tends to affect people who are older at disease onset.
- *Progressive relapsing MS* (PRMS): Progressive at onset due to neuronal damage or loss, with episodes of more severe symptoms due to periods of acute inflammation. Least common phenotype.

Sensory and Motor Symptoms

Sensory and motor disturbances are the most common initial symptoms of MS. About 14% of people with MS initially present with multiple sensory and motor symptoms (Olek, 2005). Sensory disturbances may include limb numbness and paresthesia, Lhermitte's sign (an electric shock-like sensation in the back and limbs upon flexing the neck), blurry vision, vision loss and eye pain. Approximately 60% of MS patients report pain (Roth et al., 2005). Pain may be related to trigeminal neuralgia, tonic spasms, continuous dysesthetic pain, acute radicular pain, optic neuritis, muscle cramps, headache and back pain. Motor disturbances may include paraparesis, hemiparesis, horizontal diplopia, difficulty with visually tracking high-speed objects and dizziness upon lateral gaze secondary to internuclear ophthalmoplegia (Table 22.1).

Cognitive Symptoms

The prevalence of cognitive dysfunction in MS is about 40–65% (Rao et al., 1993). Cognitive impairment is more prevalent and severe in men versus women (Donaldson et al., 2019). Cognitive decline often begins early in the course (Lyon-Caen et al.,

Table 22.1 Frequency (*f*) of MS symptoms

Symptom	*f* (%)
Sensory symptoms of limbs	30.7
Vision loss	15.9
Motor symptoms (subacute)	8.9
Diplopia	6.8
Gait disturbance	4.8
Motor symptoms (acute)	4.3
Balance problems	2.9
Sensory symptoms of face	2.8

Adapted from Olek (2005)

1986) and worsens with age and degree of cortical lesion burden (Calabrese et al., 2009) and white matter hyperintensity load (De Meo et al., 2021; Rao et al., 1989). However, there is mounting research that demonstrates that it is not only overall lesion burden, but also anatomical lesion location that is predictive of the debilitating symptoms associated with MS, including cognition (Altermatt et al. 2018).

Cognitive Symptom Profile Information processing speed and episodic memory are most commonly affected in MS, in addition to working memory, executive functioning, verbal fluency and visuospatial functioning (Amato et al. 1995, 2001; Benedict et al., 2006; Brochet & Ruet, 2019; Deloire et al., 2011; Rao et al., 1993; Rao, Leo, Bernardinet al., 1991; Ryan et al., 1996). Slow processing speed is commonly regarded as the key component underlying other cognitive deficits in MS. Slow and variable processing speed on testing are hallmarks of early cognitive changes in MS (Eilam-Stock et al., 2021). Slow processing speed may exacerbate or factor into low scores on tests in other cognitive domains. Arnett (2004) found that fewer MS patients performed poorly on a measure of story memory when the stories were presented at a slower rate. Other studies have also demonstrated that MS patients performed similar to controls on cognitive tasks when they were given adequate time to process the test stimuli (Demaree et al., 1999; Lengenfelder et al., 2006).

Memory impairment has been linked to damage to memory circuitry connecting the hippocampus, parahippocampus, fornix and cingulate (Kletenik et al., 2023). Verbal memory deficits have been associated with thalamic volume loss (Kern et al., 2014; Tremblay et al., 2018) and hippocampal atrophy (De Meo et al., 2021). It is notable that processing speed and early verbal memory impairments have also been shown to be predictive of greater disability later in the disease course (Deloire et al., 2010).

Working memory deficits are also commonly seen in individuals with MS (De Meo et al., 2021; Rao, Leo, Bernadin et al., 1991), with research noting general volume loss in neocortical gray matter as a possible underlying mechanism, though white matter integrity has also been implicated for more severe deficits (De Meo et al., 2021). In individuals with multi-domain cognitive deficits, poorer cognitive performance has also been linked to cortical volume loss, with the degree of global atrophy being highly correlated with severity of cognitive deficits (De Meo et al. 2021).

Cognitive Symptom Course Cognitive decline often starts early in the course of MS. Greater cognitive impairment severity is associated with greater age, disease duration and conversion to progressive MS (Amato et al., 2006; Brochet et al., 2022; Huijbregts et al., 2004; Ruano et al., 2017; Ruet et al., 2013; Wu et al., 2024). In a large cross-sectional study, cognition was preserved in 25% of early stage RRMS, 19% of late stage RRMS and 7% of PPMS cases (De Meo et al., 2021).

In a cross-sectional study of cognitive changes based on disease duration, researchers noted that within 5 years of disease onset, 20.9% of MS patients demonstrated cognitive declines characterized by performance 1 standard deviation below average and 6% had cognitive decline characterized by performance 2 standard deviations below average. When observing those who reported 10 years after disease onset, these values had increased to 29.3% and 9%, respectively (Achiron et al., 2013). A longitudinal study of cognitive functioning in MS patients that followed 50 patients across 10 years found no impairments in 74% of the initially recruited participants, moderate impairments in 8% and severe impairments in 18% (Amato et al., 2001). After a 10-year period, 45 of the original 50 patients were reassessed with researchers finding that 44% showed no significant impairments, 34% had moderate impairments and 22% had severe impairments (Amato et al., 2001). While there is a general trend of decline in cognitive functioning over time, there are significant differences between individual patients in terms of disease course and other modifying factors that may reduce risks of MS-related exacerbations. A greater magnitude of overall cognitive impairment has been demonstrated in SPMS and PPMS relative to RRMS, with deficits in SPMS exceeding those seen in PPMS (Brochet et al., 2022; Cavaco et al., 2022; De Meo et al., 2021; Huijbregts et al., 2004). Very little research regarding the cognitive profile of the PRMS phenotype exists, given that it is a much less common presentation of MS. A small body of research has suggested that functional deficits and outcomes are generally very similar to profiles seen in PPMS (Kremenchutzky et al., 1999; Tullman et al., 2004) (Table 22.2).

Key Points: Cognitive Changes in MS

- Information processing speed and episodic memory are most commonly impacted.
- Working memory, executive functioning, verbal fluency, visuospatial functioning may also be impacted.
- Other cognitive changes can occur, depending on anatomical sites of MS lesions.
- Progressive phenotypes show similar cognitive profile with increased severity of deficits.

Cognitive Symptoms in Pediatric-Onset MS The literature on pediatric-onset MS (POMS) is sparse given the very low prevalence of POMS (about 3% of MS cases; Chitnis et al., 2009) examining cognitive deficits and the impact of inflammation and demyelination on brain development, especially in the context of myelinogenesis that typically occurs during the post-natal period all the way through early adulthood. A review of the literature by Tan et al. (2018) outlines cognitive profiles in pediatric-onset MS and other demyelinating disorders noting that there are important differences in the outcomes for pediatric versus adult-onset MS (see Table 22.3). Blaschek et al. (2012) identified linguistic abilities as a notable difference in cognitive profiles between pediatric and adult populations, suggesting that language dysfunction may have significant functional consequences given the emphasis that is placed on verbal abilities during later academic years. Importantly, these studies highlight considerations for how outcomes in childhood onset

Table 22.2 Cognitive impairments in different MS phenotypes

	MS phenotypes				
Cognitive domain	RIS	CIS	RRMS	SPMS	PPMS
Processing speed	+	+	++	++	++
Attention & working memory[a]	–	–/+	+	++	++
Visuospatial	–	–	–	–/+	–
Language[b]	–	–/+	+	–/+	–
Verbal learning & memory	–/+	+	++	++	+
Visual learning & memory	–/+	+	++	++	–
Executive functioning	–	–/+	–/+	+	+

RIS, radiographically isolated syndrome; CIS, clinically isolated syndrome; RRMS, relapsing-remitting MS; SPMS, secondary progressive MS; PPMS, primary progressive MS; ++, typically present; +, often present; –/+, sometimes present; –, not present or not included in reviewed studies

Note:

[a]Attention/working memory was usually measured by PASAT

[b]Language skills typically measured with a verbal fluency task

Table 22.3 Cognitive profiles in pediatric-onset demyelinating disorders

	Pediatric demyelinating disorders			
Cognitive domain	MS	ADEM	NMO	TM
Visuomotor	+	–/+	++	+
Processing speed	++	++	–	–/+
Attention & working memory	++	++	+	+
Visuospatial	++	++	++	+
Language	++	++	+	–/+
Verbal learning & memory	++	++	+	+
Visual learning & memory	++	+	–	–
Executive functioning	++	+	+	+

MS, multiple sclerosis; ADEM, acute demyelinating encephalomyelitis; NMO, neuromyelitis optica; TM, transverse myelitis; ++, typically present; +, often present; –/+, sometimes present; –, not present or not included in reviewed studies

demyelinating diseases may reflect reduced developmental gains in children and noted that better neuropsychological outcomes for children with older age of onset may be a function of being further along in the development process (Blaschek et al., 2012; Tan et al., 2018).

Cognitive Symptoms and Cognitive Reserve Despite the chronic nature of MS, some research has suggested that greater cognitive reserve is a protective factor that may attenuate cognitive dysfunction, especially during earlier stages of the disease (Benedict et al., 2010; Sumowski et al., 2014). A study by Sumowski et al. (2013) investigated brain reserve (i.e., maximal lifetime brain volume) and cognitive reserve (i.e., level of early intellectual enrichment) in individuals with MS. They found that increased brain reserve was associated with less cognitive inefficiency, while increased cognitive reserve was associated with less disease-related cognitive impairment independently of brain reserve (Sumowski et al., 2013). However, the protective nature of cognitive reserve has been found to diminish with progression of disease course (Rocca et al., 2019).

Cognitive Symptoms and Functional Reorganization Many MS patients, especially early on in the course, may not have any cognitive symptoms despite having positive MR findings. Functional MRI (fMRI) research has shown considerable evidence to suggest that, to some extent, functional reorganization or recruitment of cortical regions occurs, especially during early stages of the MS disease (Nasios et al., 2020). Some researchers have suggested that differences in functional connectivity seen across time in MS patients may represent an adaptive mechanism in response to neuroinflammation that helps to preserve global brain efficiency (Fleischer et al., 2019; Koubiyr et al., 2020). Adaptive functional organization changes in the brain are associated with limiting the clinical expression of MS-related cognitive impairments (Cader et al., 2006). However, review of the literature suggests that this ability to reorganize and recruit additional areas of the brain is not universal across all individuals with MS, and while some individuals may remain cognitively intact for extended periods of time following diagnosis, there are also a number of individuals who present with cognitive deficits early on (Nasios et al., 2020).

Fatigue and Sleep Symptoms

Fatigue is the most common and often the most debilitating symptom of MS (Giovannoni, 2006; Patejdl & Zettl, 2022; Rommer et al., 2019) and can significantly impact performance on neuropsychological measures. In fact, MS patients performance on cognitive measures that were repeated worsened following an effortful cognitive task, while controls demonstrated the inverse relationship, such that their performance improved on cognitive measures that were repeated (Krupp & Elkins, 2000). Fatigue has been shown to be predictive of reduced cognitive performance beyond what might be expected related to anxiety/depression symptoms or disease progression (Guillemin et al., 2022), and has been demonstrated through induced cognitive and physical effort to assess the impact of fatigue on cognitive performance in MS patients (Claros-Salinas et al., 2013).

Sleep disturbance negatively impacts memory (Sumowski et al., 2021) and attention and information processing speed among people with MS (Hughes et al., 2018). Poor sleep is twice as prevalent in MS patients compared to controls and can be due to a variety of factors, including pain, depression, medication side effects and nocturnal movement disorders (Lobentanz et al., 2004).

Mood Symptoms

Major depressive disorder (MDD) is the most common psychiatric comorbidity of MS (DeLuca et al., 1994; Deluca & Johnson, 1993; Krupp et al., 1994; Rao et al., 1992), with a lifetime prevalence of about 50% (Siegert & Abernethy, 2005). It may be difficult to detect depression among people with MS since both syndromes present with the same or similar symptoms such as fatigue and poor concentration. Frustration and irritability are more common than feelings of worthlessness, guilt, apathy in individuals with MS and comorbid MDD (Feinstein, 2004).

Findings are mixed concerning differences in anxiety and depression symptoms in PPMS versus RRMS, with some studies showing negligible differences (Johnen et al., 2017) and some noting increased incidence of depressive symptoms in PPMS compared to RRMS (Jones et al., 2012). Brain lesions and psychosocial issues are considered risk factors for mood disturbance, while physical disability does not appear to be closely associated with depression (Goldman Consensus Group, 2005). Arnett et al. (1999) found that deficits in attention and processing speed were related to changes in affect and personality. Poor executive functioning has also linked with depressed mood in MS patients, suggesting that mood disturbance may be due to a disruption of frontal-subcortical pathways (Anderson et al., 2023; Arnett et al., 1999). In addition to this, verbal learning and memory in individuals with MS have been connected to mood related symptoms such as anhedonia, with researchers suggesting that more detailed assessment of depression may be important in these patients (Hoffmeister et al., 2021). Fortunately, mood disturbance associated with MS can be treated. Cognitive Behavioral Therapy (CBT) has been found to have a similar, positive effect to antidepressant medications (Mohr et al., 2001), and both treatments have been found to help improve quality of life (Hart et al., 2005).

Daily Functional Impacts

MS significantly impacts daily functioning (Rao, Leo, Ellington, et al., 1991). The rates of unemployment are high in MS, with some estimates as high as 70–80% just 5 years after diagnosis (Kornblith et al., 1986). Employment status for individuals with MS has been shown to be impacted by not only increased cognitive complaints, but also by reduced workplace support, higher depression and fatigue (van Egmond et al., 2024). In a longitudinal study that followed individuals with MS over 2 years, changes in physical functioning and declines in executive functioning abilities were predictive of reduced employment status (van Gorp et al., 2019). This predictive relationship between cognitive decline and employment status has also been demonstrated with processing speed changes (Jaworski et al., 2023). In addition to objective measures that assess cognitive change over time, self-reported cognitive impairment has been associated with lower vocational and health outcomes even after controlling for secondary factors like fatigue and depression (Lancia et al., 2024). Importantly, degree of cognitive impairment has been shown to have a direct impact on quality of life as well (Nabizadeh et al., 2022). Some studies have also raised concern regarding driving safety in MS patients with cognitive dysfunction since cognitive dysfunction is associated with poor driving skills and greater motor vehicle accident rates (Shawaryn et al., 2002).

Neuropsychological Assessment

Interest in cognitive assessment as part of a multidisciplinary approach to clinical management of MS has become more prominent in recent years due to the growing body of research that shows a direct correlation between presence of cognitive impairments and poorer long-term MS-related outcomes, including increased disability (Benedict et al., 2020; Meca-Lallana et al., 2021; Wu et al., 2024) and reduced survivability (Cavaco et al., 2022).

Reasons for Referral

Cognitive assessment for people with MS is important for establishing a pretreatment baseline, for informing medical treatment planning and prognosis (Deloire et al., 2010; Labiano-Fontcuberta et al., 2016; Zipoli et al., 2010) and for assisting with capacity determinations.

The assessment of cognitive functioning varies depending on the reason the MS patient is being referred for neuropsychological evaluation. Often, MS patients are referred for an evaluation in order to establish a baseline before treatment and to monitor disease progression. At other times, an evaluation is helpful in determining the reasons for difficulties at work and/or home and in determining whether changes in treatment approach are necessary. Many times, a neuropsychological evaluation is needed to determine one's work capacity and/or application for disability. Therefore, the length and depth of the evaluation may differ based on the purpose of the assessment. While some of these referral questions require comprehensive evaluation to best characterize one's cognitive status, patients with MS may fatigue easily and have difficulty tolerating testing sessions that last several hours. Extensive test batteries are not always necessary to answer referral questions. Screening batteries may be sufficient in some cases and can be a starting point for referral for more comprehensive evaluation when necessary.

Neuropsychological Test Batteries for MS

MACFIMS In 2001, an international panel was convened in order to develop an ideal, minimal record of neuropsychological function (Benedict et al. 2002). The panel developed a 90-minute neuropsychological battery called the Minimal Assessment of Cognitive Function in MS (MACFIMS). The MACFIMS is composed of seven tests designed to assess the cognitive domains commonly affected in MS (see Table 22.4). The tests included in this consensus battery are the Paced Auditory Serial Addition Task (working memory/processing speed), Symbol Digit Modalities Test (processing speed), California Verbal Learning Test-II (verbal memory), Brief Visual Memory Test-Revised (visual memory), Judgment of Line Orientation (visuospatial perception), Controlled Oral Word Test (verbal fluency/executive functioning) and Sorting subtest from DKEFS (executive functioning/novel). To date, this well-validated test battery continues to be widely utilized as a standard for validation of other briefer screening iterations.

Neuronorma Battery, Basso and Colleagues Screener, & BRB-N There are other brief neuropsychological batteries that have been suggested and/or validated for assessment of cognitive functioning in individuals with MS. This includes slightly longer batteries such as the Neuronorma Battery which was developed with a Spanish population to assess various neuropsychological concerns, but has been validated for the assessment of cognition in individuals with MS (Matías-Guiu et al., 2020), an MS screening battery proposed by Basso et al. (1996) and the Rao Brief Repeatable Battery of Neuropsychological Tests in MS (BRB-N; Rao, 1990). These batteries offer more detailed assessment of multiple domains, with the Spanish-normed Neuronorma battery representing the most comprehensive (and longest) of these.

Other Brief Screeners There are also much briefer (i.e., from 5 to 30 min screens that have been proposed, including the Brief International Cognitive Assessment for MS (BICAMS; Langdon et al., 2012), the Brief Computerized Cognitive Assessment in Multiple Sclerosis (BCCAMS; Maubeuge et al., 2022) and the TRACK-MS screen (Taranu et al., 2022). These screening batteries were designed for rapid and repeatable assessment of cognitive changes in individuals with MS. While abbreviated screening batteries are not considered a comprehensive assessment of cognition, they may be useful in helping practitioners to identify when more comprehensive neuropsychological assessment may be needed (see Table 22.5). Another method for addressing assessment of cognitive dysfunction is the use of the MS Neuropsychological Questionnaire, which is a brief screening questionnaire that can be completed by patients and/or collateral informants in the clinical setting (Benedict et al., 2003). Unlike the batteries of objective measures described above, this measure assesses subjective experience (or observed changes in the case of collateral informant) to assist the clinician in management of these symptoms. A high rate of cognitive complaints would likely trigger more comprehensive neuropsychological evaluation to better appreciate the concerns and to assist with treatment planning.

Table 22.4 Abbreviated neuropsychological assessment batteries for characterization of cognitive deficits in individuals with MS

Domain	Test	Battery			
		MACFIMS 90 mins.	Neuronorma 150 mins.	Basso 50 mins.	BRB-N 50 mins.
Processing Speed & Working Memory	PASAT	X			X
	SDMT	X	X		X
	DSF		X		
	DSB		X		
	Corsi's Test		X		
	TMT		X		
	SCWT C & W		X		
	SSRT			X	
Verbal/Auditory Learning/Memory	CVLT-2	X			X
	SRT		X		
	WMS-R LM			X	
Visual/Spatial Learning/Memory	BVMT-R	X			X
	ROFCT		X		
Language	COWAT	X		X	
	BNT		X		
	Verbal fluency		X		
	WLG				X
Visuospatial	JLO	X	X		
Executive Functioning	D-KEFS Sorting	X			
	SCWT C/W		X		
	ToL		X		
	TMT-B		X		
	SCWT C/W		X		
Sensory Perceptual Functioning	Graphethesia & Astereognosis Measures			X	

Note: MACFIMS, Minimal Assessment of Cognitive Function in Multiple Sclerosis; Basso, Cognitive screening battery by Basso et al. (1996); BRB-N, Brief Repeatable Battery of Neuropsychological Tests in MS; PASAT, Paced Auditory Serial Addition Test; SDMT, Symbol Digit Modalities Test; DSF, Digit Span Forward; DSB, Digit Span Backward; TMT-A, Trail-Making Test, part A; SCWT, Stroop Color Word Test, Color Trial and Word Trial; SSRT, Seashore Rhythm Test; CVLT-2, California Verbal Learning Test, second edition; SRT, Selective Remind Test; WMS-R LM, Wechsler Memory Scale-Revised, Logical Memory; ROCFT, Rey-Osterrieth Complex Figure Test; COWAT, Controlled Oral Word Associations Test; BNT, Boston Naming Test; WLG, Word List Generation; JLO, Judgment of Line Orientation; D-KEFS, Delis-Kaplan Executive Function System; SCWT, Stroop Color Word Test; ToL, Tower of London; SCWT C/W, Stroop Color Wort Test, Color/Word Trial

Secondary Factors of MS That Influence Cognitive Test Performance

Secondary factors of MS impact cognitive test performance and should be accommodated when possible and considered when interpreting cognitive performance test scores. While a brief screen of cognitive functions (e.g., Mini Mental State Exam) may miss or under appreciate the cognitive deficits that can be associated with MS, long and comprehensive evaluations can sometimes be difficult for MS

Table 22.5 Brief screening batteries for identification of cognitive deficits in MS

Domain	Test	Battery BICAMS 30 mins.	BCCAMS 15 mins.	TRACK-MS 5 mins.
Information Processing Speed/Working Memory	SDMT	X		X
	CSCT		X	
Verbal/Auditory Learning/Memory	CVLT-2	X		
	CVLT-M		X	
Visual/Spatial Learning/memory	BVMT-R	X		
	CEVMT		X	
Language	WLG	X		
	COWAT			X

BICAMS, Brief International Cognitive Assessment for MS; BCCAMS, Brief Computerized Cognitive Assessment in Multiple Sclerosis; SDMT, Symbol Digit Modalities Test; CSCT, Computerized Speech Cognitive Test; CVLT-2, California Verbal Learning Test, second edition; BVMT-R, Brief Visuospatial Memory Test, revised; CEVMT, Computerized Episodic Visual Memory Test; WLG, Word List Generation; COWAT, Controlled Oral Word Association Test

patients to tolerate due to issues such as fatigue and pain. The clinician is encouraged to carefully consider the reason for evaluation and to assess accordingly. In cases where the referral question relates to the individual's ability to work or engage in learning (i.e., academic assessment for accommodations in school), a more comprehensive evaluation is often necessary. Routine monitoring may require less time. Objective assessment of cognitive abilities, neuropsychiatric symptoms and clinical data related to disease duration and comorbidities has proven to be important in the evaluation of capacity to work above and beyond limitations related to physical disability (Renner et al., 2020). Therefore, a thorough assessment in these situations is warranted. In some cases, it may be prudent to complete extended testing across multiple testing sessions to limit the effects of fatigue.

Testing Considerations

While it is important for the clinician to characterize the nature and severity of cognitive problems, assessment of other issues such as depression, poor sleep pain and fatigue via clinical interview and symptom self-report measures may be helpful when developing treatment recommendations. Additionally, the importance of behavioral observations during interview and testing cannot be overstated. Clinicians should be careful to watch for indications of testing interference related to secondary factors (e.g., fatigue, pain, etcetera) on an examinee's performance and may need to train their psychometrists to watch for these signs as well. With any situation of repeat cognitive testing, clinicians must also consider issues such as test–retest reliability and practice effects in the interpretation of results. Finally, it is important to consider that the time and resource costs of comprehensive neuropsychological assessment may preclude routine neuropsychological assessment from the standard of care in MS medical clinics (Sumowski et al., 2018). Sumowski and colleagues noted that the ecological validity of conventional neuropsychological tests for characterizing typical MS difficulties is also a concern, since daily functioning does not occur in the context of a sterile, quiet testing environment.

Management of Neuropsychological Symptoms of MS

In the last two decades a significant body of research focused on pharmacological treatment of cognitive deficits in MS patients has emerged. Results of research are extremely inconsistent with some reporting benefit and others reporting no benefits, but the majority of these studies have focused on a few different classes of medications including disease modifying therapies (DMTs), acetylcholinesterase inhibitors, CNS stimulants and fampridine. While a full review of these studies is outside of the scope of this chapter, some trends have emerged that may continue to guide future research.

Medications for Neuropsychological Symptoms of MS

Disease Modifying Therapies Evidence of cognitive improvement related to use of disease modifying therapies (DMTs) commonly used in treatment of MS remains highly variable though there has been some compelling evidence of small improvements in cognitive functioning related to platform therapies such as β-interferon, glatiramer acetate, dimethyl fumarate and teriflunomide and escalation therapies such as fingolimod, alemtuzumab, rituximab, cyclophosphamide and natalizumab (Landmeyer et al., 2020). These findings are overall inconsistent and do not presently provide quality support for these medications as a treatment specifically for cognitive decline (Chen et al., 2020; Landmeyer et al., 2020). However, these medications are certainly important in prevention of MS exacerbations, and as such may be preventative of cognitive decline by nature of preventing development of new lesions.

Stimulant Medications Stimulant medications such as amphetamine salts, methylphenidate and lisdexamfetamine dimesylate have also shown highly mixed but promising results, though the extremely high variability in outcomes across studies as well as variability in study quality suggests that more research is needed to provide a more consistent understanding of how MS patient can benefit from these medications (Chen et al., 2020; Motavalli et al., 2020).

Though not a stimulant medication, some work with SNRI medications, which are sometimes utilized in place of stimulants in other conditions (e.g., ADHD), such as atomoxetine (Strattera), have also shown promise as a possible area of future research for treating cognitive deficits in MS. A recent study showed benefit to cognitive functioning in an RCT of atomoxetine (Mohammadian Nejad et al., 2023).

Acetylcholinesterase Inhibitor and NMDA Receptor Antagonist Medications Medications used for treatment of cognitive deficits in dementia patients such as donepezil, rivastigmine and memantine have undergone several high quality trials that demonstrated little to no improvement in cognitive functioning for individuals with MS (Chen et al., 2020; Motavalli et al., 2020).

Potassium Channel Blocker Fampridine, a potassium channel blocker which is primarily used to treat walking difficulties in individuals with MS, has shown more consistent evidence of cognitive improvement across trials (Chen et al., 2020; Motavalli et al., 2020), though more class I trials are needed to confirm efficacy as a primary treatment of cognitive symptoms of MS.

Other Medications Other medication classes and supplements have also been studied, though less frequently and with highly variable reported efficacy, for example modafinil/armodafinil, recombinant human erythropoietin (EPO), simvastatin, atorvastatin, methylprednisolone and estrogen supplementation (Chen et al., 2020), as well as vitamin D supplementation and herbal remedies such as Achillea millefolium and Boswellia papyrifera (Motavalli et al., 2020). Studies examining amantadine, pemoline and ginkgo biloba showed no effects (Chen et al., 2020; Motavalli et al., 2020). Across all of these trials, the primary areas of cognitive functioning that were studied usually focused on processing speed and memory difficulties, inconsistently looking at other domains of cognitive functioning. In studies that reported improvements, it is also important to note that while there were statistically significant differences in cognitive scores pre- and post-medication trials, these differences may not always constitute a clinically meaningful difference in cognitive performance.

Cognitive Rehabilitation

In addition to the abundance of research into pharmacological treatment of cognitive issues in MS, there has also been an incipient and rapidly growing interest in rehabilitative therapies to address cognitive dysfunction in individuals with MS. These therapies are focused on strategies aimed at helping patients adapt and cope with cognitive dysfunction A recent review of research from 2013 through 2021 found that studies of individual, in-person cognitive rehabilitation using the modified story memory technique (m-SMT) showed evidence of good efficacy in improving learning in MS patients, as well as improving verbal episodic memory, though there was no evidence of generalization to other domains of cognitive functioning (Brochet, 2021).

Studies examining individualized cognitive rehabilitation that utilized intensive training over a period of weeks (and for several hours a week) have shown the most promise in terms of improving cognitive functioning across multiple domains, though it is notable that the feasibility of this type of therapy may be limited as it requires a substantial commitment from patients and practitioners (Brochet, 2021). Group rehabilitation studies have shown greater feasibility, but also had more variable results with some studies showing no benefit to cognitive functioning or quality of life measures following interventions (Brochet, 2021).

Studies utilizing computerized cognitive training with individuals with MS have shown promise, with a meta-analysis showing small to medium effect sizes across computerized cognitive rehabilitation studies in the areas of processing speed, memory and executive functioning skills, though these improvements diminished over time when individuals stopped therapies (Lampit et al., 2019). Efficacy of these computerized cognitive therapy programs was also shown in a review completed by Brochet (2021), who suggested that these programs may additionally offer some benefits in terms of feasibility of implementation due to accessibility (i.e., patients can access from home without the need to travel to a facility) and ease of use.

Brochet (2021) and Benedict et al. (2020) offer more in-depth descriptions of recently studied computerized cognitive rehabilitation programs. Cognitive behavioral interventions are presently the most beneficial treatment for MS-related cognitive decline based on the available body of research (Benedict et al., 2017).

Exercise therapy is another area of research that has shown some promise in improving cognitive deficits and improving outcomes when combined with other treatment modalities, though results remain quite inconclusive due to methodological concerns (Benedict et al., 2020).

The purview of neuropsychologists in treating individuals with MS primarily lies in the identification of cognitive problems through standardized assessment, treatment of cognitive problems after-the-fact through rehabilitative strategies and assisting in care planning through recommendations and provision of patient/family education. While neuropsychologist may see patients only after cognitive problems have arisen, they may still have a role in promoting primary prevention strategies to help limit or slow further decline in cognitive functioning.

Some targets of primary prevention for cognitive problems might include promoting behavioral, cognitive and motivational strategies to facilitate medication adherence, healthy lifestyle choices, management of comorbid psychological concerns or other moderating factors that may impact not only cognition, but also quality of life. Sumowski et al. (2018) discussed primary prevention as an important piece of holistic prevention and treatment of cognitive changes for patients with MS. These are areas where neuropsychologist can assist in providing information, training or helping patients to get connected with appropriate care providers.

References

Achiron, A., Chapman, J., Magalashvili, D., Dolev, M., Lavie, M., Bercovich, E., Polliack, M., Doniger, G. M., Stern, Y., Khilkevich, O., Menascu, S., Hararai, G., Gurevich, M., & Barak, Y. (2013). Modeling of cognitive impairment by disease duration in multiple sclerosis: A cross-sectional study. *PLoS One, 8*(8), Article e71058. https://doi.org/10.1371/journal.pone.0071058

Altermatt, A., Gaetano, L., Magon, S., Häring, D. A., Tomic, D., Wuerfel, J., Radue, E. W., Kappos, L., & Sprenger, T. (2018). Clinical correlations of brain lesion location in multiple sclerosis: Voxel-based analysis of a large clinical trial dataset. *Brain Topography, 31*(5), 886–894. https://doi.org/10.1007/s10548-018-0652-9

Amato, M. P., Ponziani, G., Pracucci, G., Bracco, L., Siracusa, G., & Amaducci, L. (1995). Cognitive impairment in early-onset multiple sclerosis. Pattern, predictors, and impact on everyday life in a 4-year follow-up. *Archives of Neurology, 52*(2), 168–172. https://doi.org/10.1001/archneur.1995.00540260072019

Amato, M. P., Ponziani, G., Siracusa, G., & Sorbi, S. (2001). Cognitive dysfunction in early-onset multiple sclerosis: A reappraisal after 10 years. *Archives of Neurology, 58*(10), 1602–1606. https://doi.org/10.1001/archneur.58.10.1602

Amato, M. P., Zipoli, V., & Portaccio, E. (2006). Multiple sclerosis-related cognitive changes: A review of cross-sectional and longitudinal studies. *Journal of The Neurological Sciences, 245*(1-2), 41–46. https://doi.org/10.1016/j.jns.2005.08.019

Anderson, J. R., Fitzgerald, K. C., Murrough, J. W., Katz Sand, I. B., Sorets, T. R., Krieger, S. C., Riley, C. S., Fabian, M. T., & Sumowski, J. F. (2023). Depression symptoms and cognition in multiple sclerosis: Longitudinal evidence of a specific link to executive control. *Multiple Sclerosis, 29*(13), 1632–1645. https://doi.org/10.1177/13524585231198746

Arnett, P. A. (2004). Speed of presentation influences story recall in college students and persons with multiple sclerosis. *Archives of Clinical Neuropsychology, 19*(4), 507–523. https://doi.org/10.1016/j.acn.2003.07.006

Arnett, P. A., Higginson, C. I., Voss, W. D., Wright, B., Bender, W. I., Wurst, J. M., & Tippin, J. M. (1999). Depressed mood in multiple sclerosis: Relationship to capacity-demanding memory and attentional functioning. *Neuropsychology, 13*(3), 434–446. https://doi.org/10.1037/0894-4105.13.3.434

Barzegar, M., Najdaghi, S., Afshari-Safavi, A., Nehzat, N., Mirmosayyeb, O., & Shaygannejad, V. (2021). Early predictors of conversion to secondary progressive multiple sclerosis. *Multiple Sclerosis and Related Disorders, 54*, Article 103115. https://doi.org/10.1016/j.msard.2021.103115

Basso, M. R., Beason-Hazen, S., Lynn, J., Rammohan, K., & Bornstein, R. A. (1996). Screening for cognitive dysfunction in multiple sclerosis. *Archives of Neurology, 53*(10), 980–984. https://doi.org/10.1001/archneur.1996.00550100046014

Beatty, W. W., & Aupperle, R. L. (2002). Sex differences in cognitive impairment in multiple sclerosis. *The Clinical Neuropsychologist, 16*(4), 472–480. https://doi.org/10.1076/clin.16.4.472.13904

Benedict, R. H. B., Amato, M. P., DeLuca, J., & Geurts, J. J. G. (2020). Cognitive impairment in multiple sclerosis: Clinical management, MRI, and therapeutic avenues. *The Lancet Neurology, 19*(10), 860–871. https://doi.org/10.1016/S1474-4422(20)30277-5

Benedict, R. H. B., Cookfair, D., Gavett, R., Gunther, M., Munschauer, F., Garg, N., & Weinstock-Guttman, B. (2006). Validity of the minimal assessment of cognitive function in multiple sclerosis (MACFIMS). *Journal of the International Neuropsychological Society, 12*(4), 549–558.

Benedict, R. H. B., DeLuca, J., Enzinger, C., Geurts, J. J. G., Krupp, L. B., & Rao, S. M. (2017). Neuropsychology of multiple sclerosis: Looking back and moving forward. *Journal of the International Neuropsychological Society, 23*(9-10), 832–842. https://doi.org/10.1017/S1355617717000959

Benedict, R. H. B., Fischer, J. S., Archibald, C. J., Arnett, P. A., Beatty, W. W., Bobholz, J., Chelune, G. J., Fisk, J. D., Langdon, D. W., Caruso, L., Foley, F., LaRocca, N. G., Vowels, L.,

Weinstein, A., DeLuca, J., Rao, S. M., & Munschauer, F. (2002). Minimal neuropsychological assessment of MS patients: a consensus approach. *The Clinical Neuropsychologist, 16*(3), 381–397. https://doi.org/10.1076/clin.16.3.381.13859

Benedict, R. H. B., Morrow, S. A., Weinstock Guttman, B., Cookfair, D., & Schretlen, D. J. (2010). Cognitive reserve moderates decline in information processing speed in multiple sclerosis patients. *Journal of the International Neuropsychological Society, 16*(5), 829–835. https://doi.org/10.1017/S1355617710000688

Benedict, R. H. B., Munschauer, F., Linn, R., Miller, C., Murphy, E., Foley, F., & Jacobs, L. (2003). Screening for multiple sclerosis cognitive impairment using a self-administered 15-item questionnaire. *Multiple Sclerosis, 9*(1), 95–101. https://doi.org/10.1191/1352458503ms861oa

Blaschek, A., Storm van's Gravesande, K., Heinen, F., Pritsch, M., Mall, V., & Calabrese, P. (2012). Neuropsychological aspects of childhood multiple sclerosis: An overview. *Neuropediatrics, 43*(4), 176–183. https://doi.org/10.1055/s-0032-1315429

Brochet, B. (2021). Cognitive rehabilitation in multiple sclerosis in the period from 2013 and 2021: A narrative review. *Brain Sciences, 12*(1), Article 55. https://doi.org/10.3390/brainsci12010055

Brochet, B., Clavelou, P., Defer, G., De Seze, J., Louapre, C., Magnin, E., Ruet, A., Thomas-Anterion, C., & Vermersch, P. (2022). Cognitive impairment in secondary progressive multiple sclerosis: Effect of disease duration, age, and progressive phenotype. *Brain Sciences, 12*(2), Article 183. https://doi.org/10.3390/brainsci12020183

Brochet, B., & Ruet, A. (2019). Cognitive impairment in multiple sclerosis with regards to disease duration and clinical phenotypes. *Frontiers in Neurology, 10*, Article 261. https://doi.org/10.3389/fneur.2019.00261

Bulman, D. E., Sadovnick, A. D., & Ebers, G. C. (1991). Age of onset in siblings concordant for multiple sclerosis. *Brain, 114*(2), 937–950.

Cader, S., Cifelli, A., Abu-Omar, Y., Palace, J., & Matthews, P. M. (2006). Reduced brain functional reserve and altered functional connectivity in patients with multiple sclerosis. *Brain, 129*(2), 527–537. https://doi.org/10.1093/brain/awh670

Calabrese, M., Agosta, F., Rinaldi, F., Mattisi, I., Grossi, P., Favaretto, A., Atzori, M., Bernardi, V., Barachino, L., Rinaldi, L., Perini, P., Gallo, P., & Filippi, M. (2009). Cortical lesions and atrophy associated with cognitive impairment in relapsing-remitting multiple sclerosis. *Archives of Neurology, 66*(9), 1144–1150. https://doi.org/10.1001/archneurol.2009.174

Cavaco, S., Ferreira, I., Moreira, I., Santos, E., Samões, R., Sousa, A. P., Pinheiro, J., Teixeira-Pinto, A., & Martins da Silva, A. (2022). Cognitive dysfunction and mortality in multiple sclerosis: Long-term retrospective review. *Multiple Sclerosis, 28*(9), 1382–1391. https://doi.org/10.1177/13524585211066598

Chen, M. H., Goverover, Y., Genova, H. M., & DeLuca, J. (2020). Cognitive efficacy of pharmacologic treatments in multiple sclerosis: A systematic review. *CNS Drugs, 34*(6), 599–628. https://doi.org/10.1007/s40263-020-00734-4

Chitnis, T., Glanz, B., Jaffin, S., & Healy, B. (2009). Demographics of pediatric-onset multiple sclerosis in an MS center population from the northeastern United States. *Multiple sclerosis, 15*(5), 627–631. https://doi.org/10.1177/1352458508101933

Claros-Salinas, D., Dittmer, N., Neumann, M., Sehle, A., Spiteri, S., Willmes, K., Schoenfeld, M. A., & Dettmers, C. (2013). Induction of cognitive fatigue in MS patients through cognitive and physical load. *Neuropsychological Rehabilitation, 23*(2), 182–201. https://doi.org/10.1080/09602011.2012.726925

Compston, A., & Coles, A. (2002). Multiple sclerosis. *Lancet, 359*(9313), 1221–1231. https://doi.org/10.1016/S0140-6736(02)08220-X

Dawson, J. W. (1916). The histology of disseminated sclerosis. *Edinburgh Medical Journal, 17*(5), 311–344.

Deloire, M., Ruet, A., Hamel, D., Bonnet, M., & Brochet, B. (2010). Early cognitive impairment in multiple sclerosis predicts disability outcome several years later. *Multiple Sclerosis, 16*(5), 581–587. https://doi.org/10.1177/1352458510362819

Deloire, M. S., Ruet, A., Hamel, D., Bonnet, M., Dousset, V., & Brochet, B. (2011). MRI predictors of cognitive outcome in early multiple sclerosis. *Neurology, 76*(13), 1161–1167. https://doi.org/10.1212/WNL.0b013e318212a8be

DeLuca, J., Barbieri-Berger, S., & Johnson, S. (1994). The nature of memory impairments in multiple sclerosis: Acquisition versus retrieval. *Journal of Clinical and Experimental Neuropsychology, 16*(2), 183–189. https://doi.org/10.1080/01688639408402629

Deluca, J., & Johnson, S. K. (1993). Cognitive impairments in multiple sclerosis: Implications for rehabilitation. *NeuroRehabilitation, 3*(4), 9–16. https://doi.org/10.3233/NRE-1993-3404

Demaree, H., DeLuca, J., Gaudino, E., & Diamond, B. J. (1999). Speed of information processing as a key deficit in multiple sclerosis: Implications for rehabilitation. *Journal of Neurology, Neurosurgery and Psychiatry, 67*(5), 661–663. https://doi.org/10.1136/jnnp.67.5.661

De Meo, E., Portaccio, E., Giorgio, A., Ruano, L., Goretti, B., Niccolai, C., Patti, F., Chisari, C. G., Gallo, P., Grossi, P., Ghezzi, A., Roscio, M., Mattioli, F., Stampatori, C., Simone, M., Viterbo, R. G., Bonacchi, R., Rocca, M. A., De Stefano, N., Filippi, M., … Amato, M. P. (2021). Identifying the distinct cognitive phenotypes in multiple sclerosis. *JAMA Neurology*, *78*(4), 414–425. https://doi.org/10.1001/jamaneurol.2020.4920.

D'hooghe, M. B., Nagels, G., & Uitdehaag, B. M. (2010). Long-term effects of childbirth in MS. *Journal of Neurology, Neurosurgery, and Psychiatry, 81*(1), 38–41. https://doi.org/10.1136/jnnp.2008.163816

Donaldson, E., Patel, V. P., Shammi, P., & Feinstein, A. (2019). Why sex matters: A cognitive study of people with multiple sclerosis. *Cognitive and Behavioral Neurology, 32*(1), 39–45. https://doi.org/10.1097/WNN.0000000000000188

Doolittle, T. H., Myers, R. H., Lehrich, J. R., Birnbaum, G., Sheremata, W., Franklin, G. M., Nelson, L. M., & Hauser, S. L. (1990). Multiple sclerosis sibling pairs: clustered onset and familial predisposition. *Neurology, 40*(10), 1546–1546.

Eilam-Stock, T., Shaw, M. T., Krupp, L. B., & Charvet, L. E. (2021). Early neuropsychological markers of cognitive involvement in multiple sclerosis. *Journal of the Neurological Sciences, 423*, Article 117349. https://doi.org/10.1016/j.jns.2021.117349

Eshaghi, A., Marinescu, R. V., Young, A. L., Firth, N. C., Prados, F., Jorge Cardoso, M., Tur, C., De Angelis, F., Cawley, N., Brownlee, W. J., De Stefano, N., Laura Stromillo, M., Battaglini, M., Ruggieri, S., Gasperini, C., Filippi, M., Rocca, M. A., Rovira, A., Sastre-Garriga, J., … Ciccarelli, O. (2018). Progression of regional grey matter atrophy in multiple sclerosis. *Brain, 141*(6), 1665–1677. https://doi.org/10.1093/brain/awy088.

Feinstein, A. (2004). The neuropsychiatry of multiple sclerosis. *Canadian Journal of Psychiatry, 49*(3), 157–163. https://doi.org/10.1177/070674370404900302

Fleischer, V., Koirala, N., Droby, A., Gracien, R. M., Deichmann, R., Ziemann, U., Meuth, S. G., Muthuraman, M., Zipp, F., & Groppa, S. (2019). Longitudinal cortical network reorganization in early relapsing-remitting multiple sclerosis. *Therapeutic Advances in Neurological Disorders, 12*, Article 1756286419838673. https://doi.org/10.1177/1756286419838673

Futatsuya, K., Kakeda, S., Yoneda, T., Ueda, I., Watanabe, K., Moriya, J., Murakami, Y., Ide, S., Ogasawara, A., Ohnari, N., Okada, K., Adachi, H., & Korogi, Y. (2016). Juxtacortical lesions in multiple sclerosis: Assessment of gray matter involvement using phase difference-enhanced imaging (PADRE). *Magnetic Resonance in Medical Sciences, 15*(4), 349–354. https://doi.org/10.2463/mrms.mp.2015-0099

Gardener, H., Munger, K., Chitnis, T., Spiegelman, D., & Ascherio, A. (2009). The relationship between handedness and risk of multiple sclerosis. *Multiple Sclerosis, 15*(5), 587–592. https://doi.org/10.1177/1352458509102622

Geraldes, R., Ciccarelli, O., Barkhof, F., De Stefano, N., Enzinger, C., Filippi, M., Hofer, M., Paul, F., Preziosa, P., Rovira, A., DeLuca, G. C., Kappos, L., Yousry, T., Fazekas, F., Frederiksen, J., Gasperini, C., Sastre-Garriga, J., Evangelou, N., Palace, J., & MAGNIMS Study Group. (2018). The current role of MRI in differentiating multiple sclerosis from its imaging mimics. *Nature Reviews Neurology, 14*(4), 199–213. https://doi.org/10.1038/nrneurol.2018.14

Geurts, J. J., Bö, L., Roosendaal, S. D., Hazes, T., Daniëls, R., Barkhof, F., Witter, M. P., Huitinga, I., & van der Valk, P. (2007). Extensive hippocampal demyelination in multiple sclerosis. *Journal of Neuropathology and Experimental Neurology, 66*(9), 819–827. https://doi.org/10.1097/nen.0b013e3181461f54

Gilmore, C. P., DeLuca, G. C., Bö, L., Owens, T., Lowe, J., Esiri, M. M., & Evangelou, N. (2009). Spinal cord neuronal pathology in multiple sclerosis. *Brain Pathology, 19*(4), 642–649. https://doi.org/10.1111/j.1750-3639.2008.00228.x

Gilmore, C. P., Donaldson, I., Bö, L., Owens, T., Lowe, J., & Evangelou, N. (2009). Regional variations in the extent and pattern of grey matter demyelination in multiple sclerosis: a comparison between the cerebral cortex, cerebellar cortex, deep grey matter nuclei and the spinal cord. *Journal of Neurology, Neurosurgery, and Psychiatry, 80*(2), 182–187. https://doi.org/10.1136/jnnp.2008.148767

Gilmore, C. P., Geurts, J. J., Evangelou, N., Bot, J. C., van Schijndel, R. A., Pouwels, P. J., Barkhof, F., & Bö, L. (2009). Spinal cord grey matter lesions in multiple sclerosis detected by post-mortem high field MR imaging. *Multiple Sclerosis, 15*(2), 180–188. https://doi.org/10.1177/1352458508096876

Giovannoni, G. (2006). Multiple sclerosis related fatigue. *Journal of Neurology, Neurosurgery, and Psychiatry, 77*(1), 2–3. https://doi.org/10.1136/jnnp.2005.074948

Goldman Consensus Group. (2005). The Goldman consensus statement on depression in multiple sclerosis. *Multiple Sclerosis, 11*(3), 328–337. https://doi.org/10.1191/1352458505ms1162oa

Guillemin, C., Lommers, E., Delrue, G., Gester, E., Maquet, P., & Collette, F. (2022). The complex interplay between trait fatigue and cognition in multiple sclerosis. *Psychologica Belgica, 62*(1), 108–122. https://doi.org/10.5334/pb.1125

Haider, L., Simeonidou, C., Steinberger, G., Hametner, S., Grigoriadis, N., Deretzi, G., Kovacs, G. G., Kutzelnigg, A., Lassmann, H., & Frischer, J. M. (2014). Multiple sclerosis deep grey matter: The relation between demyelination, neurodegeneration, inflammation and iron. *Journal of Neurology, Neurosurgery, and Psychiatry, 85*(12), 1386–1395. https://doi.org/10.1136/jnnp-2014-307712

Hart, S., Fonareva, I., Merluzzi, N., & Mohr, D. C. (2005). Treatment for depression and its relationship to improvement in quality of life and psychological well-being in multiple sclerosis patients. *Quality of Life Research, 14*(3), 695–703. https://doi.org/10.1007/s11136-004-1364-z

Hittle, M., Culpepper, W. J., Langer-Gould, A., Marrie, R. A., Cutter, G. R., Kaye, W. E., Wagner, L., Topol, B., LaRocca, N. G., Nelson, L. M., & Wallin, M. T. (2023). Population-based estimates for the prevalence of multiple sclerosis in the United States by race, ethnicity, age, sex, and geographic region. *JAMA Neurology, 80*(7), 693–701. https://doi.org/10.1001/jamaneurol.2023.1135

Hoffmeister, J., Basso, M. R., Reynolds, B., Whiteside, D., Mulligan, R., Arnett, P. A., & Combs, D. R. (2021). Effects of diminished positive mood and depressed mood upon verbal learning and memory among people with multiple sclerosis. *Journal of Clinical and Experimental Neuropsychology, 43*(2), 117–128. https://doi.org/10.1080/13803395.2020.1853066

Hughes, A. J., Dunn, K. M., & Chaffee, T. (2018). Sleep disturbance and cognitive dysfunction in multiple sclerosis: A systematic review. *Current Neurology and Neuroscience Reports, 18*(1), Article 2. https://doi.org/10.1007/s11910-018-0809-7

Huijbregts, S. C., Kalkers, N. F., de Sonneville, L. M., de Groot, V., Reuling, I. E., & Polman, C. H. (2004). Differences in cognitive impairment of relapsing remitting, secondary, and primary progressive MS. *Neurology, 63*(2), 335–339. https://doi.org/10.1212/01.wnl.0000129828.03714.90

Jaworski, M. G., 3rd, Gillies, J. K., Youngs, M., Wojcik, C., Santivasci, C., Jakimovski, D., Bergsland, N., Weinstock-Guttman, B., & Benedict, R. H. (2023). Predicting employment deterioration with the Processing Speed Test (PST) and SDMT in multiple sclerosis. *Multiple Sclerosis, 29*(10), 1327–1336. https://doi.org/10.1177/13524585231187283

Johnen, A., Landmeyer, N. C., Bürkner, P. C., Wiendl, H., Meuth, S. G., & Holling, H. (2017). Distinct cognitive impairments in different disease courses of multiple sclerosis: A systematic review and meta-analysis. *Neuroscience and Biobehavioral Reviews, 83*, 568–578. https://doi.org/10.1016/j.neubiorev.2017.09.005

Jones, K. H., Ford, D. V., Jones, P. A., John, A., Middleton, R. M., Lockhart-Jones, H., Osborne, L. A., & Noble, J. G. (2012). A large-scale study of anxiety and depression in people with multiple sclerosis: A survey via the web portal of the UK MS Register. *PLoS One, 7*(7), Article e41910. https://doi.org/10.1371/journal.pone.0041910

Joy, J. E., & Johnston, R. B. (Eds.). (2001). *Multiple sclerosis: Current status and strategies for the future*. National Academies Press. https://doi.org/10.17226/10031

Kern, K. C., Gold, S. M., Lee, B., Montag, M., Horsfall, J., O'Connor, M. F., & Sicotte, N. L. (2014). Thalamic-hippocampal-prefrontal disruption in relapsing-remitting multiple sclerosis. *NeuroImage: Clinical, 8*, 440–447. https://doi.org/10.1016/j.nicl.2014.12.015

Kletenik, I., Cohen, A. L., Glanz, B. I., Ferguson, M. A., Tauhid, S., Li, J., Drew, W., Polgar-Turcsanyi, M., Palotai, M., Siddiqi, S. H., Marshall, G. A., Chitnis, T., Guttmann, C. R. G., Bakshi, R., & Fox, M. D. (2023). Multiple sclerosis lesions that impair memory map to a connected memory circuit. *Journal of Neurology, 270*(11), 5211–5222. https://doi.org/10.1007/s00415-023-11907-8

Koch-Henriksen, N., & Sorensen, P. S. (2011). Why does the north-south gradient of incidence of multiple sclerosis seem to have disappeared on the northern hemisphere? *Journal of the Neurological Sciences, 311*(1-2), 58–63. https://doi.org/10.1016/j.jns.2011.09.003

Kornblith, A. B., La Rocca, N. G., & Baum, H. M. (1986). Employment in individuals with multiple sclerosis. *International Journal of Rehabilitation Research, 9*(2), 155–165. https://doi.org/10.1097/00004356-198606000-00006

Koubiyr, I., Deloire, M., Besson, P., Coupé, P., Dulau, C., Pelletier, J., Tourdias, T., Audoin, B., Brochet, B., Ranjeva, J. P., & Ruet, A. (2020). Longitudinal study of functional brain network reorganization in clinically isolated syndrome. *Multiple Sclerosis, 26*(2), 188–200. https://doi.org/10.1177/1352458518813108

Kremenchutzky, M., Cottrell, D., Rice, G., Hader, W., Baskerville, J., Koopman, W., & Ebers, G. C. (1999). The natural history of multiple sclerosis: A geographically based study. 7. Progressive-relapsing and relapsing-progressive multiple sclerosis: A re-evaluation. *Brain, 122*(10), 1941–1950. https://doi.org/10.1093/brain/122.10.1941

Krupp, L. B., & Elkins, L. E. (2000). Fatigue and declines in cognitive functioning in multiple sclerosis. *Neurology, 55*(7), 934–939. https://doi.org/10.1212/wnl.55.7.934

Krupp, L. B., Sliwinski, M., Masur, D. M., Friedberg, F., & Coyle, P. K. (1994). Cognitive functioning and depression in patients with chronic fatigue syndrome and multiple sclerosis. *Archives of Neurology, 51*(7), 705–710. https://doi.org/10.1001/archneur.1994.00540190089021

Kurtzke, J. F. (2000). Epidemiology of multiple sclerosis. Does this really point toward an etiology? Lectio Doctoralis. *Neurological Sciences, 21*(6), 383–403. https://doi.org/10.1007/s100720070055

Kutzelnigg, A., Faber-Rod, J. C., Bauer, J., Lucchinetti, C. F., Sorensen, P. S., Laursen, H., Stadelmann, C., Brück, W., Rauschka, H., Schmidbauer, M., & Lassmann, H. (2007). Widespread demyelination in the cerebellar cortex in multiple sclerosis. *Brain Pathology, 17*(1), 38–44. https://doi.org/10.1111/j.1750-3639.2006.00041.x

Kutzelnigg, A., Lucchinetti, C. F., Stadelmann, C., Brück, W., Rauschka, H., Bergmann, M., Schmidbauer, M., Parisi, J. E., & Lassmann, H. (2005). Cortical demyelination and diffuse white matter injury in multiple sclerosis. *Brain, 128*(11), 2705–2712. https://doi.org/10.1093/brain/awh641

Labiano-Fontcuberta, A., Martínez-Ginés, M. L., Aladro, Y., Ayuso, L., Mitchell, A. J., Puertas-Martín, V., Cerezo, M., Higueras, Y., & Benito-León, J. (2016). A comparison study of cognitive deficits in radiologically and clinically isolated syndromes. *Multiple Sclerosis, 22*(2), 250–253. https://doi.org/10.1177/1352458515591072

Lampit, A., Heine, J., Finke, C., Barnett, M. H., Valenzuela, M., Wolf, A., Leung, I. H. K., & Hill, N. T. M. (2019). Computerized Cognitive Training in Multiple Sclerosis: A systematic review and meta-analysis. *Neurorehabilitation and Neural Repair, 33*(9), 695–706. https://doi.org/10.1177/1545968319860490

Lancia, S., Marrie, R. A., Cutter, G., Fox, R. J., & Salter, A. (2024). Association of patient-reported cognitive impairment with quality of life and employment in multiple sclerosis. *Multiple Sclerosis and Related Disorders, 87*, Article 105675. https://doi.org/10.1016/j.msard.2024.105675

Landmeyer, N. C., Bürkner, P. C., Wiendl, H., Ruck, T., Hartung, H. P., Holling, H., Meuth, S. G., & Johnen, A. (2020). Disease-modifying treatments and cognition in relapsing-remitting multiple sclerosis: A meta-analysis. *Neurology, 94*(22), e2373–e2383. https://doi.org/10.1212/WNL.0000000000009522

Langdon, D. W., Amato, M. P., Boringa, J., Brochet, B., Foley, F., Fredrikson, S., Hämäläinen, P., Hartung, H. P., Krupp, L., Penner, I. K., Reder, A. T., & Benedict, R. H. (2012). Recommendations for a Brief International Cognitive Assessment for Multiple Sclerosis (BICAMS). *Multiple Sclerosis, 18*(6), 891–898. https://doi.org/10.1177/1352458511431076

Lassmann, H. (2018). Multiple sclerosis pathology. *Cold Spring Harbor Perspectives in Medicine, 8*(3), Article a028936. https://doi.org/10.1101/cshperspect.a028936

Lengenfelder, J., Bryant, D., Diamond, B. J., Kalmar, J. H., Moore, N. B., & DeLuca, J. (2006). Processing speed interacts with working memory efficiency in multiple sclerosis. *Archives of Clinical Neuropsychology, 21*(3), 229–238. https://doi.org/10.1016/j.acn.2005.12.001

Liguori, M., Marrosu, M. G., Pugliatti, M., Giuliani, F., De Robertis, F., Cocco, E., Zimatore, G. B., Livrea, P., & Trojano, M. (2000). Age at onset in multiple sclerosis. *Neurological Sciences, 21*(4), S825–S829. https://doi.org/10.1007/s100720070020

Lobentanz, I. S., Asenbaum, S., Vass, K., Sauter, C., Klösch, G., Kollegger, H., Kristoferitsch, W., & Zeitlhofer, J. (2004). Factors influencing quality of life in multiple sclerosis patients: disability, depressive mood, fatigue and sleep quality. *Acta Neurologica Scandinavica, 110*(1), 6–13. https://doi.org/10.1111/j.1600-0404.2004.00257.x

Lublin, F. D., Reingold, S. C., & National Multiple Sclerosis Society (USA) Advisory Committee on Clinical Trials of New Agents in Multiple Sclerosis. (1996). Defining the clinical course of multiple sclerosis: Results of an international survey. *Neurology, 46*(4), 907–911. https://doi.org/10.1212/wnl.46.4.907

Lyon-Caen, O., Jouvent, R., Hauser, S., Chaunu, M. P., Benoit, N., Widlöcher, D., & Lhermitte, F. (1986). Cognitive function in recent-onset demyelinating diseases. *Archives of Neurology, 43*(11), 1138–1141. https://doi.org/10.1001/archneur.1986.00520110034010

Matías-Guiu, J. A., Sánchez-Benavides, G., Rivera-Àvila, N., Cortés-Martínez, A., Delgado-Alonso, C., Delgado-Álvarez, A., Montero, P., Pytel, V., Matías-Guiu, J., & Peña-Casanova, J. (2020). Validation of the Neuronorma battery for neuropsychological assessment in multiple sclerosis. *Multiple Sclerosis and Related Disorders, 42*, Article 102070. https://doi.org/10.1016/j.msard.2020.102070

Maubeuge, N., Deloire, M. S., Brochet, B., Charré-Morin, J., Saubusse, A., & Ruet, A. (2022). Validation of a Brief Computerized Cognitive Assessment in Multiple Sclerosis (BCCAMS) and comparison with reference batteries. *Multiple Sclerosis, 28*(7), 1112–1120. https://doi.org/10.1177/13524585211054006

McGinley, M. P., Goldschmidt, C. H., & Rae-Grant, A. D. (2021). Diagnosis and treatment of multiple sclerosis: a review. *JAMA, 325*(8), 765–779.

Meca-Lallana, V., Gascón-Giménez, F., Ginestal-López, R. C., Higueras, Y., Téllez-Lara, N., Carreres-Polo, J., Eichau-Madueño, S., Romero-Imbroda, J., Vidal-Jordana, Á., & Pérez-Miralles, F. (2021). Cognitive impairment in multiple sclerosis: Diagnosis and monitoring. *Neurological Sciences, 42*(12), 5183–5193. https://doi.org/10.1007/s10072-021-05165-7

Mohammadian Nejad, E., Amouzadeh, E., Kashipazha, D., Shamsaei, G., & Cheraghian, B. (2023). The effect of atomoxetine on cognitive function in patients with multiple sclerosis. *Current Journal of Neurology, 22*(3), 149–154. https://doi.org/10.18502/cjn.v22i3.13792

Mohr, D. C., Boudewyn, A. C., Goodkin, D. E., Bostrom, A., & Epstein, L. (2001). Comparative outcomes for individual cognitive-behavior therapy, supportive-expressive group psychotherapy, and sertraline for the treatment of depression in multiple sclerosis. *Journal of Consulting and Clinical Psychology, 69*(6), 942–949.

Motavalli, A., Majdi, A., Hosseini, L., Talebi, M., Mahmoudi, J., Hosseini, S. H., & Sadigh-Eteghad, S. (2020). Pharmacotherapy in multiple sclerosis-induced cognitive impairment: A systematic review and meta-analysis. *Multiple Sclerosis and Related Disorders, 46*, Article 102478. https://doi.org/10.1016/j.msard.2020.102478

Nabizadeh, F., Balabandian, M., Rostami, M. R., Owji, M., Sahraian, M. A., Bidadian, M., Ghadiri, F., Rezaeimanesh, N., & Moghadasi, A. N. (2022). Association of cognitive impairment and quality of life in patients with multiple sclerosis: A cross-sectional study. *Current Journal of Neurology, 21*(3), 144–150. https://doi.org/10.18502/cjn.v21i3.11106

Nasios, G., Bakirtzis, C., & Messinis, L. (2020). Cognitive impairment and brain reorganization in MS: underlying mechanisms and the role of neurorehabilitation. *Frontiers in Neurology, 11*, Article 147. https://doi.org/10.3389/fneur.2020.00147

Olek, M. J. (Ed.). (2005). *Multiple sclerosis: Etiology, diagnosis, and new treatment strategies*. Humana Press.

Patejdl, R., & Zettl, U. K. (2022). The pathophysiology of motor fatigue and fatigability in multiple sclerosis. *Frontiers in Neurology, 13*, Article 891415. https://doi.org/10.3389/fneur.2022.891415

Pitt, D., Lo, C. H., Gauthier, S. A., Hickman, R. A., Longbrake, E., Airas, L. M., Mao-Draayer, Y., Riley, C., De Jager, P. L., Wesley, S., Boster, A., Topalli, I., Bagnato, F., Mansoor, M., Stuve, O., Kister, I., Pelletier, D., Stathopoulos, P., Dutta, R., & Lincoln, M. R. (2022). Toward precision phenotyping of multiple sclerosis. *Neurology, Neuroimmunology & Neuroinflammation, 9*(6), Article e200025. https://doi.org/10.1212/NXI.0000000000200025

Polliack, M. L., Barak, Y., & Achiron, A. (2001). Late-onset multiple sclerosis. *Journal of the American Geriatrics Society, 49*(2), 168–171. https://doi.org/10.1046/j.1532-5415.2001.49038.x

Prosperini, L., Lucchini, M., Ruggieri, S., Tortorella, C., Haggiag, S., Mirabella, M., Pozzilli, C., & Gasperini, C. (2022). Shift of multiple sclerosis onset towards older age. *Journal of Neurology, Neurosurgery & Psychiatry, 93*(10), 1137–1139.

Rao, S. M. (1990). *A manual for the brief repeatable battery of neuropsychological test in multiple sclerosis*. Medical College of Wisconsin.

Rao, S. M., Grafman, J., DiGiulio, D., Mittenberg, W., Bernardin, L., Leo, G. J., Luchetta, T., & Unverzagt, F. (1993). Memory dysfunction in multiple sclerosis: Its relation to working memory, semantic encoding, and implicit learning. *Neuropsychology, 7*(3), 364–374. https://doi.org/10.1037/0894-4105.7.3.364

Rao, S. M., Huber, S. J., & Bornstein, R. A. (1992). Emotional changes with multiple sclerosis and Parkinson's disease. *Journal of Consulting and Clinical Psychology, 60*(3), 369–378. https://doi.org/10.1037/0022-006x.60.3.369

Rao, S. M., Leo, G. J., Bernardin, L., & Unverzagt, F. (1991). Cognitive dysfunction in multiple sclerosis. I. Frequency, patterns, and prediction. *Neurology, 41*(5), 685–691. https://doi.org/10.1212/wnl.41.5.685

Rao, S. M., Leo, G. J., Ellington, L., Nauertz, T., Bernardin, L., & Unverzagt, F. (1991). Cognitive dysfunction in multiple sclerosis. II. Impact on employment and social functioning. *Neurology, 41*(5), 692–696. https://doi.org/10.1212/wnl.41.5.692

Rao, S. M., Leo, G. J., Haughton, V. M., St Aubin-Faubert, P., & Bernardin, L. (1989). Correlation of magnetic resonance imaging with neuropsychological testing in multiple sclerosis. *Neurology, 39*(2), 161–166. https://doi.org/10.1212/wnl.39.2.161

Reipert, B. (2004). Multiple sclerosis: A short review of the disease and its differences between men and women. *Journal of Men's Health and Gender, 1*(4), 334–340. https://doi.org/10.1016/j.jmhg.2004.10.005

Renner, A., Baetge, S. J., Filser, M., & Penner, I. K. (2020). Working ability in individuals with different disease courses of multiple sclerosis: Factors beyond physical impairment. *Multiple Sclerosis and Related Disorders, 46*, Article 102559. https://doi.org/10.1016/j.msard.2020.102559

Rocca, M. A., Riccitelli, G. C., Meani, A., Pagani, E., Del Sette, P., Martinelli, V., Comi, G., Falini, A., & Filippi, M. (2019). Cognitive reserve, cognition, and regional brain damage in MS: A 2-year longitudinal study. *Multiple Sclerosis, 25*(3), 372–381. https://doi.org/10.1177/1352458517750767

Rommer, P. S., Eichstädt, K., Ellenberger, D., Flachenecker, P., Friede, T., Haas, J., Kleinschnitz, C., Pöhlau, D., Rienhoff, O., Stahmann, A., & Zettl, U. K. (2019). Symptomatology and symptomatic treatment in multiple sclerosis: Results from a nationwide MS registry. *Multiple Sclerosis, 25*(12), 1641–1652. https://doi.org/10.1177/1352458518799580

Rosati, G. (2001). The prevalence of multiple sclerosis in the world: An update. *Neurological Sciences, 22*(2), 117–139. https://doi.org/10.1007/s100720170011

Roth, R. S., Geisser, M. E., Theisen-Goodvich, M., & Dixon, P. J. (2005). Cognitive complaints are associated with depression, fatigue, female sex, and pain catastrophizing in patients with chronic pain. *Archives of Physical Medicine and Rehabilitation, 86*(6), 1147–1154. https://doi.org/10.1016/j.apmr.2004.10.041

Ruano, L., Portaccio, E., Goretti, B., Niccolai, C., Severo, M., Patti, F., Cilia, S., Gallo, P., Grossi, P., Ghezzi, A., Roscio, M., Mattioli, F., Stampatori, C., Trojano, M., Viterbo, R. G., & Amato, M. P. (2017). Age and disability drive cognitive impairment in multiple sclerosis across disease subtypes. *Multiple Sclerosis, 23*(9), 1258–1267. https://doi.org/10.1177/1352458516674367

Ruet, A., Deloire, M. S., Charré-Morin, J., Hamel, D., & Brochet, B. (2013). A new computerised cognitive test for the detection of information processing speed impairment in multiple sclerosis. *Multiple Sclerosis, 19*(12), 1665–1672. https://doi.org/10.1177/1352458513480251

Ryan, L., Clark, C. M., Klonoff, H., Li, D., & Paty, D. (1996). Patterns of cognitive impairment in relapsing–remitting multiple sclerosis and their relationship to neuropathology on magnetic resonance images. *Neuropsychology, 10*(2), 176–193. https://doi.org/10.1037/0894-4105.10.2.176

Shawaryn, M. A., Schultheis, M. T., Garay, E., & Deluca, J. (2002). Assessing functional status: exploring the relationship between the multiple sclerosis functional composite and driving. *Archives of Physical Medicine and Rehabilitation, 83*(8), 1123–1129. https://doi.org/10.1053/apmr.2002.33730

Siegert, R. J., & Abernethy, D. A. (2005). Depression in multiple sclerosis: A review. *Journal of Neurology, Neurosurgery, and Psychiatry, 76*(4), 469–475. https://doi.org/10.1136/jnnp.2004.054635

Soldan, S. S., & Lieberman, P. M. (2023). Epstein-Barr virus and multiple sclerosis. *Nature Reviews Microbiology, 21*(1), 51–64. https://doi.org/10.1038/s41579-022-00770-5

Sumowski, J. F., Benedict, R., Enzinger, C., Filippi, M., Geurts, J. J., Hamalainen, P., Hulst, H., Inglese, M., Leavitt, V. M., Rocca, M. A., Rosti-Otajarvi, E. M., & Rao, S. (2018). Cognition in multiple sclerosis: State of the field and priorities for the future. *Neurology, 90*(6), 278–288. https://doi.org/10.1212/WNL.0000000000004977

Sumowski, J. F., Horng, S., Brandstadter, R., Krieger, S., Leavitt, V. M., Katz Sand, I., Fabian, M., Klineova, S., Graney, R., Riley, C. S., Lublin, F. D., Miller, A. E., & Varga, A. W. (2021). Sleep disturbance and memory dysfunction in early multiple sclerosis. *Annals of Clinical and Translational Neurology, 8*(6), 1172–1182. https://doi.org/10.1002/acn3.51262

Sumowski, J. F., Rocca, M. A., Leavitt, V. M., Dackovic, J., Mesaros, S., Drulovic, J., DeLuca, J., & Filippi, M. (2014). Brain reserve and cognitive reserve protect against cognitive decline over 4.5 years in MS. *Neurology, 82*(20), 1776–1783. https://doi.org/10.1212/WNL.0000000000000433

Sumowski, J. F., Rocca, M. A., Leavitt, V. M., Riccitelli, G., Comi, G., DeLuca, J., & Filippi, M. (2013). Brain reserve and cognitive reserve in multiple sclerosis: What you've got and how you use it. *Neurology, 80*(24), 2186–2193. https://doi.org/10.1212/WNL.0b013e318296e98b

Tan, A., Hague, C., Greenberg, B. M., & Harder, L. (2018). Neuropsychological outcomes of pediatric demyelinating diseases: A review. *Child Neuropsychology, 24*(5), 575–597. https://doi.org/10.1080/09297049.2017.1339785

Taranu, D., Tumani, H., Holbrook, J., Tumani, V., Uttner, I., & Fissler, P. (2022). The TRACK-MS Test Battery: A very brief tool to track multiple sclerosis-related cognitive impairment. *Biomedicines, 10*(11), Article 2975. https://doi.org/10.3390/biomedicines10112975

Tremblay, A., Jobin, C., Demers, M., Dagenais, E., Narayanan, S., Araújo, D., Douglas, A. L., Roger, E., Chamelian, L., Duquette, P., & Rouleau, I. (2018). Thalamic and hippocampal volume associated with memory functions in multiple sclerosis. *Brain and Cognition, 125*, 61–68. https://doi.org/10.1016/j.bandc.2018.05.013

Trojano, M., Avolio, C., Manzari, C., Calò, A., De Robertis, F., Serio, G., & Livrea, P. (1995). Multivariate analysis of predictive factors of multiple sclerosis course with a validated method to assess clinical events. *Journal of Neurology, Neurosurgery, and Psychiatry, 58*(3), 300–306. https://doi.org/10.1136/jnnp.58.3.300

Tullman, M. J., Oshinsky, R. J., Lublin, F. D., & Cutter, G. R. (2004). Clinical characteristics of progressive relapsing multiple sclerosis. *Multiple Sclerosis, 10*(4), 451–454. https://doi.org/10.1191/1352458504ms1059oa

van Egmond, E. E. A., van der Hiele, K., de Rooij, M. J., van Gorp, D. A. M., Jongen, P. J., van der Klink, J. J. L., Reneman, M. F., Beenakker, E. A. C., van Eijk, J. J. J., Frequin, S. T. F. M., de Gans, K., Hoitsma, E., Gerlach, O. H. H., Mostert, J. P., Verhagen, W. I. M., Visser, L. H., & Middelkoop, H. A. M. (2024). Longitudinal determinants of employment status in people with relapsing-remitting multiple sclerosis. *IBRO Neuroscience Reports, 16*, 518–526. https://doi.org/10.1016/j.ibneur.2024.04.002

van Gorp, D. A. M., van der Hiele, K., Heerings, M. A. P., Jongen, P. J., van der Klink, J. J. L., Reneman, M. F., Arnoldus, E. P. J., Beenakker, E. A. C., van Eijk, J. J. J., Frequin, S. T. F. M., de Gans, K., Hoitsma, E., Mostert, J. P., Verhagen, W. I. M., Zemel, D., Visser, L. H., & Middelkoop, H. A. M. (2019). Cognitive functioning as a predictor of employment status in relapsing-remitting multiple sclerosis: A 2-year longitudinal study. *Neurological Sciences, 40*(12), 2555–2564. https://doi.org/10.1016/j.ibneur.2024.04.002

van Noort, J. M., Baker, D., Kipp, M., & Amor, S. (2023). The pathogenesis of multiple sclerosis: A series of unfortunate events. *Clinical and Experimental Immunology, 214*(1), 1–17. https://doi.org/10.1093/cei/uxad075

Vercellino, M., Masera, S., Lorenzatti, M., Condello, C., Merola, A., Mattioda, A., Tribolo, A., Capello, E., Mancardi, G. L., Mutani, R., Giordana, M. T., & Cavalla, P. (2009). Demyelination, inflammation, and neurodegeneration in multiple sclerosis deep gray matter. *Journal of Neuropathology and Experimental Neurology, 68*(5), 489–502. https://doi.org/10.1097/NEN.0b013e3181a19a5a

Vollmer, T. L. (1999). Multiple sclerosis: The disease and its diagnosis. In S. van den Noort & N. J. Holland (Eds.), *Multiple sclerosis in clinical practice* (pp. 1–22). Demos Medical.

Wu, W., Francis, H., Lucien, A., Wheeler, T. A., & Gandy, M. (2024). The prevalence of cognitive impairment in relapsing-remitting multiple sclerosis: A systematic review and meta-analysis. *Neuropsychology Review* . Advance online publication. https://doi.org/10.1007/s11065-024-09640-8

Zéphir, H. (2018). Progress in understanding the pathophysiology of multiple sclerosis. *Revue Neurologique, 174*(6), 358–363. https://doi.org/10.1016/j.neurol.2018.03.006

Zipoli, V., Goretti, B., Hakiki, B., Siracusa, G., Sorbi, S., Portaccio, E., & Amato, M. P. (2010). Cognitive impairment predicts conversion to multiple sclerosis in clinically isolated syndromes. *Multiple Sclerosis, 16*(1), 62–67. https://doi.org/10.1177/1352458509350311

Chapter 23
Sport-Related Concussion

Grant L. Iverson and Julia E. Maietta

Introduction

A sport-related concussion, by definition, is a mild traumatic brain injury (Davis, Patricios, Schneider, et al., 2023; Patricios, Schneider, Dvorak, et al., 2023; Silverberg et al., 2023). New diagnostic criteria for mild TBI, including sport-related concussion, were published in 2023 (Silverberg et al., 2023). Signs of concussion are observable by another person (e.g., a teammate, coach, family member or athletic trainer). Symptoms of concussion are subjective—they are experienced and reported by the injured athlete. Observable clinical signs of concussion include loss of consciousness (i.e., being "knocked out"), post-traumatic amnesia (i.e., complete or partial loss of memory for events following the injury) and alterations

G. L. Iverson (✉)
Department of Physical Medicine and Rehabilitation, Harvard Medical School, Boston, MA, USA

Department of Physical Medicine and Rehabilitation, Spaulding Rehabilitation Hospital, Boston, MA, USA

Schoen Adams Research Institute at Spaulding Rehabilitation, Boston, MA, USA

Mass General for Children Sports Concussion Program, Boston, MA, USA

Home Base, A Red Sox Foundation and Massachusetts General Hospital Program, Boston, MA, USA
e-mail: GIverson@mgh.harvard.edu

J. E. Maietta
Department of Physical Medicine and Rehabilitation, Harvard Medical School, Boston, MA, USA

Department of Physical Medicine and Rehabilitation, Spaulding Rehabilitation, Boston, MA, USA

Mass General for Children Sports Concussion Program, Boston, MA, USA

M. R. Schoenberg, J. G. Scott (eds.), *The Little Black Book of Neuropsychology*, https://doi.org/10.1007/978-3-032-07777-6_23

in mental status (e.g., slowness to respond to questions or disorientation to time, place or situation) (Silverberg et al., 2023) (see Fig. 23.1). Observable signs of concussion, or a suspected concussion, based on video review during televised professional sporting events, include no protective action when falling, lying motionless on the ground or ice, tonic posturing, motor incoordination or ataxia upon standing and a blank or vacant stare (Davis et al., 2019). Acute clinical symptoms experienced and reported by the injured athlete include an acute subjective alteration in

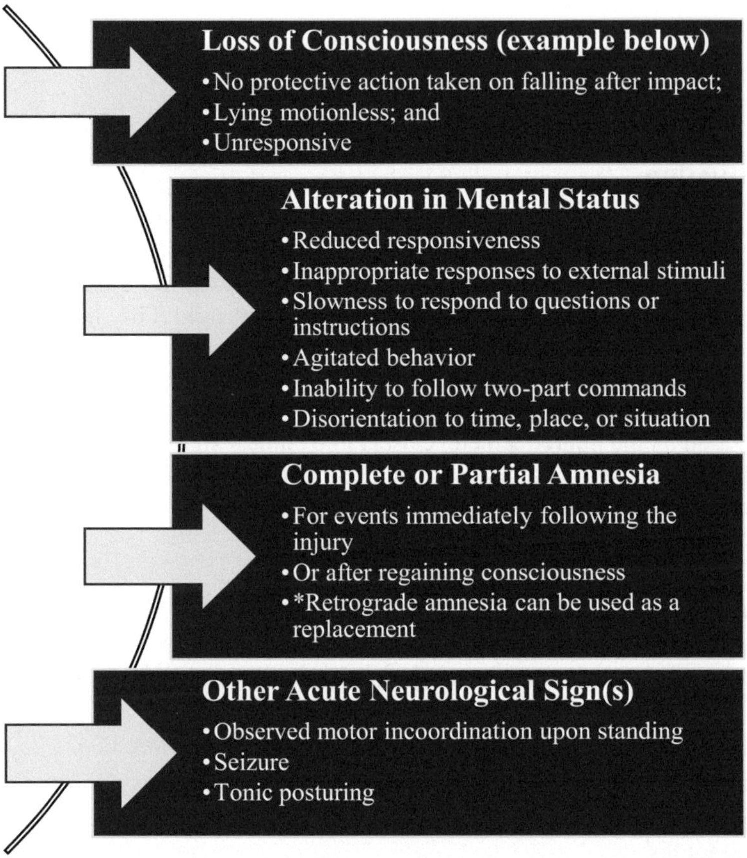

Fig. 23.1 Clinical signs used in the ACRM diagnostic criteria for mild TBI [one or more clinical signs (criterion 2) attributable to brain injury] (Silverberg et al., 2023). Note: The presence of one (or more) of these four clinical signs, following a plausible mechanism of injury and not attributable to some other factor, is sufficient for diagnosing the injury. The example for loss of consciousness is inferred from a video review of the impact. Asterisk: If post-traumatic amnesia cannot be reliably assessed, retrograde amnesia (i.e., a gap in memory for events immediately preceding the injury) can be used as a replacement for this criterion. The criteria illustrated in this figure and in Fig. 23.2 are derived from The American Congress of Rehabilitation Medicine Diagnostic Criteria for Mild Traumatic Brain Injury. Arch Phys Med Rehabil. 2023 Aug;104(8):1343–1355. doi: 10.1016/j.apmr.2023.03.036 (Silverberg et al., 2023)

mental status (e.g., feeling confused or dazed), physical symptoms (e.g., headaches, dizziness or sensitivity to light or noise), cognitive symptoms (e.g., feeling slowed down, "mental fog" or difficulty concentrating) and emotional symptoms (e.g., irritability) (Silverberg et al., 2023) (see Fig. 23.2).

Concussions are a relatively common injury in amateur and professional sports (Iverson & Gardner, 2022; Pfister et al., 2016; Prien et al., 2018; Walshe et al., 2022). The conceptual definition of concussion, from the most recent consensus statement on concussion in sport (Patricios, Schneider, Dvorak, et al., 2023), is reprinted in part below.

> Sport-related concussion is a traumatic brain injury caused by a direct blow to the head, neck or body resulting in an impulsive force being transmitted to the brain that occurs in sports and exercise-related activities. This initiates a neurotransmitter and metabolic

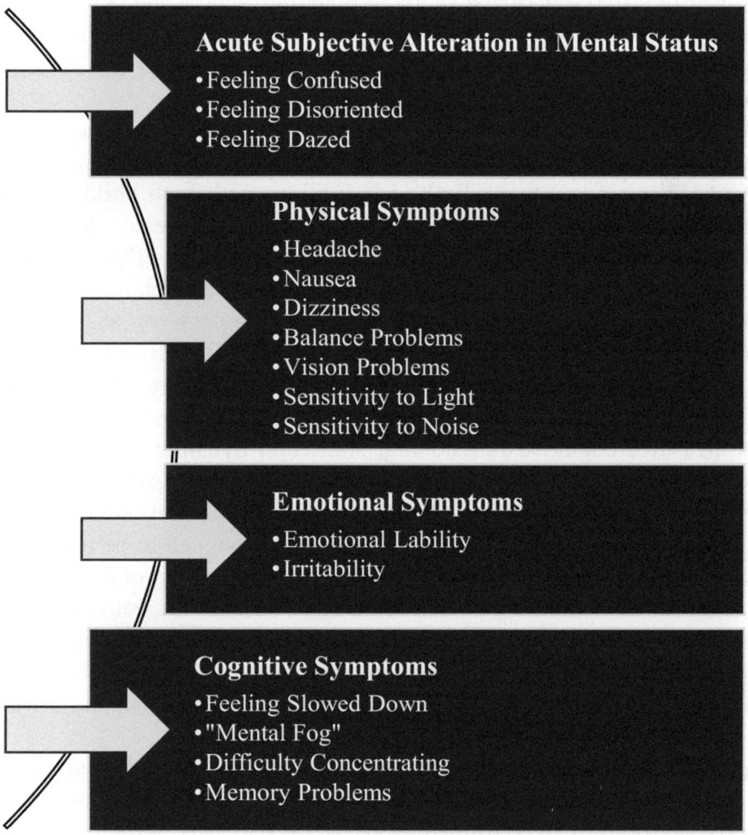

Fig. 23.2 Acute symptoms used in the ACRM diagnostic criteria for mild TBI [at least two acute symptoms (criterion 3) and at least one clinical or laboratory finding (criterion 4) attributable to brain injury] (Silverberg et al., 2023). Note: The physiological disruption of brain function from sport-related concussion is manifested by *two or more* new or worsened symptoms, from this list, present in the first 72 h following injury

cascade, with possible axonal injury, blood flow change and inflammation affecting the brain. Symptoms and signs may present immediately, or evolve over minutes or hours, and commonly resolve within days, but may be prolonged (Patricios, Schneider, Dvorak, et al., 2023).

Acute and Subacute Evaluation

Concussion is a clinical diagnosis. One of the strongest predictors of slower recovery and persisting symptoms is the severity of symptoms experienced acutely, in the first 72 h (Cook et al., 2022; Iverson et al., 2017; Iverson, Terry, et al., 2021; McAllister et al., 2023; Putukian et al., 2023). For example, there is a strong association between having a high burden of acute post-concussion symptoms and having a slower return to school and sports in both high school and collegiate athletes, and the inverse is also true—that those student athletes with a low burden of acute symptoms have a faster return to school and sports (Cook et al., 2022; Iverson, Terry, et al., 2021).

Tests and measures do not diagnose the injury—they are used to assess the clinical effects of the injury (see Table 23.1). A widely used test for this purpose is the Sport Concussion Assessment Tool—5th Edition, with both child (Davis et al., 2017; Kelshaw et al., 2022) and adult versions (Echemendia et al., 2017). The sixth edition was published in 2023 (SCAT6 and Child SCAT6) (Davis, Echemendia, Ahmed, Anderson, Blauwet, Brett, Broglio, Bruce, Burma, Gioia, Giza, Guskiewicz, Harmon, Herring, Makdissi, Master, McCrea, Meehan, et al., 2023; Davis, Echemendia, Ahmed, Anderson, Blauwet, Brett, Broglio, Bruce, Burma, Gioia, Giza, Guskiewicz, Harmon, Herring, Makdissi, Master, McCrea, Valovich McLeod, et al., 2023; Echemendia, Brett, et al., 2023; Echemendia, Burma, et al., 2023). The SCAT6 measures cognitive functioning, static and dynamic balance and subjectively experienced symptoms. A new component of the SCAT6, compared to the SCAT5, is timed tandem gait (with the option to use a dual-task timed tandem gait) (Echemendia, Burma, et al., 2023). The SCAT6 is designed to be used in the first few days following injury, as a brief evaluation. Clinical utility of the SCAT6 is best within the first 72 h after injury (Echemendia et al., 2017; Patricios, Schneider, Dvorak, et al., 2023). The SCAT can also be used up to 7 days after injury but with reduced clinical utility (Echemendia, Burma, et al., 2023; Patricios, Schneider, Dvorak, et al., 2023). The symptom scale can be used well beyond a week after injury, of course, to monitor for persisting symptoms.

In an office setting, during the subacute and post-acute time periods, a new integrated assessment called The Sport Concussion Office Assessment Tool 6 (SCOAT6) (Patricios, Davis, Ahmed, et al., 2023; Patricios, Schneider, van Ierssel, et al., 2023) and a child version (Child SCOAT6) (Davis, Patricios, Purcell, Anderson, Gioia, Giza, Yeates, Ahmed, Blauwet, Corwin, Master, Schneider, van Ierssel, Echemendia, Fremont, Fuller, Harmon, et al., 2023; Davis, Patricios, Purcell, Anderson, Gioia, Giza, Yeates, Ahmed, Blauwet, Corwin, Master,

Table 23.1 Examples of tests and measures used to measure the clinical effects of concussion

SCAT6	**Child SCOAT6**	**ImPACT Quick Test**
• Symptom Evaluation	• Symptom Evaluation (child report)	• Symptom Evaluation
• Orientation	• Symptom Evaluation (parent report)	• Attention Tracker
• Immediate Memory	• Immediate Memory	• Motor Speed
• Concentration	• Digits Backwards	• Memory
• mBESS	• Days in Reverse	**ImPACT Pediatric**
• Timed Tandem Gait	• Orthostatic Vital Signs	• Symptom Evaluation (child & parent)
• Delayed Recall	• Cervical Spine Assessment	• Sequential Memory
Child SCAT6	• Neurological Examination	• Word Memory
• Symptom Evaluation (child report)	• mBESS	• Visual Memory
• Symptom Evaluation (parent report)	• Timed Tandem Gait	• Rapid Processing
• Immediate Memory	• Complex Tandem Gait	**CNS Vital Signs**
• Concentration	• Dual-Task Tandem Gait	• Neurocognitive Index
• mBESS	• Visuo-vestibular Examination	• Composite Memory
• Timed Tandem Gait	• Mental Health & Sleep Screening	• Verbal Memory
• Complex Tandem Gait	• Delayed Word Recall	• Visual Memory
• Delayed Recall	**VOMS**	• Psychomotor Speed
SCOAT6	• Smooth pursuits	• Reaction Time
• Symptom Evaluation	• Horizontal and vertical saccades	• Complex Attention
• Immediate Memory	• Near point convergence	• Cognitive Flexibility
• Digits Backwards	• Horizontal vestibular ocular reflex	• Processing Speed
• Months in Reverse	• Visual motion sensitivity	• Executive Function
• Orthostatic Vital Signs	**ImPACT**	• Simple Attention
• Cervical Spine Assessment	• Symptom Evaluation	• Motor Speed
• Neurological Examination	• Verbal Memory	**Sway Mobile Cognitive and Balance Tests**
• mBESS	• Visual Memory	• Balance Testing
• Timed Tandem Gait	• Visual Motor Speed	• Inspection Time
• Complex Tandem Gait	• Reaction Time	• Reaction Time
• Dual-Task Gait	• Impulse Control	• Impulse Control
• Modified VOMS		• Memory
• Anxiety Screen		
• Depression Screen		
• Sleep Screen		
• Delayed Word Recall		

Note: *SCAT6* Sport Concussion Assessment Tool—6th Edition; *SCOAT6* Sport Concussion Office Assessment Tool 6; *VOMS* Vestibular Ocular Motor Screening; *ImPACT* Immediate Post-concussion Assessment and Cognitive Testing; *mBESS* Modified Balance Error Scoring System; *GAD-7* Generalized Anxiety Disorder-7; *PHQ-9* Patient Health Questionnaire-9

Schneider, van Ierssel, Echemendia, Fremont, Fuller, Herring, et al., 2023) have been developed. The SCOAT6 is designed for evaluating injured athletes aged 13 years and older three to 30 days post-injury and it includes sections on injury history; health history; current post-concussion symptoms; cognitive functioning; orthostatic vital signs; cervical spine assessment; cranial and peripheral nerve assessment; static balance and postural stability; dynamic balance; vestibular-oculomotor testing; anxiety, depression and sleep dysfunction screening; documentation of other test results; and a management and follow-up plan (Patricios, Schneider, van Ierssel, et al., 2023). Several brief batteries of tests (Wilmoth et al., 2022) used to measure the effects of concussion can be administered on electronic devices, such as computers, tablets and phones, such as ImPACT (Alsalaheen et al., 2016a, 2016b), ImPACT Pediatric (Iverson & Schatz, 2019), ImPACT Quick Test (Wallace et al., 2020), CNS Vital Signs (Prien et al., 2019; Rogers et al., 2017) and Sway Mobile Cognitive and Balance Tests (Brett et al., 2020; Caccese et al., 2022; Van Patten et al., 2021).

Rest and Return to School and Sports

A brief period of rest following injury, with gradual resumption of daily activities, is recommended (Miutz et al., 1985). Patients are *not* encouraged to engage in strict bed rest, to "cocoon," or to spend days in a dark room (Leddy et al., 2023; Patricios, Schneider, Dvorak, et al., 2023). Patients are encouraged to engage in light daily activities in the initial days following injury, but not vigorous exercise or activities that might result in additional head injury (Leddy et al., 2023; Patricios, Schneider, Dvorak, et al., 2023). Academic-related difficulties are reported by a large percentage of student athletes following injury (Putukian et al., 2023). The first priority is a swift, effective and durable return to school (Iverson & Gioia, 2016), and recommendations relating to return to school are summarized in Fig. 23.3 (Patricios, Schneider, Dvorak, et al., 2023). It is estimated that more than 90% of student athletes return to their normal educational activities within 10 days of injury (Putukian et al., 2023). Some, however, have difficulties that extend many weeks. Some of the greatest concerns for youth who are recovering from this injury include the amount of schoolwork they have and falling behind with it, their grades dropping, and when they will be able to return to sports (DeMatteo et al., 2022). Providing academic accommodations early in the recovery process may be beneficial to help students keep up with work and reduce symptom exacerbation. A stepwise progression is also recommended for return to sports (Patricios, Schneider, Dvorak, et al., 2023), which is summarized in Fig. 23.4.

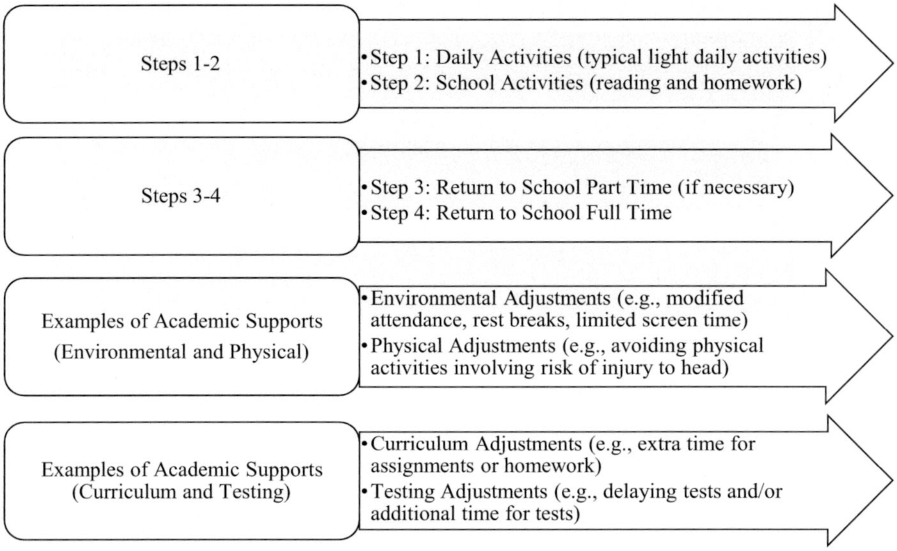

Fig. 23.3 Return to school (return to learn) strategy (adapted from the Concussion in Sport Group, Amsterdam 2022) (Patricios, Schneider, Dvorak, et al., 2023). Note: The content of this figure was extracted from the Concussion in Sport Group consensus statement (Patricios, Schneider, Dvorak, et al., 2023) and summarized in this figure. Please see the consensus statement (Patricios, Schneider, Dvorak, et al., 2023) and the supporting systematic review (McAllister et al., 2023) for the specific wording and for additional information

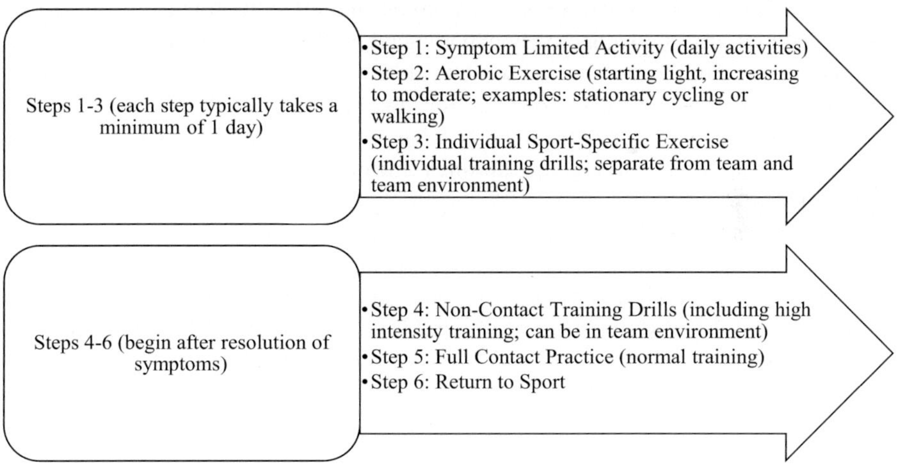

Fig. 23.4 Return to sports strategy (adapted from the Concussion in Sport Group, Amsterdam 2022) (Patricios, Schneider, Dvorak, et al., 2023). Note: The content of this figure was extracted from the Concussion in Sport Group consensus statement (Patricios, Schneider, Dvorak, et al., 2023) and summarized in this figure. Please see the consensus statement (Patricios, Schneider, Dvorak, et al., 2023) and the supporting systematic review (McAllister et al., 2023) for the specific wording and for additional information

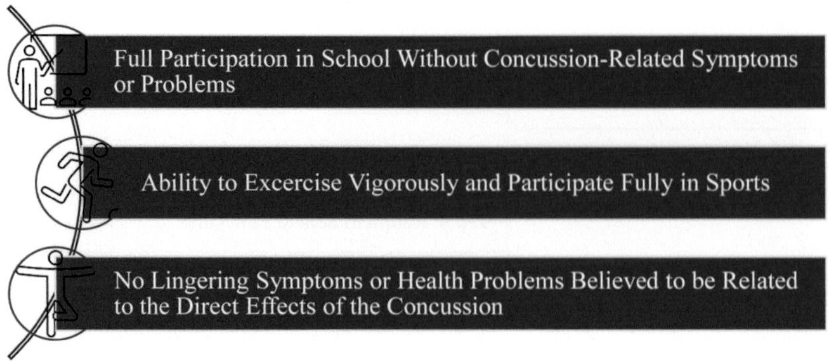

Fig. 23.5 Conceptualizing clinical recovery

Recovery Time

Most student athletes recover, from a clinical perspective, within one month of injury (Broglio et al., 2022; King et al., 2014; Manzanero et al., 2017; Putukian et al., 2023; Williams et al., 2015). There is considerable variability in recovery time, with some people experiencing symptom resolution in a few days while, *on average*, recovery takes approximately 2–3 weeks (Bretzin et al., 2022; Broglio et al., 2022; Kara et al., 2020; Purcell et al., 2016; Putukian et al., 2023; Teel et al., 2017). Clinical recovery refers to improvement and resolution of cognitive deficits, balance problems, visual oculomotor symptoms elicited with provocation, exercise-induced symptoms and subjectively experienced physical, cognitive and emotional symptoms (see Fig. 23.5). There is some evidence that physiological recovery takes longer than clinical recovery; however, the findings are mixed across studies and biomarkers—and it is currently unclear what, exactly, lingering blood or experimental neuroimaging biomarker findings mean (Kamins et al., 2017; Tabor et al., 2023).

It is important to appreciate that a substantial percentage of children, adolescents and adults do not recover swiftly following this injury and they have symptoms and problems that can persist for weeks or months following injury (Broglio et al., 2022; Broshek et al., 2022; Cancelliere et al., 2023; Ledoux et al., 2019; McCrea et al., 2013; Zemek et al., 2016). These individuals are conceptualized as having persisting symptoms.

Persisting Symptoms

The term post-concussion syndrome (PCS) has been used for decades to describe symptoms such as sleep disturbance, dizziness, headaches, fatigue, memory difficulty, irritability, anxiety and depression that can occur and persist following a concussion. This term and diagnosis have been controversial because it implies that there is a specific "syndrome" comprised of a cohesive set of symptoms that is caused directly by long lasting physiological damage or dysfunction from concussion—and, after decades of research, this has not been established. Persisting symptoms are often individualized (not clearly syndromic) and have multiple potential causal and amplifying contributing etiological factors that can be mostly or entirely unrelated to the pathophysiology of the original concussive injury. It is important to note that the symptoms of concussion are nonspecific and can occur in many other conditions including under situations of normal stress (Iverson et al., 2015; Iverson & Lange, 2003; Makdissi et al., 2017). It is important to consider a broader biopsychosocial context when conceptualizing persisting symptoms in individual patients (Fig. 23.6) (Iverson, 2019).

Children, adolescents and young adults who have symptoms lasting more than one month are now conceptualized as having "persistent" or "persisting" symptoms (Broglio et al., 2022). Using the term "persisting symptoms" implies that symptoms of concussion are recovering more slowly and have lasted longer than the typical recovery window. It does not suggest an underlying disease process or etiology for persisting symptoms but rather describes a constellation of symptoms that might be

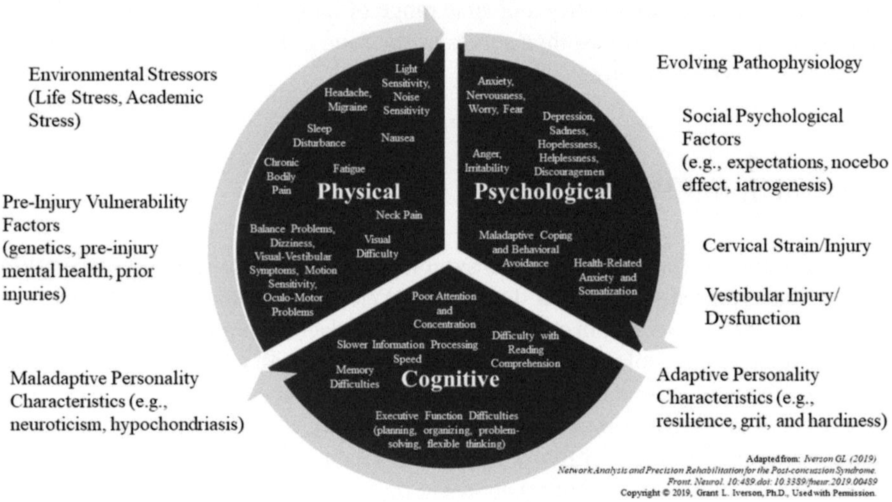

Fig. 23.6 Personal biopsychosocial context for subacute and persisting symptoms. Adapted from: Iverson, G. L. (2019). Network analysis and precision rehabilitation for the post-concussion syndrome. *Frontiers in Neurology, 10*, 489. doi: 10.3389/fneur.2019.00489. Copyright © 2019, Grant L. Iverson, Ph.D., Used with permission

linked to pre-existing, co-existing or confounding conditions or problems (Makdissi et al., 2017). Using the term persisting symptoms also places an optimistic, recovery-focused lens on other factors (e.g., pre-injury anxiety) that may need to be treated. Additionally, when athletes are identified (incorrectly) as having "post-concussion syndrome," this may lead to prolonged recovery because athletes might then expect their symptoms to linger or to become chronic.

Children and adolescents who present to the emergency department following sport-related concussion are at increased risk for experiencing persisting symptoms, with at least one third reporting symptoms lasting more than a month (Ledoux et al., 2019; Zemek et al., 2016). Youth and adults who are evaluated and treated in specialty concussion clinics are much more likely to have persisting symptoms (Chadwick et al., 2022), presumably because those on a trajectory for more rapid recovery are not referred to specialty clinics and they are more likely to be medically managed in primary care or other settings.

Clusters of post-concussion symptoms (i.e., neurocognitive, fatigue, emotional, migraine and vestibular ocular predominance) often occur acutely and in athletes with persisting symptoms (Bretzin et al., 2022; Kamins et al., 2017; Kara et al., 2020; Manzanero et al., 2017; Purcell et al., 2016; Tabor et al., 2023; Teel et al., 2017). These symptoms can be exacerbated by sleep disturbance (Kara et al., 2020; Manzanero et al., 2017). Symptoms lasting weeks or months might not be caused by lingering neurobiological effects of the original injury but instead might be maintained, at least mostly, by other factors. Concussion-like symptoms are not specific to concussion—they are considered nonspecific because they occur in daily life and in association with ADHD, learning problems, mental health problems and having a headache condition (Iverson et al., 2015). A careful multimodal clinical assessment is often needed to identify a diverse range of factors that might be causing or amplifying symptoms, which then serves as the foundation for treatment and rehabilitation recommendations.

Cervical Spine/Musculoskeletal Injury

Cervical spine dysfunction can cause symptoms similar to concussion, or amplify concussion symptoms, including dizziness, cervicogenic headaches and neck pain (Ellis et al., 2019). Neck pain and cervicogenic headaches might contribute to sleep dysfunction and psychological distress. Some athletes with cervical spine dysfunction might be at increased risk for prolonged recovery because their symptoms may be attributed to concussion rather than neck problems, leading to a delay in receiving appropriate treatment (Ellis et al., 2019). Occipital neuralgia (e.g., recurring attacks of throbbing or stabbing pain at the posterior aspect of the skull involving branches of the occipital nerve) is uncommon following concussion but can occur. Referral for multidisciplinary headache and cervical spine management can be important for some patients.

Treatment and Rehabilitation

There are effective treatment and rehabilitation strategies for symptoms and problems associated with concussion (Collins et al., 2016; Patricios, Schneider, Dvorak, et al., 2023; Schneider et al., 2017). Some people experience autonomic dysregulation, exercise intolerance and/or exercise-induced symptoms (Bishop et al., 2017; Dobson et al., 2017; Haider et al., 2023), and cardiovascular exercise is used as a rehabilitation intervention for these problems (Baker et al., 2020; Jaganathan et al., 2023; Langevin et al., 2020; Leddy et al., 2023; Miutz et al., 1985). Exercise used as a treatment and rehabilitation strategy might also have other benefits such as reducing symptoms of stress, anxiety and depression, and improving psychological well-being (Daley, 2008; Jayakody et al., 2014). The basic principle is to use daily exercise at an intensity level that is below the level that provokes significant symptom exacerbation (Jaganathan et al., 2023; Leddy et al., 2023). Athletes with cervical injuries might benefit from physical therapy (Schneider et al., 2014), and there is some evidence that vestibular therapy is useful for vestibular and oculomotor symptoms and problems (Galeno et al., 2022). Psychological treatment is recommended for those who experience problems with stress, anxiety or depression following injury (Barela et al., 2023; Makdissi et al., 2017). A coordinated and integrated collaborative care model, such as those found in some specialty clinics, can be particularly helpful for those with persisting symptoms (McCarty et al., 2016, 2021).

Retirement from Sport

Decisions to retire from sports are multi-faceted, complex and specific to the athlete. There is very little scientific literature that directly addresses this topic and, thus, it is unclear if there are factors that would unequivocally suggest that retirement should be imminent. Healthcare providers who consult on retirement decisions should have expertise in sport-related concussion (Patricios, Schneider, Dvorak, et al., 2023). Factors that are often considered in retirement decisions include (1) the presence of persisting post-concussion symptoms or increasingly severe symptoms with subsequent concussions, (2) lingering or persistent neurological or neurocognitive deficits despite sufficient post-concussion treatment, (3) concussion occurrence at presumed lower threshold impacts and (4) identified conventional neuroimaging abnormalities (Makdissi et al., 2023). There is no specific combination of these factors (including the number of concussions) that necessitates retirement, and so athletes should be informed about the realities of the unclear literature on this topic. Healthcare providers are encouraged to have a thoughtful and informed discussion about the potential future risks and benefits of continued sport participation (Makdissi et al., 2023). Retirement decisions can be extraordinarily difficult, and care should be made to respect the autonomy of athletes and to support their decision. If retirement is the outcome, then athletes should be encouraged to continue engaging in safe non-contact physical or sporting activities given the physical and mental health benefits of exercise and the role and importance of exercise in athletes' identities (Makdissi et al., 2023).

Possible Later-in-Life Mental Health and Neurological Problems

There are numerous cross-sectional studies relating to later-in-life brain health, broadly defined, in former amateur and professional athletes, and these studies have been summarized in published narrative and systematic reviews (Albayram et al., 2020; Alosco et al., 2021; Bellomo et al., 2022; Brand & Finkel, 2020; Brett et al., 2019; Cantu & Bernick, 2020; Cunningham et al., 2018, 2020; Echlin et al., 2021; Gallo et al., 2020; Iverson, Buttner, et al., 2021; Iverson et al., 2019; Lee et al., 2018; Legarreta et al., 2018; Lesman-Segev et al., 2020; LoBue et al., 2020; Manley et al., 2017; McKee, 2020; Morales et al., 2021, 2022; Murray et al., 2022; Shively et al., 2021; Smith et al., 2019; Sparks et al., 2020; Stein & Crary, 2020; Vos et al., 2018; Willer et al., 2021; Zhang et al., 2019). Cross-sectional studies, using surveys or comparing two groups on neuroimaging and neuropsychological testing, are not designed to examine causal relationships. A recent systematic review examined only case–control and cohort studies in an attempt to draw conclusions about whether sport-related concussions, and exposure to repetitive head impacts through participation in contact and collision sports during youth and young adulthood, are associated with later-in-life mental health problems, cognitive impairment and neurological diseases (Iverson et al., 2023). Based on the results from a small number of cohort studies, the authors of that review (Iverson et al., 2023) concluded that:

- (i) Former amateur athletes are not at increased risk for later-in-life depression, suicidality, cognitive impairment or neurodegenerative diseases (Bohr et al., 2019; Deshpande et al., 2017, 2020; Iverson, Merz, et al., 2021; Iverson & Terry, 2022; Janssen et al., 2017; Savica et al., 2012; Valenti et al., 2005; Weiss et al., 2021)
- (ii) Former professional soccer players are not at increased risk for psychiatric hospitalization during their adult lives (Russell et al., 2020)
- (iii) Former professional American football players and professional soccer players are not at increased risk for suicide as a manner of death (Baron et al., 2012; Lehman et al., 2016; Lincoln et al., 2018; Russell et al., 2020; Taioli, 2007)
- (iv) Former professional American football players and former professional soccer players are at increased risk for neurological problems (e.g., dementia) and neurodegenerative diseases (e.g., Alzheimer's disease and amyotrophic lateral sclerosis (Belli & Vanacore, 2005; Chio et al., 2005, 2009; Daneshvar et al., 2021; Lehman et al., 2012; Mackay et al., 2019; Pupillo et al., 2020; Taioli, 2007))

The authors of that review noted that the cohort studies were methodologically limited because, as a rule, they could not address confounding factors or consider the possible effects of genetics; demographic variables; socioeconomic status and social determinants of health; alcohol and substance use; or comorbid medical conditions, such as hypertension and cardiovascular disease (Iverson et al., 2023). They encouraged future well-designed case–control and cohort studies that take into account confounding factors such as genetics, demographic variables and environmental factors, to determine if these associations in former professional athletes are causal.

Chronic Traumatic Encephalopathy Neuropathologic Change and Traumatic Encephalopathy Syndrome

In the twentieth century, case studies and case series of current and former high exposure boxers were published, and these articles described chronic forms of traumatic brain injury and neurological problems using terms like punch drunk (Martland, 1928), dementia pugilistica (Millspaugh, 1937) and chronic traumatic encephalopathy (CTE) (Critchley, 1949, 1957). In recent years, the term "CTE" has been used to describe both a clinical condition and a post-mortem neuropathological entity, creating conceptual confusion because it is not known whether clinical signs and symptoms experienced by former athletes in middle age or older adulthood are actually related to the neuropathology (Cullum & LoBue, 2021; Iverson et al., 2023; Iverson & Gardner, 2021). Therefore, the terms CTE neuropathology (Iverson et al., 2018, 2019) and CTE neuropathologic change (CTE-NC) (Lee et al., 2019) have been encouraged to avoid conflating the pathology and possible specific clinical symptoms or disorders with the same name. The neuropathological entity CTE-NC (McKee et al., 2013, 2016) has a defining microscopic feature (i.e., the "pathognomonic" lesion) described as "p-tau aggregates in neurons, with or without thorn-shaped astrocytes, at the depth of a sulcus around a small blood vessel, deep in the parenchyma, and not restricted to the subpial or superficial region of the sulcus" (page 217) (Bieniek et al., 2021). This can only be identified after death by examining brain tissue under a microscope. At present, it is not known whether CTE-NC is inexorably progressive (Iverson et al., 2023; Patricios, Schneider, Dvorak, et al., 2023).

A clinical phenotype (i.e., clinical presentation) associated with CTE-NC during life has not been established. In recent years, authors have speculated that a very broad range of psychosocial problems (e.g., gambling, financial problems, marital problems), mental health and impulse control problems (e.g., depression, anxiety, suicidality, substance use and anger dyscontrol) and neurological conditions and problems (e.g., mild cognitive impairment, Parkinsonism and dementia) experienced during life are related to CTE-NC (Baugh et al., 2012; Gavett et al., 2011; McKee et al., 2010, 2013; Montenigro et al., 2014; Omalu, 2014; Omalu et al.,

2005, 2010, 2011; Stern et al., 2011, 2013). However, a large-scale clinicopathological study, published in 2021, did not find an association between CTE-NC and depressive symptoms, hopelessness, suicidality, anxiety, explosivity, physical violence, verbal violence, impulsivity or substance use (see online supplement, eTable 5, Mez et al., 2021).

Consensus criteria for traumatic encephalopathy syndrome (TES), a new clinical diagnosis, were published in 2021 (Katz et al., 2021). Specifically, the authors wrote that the: "Diagnosis of TES requires (1) substantial exposure to repetitive head impacts (RHIs) from contact sports, military service, or other causes; (2) core clinical features of cognitive impairment (in episodic memory and/or executive functioning), neurobehavioral dysregulation, or both; (3) a progressive course; and (4) that the clinical features are not fully accounted for by any other neurologic, psychiatric, or medical conditions" (pg. 848) (Katz et al., 2021). The new diagnosis of TES is designed to be used in research to determine the extent to which CTE-NC identified after death is associated with this new clinical diagnosis during life. Much research is needed on this because, at present, it is not known whether CTE-NC is the underlying cause of any specific neurological or psychiatric problems (Iverson et al., 2023; Patricios, Schneider, Dvorak, et al., 2023).

Conclusions and Key Points

Concussion is a commonly experienced injury in sports. Concussions are, by definition, a form of mild traumatic brain injury. Observable clinical signs of concussion include loss of consciousness, post-traumatic amnesia and alterations in mental status following injury. Concussion symptoms are subjective and can include altered mental status (reported by the person), physical symptoms, cognitive symptoms and emotional symptoms. Recovery typically occurs within 2–3 weeks and up to one month post-injury. However, some athletes can experience symptoms that persist longer than one month following concussion. Active rehabilitation including exercise, physical therapy (as needed) and vestibular therapy (as needed) are effective for promoting successful recovery. Some key points are summarized below.

- Recognize and Remove: It is important to recognize the injury (or possible injury) and remove the athlete from play. Continuing to play with a concussion is a risk factor for worse clinical outcome and taking longer to return to sports (Patricios, Schneider, Dvorak, et al., 2023; Putukian et al., 2023).
- Rest: An initial period of relative rest, for a day or two, is reasonable—especially for those who are highly symptomatic. Light daily activities are encouraged. Prolonged rest (for days or weeks) is not recommended (Leddy et al., 2023; Patricios, Schneider, Dvorak, et al., 2023).
- Exercise: Early (i.e., first 48 h), low-intensity, physical activity (e.g., walking) that does not provoke significant symptoms is likely beneficial for recovery. After 48 h, prescribed aerobic activity (e.g., stationary biking) that does not

exceed mild symptom exacerbation is likely beneficial. Aerobic exercise can be increased in a stepwise fashion (without more than mild symptom exacerbation) every few days to every week (Leddy et al., 2023; Patricios, Schneider, Dvorak, et al., 2023).

- Recovery Time: Most athletes recover within 2–3 weeks and up to one month following injury. Some athletes can experience persisting symptoms after one month. Persisting symptoms may be related to concussion or to other factors (e.g., life stress or pre-existing health or mental health conditions) (Patricios, Schneider, Dvorak, et al., 2023).
- Treatment and Rehabilitation: Prescribed exercise should be used in combination with other treatments (as needed). Multidisciplinary treatment and referral for specialty evaluation (e.g., vestibular therapy for balance difficulties; therapy for mental health difficulties) may be beneficial for those athletes who are at risk for prolonged recovery and persisting symptoms (Patricios, Schneider, Dvorak, et al., 2023).
- Return to School: The large majority of athletes are back to school without accommodations by 10 days following injury. Early return to school should be encouraged and the use of temporary accommodations is recommended to facilitate full return to learn. Return to learn should be completed before return to sport (Patricios, Schneider, Dvorak, et al., 2023; Putukian et al., 2023).
- Return to Sports: Return to sports generally occurs within one month. Graded physical activity resumption beginning within the first 48 hours of recovery is beneficial. Athletes who are not progressing toward recovery at 2–4 weeks (or whose symptoms worsen) should be referred for multidisciplinary treatment and rehabilitation (Leddy et al., 2023; Patricios, Schneider, Dvorak, et al., 2023; Putukian et al., 2023).

References

Albayram, O., Albayram, S., & Mannix, R. (2020). Chronic traumatic encephalopathy-a blueprint for the bridge between neurological and psychiatric disorders. *Translational Psychiatry, 10*, 424. https://doi.org/10.1038/s41398-020-01111-x

Alosco, M. L., Culhane, J., & Mez, J. (2021). Neuroimaging biomarkers of chronic traumatic encephalopathy: Targets for the academic memory disorders clinic. *Neurotherapeutics, 18*, 772–791. https://doi.org/10.1007/s13311-021-01028-3

Alsalaheen, B., Stockdale, K., Pechumer, D., & Broglio, S. P. (2016a). Validity of the immediate post concussion assessment and cognitive testing (ImPACT). *Sports Medicine, 46*, 1487–1501. https://doi.org/10.1007/s40279-016-0532-y

Alsalaheen, B., Stockdale, K., Pechumer, D., & Broglio, S. P. (2016b). Measurement error in the immediate postconcussion assessment and cognitive testing (ImPACT): Systematic review. *The Journal of Head Trauma Rehabilitation, 31*, 242–251. https://doi.org/10.1097/HTR.0000000000000175

Baker, B., Koch, E., Vicari, K., & Walenta, K. (2020). Mode and intensity of physical activity during the postacute phase of sport-related concussion: A systematic review. *Journal of Sport Rehabilitation, 30*, 492–500. https://doi.org/10.1123/jsr.2019-0323

Barela, M., Wong, A., & Chamberlain, R. (2023). Concussion and psychological effects: A review of recent literature. *Current Sports Medicine Reports, 22*, 24–28. https://doi.org/10.1249/JSR.0000000000001031

Baron, S. L., Hein, M. J., Lehman, E., & Gersic, C. M. (2012). Body mass index, playing position, race, and the cardiovascular mortality of retired professional football players. *The American Journal of Cardiology, 109*, 889–896. https://doi.org/10.1016/j.amjcard.2011.10.050

Baugh, C. M., Stamm, J. M., Riley, D. O., Gavett, B. E., Shenton, M. E., Lin, A., Nowinski, C. J., Cantu, R. C., McKee, A. C., & Stern, R. A. (2012). Chronic traumatic encephalopathy: neurodegeneration following repetitive concussive and subconcussive brain trauma. *Brain Imaging and Behavior, 6*, 244–254. https://doi.org/10.1007/s11682-012-9164-5

Belli, S., & Vanacore, N. (2005). Proportionate mortality of Italian soccer players: is amyotrophic lateral sclerosis an occupational disease? *European Journal of Epidemiology, 20*, 237–242. https://doi.org/10.1007/s10654-004-6879-7

Bellomo, G., Piscopo, P., Corbo, M., Pupillo, E., Stipa, G., Beghi, E., Vanacore, N., & Lacorte, E. (2022). A systematic review on the risk of neurodegenerative diseases and neurocognitive disorders in professional and varsity athletes. *Neurological Sciences*. https://doi.org/10.1007/s10072-022-06319-x

Bieniek, K. F., Cairns, N. J., Crary, J. F., Dickson, D. W., Folkerth, R. D., Keene, C. D., Litvan, I., Perl, D. P., Stein, T. D., Vonsattel, J. P., Stewart, W., Dams-O'Connor, K., Gordon, W. A., Tripodis, Y., Alvarez, V. E., Mez, J., Alosco, M. L., McKee, A. C., & TBI/CTE Research Group. (2021). The Second NINDS/NIBIB Consensus Meeting to define neuropathological criteria for the diagnosis of chronic traumatic encephalopathy. *Journal of Neuropathology and Experimental Neurology, 80*, 210–219. https://doi.org/10.1093/jnen/nlab001

Bishop, S., Dech, R., Baker, T., Butz, M., Aravinthan, K., & Neary, J. P. (2017). Parasympathetic baroreflexes and heart rate variability during acute stage of sport concussion recovery. *Brain Injury, 31*, 247–259. https://doi.org/10.1080/02699052.2016.1226385

Bohr, A. D., Boardman, J. D., & McQueen, M. B. (2019). Association of adolescent sport participation with cognition and depressive symptoms in early adulthood. *Orthopaedic Journal of Sports Medicine, 7*, 2325967119868658. https://doi.org/10.1177/2325967119868658

Brand, K. P., & Finkel, A. M. (2020). A decision-analytic approach to addressing the evidence about football and chronic traumatic encephalopathy. *Seminars in Neurology, 40*, 450–460. https://doi.org/10.1055/s-0039-1688484

Brett, B. L., Wilmoth, K., Cummings, P., Solomon, G. S., McCrea, M. A., & Zuckerman, S. L. (2019). The neuropathological and clinical diagnostic criteria of chronic traumatic encephalopathy: A critical examination in relation to other neurodegenerative diseases. *Journal of Alzheimer's Disease, 68*, 591–608. https://doi.org/10.3233/JAD-181058

Brett, B. L., Zuckerman, S. L., Terry, D. P., Solomon, G. S., & Iverson, G. L. (2020). Normative data for the sway balance system. *Clinical Journal of Sport Medicine, 30*, 458–464. https://doi.org/10.1097/JSM.0000000000000632

Bretzin, A. C., Esopenko, C., D'Alonzo, B. A., & Wiebe, D. J. (2022). Clinical recovery timelines after sport-related concussion in men's and women's collegiate sports. *Journal of Athletic Training, 57*, 678–687. https://doi.org/10.4085/601-20

Broglio, S. P., McAllister, T., Katz, B. P., LaPradd, M., Zhou, W., McCrea, M. A., & Investigators, C. C. (2022). The natural history of sport-related concussion in collegiate athletes: Findings from the NCAA-DoD CARE Consortium. *Sports Medicine, 52*, 403–415. https://doi.org/10.1007/s40279-021-01541-7

Broshek, D. K., Pardini, J. E., & Herring, S. A. (2022). Persisting symptoms after concussion: Time for a paradigm shift. *PM & R: The Journal of Injury, Function, and Rehabilitation, 14*, 1509–1513. https://doi.org/10.1002/pmrj.12884

Caccese, J. B., Teel, E., Van Patten, R., Muzeau, M. A., Iverson, G. L., & VanRavenhorst-Bell, H. A. (2022). Test-retest reliability and preliminary reliable change estimates for Sway Balance tests administered remotely in community-dwelling adults. *Frontiers in Digital Health, 4*, 999250. https://doi.org/10.3389/fdgth.2022.999250

Cancelliere, C., Verville, L., Stubbs, J. L., Yu, H., Hincapie, C. A., Cassidy, J. D., Wong, J. J., Shearer, H. M., Connell, G., Southerst, D., Howitt, S., Guist, B., & Silverberg, N. D. (2023). Post-concussion symptoms and disability in adults with mild traumatic brain injury: A systematic review and meta-analysis. *Journal of Neurotrauma, 40*, 1045–1059. https://doi.org/10.1089/neu.2022.0185

Cantu, R. C., & Bernick, C. (2020). History of chronic traumatic encephalopathy. *Seminars in Neurology, 40*, 353–358. https://doi.org/10.1055/s-0040-1713622

Chadwick, L., Sharma, M. J., Madigan, S., Callahan, B. L., & Owen, Y. K. (2022). Classification criteria and rates of persistent postconcussive symptoms in children: A systematic review and meta-analysis. *The Journal of Pediatrics, 246*(131-137), e132. https://doi.org/10.1016/j.jpeds.2022.03.039

Chio, A., Benzi, G., Dossena, M., Mutani, R., & Mora, G. (2005). Severely increased risk of amyotrophic lateral sclerosis among Italian professional football players. *Brain, 128*, 472–476. https://doi.org/10.1093/brain/awh373

Chio, A., Calvo, A., Dossena, M., Ghiglione, P., Mutani, R., & Mora, G. (2009). ALS in Italian professional soccer players: the risk is still present and could be soccer-specific. *Amyotrophic Lateral Sclerosis, 10*, 205–209. https://doi.org/10.1080/17482960902721634

Collins, M. W., Kontos, A. P., Okonkwo, D. O., Almquist, J., Bailes, J., Barisa, M., Bazarian, J., Bloom, O. J., Brody, D. L., Cantu, R., Cardenas, J., Clugston, J., Cohen, R., Echemendia, R., Elbin, R. J., Ellenbogen, R., Fonseca, J., Gioia, G., Guskiewicz, K., …, Zafonte, R. (2016). Statements of agreement from the targeted evaluation and active management (TEAM) approaches to treating concussion meeting held in Pittsburgh, October 15–16, 2015. *Neurosurgery, 79*, 912–929. https://doi.org/10.1227/NEU.0000000000001447.

Cook, N. E., Gaudet, C. E., Maxwell, B., Zafonte, R., Berkner, P. D., & Iverson, G. L. (2022). Greater acute concussion symptoms are associated with longer recovery times in adolescents. *Journal of Child Neurology, 37*, 970–978. https://doi.org/10.1177/08830738221125986

Critchley, M. (1949). Punch-drunk syndromes: The chronic traumatic encephalopathy of boxers. In Maloine (Ed.), *Hommage a Clovis Vincent* (pp. 131–145). Imprimerie Alascienne.

Critchley, M. (1957). Medical aspects of boxing, particularly from a neurological standpoint. *British Medical Journal, 1*, 357–362.

Cullum, C. M., & LoBue, C. (2021). Defining traumatic encephalopathy syndrome—Advances and challenges. *Nature Reviews. Neurology, 17*, 331–332. https://doi.org/10.1038/s41582-021-00500-0

Cunningham, J., Broglio, S., & Wilson, F. (2018). Influence of playing rugby on long-term brain health following retirement: a systematic review and narrative synthesis. *BMJ Open Sport & Exercise Medicine, 4*, e000356. https://doi.org/10.1136/bmjsem-2018-000356

Cunningham, J., Broglio, S. P., O'Grady, M., & Wilson, F. (2020). History of sport-related concussion and long-term clinical cognitive health outcomes in retired athletes: A systematic review. *Journal of Athletic Training, 55*, 132–158. https://doi.org/10.4085/1062-6050-297-18

Daley, A. (2008). Exercise and depression: a review of reviews. *Journal of Clinical Psychology in Medical Settings, 15*, 140–147. https://doi.org/10.1007/s10880-008-9105-z

Daneshvar, D. H., Mez, J., Alosco, M. L., Baucom, Z. H., Mahar, I., Baugh, C. M., Valle, J. P., Weuve, J., Paganoni, S., Cantu, R. C., Zafonte, R. D., Stern, R. A., Stein, T. D., Tripodis, Y., Nowinski, C. J., & McKee, A. C. (2021). Incidence of and mortality from amyotrophic lateral sclerosis in National Football League athletes. *JAMA Network Open, 4*, e2138801. https://doi.org/10.1001/jamanetworkopen.2021.38801

Davis, G. A., Echemendia, R. J., Ahmed, O. H., Anderson, V., Blauwet, C., Brett, B. L., Broglio, S., Bruce, J. M., Burma, J. S., Gioia, G., Giza, C. C., Guskiewicz, K. M., Harmon, K. G., Herring, S. A., Makdissi, M., Master, C. L., McCrea, M., Meehan, W. P., 3rd, Naidu, D., …, Zemek, R. (2023). Child SCAT6. *British Journal of Sports Medicine, 57*, 636–647. https://doi.org/10.1136/bjsports-2023-106982.

Davis, G. A., Echemendia, R. J., Ahmed, O. H., Anderson, V., Blauwet, C., Brett, B. L., Broglio, S., Bruce, J. M., Burma, J. S., Gioia, G. A., Giza, C. C., Guskiewicz, K. M., Harmon, K. G.,

Herring, S., Makdissi, M., Master, C. L., McCrea, M., Valovich McLeod, T. C., Meehan, W. P., 3rd, …, Zemek, R. (2023). Introducing the Child Sport Concussion Assessment Tool 6 (Child SCAT6). *British Journal of Sports Medicine, 57*, 632–635. https://doi.org/10.1136/bjsports-2023-106853.

Davis, G. A., Makdissi, M., Bloomfield, P., Clifton, P., Echemendia, R. J., Falvey, E. C., Fuller, G. W., Green, G., Harcourt, P., Hill, T., McGuirk, N., Meeuwisse, W., Orchard, J., Raftery, M., Sills, A. K., Solomon, G. S., Valadka, A., & McCrory, P. (2019). International consensus definitions of video signs of concussion in professional sports. *British Journal of Sports Medicine, 53*, 1264–1267. https://doi.org/10.1136/bjsports-2019-100628

Davis, G. A., Patricios, J., Schneider, K. J., Iverson, G. L., & Silverberg, N. D. (2023). Definition of sport-related concussion: the 6th International Conference on Concussion in Sport. *British Journal of Sports Medicine, 57*, 617–618. https://doi.org/10.1136/bjsports-2022-106650

Davis, G. A., Patricios, J. S., Purcell, L. K., Anderson, V., Gioia, G., Giza, C. C., Yeates, K. O., Ahmed, O. H., Blauwet, C., Corwin, D., Master, C. L., Schneider, G., van Ierssel, J., Echemendia, R. J., Fremont, P., Fuller, G. W., Harmon, K. G., Herring, S. A., Holte, K., …, Schneider, K. J. (2023). Child SCOAT6. *British Journal of Sports Medicine, 57*, 672–688. https://doi.org/10.1136/bjsports-2023-106984.

Davis, G. A, Patricios, J. S., Purcell, L. K., Anderson, V., Gioia, G. A., Giza, C. C., Yeates, K. O., Ahmed, O. H., Blauwet, C., Corwin, D., Master, C. L., Schneider, G. M., van Ierssel, J., Echemendia, R. J., Fremont, P., Fuller, G. W., Herring, S., Harmon, K. G., Holte, K., …, Schneider, K. J. (2023). Introducing the Child Sport Concussion Office Assessment Tool 6 (Child SCOAT6). *British Journal of Sports Medicine, 57*, 668–671. https://doi.org/10.1136/bjsports-2023-106858.

Davis, G. A., Purcell, L., Schneider, K. J., Yeates, K. O., Gioia, G. A., Anderson, V., Ellenbogen, R. G., Echemendia, R. J., Makdissi, M., Sills, A., Iverson, G. L., Dvorak, J., McCrory, P., Meeuwisse, W., Patricios, J., Giza, C. C., & Kutcher, J. S. (2017). The Child Sport Concussion Assessment Tool 5th edition (Child SCAT5): Background and rationale. *British Journal of Sports Medicine, 51*, 859–861. https://doi.org/10.1136/bjsports-2017-097492

DeMatteo, C. A., Jakubowski, J., Randall, S., Stazyk, K., Lin, C. Y., & Yakubov, R. (2022). School performance in youth after a concussion. *Frontiers in Sports and Active Living, 4*, 1008551. https://doi.org/10.3389/fspor.2022.1008551

Deshpande, S. K., Hasegawa, R. B., Rabinowitz, A. R., Whyte, J., Roan, C. L., Tabatabaei, A., Baiocchi, M., Karlawish, J. H., Master, C. L., & Small, D. S. (2017). Association of playing high school football with cognition and mental health later in life. *JAMA Neurology, 74*, 909–918. https://doi.org/10.1001/jamaneurol.2017.1317

Deshpande, S. K., Hasegawa, R. B., Weiss, J., & Small, D. S. (2020). The association between adolescent football participation and early adulthood depression. *PLoS One, 15*, e0229978. https://doi.org/10.1371/journal.pone.0229978

Dobson, J. L., Yarbrough, M. B., Perez, J., Evans, K., & Buckley, T. (2017). Sport-related concussion induces transient cardiovascular autonomic dysfunction. *American Journal of Physiology. Regulatory, Integrative and Comparative Physiology, 312*, R575–R584. https://doi.org/10.1152/ajpregu.00499.2016

Echemendia, R. J., Brett, B. L., Broglio, S., Davis, G. A., Giza, C. C., Guskiewicz, K. M., Harmon, K. G., Herring, S., Howell, D. R., Master, C., McCrea, M., Naidu, D., Patricios, J. S., Putukian, M., Walton, S. R., Schneider, K. J., Burma, J. S., & Bruce, J. M. (2023). Sport concussion assessment tool - 6 (SCAT6). *British Journal of Sports Medicine, 57*, 622–631. https://doi.org/10.1136/bjsports-2023-107036

Echemendia, R. J., Burma, J. S., Bruce, J. M., Davis, G. A., Giza, C. C., Guskiewicz, K. M., Naidu, D., Black, A. M., Broglio, S., Kemp, S., Patricios, J. S., Putukian, M., Zemek, R., Arango-Lasprilla, J. C., Bailey, C. M., Brett, B. L., Didehbani, N., Gioia, G., Herring, S. A., …, Schneider, K. J. (2023). Acute evaluation of sport-related concussion and implications for the Sport Concussion Assessment Tool (SCAT6) for adults, adolescents and children: A systematic review. *British Journal of Sports Medicine, 57*, 722–735. https://doi.org/10.1136/bjsports-2022-106661.

Echemendia, R. J., Meeuwisse, W., McCrory, P., Davis, G. A., Putukian, M., Leddy, J., Makdissi, M., Sullivan, S. J., Broglio, S. P., Raftery, M., Schneider, K., Kissick, J., McCrea, M., Dvorak, J., Sills, A. K., Aubry, M., Engebretsen, L., Loosemore, M., Fuller, G., …, Herring, S. (2017). The Sport Concussion Assessment Tool 5th Edition (SCAT5): Background and rationale. *British Journal of Sports Medicine, 51*, 848–850. https://doi.org/10.1136/bjsports-2017-097506.

Echlin, H. V., Rahimi, A., & Wojtowicz, M. (2021). Systematic review of the long-term neuroimaging correlates of mild traumatic brain injury and repetitive head injuries. *Frontiers in Neurology, 12*, 726425. https://doi.org/10.3389/fneur.2021.726425

Ellis, M. J., McDonald, P. J., Olson, A., Koenig, J., & Russell, K. (2019). Cervical spine dysfunction following pediatric sports-related head trauma. *The Journal of Head Trauma Rehabilitation, 34*, 103–110. https://doi.org/10.1097/HTR.0000000000000411

Galeno, E., Pullano, E., Mourad, F., Galeoto, G., & Frontani, F. (2022). Effectiveness of vestibular rehabilitation after concussion: A Systematic review of randomised controlled trial. *Healthcare (Basel)*, 11. https://doi.org/10.3390/healthcare11010090

Gallo, V., Motley, K., Kemp, S. P. T., Mian, S., Patel, T., James, L., Pearce, N., & McElvenny, D. (2020). Concussion and long-term cognitive impairment among professional or elite sport-persons: a systematic review. *Journal of Neurology, Neurosurgery, and Psychiatry, 91*, 455–468. https://doi.org/10.1136/jnnp-2019-321170

Gavett, B. E., Stern, R. A., & McKee, A. C. (2011). Chronic traumatic encephalopathy: a potential late effect of sport-related concussive and subconcussive head trauma. *Clinics in Sports Medicine, 30*(179-188), xi. S0278-5919(10)00086-4 [pii]. https://doi.org/10.1016/j.csm.2010.09.007

Haider, M. N., Lutnick, E., Nazir, M. S. Z., Nowak, A., Chizuk, H. M., Miecznikowski, J. C., McPherson, J. I., Willer, B. S., & Leddy, J. J. (2023). Sensitivity and specificity of exercise intolerance on graded exertion testing for diagnosing sport-related concussion: A systematic review and exploratory meta-analysis. *Journal of Neurotrauma*. https://doi.org/10.1089/neu.2022.0331

Iverson, G. L. (2019). Network analysis and precision rehabilitation for the post-concussion syndrome. *Frontiers in Neurology, 10*, 489.

Iverson, G. L., Buttner, F., & Caccese, J. B. (2021). Age of first exposure to contact and collision sports and later in life brain health: A narrative review. *Frontiers in Neurology, 12*, 727089. https://doi.org/10.3389/fneur.2021.727089

Iverson, G. L., Castellani, R. J., Cassidy, J. D., Schneider, G. M., Schneider, K. J., Echemendia, R. J., Bailes, J. E., Hayden, K. A., Koerte, I. K., Manley, G. T., McNamee, M., Patricios, J. S., Tator, C. H., Cantu, R. C., & Dvorak, J. (2023). Examining later-in-life health risks associated with sport-related concussion and repetitive head impacts: a systematic review of case-control and cohort studies. *British Journal of Sports Medicine, 57*, 810–821. https://doi.org/10.1136/bjsports-2023-106890

Iverson, G. L., & Gardner, A. J. (2021). Symptoms of traumatic encephalopathy syndrome are common in the US general population. *Brain Communications, 3*, fcab001. https://doi.org/10.1093/braincomms/fcab001

Iverson, G. L., & Gardner, A. J. (2022). Incidence of concussion and time to return-to-play in the national rugby league. *Clinical Journal of Sport Medicine, 32*, 595–599. https://doi.org/10.1097/JSM.0000000000000965

Iverson, G. L., Gardner, A. J., Shultz, S. R., Solomon, G. S., McCrory, P., Zafonte, R., Perry, G., Hazrati, L. N., Keene, C. D., & Castellani, R. J. (2019). Chronic traumatic encephalopathy neuropathology might not be inexorably progressive or unique to repetitive neurotrauma. *Brain, 142*, 3672–3693. https://doi.org/10.1093/brain/awz286

Iverson, G. L., Gardner, A. J., Terry, D. P., Ponsford, J. L., Sills, A. K., Broshek, D. K., & Solomon, G. S. (2017). Predictors of clinical recovery from concussion: a systematic review. *British Journal of Sports Medicine, 51*, 941–948. https://doi.org/10.1136/bjsports-2017-097729

Iverson, G. L., & Gioia, G. A. (2016). Returning to school following sport-related concussion. *Physical Medicine and Rehabilitation Clinics of North America, 27*, 429–436. https://doi.org/10.1016/j.pmr.2015.12.002

Iverson, G. L., Keene, C. D., Perry, G., & Castellani, R. J. (2018). The need to separate chronic traumatic encephalopathy neuropathology from clinical features. *Journal of Alzheimer's Disease, 61*, 17–28. https://doi.org/10.3233/JAD-170654

Iverson, G. L., & Lange, R. T. (2003). Examination of "postconcussion-like" symptoms in a healthy sample. *Applied Neuropsychology, 10*, 137–144. https://doi.org/10.1207/S15324826AN1003_02

Iverson, G. L., Merz, Z. C., & Terry, D. P. (2021). Playing high school football is not associated with an increased risk for suicidality in early adulthood. *Clinical Journal of Sport Medicine, 31*, 469–474.

Iverson, G. L., & Schatz, P. (2019). Brief iPad-based assessment of cognitive functioning with ImPACT(R) pediatric. *Developmental Neuropsychology, 44*, 43–49. https://doi.org/10.1080/87565641.2018.1545844

Iverson, G. L., Silverberg, N. D., Mannix, R., Maxwell, B. A., Atkins, J. E., Zafonte, R., & Berkner, P. D. (2015). Factors associated with concussion-like symptom reporting in high school athletes. *JAMA Pediatrics, 169*, 1132–1140. https://doi.org/10.1001/jamapediatrics.2015.2374

Iverson, G. L., & Terry, D. P. (2022). High school football and risk for depression and suicidality in adulthood: Findings from a national longitudinal study. *Frontiers in Neurology, 12*, 812604. https://doi.org/10.3389/fneur.2021.812604

Iverson, G. L., Terry, D. P., Maxwell, B., Zafonte, R., Berkner, P. D., & Cook, N. E. (2021). Greater acute concussion symptoms are associated with longer recovery times in NCAA Division III Collegiate Athletes. *Frontiers in Neurology, 12*, 801607. https://doi.org/10.3389/fneur.2021.801607

Jaganathan, K. S., Sullivan, K. A., Kinmond, S., Berndt, S., Street, S., Haden, C., Greenslade, J., McMahon, K., Mitchell, G., & Kerr, G. (2023). Exercise parameters for postconcussion symptom rehabilitation: A systematic review. *Journal of Sport Rehabilitation*, 1–10. https://doi.org/10.1123/jsr.2022-0122

Janssen, P. H., Mandrekar, J., Mielke, M. M., Ahlskog, J. E., Boeve, B. F., Josephs, K., & Savica, R. (2017). High school football and late-life risk of neurodegenerative syndromes, 1956-1970. *Mayo Clinic Proceedings, 92*, 66–71. https://doi.org/10.1016/j.mayocp.2016.09.004

Jayakody, K., Gunadasa, S., & Hosker, C. (2014). Exercise for anxiety disorders: systematic review. *British Journal of Sports Medicine, 48*, 187–196. https://doi.org/10.1136/bjsports-2012-091287

Kamins, J., Bigler, E., Covassin, T., Henry, L., Kemp, S., Leddy, J. J., Mayer, A., McCrea, M., Prins, M., Schneider, K. J., Valovich McLeod, T. C., Zemek, R., & Giza, C. C. (2017). What is the physiological time to recovery after concussion? A systematic review. *British Journal of Sports Medicine, 51*, 935–940. https://doi.org/10.1136/bjsports-2016-097464

Kara, S., Crosswell, H., Forch, K., Cavadino, A., McGeown, J., & Fulcher, M. (2020). Less than half of patients recover within 2 weeks of injury after a sports-related mild traumatic brain injury: A 2-year prospective study. *Clinical Journal of Sport Medicine, 30*, 96–101. https://doi.org/10.1097/JSM.0000000000000811

Katz, D. I., Bernick, C., Dodick, D. W., Mez, J., Mariani, M. L., Adler, C. H., Alosco, M. L., Balcer, L. J., Banks, S. J., Barr, W. B., Brody, D. L., Cantu, R. C., Dams-O'Connor, K., Geda, Y. E., Jordan, B. D., McAllister, T. W., Peskind, E. R., Petersen, R. C., Wethe, J. V., …, Stern, R. A. (2021). National Institute of Neurological Disorders and Stroke consensus diagnostic criteria for traumatic encephalopathy syndrome. *Neurology, 96*, 848–863. https://doi.org/10.1212/WNL.0000000000011850.

Kelshaw, P. M., Cook, N. E., Terry, D. P., Iverson, G. L., & Caswell, S. V. (2022). Child Sport Concussion Assessment Tool 5th edition: Normative reference values in demographically diverse youth. *Clinical Journal of Sport Medicine, 32*, e126–e133. https://doi.org/10.1097/JSM.0000000000000921

King, D., Brughelli, M., Hume, P., & Gissane, C. (2014). Assessment, management and knowledge of sport-related concussion: systematic review. *Sports Medicine, 44*, 449–471. https://doi.org/10.1007/s40279-013-0134-x

Langevin, P., FrEmont, P., Fait, P., Dub, E. M., Bertrand-Charette, M., & Roy, J. S. (2020). Aerobic exercise for sport-related concussion: A systematic review and meta-analysis. *Medicine and Science in Sports and Exercise, 52*, 2491–2499. https://doi.org/10.1249/MSS.0000000000002402

Leddy, J. J., Burma, J. S., Toomey, C. M., Hayden, A., Davis, G. A., Babl, F. E., Gagnon, I., Giza, C. C., Kurowski, B. G., Silverberg, N. D., Willer, B., Ronksley, P. E., & Schneider, K. J. (2023). Rest and exercise early after sport-related concussion: a systematic review and meta-analysis. *British Journal of Sports Medicine, 57*, 762–770. https://doi.org/10.1136/bjsports-2022-106676

Ledoux, A. A., Tang, K., Yeates, K. O., Pusic, M. V., Boutis, K., Craig, W. R., Gravel, J., Freedman, S. B., Gagnon, I., Gioia, G. A., Osmond, M. H., Zemek, R. L., & Pediatric Emergency Research Canada Concussion Team. (2019). Natural progression of symptom change and recovery from concussion in a pediatric population. *JAMA Pediatrics, 173*, e183820. https://doi.org/10.1001/jamapediatrics.2018.3820

Lee, B. G., Leavitt, M. J., Bernick, C. B., Leger, G. C., Rabinovici, G., & Banks, S. J. (2018). A systematic review of positron emission tomography of tau, amyloid beta, and neuroinflammation in chronic traumatic encephalopathy: The evidence to date. *Journal of Neurotrauma, 35*, 2015–2024. https://doi.org/10.1089/neu.2017.5558

Lee, E. B., Kinch, K., Johnson, V. E., Trojanowski, J. Q., Smith, D. H., & Stewart, W. (2019). Chronic traumatic encephalopathy is a common co-morbidity, but less frequent primary dementia in former soccer and rugby players. *Acta Neuropathologica, 138*, 389–399. https://doi.org/10.1007/s00401-019-02030-y

Legarreta, A. D., Monk, S. H., Kirby, P. W., Brett, B. L., Yengo-Kahn, A. M., Bhatia, A., Solomon, G. S., & Zuckerman, S. L. (2018). Long-term neuroimaging findings in American football players: Systematic review. *World Neurosurgery, 120*, e365–e379. https://doi.org/10.1016/j.wneu.2018.08.079

Lehman, E. J., Hein, M. J., Baron, S. L., & Gersic, C. M. (2012). Neurodegenerative causes of death among retired National Football League players. *Neurology, 79*, 1970–1974. https://doi.org/10.1212/WNL.0b013e31826daf50

Lehman, E. J., Hein, M. J., & Gersic, C. M. (2016). Suicide mortality among retired National Football League players who played 5 or more seasons. *The American Journal of Sports Medicine, 44*, 2486–2491. https://doi.org/10.1177/0363546516645093

Lesman-Segev, O. H., Edwards, L., & Rabinovici, G. D. (2020). Chronic traumatic encephalopathy: A comparison with Alzheimer's disease and frontotemporal dementia. *Seminars in Neurology, 40*, 394–410. https://doi.org/10.1055/s-0040-1715134

Lincoln, A. E., Vogel, R. A., Allen, T. W., Dunn, R. E., Alexander, K., Kaufman, N. D., & Tucker, A. M. (2018). Risk and causes of death among former National Football League players (1986-2012). *Medicine and Science in Sports and Exercise, 50*, 486–493. https://doi.org/10.1249/MSS.0000000000001466

LoBue, C., Schaffert, J., & Cullum, C. M. (2020). Chronic traumatic encephalopathy: understanding the facts and debate. *Current Opinion in Psychiatry, 33*, 130–135. https://doi.org/10.1097/YCO.0000000000000580

Mackay, D. F., Russell, E. R., Stewart, K., MacLean, J. A., Pell, J. P., & Stewart, W. (2019). Neurodegenerative disease mortality among former professional soccer players. *The New England Journal of Medicine, 381*, 1801–1808. https://doi.org/10.1056/NEJMoa1908483

Makdissi, M., Critchley, M. L., Cantu, R. C., Caron, J. G., Davis, G. A., Echemendia, R. J., Fremont, P., Hayden, K. A., Herring, S. A., Hinds, S. R., Jordan, B., Kemp, S., McNamee, M., Maddocks, D., Nagahiro, S., Patricios, J., Putukian, M., Turner, M., Sick, S., & Schneider, K. J. (2023). When should an athlete retire or discontinue participating in contact or collision sports following sport-related concussion? A systematic review. *British Journal of Sports Medicine, 57*, 822–830. https://doi.org/10.1136/bjsports-2023-106815

Makdissi, M., Schneider, K. J., Feddermann-Demont, N., Guskiewicz, K. M., Hinds, S., Leddy, J. J., McCrea, M., Turner, M., & Johnston, K. M. (2017). Approach to investigation and treatment of persistent symptoms following sport-related concussion: a systematic review. *British Journal of Sports Medicine, 51*, 958–968. https://doi.org/10.1136/bjsports-2016-097470

Manley, G., Gardner, A. J., Schneider, K. J., Guskiewicz, K. M., Bailes, J., Cantu, R. C., Castellani, R. J., Turner, M., Jordan, B. D., Randolph, C., Dvorak, J., Hayden, K. A., Tator, C. H., McCrory, P., & Iverson, G. L. (2017). A systematic review of potential long-term effects of sport-related concussion. *British Journal of Sports Medicine, 51*, 969–977. https://doi.org/10.1136/bjsports-2017-097791

Manzanero, S., Elkington, L. J., Praet, S., Lovell, G., Waddington, G., & Highes, D. C. (2017). Post-concussion recovery in children and adolescents: A narrative review. *Journal of Concussion, 1*, 2059700217726874.

Martland, H. S. (1928). Punch drunk. *Journal of the American Medical Association, 91*, 1103–1107.

McAllister, T. W., Broglio, S. P., Katz, B. P., Perkins, S. M., LaPradd, M., Zhou, W., McCrea, M. A., & Concussion Assessment, Research and Education (CARE) Consortium. (2023). Characteristics and outcomes of athletes with slow recovery from sports-related concussion: A CARE Consortium Study. *Neurology, 100*, e1510–e1519. https://doi.org/10.1212/WNL.0000000000206853

McCarty, C. A., Zatzick, D., Stein, E., Wang, J., Hilt, R., Rivara, F. P., & Seattle Sports Concussion Research Collaborative. (2016). Collaborative care for adolescents with persistent postconcussive symptoms: A randomized trial. *Pediatrics*, 138. https://doi.org/10.1542/peds.2016-0459

McCarty, C. A., Zatzick, D. F., Marcynyszyn, L. A., Wang, J., Hilt, R., Jinguji, T., Quitiquit, C., Chrisman, S. P. D., & Rivara, F. P. (2021). Effect of collaborative care on persistent postconcussive symptoms in adolescents: A randomized clinical trial. *JAMA Network Open, 4*, e210207. https://doi.org/10.1001/jamanetworkopen.2021.0207

McCrea, M., Guskiewicz, K., Randolph, C., Barr, W. B., Hammeke, T. A., Marshall, S. W., Powell, M. R., Woo Ahn, K., Wang, Y., & Kelly, J. P. (2013). Incidence, clinical course, and predictors of prolonged recovery time following sport-related concussion in high school and college athletes. *Journal of the International Neuropsychological Society, 19*, 22–33. https://doi.org/10.1017/S1355617712000872

McKee, A. C. (2020). The neuropathology of chronic traumatic encephalopathy: The status of the literature. *Seminars in Neurology, 40*, 359–369. https://doi.org/10.1055/s-0040-1713632

McKee, A. C., Cairns, N. J., Dickson, D. W., Folkerth, R. D., Keene, C. D., Litvan, I., Perl, D. P., Stein, T. D., Vonsattel, J. P., Stewart, W., Tripodis, Y., Crary, J. F., Bieniek, K. F., Dams-O'Connor, K., Alvarez, V. E., Gordon, W. A., & TBI/CTE Group. (2016). The first NINDS/NIBIB consensus meeting to define neuropathological criteria for the diagnosis of chronic traumatic encephalopathy. *Acta Neuropathologica, 131*, 75–86. https://doi.org/10.1007/s00401-015-1515-z

McKee, A. C., Gavett, B. E., Stern, R. A., Nowinski, C. J., Cantu, R. C., Kowall, N. W., Perl, D. P., Hedley-Whyte, E. T., Price, B., Sullivan, C., Morin, P., Lee, H. S., Kubilus, C. A., Daneshvar, D. H., Wulff, M., & Budson, A. E. (2010). TDP-43 proteinopathy and motor neuron disease in chronic traumatic encephalopathy. *Journal of Neuropathology and Experimental Neurology, 69*, 918–929. https://doi.org/10.1097/NEN.0b013e3181ee7d85

McKee, A. C., Stein, T. D., Nowinski, C. J., Stern, R. A., Daneshvar, D. H., Alvarez, V. E., Lee, H. S., Hall, G., Wojtowicz, S. M., Baugh, C. M., Riley, D. O., Kubilus, C. A., Cormier, K. A., Jacobs, M. A., Martin, B. R., Abraham, C. R., Ikezu, T., Reichard, R. R., Wolozin, B. L., …, Cantu, R. C. (2013). The spectrum of disease in chronic traumatic encephalopathy. *Brain, 136*, 43–64.

Mez, J., Alosco, M. L., Daneshvar, D. H., Saltiel, N., Baucom, Z., Abdolmohammadi, B., Uretsky, M., Nicks, R., Martin, B. M., Palmisano, J. N., Nowinski, C. J., Montenigro, P., Solomon, T. M., Mahar, I., Cherry, J. D., Alvarez, V. E., Dwyer, B., Goldstein, L. E., Katz, D. I., …, McKee, A. C. (2021). Validity of the 2014 traumatic encephalopathy syndrome criteria for CTE pathology. *Alzheimer's & Dementia, 17*, 1709–1724. https://doi.org/10.1002/alz.12338.

Millspaugh, J. A. (1937). Dementia pugilistica. *US Naval Medicine Bulletin, 35*, 297–303.
Miutz, L. N., Burma, J. S., Lapointe, A. P., Newel, K. T., Emery, C. A., & Smirl, J. D. (1985). Physical activity following sport-related concussion in adolescents: a systematic review. *Journal of Applied Physiology, 2022*(132), 1250–1266. https://doi.org/10.1152/japplphysiol.00691.2021
Montenigro, P. H., Baugh, C. M., Daneshvar, D. H., Mez, J., Budson, A. E., Au, R., Katz, D. I., Cantu, R. C., & Stern, R. A. (2014). Clinical subtypes of chronic traumatic encephalopathy: literature review and proposed research diagnostic criteria for traumatic encephalopathy syndrome. *Alzheimer's Research & Therapy, 6*, 68. https://doi.org/10.1186/s13195-014-0068-z
Morales, J. S., Castillo-Garcia, A., Valenzuela, P. L., Saco-Ledo, G., Manas, A., Santos-Lozano, A., & Lucia, A. (2021). Mortality from mental disorders and suicide in male professional American football and soccer players: A meta-analysis. *Scandinavian Journal of Medicine & Science in Sports, 31*, 2241–2248. https://doi.org/10.1111/sms.14038
Morales, J. S., Valenzuela, P. L., Saco-Ledo, G., Castillo-Garcia, A., Carabias, C. S., McCrory, P., Santos-Lozano, A., & Lucia, A. (2022). Mortality risk from neurodegenerative disease in sports associated with repetitive head impacts: Preliminary findings from a systematic review and meta-analysis. *Sports Medicine, 52*, 835–846. https://doi.org/10.1007/s40279-021-01580-0
Murray, H. C., Osterman, C., Bell, P., Vinnell, L., & Curtis, M. A. (2022). Neuropathology in chronic traumatic encephalopathy: a systematic review of comparative post-mortem histology literature. *Acta Neuropathologica Communications, 10*, 108. https://doi.org/10.1186/s40478-022-01413-9
Omalu, B. (2014). Chronic traumatic encephalopathy. *Progress in Neurological Surgery, 28*, 38–49. https://doi.org/10.1159/000358761
Omalu, B., Bailes, J., Hamilton, R. L., Kamboh, M. I., Hammers, J., Case, M., & Fitzsimmons, R. (2011). Emerging histomorphologic phenotypes of chronic traumatic encephalopathy in American athletes. *Neurosurgery, 69*, 173-183.; Discussion 183. https://doi.org/10.1227/NEU.0b013e318212bc7b
Omalu, B. I., Bailes, J., Hammers, J. L., & Fitzsimmons, R. P. (2010). Chronic traumatic encephalopathy, suicides and parasuicides in professional American athletes: the role of the forensic pathologist. *The American Journal of Forensic Medicine and Pathology, 31*, 130–132. https://doi.org/10.1097/PAF.0b013e3181ca7f35
Omalu, B. I., DeKosky, S. T., Minster, R. L., Kamboh, M. I., Hamilton, R. L., & Wecht, C. H. (2005). Chronic traumatic encephalopathy in a National Football League player. *Neurosurgery, 57*, 128–134. Discussion 128-134.
Patricios, J. S., Davis, G. A., Ahmed, O. H., Blauwet, C., Schneider, G. M., Purcell, L. K., Echemendia, R. J., Fremont, P., Fuller, G. W., Herring, S. A., Harmon, K. G., Loosemore, M., Makdissi, M., O'Halloran, P., Putukian, M., Turner, M., Webborn, N., Yeates, K. O., van Ierssel, J., & Schneider, K. J. (2023). Introducing the Sport Concussion Office Assessment Tool 6 (SCOAT6). *British Journal of Sports Medicine, 57*, 648–650. https://doi.org/10.1136/bjsports-2023-106860
Patricios, J. S., Schneider, G. M., van Ierssel, J., Purcell, L. K., Davis, G. A., Echemendia, R. J., Fremont, P., Fuller, G. W., Herring, S. A., Harmon, K. G., Holte, K., Loosemore, M., Makdissi, M., McCrea, M., Meehan, W. P., 3rd, O'Halloran, P., Premji, Z., Putukian, M., Shill, I. J., …, Schneider, K. J. (2023). Beyond acute concussion assessment to office management: A systematic review informing the development of a Sport Concussion Office Assessment Tool (SCOAT6) for adults and children. *British Journal of Sports Medicine, 57*, 737–748. https://doi.org/10.1136/bjsports-2023-106897.
Patricios, J. S., Schneider, K. J., Dvorak, J., Ahmed, O. H., Blauwet, C., Cantu, R. C., Davis, G. A., Echemendia, R. J., Makdissi, M., McNamee, M., Broglio, S., Emery, C. A., Feddermann-Demont, N., Fuller, G. W., Giza, C. C., Guskiewicz, K. M., Hainline, B., Iverson, G. L., Kutcher, J. S., …, Meeuwisse, W. (2023). Consensus statement on concussion in sport: the 6th international conference on concussion in sport-Amsterdam, October 2022. *British Journal of Sports Medicine, 57,* 695–711. https://doi.org/10.1136/bjsports-2023-106898.

Pfister, T., Pfister, K., Hagel, B., Ghali, W. A., & Ronksley, P. E. (2016). The incidence of concussion in youth sports: a systematic review and meta-analysis. *British Journal of Sports Medicine, 50*, 292–297. https://doi.org/10.1136/bjsports-2015-094978

Prien, A., Grafe, A., Rossler, R., Junge, A., & Verhagen, E. (2018). Epidemiology of head injuries focusing on concussions in team contact sports: A systematic review. *Sports Medicine, 48*, 953–969. https://doi.org/10.1007/s40279-017-0854-4

Prien, A., Junge, A., Brugger, P., Straumann, D., & Feddermann-Demont, N. (2019). Neurocognitive performance of 425 top-level football players: Sport-specific norm values and implications. *Archives of Clinical Neuropsychology, 34*, 575–584. https://doi.org/10.1093/arclin/acy056

Pupillo, E., Bianchi, E., Vanacore, N., Montalto, C., Ricca, G., Robustelli Della Cuna, F. S., Fumagalli, F., Castellani, M., Poli, F., Romeo, F., Tommasi, D., Lazzaro, P., & Beghi, E. (2020). Increased risk and early onset of ALS in professional players from Italian Soccer Teams. *Amyotrophic Lateral Sclerosis and Frontotemporal Degeneration, 21*, 403–409. https://doi.org/10.1080/21678421.2020.1752250

Purcell, L., Harvey, J., & Seabrook, J. A. (2016). Patterns of recovery following sport-related concussion in children and adolescents. *Clinical Pediatrics (Phila), 55*, 452–458. https://doi.org/10.1177/0009922815589915

Putukian, M., Purcell, L., Schneider, K. J., Black, A. M., Burma, J. S., Chandran, A., Boltz, A., Master, C. L., Register-Mihalik, J. K., Anderson, V., Davis, G. A., Fremont, P., Leddy, J. J., Maddocks, D., Premji, Z., Ronksley, P. E., Herring, S., & Broglio, S. (2023). Clinical recovery from concussion-return to school and sport: a systematic review and meta-analysis. *British Journal of Sports Medicine, 57*, 798–809. https://doi.org/10.1136/bjsports-2022-106682

Rogers, S. D., Smith, P. J., Stephenson, A. J., & Erik Everhart, D. (2017). A retrospective cross-sectional and longitudinal study of the effects of age on CNS vital signs scores in high-school athletes. *Sports Medicine, 47*, 1893–1899. https://doi.org/10.1007/s40279-017-0686-2

Russell, E. R., McCabe, T., Mackay, D. F., Stewart, K., MacLean, J. A., Pell, J. P., & Stewart, W. (2020). Mental health and suicide in former professional soccer players. *Journal of Neurology, Neurosurgery, and Psychiatry, 91*, 1256–1260. https://doi.org/10.1136/jnnp-2020-323315

Savica, R., Parisi, J. E., Wold, L. E., Josephs, K. A., & Ahlskog, J. E. (2012). High school football and risk of neurodegeneration: a community-based study. *Mayo Clinic Proceedings, 87*, 335–340. https://doi.org/10.1016/j.mayocp.2011.12.016

Schneider, K. J., Leddy, J. J., Guskiewicz, K. M., Seifert, T., McCrea, M., Silverberg, N. D., Feddermann-Demont, N., Iverson, G. L., Hayden, A., & Makdissi, M. (2017). Rest and treatment/rehabilitation following sport-related concussion: a systematic review. *British Journal of Sports Medicine, 51*, 930–934. https://doi.org/10.1136/bjsports-2016-097475

Schneider, K. J., Meeuwisse, W. H., Nettel-Aguirre, A., Barlow, K., Boyd, L., Kang, J., & Emery, C. A. (2014). Cervicovestibular rehabilitation in sport-related concussion: a randomised controlled trial. *British Journal of Sports Medicine, 48*, 1294–1298. https://doi.org/10.1136/bjsports-2013-093267

Shively, S. B., Priemer, D. S., Stein, M. B., & Perl, D. P. (2021). Pathophysiology of traumatic brain injury, chronic traumatic encephalopathy, and neuropsychiatric clinical expression. *The Psychiatric Clinics of North America, 44*, 443–458. https://doi.org/10.1016/j.psc.2021.04.003

Silverberg, N. D., Iverson, G. L., ACRM Brain Injury Special Interest Group Mild TBI Task Force Members, Cogan, A., Dams, O. C. K., Delmonico, R., Graf, M. J. P., Iaccarino, M. A., Kajankova, M., Kamins, J., McCulloch, K. L., McKinney, G., Nagele, D., Panenka, W. J., Rabinowitz, A. R., Reed, N., Wethe, J. V., Whitehair, V., ACRM Mild TBI Diagnostic Criteria Expert Consensus Group, …, Zemek, R. (2023). The American Congress of Rehabilitation Medicine diagnostic criteria for mild traumatic brain injury. *Archives of Physical Medicine and Rehabilitation, 104*, 1343–1355. https://doi.org/10.1016/j.apmr.2023.03.036.

Smith, D. H., Johnson, V. E., Trojanowski, J. Q., & Stewart, W. (2019). Chronic traumatic encephalopathy—Confusion and controversies. *Nature Reviews. Neurology, 15*, 179–183. https://doi.org/10.1038/s41582-018-0114-8

Sparks, P., Lawrence, T., & Hinze, S. (2020). Neuroimaging in the diagnosis of chronic traumatic encephalopathy: A systematic review. *Clinical Journal of Sport Medicine, 30*(Suppl 1), S1–S10. https://doi.org/10.1097/JSM.0000000000000541

Stein, T. D., & Crary, J. F. (2020). Chronic traumatic encephalopathy and neuropathological comorbidities. *Seminars in Neurology, 40*, 384–393. https://doi.org/10.1055/s-0040-1713628

Stern, R. A., Daneshvar, D. H., Baugh, C. M., Seichepine, D. R., Montenigro, P. H., Riley, D. O., Fritts, N. G., Stamm, J. M., Robbins, C. A., McHale, L., Simkin, I., Stein, T. D., Alvarez, V. E., Goldstein, L. E., Budson, A. E., Kowall, N. W., Nowinski, C. J., Cantu, R. C., & McKee, A. C. (2013). Clinical presentation of chronic traumatic encephalopathy. *Neurology, 81*, 1122–1129. https://doi.org/10.1212/WNL.0b013e3182a55f7f

Stern, R. A., Riley, D. O., Daneshvar, D. H., Nowinski, C. J., Cantu, R. C., & McKee, A. C. (2011). Long-term consequences of repetitive brain trauma: chronic traumatic encephalopathy. *PM & R: The Journal of Injury, Function, and Rehabilitation, 3*, S460–S467. https://doi.org/10.1016/j.pmrj.2011.08.008

Tabor, J. B., Brett, B. L., Nelson, L., Meier, T., Penner, L. C., Mayer, A. R., Echemendia, R. J., McAllister, T., Meehan, W. P., 3rd, Patricios, J., Makdissi, M., Bressan, S., Davis, G. A., Premji, Z., Schneider, K. J., Zetterberg, H., & McCrea, M. (2023). Role of biomarkers and emerging technologies in defining and assessing neurobiological recovery after sport-related concussion: a systematic review. *British Journal of Sports Medicine, 57*, 789–797. https://doi.org/10.1136/bjsports-2022-106680

Taioli, E. (2007). All causes of mortality in male professional soccer players. *European Journal of Public Health, 17*, 600–604. https://doi.org/10.1093/eurpub/ckm035

Teel, E. F., Marshall, S. W., Shankar, V., McCrea, M., & Guskiewicz, K. M. (2017). Predicting recovery patterns after sport-related concussion. *Journal of Athletic Training, 52*, 288–298. https://doi.org/10.4085/1062-6050-52.1.12

Valenti, M., Pontieri, F. E., Conti, F., Altobelli, E., Manzoni, T., & Frati, L. (2005). Amyotrophic lateral sclerosis and sports: a case-control study. *European Journal of Neurology, 12*, 223–225. https://doi.org/10.1111/j.1468-1331.2004.00978.x

Van Patten, R., Iverson, G. L., Muzeau, M. A., & VanRavenhorst-Bell, H. A. (2021). Test-retest reliability and reliable change estimates for four mobile cognitive tests administered virtually in community-dwelling adults. *Frontiers in Psychology, 12*, 734947. https://doi.org/10.3389/fpsyg.2021.734947

Vos, B. C., Nieuwenhuijsen, K., & Sluiter, J. K. (2018). Consequences of traumatic brain injury in professional American football players: A systematic review of the literature. *Clinical Journal of Sport Medicine, 28*, 91–99. https://doi.org/10.1097/JSM.0000000000000432

Wallace, J., Schatz, P., Covassin, T., & Iverson, G. L. (2020). Brief iPad-based assessment of cognitive functioning with ImPACT(R) quick test: Prevalence of low scores using multivariate base rates. *Archives of Clinical Neuropsychology, 35*, 1276–1282. https://doi.org/10.1093/arclin/acaa078

Walshe, A., Daly, E., & Ryan, L. (2022). Epidemiology of sport-related concussion rates in female contact/collision sport: a systematic review. *BMJ Open Sport & Exercise Medicine, 8*, e001346. https://doi.org/10.1136/bmjsem-2022-001346

Weiss, J., Rabinowitz, A. R., Deshpande, S. K., Hasegawa, R. B., & Small, D. S. (2021). Participation in collision sports and cognitive aging among Swedish twins. *American Journal of Epidemiology, 190*, 2604–2611. https://doi.org/10.1093/aje/kwab177

Willer, B. S., Haider, M. N., Wilber, C., Esopenko, C., Turner, M., & Leddy, J. (2021). Long-term neurocognitive, mental health consequences of contact sports. *Clinics in Sports Medicine, 40*, 173–186. https://doi.org/10.1016/j.csm.2020.08.012

Williams, R. M., Puetz, T. W., Giza, C. C., & Broglio, S. P. (2015). Concussion recovery time among high school and collegiate athletes: a systematic review and meta-analysis. *Sports Medicine, 45*, 893–903. https://doi.org/10.1007/s40279-015-0325-8

Wilmoth, K., Brett, B. L., Emmert, N. A., Cook, C. M., Schaffert, J., Caze, T., 2nd, Kotsonis, T., Cusick, M., Solomon, G., Resch, J. E., Cullum, C. M., Nelson, L. D., & McCrea, M. (2022).

Psychometric properties of computerized cognitive tools and standard neuropsychological tests used to assess sport concussion: A systematic review. *Neuropsychology Review*. https://doi.org/10.1007/s11065-022-09553-4

Zemek, R., Barrowman, N., Freedman, S. B., Gravel, J., Gagnon, I., McGahern, C., Aglipay, M., Sangha, G., Boutis, K., Beer, D., Craig, W., Burns, E., Farion, K. J., Mikrogianakis, A., Barlow, K., Dubrovsky, A. S., Meeuwisse, W., Gioia, G., Meehan, W. P., 3rd, …, Osmond, M. H. (2016) Pediatric Emergency Research Canada Concussion Team. Clinical risk score for persistent postconcussion symptoms among children with acute concussion in the ED. *Journal of the American Medical Association, 315*, 1014–1025. https://doi.org/10.1001/jama.2016.1203.

Zhang, Y., Ma, Y., Chen, S., Liu, X., Kang, H. J., Nelson, S., & Bell, S. (2019). Long-term cognitive performance of retired athletes with sport-related concussion: A systematic review and meta-analysis. *Brain Sciences*, 9. https://doi.org/10.3390/brainsci9080199

Chapter 24
Mild Traumatic Brain Injury

Grant L. Iverson and Julia E. Maietta

Key Points and Chapter Summary

- Mild traumatic brain injury (mTBI) includes a broad spectrum of injuries that are characterized by a Glasgow Coma Scale score of 13–15, duration of loss of consciousness (LOC) from not present to 30 min, and duration of post-traumatic amnesia (PTA) from not present to 24 h.
- Clinical signs of mTBI may include LOC, alteration of mental status, complete or partial PTA and other neurological signs such as seizure or tonic posturing immediately following injury or motor incoordination upon standing and walking.
- Acute symptoms of mTBI may include subjective alteration in mental status, physical symptoms (i.e., headache, nausea, dizziness, balance problems, vision problems, sensitivity to light and/or noise), cognitive symptoms (i.e., feeling slowed down, mentally foggy, having difficulty concentrating, memory problems) and emotional symptoms (i.e., uncharacteristic emotional lability and/or irritability).
- A concussion, by definition, is an mTBI.
- An important subtype of injury within the mTBI spectrum is defined by the presence of a trauma-related structural intracranial abnormality on day-of-injury computed tomography or later magnetic resonance imaging.
- Cognitive impairment may be present within the initial hours, days and weeks after injury. Deficits on neuropsychological testing are not generally seen 1–3 months after mTBI. Those with neuroimaging evidence of intracranial injury may have, on average, modestly worse cognitive functioning after 3 months but these differences may not be present 6 or more months after injury.
- An initial brief period of rest (but not prolonged rest) and a gradual stepwise return to activities is beneficial for recovery. Early intervention, including education about the positive prognosis in mTBI, in combination with treatment and rehabilitation, may help to reduce the risk of persisting symptoms.

M. R. Schoenberg, J. G. Scott (eds.), *The Little Black Book of Neuropsychology*,
https://doi.org/10.1007/978-3-032-07777-6_24

Introduction and Epidemiology

Traumatic brain injuries (TBI) occur on an extraordinarily broad spectrum, from very mild to severe to catastrophic. Mild traumatic brain injury (mTBI) is the most common severity of injury. Estimates vary depending on the study methodology and where the sample is being recruited from, with approximately 60 to 95% of all TBIs classified within the mild range (Capizzi et al., 2020; Cassidy et al., 2004; Dewan et al., 2016; Lefevre-Dognin et al., 2021; Voss et al., 2015). Worldwide, the pooled annual incidence of mTBI is approximately 200–300 per 100,000, although these rates can vary dramatically by country (Cassidy et al., 2004; Lefevre-Dognin et al., 2021; Nguyen et al., 2016)—and those statistics are generally derived from hospital data which seriously underestimates the true incidence.

In epidemiological studies, data on the incidence of mTBI is usually estimated from research on patients in emergency departments who are diagnosed with mTBI. Many individuals who sustain an mTBI do not seek medical attention after their injury and are not evaluated in the emergency department or admitted to the hospital, and are therefore not captured in studies that rely on hospital-based data (Cassidy et al., 2004; Lefevre-Dognin et al., 2021; Nguyen et al., 2016). For example, in one retrospective study of patients in Australia with self-reported mTBI, 24% reported seeking no healthcare after their injury (Thorne et al., 2022). Another hospital-system-wide study of pediatric mTBI in the United States found that 82% of patients seek care from their primary care physician, not from the emergency room (Arbogast et al., 2016). Therefore, published incidence rates *underestimate* the true population incidence of mTBI. Some researchers suggest that the incidence is likely 600 per 100,000 or greater, but the annual incidence of mTBI remains unknown (Cassidy et al., 2004; Lefevre-Dognin et al., 2021).

Young children (infants to age 4), late adolescents/young adults (ages 15–24) and older adults (greater than 65 years) have the highest incidence rates of mTBI

G. L. Iverson (✉)
Department of Physical Medicine and Rehabilitation, Harvard Medical School, Boston, MA, USA

Department of Physical Medicine and Rehabilitation, Spaulding Rehabilitation, Boston, MA, USA

Schoen Adams Research Institute at Spaulding Rehabilitation, Boston, MA, USA

Mass General for Children Sports Concussion Program, Boston, MA, USA

Home Base, A Red Sox Foundation and Massachusetts General Hospital Program, Boston, MA, USA
e-mail: GIverson@mgh.harvard.edu

J. E. Maietta
Department of Physical Medicine and Rehabilitation, Harvard Medical School, Boston, MA, USA

Department of Physical Medicine and Rehabilitation, Spaulding Rehabilitation, Boston, MA, USA

Mass General for Children Sports Concussion Program, Boston, MA, USA

(Cancelliere et al., 2017; Lefevre-Dognin et al., 2021). The most common mechanism of mTBI in children and older adults (55 years and older) is falls while motor vehicle collisions are the most common mechanism for adults and young adults (Capizzi et al., 2020; Lefevre-Dognin et al., 2021; Voss et al., 2015). Blast-related mechanisms can occur in military service members (Allan & Lippa, 2022). Blast injury will not be covered in-depth here and interested readers are referred to Allan and Lippa (2022), Kim et al. (2023), Phipps et al. (2020), Robinson-Freeman et al. (2020) for further discussion. There is a separate chapter on sport-related concussion in this book.

It is not known, precisely, how common it is to sustain an mTBI over the course of a lifetime. Lifetime history of mTBI can vary considerably based on the age of the subjects at the time they are asked and how the injury is defined. Estimates of the prevalence of lifetime history of concussion ranged from 6.5 to 18.3% for adolescents 13–17 years across three national surveys (Haarbauer-Krupa et al., 2020). The prevalence varies considerably based on who answered the question, with parents reporting that 6.5–10.2% of their adolescent children have a prior history of concussion, whereas 18.3% of adolescents who were directly surveyed reported a lifetime history of concussion (Haarbauer-Krupa et al., 2020). In a sample of more than 27,000 adolescents from the state of Maine who completed a health survey prior to participating in sports, 16.1% (18.7% of boys and 13.4% of girls) reported a personal history of concussion (Iverson et al., 2020). In a sample of convenience of 6427 adults from the US general population, 28.9% reported a lifetime history of concussion (34.8% of men and 24.0% of women; Daugherty et al., 2020). Two recent longitudinal, prospective, cohort studies in New Zealand and the UK reported lifetime mTBI prevalence rates of 36.3 and 59.5% in their samples of middle and older aged adults (Lennon et al., 2023; Theadom et al., 2024). Other US-based population survey studies have primarily used the presence of loss of consciousness (LOC) to operationalize occurrence of TBI in their respondents, so these estimates do not generalize to the lifetime prevalence of mTBI without LOC. The results of these surveys have generally reported lifetime prevalence rates of mTBI (with LOC) to be between 16 and 20% (Bogner et al., 2020; Manchester et al., 2020; Sarmiento et al., 2022; Waltzman et al., 2022; Whiteneck et al., 2016a, 2016b; Yi et al., 2018).

Definitions and Diagnostic Criteria for mTBI

There are several definitions and diagnostic criteria for mTBI and none of these are universally accepted. Most criteria are based on initial severity indicators such as duration of LOC, Glasgow Coma Scale (GCS) and duration of post-traumatic amnesia (PTA). Definitions have been created by the Centers for Disease Control and Prevention working group (Center for Disease Control and Prevention, 2003), the World Health Organization (WHO) Collaborating Centre for Neurotrauma Task Force (Holm et al., 2005), the Concussion in Sport Group (Aubry et al., 2002; McCrory et al., 2005, 2009, 2013, 2017; Patricios et al., 2023), the Department of Veterans Affairs and Department of Defense (Management of Concussion/mTBI Working Group, 2009, 2016) and the

Mild Traumatic Brain Injury Committee of the Head Injury Interdisciplinary Special Interest Group of the American Congress of Rehabilitation Medicine (ACRM; Silverberg et al., 2023). Most commonly used definitions of mTBI are relatively similar and these similarities have been reviewed elsewhere (Silverberg et al., 2021). The new ACRM diagnostic criteria for mTBI were published in 2023, after several years in development, and they are described in detail below.

American Congress of Rehabilitation Medicine (ACRM) Diagnostic Criteria for Mild Traumatic Brain Injury

The 2023 ACRM diagnostic criteria for mTBI are presented in Tables 24.1 and 24.2 (Silverberg et al., 2023). One or more of the following three criteria must be met. The patient must present with (1) one or more clinical sign(s) attributable to brain injury, (2) at least two or more acute symptoms and one or more clinical or laboratory finding attributable to brain injury and/or (3) neuroimaging evidence of TBI that is apparent on computed tomography (CT) or magnetic resonance imaging (MRI) and is unambiguously trauma related. The mechanism of injury must be biomechanically plausible, and possible confounding factors for clinical signs and symptoms must be considered. Table 24.2 provides definitions, explanatory notes and qualifiers for the ACRM diagnostic criteria presented in Table 24.1.

A "mild" qualifier is added to the diagnosis of TBI (i.e., mTBI) only if the injury criteria do not meet threshold for a moderate or severe TBI. Specifically, LOC must be less than 30 min, GCS must be greater than or equal to 13 out of 15 (30 min after injury) and PTA cannot exceed 24 h. If any of these criteria exceed the listed thresholds, then a TBI is diagnosed without the "mild" qualifier and the injury is considered to be moderate or severe (depending on severity of the clinical signs). In the case of mTBI with abnormal neuroimaging, a qualifier of "with neuroimaging evidence of structural intracranial injury" may be used to describe what was previously termed a *complicated* mTBI. Similarly, when there is a normal neuroimaging result, "without neuroimaging evidence of structural intracranial injury" would be used as a qualifier instead to indicate what was previously described as *uncomplicated* mTBI.

Diagnostic Challenges

Sometimes it can be difficult to distinguish between LOC and PTA. When people experience a period of LOC, they will be amnestic for that period, and as they regain arousal and awareness they will usually experience at least brief post-traumatic confusion or PTA. A person cannot know with reasonable certainty if they experienced LOC—reliable documentation of that is from a witness or if captured on video (such as in sports films or on a surveillance camera). Sometimes a patient in a car

Table 24.1 American congress of rehabilitation medicine diagnostic criteria for mild traumatic brain injury

Mild traumatic brain injury (TBI) is diagnosed when, following a biomechanically plausible mechanism of injury (Criterion 1) *one or more* of the criteria (i-iii) listed below are met. i. One or more clinical signs (Criterion 2) attributable to brain injury ii. At least two acute symptoms (Criterion 3) and at least one clinical or laboratory finding (Criterion 4) attributable to brain injury. iii. Neuroimaging evidence of TBI, such as unambiguous trauma-related intracranial abnormalities on computed tomography or structural magnetic resonance imaging (Criterion 5). Confounding factors do not fully account for the clinical signs (Criterion 2), acute symptoms (Criterion 3) and clinical examination and laboratory findings (Criterion 4) that are necessary for the diagnosis (Criterion 6).
Mild Qualifier: The 'mild' qualifier is not used if any of the injury severity indicators listed below are present. Instead, traumatic brain injury (TBI) is diagnosed (without the 'mild' qualifier). i. Loss of consciousness duration greater than 30 minutes. ii. After 30 minutes, a Glasgow Coma Scale (GCS) of less than 13. iii. Post-traumatic amnesia greater than 24 hours.
Neuroimaging Qualifier: If neuroimaging is abnormal (Criterion 5), the qualifier mild TBI 'with neuroimaging evidence of structural intracranial injury' may be used. When neuroimaging is completed and found to be normal, the qualifier mild TBI 'without neuroimaging evidence of structural intracranial injury' may be used. If neuroimaging is not completed, no qualifier is used.
Concussion: The diagnostic label 'concussion' may be used interchangeably with 'mild TBI' when neuroimaging is normal or not clinically indicated.
Suspected Mild TBI: A mild TBI is suspected when, following abiomechanically plausible mechanism of injury (Criterion 1), one or more of the three criteria listed below are met. i. At least two acute symptoms (Criterion 3) and the person does not meet other criteria sufficient for diagnosing mild TBI. ii. At least two clinical examination or laboratory findings (Criterion 4) but the person does not meet other criteria for diagnosing mild TBI. iii. It is unclear whether signs (Criterion 2), acute symptoms (Criterion 3) and available clinical or laboratory findings (Criterion 4) are accounted for by confounding factors (i.e., it is unclear if Criterion 6 is met).
See Table 24.2 for definitions and explanatory notes.

Note: See the **2023** article, Box **1** and Box **2**, for a specific description of the criteria. This table is reprinted with permission from Silverberg ND, Iverson GL; ACRM Brain Injury Special Interest Group Mild TBI Task Force and the ACRM Mild TBI Definition Expert Consensus Group, ACRM Brain Injury Special Interest Group Mild TBI Task Force members; Cogan A, Dams-O'Connor K, Delmonico R, Graf MJP, Iaccarino MA, Kajankova M, Kamins J, McCulloch KL, McKinney G, Nagele D, Panenka WJ, Rabinowitz AR, Reed N, Wethe JV, Whitehair V; ACRM Mild TBI Diagnostic Criteria Expert Consensus Group; Anderson V, Arciniegas DB, Bayley MT, Bazarian JJ, Bell KR, Broglio SP, Cifu D, Davis GA, Dvorak J, Echemendia RJ, Gioia GA, Giza CC, Hinds SR **2**nd, Katz DI, Kurowski BG, Leddy JJ, Sage NL, Lumba-Brown A, Maas AIR, Manley GT, McCrea M, Menon DK, Ponsford J, Putukian M, Suskauer SJ, van der Naalt J, Walker WC, Yeates KO, Zafonte R, Zasler ND, Zemek R. The American Congress of Rehabilitation Medicine Diagnostic Criteria for Mild Traumatic Brain Injury. Arch Phys Med Rehabil. **2023** Aug;**104(8)**:**1343–1355**. doi: **10.1016**/j.apmr.**2023.03.036**

Table 24.2 Definitions, explanatory notes and qualifiers for the ACRM diagnostic criteria for mild traumatic brain injury

Criterion 1: Mechanism of Injury
Traumatic brain injury (TBI) results from a transfer of mechanical energy to the brain from external forces resulting from the (1) head being struck with an object, (2) head striking a hard object or surface, (3) brain undergoing an acceleration/deceleration movement without direct contact between the head and an object or surface and/or (4) forces generated from a blast or explosion
Notes: Criterion 1 can be met by direct observation (in person or video review) or collateral (witness) report of the injury event, review of acute care records or the person's recount of the injury event during an interview
Criterion 2: Clinical Signs
The injury event causes an acute physiological disruption of brain function, as manifested by *one or more* of the clinical signs listed below
1. Loss of consciousness immediately following injury (e.g., no protective action taken on falling after impact or lying motionless and unresponsive)
2. Alteration of mental status immediately following the injury (or upon regaining consciousness), evidenced by reduced responsiveness or inappropriate responses to external stimuli; slowness to respond to questions or instructions; agitated behavior; inability to follow two-part commands; or disorientation to time, place or situation
3. Complete or partial amnesia for events immediately following the injury (or after regaining consciousness). If post-traumatic amnesia cannot be reliably assessed (e.g., due to polytrauma or sedating analgesics), retrograde amnesia (i.e., a gap in memory for events immediately preceding the injury) can be used as a replacement for this criterion
4. Other acute neurological sign(s) (e.g., observed motor incoordination upon standing, seizure or tonic posturing immediately following injury)
Notes: Criterion 2 can be met by direct observation (in person or video review), collateral (witness) report, review of acute care records, or when none of these are available, the person's recount of the injury event
Criterion 3: Acute Symptoms
The physiological disruption of brain function is manifested by *two or more* new or worsened symptoms from the list below
1. Acute subjective alteration in mental status: feeling confused, feeling disoriented and/or feeling dazed
2. Physical symptoms: headache, nausea, dizziness, balance problems, vision problems, sensitivity to light and/or sensitivity to noise
3. Cognitive symptoms: feeling slowed down, "mental fog," difficulty concentrating and/or memory problems
4. Emotional symptoms: uncharacteristic emotional lability and/or irritability
The symptoms may be from one or more categories (i.e., experiencing two symptoms within a single category is sufficient). Other symptoms may be present, but they should not be counted toward Criterion 3. The onset of acute subjective alteration in mental status occurs immediately following the impact or after regaining consciousness. The onset of other symptoms (physical, cognitive and emotional) may be delayed by a few hours, but they nearly always appear less than 72 h from injury
Notes: Criterion 3 can be met by (1) review of acute care documentation of the injured person's acute symptoms, (2) interviewing the injured person about the first few days following injury; (3) having the injured person complete a self-report rating scale documenting symptoms during the first few days following injury; or (4) collateral observation for an individual who cannot accurately report symptoms due to developmental stage (e.g., children under 5 years old) or pre-injury disability
Criterion 4: Clinical Examination and Laboratory Findings
The assessment findings listed below can also provide supportive evidence of brain injury
1. Cognitive impairment on acute clinical examination
2. Balance impairment on acute clinical examination

(continued)

Table 24.2 (continued)

3. Oculomotor impairment or symptom provocation in response to vestibular-oculomotor challenge on acute clinical examination
4. Elevated blood biomarker(s) indicative of intracranial injury

Notes: Clinical and laboratory tests that meet standards of reliability and diagnostic accuracy should be considered for Criterion 4. Impairment in Criterion 4(1–3) is defined as a clinically meaningful discrepancy between post-injury test performance and age-appropriate normative reference data, or where available, pre-injury test performance. The diagnostic sensitivity of most clinical and laboratory tests decreases over the first 72 h following injury and the rate of sensitivity decline differs between specific tests

Criterion 5: Neuroimaging

Trauma-related intracranial abnormalities on computed tomography or structural magnetic resonance imaging

Notes: Neuroimaging is not necessary to diagnose mild TBI. Its primary clinical role is to rule out head and brain injuries that might require neurosurgical or other medical intervention in an acute care setting. When obtained, neuroimaging may reveal intracranial abnormalities indicative of TBI such as contusion(s) or intracranial hemorrhage

Criterion 6: Not Better Accounted for by Confounding Factors

Confounding factors, including pre-existing and co-occurring health conditions, have been considered and determined to not fully account for the clinical signs, acute symptoms and clinical examination and laboratory findings that are necessary for the diagnosis

Notes: A clinical sign only qualifies for Criterion 2 when it is not better accounted for by acute musculoskeletal pain, psychological trauma, alcohol or substance intoxication, pulmonary or circulatory disruption, syncope prior to fall or other confounding factors. Symptoms should only be counted toward Criterion 3 when they are not better accounted for by drug, alcohol or medication use; co-occurring physical injuries (e.g., musculoskeletal injury involving the neck or peripheral vestibular dysfunction) or psychological conditions (e.g., an acute stress reaction to trauma); pre-existing health conditions; or symptom exaggeration. Criterion 4 findings must not be better accounted for by drug, alcohol or medication use; co-occurring physical injuries or psychological conditions; pre-existing health conditions; or factors influencing the validity of the symptom reporting or test results

General Notes: Consideration should be given to cultural and linguistic differences in symptom reporting and test performance. Caution is warranted when applying the diagnostic criteria for mild TBI to young children and individuals with pre-injury cognitive and/or communication impairments. Due to developmental stage (e.g., children under 5 years old) or pre-injury disability, an individual may not be able to accurately report symptoms in Criterion 3; thus, this criterion could be met based on proxy report or observation of related behaviors (e.g., changes in appetite or behaving out of character). An injured person's behavior should also be interpreted in the context of their developmental stage and pre-injury functioning. Clinical and laboratory test interpretation requires age-appropriate scales and/or cut-off scores

Note: See the 2023 article, Box 1 and Box 2, for a specific description of the criteria. This table is reprinted with permission from Silverberg ND, Iverson GL; ACRM Brain Injury Special Interest Group Mild TBI Task Force and the ACRM Mild TBI Definition Expert Consensus Group, ACRM Brain Injury Special Interest Group Mild TBI Task Force members; Cogan A, Dams-O'Connor K, Delmonico R, Graf MJP, Iaccarino MA, Kajankova M, Kamins J, McCulloch KL, McKinney G, Nagele D, Panenka WJ, Rabinowitz AR, Reed N, Wethe JV, Whitehair V; ACRM Mild TBI Diagnostic Criteria Expert Consensus Group; Anderson V, Arciniegas DB, Bayley MT, Bazarian JJ, Bell KR, Broglio SP, Cifu D, Davis GA, Dvorak J, Echemendia RJ, Gioia GA, Giza CC, Hinds SR 2nd, Katz DI, Kurowski BG, Leddy JJ, Sage NL, Lumba-Brown A, Maas AIR, Manley GT, McCrea M, Menon DK, Ponsford J, Putukian M, Suskauer SJ, van der Naalt J, Walker WC, Yeates KO, Zafonte R, Zasler ND, Zemek R. The American Congress of Rehabilitation Medicine Diagnostic Criteria for Mild Traumatic Brain Injury. Arch Phys Med Rehabil. 2023 Aug;104(8):1343–1355. doi: 10.1016/j.apmr.2023.03.036

crash may report that he or she "woke up 45 min later in the hospital" despite the fact that they were conscious and responding to emergency personnel's questions immediately at the time of the accident (according to the ambulance crew report). In this case, PTA (i.e., amnesia for events following the accident) could be mistakenly labeled as possible LOC of up to 45 min, which is not only incorrect, but also greater than the LOC duration threshold for mTBI. It is best to assess PTA and LOC using all available sources of information including, but not limited to, the patient's report, collateral report and medical records.

It is important to consider the impact of possible confounding medical and psychological factors on the assessment of mental status. For example, acute alcohol or other substance intoxication can contribute to confusion and memory lapses, and acute stress reactions may result in difficulty remembering the circumstances around the injury event. Additionally, orthopedic injuries requiring sedation or respiratory distress requiring intubation can make it challenging to document GCS, PTA and mental status changes attributable to mTBI versus to other medical comorbidities. Mild TBI may not be identified in situations where urgent and traumatic bodily injuries take precedence at the scene and in acute care.

mTBI Versus Concussion

A concussion is, by definition, a mild TBI. Concussion is usually the preferred term in sports, both in clinical practice and in research. The term concussion is frequently used in clinical practice in civilian trauma cases, especially for injuries that seem to fall on the milder end of the mTBI spectrum. An exception would be if an athlete or civilian sustained an injury characterized by prolonged LOC, prolonged PTA or visible intracranial injury on CT or MRI. Some have suggested that the term concussion (versus mTBI) may be more useful to avoid potential iatrogenic effects of dwelling on having a brain injury (Gordon et al., 2010; Kelly & Erdal, 2017; Kempe et al., 2013; Sullivan et al., 2014; Vanderploeg et al., 2014). The term concussion should not be used when there is neuroimaging evidence of structural intracranial lesions (Silverberg et al., 2023).

mTBI with Neuroimaging Evidence of Structural Intracranial Injury

The ACRM diagnostic criteria for mTBI includes the qualifier "with neuroimaging evidence of structural intracranial injury" when a previously termed *complicated* mTBI is identified. Intracranial injury can include edema, hematoma, hemorrhage or contusion. The presence of skull fracture is predictive of increased risk for mTBI with neuroimaging evidence of structural intracranial injury (Lumba-Brown et al., 2018; Pandor et al., 2011; Teeratakulpisarn et al., 2021; Vaniyapong et al., 2019; Zia Ziabari et al., 2022). In general, the most common intracranial abnormalities identified on CT scans in individuals following mTBI include subarachnoid hemorrhage, subdural hematoma and contusion (Isokuortti et al., 2018; Orlando et al., 2023; Riemann et al., 2023; Vande Vyvere et al., 2024; Yuh et al., 2021). Although epidural hematoma is associated with a higher need for neurosurgical intervention, patients with subarachnoid hemorrhage (alone or in combination with other intracranial pathologies) appear to have worse functional outcomes (Marincowitz et al., 2018; Yuh et al., 2021).

Evidence of Intracranial Injury on CT

Intracranial injury may be present on acute or early CT imaging (e.g., same day CT scan or imaging less than 48 h after injury). Delayed intracranial hemorrhage is uncommon and it may be identified on repeat or CT imaging that is obtained days or weeks after the initial mTBI. Rates of acute intracranial injury vary widely depending on the study inclusion criteria and age range of the patients included. Table 24.3 presents the rates of intracranial injury identified on CT in a few selected studies of children, adults and older adults.

The likelihood of positive CT scan following mTBI differs considerably by level of GCS score such that a GCS of 15 is associated with the lowest likelihood of acute intracranial injury and need for neurosurgical intervention (Greenberg et al., 2017; Hageman & Nihom, 2022; Ibañez Pérez De La Blanca et al., 2018; Isokuortti et al., 2018; Marincowitz et al., 2018; Pandor et al., 2011; Sadegh et al., 2016; Shafie et al., 2023; Teeratakulpisarn et al., 2021; Vaniyapong et al., 2019; Zia Ziabari et al., 2022). Table 24.4 shows the rates of positive CT scan by GCS score in several recent studies and Table 24.5 presents the evidence for different predictors of positive acute CT scan.

Need for Neurosurgery

Delayed intracranial hemorrhage after initial negative acute CT scan is rare (0.05–0.77%; Bergenfeldt et al., 2023; Colombo et al., 2021; Heinonen et al., 2022), while progression/worsening of acute intracranial injury is more common, but still an unlikely outcome (3–18% of those with positive acute CT findings; Fadzil et al., 2022; Joseph et al., 2015; Pruitt et al., 2017; Root et al., 2020). The need for neurosurgical intervention in those with intracranial injury is also an uncommon outcome (1–8% of cases; Foks et al., 2018; Hageman & Nihom, 2022; Joseph et al., 2015; Orlando et al., 2023; Pandor et al., 2011; Patel et al., 2023; Sadegh et al., 2016; Schwed et al., 2016; Tourigny et al., 2021; Vaniyapong et al., 2019). Predictors of neurosurgery include greater midline shift and evidence of epidural hematoma on CT imaging (Greenberg et al., 2017; Marincowitz et al., 2018; Patel et al., 2023; Tourigny et al., 2021). Subarachnoid hemorrhage is associated with the lowest risk with only 0.01% requiring neurosurgical intervention (Marincowitz et al., 2018).

Table 24.3 Examples of rates of CT evidence of acute intracranial injury following mTBI

Study	Study type	Location	Population	Ages [mean (SD) or range]	Sample size	Rate of acute intracranial injury (%)
Adults						
Isokuortti et al. (2014)	Retrospective	Finland	ED patients	34–76	3023	19
Pandor et al. (2011)	Systematic Review & MA	–	–	–	19 studies	7
Pozzato et al. (2020)	Retrospective	Australia	ED patients	18–65	351	9
Yue et al. (2018)	Prospective	USA (TRACK-TBI)	ED patients	44.4 (18.1)	260	37
Children						
Dunning et al. (2006)	Prospective	England	ED patients	<16	22,772	1
Greenberg et al. (2017)	Retrospective	North America	ED patients	<18	15,162	6
Lumba-Brown et al. (2018)	Systematic Review	–	–	<18	16 studies	8
Naghibi et al. (2021)	Prospective	Iran	ED patients	2–14	200	4
Pandor et al. (2011)	Systematic Review & MA	–	–	–	14 studies	7
Older adults						
Barrett et al. (2023)	Retrospective	United Kingdom	ED patients	>60	2111	8
Ibañez Pérez De La Blanca et al. (2018)	Prospective	Spain	ED patients	>60	504	20
Lifespan						
Foks et al. (2018)	Prospective	Netherlands	ED patients	16–101	3742	8
Isokuortti et al. (2018)	Retrospective	Finland	ED patients	<1–103	1990	16
Lannsjö et al. (2013)	Prospective	Sweden	ED patients	6–94	1262	4
Mishra et al. (2017)[a]	Prospective	India	ED patients	32.8 (17.5)	453	43
Riemann et al. (2023)	Prospective	Europe (CENTER-TBI)	ED patients	≤24	462	37
Sadegh et al. (2016)[b]	Prospective	Iran	ED patients	37.1 (14.5)	500	13

(continued)

Table 24.3 (continued)

Study	Study type	Location	Population	Ages [mean (SD) or range]	Sample size	Rate of acute intracranial injury (%)
Shafie et al. (2023)	Cross-sectional	Iran	ED patients	33.4 (19.7)	498	20
Vaniyapong et al. (2019)	Prospective	Thailand	ED patients	15–98	1164	21
Waganekar et al. (2018)	Prospective	India	ED patients	36.2 (17.0)	1341	38

Note: MA: meta-analysis. TRACK-TBI: Transforming Research and Clinical Knowledge in Traumatic Brain Injury study. TRACK-TBI is a multi-center, prospective study which collected observational data from 18 trauma centers in the United States between 2014 and 2018. Inclusion criteria for TRACK-TBI was 16+ years old, head trauma, presentation at one of the trauma centers, diagnosis of TBI using 1993 ACRM criteria (Kay et al., 1993) and performance of a head CT within 24 h of injury. CENTER-TBI: Collaborative European NeuroTrauma Effectiveness Research in Traumatic Brain Injury. CENTER-TBI is a multi-center, prospective study which collected observational data from 68 centers across 20 countries in Europe between 2014 and 2017. Patients in the core study were identified by presentation to the emergency department, admission to the hospital and admission to the ICU at the participating hospitals. Inclusion criteria were patients who had a clinical diagnosis of TBI who presented within 24 h of injury and had a clinical indication for head CT

[a]This study only included patients with Glasgow Coma Scale scores of 15

[b]This study only included patients with Glasgow Coma Scale scores of 14–15

MRI Findings in mTBI

CT is used in the acute phase of mTBI given its widespread availability in emergency departments and its relative cost-effectiveness for emergency triage decisions. This imaging modality, however, has false negatives for identifying smaller parenchymal injuries, especially those that are not hemorrhagic. Studies have reported that between 5 and 27% of those with negative CT imaging studies have abnormal MRI findings (Einarsen et al., 2019; Yue, Yuh, et al., 2019; Yuh et al., 2021), and MRI findings have been associated with worse functional outcomes after injury (Burrowes et al., 2020; Einarsen et al., 2019; Huovinen et al., 2022; Imms et al., 2024; Richter et al., 2021; Sibilia et al., 2023; Wiegand et al., 2022; Yuh et al., 2013). Even with positive acute CT scan, MRI tends to detect more intracranial pathology than CT alone (Buttram et al., 2015; Lee et al., 2008; Yue et al., 2024). For example, in those patients with a single subarachnoid hemorrhage on initial CT scan, 46% evidence more extensive intracranial pathology on follow-up MRI sequencing (Yue et al., 2024). It should be noted that less than 1% of sport-related concussions have positive imaging findings on MRI, again suggesting that sport concussion is likely on the milder end of the mTBI spectrum (Klein et al., 2019; Mayer et al., 2020).

Table 24.4 Examples of rates of CT evidence of acute intracranial injury by Glasgow Coma Scale (GCS) score

Study	Study type	Ages [mean (SD) or range]	Sample size	GCS Score		
				15	14	13
Foks et al. (2018)	Prospective	56.9 (16–101)	3742	8%	18%	33%
Isokuortti et al. (2018)	Retrospective	56.4 (34.2–77.1)[b]	1990	10%	36%	48%
Riemann et al. (2023)	Prospective[a]	<24	462	31%	54%	63%
Stein and Ross (1992)	Retrospective	Adults	1538	13%	24%	38%
Thiruppathy and Muthukumar (2004)	Prospective	3 months–78 years	381	34%	52%	51%
Livingston et al. (1991)	Retrospective	29 (16–70)	111	10%	30%	–
Ono et al. (2007)	Prospective	46 (23)	1064	4%	36%	–
Sadegh et al. (2016)	Prospective	37.1 (14.5)	500	9%	20%	–
Jeret et al. (1993)	Prospective	35.6 (14.1)	712	9%	–	–
Kisat et al. (2012)	Retrospective	39 (24–55)[b]	83,566	4%	–	–
Saboori et al. (2007)	Prospective	29 (6–85)	682	7%	–	–
Shafie et al. (2023)	Cross-sectional	33.4 (19.7)	498	15%	–[c]	–[c]
Stiell et al. (2005)	Prospective	37.7 (18)	1822	5%	–	–
				GCS = 14–15		
Atabaki et al. (2016)	Prospective	<18	8496	6%		
Ibañez Pérez De La Blanca et al. (2018)	Prospective	79.4 (8.1)	504	20%		
Naghibi et al. (2021)	Prospective	2–14	200	4%		
Nigrovic et al. (2012)	Prospective	<18	14,696	1%		

Note: These studies only include patients who underwent CT scan (either as part of the study inclusion criteria or due to clinical indication for CT scan) and so results will not generalize to those patients with GCS 13–15 who did not receive CT scan

[a]CENTER-TBI is a multi-center, prospective study which collected observational data from 68 centers across 20 countries in Europe between 2014 and 2017. Patients in the core study were identified by presentation to the emergency department, admission to the hospital, and admission to the ICU at the participating hospitals. Inclusion criteria were patients who had a clinical diagnosis of TBI who presented within 24 h of injury and had a clinical indication for head CT

[b]This study presented median and interquartile ranges for age of participants with suspected or confirmed mTBI

[c]This study had small sample sizes ($n = 14$) with high rates of CT positivity for both the GCS 13 and GCS 14 groups

Experimental Neuroimaging in mTBI

Compared to CT and structural MRI, advanced experimental neuroimaging techniques are more sensitive for detecting changes to the structure or neurobiology of the brain (Bigler, 2023). There is some evidence for changes in white matter acutely, sub-acutely and chronically following mTBI (Lindsey et al., 2023). Examples of advanced multimodal imaging techniques include resting-state and task-based functional MRI (fMRI; Dogra et al., 2024), perfusion weighted imaging, magnetic resonance spectroscopy (MRS; Joyce et al., 2022), arterial spin labeling (ASL; Wang

Table 24.5 Risk factors associated with positive acute computed tomography (CT) scan

Risk factor	Selected study evidence in support	Selected study evidence against
Acute drug or alcohol intoxication	Pandor et al. (2011)[a]—in children	Vaniyapong et al. (2019)
Chronic alcohol use	Isokuortti et al. (2018); Pandor et al. (2011)	
Antithrombotic medication	Barrett et al. (2023); Fiorelli et al. (2020); Ibañez Pérez De La Blanca et al. (2018); Sadegh et al. (2016)	
Decreased level of consciousness/a decrease in GCS score while under observation	Naghibi et al. (2021); Pandor et al. (2011)[a] —in children and adults	
Evidence of skull fracture	Lumba-Brown et al. (2018)—systematic review in children; Pandor et al. (2011)[a]—in children and adults; Sadegh et al. (2016); Shafie et al. (2023); Teeratakulpisarn et al. (2021); Vaniyapong et al. (2019); Zia Ziabari et al. (2022)	
GCS score of 13 or 14	Greenberg et al. (2017); Ibañez Pérez De La Blanca et al. (2018); Isokuortti et al. (2018); Pandor et al. (2011)[a]—in children and adults; Sadegh et al. (2016); Shafie et al. (2023); Teeratakulpisarn et al. (2021); Vaniyapong et al. (2019); Zia Ziabari et al. (2022)	
Headache	Lumba-Brown et al. (2018)—systematic review, severe/worsening headache in children; Naghibi et al. (2021); Pandor et al. (2011)[a]— severe and persistent headache in children; Vaniyapong et al. (2019)	Pandor et al. (2011)[a]—in adults
Identified neurologic deficit	Pandor et al. (2011)[a]—in both chilren and adults; Sadegh et al. (2016); Vaniyapong et al. (2019)	
LOC	Ibañez Pérez De La Blanca et al. (2018); Lumba-Brown et al. (2018)—systematic review in children; Pandor et al. (2011)[a]—in children; Waganekar et al. (2018)—LOC >5 min	Pandor et al. (2011)[a]—in adults
Motor vehicle accident	Ibañez Pérez De La Blanca et al. (2018); Pandor et al. (2011)[a]—in both children and adults (as a pedestrian/biker)	
Older age	Isokuortti et al. (2018); Pandor et al. (2011)[a]—in adults (>60 years old); Sadegh et al. (2016)	Vaniyapong et al. (2019)
Post-traumatic seizure	Pandor et al. (2011)[a]—in children and adults; Waganekar et al. (2018)	
Vomiting	Lumba-Brown et al. (2018)—systematic review in children; Mishra et al. (2017); Naghibi et al. (2021)—2+ episodes of vomiting; Pandor et al. (2011)[a]—in children and adults; Sadegh et al. (2016); Shafie et al. (2023); Vaniyapong et al. (2019)—2+ episodes of vomiting; Waganekar et al. (2018); Zia Ziabari et al. (2022)	

(continued)

Table 24.5 (continued)

Risk factor	Selected study evidence in support	Selected study evidence against
PTA	Lumba-Brown et al. (2018)—systematic review in children; Shafie et al. (2023)	Vaniyapong et al. (2019)
Scalp laceration	Lumba-Brown et al. (2018)—systematic review in children; Vaniyapong et al. (2019)	Pandor et al. (2011)[a]—in children

Note: *GCS* Glasgow Coma Scale score, *LOC* loss of consciousness, *PTA* post-traumatic amnesia
[a]Pandor et al. (2011) is a systematic review and meta-analysis that included 93 studies (retrospective and prospective cohort studies) published before March 2010. They included 42 studies of adults following mTBI and 29 studies of children following mTBI. This is not meant to be a comprehensive review of the literature on risk factors for intracranial abnormalities on head CT. This simply illustrates some of the more commonly reported risk factors

et al., 2023), electroencephalography (EEG), positron emission tomography (PET), single photon emission computed tomography (SPECT) and diffusion weighted imaging (including diffusion tensor imaging analysis; DTI; Lindsey et al., 2023; van Rhijn et al., 2024). The interested reader is referred to the following resources for an overview of findings in experimental neuroimaging following mTBI: Bartnik-Olson et al. (2021); Bigler (2023); Kim et al. (2022); Lindsey et al. (2023); Lunkova et al. (2021); Wiegand et al. (2022).

Neuropsychological Outcome

Cognitive symptoms are common following mTBI (Levy et al., 2023). The natural history of neurocognitive outcome from mTBI, as measured by using neuropsychological tests, is reasonably well understood. Cognitive impairment may be present in the acute phases of injury and it is likely to resolve in the days, weeks and months after injury (de Freitas Cardoso et al., 2019; Iverson et al., 2019; Karr et al., 2014; Ritchie & Slomine, 2022). Systematic reviews and meta-analyses on neuropsychological testing after mTBI have been somewhat heterogeneous in regard to domain-specific deficits that may be present in the acute phases after injury (Karr et al., 2014). In general, by 3 months after mTBI, identifiable deficits on neuropsychological testing are unlikely to be seen in group studies (Belanger et al., 2005; Carroll et al., 2014; Hume et al., 2022; Iverson et al., 2019; Karlsen et al., 2020; Karr et al., 2014; McCrea et al., 2009; Ritchie & Slomine, 2022; Rohling et al., 2011, 2012).

Figure 24.1 was created using meta-analytic reviews of the literature in this area and it demonstrates the effects of mTBI on cognitive functioning over time. As can

(continued) disorder (Kurtz & Gerraty, 2009), ADHD in adults (Alderson et al., 2013), cannabis (Figueiredo et al., 2020), tobacco (Conti et al., 2019), cocaine (Hall et al., 2018), ecstasy-MDMA (Zakzanis et al., 2007), methamphetamine (Hall et al., 2018), alcohol use disorder (Stephan et al., 2017), long-term opioid use for chronic pain (Allegri et al., 2019), opioid use disorder (Wollman et al., 2019), benzodiazepine withdrawal (Barker et al., 2004), chronic benzodiazepine use (Barker et al., 2004)

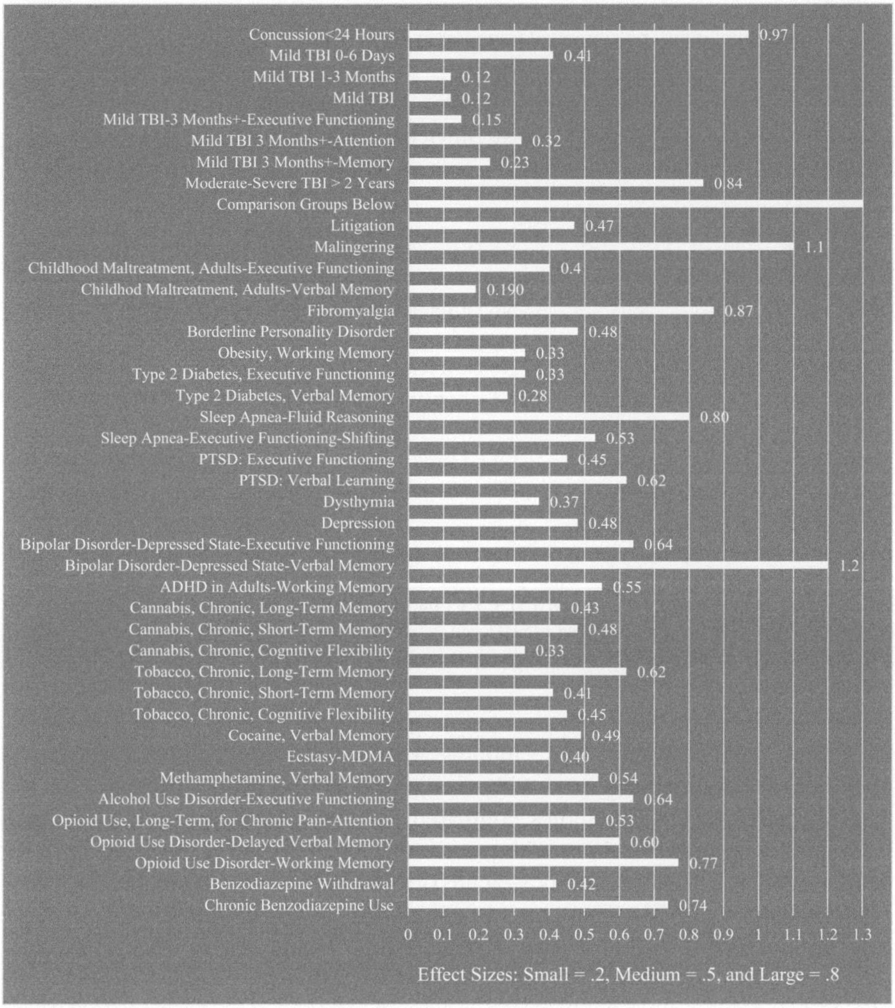

Fig. 24.1 Meta-analytic effect sizes: Adverse effects on neuropsychological functioning. Note: Copyright (2021, 2024) Grant L. Iverson, Ph.D., used with permission. Effect sizes less than .3 should be considered very small and difficult to detect in individual patients because the patient and control groups largely overlap. Effect sizes typically are expressed in pooled, weighted standard deviation units. However, across studies, there are variations in the methods of calculation. For this figure, the overall effect on cognitive or neuropsychological functioning is reported, unless otherwise noted. Sport-related concussion <24 h (Belanger & Vanderploeg, 2005); Mild TBI 0–6 days (Schretlen & Shapiro, 2003), Mild TBI 1–3 months (Schretlen & Shapiro, 2003), Mild TBI (Binder et al., 1997), Mild TBI 3 months+-executive functioning (Belanger et al., 2005), MTBI 3 months+-attention (Belanger et al., 2005), MTBI 3 months+-memory (Belanger et al., 2005), moderate-severe > 24 months (Schretlen & Shapiro, 2003), litigation (Binder & Rohling, 1996), malingering (Vickery et al., 2001), adults with childhood maltreatment (Masson et al., 2015), fibromyalgia (Wu et al., 2018), borderline personality disorder (Unoka & Richman, 2016), obesity (Yang et al., 2018), diabetes (Palta et al., 2014), sleep apnea (Olaithe & Bucks, 2013), PTSD (Scott et al., 2015), dysthymia (Christensen et al., 1997), depression (Christensen et al., 1997), bipolar

Table 24.6 Meta-analysis of neuropsychological functioning following mTBI in people with and without intracranial injury on computed tomography (CT)

Cognitive domain	Acute differences (<3 months)	Group differences	Post-acute differences (>3 months)	Group differences
General Memory	–	No Difference	3.30 points	CT+ Lower
Immediate Memory	–	No Difference	3.75 points	CT+ Lower
Delayed Memory	–	No Difference	3.30 points	CT+ Lower
Working Memory	–	No Difference	[a]	[a]
Attention	–	No Difference	–	No Difference
Processing Speed	7.80 points	CT+ Lower	3.50 points	CT+ Lower
Language	6.60 points	CT+ Lower	–	No Difference
Executive Functioning	4.20 points	CT+ Lower	2.55 points	CT+ Lower

Note: Data based on pooled mean differences in performance found in the meta-analysis performed by Hacker et al. (2023). Points presented are IQ-type points (standard score points with mean of 100 and standard deviation of 15). CT+ : patients with intracranial injury identified on CT scan (previously termed *complicated* mTBI)

[a]No studies were available for this recovery time period

be seen in the figure, these effects are more pronounced in the acute period directly after injury and disappear after 3 months. This figure also illustrates other health conditions and their associations with neuropsychological test scores.

A meta-analysis of 23 studies compared patients who had negative CT scans (CT-) following mTBI to those with positive CT scans (CT+) at the acute and subacute (less than 3 months) and post-acute (greater than 3 months) phases of recovery (Hacker et al., 2023). These authors found that, in the acute and subacute phase following injury, the CT+ patients tended to have worse performance in the language, processing speed and executive functioning domains. Table 24.6 presents the pooled mean differences between the groups in terms of IQ-type points (standard score points with mean of 100 and standard deviation of 15). After 3 months following injury, those with CT+ had lower scores on tests of general memory, immediate and delayed memory, processing speed and executive functioning. These differences were generally small (3 standard score points on average; approximately one-fifth of a standard deviation). Hacker et al. (2023) also compared the performance of individuals with CT+ mTBI to those with moderate-to-severe TBI.

In the acute and subacute phase of recovery (less than 3 months), patients with moderate-to-severe TBIs had lower scores on tests of general memory (composite difference of 8.85 standard score points), immediate memory (difference of 6.60 points) and delayed memory (difference of 8.7 points). There was a non-significant trend toward lower scores on tests of executive functioning in the acute phase (difference of 7.20 points). In the post-acute phase (greater than 3 months), those with moderate-to-severe TBI had lower scores on immediate and delayed memory (3.90

and 5.0 points), processing speed (3.50 points), and there was a non-significant trend toward lower executive functioning performance (4.40 points). Overall, the literature suggests that those with CT+ mTBI obtain lower scores than those with CT- mTBI in the acute, subacute and post-acute phases of recovery, with small to medium effect sizes, but obtain higher scores, on average, than those with moderate-to-severe TBI at all phases of recovery (Bryant et al., 2023; Hacker et al., 2023; Iverson et al., 2019). Additionally, by 6 months, having CT+ mTBI may not be associated with higher rates of cognitive deficits (Bryant et al., 2023; Iverson et al., 2019).

Return to Work

Most people who sustain an mTBI return to work within the first month; however, this timeline varies considerably among people and across studies (Iverson et al., 2022). Those with milder mTBIs tend to have a higher return to work rates than those with greater injury severity—although there is considerable variability in the literature relating to associations between injury severity indicators and time to return to work (Iverson et al., 2022). Researchers have reported that 22–84% of mTBI patients return to work within the first week and 53–90% return within 6 months after mTBI (Bloom et al., 2018; Kristman et al., 2010; Snell et al., 2023). Those who suffer with persisting symptoms or who have high fear avoidance behaviors may take longer to return to work, which can result in economic, family and other interpersonal problems (Snell et al., 2023).

Medical Management, Treatment and Rehabilitation

Rest and Activity Resumption

Rest has long been considered an integral part of recovery from mTBI; however, there have been considerable changes in the recommendations for rest after mTBI in the past 20 years. The interested reader is referred to Silverberg and Iverson (2013) for a review of the history of rest recommendations in mTBI. It is now clear that *prolonged rest* is not the best course of action after mTBI and may even be harmful for clinical recovery (Grool et al., 2016; de Kruijk et al., 2002; Silverberg & Otamendi, 2019; Thomas et al., 2015). Current recommendations are to rest for 24–48 h and reintroduce work, school and other responsibilities in a gradual, step-wise manner (Patricios et al., 2023; Schneider et al., 2017; Silverberg, Iaccarino, et al., 2020). As cognitive demand increases, mild symptom exacerbation may occur. Patients should be counseled to take breaks from cognitive and/or physical exertion if significant symptom exacerbation occurs. Increasing cognitive and/or physical demands should be encouraged, and it is usually best if there is only mild change in symptoms during or after the activity. As symptoms improve, more activities can be added in a stepwise manner until final symptom resolution and full return-to-activities occur.

Early Education

There is some evidence to support the use of early education to promote recovery and reduce the likelihood that a person might develop persisting symptoms following mTBI (Belanger et al., 2013; Comper et al., 2005; Cooper et al., 2015; Prince & Bruhns, 2017; Snell et al., 2009). Formalized educational brochures or sessions typically provide information regarding common symptoms, the likely time course of recovery, reassurance of recovery and suggested coping strategies following mTBI (e.g., McNally et al., 2018; Mittenberg et al., 1996; Paniak et al., 2000; Ponsford et al., 2002; Wade et al., 1998). These interventions often also focus on instilling hope and helping patients to feel optimistic about their potential recovery outcomes. Guidance can also be given on resumption of normal activities in a gradual, stepwise manner. These types of educational programs may convey some positive benefit (Hanks et al., 2019; McNally et al., 2018; Mittenberg et al., 1992, 1996; Ponsford et al., 2002; Prince & Bruhns, 2017) and may reduce the likelihood of pessimistic expectations and misattribution of stress-related symptoms to mTBI, both of which have been associated with increased risk for the development of persisting symptoms (Cassidy, Boyle, et al., 2014; Snell et al., 2013; Terry et al., 2018; Whittaker et al., 2007). Education, in combination with other treatments (e.g., rehabilitation, specialty clinic consultation, psychotherapy) may provide positive benefit (Arbabi et al., 2020; Teo et al., 2020).

Treatment and Rehabilitation

Proactive treatment of headache, sleep problems and comorbid anxiety or depression is important (Silverberg, Panenka, et al., 2020). Anxiety, depressive symptoms and emotional distress early after injury is associated with worse outcomes during the first year following injury (de Neeling et al., 2023). Some patients might benefit from vestibular rehabilitation (Aljabri et al., 2023; Babula et al., 2023). There has also been considerable focus on early aerobic exercise as treatment for mTBI. Much of this literature has been focused on youth and adult athletes rather than civilian mTBI patients this literature has broadly shown positive effects on recovery time in athlete populations (Chrisman et al., 2019; De Luigi et al., 2023; Langevin et al., 2020; Leddy et al., 2019; Leddy & Willer, 2013; McIntyre et al., 2020; Rytter et al., 2021). Psychological interventions (i.e., cognitive behavioral therapy, problem solving therapy, acceptance and commitment therapy) have also been shown to reduce post-acute mTBI symptom severity and improve functional outcomes

(Arbabi et al., 2020; Marshall et al., 2015; Sullivan et al., 2020; Teo et al., 2020). There is some evidence that multidisciplinary treatment, using a needs-based approach, can be useful for reducing symptoms and improving functioning (Moore et al., 2024).

Persisting Symptoms

While most individuals who sustain an mTBI recover within 3 months, there is a substantial minority of people who report symptoms months, and even years, after injury. In the past, this group of patients was sometimes referred to as having a "post-concussion syndrome" because this term has been used for decades to describe prolonged symptoms following mTBI. This term is problematic because it implies that there is a specific "syndrome" that is *caused* by mTBI, which has not been established. Those who have symptoms lasting more than 3 months are now conceptualized as having "persisting" symptoms. It is important to appreciate that physical, emotional and cognitive symptoms are non-specific and have been commonly identified in the general population as well as in patients with no history of mTBI who have experienced orthopedic injuries, life stress, sleep problems, depression and chronic pain (Dean et al., 2012; Gasquoine, 2000; Iverson, 2006; Iverson & Lange, 2003; Iverson & McCracken, 1997; Machulda et al., 1998; Silverberg et al., 2016; Smith-Seemiller et al., 2003; Suhr & Gunstad, 2002b; Trahan et al., 2001; Voormolen et al., 2019). Therefore, there might be many factors that contribute to the experience and reporting of physical, cognitive and emotional symptoms by people who sustained an mTBI months or years in the past.

Persisting symptoms tend to wax and wane over time (Iverson et al., 2022). Persisting symptoms can be related, at least in part, to premorbid mental and physical health status as well as increased distress about mTBI injury (Booker et al., 2019a; Cassidy, Cancelliere, et al., 2014; Losoi et al., 2016; Ponsford et al., 2019; Silverberg et al., 2015). A biopsychosocial model may be useful for conceptualizing predisposing and maintaining factors for persisting symptoms after mTBI (Evered et al., 2003; Ruff et al., 1996). Figure 24.2 shows biopsychosocial contributors to persisting symptoms, including possible neurobiological effects of mTBI, psychosocial factors and other physical or mental health factors, some of which are described further below.

Psychosocial Factors That Might Contribute to Persisting Symptoms

It is important to consider a broader biopsychosocial context when conceptualizing why a patient, or research subject, is experiencing physical, emotional and/or cognitive symptoms in the weeks, months or years following an mTBI. There are a large

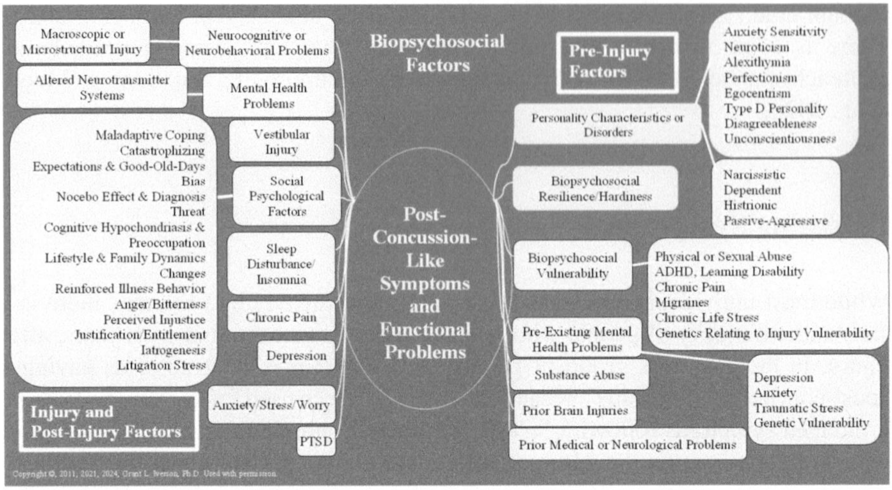

Fig. 24.2 Biopsychosocial factors associated with persisting symptoms after mild traumatic brain injury. Copyright ©, 2011, 2021, 2024, Grant L. Iverson, Ph.D. Used with permission

number of psychosocial factors that might contribute to the experience and reporting of these symptoms.

Personality Factors

Personality factors can influence the way that individuals approach recovery and its associated stressors. Pre-injury personality characteristics may be associated with the development of persisting symptoms. These personality characteristics may include compulsivity, histrionic presentations, social inhibition, negative affectivity, insecurity and borderline personality traits (Evered et al., 2003; Kay et al., 1992; Ruff et al., 1996; Stulemeijer, Andriessen, et al., 2007; Stulemeijer, Vos, et al., 2007). Table 24.7 shows different psychosocial and personality factors that may be associated with increased risk for persisting symptoms after mTBI.

Mental Health Factors

Depression, anxiety and traumatic stress are important to consider following mTBI. Pre-injury mental health difficulties are a risk factor for persisting symptoms after mTBI (Evered et al., 2003; Greiffenstein & Baker, 2001; Meares et al., 2011; Mooney et al., 2005; Ponsford et al., 2019). In prospective mTBI studies, a pre-injury history of psychiatric diagnosis was associated with worse outcomes in most

Table 24.7 Personality and social psychological factors that might be associated with persistent symptom reporting

Personality and behavioral factors	
Alexithymia	A cluster of traits characterized by difficulty identifying feelings, difficulty describing feelings to others, externally oriented thinking and limited capacity for imaginal thinking (Hogeveen & Grafman, 2021)
Anxiety Sensitivity	A trait composed of physical, psychological and social pre-occupations and concerns is characterized by fear of anxiety-related bodily sensations
Cognitive Hypochondriasis & Preoccupation	Hypochondriasis and somatic preoccupation have been recognized as dysfunctional behavior patterns for decades. They are associated with a magnified perception of bodily sensations and symptoms, fear of having serious health problems or disease and extensive contact with health care providers. By extension, Boone (2009) discussed a form of cognitive hypochondriasis that sometimes occurs in patients with poor outcome following MTBI. These patients have a fixed belief that they are significantly cognitively impaired, despite normal neuropsychological test performance, and that this impairment reflects permanent brain damage. Delis and Wetter (2007) proposed a "Cogniform Disorder," a Somatoform Disorder Subtype, characterized by pervasive and excessive cognitive symptoms and conversion-like adoption of the sick role
Disagreeableness	A personality trait characterized by antagonism, skepticism and egocentrism
Egocentrism	A personality characteristic relating to the tendency to perceive, understand and interpret one's social interactions from a highly personalized frame of reference. This personality characteristic is related to selfishness, self-centeredness and narcissism
Hardiness	A personality characteristic consisting of three psychological attitudes and beliefs: commitment, challenge and control. Through commitment, a person turns events into something meaningful and important. Control refers to the belief that one can influence the course of events. Challenge refers to a belief system in which wisdom and growth are gained from difficult experiences
Neuroticism	A personality trait characterized by a strong tendency to experience negative emotions such as anxiety, depression, anger and self-consciousness. Individuals with this trait have considerable difficulty coping with stress
Perfectionism	A personality characteristic characterized by an organized, disciplined and focused striving toward perfection in behavior and activities. It can be particularly pathological when a person with high levels of neuroticism believes firmly that anything less than perfection is unacceptable
Reinforced Illness Behavior	Some patients with chronic pain conditions and somatoform disorders develop entrenched reinforced illness behaviors and evolve into describing their symptoms and problems in a dramatic or exaggerated manner. That is, their behavior and interpersonal style changes over time, through environmental factors and social reinforcement, to include verbal and nonverbal illness behaviors

(continued)

Table 24.7 (continued)

Resilience	This is composed of a diverse set of biological, psychological and social factors that confer some degree of protection from physical and mental health problems. From a psychological perspective, resilience is an intrinsic characteristic underlying a person's ability to successfully adapt to acute stress and more chronic forms of adversity
Type D Personality	This personality pattern is characterized by two stable personality traits: negative affectivity and social inhibition
Unconscientiousness	A personality trait characterized by reduced self-discipline and ambition, disorganization and a more lackadaisical approach to life
Vulnerability	Conceptualized as a superordinate composition of individual risk factors for physical and mental health problems
Social psychological factors	
Diagnosis Threat	This term, proposed by Suhr and Gunstad (2002a), was adapted from the social psychological concept of *stereotype threat* Steele and Aronson (1995). Specifically, if told the reason for neuropsychological testing is because you might have problems due to a past head trauma, a person might perform more poorly than if given a more benign explanation for the purpose of testing
Expectation as Etiology	An expression coined by Mittenberg et al. (1992). Following an injury, people's anticipation or expectation of certain symptoms might cause them to misattribute future normal, everyday symptoms to the remote injury—or fail to appreciate the relation between more proximal factors (e.g., life stress, poor sleep and mild depression) and their symptoms
Good-Old-Days Bias	This refers to the tendency to view oneself as healthier in the past and underestimate past problems. This response bias, combined with an expectation of certain symptoms following mTBI, can have a potent impact on symptom reporting
Iatrogenesis	A state of ill health or adverse effect caused by medical treatment. For example, diagnosing "brain damage" as an explanation for persistent problems seen long after a mild concussion can be iatrogenic for some people
Nocebo Effect	The nocebo effect is the causation of sickness by the expectations of sickness and by associated emotional states. That is, the sickness is, essentially, caused by expectation of sickness (Hahn, 1997)
Perceived Injustice	A strongly held belief that one has been treated unfairly, disrespectfully and/or thwarted in what one feels entitled to. Believing that one is suffering unnecessarily as a result of another's actions can underlie perceived injustice. This can be a firmly entrenched belief system that can influence the perception and reporting of symptoms, treatment adherence and health-related behaviors

Note: Adapted with modifications from: Silverberg, N.D., & Iverson, G.L. (2011). Etiology of the post-concussion syndrome: Physiogenesis and psychogenesis revisited. *NeuroRehabilitation: An International Journal, 29(4)*, 317–329. The material above was reformatted and re-organized compared to how it was presented in Table 2 of Silverberg and Iverson (2011)

studies (Booker et al., 2019b; Lingsma et al., 2015; Luis et al., 2003; Meares et al., 2011; Mikolić et al., 2021; Mooney et al., 2005; Ponsford et al., 2000, 2019; Stein et al., 2016; van der Naalt et al., 2017; Yue, Cnossen, et al., 2019); however, some studies have not shown this association (Snell et al., 2011; Stulemeijer et al., 2008). Symptoms such as worry, increased distress and anxiety can also be associated with persisting symptoms (de Koning et al., 2016; Kay et al., 1992; Stein et al., 2016; Stulemeijer, Vos, et al., 2007; Wood, 2004).

There is evidence that the earlier the patient's depression or anxiety presents, the higher the likelihood of later functional disability as compared to those who have later-onset mood symptoms (Zahniser et al., 2019). Depression is common following TBI of all severity levels, including mTBI (Fakhoury et al., 2020; Hellewell et al., 2020; Juengst et al., 2017; Rapoport, 2012; Scholten et al., 2016; Singh et al., 2018). This may be due, directly or indirectly, to the pathophysiology of mTBI; however, it could also be related to psychological reactions to the life disruption that comes along with mTBI recovery. Depressed mood is important to consider because (a) cognitive symptoms may be strongly associated with mood difficulties, (2) depression is treatable and (3) improvement in depression may also lead to overall improvement in those with persisting physical, emotional and cognitive symptoms.

Traumatic stress is important to consider after mTBI. Approximately 12–27% of civilians who sustain mTBIs and 33–39% of military service members who sustain mTBIs experience traumatic stress (Carlson et al., 2011; Hoffman et al., 2012; Iljazi et al., 2020; Lai et al., 2024). Differential diagnosis of post-traumatic stress disorder (PTSD) versus persisting mTBI symptoms can be challenging because many of the symptoms overlap (e.g., difficulty concentrating, memory problems, irritability, sleep disturbance). Comorbid PTSD may also have an exacerbating effect on symptom reporting (Brenner et al., 2010; Combs et al., 2015; Jamora et al., 2012; Vanderploeg et al., 2009). Anxiety after mTBI may also be contributory to persisting symptoms. It is unclear whether PTSD or anxiety disorders are more common after mTBI than in the general population (Iverson et al., 2022); however, careful differential diagnosis and proactive treatment of comorbid mental health problems is likely beneficial.

Psychological distress is also an important factor to consider following mTBI. Within the literature on persisting symptoms, increased distress in the initial days or weeks following mTBI is a consistent predictor of both symptoms and functional outcome (Booker et al., 2019a; Cassidy, Cancelliere, et al., 2014; Hellstrøm et al., 2017; Losoi et al., 2016; Ponsford et al., 2019; Scheenen et al., 2017; Silverberg et al., 2015; van der Naalt et al., 2017). As noted previously, anxiety, depressive symptoms and emotional distress early after injury are associated with worse outcomes during the first year following injury (de Neeling et al., 2023).

Expectations and Misattribution

There is evidence to suggest that negative expectations about recovery can also influence the development of persisting mTBI symptoms (Carter-Allison et al., 2016; Hou et al., 2012; Mittenberg et al., 1992, 1996; Ozen & Fernandes, 2011; Polich et al., 2020; Suhr & Gunstad, 2002a; Vanderploeg et al., 2014; Whittaker et al., 2007). Patients who misattribute normal cognitive lapses (e.g., "where did I put my glasses?") as symptoms of underlying brain damage secondary to their mTBI tend to have longer recovery times (Carter-Allison et al., 2016; Hou et al., 2012; Mittenberg et al., 1992, 1996; Ozen & Fernandes, 2011; Picon et al., 2022; Polich et al., 2020; Suhr & Gunstad, 2002a; Vanderploeg et al., 2014; Whittaker et al., 2007). A "good-old-days" bias can also develop where patients may reflect on their cognitive status before mTBI as being superior to their current (recovered) status, which can interact with misattribution errors and fear avoidance behaviors to increase the likelihood of persisting symptoms (Davis, 2002; Gunstad & Suhr, 2001, 2004; Hilsabeck et al., 1998; Iverson et al., 2010; Lange et al., 2010; Mittenberg et al., 1992; Silverberg et al., 2018; Wijenberg et al., 2017).

Litigation

Litigation status is an important consideration in mTBI. Several studies have identified both more severe subjective complaints and lower scores on neuropsychological testing in individuals who are involved in litigation or have other external incentives following mTBI (Belanger et al., 2005; Binder & Rohling, 1996; Cassidy et al., 2004; Hanks et al., 2019; Mavroudis et al., 2024; Paniak et al., 2002; Uiterwijk et al., 2022; Vanderploeg et al., 2014). In these cases, it is, of course, important to evaluate for possible symptom exaggeration.

Conclusions

Mild TBIs fall on a very broad spectrum, from those that are difficult to detect and are associated with symptoms that resolve quickly to those involving macrostructual and microstructural damage to the brain and persisting symptoms and functional problems. Clinical signs of mTBI may include LOC, alteration of mental status, complete or partial PTA and other acute neurological signs such as seizure or tonic posturing immediately following injury or motor incoordination upon standing and walking. TBIs are not considered to be in the mild classification if they are characterized by a GCS score of less than 13 (after 30 min), duration of LOC greater than 30 min and duration of PTA greater than 24 h. Acute symptoms of mTBI may include subjective alteration in mental status, physical symptoms (i.e., headache, nausea, dizziness, balance problems, vision problems, sensitivity to light and/or noise), cognitive symptoms (i.e., feeling slowed down, mentally foggy, having difficulty concentrating, memory problems) and emotional symptoms (i.e., uncharacteristic emotional lability and/or irritability). New diagnostic criteria for mTBI were published in 2023 (Silverberg et al., 2023).

A concussion, by definition, is an mTBI. The term concussion is frequently used in clinical practice and civilian trauma cases, especially for injuries that seem to fall on the milder end of the mTBI spectrum. An important consideration within the mTBI spectrum is defined by the presence or absence of structural intracranial abnormality visible on CT or MRI. When imaging is done, these injuries are termed mTBI "with neuroimaging evidence of structural intracranial injury" (previously called complicated mTBI), and mTBI "without neuroimaging evidence of structural intracranial injury" (previously called uncomplicated mTBI). For patients who have a mTBI *with* neuroimaging evidence of structural intracranial injury, the term concussion is not recommended (Silverberg et al., 2023).

The course of neurocognitive recovery from mTBI is reasonably well understood. Cognitive impairment may be present within the first hours, days and weeks after injury; however, deficits on neuropsychological testing are not generally seen after 1–3 months after mTBI. Those with neuroimaging evidence of intracranial injury may demonstrate worse cognitive functioning, in group studies, after 3 months but these differences may not be present 6 or more months after injury.

Those with symptoms lasting longer than 3 months are characterized as having persisting symptoms. These symptoms may wax and wane over time, they might be related at least in part to pre-injury mental health status, and they can be amplified by ongoing psychological distress. A biopsychosocial model is useful for conceptualizing persisting symptoms after mTBI. Early intervention, including education about the positive prognosis in mTBI, in combination with treatment and rehabilitation, may help to reduce the risk of persisting symptoms.

References

Alderson, R. M., Kasper, L. J., Hudec, K. L., & Patros, C. H. G. (2013). Attention-deficit/hyperactivity disorder (ADHD) and working memory in adults: A meta-analytic review. *Neuropsychology, 27*(3), 287–302. https://doi.org/10.1037/a0032371

Aljabri, A., Halawani, A., Ashqar, A., Alageely, O., & Alhazzani, A. (2023). The efficacy of vestibular rehabilitation terapy for mild traumatic brain injury: A systematic review and meta-analysis. *The Journal of Head Trauma Rehabilitation*. https://doi.org/10.1097/HTR.0000000000000882

Allan, L. M., & Lippa, S. (2022). Military traumatic brain injury: Special considerations. In N. D. Zasler, D. I. Katz, R. D. Zafonte, D. B. Arciniegas, M. R. Bullock, F. M. Hammond, J. S. Kreutzer, R. Nakase-Richardson, & T. K. Watanabe (Eds.), *Brain injury medicine: Principles and practice* (3rd ed., pp. 462–474). Springer.

Allegri, N., Mennuni, S., Rulli, E., Vanacore, N., Corli, O., Floriani, I., De Simone, I., Allegri, M., Govoni, S., Vecchi, T., Sandrini, G., Liccione, D., & Biagioli, E. (2019). Systematic review and meta-analysis on neuropsychological effects of long-term use of opioids in patients with chronic noncancer pain. *Pain Practice, 19*(3), 328–343. https://doi.org/10.1111/papr.12741

Arbabi, M., Sheldon, R., Bahadoran, P., Smith, J. G., Poole, N., & Agrawal, N. (2020). Treatment outcomes in mild traumatic brain injury: A systematic review of randomized controlled trials. *Brain Injury, 34*(9), 1139–1149. https://doi.org/10.1080/02699052.2020.1797168

Arbogast, K. B., Curry, A. E., Pfeiffer, M. R., Zonfrillo, M. R., Haarbauer-Krupa, J., Breiding, M. J., Coronado, V. G., & Master, C. L. (2016). Point of health care entry for youth with concussion within a large pediatric care network. *JAMA Pediatrics, 170*(7), e160294. https://doi.org/10.1001/jamapediatrics.2016.0294

Atabaki, S. M., Hoyle, J. D., Schunk, J. E., Monroe, D. J., Alpern, E. R., Quayle, K. S., Glass, T. F., Badawy, M. K., Miskin, M., Schalick, W. O., Dayan, P. S., Holmes, J. F., & Kuppermann, N. (2016). Comparison of prediction rules and clinician suspicion for identifying children with clinically important brain injuries after blunt head trauma. *Academic Emergency Medicine: Official Journal of the Society for Academic Emergency Medicine, 23*(5), 566–575. https://doi.org/10.1111/acem.12923

Aubry, M., Cantu, R., Dvorak, J., Graf-Baumann, T., Johnston, K., Kelly, J., Lovell, M., McCrory, P., Meeuwisse, W., Schamasch, P., & Concussion in Sport Group. (2002). Summary and agreement statement of the First International Conference on Concussion in Sport, Vienna 2001. Recommendations for the improvement of safety and health of athletes who may suffer concussive injuries. *British Journal of Sports Medicine, 36*(1), 6–10. https://doi.org/10.1136/bjsm.36.1.6

Babula, G., Warunek, E., Cure, K., Nikolski, G., Fritz, H., & Barker, S. (2023). Vestibular rehabilitation as an early intervention in athletes who are post-concussion: A systematic review. *International Journal of Sports Physical Therapy, V18*(3), 577–586. https://doi.org/10.26603/001c.75369

Barker, M. J., Greenwood, K. M., Jackson, M., & Crowe, S. F. (2004). Persistence of cognitive effects after withdrawal from long-term benzodiazepine use: A meta-analysis. *Archives of Clinical Neuropsychology, 19*(3), 437–454. https://doi.org/10.1016/S0887-6177(03)00096-9

Barrett, J. W., Williams, J., Skene, S. S., Griggs, J. E., Bootland, D., Leung, J., Da Costa, A., Ballantyne, K., Davies, R., & Lyon, R. M. (2023). Head injury in older adults presenting to the ambulance service: Who do we convey to the emergency department, and what clinical variables are associated with an intracranial bleed? A retrospective case-control study. *Scandinavian Journal of Trauma, Resuscitation and Emergency Medicine, 31*(1), 65. https://doi.org/10.1186/s13049-023-01138-1

Bartnik-Olson, B. L., Alger, J. R., Babikian, T., Harris, A. D., Holshouser, B., Kirov, I. I., Maudsley, A. A., Thompson, P. M., Dennis, E. L., Tate, D. F., Wilde, E. A., & Lin, A. (2021). The clinical utility of proton magnetic resonance spectroscopy in traumatic brain injury: Recommendations from the ENIGMA MRS Working Group. *Brain Imaging and Behavior, 15*(2), 504–525. https://doi.org/10.1007/s11682-020-00330-6

Belanger, H. G., Barwick, F. H., Kip, K. E., Kretzmer, T., & Vanderploeg, R. D. (2013). Postconcussive symptom complaints and potentially malleable positive predictors. *The Clinical Neuropsychologist, 27*(3), 343–355. https://doi.org/10.1080/13854046.2013.774438

Belanger, H. G., Curtiss, G., Demery, J. A., Lebowitz, B. K., & Vanderploeg, R. D. (2005). Factors moderating neuropsychological outcomes following mild traumatic brain injury: A meta-analysis. *Journal of the International Neuropsychological Society: JINS, 11*(3), 215–227. https://doi.org/10.1017/S1355617705050277

Belanger, H. G., & Vanderploeg, R. D. (2005). The neuropsychological impact of sports-related concussion: A meta-analysis. *Journal of the International Neuropsychological Society: JINS, 11*(4), 345–357. https://doi.org/10.1017/s1355617705050411

Bergenfeldt, H., Forberg, J. L., Lehtinen, R., Anefjäll, E., & Vedin, T. (2023). Delayed intracranial hemorrhage after head trauma seems rare and rarely needs intervention-even in antiplatelet or anticoagulation therapy. *International Journal of Emergency Medicine, 16*(1), 54. https://doi.org/10.1186/s12245-023-00530-z

Bigler, E. D. (2023). Volumetric MRI findings in mild traumatic brain injury (mTBI) and neuropsychological outcome. *Neuropsychology Review, 33*(1), 5–41. https://doi.org/10.1007/s11065-020-09474-0

Binder, L. M., & Rohling, M. L. (1996). Money matters: A meta-analytic review of the effects of financial incentives on recovery after closed-head injury. *The American Journal of Psychiatry, 153*(1), 7–10. https://doi.org/10.1176/ajp.153.1.7

Binder, L. M., Rohling, M. L., & Larrabee, G. J. (1997). A review of mild head trauma. Part I: Meta-analytic review of neuropsychological studies. *Journal of Clinical and Experimental Neuropsychology, 19*(3), 421–431. https://doi.org/10.1080/01688639708403870

Bloom, B., Thomas, S., Ahrensberg, J. M., Weaver, R., Fowler, A., Bestwick, J., Harris, T., & Pearse, R. (2018). A systematic review and meta-analysis of return to work after mild Traumatic brain injury. *Brain Injury, 32*(13–14), 1623–1636. https://doi.org/10.1080/02699052.2018.1532111

Bogner, J., Corrigan, J. D., Yi, H., Singichetti, B., Manchester, K., Huang, L., & Yang, J. (2020). Lifetime history of traumatic brain injury and behavioral health problems in a population-based sample. *The Journal of Head Trauma Rehabilitation, 35*(1), E43–E50. https://doi.org/10.1097/HTR.0000000000000488

Booker, J., Sinha, S., Choudhari, K., Dawson, J., & Singh, R. (2019a). Description of the predictors of persistent post-concussion symptoms and disability after mild traumatic brain injury: The SHEFBIT cohort. *British Journal of Neurosurgery, 33*(4), 367–375. https://doi.org/10.1080/02688697.2019.1598542

Booker, J., Sinha, S., Choudhari, K., Dawson, J., & Singh, R. (2019b). Predicting functional recovery after mild traumatic brain injury: The SHEFBIT cohort. *Brain Injury, 33*(9), 1158–1164. https://doi.org/10.1080/02699052.2019.1629626

Boone, K. B. (2009). Fixed belief in cognitive dysfunction despite normal neuropsychological scores: Neurocognitive hypochondriasis? *The Clinical Neuropsychologist, 23*(6), 1016–1036. https://doi.org/10.1080/13854040802441135

Brenner, L. A., Ivins, B. J., Schwab, K., Warden, D., Nelson, L. A., Jaffee, M., & Terrio, H. (2010). Traumatic brain injury, posttraumatic stress disorder, and postconcussive symptom reporting among troops returning from Iraq. *The Journal of Head Trauma Rehabilitation, 25*(5), 307. https://doi.org/10.1097/HTR.0b013e3181cada03

Bryant, A. M., Rose, N. B., Temkin, N. R., Barber, J. K., Manley, G. T., McCrea, M. A., Nelson, L. D., TRACK-TBI Investigators, Badjatia, N., Gopinath, S., Keene, C. D., Madden, C., Ngwenya, L. B., Puccio, A., Robertson, C., Schnyer, D., Taylor, S. R., & Yue, J. K. (2023). Profiles of cognitive functioning at 6 months after traumatic brain injury among patients in level I trauma centers: A TRACK-TBI study. *JAMA Network Open, 6*(12), e2349118. https://doi.org/10.1001/jamanetworkopen.2023.49118

Burrowes, S. A. B., Rhodes, C. S., Meeker, T. J., Greenspan, J. D., Gullapalli, R. P., & Seminowicz, D. A. (2020). Decreased grey matter volume in mTBI patients with post-traumatic headache compared to headache-free mTBI patients and healthy controls: A longitudinal MRI study. *Brain Imaging and Behavior, 14*(5), 1651–1659. https://doi.org/10.1007/s11682-019-00095-7

Buttram, S. D. W., Garcia-Filion, P., Miller, J., Youssfi, M., Brown, S. D., Dalton, H. J., & Adelson, P. D. (2015). Computed tomography vs magnetic resonance imaging for identifying acute lesions in pediatric traumatic brain injury. *Hospital Pediatrics, 5*(2), 79–84. https://doi.org/10.1542/hpeds.2014-0094

Cancelliere, C., Coronado, V. G., Taylor, C. A., & Xu, L. (2017). Epidemiology of isolated versus nonisolated mild traumatic brain injury treated in emergency departments in the United States, 2006-2012: Sociodemographic characteristics. *The Journal of Head Trauma Rehabilitation, 32*(4), E37–E46. https://doi.org/10.1097/HTR.0000000000000260

Capizzi, A., Woo, J., & Verduzco-Gutierrez, M. (2020). Traumatic brain injury: An overview of epidemiology, pathophysiology, and medical management. *Medical Clinics of North America, 104*(2), 213–238. https://doi.org/10.1016/j.mcna.2019.11.001

Carlson, K. F., Kehle, S. M., Meis, L. A., Greer, N., MacDonald, R., Rutks, I., Sayer, N. A., Dobscha, S. K., & Wilt, T. J. (2011). Prevalence, assessment, and treatment of mild traumatic brain injury and posttraumatic stress disorder: A systematic review of the evidence. *The Journal of Head Trauma Rehabilitation, 26*(2), 103. https://doi.org/10.1097/HTR.0b013e3181e50ef1

Carroll, L. J., Cassidy, J. D., Cancelliere, C., Côté, P., Hincapié, C. A., Kristman, V. L., Holm, L. W., Borg, J., Nygren-de Boussard, C., & Hartvigsen, J. (2014). Systematic review of the prognosis after mild traumatic brain injury in adults: Cognitive, psychiatric, and mortality outcomes: Results of the international collaboration on mild traumatic brain injury prognosis. *Archives of Physical Medicine and Rehabilitation, 95*(3 Suppl), S152–S173. https://doi.org/10.1016/j.apmr.2013.08.300

Carter-Allison, S. N., Potter, S., & Rimes, K. (2016). Diagnosis threat and injury beliefs after mild traumatic brain injury. *Archives of Clinical Neuropsychology, 31*(7), 727–737. https://doi.org/10.1093/arclin/acw062

Cassidy, J. D., Boyle, E., & Carroll, L. J. (2014). Population-based, inception cohort study of the incidence, course, and prognosis of mild traumatic brain injury after motor vehicle collisions. *Archives of Physical Medicine and Rehabilitation, 95*(3), S278–S285. https://doi.org/10.1016/j.apmr.2013.08.295

Cassidy, J. D., Cancelliere, C., Carroll, L. J., Côté, P., Hincapié, C. A., Holm, L. W., Hartvigsen, J., Donovan, J., Nygren-de Boussard, C., Kristman, V. L., & Borg, J. (2014). Systematic review of the prognosis after mild traumatic brain injury in adults: Cognitive, psychiatric, and mortality outcomes: Results of the international collaboration on mild traumatic brain injury prognosis. *Archives of Physical Medicine and Rehabilitation, 95*(3, Suppl), S132–S151. https://doi.org/10.1016/j.apmr.2013.08.299

Cassidy, J. D., Carroll, L., Côté, P., Holm, L., & Nygren, A. (2004). Mild traumatic brain injury after traffic collisions: A population-based inception cohort study. *Journal of Rehabilitation Medicine, 43*(*Suppl*), 15–21. https://doi.org/10.1080/16501960410023688

Center for Disease Control and Prevention. (2003). *Report to Congress on mild traumatic brain injury in the United States: Steps to prevent a serious public health problem.* Centers for Disease Control and Prevention. http://www.cdc.gov/traumaticbraininjury/pdf/mtbireport-a.pdf.

Chrisman, S. P. D., Whitlock, K. B., Mendoza, J. A., Burton, M. S., Somers, E., Hsu, A., Fay, L., Palermo, T. M., & Rivara, F. P. (2019). Pilot randomized controlled trial of an exercise program requiring minimal in-person visits for youth with persistent sport-related concussion. *Frontiers in Neurology, 10*. https://www.frontiersin.org/articles/10.3389/fneur.2019.00623

Christensen, H., Griffiths, K., Mackinnon, A., & Jacomb, P. (1997). A quantitative review of cognitive deficits in depression and Alzheimer-type dementia. *Journal of the International Neuropsychological Society: JINS, 3*(6), 631–651.

Colombo, G., Bonzi, M., Fiorelli, E., Jachetti, A., Bozzano, V., Casazza, G., Solbiati, M., & Costantino, G. (2021). Incidence of delayed bleeding in patients on antiplatelet therapy after mild traumatic brain injury: A systematic review and meta-analysis. *Scandinavian Journal of Trauma, Resuscitation and Emergency Medicine, 29*(1), 123. https://doi.org/10.1186/s13049-021-00936-9

Combs, H. L., Berry, D. T. R., Pape, T., Babcock-Parziale, J., Smith, B., Schleenbaker, R., Shandera-Ochsner, A., Harp, J. P., & High, W. M. (2015). The effects of mild traumatic brain injury, post-traumatic stress disorder, and combined mild traumatic brain injury/post-traumatic stress disorder on returning veterans. *Journal of Neurotrauma, 32*(13), 956–966. https://doi.org/10.1089/neu.2014.3585

Comper, P., Bisschop, S. M., Carnide, N., & Tricco, A. (2005). A systematic review of treatments for mild traumatic brain injury. *Brain Injury, 19*(11), 863–880. https://doi.org/10.1080/02699050400025042

Conti, A. A., McLean, L., Tolomeo, S., Steele, J. D., & Baldacchino, A. (2019). Chronic tobacco smoking and neuropsychological impairments: A systematic review and meta-analysis. *Neuroscience and Biobehavioral Reviews, 96*, 143–154. https://doi.org/10.1016/j.neubiorev.2018.11.017

Cooper, D. B., Bunner, A. E., Kennedy, J. E., Balldin, V., Tate, D. F., Eapen, B. C., & Jaramillo, C. A. (2015). Treatment of persistent post-concussive symptoms after mild traumatic brain injury: A systematic review of cognitive rehabilitation and behavioral health interventions in military service members and veterans. *Brain Imaging and Behavior, 9*(3), 403–420. https://doi.org/10.1007/s11682-015-9440-2

Daugherty, J., DePadilla, L., Sarmiento, K., & Breiding, M. J. (2020). Self-reported lifetime concussion among adults: Comparison of 3 different survey questions. *The Journal of Head Trauma Rehabilitation, 35*(2), E136–E143. https://doi.org/10.1097/HTR.0000000000000534

Davis, C. H. (2002). Self-perception in mild traumatic brain injury. *American Journal of Physical Medicine & Rehabilitation, 81*(8), 609–618.

Dean, P. J. A., O'Neill, D., & Sterr, A. (2012). Post-concussion syndrome: Prevalence after mild traumatic brain injury in comparison with a sample without head injury. *Brain Injury, 26*(1), 14–26. https://doi.org/10.3109/02699052.2011.635354

de Freitas Cardoso, M. G., Faleiro, R. M., de Paula, J. J., Kummer, A., Caramelli, P., Teixeira, A. L., de Souza, L. C., & Miranda, A. S. (2019). Cognitive impairment following acute mild traumatic brain injury. *Frontiers in Neurology, 10*, 198. https://doi.org/10.3389/fneur.2019.00198

de Koning, M. E., Gareb, B., El Moumni, M., Scheenen, M. E., van der Horn, H. J., Timmerman, M. E., Spikman, J. M., & van der Naalt, J. (2016). Subacute posttraumatic complaints and psychological distress in trauma patients with or without mild traumatic brain injury. *Injury, 47*(9), 2041–2047. https://doi.org/10.1016/j.injury.2016.04.036

de Kruijk, J. R., Leffers, P., Meerhoff, S., Rutten, J., & Twijnstra, A. (2002). Effectiveness of bed rest after mild traumatic brain injury: A randomised trial of no versus six days of bed rest. *Journal of Neurology, Neurosurgery & Psychiatry, 73*(2), 167–172. https://doi.org/10.1136/jnnp.73.2.167

Delis, D. C., & Wetter, S. R. (2007). Cogniform disorder and cogniform condition: Proposed diagnoses for excessive cognitive symptoms. *Archives of Clinical Neuropsychology, 22*(5), 589–604. https://doi.org/10.1016/j.acn.2007.04.001

De Luigi, A. J., Bell, K. R., Bramhall, J. P., Choe, M., Dec, K., Finnoff, J. T., Halstead, M., Herring, S. A., Matuszak, J., Raksin, P. B., Swanson, J., & Millett, C. (2023). Consensus statement: An evidence-based review of exercise, rehabilitation, rest, and return to activity protocols for the treatment of concussion and mild traumatic brain injury. *PM&R, 15*(12), 1605–1642. https://doi.org/10.1002/pmrj.13070

de Neeling, M., Liessens, D., & Depreitere, B. (2023). Relationship between psychosocial and psychiatric risk factors and poor long-term outcome following mild traumatic brain injury: A systematic review. *European Journal of Neurology, 30*(5), 1540–1550. https://doi.org/10.1111/ene.15713

Dewan, M. C., Mummareddy, N., Wellons, J. C., & Bonfield, C. M. (2016). Epidemiology of global pediatric traumatic brain injury: Qualitative review. *World Neurosurgery, 91*, 497–509.e1. https://doi.org/10.1016/j.wneu.2016.03.045

Dogra, S., Arabshahi, S., Wei, J., Saidenberg, L., Kang, S. K., Chung, S., Laine, A., & Lui, Y. W. (2024). Functional connectivity changes on resting-state fMRI after mild traumatic brain injury: A systematic review. *AJNR. American Journal of Neuroradiology, 45*(6), 795–801. https://doi.org/10.3174/ajnr.A8204

Dunning, J., Daly, J. P., Lomas, J.-P., Lecky, F., Batchelor, J., Mackway-Jones, K., & Children's Head Injury Algorithm for the Prediction of Important Clinical Events Study Group. (2006). Derivation of the children's head injury algorithm for the prediction of important clinical events decision rule for head injury in children. *Archives of Disease in Childhood, 91*(11), 885–891. https://doi.org/10.1136/adc.2005.083980

Einarsen, C. E., Moen, K. G., Håberg, A. K., Eikenes, L., Kvistad, K. A., Xu, J., Moe, H. K., Tollefsen, M. H., Vik, A., & Skandsen, T. (2019). Patients with mild traumatic brain injury recruited from both hospital and primary care settings: A controlled longitudinal magnetic resonance imaging study. *Journal of Neurotrauma, 36*(22), 3172–3182. https://doi.org/10.1089/neu.2018.6360

Evered, L., Ruff, R., Baldo, J., & Isomura, A. (2003). Emotional risk factors and postconcussional disorder. *Assessment, 10*(4), 420–427. https://doi.org/10.1177/1073191103259539

Fadzil, F., Mei, A. K. C., Mohd Khairy, A., Kumar, R., & Mohd Azli, A. N. (2022). Value of repeat CT brain in mild traumatic brain injury patients with high risk of intracerebral hemorrhage progression. *International Journal of Environmental Research and Public Health, 19*(21), 14311. https://doi.org/10.3390/ijerph192114311

Fakhoury, M., Shakkour, Z., Kobeissy, F., & Lawand, N. (2020). Depression following traumatic brain injury: A comprehensive overview. *Reviews in the Neurosciences, 1*(ahead-of-print). https://doi.org/10.1515/revneuro-2020-0037

Figueiredo, P. R., Tolomeo, S., Steele, J. D., & Baldacchino, A. (2020). Neurocognitive consequences of chronic cannabis use: A systematic review and meta-analysis. *Neuroscience and Biobehavioral Reviews, 108*, 358–369. https://doi.org/10.1016/j.neubiorev.2019.10.014

Fiorelli, E. M., Bozzano, V., Bonzi, M., Rossi, S. V., Colombo, G., Radici, G., Canini, T., Kurihara, H., Casazza, G., Solbiati, M., & Costantino, G. (2020). Incremental risk of intracranial hemorrhage after mild traumatic brain injury in patients on antiplatelet therapy: Systematic review and meta-analysis. *The Journal of Emergency Medicine, 59*(6), 843–855. https://doi.org/10.1016/j.jemermed.2020.07.036

Foks, K. A., van den Brand, C. L., Lingsma, H. F., van der Naalt, J., Jacobs, B., de Jong, E., den Boogert, H. F., Sir, Ö., Patka, P., Polinder, S., Gaakeer, M. I., Schutte, C. E., Jie, K. E., Visee, H. F., Hunink, M. G. M., Reijners, E., Braaksma, M., Schoonman, G. G., Steyerberg, E. W., … Dippel, D. W. J. (2018). External validation of computed tomography decision rules for minor head injury: Prospective, multicentre cohort study in the Netherlands. *BMJ (Clinical Research Ed.), 362*, k3527. https://doi.org/10.1136/bmj.k3527.

Gasquoine, P. G. (2000). Postconcussional symptoms in chronic back pain. *Applied Neuropsychology, 7*(2), 83–89. https://doi.org/10.1207/S15324826AN0702_3

Gordon, K. E., Dooley, J. M., Fitzpatrick, E. A., Wren, P., & Wood, E. P. (2010). Concussion or mild traumatic brain injury: Parents appreciate the nuances of nosology. *Pediatric Neurology, 43*(4), 253–257. https://doi.org/10.1016/j.pediatrneurol.2010.05.012

Greenberg, J. K., Yan, Y., Carpenter, C. R., Lumba-Brown, A., Keller, M. S., Pineda, J. A., Brownson, R. C., & Limbrick, D. D. (2017). Development and internal validation of a clinical risk score for treating children with mild head trauma and intracranial injury. *JAMA Pediatrics, 171*(4), 342–349. https://doi.org/10.1001/jamapediatrics.2016.4520

Greiffenstein, M. F., & Baker, W. J. (2001). Comparison of premorbid and postinjury MMPI-2 profiles in late postconcussion claimants. *The Clinical Neuropsychologist, 15*(2), 162–170. https://doi.org/10.1076/clin.15.2.162.1895

Grool, A. M., Aglipay, M., Momoli, F., Meehan, W. P., III, Freedman, S. B., Yeates, K. O., Gravel, J., Gagnon, I., Boutis, K., Meeuwisse, W., Barrowman, N., Ledoux, A.-A., Osmond, M. H., Zemek, R., & for the Pediatric Emergency Research Canada (PERC) Concussion Team. (2016). Association between early participation in physical activity following acute concussion and persistent postconcussive symptoms in children and adolescents. *JAMA, 316*(23), 2504–2514. https://doi.org/10.1001/jama.2016.17396

Gunstad, J., & Suhr, J. A. (2001). "Expectation as etiology" versus "the good old days": Postconcussion syndrome symptom reporting in athletes, headache sufferers, and depressed individuals. *Journal of the International Neuropsychological Society: JINS, 7*(3), 323–333. https://doi.org/10.1017/s1355617701733061

Gunstad, J., & Suhr, J. A. (2004). Cognitive factors in postconcussion syndrome symptom report. *Archives of Clinical Neuropsychology, 19*(3), 391–405. https://doi.org/10.1016/S0887-6177(03)00073-8

Haarbauer-Krupa, J., Lebrun-Harris, L. A., Black, L. I., Veliz, P., Daugherty, J., Desrocher, R., Schulenberg, J., Pilkey, D., & Breiding, M. (2020). Comparing prevalence estimates of concussion/head injury in U.S. children and adolescents in national surveys. *Annals of Epidemiology*. https://doi.org/10.1016/j.annepidem.2020.11.006

Hacker, D., Jones, C. A., Yasin, E., Preece, S., Davies, H., Hawkins, A., Belli, A., & Paton, E. (2023). Cognitive outcome after complicated mild traumatic brain injury: A literature review and meta-analysis. *Journal of Neurotrauma, 40*(19–20), 1995–2014. https://doi.org/10.1089/neu.2023.0020

Hageman, G., & Nihom, J. (2022). A child presenting with a Glasgow Coma Scale score of 13: Mild or moderate traumatic brain injury? A narrative review. *Neuropediatrics, 53*(2), 83–95. https://doi.org/10.1055/s-0041-1740455

Hahn, R. A. (1997). The nocebo phenomenon: Concept, evidence, and implications for public health. *Preventive Medicine, 26*(5), 607–611. https://doi.org/10.1006/pmed.1996.0124

Hall, M. G., Hauson, A. O., Wollman, S. C., Allen, K. E., Connors, E. J., Stern, M. J., Kimmel, C. L., Stephan, R. A., Sarkissians, S., Barlet, B. D., & Grant, I. (2018). Neuropsychological comparisons of cocaine versus methamphetamine users: A research synthesis and meta-analysis. *The American Journal of Drug and Alcohol Abuse, 44*(3), 277–293. https://doi.org/10.1080/00952990.2017.1355919

Hanks, R. A., Rapport, L. J., Seagly, K., Millis, S. R., Scott, C., & Pearson, C. (2019). Outcomes after concussion recovery education: Effects of litigation and disability status on maintenance of symptoms. *Journal of Neurotrauma, 36*(4), 554–558. https://doi.org/10.1089/neu.2018.5873

Heinonen, A., Rauhala, M., Isokuortti, H., Kataja, A., Nikula, M., Öhman, J., Iverson, G. L., & Luoto, T. (2022). Incidence of surgically treated post-traumatic hydrocephalus 6 months following head injury in patients undergoing acute head computed tomography. *Acta Neurochirurgica, 164*(9), 2357–2365. https://doi.org/10.1007/s00701-022-05299-3

Hellewell, S. C., Beaton, C. S., Welton, T., & Grieve, S. M. (2020). Characterizing the risk of depression following mild traumatic brain ijury: A meta-analysis of the literature comparing chronic mTBI to non-mTBI populations. *Frontiers in Neurology, 11*, 350. https://doi.org/10.3389/fneur.2020.00350

Hellstrøm, T., Kaufmann, T., Andelic, N., Soberg, H. L., Sigurdardottir, S., Helseth, E., Andreassen, O. A., & Westlye, L. T. (2017). Predicting outcome 12 months after mild traumatic brain injury in patients admitted to a neurosurgery service. *Frontiers in Neurology, 8*. https://www.frontiersin.org/articles/10.3389/fneur.2017.00125

Hilsabeck, R. C., Gouvier, W. D., & Bolter, J. F. (1998). Reconstructive memory bias in recall of neuropsychological symptomatology. *Journal of Clinical and Experimental Neuropsychology, 20*(3), 328–338. https://doi.org/10.1076/jcen.20.3.328.813

Hoffman, J. M., Dikmen, S., Temkin, N., & Bell, K. R. (2012). Development of posttraumatic stress disorder after mild traumatic brain injury. *Archives of Physical Medicine and Rehabilitation, 93*(2), 287–292. https://doi.org/10.1016/j.apmr.2011.08.041

Hogeveen, J., & Grafman, J. (2021). Alexithymia. In K. M. Heilman & S. E. Nadeau (Eds.), *Handbook of clinical neurology* (Vol. 183, pp. 47–62). Elsevier. https://doi.org/10.1016/B978-0-12-822290-4.00004-9

Holm, L., Cassidy, J. D., Carroll, L. J., Borg, J., & Neurotrauma Task Force on Mild Traumatic Brain Injury of the WHO Collaborating Centre. (2005). Summary of the WHO collaborating centre for neurotrauma task force on mild traumatic brain injury. *Journal of Rehabilitation Medicine, 37*(3), 137–141. https://doi.org/10.1080/16501970510027321

Hou, R., Moss-Morris, R., Peveler, R., Mogg, K., Bradley, B. P., & Belli, A. (2012). When a minor head injury results in enduring symptoms: A prospective investigation of risk factors for post-concussional syndrome after mild traumatic brain injury. *Journal of Neurology, Neurosurgery & Psychiatry, 83*(2), 217–223. https://doi.org/10.1136/jnnp-2011-300767

Hume, C. H., Wright, B. J., & Kinsella, G. J. (2022). Systematic review and meta-analysis of outcome after mild traumatic brain injury in older people. *Journal of the International Neuropsychological Society, 28*(7), 736–755. https://doi.org/10.1017/S1355617721000795

Huovinen, A., Marinkovic, I., Isokuortti, H., Korvenoja, A., Mäki, K., Nybo, T., Raj, R., & Melkas, S. (2022). Return to work after mild traumatic brain injury: Association with positive CT and MRI findings. *Acta Neurochirurgica, 164*(7), 1707–1717. https://doi.org/10.1007/s00701-022-05244-4

Ibañez Pérez De La Blanca, M. A., Fernández Mondéjar, E., Gómez Jimènez, F. J., Alonso Morales, J. M., Lombardo, M. D. Q., & Viso Rodriguez, J. L. (2018). Risk factors for intracranial lesions and mortality in older patients with mild traumatic brain injuries. *Brain Injury, 32*(1), 99–104. https://doi.org/10.1080/02699052.2017.1382716

Iljazi, A., Ashina, H., Al-Khazali, H. M., Lipton, R. B., Ashina, M., Schytz, H. W., & Ashina, S. (2020). Post-traumatic stress disorder after traumatic brain injury—A systematic review and meta-analysis. *Neurological Sciences, 41*(10), 2737–2746. https://doi.org/10.1007/s10072-020-04458-7

Imms, P., Chowdhury, N. F., Chaudhari, N. N., Amgalan, A., Poudel, G., Caeyenberghs, K., & Irimia, A. (2024). Prediction of cognitive outcome after mild traumatic brain injury from acute measures of communication within brain networks. *Cortex, 171*, 397–412. https://doi.org/10.1016/j.cortex.2023.10.022

Isokuortti, H., Iverson, G. L., Silverberg, N. D., Kataja, A., Brander, A., Öhman, J., & Luoto, T. M. (2018). Characterizing the type and location of intracranial abnormalities in mild traumatic brain injury. *Journal of Neurosurgery, 129*(6), 1588–1597. https://doi.org/10.3171/2017.7.JNS17615

Isokuortti, H., Luoto, T. M., Kataja, A., Brander, A., Siironen, J., Liimatainen, S., Iverson, G. L., Ylinen, A., & Ohman, J. (2014). Necessity of monitoring after negative head CT in acute head injury. *Injury, 45*(9), 1340–1344. https://doi.org/10.1016/j.injury.2014.04.012

Iverson, G. L. (2006). Misdiagnosis of the persistent postconcussion syndrome in patients with depression. *Archives of Clinical Neuropsychology, 21*(4), 303–310. https://doi.org/10.1016/j.acn.2005.12.008

Iverson, G. L., Karr, J. E., Gardner, A. J., Silverberg, N. D., & Terry, D. P. (2019). Results of scoping review do not support mild traumatic brain injury being associated with a high incidence of chronic cognitive impairment: Commentary on McInnes et al. 2017. *PLoS One, 14*(9), e0218997. https://doi.org/10.1371/journal.pone.0218997

Iverson, G. L., & Lange, R. T. (2003). Examination of "postconcussion-like" symptoms in a healthy sample. *Applied Neuropsychology, 10*(3), 137–144. https://doi.org/10.1207/S15324826AN1003_02

Iverson, G. L., Lange, R. T., Brooks, B. L., & Lynn Ashton Rennison, V. (2010). "Good old days" bias following mild traumatic brain injury. *The Clinical Neuropsychologist, 24*(1), 17–37. https://doi.org/10.1080/13854040903190797

Iverson, G. L., & McCracken, L. M. (1997). 'Postconcussive' symptoms in persons with chronic pain. *Brain Injury, 11*(11), 783–790. https://doi.org/10.1080/026990597122990

Iverson, G. L., Silverberg, N. D., & Zasler, N. D. (2022). Mild traumatic brain injury. In N. D. Zasler, D. I. Katz, R. D. Zafonte, D. B. Arciniegas, M. R. Bullock, F. M. Hammond, J. S. Kreutzer, R. Nakase-Richardson, & T. K. Watanabe (Eds.), *Brain injury medicine: Principles and practice* (3rd ed., pp. 414–424). Springer.

Iverson, G. L., Wojtowicz, M., Brooks, B. L., Maxwell, B. A., Atkins, J. E., Zafonte, R., & Berkner, P. D. (2020). High school athletes with ADHD and learning difficulties have a greater lifetime concussion history. *Journal of Attention Disorders, 24*(8), 1095–1101. https://doi.org/10.1177/1087054716657410

Jamora, C. W., Young, A., & Ruff, R. M. (2012). Comparison of subjective cognitive complaints with neuropsychological tests in individuals with mild vs more severe traumatic brain injuries. *Brain Injury, 26*(1), 36–47. https://doi.org/10.3109/02699052.2011.635352

Jeret, J. S., Mandell, M., Anziska, B., Lipitz, M., Vilceus, A. P., Ware, J. A., & Zesiewicz, T. A. (1993). Clinical predictors of abnormality disclosed by computed tomography after mild head trauma. *Neurosurgery, 32*(1), 9–15.; Discussion 15–16. https://doi.org/10.1227/00006123-199301000-00002

Joseph, B., Pandit, V., Aziz, H., Kulvatunyou, N., Zangbar, B., Green, D. J., Haider, A., Tang, A., O'Keeffe, T., Gries, L., Friese, R. S., & Rhee, P. (2015). Mild traumatic brain injury defined by Glasgow Coma Scale: Is it really mild? *Brain Injury, 29*(1), 11–16. https://doi.org/10.3109/02699052.2014.945959

Joyce, J. M., La, P. L., Walker, R., & Harris, A. D. (2022). Magnetic resonance spectroscopy of traumatic brain injury and subconcussive hits: A systematic review and meta-analysis. *Journal of Neurotrauma, 39*(21–22), 1455–1476. https://doi.org/10.1089/neu.2022.0125

Juengst, S. B., Kumar, R. G., & Wagner, A. K. (2017). A narrative literature review of depression following traumatic brain injury: Prevalence, impact, and management challenges. *Psychology Research and Behavior Management, 10*, 175–186. https://doi.org/10.2147/PRBM.S113264

Karlsen, R. H., Saksvik, S. B., Stenberg, J., Lundervold, A. J., Olsen, A., Rautio, I. V., Folvik, L., Håberg, A. K., Vik, A., Karr, J. E., Iverson, G. L., & Skandsen, T. (2020). Examining the subacute effects of mild traumatic brain injury with the CENTER-TBI neuropsychological test battery. *Journal of Neurotrauma*. https://doi.org/10.1089/neu.2019.6922

Karr, J. E., Areshenkoff, C. N., & Garcia-Barrera, M. A. (2014). The neuropsychological outcomes of concussion: A systematic review of meta-analyses on the cognitive sequelae of mild traumatic brain injury. *Neuropsychology, 28*(3), 321–336. https://doi.org/10.1037/neu0000037

Kay, T., Harrington, D. E., Adams, R., Anderson, T., Berrol, S., Cicerone, K., Dahlberg, C., Gerber, D., Goka, R., Harley, P., Hilt, J., Horn, L., Lehmkuhl, D., & Malec, J. (1993). Definition of mild traumatic brain injury. *The Journal of Head Trauma Rehabilitation, 8*(3), 86–87. https://doi.org/10.1097/00001199-199309000-00010

Kay, T., Newman, B., Cavallo, M., Ezrachi, O., & Resnick, M. (1992). Toward a neuropsychological model of functional disability after mild traumatic brain injury. *Neuropsychology, 6*(4), 371–384. https://doi.org/10.1037/0894-4105.6.4.371

Kelly, K., & Erdal, K. (2017). Diagnostic terminology, athlete status, and history of concussion affect return to play expectations and anticipated symptoms following mild traumatic brain injury. *Journal of Clinical and Experimental Neuropsychology, 39*(6), 587–595. https://doi.org/10.1080/13803395.2016.1250870

Kempe, C. B., Sullivan, K. A., & Edmed, S. L. (2013). The effect of varying diagnostic terminology within patient discharge information on expected mild traumatic brain injury outcome. *The Clinical Neuropsychologist, 27*(5), 762–778. https://doi.org/10.1080/13854046.2013.795245

Kim, E., Yoo, R.-E., Seong, M. Y., & Oh, B.-M. (2022). A systematic review and data synthesis of longitudinal changes in white matter integrity after mild traumatic brain injury assessed by diffusion tensor imaging in adults. *European Journal of Radiology, 147*, 110117. https://doi.org/10.1016/j.ejrad.2021.110117

Kim, S., Yeh, P.-H., Ollinger, J. M., Morris, H. D., Hood, M. N., Ho, V. B., & Choi, K. H. (2023). Military-related mild traumatic brain injury: Clinical characteristics, advanced neuroimaging, and molecular mechanisms. *Translational Psychiatry, 13*(1), Article 1. https://doi.org/10.1038/s41398-023-02569-1

Kisat, M., Zafar, S. N., Latif, A., Villegas, C. V., Efron, D. T., Stevens, K. A., Haut, E. R., Schneider, E. B., Zafar, H., & Haider, A. H. (2012). Predictors of positive head CT scan and neurosurgical procedures after minor head trauma. *The Journal of Surgical Research, 173*(1), 31–37. https://doi.org/10.1016/j.jss.2011.04.059

Klein, A. P., Tetzlaff, J. E., Bonis, J. M., Nelson, L. D., Mayer, A. R., Huber, D. L., Harezlak, J., Mathews, V. P., Ulmer, J. L., Sinson, G. P., Nencka, A. S., Koch, K. M., Wu, Y.-C., Saykin, A. J., DiFiori, J. P., Giza, C. C., Goldman, J., Guskiewicz, K. M., Mihalik, J. P., … Meier, T. B. (2019). Prevalence of potentially clinically significant magnetic resonance imaging findings in athletes with and without sport-related concussion. *Journal of Neurotrauma, 36*(11), 1776–1785. https://doi.org/10.1089/neu.2018.6055.

Kristman, V. L., Côté, P., Hogg-Johnson, S., Cassidy, J. D., Eerd, D. V., Vidmar, M., Rezai, M., & Wennberg, R. A. (2010). The burden of work disability associated with mild traumatic brain injury in Ontario compensated workers: A prospective cohort study. *The Open Occupational Health & Safety Journal, 2*(1) https://benthamopen.com/ABSTRACT/TOOHSJ-2-1

Kurtz, M. M., & Gerraty, R. T. (2009). A meta-analytic investigation of neurocognitive deficits in bipolar illness: Profile and effects of clinical state. *Neuropsychology, 23*(5), 551–562. https://doi.org/10.1037/a0016277

Lai, C., Kostas-Polston, E. A., Engler, M. B., Capple, K. A., & Froelicher, E. S. (2024). Prevalence of PTSD in active duty members with mild traumatic brain injury: Systematic review and meta-analysis. *Military Medicine*. https://doi.org/10.1093/milmed/usae272

Lange, R. T., Iverson, G. L., & Rose, A. (2010). Post-concussion symptom reporting and the "good-old-days" bias following mild traumatic brain injury. *Archives of Clinical Neuropsychology, 25*(5), 442–450. https://doi.org/10.1093/arclin/acq031

Langevin, P., FrÉmont, P., Fait, P., DubÉ, M.-O., Bertrand-Charette, M., & Roy, J.-S. (2020). Aerobic exercise for sport-related concussion: A systematic review and meta-analysis. *Medicine and Science in Sports and Exercise, 52*(12), 2491–2499. https://doi.org/10.1249/MSS.0000000000002402

Lannsjö, M., Backheden, M., Johansson, U., Af Geijerstam, J. L., & Borg, J. (2013). Does head CT scan pathology predict outcome after mild traumatic brain injury? *European Journal of Neurology, 20*(1), 124–129. https://doi.org/10.1111/j.1468-1331.2012.03813.x

Leddy, J. J., Haider, M. N., Ellis, M. J., Mannix, R., Darling, S. R., Freitas, M. S., Suffoletto, H. N., Leiter, J., Cordingley, D. M., & Willer, B. (2019). Early subthreshold aerobic exercise for sport-related concussion: A randomized clinical trial. *JAMA Pediatrics, 173*(4), 319–325. https://doi.org/10.1001/jamapediatrics.2018.4397

Leddy, J. J., & Willer, B. (2013). Use of graded exercise testing in concussion and return-to-activity management. *Current Sports Medicine Reports, 12*(6), 370. https://doi.org/10.1249/JSR.0000000000000008

Lee, H., Wintermark, M., Gean, A. D., Ghajar, J., Manley, G. T., & Mukherjee, P. (2008). Focal lesions in acute mild traumatic brain injury and neurocognitive outcome: CT versus 3T MRI. *Journal of Neurotrauma, 25*(9), 1049–1056. https://doi.org/10.1089/neu.2008.0566

Lefevre-Dognin, C., Cogné, M., Perdrieau, V., Granger, A., Heslot, C., & Azouvi, P. (2021). Definition and epidemiology of mild traumatic brain injury. *Neurochirurgie, 67*(3), 218–221. https://doi.org/10.1016/j.neuchi.2020.02.002

Lennon, M. J., Brooker, H., Creese, B., Thayanandan, T., Rigney, G., Aarsland, D., Hampshire, A., Ballard, C., Corbett, A., & Raymont, V. (2023). Lifetime traumatic brain injury and cognitive domain deficits in late life: The PROTECT-TBI cohort study. *Journal of Neurotrauma*. https://doi.org/10.1089/neu.2022.0360

Levy, A. M., Saling, M. M., & Anderson, J. F. I. (2023). Frequency and extent of cognitive complaint following adult civilian mild traumatic brain injury: A systematic review and meta-analysis. *Brain Impairment: A Multidisciplinary Journal of the Australian Society for the Study of Brain Impairment, 24*(2), 309–332. https://doi.org/10.1017/BrImp.2022.19

Lindsey, H. M., Hodges, C. B., Greer, K. M., Wilde, E. A., & Merkley, T. L. (2023). Diffusion-weighted imaging in mild traumatic brain injury: A systematic review of the literature. *Neuropsychology Review, 33*(1), 42–121. https://doi.org/10.1007/s11065-021-09485-5

Lingsma, H. F., Yue, J. K., Maas, A. I. R., Steyerberg, E. W., Manley, G. T., Cooper, S. R., Dams-O'Connor, K., Gordon, W. A., Menon, D. K., Mukherjee, P., Okonkwo, D. O., Puccio, A. M., Schnyer, D. M., Valadka, A. B., Vassar, M. J., & Yuh, E. L. (2015). Outcome prediction after mild and complicated mild traumatic brain injury: External validation of existing models and identification of new predictors using the TRACK-TBI pilot study. *Journal of Neurotrauma, 32*(2), 83–94. https://doi.org/10.1089/neu.2014.3384

Livingston, D. H., Loder, P. A., Koziol, J., & Hunt, C. D. (1991). The use of CT scanning to triage patients requiring admission following minimal head injury. *The Journal of Trauma, 31*(4), 483–487. Discussion 487–489.

Losoi, H., Silverberg, N. D., Wäljas, M., Turunen, S., Rosti-Otajärvi, E., Helminen, M., Luoto, T. M., Julkunen, J., Öhman, J., & Iverson, G. L. (2016). Recovery from mild traumatic brain injury in previously healthy adults. *Journal of Neurotrauma, 33*(8), 766–776. https://doi.org/10.1089/neu.2015.4070

Luis, C. A., Vanderploeg, R. D., & Curtiss, G. (2003). Predictors of postconcussion symptom complex in community dwelling male veterans. *Journal of the International Neuropsychological Society, 9*(7), 1001–1015. https://doi.org/10.1017/S1355617703970044

Lumba-Brown, A., Yeates, K. O., Sarmiento, K., Breiding, M. J., Haegerich, T. M., Gioia, G. A., Turner, M., Benzel, E. C., Suskauer, S. J., Giza, C. C., Joseph, M., Broomand, C., Weissman, B., Gordon, W., Wright, D. W., Moser, R. S., McAvoy, K., Ewing-Cobbs, L., Duhaime, A.-C., … Timmons, S. D. (2018). Diagnosis and management of mild traumatic brain injury in children: A systematic review. *JAMA Pediatrics*, *172*(11), e182847. https://doi.org/10.1001/jamapediatrics.2018.2847.

Lunkova, E., Guberman, G. I., Ptito, A., & Saluja, R. S. (2021). Noninvasive magnetic resonance imaging techniques in mild traumatic brain injury research and diagnosis. *Human Brain Mapping, 42*(16), 5477–5494. https://doi.org/10.1002/hbm.25630

Machulda, M. M., Bergquist, T. F., Ito, V., & Chew, S. (1998). Relationship between stress, coping, and postconcussion symptoms in a healthy adult population. *Archives of Clinical Neuropsychology, 13*(5), 415–424. https://doi.org/10.1093/arclin/13.5.415

Management of Concussion/mTBI Working Group. (2009). VA/DoD clinical practice guideline for the management of concussion/mild traumatic brain injury (mTBI). *Journal of Rehabilitation Research and Development, 46*(6), CP1-68.

Management of Concussion/mTBI Working Group. (2016). *VA/DoD clinical practice guideline for the management of concussion-mild traumatic brain injury*. https://www.healthquality.va.gov/guidelines/rehab/mtbi/mtbicpgfullcpg50821816.pdf.

Manchester, K., Corrigan, J. D., Singichetti, B., Huang, L., Bogner, J., Yi, H., & Yang, J. (2020). Current health status and history of traumatic brain injury among Ohio adults. *Injury Prevention: Journal of the International Society for Child and Adolescent Injury Prevention, 26*(2), 129–137. https://doi.org/10.1136/injuryprev-2018-043056

Marincowitz, C., Lecky, F. E., Townend, W., Borakati, A., Fabbri, A., & Sheldon, T. A. (2018). The risk of deterioration in GCS 13-15 patients with traumatic brain injury identified by computed tomography imaging: A systematic review and meta-analysis. *Journal of Neurotrauma, 35*(5), 703–718. https://doi.org/10.1089/neu.2017.5259

Marshall, S., Bayley, M., McCullagh, S., Velikonja, D., Berrigan, L., Ouchterlony, D., & Weegar, K. (2015). Updated clinical practice guidelines for concussion/mild traumatic brain injury and persistent symptoms. *Brain Injury, 29*(6), 688–700. https://doi.org/10.3109/02699052.2015.1004755

Masson, M., Bussières, E.-L., East-Richard, C., R-Mercier, A., & Cellard, C. (2015). Neuropsychological profile of children, adolescents and adults experiencing maltreatment: A meta-analysis. *The Clinical Neuropsychologist, 29*(5), 573–594. https://doi.org/10.1080/13854046.2015.1061057

Mavroudis, I., Balmus, I.-M., Ciobica, A., & Hogas, M. (2024). A narrative review of risk factors and predictors for poor outcome and prolonged recovery after a mild traumatic brain injury. *The International Journal of Neuroscience*, 1–10. https://doi.org/10.1080/00207454.2024.2328710

Mayer, A. R., Cohen, D. M., Wertz, C. J., Dodd, A. B., Shoemaker, J., Pluto, C., Zumberge, N. A., Park, G., Bangert, B. A., Lin, C., Minich, N. M., Bacevice, A. M., Bigler, E. D., Campbell, R. A., Hanlon, F. M., Meier, T. B., Oglesbee, S. J., Phillips, J. P., Pottenger, A., … Yeates, K. O. (2020). Radiologic common data elements rates in pediatric mild traumatic brain injury. *Neurology*, *94*(3), e241–e253. https://doi.org/10.1212/WNL.0000000000008488.

McCrea, M. C., Iverson, G. L., McAllister, T. W., Hammeke, T. A., Powell, M. R., Barr, W. B., & Kelly, J. P. (2009). An integrated review of recovery after mild traumatic brain injury (MTBI): Implications for clinical management. *The Clinical Neuropsychologist, 23*(8), 1368–1390. https://doi.org/10.1080/13854040903074652

McCrory, P., Johnston, K., Meeuwisse, W., Aubry, M., Cantu, R., Dvorak, J., Graf-Baumann, T., Kelly, J., Lovell, M., & Schamasch, P. (2005). Summary and agreement statement of the 2nd International Conference on Concussion in Sport, Prague 2004. *British Journal of Sports Medicine, 39*(4), 196–204. https://doi.org/10.1136/bjsm.2005.018614

McCrory, P., Meeuwisse, W., Dvorak, J., Aubry, M., Bailes, J., Broglio, S., Cantu, R. C., Cassidy, D., Echemendia, R. J., Castellani, R. J., Davis, G. A., Ellenbogen, R., Emery, C., Engebretsen, L., Feddermann-Demont, N., Giza, C. C., Guskiewicz, K. M., Herring, S., Iverson, G. L., … Vos, P. E. (2017). Consensus statement on concussion in sport—The 5th international conference on concussion in sport held in Berlin, October 2016. *British Journal of Sports Medicine*. https://doi.org/10.1136/bjsports-2017-097699.

McCrory, P., Meeuwisse, W., Johnston, K., Dvorak, J., Aubry, M., Molloy, M., & Cantu, R. (2009). Consensus statement on concussion in sport: The 3rd international conference on concussion in sport held in Zurich, November 2008. *British Journal of Sports Medicine, 43*(Suppl 1), i76–i90. https://doi.org/10.1136/bjsm.2009.058248

McCrory, P., Meeuwisse, W. H., Aubry, M., Cantu, R. C., Dvořák, J., Echemendia, R. J., Engebretsen, L., Johnston, K., Kutcher, J. S., Raftery, M., Sills, A., Benson, B. W., Davis, G. A., Ellenbogen, R., Guskiewicz, K. M., Herring, S. A., Iverson, G. L., Jordan, B. D.,

Kissick, J., … Turner, M. (2013). Consensus statement on concussion in sport: The 4th international conference on concussion in sport, Zurich, November 2012. *Journal of Athletic Training, 48*(4), 554–575. https://doi.org/10.4085/1062-6050-48.4.05.

McIntyre, M., Kempenaar, A., Amiri, M., Alavinia, S. M., & Kumbhare, D. (2020). The role of subsymptom threshold aerobic exercise for persistent concussion symptoms in patients with postconcussion syndrome: A systematic review. *American Journal of Physical Medicine & Rehabilitation, 99*(3), 257. https://doi.org/10.1097/PHM.0000000000001340

McNally, K. A., Patrick, K. E., LaFleur, J. E., Dykstra, J. B., Monahan, K., & Hoskinson, K. R. (2018). Brief cognitive behavioral intervention for children and adolescents with persistent post-concussive symptoms: A pilot study. *Child Neuropsychology, 24*(3), 396–412. https://doi.org/10.1080/09297049.2017.1280143

Meares, S., Shores, E. A., Taylor, A. J., Batchelor, J., Bryant, R. A., Baguley, I. J., Chapman, J., Gurka, J., & Marosszeky, J. E. (2011). The prospective course of postconcussion syndrome: The role of mild traumatic brain injury. *Neuropsychology, 25*, 454–465. https://doi.org/10.1037/a0022580

Mikolić, A., Polinder, S., Steyerberg, E. W., Retel Helmrich, I. R. A., Giacino, J. T., Maas, A. I. R., van der Naalt, J., Voormolen, D. C., von Steinbüchel, N., Wilson, L., Lingsma, H. F., van Klaveren, D., Åkerlund, C., Amrein, K., Andelic, N., Andreassen, L., Anke, A., Antoni, A., Audibert, G., … Zoerle, T. (2021). Prediction of global functional outcome and post-concussive symptoms after mild traumatic brain injury: External validation of prognostic models in the collaborative European neurotrauma effectiveness research in traumatic brain injury (CENTER-TBI) study. *Journal of Neurotrauma, 38*(2), 196–209. https://doi.org/10.1089/neu.2020.7074.

Mishra, R. K., Munivenkatappa, A., Prathyusha, V., Shukla, D. P., & Devi, B. I. (2017). Clinical predictors of abnormal head computed tomography scan in patients who are conscious after head injury. *Journal of Neurosciences in Rural Practice, 8*(1), 64–67. https://doi.org/10.4103/0976-3147.193538

Mittenberg, W., DiGiulio, D. V., Perrin, S., & Bass, A. E. (1992). Symptoms following mild head injury: Expectation as aetiology. *Journal of Neurology, Neurosurgery & Psychiatry, 55*(3), 200–204. https://doi.org/10.1136/jnnp.55.3.200

Mittenberg, W., Tremont, G., Zielinski, R. E., Fichera, S., & Rayls, K. R. (1996). Cognitive-behavioral prevention of postconcussion syndrome. *Archives of Clinical Neuropsychology, 11*(2), 139–145.

Mooney, G., Speed, J., & Sheppard, S. (2005). Factors related to recovery after mild traumatic brain injury. *Brain Injury, 19*(12), 975–987. https://doi.org/10.1080/02699050500110264

Moore, B. M., Stark, R. K., & D'Angelo, E. C. (2024). Multidisciplinary care for patients with persistent symptoms following concussion: A systematic review. *Disability and Rehabilitation, 46*(9), 1760–1775. https://doi.org/10.1080/09638288.2023.2205663

Naghibi, T., Rostami, M., Jamali, B., Karimimoghaddam, Z., Zeraatchi, A., & Rouhi, A. J. (2021). Predicting factors for abnormal brain computed tomography in children with minor head trauma. *BMC Emergency Medicine, 21*(1), 142. https://doi.org/10.1186/s12873-021-00540-1

Nguyen, R., Fiest, K. M., McChesney, J., Kwon, C.-S., Jette, N., Frolkis, A. D., Atta, C., Mah, S., Dhaliwal, H., Reid, A., Pringsheim, T., Dykeman, J., & Gallagher, C. (2016). The international incidence of traumatic brain injury: A systematic review and meta-analysis. *The Canadian Journal of Neurological Sciences, 43*(6), 774–785. https://doi.org/10.1017/cjn.2016.290

Nigrovic, L. E., Lee, L. K., Hoyle, J., Stanley, R. M., Gorelick, M. H., Miskin, M., Atabaki, S. M., Dayan, P. S., Holmes, J. F., Kuppermann, N., & Traumatic Brain Injury (TBI) Working Group of Pediatric Emergency Care Applied Research Network (PECARN). (2012). Prevalence of clinically important traumatic brain injuries in children with minor blunt head trauma and isolated severe injury mechanisms. *Archives of Pediatrics & Adolescent Medicine, 166*(4), 356–361. https://doi.org/10.1001/archpediatrics.2011.1156

Olaithe, M., & Bucks, R. S. (2013). Executive dysfunction in OSA before and after treatment: A meta-analysis. *Sleep, 36*(9), 1297–1305. https://doi.org/10.5665/sleep.2950

Ono, K., Wada, K., Takahara, T., & Shirotani, T. (2007). Indications for computed tomography in patients with mild head injury. *Neurologia Medico-Chirurgica, 47*(7), 291–297.; Discussion 297–298. https://doi.org/10.2176/nmc.47.291

Orlando, A., Coresh, J., Carrick, M. M., Quan, G., Berg, G. M., Dhakal, L., Hamilton, D., Madayag, R., Lascano, C. H. P., & Bar-Or, D. (2023). Significant national declines in neurosurgical intervention for mild traumatic brain injury with intracranial hemorrhage: A 13-year review of the national trauma data bank. *Neurotrauma Reports, 4*(1), 137–148. https://doi.org/10.1089/neur.2022.0077

Ozen, L. J., & Fernandes, M. A. (2011). Effects of "diagnosis threat" on cognitive and affective functioning long after mild head injury. *Journal of the International Neuropsychological Society: JINS, 17*(2), 219–229. https://doi.org/10.1017/S135561771000144X

Palta, P., Schneider, A. L. C., Biessels, G. J., Touradji, P., & Hill-Briggs, F. (2014). Magnitude of cognitive dysfunction in adults with type 2 diabetes: A meta-analysis of six cognitive domains and the most frequently reported neuropsychological tests within domains. *Journal of the International Neuropsychological Society: JINS, 20*(3), 278–291. https://doi.org/10.1017/S1355617713001483

Pandor, A., Goodacre, S., Harnan, S., Holmes, M., Pickering, A., Fitzgerald, P., Rees, A., & Stevenson, M. (2011). Diagnostic management strategies for adults and children with minor head injury: A systematic review and an economic evaluation. *Health Technology Assessment, 15*(27), 1–202. https://doi.org/10.3310/hta15270

Paniak, C., Reynolds, S., Toller-Lobe, G., Melnyk, A., Nagy, J., & Schmidt, D. (2002). A longitudinal study of the relationship between financial compensation and symptoms after treated mild traumatic brain injury. *Journal of Clinical and Experimental Neuropsychology, 24*(2), 187–193. https://doi.org/10.1076/jcen.24.2.187.999

Paniak, C., Toller-Lobe, G., Reynolds, S., Melnyk, A., & Nagy, J. (2000). A randomized trial of two treatments for mild traumatic brain injury: 1 year follow-up. *Brain Injury, 14*(3), 219–226. https://doi.org/10.1080/026990500120691

Patel, P. D., Broadwin, M., Stansbury, T., Brown, J. B., Kincaid, H., Duka, S., Pasquale, J., Cipolle, M., & Shah, K. (2023). Risk factors associated with neurosurgical intervention in patients with mild traumatic intracranial hemorrhage. *The Journal of Surgical Research, 283*, 137–145. https://doi.org/10.1016/j.jss.2022.10.042

Patricios, J. S., Schneider, K. J., Dvorak, J., Ahmed, O. H., Blauwet, C., Cantu, R. C., Davis, G. A., Echemendia, R. J., Makdissi, M., McNamee, M., Broglio, S., Emery, C. A., Feddermann-Demont, N., Fuller, G. W., Giza, C. C., Guskiewicz, K. M., Hainline, B., Iverson, G. L., Kutcher, J. S., … Meeuwisse, W. (2023). Consensus statement on concussion in sport: The 6th international conference on concussion in sport–Amsterdam, October 2022. *British Journal of Sports Medicine, 57*(11), 695–711. https://doi.org/10.1136/bjsports-2023-106898.

Phipps, H., Mondello, S., Wilson, A., Dittmer, T., Rohde, N. N., Schroeder, P. J., Nichols, J., McGirt, C., Hoffman, J., Tanksley, K., Chohan, M., Heiderman, A., Abou Abbass, H., Kobeissy, F., & Hinds, S. (2020). Characteristics and impact of U.S. military blast-related mild traumatic brain injury: A systematic review. *Frontiers in Neurology, 11*(559318), 1–22. https://doi.org/10.3389/fneur.2020.559318

Picon, E. L., Todorova, E. V., Palombo, D. J., Perez, D. L., Howard, A. K., & Silverberg, N. D. (2022). Memory perfectionism is associated with persistent memory complaints after concussion. *Archives of Clinical Neuropsychology, 37*(6), 1177–1184. https://doi.org/10.1093/arclin/acac021

Polich, G., Iaccarino, M. A., Kaptchuk, T. J., Morales-Quezada, L., & Zafonte, R. (2020). Nocebo effects in concussion: Is all that is told beneficial? *American Journal of Physical Medicine & Rehabilitation, 99*(1), 71. https://doi.org/10.1097/PHM.0000000000001290

Ponsford, J. L., Nguyen, S., Downing, M., Bosch, M., McKenzie, J. E., Turner, S., Chau, M., Mortimer, D., Gruen, R. L., Knott, J., & Green, S. (2019). Factors associated with persistent post-concussion symptoms following mild traumatic brain injury in adults. *Journal of Rehabilitation Medicine, 51*(1), Article 1. https://doi.org/10.2340/16501977-2492

Ponsford, J. L., Willmott, C., Rothwell, A., Cameron, P., Kelly, A., Nelms, R., & Curran, C. (2002). Impact of early intervention on outcome following mild head injury in adults. *Journal of Neurology, Neurosurgery, and Psychiatry, 73*(3), 330–332. https://doi.org/10.1136/jnnp.73.3.330

Ponsford, J. L., Willmott, C., Rothwell, A., Cameron, P., Kelly, A.-M., Nelms, R., Curran, C., & Ng, K. (2000). Factors influencing outcome following mild traumatic brain injury in adults. *Journal of the International Neuropsychological Society, 6*(5), 568–579. https://doi.org/10.1017/S1355617700655066

Pozzato, I., Meares, S., Kifley, A., Craig, A., Gillett, M., Vu, K. V., Liang, A., Cameron, I., & Gopinath, B. (2020). Challenges in the acute identification of mild traumatic brain injuries: Results from an emergency department surveillance study. *BMJ Open, 10*(2), e034494. https://doi.org/10.1136/bmjopen-2019-034494

Prince, C., & Bruhns, M. E. (2017). Evaluation and treatment of mild traumatic brain injury: The role of neuropsychology. *Brain Sciences, 7*(8), 1–14. https://doi.org/10.3390/brainsci7080105

Pruitt, P., Penn, J., Peak, D., & Borczuk, P. (2017). Identifying patients with mild traumatic intracranial hemorrhage at low risk of decompensation who are safe for ED observation. *The American Journal of Emergency Medicine, 35*(2), 255–259. https://doi.org/10.1016/j.ajem.2016.10.064

Rapoport, M. J. (2012). Depression following traumatic brain injury. *CNS Drugs, 26*(2), 111–121. https://doi.org/10.2165/11599560-000000000-00000

Richter, S., Winzeck, S., Kornaropoulos, E. N., Das, T., Vande Vyvere, T., Verheyden, J., Williams, G. B., Correia, M. M., Menon, D. K., Newcombe, V. F. J., & Collaborative European NeuroTrauma Effectiveness Research in Traumatic Brain Injury Magnetic Resonance Imaging (CENTER-TBI MRI) Substudy Participants and Investigators. (2021). Neuroanatomical substrates and symptoms associated with magnetic resonance imaging of patients with mild traumatic brain injury. *JAMA Network Open, 4*(3), e210994. https://doi.org/10.1001/jamanetworkopen.2021.0994

Riemann, L., Mikolic, A., Maas, A., Unterberg, A., Younsi, A., & Collaborative European NeuroTrauma Effectiveness Research in Traumatic Brain Injury (CENTER-TBI) Investigators and Participants. (2023). Computed tomography lesions and their association with global outcome in young people with mild traumatic brain injury. *Journal of Neurotrauma, 40*(11–12), 1243–1254. https://doi.org/10.1089/neu.2022.0055

Ritchie, K. A., & Slomine, B. S. (2022). Neuropsychological and neuropsychiatric recovery from mild traumatic brain injury. *Current Opinion in Psychiatry, 35*(2), 83–89. https://doi.org/10.1097/YCO.0000000000000776

Robinson-Freeman, K. E., Collins, K. L., Garber, B., Terblanche, R., Risling, M., Vermetten, E., Besemann, M., Mistlin, A., & Tsao, J. W. (2020). A decade of mTBI experience: What have we learned? A summary of proceedings from a NATO lecture series on military mTBI. *Frontiers in Neurology, 11*, 836. https://doi.org/10.3389/fneur.2020.00836

Rohling, M. L., Binder, L. M., Demakis, G. J., Larrabee, G. J., Ploetz, D. M., & Langhinrichsen-Rohling, J. (2011). A meta-analysis of neuropsychological outcome after mild traumatic brain injury: Re-analyses and reconsiderations of Binder et al. (1997), Frencham et al. (2005), and Pertab et al. (2009). *The Clinical Neuropsychologist, 25*(4), 608–623. https://doi.org/10.1080/13854046.2011.565076

Rohling, M. L., Larrabee, G. J., & Millis, S. R. (2012). The "miserable minority" following mild traumatic brain injury: Who are they and do meta-analyses hide them? *The Clinical Neuropsychologist, 26*(2), 197–213. https://doi.org/10.1080/13854046.2011.647085

Root, B. K., Kanter, J. H., Calnan, D. C., Reyes-Zaragosa, M., Gill, H. S., & Lanter, P. L. (2020). Emergency department observation of mild traumatic brain injury with minor radiographic findings: Shorter stays, less expensive, and no increased risk compared to hospital admission. *Journal of the American College of Emergency Physicians Open, 1*(4), 609–617. https://doi.org/10.1002/emp2.12124

Ruff, R. M., Camenzuli, L., & Mueller, J. (1996). Miserable minority: Emotional risk factors that influence the outcome of a mild traumatic brain injury. *Brain Injury, 10*(8), 551–566. https://doi.org/10.1080/026990596124124

Rytter, H. M., Graff, H. J., Henriksen, H. K., Aaen, N., Hartvigsen, J., Hoegh, M., Nisted, I., Næss-Schmidt, E. T., Pedersen, L. L., Schytz, H. W., Thastum, M. M., Zerlang, B., & Callesen, H. E. (2021). Nonpharmacological treatment of persistent postconcussion symptoms in adults: A systematic review and meta-analysis and guideline recommendation. *JAMA Network Open, 4*(11), e2132221. https://doi.org/10.1001/jamanetworkopen.2021.32221

Saboori, M., Ahmadi, J., & Farajzadegan, Z. (2007). Indications for brain CT scan in patients with minor head injury. *Clinical Neurology and Neurosurgery, 109*(5), 399–405. https://doi.org/10.1016/j.clineuro.2007.01.013

Sadegh, R., Karimialavijeh, E., Shirani, F., Payandemehr, P., Bahramimotlagh, H., & Ramezani, M. (2016). Head CT scan in Iranian minor head injury patients: Evaluating current decision rules. *Emergency Radiology, 23*(1), 9–16. https://doi.org/10.1007/s10140-015-1349-y

Sarmiento, K., Waltzman, D., Daugherty, J., Okoro, C. A., & Proescholdbell, S. (2022). Association between self-reported disability and lifetime history of traumatic brain injury with loss of consciousness among veterans and nonveterans in North Carolina. *The Journal of Head Trauma Rehabilitation, 37*(6), E428–E437. https://doi.org/10.1097/HTR.0000000000000753

Scheenen, M. E., Spikman, J. M., de Koning, M. E., van der Horn, H. J., Roks, G., Hageman, G., & van der Naalt, J. (2017). Patients "at risk" of suffering from persistent complaints after mild traumatic brain injury: The role of coping, mood disorders, and post-traumatic stress. *Journal of Neurotrauma, 34*(1), 31–37. https://doi.org/10.1089/neu.2015.4381

Schneider, K. J., Leddy, J. J., Guskiewicz, K. M., Seifert, T., McCrea, M., Silverberg, N. D., Feddermann-Demont, N., Iverson, G. L., Hayden, A., & Makdissi, M. (2017). Rest and treatment/rehabilitation following sport-related concussion: A systematic review. *British Journal of Sports Medicine, 51*(12), 930–934. https://doi.org/10.1136/bjsports-2016-097475

Scholten, A. C., Haagsma, J. A., Cnossen, M. C., Olff, M., van Beeck, E. F., & Polinder, S. (2016). Prevalence of and risk factors for anxiety and depressive disorders after traumatic brain injury: A systematic review. *Journal of Neurotrauma, 33*(22), 1969–1994. https://doi.org/10.1089/neu.2015.4252

Schretlen, D. J., & Shapiro, A. M. (2003). A quantitative review of the effects of traumatic brain injury on cognitive functioning. *International Review of Psychiatry, 15*(4), 341–349. https://doi.org/10.1080/09540260310001606728

Schwed, A. C., Boggs, M. M., Watanabe, D., Plurad, D. S., Putnam, B. A., & Kim, D. Y. (2016). Admission variables associated with a favorable outcome after mild traumatic brain injury. *The American Surgeon, 82*(10), 898–902.

Scott, J. C., Matt, G. E., Wrocklage, K. M., Crnich, C., Jordan, J., Southwick, S. M., Krystal, J. H., & Schweinsburg, B. C. (2015). A quantitative meta-analysis of neurocognitive functioning in posttraumatic stress disorder. *Psychological Bulletin, 141*(1), 105–140. https://doi.org/10.1037/a0038039

Shafie, M., Mahmoodkhani, M., Salehi, I., & Dehghan, A. (2023). Clinical predictors of abnormal brain computed tomography findings in mild traumatic brain injury: A cross-sectional study. *Medicine, 102*(26), e34167. https://doi.org/10.1097/MD.0000000000034167

Sibilia, F., Custer, R. M., Irimia, A., Sepehrband, F., Toga, A. W., Cabeen, R. P., & TRACK-TBI Investigators. (2023). Life after mild traumatic brain injury: Widespread structural brain changes associated with psychological distress revealed with multimodal magnetic resonance imaging. *Biological Psychiatry Global Open Science, 3*(3), 374–385. https://doi.org/10.1016/j.bpsgos.2022.03.004

Silverberg, N. D., Berkner, P. D., Atkins, J. E., Zafonte, R., & Iverson, G. L. (2016). Relationship between short sleep duration and preseason concussion testing. *Clinical Journal of Sport Medicine, 26*(3), 226. https://doi.org/10.1097/JSM.0000000000000241

Silverberg, N. D., Gardner, A. J., Brubacher, J. R., Panenka, W. J., Li, J. J., & Iverson, G. L. (2015). Systematic review of multivariable prognostic models for mild traumatic brain injury. *Journal of Neurotrauma, 32*(8), 517–526. https://doi.org/10.1089/neu.2014.3600

Silverberg, N. D., Iaccarino, M. A., Panenka, W. J., Iverson, G. L., McCulloch, K. L., Dams-O'Connor, K., Reed, N., McCrea, M., Cogan, A. M., Park Graf, M. J., Kajankova, M., McKinney,

G., & Weyer Jamora, C. (2020). Management of concussion and mild traumatic brain injury: A synthesis of practice guidelines. *Archives of Physical Medicine and Rehabilitation, 101*(2), 382–393. https://doi.org/10.1016/j.apmr.2019.10.179

Silverberg, N. D., & Iverson, G. L. (2011). Etiology of the post-concussion syndrome: Physiogenesis and psychogenesis revisited. *NeuroRehabilitation, 29*(4), 317–329. https://doi.org/10.3233/NRE-2011-0708

Silverberg, N. D., & Iverson, G. L. (2013). Is rest after concussion "the best medicine?": Recommendations for activity resumption following concussion in athletes, civilians, and military service members. *The Journal of Head Trauma Rehabilitation, 28*(4), 250. https://doi.org/10.1097/HTR.0b013e31825ad658

Silverberg, N. D., Iverson, G. L., & ACRM Brain Injury Special Interest Group, & ACRM Mild TBI Definition Expert Consensus Group. (2023). The American Congress of Rehabilitation Medicine diagnostic criteria for mild traumatic brain injury. *Archives of Physical Medicine and Rehabilitation, 104*(8), 1343–1355. https://doi.org/10.1016/j.apmr.2023.03.036

Silverberg, N. D., Iverson, G. L., & ACRM Mild TBI Definition Expert Consensus Group and the ACRM Brain Injury Special Interest Group Mild TBI Task Force. (2021). Expert panel survey to update the American congress of rehabilitation medicine definition of mild traumatic brain injury. *Archives of Physical Medicine and Rehabilitation, 102*(1), 76–86. https://doi.org/10.1016/j.apmr.2020.08.022

Silverberg, N. D., & Otamendi, T. (2019). Advice to rest for more than 2 days after mild traumatic brain injury is associated with delayed return to productivity: A case-control study. *Frontiers in Neurology, 10*. https://www.frontiersin.org/articles/10.3389/fneur.2019.00362

Silverberg, N. D., Panenka, W. J., & Iverson, G. L. (2018). Fear avoidance and clinical outcomes from mild traumatic brain injury. *Journal of Neurotrauma, 35*(16), 1864–1873. https://doi.org/10.1089/neu.2018.5662

Silverberg, N. D., Panenka, W. J., Lizotte, P.-P., Bayley, M. T., Dance, D., & Li, L. C. (2020). Promoting early treatment for mild traumatic brain injury in primary care with a guideline implementation tool: A pilot cluster randomised trial. *BMJ Open, 10*(10), e035527. https://doi.org/10.1136/bmjopen-2019-035527

Singh, R., Mason, S., Lecky, F., & Dawson, J. (2018). Prevalence of depression after TBI in a prospective cohort: The SHEFBIT study. *Brain Injury, 32*(1), 84–90. https://doi.org/10.1080/02699052.2017.1376756

Smith-Seemiller, L., Fow, N. R., Kant, R., & Franzen, M. D. (2003). Presence of post-concussion syndrome symptoms in patients with chronic pain vs mild traumatic brain injury. *Brain Injury, 17*(3), 199–206. https://doi.org/10.1080/0269905021000030823

Snell, D. L., Faulkner, J. W., Williman, J. A., Silverberg, N. D., Theadom, A., Surgenor, L. J., Hackney, J., & Siegert, R. J. (2023). Fear avoidance and return to work after mild traumatic brain injury. *Brain Injury*, 1–10. https://doi.org/10.1080/02699052.2023.2180663

Snell, D. L., Hay-Smith, E. J. C., Surgenor, L. J., & Siegert, R. J. (2013). Examination of outcome after mild traumatic brain injury: The contribution of injury beliefs and Leventhal's common sense model. *Neuropsychological Rehabilitation, 23*(3), 333–362. https://doi.org/10.1080/09658211.2012.758419

Snell, D. L., Siegert, R. J., Hay-Smith, E. J. C., & Surgenor, L. J. (2011). Associations between illness perceptions, coping styles and outcome after mild traumatic brain injury: Preliminary results from a cohort study. *Brain Injury, 25*(11), 1126–1138. https://doi.org/10.3109/02699052.2011.607786

Snell, D. L., Surgenor, L. J., Hay-Smith, E. J. C., & Siegert, R. J. (2009). A systematic review of psychological treatments for mild traumatic brain injury: An update on the evidence. *Journal of Clinical and Experimental Neuropsychology, 31*(1), 20–38. https://doi.org/10.1080/13803390801978849

Steele, C. M., & Aronson, J. (1995). Stereotype threat and the intellectual test performance of African Americans. *Journal of Personality and Social Psychology, 69*(5), 797–811. https://doi.org/10.1037/0022-3514.69.5.797

Stein, M. B., Ursano, R. J., Campbell-Sills, L., Colpe, L. J., Fullerton, C. S., Heeringa, S. G., Nock, M. K., Sampson, N. A., Schoenbaum, M., Sun, X., Jain, S., Kessler, R. C., Cersovsky, S., Cox, K., Aliaga, P. A., Benedek, D. M., Benevides, K. N., Bliese, P. D., Borja, S., … Ressler, K. (2016). Prognostic indicators of persistent post-concussive symptoms after deployment-related mild traumatic brain injury: A prospective longitudinal study in U.S. army soldiers. *Journal of Neurotrauma, 33*(23), 2125–2132. https://doi.org/10.1089/neu.2015.4320.

Stein, S. C., & Ross, S. E. (1992). Mild head injury: A plea for routine early CT scanning. *The Journal of Trauma, 33*(1), 11–13.

Stephan, R. A., Alhassoon, O. M., Allen, K. E., Wollman, S. C., Hall, M., Thomas, W. J., Gamboa, J. M., Kimmel, C., Stern, M., Sari, C., Dalenberg, C. J., Sorg, S. F., & Grant, I. (2017). Meta-analyses of clinical neuropsychological tests of executive dysfunction and impulsivity in alcohol use disorder. *The American Journal of Drug and Alcohol Abuse, 43*(1), 24–43. https://doi.org/10.1080/00952990.2016.1206113

Stiell, I. G., Clement, C. M., Rowe, B. H., Schull, M. J., Brison, R., Cass, D., Eisenhauer, M. A., McKnight, R. D., Bandiera, G., Holroyd, B., Lee, J. S., Dreyer, J., Worthington, J. R., Reardon, M., Greenberg, G., Lesiuk, H., MacPhail, I., & Wells, G. A. (2005). Comparison of the Canadian CT Head Rule and the New Orleans Criteria in patients with minor head injury. *JAMA, 294*(12), 1511–1518. https://doi.org/10.1001/jama.294.12.1511

Stulemeijer, M., Andriessen, T. M. J. C., Brauer, J. M. P., Vos, P. E., & Van Der Werf, S. (2007). Cognitive performance after mild traumatic brain injury: The impact of poor effort on test results and its relation to distress, personality and litigation. *Brain Injury, 21*(3), 309–318. https://doi.org/10.1080/02699050701209980

Stulemeijer, M., van der Werf, S., Borm, G. F., & Vos, P. E. (2008). Early prediction of favourable recovery 6 months after mild traumatic brain injury. *Journal of Neurology, Neurosurgery & Psychiatry, 79*(8), 936–942. https://doi.org/10.1136/jnnp.2007.131250

Stulemeijer, M., Vos, P. E., Bleijenberg, G., & van der Werf, S. P. (2007). Cognitive complaints after mild traumatic brain injury: Things are not always what they seem. *Journal of Psychosomatic Research, 63*(6), 637–645. https://doi.org/10.1016/j.jpsychores.2007.06.023

Suhr, J. A., & Gunstad, J. (2002a). "Diagnosis threat": The effect of negative expectations on cognitive performance in head injury. *Journal of Clinical and Experimental Neuropsychology, 24*(4), 448–457. https://doi.org/10.1076/jcen.24.4.448.1039

Suhr, J. A., & Gunstad, J. (2002b). Postconcussive symptom report: The relative influence of head injury and depression. *Journal of Clinical and Experimental Neuropsychology, 24*(8), 981–993. https://doi.org/10.1076/jcen.24.8.981.8372

Sullivan, K. A., Edmed, S. L., & Kempe, C. (2014). The effect of injury diagnosis on illness perceptions and expected postconcussion syndrome and posttraumatic stress disorder symptoms. *The Journal of Head Trauma Rehabilitation, 29*(1), 54. https://doi.org/10.1097/HTR.0b013e31828c708a

Sullivan, K. A., Kaye, S.-A., Blaine, H., Edmed, S. L., Meares, S., Rossa, K., & Haden, C. (2020). Psychological approaches for the management of persistent postconcussion symptoms after mild traumatic brain injury: A systematic review. *Disability and Rehabilitation, 42*(16), 2243–2251. https://doi.org/10.1080/09638288.2018.1558292

Teeratakulpisarn, P., Angkasith, P., Wannakul, T., Tanmit, P., Prasertcharoensuk, S., Thanapaisal, C., Wongkonkitsin, N., Kitkhuandee, A., Sukeepaisarnjaroen, W., Phuttharak, W., & Sawanyawisuth, K. (2021). What are the strongest indicators of intracerebral hemorrhage in mild traumatic brain injury? *Trauma Surgery & Acute Care Open, 6*(1), e000717. https://doi.org/10.1136/tsaco-2021-000717

Teo, S. H., Fong, K. N. K., Chen, Z., & Chung, R. C. K. (2020). Cognitive and psychological interventions for the reduction of post-concussion symptoms in patients with mild traumatic brain injury: A systematic review. *Brain Injury, 34*(10), 1305–1321. https://doi.org/10.1080/02699052.2020.1802668

Terry, D. P., Iverson, G. L., Panenka, W., Colantonio, A., & Silverberg, N. D. (2018). Workplace and non-workplace mild traumatic brain injuries in an outpatient clinic sample: A case-control study. *PLoS One, 13*(6), e0198128. https://doi.org/10.1371/journal.pone.0198128

Theadom, A., Barker-Collo, S., Parag, V., Caspi, A., Moffitt, T. E., Hogan, S., Ramrakha, S., & Poulton, R. (2024). Mild traumatic brain injury does not significantly affect midlife cognitive functioning within the general population: Findings from a prospective longitudinal birth cohort study. *The Journal of Head Trauma Rehabilitation, 39*(2), E70–E82. https://doi.org/10.1097/HTR.0000000000000875

Thiruppathy, S. P., & Muthukumar, N. (2004). Mild head injury: Revisited. *Acta Neurochirurgica, 146*(10), 1075–1082.; Discussion 1082–1083.. https://doi.org/10.1007/s00701-004-0335-z

Thomas, D. G., Apps, J. N., Hoffmann, R. G., McCrea, M., & Hammeke, T. (2015). Benefits of strict rest after acute concussion: A randomized controlled trial. *Pediatrics, 135*(2), 213–223. https://doi.org/10.1542/peds.2014-0966

Thorne, J., Markovic, S., Chih, H., Thomas, E., Jefferson, A., Aoun, S., Fitzgerald, M., & Hellewell, S. (2022). Healthcare choices following mild traumatic brain injury in Australia. *BMC Health Services Research, 22*(1), 858. https://doi.org/10.1186/s12913-022-08244-3

Tourigny, J.-N., Paquet, V., Fortier, É., Malo, C., Mercier, É., Chauny, J.-M., Clark, G., Blanchard, P.-G., Boucher, V., Carmichael, P.-H., Gariépy, J.-L., & Émond, M. (2021). Predictors of neurosurgical intervention in complicated mild traumatic brain injury patients: A retrospective cohort study. *Brain Injury, 35*(10), 1267–1274. https://doi.org/10.1080/02699052.2021.1972147

Trahan, D. E., Ross, C. E., & Trahan, S. L. (2001). Relationships among postconcussional-type symptoms, depression, and anxiety in neurologically normal young adults and victims of mild brain injury. *Archives of Clinical Neuropsychology, 16*(5), 435–445. https://doi.org/10.1016/S0887-6177(00)00051-2

Uiterwijk, D., Stargatt, R., & Crowe, S. F. (2022). Objective cognitive outcomes and subjective emotional sequelae in litigating adults with a traumatic brain injury: The impact of performance and symptom validity measures. *Archives of Clinical Neuropsychology, 37*(8), 1662–1687. https://doi.org/10.1093/arclin/acac039

Unoka, Z., & Richman, M. J. (2016). Neuropsychological deficits in BPD patients and the moderator effects of co-occurring mental disorders: A meta-analysis. *Clinical Psychology Review, 44*, 1–12. https://doi.org/10.1016/j.cpr.2015.11.009

van der Naalt, J., Timmerman, M. E., de Koning, M. E., van der Horn, H. J., Scheenen, M. E., Jacobs, B., Hageman, G., Yilmaz, T., Roks, G., & Spikman, J. M. (2017). Early predictors of outcome after mild traumatic brain injury (UPFRONT): An observational cohort study. *The Lancet Neurology, 16*(7), 532–540. https://doi.org/10.1016/S1474-4422(17)30117-5

Vanderploeg, R. D., Belanger, H. G., & Curtiss, G. (2009). Mild traumatic brain injury and post-traumatic stress disorder and their associations with health symptoms. *Archives of Physical Medicine and Rehabilitation, 90*(7), 1084–1093. https://doi.org/10.1016/j.apmr.2009.01.023

Vanderploeg, R. D., Belanger, H. G., & Kaufmann, P. M. (2014). Nocebo effects and mild traumatic brain injury: Legal implications. *Psychological Injury and Law, 7*(3), 245–254. https://doi.org/10.1007/s12207-014-9201-3

Vande Vyvere, T., Pisică, D., Wilms, G., Claes, L., Van Dyck, P., Snoeckx, A., van den Hauwe, L., Pullens, P., Verheyden, J., Wintermark, M., Dekeyzer, S., Mac Donald, C. L., Maas, A. I. R., & Parizel, P. M. (2024). Imaging findings in acute traumatic brain injury: A National Institute of Neurological Disorders and Stroke common data element-based pictorial review and analysis of over 4000 admission brain computed tomography scans from the Collaborative European NeuroTrauma Effectiveness Research in Traumatic Brain Injury (CENTER-TBI) study. *Journal of Neurotrauma*. Online ahead of print. https://doi.org/10.1089/neu.2023.0553

Vaniyapong, T., Patumanond, J., Ratanalert, S., & Limpastan, K. (2019). Clinical indicators for traumatic intracranial findings in mild traumatic brain injury patients. *Surgical Neurology International, 10*, 64. https://doi.org/10.25259/SNI-101-2019

van Rhijn, S., Teixeira-Dias, M., Medford, N., Nicholson, T., Okai, D., Shotbolt, P., & Deeley, Q. (2024). Predictive utility of diffusion MRI after mild traumatic brain injury in civilian populations: A systematic review. *The Journal of Neuropsychiatry and Clinical Neurosciences*. https://doi.org/10.1176/appi.neuropsych.20230122

Vickery, C. D., Berry, D. T., Inman, T. H., Harris, M. J., & Orey, S. A. (2001). Detection of inadequate effort on neuropsychological testing: A meta-analytic review of selected procedures. *Archives of Clinical Neuropsychology, 16*(1), 45–73.

Voormolen, D. C., Cnossen, M. C., Polinder, S., Gravesteijn, B. Y., Von Steinbuechel, N., Real, R. G. L., & Haagsma, J. A. (2019). Prevalence of post-concussion-like symptoms in the general population in Italy, The Netherlands and the United Kingdom. *Brain Injury, 33*(8), 1078–1086. https://doi.org/10.1080/02699052.2019.1607557

Voss, J. D., Connolly, J., Schwab, K. A., & Scher, A. I. (2015). Update on the epidemiology of concussion/mild traumatic brain injury. *Current Pain and Headache Reports, 19*(7), 32. https://doi.org/10.1007/s11916-015-0506-z

Wade, D., King, N., Wenden, F., Crawford, S., & Caldwell, F. (1998). Routine follow up after head injury: A second randomised controlled trial. *Journal of Neurology, Neurosurgery, and Psychiatry, 65*(2), 177–183.

Waganekar, A., Sadasivan, J., Prabhu, A. S., & Harichandrakumar, K. T. (2018). Computed tomography profile and its utilization in head injury patients in emergency department: A prospective observational study. *Journal of Emergencies, Trauma, and Shock, 11*(1), 25–30. https://doi.org/10.4103/JETS.JETS_112_17

Waltzman, D., Sarmiento, K., Daugherty, J., & Proescholdbell, S. (2022). Examination of behaviors and health indicators for individuals with a lifetime history of traumatic brain injury with loss of consciousness: 2018 BRFSS North Carolina. *North Carolina Medical Journal, 83*(3), 206–213. https://doi.org/10.18043/ncm.83.3.206

Wang, Y., Bartels, H. M., & Nelson, L. D. (2023). A systematic review of ASL perfusion MRI in mild TBI. *Neuropsychology Review, 33*(1), 160–191. https://doi.org/10.1007/s11065-020-09451-7

Whiteneck, G. G., Cuthbert, J. P., Corrigan, J. D., & Bogner, J. A. (2016a). Prevalence of self-reported lifetime history of traumatic brain injury and associated disability: A statewide population-based survey. *The Journal of Head Trauma Rehabilitation, 31*(1), E55–E62. https://doi.org/10.1097/HTR.0000000000000140

Whiteneck, G. G., Cuthbert, J. P., Corrigan, J. D., & Bogner, J. A. (2016b). Risk of negative outcomes after traumatic brain injury: A statewide population-bsed survey. *The Journal of Head Trauma Rehabilitation, 31*(1), E43–E54. https://doi.org/10.1097/HTR.0000000000000141

Whittaker, R., Kemp, S., & House, A. (2007). Illness perceptions and outcome in mild head injury: A longitudinal study. *Journal of Neurology, Neurosurgery & Psychiatry, 78*(6), 644–646. https://doi.org/10.1136/jnnp.2006.101105

Wiegand, T. L. T., Sollmann, N., Bonke, E. M., Umeasalugo, K. E., Sobolewski, K. R., Plesnila, N., Shenton, M. E., Lin, A. P., & Koerte, I. K. (2022). Translational neuroimaging in mild traumatic brain injury. *Journal of Neuroscience Research, 100*(5), 1201–1217. https://doi.org/10.1002/jnr.24840

Wijenberg, M. L. M., Stapert, S. Z., Verbunt, J. A., Ponsford, J. L., & Van Heugten, C. M. (2017). Does the fear avoidance model explain persistent symptoms after traumatic brain injury? *Brain Injury, 31*(12), 1597–1604. https://doi.org/10.1080/02699052.2017.1366551

Wollman, S. C., Hauson, A. O., Hall, M. G., Connors, E. J., Allen, K. E., Stern, M. J., Stephan, R. A., Kimmel, C. L., Sarkissians, S., Barlet, B. D., & Flora-Tostado, C. (2019). Neuropsychological functioning in opioid use disorder: A research synthesis and meta-analysis. *The American Journal of Drug and Alcohol Abuse, 45*(1), 11–25. https://doi.org/10.1080/00952990.2018.1517262

Wood, R. L. (2004). Understanding the 'miserable minority': A diathesis-stress paradigm for post-concussional syndrome. *Brain Injury, 18*(11), 1135–1153. https://doi.org/10.1080/02699050410001675906

Wu, Y.-L., Huang, C.-J., Fang, S.-C., Ko, L.-H., & Tsai, P.-S. (2018). Cognitive impairment in fibromyalgia: A meta-analysis of case-control studies. *Psychosomatic Medicine, 80*(5), 432–438. https://doi.org/10.1097/PSY.0000000000000575

Yang, Y., Shields, G. S., Guo, C., & Liu, Y. (2018). Executive function performance in obesity and overweight individuals: A meta-analysis and review. *Neuroscience and Biobehavioral Reviews, 84*, 225–244. https://doi.org/10.1016/j.neubiorev.2017.11.020

Yi, H., Corrigan, J. D., Singichetti, B., Bogner, J. A., Manchester, K., Guo, J., & Yang, J. (2018). Lifetime history of traumatic brain injury and current disability among Ohio adults. *The Journal of Head Trauma Rehabilitation, 33*(4), E24–E32. https://doi.org/10.1097/HTR.0000000000000352

Yue, J. K., Cnossen, M. C., Winkler, E. A., Deng, H., Phelps, R. R. L., Coss, N. A., Sharma, S., Robinson, C. K., Suen, C. G., Vassar, M. J., Schnyer, D. M., Puccio, A. M., Gardner, R. C., Yuh, E. L., Mukherjee, P., Valadka, A. B., Okonkwo, D. O., Lingsma, H. F., Manley, G. T., … Morabito, D. J. (2019). Pre-injury comorbidities are associated with functional impairment and post-concussive symptoms at 3- and 6-months after mild traumatic brain injury: A TRACK-TBI study. *Frontiers in Neurology, 10*. https://www.frontiersin.org/articles/10.3389/fneur.2019.00343.

Yue, J. K., Winkler, E. A., Puffer, R. C., Deng, H., Phelps, R. R. L., Wagle, S., Morrissey, M. R., Rivera, E. J., Runyon, S. J., Vassar, M. J., Taylor, S. R., Cnossen, M. C., Lingsma, H. F., Yuh, E. L., Mukherjee, P., Schnyer, D. M., Puccio, A. M., Valadka, A. B., Okonkwo, D. O., … The TRACK-TBI Investigators. (2018). Temporal lobe contusions on computed tomography are associated with impaired 6-month functional recovery after mild traumatic brain injury: A TRACK-TBI study. *Neurological Research, 40*(11), 972–981. https://doi.org/10.1080/01616412.2018.1505416.

Yue, J. K., Yuh, E. L., Elguindy, M. M., Sun, X., Van Essen, T. A., Deng, H., Belton, P. J., Satris, G. G., Wong, J. C., Valadka, A., Korley, F. K., Robertson, C. S., McCrea, M., Stein, M. B., Diaz-Arrastia, R., Wang, K. K. W., Temkin, N., DiGiorgio, A. M., Tarapore, P. E., … Manley, G. T. (2024). Isolated traumatic subarachnoid hemorrhage on head computed tomography scan may not be isolated: A TRACK-TBI study. *Journal of Neurotrauma*. https://doi.org/10.1089/neu.2023.0253.

Yue, J. K., Yuh, E. L., Korley, F. K., Winkler, E. A., Sun, X., Puffer, R. C., Deng, H., Choy, W., Chandra, A., Taylor, S. R., Ferguson, A. R., Huie, J. R., Rabinowitz, M., Puccio, A. M., Mukherjee, P., Vassar, M. J., Wang, K. K. W., Diaz-Arrastia, R., Okonkwo, D. O., … TRACK-TBI Investigators. (2019). Association between plasma GFAP concentrations and MRI abnormalities in patients with CT-negative traumatic brain injury in the TRACK-TBI cohort: A prospective multicentre study. *The Lancet. Neurology, 18*(10), 953–961. https://doi.org/10.1016/S1474-4422(19)30282-0.

Yuh, E. L., Jain, S., Sun, X., Pisică, D., Harris, M. H., Taylor, S. R., Markowitz, A. J., Mukherjee, P., Verheyden, J., Giacino, J. T., Levin, H. S., McCrea, M., Stein, M. B., Temkin, N. R., Diaz-Arrastia, R., Robertson, C. S., Lingsma, H. F., Okonkwo, D. O., Maas, A. I. R., … TRACK-TBI Investigators for the CENTER-TBI Investigators. (2021). Pathological computed tomography features associated with adverse outcomes after mild traumatic brain injury: A TRACK-TBI study with external validation in CENTER-TBI. *JAMA Neurology, 78*(9), 1137–1148. https://doi.org/10.1001/jamaneurol.2021.2120.

Yuh, E. L., Mukherjee, P., Lingsma, H. F., Yue, J. K., Ferguson, A. R., Gordon, W. A., Valadka, A. B., Schnyer, D. M., Okonkwo, D. O., Maas, A. I. R., Manley, G. T., & TRACK-TBI Investigators. (2013). Magnetic resonance imaging improves 3-month outcome prediction in mild traumatic brain injury. *Annals of Neurology, 73*(2), 224–235. https://doi.org/10.1002/ana.23783

Zahniser, E., Nelson, L. D., Dikmen, S. S., Machamer, J. E., Stein, M. B., Yuh, E., Manley, G. T., Temkin, N. R., Adeoye, O., Badjatia, N., Boase, K., Bodien, Y., Ross Bullock, M., Chesnut, R., Corrigan, J. D., Crawford, K., Diaz-Arrastia, R., Duhaime, A.-C., Ellenbogen, R., … Zafonte, R. (2019). The temporal relationship of mental health problems and functional limitations following mTBI: A TRACK-TBI and TED study. *Journal of Neurotrauma, 36*(11), 1786–1793. https://doi.org/10.1089/neu.2018.6172.

Zakzanis, K. K., Campbell, Z., & Jovanovski, D. (2007). The neuropsychology of ecstasy (MDMA) use: A quantitative review. *Human Psychopharmacology, 22*(7), 427–435. https://doi.org/10.1002/hup.873

Zia Ziabari, S. M., Asadi, P., Reihanian, Z., Rafieezadeh, A., Noori Roodsari, N., Tavakoli, I., Eslami-Kenarsari, H., & Seifi, G. (2022). Investigation of clinical findings and CT scan in children with minor head trauma. *International Journal of Burns and Trauma, 12*(6), 261–268.

Chapter 25
Moderate and Severe Traumatic Brain Injury

Grant L. Iverson, Julia Cho, Emily N. Vanderbleek, Julia E. Maietta, and Rael T. Lange

Key Points and Chapter Summary

- Traumatic brain injuries (TBI) occur on a broad continuum of severity, from very mild transient injuries to catastrophic injuries resulting in severe disability or death.
- The severity of TBI is typically classified using the Glasgow Coma Scale, duration of unconsciousness and duration of posttraumatic amnesia/confusion.
- TBI-associated impairment may be caused by primary (hemorrhage, herniation, axonal injury) and secondary (ischemia, edema, inflammation, excitotoxicity) pathophysiology. Most parts of the brain are vulnerable to traumatic injury.
- Moderate and severe TBIs can result in temporary, prolonged or permanent neurological or neuropsychiatric problems such as (a) motor impairments and movement disorders; (b) visual impairments; (c) auditory impairments; (d) cranial nerve impairments; (e) speech, language and swallowing problems; (f) imbalance and dizziness; (g) headaches; (h) posttraumatic seizures; (i) fatigue and sleep problems; (j) psychotic disorders; (k) lack of awareness; (l) personality changes and apathy; and (m) sexual dysfunction.
- Moderate or severe TBIs frequently result in permanent neurocognitive and neurobehavioral impairments, although some people have a very good outcome. As a general rule, as injury severity increases, the magnitude of impairment increases.
- The vast majority of recovery from moderate to severe TBI occurs within the first year, although additional recovery can occur thereafter.
- The short- and long-term effects of moderate and severe TBI present a number of challenges that make adjustment back to everyday life difficult for both patients and family members. Some of the most common issues relate to substance use, family and marital issues, return to work and community integration.

M. R. Schoenberg, J. G. Scott (eds.), *The Little Black Book of Neuropsychology*, https://doi.org/10.1007/978-3-032-07777-6_25

Overview

Traumatic brain injury (TBI), a form of acquired brain injury, occurs as a result of a disruption in the normal function of the brain due to an external force. This may include blunt trauma, an object penetrating the skull (i.e., open head injury), acceleration–deceleration forces or forces generated from a blast or explosion. TBIs occur on a broad continuum of severity, from very mild transient injuries to catastrophic injuries resulting in severe disability or death.

Epidemiology

In the United States, an estimated 2.5–3.5 million people sustain a TBI of all severity levels each year (Capizzi et al., 2020; Lefevre-Dognin et al., 2021), and approximately 20% are categorized as moderate or severe TBI (Capizzi et al.,

G. L. Iverson (✉)
Department of Physical Medicine and Rehabilitation, Harvard Medical School, Boston, MA, USA

Department of Physical Medicine and Rehabilitation, Spaulding Rehabilitation Hospital, Boston, MA, USA

Schoen Adams Research Institute at Spaulding Rehabilitation, Boston, MA, USA

Mass General for Children Sports Concussion Program, Boston, MA, USA

Home Base, A Red Sox Foundation and Massachusetts General Hospital Program, Boston, MA, USA
e-mail: GIverson@mgh.harvard.edu

J. Cho
Harvard Medical School, Boston, MA, USA

E. N. Vanderbleek
Departments of Psychiatry and Neurosciences, Neurology, and Neurosurgery, University of South Florida College of Medicine, Tampa, FL, USA

J. E. Maietta
Department of Physical Medicine and Rehabilitation, Harvard Medical School, Boston, MA, USA

Department of Physical Medicine and Rehabilitation, Spaulding Rehabilitation Hospital, Boston, MA, USA

Mass General for Children Sports Concussion Program, Boston, MA, USA

R. T. Lange
British Columbia Mental Health and Addiction Services, Coquitlam, BC, Canada
e-mail: rlange@dvbic.org

2020). There are approximately 227,000 hospitalizations related to TBI and 61,000 TBI-related deaths each year (Centers for Disease Control and Prevention, 2021). In the United States military, between 2000 and the third quarter of 2022, there were more than 468,000 documented TBIs, with 11% being classified as moderate and 1% being classified as severe (Traumatic Brain Injury Center of Excellence Annual Report: DoD Numbers for Traumatic Brain Injury Worldwide, 2022). Across all severity levels of TBI, the most common mechanisms of injury include falls, being struck by (or striking) an object accidentally and motor vehicle accidents. The most common lethal mechanisms of injury contributing to TBI-related death include suicide, unintentional falls and motor vehicle accidents (Breiding et al., 2022). Older adults (ages 55 and up) have the highest rates of TBI-related deaths as well as TBI-related hospitalizations (Centers for Disease Control and Prevention, 2021). Advanced age is generally associated with worse outcomes after TBI due to complications associated with mechanism of injury (e.g., subdural hematoma), medical comorbidities (e.g., hypertension) and lower levels of neural plasticity in the aging brain (Breiding et al., 2022). Overall, males have a higher rate of TBI than females and they are more likely to sustain a moderate or severe TBI; death rates from TBI are over two times higher among males compared to females (Daugherty, 2019).

Classification Considerations

Traumatic brain injuries are typically classified as mild, moderate or severe. There are no universally accepted classification criteria, but the most commonly used indicators of injury severity are the Glasgow Coma Scale, duration of unconsciousness and duration of posttraumatic amnesia/confusion. An example of one commonly used classification system for mild, moderate and severe TBI is summarized in Fig. 25.1 (Table 25.1).

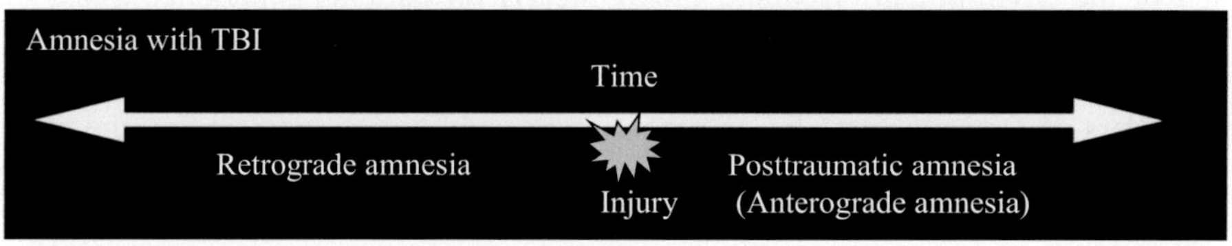

Fig. 25.1 Retrograde and posttraumatic (anterograde) amnesia

Table 25.1 Common classification system for traumatic brain injury

Classification	Duration of unconsciousness	Glasgow Coma Scale	Posttraumatic amnesia
Mild	<30 min	13–15	<24 h
Moderate	30 min–24 h	9–12	1–7 days
Severe	>24 h	3–8	>7 days

Note: This is not a universally agreed-upon classification system

Glasgow Coma Scale

The Glasgow Coma Scale (GCS) is the most widely used rapid screening instrument for evaluating brain injury severity and is used often by emergency medical technicians and personnel at the scene of an accident or in the emergency room (Brennan et al., 2020; Jain & Iverson, 2023; Teasdale & Jennett, 1974, 1976). The GCS is used to evaluate three components of arousal: eye opening, verbal response and motor response to stimuli. Scores on the GCS range from 3 to 15, with higher scores indicating better functioning. Because intubated patients cannot respond verbally, the scoring is adapted to range from 2T to 10T (only including eye opening and motor response), with the "T" indicating intubation. The TBI severity classification ranges for GCS scores are as follows: Mild = 13–15, Moderate = 9–12 and Severe = 3–8. The classification system based on GCS is widely, but not universally, used in clinical practice and research. There are several factors that can impact GCS and may lead to overestimating injury severity, including medical sedation, drug or alcohol intoxication, preexisting neurological impairment, other physical injuries affecting vital functions and language or cultural barriers (Jain & Iverson, 2023) (Table 25.2).

Loss of Consciousness

Technically, the term *unconsciousness* "is taken to imply lack of awareness of the self or the environment" (Jennett, 1996). Nearly all patients experience a loss or alteration of consciousness following a moderate to severe TBI. The return to a conscious state is most often indicated by the ability to follow simple commands. Disorders of consciousness lie on a continuum, with *coma* representing the most severe. *Coma* is a state of unconsciousness characterized by a lack of arousal. There are no sleep–wake cycles, expressive or receptive language or purposeful motor activity. Some patients emerge from a coma to a *vegetative state*. There is still no evidence of awareness or purposeful response to stimuli, but there may be intermittent periods of wakefulness and some involuntary movements. Most individuals do not remain in a vegetative state and progress to a *minimally conscious state*. In this state, patients show inconsistent but clear signs of awareness such as following commands, vocalizations, visual pursuit, localized motor responses or object manipulation (Giacino et al., 2002, 2018).

Table 25.2 Glasgow Coma Scale (GCS) scoring system

Patient opens eyes	Spontaneously	4
	In response to speech	3
	In response to pain	2
	Never	1
Patient responds verbally	Oriented to person, place, time	5
	With confusion	4
	Inappropriately	3
	Incomprehensibly	2
	Never	1
Patient responds with movement	Obeying commands	6
	Localizing pain	5
	Withdrawing from pain	4
	Flexion from pain	3
	Extension from pain	2
	Never	1
Total Score	Mild	13–15
	Moderate	9–12
	Severe	3–8

Note: This scale was published by Teasdale and Jennett (1974)

Amnesias and Posttraumatic Confusional State

Individuals who experience TBIs often demonstrate different forms of memory disruption. Some patients are unable to remember events that occur immediately after their injury. They may not be able to keep track of the day of the week or remember if a family member visited them in the hospital. This memory disturbance, called *posttraumatic amnesia* (PTA), may last for minutes, hours, days, weeks or months. It is important to realize that a patient's experience of PTA can be adversely impacted by several factors, including intoxication, pain medication or the effects of general anesthesia. The duration of PTA is commonly used in the classification of injury severity. The duration of *retrograde amnesia* (RTA) refers to the loss of memory for events prior to the TBI. The duration of RTA is related to the severity of the injury; for example, a person may have no memory for what they did an hour or a week prior to the injury. The change in functioning following TBI can also be described as a "posttraumatic confusional state," which encompasses not only memory difficulties but also disorientation, distractibility, perceptual disturbances, sleep disturbance, delusional beliefs and emotional lability—akin to delirium (Bodien et al., 2020; Sherer et al., 2020).

Pathoanatomy and Pathophysiology

Most parts of the brain are vulnerable to traumatic injury. However, the anterior portion of the brain is most likely to be affected (i.e., frontal and temporal regions). There are primary and secondary pathophysiologies that contribute to TBI-associated cognitive and neurobehavioral impairment. Primary damage involves hemorrhage, herniation and axonal injury. Secondary damage can arise from the endogenous evolution of cellular damage or from secondary systemic processes, such as hypotension or hypoxia (Close et al., 2022).

Terminology for Injuries to the Head and Brain

Most skull fractures resulting from head injuries are of two types, linear or depressed. *Linear fractures* are usually thin and straight, ranging the entire thickness of the skull. A dent in the skull is referred to as a *depressed skull fracture*. A *diastatic fracture* is a linear fracture that extends into a suture (the line where two skull bones join).

A *contusion* is a bruise on the brain that is usually associated with swelling and some bleeding. A *coup/contrecoup injury* is a classic lesion pattern resulting from serious falls or motor vehicle accidents (Payne et al., 2023). If a person falls backward and hits the back of her head, she may have a relatively small contusion at the site of impact ("coup") and a large contusion at the opposite side of the brain (front; "contrecoup"). This is due to the physics of translational forces on the brain (see Fig. 25.2). The areas of the brain most likely to be contused are illustrated in Fig. 25.3.

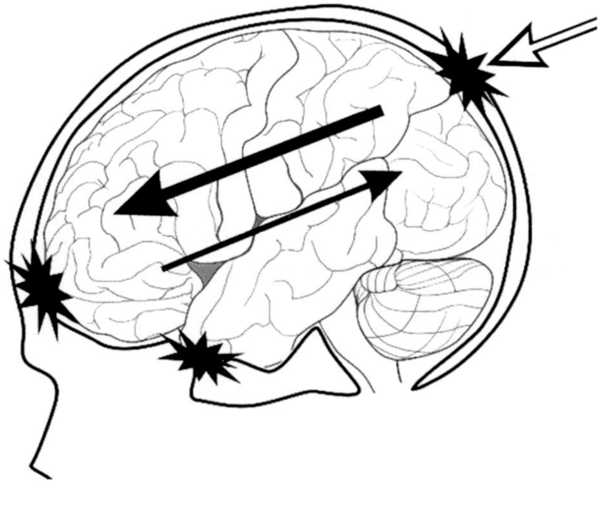

Fig. 25.2 Coup/contrecoup brain injury. The authors thank Ms. Elena Dupont for providing this figure

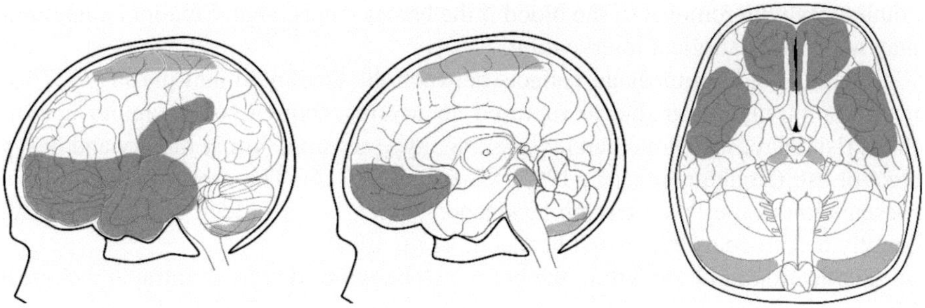

Fig. 25.3 Areas affected by contusions. Note: These schematic diagrams of contusion locations in lateral, sagittal midline and base views show the areas most commonly affected by contusions (dark gray) and those that are occasionally affected by contusions (light gray). Areas commonly affected by contusions include the orbitofrontal cortex, anterior temporal lobe and posterior portion of the superior temporal gyrus area, with the adjacent parietal opercular area. Areas that are less commonly affected include the lateral midbrain, inferior cerebellum and adjacent tonsil and the midline superior cerebral cortex. These drawings were remade from drawings presented in Morales et al. (2007). The authors thank Ms. Elena Dupont for providing this figure

Hemorrhage represents bleeding in or around the brain. Hemorrhages within the brain are caused by damage to an artery or vein. Increased symptom onset 2–4 days after the trauma can occur, presenting as a patient who initially shows good functional recovery from the injury, but then deteriorates over a period of several hours with confusion and obtundation (i.e., increased drowsiness and decreased responsiveness to the environment).

A *hematoma* is an accumulation of blood in a specific location. Hematomas around the brain may be in three locations: epidural, subdural and subarachnoid. Epidural hematomas are located between the skull and the dura and they can be life-threatening. A blow to the side of the head may damage the middle meningeal artery causing an epidural hematoma. Classically, the clinical presentation involves an initial loss of consciousness, followed by recovery of consciousness and a return to broadly normal function (patient appears lucid and walks and talks normally) for a few hours. This is followed by rapid, life-threatening deterioration in function (hours to a day). Epidural hematomas caused by damage to a vein result in slower progression of symptoms while arterial hemorrhages tend to exhibit faster progression of symptoms and greater likelihood for brain herniation.

Subdural hematomas can present similarly to epidural hematomas, with initial traumatic loss of consciousness, followed by return to broadly normal function, then a deterioration in function over several hours to days. Subdural hematomas collect between the dura and the arachnoid mater, generally along the brain convexities. They are typically the consequence of head trauma, but sometimes no causal injury can be identified. Older adults are at increased risk for these hematomas following even relatively minor head trauma. In addition, deterioration in function following subdural hematomas in older adults can progress very slowly, such that the presentation of neuropsychological dysfunction can be mistaken for dementia. Treatment for both subdural hematomas and epidural hematomas may involve craniotomy with removal of the blood if the hematoma is large. Smaller hematomas may not require surgical intervention.

Subarachnoid hemorrhage collects between the arachnoid and pia mater. They most commonly occur due to ruptured aneurysms, though subarachnoid hemorrhage risk increases with cigarette smoking, hypertension, family history and heavy alcohol use (Ronkainen et al., 1997; Vlak et al., 2013). The most notable clinical presentation is the "thunderclap headache," which has a sudden onset and is frequently described as "the worst headache of my life."

A collection of blood within the brain may be referred to as an intraparenchymal (i.e., within the parenchyma, or "brain tissue") hematoma. Serial CT studies show that this type of hemorrhage can enlarge over time and/or several smaller hemorrhages may coalesce into a single larger pool of blood. Additionally, blood is an irritating substance for the brain parenchyma and it may trigger vasospasm and stroke. Small hemorrhages may be broken down by the body, resulting in minimal or no obvious encephalomalacia (i.e., loss of brain tissue after brain injury) visible on imaging at the site of hemorrhage.

Edema is the term used to describe swelling in the brain. Swelling can be minor, as in the case of a small contusion, or severe, when associated with multiple or severe contusions. Diffuse brain swelling can cause compression or *herniation*. Herniation is best understood by considering the basic anatomy of the skull. Within the skull, the brain is divided into compartments formed by structural dividers, such as the falx which separates the left and right hemispheres of the cerebral cortex. The tentorium, another structural divider, is like a roof above the posterior and inferior portions of the brain (e.g., brainstem and cerebellum). Major edema or a large hematoma can cause the brain to compress, or herniate, against these structural dividers. This compression, and the subsequently increased pressure on adjacent brain regions, leads to damage and death of brain tissue. In some cases, the brain can also herniate through natural openings in the skull (e.g., tonsillar herniation). Herniation is more likely when diffuse edema is coupled with a hemorrhage.

Figure 25.4 illustrates several possible types of brain herniation (Riveros Gilardi et al., 2019), as listed below.

1. Subfalcine herniation, involving the cingulate gyrus and related structures compressing against the falx cerebri.
2. Central herniation, involving descent of parts of the brainstem and diencephalon.
3. Uncal herniation, involving the uncus (medial temporal lobe) compressing downward against the tentorium.
4. Tonsillar herniation, involving the brainstem and cerebellum herniating through the foramen magnum.

Uncal herniation is notable for a classic triad of clinical features: hemiplegia, dilated ipsilateral pupil and coma. Hemiplegia, or paresis of the left or right half of the body, occurs on the contralateral side of the injury due to compression of the ipsilateral corticospinal tract. Rarely, extreme mass effect can damage the contralateral corticospinal tract as well, leading to ipsilateral hemiparesis called Kernohan

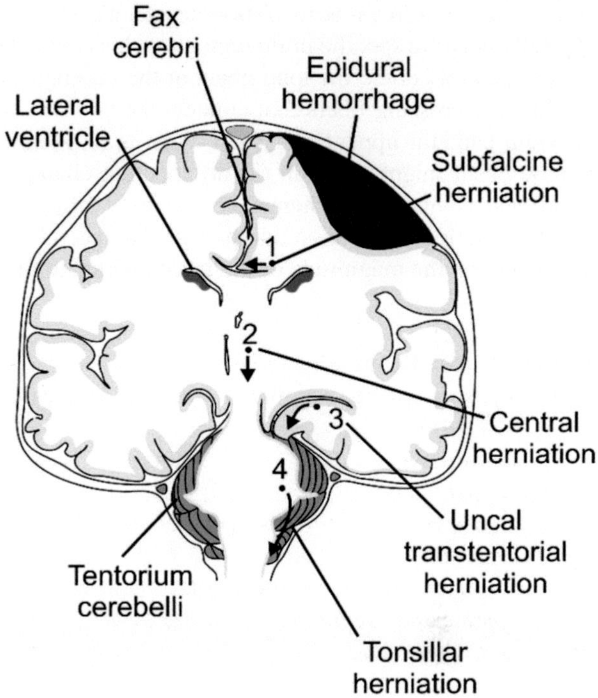

Fig. 25.4 Brain herniations. The authors thank Ms. Elena Dupont for providing this figure

phenomenon (Beucler et al., 2022). The ipsilateral pupil becomes dilated due to compression of the oculomotor nerve (cranial nerve III), and may be the first presenting sign of uncal herniation. Coma or loss of consciousness arises due to compression of ascending arousal pathways from the brainstem (Decker & Pearson-Shaver, 2023).

Ventricular dilation, also referred to as ventriculomegaly or hydrocephalus *ex vacuo*, can occur following severe TBI for multiple reasons. Cerebrospinal fluid (CSF) is produced in the ventricles and it circulates within and around the brain. A TBI can cause blockage of the small passages or holes through which the CSF circulates. This results in hydrocephalus (i.e., buildup of CSF in the ventricles) and consequently, ventricular dilation. Ventricular dilation also may result from the gradual dying off and removal of brain cells. That is, after a TBI, damaged cells essentially shrink and then are removed, with the residual space filled passively by the ventricles expanding. Asymmetry is often observed, reflecting regions with greater volume loss. *Cortical atrophy* (e.g., ventricular dilation, widening of the sulci and cortical thinning) has been identified in patients with traumatic brain injuries through neuroimaging conducted 6 weeks to 1 year following injury (Harris et al., 2019). Atrophy may be generalized or focal, with the hippocampus often affected disproportionately (Ariza et al., 2006; Green et al., 2014).

Traumatic axonal injuries are often referred to as diffuse axonal injuries, shearing injuries or deep white matter injuries. Axonal injuries result from severe rotational and/or linear acceleration/deceleration forces on the brain. These injuries typically occur in specific brain regions such as the gray and white matter interfaces of the cerebral cortex, the long fibers of the internal capsule that carry motor information, the crossing fibers that connect the two cerebral hemispheres (i.e., corpus callosum) and the upper brainstem (Wilde et al., 2022). A single acceleration/deceleration event might result in (a) no apparent change in structure or function, (b) functional or metabolic change, (c) eventual structural change in the axon or (d) frank separation of the axon into proximal and distal segments. These outcomes are dependent on the magnitude of the force applied to the brain.

Key Points: Terminology

- Skull fractures can be linear (straight), depressed ('caved in') or diastatic (linear to suture).
- Hemorrhages can be epidural, subdural, subarachnoid or intraparenchymal.
- Edema (swelling) of the parenchyma combined with hemorrhage can result in herniation.
- Traumatic axonal injury is a complex process where damaged axons swell, separate and eventually degenerate.

Neuroimaging

On neuroimaging, macroscopic abnormalities can be seen within the brain tissue or outside the brain, in what is often referred to as the extra-axial space. Within the brain, injuries include hemorrhagic or non-hemorrhagic contusions, hemorrhagic or non-hemorrhagic shearing injuries, herniations and cerebral edema. Outside the brain tissue, injuries include epidural hematomas, subdural hematomas, subdural hygromas (collection of CSF), subarachnoid hemorrhage, intraventricular hemorrhage and hydrocephalus (Close et al., 2022). As described previously, cortical atrophy is common following TBI.

Computed tomography (CT) is the most commonly utilized neuroimaging technique, particularly in acute settings (Wilde et al., 2022). CT machines are widely available, relatively low cost, and provide information quickly. CTs are best for imaging skull fractures and intracranial bleeds with high sensitivity and specificity (Wilde et al., 2022). Magnetic resonance imaging (MRI) is often used after or in conjunction with CT to image more subtle injuries such as microhemorrhages and contusions. MRI is more often used in chronic monitoring or in cases when there is an acute deterioration of the patient's status with no identifiable cause on CT. MRI findings that may be associated with poorer outcomes are brainstem lesions, cortical lesions with hemorrhage, contusions and white matter changes within the corpus callosum; however, there is significant heterogeneity in the research on the prognostic indicators in MRI (Wilde et al., 2022).

Table 25.3 Summary of neurological and neuropsychiatric problems associated with TBI

Balance Problems & Dizziness	
Cranial Nerve Impairments (e.g., olfactory, ocular/optic, face movement/sensation and auditory/balance) Speech, Language and Swallowing Problems Posttraumatic Seizures	
Depression, Anxiety and Traumatic Stress	
Fatigue & Sleep Disturbance	
Headaches	
Lack of Awareness (e.g., anosognosia, anosodiaphoria, lack of insight/judgment)	
Movement Disorders (e.g., bradykinesia, tremor, dystonia, myoclonus)	
Motor Impairments (e.g., hemiparesis, ataxia, apraxia)	
Psychotic Disorders	
Personality Changes, Apathy and Decreased Motivation	
Sexual Dysfunction	
Visual Impairments (blurred vision, double vision) Auditory Impairments (e.g., hearing loss)	

Neurological Complications

Moderate and severe traumatic brain injuries can result in temporary, prolonged or permanent neurological or neuropsychiatric problems. A summary of the neurological and neuropsychiatric problems associated with TBI is provided in Table 25.3. These problems are described in the sections below.

Motor Impairments and Movement Disorders

Voluntary movement is a complex function governed by different parts of the nervous system, such as upper and lower motor neurons (motor cortex of the frontal lobe, corticospinal tract of the spinal cord, peripheral motor nerves), the basal ganglia, cerebellum and many others. Damage to upper or lower motor neurons can lead to motor impairments such as paresis (weakness), spasticity (increased muscle tone and exaggerated reflexes) or ataxia (loss of muscle coordination). On the other hand, damage to the basal ganglia can result in movement disorders; these manifest as either slowness or poverty of movement (hypokinesia) or excessive involuntary movements (hyperkinesia). Most posttraumatic movement disorders are caused by severe TBI; however, significant improvement has been seen in the incidence and outcomes for patients with posttraumatic movement disorders with the rise of decompressive craniectomies (Krauss et al., 2022).

The two most common presentations of movement disorders are tremors and dystonia (Krauss et al., 2022). Tremors are characterized by rhythmic, oscillatory movements; some tremor types include (a) *resting* (seen when the body part is at rest), (b) *postural* (seen when holding a body part out, such as outstretched arms) and (c) *intention* (seen at the end of purposeful movement, such as during the finger-to-nose test). Dystonia is characterized by sustained contractions of opposing muscles that cause repetitive twisting or abnormal posturing. Posttraumatic dystonias can affect any part of the body (e.g., arms and legs, trunk, neck, head or face) and sometimes co-occur with tremors.

Visual Impairments

Visual impairments are seen commonly in patients with TBI, given that numerous structures contribute to vision and may become injured; the reported incidence varies widely from 10 to 70% (Ciufreda et al., 2022). The consequences of TBI can disrupt vision from direct damage to the (a) eye, orbit or surrounding structures and/or (b) components of the visual pathway of the nervous system (e.g., cranial nerves, subcortical, cortical or brainstem regions involved with vision). Such damage may lead to blurred vision, binocular vision problems (e.g., diplopia, changes in depth perception, difficulty localizing objects in space), visual field deficits, difficulty with visual tracking (e.g., deficit of smooth pursuit), a vergence deficit, photosensitivity, nystagmus (rhythmic regular oscillation of the eyes) or saccadic intrusions (irregular and rapid bursts of eye movements; Ciufreda et al., 2022).

Auditory Impairments

Many patients with TBI concurrently suffer from hearing loss or auditory impairment, with one study showing a 74% prevalence of hearing loss in a population of post-TBI civilians (Bergemalm, 2003). Hearing loss has a high level of burden on quality of life and the healthcare system, as it has been associated with a significant decline in executive functioning and more than one billion dollars annually in healthcare costs for US veterans (Fausti et al., 2009; Hwang et al., 2022). Given its high prevalence, it is important for clinicians to detect hearing loss; at times, hearing loss can be misdiagnosed as unresponsiveness in a post-TBI population (Chandler, 2006; Coelho et al., 2022; Dougherty et al., 2013).

Hearing loss can be broadly categorized into conductive hearing loss (prevention of physical transmission of sound energy from the external/middle to the inner ear), sensorineural hearing loss (prevention of conversion of mechanical sound energy to, or interpretation of, neural signal due to damage in the inner ear or central auditory system) or a mixed picture (components of both conductive and sensorineural hearing loss). TBI can cause any of these types of hearing loss depending on which structures are injured.

The structures involved in hearing can be broadly divided into peripheral (external, middle and inner ear) and central structures (brainstem, thalamus, auditory cortex of the temporal lobe); any of these may be damaged in TBI. Generally, external and middle ear injuries are more likely to cause conductive hearing loss, and inner ear injuries are more likely to cause sensorineural hearing loss (Coelho et al., 2022). However, research into central auditory system damage has been limited to date; it is thought that damage here impairs auditory processing, localization and word discrimination, rather than pure hearing loss.

Cranial Nerve Impairments

The cranial nerves provide motor and sensory innervation to the head and neck and can be damaged as a result of traumatic injuries to the head or brain. Certain cranial nerves are more likely to be damaged in different mechanisms of injury, such as skull fractures (e.g., olfactory, optic, oculomotor, trigeminal, facial and auditory-vestibular), shearing forces (e.g., olfactory, optic), intracranial hemorrhages (e.g., olfactory, oculomotor), uncal herniation (e.g., oculomotor) or infarcts (Hammond & Katta-Charles, 2022). Damage to a cranial nerve can cause problems with olfaction, vision, eye movements, facial sensation and movements, hearing, balance, swallowing, tongue movements and neck strength, among others. Despite being the most common cranial nerve injury in TBI, damage to the olfactory nerve (cranial nerve I) is often missed simply because olfaction is infrequently tested in acute trauma settings (Hammond & Katta-Charles, 2022).

Speech, Language and Swallowing Problems

It is important to consider the speech, language and swallowing disorders that may occur after TBI, given their potential impact on recovery and quality of life. All three of these processes are governed by a multitude of nervous system structures, including the cerebrum, midbrain, brainstem, cerebellum, cranial nerves and peripheral nerves; therefore, TBI may interrupt function at any point along these pathways. The most common form of speech dysfunction after TBI is dysarthria, which is a disorder in the motor control of the muscles of speech which leads to difficulty executing speech (Morgan, 2014; Togher et al., 2022). This is different than apraxia (disorder of speech movement planning) and aphasia (disorder of speech comprehension and expression), both of which are much less common following TBI (Togher et al., 2022). Regardless of the type, speech disorders can complicate a patient's relationship with their loved ones, co-workers and communities (Elbourn et al., 2019), in addition to leading to higher rates of caregiver fatigue and depression from their higher dependency for care (Holloway et al., 2019; Togher et al., 2022).

Similarly, dysfunctional swallowing impacts quality of life by limiting what a patient can eat and potentially causing malnutrition (Miles, 2022). Swallowing dysfunction is also a negative prognostic factor, because it is associated with longer hospitalizations and increased likelihood of death from aspiration pneumonia (Howle et al., 2014). With the guidance of a speech-language pathologist and dietician, the thickness of food may be altered (thin liquid, mildly thick liquid, puree, etc.) to help a patient swallow safely.

Dizziness and Imbalance

Dizziness is a common complaint in patients with TBIs of all severities and it is a predictor of prolonged recovery (Corwin et al., 2015; Kleffelgaard et al., 2017; Lau et al., 2011; Maskell et al., 2006; Whitney & Furman, 2022). It is important to note that "dizziness" is a nonspecific term that patients may use to refer to lightheadedness, balance deficits, disorientation or true "vertigo" (i.e., sensation of spinning). The vestibular (balance) system is controlled by multiple anatomical areas ranging from peripheral structures (inner ear, eyes, cranial nerves, vestibular and proprioceptive end organs) to central structures (brainstem, cerebellum, cerebral cortex). The most common cause of balance and dizziness complaints from peripheral vestibular origin is benign paroxysmal positional vertigo, which has been reported in up to 38% of patients with moderate to severe TBI (Marcus et al., 2019). Benign paroxysmal positional vertigo is caused by crystals normally present along the surface of the inner ear becoming dislodged and disrupting the flow of inner ear fluid; this causes brief (<1 min) episodes of vertigo triggered by head movements (Bhattacharyya et al., 2017). Cervicogenic dizziness, which may be caused by blunt force trauma or whiplash, is related to changes in cervical spine position or joint movement (Reiley et al., 2017).

Headaches

Posttraumatic headaches are defined as new-onset secondary headaches that emerge within seven days of TBI without loss of consciousness or seven days following recovery of consciousness after TBI (Katta-Charles et al., 2022). Posttraumatic headaches are conceptualized as acute if they last for fewer than 3 months and chronic if longer than 3 months; fortunately, most resolve within the first 3 months. The most common phenotypes of headaches seen after TBI are migraine-like (unilateral throbbing sometimes followed by nausea and/or vomiting) and tension-type (bilateral band-like, squeezing pain in the temporal regions). Less common are cluster-like headaches (unilateral, stabbing pain in the periorbital or temporal region often repeating multiple times per day), cervicogenic-like (unilateral sub-occipital head pain worsened by neck movement) and neuritic and neuralgic head pain (sharp and shooting pain arising from the development of a neuroma in the occipital or parietal region of the scalp; Katta-Charles et al., 2022). Posttraumatic headaches can also be associated with somatic symptoms like nausea, vomiting, photo- or phonophobia and psychological symptoms like depression, anxiety and posttraumatic stress disorder (PTSD; Ashina et al., 2019); the latter may be mutually reinforcing with headaches, thus worsening both posttraumatic headaches and psychological symptoms.

Posttraumatic Seizures

Some important consequences of TBI to keep in mind are posttraumatic seizures and epilepsy. In fact, TBI is a leading cause of epilepsy in young adults (Towne & Yablon, 2022). In addition to the pathologic effects of neurotrauma, other factors may precipitate seizure development in TBI populations. These include drugs such as alcohol, psychiatric medications (tricyclic antidepressants, bupropion, clozapine), antibiotics, dopamine receptor antagonists, high doses of caffeine and cocaine (Towne & Yablon, 2022). In some high-risk patients (history of alcohol use disorder, older age, prolonged posttraumatic amnesia), antiepileptic drugs are sometimes used as seizure prophylaxis following a TBI to prevent secondary injury from seizures or preserve quality of life; however, research shows only modest evidence for the efficacy of seizure prophylaxis in preventing posttraumatic seizures (Wat et al., 2019). Additionally, antiepileptic drugs can have adverse effects (e.g., sedation). Some of these medications can have cognitive side effects that may impact neuropsychological test results.

Neuropsychiatric Problems

Fatigue and Sleep Problems

Post-TBI fatigue is a commonly reported symptom following TBI, with incidence as high as 80% in some studies (Lequerica et al., 2017; Mollayeva et al., 2014). The severity and chronicity of this fatigue seem to depend on the severity of brain injury, with prolonged recovery reported in moderate and severe TBI compared to mild TBI (Beaulieu-Bonneau & Ouellet, 2017). Post-TBI fatigue can trigger a "vicious cycle" of worsening quality of life; for example, a tired patient may nap during the day, leading to an irregular sleep–wake cycle and progressive withdrawal from daily activities (Ripley & Greenwald, 2022). Other sleep disturbances following TBI are also common, typically characterized as (a) insomnia (difficulty initiating or maintaining sleep), (b) hypersomnia (excessive sleep or excessive daytime sleepiness), or (c) disturbed sleep–wake (circadian) cycles (Nakase-Richardson et al., 2022). Of note, fatigue and sleep disturbances can be related to traumatic brain damage, co-occurring depression or both.

Depression, Anxiety and Traumatic Stress

Patients with TBI are at risk for developing depressive, anxiety and trauma-related disorders. Multiple factors contribute, as early presentation of psychiatric conditions can be influenced by neurotrauma and biological changes, whereas later presentations can be precipitated by the psychosocial stressors associated with TBI recovery (Wortzel & Brenner, 2022). Depressive disorders are more prevalent after TBI compared to orthopedic injuries of similar severity, highlighting the possible pathologic role that neurotrauma may play (Jorge et al., 2004).

The estimated prevalence of depression following TBI varies widely, ranging from 6 to 77% (Jorge & Arciniegas, 2014; Seel et al., 2010). It is also highly comorbid with anxiety and substance use disorders, with rates of new-onset anxiety disorders after TBI ranging from 19 to 50% (Ponsford et al., 2018). Given the significant negative impact that depression and anxiety can have on quality of life, it is important for clinicians to identify and address mood symptoms and common somatic symptoms like sleep disturbance, fatigue, weight changes, headache, dizziness or paresthesia.

A somewhat controversial issue is whether a person who sustains a TBI can develop PTSD when that person has no memory for the traumatic event. It has been hypothesized that some injured people can experience a degree of fear conditioning even while in a state of posttraumatic amnesia or confusion. Moreover, they can reconstruct their traumatic experiences over time, with a combination of accurate and possibly inaccurate information, and this might intermingle with the original fear conditioning to perpetuate anxiety symptoms. These reconstructed memories might be re-experienced, fulfilling one of the hallmark criteria for PTSD (Choi & Stein, 2022).

One other notable neuropsychiatric consequence of TBI is emotional dyscontrol, which refers to symptoms of unpredictable and rapid change in emotion (Wortzel & Brenner, 2022). Some examples include pathological laughing and crying, affective lability and irritability. Emotional dyscontrol is more common early in the course of recovery after TBI, though it can become persistent following moderate to severe TBI. While pathologic laughing or crying and affective lability both involve uncontrolled and intense expressions of laughter and crying, the interesting difference between the two is that the laughter or crying does not necessarily coincide with the underlying experienced emotion in pathologic laughing or crying (Wortzel & Brenner, 2022). For example, the patient may unexpectedly begin laughing during a somber moment; on the other hand, in affective lability, the patient's emotional expressivity is enhanced (e.g., they are more likely to cry excessively when sad).

Psychotic Disorders

Psychotic disorders following TBI are generically referred to as *posttraumatic psychosis*. Posttraumatic psychosis is relatively rare, occurring in 0.9–8.5% of patients after TBI, and is typically of delayed onset, most commonly 4 or more years later (Batty et al., 2013; Fujii & Ahmed, 2014). However, it is difficult for a clinician to definitively demonstrate that any case of posttraumatic psychosis is directly caused by TBI. Some factors that increase the likelihood of TBI's involvement include a strong temporal relationship between injury and psychosis, a lack of family history of psychosis and atypical features of psychosis (e.g., older age of onset, visual or olfactory hallucinations; Wortzel & Brenner, 2022). Posttraumatic psychosis can present similarly to a delusional disorder or a schizophrenia-like psychosis.

Lack of Awareness

Individuals who sustain moderate to severe TBIs, especially those involving the frontal lobes and right hemisphere, can have reduced awareness of medical, physical and/or cognitive deficits (Steward & Kretzmer, 2022). This can result in delayed or inadequate presentation for healthcare, safety risks such as increased falls or frank denial of any cognitive deficits (Eslinger et al., 2022). In addition, although many patients tend to exhibit some awareness of cognitive and speech deficits, they are less likely to report changes in personality and behavior (Eslinger et al., 2022). Lack of awareness has been described using the neurologic and psychodynamic terminology listed below (Eslinger et al., 2022).

- *Agnosia:* Impaired recognition of previously meaningful stimuli that cannot be attributed to primary sensory defects, attentional disturbances or a naming disorder.
- *Anosognosia:* A lack of knowledge, or unawareness of cognitive, linguistic, sensory and motor deficits following neurological injury.
- *Anosodiaphoria:* Lack of emotional concern for serious neurological impairments, despite recognizing their existence.
- *Denial of Insight:* A psychological explanation to account for symptoms of anosognosia. Patients with anosognosia are thought to be motivated to block distressing symptoms from awareness by using a defense mechanism (denial).
- *Lack of Insight:* A multidimensional construct that describes a spectrum of concepts, ranging from a psychological defense mechanism to lack of cognitive skills that permit understanding of deficits (Flashman & McAllister, 2002).

Though it had previously been suggested that lack of awareness was a psychologic defense mechanism in the aftermath of TBI, the time course of these symptoms suggests otherwise. Unlike a defense mechanism, which would be employed more as the patient regained consciousness and recognized their chronic disabilities, symptoms of impaired awareness are most apparent immediately after injury and gradually fade, presumably as the brain recovers (Eslinger et al., 2022). Lack of awareness impacts health in a multitude of ways, from delayed patient presentation for healthcare to patient denial of essential medical or rehabilitation services.

Personality and Behavioral Changes

TBIs can often cause changes in personality and behavior, which pose challenges to caregivers and potential barriers to rehabilitation. Personality changes can result from damage to specific regions of the brain. For example, damage to the frontal lobes can result in agitation, impulsivity, emotional lability, socially inappropriate behaviors, apathy, decreased spontaneity, lack of interest or emotional blunting. Damage to the temporal lobes can result in episodic hyper-irritability, aggressive outbursts or dysphoric mood states. However, personality changes can also manifest as a consequence of individuals' reactions to their injury as they experience cognitive and behavioral deficits and major changes in their lifestyle. Depression, anxiety, irritability or aggression, decreased empathy, low frustration tolerance and apathy are common in this regard (Ponsford, 2022; Svensson et al., 2023; Weddell & Wood, 2018). Personality changes can be considered a consequence of a complex interaction between the direct consequences of the brain injury and secondary reactions to impairment or loss (Ponsford, 2022).

Sexual Dysfunction

Changes in sexuality and sexual functioning are commonly reported by patients or spouses following TBI (Sander et al., 2022). These changes can involve desire, drive, arousal, orgasm and other sexual behaviors. Human sexuality is influenced by physical, cognitive, emotional and social factors. Sexual dysfunction might be related to many factors, such as damage to specific brain regions, neurochemical changes relating to brain damage, endocrinologic abnormalities, medication side effects, secondary medical conditions, physical limitations, cognitive impairments, emotional problems, behavioral problems and interpersonal difficulties (Sander, 2019). Disinhibited sexual behavior can occur after TBI and may be a barrier to caregiving, but hyposexuality is much more frequent (Sander et al., 2022; Simpson et al., 2013).

Functional and Neuropsychological Outcome

All aspects of recovery and outcome are affected by injury severity. Many individuals with severe brain injuries have persistent neuropsychological impairments, functional disability (e.g., difficulty managing day-to-day affairs) and poor return to work rates (Cuthbert et al., 2015; Eslinger et al., 2022). The Glasgow Outcome Scale (Jennett & Bond, 1975) was designed to categorize global functional outcome following TBI. The five outcome categories are: (a) dead, (b) vegetative state, (c) severe disability (unable to live alone for more than 24 h), (d) moderate disability (independent at home, able to utilize public transportation, able to work in a supported environment) and (e) good recovery (capable of resuming normal occupational and social functioning, although there might be minor residual physical or mental deficits). Patients who sustain severe TBIs are at risk for moderate or severe disability. A substantial percentage, however, have good recovery (Lu et al., 2018). In predicting those who will have a good recovery versus a poor outcome, lower initial GCS scores are generally associated with worse outcomes; however, there are no specific cutoff thresholds that exist in the literature. Older age (65+) and bilateral brainstem injury are also associated with poorer outcomes. Good recovery is less likely when time to follow commands is greater than 4 weeks and PTA is greater than 3 months (Kothari & Zhang, 2022).

Cognitive impairment following TBI is highly individualized and difficult to predict. When considering groups of patients, those with severe TBIs are likely to have some degree of persisting impairment and those with mild TBIs are unlikely to have persisting impairment on neuropsychological testing (Dikmen et al., 2001; Eslinger et al., 2022; Schretlen & Shapiro, 2003).

Moderate or severe TBIs frequently result in permanent neurocognitive and neurobehavioral impairments. A minority, however, have a very good outcome (Lippa et al., 2020). As mentioned, neurobehavioral changes can include personality changes, problems regulating one's emotions, apathy, disinhibition and anosognosia. From a neurocognitive perspective, impairments are most notable in attention, working memory, processing speed, declarative memory, executive functioning and social cognition (Arciniegas & Wortzel, 2019; Eslinger et al., 2022). However, impairments are certainly not restricted to these domains. As injury severity increases, there is a greater likelihood of global cognitive deficits that may include motor skills, visuospatial ability and language (Dikmen et al., 1995; Eslinger et al., 2022). As a rule, the vast majority of recovery from moderate to severe TBI occurs within the first year, although some additional recovery can occur in the years thereafter. Substantial improvements after 2 years are not expected for most patients. However, improvement in functioning can and does occur as the result of learned accommodations and compensations in the years following injury.

Key Points: Functional and Neuropsychological Outcome

- Neuropsychological and functional outcome is related to injury severity.
- Acquired long-term deficits are common in moderate and severe brain injuries, but uncommon in mild brain injuries.
- Most recovery from moderate to severe TBI occurs within the first year.
  - Additional recovery is possible in the years thereafter.
  - Substantial recovery of function after 2 years is not generally present, although accommodations and compensatory strategies can improve daily functioning.

Outcomes can be improved with effective rehabilitation. Access to rehabilitation care has been shown to positively impact functional outcomes and recovery (Greiss et al., 2016). In the acute phase, early rehabilitative efforts will focus on medical interventions, preventing morbidity and minimizing future complications—for example, tracheostomy, preventing skin breakdown, bladder management, optimizing nutrition and maintaining joint mobility. Therapy may include physical therapy, occupational therapy, speech therapy (for language and/or swallowing), cognitive rehabilitation and recreational therapy. A team-based approach is an integral part of rehabilitation efforts. Participation in residential, outpatient and home rehabilitation programs has also been shown to have a positive effect on quality of life, activities of daily living, self-efficacy and community functioning (Glenn & Shih, 2020; Ivanhoe et al., 2022).

Psychosocial Outcome

The short- and long-term effects of moderate and severe TBI present a number of challenges that make adjustment back to everyday life difficult for both patient and family members. Some of the most common issues relate to substance use disorder, family and marital issues, return to work and community integration.

Problematic Substance Use

Substance misuse both before and after TBI can complicate medical recovery and rehabilitation. Some studies show a potential bidirectional association: people with substance use disorder are more likely to experience TBI, and people who sustain a TBI might be at increased risk for developing a substance use disorder starting in the second year following injury (Gould et al., 2011; Olsen & Corrigan, 2022; Pagulayan et al., 2016; Ponsford et al., 2018; Weil et al., 2018). During the first year following injury, rates of substance misuse can be lower for individuals than their pre-injury rates, usually due to extended hospitalizations or recommendations for abstinence (Bombardier et al., 2003; Corrigan et al., 2022; Ponsford et al., 2007). Additionally, there is some conflicting evidence on whether the rate of substance use disorder is higher in people who have had TBIs relative to the general population, with one prospective study showing return to national rates 3 years or more following injury (Alway et al., 2016).

One study of the National Trauma Data Bank which included nearly 104,000 TBI patients showed that having an elevated blood alcohol level at the time of injury increased the chances of sustaining a TBI (Chen et al., 2012). Additionally, patients who were actively intoxicated at the time of their TBI were more likely to have more severe injuries, more complicated medical course, longer hospitalizations and greater chronic neurological impairments (Corrigan et al., 2022).

Problematic substance use can also follow TBI, though it is unclear whether there is a mechanistic versus social connection between the two. Regardless, substance misuse during recovery from TBI is a serious issue that can interfere with rehabilitation. One study of combat-related TBI showed that military personnel with a history of TBI were more likely than uninjured personnel to binge drink (Adams et al., 2012). Additionally, several studies have shown that experiencing a TBI in childhood is associated with greater likelihood of developing alcohol use disorder later in life (McKinlay et al., 2009; Wu et al., 2016).

Increases in alcohol use following injury may be related, in part, to self-medication attempts to alleviate pain, depression and/or anxiety (Corrigan et al., 2022), though this issue has received little research to date and is poorly understood. Some risk factors for developing a substance use disorder following TBI include pre-injury history of problematic substance use, onset of depression since injury, chronic pain and male gender (Corrigan et al., 2022).

Return to Work

Vocational outcome following TBI is important for patients and society as a whole. For many individuals, the inability to return to work results in a number of economic, social, family and interpersonal problems. In addition, the economic burden placed on society is of concern (e.g., long-term illness and unemployment benefits), particularly because many individuals who sustain a TBI tend to be young and have their whole working lives ahead of them (Georges & Das, 2023).

Unfortunately, failure to return to work is a common issue for patients who have experienced TBI; the prevalence of unemployment 1 year following injury was between 45.5 and 60% compared to 3.9% nationally today (Hart et al., 2019; Sigurdardottir et al., 2020; U.S. Department of Labor Bureau of Labor Statistics, 2023).

Successful return to work is related to injury severity. Individuals who have sustained moderate or severe TBIs have generally lower return to work rates when compared to individuals who have sustained a mild TBI (Hart et al., 2019; Saltychev et al., 2013). Other evidence-based factors that statistically increase the risk of poor return to work include: (a) male gender; (b) older age at time of injury; (c) minority group membership; (d) low educational/occupational attainment; (e) low level of social support; (f) greater cognitive, physical and psychosocial impairment; (g) depression or changes in personality; (h) a history of substance use disorder; and (i) lack of independent transportation (Avellone & Wehman, 2022).

Marital and Family Issues

Many report worse family functioning when a family member has sustained a severe TBI and the impact of TBI on the family varies depending on the relationship between injured and uninjured family members. The greatest burden is usually placed on the spouse. The uninjured spouse typically assumes some caregiver or supervision responsibilities which can come with associated caregiver burdens. Couples may additionally be faced with increased financial burden, changes of lifestyle, loss of financial and other support from the injured spouse, sexuality and intimacy problems and separation/divorce. When a child is injured, parents may be impacted by increased tension in their marital relationship, neglect of their other children and decreased adult social interaction with friends. Children of parents with brain injury may be faced with the loss of nurturance and love from the parent or emergence of behavioral problems due to changes in their family situation. Uninjured siblings may feel neglected by their parents and develop behavioral problems. Adult children and adult siblings are often torn between the needs of their own lives and the needs of the injured parent or sibling.

Regardless of the family relationship, there is an obvious increased burden for those family members who have assumed the role of caregiver. A healthy versus unhealthy family environment can contribute to how well the injured person functions psychologically in daily life. Emotional and behavioral changes, level of cognitive functioning, financial security and premorbid relationship quality have been shown to be strong predictors of family functioning following injury (Carnes & Quinn, 2005; Hanks et al., 2007).

Community Integration

Community integration following TBI is important for improving quality of life. The most common community integration issues are: (a) family adjustment, (b) social isolation, (c) limited community mobility and (d) returning to work. Family adjustment and return to work issues have been discussed in previous sections. Social isolation commonly manifests as a consequence of the person not being able to fulfill or resume a social role following injury. This may be caused by psychosocial or emotional problems (e.g., depression, anxiety, fatigue), or a loss of other skills to develop and maintain personal relationships (e.g., language deficits and personality changes). Limited community mobility is related to transportation problems, such as driving restrictions or inability to independently use public transportation due to physical or sensory impairments (e.g., motor incoordination, visual deficits, posttraumatic epilepsy), cognitive deficits (e.g., distractibility, judgment problems) and/or behavioral changes (e.g., impulsivity).

Conclusion

TBIs are common and occur on a broad continuum of severity, from very mild to catastrophic. The vast majority (at least 80%) are mild in severity. The severity of injury typically is classified based on combinations of severity criteria derived from the duration of unconsciousness, Glasgow Coma Scale score and duration of posttraumatic amnesia/confusion.

Moderate and severe TBIs can result in temporary, prolonged or permanent neurological or neuropsychiatric problems. These problems may include motor impairments, movement disorders, visual impairments, auditory impairments, cranial nerve impairments, speech/language/swallowing problems, poor balance and dizziness, headaches, posttraumatic seizures, fatigue and sleep problems, depression, anosognosia, personality changes, apathy and sexual dysfunction.

In general, greater injury severity is associated with greater magnitude and breadth of cognitive abilities affected. Impairments are most notable in attention, working memory, processing speed, declarative memory, executive functioning and social cognition, but as injury severity increases, there is a greater likelihood of widespread cognitive deficits. As a rule, the vast majority of recovery from moderate to severe TBI occurs within the first year, with some additional recovery in the years thereafter. Substantial improvements after 2 years are not expected for most patients and lower initial GCS scores, older age (65+) and bilateral brainstem injury are generally associated with worse outcomes. Additionally, severe disability is likely when time to follow commands is greater than 4 weeks and PTA is greater than 3 months. However, improvement in functioning can and does occur as the result of learned accommodations and compensations in the years following injury.

Many individuals with severe brain injuries have persistent functional disabilities (e.g., managing day-to-day affairs) and poor return to work rates. Problems with returning to work results in a number of economic, social, family and interpersonal problems for the patients. In addition, there is an increased economic burden on society because many of these individuals are young and have their whole working lives ahead of them. It is important to appreciate that the long-term neurological, neuropsychiatric, functional and neurocognitive deficits and problems associated with moderate to severe TBI are not restricted to the injured person. TBI in a family member results in adverse effects for the entire family system. The greatest burden is typically placed on those family members that assume the role of caregiver. The level of burden placed on the caregiver is significantly influenced by changes in the family system and role responsibilities, financial difficulties and the level of independence exhibited by the injured person as they attempt to integrate back into the community.

References

Adams, R. S., Larson, M. J., Corrigan, J. D., Horgan, C. M., & Williams, T. V. (2012). Frequent binge drinking after combat-acquired traumatic brain injury among active duty military personnel with a past year combat deployment. *Journal of Head Trauma Rehabilitation, 27*(5), 349–360. https://doi.org/10.1097/HTR.0b013e318268db94

Alway, Y., Gould, K. R., Johnston, L., McKenzie, D., & Ponsford, J. (2016). A prospective examination of Axis I psychiatric disorders in the first 5 years following moderate to severe traumatic brain injury. *Psychological Medicine, 46*(6), 1331–1341. https://doi.org/10.1017/S0033291715002986

Arciniegas, D. B., & Wortzel, H. (2019). Neurocognitive disorders. In J. M. Silver, T. W. McAllister, & D. B. Arciniegas (Eds.), *Textbook of traumatic brain injury* (3rd ed., pp. 247–268). American Psychiatric Association.

Ariza, M., Serra-Grabulosa, J. M., Junqué, C., Ramírez, B., Mataró, M., Poca, A., Bargalló, N., & Sahuquillo, J. (2006). Hippocampal head atrophy after traumatic brain injury. *Neuropsychologia, 44*(10), 1956–1961. https://doi.org/10.1016/j.neuropsychologia.2005.11.007

Ashina, H., Porreca, F., Anderson, T., Amin, F. M., Ashina, M., Schytz, H. W., & Dodick, D. W. (2019). Post-traumatic headache: Epidemiology and pathophysiological insights. *Nature Reviews. Neurology, 15*(10), 607–617. https://doi.org/10.1038/s41582-019-0243-8

Avellone, L., & Wehman, P. (2022). Return to work following traumatic brain injury. In N. D. Zasler, D. I. Katz, R. D. Zafonte, D. B. Arciniegas, M. R. Bullock, F. M. Hammond, J. S. Kreutzer, R. Nakase-Richardson, & T. K. Watanabe (Eds.), *Brain injury medicine: Principles and practice* (3rd ed.). Springer.

Batty, R. A., Rossell, S. L., Francis, A. J. P., & Ponsford, J. (2013). Psychosis following traumatic brain injury. *Brain Impairment, 14*(1), 21–41. https://doi.org/10.1017/BrImp.2013.10

Beaulieu-Bonneau, S., & Ouellet, M.-C. (2017). Fatigue in the first year after traumatic brain injury: Course, relationship with injury severity, and correlates. *Neuropsychological Rehabilitation, 27*(7), 983–1001. https://doi.org/10.1080/09602011.2016.1162176

Bergemalm, P.-O. (2003). Progressive hearing loss after closed head injury: A predictable outcome? *Acta Oto-Laryngologica, 123*(7), 836–845. https://doi.org/10.1080/00016480310002474

Beucler, N., Cungi, P.-J., Baucher, G., Coze, S., Dagain, A., & Roche, P.-H. (2022). The Kernohan-Woltman Notch phenomenon: A systematic review of clinical and radiologic presentation, surgical management, and functional prognosis. *Journal of Korean Neurosurgical Society, 65*(5), 652–664. https://doi.org/10.3340/jkns.2022.0002

Bhattacharyya, N., Gubbels, S. P., Schwartz, S. R., Edlow, J. A., El-Kashlan, H., Fife, T., Holmberg, J. M., Mahoney, K., Hollingsworth, D. B., Roberts, R., Seidman, M. D., Steiner, R. W. P., Do, B. T., Voelker, C. C. J., Waguespack, R. W., & Corrigan, M. D. (2017). Clinical practice guideline: Benign paroxysmal positional vertigo (update). *Otolaryngology–Head and Neck Surgery, 156*(S3). https://doi.org/10.1177/0194599816689667

Bodien, Y. G., Martens, G., Ostrow, J., Sheau, K., & Giacino, J. T. (2020). Cognitive impairment, clinical symptoms and functional disability in patients emerging from the minimally conscious state. *NeuroRehabilitation, 46*(1), 65–74. https://doi.org/10.3233/NRE-192860

Bombardier, C. H., Temkin, N. R., Machamer, J., & Dikmen, S. S. (2003). The natural history of drinking and alcohol-related problems after traumatic brain injury. *Archives of Physical Medicine and Rehabilitation, 84*(2), 185–191. https://doi.org/10.1053/apmr.2003.50002

Breiding, L. M., Peterson, S., Waltzman, D., & Daugherty, J. (2022). Traumatic brain injury epidemiology and public health issues. In N. D. Zasler, D. I. Katz, R. D. Zafonte, D. B. Arciniegas, M. R. Bullock, F. M. Hammond, J. S. Kreutzer, R. Nakase-Richardson, & T. K. Watanabe (Eds.), *Brain injury medicine: Principles and practice* (3rd ed., pp. 92–108). Springer.

Brennan, P. M., Murray, G. D., & Teasdale, G. M. (2020). A practical method for dealing with missing Glasgow Coma Scale verbal component scores. *Journal of Neurosurgery, 135*(1), 214–219. https://doi.org/10.3171/2020.6.JNS20992

Capizzi, A., Woo, J., & Verduzco-Gutierrez, M. (2020). Traumatic brain injury: An overview of epidemiology, pathophysiology, and medical management. *Medical Clinics of North America, 104*(2), 213–238. https://doi.org/10.1016/j.mcna.2019.11.001

Carnes, S. L., & Quinn, W. H. (2005). Family adaptation to brain injury: Coping and psychological distress. *Families, Systems, & Health, 23*(2), 186–203. https://doi.org/10.1037/1091-7527.23.2.186

Centers for Disease Control and Prevention. (2021). *Traumatic brain injury-related hospitalizations and deaths by age group, sex, and mechanism of injury—United States, 2016 and 2017.* Centers for Disease Control and Prevention, U.S. Department of Health and Human Services.

Chandler, C. D. W. (2006). Blast-related ear injury in current U.S. military operations. *The ASHA Leader*. https://doi.org/10.1044/leader.FTR4.11092006.8

Chen, C. M., Yi, H.-Y., Yoon, Y.-H., & Dong, C. (2012). Alcohol use at time of injury and survival following traumatic brain injury: Results from the national trauma data bank. *Journal of Studies on Alcohol and Drugs, 73*(4), 531–541. https://doi.org/10.15288/jsad.2012.73.531

Choi, S.-H., & Stein, M. (2022). Posttraumatic stress disorder and traumatic brain injury. In N. D. Zasler, D. I. Katz, R. D. Zafonte, D. B. Arciniegas, M. R. Bullock, F. M. Hammond, J. S. Kreutzer, R. Nakase-Richardson, & T. K. Watanabe (Eds.), *Brain injury medicine: Principles and practice* (3rd ed.). Springer.

Ciufreda, K., Tannen, B., Singman, J., & Han, E. (2022). Evaluation and treatment of visual dysfunction. In N. D. Zasler, D. I. Katz, R. D. Zafonte, D. B. Arciniegas, M. R. Bullock, F. M. Hammond, J. S. Kreutzer, R. Nakase-Richardson, & T. K. Watanabe (Eds.), *Brain injury medicine: Principles and practice* (3rd ed.). Springer.

Close, L., Quesada, L., & Bullock, M. (2022). Pathobiology of traumatic brain injury. In N. D. Zasler, D. I. Katz, R. D. Zafonte, D. B. Arciniegas, M. R. Bullock, F. M. Hammond, J. S. Kreutzer, R. Nakase-Richardson, & T. K. Watanabe (Eds.), *Brain injury medicine: Principles and practice* (3rd ed.). Springer.

Coelho, D., Williams, E., Bauschard, M., & Hoffer, M. (2022). Audiological impairment. In N. D. Zasler, D. I. Katz, R. D. Zafonte, D. B. Arciniegas, M. R. Bullock, F. M. Hammond, J. S. Kreutzer, R. Nakase-Richardson, & T. K. Watanabe (Eds.), *Brain injury medicine: Principles and practice* (3rd ed.). Springer.

Corrigan, J., Adams, R., & Dams-O'Connor, K. (2022). At-risk substance use and substance use disorders. In N. D. Zasler, D. I. Katz, R. D. Zafonte, D. B. Arciniegas, M. R. Bullock, F. M. Hammond, J. S. Kreutzer, R. Nakase-Richardson, & T. K. Watanabe (Eds.), *Brain injury medicine: Principles and practice* (3rd ed.). Springer.

Corwin, D. J., Wiebe, D. J., Zonfrillo, M. R., Grady, M. F., Robinson, R. L., Goodman, A. M., & Master, C. L. (2015). Vestibular deficits following youth concussion. *The Journal of Pediatrics, 166*(5), 1221–1225. https://doi.org/10.1016/j.jpeds.2015.01.039

Cuthbert, J. P., Harrison-Felix, C., Corrigan, J. D., Bell, J. M., Haarbauer-Krupa, J. K., & Miller, A. C. (2015). Unemployment in the United States after traumatic brain injury for working-age individuals: Prevalence and associated factors 2 years postinjury. *The Journal of Head Trauma Rehabilitation, 30*(3), 160–174. https://doi.org/10.1097/HTR.0000000000000090

Daugherty, J. (2019). Traumatic brain injury–related deaths by race/ethnicity, sex, intent, and mechanism of injury—United States, 2000–2017. *MMWR. Morbidity and Mortality Weekly Report, 68*. https://doi.org/10.15585/mmwr.mm6846a2

Decker, R., & Pearson-Shaver, A. (2023). *Uncal Herniation*. StatPearls.

Dikmen, S., Machamer, J., & Temkin, N. (2001). Mild head injury: Facts and artifacts. *Journal of Clinical and Experimental Neuropsychology, 23*(6), 729–738. https://doi.org/10.1076/jcen.23.6.729.1019

Dikmen, S. S., Machamer, J. E., Winn, H. R., & Temkin, N. R. (1995). Neuropsychological outcome at 1-year post head injury. *Neuropsychology, 9*(1), 80–90. https://doi.org/10.1037/0894-4105.9.1.80

Dougherty, A. L., MacGregor, A. J., Han, P. P., Viirre, E., Heltemes, K. J., & Galarneau, M. R. (2013). Blast-related ear injuries among U.S. Military personnel. *Journal of Rehabilitation Research and Development, 50*(6), 893–904. https://doi.org/10.1682/JRRD.2012.02.0024

Elbourn, E., Kenny, B., Power, E., & Togher, L. (2019). Psychosocial outcomes of severe traumatic brain injury in relation to discourse recovery: A longitudinal study up to 1 year post-injury. *American Journal of Speech-Language Pathology, 28*(4), 1463–1478. https://doi.org/10.1044/2019_AJSLP-18-0204

Eslinger, P. J., Zappala, G., & Chakara, F. (2022). Cognitive impairments. In N. D. Zasler, D. I. Katz, R. D. Zafonte, D. B. Arciniegas, M. R. Bullock, F. M. Hammond, J. S. Kreutzer, R. Nakase-Richardson, & T. K. Watanabe (Eds.), *Brain injury medicine: Principles and practice* (3rd ed., pp. 932–944). Springer.

Fausti, S. A., Wilmington, D. J., Gallun, F. J., Myers, P. J., & Henry, J. A. (2009). Auditory and vestibular dysfunction associated with blast-related traumatic brain injury. *The Journal of Rehabilitation Research and Development, 46*(6), 797. https://doi.org/10.1682/JRRD.2008.09.0118

Flashman, L. A., & McAllister, T. W. (2002). Lack of awareness and its impact in traumatic brain injury. *NeuroRehabilitation, 17*(4), 285–296.

Fujii, D. E., & Ahmed, I. (2014). Psychotic disorder caused by traumatic brain injury. *The Psychiatric Clinics of North America, 37*(1), 113–124. https://doi.org/10.1016/j.psc.2013.11.006

Georges, A., & Das, J. (2023). *Traumatic brain injury*. StatPearls. Retrieved November 29, 2023, from http://www.ncbi.nlm.nih.gov/books/NBK459300/

Giacino, J. T., Ashwal, S., Childs, N., Cranford, R., Jennett, B., Katz, D. I., Kelly, J. P., Rosenberg, J. H., Whyte, J., Zafonte, R. D., & Zasler, N. D. (2002). The minimally conscious state: Definition and diagnostic criteria. *Neurology, 58*(3), 349–353. https://doi.org/10.1212/wnl.58.3.349

Giacino, J. T., Katz, D. I., Schiff, N. D., Whyte, J., Ashman, E. J., Ashwal, S., Barbano, R., Hammond, F. M., Laureys, S., Ling, G. S. F., Nakase-Richardson, R., Seel, R. T., Yablon, S., Getchius, T. S. D., Gronseth, G. S., & Armstrong, M. J. (2018). Comprehensive systematic review update summary: Disorders of consciousness: Report of the guideline development, dissemination, and implementation Subcommittee of the American Academy of Neurology; the American Congress of Rehabilitation Medicine; and the National Institute on Disability, Independent Living, and Rehabilitation Research. *Neurology, 91*(10), 461–470. https://doi.org/10.1212/WNL.0000000000005928

Glenn, M. B., & Shih, S. L. (2020). Rehabilitation following TBI. In J. W. Tsao (Ed.), *Traumatic brain injury: A clinician's guide to diagnosis, management, and rehabilitation* (pp. 293–328). Springer.

Gould, K. R., Ponsford, J. L., Johnston, L., & Schönberger, M. (2011). The nature, frequency and course of psychiatric disorders in the first year after traumatic brain injury: A prospective study. *Psychological Medicine, 41*(10), 2099–2109. https://doi.org/10.1017/S003329171100033X

Green, R. E. A., Colella, B., Maller, J. J., Bayley, M., Glazer, J., & Mikulis, D. J. (2014). Scale and pattern of atrophy in the chronic stages of moderate-severe TBI. *Frontiers in Human Neuroscience, 8*, 67. https://doi.org/10.3389/fnhum.2014.00067

Greiss, C., Yonclas, P. P., Jasey, N., Lequerica, A., Ward, I., Chiaravalloti, N., Felix, G., Dabaghian, L., & Livingston, D. H. (2016). Presence of a dedicated trauma center physiatrist improves functional outcomes following traumatic brain injury. *The Journal of Trauma and Acute Care Surgery, 80*(1), 70–75. https://doi.org/10.1097/TA.0000000000000890

Hammond, F., & Katta-Charles, S. (2022). Cranial nerve disorders. In N. D. Zasler, D. I. Katz, R. D. Zafonte, D. B. Arciniegas, M. R. Bullock, F. M. Hammond, J. S. Kreutzer, R. Nakase-Richardson, & T. K. Watanabe (Eds.), *Brain injury medicine: Principles and practice* (3rd ed.). Springer.

Hanks, R. A., Rapport, L. J., & Vangel, S. (2007). Caregiving appraisal after traumatic brain injury: The effects of functional status, coping style, social support and family functioning. *NeuroRehabilitation, 22*(1), 43–52. https://doi.org/10.3233/NRE-2007-22105

Harris, T. C., de Rooij, R., & Kuhl, E. (2019). The shrinking brain: Cerebral atrophy following traumatic brain injury. *Annals of Biomedical Engineering, 47*(9), 1941. https://doi.org/10.1007/s10439-018-02148-2

Hart, T., Ketchum, J. M., O'Neil-Pirozzi, T. M., Novack, T. A., Johnson-Greene, D., & Dams-O'Connor, K. (2019). Neurocognitive status and return to work after moderate to severe traumatic brain injury. *Rehabilitation Psychology, 64*(4), 435–444. https://doi.org/10.1037/rep0000290

Holloway, M., Orr, D., & Clark-Wilson, J. (2019). Experiences of challenges and support among family members of people with acquired brain injury: A qualitative study in the UK. *Brain Injury, 33*(4), 401–411. https://doi.org/10.1080/02699052.2019.1566967

Howle, A. A., Baguley, I. J., & Brown, L. (2014). Management of dysphagia following traumatic brain injury. *Current Physical Medicine and Rehabilitation Reports, 2*(4), 219–230. https://doi.org/10.1007/s40141-014-0064-z

Hwang, P. H., Nelson, L. D., Sharon, J. D., McCrea, M. A., Dikmen, S. S., Markowitz, A. J., Manley, G. T., Temkin, N. R., & TRACK-TBI Investigators. (2022). Association between TBI-related hearing impairment and cognition: A TRACK-TBI study. *The Journal of Head Trauma Rehabilitation, 37*(5), E327–E335. https://doi.org/10.1097/HTR.0000000000000735

Ivanhoe, C. B., Durand-Sanchez, A., & Spier, F. (2022). Acute rehabilitation. In N. D. Zasler, D. I. Katz, R. D. Zafonte, D. B. Arciniegas, M. R. Bullock, F. M. Hammond, J. S. Kreutzer, R. Nakase-Richardson, & T. K. Watanabe (Eds.), *Brain injury medicine: Principles and practice* (3rd ed., pp. 366–384). Springer.

Jain, S., & Iverson, L. (2023). *Glasgow Coma Scale*. StatPearls. https://www.ncbi.nlm.nih.gov/books/NBK513298/.

Jennett, B. (1996). Clinical and pathological features of vegetative survival. In H. S. Levin, A. L. Benton, J. P. Muizelaar, & H. M. Eisenberg (Eds.), *Catastrophic brain injury*. Oxford University Press.

Jennett, B., & Bond, M. (1975). Assessment of outcome after severe brain damage. *Lancet (London, England), 1*(7905), 480–484. https://doi.org/10.1016/s0140-6736(75)92830-5

Jorge, R. E., & Arciniegas, D. B. (2014). Mood disorders after TBI. *The Psychiatric Clinics of North America, 37*(1), 13–29. https://doi.org/10.1016/j.psc.2013.11.005

Jorge, R. E., Robinson, R. G., Moser, D., Tateno, A., Crespo-Facorro, B., & Arndt, S. (2004). Major depression following traumatic brain injury. *Archives of General Psychiatry, 61*(1), 42–50. https://doi.org/10.1001/archpsyc.61.1.42

Katta-Charles, S., Tessler, J., & Horn, L. (2022). Possttraumatic headaches. In N. D. Zasler, D. I. Katz, R. D. Zafonte, D. B. Arciniegas, M. R. Bullock, F. M. Hammond, J. S. Kreutzer, R. Nakase-Richardson, & T. K. Watanabe (Eds.), *Brain injury medicine: Principles and practice* (3rd ed., pp. 366–384). Springer.

Kleffelgaard, I., Langhammer, B., Hellstrom, T., Sandhaug, M., Tamber, A. L., & Soberg, H. L. (2017). Dizziness-related disability following mild–moderate traumatic brain injury. *Brain Injury, 31*(11), 1436–1444. https://doi.org/10.1080/02699052.2017.1377348

Kothari, S., & Zhang, S. (2022). Prognosis after moderate to severe traumatic brain injury: A practical, evidence-based approach. In N. D. Zasler, D. I. Katz, R. D. Zafonte, D. B. Arciniegas, M. R. Bullock, F. M. Hammond, J. S. Kreutzer, R. Nakase-Richardson, & T. K. Watanabe (Eds.), *Brain injury medicine: Principles and practice* (3rd ed., pp. 248–266). Springer.

Krauss, J., Polemikos, M., & Jankovic, J. (2022). Movement disorders after traumatic brain injury. In N. D. Zasler, D. I. Katz, R. D. Zafonte, D. B. Arciniegas, M. R. Bullock, F. M. Hammond,

J. S. Kreutzer, R. Nakase-Richardson, & T. K. Watanabe (Eds.), *Brain injury medicine: Principles and practice* (3rd ed.). Springer.

Lau, B. C., Kontos, A. P., Collins, M. W., Mucha, A., & Lovell, M. R. (2011). Which on-field signs/symptoms predict protracted recovery from sport-related concussion among high school football players? *The American Journal of Sports Medicine, 39*(11), 2311–2318. https://doi.org/10.1177/0363546511410655

Lefevre-Dognin, C., Cogné, M., Perdrieau, V., Granger, A., Heslot, C., & Azouvi, P. (2021). Definition and epidemiology of mild traumatic brain injury. *Neurochirurgie, 67*(3), 218–221. https://doi.org/10.1016/j.neuchi.2020.02.002

Lequerica, A. H., Botticello, A. L., Lengenfelder, J., Chiaravalloti, N., Bushnik, T., Dijkers, M. P., Hammond, F. M., Kolakowsky-Hayner, S. A., & Rosenthal, J. (2017). Factors associated with remission of post-traumatic brain injury fatigue in the years following traumatic brain injury (TBI): A TBI model systems module study. *Neuropsychological Rehabilitation, 27*(7), 1019–1030. https://doi.org/10.1080/09602011.2016.1231120

Lippa, S. M., French, L. M., Bell, R. S., Brickell, T. A., & Lange, R. T. (2020). United States military service members demonstrate substantial and heterogeneous long-term neuropsychological dysfunction after moderate, severe, and penetrating traumatic brain injury. *Journal of Neurotrauma, 37*(4), 608–617. https://doi.org/10.1089/neu.2019.6696

Lu, J., Roe, C., Sigurdardottir, S., Andelic, N., & Forslund, M. (2018). Trajectory of functional independent measurements during first five years after moderate and severe traumatic brain injury. *Journal of Neurotrauma, 35*(14), 1596. https://doi.org/10.1089/neu.2017.5299

Marcus, H. J., Paine, H., Sargeant, M., Wolstenholme, S., Collins, K., Marroney, N., Arshad, Q., Tsang, K., Jones, B., Smith, R., Wilson, M. H., Rust, H. M., & Seemungal, B. M. (2019). Vestibular dysfunction in acute traumatic brain injury. *Journal of Neurology, 266*(10), 2430–2433. https://doi.org/10.1007/s00415-019-09403-z

Maskell, F., Chiarelli, P., & Isles, R. (2006). Dizziness after traumatic brain injury: Overview and measurement in the clinical setting. *Brain Injury, 20*(3), 293–305. https://doi.org/10.1080/02699050500488041

McKinlay, A., Grace, R., Horwood, J., Fergusson, D., & MacFarlane, M. (2009). Adolescent psychiatric symptoms following preschool childhood mild traumatic brain injury: Evidence from a birth cohort. *Journal of Head Trauma Rehabilitation, 24*(3), 221–227. https://doi.org/10.1097/HTR.0b013e3181a40590

Miles, A. (2022). Evaluation and treatment of swallowing problems. In N. D. Zasler, D. I. Katz, R. D. Zafonte, D. B. Arciniegas, M. R. Bullock, F. M. Hammond, J. S. Kreutzer, R. Nakase-Richardson, & T. K. Watanabe (Eds.), *Brain injury medicine: Principles and practice* (3rd ed.). Springer.

Mollayeva, T., Kendzerska, T., Mollayeva, S., Shapiro, C. M., Colantonio, A., & Cassidy, J. D. (2014). A systematic review of fatigue in patients with traumatic brain injury: The course, predictors and consequences. *Neuroscience & Biobehavioral Reviews, 47*, 684–716. https://doi.org/10.1016/j.neubiorev.2014.10.024

Morales, D. L., Diaz-Daza, O., Hlatky, R., & Hayman, L. A. (2007). *Brain, contusion*. http://emedicine.medscape.com/article/337782-overview.

Morgan, A. (2014). Dysarthria in children and adults with TBI. In S. McDonald, L. Togher, & C. Code (Eds.), *Social and communication disorders following traumatic brain injury* (2nd ed., pp. 218–257). Psychology Press.

Nakase-Richardson, R., Silva, M., Garcia, A., & Wittine, L. (2022). Sleep management after traumatic brain injury. In N. D. Zasler, D. I. Katz, R. D. Zafonte, D. B. Arciniegas, M. R. Bullock, F. M. Hammond, J. S. Kreutzer, R. Nakase-Richardson, & T. K. Watanabe (Eds.), *Brain injury medicine: Principles and practice* (3rd ed.). Springer.

Olsen, C. M., & Corrigan, J. D. (2022). Does traumatic brain injury cause risky substance use or substance use disorder? *Biological Psychiatry, 91*(5), 421–437. https://doi.org/10.1016/j.biopsych.2021.07.013

Pagulayan, K. F., Temkin, N. R., Machamer, J. E., & Dikmen, S. S. (2016). Patterns of alcohol use after traumatic brain injury. *Journal of Neurotrauma, 33*(14), 1390–1396. https://doi.org/10.1089/neu.2015.4071

Payne, W., De Jesus, O., & Payne, A. (2023, May 22). *Contrecoup brain injury*. StatPearls. Retrieved November 8, 2023, from https://www.ncbi.nlm.nih.gov/books/NBK536965/.

Ponsford, J. (2022). Psychological interventions for emotional and behavioral problems following traumatic brain injury. In N. D. Zasler, D. I. Katz, R. D. Zafonte, D. B. Arciniegas, M. R. Bullock, F. M. Hammond, J. S. Kreutzer, R. Nakase-Richardson, & T. K. Watanabe (Eds.), *Brain injury medicine: Principles and practice* (3rd ed.). Springer.

Ponsford, J., Alway, Y., & Gould, K. R. (2018). Epidemiology and natural history of psychiatric disorders after TBI. *The Journal of Neuropsychiatry and Clinical Neurosciences, 30*(4), 262–270. https://doi.org/10.1176/appi.neuropsych.18040093

Ponsford, J., Whelan-Goodinson, R., & Bahar-Fuchs, A. (2007). Alcohol and drug use following traumatic brain injury: A prospective study. *Brain Injury, 21*(13–14), 1385–1392. https://doi.org/10.1080/02699050701796960

Reiley, A. S., Vickory, F. M., Funderburg, S. E., Cesario, R. A., & Clendaniel, R. A. (2017). How to diagnose cervicogenic dizziness. *Archives of Physiotherapy, 7*(1), 12. https://doi.org/10.1186/s40945-017-0040-x

Ripley, D., & Greenwald, B. (2022). Posttraumatic brain injury fatigue: Assessment and treatment. In N. D. Zasler, D. I. Katz, R. D. Zafonte, D. B. Arciniegas, M. R. Bullock, F. M. Hammond, J. S. Kreutzer, R. Nakase-Richardson, & T. K. Watanabe (Eds.), *Brain injury medicine: Principles and practice* (3rd ed.). Springer.

Riveros Gilardi, B., Muñoz López, J. I., Hernández Villegas, A. C., Garay Mora, J. A., Rico Rodríguez, O. C., Chávez Appendini, R., De la Mora Malváez, M., & Higuera Calleja, J. A. (2019). Types of cerebral herniation and their imaging features. *RadioGraphics, 39*(6), 1598–1610. https://doi.org/10.1148/rg.2019190018

Ronkainen, A., Hernesniemi, J., Puranen, M., Niemitukia, L., Vanninen, R., Ryynänen, M., Kuivaniemi, H., & Tromp, G. (1997). Familial intracranial aneurysms. *Lancet, 349*(9049), 380–384. https://doi.org/10.1016/S0140-6736(97)80009-8

Saltychev, M., Eskola, M., Tenovuo, O., & Laimi, K. (2013). Return to work after traumatic brain injury: Systematic review. *Brain Injury, 27*(13–14), 1516–1527. https://doi.org/10.3109/02699052.2013.831131

Sander, A. M. (2019). Sexual functioning. In J. M. Silver, T. W. McAllister, & D. B. Arciniegas (Eds.), *Textbook of traumatic brain injury* (3rd ed., pp. 535–544). American Psychiatric Association.

Sander, A. M., Sandel, E., Moreno, A., & Delmonico, R. (2022). Sexuality and intimacy following traumatic brain injury. In N. D. Zasler, D. I. Katz, R. D. Zafonte, D. B. Arciniegas, M. R. Bullock, F. M. Hammond, J. S. Kreutzer, R. Nakase-Richardson, & T. K. Watanabe (Eds.), *Brain injury medicine: Principles and practice* (3rd ed.). Springer.

Schretlen, D. J., & Shapiro, A. M. (2003). A quantitative review of the effects of traumatic brain injury on cognitive functioning. *International Review of Psychiatry, 15*(4), 341–349. https://doi.org/10.1080/09540260310001606728

Seel, R. T., Macciocchi, S., & Kreutzer, J. S. (2010). Clinical considerations for the diagnosis of major depression after moderate to severe TBI. *The Journal of Head Trauma Rehabilitation, 25*(2), 99–112. https://doi.org/10.1097/HTR.0b013e3181ce3966

Sherer, M., Katz, D. I., Bodien, Y. G., Arciniegas, D. B., Block, C., Blum, S., Doiron, M., Frey, K., Giacino, J. T., Graf, M. J. P., Greenwald, B., Hammond, F. M., Kalmar, K., Kean, J., Kraus, M. F., Nakase-Richardson, R., Pavawalla, S., Rosenbaum, A., Stuss, D. T., & Yablon, S. A. (2020). Post-traumatic confusional state: A case definition and diagnostic criteria. *Archives of Physical Medicine and Rehabilitation, 101*(11), 2041–2050. https://doi.org/10.1016/j.apmr.2020.06.021

Sigurdardottir, S., Andelic, N., Wehling, E., Anke, A., Skandsen, T., Holthe, O. O., Manskow, U. S., & Roe, C. (2020). Return to work after severe traumatic brain injury: A national study with a one-year follow-up of neurocognitive and behavioural outcomes. *Neuropsychological Rehabilitation, 30*(2), 281–297. https://doi.org/10.1080/09602011.2018.1462719

Simpson, G. K., Sabaz, M., & Daher, M. (2013). Prevalence, clinical features, and correlates of inappropriate sexual behavior after traumatic brain injury: A multicenter study. *The Journal of Head Trauma Rehabilitation, 28*(3), 202–210. https://doi.org/10.1097/HTR.0b013e31828dc5ae

Steward, K. A., & Kretzmer, T. (2022). Anosognosia in moderate-to-severe traumatic brain injury: A review of prevalence, clinical correlates, and diversity considerations. *The Clinical Neuropsychologist, 36*(8), 2021–2040. https://doi.org/10.1080/13854046.2021.1967452

Svensson, F., Much, A., & Exner, C. (2023). Personality changes after acquired brain injury and their effects on rehabilitation outcomes. *Neuropsychological Rehabilitation, 33*(2), 305–324. https://doi.org/10.1080/09602011.2021.2011749

Teasdale, G., & Jennett, B. (1974). Assessment of coma and impaired consciousness. A practical scale. *Lancet, 2*(7872), 81–84. https://doi.org/10.1016/s0140-6736(74)91639-0

Teasdale, G., & Jennett, B. (1976). Assessment and prognosis of coma after head injury. *Acta Neurochirurgica, 34*(1–4), 45–55. https://doi.org/10.1007/BF01405862

Togher, L., Keegan, L., & Elbourn, E. (2022). Assessment and treatment of speech and language disorders following traumatic brain injury. In N. D. Zasler, D. I. Katz, R. D. Zafonte, D. B. Arciniegas, M. R. Bullock, F. M. Hammond, J. S. Kreutzer, R. Nakase-Richardson, & T. K. Watanabe (Eds.), *Brain injury medicine: Principles and practice* (3rd ed., pp. 192–214). Springer.

Towne, A., & Yablon, S. (2022). Posttraumatic seizures and epilepsy. In N. D. Zasler, D. I. Katz, R. D. Zafonte, D. B. Arciniegas, M. R. Bullock, F. M. Hammond, J. S. Kreutzer, R. Nakase-Richardson, & T. K. Watanabe (Eds.), *Brain injury medicine: Principles and practice* (3rd ed.). Springer.

Traumatic Brain Injury Center of Excellence Annual Report: DoD numbers for traumatic brain injury worldwide. (2022). Annual report. Defense Health Agency. https://health.mil/Military-Health-Topics/Centers-of-Excellence/Traumatic-Brain-Injury-Center-of-Excellence.

U.S. Department of Labor Bureau of Labor Statistics. (2023). *The employment situation*.

Vlak, M. H. M., Rinkel, G. J. E., Greebe, P., Greving, J. P., & Algra, A. (2013). Lifetime risks for aneurysmal subarachnoid haemorrhage: Multivariable risk stratification. *Journal of Neurology, Neurosurgery & Psychiatry, 84*(6), 619. https://doi.org/10.1136/jnnp-2012-303783

Wat, R., Mammi, M., Paredes, J., Haines, J., Alasmari, M., Liew, A., Lu, V. M., Arnaout, O., Smith, T. R., Gormley, W. B., Aglio, L. S., Mekary, R. A., & Zaidi, H. (2019). The effectiveness of antiepileptic medications as prophylaxis of early seizure in patients with traumatic brain injury compared with placebo or no treatment: A systematic review and meta-analysis. *World Neurosurgery, 122*, 433–440. https://doi.org/10.1016/j.wneu.2018.11.076

Weddell, R. A., & Wood, R. L. (2018). Perceived personality change after traumatic brain injury II: comparing participant and informant perspectives. *Brain Injury, 32*(4), 442–452. https://doi.org/10.1080/02699052.2018.1429657

Weil, Z. M., Corrigan, J. D., & Karelina, K. (2018). Alcohol use disorder and traumatic brain injury. *Alcohol Research: Current Reviews, 39*(2), 171–180.

Whitney, S., & Furman, J. (2022). Dizziness and imbalance. In N. D. Zasler, D. I. Katz, R. D. Zafonte, D. B. Arciniegas, M. R. Bullock, F. M. Hammond, J. S. Kreutzer, R. Nakase-Richardson, & T. K. Watanabe (Eds.), *Brain injury medicine: Principles and practice* (3rd ed.). Springer.

Wilde, E. A., Hovenden, S., Finuf, C. S., Bigler, E. D., Shenton, M. E., Tate, D. F., & Hunter, J. V. (2022). Structural neuroimaging. In N. D. Zasler, D. I. Katz, R. D. Zafonte, D. B. Arciniegas, M. R. Bullock, F. M. Hammond, J. S. Kreutzer, R. Nakase-Richardson, & T. K. Watanabe (Eds.), *Brain injury medicine: Principles and practice* (3rd ed.). Springer.

Wortzel, H., & Brenner, L. (2022). Neuropsychiatric symptoms and syndromes. In N. D. Zasler, D. I. Katz, R. D. Zafonte, D. B. Arciniegas, M. R. Bullock, F. M. Hammond, J. S. Kreutzer, R. Nakase-Richardson, & T. K. Watanabe (Eds.), *Brain injury medicine: Principles and practice* (3rd ed.). Springer.

Wu, C.-H., Tsai, T.-H., Su, Y.-F., Zhang, Z.-H., Liu, W., Wu, M.-K., Chang, C.-H., Kuo, K.-L., Lu, Y.-Y., & Lin, C.-L. (2016). Traumatic brain injury and substance related disorder: A 10-year nationwide cohort study in Taiwan. *Neural Plasticity, 2016*, 1–8. https://doi.org/10.1155/2016/8030676

Chapter 26
Paediatric Traumatic Brain Injury (TBI): Overview

Cathy Catroppa, Louise Crowe, Nicholas P. Ryan, Edith N. Botchway, Nikita Sood, and Vicki A. Anderson

Key Points and Chapter Summary

- The most common type of TBI in children and adolescents is a closed head injury.
- Paediatric traumatic brain injury (TBI) can result in long-term cognitive, behavioural, social and functional difficulties, particularly for those sustaining more severe injuries.
- Neuropsychological testing is important in identifying residual deficits and assisting in designing rehabilitation and educational programs to address deficits.
- More research is needed to adapt and develop intervention programs and to then evaluate the feasibility and efficacy of these programs.

C. Catroppa (✉)
Department of Psychology, Australian Centre for Child Neuropsychology Studies, Murdoch Children's Research Institute, Royal Children's Hospital, University of Melbourne, Melbourne, Australia
e-mail: cathy.catroppa@mcri.edu.au

L. Crowe · E. N. Botchway · N. Sood
Australian Centre for Child Neuropsychology Studies, Murdoch Children's Research Institute, Melbourne, VIC, Australia

N. P. Ryan
Australian Centre for Child Neuropsychology Studies, Murdoch Children's Research Institute, Melbourne, Australia

M. R. Schoenberg, J. G. Scott (eds.), *The Little Black Book of Neuropsychology*,
https://doi.org/10.1007/978-3-032-07777-6_26

Overview

The aim of this chapter is to provide an overview of the: (1) prevalence of paediatric TBI; (2) the symptoms associated with paediatric TBI; (3) outcomes and predictors of paediatric TBI; and (4) rehabilitation in this area.

Definition and Prevalence of Paediatric TBI

TBI is a major cause of mortality and disability worldwide, and is associated with a three-fold increase in cognitive, behavioural, social and vocational difficulties (Corrigan et al., 2010; Mathers & Loncar, 2006). The incidence of TBI based on hospital admissions has been reported to be between 100 and 300 per 100,000 per year for children and young adults (Cassidy et al., 2004; Crowe et al., 2009; Goldstein & Levin, 1987; Langlois et al., 2006).

The most common type of TBI in children and adolescents is a closed head injury (Andriessen et al., 2010; Feng et al., 2010; Gaetz, 2004). Specifically, closed head injuries (CHI) lead to brain damage because of the initial compression of the head against an object and also because the brain can move forward, backward and side-to-side (a rotational effect) within the skull. The movements can lead to brain damage at the site of impact (coup) and opposite to the point of impact (contre-coup), as well as stretching and damaging nerve axons and blood vessels, contributing to diffuse axonal injury (Andriessen et al., 2010; Barkhoudarian et al., 2011; Sharp et al., 2014).

Primary brain injury is due to mechanical damage that occurs at the time of injury as a result of contact between brain matter and the interior skull (e.g., lacerations, contusions, fractures, haemorrhage). Internal rotational and velocity forces can also lead to tearing and stretching of axons within white matter (Cloots et al., 2011; Levin et al., 2010; Matsukawa et al., 2011; Wilde et al., 2006). Following the primary injury, secondary effects, such as hypoxia, seizures and oedema, may also occur. An increase in cerebro-spinal fluid or cerebral blood or extracellular fluid will result in raised intracranial pressure (ICP; Greve & Zink, 2009; Papoutsis et al., 2014; Shlosberg et al., 2010). Neurochemical processes involving elevated glutamate, aspirate and excitatory amino acids also disrupt cell function (Farkas & Povlishock, 2007; Greve & Zink, 2009; Ichkova et al., 2017; Popernack et al., 2014; Richards et al., 2003).

V. A. Anderson
Department of Psychology, Australian Centre for Child Neuropsychology Studies, Murdoch Children's Research Institute, Royal Children's Hospital, University of Melbourne, Parkville, Melbourne, Australia
e-mail: Vicki.anderson@rch.org.au

Key Points: Pediatric TBI Mechanisms of Brain Damage

- Primary brain injury is due to mechanical damage that occurs at the time of injury as a result of contact between brain matter and the interior skull.
- Brain injury may also result from secondary factors such as hypoxia, seizures, oedema, ICP and neurochemical changes—it is these factors that medical staff treat in order to minimize/prevent further brain injury.

Symptoms of TBI

Review of Symptoms of Mild TBI

Mild TBI is most prevalent in the 5–14 age range (Crowe et al., 2009; Russo et al., 2012; Valerio & Illes, 2012). In the weeks post-injury, fatigue, sleep disturbance, headache, drowsiness, irritability, labile mood, dizziness and nausea and emesis may occur (Eisenberg et al., 2014; Nacajauskaite et al., 2006). Research suggests these physical, psychological and cognitive symptoms resolve by 3–6 months post-injury (Belanger & Vanderploeg, 2005; Carroll et al., 2004; Rohling et al., 2011). However, a group, both children and adults continue to experience such symptoms, and go on to develop psychological and cognitive problems including anxiety, irritability, depression, reduced speed of information processing, attention, memory, executive control academic performance and social withdrawal (Anderson et al., 2001; Catale et al., 2009; Li et al., 2017; McCrory et al., 2013). This has led to the inclusion of a subdivision into mild and mild complicated TBI. Mild complicated TBI is distinguished from mild TBI by the presence of subtle structural brain abnormalities and the possibility of neurochemical effects, hence more at the 'severe' extreme of the mild TBI spectrum (McKinlay, 2010; Roberts et al., 1995; Yeates, 1999).

Review of Symptoms of Moderate–Severe TBI

Moderate–severe TBI is often associated with loss of consciousness (LOC), post-traumatic amnesia (PTA) and/or focal or diffuse neurological signs. Early assessment of the level of consciousness is essential, as it gives an indication of how the initial brain injury is impacting brain function (Miller, 1991). The Glasgow Coma Scale (GCS; Teasdale & Jennett, 1974) is widely used as a measure of responsiveness/consciousness. The GCS measures three aspects of behaviour—eye opening, motor responses and verbal responses (see Table 26.1). When using the GCS, the

Table 26.1 Glasgow Coma Scale (GCS)

Category	Description	Score
Eye opening	Spontaneous	4
	To command	3
	To pain	2
	Nil	1
Motor Response	Obeys commands	6
	Localizes pain	5
	Normal flexion	4
	Abnormal flexion	3
	Extension	2
	Nil	1
Verbal Response	Oriented	5
	Disoriented	4
	Words only	3
	Sounds only	2
	Nil	1
Behavioural response[a]	Smiles, oriented to sound, follows objects	5
	Consolable crying, inappropriate interactions	4
	Inconsistently consolable, moaning	3
	Inconsolable, restless and irritable	2
	No response	1

[a]Behavioural response replaces Verbal Response for children of preschool age and below (adapted from Teasdale & Jennett, 1974)

duration of coma (length of time the GCS is less than or equal to eight) is calculated by serial observations (usually 4 hourly), and consists of the time span in which there is no eye opening, an inability to obey commands and the absence of comprehensible speech.

The duration of post-traumatic amnesia (PTA) has also been argued to be a useful measure of the severity of diffuse brain damage (Brown et al., 2005; Rutter et al., 1983); The PTA period refers to a post-injury period of confusion and memory loss, after regaining consciousness, during which the patient is disoriented and unable to register day-to-day information, with older memories relatively resistant to cerebral insult. Therefore, PTA is usually measured up to the point where memory for everyday ongoing events is continuous and reliable (Ahmed et al., 2000).

Table 26.2 Symptoms/categorization of childhood TBI

	Mild TBI	Mild–complicated	Moderate TBI	Severe TBI
GCS	13–15	13–15	9–12	8 or less
LOC	Less than 1 h	Less than 1 h	1–24 h	Greater than 24 h
PTA	Less than 24 h	Less than 24 h	1–7 days	Greater than 7 days
Neurological Signs	No	Yes[a]	Yes[a]	Yes[a]
Abnormal Imaging	No	Yes[a]	Yes[a]	Yes[a]

Based/adapted from Begali (1992); Goldstein and Harvey (1992); Yeates (1999)
[a]May be present

The presence of neurological signs is an indicator of a moderate–severe TBI. Such neurological signs, as reported in research conducted by our research group (Anderson & Catroppa, 2006; Catroppa & Anderson, 2003), may include children with differing degrees of hemiparesis, poor motor control, post-injury seizures and hearing loss. Additionally, children with a moderate–severe TBI often have abnormalities revealed by imaging techniques such as X-ray, computed tomography (CT) and magnetic resonance imaging (MRI; Wilde et al., 2006; Wilson et al., 1988). Table 26.2 provides a summary of symptoms used to classify (and distinguish between) mild, moderate and severe TBI.

Differences Between Paediatric TBI and Adult TBI

As in the adult literature, residual physical, cognitive, psychological/psychiatric, social, educational and vocational problems can occur following a diffuse brain injury sustained in childhood (Engberg & Teasdale, 2004; Hoofien et al., 2001). However, unlike TBI in adults, the developmental level of the child, in addition to the child's family and psychosocial support base, is of extreme importance with regard to long-term outcome (Catroppa et al., 2008, 2012; Finnanger et al., 2015; Kurowski et al., 2011; Yeates et al., 2010). It has been argued that the developing brain is particularly vulnerable to brain trauma, therefore derailing normal developmental processes (Anderson et al., 2010; Catroppa et al., 2012), where skills not developed at the time of injury may be at most risk (Dennis, 1989). Several demographic variables have also been shown to significantly affect recovery from TBI among children. Such factors include age at the time of injury, family support, access to educational accommodation and appropriate intervention in psychological or psychosocial difficulties post-TBI (Anderson et al., 2001, 2005, 2011, 2012).

Proposed Neuropsychological Assessment Protocol Post Childhood TBI (Clinical/Research)

Important factors to consider when conducting all assessments in paediatric TBI:

- Develop and maintain good rapport
- Monitor the child/adolescent for fatigue and anxiety/frustration
- Allow for short breaks during the assessment to ensure attention and motivation are maintained.
- Test in rooms that minimize noise

Clinical Assessment

The clinician will decide on an assessment battery taking into account: (1) the referral question(s); (2) the child's areas of difficulty as well as the child's age; (3) questions or concerns of the child's primary care giver(s). Referral may be from various sources including a neurologist, a neurosurgeon, a general practitioner, a teacher or the parents. Common purposes for referral include the identification and description of neuropsychological deficits (and preserved functions) following TBI to assist with diagnosis and rehabilitative efforts (and/or academic programming). Assessments may indicate whether specific skills (e.g., writing, reading, memory, attention) have been 'damaged' due to the injury. Such evaluations are useful in guiding interventions in academic and behavioural management treatments.

When planning the assessment, it is essential that the referral question has been addressed (e.g., identify cognitive deficits, assist in developing rehabilitation programming and/or aid in school re-integration). We generally encourage the clinical assessment to incorporate a measure of general cognitive functioning (i.e., intellectual functioning) along with assessment of attention/executive, memory/learning, language, visuoperceptual/visuoconstructional skills and an assessment of mood/affect. After evaluation of common neuropsychological domains (and identifying areas of strengths and weakness) the clinician can assess for specific processes or skills which are dysfunctional. We also undertake a qualitative assessment of the child's behaviour, for example, whether the child is fidgeting, anxious/depressed, withdrawn, as this may provide assessment of brain–behaviour relationships not easily measured by currently available psychometric instruments.

Research Assessment

A neuropsychological assessment protocol for research purposes will be determined by the hypothesis(es) of the study. When conducting research in our laboratory, feedback is provided to the family and child, and this is often in the form of a neuropsychological report. When required, and with consent from the family, a child may be referred to other clinicians for further assessment or intervention and the researcher may liaise with the child's school and provide information regarding the child's needs.

Outcome and Recovery from TBI

Outcome Following Mild TBI

Outcome from mild head injury in children, which comprises up to 90% of all paediatric TBI (McKinlay et al., 2008), is not well defined. Some argue mild TBI in children/adolescents is associated with either no detectable sequelae or full recovery (Giza & Prins, 2006), while others report significant, ongoing problems (Anderson et al., 2011; Barlow et al., 2010; McKinlay et al., 2002, 2009; Yeates et al., 2009), perhaps dependent upon whether the injury is at the more 'severe' extreme of the mild TBI spectrum.

Cognitive aspects of post-concussion syndrome include deficits in speed of information processing, memory and attention/executive control functions (Babikian et al., 2011; Catale et al., 2009; Königs et al., 2015; Papoutsis et al., 2014). Deficits in functional outcomes such as sleep are also reported in childhood mild TBI, and can cause physical, psychological or physiological distress and impairments in daytime functioning (Gagner et al., 2015). Recent evidence suggests a high prevalence (30–90%) of sleep disturbances in this TBI population (Kaufman et al., 2001; Landry-Roy et al., 2017; Tham et al., 2015), and while some children recover from sleep disturbances by 3 months post-injury (Schmidt et al., 2015), others experience difficulties several years post-injury (Pillar et al., 2003; Theadom et al., 2016). Insomnia and excessive daytime sleepiness are the most sleep disturbances reported in children with TBI. Although the reasons for these disturbances are not fully understood, emerging evidence suggests factors such as pre-existing sleep disturbances, depressive symptoms, pain, gender and high body mass index (Landry-Roy et al., 2017; Pillar et al., 2003; Tham et al., 2015, 2012).

Moderate–Severe TBI Outcome

Studies of outcome and recovery from TBI based on preschool children and school-aged children have identified acute and long-term (up to 16 years post-injury) impairments in many areas including attentional capacity (Anderson et al., 2005; Catroppa et al., 2007, 2011), memory and learning (Anderson & Catroppa, 2007; Levin et al., 2004), psychomotor skills (Bawden et al., 1985), linguistic abilities (Crowe et al., 2014), executive functions (Beauchamp et al., 2011; Ganesalingam et al., 2011; Muscara et al., 2008a; Nadebaum et al., 2007), social competence (Ganesalingam et al., 2011; Muscara et al., 2008b), functional skills (Anderson et al., 2005; Catroppa et al., 2008), educational ability (Ewing-Cobbs et al., 2004), vocational outcome (Hoofien et al., 2001) and psychosocial outcomes (Rosema et al., 2014). (Refer to Table 26.3). The recovery of these skills may differ depending on severity and age at injury as well as environmental factors (Anderson et al., 2000; Anderson et al., 2005).

Table 26.3 Common consequences of childhood traumatic brain injury

Domain	Specific skills
Neurological impairment	Gross and fine-motor incoordination Cranial nerve function/sensory loss Speech: e.g., dysarthria, aphasia Medical complications: e.g., epilepsy, hydrocephalus
Cognitive impairment	Intellectual impairment Attention Memory and learning Executive function Speed of processing
Educational impairment	Reduced progress in content-related areas, e.g., reading, mathematics, Processing/retention difficulties, e.g., attention, processing speed, memory Writing difficulties Need for specialist educational placement or support
Emotional/behavioural	Adjustment difficulties, e.g., reduced self-esteem Psychiatric disorders: e.g., depression, anxiety, post-traumatic stress Regulatory dysfunction: disinhibition, impulsivity, apathy, reduced insight
Social consequences	Social withdrawal and isolation Social anxiety Inappropriate social skills, reduced social awareness
Lifestyle change	Reduced independence Impaired functional communication and mobility Increased need for additional assistance Reduced recreational options Difficulties maintaining pre-injury relationships

From Anderson and Catroppa (2006)

Children who suffer a moderate–severe TBI often exhibit deficits in neuropsychological, behavioural and social areas of functioning. Findings from our laboratory give an indication of the possible recovery of skills in these areas over time (Anderson et al., 2005). Figures 26.1, 26.2, and 26.3 show recovery in the areas of intellectual, adaptive, educational skills and memory, for a paediatric group with TBI (injured between the ages of 1 and 7 years). These data illustrate the vulnerability of children injured at this young age, with the severe TBI injury group generally performing below the level of the control children and those with a mild and also moderate TBI. Figure 26.4 was included to demonstrate the possible impact of age at injury on full scale intellectual ability (FSIQ), where those with a severe injury perform poorer when compared to children with mild or moderate injuries, regardless of age at injury. However, children sustaining an injury earlier in life tend to exhibit poorer outcomes, with younger children who sustain a severe TBI exhibiting the least recovery (poorest outcome) (figures adapted from Anderson et al., 2005, 2006).

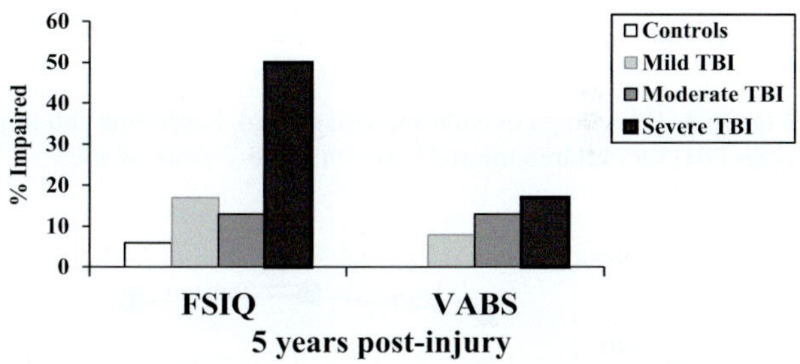

Fig. 26.1 Percentage impaired for full-scale intellectual quotient (FSIQ) and adaptive functioning (VABS) at 5 years post-injury for children injured between 1 and 7 years of age

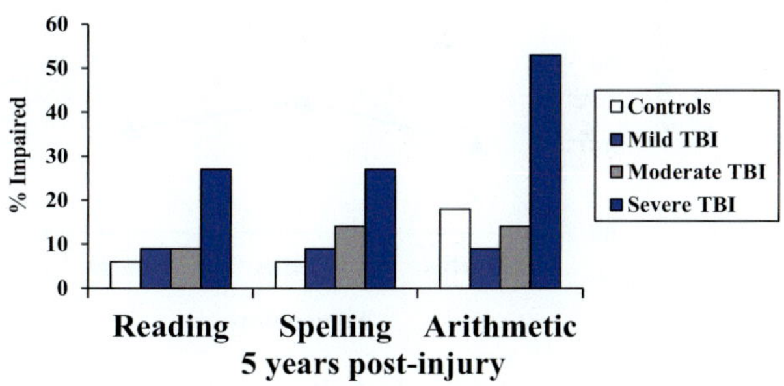

Fig. 26.2 Percentage impaired for educational skills at 5 years post-injury for children injured between 1 and 7 years of age

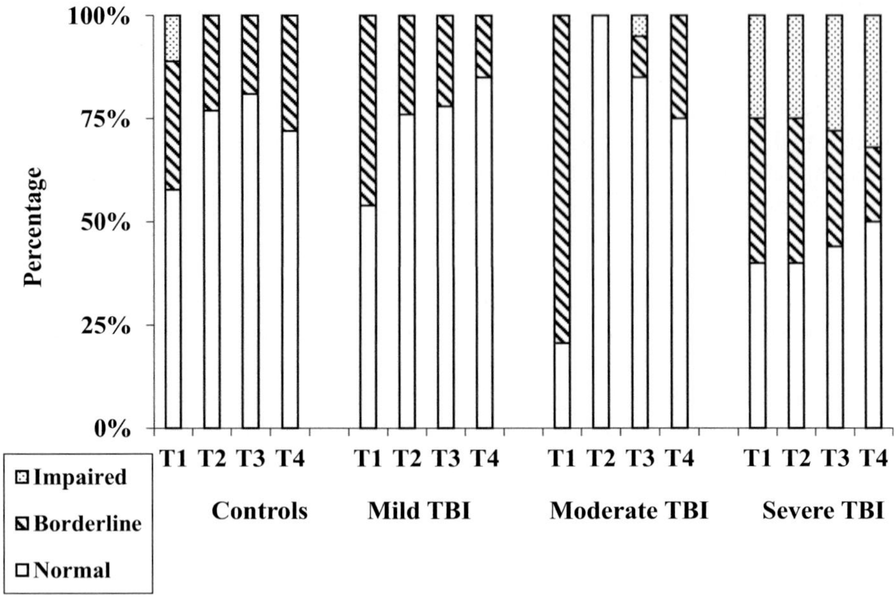

Fig. 26.3 Percentage of children with normal, borderline and impaired memory (acute 18 months post-TBI) for children injured between 1 and 7 years of age

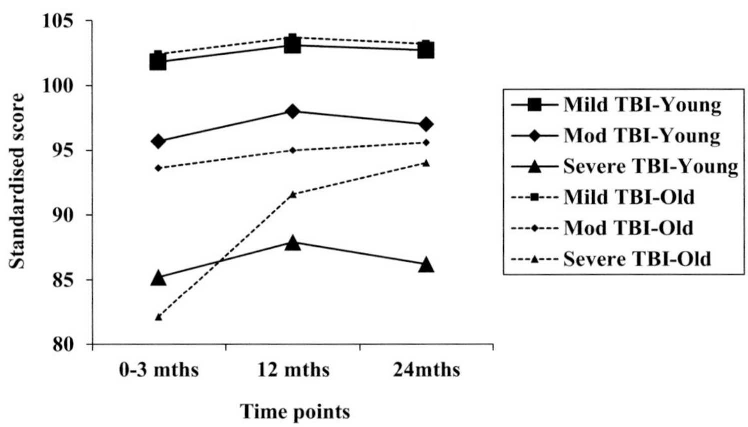

Fig. 26.4 Recovery trajectory for FSIQ for children injured between 1 and 7 years of ages (TBI-young) and between 8 and 12 years of age (TBI-old)

Developmental Considerations

Traumatic Brain Injury Sustained in Infancy and Preschool Years

The outcomes of TBI in children have long been dominated by a focus on school-aged children and adolescents. This is despite TBI occurring at high frequencies in babies and young children. Whilst inflicted injury sometimes referred to as 'shaken-baby' is highlighted in this age group, the major causes of TBI are accidental. For this age group, falls tops the list as the most common cause, responsible for between 75 and 90% of all TBI (Crowe, Catroppa, Anderson, et al., 2012). Consistent with other age groups, the majority of injuries sustained are mild. Children younger than 6 months of age have the highest risk of moderate to severe TBI, with rolling or falling off furniture over 1 m and being dropped by a caregiver, the two main mechanisms (Crowe et al., 2012). Severity of TBI in this age groups is typically defined by Glasgow Coma Scale (GCS); however, a modified version is used to account for language limitations (Reilly et al., 1988).

Sequelae following TBI in young children are somewhat under-researched. This is likely because of the difficulty in obtaining a premorbid level of functioning, the vast developmental changes that occur month to month, and the widely accepted variation in ascertainment of developmental milestones. Long-term follow-up of this group is also difficult as families are often quite mobile before children start school and loss to follow-up is common. From the research available, in terms of intellectual function (IQ), there tends to be a dose–response relationship, that is, greater severity of TBI pairs with greater impairments (Crowe, Catroppa, Babl, et al., 2012; Ewing-Cobbs et al., 1997). Children with moderate to severe TBI tend to perform below children with mild TBI and typically developing children on measures of IQ, language, attention and executive function (Crowe et al., 2013, 2014; Ewing-Cobbs et al., 2006; Treble-Barna et al., 2017). Further investigation for children with mild TBI has shown impairments in specific skills such as attention (Crowe et al., 2013), executive functions including verbal fluency (Anderson et al., 2001) and narrative memory (Anderson et al., 2001).

Poor functional outcomes and behavioural difficulties have also been highlighted as being associated with TBI at an early age (Karver et al., 2012; Wade et al., 2016), however for those injured at the youngest ages these are not always apparent early on (Crowe et al., 2012; Wetherington et al., 2010). A recent focus on social competence and social cognition has suggested that children with TBI of all severities, injured in the preschool years, are at risk for deficits in these areas (Robinson et al., 2014; Walz et al., 2009). Children with TBI display deficits in executive function, attention and language, all of which contribute to social skills. Additionally, from work on older children, TBI results in disruption in the connectivity of cortical, subcortical and limbic brain regions which has ongoing impacts on social competence (Ryan et al., 2016).

Much has been made of whether younger children have a greater vulnerability to ongoing difficulties. Physiologically, young children and infants may be particularly susceptible to damage after TBI. Babies and young children have a thin and pliable skull and a disproportionately large and heavy head with weak neck muscles, and increased elasticity of blood vessels, which intensifies susceptibility to rotational and shearing forces (Case, 2008; Hahn et al., 1988; Margulies & Thibault, 2000). The first 2 years of life are also a period of increased dendritization and synaptogenesis (Huttenlocher & Dabholkar, 1997). Work by Kriel et al. (1989), highlighted that children injured before school age (6 years) had poorer cognitive and motor outcomes than children injured over 6 years. This finding has been replicated by some (Anderson & Moore, 1995; Karver et al., 2012; Verger et al., 2000), and contradicted by others (Ewing-Cobbs et al., 1997). When a critical period model is considered, with recovery dependent on neurological and cognitive development at the time of injury rather than a focus on early vulnerability, children in the infant (0–2 years) and preschool group (3–6 years) performed below older children on measures of processing speed and performance IQ, but had comparable performance to the middle childhood group (7–9 years, Crowe et al., 2012). Other than age and injury severity, the environment including family resources, parent education and levels of family conflict all influence outcomes of TBI. Children from families of greater social disadvantage and family dysfunction are at greatest risk of poor outcomes (Crowe et al., 2012)

From what is known, TBI in the early years, that is before school age, is associated with impairments across cognitive and social domains. Recovery is influenced by injury severity and environmental factors. Longitudinal research in this area is limited, so the long-term impacts are unclear. Research by McKinlay et al. (2009), focused on the outcomes of mild TBI in this age group, suggested the presence of attention and behavioural symptoms long-term. It is likely that this is true for cognition and also for children who sustain more severe TBIs. Previous longitudinal research studies following paediatric TBI underline the importance of long-term follow-up as children transition into adolescence and adulthood.

Injuries Sustained in Childhood

Long-term neurobehavioural consequences have been reported in children post-TBI across severity groups, but especially for those of more severe injury (Hessen et al., 2008, 2007; Treble-Barna et al., 2017). Findings suggest lingering long-term deficits in several domains such as cognition (Jonsson et al., 2004; Yeates et al., 2002), education and vocation (Anderson et al., 2012; Catroppa et al., 2008), psychological outcomes including emotional, social and behavioural problems (Anson & Ponsford, 2006; Cooper et al., 2014; Ponsford et al., 2008) and general quality of life in children post severe TBI. Prospective longitudinal study, at 16 years post childhood TBI, from our research lab has reported higher risk of developing psychological problems specifically internalizing symptoms such as depression, anxiety and withdrawal (Rosema et al., 2014), as well as externalizing symptoms such as aggression and hyperactivity (Rosema et al., 2014). This research highlights that planning for evaluation of adult outcomes of child TBI is crucial. This evaluation must take into account developmental trajectories, reorganization of structure and function, compensatory mechanisms, habituation, practice effects, real-world functioning, changing life situations and the demands of the current environment (Catroppa et al., 2016). Collaboration with health professionals and rehabilitation workers is imperative for life-long management of impairments caused by paediatric TBI.

Predictors of Outcome

Injury Severity and Environmental Factors

Injury severity (as indicated by the GCS, length of PTA, neurological signs and imaging techniques—see section "Imaging Techniques" below in this chapter) has been identified as a reliable predictor of impairment in physical, cognitive and educational domains, with more severe TBI related to greater problems across all age groups (Kinsella et al., 1997; Königs et al., 2012; Smitherman et al., 2016). However, behavioural outcome may be better predicted by environmental factors, such as socioeconomic status (SES) and family functioning (Anderson et al., 2001; Bedell, 2008; Chapman et al., 2010).

Premorbid and Developmental Factors

Premorbid factors (Johnson et al., 2009; Kaldoja & Anneli, 2012) also contribute to long-term outcome. A clear relationship has been found between pre-injury learning and behavioural problems post-injury (Anderson & Catroppa, 2006). Psychiatric problems may increase post-injury for children where such problems were present pre-injury (Gerring & Wade, 2012). Also, as discussed above, younger age, or developmental level, at the time of injury (Anderson, Catroppa, Haritou, et al., 2005; Donders & Warschausky, 2007; Johnson et al., 2009; Senathi-Raja et al., 2010) has also been found to predict outcome. See Table 26.4.

Table 26.4 Predictors of outcome from childhood brain injury

Factors found to contribute to outcome from childhood brain injury
Injury factors
Severity (mild, moderate, severe)
Nature (diffuse, focal)
Disability (post-traumatic epilepsy, neurological signs, physical/speech impairment)
Developmental factors
Age at injury
Developmental stage
Pre-injury factors
Pre-injury child function: cognitive ability, personality
Pre-injury family factors: family function, parent mental health
Gender
Environmental factors
Socioeconomic status
Access to resources—educational, rehabilitation

From Anderson and Catroppa (2006)

Key Points: Variables Affecting Outcome from TBI

- Severity of injury
- Environmental factors
- Premorbid status
- Developmental considerations

Imaging Techniques

(a) *High-Resolution Morphometric MRI*

Recent advances in neuroimaging may assist in identifying alterations in the structural architecture following traumatic brain injury, in a brain that may appear deceptively 'normal' on conventional imaging sequences, such as computed tomography. Morphometric MRI permits quantitative characterization of the volume, shape and composition of regions within the immature brain.

In the first of a series of landmark studies in this area, Wilde et al. (2012) employed a longitudinal prospective design to evaluate the extent and neuroanatomical distribution of structural changes to the cortical mantle from 3- to 18-months post-TBI. Results from the 3-month time interval revealed that compared to age-matched orthopaedic injury controls, children with moderate–severe TBI demonstrate reduced cortical thickness bilaterally in a distributed network of regions, including superior frontal, dorsolateral frontal, orbital frontal and anterior cingulate areas, a pattern of changes which were suggested to reflect neuronal loss demonstrated in postmortem brains. Moreover, analysis of longitudinal change in the TBI versus an orthopaedic injury (OI) group revealed that, despite evidence for progressive injury-induced atrophic change in large areas of the parietal and occipital lobes, cortical thinning in the anterior brain regions was notably absent following TBI, with some evidence of cortical thickness increases in these areas. This finding suggests that, brain insult during a critical period of brain development, may alter the internal signalling processes that initiate programmed cell death at a developmentally typical stage. Furthermore, failure of the medial frontal regions to undergo typical patterns of thinning over time in the TBI group was correlated with poorer emotional control and behavioural regulation.

(b) *Diffusion Weighted Imaging*

Diffusion weighted imaging (DWI) measures the magnitude and directionality of water diffusion in tissue, notably of white matter tracts, and represents a sensitive biomarker of diffuse white matter injury in TBI via detection of traumatic axonal injury (Wilde et al., 2012). This technique enables evaluation of white matter fibre tracts by taking advantage of the intrinsic directionality of water diffusion in the immature brain. Several commonly derived measures of diffusion anisotropy have proved useful in quantifying white matter injury in child TBI (Wilde et al., 2012). Fractional anisotropy (FA) is derived from the tendency of water molecules to move preferentially in parallel (rather than perpendicular) to barriers to free diffusion such as axons, fibres or other support cells. A high degree of anisotropic diffusion is related to homogeneity of fibre orientation, increased fibre density or axonal diameter and the ratio of intracellular/extracellular space (Wilde et al., 2012). Conversely, apparent diffusion coefficient (ADC) represents the average diffusivity of free water movement within tissue, which also permits inferences regarding the microstructure in tissue; higher average diffusivity is indicative of decreased fibre density, axonal diameter, decreased myelination and/or increased extracellular space (Wilde et al., 2012).

In applying this technique to children and adolescents with moderate–severe injuries there is evidence of decreased FA and/or increased ADC in numerous white matter fibre bundles including the corpus callosum, inferior and superior frontal and supracallosal white matter, internal capsule, superior longitudinal fasciculus and orbitofrontal white matter, cingulum bundles and uncinate fasciculus (Wilde et al., 2012). It has been hypothesized that reductions in FA and increased ADC reflect axonal disconnection or damage to myelin sheaths; however, the implications of these findings remain unclear.

A number of studies report robust associations between DWI metrics and outcomes across the domains of memory, executive function and fine motor and processing speed, suggesting that DTI may be a useful structural biomarker to identify children at elevated risk for a range of unfavourable neurodevelopmental outcomes (Wilde et al., 2006).

Management and Rehabilitation Issues

It is clear that childhood TBI can have long-term adverse effects on neuropsychological, academic and behavioural functioning. Research indicates children most 'at risk' for poor outcome are those who: (1) have more severe injuries at a younger age (Anderson & Moore, 1995); (2) have a pre-injury history of developmental or behavioural problems (Ponsford et al., 1997) and/or (3) live in poorer functioning and less advantaged families (Rivara et al., 1994). 'At risk' children are the most vulnerable, and therefore, most appropriate for rehabilitation efforts. Thus, we argue different models of intervention post-TBI should be considered.

Rehabilitation can be divided according to the goal of the intervention, reflecting either (1) restitution/restorative or (2) substitution/adaptation. Restitution/restorative rehabilitation focuses on restoring function via re-establishment of impaired functions and/or regaining lost skills (Cicerone & Tupper, 1991). Although there is little evidence base for such interventions in children, restitution/restorative approaches have shown significant improvements in executive function/cognitive outcomes such as attention, memory and working memory (see Table 26.5 for intervention approaches).

Cognitive Interventions

In one of such studies, our research lab conducted a pilot study of The Amsterdam Memory and Attention Training for children (Amat-c) to enhance attention and memory skills in children presenting with difficulties in these domains (Catroppa et al., 2014, 2015).

Table 26.5 Phases/models of intervention

Phase	Intervention
1. During coma	Sensory stimulation
2. Short-term post-injury (e.g., 6 h)	Hypothermia
3. Post-Coma/PTA	Intervention for difficulties in cognition and behaviour
4. Outpatient therapy	Intervention to assist re-entry into home/school/community: Direct approach Behavioural compensation Environmental modifications and supports Behavioural interventions Psych-educational approaches Psychological treatments Family-based interventions

Adapted from Catroppa and Anderson (2010)

Results from this pilot supported the feasibility and efficacy of the intervention, reflected in significant improvements maintained to 6 months post-treatment in areas of attention and memory, with generalization to everyday life. An online clinician support version of this program is currently in progress. Currently, our research lab is also investigating the efficacy of Cogmed Working Memory Intervention Training in improving executive function skills such as working memory and decision-making and everyday functional outcomes in paediatric TBI. To date only a single study has reported promising preliminary data suggesting that Cogmed is an efficacious treatment program for children post-TBI (Phillips et al., 2016). Therefore, our project aims not only to extend and support the findings from this study.

Substitution/adaptation focuses on functional adaptation, where intact abilities are utilized to 're-route' skills that have been disrupted. Our group is running a 'diary training intervention for memory problems', initially developed by Ho et al. (2011). This intervention aims to implement a structured evidence-based clinical rehabilitation program for memory into clinical paediatric rehabilitation practice. In the current study, children with ABI aged 11–18 years were invited to participate in group memory training (5 weekly sessions) as a part of clinical care, across a statewide paediatric rehabilitation service, if they presented with reduced everyday memory on screening questionnaires (<1 SD). It is anticipated that children will demonstrate gains in everyday memory.

Behavioural/Psychosocial Interventions

Providing parent support to families of children with TBI is essential. The 'Signposts for Building Better Behaviour' program (Woods et al., 2007) is a modified cognitive behavioural intervention targeting parents of children with TBI. Originally developed by Hudson et al. (2003), this program relies on training parents to implement behaviour change strategies at home (Gavidia-Payne & Hudson, 2002). We expected that parents of children with TBI would benefit from the adapted program (inclusion of a TBI module), and pilot data (Woods et al., 2007) has shown benefit to both parents and children post-TBI, with parent coping strategies improved and child behaviour enhanced.

Anxiety is a prevalent comorbidity in child TBI. The Cool Kids program (Rapee et al., 2006) is a structured cognitive behavioural therapy program developed for treating anxiety in children and adolescents. Our lab has evaluated the program in adolescents with acquired brain injury (ABI) using a case study approach (Soo et al., 2012) and found improved anxiety levels. Results from a randomized controlled trial examining the efficacy of the Cool Kids program for adolescents with ABI and anxiety are currently being analysed.

Key Points: Rehabilitation Approaches

- Restitution/restorative—procedures and interventions designed to restore function of a previously lost skill or behaviour
- Substitution/adaptation—procedures where intact abilities are used to develop adaptations to perform skills that have been disrupted

Academic/Vocational Considerations

For the child, return to school is frequently a major goal of outpatient rehabilitation (Glang et al., 2008; Hawley, 2004). Prior to school return, a number of issues must be considered (Anderson & Catroppa, 2006) including the physical incorporation of adaptive equipment, environmental aspects and instructional adaptations or accommodations that may be necessary. Physical incorporation of adaptive equipment involves consideration of including wheelchairs, special desks, computers and/or communication devices. Environmental aspects for return to school include the provision of extra time for assignments, instruction and/or taking exams, providing a quiet, well-structured classroom and/or opportunity for the child to receive increased repetition of material and/or opportunities to practice skills and revision of assignments, classwork, etc. Instructional aspects to consider in returning to school include inclusion of specific educational programming, individual tuition and social skills retraining. These modifications should be negotiated prior to school return to allow the transition to be as smooth as possible.

For the adolescent or young adult who has sustained a TBI, the completion of education and entering the workforce is often a time of significant stress. This process may be supported by: (a) providing training for the individual to prepare curriculum vitae/resume; (b) furnishing training to perform adequately in interviews (e.g., behavioural training in social skills, interview skills, relaxation skills, etc.); (c) consultation with liaison services where counsellors discuss the individual's needs with potential employers, or conduct site visits to determine any environmental modifications which may be required to enhance the individual's performance (e.g., provide referral to vocational counsellors/therapists).

Key Points: Factors That May Support Recovery from TBI

- Assure premorbid and comorbid injury variables (post-traumatic epilepsy, mood disruption, focal neurologic signs) are being treated
- Implementation of an intervention program (child/parent)
- Consider physical, environmental and instructional variables for return to school
- Consider vocational counselling/therapy evaluation to plan for work skill development, particularly for adolescents/young adults completing education

Conclusions

This chapter has provided a brief summary of a number of areas associated with paediatric TBI, commencing with the prevalence of the injuries to rehabilitation issues. This chapter has highlighted the complexities following a TBI in childhood and the need for future research in the area of intervention post childhood TBI, in order to develop evidence-based treatments.

References and Recommended Further Reading

Ahmed, S., Bierley, R., Sheikh, J. I., & Date, E. S. (2000). Post-traumatic amnesia after closed head injury: a review of the literature and some suggestions for further research. *Brain Injury, 14*(9), 765–780.

Anderson, V., Brown, S., & Newitt, H. (2010). What contributes to quality of life in adult survivors of childhood traumatic brain injury? *Journal of Neurotrauma, 27*, 863–870.

Anderson, V., Brown, S., Newitt, H., & Hoile, H. (2011). Long-term outcome from childhood traumatic brain injury: intellectual ability, personality, and quality of life. *Neuropsychology, 25*, 176–184.

Anderson, V., & Catroppa, C. (2006). Advances in postacute rehabilitation after childhood-acquired brain injury. *American Journal of Physical Medicine & Rehabilitation, 85*, 767–778.

Anderson, V., & Catroppa, C. (2007). Memory outcome at 5 years post-childhood traumatic brain injury. *Brain Injury, 21*, 1399–1409.

Anderson, V., Catroppa, C., Godfrey, C., & Rosenfeld, J. V. (2012). Intellectual ability 10 years after traumatic brain injury in infancy and childhood: What predicts outcome? *Journal of Neurotrauma, 29*, 143–153.

Anderson, V., Catroppa, C., Morse, S., Haritou, F., & Rosenfeld, J. (2001). Outcome from mild head injury in young children: a prospective study. *Journal of Clinical and Experimental Neuropsychology, 23*, 705–717.

Anderson, V., Catroppa, C., Morse, S., Haritou, F., & Rosenfeld, J. (2005a). Attentional and processing skills following traumatic brain injury in early childhood. *Brain Injury, 19*, 699–710.

Anderson, V., Catroppa, C., Morse, S., Haritou, F., & Rosenfeld, J. (2005b). Functional plasticity or vulnerability after early brain injury? *Pediatrics, 116*, 1374–1382.

Anderson, V., & Moore, C. (1995). Age at injury as a predictor of outcome following pediatric head injury: A longitudinal perspective. *Child Neuropsychology, 1*, 187–202.

Anderson, V. A., Catroppa, C., Haritou, F., Morse, S., Pentland, L., Rosenfeld, J., & Stargatt, R. (2001). Predictors of acute child and family outcome following traumatic brain injury in children. *Pediatric Neurosurgery, 34*, 138–148.

Anderson, V. A., Catroppa, C., Haritou, F., Morse, S., & Rosenfeld, J. V. (2005). Identifying factors contributing to child and family outcome 30 months after traumatic brain injury in children. *Journal of Neurology, Neurosurgery, and Psychiatry, 76*, 401–408.

Anderson, V. A., Catroppa, C., Morse, S. A., Haritou, F., & Rosenfeld, J. (2000). Recovery of intellectual ability following traumatic brain injury in childhood: impact of injury severity and age at injury. *Pediatric Neurosurgery, 32*, 282–290.

Andriessen, T. M. J. C., Jacobs, B., & Vos, P. E. (2010). Clinical characteristics and pathophysiological mechanisms of focal and diffuse traumatic brain injury. *Journal of Cellular and Molecular Medicine, 14*, 2381–2392.

Anson, K., & Ponsford, J. (2006). Coping and emotional adjustment following traumatic brain injury. *The Journal of Head Trauma Rehabilitation, 21*, 248–259.

Babikian, T., Satz, P., Zaucha, K., Light, R., Lewis, R., & Asarnow, R. (2011). The UCLA longitudinal study of neurocognitive outcomes following mild pediatric traumatic brain injury. *Journal of the International Neuropsychological Society, 17*, 886–895.

Barkhoudarian, G., Hovda, D. A., & Giza, C. C. (2011). The molecular pathophysiology of concussive brain injury. *Clinics in Sports Medicine, 30*, 33–48.

Barlow, K. M., Crawford, S., Stevenson, A., Sandhu, S. S., Belanger, F., & Dewey, D. (2010). Epidemiology of postconcussion syndrome in pediatric mild traumatic brain injury. *Pediatrics, 126*, e374–e381.

Bawden, H. N., Knights, R. M., & Winogron, H. W. (1985). Speeded performance following head injury in children. *Journal of Clinical and Experimental Neuropsychology, 7*, 39–54.

Beauchamp, M., Catroppa, C., Godfrey, C., Morse, S., Rosenfeld, J. V., & Anderson, V. (2011). Selective changes in executive functioning ten years after severe childhood traumatic brain injury. *Developmental Neuropsychology, 36*, 578–595.

Bedell, G. M. (2008). Functional outcomes of school-age children with acquired injuries at discharge from inpatient rehabilitation. *Brain Injury, 22*, 313–324.

Begali, V. (1992). *Head injury in children and adolescents: A resource and review for school and allied professionals* (2nd ed.). Clinical Psychology.

Belanger, H. G., & Vanderploeg, R. D. (2005). The neuropsychological impact of sports-related concussion: A meta-analysis. *Journal of the International Neuropsychological Society, 11*, 345–357.

Brown, A. W., Malec, J. F., McClelland, R. L., Diehl, N. N., Englander, J., & Cifu, D. X. (2005). Clinical elements that predict outcome after traumatic brain injury: a prospective multicenter recursive partitioning (decision-tree) analysis. *Journal of Neurotrauma, 22*, 1040–1051.

Carroll, L., Cassidy, J. D., Peloso, P., Borg, J., von Holst, H., Holm, L., Paniak, C., & Pépin, M. (2004). Prognosis for mild traumatic brain injury: results of the WHO collaborating centre task force on mild traumatic brain injury. *Journal of Rehabilitation Medicine, 36*, 84–105.

Case, M. E. (2008). Accidental traumatic head injury in infants and young children. *Brain Pathology, 18*(4), 583–589.

Cassidy, J. D., Carroll, L. J., Peloso, P. M., Borg, J., Von Holst, H., Holm, L., Kraus, J., & Coronado, V. G. (2004). Incidence, risk factors and prevention of mild traumatic brain injury: Results of the WHO Collaborating Centre Task Force on mild traumatic brain injury. *Journal of Rehabilitation Medicine, 36*, 28–60.

Catale, C., Marique, P., Closset, A., & Meulemans, T. (2009). Attentional and executive functioning following mild traumatic brain injury in children using the Test for Attentional Performance (TAP) battery. *Journal of Clinical and Experimental Neuropsychology, 31*, 331–338.

Catroppa, C., & Anderson, V. (2003). Recovery and predictors of intellectual ability two years following paediatric traumatic brain injury. *Neuropsychological Rehabilitation, 13*, 517–536.

Catroppa, C., & Anderson, V. (2010). Cognitive rehabilitation following paediatric traumatic brain injury. In V. Anderson & K. O. Yeates (Eds.), *New frontiers in paediatric traumatic brain injury*. Cambridge University Press.

Catroppa, C., Anderson, V., Beauchamp, M. H., & Yeates, K. O. (2016). *New frontiers in pediatric traumatic brain injury: An evidence based for clinical practice*. Routledge.

Catroppa, C., Anderson, V., Godfrey, C., & Rosenfeld, J. V. (2011). Attentional skills 10 years post-paediatric traumatic brain injury (TBI). *Brain Injury, 25*, 858–869.

Catroppa, C., Anderson, V. A., Morse, S. A., Haritou, F., & Rosenfeld, J. V. (2007). Children's attentional skills 5 years post-TBI. *Journal of Pediatric Psychology, 32*, 354–369.

Catroppa, C., Anderson, V. A., Morse, S. A., Haritou, F., & Rosenfeld, J. V. (2008). Outcome and predictors of functional recovery 5 years following pediatric traumatic brain injury (TBI). *Journal of Pediatric Psychology, 33*, 707–718.

Catroppa, C., Godfrey, C., Rosenfeld, J. V., Hearps, S. S. J., & Anderson, V. A. (2012). Functional recovery ten years after pediatric traumatic brain injury: Outcomes and predictors. *Journal of Neurotrauma, 29*, 2539–2547.

Catroppa, C., Stone, K., Hearps, S. J. C., Soo, C., Anderson, V., & Rosema, S. (2015). Evaluation of an attention and memory intervention post-childhood acquired brain injury: Preliminary efficacy, immediate and 6 months post-intervention. *Brain Injury, 29*, 1317–1324.

Catroppa, C., Stone, K., Rosema, S., Soo, C., & Anderson, V. (2014). Preliminary efficacy of an attention and memory intervention post-childhood brain injury. *Brain Injury, 28*, 252–260.

Chapman, L. A., Wade, S. L., Walz, N. C., Taylor, H. G., Stancin, T., & Yeates, K. O. (2010). Clinically significant behavior problems during the initial 18 months following early childhood traumatic brain injury. *Rehabilitation Psychology, 55*, 48–57.

Cicerone, K. D., & Tupper, D. E. (1991). *Neuropsychological rehabilitation: Treatment on errors in everyday function, The neuropsychology of everyday life: Issues in development and rehabilitation*. Springer.

Cloots, R. J. H., Van Dommelen, J. A. W., Nyberg, T., Kleiven, S., & Geers, M. G. D. (2011). Micromechanics of diffuse axonal injury: Influence of axonal orientation and anisotropy. *Biomechanics and Modeling in Mechanobiology, 10*, 413–422.

Cooper, J. M., Catroppa, C., Beauchamp, M. H., Eren, S., Godfrey, C., Ditchfield, M., & Anderson, V. A. (2014). Attentional control ten years post-childhood traumatic brain injury: The impact of lesion presence, location, and severity in adolescence and early adulthood. *Journal of Neurotrauma, 31*, 713–721.

Corrigan, J. D., Selassie, A. W., & Orman, J. A. L. (2010). The epidemiology of traumatic brain injury. *The Journal of Head Trauma Rehabilitation, 25*, 72–80.

Crowe, L. M., Anderson, V., Barton, S., Babl, F. E., & Catroppa, C. (2014). Verbal ability and language outcome following traumatic brain injury in early childhood. *The Journal of Head Trauma Rehabilitation, 29*, 217–223.

Crowe, L. M., Babl, F., Anderson, V., & Catroppa, C. (2009). The epidemiology of paediatric head injuries: Data from a referral centre in Victoria, Australia. *Journal of Paediatrics and Child Health, 45*, 346–350.

Crowe, L. M., Catroppa, C., Anderson, V., & Babl, F. E. (2012). Head injuries in children under 3 years. *Injury, 43*, 2141–2145.

Crowe, L. M., Catroppa, C., Babl, F. E., & Anderson, V. (2012). Intellectual, behavioral, and social outcomes of accidental traumatic brain injury in early childhood. *Pediatrics, 129*, e262–e268.

Crowe, L. M., Catroppa, C., Babl, F., & Anderson, V. (2013). Executive function outcomes of children with traumatic brain injury sustained in infancy. *Child Neuropsychology, 19*, 113–126.

Dennis, M. (1989). Language and the young damaged brain. In T. Boll & B. Bryant (Eds.), *Clinical neuoropsychology and brain function: Research, measurement and practice*. American Psychological Association.

Donders, J., & Warschausky, S. (2007). Neurobehavioral outcomes after early versus late childhood traumatic brain injury. *The Journal of Head Trauma Rehabilitation, 22*, 296–302.

Eisenberg, M. A., Meehan, W. P., & Mannix, R. (2014). Duration and course of post-concussive symptoms. *Pediatrics, 133*, 999–1006.

Engberg, A. W., & Teasdale, T. W. (2004). Psychosocial outcome following traumatic brain injury in adults: a long-term population-based follow-up. *Brain Injury, 18*, 533–545.

Ewing-Cobbs, L., Barnes, M., Fletcher, J. M., Levin, H. S., Swank, P. R., & Song, J. (2004). Modeling of longitudinal academic achievement scores after pediatric traumatic brain injury. *Developmental Neuropsychology, 25*, 107–133.

Ewing-Cobbs, L., Fletcher, J. M., Levin, H. S., Francis, D. J., Davidson, K., & Miner, M. E. (1997). Longitudinal neuropsychological outcome in infants and preschoolers with traumatic brain injury. *Journal of the International Neuropsychological Society, 3*, 581–591.

Ewing-Cobbs, L., Prasad, M. R., Kramer, L., Cox, C. S., Baumgartner, J., Fletcher, S., Mendez, D., Barnes, M., Zhang, X., & Swank, P. (2006). Late intellectual and academic outcomes following traumatic brain injury sustained during early childhood. *Journal of Neurosurgery, 105*, 287–296.

Farkas, O., & Povlishock, J. T. (2007). Cellular and subcellular change evoked by diffuse traumatic brain injury: a complex web of change extending far beyond focal damage. *Progress in Brain Research, 161*, 43–59.

Feng, Y., Abney, T. M., Okamoto, R. J., Pless, R. B., Genin, G. M., & Bayly, P. V. (2010). Relative brain displacement and deformation during constrained mild frontal head impact. *Journal of the Royal Society Interface, 7*, 1677–1688.

Finnanger, T. G., Olsen, A., Skandsen, T., Lydersen, S., Vik, A., Evensen, K. A. I., Catroppa, C., Håberg, A. K., Andersson, S., & Indredavik, M. S. (2015). Life after adolescent and adult moderate and severe traumatic brain injury: Self-reported executive, emotional, and behavioural function 2–5 years after injury. *Behavioural Neurology*. https://doi.org/10.1155/2015/329241

Gaetz, M. (2004). The neurophysiology of brain injury. *Clinical Neurophysiology, 115*(1), 4–18.

Gagner, C., Landry-roy, C., & Laine, F. (2015). Sleep-wake disturbances and fatigue after pediatric traumatic brain injury: A systematic review of the literature. *Journal of Neurotrauma, 32*, 1539–1552.

Ganesalingam, K., Yeates, K. O., Taylor, H. G., Walz, N. C., Stancin, T., & Wade, S. (2011). Executive functions and social competence in young children 6 months following traumatic brain injury. *Neuropsychology, 25*, 466–476.

Gavidia-Payne, S., & Hudson, A. (2002). Behavioural supports for parents of children with an intellectual disability and problem behaviours: An overview of the literature. *Journal of Intellectual & Developmental Disability, 27*, 31–55.

Gerring, J. P., & Wade, S. (2012). The essential role of psychosocial risk and protective factors in pediatric traumatic brain injury research. *Journal of Neurotrauma, 29*, 621–628.

Giza, C. C., & Prins, M. L. (2006). Is being plastic fantastic? Mechanisms of altered plasticity after developmental traumatic brain injury. *Developmental Neuroscience, 28*(4–5), 364–379.

Glang, A., Todis, B., Thomas, C. W., Hood, D., Bedell, G., & Cockrell, J. (2008). Identification and appropriate service deliveary for children who have TBI in schools. *NeuroRehabilitation, 23*, 477–486.

Goldstein, F. C., & Harvey, S. L. (1992). Cognitive function after closed head injury: Sequelae and outcome. In L. J. Thal, W. H. Moos, & E. R. Gamzu (Eds.), *Cognitive disorders: Pathophysiology and treatment* (pp. 61–92). Marcel Dekker.

Goldstein, F. C., & Levin, H. S. (1987). Epidemiology of pediatric closed head injury: Incidence, clinical characteristics, and risk factors. *Journal of Learning Disabilities, 20*, 518–525.

Greve, M. W., & Zink, B. J. (2009). Cognitive rehabilitation following traumatic brain injury: assessment to treatment. *Mount Sinai Journal of Medicine, 76*, 173–181.

Hahn, Y. S., Chyung, C., Barthel, M. J., Bailes, J., Flannery, A. M., & McLone, D. G. (1988). Head injuries in children under 36 months of age. Demography and outcome. *Child's Nervous System, 4*, 34–40.

Hawley, C. A. (2004). Behaviour and school performance after brain injury. *Brain Injury, 18*, 645–659.

Hessen, E., Anderson, V., & Nestvold, K. (2008). MMPI-2 profiles 23 years after paediatric mild traumatic brain injury. *Brain Injury, 22*, 39–50.

Hessen, E., Nestvold, K., & Anderson, V. (2007). Neuropsychological function 23 years after mild traumatic brain injury: a comparison of outcome after paediatric and adult head injuries. *Brain Injury, 21*, 963–979.

Ho, J., Epps, A., Parry, L., Poole, M., & Lah, S. (2011). Rehabilitation of everyday memory deficits in paediatric brain injury: self-instruction and diary training. *Neuropsychological Rehabilitation, 21*, 183–207.

Hoofien, D., Gilboa, A., Vakil, E., & Donovick, P. J. (2001). Traumatic brain injury (TBI) 10-20 years later: a comprehensive outcome study of psychiatric symptomatology, cognitive abilities and psychosocial functioning. *Brain Injury, 15*, 189–209.

Hudson, A. M., Matthews, J. M., Gavidia-Payne, S. T., Cameron, C. A., Mildon, R. L., Radler, G. A., & Nankervis, K. L. (2003). Evaluation of an intervention system for parents of children with intellectual disability and challenging behaviour. *Journal of Intellectual Disability Research, 47*, 238–249.

Huttenlocher, P. R., & Dabholkar, A. S. (1997). Regional differences in synaptogenesis in human cerebral cortex. *Journal of Comparative Neurology, 387*, 167–178.

Ichkova, A., Rodriguez-Grande, B., Bar, C., Villega, F., Konsman, J. P., & Badaut, J. (2017). Vascular impairment as a pathological mechanism underlying long-lasting cognitive dysfunction after pediatric traumatic brain injury. *Neurochemistry International, 111*, 93–102.

Johnson, A. R., DeMatt, E., & Salorio, C. F. (2009). Predictors of outcome following acquired brain injury in children. *Developmental Disabilities Research Reviews, 5*(2), 124–132.

Jonsson, C. A., Horneman, G., & Emanuelson, I. (2004). Neuropsychological progress during 14 years after severe traumatic brain injury in childhood and adolescence. *Brain Injury, 18*, 921–934.

Kaldoja, M.-L., & Anneli, K. (2012). Social-emotional behaviour in infants and toddlers with mild traumatic brain injury. *Brain Injury, 26*, 1005–1013.

Karver, C. L., Wade, S. L., Cassedy, A., Taylor, H. G., Stancin, T., Yeates, K. O., & Walz, N. C. (2012). Age at injury and long-term behavior problems after traumatic brain injury in young children. *Rehabilitation Psychology, 57*, 256–265.

Kaufman, Y., Tzischinsky, O., Epstein, R., Etzioni, A., Lavie, P., & Pillar, G. (2001). Long-term sleep disturbances in adolescents after minor head injury. *Pediatric Neurology, 24*, 129–134.

Kinsella, G. J., Prior, M., Sawyer, M., Ong, B., Murtagh, D., Eisenmajer, R., Bryan, D., Anderson, V., & Klug, G. (1997). Predictors and indicators of academic outcome in children 2 years following traumatic brain injury. *Journal of the International Neuropsychological Society, 3*, 608–616.

Königs, M., de Kieviet, J. F., & Oosterlaan, J. (2012). Post-traumatic amnesia predicts intelligence impairment following traumatic brain injury: a meta-analysis. *Journal of Neurology, Neurosurgery, and Psychiatry, 83*, 1048–1055.

Königs, M., Heij, H. A., van der Sluijs, J. A., Vermeulen, R. J., Goslings, J. C., Luitse, J. S. K., Poll-Thé, B. T., Beelen, A., van der Wees, M., Kemps, R. J. J. K., Catsman-Berrevoets, C. E., & Oosterlaan, J. (2015). Pediatric traumatic brain injury and attention deficit. *Pediatrics, 136*, 534–541.

Kriel, R. L., Krach, L. E., & Panser, L. A. (1989). Closed head injury: Comparison of children younger and older than 6 years of age. *Pediatric Neurology, 5*, 296–300.

Kurowski, B. G., Taylor, H. G., Yeates, K. O., Walz, N. C., Stancin, T., & Wade, S. L. (2011). Caregiver ratings of long-term executive dysfunction and attention problems after early childhood traumatic brain injury: family functioning is important. *PM & R : The Journal of Injury, Function, and Rehabilitation, 3*, 836–845.

Landry-Roy, C., Bernier, A., Gravel, J., & Beauchamp, M. H. (2017). Predictors of sleep outcomes following mild traumatic brain injury in preschoolers. *The Journal of Head Trauma Rehabilitation*, 1–11.

Langlois, J. A., Rutland-Brown, W., & Thomas, K. E. (2006). Traumatic brain injury in the United States: Emergency department visits, hospitalizations, and deaths. *Brain Injury, 21*, 357–378.

Levin, H. S., Hanten, G., Zhang, L., Swank, P. R., Ewing-Cobbs, L., Dennis, M., Barnes, M. A., Max, J., Schachar, R., Chapman, S. B., & Hunter, J. V. (2004). Changes in working memory after traumatic brain injury in children. *Neuropsychology, 18*, 240–247.

Levin, H. S., Wilde, E., Troyanskaya, M., Petersen, N. J., Scheibel, R., Newsome, M., Radaideh, M., Wu, T., Yallampalli, R., & Chu, Z. (2010). Diffusion tensor imaging of mild to moderate blast-related traumatic brain injury and its sequelae. *Journal of Neurotrauma, 27*, 683–694.

Li, W., Risacher, S. L., McAllister, T. W., & Saykin, A. J. (2017). Age at injury is associated with the long-term cognitive outcome of traumatic brain injuries. *Alzheimer's & Dementia: Diagnosis, Assessment & Disease Monitoring, 6*, 196–200.

Margulies, S. S., & Thibault, K. L. (2000). Infant skull and suture properties: measurements and implications for mechanisms of pediatric brain injury. *Journal of Biomechanical Engineering, 122*, 364–371.

Mathers, C. D., & Loncar, D. (2006). Projections of global mortality and burden of disease from 2002 to 2030. *PLoS Medicine, 3*, 2011–2030.

Matsukawa, H., Shinoda, M., Fujii, M., Takahashi, O., Yamamoto, D., Murakata, A., & Ishikawa, R. (2011). Genu of corpus callosum as a prognostic factor in diffuse axonal injury: Clinical article. *Journal of Neurosurgery, 115*(5), 1019–1024.

McCrory, P., Meeuwisse, W. H., Aubry, M., Cantu, B., Dvořák, J., Echemendia, R. J., Engebretsen, L., Johnston, K., Kutcher, J. S., Raftery, M., Sills, A., Benson, B. W., Davis, G. A., Ellenbogan, R., Guskiewicz, K., Herring, S. A., Iverson, G. L., Jordan, B. D., Kissick, J., …, Turner, M. (2013). Consensus statement on concussion in sport: The 4th international conference on concussion in sport held in Zurich, November 2012. *Journal of the American College of Surgeons, 216*, 55–71.

McKinlay, A. (2010). Controversies and outcomes associated with mild traumatic brain injury in childhood and adolescences. *Child: Care, Health and Development, 36*(1), 3–21.

McKinlay, A., Grace, R., Horwood, J., Fergusson, D., & MacFarlane, M. (2009). Adolescent psychiatric symptoms following preschool childhood mild traumatic brain injury: Evidence from a birth cohort. *The Journal of Head Trauma Rehabilitation, 24*, 221–227.

McKinlay, A., Grace, R. C., Horwood, L. J., Fergusson, D. M., Ridder, E. M., & MacFarlane, M. R. (2008). Prevalence of traumatic brain injury among children, adolescents and young adults: Prospective evidence from a birth cohort. *Brain Injury, 22*, 175–181.

McKinlay, A., Horwood, L. J., & Fergusson, D. M. (2002). Long term psychosocial outcomes after mild head injury in early childhood. *Journal of Neurology, Neurosurgery and Psychiatry, 73*(3), 281–289.

Miller, J. D. (1991). Pathophysiology and management of head injury. *Neuropsychology, 5*, 235–251.

Muscara, F., Catroppa, C., & Anderson, V. (2008a). The impact of injury severity on executive function 7-10 years following pediatric traumatic brain injury. *Developmental Neuropsychology, 33*, 623–636.

Muscara, F., Catroppa, C., & Anderson, V. (2008b). Social problem-solving skills as a mediator between executive function and long-term social outcome following paediatric traumatic brain injury. *Journal of Neuropsychology, 2*, 445–461.

Nacajauskaite, O., Endziniene, M., Jureniene, K., & Schrader, H. (2006). The validity of postconcussion syndrome in cahildren: A controlled historical cohort study. *Brain & Development, 28*, 507–514.

Nadebaum, C., Anderson, V., & Catroppa, C. (2007). Executive function outcomes following traumatic brain injury in young children: a five year follow-up. *Developmental Neuropsychology, 32*, 703–728.

Papoutsis, J., Stargatt, R., & Catroppa, C. (2014). Long-term executive functioning outcomes for complicated and uncomplicated mild traumatic brain injury sustained in early childhood. *Developmental Neuropsychology, 39*, 638–645.

Phillips, N. L., Mandalis, A., Benson, S., Parry, L., Epps, A., Morrow, A., & Lah, S. (2016). Computerized working memory training for children with moderate to severe traumatic brain injury: A double-blind, randomized, placebo-controlled trial. *Journal of Neurotrauma, 8*, 1–8.

Pillar, G., Averbooch, E., Katz, N., Peled, N., Kaufman, Y., & Shahar, E. (2003). Prevalence and risk of sleep disturbances in adolescents after minor head injury. *Pediatric Neurology, 29*, 131–135.

Ponsford, J., Draper, K., & Schönberger, M. (2008). Functional outcome 10 years after traumatic brain injury: Its relationship with demographic, injury severity, and cognitive and emotional status. *Journal of the International Neuropsychological Society, 14*, 233–242.

Ponsford, J., Willmott, C., Rothwell, A., Cameron, P., Kelly, A., Ayton, G., Curran, C., & Nelms, R. (1997). Cognitive and behavioural outcome following mild traumatic brain injury in children. *Journal of the International Neuropsychological Society, 3*, 225.

Popernack, M. L., Gray, N., & Reuter-Rice, K. (2014). Moderate-to-severe traumatic brain injury in children: complications and rehabilitation strategies. *Journal of Pediatric Health Care, 29*, 1–7.

Rapee, R., Lyneham, H., Schniering, C., Wuthrich, V., Abbott, M., Hudson, J., & Wignall, A. (2006). *The cool kids child and adolescent anxiety program therapist manual*. Centre for Emotional Health, Macquarie University.

Reilly, P. L., Simpson, D. A., Sprod, R., & Thomas, L. (1988). Assessing the conscious level in infants and young children: a pediatric version of the Glasgow Coma Scale. *Child's Nervous System, 4*, 30–33.

Richards, D. A., Tolias, C. M., Sgouros, S., & Bowery, N. G. (2003). Extracellular glutamine to glutamate ratio may predict outcome in the injured brain: A clinical microdialysis study in children. *Pharmacological Research, 48*, 101–109.

Rivara, J. B., Jaffe, K. M., Polissar, N. L., Fay, G. C., Martin, K. M., Shurtleff, H. A., & Liao, S. (1994). Family functioning and children's academic performance and behavior problems in the year following traumatic brain injury. *Archives of Physical Medicine and Rehabilitation, 75*, 369–379.

Roberts, M. A., Manshadi, F. F., Bushnell, D. L., & Hines, M. E. (1995). Neurobehavioural dysfunction following mild traumatic brain injury in childhood: A case report with positive findings on positron emission tomography (PET). *Brain Injury, 9*, 427–436.

Robinson, K. E., Fountain-Zaragoza, S., Dennis, M., Taylor, H. G., Bigler, E. D., Rubin, K., Vannatta, K., Gerhardt, C. A., Stancin, T., & Yeates, K. O. (2014). Executive functions and theory of mind as predictors of social adjustment in childhood traumatic brain injury. *Journal of Neurotrauma, 31*, 1835–1842.

Rohling, M. L., Binder, L. M., Demakis, G. J., Larrabee, G. J., Ploetz, D. M., & Langhinrichsen-Rohling, J. (2011). A meta-analysis of neuropsychological outcome after mild traumatic brain injury: Re-analyses and reconsiderations of Binder et al. (1997), Frencham et al. (2005), and Pertab et al. (2009). *The Clinical Neuropsychologist, 25*, 608–623.

Rosema, S., Muscara, F., Godfrey, C., & Catroppa, C. (2014). Young adults' perspectives on their psychosocial outcomes 16 years following childhood traumatic brain injury. *Social Care and Neurodisability, 5*, 135–144.

Russo, R. N., Rice, J., Chern, P. M., & Raftos, J. (2012). Minimal and mild paediatric brain injury: A 3-year cohort of consecutive presentations. *Developmental Neurorehabilitation, 15*, 13–18.

Rutter, M., Chadwick, O., & Shaffer, D. (1983). Head injury. In M. Rutter (Ed.), *Developmental neuropsychiatry* (pp. 83–111). Churchill Livingstone.

Ryan, N. P., Beauchamp, M. H., Beare, R., Coleman, L., Ditchfield, M., Kean, M., Silk, T. J., Genc, S., Catroppa, C., & Anderson, V. A. (2016). Uncovering cortico-striatal correlates of cognitive fatigue in pediatric acquired brain disorder: Evidence from traumatic brain injury. *Cortex, 83*, 222–230.

Schmidt, A. T., Li, X., Hanten, G. R., Mccauley, S. R., Faber, J., & Levin, H. S. (2015). A longitudinal investigation of sleep quality in adolescents and young adults after mild traumatic brain injury. *Cognitive and Behavioral Neurology, 28*, 53–62.

Senathi-Raja, D., Ponsford, J., & Schönberger, M. (2010). The association of age and time postinjury with long-term emotional outcome following traumatic brain injury. *The Journal of Head Trauma Rehabilitation, 25*, 330–338.

Sharp, D. J., Scott, G., & Leech, R. (2014). Network dysfunction after traumatic brain injury. *Nature Reviews. Neurology, 10*, 156–166.

Shlosberg, D., Benifla, M., Kaufer, D., & Friedman, A. (2010). Blood–brain barrier breakdown as a therapeutic target in traumatic brain injury. *Nature Reviews. Neurology, 6*, 393–403.

Smitherman, E., Hernandez, A., Stavinoha, P. L., Huang, R., Kernie, S. G., Diaz-Arrastia, R., & Miles, D. K. (2016). Predicting outcome after pediatric traumatic brain injury by early magnetic resonance imaging lesion location and volume. *Journal of Neurotrauma, 33*, 35–48.

Soo, C., Tate, R. L., & Rapee, R. M. (2012). Social anxiety and its treatment in children and adolescents with acquired brain injury. In V. Anderson & M. H. Beauchamp (Eds.), *Developmental social neuroscience and childhood brain insult: Theory and practice* (pp. 370–388). Guilford Press.

Teasdale, G., & Jennett, B. (1974). Assessment of coma and impaired consciousness. A practical scale. *Lancet, 2*, 81–84.

Tham, S. W., Fales, J., & Palermo, T. M. (2015). Subjective and objective assessment of sleep in adolescents with mild traumatic brain injury. *Journal of Neurotrauma, 32*, 847–852.

Tham, S. W., Palermo, T. M., Vavilala, M. S., Wang, J., Jaffe, K. M., Koepsell, T. D., Dorsch, A., Temkin, N., Durbin, D., & Rivara, F. P. (2012). The longitudinal course, risk factors, and impact of sleep disturbances in children with traumatic brain injury. *Journal of Neurotrauma, 29*, 154–161.

Theadom, A., Starkey, N., Jones, K., Cropley, M., Parmar, P., Barker-Collo, S., & Feigin, V. L. (2016). Sleep difficulties and their impact on recovery following mild traumatic brain injury in children. *Brain Injury, 30*, 1243–1248.

Treble-Barna, A., Zhang, N., Zang, H., Taylor, H. G., Yeates, K. O., & Wade, S. L. (2017). Long-term neuropsychological profiles and their role as mediators of adaptive functioning following traumatic brain injury in early childhood. *Journal of Neurotrauma, 34*, 353–362.

Valerio, J., & Illes, J. (2012). Ethical implications of neuroimaging in sports concussion. *The Journal of Head Trauma Rehabilitation, 27*, 216–221.

Verger, K., Junqué, C., Jurado, M. A., Tresserras, P., Bartumeus, F., Nogués, P., & Poch, J. M. (2000). Age effects on long-term neuropsychological outcome in paediatric traumatic brain injury. *Brain Injury, 14*, 495–503.

Wade, S. L., Zhang, N., Yeates, K. O., Stancin, T., & Taylor, H. G. (2016). Social environmental moderators of long-term functional outcomes of early childhood brain injury. *JAMA Pediatrics, 170*, 343.

Walz, N. C., Yeates, K. O., Taylor, H. G., Stancin, T., & Wade, S. L. (2009). First-order theory of mind skills shortly after traumatic brain injury in 3- to 5-year-old children. *Developmental Neuropsychology, 34*, 507–519.

Wetherington, C. E., Hooper, S. R., Keenan, H. T., Nocera, M., & Runyan, D. (2010). Parent ratings of behavioral functioning after traumatic brain injury in very young children. *Journal of Pediatric Psychology, 35*, 662–671.

Wilde, E. A., Chu, Z., Bigler, E. D., Hunter, J. V., Fearing, M. A., Hanten, G., Newsome, M. R., Scheibel, R. S., Li, X., & Levin, H. S. (2006). Diffusion tensor imaging in the corpus callosum in children after moderate to severe traumatic brain injury. *Journal of Neurotrauma, 23*, 1412–1426.

Wilde, E. A., Merkley, T. L., Bigler, E. D., Max, J. E., Schmidt, A. T., Ayoub, K. W., McCauley, S. R., Hunter, J. V., Hanten, G., Li, X., Chu, Z. D., & Levin, H. S. (2012). Longitudinal changes in cortical thickness in children after traumatic brain injury and their relation to behavioral regulation and emotional control. *International Journal of Developmental Neuroscience, 30*, 267–276.

Wilson, J. T., Wiedmann, K. D., Hadley, D. M., Condon, B., Teasdale, G., & Brooks, D. N. (1988). Early and late magnetic resonance imaging and neuropsychological outcome after head injury. *Journal of Neurology, Neurosurgery, and Psychiatry, 51*, 391–396.

Woods, D., Catroppa, C., Anderson, V., Godfrey, C., Matthews, J., Giallo, R., & Barnett, P. (2007). Treatment acceptability of a family-centred intervention for parents of children with an acquired brain injury (ABI)—Pilot study. In *New frontiers in pediatric traumatic brain injury*.

Woods, D. T., Catroppa, C., Barnett, P., & Anderson, V. A. (2011). Parental disciplinary practices following acquired brain injury in children. *Developmental Neurorehabilitation, 14*, 274–282.

Yeates, K. O. (1999). Closed head injury. In K. O. Yeates, M. D. Ris, & H. G. Taylor (Eds.), *Pediatric neuropsychology: Research, theory and practice* (pp. 192–218). Guilford Press.

Yeates, K. O., Taylor, H. G., Rusin, J., Bangert, B., Dietrich, A., Nuss, K., Wright, M., Nagin, D. S., & Jones, B. L. (2009). Longitudinal trajectories of postconcussive symptoms in children with mild brain injuries and their relationship to acute clinical status. *Pediatrics, 123*, 735–743. https://doi.org/10.1542/peds.2008-1056.Longitudinal

Yeates, K. O., Taylor, H. G., Wade, S. L., Drotar, D., Stancin, T., & Minich, N. (2002). A prospective study of short- and long-term neuropsychological outcomes after traumatic brain injury in children. *Neuropsychology, 16*, 514–523.

Yeates, K. O., Taylor, H. G., Walz, N. C., Stancin, T., & Wade, S. L. (2010). The family environment as a moderator of psychosocial outcomes following traumatic brain injury in young children. *Neuropsychology, 24*, 345–356.

Chapter 27
Cognitive Decline in Childhood or Young Adulthood

Michael R. Schoenberg and James G. Scott

Key Points & Chapter Summary

- Cognitive decline in children is rare, but can be caused by many disorders
- Suspected cognitive decline or regression in children should be investigated aggressively as many causes can be treated effectively if identified early
- Neuropsychological assessment is essential in differentiating between developmental delays, intellectual disability and cognitive decline
- Repeated assessment may be necessary to measure the effectiveness of intervention or document magnitude of any further decline or recovery
- Similar to adults, causes can include genetic, infectious, metabolic, structural abnormalities, immune dysfunction and neurotoxic etiologies

Overview

Childhood major neurocognitive disorders/dementias are rare, occurring at an incidence rate of 5.6/100,000 (.0056% point prevalence). Many medical disorders can contribute to deterioration in children where a previously acquired skill is lost or negatively compromised. Such diseases would technically be termed a Major Neurocognitive Disorder (DSM-5-TR) or dementia or dementing illness; however, this term is controversial in children. The term controversy stems from the opposing

M. R. Schoenberg (✉)
Department of Neurology, and Neurosurgery, University of South Florida College of Medicine, Tampa, FL, USA
e-mail: Mschoenb@health.usf.edu

J. G. Scott
Department of Psychiatry and Behavioral Sciences, University of Oklahoma, Health Sciences, Center College of Medicine, Oklahoma City, OK, USA

M. R. Schoenberg, J. G. Scott (eds.), *The Little Black Book of Neuropsychology*,
https://doi.org/10.1007/978-3-032-07777-6_27

interactive forces of continued developmental progress in a child/adolescent and the counter developmental effect of ongoing or chronic illness. This controversy aside, this chapter discusses illnesses and issues of deterioration in childhood neuropsychological functions. This is an often-neglected issue in Neuropsychology and the interested reader is guided to in-depth descriptions of many of the diseases discussed in comprehensive texts in pediatric neuropsychology (see Baron, 2018; Baron & Rey-Casserly, 2013; Beauchamp et al., 2022; Lezak et al., 2012; Yeates et al., 2010. See also Heilman & Valenstein, 2012).

Cognitive deterioration (i.e., technically a "dementia" (major neurocognitive disorder) in childhood is difficult to identify and diagnose. The DSM-5-TR provides for diagnosis of major neurocognitive disorder in children, which is based on the same criteria as in adults (see Chap. 15, this volume). Briefly, the diagnosis of major neurocognitive disorder requires the presence of significant deterioration in memory and at least one other cognitive domain, which results in difficulty in functioning in social, interpersonal, educational and/or occupational (for adolescents) domains. In children, deterioration in cognitive and motor skills from a neurodegenerative condition or disease is opposed by neurodevelopmental forces, making it challenging to determine if cognitive and/or motor skills have worsened. The process of acquired neuropsychological deficit may be insidious or acute depending upon the neuropathological process. Other chapters have focused on acute processes for onset of childhood dementias that include traumatic brain injuries, stroke and some cancers. This chapter will focus on those neuropathological processes that present with acquired neuropsychological deficits that are more neurodegenerative. In cases of insidious onset, it is difficult to ascertain a baseline level of development (premorbid neurocognitive comparison standard) from which to establish what level (and which) cognitive skills have deteriorated. Thus, the determination of cognitive deterioration can be challenging with children, particularly for those under the age of 6 years old. It is often difficult to identify if pediatric patients are experiencing ongoing decline from acquired levels of function, particularly among younger children in which academic skills are emerging or yet to developmentally emerge. Therefore, the determination of particular academic deficits may have to wait until an adequate repeat evaluation can be obtained and/or maturation of particular academic or neurocognitive functions are expected to develop (e.g., reading/writing/spelling and arithmetic skills in young children and geometry, affective prosody perception and advanced social skill development in older children/adolescents). In these pediatric cases, it is critical to evaluate the patient's level of function both relative to developmentally similar peers and relative to changes in performance over time in absolute terms. This affords both the evaluation of the relative levels of functioning relative to same aged peers and the evaluation of developmental progress over time relative to same aged peers. For example, a child can make absolute progress in a test performance across repeated assessment, yet statistically continue to decline relative to same aged peers thus indicating no absolute decline, but failure to make expected developmental progress relative to their peers.

There are several conditions in which it is recognized that cognitive and motor skills may be expected to deteriorate in childhood (e.g., hydrocephalus, Rett's disorder, type 1 diabetes, seizures/epilepsy and some genetic disorders). This chapter reviews some of the more common and distinct syndromes leading to deterioration of cognitive functioning in childhood or early adulthood. A detailed review of all of the childhood disorders that can include loss of cognitive or motor functions is beyond the scope of this book, and interested readers are referred to the comprehensive texts of Baron, 2018; Baron & Rey-Casserly, 2013; Beauchamp et al., 2022; Yeates et al. (2010) and Adams and Victor's Principles of Neurology (12th Ed., Ropper et al., 2023).

Four general patterns of neuropsychological deterioration have been identified in children reflecting the differing effects of the disease/condition and neurodevelopmental forces (1).

1. Normal development slows, plateaus and then declines as the disease progresses. When viewed over short periods (e.g., weeks to months), then it follows a step-like progression, but when viewed over longer periods (e.g., months to years), then loss of function appears more linear.
2. Normal cognitive and motor skill development gradually slows without any actual loss of an obtained developmental milestone or cognitive function. The rate of development is slowed and significantly lags behind healthy peers (and presumed trajectory based on premorbid estimates). As an example, children and adolescents with untreated HIV (AIDS) can present with this course.
3. An acute and rapid decline followed by a cessation of any further cognitive or motor development. Examples of diseases reflecting this pattern are severe traumatic brain injuries, some epileptic encephalopathies and some brain tumors. Rett syndrome also results in this pattern of functional deterioration.
4. An acute and rapid decline followed by a very slow, but otherwise normal, development of cognitive and motor skills. Conditions that can result in this pattern include some neurotoxins, traumatic brain injuries, infections and inflammatory diseases.

Key Points: Cognitive Decline in Childhood

- Progressive cognitive decline is rare and must be distinguished from developmental delays and intellectual disabilities
- May be due to a variety of acquired brain injury, but we consider this separate from cognitive deficits due to head injury, stroke, epilepsy, brain tumors or infections.
- Decline should be documented and can be gradual or more rapid/step like over time
- Deficits must pertain to multiple domains of cognitive functioning and psychosocial functioning
- Deficits should be expected to decline with persistence of the etiological factor
- Earlier onset of cognitive decline typically predicts poorer outcomes
- Many etiologies affect cerebral white matter more than gray matter and thus produce focal deficits or general cognitive slowing and inefficiency without frank aphasias or amnesia

The more common conditions that can present with cognitive deterioration in childhood or early adulthood are reviewed below.

Metabolic Diseases

Lysosomal Storage Diseases (LSDs)

Collectively, LSDs are due to deficiencies of various lysomal enzymes caused by mutations of genes involved in production of enzyme proteins and/or related cofactors. Lysosome enzymes degrade and recycle most biomolecules and are crucial for cellular health. Disruption of lysosome enzymes results in the storage (accumulation) of products in lysosomes leading to cellular dysfunction, enlargement (ballooning) and, eventually, death. Some of the more commonly occurring (but rare nonetheless) lysosomal storage diseases are reviewed below.

Tay-Sachs Disease:

Prevalence: 1/300,000, but is 100 times more common in Ashkenazi Jews.

Onset: Typically in early infancy. Due to deficiency of enzyme that breaks down fatty substance in brain that is called GN12 ganglioside. The enzyme is called hexosaminidase A (HEX A). Deficient HEX A results in the fatty substance accumulating in the brain.

Behavioral Symptoms/Clinical Presentation: Red spot in the macula along with motor weakness (hypotonia), irritability, increased startle reflex, reduced responsiveness and voluntary movements within 8–10 months. Progression of disease leads to blindness, myoclonic seizures and macrocephaly. Mortality typically occurs by 2–4 years old.

Neuropathology: Initially, abnormality of white matter and basal ganglia, followed by enlargement of caudate nucleus and further white matter degeneration. The last changes reflect general cerebral atrophy.

Juvenile Onset Tay-Sachs:

Prevalence: Less common than Tay-Sachs type 1. Inefficient hex A enzyme.

Onset: Typically age 2 to 5 years old, although onset in early adulthood has been reported.

Behavioral Symptoms/Clinical Presentation: Gait ataxia and incoordination, along with speech and language deficits. Additional deficits in cognitive functions (attention/executive, memory and visuoperceptual skills) can occur along with apraxias. Patients develop spasticity and seizures later in the course of the disease. A "vegetative" state ensues that can last years. Mortality usually occurs before age 20, but is later in those with adult onset.

Neuropathology: Primarily cerebellar atrophy (particularly of the vermis). Cerebral atrophy is found less consistently.

Niemann-Pick Disease

A group of inherited disorders causing disruption in the individual's ability to metabolize cholesterol (and other lipids). Three subtypes have been reported: Types A, B and C (type D was found to have gene mutation of type C). Types A and B are caused by an enzyme deficiency resulting in poor metabolism of lipids. Type C is due to a disruption in ability to metabolize cholesterol, with accumulation in lysosomes.

Prevalence: Type A & B is about 1:250,000 (1:40,000 in Ashkenazi Jew population), and Type C is about 1:150,000

Onset: Infancy to early adulthood.

Behavioral Symptoms/Clinical Presentation: Type A symptoms include failure to thrive, jaundice, ascites (fluid in abdomen), respiratory problems, vision loss and ophthalmoplegia (gaze paralysis), ataxia, myoclonus and mental retardation. Seizure disorders have been reported, but are more commonly associated with Type C (below). Patients with Type A typically present with early severe neurological and physical deficits and mortality occurs by age 4 years old. Patients with Type B, known as the visceral (organ) form, have less severe symptom presentation, with little to no neurological involvement. Patients with Type B have enlarged liver and spleens with respiratory problems with onset of cardiovascular disease as the disease progresses. Mortality of patients with Type B occurs later with survival into teens or early adulthood. Type C symptoms reflect accumulation of cholesterol in the liver and spleen while other lipids accumulate in the brain. Symptom onset usually occurs in young school age children, but may occur within first year of life or not until early adulthood. Symptom presentation may initially be limited to jaundice (enlarged liver and/or spleen) and/or vertical gaze palsy. Seizures may be present and are often refractory to antiepileptic medications. Onset of dementia occurs gradually. Motor abnormalities can also include dystonia, incoordination and breathing difficulties. Mortality often occurs by age 40 years.

Neuropathology: Type C includes diffuse atrophy with neurofibrillary tangles throughout the cerebral cortex and cerebellum.

Metachromatic Leukodystrophy (MLD)

An autosomal recessive lysosomal storage disease resulting in demyelination of the CNS. There are three forms of MLD: early (late infantile) onset type (before age 6 years old), juvenile onset (after age 6 but before adulthood) and adult forms (onset in early adulthood).

Prevalence: 1/100,000.

Behavioral Symptoms/Clinical Presentation: Early onset type is characterized by predominate motor symptoms early in the course of the disease, followed by cognitive deterioration of memory and visuoperceptual skills. Language skills (receptive and expressive speech and reading) are relatively spared until late. Social and emotional functioning is generally adequate in these children. Children can present with features of nonverbal learning disorder. Nonverbal learning disorder symptoms typically involve three areas: cognitive deficits, academic problems and social-emotional difficulties. Individuals may have deficits in attention (visual), memory (visual), executive functions (nonverbal reasoning, sequencing, etc.), language (reading comprehension, writing), fine motor skills/ psychomotor speed. Arithmetic skills are commonly disrupted and individuals often have a poor appreciation of social cues and appreciating intent with change in prosody in speech.

Juvenile and adult onset type is characterized by more prominent behavioral and cognitive problems, with features of frontal lobe syndromes. Neuropsychological deficits include pronounced attention problems, memory deficits (verbal more impaired than visual/nonverbal memory) and some deficits in executive functions. Language functions were generally intact. Motor deficits can be present, but not predominate.

Neuropathology: Similar for both early and late onset types, with diffuse deymyelination involving CNS, in which frontal lobe involvement is more affected.

*Hurler Syndrome [*Mucopolysaccharidosis (MPS) disorder (*MPS I])*

Autosomal recessive disease with genetic abnormality on chromosome 4. Results in glycosaminoglycans (GAGs) not being degraded properly by lysosomes. Accumulation occurs in virtually all organ systems.

Onset: Late infancy (after first year of life).

Behavioral Symptoms/Clinical Presentation: Early in infancy, children may appear normal and have normal neurodevelopment. Onset of a variety of abnormalities in motor, sensory, physical functioning begins by 1–2 years of life. Patients present with hepatosplenomegaly, corneal clouding, macrocephaly, hearing loss, respiratory insufficiency, heart disease, enlarged tongue and hip contractures. Hydrocephalus can be present due to blockage (noncommunicating). Cognitive development and obtaining basic milestones can be normal through year 1, but rate of development slows during the second year, and by age 3 years old, loss of previously acquired developmental milestones is apparent. Thus, cognitive function develops normally, slows, plateaus and then declines. Mortality generally occurs by 10 years of age.

Neuropathology: Ventriculomegaly is common. White matter may have "Swiss cheese" appearance due to accumulation of CAG.

Neuronal Ceroid Lipofuscinosis (NCL) Disorders

NCL are a group of neurodegenerative disorders resulting from excessive accumulation of lipopigments in body tissues. At present, there are eight distinct disorders; we review three of the most common.

Jansky-Bielschowsky Disease (Infantile NCL):

Fatal autosomal recessive disease (gene location 11p15) characterized by loss of cerebral grey matter neurons and accumulation of lipopigments in the neurons and glial cells in the CNS and PNS.

Onset: Late infancy to age 2–3 years of age.

Prevalence: 1:20,000

Behavioral Symptoms/Clinical Presentation: Early development is normal. Beginning around age 1–2 years old, infants typically present with hyperexcitability, muscular hypotonia and slowing of fine motor development. Microcephaly is also typically noted (called Stage 1), but children will initially continue to acquire developmental milestones. Symptoms progress with slowing in acquiring developmental milestones (stage 2). Subsequently, seizure disorder and deterioration of visual, motor and cognitive functioning occurs over a period of months (stage 3). Seizures typically present 1–3 years of age, and seizure types include myoclonic, complex partial or absence seizures. Visual loss is being unable to appreciate light. Other symptoms that may present include choreoathetosis, dystonias, truncal ataxia and myoclonic jerks. This is followed by further loss of visual, motor and cognitive functioning (stage 4). A vegetative state may ensue for several years before death. Mortality generally occurs by age 11 years, but survival to 16 years old has been reported.

Neuropathology: Thalamic T2 hypointensity is the first abnormality typically appreciated, but only after the first 6 months of age (no abnormalities are present early). White matter lesions, particularly involving the periventricular white matter surrounding the lateral ventricle, are next appreciated. Cerebral and cerebellar atrophy can be found after age 13 months. After age 2 years old, the macula is often discolored a brownish color along with degeneration of the retina and optic nerve.

Batten Disease (Juvenile NCL):

Fatal autosomal recessive disease (gene location 1p32) characterized by loss of cerebral grey matter neurons and accumulation of lipopigments in the neurons and glial cells in the CNS and PNS. It includes myoclonic epilepsy

Onset: 4–9 years of age. Mortality generally occurs by late teens or 20 s.

Prevalence: 1/21,000

Behavioral Symptoms/Clinical Presentation: The initial symptom is commonly progressive visual loss beginning at age 4–8 years old, such that children are functionally blind by their 20 s. Other changes early in course of disease are neuropsychological deficits, behavioral/personality changes and motor deficits presenting as truncal ataxia and other parkinsonian symptoms. Seizures typically present at age 10–11 years, but can be subtle and occur predominately at night, particularly when treated with anti-epileptic medication. Seizures are typically primary or secondary generalized seizures along with complex partial seizures. Seizure frequency can be low, with 1–8 seizures per year. Vision loss may be the initial symptom due to retinal pigmentation. Children may appear increasingly clumsy and uncoordinated with shortened and shuffling gait as parkinsonism worsens. Progression of cognitive deterioration occurs over years and progresses to blindness, global dementia and gross motor impairments. Neuropsychological deficits include attention, memory and speech deficits (dysarthria). Motor impairments lead individuals to become wheel chair bound, typically in adolescence or early adulthood.

Neuropathology: No structural abnormalities observed early (until after age 10 years old). Cerebral and/or cerebellar atrophy that progresses is observed after age 10 years old (typically in early adolescence).

Kuf's Disease aka Parry's Disease (Adult NCL):

Onset: Typically occurs before age 40 years (usually 15–25 years of age).

Incidence: 1/1,000,000

Behavioral Symptoms/Clinical Presentation: Two subtypes described. One presenting with progressive myoclonic epilepsy. Another subtype presents with early personality/behavioral changes (e.g., apathy, increased irritability, depressive features or emotional liability), cognitive decline (dementia) and facial dyskinesias, which may be initial symptoms. While visual problems may be present, patients have not progressed to blindness. Cognitive deterioration leading to dementia occurs. Disease course progresses slowly (e.g., 10 years).

Neuropathology: Neuroimaging can also be normal. Atrophy of brain stem, cerebellum and subcortical grey matter (thalamus and striatum) is also observed.

Aminoacidopathies

A group of 48 inherited aminoacidopathies in which disruption of various amino acids occurs. We review the most clinically visible of these, the phenylketonurias (PKUs).

Phenylketonurias (PKUs)

Autosomal recessive disease (gene location chromosome 12) characterized by a deficiency of a hepatic enzyme phenylalanine hydroxylase leading to failure to metabolize the amino acid phenylalanine to tyrosine. This results in patients excreting phenylpyruvic acid.

Prevalence: Varies among ethnic groups. 1:10,000 for Caucasians. Much lower in Japanese, Ashkenazi Jewish, Finish and African ethnic groups. Rates in Turkey is reported the highest, 1: 2600.

Onset: Disorder present at birth. Symptom onset typically occurs within first year of life in undetected children. However, there are considerable variations in severity of PKU, with mild and moderately affected individuals. Children with severe form with autosomal mothers are born with mental retardation. Alternatively, some children with milder forms may not exhibit symptoms until early school age or even early adolescence or not at all. Some patients with very mild forms do not require diet changes.

Behavioral Symptoms/Clinical Presentation: Affected children will present with lighter colored skin, eyes and hair than siblings/parents. Children may have a unique odor due to phenylpyruvic acid in urine. In untreated children, development is typically normal initially, but after several months, progressive decline in motor skills and deterioration in global cognitive function occurs. Infants may exhibit weight loss, frequent vomiting (emesis), diarrhea, and be sensitive to bright light. Motor abnormalities, with myoclonus, tremors and seizures can occur. In older children, symptoms can progress with repetitive behaviors (rocking, head banging) and self-injurious behaviors. Growth is often slowed and seizures develop if disease is not treated. Progression of untreated disease leads to severe cognitive impairment (mental retardation) with seizures.

Neuropsychological symptoms: Adolescents and young adults with early treated PKU have been found to exhibit normal or near normal general cognitive (intellectual) function with deficits in attention/executive function, verbal fluency and word retrieval problems and memory. Neuropsychological deficits are associated with childhood treatment indicators (e.g., level of phenylalanine).

Neuropathology: Cerebral and/or cerebellar atrophy can be found, but more often among patients with longer disease course. Early onset neuroimaging is often normal.

Acute Disseminated Encephalomyelitis (ADEM)

This is an acute demyelinating disease that typically follows infection, immunization (rare), or, occasionally no known precipitating infection. In developed countries mortality is now generally rare (~2%), but can be as high as 10–20% in undeveloped countries. Recovery is classically described as complete after several months, with no residual deficits after one year. However, about a third of patients can exhibit permanent neurological and/or neuropsychological deficits. Adults with ADEM who survive tend to present with fewer permanent neurological or neuropsychological deficits.

Prevalence: 3:100,000 for first decade of life. 1:100,000 for second decade of life. In North America, incidence increases during February/March and is less frequent in July/August. Incidence may be decreasing as worldwide use of immunization to pathogens known to be associated with ADEM has increased, resulting in less ADEM.

Onset: ADEM in childhood occurs most often (80%) before 10 years old. Symptoms typically present within days or weeks following exposure to virus/bacteria, and often when other symptoms of infection have resolved or are resolving.

Behavioral Symptoms/Clinical Presentation: Symptoms present acutely and include confusion, somnolence, seizures, fever and/or stiffness of the neck. Ataxia, myoclonus and choreoathetosis have been reported. Classically, ADEM shares a clinical and pathological resemblance to Multiple Sclerosis (MS), but generally has clinical and pathological features which differentiates ADEM from MS. Typically, ADEM in children occurs as a progressive decline in function in school age children, while MS more typically occurs in late adolescence/early adulthood. There is, however, overlap and ADEM and MS may reflect conditions of a clinical continuum. A form affecting only the cerebellum has been reported (particularly with Varicella (chicken pox)), presenting with predominate ataxia. The syndrome can rapidly progress over hours to days with headache, confusion and neck stiffness being more common. Less commonly, patients will experience stupor, decerebrate rigidity and coma.

Neuropsychological deficits are associated with the extent of underlying neuropathology present, which can range from none to significant. Children with severe ADEM can present with global cognitive impairment after recovery, with scores on intelligence based tests at or below 70. Less profound neuropsychological impairments can include deficits in attention/concentration, memory, language, visuoperception, executive and/or motor skills. Learning and memory scores may fall below normal, but recognition memory is usually better and normal or nearly normal. In some cases, residual ataxia and/or hemiparesis are possible.

Neuropathology: Can exhibit variable bilateral white matter lesions. Classically, ADEM will result in bilateral diffuse white matter lesions early in symptom course that than resolve over time, with little residual pathological evidence of ADEM. Chemokines concentrations elevated in CSF of patients with ADEM.

Rasmussen's Encephalopathy

Rasmussen's syndrome is an autoimmune disorder which causes severe deficits that start unilaterally, but spread bilaterally if not arrested. The mechanism of immune dysfunction in Rasmussen's syndrome is unknown. It typically leads to hemispheric atrophy.

Prevalence: very rare (less than 1:100,000).

Onset: The onset of the disease is typically in middle childhood (mean onset peaks at age 6 years old), but can be quite variable (Bien et al., 2005). The onset is marked by unilateral seizures, hemiparesis and lateralized cognitive and motor symptoms. Progression is insidious and often includes increased seizure frequency, hemiplegia and marked cognitive and less frequently sensory deficits over 8- to 12-month time period.

Behavioral Symptoms/Clinical Presentation: As noted, the initial symptoms are often seizures of unknown etiology and hemiparesis. These symptoms are progressive and lead to increased seizure frequency, duration and severity as well as associated hemiplegia. Bien et al. (2005) describes three phases, the first of which is the prodromal phase. The prodromal phase is associated with the initial onset of mild infrequent seizures and, often gradually, hemiparesis that develops often in less than a year (median duration was 7.1 months). The second phase, termed acute phase, results in more frequent and severe seizures, evolving from frequent simple seizures to more complex partial seizures. This stage is also marked by greater hemiparesis or frank hemiplegia, cognitive deterioration (see below) and occasional hemianopsia. This stage is noted to last a median of 8 months. The third stage, or residual stage, is characterized by a decrease in seizure frequency, relatively stable neurological deficits and additional cognitive decline. In this last stage, some patients may recover from hemiplegia and exhibit a spastic hemiparesis. Diagnosis is made using criteria of unilateral seizures, unilateral focal physical of cognitive symptoms, and unilateral hyperintensities in the cortex and underlying white matter and caudate. Treatment with antiepileptic drugs is typically unsuccessful both in monotherapy and poly-therapy. Clinical monitoring of the disease course may be achieved by assessing extent of hemiparesis. Hemispherectomy has demonstrated the only effective treatment in controlling seizures, but is not without its residual consequences of spastic hemiplegia and homonymous hemianopsia. Outcomes from immunotherapy with corticosteroids, immunoglobulins (IVIG) and plasmapheresis have been mixed with some patients responding well if these therapies are administered early in the course of the disease.

Neuropsychological deficits are typically striking unilateral deficits in the cognitive domains in the effected hemisphere. In addition to the contralateral motor and sensory symptoms, patients with left hemisphere onset typically have language and verbal memory deficits. Language-based deficits may initially be fluency and naming deficits and progress to frank expressive and/or receptive aphasias (see Chaps. 7 and 12, this volume). As these symptoms progress, these patients may have a right hemianopsia, apraxias and language-based reasoning and problem-solving deficits. In contrast, patients with right hemisphere onset typically have visuospatial processing, left neglect and visual (nonverbal) memory deficits in addition to left-sided motor impairments. As these symptoms progress, both nonverbal reasoning and expressive and receptive prosody deficits may emerge in addition to a left hemianopsia. Regardless of the side of onset, these patients demonstrate non-focal or lateralizing neuropsychological deficits in attention and processing speed. If the disease progression is arrested (often following hemispherectomy) and seizure control can be gained, some recovery of lost functions may be possible. However, residual neurologic and neuropsychological deficits remain and can be severe. Recovery of function (both motor and neuropsychological) is typically better when treated in younger children. Adolescents and younger adults tend to exhibit less recovery of function, although some recovery may occur. For example, the patient may be ambulatory with a spastic gait and gain some gross motor function of arm and hand. Some neuropsychological recovery of function may occur, including development of some language skills in younger patients (particularly patients younger than 6 years old) as well as attention/executive, memory and visuoconstructional skills. Compared to baseline, left hemispherectomy patients exhibited a post-surgical decline in expressive speech, but no other domain, including receptive language functions. The patient's academic functioning may be delayed, but some academic skill acquisition often occurs.

Neuropathology: The etiology remains to be well understood. Originally thought to be due to a virus, data suggest it is an autoimmune disease, with involvement of autoantibodies and T-lymphocyte-mediated cytotoxicity. Grossly, most of the brain damage occurs over an 8- to 12-month time frame. MRI findings indicate unilateral cerebral atrophy, particularly involving the insular and peri-insular regions, diffuse and patchy subcortical white matter T2 hyperintensities and often atrophy of the caudate. FDG PET scans show predominant hypometabolism of the frontotemporal regions during the early stages of disease, but involve more posterior cortex later in the disease course.

Vitamin B12 Deficiency (Cobalamin Disorders)

Deficiency in vitamin B12 (cobalamin) can be due to a number of autosomal recessive metabolic disorders and environmental causes.

Prevalence: True prevalence is unknown and varies substantially among populations. Depending upon the assay used and cut-off threshold (e.g., less than 200 pg/ml vs. 300 pg/ml), estimates vary from 3–16% of adults in the USA. Prevalence in Europe has been reported to vary from 1.6–10%. Rates in developing countries can be higher and is higher in subpopulations at risk, including the elderly, vegetarians and those with diabetes. Recommended daily intake of B12 is 2 mcg for adults and adolescents, and 0.7 mcg for children.

Onset: Most common across age groups is due to poor absorption. May be present at birth due to variety of intrinsic factors: Juvenile/congenital pernicious anemia (unable to absorb B12 due to lack of intrinsic factor in gastric secretions), transport protein abnormalities (e.g., Imerslund-Grasbeck syndrome), abnormalities of intracellular B12 metabolism (methylmalonic aciduria, homocystinuria), pancreatic deficiency, Zollinger-Ellison syndrome, disorders of terminal ileum (e.g., celiac disease, Whipple disease, etc.), etc. Extrinsic factors include: competition for B12 due to tapeworms, medications (e.g., neomycin), deficient B12 intake, etc. Abnormal B12 metabolism noted for infants born to mothers with B12 deficiency. While onset is rare in children/adolescents, it may occur at any time. For infants, symptoms present after store of B12 obtained in utero is exhausted. Symptoms present more rapidly and more intensely in infancy and early childhood than in adults, as liver stores from in utero development are substantially less than the 2- to 5-year store typical for adults. Treatment often results in rapid improvement, although initial worsening immediately after treatment is initiated has been reported. Outcome is variable, but decreased overall cognitive functioning has been observed relative to the normal population.

Behavioral Symptoms/Clinical Presentation: B12 deficiency in infancy presents with failure to thrive, poor feeding, edema, abdominal pain, pallor, irritability, developmental delays, lethargy, respiratory distress, megaloblastic anemia and pigmentary retinopathy. Rarely, cobalamin metabolic defects can present in later childhood, and present with a decline in cognitive and motor skills and choreoathetoid movements. Among adults the classic presentation is triad of weakness, sore tongue and paresthesias, but these symptoms are rarely the chief complaints (or noted) in children. In adolescence/adulthood early symptoms include weakness, fatigue, loss of appetite (anorexia), nausea, constipation and paresthesias of the toes and fingers. Other symptoms include brittle nails, dry lips, large spleen and low grade fever. If not treated, paresthesias may extend to limbs along with onset of limb weakness and ataxia. Autonomic nervous system dysfunction (syncope, heart palpitations, constipation, dyspnea, heartburn, etc.) as well as cognitive/neuropsychological deficits may occur. Common neuropsychological deficits include mental retardation along with impaired attention/executive, memory, language and visuoperceptual functions. Developmental delays are often present. In older children and young adults (and older adults) general cognitive deterioration from previous ability level occurs. Increased irritability, labile mood, anxiety, paranoia and hallucinations can occur.

Neuropathology: Diffuse cerebral atrophy with widening of sulci (narrowing of gyri) as well as basal ganglia. Other manifestations include pathology in peripheral and optic nerves, posterior column and lateral corticospinal tract (subacute combined degeneration of spinal cord).

Galactosemia

Prevalence: Incidence rate is 1/62,000 live births. Carrier frequency is 1/125.

Onset: Autosomal recessive disorder of carbohydrate metabolism with symptoms presenting within weeks of birth.

Behavioral Symptoms/Clinical Presentation: First symptoms are typically jaundice and anorexia. Failure to thrive in infancy, cataracts and hepatomegaly. Without treatment, symptoms worsen to include emesis, diarrhea, lethargy, poor growth, septicemia, hepatomegaly, aminoaciduria, Often identified as failure to thrive infants. Ataxia, tremor, dysarthria and hypotonia can be present. Along with cognitive deficits, physical development is diminished. Neuropsychological deficits in intellectual functioning, academic problems, language and visuoperceptual functions. Treatment is lactose-free diet. Despite strict adherence, neuropsychological deficits remain and progressive neuropsychological deficits occur. Mild deficits in mean intellectual function have been identified in groups (Mean FSIQ = 85) (Schweitzer et al., 1993).

Neuropathology: Cerebral and cerebellar atrophy with demyelination (multiple white matter lesions).

Hallervorden-Spatz Syndrome

Fatal disorder thought to be related to disorder of iron metabolism, with mutation of the PANK2 gene. Could be autosomal recessive disorder, but some cases appear sporadic.

Prevalence: 1–3:1,000,000.

Onset: Highly variable, but commonly symptoms present by late childhood or early adolescent.

Behavioral Symptoms/Clinical Presentation: Progressive onset of movement disorder and in some patients, cognitive deterioration. Initial symptom may be optic atrophy (retinal pigment found in 20% of patients) followed by movement disorder and/or cognitive deficits. Motor disorder typically involves a progressive dystonia (particularly involving the feet) with gait ataxia, and dysarthria. Choreoathetosis has been reported in 50% patients.

Cognitive deterioration is slow and progressive. Pattern similar to a "subcortical" dementia pattern with early deficits in fine motor deficits, attention/executive dysfunction, memory loss (recognition cues can improve recall). Visuoperceptual/visuospatial deficits and acalculia may be present. Mood/personality changes occur later in the disease and can include stereotyped and compulsive behaviors and irritability.

Neuropathology: Excessive iron deposition in the globus pallidus, pars reticulata of the substantia nigra (SNr) and red nucleus. Neuroimaging frequently reveals "eye of the tiger" sign in which bilateral hyperintensities are found above globus pallidus and substantia nigra.

Hashimoto's Encephalopathy

Hashimoto's encephalopathy is due to Hashimoto's disease, which reflects onset of hypothyroidism due to the person's immune system attacking the thyroid gland. Hashimoto's disease is also termed chronic lymphocytic thyroiditis. Importantly, Hashimoto's encephalopathy responds very well to steroid therapy, and return to baseline or near baseline cognitive functioning has been reported following cessation of steroid treatment for many, but not all cases.

Prevalence: Rare. Less than 50 cases have been reported worldwide, but prevalence may be higher as the etiology for encephalopathy due to hypothyroidism has only recently been reported.

Onset: Range of onset varies from 14 years old to 78 years. Average age is about 47 years old.

Behavioral Symptoms/Clinical Presentation:

Neuropathology: Hashimoto's encephalopathy has been found in patients with blood studies indicating a euthyroid state. Positive antithyroid antibody titer is present. MRI studies frequently identify bilateral hyperintensities of the cerebral white matter and/or mild cortical atrophy.

Rett Syndrome

A progressive dementia originally thought to only affect young females, but a form also found for young males.

Prevalence: 1/15,000-20,000.

Onset: Symptoms present typically by 18 months of age.

Behavioral Symptoms/Clinical Presentation: A period of normal development followed by reversal and deterioration of cognitive and motor skills. Patients present with autistic features, loss of use of purposeful hand movements, seizures and ataxia. Children can present with a characteristic hand wringing movements. Spastic paraparesis develops and physical growth is decreased.

Neuropathology: Cessation or severe reduction in axo-dendritic connections in the CNS. Initially no clear abnormality on neuroimaging, except for volumetric reductions of frontal parenchyma, caudate nucleus and mid brain. Microcephaly develops.

Hydrocephalus

Hydrocephalus refers to an increase volume of cerebrospinal fluid (CSF) in the ventricles leading to increased intracerebral pressure. Hydrocephalus is not a disease entity, but rather a symptom with many causes (over 180 different causes have been identified). Hydrocephalus can be divided into two categories; (1) congenital hydrocephalus, or (2) acquired hydrocephalus. Another division is by presumed etiology and includes: (a) communicating hydrocephalus and (b) noncommunicating hydrocephalus. Congenital hydrocephalus is present at birth and is most often due to neural tube defects, including spina bifida, Dandy-Walker syndrome, congenital foraminal stenosis and meningomyelocele. In addition, congenital hydrocephalus can develop following infection such as meningitis or cyst, or in utero trauma such as hemorrhagic stroke or intraventricular bleeding. Other causes may produce hydrocephalus such as space occupying (tumor or arteriovenous malformation). Hydrocephalus is often treated with ventricular-peritoneal (VP) shunt in which CSF is drained into the peritoneum via a shunt inserted into the affected ventricular system (often lateral ventricle).

Prevalence: 1–2 per 1000 live births secondary to neural tube defects and 0.5 per 1000 due to other causes.

Onset: May begin as early as in utero through childhood; however, the incidence after infancy is roughly half of that during infancy. Progression can be relatively rapid (days) to chronic (months to years).

Behavioral Symptoms/Clinical Presentation: Varies by age and etiology (congenital versus acquired). Onset of symptoms is slower in children than adults, and may be quite subtle. Children with congenital hydrocephalus can be more difficult to identify in some cases, as a change in clinical status after a period of normal development is not present, and an infant with congenital hydrocephalus may not present with pronounced symptoms. Symptoms may be limited, and appear grossly normal, save for a larger than normal head. Other symptoms can include low energy, poor feeding and/or irritability. Infants with acquired hydrocephalus, even at birth, can be difficult to readily identify as well, but there may be more clinical symptoms, particularly if hydrocephalus is secondary to stroke. As the patients become older, onset of acquired hydrocephalus will typically result in more pronounced clinical changes as reviewed below.

- Infants and young children typically present with lethargy, poor feeding, emesis and irritability. Acquired developmental milestones can be lost. Other features include separation of skull sutures, increased head circumference, bulging fontanelle, frontal "bossing," downward gaze paralysis (so-called "setting sun sign") and distortion of skull shape, appearing "globular." Seizures may also occur. Head circumference can rapidly increase over days to weeks.

- Children and adolescents/young adults (age 6 years and older) present with headache involving nausea (often with emesis) that is worse in the morning (and affected by head position), diplopia, gait apraxia, reduced fine motor coordination, papilledema, CN VI palsy, urinary incontinence, lethargy and social withdraw, increased irritability and decreased academic performance/loss of academic skills.

Early neuropsychological impairments can be mild (or completely missed). In general, children with hydrocephalus present with mild neuropsychological deficits in psychomotor slowing, attention/executive, memory and visuospatial functions. Deficits can fluctuate over time. Progression of hydrocephalus can lead to global cognitive impairments, in which some individuals may exhibit profound mental retardation. However, children treated early in course of acquired hydrocephalus can show recovery of neuropsychological function. Paradoxically, individuals with congenital or slowly developing hydrocephalus may show less severe neuropsychological deficits, but exhibit less recovery of cognitive functions with treatment (VP shunting). Recovery of function is also dependent on any comorbid conditions/disease affecting the brain (e.g., previous stroke, traumatic brain injury, space occupying lesions vs. congenital defects, infection, etc.). There have been case reports of individuals with marked hydrocephalus exhibiting normal function in everyday life with mild to moderate neuropsychological deficits, despite extreme hydrocephalus (e.g., Feuillet et al., 2007).

Neuropathology: Hydrocephalus can result from three etiologies: (1) obstruction of CSF flow in the ventricles, (2) insufficient absorption of CSF and (3) excessive secretion of CSF by choroid plexus (see Chap. 3 for review of CSF pathway). In general, hydrocephalus is categorized as *communicating* or *noncommunicating.*

Communicating hydrocephalus occurs when there is insufficient re-absorption of CSF due to obstruction of arachnoid villi, draining veins or subarachnoid space. Termed "communicating" because CSF flow is not obstructed between the ventricles. Causes include intraventricular/subarachnoid hemorrhage or infectious process that irritates the leptomeninges, congenital malformations (i.e., Arnold-Chiari malformation), posttraumatic obstruction, or tumors.

Normal pressure hydrocephalus is a particular subtype of communicating hydrocephalus that is characteristically associated with the elderly, but has been reported in adults. It is characterized by normal CSF pressure but imaging demonstrates enlarged ventricles (particularly lateral ventricles). The exact mechanism remains unknown, but theorized due to dysfunction of the arachnoid granulations located within the superior sagittal sinus.

Noncommunicating hydrocephalus occurs when CSF flow is blocked (or diminished) by intraventricular obstruction involving the foramen of Monro, third ventricle, aqueduct and/or the foramen of Magendie or Luschka. Common etiologies include aqueductal stenosis, congenital malformations (i.e., aqueductal stenosis) or cysts/tumors (extra- or intra-ventricular). The enlarged ventricles observed with structural neuroimaging is often marked, but may not include the entire ventricular system (will not in cases of noncommunicating hydrocephalus).

Pseudotumor Cerebri (Idiopathic Intracranial Hypertension)

Pseudotumor cerebri or idiopathic intracranial hypertension (IIH) is a progressive disorder marked by increased intracranial pressure without a known cause. Some divide pseudotumor cerebri into primary (idiopathic) and secondary forms. In primary pseudotumor cerebri, there is no clear cause, but it has a higher prevalence in obese young adult women. Secondary pseudotumor cerebri is not firmly established, but some potential cause(s) are identified, such as venous sinus thrombosis and increased venous sinus pressure as well as some medications such as retinoic acid, antibiotics, steroids and vitamin A.

Prevalence: In children, it is unknown, but "secondary" pseudotumor cerebri has been reported in children younger than 6 years old. Cases of primary (idiopathic) pseudotumor cerebri are very rare in young children, and more common after age 11 years old. Increasing frequency of pseudotumor cerebri is suspected in children. There is no sex discrepancy in prevalence in children. Highest prevalence is in obese women of childbearing age. Overall incidence rate is 0.9 per 100,000. Incidence in women is 1.6 per 100,000 and 7.9 to 19.3 cases per 100,000 in obese women (aged 15–44). More common in women than men (8:1). Risk increased with female gender, reproductive age group, obesity, menstrual irregularity. There is some evidence of increased risk in children with low thyrotropin levels who are treated with excessive thyroxine replacement therapy.

Behavioral Symptoms/Clinical Presentation: In children, presenting symptoms usually include headache, fatigue, blurred vision and nausea/vomiting. In adolescents/young adults, associated with headache, vision loss, papilledema and horizontal diplopia. Most common symptoms in children and adults are nonspecific headache, fatigue, blurred vision and nausea/vomiting. Other symptoms include horizontal diplopia (with some having a false-localizing CN VI nerve palsy), papilledema (transient visual loss, in which vision blacks out or dims in one or both eyes for short periods of time, often after leaning or bending down; loss of visual fields beginning in the nasal inferior quadrants; blurring or visual distortions—metamorphopsia; or sudden vision loss in one eye—due to intraocular hemorrhage) and pulsatile tinnitus (ringing in one or both ears often in association with heart beat). If untreated, symptoms progress to include lethargy, acute cognitive decline and, rarely, radiculopathy. Papilledema present in 22–96% of cases. Cases of reduced abduction of one or both eyes (eyes looking away from body) reported. Optic nerve damage can be persistent even if ICP is controlled. Treatment usually consists of diuretics and weight loss if no occult cause can be found. Shunting is also common in cases that do not respond to diuretics and weight loss.

Neuropathology: Unknown. Research has demonstrated an increased resistance in arachnoid granulations for absorption of CSF. Some data suggest increased intracranial pressure results in narrowing of the transverse dural venous sinus, which exacerbates the pressure elevation by increasing venous pressure in the superior sagittal sinus. Alternatively, arterial inflow has shown to be elevated in patients with pseudotumor cerebri (21%), while drainage via the superior sagittal sinus was normal (net increase in pressure due to increased arterial inflow).

Sickle Cell Disease

Prevalence: One in six-hundred (1:600) newborn African-American children, but is present in many ethnic populations to a lesser degree.

Onset: Systematic testing of newborns in the USA has led to identification of the gene at birth. SSD is an autosomal recessive pattern of inheritance and thus would be expected to be carried by 25% of children who have a parent with the gene. For individuals with both parents having the trait, 50% would be expected to manifest the disease. The course is often waxing and waning and can be marked by medical complications in multiple systems (i.e., renal, hepatic, pulmonary, cardiac). The course of Neuropsychological function can also be quite variable and is determined by the interplay or the effect of CNS involvement as well as the effect of other systems on CNS functioning over time. Sickle cell anemia is present at birth, and symptoms typically present in infants in which sickle cell disease is not identified/treated after 4 months of age. Infants diagnosed with sickle cell anemia will typically have transcranial Doppler ultrasounds of arteries to identify and reduce risk for strokes.

Behavioral Symptoms/Clinical Presentation:. Early in the course, undetected newborns may develop colic symptoms or fever. Other symptoms include headache, dizziness, shortness of breath, swelling/pain/coldness in hands/feet and pale skin. Swelling and pain of the hands and/or feet may be the first symptom of a sickle cell crisis in infants. A sickle cell "crisis" is associated with sudden pain throughout the body, and occurs when red blood cells clump together. The clumps of red blood cells can obstruct small arteries and veins throughout the body, including the brain. The obstruction of small arteries can lead to damage of organs and tissues throughout the body, and either TIA or clear stroke (see Chap. 13, this volume for detailed description). The pain of a sickle cell crisis can vary from person to person from mild to severe, intense pain that typically lasts several hours to several days in duration. Obstruction of arterial blood can damage any organ, and patients may present with TIA/stroke, vision loss/blindness, and damage to lungs, liver, kidney, stomach and/or heart. Splenic crisis may occur, and result in a blood transfusion. Patients suffering a stroke may present with either or both ischemic and/or hemorrhagic stroke.

Neuropathology: The primary neuropathology includes the cumulative effect of microvascular cerebral lesions and possibly larger strokes. The associated area of infarct predicts the extent and nature of the deficit seen in these children. Studies consistently demonstrate wide ranging and variable neuropsychological deficits in attention, memory, processing speed, visuospatial skill and executive (e.g., reasoning/problem solving, sequencing) skills. These are often accompanied by deficits in academic skill development or frank regression.

Lafora Disease (aka Lafora Progressive Myoclonic Epilepsy)

Lafora is an autosomal recessive genetic disorder marked by inclusion bodies (Lafora) in the brain, skin, liver and muscles. It is one of five inherited progressive myoclonus epilepsy syndromes. It is ultimately a fatal disease, and mortality generally occurs within 2 to10 years of symptom onset. Few individuals with Lafora disease live to be 30 years old.

Prevalence: Unknown, and classified as a "rare" disease, affecting less than 200,000 in the entire USA population. Incidence rate is equal for males and females. May be more common among children of Middle Eastern, Southern European, South Asian and North African descent.

Onset: Typically in adolescents, but may develop in childhood. While frequently after the first decade of life, a few cases of Lafora disease onset have been reported in early childhood (ages 5 and 6 years old).

Behavioral Symptoms/Clinical Presentation: Initial presenting symptom is often a seizure in late childhood or early adolescence (after age 10 years old). If onset in early childhood, first symptoms tend to be learning problems and onset of neuropsychological deficits. In both cases, the initial symptom is quickly followed by onset of other common symptoms including myoclonus (muscle spasms), ataxic gait, rapidly progressive dementia, temporary blindness, visual hallucinations and/or depression. Patients with Lafora disease develop several seizures types (myoclonic seizures, generalized tonic-clonic seizures, focal seizures) and the myoclonus is progressive and severe such that the individual may appear to be having nearly continuous myoclonus along with progressive motor ataxia and dementia. There are broad and marked neuropsychological deficits, but some data suggest a common neuropsychological pattern. Most profound deficits observed in visuoperceptual/visuoperceptual and attention/executive functions. Memory is impaired. Phonemic verbal fluency more impaired than semantic verbal fluency. Verbal abilities can be initially somewhat spared, although verbal intellectual function was impaired compared to controls. There is no known treatment for Lafora disease and treatment is usually symptomatic relief for seizures and myoclonus.

Neuropathology: Most cases of Lafora disease are caused by genetic mutation of EPM2A and EPM2B on chromosome 6, which code for protein laforin and malin. Most patients (75–85%) with Lafora disease have the EPM2A mutation. Most of the remaining cases are thought to be due to mutations of EPM2B. A few cases are due to an as yet unidentified gene. The mutations lead to formation of Lafora bodies within cellular cytoplasm. Formation of these bodies leads to buildup of polyglucosans within cells and compromise cell function ultimately leading to cell death. Neuroanatomic studies demonstrates greater metabolic dysfunction of the frontal, parietal, basal ganglia and cerebellum regions using proton magnetic resonance spectroscopy (^{1}[H]MRS) (Pichiecchio et al., 2008; Villanueva et al., 2006).

HIV-associated Progressive Encephalopathy (HPE)/ HIV-associated Neurocognitive Disorders

The vast majority of children infected with HIV are born to infected mothers, with exposure either in utero, during delivery or from breast milk. HIV infections occur in about 10–30% of infants born to women infected with HIV. HIV-associated progressive encephalopathy is a term used to describe a constellation of neurocognitive, motor and behavioral symptoms in children mirroring the termed HIV-associated neurocognitive disorders (HAND) in adults. As noted above, there are a number of direct and indirect complications with HIV infection and AIDS that can lead to transitory or permanent neuropsychological deficits.

Prevalence: HPE has been reported in 10–67% of children as the first presenting symptom of HIV infection. In untreated children, the prevalence of HPE is 50–67%, but reports of up to 90% of pediatric samples have exhibited some cognitive dysfunction. In children receiving antiretroviral therapy, the prevalence rate is low 1.6%.

Risk factors: HIV infection in general, especially with lower CD4 counts.

Onset: Most cases present at infancy. Progression when HIV infection is present in infancy is faster than in adults. Some form of symptoms (whether neurocognitive or not) are usually present by 3 years old. The majority (about 80%) will exhibit clinical symptomatology by 6 months of age. Onset and progression varies, but once AIDS symptoms have started, progression is similar to that of adults. Like adults, course is usually progressive, but reduction in symptoms with antiviral therapy and protease inhibitors (i.e., highly active antiviral therapy) among untreated children has been reported.

Behavioral Symptoms/Clinical Presentation: Among infants, the first manifestation of HPE is often delays in reaching psychomotor developmental milestones and slowing of global functioning. In young children, developing new motor skills and learning rates is slowed. Fine motor skills and motor coordination development slows, and is often impaired. Behavioral abnormalities with social withdraw, apathy or emotional liability may occur. Learning disorders may be identified. If infection (or symptom onset) occurs in late childhood and/or adolescence, symptoms mirror that of the adults (see Chap. 14, this volume). Neuropsychological deficits mirror those of adults with deficits in attention/executive, visuoperceptual/visuospatial, language (verbal fluency and confrontation naming) and memory functions. Recognition memory likely will be better than delayed recall. As disease progresses, patients often present with seizures, prominent motor deficits, increasing cognitive deterioration (worsening dementia), mutism, incontinence and coma.

Neuropathology: Cerebral atrophy largely due to prominent lesions of subcortical white matter and subcortical grey matter structures.

Cerebral Autosomal Dominant Arteriopathy with Subcortical Infarcts and Leukoencephalopathy (CADISIL)

Autosomal dominate disorder presenting in early adulthood with headaches (typically migrainous in nature) and recurrent small strokes that culminate in a dementia syndrome.

Prevalence: 1–9:1,000,000.

Onset: Variable, but typically early adulthood. Symptoms present by early 60 s.

Behavioral Symptoms/Clinical Presentation: Patients may present with initial cognitive deterioration and/or transient neurological symptoms such as hemiparesis or sensory losses consistent with TIAs and small strokes. Ischemic strokes tend to predominate in the subcortical white matter and basal ganglia. Neuropsychological deficits typically exhibit as a progressive "subcortical dementia pattern" in early to middle adulthood. Patients may present with early attention/executive dysfunction, psychomotor slowing, verbal fluency, and word finding problems, and memory deficits. Motor deficits are common, with reduced fine motor coordination, which can be asymmetric. In addition, sensory loss, with hemi-inattention and/or the presence of sensory extinction, may also be present.

Neuropathology: MRI/CT studies identify multiple confluent white matter lesions of various sizes, predominantly involving the subcortical white matter and basal ganglia.

Wilson's Disease (Hepatolenticular Degeneration)

Autosomal recessive disorder of copper metabolism mapped to chromosome 13 (13q14.3). Results in the accumulation of copper in the brain, eyes, kidney and liver. Can be fatal if not detected.

Prevalence: 1:30,000.

Onset: Highly variable, ranging from middle childhood to middle adulthood (e.g., 5–50 years old). Typical symptom onset is 10–21 years old. Onset in early childhood (before age 5 years) is very rare.

Behavioral Symptoms/Clinical Presentation: Symptoms involve two prominent types; complications related to hepatic (liver) dysfunction and symptoms due to neurological dysfunction. Hepatic-based symptom onset typically occurs in late childhood early teens (10–14), while neurological-based symptom onset is often later, occurring in late teens to early 20 s. Classically, Wilson's disease is associated with jaundice, a greenish-brown ring around the cornea (Kayser-Fleischer rings) due to copper accumulation, motor abnormalities and cognitive/behavioral problems. While Kayser-Fleischer rings are often thought of as diagnostic of Wilson's disease, they are not (Kayser-Fleischer rings not specific to Wilson's disease and not found in all cases). Jaundice with unknown etiology for acute hepatitis and elevated liver enzymes are found in Wilson's disease and are often first symptoms. Liver cirrhosis is often found among patients with cognitive and behavioral symptoms. Motor symptoms include asymmetric tremor (may be postural, resting or kinetic), dysarthria, and Parkinsonian symptoms (masked facies, bradykinesia, ataxia, dyskinesias and rigidity). Asterixis (hand flapping tremor) and chorea may also be present. Cognitive and psychiatric symptoms are found in neurologically symptomatic individuals (but few deficits have been found in asymptomatic individuals). Neuropsychological deficits involve complex attention/executive functions, memory and visuoconstructional skills. Fine motor deficits are frequently observed. Dysarthria is not uncommon. Language functions generally remain grossly intact. Mood/personality changes include affective labiality, impulsivity, disinhibition, depression, anxiety symptoms, and psychosis in some patients. Up to 50% of patients with Wilson's disease were diagnosed with psychiatric disorders before Wilson's disease was identified.

Neuropathology: Diffuse atrophy may be present, with greater atrophy of the striatum. There are neuronal loss, astrocytic gliosis, and Opalski cells.

22q11.2 Deletion Syndrome (Also Termed DiGeorge Syndrome, Conotruncal Anomaly Face, Cayler Cardiofacial Syndrome, Velo-cardio-facial Syndrome, Opitz G/BBB Depending Upon Various Symptom Cluster Phenotypes with Shared Genetic Pathology)

Disorder caused by the deletion of a small part of chromosome 22 at location designated q11.2.

Prevalence: 1:4000 live births. It is the most common microdeletion syndrome. It is the second most common cause of developmental delays and congenital heart disease. It is the most common cause of syndromic cleft palate and schizophrenia.

Onset: Birth abnormalities common, but highly variable, and clinical symptoms may not be recognized until childhood and even adulthood.

Behavioral Symptoms/Clinical Presentation: 22q11.2 deletion syndrome can result in a vast array of symptoms and signs that can affect many parts of the body and symptoms and signs differ markedly among individuals affected. DiGeorge syndrome is associated with a classic triad of symptoms including congenital heart disease, hypocalcemia, and immunodeficiency; but multiple different symptoms and signs are known to occur. Different sizes and locations of microdeletion of 22q11 are known to occur and are thought to account for the variability in symptoms and signs. Most common systems affected include heart abnormalities, recurrent infections (can include recurrent otitis media) and distinct facial features (small ears with squared upper ear, hooded eyelids, asymmetric facial appearance when tearful, small mouth, chin and nose tip) and/or cleft palate. Other symptoms and medical disorders include submucosal cleft palate (muscles in the roof of the mouth does not close completely), breathing problems, dysphagia, nasal quality to speech due to submucosal cleft palate, kidney abnormalities, thrombocytopenia, gastrointestinal problems, (conductive) hearing loss, seizures, low muscle tone and neuropsychological and behavioral deficits. Skeletal abnormalities can also present with individuals having a short stature and, sometimes, abnormalities of the spinal bones.

Cognitive and psychiatric symptoms are found in neurologically symptomatic individuals with a distinct neuropsychological profile classically described as involving deficits in attention/executive, visual-spatial/constructional and aspects of memory and speech/language functions. Verbal (auditory) memory may be better than nonverbal (visual) memory, and deficits in facial memory are a recognized weakness. Deficits in speech/language include impaired verbal comprehension for complex syntax, decreased verbal fluency and pragmatic language use. Children and adolescents with 22q11.2 deletion syndrome often meet criteria for Attention Deficit Hyperactivity Disorder (ADHD), learning disorders (mathematics and reading comprehension/language pragmatics) and/or a Nonverbal Learning Disorder (DSM-5-TR Autism Spectrum Disorder) that include problems in communication and social interactions (and neurocognitive features as above). Psychiatric/Mood conditions are common and 22q11.2 deletion syndrome is one of the highest known risk factors for developing schizophrenia with a 25–30% lifetime prevalence rate (which is 1% in the general population). Interestingly, the presence of 22q11.2 deletions among individuals with schizophrenia has been found to occur at higher rates than in the general population. The symptomatic features of schizophrenia among individuals with 22q11.2 deletion syndrome mirror the core symptoms of schizophrenia that develop in this population, but individuals with 22q11.2 deletion syndrome have characteristic physical features, heart conditions and lower intellectual functions (high rates of learning disorders), and include anxiety disorders, obsessive and compulsive behaviors, as well as difficulties in social interactions and communication. Some individuals can develop symptoms meeting criteria for schizophrenia. Children/adolescents with 22q11.2 deletion syndrome are noted to have higher rates of depression than anxiety (50–67% of samples have been reported) while those with both clinical anxiety and comorbid clinical depression were less common (e.g., less than 20% of samples).

Neuropathology: Diffuse reduced grey and white matter volumes. Compared to control subjects (children/adolescents), decreased average volume has been found in the frontal lobes, temporal lobes, parietal lobes, cerebellum and hippocampi. The reduced brain volumes reported above are found across variable clinical presentations, with the exception of hippocampal volume/abnormalities that are variable along with abnormal volume of the lateral ventricles. The presentation of reduced hippocampal volume/abnormalities is not consistent (variable).

References

Baron, I. S. (2018). *Neuropsychological evaluation of the child: Domains, methods and case studies*. Oxford University Press.

Baron, I. S., & Rey-Casserly, C. (2013). *Pediatric neuropsychology: Medical advances and lifespan outcomes*. Oxford University Press.

Beauchamp, R. L., Peterson, R. L., Ris, M. D., Taylor, H. G., & Yeates, K. O. (2022). *Pediatric neuropsychology: Research, theory and practice* (3rd ed.). The Guilford Press.

Bien, C. G., Granata, T., Antozzi, C., Cross, J., et al. (2005). Pathogenesis, diagnosis and treatment of Rasmussen encephalitis. *Brain, 128*, 454–471.

Feuillet, L., Dufour, H., & Pelletier, J. (2007). Brain of a white-collar worker. *The Lancet, 370*(9583), 262.

Heilman, K. M., & Valenstein, E. (2012). *Clinical neuropsychology* (5th ed.). Oxford University Press.

Lezak, M. D., Howieson, D. B., Bigler, E. D., & Tranel, D. (2012). *Neuropsychological assessment* (5th ed.). Oxford University Press.

Pichiecchio, A., Veggiotti, P., Cardinali, S., Longaretti, F., Poloni, G. U., & Uggetti, C. (2008). Lafora disease: Spectroscopy study correlated with neuropsychological findings. *European Journal of Paediatric Neurology, 12*, 342–347.

Ropper, A. H., Samuels, M. A., Klein, J. P., & Prasad, S. (2023). *Adams and Victor's principals of neurology* (12th ed.). The McGraw-Hill Companies.

Schweitzer, S., Shin, Y., Jakobs, C., & Brodehl, J. (1993). Long term outcome in 134 patients with galactocemia. *European Journal of Pediatrics., 152*, 36–43.

Villanueva, V., Alvarez-Linera, J., Gomez-Garre, P., Gutierrez, J., & Serratosa, J. M. (2006). MRI volummetry and proton MR spectroscopy of the brain in Lafora disease. *Epilepsia, 47*, 788–792.

Yeates, K. O., Ris, M. D., Taylor, H. G., & Pennington, B. F. (2010). *Pediatric neuropsychology: Research, theory and practice*. Guilford Press.

Chapter 28
Brain Tumors

Catherine Dion and David S. Sabsevitz

Key Points and Chapter Summary

- A brain tumor is the abnormal proliferation of cells inside the skull cavity. Brain tumors are either malignant (cancerous) or non-malignant (non-cancerous).
- Both malignant and non-malignant tumors can be life-threatening depending on location and size.
- Brain tumors are either primary or metastatic.
  - Primary tumors are those that originate from and grow within the brain. The most common primary brain tumors are gliomas, which arise from glial cells.
  - Metastatic brain tumors are those that originate systemically and spread hemodynamically to the brain. Brain metastases are far more common than primary brain tumors. Common sites of origin include lungs, breasts, kidneys and skin.
- The signs and symptoms of a brain tumor vary from asymptomatic to considerable cognitive and behavioral impairment, with tumor location and size, growth rate and individual characteristics impacting this variability. Headaches and seizures are the most common neurologic presenting symptom, but neurocognitive impairment and focal neurologic deficits are often present.

(continued)

C. Dion (✉) · D. S. Sabsevitz
Department of Psychiatry and Psychology, Mayo Clinic–Jacksonville, Jacksonville, FL, USA
e-mail: Catherine.Dion@mayo.edu

M. R. Schoenberg, J. G. Scott (eds.), *The Little Black Book of Neuropsychology*,
https://doi.org/10.1007/978-3-032-07777-6_28

(continued)

- Brain tumors are diagnosed by histopathological analyses. The World Health Organization (WHO) now classifies brain tumors and tumor grading using molecular parameters in addition to histological findings.
- The first line of treatment for primary brain tumors is surgical resection, and depending on the tumor characteristics and grade, this is often followed by radiation and chemotherapy or immunotherapy. The treatment goal for most lower-grade brain tumors is curative, while for higher grade it is palliative, focused on prolonging survival and managing symptoms.
- Neuropsychologists are becoming increasingly involved in the assessment and management of behavioral and cognitive symptoms at all stages of the treatment course, whether it be preoperatively, intraoperatively or to monitor effects from chemotherapy and radiation and disease progression.

Overview

Cognitive dysfunction in individuals with brain tumors is common, and the cognitive trajectory of those individuals can change dramatically throughout the disease course. Cognitive dysfunction may result from various contributing factors, including the tumor itself, treatments such as surgery, radiation and/or chemotherapy or other associated morbidities such as seizures or mood disturbances. All of these factors can, in turn, impact functional independence and quality of life.

The economic burden of brain tumors includes substantial healthcare costs, including diagnostic procedures, surgery, radiation therapy, and ongoing medical care. Additionally, indirect costs arise secondary to disability particularly in low-grade gliomas, since the highest incidence occurs between the 20 s and 40 s, during peak participation in the workforce and career development (Grier & Batchelor, 2006). In glioma patients who survive past the first stage of treatment and experience a period of stability in the disease course, the majority of them experience ongoing loss of productivity, a negative effect on their employment status, high out-of-pocket expenses, increased debt and anxiety about their financial stability (Haider et al., 2020). Neuropsychologists are increasingly involved in the assessment and management of cognitive and emotional changes in patients with brain tumors at all stages of care, from the presurgical workup to assisting neurosurgery with intraoperative mapping and testing, to following patients after adjuvant therapies to monitor for potential neurotoxicity and disease progression. Monitoring of cognition and provision of tailored recommendations has the potential to optimize quality of life.

This chapter aims to provide a broad yet up-to-date understanding of brain tumors including terminology, epidemiology and tumor classification and grading and help define the role of neuropsychologists in the care of brain tumor patients. The chapter is organized into the following sections: definition of brain tumors, signs and symptoms, epidemiology, classification of brain tumors, paraneoplastic neurological syndromes, neuroimaging, treatments, neuropsychological evaluation and presentation of an illustrative case example.

Definition of Brain Tumors

Brain tumors represent a heterogeneous group of neoplasms that can arise from the meninges (extra-axial) or the brain parenchyma (intra-axial). Greater than 90% of intra-axial tumors arise from supportive glial cells (e.g., astrocytes, oligodendrocytes, microglia—collectively referred to as gliomas) or, more rarely from neuronal cells (1%) (Victor & Ropper, 2002; Davis et al., 2005; El-Zein et al., 2005; Kaye, 2009). Glial cells contribute to synaptic communication, plasticity, homeostasis and network-level activity (Allen & Lyons, 2018). Sequential steps in the growth of brain tumors differ, but generally include cellular gene mutation, uncontrolled cell division, invasion into normal brain, formation of a blood supply for the tumor (i.e., angiogenesis) and disruption of the blood–brain barrier resulting in edema (DeAngelis et al., 2001). Epidemiological research studies have investigated numerous potential risk factors for brain tumors; however, to date, the only validated risk factors for brain tumors are: a history of allergies, which lowers risk in adults, and ionizing radiation, which raises risk in both adults and children (Ostrom et al., 2019). Studies of genetic risk factors have identified 32 germline variants, two of which have been linked to meningiomas, three to pituitary adenomas and two to primary CNS lymphoma. These germline variants are associated with an increased risk for these tumors in adulthood (Ostrom et al., 2019).

Brain tumors can be either primary or metastatic. Primary tumors are those that grow from their site of origin within the brain but can sometimes metastasize to the spine. Among the primary brain tumors, they can be intra-axial, meaning they grow from within the brain, or extra-axial, referring to those that grow outside the brain parenchyma from the meninges. In adults, primary malignant brain tumors are most frequently located in the frontal and temporal lobes, whereas in childhood, they are usually found in the posterior fossa/infratentorial region (Ostrom et al., 2014). Some primary brain tumors can spread via the CSF to the spinal cord, such as medulloblastomas, which then require cranial and spinal radiation. Metastatic tumors are those that have spread hematologically from other parts of the body to the brain and are far more common than primary brain tumors. Brain metastases are a common complication from cancer, impacting on average one fifth of cancer patients with the most common sites of origin including the lungs, breasts, kidneys or skin (Sacks & Rahman, 2020). Brain metastases tend to grow at the gray-white matter junction, though they can occur in any part of the brain (Hwang et al., 1996).

The term "benign," often used to describe non-malignant tumors, is an unfortunate misnomer since benign tumors are not harmless, can be very symptomatic and can undergo malignant transformations. Consequently, benign tumors will be referred to as "non-malignant" in this chapter. Non-malignant brain tumors are those that are less aggressive and slow growing, while malignant brain tumors are often called "cancerous" and grow rapidly.

Signs and Symptoms

Brain tumors in adults can present with a variety of signs and symptoms, which are often related to the anatomical location of the tumor within the brain. Common neurologic symptoms of brain tumors include headache (reported in approximately 50% of patients), seizures (20%–50%) and focal neurologic deficits (10%–40%) (Schaff & Mellinghoff, 2023). Notably, the rise in intracranial pressure caused by the tumor and the edema can lead to false localizing signs from a shift in distal intracranial structures. Focal tumor growth can also cause herniations in the mesial frontal (under the falx cerebri), temporal (forced through the tentorium cerebelli) and cerebellar tonsils (depressed through the foramen magnum) due to a shift in tissue to compartments where the pressure is lower (DeAngelis et al., 2001). The resulting increased tissue pressure may also cause symptoms via interference with local blood supply. High-grade gliomas are infiltrative and can spread via white matter pathways potentially resulting in more diffuse or distant cognitive effects that can be fully appreciated on conventional imaging.

Neurocognitive impairment is common during the course of a brain tumor, with reported rates in the literature in up to 91% of cases (Tucha et al., 2000; Meyers & Hess, 2003; Taphoorn & Klein, 2004; Noll et al., 2016). There are many different factors that can contribute to cognitive complications in this population. The tumor itself can impact cognitive profiles depending on the tumor location, its size and its growth momentum. Growth momentum refers to how rapidly tumors grow, with higher grade tumors growing more rapidly and being associated with higher cognitive morbidity compared to lower-grade tumors. Brain tumor patients will also undergo a variety of different treatments. The cognitive impact of these different treatments will vary in terms of their onset and course. Surgery can be associated with cognitive morbidity and when cognitive complications are seen from surgery they occur acutely and, in many cases, will improve to some degree over time, assuming good tumor control. After surgery many patients will undergo concurrent chemotherapy and radiation, with both acute and delayed presentations of cognitive symptoms. This will be discussed later in the chapter. Patients are often prescribed antiseizure medications to control seizures, as well as steroids to help control vasogenic edema. Some antiseizure medications have associated behavioral and cognitive side effects. Most notably, levetiracetam is often used in brain tumor patients, and it has been associated with behavioral irritability. Steroids can cause a variety of side effects, including insomnia and mood changes. There is a high rate of medical complications in this population including seizures, endocrine dysfunction and sleep disturbance, all of which can be associated with cognitive symptoms. Patients with brain tumors also often present with pre-existing medical and neurological conditions that need to be considered. For example, certain older patients may have cerebrovascular disease that can contribute to the neuropsychological profiles. Emotionally, there are much higher rates of depression and anxiety in patients with brain tumors, and mood can impact cognition. Fatigue, pain and other physical symptoms can also play a role in cognition. Brain tumors can affect cognition by damaging brain tissue by invading it, increasing intracranial pressure, inducing seizures, secreting hormones, altering endocrine functions or inducing midline shift or hydrocephalus. The age of the patient is also predictive of cognitive status, with higher likelihood of cognitive impairment in older age. There is no single neuropsychological profile seen in all brain tumors since there are a multitude of factors that can impact cognition and all of these factors should be considered when conceptualizing a patient's cognitive presentation (see Fig. 28.1). A thorough history and clinical assessment, understanding the onset and course of the symptom presentation and careful review of imaging over time can help differentiate between these

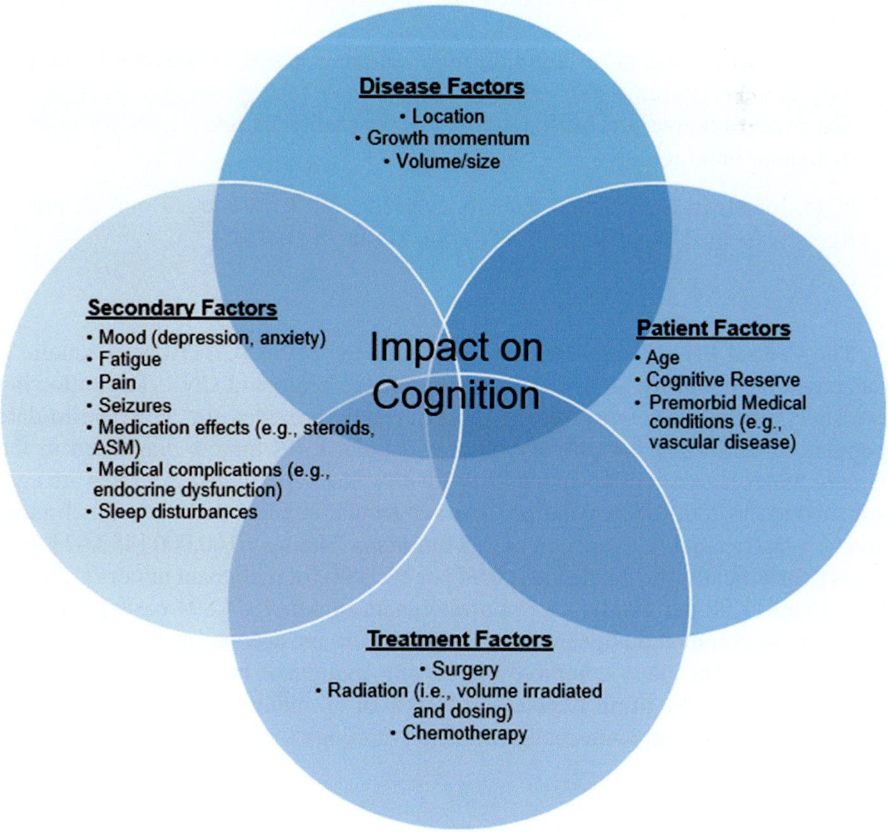

Fig. 28.1 Factors impacting cognitive functioning in patients with brain tumors

possible contributing factors. Patients with tumors in the dominant hemisphere tend to have more cognitive deficits. Although there can be focal impairment, cognitive deficits can also be non-focal, which may be due to the infiltrative nature of certain tumors, associated edema and mass effect that may disrupt broader networks.

Epidemiology

Quick facts about brain tumors

- Rates for CNS tumors are highest in females and non-Hispanic individuals.

Malignant tumors of the brain are more common in males.

Non-malignant tumors of the brain are more common in females.

Gliomas account for 26.3% of all brain tumors and are the most common tumor.

Glioblastoma is the most common malignant CNS histopathology and most common in males.

Meningioma is the most common non-malignant CNS histopathology and most common in females.

The 5-year relative survival rate is 35.7% for malignant and 91.8% for non-malignant brain tumors.

Note: Information for Quick facts is derived from the Central Brain Tumor Registry of the United States CBTRUS (Ostrom et al., 2023).

The Central Brain Tumor Registry of the United States (CBTRUS) maintains a database and publishes statistics on tumors of the brain and CNS. The following statistics reflect their most recent report, which provides the most up-to-date population-based data on primary brain and other CNS tumors diagnosed in the United States between 2016 and 2020, with all states represented. All rates are age-adjusted to the 2000 US population. Average annual incidence rate of all malignant and non-malignant brain and other CNS tumors is 24.83 per 100,000 [453,623 total cases]. Specifically, the incidence is 6.94 per 100,000 for malignant tumors [126,729 cases] and 17.88 per 100,000 for non-malignant tumors [326,894 cases]. Gliomas are the most common malignant brain and CNS tumors, accounting for 26.3% of all brain tumors. The most commonly occurring malignant brain histopathology is glioblastoma (14.2% of all tumors and 50.9% of all malignant tumors). The most common predominantly non-malignant histopathology is meningioma (40.8% of all tumors and 56.2% of all non-malignant tumors). The five-year relative survival rate following diagnosis of a malignant brain tumor is 35.7% and for a non-malignant brain tumor, the five-year relative survival rate is 91.8%.

Sex Differences

The overall rates of brain tumors are higher in females than males (27.85 versus 21.62 per 100,000). Glioblastomas are more common in males, while meningiomas are more common in females. In the United States, lifetime risk of being diagnosed with a primary malignant brain and other CNS (excluding lymphomas, leukemias, tumors of pituitary and pineal glands and olfactory tumors of the nasal cavity) is overall 0.6% (0.75% for males and 0.54% for females) and the risk of associated death is overall 0.5% (0.56% for males and 0.42% for females).

Ethnoracial Differences

The incidence of brain tumors is higher among non-Hispanic individuals (of any race) compared to Hispanics (25.24 versus 22.61 per 100,000). For non-Hispanic White individuals, the risk of developing a primary malignant brain tumor is 0.7%, and the risk of death from a primary brain tumor is 0.6%, compared to 0.5% and 0.4%, respectively, in White Hispanic individuals. For Black individuals (both ethnicities), the risk of developing and dying from a primary brain tumor is 0.3% and 0.3%, respectively. In Asian/Pacific Islanders (both ethnicities), the risk of developing and dying from a primary brain tumor is 0.4% and 0.3%, respectively.

Age Differences in the Incidence of All Brain Tumors

- Pediatric incidence (ages 0–14): 5.67 per 100,000 population
- Adolescents and young adults incidence (ages 15–39): 12 per 100,000 population
- Adults incidence (ages 40+): 44.97 per 100,000 population

Although brain cancer is the most common form of cancer in pediatric populations, it remains a rare occurrence. For malignant brain tumors, the five-year survival is highest in persons aged 0–14 years (75.0%) and aged 15–39 years (71.9%) as compared to those aged 40+ years (21.1%).

Classification of Brain Tumors

Classification of brain tumors

- Brain tumors are now classified based on a combination of histological and molecular features
- Tumor grading is done within tumor types
- Molecular genetics are increasingly important in determining the prognosis and treatability of different brain tumors
- Since 2021, tumors of the CNS include the following:
  - Gliomas, glioneuronal tumors and neuronal tumors
  - Choroid plexus tumors
  - Embryonal tumors
  - Pineal tumors
  - Cranial and paraspinal nerve tumors
  - Meningiomas
  - Mesenchymal, non-meningothelial
  - Melanocytic tumors
  - Hematolymphoid tumors
  - Germ cell tumor
  - Tumors of the sellar region
  - Metastases to the CNS

Up until recently, brain tumors were classified using only histopathological features (e.g., atypia, cell proliferation) from microscopic examination of the tissue. In 2016, the World Health Organization (WHO) introduced a significant shift in the approach to classifying brain tumors, such that, for the first time, molecular parameters were used in addition to histological findings to define many tumor entities (Louis et al., 2016). Molecular profiling refers to the form of testing that classifies tumors based on their genetic makeup, while histology is a branch of biology that studies microscopic anatomy of biological tissues. In 2021, the system expanded this approach by further integrating molecular diagnostics and introducing a more nuanced approach to tumor taxonomy and nomenclature (Louis et al., 2021). Tumor grading is now done within rather than across tumor types and Arabic numerals have replaced roman numerals. Tumors are still graded 1–4 based on the expected natural history of the tumor with a newer emphasis on consideration of both histological features and molecular markers. Although tumor grading is generally useful in predicting growth rates and potential spread outside the tumor boundaries and can be used to guide treatment recommendations, the clinical manifestation of different tumor types with the same WHO grade can vary significantly. For example, an astrocytoma IDH-mutant WHO grade 3 may show a markedly different survival time when compared to a meningioma WHO grade 3 (Park et al., 2023). Similarly, given recent advancements in molecular genetics and treatments, WNT-activated medulloblastomas WHO grade 4 have a survival rate of over 90% with modern treatments (Cotter & Hawkins, 2022).

Tumors of the CNS are divided into the following categories: Gliomas, glioneuronal tumors and neuronal tumors; choroid plexus tumors; embryonal tumors; pineal tumors; cranial and paraspinal nerve tumors; meningiomas; mesenchymal, non-meningothelial; melanocytic tumors; hematolymphoid tumors; germ cell tumor; tumors of the sellar region; and metastases to the CNS. The following section will focus on the most common types of brain tumors encountered clinically, since a comprehensive discussion of all tumor types is beyond the scope of this chapter (Table 28.1).

Common Pediatric Tumors

Childhood brain cancer is the most common cause of cancer-related mortality in children aged 0–14. Most primary brain tumors in childhood are found in the posterior fossa (posterior 1/third of the skull). Tumors commonly seen in childhood include circumscribed astrocytic gliomas, embryonal tumors and ependymomas.

Table 28.1 Common brain tumors

Type of brain tumor	WHO grade	Populations affected	Lesion site
Pilocytic astrocytoma	1	Mostly <19 years of age	Mostly in the cerebellum but can be found anywhere in the neuroaxis.
Medulloblastoma	4	Varies based on subtype, but mostly seen in children aged 0–17 (WNT), aged 0–10 (SHH), aged 3–10 (group 3) and aged 3–10 (group 4).	Tend to originate in the cerebellum and spread to the neuraxis via the cerebrospinal fluid.
Astrocytoma, IDH-mutant	2, 3, 4	Most common in adults aged 40–50.	Mostly found in the frontal lobes.
Oligodendroglioma, IDH-mutant and 1p/19q-codeleted	2, 3	Most common in adults aged 40–50.	Mostly found in the frontal lobes.
Glioblastoma, IDH-wildtype	4	Most common in adults age > 50 and peaks around age 75–84 years.	Most likely to have a multifocal and non-lobar location in the supratentorial region.
Meningioma	1, 2, 3	Most common in adults and older adults. The median age at diagnosis is 65 years old.	Supratentorial region and posterior fossa.
Ependymoma	2, 3	Most common in children and young adults.	Supratentorial brain, posterior fossa and spine.

Information derived from Louis et al. (2021), Cotter and Hawkins (2022), Funakoshi et al. (2023), Ostrom et al. (2023)
WNT wingless pathway-activated, *SHH* sonic hedgehog-activated, *IDH* isocitrate dehydrogenase

Of the circumscribed astrocytic gliomas, pilocytic astrocytoma is a slow-growing tumor arising from astrocytes that is usually well-defined and cystic. The approach to treatment generally involves surgical removal of the tumor. The prognosis tends to be more favorable compared to other types of brain tumors.

Of the embryonal tumors, medulloblastoma is the most common type. Medulloblastomas originate in the cerebellum and tend to spread to the neuraxis via the cerebrospinal fluid (CSF). They are now classified using specific genetic and molecular characteristics (i.e., medulloblastoma, wingless pathway (WNT)-activated; medulloblastoma, sonic hedgehog (SHH)-activated and tumor protein (TP53)-wildtype; medulloblastoma SHH-activated and TP53-mutant; and medulloblastoma, non-WNT/non-SHH). Medulloblastomas are typically treated with surgical resection followed by radiation therapy and chemotherapy. Craniospinal irradiation has been shown to improve overall survival rates, prevent leptomeningeal spread, reduce the risk for metastases and minimize radiation-related toxicity to normal brain tissue in medulloblastomas.

Ependymomas originate from the ependymal cells that line the ventricles and the central canal of the spinal cord. They are found in the supratentorial region, posterior fossa and spinal cord and are generally treated with surgical resection followed by radiation. In some instances, chemotherapy is used to shrink the tumor before surgery (neoadjuvant chemotherapy) or to treat residual disease after surgery or radiation therapy (adjuvant chemotherapy).

Cognitive side effects of treatment in primary pediatric brain tumors include poorer processing speed, attention, working memory, executive functioning and learning and memory (Olsson et al., 2014; Jayakar et al., 2015; King et al., 2019). Children with primary brain tumors tend to have poorer health related quality of life as it pertains to physical, psychosocial, social and cognitive well-being (Macartney et al., 2014).

Gliomas

The updated WHO classification system for brain tumors also introduced a restructuring of the tumor categories, particularly for gliomas, which now includes adult-type diffuse gliomas, pediatric-type diffuse low and high-grade gliomas and circumscribed astrocytic gliomas. Diffuse gliomas, the most common CNS tumors in adults, are now assigned to three different tumor types: Astrocytoma, isocitrate dehydrogenase (IDH)-mutant; Oligodendroglioma, IDH-mutant and 1p/19q-deleted; and Glioblastoma, IDH-wildtype (Louis et al., 2021).

Molecular genetics are increasingly important in diagnosing and determining the prognosis and treatability of different brain tumors. The most common molecular alteration driving diagnostics is the mutation status of the enzyme isocitrate dehydrogenase (IDH) (i.e., IDH-mutant vs IDH-wildtype). Tumors that harbor IDH mutation are usually less aggressive and predictive of better prognosis compared to IDH-wildtype tumors. With regard to treatability, molecular genetics help guide decision-making on what agents to use in treatment. For example, 1p/19q codeletions tend to respond more favorably to alkylating agents. Methylation status of O6-methylguanine-DNA methyltransferase (MGMT) genes helps predict response to alkylating agents as well. Patients with unmethylated MGMT genes express more DNA repair proteins, which reduce the efficiency of alkylating agents in eliminating tumor cells. Neuropsychologists who work with neuro-oncology populations may wish to familiarize themselves with these genetic markers. The table below highlights genetic and molecular features relevant to the prognosis of gliomas (Table 28.2).

Below are the main clinical and imaging characteristics of the three adult diffuse gliomas. Although several features on neuroimaging can help predict the type of glioma, tissue sampling is required for diagnostics. Generally, higher-grade tumors are predictive of poorer prognosis; however, low-grade gliomas can evolve into higher-grade tumors. More details about survival rates by specific tumor type are available in the CBTRUS.

Table 28.2 Genetic and molecular features relevant to gliomas

Marker	Positive Prognosis	Negative Prognosis	Relevance
1p/19q	Deleted	Intact	Deletion is diagnostic of oligodendroglioma and predictive of better treatment response to alkylating agents
IDH	Mutated/ positive	Wildtype/ negative	Predictive of aggressiveness in subtypes of astrocytoma, such that IDH mutation confers better prognosis and less cognitive impairment than IDH wildtype. For a tumor to be considered glioblastoma, it requires IDH wildtype.
MGMT	Methylated	Unmethylated	Methylation predicts better response to alkylating chemotherapy agents and better prognosis compared to unmethylated.
ATRX	Mutated	Wildtype	Predictive of aggressiveness such that ATRX mutation confers better prognosis than ATRX wildtype.
TERT	Wildtype	Mutated	Predictive of aggressiveness, such that TERT mutation confers worse prognosis compared to wildtype.
EGFR	Not amplified	Amplified	Predictive of aggressiveness such that EGFR not amplified confers better prognosis compared to EGFR amplified.
TP53	Intact	Deleted	Predictive of poorer prognosis, particularly in astrocytoma.
CDKN2A	Intact	Deleted (loss)	Predictive of aggressiveness and astrocytoma IDH mutant
Ki-67	Lower (e.g., <5%)	Higher %	Indicator of rate of mitosis.

IDH Isocitrate dehydrogenase, *MGMT* O6-methylguanine-DNA methyltransferase, *ATRX* alpha-thalassemia/mental retardation, X-linked, *TERT* Telomerase reverse transcriptase, *EGFR* epidermal growth factor receptor, *TP53* tumor protein 53, *CDKN2A* cyclin-dependent kinase inhibitor 2A

Oligodendrogliomas are defined by IDH mutation and 1p/19q codeletion and they arise from oligodendrocytes. They are most commonly found in the frontal lobes and manifest around the fourth and fifth decades of life. These tumors can be of grades 2 or 3. Common radiological characteristics include well-defined borders, heterogeneous signal, calcification, cystic changes and variable contrast enhancement with greater contrast enhancement in WHO grade 3 tumors. Of the adult diffuse gliomas, oligodendroglioma IDH-mutant has the most favorable prognosis.

Astrocytomas are defined by IDH mutation, and they arise from astrocytes. They are most commonly found in the frontal lobes and manifest around the fourth and fifth decades of life. These tumors can be of WHO grades 2, 3 or 4. Lower-grade astrocytomas have better defined borders than high-grade astrocytomas. IDH-mutant astrocytomas can show the T2/Fluid Attenuated Inversion Recovery (FLAIR) mismatch sign where tumors have markedly hyperintense signal on T2-weighted imaging while showing hypodense signal on T2/FLAIR. This can help differentiate this tumor from other low-grade gliomas (e.g., oligodendroglioma). Occasionally, a rim of hyperintensity can be seen at the tumor margin. Contrast enhancement is variable, with higher-grade astrocytomas tend to be larger, more infiltrative, greater enhancement and showing higher cerebral blood volume. Of the adult diffuse gliomas, astrocytomas IDH-mutant have the second most favorable prognosis after oligodendroglioma IDH-mutant.

Glioblastomas are defined by IDH wildtype, and they arise from astrocytes. They are found anywhere in the supratentorial region and generally manifest in the sixth and seventh decades of life. These tumors are always WHO grade 4. They have significant contrast enhancement and are highly infiltrative. There is usually heterogeneous signal intensity, and sometimes a peripheral rim enhancement with central necrosis, hemorrhage and high cerebral blood volume is seen on neuroimaging. The average survival time for glioblastoma IDH wildtype is 12–18 months with standard of care and represents the worst prognosis out of all adult-type diffuse gliomas. The extent of resection contributes to the optimization of survival in glioblastoma, with a longer survival time for those who receive a gross total resection.

Patients with gliomas that possess an IDH mutation (IDH-mutant) are generally younger, and the pathology of these tumors is less aggressive than IDH-wildtype gliomas. Both IDH-mutant and IDH-wildtype gliomas occur more predominantly in the frontal and temporal lobes and typically show a pattern of infiltration along white matter structures. Although it is well known that gliomas have focal effects on neural structures in which the mass arises, growing evidence suggests accompanying neural network disruption. Specifically, IDH-wildtype gliomas tend to cause more disruption of functional connectivity than IDH-mutant gliomas (Parsons & Sabsevitz, 2023).

The neuropsychological profile of individuals with IDH-mutant gliomas is generally more favorable than those with IDH-wildtype tumors. Wefel and colleagues showed that cognitive impairment is more frequent in patients with IDH-wildtype compared to IDH-mutant tumors across most cognitive domains, including language comprehension, recent memory, information processing speed, executive functions and fine motor dexterity/speed (Wefel et al., 2016). The authors also showed that those with IDH-wildtype tend to have more widespread cognitive deficits across domains. This difference in performance across IDH status may be explained by growth momentum where the slower growth in IDH-mutant tumors allows for more reorganization or compensation of function than quicker growing IDH-wildtype tumors. For a thorough review on the subject matter, please see Parsons and Sabsevitz (2023).

Meningiomas

Meningiomas are the most common non-malignant brain tumor in adults and the most common tumor of the meninges. They can be found anywhere in the meninges and arise from arachnoid cap cells. They are extra-axial tumors as they grow outside the brain parenchyma but in some cases can intrude into the brain tissue. Although most meningiomas are non-malignant, more aggressive phenotypic presentations can include multiple recurrences and invasion into the brain, dura and adjacent bone. Meningiomas of WHO grade 1 are non-malignant, grade 2 are atypical and grade 3 are malignant. Genetic and molecular features play a role in grading and classifying subtypes of meningiomas. For example, mutations of SMARCE1 suggest a clear cell subtype, BAP1 suggests rhabdoid and papillary subtypes and KLF4/TRAF7 suggests a secretory subtype. TERT promoter mutation and/or homozygous deletion of CDKN2A/B62 are seen in WHO grade 3, loss of nuclear expression in H3K27me3 suggests a potentially worse prognosis and methylome profiling offers prognostic subtyping (Louis et al., 2021). On neuroimaging, meningiomas usually demonstrate the common features of extra-axial tumors. These include the CSF cleft sign, which is a clear space between the tumor and the brain interface best visualized on T2-weighted scans as hyperintense signal; the dural tail sign, which is a thickening of the dura mater immediately adjacent to the tumor (can be seen in other tumor types, even intra-axial tumors); and bony changes in the overlying skull due to their superficial location and proximity to the skull. Surgery is often considered in meningiomas that are symptomatic and in areas with high risk for complications with further growth (e.g., venous sinuses). Radiation can also be used to manage meningiomas. One long-term side effect of brain radiation is developing meningiomas and other gliomas.

Paraneoplastic Neurological Syndromes

Paraneoplastic neurological syndromes refer to a group of immune-mediated disorders that occur in cancer patients, where the cancer-fighting antibodies or white blood cells mistakenly attack healthy cells in the nervous system, resulting in neurological symptoms. Importantly, these neurological symptoms are not better explained by tumors, metastases, ischemia or infections and generally occur before clinical manifestations of the cancer. Below are the most common paraneoplastic neurological syndromes. See Honnorat and Antoine (2007) for a thorough review of paraneoplastic syndromes.

1. Limbic encephalitis: characterized by inflammation and damage of the limbic system. Symptoms typically include confusion, memory impairment and seizures. In some cases, there is an insidious onset of depression and hallucinations.
2. Subacute cerebellar ataxia: characterized by cerebellar dysfunction induced by a disproportionate loss of Purkinje neurons and eventually with cerebellar atrophy. Symptoms include difficulties with coordination, balance, gait, tremors and slurred speech.
3. Opsoclonus-myoclonus: characterized by rapid involuntary eye movements (opsoclonus) and muscle twitching or jerking (myoclonus).
4. Retinopathies: group of three disorders affecting the integrity of the retina including cancer-associated retinopathy, melanoma-associated retinopathy, uveitis, optic neuropathy or retinopathy.
5. Chronic gastrointestinal pseudo-obstruction: characterized by impaired movement of the muscles in the gastrointestinal tract with symptoms such as severe abdominal pain, bloating, nausea, vomiting, constipation and malnutrition.
6. Sensory neuropathy: characterized by pain and paresthesias resulting from damage to the cell body of the dorsal root ganglia. In more advanced cases, there can be limb ataxia.
7. Lambert-Eaton myasthenic syndrome is characterized by a neuromuscular junction disorder resulting in muscle weakness and fatigue.

Neuroimaging

Neuroimaging, including computed tomography (CT) and magnetic resonance imaging (MRI), is essential for screening and monitoring brain tumors. Although non-diagnostic, tumor characteristics on neuroimaging can provide helpful information about a given tumor type. Brain tumors can either be intra-axial, meaning they grow from within the brain, or extra-axial, referring to those that grow outside the brain parenchyma. Common features of extra-axial tumors on neuroimaging include the cerebrospinal fluid (CSF)-cleft sign (i.e., clear rim between the tumor and the brain), the dural tail sign (i.e., thickening of the dura mater immediately next to the tumor) and bony changes in the overlying skull which are due to extra-axial tumors' superficial location and proximity to the skull. Certain imaging features can help infer tumor aggressiveness (see Fig. 28.2). More aggressive brain tumors tend to show contrast enhancement. Contrast enhancement occurs by way of angiogenesis that is disrupting the blood–brain barrier (BBB), thereby allowing contrast agents to penetrate it and enhance on MRI. Vasogenic edema, which also results from damage to the BBB, mainly affects the white matter via leakage of fluid from

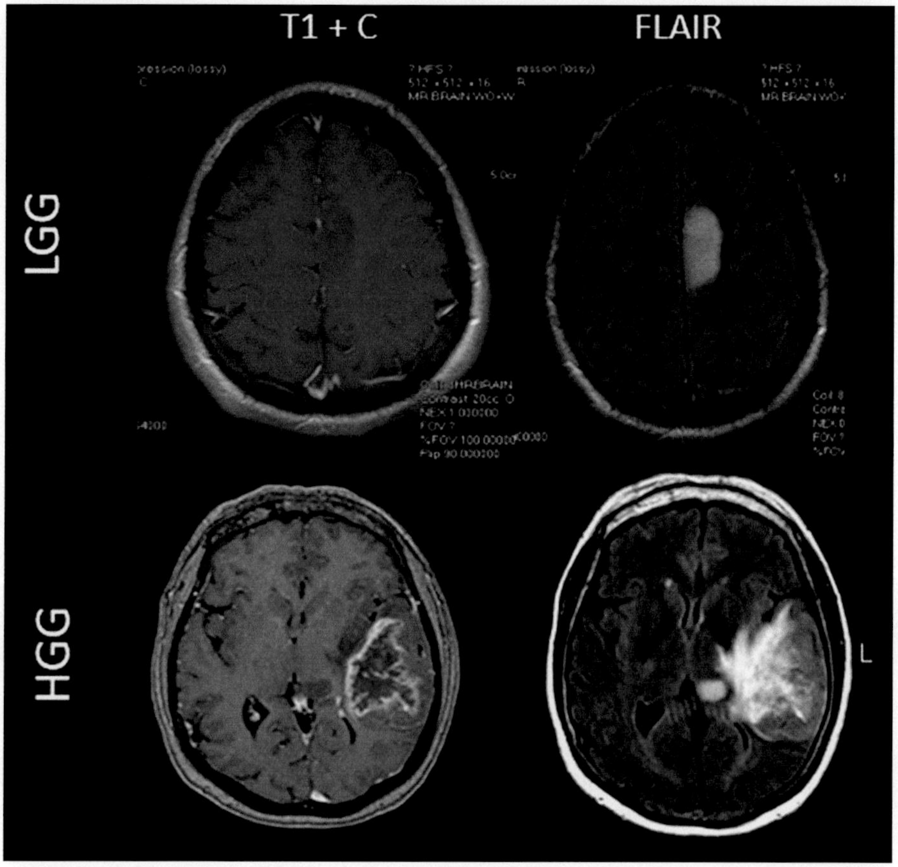

Fig. 28.2 T1 with contrast and FLAIR imaging characteristics of low- vs high-grade gliomas. Note the well-defined area of hypo-intensity and FLAIR signal without any contrast enhancement and no apparent mass effect in the low-grade glioma while the high-grade glioma has ill-defined borders, enhances with contrast, has a cystic necrotic center and produces more apparent mass effect and edema

capillaries. Vasogenic edema generally develops in the white matter and travels along these tracts (DeAngelis et al., 2001). Of note, the degree to which angiogenesis, contrast enhancement and vasogenic edema correlate with one another varies across tumor types. High-grade gliomas tend to enhance, produce more significant vasogenic edema, have irregular borders, have cystic necrotic components and show faster growth rate on serial imaging. Low-grade gliomas typically do not enhance, have more clear and regular borders, no necrosis and are slower growing on serial imaging. Regarding contrast enhancement, it is important to note that meningiomas intensely and homogeneously enhance with contrast as do other types of brain cancer (e.g., CNS lymphoma). Generally, the presence of multiple contrast enhancing lesions on neuroimaging favors metastases, but gliomas can be multifocal and look similar on neuroimaging. The T2/FLAIR mismatch sign is a radiographic feature useful in distinguishing astrocytoma, IDH-mutant from oligodendroglioma, IDH-mutant 1p/19q codeletion. IDH-mutant astrocytomas can have markedly hyperintense signal on T2-weighted imaging while showing hypodense signal on T2/FLAIR, with a hyperintense rim at the tumor margin. Oligodendrogliomas and meningiomas can show calcification (hyperdense signal on CT, hyperintense signal on T1). Neuroimaging is also helpful in distinguishing treatment-related effects (e.g., blood products from the surgical resection) from tumor recurrence. Subacute blood products appear hyperintense on both T1 and T1 with contrast, whereas residual tumors would not appear hyperintense on T1 without contrast but would with contrast. Similarly, cerebral blood volume studies can help differentiate radiation-induced damage (i.e., radiation necrosis) from tumor recurrence in that radiation damage would show decreased/absent cerebral blood volume (CBV) while tumor can show increased CBV. This is especially important in patients who show pseudoprogression on imaging where there is an increase in FLAIR and contrast enhancement without increased perfusion. This is due to the treatment effect, in particular, temozolomide on the Stupp protocol.

Diffusion weighted imaging (DWI), an MR technique that assesses microscopic rate of water movement in tissue, can be used to evaluate tumor cellularity, track tumor growth and differentiate between progression and treatment effect. Apparent diffusion coefficient (ADC) images, which are generated from DWI, correlate with areas of hypercellularity in the tumor by highlighting restricted diffusion. However, autopsy studies have shown that infiltrative tumors can extend up to 10 cm beyond the T1 with contrast and FLAIR margins (LaViolette et al., 2014; Bobholz et al., 2022). When analyzing tissue samples obtained from regions beyond the suspected tumor area, studies have shown only weak relationships between the ADC and hypercellularity (Eidel et al., 2016; Chenevert et al., 2019; Bobholz et al., 2020). Radiopathomic mapping involves correlating radiological features with histopathological findings to identify associations between imaging characteristics and underlying tissue properties. Autopsy-based radiopathomic tumor probability maps have been shown to accurately identify areas of infiltrative tumor beyond traditional imaging signatures in glioma patients (Bobholz et al., 2024).

Neuroimaging also plays a critical role in presurgical planning. Functional MRI (fMRI) is used preoperatively to map functions of various cortical brain regions. Task-based fMRI maps changes in blood oxygen level-dependent (BOLD) signal during cognitive and motor tasks, which helps inform the surgical team in planning for the intraoperative mapping and surgical approach. While fMRI can provide important information about function localization in gray matter structures, diffusion tensor imaging (DTI) provides a more complete picture of the integrity of various brain systems. Generally, the combination of preoperative task-based fMRI, DTI with MR tractography and intraoperative cortical and/or subcortical stimulation allows for a greater extent of resection, improved survival and better functional outcomes (Lakhani et al., 2023).

Treatments

Key Points: Treatments of Brain Tumors

- Surgery is the first line of treatment with the goal of obtaining tissue for diagnosis, resecting as much tumor as possible to alleviate symptoms and decrease steroid dependency.
- Adjuvant radiation and chemotherapy are typically prescribed for higher-grade tumors or high-risk low-grade tumors.
- The treatment goal for higher-grade tumors is palliative to prolong survival and manage symptoms.

Surgery

Surgical intervention is the first line of treatment for most brain tumors. Surgery can be done asleep under general anesthesia or awake to allow for intraoperative mapping to guide the surgical resection. While many surgical centers opt to perform non-dominant tumor resections asleep, there has been a push to keep patients awake in non-dominant resections, especially if eloquent areas are suspected to be near the area of resection.

Awake surgical resections require carefully balancing levels of sedation, anxiolysis and analgesia, to facilitate intraoperative mapping. Awake craniotomies for tumor resection require highly experienced surgical teams. Different variations in types of awake craniotomies exist including asleep–awake–asleep or awake–awake–awake formats. In an asleep–awake–asleep approach, the patient is given anesthesia during the opening and craniotomy, which is subsequently withheld, allowing the patient to regain an appropriate level of arousal to engage in cognitive testing. After completion of the intraoperative mapping and resection, the patient is most often sedated again to return to sleep for the closing. In cases where the patient is comfortable and tolerating the procedure well, the team may opt to keep the patient awake during the opening and closing. The patient typically undergoes a scalp block to numb the pain receptors in the scalp before the incision is made. Surgical incision is made followed by a craniotomy which consists of removing a section of the skull and opening of the dura to gain access to the brain and the tumor. Neuronavigation systems can be used to guide the surgeon to the location of the tumor.

Based on the tumor location, cortical mapping of the surface with electrical stimulation is often performed to help determine the most optimal surgical approach while avoiding functionally eloquent regions. Stimulation mapping can also be performed at the borders of the tumor to help achieve gross total or even supramaximal resections (i.e., removal of tissue past the area of contrast enhancement). The main goal of surgery is to obtain tissue for diagnostics and, in symptomatic patients, reduce symptoms that result from mass effect and edema and to decrease the need for corticosteroids. During surgery, the tissue is removed and sent to pathology to determine molecular profiling and histopathology. Although neuroimaging features provide guidance regarding the tumor type and grade, diagnosis can only be achieved after careful consideration of molecular and histological features. Newer techniques have been developed to help improve visualization of tumor cells to optimize extent of resection. Fluorescence-guided surgery using 5-aminolevulinic acid (5-ALA) is such a technique that allows for intraoperative visualization of malignant glioma infiltrated tissue. 5-ALA is administered orally before surgery and selectively accumulates in tumor cells such that under blue light, the tumor fluoresces, aiding neurosurgeons in precisely removing affected tissue, while sparing healthy adjacent brain tissue. 5-ALA has been shown to ultimately contribute to better patient outcome and prognosis. For some low-grade gliomas, surgical resection can be curative if gross total resection is achieved, but more often than not, there will be tumor recurrence, and adjuvant therapies will be needed. In high-grade tumors, repeated surgical resections may be indicated after tumor recurrence to increase survival. Of note, a recent study showed that repeated surgical resections did not adversely impact quality of life and perceived cognitive functioning in carefully selected high-grade glioma patients (Koay et al., 2024).

A delicate balance must be achieved between maximizing tumor removal while minimizing neurologic deficits, which is essential for maintaining quality of life, a term that has been coined "the onco-functional balance" (Duffau & Mandonnet, 2013). Neuropsychologists play an important role in preservation of such functions. Sparing cognitive functions is achieved with close communication between neuropsychology, neurosurgery and anesthesiology. Consideration of potential damage inflicted to gray matter structures as well as white matter tracts is key. As neuropsychologists, having an adequate understanding of white matter organization and potential resulting cognitive and sensory impairment is essential for effective communication with the surgical team. Neuropsychologists collaborate with the medical team to assess and monitor cognitive functions perioperatively. Preoperatively, they evaluate cognitive functioning, identify potential surgical risks based on potential damage to given structures and white matter tracts. Intraoperatively, the role of neuropsychologists is to assist with mapping of the eloquent cortex and subcortical white matter tracts that are susceptible to cause functional impairment if damaged.

Chemotherapy and Cognitive Side Effects

While some providers opt to treat low-grade gliomas with adjuvant therapies after resection, others prefer to monitor the tumor on neuroimaging overtime and prescribe adjuvant treatments only if and when it is needed. Vorasidenib is a new treatment drug that has shown promise in the treatment of lower-grade gliomas that harbor an IDH mutation. The drug works by blocking the activity of the mutated IDH enzyme to disrupt the abnormal metabolic pathways that contribute to tumor growth and progression. In patients with grade 2 IDH-mutant glioma, Vorasidenib significantly increased progression-free survival and delayed the time to the next intervention (Mellinghoff et al., 2023). For higher-grade gliomas, such as glioblastoma, the standard treatment is to proceed with concurrent chemotherapy with the alkylating chemotherapeutic agent temozolomide and radiation therapy following the surgical resection (Stupp protocol). This approach has been shown to improve survival rates compared to radiation therapy on its own in patients with glioblastoma (Schaff & Mellinghoff, 2023). Despite chemotherapy with temozolomide generally being well-tolerated, it confers risk for associated cognitive changes. In fact, about 30% of patients with glioblastoma who are stable clinically and radiographically experience cognitive decline during chemoradiation treatment with temozolomide (Wefel & Schagen, 2012; Prust et al., 2015; Prust et al., 2018). A review by Wefel and Shagen showed that after treatment, the incidence of cognitive decline ranged from 19% to 78% across studies and involved changes in processing speed, learning and memory and executive functioning (Wefel & Schagen, 2012).

Radiation Therapy and Cognitive Effects

When it comes to radiation therapy, treatment is delivered in fractions, which refer to the number of radiation sessions a patient receives. Patients can undergo single fraction (e.g., radiosurgery) or multiple fractions (e.g., fractionated radiation for gliomas). Grays (Gy) refer to the total dose of radiation delivered. For example, if a patient receives 30 fractions at 2 Gy per fraction, they are undergoing 30 sessions of radiation to a total dose of 60 Gy. Fractionated radiation can be done to specific areas of the brain where tumors are located or can be done to the whole brain. Fractionated partial brain radiation is often used to treat primary brain tumors while whole-brain radiation is reserved for patients with a high number of metastatic lesions to the brain and in some cases prophylactically in high-risk cancers that tend to metastasize to the brain (Sun et al., 2011) and in certain pediatric tumors that can spread to the spine (e.g., medulloblastomas). There are well-documented neurotoxic effects of radiation to the brain that can present at different time windows including acute, early delayed and late. Late delayed brain injury is characterized histopathologically by vascular abnormalities, demyelination, gliosis and ultimately white matter necrosis and generalized cognitive impairment (Tofilon & Fike, 2000; Greene-Schloesser et al., 2012) and tend to be more refractory than acute or early effects. The most affected cognitive domains are processing speed, attention, executive functioning and learning and memory, but it is likely that radiation-induced cognitive impairment varies based on the volume and area irradiated. The main risk factors for radiation-induced cognitive decline are a larger amount of radiation delivered at each dose, larger volume irradiated and later age of the patient. Hippocampal-sparing during whole-brain radiation can help reduce cognitive morbidity. Hippocampal-sparing effectively limits memory decline associated with whole-brain radiation therapy, in turn helping maintain quality of life in patients with brain metastasis. Preclinical studies suggest that anti-inflammatory drugs may prevent/reduce radiation-induced cognitive impairment. Other studies have found limited benefits from methylphenidate (Meyers et al., 1998) and donepezil (Shaw et al., 2006). Prophylactic use of memantine has been shown to delay and reduce the rate of cognitive decline in processing speed, executive function and memory after whole-brain radiation therapy (Brown et al., 2013).

Other Types of Treatments

In certain cases, brain tumors are treated with antiangiogenic therapy. Bevacizumab (Avastin) is a monoclonal antibody designed to target vascular endothelial growth factor (VEGF), which is a key promoter of angiogenesis, particularly in glioblastoma. Bevacizumab has the ability to bind to VEGF and block the downstream signaling pathway that leads to endothelial cell proliferation, migration and formation of new blood vessels that feed the tumor (Wedam et al., 2006). Bevacizumab has been shown to delay tumor revascularization but does not prolong survival (Tan et al., 2020). In a study of recurrent glioblastoma treated with bevacizumab, the authors found stable or improved cognitive functioning in patients who showed no disease progression on imaging. Similarly, they identified cognitive decline in those with imaging suggestive of disease progression (Wefel et al., 2011). Tumor treating fields (TTFields) are a newer and non-invasive treatment modality approved for patients with newly diagnosed or recurrent glioblastoma. The Optune device, which is worn as a cap, delivers transcranial low-intensity and intermediate-frequency electric fields that disrupt the mitotic activity of glioblastoma and is FDA-approved for the treatment for newly diagnosed and recurrent glioblastoma. Some patients find it difficult to tolerate the device as it must be worn for a minimum of 18 hours per day. Studies on the clinical effectiveness of TTFields have shown mixed results. Studies examining the effectiveness of TTFields have yielded mixed results. However, recent research by Hong and colleagues found that combining TTFields with temozolomide after the first recurrence led to a significant increase in median overall survival, with patients living for an average of 11.8 months compared to the 9.2 months seen with temozolomide alone (Hong et al., 2022).

Long-term Cognitive Monitoring

Cognition has been shown to be a predictor of brain tumor progression and survival in glioma patients. In a sample of patients with glioblastoma, Meyers and Hess showed that greater cognitive deterioration preceded radiographic evidence of tumor progression by 6 weeks (Meyers & Hess, 2003). Decline in cognitive testing occurred earlier than neuroimaging evidence of progression and has been shown to be highly correlated with disease progression. Tests of memory and fine motor coordination were the most sensitive to decline in this group. These findings have since been supported by others (Johnson et al., 2012; Noll et al., 2019) showing that decline in cognition is predictive of progression and overall survival. These findings support the implementation of routine neuropsychological testing in assessing neurotoxic effects of adjuvant therapies, but also in detecting early signs of disease progression.

Neuropsychological Evaluation

There is no standard neuropsychological battery for the assessment of patients with brain tumors. We recommend using a battery that covers a variety of cognitive domains, is sensitive to both dominant and non-dominant hemisphere functioning and is repeatable (alternate forms where possible) to reduce practice effects. This approach provides the best coverage for the wide variety of locations where the tumor can appear. Specifically, assessment of the following neuropsychological domains is highly recommended: attention/concentration, speeded processing, motor speed, language (receptive and expressive), verbal and visual learning and memory, executive functioning, emotional functioning and quality of life.

An example of such a battery is as follows: Wechsler Test of Adult Reading (WTAR), Hopkins Verbal Learning Test-Revised (HVLT-R), Brief Visuospatial Memory Test-Revised (BVMT-R), Wechsler Adult Intelligence Scale (WAIS) Processing Speed Index, WAIS Digit span, Wechsler Memory Scale (WMS) Spatial Span, Boston Naming Test (short or long forms), Trail Making Test, Delis-Kaplan Executive Functions System (DKEFS) Verbal Fluency and Color-Word Interference, Grooved Pegboard Test, Beck Depression Inventory, Beck Anxiety Inventory, Functional Assessment of Cancer Therapy - Brain (FACT-Br). Additional measures can be added depending on the anatomical location of the tumor (e.g., line bisection and random letter cancellation for right fronto-parietal-temporal tumors, Benton Facial Recognition Test (BFRT) for right fusiform tumors). When selecting an appropriate neuropsychological battery for patients with brain tumors, special considerations and accommodations should be made with regard to sensorimotor deficits and battery length, as some patients struggle with fatigue from their disease (Table 28.3).

Preoperatively, our goal as neuropsychologists is to determine the impact of the tumor on cognitive and emotional functions, which allows for easier differentiation between the cognitive manifestation of the disease from interventions (e.g., surgery, radiation, etc.) later on. Some neuropsychologists are involved in surgical planning and intraoperative brain mapping. Preoperative neuropsychological test data can help inform the approach and selection of intraoperative brain mapping paradigms and contribute to developing a comprehensive risk model that the surgeon can use in planning.

Intraoperatively, the surgical goals are to obtain tissue for diagnostics and perform a maximal safe total resection when possible. Based on the tumor location, cortical mapping with electrical stimulation is often performed to help determine the most optimal surgical approach or trajectory by avoiding functionally eloquent

Table 28.3 Recommended neuropsychological test by cognitive domain

Cognitive domain	Neuropsychological test
Premorbid Intellectual Functioning	Wechsler Test of Adult Reading
Attention/Concentration	Wechsler Adult Intelligence Scale-IV Digit Span (Forward, Backward, Sequencing) Processing Speed Index (Coding, Symbol Search) Wechsler Memory Scale-III Spatial Span
Learning and Memory	Hopkins Verbal Learning Test-R Total Learning, Delay Recall, Recognition Brief Visuospatial Memory Test-R Total Learning, Delay Recall, Recognition
Executive Functioning	Delis-Kaplan Executive Functions System Letter Fluency, Category Fluency, Color-Word Inhibition Trail Making Test - Part A Trail Making Test - Part B
Speech/Language	Boston Naming Test Quick Aphasia Battery
Motor Speed	Grooved Pegboard
Additional Measures To Consider (depending on anatomy of tumor)	Benton Facial Recognition Test Line Bisection Random Letter Cancellation Test Calculations

regions. Stimulation mapping can also be performed at the tumor borders to help map subcortical areas and achieve gross total or even super maximal resections, which refers to removing tissue past the tumor border. Outside of stimulation, it is also important to continuously assess for any cognitive changes during active surgical resection and report such changes as soon as possible to the surgeon to prevent more significant deficits from developing. Some centers also use continuous monopolar stimulation mapping while resection is being performed to map tissue as the resection advances.

Postoperatively, patients should be re-evaluated after surgery but prior to initiation of adjuvant therapies. Re-evaluation 4 to 5 weeks after surgery allows for surgical edema and effects of surgical traction and mechanical manipulation to resolve, providing a better clinical picture of the effects of surgery. The neuropsychological battery used at baseline can be repeated postoperatively. Alternate forms should be used where possible to reduce practice effects. The goal is to characterize potential acute and subacute deficits that may require rehabilitation or additional support for completing activities of daily living. Neuropsychological testing can assist with making decisions about returning to work and driving and identifying emotional issues that should be treated to optimize quality of life.

Illustrative Case

What follows is a case presentation that illustrates the various roles of neuropsychology in the management of brain tumors. The presentation consists of an introduction to the patient's presenting concerns, review of the presurgical imaging and a report on the patient's neuropsychological test results, followed by a neuropsychological interpretation and conceptualization of the data and how it is integrated in patient care.

A 35-year-old, right-handed male with 12 years of education and no previous medical history presented to his primary care physician with complaints of new onset headache and staring episodes where he would "go blank" and be unable to speak for up to a minute. During some events, he would exhibit some mouth movements. He underwent a brain MRI, which revealed a T2 hyperintense lesion in the inferior frontal gyrus (IFG) and heterogeneous contrast enhancement (see Fig. 28.3).

Case Conceptualization: Patient is right-handed and approximately 95% of right handers are left hemisphere dominant for language. The patient appears to be experiencing focal impaired aware seizures with speech/language disruption further implicating dominant hemisphere involvement. His mouth movements during his seizures may reflect some spread to the adjacent mouth motor area in the premotor/motor cortex. Imaging shows a clear intra-axial lesion with some contrast enhancement, which was concerning for a higher-grade glioma.

The patient was evaluated by the Neurosurgery, and given the location of the mass in known eloquent regions of the brain, an awake craniotomy with resection was recommended. The patient underwent advanced imaging, including fMRI and DTI to inform surgical planning. fMRI motor mapping showed expected areas of activation in precentral gyrus and supplemental motor area (SMA) with tongue, finger and foot movement protocols with no immediate or close proximity to the tumor. Language mapping, using a panel of tasks including sentence completion, reading comprehension, rhyming and semantic decision-making about auditory presented words, showed significant overlap of activation in the left fronto-parieto-temporal language areas, supporting strong left hemisphere dominance. There was some activation at the superior border of the tumor along the inferior frontal sulcus. Diffusion tensor imaging showed intact fractional anisotropy of the left superior longitudinal (SLF-III) and arcuate fasciculus (AF) with immediate proximity at the deep medial border. The mass also involved the IFG termination point for the frontal aslant tract (FAT).

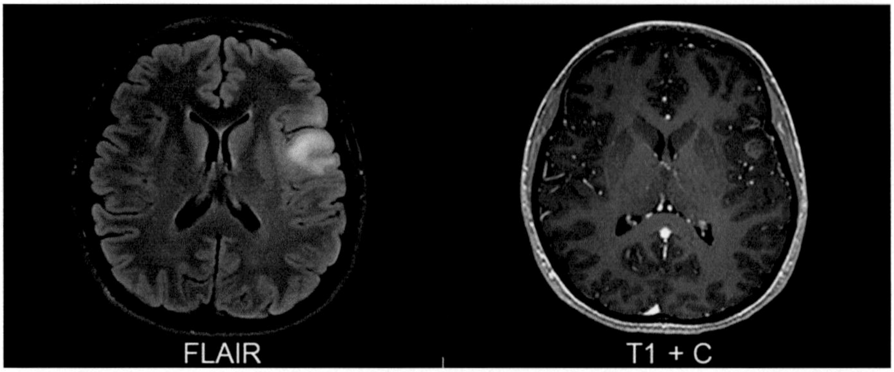

Fig. 28.3 (Left) MRI FLAIR showing T2 hyperintense signal in the left inferior frontal gyrus, specifically pars operculum, likely reflecting combination of tumor infiltration and vasogenic edema. (Right) T1 with contrast showing bright signals indicating enhancement in the mass

Case Conceptualization: fMRI motor mapping indicates little risk to motor functions given that primary and premotor areas are at least one gyrus posterior to the mass nor does the mass have close proximity to the corticospinal tract. Language mapping confirmed left hemisphere dominance for language placing the patient at some risk for language decline with resection. Specifically, the ventral premotor cortex, which is located just posterior to the mass, and the primary motor cortex posterior to that are important for the planning and execution of speech motor output. While the exact function of pars operculum is not fully understood, there is converging evidence from clinical and imaging studies suggesting that this area is not responsible for motor functions but rather phonological related processes (e.g., gating the flow or release of phonological information to speech motor centers). The IFG has also been implicated in verbal working memory and grammatical processing (perhaps via working memory contribution). There was only minimal language-related BOLD signal in close proximity to the tumor, but the absence of BOLD activation does not equate to the absence of function as tumors can alter vascular dynamics and cause neurovascular uncoupling, increasing the chance for false negative findings. For this reason, fMRI should not be used alone for surgical planning. DTI showed immediate proximity of the mass to the SLF-III and AF, both of which connect posterior cortical language areas to speech centers in the IFG and ventral premotor cortex. These tracts are part of the dorsal phonological pathway and have been implicated in conveying phonological information. The mass involves the FAT, which connects the supplementary motor area to the IFG, and has been implicated in verbal initiation and fluency. Careful intraoperative mapping would be needed to guide the surgical resection at these borders to minimize language morbidity.

The patient underwent presurgical neuropsychological testing three days before his surgery to educate and counsel the patient on his upcoming surgical procedure, evaluate his candidacy for an awake craniotomy, establish a baseline that would allow for better evaluation of surgical outcomes, develop a comprehensive risk model, assist with surgical planning and to train and establish a baseline for the patient on intraoperative cognitive mapping paradigms. A similar neuropsychological battery to the one outlined in the Neuropsychological Evaluation section above was used. Performance test results are presented in Table 28.4.

Table 28.4 Neuropsychological test performance of case example

Cognitive domain	Neuropsychological test	Standardized score (percentile ranks)
Premorbid Intellectual Functioning	WTAR	SS = 102 (55%)
Attention/concentration	Digit span (WAIS-IV)	Sc = 4 (2%)
	Forward	Sc = 6 (9%)
	Backward	Sc = 5 (5%)
	Sequencing	Sc = 5 (5%)
	Spatial span (WMS-III)	Sc = 11 (63%)
Processing Speed	Coding (WAIS-IV)	Sc = 9 (37%)
	Symbol Search (WAIS-IV)	Sc = 10 (50%)
	Trail Making Test - Part A	T = 52 (58%)
Learning and Memory	HVLT-R Total Learning	SS = 63 (1%)
	Delay Recall	SS = 79 (8%)
	Retention %	100%
	Recognition	12 TP, 0 FP
	BVMT-R Total Learning	SS = 96 (39%)
	Delay Recall	SS = 102 (55%)
	Recognition	(>16%)
Executive Functioning	DKEFS	
	Letter Fluency	Sc = 6 (9%)
	Category Fluency	Sc = 7 (16%)
	Color Naming	Sc = 10 (50%)
	Word Reading	Sc = 9 (37%)
	Color-Word Interference	Sc = 10 (50%)
	Trail Making Test - Part B	T = 51 (55%)
Speech/Language	Boston Naming Test	T = 38 (12%)
Motor Speed	Grooved pegboard	
	Dominant (right) hand	T = 46 (34%)
	Non-dominant hand	T = 47 (39%)

DKEFS Delis-Kaplan Executive Function System, *HVLT-R* Hopkins Verbal Learning Test, revised, *WAIS-IV* Wechsler Adult Intelligence Scale, Fourth Edition, *WMS-III* Wechsler Memory Scale-Third Edition, *WTAR* Wechsler Test of Adult Reading

Test results revealed weaknesses in verbal fluency (DKEFS verbal fluency) and verbal working memory (WAIS-IV Digit Span) as well as some inefficiencies in registration and learning of a word list (HVLT). There was no evidence of any forgetting as retention of the learned material was intact. Processing speed (WAIS Coding and Symbol Search, DKEFS Color Naming and Word Reading and TMT-A) was average. Non-dominant hemisphere mediated functions, such as spatial working memory (WMS-III Spatial Span) and visual learning and memory (BVMT), were all average. Executive functions, including divided attention (TMT-B), and inhibitory control (DKEFS Color Word) were low average to average. Fine motor dexterity was symmetric and average in both hands. The patient was baselined on several intraoperative cognitive paradigms for mapping and continuous monitoring or testing during surgery using the NeuroMapper testing platform (developed by David Sabsevitz, Ph.D.) Given the role of the IFG in speech/phonological process, both a picture naming and nonword and phrase repetition tasks were selected. A digit span test was used to interrogate verbal working memory functions and matching sentences that varied in grammatical complexity to pictures depicting an action (e.g., "the boy in the green shirt was kicked by the girl") was used to evaluate sentence-level semantics and to analyze grammatical structure.

Conceptualization: The patient showed expected weaknesses in verbal fluency thought likely from disruption of the IFG-frontal aslant network and in verbal working memory from involvement of the pars operculum. HVLT learning was thought to be low secondary to the patient's working memory issues. The finding of weaknesses in these areas supports the presence of functional eloquence in the surgical field and highlights the need to map these functions with neuroanatomically informed paradigms both at the surface to guide surgical trajectory and during the resection and at its border to guide extent of resection. The patient was able to perform well on the intraoperative paradigms and no obvious emotional contraindications were identified so the surgical team was notified that he appeared to be a good candidate for awake surgery. Based on the presurgical workup (imaging, neuropsychological testing), the neuropsychologist developed a comprehensive risk model that included both cortical and subcortical anatomy. The functions of the IFG and surrounding white matter tracts and planned intraoperative paradigms were reviewed with the neurosurgical team.

The patient underwent craniotomy and tumor resection using an asleep–awake–asleep protocol, which involved sedation using propofol and dexmedetomidine during the scalp incision. He was woken up once the bone was removed and prior to the opening of the dura. The surgical team used a circular grid with 360 degrees of coverage to monitor for afterdischarges and seizures during surgical mapping (see Fig. 28.4 below). The team initiated bipolar stimulation at 2 mA and increased in 1 mA intervals until reaching 10 mA, just below the threshold for afterdischarges.

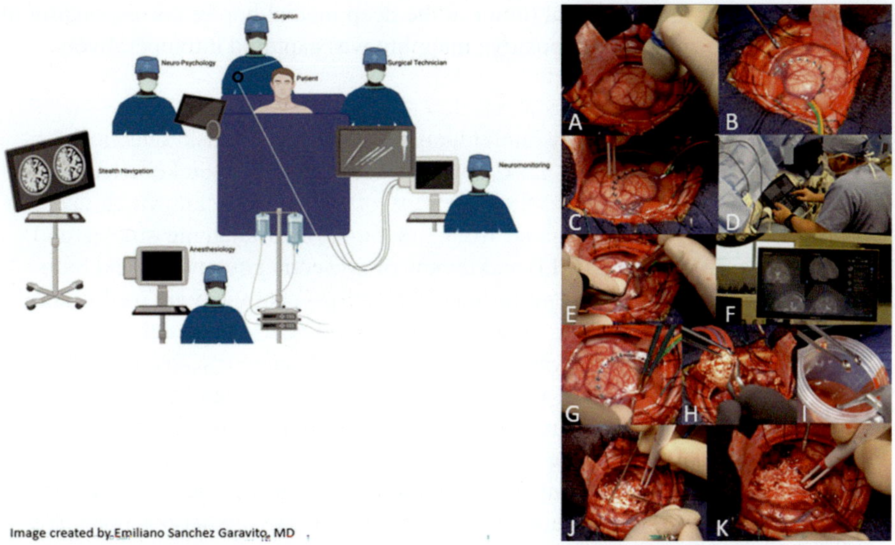

Fig. 28.4 Awake Craniotomy for Tumor Resection. (**a**) Navigated intraoperative Ultrasonography. (**b**) Placement of the high-density circular grid during direct cortical electrical stimulation for active stimulation and mapping. (**c**) Identification of areas of eloquence through active stimulation. (**d**) Neuropsychological testing during cortical stimulation and monitoring with NeuroMapper with iPad technology. (**e**) and (**f**) Use of intraoperative Stealth Neuro-navigation. (**g**, **h**) Tumor resection through the high-density circular array. (**i**) Collection of tissue samples for histopathological studies and biorepository. (**j** and **k**) Subcortical stimulation

The cortical surface was mapped first using picture naming and no disruptions in speech motor or naming abilities up to 10 mA. Speech arrest was found posterior to the tumor in the ventral premotor cortex. This area was marked with a sterile numbered tag. The surface was also mapped with the digit span paradigm. There were some variable and inconsistent sequencing errors observed along the superior bank of the mass. This area was marked with a sterile numbers tag. Surgical entry was made, and continuous monopolar mapping was used as the neuropsychologist simultaneously tested picture naming, repetition, verbal working memory and grammatical comprehension. Upper and lower extremity motor strength and coordination were also monitored. As the surgeon approached the deep medial border of the tumor, the patient exhibited some naming issues without speech motor deficits (i.e., inability to name pictures but able to say the carrier phrase "This is a .."). This approximated the location of SLF-III/AF on the neuronavigation system and determined the extent of that surgical border. The surgeon continued the resection at other borders with careful monopolar mapping without any observed behavioral changes. The patient was sedated at the end of the resection for the closing and sent to recovery. Tissue was sent to pathology for diagnosis. Preliminary pathology indicated a glioma. Permanent pathology about a week later revealed a WHO grade 3 astrocytoma, IDH-mutant. Postoperative neuroimaging showed near gross total resection, with minimal residual tumor at the deep medial border corresponding to the anatomical location where positive mapping was captured intraoperatively.

Conceptualization: A highly individualized approach to task selection for brain mapping is advocated. Tasks should be selected based on knowledge of functional neuroanatomy and the proximity of the tumor to known eloquent areas, localization data obtained from functional neuroimaging studies and diffusion tensor imaging (DTI) and review of presenting symptoms and baseline neuropsychological test performance. Neuropsychologists are well suited in advising the surgical team on what tasks should be used given their expertise in brain behavior relationships and functional anatomy. Testing should also be multidimensional in nature as tumors can be located in areas where more than one function has proximity to the tumor border. In addition to stimulation mapping, monitoring cognition in real-time during awake brain surgery offers the surgeon continuous feedback to guide surgical decision-making (Skrap et al., 2016) and intraoperative performance can predict postoperative language changes (Chang et al., 2018). Continuous monitoring was performed in this patient, and by cycling through the multiple pre-selected paradigms to assess the different cognitive functions of the area being resected, the likelihood of missing a developing deficit is minimized. Further, the use of a combined suction and monopolar stimulator that provides constant electrical stimulation mapping further reduces risk by being able to identify functional eloquence before resecting that area. In this case example, when electrical stimulation was applied to the SLF-III, a white matter tract known to be involved in phonological processing, the patient became unable to name objects presented on the screen, but basic speech motor functions were preserved. The neurosurgical team opted to spare this white matter tract to minimize the risk for language morbidity.

The patient returned for postoperative neuropsychological testing 4 weeks after surgery to allow for some time for acute/subacute surgical effects (e.g., edema) to resolve. The same battery that was given preoperatively was re-administered with alternate forms where possible. The patient showed stable cognition with no evidence of any worsening. Continued mild weaknesses in verbal working memory, verbal fluency and learning of new material were observed. Speech therapy was recommended to help optimize his cognition. Supportive counseling was provided, and the patient was given with the names of local psychotherapists that work with cancer patients. Compensatory cognitive strategies were also discussed, and examples provided.

The patient proceeded with a course of concurrent chemoradiation. Radiation was given to a total dose of 60 Gy in 30 fractions with temozolomide chemotherapy. The patient tolerated it well. He then started adjuvant temozolomide for 12 planned cycles. He was seen for repeat neuropsychological testing approximately 4 months after completing radiation. Some mild declines were seen in processing speed and verbal fluency but otherwise cognition was stable. Imaging showed increased FLAIR in the frontal region with no areas of new contrast nor any increased perfusion on perfusion MR, suggesting treatment effects from radiation with no tumor recurrence or progression. The patient was interested in returning to work in construction. It was recommended that the patient could return to work with some limitations and accommodations; mainly, avoiding aspects of his job that would pose an increased risk for harm given his psychomotor slowing (e.g., being on roofs, operating heavy machinery and other dangerous equipment). Again, cognitive compensatory strategies and suggestions to help him minimize the impact of psychomotor slowing on day-to-day functioning were reviewed with the patient. The patient endorsed some mild depression and anxiety consistent with an Adjustment Disorder. The patient was referred to Cognitive Behavioral Therapy to help cope with his diagnosis. Neuropsychological re-evaluation was recommended in another 3 months to assess cognitive trajectory.

Conceptualization: The patient experienced some decline in select frontal-subcortical mediated functions on his 4-month post-radiation follow-up. Imaging showed no evidence of tumor progression. Cognitive effects of radiation can occur at different time points following radiotherapy (e.g., acute, early and late delayed). He is well within the early delayed period and often these changes can improve assuming good tumor control. These changes are thought secondary to transient demyelination and disruption of the blood–brain barrier resulting in vasogenic edema, likely driving his T2/FLAIR changes on imaging. Re-evaluation in another 3 months would allow for further time to better determine if his decline is transient and due to early radiation effects or more permanent and/or progressive, which might suggest impending tumor progression or more intractable radiation effects.

The patient returned for follow-up neuropsychology 3 months later. Imaging showed no evidence of tumor progression or worsening T2/FLAIR signal. Testing results showed improvements in processing speed and verbal fluency with otherwise stable cognition. He reported less anxiety and depression and attributed this to his efforts in psychotherapy. Given his normalization of processing speed, return to his normal work duties with the recommendation of continuing to avoid climbing ladders and working on roofs given his seizure history was given.

This case example illustrates the role of neuropsychology in presurgical planning and intraoperative mapping and postsurgical management and highlights the need for having a more nuanced and comprehensive understanding of functional neuroanatomy, brain behavior relationships and imaging methods when working in this capacity.

Summary and Conclusions

Brain tumors are abnormal growths of cells in the skull cavity that can be primary vs. metastatic, referring to the site of origin, and malignant vs. non-malignant, referring to the tumor's aggressiveness. Brain tumors are now classified based on histological and molecular features, with the most recent classification published by the WHO in 2021. Most primary brain tumors in childhood are in the posterior fossa and include circumscribed astrocytic gliomas, embryonal tumors and ependymomas. In adulthood, meningiomas are the most common non-malignant brain tumors in adults, while glioblastomas are the most common malignant brain tumors. Molecular genetics assist with diagnosing and determining the prognosis and treatability of different brain tumors. The signs and symptoms of brain tumors vary depending on the location and aggressiveness of the tumor and can include headaches, seizures and cognitive and behavioral impairment, among others. Cognitive impairment is common among brain tumor patients at some point during the disease course. Therefore, it is essential to assess and monitor cognitive functioning in this population to minimize deficits and optimize quality of life. In most cases, surgery is the first-line treatment with the goal of obtaining tissue for diagnosis, resecting as much tumor as possible to alleviate symptoms and decreasing steroid dependency. Neuroimaging is essential for screening and monitoring brain tumors. CT and MRI can provide helpful information about a given tumor type, as well as infer tumor aggressiveness, but tissue sampling is ultimately required for diagnostics. Functional MRI and DTI are also important for presurgical planning. Neuropsychological assessment during the preoperative stage can assist with surgical planning and pre- and intraoperative brain mapping. In cases where the tumor lies near eloquent regions, performing awake surgical resections can lower the risk of cognitive complications and maximize the extent of the surgical resection. Postoperatively, neuropsychological assessment can guide the rehabilitation process and monitor the disease course and response to treatment. The treatment options for brain tumors include surgical resection, radiation and chemotherapy. Neuropsychologists are increasingly involved in managing cognitive and emotional changes in brain tumor patients at all stages of care.

References

Allen, N. J., & Lyons, D. A. (2018). Glia as architects of central nervous system formation and function. *Science, 362*(6411), 181–185.

Bobholz, S., et al. (2022). Radio-pathomic maps of cell density identify brain tumor invasion beyond traditional MRI-defined margins. *American Journal of Neuroradiology, 43*(5), 682–688.

Bobholz, S., et al. (2024). Noninvasive autopsy-validated tumor probability maps identify glioma invasion beyond contrast enhancement. *Neurosurgery, 10*, 1227.

Bobholz, S. A., et al. (2020). Radiomic features of multiparametric MRI present stable associations with analogous histological features in patients with brain cancer. *Tomography, 6*(2), 160–169.

Brown, P. D., et al. (2013). Memantine for the prevention of cognitive dysfunction in patients receiving whole-brain radiotherapy: A randomized, double-blind, placebo-controlled trial. *Neuro-Oncology, 15*(10), 1429–1437.
Chang, W.-H., et al. (2018). Intraoperative linguistic performance during awake brain surgery predicts postoperative linguistic deficits. *Journal of Neuro-Oncology, 139*, 215–223.
Chenevert, T. L., et al. (2019). Comparison of voxel-wise and histogram analyses of glioma ADC maps for prediction of early therapeutic change. *Tomography, 5*(1), 7–14.
Cotter, J. A., & Hawkins, C. (2022). Medulloblastoma: WHO 2021 and beyond. *Pediatric and Developmental Pathology, 25*(1), 23–33.
Davis, L. E., et al. (2005). *Fundamentals of neurologic disease*. Demos Medical Publishing.
DeAngelis, L. M., et al. (2001). *Intracranial tumors: Diagnosis and treatment*. CRC Press.
Duffau, H., & Mandonnet, E. (2013). The "onco-functional balance" in surgery for diffuse low-grade glioma: Integrating the extent of resection with quality of life. *Acta Neurochirurgica, 155*, 951–957.
Eidel, O., et al. (2016). Automatic analysis of cellularity in glioblastoma and correlation with ADC using trajectory analysis and automatic nuclei counting. *PLoS One, 11*(7), e0160250.
El-Zein, R., et al. (2005). *Epidemiology of brain tumors* (pp. 3–18). Springer.
Funakoshi, Y., et al. (2023). Recent advances in the molecular understanding of medulloblastoma. *Cancer Science, 114*(3), 741–749.
Greene-Schloesser, D., et al. (2012). Radiation-induced brain injury: A review. *Frontiers in Oncology, 2*, 73.
Grier, J. T., & Batchelor, T. (2006). Low-grade gliomas in adults. *The Oncologist, 11*(6), 681–693.
Haider, S. A., et al. (2020). The economic impact of glioma survivorship: The cost of care from a patient perspective. *Neurology, 95*(11), e1575–e1581.
Hong, P., et al. (2022). Tumor treating fields: A comprehensive overview of the underlying molecular mechanism. *Expert Review of Molecular Diagnostics, 22*(1), 19–28.
Honnorat, J., & Antoine, J.-C. (2007). Paraneoplastic neurological syndromes. *Orphanet Journal of Rare Diseases, 2*, 1–8.
Hwang, T. L., et al. (1996). Predilection of brain metastasis in gray and white matter junction and vascular border zones. *Cancer: Interdisciplinary International Journal of the American Cancer Society, 77*(8), 1551–1555.
Jayakar, R., et al. (2015). Hippocampal volume and auditory attention on a verbal memory task with adult survivors of pediatric brain tumor. *Neuropsychology, 29*(2), 303.
Johnson, D. R., et al. (2012). Early measures of cognitive function predict survival in patients with newly diagnosed glioblastoma. *Neuro-Oncology, 14*(6), 808–816.
Kaye, A. H. (2009). *Essential neurosurgery*. Wiley.
King, T. Z., et al. (2019). Neurodevelopmental model of long-term outcomes of adult survivors of childhood brain tumors. *Child Neuropsychology, 25*(1), 1–21.
Koay, J. M., et al. (2024). Repeated surgical resections for management of high-grade glioma and its impact on quality of life. *Journal of Neuro-Oncology, 167*, 267–273.
Lakhani, D. A., et al. (2023). Current state of functional MRI in the presurgical planning of brain tumors. *Radiology: Imaging Cancer, 5*(6), e230078.
LaViolette, P. S., et al. (2014). Precise ex vivo histological validation of heightened cellularity and diffusion-restricted necrosis in regions of dark apparent diffusion coefficient in 7 cases of high-grade glioma. *Neuro-Oncology, 16*(12), 1599–1606.
Louis, D. N., et al. (2016). The 2016 World Health Organization classification of tumors of the central nervous system: A summary. *Acta Neuropathologica, 131*, 803–820.
Louis, D. N., et al. (2021). The 2021 WHO classification of tumors of the central nervous system: A summary. *Neuro-Oncology, 23*(8), 1231–1251.
Macartney, G., et al. (2014). Quality of life and symptoms in pediatric brain tumor survivors: A systematic review. *Journal of Pediatric Oncology Nursing, 31*(2), 65–77.

Mellinghoff, I. K., et al. (2023). Vorasidenib in IDH1-or IDH2-mutant low-grade glioma. *New England Journal of Medicine, 389*(7), 589–601.
Meyers, C. A., & Hess, K. R. (2003). Multifaceted end points in brain tumor clinical trials: Cognitive deterioration precedes MRI progression. *Neuro-Oncology, 5*(2), 89–95.
Meyers, C. A., et al. (1998). Methylphenidate therapy improves cognition, mood, and function of brain tumor patients. *Journal of Clinical Oncology, 16*(7), 2522–2527.
Noll, K. R., et al. (2019). Monitoring of neurocognitive function in the care of patients with brain tumors. *Current Treatment Options in Neurology, 21*, 1–14.
Noll, K. R., et al. (2016). Neurocognitive functioning in patients with glioma of the left and right temporal lobes. *Journal of Neuro-Oncology, 128*, 323–331.
Olsson, I. T., et al. (2014). Long-term cognitive sequelae after pediatric brain tumor related to medical risk factors, age, and sex. *Pediatric Neurology, 51*(4), 515–521.
Ostrom, Q. T., et al. (2019). Risk factors for childhood and adult primary brain tumors. *Neuro-Oncology, 21*(11), 1357–1375.
Ostrom, Q. T., et al. (2014). The epidemiology of glioma in adults: A "state of the science" review. *Neuro-Oncology, 16*(7), 896–913.
Ostrom, Q. T., et al. (2023). CBTRUS Statistical Report: Primary brain and other central nervous system tumors diagnosed in the United States in 2016—2020. *Neuro-Oncology, 25*(Supplement_4), iv1–iv99.
Park, Y. W., et al. (2023). The 2021 WHO classification for gliomas and implications on imaging diagnosis: Part 1—Key points of the fifth edition and summary of imaging findings on adult-type diffuse gliomas. *Journal of Magnetic Resonance Imaging, 58*(3), 677–689.
Parsons, M. W., & Sabsevitz, D. S. (2023). Cognitive issues in patients with IDH mutant gliomas: From neuroscience to clinical neuropsychology. *Journal of Neuro-Oncology, 162*(3), 525–533.
Prust, M. J., et al. (2015). Standard chemoradiation for glioblastoma results in progressive brain volume loss. *Neurology, 85*(8), 683–691.
Prust, M. L., et al. (2018). Standard chemoradiation in combination with VEGF targeted therapy for glioblastoma results in progressive gray and white matter volume loss. *Neuro-Oncology, 20*(2), 289–291.
Sacks, P., & Rahman, M. (2020). Epidemiology of brain metastases. *Neurosurgery Clinics, 31*(4), 481–488.
Schaff, L. R., & Mellinghoff, I. K. (2023). Glioblastoma and other primary brain malignancies in adults: A review. *JAMA, 329*(7), 574–587.
Shaw, E. G., et al. (2006). Phase II study of donepezil in irradiated brain tumor patients: Effect on cognitive function, mood, and quality of life. *Journal of Clinical Oncology, 24*(9), 1415–1420.
Skrap, M., et al. (2016). Brain mapping: A novel intraoperative neuropsychological approach. *Journal of Neurosurgery, 125*(4), 877–887.
Sun, A., et al. (2011). Phase III trial of prophylactic cranial irradiation compared with observation in patients with locally advanced non–small-cell lung cancer: Neurocognitive and quality-of-life analysis. *Journal of Clinical Oncology, 29*(3), 279.
Tan, A. C., et al. (2020). Management of glioblastoma: State of the art and future directions. *CA: A Cancer Journal for Clinicians, 70*(4), 299–312.
Taphoorn, M. J., & Klein, M. (2004). Cognitive deficits in adult patients with brain tumours. *The Lancet Neurology, 3*(3), 159–168.
Tofilon, P. J., & Fike, J. R. (2000). The radioresponse of the central nervous system: A dynamic process. *Radiation Research, 153*(4), 357–370.
Tucha, O., et al. (2000). Cognitive deficits before treatment among patients with brain tumors. *Neurosurgery, 47*(2), 324–334.
Victor, M., & Ropper, A. H. (2002). *Adams and Victor's manual of neurology*.
Wedam, S. B., et al. (2006). Antiangiogenic and antitumor effects of bevacizumab in patients with inflammatory and locally advanced breast cancer. *Journal of Clinical Oncology, 24*(5), 769–777.

Wefel, J. S., et al. (2011). Neurocognitive function in patients with recurrent glioblastoma treated with bevacizumab. *Neuro-Oncology, 13*(6), 660–668.

Wefel, J. S., et al. (2016). Neurocognitive function varies by IDH1 genetic mutation status in patients with malignant glioma prior to surgical resection. *Neuro-Oncology, 18*(12), 1656–1663.

Wefel, J. S., & Schagen, S. B. (2012). Chemotherapy-related cognitive dysfunction. *Current Neurology and Neuroscience Reports, 12*, 267–275.

Chapter 29
Normal Pressure Hydrocephalus

Rachel L. Fazio

Key Point

- Normal Pressure Hydrocephalus (NPH) occurs with increasing prevalence starting at 1.3% in the general population age 65+, and up to 5.9% in those age 80+. Prevalence rates are even higher among those in extended care (>10%). It is a common reversible cause of dementia among the elderly.
- The cause is still unknown, but is believed to relate to history of hydrocephalus as a child and vascular risk factors which cause damage to the interstitial mechanism of cerebrospinal fluid resorption, which eventually leads to compensated hydrocephalus.
- Initial diagnosis is typically from CT of the head with findings of disproportionately enlarged ventricles, but is increasingly done with advanced neuroimaging and neuroradiological indices/measurements.
- Treatment is typically ventriculoperitoneal shunt, although other shunt types are available. There is also medication which can provide some minimal improvement for individuals who are not surgical candidates.
- Shunt appropriateness is often determined by spinal tap tests or external lumbar drainage.
- Clinical symptoms include the classic triad of urinary incontinence, abnormal gait with falls and changes in mental status.
- Neuropsychologically, there are often motor and gait changes and a subcortical-type cognitive pattern due to the stretching of the white matter surrounding the ventricles. This improves with treatment and there is a positive correlation between rapid onset of treatment and clinical outcomes.

R. L. Fazio (✉)
Central Arkansas VA Healthcare System, North Little Rock, AR, USA

M. R. Schoenberg, J. G. Scott (eds.), *The Little Black Book of Neuropsychology*, https://doi.org/10.1007/978-3-032-07777-6_29

Introduction

Normal Pressure Hydrocephalus (NPH) was first identified as a clinical syndrome in 1965 (Hakim & Adams). That case series involved three rather young patients, all with Cerebrospinal Fluid (CSF) pressure readings upon lumbar puncture in the normal range, who only demonstrated clinically significant symptomatic improvement when pressures were reduced to low normal or below normal range. Since that time, it has been referred to largely as "idiopathic normal pressure hydrocephalus" due to the lack of obviously identifiable etiology. Recently, however, NPH has become less idiopathic as neuroimaging and medical technology have more generally advanced (Graff-Radford, 2016), leading simply to the use of the term NPH throughout this chapter rather than iNPH. Interestingly, Hakim and Adams foreshadowed this development when they stated in 1965, "It would seem that the ventricles, once having expanded, may be maintained in this state by CSF pressures which are lower than those which caused the initial enlargement" (p. 322).

The term "NPH" is somewhat loosely defined and still evolving, but essentially refers to a clinical symptom presentation, which looks like non-communicating hydrocephalus, but in the absence of an identifiable cause. The current American-European diagnostic guidelines for NPH indicate that documentation of ventricular enlargement alone is necessary but not sufficient for diagnosis (Relkin et al., 2005). Diagnosis requires both positive neuroimaging findings and clinical confirmation of symptoms; either of these, on their own, does not constitute NPH. Currently diagnosis is split into the categories of Probable, Possible and Unlikely. All take history, imaging, clinical findings and physiological findings into account. Essentially, for a diagnosis of Probable NPH, the individual must be older than 40 years, the symptoms must be insidious and last a minimum of three months, and there can be no other conditions sufficient to explain the symptoms. Brain imaging must show ventricular enlargement with no observable obstruction to CSF flow. Clinical symptoms need to include gait abnormalities (nine separate abnormalities are listed; two must be present and not attributable to other conditions); cognitive abnormalities, including motor slowing, difficulties with attention, impaired recall, executive dysfunction or personality changes; and difficulties with sphincter control, typically, urinary incontinence of various types, which are often present. Physiologically, opening pressure for lumbar puncture should be in the normal range, defined as approximately 70–245 mm H_2O (Relkin et al., 2005). Per these guidelines, gait disorder and either cognitive or urinary abnormalities must be present; it is not necessary to have both. Some more recent studies have defined NPH more loosely, with emphasis placed on the neuroimaging and only one clinical feature necessary for diagnosis.

Epidemiology

The estimated prevalence of NPH has varied widely, primarily due to methodological differences between studies. The age of the population sampled, whether it is prospective or retrospective, and the diagnostic definitions used have all created disparity in these estimates (Martin-Laez et al., 2015). On the lower end, the prevalence amongst those in their 70 s may be only .2%, while those ages 80+ demonstrated the symptoms of hydrocephalic ventricular enlargement with either gait disturbance, dementia-level functioning or urinary incontinence at a rate of 5.9% in the general population (Jaraj et al., 2014). A systematic review of the literature estimated a pooled prevalence of 1.3% in those over age 65 (Martin-Laez et al., 2015). There is a slight trend for NPH to be more common in men than women (Jaraj et al., 2014). There is also a strong suggestion that NPH is vastly under-diagnosed and under-treated; of the 26 individuals identified as having probable NPH in one study, only two had history of placement of a shunt (approximately 8%; Jaraj et al., 2014). This may vary based on the environment and health system, however, with one study estimating 25% of those with NPH having placement of a shunt (see Martin-Laez et al., 2015, for a discussion of treatment rate variability).

Key Point

- Hydrocephalically enlarged ventricles on neuroimaging should flag clinicians to a possible diagnosis of NPH; thoroughly evaluate for mental status changes, gait disturbance and urinary incontinence, particularly in patients age 80+.
- It is not necessary to have all three symptoms of the classic triad for diagnosis.

In the population studies evaluating for probable NPH, evidence of hydrocephalic ventricular enlargement (i.e., enlargement of all four ventricles for no obvious reason, such as severe atrophy or other loss of tissue) correlated most strongly with clinical symptoms of NPH, whereas other radiological measures were much less predictive (Jaraj et al., 2014). Nearly half of those with ventricular enlargement met diagnostic criteria for probable NPH. See the Medical Evaluation section for more information on neuroradiological markers of NPH and their predictive properties for both diagnosis and treatment.

Etiology

For many years, NPH was believed to be of a familial/genetic origin in only a small number of documented cases. While there is still no known genetic marker for NPH, there is increasing evidence that there is a higher than expected familial aggregation (McGirr & Cusimano, 2016). Essentially, those with NPH are three times more likely than the average patient to have a first-degree relative who had diagnosed or shunted NPH, although the absolute risk remains low.

At various points in time, it has been hypothesized that NPH and Alzheimer disease (AD) may have high comorbidity, either due to AD preventing proper CSF resorption due to buildup of amyloid-beta plaques, or alternately, the poor flow of CSF in NPH allowing more amyloid plaques to accumulate. Numerous studies have showed no link between APOE4 and development of NPH, or the response to shunting in those with NPH (Pyykkö et al., 2012; Yang, Tullberg, et al., 2016). As such, it can be said with increasing confidence that NPH is a disorder distinct from a neurodegenerative disease processes.

With the advent of modern neuroimaging techniques, there has been a new dawn of theories regarding the etiological underpinnings of NPH. Perhaps the most convincing is what has been colloquially called the "two hit" hypothesis; namely, that individuals who have hydrocephalus as children continue to have poorly functioning arachnoid granulations as adults, with this difficulty resorbing CSF then exacerbated when vascular risk factors cause the backup resorption mechanisms to also malfunction (Bradley, 2015).

Regarding normal flow of CSF, this is largely produced by the choroid plexus in the ventricles. Typically, the primary resorption system is the arachnoid granulations placed bilaterally around the superior sagittal sinus. Non-communicating hydrocephalus is seen when this primary CSF resorption mechanism is blocked, which in adults is typically due to a tumor blocking the foramen of the fourth ventricle. What is often called "secondary hydrocephalus" can also occur with an arachnoid hemorrhage or another process, which directly affects this resorption mechanism.

A second system was also recently discovered, however, deemed the "glymphatic system," due to the astroglial cells acting in a manner similar to the traditional lymphatic system. Essentially, in this secondary system, CSF flows through the perivascular Virchow-Robin spaces near the arteries which feed the subarachnoid space. The CSF is then transported from the Virchow-Robin spaces to the interstitial space of the brain via the lining of these arteries, which consist of the astrocytic end feet of the glia limitans. The fluid exits the interstitial space through the veins via the same mechanism. It may be that "communicating hydrocephalus," a term often used interchangeably with NPH, occurs when this second system also starts to malfunction (Bradley, 2015).

Patients diagnosed with NPH have numerous features in common besides their disproportionately enlarged ventricles on MRI; they nearly all have higher than average intracranial volumes and significant deep white matter ischemia (Bradley,

2015). This implicates benign hydrocephalus of childhood as the mechanism by which they have an enlarged intracranial volume, and therefore also poorly developed or otherwise malfunctioning subarachnoid granulations. The deep white matter changes then cause the secondary resorption system, the interstitial spaces, to "back up" due to the damage to the myelin; these are the "two hits" of the previously mentioned theory (Bradley, 2015).

The vascular mechanisms contributing to NPH have recently been thoroughly studied, with quite striking results; indeed, it was suggested that NPH may be considered a subtype of vascular dementia (Israelsson et al., 2017). A population-based study found that probable NPH was related strongly to the presence of moderate to severe white matter lesions on CT scan (Jaraj et al., 2016). Hydrocephalic ventricular enlargement with fewer accompanying symptoms of NPH (i.e., possible NPH) was independently related to several indicators of vascular disease, including not only the previously mentioned white matter lesions, but also history of hypertension and diabetes (Jaraj et al., 2016). This increased pulse pressure from the hypertension and stiffening of the arteries as a consequence of diabetes was hypothesized to be a factor in the development of NPH, and increased pulse pressure as a diagnostic marker of NPH is discussed more in the Medical Evaluation section, below.

Israelsson et al. (2017) took a slightly different approach to the question of vascular risk factors contributing to NPH. They examined only individuals who had received shunts for NPH as compared to non-symptomatic controls. Their cohort was approximately 10 years younger than that used in the previously mentioned study; they may also have been healthier given that they were inherently considered surgical candidates. This study linked several vascular risk factors strongly to the occurrence of NPH. Diabetes was again a strongly significant predictive variable, but this time, obesity, hyperlipidemia and psychosocial factors such as depression demonstrated stronger links than did hypertension and cerebrovascular disease (defined as history of stroke or TIA), although these relationships persisted. Moderate alcohol consumption and regular exercise seemed to offer somewhat of a protective effect from the development of NPH. Taken together, the authors concluded the ten vascular risk factors they examined accounted for approximately 25% of cases of NPH and suggested that perhaps NPH should be considered a subtype of vascular dementia in the future. It should be noted these authors performed their research after the shunt surgery had already been performed, and they did not examine the presence of white matter disease on pre-surgical neuroimaging; the vascular risk factors they examined, however, indicate there likely would have been substantial evidence of such if neuroimaging had been examined.

Key Point

- Those with hypertension, diabetes and other vascular risk factors may be at particularly high risk of developing NPH.
- Exercise, moderate alcohol use and good mental health may offer some protective effect.

Medical Evaluation

An important part of the diagnostic process in NPH is differentiation of the symptoms of NPH from other conditions which are highly prevalent in older populations. This includes, for example, ruling out urinary dysfunction due to urinary tract infection or prostate problems, shuffling gait due to Parkinson disease or spinal stenosis and cognitive changes due to neurodegenerative conditions such as Alzheimer disease (Relkin et al., 2005; Williams & Malm, 2016). It is also important to note that some individuals may have enlarged ventricles but be completely asymptomatic, which is therefore typically an incidental finding on neuroimaging performed for other reasons. This can suggest that the individual, however, is at increased risk of developing symptoms of NPH in the near future; this would warrant periodic monitoring (Williams & Malm, 2016).

As outlined briefly in the Introduction, the American-European diagnostic guidelines for NPH are the current prevailing criteria for diagnosis (Relkin et al., 2005). Gait difficulties must be present, which could include any two or more of the following: decreased step height or length, slowed speed of walking, excessive trunk sway during ambulation, wide-based stance, outward-pointed toes while walking, retropulsion (whether spontaneous or provoked), turning *en bloc* and impaired walking balance as evidenced by corrections during tandem gait testing. Cognitively, again two of the following symptoms should be present: psychomotor slowing, decreased fine motor speed or dexterity, difficulty with divided or sustained attention, impaired recall, any executive dysfunction and behavioral or personality changes. Regarding urinary problems, the hallmark sign of NPH was typically considered urinary incontinence, but actually, urinary symptoms can include not only urinary incontinence, but also urinary urgency, urinary frequency and nocturia (two or more times per night). The above symptoms must occur in the context of insidious onset, age over 40 years, a duration of symptoms of at least three months, lack of antecedent events such as head trauma, report of progression of symptoms over time and lack of other medical or neurological diagnoses which could explain the symptoms (Relkin et al., 2005). It is noted that due to the cognitive changes often present in NPH, the history should be obtained from or corroborated by an informant if at all possible. If the above are present, along with ventricular enlargement on neuroimaging without obvious obstruction to CSF flow, and opening pressure on a spinal tap test is within the normal range (5–18 mm Hg or 70–245 mm H_2O), NPH is a highly probable diagnosis.

Although the above diagnostic criteria refer to changes in gait, urinary function and cognition, there is no universally utilized scale to quantify these changes (Shprecher et al., 2008). Scales to do this have been proposed and validated (Hellström et al., 2012; Kubo et al., 2008) and are used in some studies. Other studies, however, continue to utilize qualitative ratings or freestanding measures not specifically designed for NPH, including relatively obtuse measures such as the modified Rankin Scale. This makes it difficult to compare studies on NPH, whether they pertain to diagnostic classification accuracy, treatment outcomes or other matters.

Even though spinal tap tests are considered a mandatory part of the diagnostic workup of NPH and are often considered in regard to treatment prognosis (discussed in much more detail in the Treatment section, below), it is of interest that there is no definitive CSF biomarker to diagnose NPH (Ghosh & Lippa, 2014). Opening pressure on spinal tap remains a definitive diagnostic feature of NPH. If pressure upon opening is substantially above normal, it is likely that the individual does not have NPH, but rather has a form of obstructive or secondary hydrocephalus; in this scenario, neuroimaging and other tests should be re-reviewed to try to identify the previously missed etiology.

Perhaps most importantly for the diagnosis of NPH, ventricles must be demonstrably enlarged, and this should be out of proportion to any evident brain atrophy. The most-often used measure of this is Evans Index, and indeed an Evans Index of >.3 is specifically mentioned in the diagnostic criteria (Relkin et al., 2005). Evans Index is calculated by measuring the diameter of the frontal horns of the lateral ventricles at their widest point divided by the internal diameter of the skull at its widest point through an axial image (Evans, 1942). This results in a ratio score with the normal range originally established as about .2–.26. Values above this suggest borderline enlargement, with > .3 representative of definite ventricular enlargement, and > .33 representing greatly enlarged ventricles (Evans, 1942; Williams & Malm, 2016). See Fig. 29.1 for an example calculation of this index. It should be noted this index is not specific to NPH, but is used to quantify ventricular enlargement due to any cause. There is evidence, however, that values may typically be greater than the

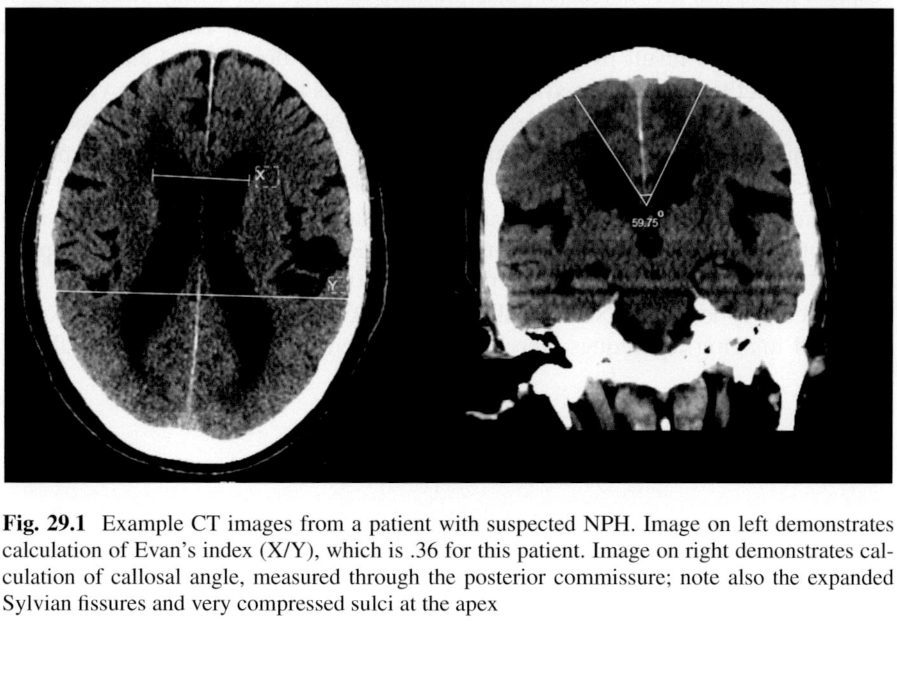

Fig. 29.1 Example CT images from a patient with suspected NPH. Image on left demonstrates calculation of Evan's index (X/Y), which is .36 for this patient. Image on right demonstrates calculation of callosal angle, measured through the posterior commissure; note also the expanded Sylvian fissures and very compressed sulci at the apex

originally established reference ranges in older adults. In healthy adults ages 70+, the average value is .27; this increases with age and tends to be slightly higher in men than women (Jaraj et al., 2017). In that sample, those with other features of NPH had a median Evans Index of .35.

An alternate imaging-based diagnostic schema for NPH has also been proposed. This was called "DESH," which stands for Disproportionately Enlarged Subarachnoid-space Hydrocephalus (Hashimoto et al., 2010). This involves examination of a coronal image through the lateral ventricles. Positive findings include a tight high-convexity (i.e., crowding of the gyri at the apex of the skull) and therefore also tightness in the medial subarachnoid space in that area. Enlarged Sylvian fissures, bilaterally, are also needed for diagnosis, which are rated per a previously established rating scale (Hashimoto et al., 2010).

Recently, a new scale was proposed combining the imaging features common in NPH into a single index, called the iNPH Radscale (Kockum et al., 2018). Although seven of eight features examined were significant in original analyses, adjusting for age and gender (consistent with the previous findings of larger ventricles in men and those who are older) resulted in only the size of the temporal horns being significantly predictive of diagnosis of NPH. There was, however, a correlation between the Radscale score and clinical symptoms of NPH. As such, this is a promising new index, which hopefully will be further validated in future research.

For suspected new-onset hydrocephalus, FLAIR MRI may play an integral role, as it is most sensitive to the interstitial edema which marks the early development of this disorder (Bradley, 2015). As the brain accommodates and the ventricles enlarge, however, this edema will dissipate, leaving the enlarged ventricles which are the hallmark of the disorder. It is suspected that the stretching of the fibers of the corticospinal tracts and the increased pulse pressure on these tracts may cause the gait disturbances also so commonly seen in NPH (Bradley, 2015). The increased pulse pressure may also result in flow voids (or alternately, flow-related enhancement, depending on the sequence used) on MRI. Flow voids have become less visualized as MRI techniques have become increasingly flow-compensated, necessitating phase-contrast techniques to evaluate CSF flow (Bradley, 2015). These phase-contrast studies, from which aqueductal CSF stroke volume (i.e., flow up and flow down during systole and diastole) can be calculated, may be predictive to some extent of response to shunting. At the time of publication of the American-European criteria for NPH diagnosis, aqueductal or fourth ventricle flow void on MRI was included as supportive of NPH (Relkin et al., 2005), although some of these other advanced imaging techniques were not yet well-enough established to be firmly included.

Treatment

Ventriculoperitoneal shunt (VPS) placement is currently the most common treatment for NPH. Ventriculoatrial and lumboperitoneal shunting have also been used. Ventriculoatrial shunting has largely been abandoned due to higher rates of complications (Ghosh & Lippa, 2014), but lumboperitoneal shunting has become an increasingly common treatment in some regions of the world. The first question to ask, however, is: What happens in NPH without treatment?

In individuals who have treatment of NPH delayed, although there is some variability, the overall course involves dramatic decline. When treatment by shunting was delayed by more than six months, one study demonstrated that untreated patients' MMSE scores dropped three points during that time, they went from the majority being able to live independently (55%) to only 39% being able to live independently, and several became "severely disabled" (Andren et al., 2014). These patients were compared to patients who were treated via shunt placement anywhere from six days to three months after diagnosis. Of those who were treated early, 78% demonstrated clinically significant improvement as compared to 48% of those whose treatment was delayed. Those treated early also had higher MMSE scores, both before and after treatment, than those whose treatment was delayed. After treatment, 80% of those treated early were able to live independently, as opposed to only 48% of those with delayed treatment (Andren et al., 2014). It should be noted that even after successful treatment, this is a lower percentage living independently than when they were initially diagnosed, indicating precipitous decline and poor recovery—largely attributable to the interim amount of decline—with treatment delay.

Despite shunt placement being considered the standard treatment for most cases of NPH, not all patients have a favorable outcome. As such, there has been a great volume of research dedicated to predicting outcomes for shunt placement. Historically, this research has typically consisted of looking at the predictive power of a large volume spinal tap or repeated taps, although more recently, increased predictive power has been found when pre-surgical testing is performed using an External Lumbar Drainage (ELD) procedure. This is performed over several days. This may have better predictive accuracy due to the extended nature of the procedure, as some patients do improve immediately afterward, but others fail to improve until several days later (Yang, Hickman, et al., 2016), which was not as easily assessed with the usual tap test. Although these procedures are known to identify individuals who will respond well to shunt placement, they are also known for their poor negative predictive power; i.e., many individuals who do not respond to CSF drainage will still show favorable outcomes with shunt placement (Halperin et al., 2015). This has led to the suggestion that all individuals with definitive clinical symptoms should undergo shunting regardless given that poor results from the test do not necessarily indicate the procedure will not benefit them. Research is starting to hint that the predictive accuracy of the tap test may have to do with disease duration, with the test having much improved classification accuracy for those whose symptoms have only been reported as occurring for the past 12 months or fewer (Yamada et al., 2017). A very detailed discussion regarding the lack of standardization in the tap procedures and outcome measures and how these affect the classification statistics of extant studies is available to the interested reader (Mihalj et al., 2016).

With the advent of MRI, well over a dozen imaging variables have been examined for their predictive utility for shunt responsiveness. Measurement of the callosal angle at the level of the posterior commissure has shown some positive predictive utility, as has the presence of DESH. Alternately, Evans Index did not correlate strongly with outcomes (Virhammar et al., 2014). Although MRI may eventually prove to be as effective and less invasive than some sort of tap test, at least at present, it shows similar limitations in terms of having good positive predictive power but poor negative predictive power, as nearly 60% of those who did not have the MRI findings most indicative of positive outcome still showed significant benefit from placement of a shunt (Virhammar et al., 2014).

Key Point

- Tests to predict shunt responsiveness may not be of much clinical utility given that a substantial portion of individuals with a negative test still benefit from intervention.
- Those with NPH should have treatment as soon as possible after diagnosis to increase the odds of good long-term clinical outcomes.
- This treatment will likely include surgical implantation of a programmable ventriculoperitoneal shunt.

Shunt surgery in NPH can be quite complicated from a technical perspective. In basic terms, a catheter is introduced typically to the right lateral ventricle which runs through a shunt valve; the valve consists of a mechanism that opens when the pressure exceeds a certain set threshold. This triggers drainage of CSF through the catheter and valve into the abdominal cavity (peritoneum) through a distal catheter (Williams & Malm, 2016). Regarding the valves available, there are gravitational valves; low, medium and high-pressure valves (i.e., “fixed valves”); programmable valves (which can be adjusted magnetically); and many these valves are available with or without an anti-siphon mechanism. An anti-siphon mechanism is intended to reduce the odds of over-drainage when the patient is standing, as standing intracranial pressure is naturally higher than is reclining pressure. The choice of mechanism for shunt surgery is still quite variable, with programmable valves seen as the most desirable due to their flexibility (Miyake, 2016), but studies have not consistently demonstrated better clinical outcomes with the more gradual reduction in

CSF that these valves can provide (Farahmand et al., 2016). Where they do have better outcomes, however, is in reducing surgical revisions to change fixed-differential pressure valves when complications arise. Another benefit of programmable valves is that they may also reduce the incidence of subdural hematoma after surgery, with reduced incidence of need for surgical removal of subdural hematoma, specifically (Sundström et al., 2018). Programmable valves are now also available with magnetic resistance up to 3T, making them MRI compatible (Ghosh & Lippa, 2014).

The primary risk of shunt placement is development of subdural hematoma due to the relatively quick change in CSF volume; as alluded to above, these sometimes are of great enough severity that they must be surgically evacuated. They may also lead to placement of a higher-pressure shunt (for cases where programmable shunts are not available), or they can be treated with a programmable valve with adjustment of shunt settings to prevent further complications. Other shunting risks include the standard surgical risk of infection, but also, as with any brain surgery, development of epilepsy and increase in headaches (Larsson et al., 2018). Shunts also frequently become obstructed (~30%), and this typically requires surgical revision (Williams & Malm, 2016).

Regarding shunt outcome, the previously mentioned studies cited for response rates have typically had a relatively short follow-up period of a year or less. Longer-term studies, however, have demonstrated good outcomes of shunting over longer periods of time. This has included 74% demonstrating a satisfactory or better outcome in a study which followed patients for a minimum of six years (Gölz et al., 2014). Other studies of long duration have demonstrated similar results, with a low of 56% improvement at just over five years, to a high of 87% improvement at seven years (as summarized in Gölz et al.). Again, the variability is likely due to methodological differences between sites, with different variables used to select patients, different shunts used and differential measurement of outcomes. Regardless, it is definitive that shunting is beneficial in NPH for elderly patients, as it helps preserve their functioning and independence for at least several years, lowering economic burden of the disease as a whole (Williams et al., 2012) as well as improving individual outcomes. Another important outcome variable has to do with caregiver burden. One year after shunt surgery, caregivers of those with NPH reported reduced stress, and this was correlated with their family member's cognitive improvement after surgery more so than improvement in gait or urinary symptoms (Kazui et al., 2011). As the authors thoughtfully noted, "Even if the patient has gait and urinary disturbances but does not have cognitive impairment, then the patient can likely handle the problems by him/herself and avoid danger, and thus there may be less effect of burden on the caregiver" (p. 368).

Some studies have suggested that Endoscopic Third Ventriculostomy (ETV) may be an effective treatment for NPH (Gangemi et al., 2008); this is despite the fact this procedure is typically used when there is a blockage of the flow of CSF between the third and fourth ventricles preventing drainage, and there is intrinsically no such blockage in NPH. The suggested mechanism behind the improvement seen in this study is that, essentially, fenestration of the floor of the third ventricle allows for increased systolic outflow from the ventricles, decreasing the intraventricular pulse pressure. Although this study demonstrated improvement in a percentage of patients similar to that seen in studies of shunting in NPH, there were significant methodological limitations which reduced its generalizability. These included the patient being unusually young and with good vascular health, as well as the lack of a comparison group of individuals treated with shunts; due to this lack of comparison group, whether as individuals improved or improved to the same or greater extent than those with shunts could not be ascertained (Gangemi et al., 2008). A follow-up study indicated that ETV does offer clinical improvement for some individuals, although results may not be as dramatic or as sustained as those obtained with VPS (Pinto et al., 2013). As such, ETV is not generally a recommended or performed treatment for NPH, although it may be beneficial for selected individuals (particularly those who demonstrate normal pulsation of the floor of the third ventricle during the procedure after fenestration; Pinto et al., 2013) or in scenarios where shunt placement is not possible or available for various reasons.

Another possible alternative to shunt surgery for patients who have a contraindication for such would be the use of low-dose acetazolamide. Acetazolamide is a diuretic which is used for other conditions, including idiopathic intracranial hypertension (pseudotumor cerebri), and has been used off-label for selected cases of NPH as well. Some early, small studies have demonstrated improvement in patients' gait and neuroimaging markers such as periventricular white matter intensities (Alperin et al., 2014). This remains a promising area for future research, as a non-surgical intervention would certainly be preferable for many individuals due to possibility of lower cost, avoidance of an invasive procedure and potentially lower rate of complications/side effects (McAllister et al., 2015).

Psychiatric Features

Although not a key diagnostic feature, it has long been recognized that psychiatric disturbances can be a part of the clinical picture of NPH. The literature has included largely case studies of individuals with NPH who also experience depression, anxiety, bipolar disorder, disinhibited behavior, aggression and various features of psychotic disorders (Relkin et al., 2005). More recently, there have been some larger-scale studies of psychiatric manifestations of NPH. Despite very discrepant methodology and locations halfway around the world from each other, several studies have consistently found the neuropsychiatric symptoms of NPH to be in the range of 71–73% (Kito et al., 2009; Oliveira et al., 2014). Notwithstanding the methodological differences, results suggest that symptoms of depression, specifically manifested as apathy, are the most common symptom in those with NPH.

Subsequently, another study specifically investigated the prevalence of depression in those who had received shunt treatment of NPH (Israelsson et al., 2016). This group demonstrated that even after shunting, symptoms of depression are approximately four times more prevalent than in matched controls, and severe depression is seven times more common. Although structured research in this area is still in its infancy, there is enough evidence at this point to confidently conclude that psychiatric symptoms are more common in those with NPH than the wider elderly population, although they are not quite as common as in those with neurodegenerative dementing disorders, specifically Alzheimer disease (Kito et al., 2009). That those with NPH have higher rates of symptoms of vegetative-type depression implicates the role of vascular risk factors as a potential contributor, as well as the structural changes present in NPH affecting connections to the frontal lobes (Israelsson et al., 2016). It is also important to note that due to depression possibly being one of the more prominent and identifiable features of NPH, those with the disorder may present to a variety of settings for initial diagnosis. In other words, if they have urinary incontinence as their most noticeable or bothersome symptom they may first present to a urologist; gait problems, a neurologist; but depressive symptoms, a psychiatrist or primary care provider. Indeed, those who presented to a psychiatric clinic initially who were eventually diagnosed with NPH had a higher rate of psychiatric symptoms than those presenting through other routes, such as a referral to a neurosurgical clinic or dementia center (Kito et al., 2009).

Importantly, although symptoms of depression and apathy may improve after shunting, they are rarely eliminated entirely and still persist as a high rate after (Israelsson et al., 2016; Kanemoto et al., 2016). This speaks to the need for repeated evaluation for and treatment of depression throughout the diagnostic and treatment process in those with NPH, as depression can either mask or contribute to the symptoms of NPH in terms of cognitive inefficiency and bradyphrenia, in particular.

Neuropsychological Findings

Neuropsychological testing is believed to hold "limited value" in NPH, except as to distinguish NPH from cortical neurodegenerative disorders (Ghosh & Lippa, 2014). It has been described, however, as having a pattern of frontal-subcortical dysfunction involving cognitive and motor slowing, problems with divided attention and other aspects of executive functioning and memory recall with preserved recognition. Physicians primarily seem to hold value in neuropsychological testing as a baseline, against which post-shunt testing can be compared; much more emphasis in the medical literature is placed on the gait changes in NPH.

One thing important to keep in mind is that the presence of NPH does not rule out the possibility of co-occurring pathologies. In the literature, one can easily find cases of NPH comorbid with Lewy Body dementia, Huntington's disease and Alzheimer disease (AD), among others. As such, neuropsychological testing may also be useful in regard to managing expectations of treatment outcomes for NPH, if it co-occurs in the context of a clear and advanced AD. In such a case, the individual's surgical candidacy may also be an issue as they would likely have a higher complication rate and need to be able to cooperate with shunt adjustment (in the case of a programmable shunt) at follow-up appointments. Indeed, one study demonstrated support for the hypothesis that co-existing AD may be a factor in prediction of cognitive improvement after shunt surgery. In those who demonstrated cognitive improvement after shunting, their immediate recall scores were higher on several tests than those who failed to improve; this argues for the possible comorbidity of AD in the non-responders (Thomas et al., 2005).

Key Point

- Evaluate for symptoms of depression throughout the diagnostic and treatment process in NPH.
- Symptoms of NPH can masquerade as depression and vice versa.
- Failure to identify and treat depression in those with NPH can contribute to poorer treatment outcomes.

Early research regarding cognitive patterns in NPH offered support that those with NPH tend to have problems with attention/concentration and processing speed in the context of relatively intact orientation and memory (Ogino et al., 2006). Interestingly, the baseline characteristics of samples in other studies have been highly variable, and few studies have ruled out those with comorbid neurodegenerative pathology, making results difficult to generalize. For example, in one study, recognition memory started in the impaired range, suggesting the presence of comorbid AD in some of the sample (Chaudhry et al., 2007). Alternately, in this same sample, 54% produced a normal score on Trail Making Test B; although education level was not stated, this also implies the possibility this sample was particularly educated and had high premorbid levels of executive functioning. This contrasted with another large sample, where nearly all of the sample produced a score on TMTB which would be considered poorer than the cutoff generally used to discontinue the test (Solana et al., 2012). Despite these major differences in the studies, both groups demonstrated substantial improvement in immediate and delayed recall on a list learning test post-shunt, although other results were much more variable. Adding to this confusion, however, some studies have also demonstrated global cognitive impairment or more pronounced visuospatial disturbances. Although not reported in every study, one study demonstrating this pattern (Bugalho et al., 2014) also had numerous patients with very long delay between symptom onset and evaluation. This would be supportive of studies discussed earlier in this chapter emphasizing the need for swift treatment of NPH to improve functional outcomes. This hypothesis was later supported. In 2016, Picascia and colleagues examined this variable as part of a larger study on cognition in NPH. In addition to finding individuals with the various patterns of cognitive impairment discussed above, they determined that those who had a longer disease duration were the most likely to demonstrate global cognitive impairment; this was also associated with older age. Interestingly, those with greater cognitive impairment also had poorer gait, suggesting that these symptoms progress in tandem (Picascia et al., 2016).

Studies have shown that approximately 50% of those who undergo shunting for NPH demonstrate cognitive improvement, whether this is evaluated with gross measures such as MMSE score or more elaborate neuropsychological testing (Thomas et al., 2005). This improvement tends to be in the domains of immediate and delayed recall as well as fine motor speed and dexterity; it is less often documented in the domain of executive functions, arguing that perhaps the damage NPH causes to the frontostriatal pathways is not reversible, particularly with delayed treatment (Thomas et al., 2005). Relatively speaking, however, much less is known about cognitive response to shunting in NPH than about cognition in NPH more generally. A summary of both is presented in an easily referenced table format in Picascia et al. (2015). In this format, the discrepancies in the outcome studies are easily identified in terms of what the outcome period was, what tests were used and how "improvement" in cognition was defined.

In summary, cognition in NPH is likely to be affected, although this varies based on the person's age, likely cognitive reserve, duration of the disease process and severity of the damage which has occurred, which is complicated by other factors, such as cerebrovascular risk factors and possible comorbid neuropathological conditions. These factors also impact the response to shunting. Cognitive dysfunction and subsequent improvement post-shunting have been hard to evaluate consistently due to demographic differences in population studied, varying disease characteristics, which measures were used and the timing of the various evaluations (including the possibility of test-retest effects). Overall, however, it is expected that early in the process of NPH, an individual may have no cognitive impairment or have fronto-subcortical dysfunction; as the disease progresses, more global cognitive decline would be expected. It may be more important, however, in cases of suspected NPH, to rule out well-established cognitive patterns for neurodegenerative conditions since the presentation of NPH can be so variable.

Future Directions

One promising arena for the progression of research in NPH appears to be in advanced neuroimaging techniques, including Diffusion Tensor Imaging (DTI) and fMRI. Early evidence indicates DTI is sensitive to white matter microstructural changes seen in NPH, and may be useful to differentiate it from a variety of neurodegenerative conditions (Keong et al., 2016). Indeed, DTI has illustrated the hypothesized damage to the corticospinal tract microstructure which may be responsible for the changes of gait seen in NPH. Additionally, DTI has a great enough sensitivity to show decrease in mean diffusivity after external lumbar drainage (Keong et al., 2016). It remains undetermined at this point, however, if DTI can be used as a prognosticator of shunt or other treatment responsiveness.

As may have been surmised from the discussion in the earlier sections regarding lack of standardization of diagnostic criteria, CSF drainage procedures, initial assessment and outcome measures, surgical shunting techniques, etc., standardization across all these areas is an aim not only for NPH, but hydrocephalus research generally (McAllister et al., 2015). Identification of biomarkers—CSF or otherwise—to improve the diagnostic accuracy for NPH, and to potentially provide opportunities to translate these biomarker findings into therapeutic interventions, is another area of burgeoning importance. At the present time, however, efforts may need to be focused on shunt improvement and development of "smart shunts" that can communicate problems given that shunt treatment is the most effective therapy available, but shunt failure occurs on average at about the rate of 40% in the first two years after implantation (McAllister et al., 2015). Neuropsychological evaluation, in regard to refinement and standardization of neuropsychological batteries to detect treatment change in NPH, to correlate cognitive findings with imaging and to predict outcomes, is another area of promise identified in the recent NIH symposium on NPH. A computerized testing battery for NPH was also recently developed and psychometric properties investigated (Behrens et al., 2014), which may expedite this process if further research indicates its usefulness.

Summary

Given the increasing aging population, the prevalence of NPH is likely to increase as well. It is important for neuropsychologists to carefully consider NPH among their list of differential diagnosis with patients from late middle age onward, but particularly in the most elderly. NPH is a condition which can be catastrophic, but also can be easily treated with sometimes miraculous recovery, particularly if caught early. Unfortunately, due to this being a relatively "new" condition in the grand scheme of medicine, some health providers may not be adept at its identification and treatment, leading to a more involved role for the neuropsychologist in regard to psychoeducation and patient advocacy. The Hydrocephalus Association (www.hydroassoc.org) has reference material which providers may find useful to provide to patients explaining the condition, treatments, natural course and other issues.

References

Alperin, N., Oliu, C. J., Bagci, A. M., Lee, S. H., Kovanlikaya, I., Adams, D., et al. (2014). Low-dose acetazolamide reverses periventricular white matter hyperintensities in iNPH. *Neurology, 82*(15), 1347–1351.

Andren, K., Wikkelso, C., Tisell, M., & Hellstrom, P. (2014). Natural course of idiopathic normal pressure hydrocephalus. *Journal of Neurology, Neurosurgery, & Psychiatry, 85*, 806–810.

Behrens, A., Eklund, A., Elgh, E., Smith, C., Williams, M. A., & Malm, J. (2014). A computerized neuropsychological test battery designed for idiopathic normal pressure hydrocephalus. *Fluids and Barriers of the CNS, 11*(1), 22.

Bradley, W. G. (2015). CSF flow in the brain in the context of normal pressure hydrocephalus. *American Journal of Neuroradiology, 36*, 831–838.

Bugalho, P., Alves, L., Miguel, R., & Ribeiro, O. (2014). Profile of cognitive dysfunction and relation with gait disturbance in Normal Pressure Hydrocephalus. *Clinical Neurology and Neurosurgery, 118*, 83–88.

Chaudhry, P., Kharkar, S., Heidler-Gary, J., Hillis, A. E., Newhart, M., Kleinman, J. T., et al. (2007). Characteristics and reversibility of dementia in normal pressure hydrocephalus. *Behavioural Neurology, 18*(3), 149–158.

Evans, W. A. (1942). An encephalographic ratio for estimating ventricular enlargement and cerebral atrophy. *Archives of Neurology and Psychiatry, 47*(6), 931–937.

Farahmand, D., Sæhle, T., Eide, P. K., Tisell, M., Hellström, P., & Wikkelsö, C. (2016). A double-blind randomized trial on the clinical effect of different shunt valve settings in idiopathic normal pressure hydrocephalus. *Journal of Neurosurgery, 124*(2), 359–367.

Gangemi, I., Maiuri, F., Naddeo, M., Godano, U., Mascari, C., Broggi, G., & Ferroli, P. (2008). Endoscopic third ventriculostomy in idiopathic normal pressure hydrocephalus: An Italian multicenter study. *Neurosurgery, 63*(1), 62–69.

Ghosh, S., & Lippa, C. (2014). Diagnosis and prognosis in idiopathic normal pressure hydrocephalus. *American Journal of Alzheimer's Disease & Other Dementias, 29*(7), 583–589.

Gölz, L., Ruppert, F. H., Meier, U., & Lemcke, J. (2014). Outcome of modern shunt therapy in patients with idiopathic normal pressure hydrocephalus 6 years postoperatively. *Journal of Neurosurgery, 121*(4), 771–775.

Graff-Radford, N. R. (2016). Is normal pressure hydrocephalus becoming less idiopathic? *Neurology, 86*, 588–589.

Hakim, S., & Adams, R. D. (1965). The special clinical problem of symptomatic hydrocephalus with normal cerebrospinal fluid pressure: Observations on cerebrospinal fluid hydrodynamics. *Journal of the Neurological Sciences, 2*, 307–327.

Halperin, J. J., Kurlan, R., Schwalb, J. M., Cusimano, M. D., Gronseth, G., & Gloss, D. (2015). Practice guideline: Idiopathic normal pressure hydrocephalus: Response to shunting and predictors of response. *Neurology, 85*(23), 2063–2071.

Hashimoto, M., Ishikawa, M., Mori, E., & Kuwana, N. (2010). Diagnosis of idiopathic normal pressure hydrocephalus is supported by MRI-based scheme: A prospective cohort study. *Cerebrospinal Fluid Research, 7*(1), 1–10.

Hellström, P., Klinge, P., Tans, J., & Wikkelsø, C. (2012). A new scale for assessment of severity and outcome in iNPH. *Acta Neurologica Scandinavica, 126*(4), 229–237.

Israelsson, H., Allard, P., Eklund, A., & Malm, J. (2016). Symptoms of depression are common in patients with idiopathic normal pressure hydrocephalus: The INPH-CRasH study. *Neurosurgery, 78*(2), 161–168.

Israelsson, H., Carlberg, B., Wikkelsö, C., Laurell, K., Kahlon, B., Leijon, G., et al. (2017). Vascular risk factors in INPH: A prospective case-control study (the INPH-CRasH study). *Neurology, 88*(6), 577–585.

Jaraj, D., Agerskov, S., Rabiei, K., Marlow, T., Jensen, C., Guo, X., et al. (2016). Vascular factors in suspected normal pressure hydrocephalus: A population-based study. *Neurology, 86*(7), 592–599.

Jaraj, D., Rabiei, K., Marlow, T., Jensen, C., Skoog, I., & Wikkelso, C. (2014). Prevalence of idiopathic normal-pressure hydrocephalus. *Neurology, 82*(16), 1449–1454.

Jaraj, D., Rabiei, K., Marlow, T., Jensen, C., Skoog, I., & Wikkelso, C. (2017). Estimated ventricle size using Evans index: Reference values from a population-based sample. *European Journal of Neurology, 24*, 468–474.

Kanemoto, H., Kazui, H., Suzuki, Y., Sato, S., Kishima, H., Yoshimine, T., & Yoshiyama, K. (2016). Effect of lumbo-peritoneal shunt surgery on neuropsychiatric symptoms in patients with idiopathic normal pressure hydrocephalus. *Journal of the Neurological Sciences, 361*, 206–212.

Kazui, H., Mori, E., Hashimoto, M., Ishikawa, M., Hirono, N., & Takeda, M. (2011). Effect of shunt operation on idiopathic normal pressure hydrocephalus patients in reducing caregiver burden: Evidence from SINPHONI. *Dementia and Geriatric Cognitive Disorders, 31*(5), 363–370.

Keong, N. C., Pena, A., Price, S. J., Czosnyka, M., Czosnyka, Z., & Pickard, J. D. (2016). Imaging normal pressure hydrocephalus: Theories, techniques, and challenges. *Neurosurgical Focus, 41*(3), E11.

Kito, Y., Kazui, H., Kubo, Y., Yoshida, T., Takaya, M., Wada, T., et al. (2009). Neuropsychiatric symptoms in patients with idiopathic normal pressure hydrocephalus. *Behavioural Neurology, 21*(3–4), 165–174.

Kockum, K., Lilja-Lund, O., Larsson, E. M., Rosell, M., Söderström, L., Virhammar, J., & Laurell, K. (2018). The iNPH Radscale; a radiological scale for structured evaluation of idiopathic normal pressure hydrocephalus. *European Journal of Neurology, 25*, 569–576.

Kubo, Y., Kazui, H., Yoshida, T., Kito, Y., Kimura, N., Tokunaga, H., et al. (2008). Validation of grading scale for evaluating symptoms of idiopathic normal-pressure hydrocephalus. *Dementia and Geriatric Cognitive Disorders, 25*(1), 37–45.

Larsson, J., Israelsson, H., Eklund, A., & Malm, J. (2018; Online ahead of print). Epilepsy, headache, and abdominal pain after shunt surgery for idiopathic normal pressure hydrocephalus: The INPH-CRasH study. *Journal of Neurosurgery*, *128*(6):1674–1683.

Martin-Laez, R., Cballero-Arzapalo, H., Lopez-Menendez, L. A., Arango-Lasprilla, J. C., & Vazquez-Barquero, A. (2015). Epidemiology of idiopathic normal pressure hydrocephalus: A systematic review of the literature. *World Neurosurgery, 84*(6), 2002–2009.

McAllister, J. P., Williams, M. A., Walker, M. L., Kestle, J. R., Relkin, N. R., Anderson, A. M., et al. (2015). An update on research priorities in hydrocephalus: Overview of the third National Institutes of Health-sponsored symposium "Opportunities for hydro-cephalus research: Pathways to better outcomes". *Journal of Neurosurgery, 123*(6), 1427–1438.

McGirr, A., & Cusimano, M. D. (2016). Editorial: Does idiopathic normal pressure hydrocephalus run in families? *Journal of the Neurological Sciences, 368*, 128–129.

Mihalj, M., Dolić, K., Kolić, K., & Ledenko, V. (2016). CSF tap test—Obsolete or appropriate test for predicting shunt responsiveness? A systemic review. *Journal of the Neurological Sciences, 362*, 78–84.

Miyake, H. (2016). Shunt devices for the treatment of adult hydrocephalus: Recent progress and characteristics. *Neurologia Medico-Chirurgica, 56*(5), 274–283.

Ogino, A., Kazui, H., Miyoshi, N., Hashimoto, M., Ohkawa, S., Tokunaga, H., et al. (2006). Cognitive impairment in patients with idiopathic normal pressure hydrocephalus. *Dementia and Geriatric Cognitive Disorders, 21*(2), 113–119.

Oliveira, M. F., Oliveira, J. R., Rotta, J. M., & Pinto, F. C. (2014). Psychiatric symptoms are present in most of the patients with idiopathic normal pressure hydrocephalus. *Arquivos de Neuro-Psiquiatria, 72*(6), 435–438.

Picascia, M., Minafra, B., Zangaglia, R., Gracardi, L., Pozzi, N. G., Sinforiani, E., & Pacchetti, C. (2016). Spectrum of cognitive disorders in idiopathic normal pressure hydrocephalus. *Functional Neurology, 31*(3), 143–147.

Picascia, M., Zangaglia, R., Bernini, S., Minafra, B., Sinforiani, E., & Pacchetti, C. (2015). A review of cognitive impairment and differential diagnosis in idiopathic normal pressure hydrocephalus. *Functional Neurology, 30*(4), 217.

Pinto, F. C. G., Saad, F., Oliveira, M. F. D., Pereira, R. M., Miranda, F. L. D., Tornai, J. B., et al. (2013). Role of endoscopic third ventriculostomy and ventriculoperitoneal shunt in idiopathic normal pressure hydrocephalus: Preliminary results of a randomized clinical trial. *Neurosurgery, 72*(5), 845–854.

Pyykkö, O. T., Helisalmi, S., Koivisto, A. M., Mölsä, J. A., Rummukainen, J., Nerg, O., et al. (2012). APOE4 predicts amyloid-β in cortical brain biopsy but not idiopathic normal pressure hydrocephalus. *Journal of Neurology, Neurosurgery, and Psychiatry, 83*(11), 1119–1124.

Relkin, N., Marmarou, A., Klinge, P., Bergsneider, M., & Black, P. M. (2005). Diagnosing idiopathic normal-pressure hydrocephalus: INPH guidelines, Part II. *Neurosurgery*, *57*(3), S2, 4–16.

Shprecher, D., Schwalb, J., & Kurlan, R. (2008). Normal pressure hydrocephalus: Diagnosis and treatment. *Current Neurology and Neuroscience Reports, 8*(5), 371–376.

Solana, E., Sahuquillo, J., Junqué, C., Quintana, M., & Poca, M. A. (2012). Cognitive disturbances and neuropsychological changes after surgical treatment in a cohort of 185 patients with idiopathic normal pressure hydrocephalus. *Archives of Clinical Neuropsychology, 27*(3), 304–317.

Sundström, N., Lagebrant, M., Eklund, A., Koskinen, L. O. D., & Malm, J. (2018; Online ahead of print). Subdural hematomas in 1846 patients with shunted idiopathic normal pressure hydrocephalus: Treatment and long-term survival. *Journal of Neurosurgery, 129*(3), 797–804.

Thomas, G., McGirt, M. J., Woodworth, G., Heidler, J., Rigamonti, D., Hillis, A. E., & Williams, M. A. (2005). Baseline neuropsychological profile and cognitive response to cerebrospinal fluid shunting for idiopathic normal pressure hydrocephalus. *Dementia and Geriatric Cognitive Disorders, 20*(2–3), 163–168.

Virhammar, J., Laurell, K., Cesarini, K. G., & Larsson, E. M. (2014). Preoperative prognostic value of MRI findings in 108 patients with idiopathic normal pressure hydrocephalus. *American Journal of Neuroradiology, 35*(12), 2311–2318.

Williams, M. A., & Malm, J. (2016). Diagnosis and treatment of idiopathic normal pressure hydrocephalus. *Continuum, 22*(2), 579–599.

Williams, M. A., Sharkey, P., Van Doren, D., Thomas, G., & Rigamonti, D. (2012). Influence of shunt surgery on healthcare expenditures of elderly fee-for-service Medicare beneficiaries with hydrocephalus. *Journal of Neurosurgery, 107*(1), 21–28.

Yamada, S., Ishikawa, M., Miyajima, M., Atsuchi, M., Kimura, T., Kazui, H., & Mori, E. (2017). Disease duration: The key to accurate CSF tap test in iNPH. *Acta Neurologica Scandinavica, 135*(2), 189–196.

Yang, F., Hickman, T. T., Tinl, M., Iracheta, C., Chen, G., Flynn, P., et al. (2016). Quantitative evaluation of changes in gait after extended cerebrospinal fluid drainage for normal pressure hydrocephalus. *Journal of Clinical Neuroscience, 28*, 31–37.

Yang, Y., Tullberg, M., Mehlig, K., Rosengren, A., Torén, K., Zetterberg, H., & Wikkelsö, C. (2016). The APOE genotype in idiopathic normal pressure hydrocephalus. *PLoS One, 11*(7), e0158985.

Chapter 30
Psychometric Foundations for the Interpretation of Neuropsychological Test Results

Brian L. Brooks, Elisabeth M. S. Sherman, Grant L. Iverson, Daniel J. Slick, and Esther Strauss

Key Points and Chapter Summary

- Interpreting and communicating test performance depends on having an appropriate (comparative) sample and a common "language" of descriptors.
- Sample characteristics, such as non-normal distributions, skew or truncated samples, will impact interpretation of test performance.
- Comparison of performance across tests is affected by normative sample differences, measurement error, score magnitude and rank in the distribution, extreme scores, ceiling and floor effects and extrapolation/interpolation of derived scores.
- It is normal for healthy children, adolescents, adults and older adults to have some variability across tests, to have some low scores and to have change over time on a battery of neuropsychological tests. This normal variability when

B. L. Brooks (✉) · D. J. Slick
Alberta Children's Hospital, University of Calgary, Calgary, AB, Canada
e-mail: Brian.brooks@albertahealthservices.ca

E. M. S. Sherman
Alberta Children's Hospital, University of Calgary, Calgary, AB, Canada

G. L. Iverson
Department of Physical Medicine and Rehabilitation, Harvard Medical School, Boston, MA, USA

Department of Physical Medicine and Rehabilitation, Spaulding Rehabilitation Hospital, Boston, MA, USA

Schoen Adams Research Institute at Spaulding Rehabilitation, Boston, MA, USA

Mass General for Children Sports Concussion Program, Boston, MA, USA

Home Base, A Red Sox Foundation and Massachusetts General Hospital Program, Boston, MA, USA

E. Strauss
Department of Psychology, University of Victoria, Victoria, BC, Canada

M. R. Schoenberg, J. G. Scott (eds.), *The Little Black Book of Neuropsychology*,
https://doi.org/10.1007/978-3-032-07777-6_30

administering and interpreting multiple scores must be considered in the interpretation of isolated low test scores or a single score that changes over time.
- Interpreting test scores over time requires sophisticated psychometric models to minimize clinical bias and error and supplement clinical judgment.

Overview

The purpose of this chapter is to illustrate how an understanding of the psychometric properties of tests, normative samples and test scores is an essential foundation for meaningful and accurate clinical interpretations and reduces the likelihood of misinterpreting test results. Our goal is to present this information in an easy-to-understand format that facilitates clinicians' knowledge of basic psychometrics in the context of test score interpretation. Clinical examples using commonly used tests will be provided throughout to illustrate the relevance and utility of these concepts in clinical practice.

With regard to sample distributions, we will review concepts relating to non-normality and the influence of score distribution characteristics on derived scores. Floor and ceiling effects, equivalence of normative data sets and truncated distributions will be discussed with regard to test items and test norms. When comparing scores between tests, we will review the role of test measurement error. We will also discuss normal variability and briefly comment on the prevalence of low test scores in healthy people, and how to use this information for supplementing clinical judgment. Finally, we will provide an overview of various methods for interpreting change in test performance over time.

Interpreting and Communicating Test Performance in Clinical Practice

A person's raw score on a neuropsychological test does not obtain meaning until there is (a) a comparison to a normative sample and (b) a method for interpreting and communicating the meaning of that comparison. For example, if Ms. Jane Doe, a 75-year-old female, obtains a raw score of 19 on a test of delayed memory, this fact does not hold much meaning by itself. However, if a sample of 200 women between the ages of 70 and 80 years obtain a mean score of 20 on the same test, with a standard deviation (SD) of 5.0 points,[1] then two things become readily apparent. First, Ms. Doe's performance is within one SD of the mean for her age group. Second, it is unlikely that Ms. Doe has a clinically significant problem with memory as measured by this test. In short, the performance of a normative sample allows clinicians to determine the relative standing of an individual's performance. Overall, the notion of relative standing is a key concept in neuropsychology and serves as the

[1] This example assumes that the scores are normally distributed. This example also assumes that higher raw scores reflect better performance.

basis for all test score interpretations. Almost all scores used by neuropsychologists provide information on relative standing, whether these consist of z scores (mean = 0, SD = 1), scaled scores (mean = 10, SD = 3), T scores (mean = 50, SD = 10), Index scores (mean = 100, SD = 15) or percentiles.

Having a methodology for comparing performance on a test to a representative sample is an important step in understanding a person's ability on a test of a cognitive ability. However, the result of a person's performance on the test needs to be communicated to other neuropsychologists, to other professionals, to the patient and to others involved in the patient's care. Without a system for interpreting and communicating the results, again, the patient's performance on the test remains meaningless.

A psychometric approach, based on the theoretical normal distribution, has been used for the interpretation of intelligence test results for decades. The modern version of this psychometric approach is based on the Wechsler classification system and is illustrated in Table 30.1. This classification scheme is based on fairly precise estimates of where a person falls in the distribution of scores obtained by healthy persons with no cognitive, psychiatric or neurological problems. Another classification and interpretation system, based on a system popularized by Heaton and colleagues (Heaton et al., 1991, 1993, 2004) and used for the Neuropsychological Assessment Battery (NAB; Stern & White, 2003a), is also presented in Table 30.1. Considering the above example with Ms. Doe's performance on the memory test (i.e., her performance is equal to a z score of −0.2, a T score of 48, and is at the 42nd percentile), the clinician is able to interpret and communicate that this performance is "average" compared to 70–80 year olds according to both the Wechsler and Heaton-NAB classification systems (Note: we do not advocate one classification system over the other, but we do suggest that clinicians use the same system throughout a report. Reporting scores using different classification systems, within the same report, can be conceptually confusing for readers).

Key Points: Interpreting and communicating test performance depends on having an appropriate comparative sample and a common "language" of descriptors (i.e., classification system). Regardless of the classification system that is used, it is recommended clinicians be consistent throughout a report.

Sample Characteristics and Test Score Interpretation

The Adequacy of the Normative Sample

Neuropsychological tests typically provide numerous test scores that are derived from a comparison of a person's performance to the performance of a representative normative sample, including z scores, T scores, scaled scores, index scores, IQ scores and percentiles (for a discussion on the derivation of each of these score types, see Sattler, 2001; Strauss et al., 2006; Urbina, 2004). All of these scores are

Table 30.1 Commonly used classification ranges, along with their corresponding standard scores and percentile ranks

Wechsler classification ranges[a]	Scaled score range $M = 10$, SD = 3	IQ/Index score range $M = 100$, SD = 15	T score range $M = 50$, SD = 10	Percentile ranks
Very Superior	16+	130 +	70 +	98 +
Superior	14–15	120–129	64–69	91–97
High Average	13	110–119	57–63	75–90
Average	8–12[b]	90–109	44–56	25–74
Low Average	7	80–89	37–43	9–24
Unusually Low (Borderline)[c]	5–6[d]	70–79	30–36	2–8
Extremely Low	≤4[e]	<70	<30	< 2
Heaton-NAB Classification Ranges[f]		Index Score Range $M = 100$, SD = 15	T Score Range $M = 50$, SD = 10	Percentile Ranks
Very superior		130–155	70–81	98+
Superior		115–129	60–69	84–97
Above average		107–114	55–59	68–82
Average		92–106	45–54	30–67
Below average		85–91	40–44	16–27
Mildly impaired		77–84	35–39	6–15
Mildly-to-moderately impaired		70–76	30–34	2–5
Moderately impaired		62–69	25–29	0.6–1.9
Moderately-to-severely impaired		55–61	20–24	0.13–0.5
Severely impaired		45–54	19	< .12

Table notes: *M* mean, *SD* standard deviation. [a]Note that this is similar to the Wechsler system of classification; [b]A scaled score of 12 is at the 75th percentile, but is described as being "average" in this classification system; [c]The Wechsler system refers to scores between the second and eighth percentiles as "borderline"; [d]A scaled score = 6 at the ninth percentile, but is classified as being "unusually low" (borderline); [e]A scaled score is at the second percentile, but is considered "extremely low"; [f]Note that this is similar to the Heaton system of classification. Classifications for interpreting scores according to the Wechsler system were derived from Tables 2.2 and 2.3 in the WAIS-III technical manual (Wechsler, 1997). Classifications for interpreting Index and T scores according to the NAB-Heaton method were derived from Tables 6.8 and 6.9, respectively, from the NAB Administration, Scoring, and Interpretation Manual (Stern & White, 2003b)

derived from *samples*. Importantly, these scores are not population values, and any limitations of generalizability due to normative sample composition or testing circumstances must be taken into consideration when standardized scores are interpreted. Some tests, for example, may have normative samples that are (a) limited in heterogeneity, (b) samples of convenience, (c) small in size and (d) outdated. The first consideration when using norms should be: does the test have an adequate normative sample and what are the limitations of this sample?

The Boston Naming Test (BNT) is a good example of a test in widespread use that, historically, has had problems with inadequate normative data. For example, the original normative data for adults were based on 178 adults (Kaplan et al., 1978).

Although this is a respectable number overall, the age range covered by the norms is large. Thus, the actual cell sizes when broken down by age are as low as 11 individuals in some age groups. Moreover, it turned out to be inappropriate to apply the original normative information to adults 60 years and older (i.e., the highest age group was 50–59 years, $n = 22$). Van Gorp et al. (1986) extended normative data for older adults up to 95 years of age, although the sample was small in size ($n = 78$) and was high functioning (i.e., mean Verbal IQ scores were in the high average to superior ranges). The Tombaugh and Hubley (1997) norms consisted of only 219 people between 25 and 88 years of age (cell sizes for age ranged from $n = 18$–33; cell sizes for age x education ranged from $n = 26$–78), although once again the sample was relatively well educated. Further improvements on the BNT normative data have been published, and include the Mayo's Older Americans Normative Studies (i.e., $n = 663$, ages 57–97; Ivnik et al., 1996) and the Mayo's Older African Americans Normative Studies (i.e., $n = 309$ ages 56–94; Lucas et al., 2005) and the Expanded Halstead-Reitan Neuropsychological Battery norms (i.e., $n = 1000$; Heaton et al., 2004).

Although there have been some improvements in the adequacy of the BNT normative data, having numerous (and different) comparative groups creates a problem for the clinician. Do meaningful interpretive differences exist, depending on which normative data is used? Figure **30.1** illustrates the differences in obtained percentiles that occur based on the use of different comparative normative samples. Consider the interpretation of a raw score of 51 for a 72-year-old African American woman with 10 years of education using the MOANS and MOAANS normative samples. According to the MOANS norms, this would be at the 37th percentile (scaled score = 9). However, according to the MOAANS norms, this would be at the 75th percentile (scaled score = 12). This difference in normative scores can create substantial interpretive differences, particularly as the performance declines below clinically meaningful cutoff scores. These differences can be at least partially accounted for by the nearly all Caucasian (i.e., 99.1%) and relatively well-educated (i.e., 83.6% had at least high school, 50.3% had at least some post-secondary education and 26.0% had at least a bachelor's degree) MOANS sample for the BNT normative data. Importantly, as seen for the BNT scores of 43 and 40, normative systems that are not adjusted for ethnicity will yield scores that are "impaired," whereas ethnicity-adjusted systems will yield scores that are average.

The quality and representativeness of normative data can have a dramatic effect on the clinical interpretation of test scores. For example, it is well understood that education is related to test performance. Moreover, ethnicity is related to test performance (perhaps as a surrogate for factors such as quality of education). However, many neuropsychological tests do not have education- or ethnicity-adjusted normative data—or, if it is available, it is not commonly used. The effects of education and ethnicity, on WTAR-demographics predicted Full Scale IQ, are illustrated in Fig. 30.2. As seen in this figure, estimated Full Scale IQ is positively associated with years of education and varies by ethnicity. The direction of difference between ethnic groups is consistent across all levels of education and is quite large, exceeding one standard deviation for some comparisons.

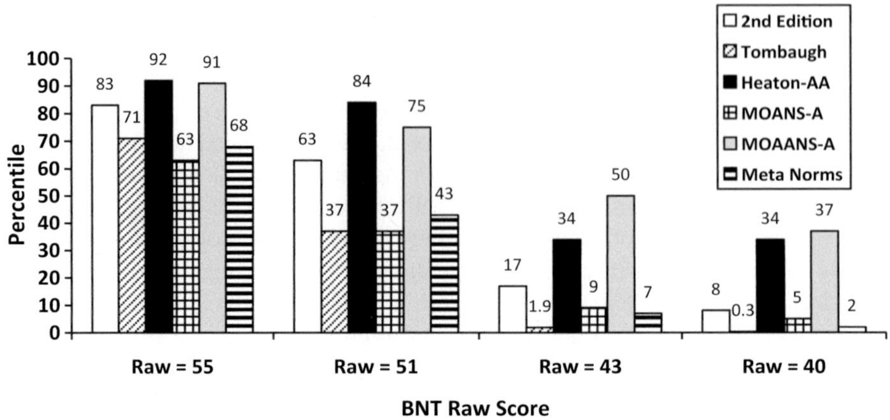

Fig. 30.1 Comparison of normative systems for the Boston Naming Test: 72-year-old African American woman with 10 years of education (percentile ranks). Figure Notes: Percentile ranks are presented. If a percentile rank included a range (e.g., 10–25%ile), then the highest value in the range is presented in the figure. Second edition = BNT-Second Edition, which includes normative data obtained from Kaplan et al. (2001). Tombaugh = Tombaugh and Hubley (1997) sample, which was relatively well-educated and had small sample sizes. To calculate the percentiles presented for the Tombaugh and Hubley (1997) norms, z scores were calculated using the age-adjusted mean (M = 52.5) and standard deviation (SD = 4.6) from Table 1 in the manuscript (despite the raw scores *not* being normally distributed). Heaton-AA = African American normative data from the Expanded Norms for the Halstead-Reitan Neuropsychological Battery (Heaton et al., 2004). MOANS-A = Age-adjusted normative data from the Mayo's Older Americans Normative Studies (Ivnik et al., 1996). MOAANS-A = Age-adjusted normative data from the Mayo's Older African Americans Normative Studies (Lucas et al., 2005). Normative data for MOANS-A and MOAANS-A were derived from page 906–907 of Strauss et al. (2006). Meta Norms = Meta-normative data from Mitrushina et al. (2005) on page 725

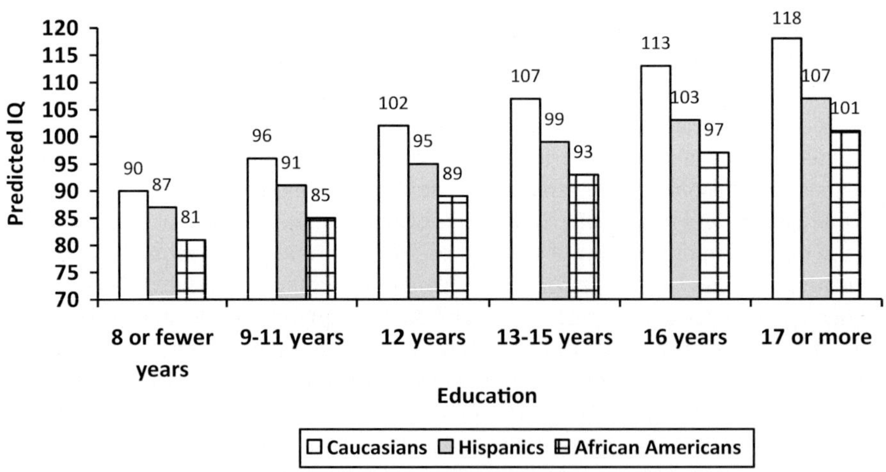

Fig. 30.2 Effects of education and ethnicity on demographics-predicted Full Scale IQ in men. Figure Note: Demographics-predicted WAIS-III FSIQ scores were derived from page 114 of the Wechsler Test of Adult Reading manual (The Psychological Corporation, 2001)

What are the clinical and interpretive implications of Fig. 30.2? First, Full Scale IQ scores are related to education and ethnicity. Second, as discussed in more detail later in this chapter, Full Scale IQ is positively correlated with other cognitive test scores. Therefore, those individuals with below average IQ are expected to have far more low neuropsychological test scores than those with above average IQ. Finally, many normative sets used in clinical practice are adjusted for age only. Therefore, variables such as education, IQ and ethnicity are left uncontrolled and must be subject to clinical judgment, as opposed to being considered psychometrically.

The Shape of the Distribution: Non-Normality and Skew

The normal curve is the basis of most commonly used (parametric) statistical and psychometric models in neuropsychology. When a new test is constructed, non-normality can be "corrected" by examining the distribution of scores on the prototype test, adjusting its properties and re-sampling until a normal distribution is reached. More commonly, normality is achieved by various "smoothing" procedures. This facilitates clinical interpretation, for reasons that we will discuss below.

A true normal distribution is perfectly symmetrical about the mean and has a skewness close to zero (see Fig. 30.3A). Positive skew indicates a frequency distribution where more scores fall below the mean compared to above the mean (Fig. 30.3B). Negative skew refers to distributions where more scores fall above the mean compared to below the mean (Fig. 30.3C). Many distributions of test scores deviate somewhat from the normal distribution that we have come to expect. What happens when scores for a test are not normally distributed?

Key Points: Distribution Descriptors

- Direction of the tail that tells the tale

- Tail 'pointing' to the right (positive) is a positively skewed distribution
- Tail 'pointing' to the left (negative) is a negatively skewed distribution
- Sample characteristics, such as non-normal distributions, skew or truncated samples, can impact interpretation of test performance

First, when distributions are skewed, the mean and median are not identical (i.e., the mean will not be at the midpoint in rank) and z scores will not accurately translate into sample percentile rank values. The error in mapping of z scores to sample percentile rank increases as skew increases. Self-report questionnaires typically have positively skewed distributions in healthy people because they are assessing problem behaviors that are typically found at a higher frequency or severity in clinical populations. Second, tests with a normal distribution of scores in samples from the general population may show significant skew or other divergence from

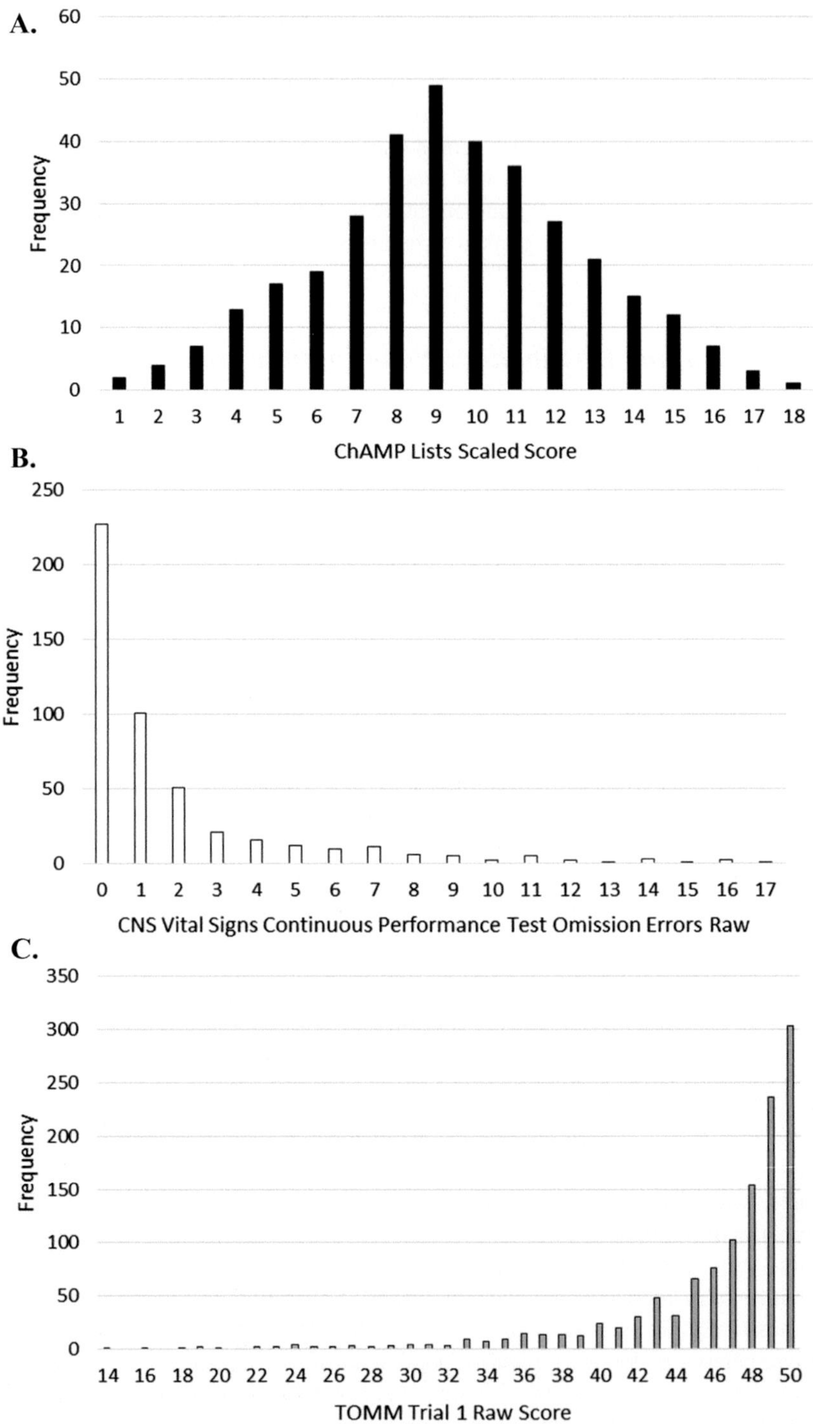
A.
Frequency
0
10
20
30
40
50
60
1 2 3 4 5 6 7 8 9 10 11 12 13 14 15 16 17 18
ChAMP Lists Scaled Score
B.
Frequency
0
50
100
150
200
250
0 1 2 3 4 5 6 7 8 9 10 11 12 13 14 15 16 17
CNS Vital Signs Continuous Performance Test Omission Errors Raw
C.
Frequency
0
50
100
150
200
250
300
350
14 16 18 20 22 24 26 28 30 32 34 36 38 40 42 44 46 48 50
TOMM Trial 1 Raw Score

(continued)

normality when given to a population that differs considerably from the average individual. For example, the performances of elderly Hispanic persons on an English Vocabulary test might result in scores clustering at the low end of the distribution. These scores are unlikely to reflect actual impairment or decline. Thus, the distribution of scores on a test's normative sample should be evaluated for congruence with the individual being assessed to determine whether there are factors that might skew score distributions (e.g., in this example, English fluency and possible cultural differences).

In some circumstances, a normal distribution of scores simply does not exist and an ability being measured may not be normally distributed in the population. An example of this might be a test of orientation, where almost all healthy individuals score almost perfectly (i.e., a negatively skewed distribution). Alternatively, one may want only to identify and/or discriminate between patients who have known cognitive impairment (i.e., identify differences between groups at one end of the normal distribution only). Thus, the measure might be designed specifically to sample a range of abilities in patients with impairments. If one is not interested in the rest of the distribution, items that would provide discrimination in that region can be omitted to save administration time.

In general, the degree to which a sample distribution approximates the underlying population distribution increases as sample size increases, and becomes less accurate as sample size decreases. This has important implications for norms comprised of small samples. Thus, a larger sample will, on average, produce a more normal distribution, but only if the underlying population distribution from which the sample is obtained is normal (i.e., a large N does not "correct" for non-normality of an underlying population distribution). Small samples may yield a non-normal distribution due to random sampling effects, even though the population from which the sample is drawn has a normal distribution. As a result, clinicians should be cautious when interpreting tests with normative samples less than 50 per age group.

The Range of the Distribution: Truncated Distributions

Significant skew often indicates the presence of a truncated distribution. This may occur when the range of scores is restricted on one side of the distribution but not the other. Truncated distributions are also present for certain neuropsychological tests, such as those involving tests that healthy people accomplish almost perfectly (e.g., orientation, recognition memory, validity testing). Some tests do not include a

Fig. 30.3 Examples of (A) normal, (B) positively skewed and (C) negatively skewed distributions. (a) Note. Distribution of ChAMP Lists Scaled Scores in a sample of $N = 342$ children with neurological diagnoses. Skewness = −0.41 (SE = .13). (b) Note. Distribution of CNS Vital Signs Continuous Performance Test Omission Errors raw scores in a sample of $N = 477$ children with neurological diagnoses. Skewness = 4.01 (SE = 0.11). (c) Note. Distribution of TOMM Trial 1 raw scores in a sample of N = 1209 children with neurological diagnoses. Skewness = −1.61 (SE = 0.17)

high enough ceiling to allow for discrimination between higher functioning individuals and to detect cognitive deficits in some cases. This can translate into a truncated distribution for such a population. A good example of this is the Failure to Maintain Set (FMS) score on the Wisconsin Card Sorting Test (WCST; Heaton et al., 1993). In the normative sample of 30–39-year-old persons, observed raw scores ranged from 0 to 21, but the majority of persons (84%) obtained scores of 0 or 1 and less than 1% obtained scores greater than 3 (see Tables D20–D25 in the WCST manual). What happens when an individual obtains a low score on a test with a truncated distribution? The clinician might calculate an extreme z or T score with a percentile rank that would not actually exist in the normative sample because the assumption of normality has not been met. Care is therefore required so as not to over-interpret abnormally low score differences based on truncated distributions.

Truncated distributions also occur when specific subgroups are purposefully (or unintentionally) excluded from inclusion in the normative sample. Purposeful exclusion of subgroups occurs when exclusion criteria are used in creating normative samples. This might include omitting persons with cognitive impairments, learning difficulties or medical conditions to create normative samples composed exclusively of healthy subjects. One of the problems with this approach is that the general population includes a certain proportion of persons falling in the low end of the distribution. Excluding these individuals therefore creates norms that are missing the left tail of the distribution or have a left tail that is not heavy enough (as opposed to full-range normative sampling). When these distributions are used for standardized testing, because low-functioning individuals have been excluded from the norms, the resulting low end of the distribution (or lowest percentiles) is now occupied by persons who would have populated higher percentiles in the full distribution. This can potentially lead to (a) identification of normal individuals as low functioning, (b) difficulties estimating the severity of impaired performance and (c) potentially, an increase in the number of persons identified as impaired with subsequent test re-norming (e.g., if the test itself is used to consecutively exclude the lowest percentile members each time new norms are created; McFadden, 1996).

The PPVT-4 (Dunn & Dunn, 2007) is an example of a test with a full-range normative sample, whereas the WCST excluded children with a variety of conditions potentially affecting cognition (Strauss et al., 2006). The WISC-V is an example of a test that screened the sample for conditions, but then re-inserted a specific proportion of special needs children into the sample (8–10%) so that it would reflect the full range of abilities in the general population (Wechsler, 2014). Knowing the inclusion and exclusion criteria that were used in creating normative samples allows better comparison between scores obtained from different measures.

Comparing Scores Between Tests

Standardizing test scores facilitates comparison of scores across measures. This is most useful, of course, when (a) the raw score distributions for tests that are being compared are approximately normal in the population, and (b) the scores being compared are derived from similar samples, or more ideally, from the same sample (i.e., co-norming).

Measurement Error

When comparing test scores, it is important to consider the reliability of the two measures and their intercorrelation before determining if a reliable or clinically meaningful difference exists (see Crawford & Garthwaite, 2002). In some cases, relatively large discrepancies between scores may not actually reflect reliable differences. Moreover, a statistically significant or reliable difference between test scores might occur frequently in a given population, and thus not necessarily be clinically meaningful (e.g., Crawford et al., 2007). For example, large differences between attention (normal range) and IQ (superior range) may occur in some gifted individuals, but this would not necessarily constitute evidence of cognitive dysfunction. Rather, it could be a normal pattern of scores for some gifted individuals.

Score Magnitude and Rank in the Score Distribution

The level of the two scores being compared should also be considered. That is, an absolute difference between two standard scores may be common or uncommon, depending on the level of the scores (e.g., T score of 30 versus 40 as compared to 60 versus 70). One should also keep in mind that when test scores are not normally distributed, standardized scores may not accurately reflect actual population rank. In these circumstances, differences between standard scores may be misleading.

The relationship between normative scores (e.g., z scores or T scores) and percentiles is not linear. That is, a constant difference between z scores will be associated with a variable difference in percentile scores, as a function of the distance of the two scores from the mean. This is because there are proportionally more scores closer to the mean than farther from the mean (i.e., otherwise, the distribution would be rectangular, or non-normal).

The nonlinear relation between z scores and percentiles has important interpretive implications. For example, a one-point difference between two z scores may be interpreted differently, depending on where the two scores fall on the normal curve. The difference between a z score of 0 and a z score of +1 is 34 percentile points, because 34% of scores fall between these two z scores (i.e., the scores being compared are at the 50th and 84th percentile). However, the difference between a z score of +2 and a z score of +3 is less than 3 percentile points, because only 2.2% of the distribution falls between these two points (i.e., the scores being compared are at the 97.7th and 99.9th percentile).

The interpretation of percentile scores with an equivalent "difference" between two percentile rankings might have very different clinical implications if the scores occur at the tail end of the curve versus near the middle of the distribution. For example, an improvement in a standard score from the fifth percentile to the 30th percentile (25 percentile points), compared to an improvement from the 37th to the 62nd percentile (25 percentile points), (a) requires a greater improvement in performance from a *standard score* perspective (i.e., going from the fifth to the 30th percentile is an Index score improvement from 76 to 92, which is more than one standard deviation; going from the 37th to the 62nd percentile is an Index score improvement from 95 to 105, which is two-thirds of a standard deviation) and (b) might be much more clinically and functionally meaningful (i.e., going from the fifth percentile to the 30th percentile is going from an unusually low score to an average score; scores at the 37th and the 62nd percentile are both in the average range).

Ceiling/Floor Effects and Score Comparisons

Floor and ceiling effects may be defined as the presence of truncated tails in the context of limitations in range of item difficulty. For example, a test may be said to have a *high floor* when a large proportion of the examinees obtain raw scores at or near the lowest possible score. This may indicate that the test lacks a sufficient number and range of easier items. Conversely, a test may be said to have a *low ceiling* when the opposite pattern is present. Floor and ceiling effects may significantly limit the usefulness of a measure. A measure with a high floor may not be suitable for use with low functioning examinees, particularly if one wishes to delineate level of impairment. Misinterpreting results obtained from tests with low ceilings is common too. For example, a perfect score of 60/60 on the Boston Naming Test should be considered as reflecting average, not excellent, naming ability.

If a clinician is not well informed of the distribution of test scores, floor and ceiling effects can potentially lead to misinterpretations when comparing across tests. For instance, on the Wechsler Memory Scale—Third Edition (WMS-III; Wechsler, 1997), the distribution varies by (a) subtest, and (b) age. A clinician who is not aware of these normative distribution characteristics might inadvertently conclude that a very high functioning examinee who scores in the superior range on the delayed portion of Logical Memory (LMII) performs less well, or has a "relative weakness", on the delayed portion of Verbal Paired Associates (VPAII; note that the maximum possible normative score for VPAII in 20–24 year olds is 12, which is at the 75th percentile).

Extrapolation/Interpolation of Derived Scores

There are times when norms fall short in terms of range or cell size. This includes missing data in some cells, inconsistent age coverage or inadequate demographic composition of some cells compared to the population. In these cases, data are often extrapolated or interpolated using the existing score distribution and techniques such as multiple regression. For example, Heaton and colleagues have published sets of norms that use multiple regression to correct for demographic characteristics and compensate for few subjects in some cells (Heaton et al., 1991, 2004). Although multiple regression is robust to slight violations of assumptions, estimation errors can occur when using normative data if they violate the assumptions of homoscedasticity (uniform variance across the range of scores) and the distribution of residuals that are necessary for multiple regression are non-normal (Fastenau & Adams, 1996).

Extrapolation methods, such as those that employ regression techniques, depend on the shape of the distribution of scores. Thus, including only a subset of the distribution of age scores in the regression (e.g., by omitting very young or very old individuals) may change the projected developmental slope of certain tests dramatically. Tests that appear to have linear relationships, when considered only in adulthood, may actually have highly nonlinear relationships when the entire age range is considered. One example is vocabulary, which tends to increase exponentially during the preschool years, shows a slower rate of progress during early adulthood, remains relatively stable with continued gradual increase and then shows a minor decrease with advancing age. If only a subset of the age range (e.g., adults) is used to estimate performance at the tail ends of the distribution (e.g., preschoolers and elderly), the estimation will not fit the shape of the actual distribution.

Key Points: Comparison of performance across tests is affected by measurement error, score magnitude and rank in the distribution, extreme scores, ceiling and floor effects and extrapolation/interpolation of derived scores.

Normal Variability Across Test Batteries and the Prevalence of Low Scores

It is important for clinicians to carefully consider how they interpret an isolated low score or a small number of low scores obtained on a battery of neuropsychological measures. This is because healthy people have variable performance on a battery of tests and the likelihood of obtaining low scores increases (a) as the number of tests increases, (b) as the cutoff for defining a low score becomes more liberal (i.e., the 16th percentile compared to the fifth percentile) and (c) with lower levels of baseline cognitive functioning (i.e., as determined by fewer years of education and/or lower intelligence). The prevalence of low scores on a neuropsychological battery is knowable when considering all test scores *simultaneously* in a co-normed sample, which has been referred to as "multivariate base rates of low scores". The fact that healthy children, adolescents, adults and older adults obtain some low scores is not a feature of any particular battery but is a psychometric reality that is found across all cognitive batteries for all ages (see Iverson and Brooks, this volume, for detailed information on prevalence of low scores). In fact, interpretation of more than one test score in any context, not just low scores, will result in a higher-than-expected rate of identification. For example, when interpreting reliable change scores on test batteries, it is common for healthy children (Brooks et al., 2017) and adults (Brooks et al., 2016) to have several scores reliably change over time.

Although it is important for clinicians to understand that low scores are common, it can be challenging to use this information in everyday clinical practice. The goal is to have interpretive tables that allow clinicians to simply and rapidly look up the prevalence of low scores on a battery of tests using various cutoff scores and to move toward publishers including this information as part of a test battery's technical manual (Sherman & Brooks, 2015).

Key Points: It is normal for healthy people to have variability and some low scores across a battery of neuropsychological tests. The number of low scores found in healthy people increases with the number of tests being administered and interpreted, fewer years of education, lower levels of intelligence at baseline, and in ethnic minorities. These principles must be considered when interpreting performance.

Assessing Change Over Time

Serial assessment in neuropsychology is used to monitor cognition over time and to make inferences regarding improvement or decline in functioning. The fundamental question, of course, is to what degree do changes in test scores reflect "real" changes in function as opposed to measurement error? To what degree do real changes in test scores reflect clinically significant changes in function as opposed to clinically trivial changes? To what degree do changes in test scores conform to expectations, given the application of treatments or the occurrence of other events or processes occurring between test and retest, such as brain injury, dementia or brain surgery?

A number of statistical/psychometric methods have been developed for assessing changes observed over repeated administrations of neuropsychological tests and these differ considerably with respect to mathematical models and assumptions regarding the nature of test data. As with most areas of psychometrics, the problems and processes involved in decomposing observed scores (i.e., change scores) into measurement error and "true" scores are often complex. Moreover, it is important to remember that a statistically meaningful change does not necessarily translate into a clinically meaningful change, and as noted above, it may take having change on multiple scores for it to be considered a clinically meaningful change (Brooks et al., 2016, 2017). A brief overview of the issues and methods is presented below.

Reference Group Change Score Distributions

If a clinical or normative sample is administered a test twice, the distribution of observed change scores can be quantified. When such information is available, individual examinee change scores can be transformed into standardized change scores, thus providing information on the degree of unusualness of any observed change in score. Unfortunately, it is rarely possible for clinicians to use this method of evaluating change due to major limitations in most data available in test manuals. Retest samples tend to be relatively small for many tests, thus limiting generalizability. This is particularly important when change scores may vary with demographic variables (e.g., age and level of education) and/or initial test score level (e.g., normal vs. abnormal), because retest samples typically are restricted with respect to both. Second, retest samples are often obtained within a short period of time after initial testing, typically less than two months, whereas in clinical practice typical test–retest intervals are often much longer. Therefore, any effects of extended test–retest intervals on change score distributions are not reflected in most change-score data presented in test manuals. Lastly, change score information is typically presented in the form of summary statistics (e.g., mean and SD) that have limited utility if change scores are not normally distributed (in which case percentile tables would be much preferable). As a result of these limitations, clinicians often must turn to other methods for analyzing change scores.

Reliable Change

Jacobson and Truax (1991; see also Jacobson et al., 1999) proposed a psychometric method for determining if changes in test scores over time are reliable (i.e., not an artifact of imperfect test reliability). This method involves calculation of a *Reliable Change Index* (RCI). The RCI is an indicator of the probability that an observed difference between two scores from the same examinee on the same test can be attributed to measurement error (i.e., to imperfect reliability). When there is a low probability that the observed change is due to measurement error, one may infer that it reflects other factors, such as progression of illness, treatment effects, motivational defects and/or prior exposure to the test.

The RCI is calculated using the *Standard Error of the Difference* (SE_{diff}), an index of measurement error derived from classical test theory. It is the standard deviation of expected test–retest difference scores about a mean of zero given an assumption that no actual change has occurred. The original formula by Jacobson and Truax (1991) used the internal consistency reliability coefficient at a single point in time for calculating the SE_{diff}, whereas more recent versions have used the test–retest reliability coefficients from time 1 and time 2. Moreover, the original formula used the standard deviation from a single point in time, whereas authors using modified formulas have used the standard deviation from both test and retest. The formulas for the SE_{diff} are:

Using internal consistency reliability (Jacobson & Truax, 1991):
$SEM = SD\sqrt{1-\alpha}$ → Standard deviation multiplied by the square root of 1 minus the internal consistency reliability coefficient (Cronbach's α).
$SE_{diff} = \sqrt{2 \bullet (SEM)^2}$ → Square root of the product of two times the squared SEM.
Using test–retest reliability:
$SEM_1 = SD1\sqrt{1-r_{12}}$ → Standard deviation from time 1, multiplied by the square root of 1 minus the test–retest reliability coefficient.
$SEM_2 = SD2\sqrt{1-r_{12}}$ → Standard deviation from time 2, multiplied by the square root of 1 minus the test–retest coefficient.
$SE_{diff} = \sqrt{(SEM_1)^2 + (SEM_2)^2}$ → Square root of the sum of the square of SEM_1 and the square of SEM_2.

The reliable change methodology has the potential to allow the clinician to reduce the adverse impact of measurement error on test interpretation. To represent clinically significant improvement, the change score must be statistically reliable. Thus, the reliable change methodology is used to *supplement* clinical judgment. For neurocognitive assessments, reliable change is used to determine if there has been improvement or deterioration in functioning that exceeds the probable range of measurement error. For example, when the SE_{diff} is multiplied by 1.64, the clinician knows that scores *outside of that range* would be found in fewer than 5% of subjects in each tail of the distribution (i.e., 90% confidence interval). Table 30.2 presents examples of reliable change values, based on the test–retest information, for use with the NAB. A change in performance on the NAB Attention Index of 14 points would be considered reliable at a 90% confidence interval.

There are, however, some drawbacks to the reliable change methodology. First, the reliable change formula implicitly assumes that no practice effects have occurred. When practice effects are present (and they frequently are present), "reliable" improvements may partially or wholly reflect effects of prior test exposure rather than a change in underlying functional level. Second, the reliable change information is typically derived from retest performance in healthy participants but is often applied to retest performance in patients. Third, the time between test and retest, which is used to derive the reliable change information, is often substantially shorter (e.g., 1–2 months for most tests) than the actual retest duration in clinical practice (e.g., one year retest is often used for traumatic brain injury reassessment; see the chapter by Sherman, Brooks, Iverson, Slick, & Strauss in this book for further discussion on retest data).

Table 30.2 Examples of reliable change values for the NAB Indexes in 18–59 year olds

NAB Indexes	SD_1	SD_2	r_{12}	SEM_1	SEM_2	SE_{diff}	RCI Index 80% Confidence Interval	RCI Index 90% Confidence Interval
Attention	16.6	16.0	0.88	5.75	5.54	7.99	10.2	13.1
Language	14.0	14.3	0.55	9.39	9.59	13.42	17.2	22.0
Memory	14.9	15.2	0.74	7.60	7.75	10.85	13.9	17.8
Spatial	16.7	16.3	0.66	9.74	9.50	13.61	17.4	22.3
Executive Functions	16.2	18.2	0.68	9.16	10.30	13.78	17.6	22.6
Total Index	15.1	17.0	0.80	6.75	7.60	10.17	13.0	16.7

Table Notes: The formula used for calculating the SE_{diff} was: $SE_{diff} = \sqrt{SEM_1^2 + SEM_2^2}$, where $SEM_1 = SD1\sqrt{1-r_{12}}$ and $SEM_2 = SD2\sqrt{1-r_{12}}$. Standard deviations (SD) and test–retest correlations were obtained from Table 5.15 in the NAB Psychometric and Technical Manual (White & Stern, 2003)

Reliable change estimates are not presented in the vast majority of test manuals, although some publishers are increasingly providing this information to the user through their technical manuals and scoring programs (Sherman & Brooks, 2015). Thus, they must be calculated by clinicians or researchers and are sometimes published as part of chapters or books on this topic. We have calculated reliable change estimates for the WAIS-IV, WMS-IV, and selected D-KEFS subtests and presented them in Tables 30.3, 30.4, 30.5. We have also computed the average practice effects. By examining these tables, clinicians can gain a better understanding of the probable range of measurement error, in healthy adults, over relatively brief retest intervals. For example, on the WMS-IV, Index scores on the adult battery need to change by 11.2–12.7 points to be considered reliably higher or lower at the 80% confidence interval. These confidence intervals can be adjusted, if desired, by adding or subtracting the average practice effects.

Reliable Change Adjusted for Practice Effects

Chelune (2003) suggested a modification to the calculation of the RCI in which the mean change score for a reference group [i.e., mean change score = (mean score at time 2) – (mean score at time 1)] is subtracted from the observed change score of an individual examinee and the result used as an Adjusted Change Score for purposes of calculating reliable change adjusted for practice effects. Table 30.7 presents data that involves change scores for the NAB using this methodology. For example, if we subtract the practice effect of 6.5 index points from 10.2 (i.e., this is the 80% confidence interval for a reliable decline; that is, $1.28 \times SE_{diff}$), then a decline greater than 3.7 index points (i.e., 10.2–6.5) would be considered reliable at the 80% confidence interval. Likewise, if we add the practice effect of 6.5 points to 10.2 (80%

Table 30.3 Reliable change on the WAIS-IV

WAIS-IV IQ, Indexes and Subtests	Age: 16–29 years				Age: 30–54 years				Age: 55–69 years				Age: 70–90 years			
	SE_{diff}	80% CI	90% CI	Average Practice Effect	SE_{diff}	80% CI	90% CI	Average Practice Effect	SE_{diff}	80% CI	90% CI	Average Practice Effect	SE_{diff}	80% CI	90% CI	Average Practice Effect
FSIQ	5.0	6.4	8.2	4.4	4.3	5.5	7.1	4.4	4.2	5.4	6.9	4.9	4.6	5.9	7.6	3.5
VCI	4.8	6.1	7.9	2.2	4.3	5.6	7.1	2.7	5.1	6.5	8.3	3.3	4.6	5.9	7.6	2.1
PRI	8.0	10.2	13.1	4.6	7.7	9.8	12.6	4.5	7.2	9.2	11.8	3.6	7.9	10.2	13.0	3.2
WMI	8.8	11.2	14.4	2.7	8.6	11.0	14.1	1.9	6.2	8.0	10.2	4.3	6.6	8.5	10.9	3.2
PSI	7.9	10.1	12.9	4.8	9.8	12.6	16.1	5.3	6.6	8.5	10.8	5.0	7.8	9.9	12.7	2.7
Block Design	1.8	2.3	3.0	1.2	1.9	2.4	3.1	1.0	2.0	2.6	3.3	0.6	1.7	2.1	2.7	0.4
Similarities	1.9	2.4	3.1	0.4	1.4	1.8	2.3	0.6	1.5	2.0	2.5	0.7	1.6	2.0	2.6	0.5
Digit Span	2.2	2.8	3.6	0.6	1.9	2.5	3.2	0.5	1.4	1.8	2.3	0.8	1.6	2.1	2.7	0.7
Matrix Reasoning	2.4	3.1	3.9	0.2	1.9	2.4	3.1	0.1	2.4	3.0	3.9	0.8	2.1	2.6	3.4	0.3
Vocabulary	1.3	1.7	2.2	0.2	1.4	1.7	2.2	0.1	1.5	1.9	2.5	0.2	1.2	1.5	1.9	0.0
Arithmetic	1.6	2.1	2.7	0.5	2.0	2.5	3.2	0.3	1.8	2.3	2.9	0.8	1.8	2.3	2.9	0.4
Symbol Search	1.9	2.4	3.1	1.2	2.3	2.9	3.8	1.1	1.9	2.5	3.2	1.1	1.7	2.2	2.8	0.2
Visual Puzzles	2.0	2.6	3.3	1.1	2.4	3.0	3.9	1.1	2.2	2.8	3.6	0.4	2.6	3.3	4.2	1.0
Information	1.3	1.7	2.2	0.7	1.5	1.9	2.5	0.8	1.3	1.7	2.1	0.9	1.2	1.5	2.0	0.6
Coding	1.6	2.1	2.7	0.5	1.6	2.1	2.7	0.9	1.5	2.0	2.5	0.6	1.6	2.1	2.6	0.6
Letter-Number Sequencing	2.1	2.6	3.4	0.7	1.8	2.2	2.9	0.5	2.2	2.8	3.6	0.1	–	–	–	–
Figure Weights	2.2	2.8	3.6	1.0	2.0	2.6	3.3	1.0	2.1	2.7	3.5	0.6	–	–	–	–
Comprehension	1.6	2.1	2.7	0.0	1.3	1.7	2.2	0.2	1.6	2.1	2.7	0.0	1.6	2.1	2.7	0.4
Cancellation	2.0	2.5	3.2	1.1	2.3	2.9	3.7	0.5	1.9	2.4	3.1	0.2	–	–	–	–
Picture Completion	2.1	2.7	3.5	2.4	2.5	3.2	4.1	2.3	2.1	2.7	3.5	1.8	2.0	2.6	3.3	1.2

Table Notes: $N = 228$. Mean test interval was 22 days (range = 8–82 days). SE_{diff} = Standard error of difference. The formula used for calculating the SE_{diff} was:

$SE_{diff} = \sqrt{SEM_1^2 + SEM_2^2}$, where $SEM_1 = SD1\sqrt{1-r_{12}}$ and $SEM_2 = SD2\sqrt{1-r_{12}}$. The correlations used were the uncorrected "average stability coefficients". *CI* confidence interval. The standard deviations and correlations used to calculate these reliable change estimates are presented on pages 49–52 in the WAIS-IV technical and interpretive manual (Wechsler et al., 2008). Average practice effects are calculated by subtracting the age-adjusted mean score at time 2—mean score at time 1

Table 30.4 Reliable change on the WMS-IV

	Age: 16–69 years (Adult Battery)				Age: 65–90 years (Older Adult Battery)			
WMS-IV Indexes and Subtests	SE_{diff}	80% CI	90% CI	Average Practice Effect	SE_{diff}	80% CI	90% CI	Average Practice Effect
Auditory Memory Index	8.8	11.2	14.4	11.5	8.2	10.5	13.5	10.6
Visual Memory Index	9.9	12.7	16.3	12.1	10.3	13.1	16.8	11.0
Visual Working Memory Index	9.0	11.5	14.8	4.3	–	–	–	–
Immediate Memory Index	9.4	12.0	15.4	12.4	7.9	10.2	13.0	12.4
Delayed Memory Index	9.4	12.0	15.4	13.7	8.7	11.1	14.3	11.0
Logical Memory I	2.1	2.6	3.4	1.9	2.1	2.7	3.5	2.0
Logical Memory II	2.3	3.0	3.8	2.3	2.1	2.7	3.4	2.1
Verbal Paired Associates I	2.3	2.9	3.7	2.3	2.0	2.5	3.2	1.7
Verbal Paired Associates II	2.0	2.5	3.2	1.0	1.8	2.3	3.0	1.1
Designs I	2.3	3.0	3.8	1.1	–	–	–	–
Designs II	2.2	2.8	3.6	1.7	–	–	–	–
Visual Reproduction I	2.4	3.1	4.0	1.9	2.0	2.6	3.3	1.8
Visual Reproduction II	2.6	3.4	4.3	2.8	2.5	3.2	4.1	1.8
Spatial Addition	2.1	2.7	3.4	0.8	–	–	–	–
Symbol Span	2.3	2.9	3.7	0.6	2.3	2.9	3.7	0.6

Table Notes: Adult battery, n = 144–173. Older adult battery, n = 69–71. Mean test interval was 23 days (range = 14–84 days). SE_{diff} = Standard error of difference. The formula used for calculating the SE_{diff} was: $SE_{diff} = \sqrt{SEM_1^2 + SEM_2^2}$, where $SEM_1 = SD1\sqrt{1-r_{12}}$ and $SEM_2 = SD2\sqrt{1-r_{12}}$. The correlations used were the uncorrected "average stability coefficients". *CI* confidence interval. The standard deviations and correlations used to calculate these reliable change estimates are presented on page 51 in the WMS-IV technical and interpretive manual (Wechsler et al., 2009). Average practice effects are calculated by subtracting the age-adjusted mean score at time 2—mean score at time 1

confidence interval for a reliable improvement), then an increase greater than 16.7 index points (10.2 + 6.5) would be considered reliable (80% confidence interval). When considering the previous example of a 14-point change on the NAB Attention Index, a decline of this amount would be reliable at the 90% confidence interval if it is adjusted for practice effects. However, if the 14-point change was an

Table 30.5 Reliable change on selected D-KEFS subtests

Selected D-KEFS Subtests	Ages: 8–19 years				Ages: 20–49 years				Ages: 50–89 years			
	SE_{diff}	80% CI	90% CI	Average Practice Effect	SE_{diff}	80% CI	90% CI	Average Practice Effect	SE_{diff}	80% CI	90% CI	Average Practice Effect
Visual Scanning	2.3	3.0	3.8	2.0	2.6	3.4	4.3	0.7	2.3	3.0	3.8	0.4
Number Sequencing	1.7	2.1	2.7	1.0	2.6	3.4	4.3	1.3	2.9	3.7	4.8	1.8
Letter Sequencing	2.7	3.5	4.5	1.7	2.9	3.7	4.8	0.9	2.4	3.1	4.0	0.9
Number-Letter Sequencing	3.8	4.8	6.2	1.1	2.7	3.4	4.4	1.3	3.0	3.8	4.9	0.3
Motor Speed	1.6	2.0	2.6	0.4	2.5	3.1	4.0	0.7	2.0	2.6	3.4	0.0
Letter Fluency	2.2	2.8	3.6	0.8	2.3	3.0	3.8	0.6	1.8	2.3	3.0	0.3
Category Fluency	2.1	2.7	3.5	1.0	2.1	2.7	3.4	0.5	2.2	2.8	3.6	0.1
Category Switching-Correct	2.2	2.8	3.6	1.3	3.7	4.7	6.0	−1.2	3.6	4.6	5.9	0.1
Category Switching-Accuracy	2.9	3.7	4.7	0.7	4.3	5.5	7.0	−1.1	3.7	4.7	6.1	0.7
CW: Color Naming	1.7	2.2	2.8	1.1	1.5	2.0	2.5	1.0	3.0	3.9	5.0	0.5
CW: Word Reading	2.2	2.8	3.6	0.0	2.6	3.3	4.3	0.6	2.7	3.4	4.4	0.5
CW: Inhibition	1.3	1.7	2.1	1.5	1.8	2.4	3.0	1.2	3.3	4.2	5.4	0.5
CW: Inhibition/ Switching	2.0	2.5	3.2	1.8	2.2	2.8	3.6	1.1	2.9	3.7	4.7	0.5

Table Notes: Sample sizes were as follows: ages 18–19, $n = 26–28$; ages 20–49, $n = 35$; and ages 50–89, $n = 36–38$. Mean test interval was 25 days (range = 9–74 days). SE_{diff} = Standard error of difference. The formula used for calculating the SE_{diff} was: $SE_{diff} = \sqrt{SEM_1^2 + SEM_2^2}$, where $SEM_1 = SD1\sqrt{1 - r_{12}}$ and $SEM_2 = SD2\sqrt{1 - r_{12}}$. *CI* confidence interval, *CW* Color-Word Interference subtest. The standard deviations and correlations used to calculate these reliable change estimates are presented on pages 21, 23 and 29 in the D-KEFS technical manual (Delis et al., 2001). Average practice effect is calculated by subtracting the mean age-adjusted score at time 2—mean score at time 1

Table 30.6 Example of reliable change corrected for practice effects: NAB Attention Index in 18–59 year olds

								Confidence Intervals			
	Time 1		Time 2		Practice Effect			Reliable Decline		Reliable Improvement	
NAB Index	$Mean_1$	SD_1	$Mean_2$	SD_2	$Mean_2$-$Mean_1$	r_{12}	SE_{diff}	80%	90%	80%	90%
Attention	96.2	16.6	102.7	16	6.5	0.88	7.99	3.7	6.6	16.7	19.6

Table Notes: The formula used for calculating the SE_{diff} was: $SE_{diff} = \sqrt{SEM_1^2 + SEM_2^2}$, where $SEM_1 = SD1\sqrt{1-r_{12}}$ and $SEM_2 = SD2\sqrt{1-r_{12}}$. The practice effect was either subtracted from (reliable decline) or added to (reliable improvement) the confidence interval for the SE_{diff}. Means, standard deviations (SD) and test–retest correlations were obtained from Table 5.15 in the NAB Psychometric and Technical Manual (White & Stern, 2003)

improvement on the Attention Index, then this would not be considered reliable at either the 80% or 90% confidence intervals adjusted for practice effects.

Reliable change corrected for practice effects seems more appropriate for tests where large practice effects are expected. However, it is problematic in a number of ways, first and foremost of which is the use of a constant (group mean) term for the practice effect, which does not take into account the range of practice effects that are actually present in a sample of people tested twice. For example, there is evidence that more able people typically gain more on retesting than less able people (Rapport et al., 1997). Second, the calculation of practice effects is typically based on relatively short retest durations (e.g., one to two months). Therefore, practice effects might be overestimated because of the brief retest interval. Third, average practice effects (typically calculated over brief retest intervals) are computed from healthy subjects in normative samples. Practice effects in clinical groups might be different. Fourth, neither standard nor adjusted RCIs account for regression toward the mean (i.e., estimated measurement error is not proportional to extremity of observed change). Finally, the use of practice effects when calculating change scores has been recommended *only* when 75% or more of the sample showed at least some improvement on the test score (Iverson & Green, 2001).

Regression Methods

The reliable change methodology may provide useful information regarding the likelihood of a meaningful change in test performance, but it can have limited validity when various variables are systematically associated with changes in scores over time. These variables include: test–retest interval; scores from other tests; examinee characteristics such as baseline ability level (Time 1 score), gender, education, age and acculturation; and neurological or medical conditions. In addition, although this methodology factors in test reliability, this is operationalized as a constant error term that does not account for regression to the mean (although some reliable change methods used in clinical psychology have been adjusted for regression to the mean). One method for evaluating change that does allow clinicians to account for additional predictors and also controls for regression to the mean is the use of linear regression models (Crawford & Howell, 1998; Hermann et al., 1991).

With linear regression models, *predicted* retest scores are derived and these are compared with *observed* retest scores for purposes of determining if deviations are "significant." This is accomplished by dividing the difference between obtained retest scores and regression-predicted retest scores by the *Standard Error for Individual Predicted Scores* ($SE_{\hat{Y}}$). Because score differences are divided by a standard error measure, the resulting value is considered to be standardized. The resulting standardized score is in fact a t statistic that can be translated into a probability value using an appropriate program or table. As with other standardized scores (e.g., z scores), standardized regression-based change scores from different measures can be directly compared, regardless of the original test score metric. Regression models can also be used when one wishes to consider change scores from multiple tests simultaneously (see McCleary et al., 1996).

It is important to understand the limitations of regression methods. Regression equations based on smaller sample sizes can lead to large error terms so that meaningful predicted-obtained differences may be missed. However, attenuation of reliability in small samples *is also not factored into reliable change calculations*, which might be based on spuriously low or high test–retest correlations obtained from small samples. Regression equations from large studies, or that have been cross-validated, are therefore preferred. In order to maximize utility, sample characteristics should match populations seen clinically and predictor variables should be carefully chosen to match data that will likely be available to clinicians. Test users should generally avoid interpolation—that is, they should avoid applying a regression equation to an examinee's data (predictor variables and test–retest scores) when the data values fall outside the ranges for corresponding variables comprising the regression equation. For example, if a regression equation is developed for predicting IQ at retest from a sample with initial IQ scores ranging from 85 to 125, it should not be applied to an examinee whose initial IQ is 65. Finally, regression-based change scores should only be derived and used when necessary assumptions concerning residuals are met (see Pedhazur, 1997, p. 33–34).

Key Points: Interpreting change in test performance over time requires sophisticated psychometric models to minimize clinical bias and error associated with clinical judgment.

Summary and Conclusions

The purpose of this chapter was to provide an overview of the basic psychometric properties that are necessary for proper neuropsychological test interpretation. Moreover, our goal was to provide this information in a manner that would be easily understood by clinicians. To achieve this goal, we illustrated various psychometric concepts using tests that are commonly used by clinicians in everyday practice.

It was not our intention to suggest that certain cognitive measures, which were used as examples, have better or worse psychometric properties or normative samples than other measures that were not presented. It was also not our intention to suggest that clinicians should not use the tests that were used to illustrate some of the psychometric concepts in this chapter.

It was our intention, however, to draw attention to *all* psychological and neuropsychological tests and to have clinicians carefully consider the psychometric foundations presented in this chapter when interpreting test performance. The highlighted problems with psychometric properties, which can lead to inaccurate interpretation of test performance in some situations, are a reality of many tests in psychology and neuropsychology. However, having these issues addressed has often resulted in test developers and publishers becoming more aware of the problems and striving to address, correct and/or eliminate these problems on subsequent versions of the tests or on newly developed tests.

Based on our review, we offer a number of suggestions for best practice when interpreting test performance. These are presented in Table 30.7. We suggest that clinicians carefully consider the normative data for tests that they administer and interpret, the psychometric properties of the tests and other psychometrically based strategies that are designed to improve our interpretation of these tests. The composition of normative samples, in some cases, can have a major effect on test interpretation (e.g., see Fig. 30.2).

There were five main themes discussed in this chapter. First, we believe that interpreting and communicating test performance is facilitated by having a common "language" of descriptors (i.e., classification system). Regardless of the classification system that is used (see Table 30.1), it is recommended that clinicians be consistent throughout a report (See also Chap. 1, this volume). Second, sample characteristics, such as non-normal distributions and truncated samples, can impact interpretation of test performance. Third, comparison of performance across tests is affected by measurement error and ceiling and floor effects. Fourth, it is normal for healthy people to have variability and some low scores across a battery of neuropsychological tests. The number of low scores found in healthy people increases with the number of tests being administered, fewer years of education, lower levels of premorbid intelligence and in ethnic minorities. These principles should be

Table 30.7 Points to consider in the interpretation of test scores

• Are the norms adequate (i.e., sufficient sample size; representative of the larger population)?
• Is this individual from a group with a non-normal distribution?
• Is this individual likely from the ends/tails of the normal distribution?
• Does this test have floor effects?
• Does this test have ceiling effects?
• Was score extrapolation/interpolation used in the creation of derived scores?
• When considering scores on two or more tests, are the normative samples equivalent in terms of demographics?
• Does either test have a normative sample with a truncated distribution? (i.e., what were the screening methods used in the recruitment for the normative samples?)
• When comparing two tests, are they equally reliable?
• Does one of the tests have a small normative sample size?
• Is one of the scores an extreme score (i.e., is the magnitude of score size the same)?
• What is the likelihood that having a low score, when interpreting multiple test scores, is considered "broadly normal" compared to healthy people with similar intelligence?
• What is the likelihood that a change over time represents a real change or an artifact?
• What classification system will be used to communicate the results?
• Has the same classification system been used for interpretation of all tests?

considered when interpreting performance. Finally, interpreting change in test performance over time requires sophisticated psychometric models.

Key Points: General Guidelines for Interpreting Neuropsychological Data

- A common language of descriptors is needed to describe performance (the same descriptors should be used throughout a report)
- Sample characteristics can impact test interpretation
- Measurement error, ceiling effects and floor effects can impact comparisons of performance across different tests
- It is normal for healthy children, adolescents, adults and older adults to have variability in test performance, some low scores and some scores that change over time
- Interpreting test performance over time should include psychometric methods for determining change

References

Brooks, B. L., Holdnack, J. A., & Iverson, G. L. (2016). To change is human: "Abnormal" reliable change memory scores are common in healthy adults and older adults. *Archives of Clinical Neuropsychology, 31*(8), 1026–1036. https://doi.org/10.1093/arclin/acw079. Advance online publication.

Brooks, B. L., Holdnack, J. A., & Iverson, G. L. (2017). Reliable change on memory tests is common in healthy children and adolescents. *Archives of Clinical Neuropsychology, 32*(8), 1001–1009.

Chelune, G. J. (2003). Assessing reliable neuropsychological change. In R. D. Franklin (Ed.), *Prediction in forensic and neuropsychology: Sound statistical practices* (pp. 65–88). Lawrence Erlbaum Associates.

Cohen, M. J. (1997). *Children's Memory Scale (CMS) manual.* The Psychological Corporation.

Crawford, J. R., & Garthwaite, P. H. (2002). Investigation of the single case in neuropsychology: Confidence limits on the abnormality of test scores and test score differences. *Neuropsychologia, 40*(8), 1196–1208.

Crawford, J. R., Garthwaite, P. H., & Gault, C. B. (2007). Estimating the percentage of the population with abnormally low scores (or abnormally large score differences) on standardized neuropsychological test batteries: a generic method with applications. *Neuropsychology, 21*(4), 419–430.

Crawford, J. R., & Howell, D. C. (1998). Regression equations in clinical neuropsychology: An evaluation of statistical methods for comparing predicted and obtained scores. *Journal of Clinical and Experimental Neuropsychology, 20*(5), 755–762.

Delis, D. C., Kaplan, E., & Kramer, J. H. (2001). *Delis Kaplan Executive Function System technical manual.* The Psychological Corporation.

Dunn, L. M., & Dunn, D. M. (2007). *Peabody picture vocabulary test* (4th ed.). Pearson Assessments.

Fastenau, P. S., & Adams, K. M. (1996). Heaton, Grant, and Matthew's comprehensive norms: An overzealous attempt. *Journal of Clinical and Experimental Neuropsychology, 18*(3), 444–448.

Heaton, R. K., Chelune, G. J., Talley, J. L., Kay, G. G., & Curtiss, G. (1993). *Wisconsin card sorting test manual.* Psychological Assessment Resources.

Heaton, R. K., Grant, I., & Matthews, C. G. (1991). *Comprehensive norms for an extended Halstead-Reitan Battery: Demographic corrections, research findings, and clinical applications.* Psychological Assessment Resources.

Heaton, R. K., Miller, S. W., Taylor, M. J., & Grant, I. (2004). *Revised comprehensive norms for an expanded Halstead-Reitan Battery: Demographically adjusted neuropsychological norms for African American and Caucasian Adults professional manual.* Psychological Assessment Resources.

Hermann, B. P., Wyler, A. R., VanderZwagg, R., LeBailey, R. K., Whitman, S., Somes, G., et al. (1991). Predictors of neuropsychological change following anterior temporal lobectomy: Role of regression toward the mean. *Journal of Epilepsy, 4*, 139–148.

Iverson, G. L., & Green, P. (2001). Measuring improvement or decline on the WAIS-R in inpatient psychiatry. *Psychological Reports, 89*(2), 457–462.

Ivnik, R. J., Makec, J. F., Smith, G. E., Tangolos, E. G., & Peterson, R. C. (1996). Neuropsychological tests' norms above age 55: COWAT, BNT, MAE Token, WRAT-R Reading, AMNART, STROOP, TMT, and JLO. *The Clinical Neuropsychologist, 10*, 262–278.

Jacobson, N. S., Roberts, L. J., Berns, S. B., & McGlinchey, J. B. (1999). Methods for defining and determining the clinical significance of treatment effects: Description, application, and alternatives. *Journal of Consulting and Clinical Psychology, 67*(3), 300–307.

Jacobson, N. S., & Truax, P. (1991). Clinical significance: A statistical approach to defining meaningful change in psychotherapy research. *Journal of Consulting and Clinical Psychology, 59*(1), 12–19.

Kaplan, E. F., Goodglass, H., & Weintraub, S. (1978). *The Boston Naming Test.* E. Kaplan & H. Goodglass.

Kaplan, E. F., Goodglass, H., & Weintraub, S. (2001). *The Boston Naming Test* (2nd ed.). Lippincott Williams & Wilkins.

Lucas, J. A., Ivnik, R. J., Smith, G. E., Ferman, T. J., Willis, F. B., Petersen, R. C., et al. (2005). Mayo's Older African Americans Normative Studies: Norms for Boston Naming Test, Controlled Oral Word Association, Category Fluency, Animal Naming, Token Test, Wrat-3 Reading, Trail Making Test, Stroop Test, and Judgment of Line Orientation. *The Clinical Neuropsychologist, 19*(2), 243–269.

McCleary, R., Dick, M. B., Buckwalter, G., Henderson, V., & Shankle, W. R. (1996). Full-information models for multiple psychometric tests: Annualized rates of change in normal aging and dementia. *Alzheimer's Disease and Associated Disorders, 10*(4), 216–223.

McFadden, T. U. (1996). Creating language impairments in typically achieving children: The pitfalls of "normal" normative sampling. *Language, Speech, and Hearing Services in Schools, 27*, 3–9.

Mitrushina, M. N., Boone, K. B., Razani, J., & D'Elia, L. F. (2005). *Handbook of normative data for neuropsychological assessment*. Oxford University Press.

Pedhazur, E. J. (1997). *Multiple regression in behavioral research*. Harcourt Brace.

Rapport, L. J., Brines, D. B., Theisen, M. E., & Axelrod, B. N. (1997). Full scale IQ as a mediator of practice effects: The rich get richer. *The Clinical Neuropsychologist, 11*(4), 375–380.

Sattler, J. M. (2001). *Assessment of children: Cognitive applications* (4th ed.). Jerome M. Sattler Publisher.

Sherman, E. M. S., & Brooks, B. L. (2015). *Child and Adolescent Memory Profile (ChAMP)*. Psychological Assessment Resources.

Stern, R. A., & White, T. (2003a). *Neuropsychological assessment battery*. Psychological Assessment Resources.

Stern, R. A., & White, T. (2003b). *Neuropsychological assessment battery: Administration, scoring, and interpretation manual*. Psychological Assessment Resources.

Strauss, E., Sherman, E. M. S., & Spreen, O. (2006). *A compendium of neuropsychological tests: Administration, norms, and commentary* (3rd ed.). Oxford University Press.

The Psychological Corporation. (2001). *Wechsler Test of Adult Reading manual*. Author.

Tombaugh, T. N., & Hubley, A. M. (1997). The 60-item Boston Naming Test: Norms for cognitively intact adults aged 25 to 88 years. *Journal of Clinical and Experimental Neuropsychology, 19*(6), 922–932.

Urbina, S. (2004). *Essentials of psychological testing*. Wiley.

Van Gorp, W. G., Satz, P., Kiersch, M. E., & Henry, R. (1986). Normative data on the Boston Naming Test for a group of normal older adults. *Journal of Clinical and Experimental Neuropsychology, 8*, 702–705.

Wechsler, D. (1997). *Wechsler memory scale* (3rd ed.). The Psychological Corporation.

Wechsler, D. (2014). *Wechsler Intelligence Scale for Children, Fifth Edition (WISC-V)*. NCS Pearson.

Wechsler, D., Coalson, D. L., & Raiford, S. E. (2008). *Wechsler Adult Intelligence Scale – 4th ed., technical and interpretive manual*. NCS Pearson.

Wechsler, D., Holdnack, J. A., & Drozdick, L. W. (2009). *Wechsler Memory Scale – 4th ed., technical and interpretive manual*. NCS Pearson.

White, T., & Stern, R. A. (2003). *Neuropsychological assessment battery: Psychometric and technical manual*. Psychological Assessment Resources.

Chapter 31
Reliability and Validity in Neuropsychology

Elisabeth M. S. Sherman, Brian L. Brooks, Grant L. Iverson, Daniel J. Slick, and Esther Strauss

There are now literally hundreds of neuropsychological tests designed for evaluating cognitive abilities in children, adolescents and adults. Given this vast library of instruments, how do clinicians decide which neuropsychological tests to choose? Two critical sources of information for making that decision are evidence of a test's reliability and validity. This seems like a straightforward task for most neuropsychologists, who have typically covered basic concepts of reliability and validity throughout their training. Yet, a common mistake is to ask an all-or-none question, such as "is this test reliable?" or "has this test been validated?"

The goal of this chapter is to facilitate the process of assessing the reliability and validity of tests for clinical use and highlight subtleties and raise awareness of factors that influence reliability and validity. We will provide an overview of reliability, including different types of reliability, methods for determining reliability, factors

Some elements from this chapter originally appeared in Strauss et al. (2006).

E. M. S. Sherman (✉) · B. L. Brooks · D. J. Slick
Alberta Children's Hospital, University of Calgary, Calgary, AB, Canada
e-mail: elisabeth.sherman@albertahealthservices.ca

G. L. Iverson
Department of Physical Medicine and Rehabilitation, Harvard Medical School, Boston, MA, USA

Department of Physical Medicine and Rehabilitation, Spaulding Rehabilitation Hospital, Boston, MA, USA

Schoen Adams Research Institute at Spaulding Rehabilitation, Boston, MA, USA

Mass General for Children Sports Concussion Program, Boston, MA, USA

Home Base, A Red Sox Foundation and Massachusetts General Hospital Program, Boston, OK, USA

E. Strauss
Department of Psychology, University of Victoria, Victoria, BC, Canada
e-mail: jim-scott@ouhsc.edu

M. R. Schoenberg, J. G. Scott (eds.), *The Little Black Book of Neuropsychology*, https://doi.org/10.1007/978-3-032-07777-6_31

that affect reliability and limits to reliability. We will also cover basic concepts relating to validity, including specific kinds of evidence contributing to validity, ways of evaluating validity and basic guidelines for interpreting validity. We will do this while keeping the context focused as much as possible on everyday clinical practice.

Key Points and Chapter Summary

- Understanding the concepts of reliability and validity is a prerequisite for skilled use of tests in clinical and research settings.
- Reliability refers to consistency of measurement, and is not an "all-or-none" property of tests. Rather, reliability refers to test scores, determined through evaluation of different kinds of reliability evidence (e.g., internal, test–retest, alternate form and interrater) in conjunction with the concept being measured and its stability over time.
- Determining the reliability of a test score is an ongoing process based on information gathered in healthy individuals and clinical populations.
- Similarly, validity is not an "all-or-none" property of a test. Validity is a property of the meaning attached to a test score in the specific context of test usage. That is, test scores have varying degrees of validity, for specific uses, with specific populations.
- In the tripartite model of validity, there are three broad categories of validity evidence to consider: content-related, construct-related, and criterion-related.
- Within these broad categories, there are many ways of estimating the validity of test scores.
- Similar to reliability, determining the validity of a test score is an ongoing process based on evidence gathered in healthy individuals and clinical populations.
- The process of appropriately selecting neuropsychological tests requires a careful and thoughtful process that involves sifting through multiple sources of psychometric evidence.

Reliability in Neuropsychology

Reliability refers to the *consistency of measurement* of a given score. Reliability is not a unitary psychometric construct. Instead, it is determined through evaluation of different kinds of reliability evidence (see Fig. 31.1), applied in different clinical contexts, to diverse groups. Reliability also relates to the clinical inferences derived from tests (c.f., Franzen, 1989, 2000). Types of reliability include the consistency across test items (*internal reliability* or internal consistency), consistency over time (*test–retest reliability* or test stability), consistency across alternate forms (*alternate form reliability*) and consistency across raters (*interrater reliability*). All these different kinds of reliabilities contribute to an overall assessment of a particular test's reliability, which is simply an estimate of the degree to which a test is free from

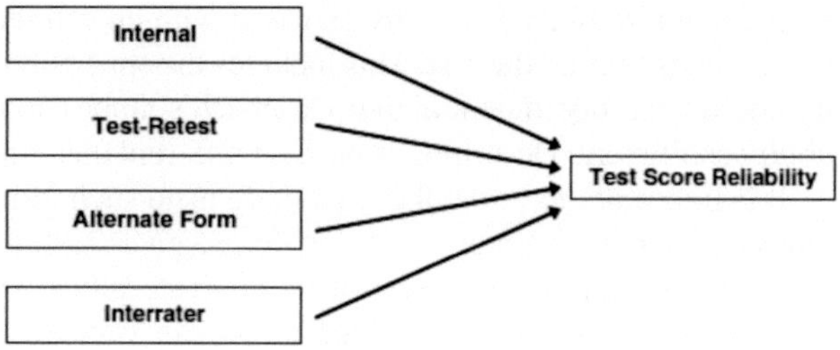

Fig. 31.1 Types of reliability *evidence* to consider for test scores

measurement error. By measurement error, we refer to "fluctuation in scores that results from factors related to the measurement process that are irrelevant to what is being measured"; reliability is therefore a property of test *scores*, not of tests (Urbina, 2004). Reliability coefficients therefore fall somewhere between perfectly reliable ($r = 1.00$) and completely unreliable ($r = .00$).

Key Points: Reliability

- Reliability refers to the consistency of measurement of a given score.
- Reliability is not an "all-or-none" property.
- Reliability refers to test scores, not to tests.
- Reliability is determined through evaluation of different kinds of reliability evidence.
- There are four types of reliability evidence to consider: Internal, test–retest, alternate form and interrater reliability.
- Determining the reliability of a test score is an ongoing process based on information gathered in both healthy individuals and clinical populations.

Internal Reliability

Internal reliability, a core concept in classical test theory, reflects the *extent to which the individual items within a test measure the same cognitive domain or construct.* For example, the internal reliability of the WAIS-IV Information subtest is an estimate of the extent to which all of the items on this subtest measure a person's fund of knowledge. It has a high coefficient ($r = .93$) because it has good item cohesiveness and common content. In contrast, low internal consistency generally means that a test is made up of items that do not measure the same construct, or are more heterogeneous than those of tests with high internal consistency. IQ tests are a class of tests that typically are designed to have scores with very high internal reliability (e.g., for the WAIS-IV: $r = .94$ for Vocabulary, $r = .90$ for Matrix Reasoning; Wechsler et al., 2008), whereas instruments designed to sample a variety of content domains over few items will have lower internal reliabilities (e.g., Mini Mental State Exam; MMSE, $r = .31–.96$; Strauss et al., 2006). Internal reliability estimates for the standardization sample and clinical samples for the WAIS-IV are presented in Fig. 31.2.

Internal reliability is usually assessed with an estimate of the average correlation among items within the test. This includes the split-half or Spearman–Brown reliability coefficient, coefficient alpha (Cronbach's alpha) and the Kuder–Richardson reliability coefficient. Descriptions of these different methods are presented in Table 31.1.

It is important to remember that there is no such thing as a single internal consistency estimate for a given score, let alone a given test. Like other kinds of reliability, internal reliability varies with sample characteristics. This is why the strength of the correlations between items within a test can vary across different age groups and

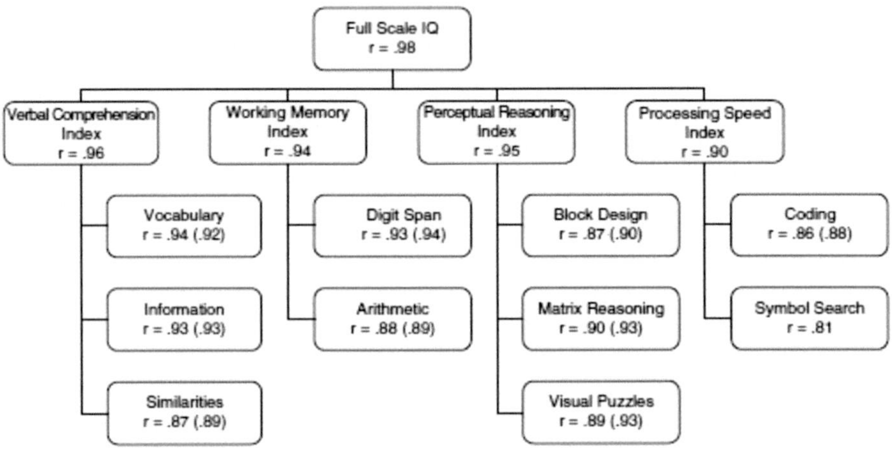

Fig. 31.2 Internal reliability coefficients of the Wechsler adult intelligence scale—Fourth Edition (WAIS-IV). Internal consistency reliability estimates for the total WAIS-IV standardization sample were obtained from p. 42 of the Technical Manual (Wechsler et al., 2008). The reliability estimates in parentheses are averaged for 13 clinical groups; available values were obtained from p. 44 of the Technical Manual. Reliability estimates for the FSIQ or Index scores were not presented for the clinical groups

Table 31.1 Methods for evaluating internal reliability

Method	Description
Split-half or Spearman–Brown reliability coefficient	• Obtained by correlating two halves of items from the same test
Coefficient alpha (Cronbach's alpha)	• Provides a general estimate of reliability based on all the possible ways of splitting test items.
	• Based on the average intercorrelation between test items and any other set of items, and is used for tests with items that yield more than two response types (e.g., items are scored 0, 1 or 2).
Kuder–Richardson reliability coefficient	• Used for items with dichotomous answers (i.e., yes/no, true/false), or heterogeneous tests where split-half methods must be used (i.e., the mean of all the different split-half coefficients if the test were split into all possible ways).
	• Generally, Kuder–Richardson coefficients will be lower than split-half coefficients when tests are heterogeneous in terms of content (Anastasi & Urbina, 1997)

different clinical groups. For example, for the Verbal Comprehension Index subtests of the WISC-IV (Similarities, Vocabulary and Comprehension), there is a trend toward an overall increase in split-half correlations with increasing age (see Fig. 31.3).

Greater variability in internal consistency reliability is expected across tests when measuring more variable or less stable cognitive abilities, such as memory and executive functioning. For example, variability in internal consistency reliability across different tests from the Delis-Kaplan Executive Function System (D-KEFS; Delis et al., 2001), by age group, is presented in Fig. 31.4.

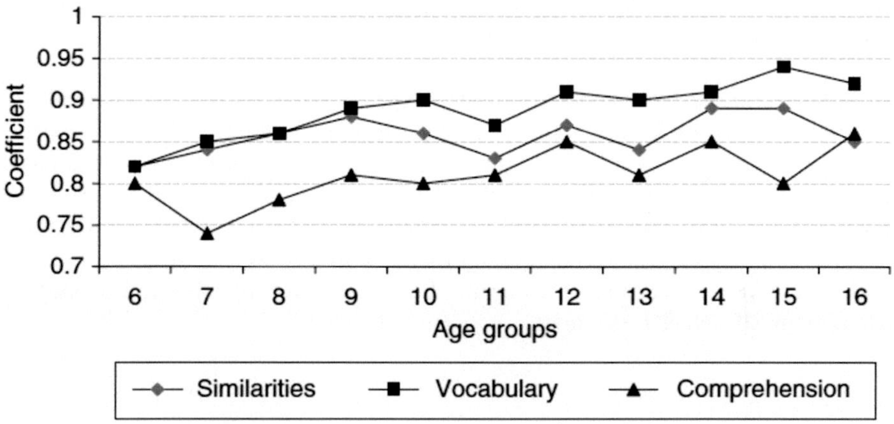

Fig. 31.3 Split-half reliability coefficients for the WISC-IV verbal comprehension index subtests across age groups. This information is adapted from Table 4.1 in the WISC-IV integrated technical and interpretive manual (Wechsler, 2004). Each age group has $n = 200$

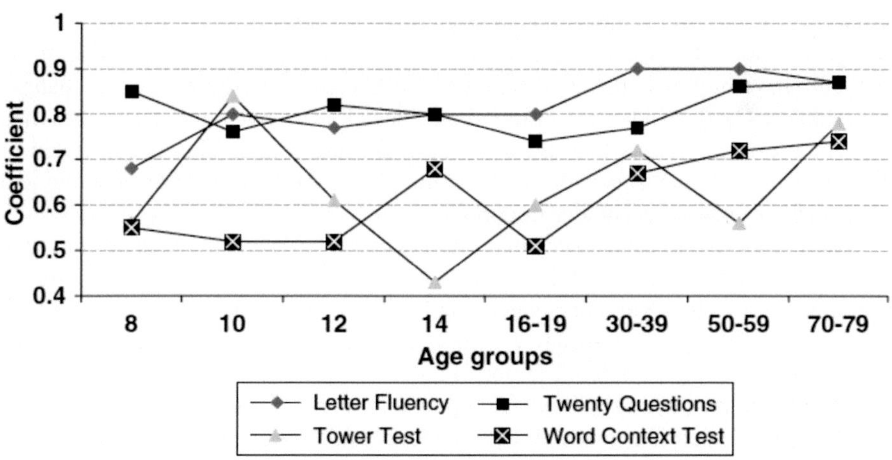

Fig. 31.4 Internal consistency reliability coefficients for selected D-KEFS subtests across age groups. This information is adapted from tables on pp. 22, 34, 37 and 40 of the D-KEFS Technical Manual (Delis et al., 2001)

Table 31.2 Internal consistency estimates for the Ruff Neurobehavioral Inventory (RNBI)

Scale	Number of items	Standardization sample	Mixed clinical sample
RNBI composite score			
Cognitive domain	24	.90	.93
RNBI subscales			
Attention and concentration	6	.88	.90
Executive functions	6	.79	.80
Learning and memory	6	.81	.87
Speech and language	6	.82	.87

Note: The Ruff Neurobehavioral Inventory (RNBI) standardization sample ($N = 1024$) reliability estimates are for "postmorbid" ratings. All coefficients were taken from the test manual (Ruff & Hibbard, 2003)

Internal consistency is reported for most types of cognitive tests and virtually all self-report measures. Examples of reliability estimates for the Ruff Neurobehavioral Inventory (Ruff & Hibbard, 2003) for normative and clinical groups are presented in Table 31.2. This example illustrates the basic principle that, all things being equal, a scale with more items such as a composite score (i.e., Cognitive Domain) tends to have higher internal consistency than a scale with few items, such as a subscale score (i.e., Attention & Concentration, Executive Functions, Learning & Memory or Speech & Language).

Test–Retest Reliability

Test–retest reliability provides an *estimate of the correlation between scores on a test administered twice* over a given time interval. A test score with high test–retest reliability would show little change over time. IQ tests are an example of tests designed a priori to capture stable estimates of an individual's ability levels; these typically have high test–retest correlations. Tests measuring dynamic (i.e., changeable) abilities such as attention or mood may have lower test–retest reliabilities than tests measuring domains that are more trait-like and stable. This is illustrated in Fig. 31.5. In most neuropsychological contexts, the evaluation of both stable and changeable functions is equally important.

The size of test–retest coefficients is influenced by subject characteristics as well as the length of the time interval between test and retest. For example, the test–retest coefficient for Letter-Number Sequencing is .48 for 16–29 year olds versus .77 for 55–74 year olds in the normative sample. Other subtests show few differences across adult age (e.g., Logical Memory 1).

The test–retest interval will depend upon a number of factors, including the particular clinical situation, research question and availability of relevant retest data. Across tests, there is no standard time interval for determining test–retest reliability coefficients. This complicates score comparisons between tests. Retest periods for different tests range from days (e.g., Comprehensive Trail Making Test, Reynolds,

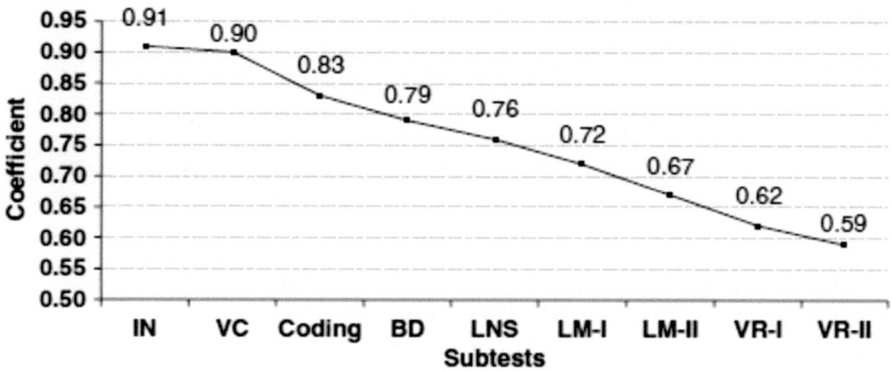

Fig. 31.5 Test–retest correlation coefficients for selected WAIS-IV and WMS-IV subtests. WMS-IV—Wechsler Memory Scale, Fourth Edition (Wechsler et al., 2009). Test–retest coefficients were obtained from p. 48 of the WAIS-IV Technical Manual (Wechsler et al., 2008) and from p. 51 of the WMS-IV Technical Manual (Wechsler et al., 2009). WAIS-IV Subtests: *IN* Information, *VC* vocabulary, *BD* block design and *LN* letter-number sequencing. WMS-IV Subtests: *LM-I* logical memory-I, *LM-II* logical memory-II, *VR-I* visual reproduction-I and *VR-II* visual reproduction-II

2002) to months (e.g., Paced Auditory Serial Addition Test, Sjögren et al., 2000) to years (e.g., Woodcock-Johnson III Tests of Cognitive Abilities, WJIII-COG, McGrew & Woodcock, 2001). Many standardized tests provide reliability information for intervals ranging from 2 to 12 weeks, although some tests provide reliability estimates over longer intervals. In particular, the 6-month retest interval for the Neuropsychological Assessment Battery (White & Stern, 2003) and the 1-, 3- and 10-year retest intervals for the WJIII-COG are especially noteworthy.

In most cases, the shorter the time interval between test and retest, the higher the retest reliability coefficient will be. However, the extent to which the time interval affects the test–retest coefficient will depend on the type of ability evaluated (i.e., stable vs more variable) and the type of individual being assessed, because some groups are intrinsically more variable than others. Score fluctuations over time may depend on subject characteristics, including age (e.g., preschoolers vs adults) and neurological status (e.g., brain injured vs healthy). Because this may not necessarily occur in expected patterns across age or demographics, reliability estimates should ideally be provided for both a range of normal individuals and a range of clinical populations.

Alternate Form Reliability

Alternate forms are designed to eliminate the confounding effects of practice when a test must be administered more than once. However, alternate forms can introduce another type of error variance, called content sampling error, in addition to the time

Table 31.3 Factors that increase the reliability of alternate forms

Very high correlations between forms
Very high test–retest reliability for both forms
Equivalence in terms of mean scores from test to retest for both forms
Consistency in score classification within individuals from test to retest

sampling error that accumulates when a test is repeatedly administered over time (see Lineweaver & Chelune, 2003). Thus, tests with alternate forms must employ rigorous psychometric standards to avoid introducing new sources of error (see Table 31.3). For example, the Neuropsychological Assessment Battery (Stern & White, 2003) was designed to have two parallel alternate forms. A generalizability study was conducted to evaluate the two alternate forms. Of the 36 primary test scores generated from the NAB battery, only 5 fell below the level that would be considered very good reliability (White & Stern, 2003). Nevertheless, even though psychometrically equivalent alternate forms may be designed to eliminate practice effects, prior exposure to similar stimuli and procedures can improve retest scores because of format familiarity and procedural learning despite the use of a different set of items. Thus, it is possible for mean scores to be higher when retesting with an alternate form even though the examinee may not have been previously exposed to the actual content of the test items. See Table 31.3 for factors relevant to constructing good alternate test forms.

Interrater Reliability

Interrater reliability refers to the *degree of consensus between different raters* in scoring items. Test manuals provide specific and detailed instructions on how to administer and score tests according to standard procedures in order to reduce the chances of introducing additional error due to different examiners and scorers. However, some degree of examiner variance remains in individually administered tests, particularly when scores involve a degree of judgment in the scoring procedure. Although many tests are administered and scored in a straightforward manner such that a wrong answer is unequivocally wrong (e.g., Wechsler Digit Symbol), there are other tests that have a subjective component that requires detailed scoring instructions because of the potential for examiner variance (e.g., Wechsler verbal subtests, Rey–Osterrieth Complex Figure, Verbal Fluency). When this is the case, an estimate of the consistency of scores across examiners is needed as additional evidence for the reliability of the test. See Table 31.4 for examples of statistical methods for evaluating interrater reliability.

Table 31.4 Statistical methods for evaluating interrater reliability

Method	Explanation
Percent agreement	This technique is used for nominal data such as classifications or ratings. The number of times each rating is assigned by each rater is divided by the total number of ratings. This method assumes that the data are nominal and it does not adjust for chance agreement between raters.
Kappa	Cohen's kappa is used for comparing two raters; Fleiss' kappa for more than two raters. This technique takes into account the amount of agreement that would be expected to occur by chance. However, the data are treated as nominal.
Pearson's product-moment correlation Spearman's rank correlation	Pearson's coefficient is used for continuous data, Spearman's for ordinal data. Both involve pairwise correlations between the scores of raters. However, because this technique does not take into account the magnitude of the score differences between raters, the scores of two raters could yield a perfect correlation, yet not agree (e.g., Rater 1 = 1, 2, 3, 4; Rater 2 = 7, 8, 9, 10).
Intraclass correlation coefficient (ICC)	The ICC reflects the proportion of variance of an observation due to between-subject variability in the true scores. The ICC will be high when there is little variation between the scores assigned to each item by the raters.
Mean differences and confidence intervals (Bland-Altman plot)	This technique provides information on agreement between raters and identifies any biases among raters through the derivation of two indices: (1) the mean of the differences between the two raters, and (2) confidence intervals reflecting agreement. If the raters tend to agree, the mean will be near zero. If one rater is usually higher than the other by a consistent amount, the mean will be greater than zero, but the confidence interval will be narrow. If the raters tend to disagree, but without a consistent pattern of one rating higher than the other, the mean will be near zero but the confidence interval will be wide. This information can be graphed using a Bland-Altman plot.

Source: Bland and Altman (1986), Cicchetti and Sparrow (1981), Fastenau et al. (1996), Sattler (2001)

Evaluating a Test's Reliability

As we have discussed, tests cannot be described simply as "reliable" or "unreliable." Rather, test scores can be said to possess different kinds and degrees of reliability. The relative importance of one kind of reliability over another will depend on how the test score will be used, with whom and for what purpose. For instance, a demanding attention test may be highly reliable in normally functioning adults, but yield unreliable scores in young children or in individuals with severe neurological illness. Importantly, high reliability does not necessarily translate into high validity; some constructs that can be measured with a high degree of precision may be of little use clinically. When faced with deciding between tests with varying reliability, it is usually preferable to choose a test that has slightly lower evidence of reliability if that test has evidence of superior validity (Nunnally & Bernstein, 1994).

Given the different kinds of reliabilities, which one matters most when choosing a test? Some have argued that internal reliability is the most important kind of reliability; thus, if alpha is low (regardless of other levels of reliability evidence), a test score should not be considered reliable. Some tests yield scores with relatively lower alpha values yet possess high test–retest reliability. Examples are tests that are made up of heterogeneous items that yield stable scores at retest, such as certain dementia screening instruments. Internal consistency is therefore not necessarily the primary index of reliability, but should be evaluated within the broader context of test–retest and interrater reliability (Cicchetti, 1994).

What about test–retest reliability? Does it need to be considered if the test will only be used once and is not likely to be administered again in future? Stability coefficients are essential for evaluating a test's utility because they provide a measure of the degree to which test scores are replicable and stable. For example, a clinician must be reasonably certain that the IQ or memory score obtained now is a good estimate of that person's functioning in future, if that score is to be used for educational planning, or for making a diagnosis regarding a permanent condition such as cognitive disability or dementia. Test scores will have limited clinical utility if they cannot be trusted to give a reasonable estimate of a person's functioning in the future.

Overall, selecting tests—and equally important, selecting test scores—requires that a clinician use an informed and pragmatic (rather than dogmatic) approach to evaluating the reliability of tests for clinical decision making (see Table 31.5). If the goal is to measure a specific, narrowly defined construct, then high internal reliability might be the most important consideration. High test–retest reliability is usually a requirement of most clinical situations, but may be considered less important if the test is specifically designed to measure state variables that fluctuate. For example, if a depression symptom scale is composed entirely of extremely stable items that are completely resistant to change, it will not be sensitive to treatment-related effects and would be a poor choice for determining whether a patient has benefited from an antidepressant drug regimen. One way around the problem of low test–retest reliability may be to use multiple measures of the specific construct and seek converging evidence to support clinical inferences. In the end, when test scores have lesser reliability in one domain versus another, such as high internal consistency but low test–retest reliability, there are usually no clear-cut guidelines on how to interpret

Table 31.5 Examples of interpretations of different patterns of reliability evidence

Reliability			Interpretation of reliability evidence	
Internal	Test–retest	Interrater	Positive interpretation	Negative interpretation
High	High	High	An ideal test for most purposes	None
Low	High	High	Scores reflect a test with heterogeneous item content	Scores are based on items that are measuring something other than the construct the test is designed to measure
High	Low	High	Scores reflect a test measuring a fluctuating ability	Scores are too vulnerable to the effects of normal variability and time

test scores, or whether the test is appropriate for the specific test usage. It is up to the user to consider all the available evidence and make an informed interpretation of the possible strengths and weaknesses of the test and its scores (see Table 31.5 for examples).

Key Points: Reliability Coefficients

- High reliability coefficients are generally preferable, but there are circumstances where lower coefficients may be acceptable, particularly when measuring conditions that are likely to change (i.e., depression)
- Low internal consistency may mean that a test is made up of items that do not measure the same construct, or it could mean that the test is designed to measure a broad set of heterogeneous domains (e.g., dementia screening).
- Low test–retest stability may mean that a test is poorly designed and unstable over time, or it could mean that the trait being measured is changeable and dynamic.
- Alternate forms do not eliminate practice effects, and may introduce content sampling error and/or time sampling error.
- It is up to the user to review available evidence on reliability and make an informed interpretation of the strengths and weaknesses of tests

Limits to Reliability, Practice Effects and Effects of Prior Exposure

Although it is possible to have a reliable test score that is not valid for some purpose, it is *not possible to have a valid test score that is highly unreliable*. Despite this statement, it is also conceivable that there are some neuropsychological domains that are very difficult to measure in a highly reliable manner. Thus, even though there is the assumption that questionable reliability is always a function of poor test construction, reliability may depend on the nature of the cognitive process measured and on the nature of the population evaluated. For example, many executive functioning tests scores have relatively modest reliabilities, suggesting that this ability is difficult to assess reliably. Other tests measuring domains such as reaction time or processing speed may yield low coefficients in groups with high response variability, such as preschoolers, elderly individuals or individuals with brain disorders. Lastly, like validity, reliability is a matter of degree rather than an all-or-none property. Reliability is therefore never actually final. Test scores must be continually re-evaluated from the standpoint of reliability as populations and testing contexts change over time.

One of the most significant influences on test scores re-administered after a period of time is the practice effect. Re-administering a test would be expected to yield better performance at retest, and this is the case in most instances. For example, mean practice effects on the WISC-IV FSIQ range from 4.2 to 8.3 index points

(Table 4.4; Wechsler, 2004) and on the WAIS-IV FSIQ range from 3.5 to 4.9 index points (Table 4.5; Wechsler et al., 2008). However, not all persons necessarily show a positive practice effect on retest. An examinee may approach tests that he or she had difficulty with previously with heightened anxiety that leads to decreased performance.

The size of a retest reliability coefficient does not indicate the magnitude of practice effects. A test score can have a high stability coefficient, yet have an average retest mean that is several points higher than baseline scores. For example, the WMS-IV Auditory Memory Index has a test–retest reliability estimate of .81, yet has an 11.5 point practice effect over a brief retest interval in healthy adults (Wechsler et al., 2009).

Overall, two main questions must be answered to properly interpret scores in a retest situation: (1) what is the magnitude of the typical expected practice effect, and (2) is the practice effect expected to be consistent across individuals in the group from which the examinee originates? The practical problem for clinicians is that, while most test manuals provide some information on mean practice effects across groups, there is limited information in test manuals for determining the probability of a known practice effect occurring for an individual patient. This is because the majority of practice effects are estimated in healthy subjects, not clinical subjects, and are *averaged* for a group with little information provided regarding the distribution of practice effects across individuals. Therefore, when considering a large group of subjects tested twice, some will likely perform worse, some similarly, some better and some much better on retest. The *average* practice effect found in a test manual may only apply for an unknown proportion of the sample itself. Reliability coefficients do not provide information on which individuals retain their relative place in the distribution from baseline to retest and which individuals encounter score increases or decreases on retesting. Certain subgroups may benefit more from prior exposure than others (e.g., individuals with above average intelligence; Rapport et al., 1997), or some subgroups may demonstrate more stable scores or consistent practice effects than others. This causes the score distribution to change at retest which will attenuate the correlation. In these cases, the test, retest correlation may vary significantly across subgroups and the correlation for the entire sample will not be the best estimate of reliability for subgroups, overestimating reliability for some and underestimating reliability for others. Despite all these caveats, practice effects, as long as they are relatively systematic and accurately assessed, do not necessarily make a test unusable for clinical practice. Ideally, change scores can be evaluated against a cumulative frequency distribution of test–retest difference scores to determine how frequently a particular test–retest difference occurs in the normative sample (see Brooks et al., 2009). Practically speaking, for most available tests, the *average* difference score will be the only information available on expected practice effects in healthy people.

Further complicating this situation is the fact that most stability coefficients and practice effects provided in test manuals are based on a single sample of healthy adults retested over a relatively brief interval. This contrasts with the typical clinical scenario of a patient from a specific clinical group tested over longer time intervals.

As noted above, test–retest reliability should not be considered an immutable psychometric property of a test, and this is also true of practice effects. Research is needed on the psychometric properties of tests in clinical subjects who are tested over clinically relevant retest intervals.

Consider the following clinical situation as an example. A 34-year-old man who sustained a moderate traumatic brain injury is assessed with the WMS-III at 1-year post-injury and then again 1 year later. In the test manual, the average practice effect for the WMS-III Logical Memory-I subtest in 16–54 year olds tested between 2 and 12 weeks apart is 1.9 scaled score points (Psychological Corporation, 2002). If this patient does not show a 1.9 point increase in scores, is this because there was a longer time interval between baseline and retest compared to the normative sample, or was it because the patient had difficulty remembering information and thus did not benefit from re-exposure to the same test items because of his brain injury? These are questions that are not currently well answered by the available data on practice effects for the majority of neuropsychological tests.

It is also essential to note that the actual nature of the test may change with exposure. For instance, tests that rely on a "novelty effect" and/or require deduction of a strategy or problem solving (e.g., Wisconsin Card Sorting Test, Heaton et al., 1993; Tower of London, Culbertson & Zillmer, 2005) may not be performed in the same way once the examinee has prior familiarity with the testing paradigm. Practice effects and other effects of prior exposure may plateau after several exposures, and are one reason for including a minimum of test exposures when designing research involving repeated administration of cognitive or psychological tests. Conversely, other tests may simply not be amenable to be administered multiple times in the same patient.

Lastly, it must be kept in mind that factors other than prior exposure may affect test–retest reliability. Variability in scores on the same measure over time can be related to situational variables such as examinee state, examiner state, examiner identity (same vs different at retest) or environmental conditions. With all the different sources of error that can potentially confound measurement at retest, it is quite remarkable that several tests have strong test–retest reliability coefficients.

Validity in Neuropsychology

Test validity may be defined at its most basic level as *the degree to which a test actually measures what it is intended to measure*. Consistent with the construct of reliability, an important point to be made here is that a test cannot be said to have one single level of validity. Rather, it can be said to possess various types and levels of validity across a spectrum of usage and populations. That is, *validity is not a property of a test*, but rather, *validity is a property of the meaning attached to a test score in the specific context of test usage* (c.f., Franzen, 1989, 2000). This is a key concept: like reliability, validity relates to test *scores*, not tests (Urbina, 2004). As a result, there can be unique factors that can affect validity at the level of individual assessment, such as deviations from standard administration, unusual testing environments and variable or poor examinee cooperation.

Working knowledge of validity models and the validity characteristics of test scores are a central requirement for responsible and competent test use. From a practical perspective, a working knowledge of validity allows clinicians to choose which tests are appropriate for different uses. For instance, some test scores fail to reach standards for clinical diagnostic purposes of individual patients, but would be perfectly appropriate for research using group data.

Validity Models

Since Cronbach and Meehl (1955), various models of validity have been proposed. The most frequently encountered is the traditional tripartite model (see Fig. 31.6), whereby validity is divided into three core components: content-related, criterion-related and construct validity (e.g., Anastasi & Urbina, 1997; Mitrushina et al., 2005; Nunnally & Bernstein, 1994; Sattler, 2001). Other validity subtypes, including convergent, divergent, predictive, treatment, clinical and face validity are subsumed within these three domains. For example, convergent and divergent validity are most often treated as subsets of construct validity (Sattler, 2001), and concurrent and predictive validity as subsets of criterion-validity (e.g., Mitrushina et al., 2005). Concurrent and predictive validity differ in terms of a temporal gradient. Concurrent validity is relevant for tests used to identify existing diagnoses or conditions, whereas predictive validity applies when determining whether a test predicts future outcomes (Urbina, 2004).

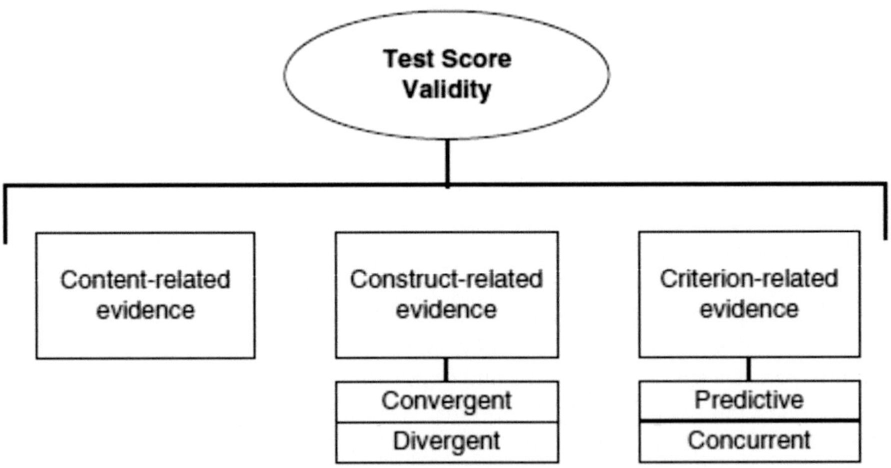

Fig. 31.6 Tripartite model of different types of *evidence* for determining validity of a test score

Although face validity is less studied, the extent to which examinees believe a test measures what it appears to measure can affect motivation, self-disclosure and effort; consequently, face validity can be seen as a moderator variable affecting concurrent and predictive validity that can be operationalized and measured (Bornstein, 1996; Nevo, 1985). Face validity matters because it encourages rapport between examiner and examinee, as well as openness and acceptance about test results and their implications (Urbina, 2004).

Again, all these labels for distinct categories of validity are ways of providing different types of validity *evidence for test scores*, not different types of validity per se. Lastly, validity is a matter of degree rather than an all-or-none property. Therefore, validity is never actually finalized because test scores must be continually re-evaluated as populations and testing contexts change over time (Nunnally & Bernstein, 1994).

Key Points: Validity

- Validity is not an "all-or-none" property.
- Validity is not a property of tests; it is a property of the meaning attached to a test score in the specific context of test usage.
- There are three broad categories of validity evidence to consider (tripartite model): Content-Related; Construct-Related; and Criterion-Related, but many different ways of determining the validity of test scores.
- Determining validity of a test score is an ongoing process based on information gathered in both healthy individuals and clinical populations.

How to Evaluate the Validity of a Test

There are different kinds and degrees of validity attached to different neuropsychological test scores, and there are numerous features that neuropsychologists can look for when evaluating a test and reviewing test manuals. Not all will have sufficient evidence to satisfy all aspects of validity, but clinicians should have a sufficiently broad knowledge of neuropsychological measures to be able to select one test over another (and one score over another within the same test), based on the quality of the validation evidence available.

Tables 31.6, 31.7, 31.8 present sources of evidence and techniques for critically evaluating the validity of neuropsychological test scores, abstracted from key sources such as Urbina (2004), the American Educational Research Association, American Psychological Association and National Council on Measurement in Education (1999), Messick (1996) and Yun and Ulrich (2002). Note that there is overlap between the sources of evidence presented in Tables 31.6, 31.7, 31.8. For example, correlations between a specific IQ score and another IQ score can simultaneously provide construct-related and criterion-related evidence of validity.

Table 31.6 Questions to ask for evaluating *content-related evidence for validity*

• Is the test based on a theoretical model?
• Is there a literature review with supporting evidence?
• Has the construct being measured been well defined?
• Has the operationalization of the construct (i.e., the translation of theory into test items) been done carefully (e.g., systematic review of the domain from which items are to be sampled)?
• Does the test have a large enough sample of items to be representative of the domain measured?
• Do the items have sufficient range of difficulty for the target population?
• Were items generated with care, using experts in the field or items from previously validated scales?
• Was the final item pool evaluated by experts in the field for accuracy and relevance?
• Will examinees think the test seems valid at face value?

Table 31.7 Questions to ask for evaluating *construct-related evidence for validity*

• Were hypotheses generated to measure the construct?
• Is the construct reliably measured as demonstrated by high reliability coefficients?
• Does it correlate highly with other test scores measuring the same construct?
• Does it have low correlations with test scores measuring different constructs?
• Do factor analytic studies support the construct measured by the test score as it is operationalized in the test?
• Are factor analytic and correlational findings consistent with the theoretical background for the construct measured?

Table 31.8 Questions to ask for evaluating the *criterion-related evidence for validity*

• Is the test score sensitive to expected developmental, demographic or other differences in the sample?
• Do group difference studies support the test score?
• Is the test score sensitive to treatment effects (e.g., responsiveness)?
• Do classification accuracy statistics (e.g., positive and negative predictive power) support the use of the test score?
• Are there meta-analytic studies on the test score's usage in the population of interest?

Content-Related Evidence for Validity

Content-related evidence for validity provides information on whether the test items actually measure the construct they are intended to measure. Content-based sources of information for determining this might include whether test items were generated based on a theoretical model for the construct in question and whether that theoretical model reflects current empirical research on the construct. Additionally, it is important to determine whether the construct has been adequately operationalized in the test's items, and whether the test developers adequately defined the specific construct to be measured by the test. One way in which this is accomplished occurs when a test developer conducts a systematic review of the literature before generating test items, and by employing experts in the field to generate items and/or review item content, ideally after consensus. The goal is to refine the item pool while also balancing the need for a sufficiently broad set of items capable of capturing a range of function across the target group, and retaining good face validity.

Table 31.6 lists some basic questions to aid in determining whether a test has sufficient evidence for content-related validity. Few tests will satisfy each condition in Table 31.6, but a good test should have sufficient evidence satisfying a number of points in the table.

Construct-Related Evidence for Validity

Construct-related evidence for validity overlaps with content-related evidence for validity, as both pertain to what is being measured by the test itself (as opposed to what the test might predict, or have utility for clinically). Table 31.7 shows specific examples of ways in which the construct validity evidence for a test can be evaluated. As with content-related evidence, the presence of a theoretical model or theoretical background supported by empirical evidence is important in test item content, test structure and test format, but equally important is whether that construct was reliably measured. Examination of reliability evidence therefore becomes crucial for determining construct validity. At the same time, a test that measures a specific construct well should overlap with other tests measuring a similar construct, and show some differentiation in terms of tests measuring different constructs. Methods such as the multitrait/multimethod matrix, factor analysis and structural equation modeling are ways in which the construct validity of tests is evaluated. These methods answer specific questions such as, is there sufficient empirical evidence for grouping test items hierarchically into specific levels, such as subscales, index scores for specific domains and global composites?

One common method for presenting validity evidence is through intercorrelations among tests that are believed to measure similar and dissimilar constructs. Realistically, many tests do not yield clear-cut correlation matrices with high correlations to similar tests and low correlations to dissimilar tests. Whenever large numbers of correlations among measures are presented, there tends to be expected and unexpected relationships between variables, and dissociable relations between tests may not occur in a clear-cut manner. Some of the overlapping variance to consider may be due to global factors such as underlying innate intelligence, or to the fact that most neuropsychological tests require multiple basic abilities.

Criterion-Related Evidence for Validity

Content and construct validity are aimed at increasing our understanding of the psychological construct being measured and how a person's performance fits within that frame of reference. A further question asks "what are the criteria that are related to the test score?". In its most basic sense, criterion-related evidence for validity refers to the sensitivity and utility of the test (see Table 31.8). For clinical neuropsychologists, this is the most important aspect of validity. The clinical sensitivity of tests can be assessed by examining whether scores follow an expected developmental curve across age, or show expected gender differences, or are sensitive to expected demographic differences across groups with known differences. Also crucial is whether the test is capable of detecting changes in performance after treatment or intervention (responsiveness), and whether it is sensitive to the expected natural course of neurological, medical or psychiatric conditions (e.g., fluctuating, declining or stable). Classification accuracy statistics relating to test scores are also used to determine the validity of test scores. Although a detailed discussion is beyond the scope of this chapter, this relates to the adequacy of statistics such as positive and negative predictive power in predicting the presence or absence of specific diagnoses or conditions based on test scores. Ideally, well-validated test scores have also been tested through meta-analytic studies to determine effect sizes describing the sensitivity of different neuropsychological tests in different contexts and with different groups.

Conclusions

The goal of this chapter was to help clinicians and researchers in assessing the reliability and validity of tests for clinical use. We discussed different types of reliability, factors that affect reliability and limits to reliability. Reliability refers to the consistency of measurement of a given score. It is not an "all-or-none" property of a test. Rather, reliability refers to test scores, determined through evaluation of different kinds of reliability evidence (e.g., internal, test–retest, alternate form and interrater). Determining the reliability of a test score is an ongoing process based on information gathered in both healthy individuals and clinical populations.

Similarly, validity is not an "all-or-none" property of a test. Validity is a property of the meaning attached to a test score in the specific context of test usage. That is, test scores have varying degrees of validity, for specific uses, with specific populations. There are three broad categories of validity evidence to consider (tripartite model): content-related, construct-related and criterion-related. Within these broad categories, there are many ways of estimating the validity of test scores. Similar to reliability, determining the validity of a test score is an ongoing process based on information gathered in both healthy individuals and clinical populations.

The selection of neuropsychological measures requires a careful and thoughtful process that involves sifting through multiple sources of psychometric evidence. The process depends heavily on test publishers' ability to include comprehensive information in test manuals that clinicians need for selecting and administering tests, but it is equally critical for clinicians to review test manuals carefully and scrutinize the information that is being presented. In the end, evaluating the reliability and validity of neuropsychological tests is a gradual process involving numerous studies over extended periods of time. Perhaps one of the most important components of reliability and validity is the *clinical inferences derived from tests* (see Franzen, 1989, 2000; Strauss et al., 2006). Our field has come a long way but there is still much progress to make in this domain.

References

American Educational Research Association, American Psychological Association, & National Council on Measurement in Education. (1999). *Standards for educational and psychological testing*. Washington, DC: American Psychological Association.

Anastasi, A., & Urbina, S. (1997). *Psychological testing* (7th ed.). Prentice-Hall.

Bland, J. M., & Altman, D. G. (1986). Statistical methods for assessing agreement between two methods of clinical measurement. *Lancet, i*, 307–310.

Bornstein, R. F. (1996). Face validity in psychological assessment: Implications for a unified model of validity. *American Psychologist, 51*(9), 983–984.

Brooks, B. L., Iverson, G. L., & White, T. (2009). *Advanced interpretation of the Neuropsychological Assessment Battery (NAB) with older adults: Base rate analyses, discrepancy scores, and interpreting change*. Unpublished manuscript.

Cicchetti, D. V. (1994). Guidelines, criteria, and rules of thumb for evaluating normed and standardized assessment instruments in psychology. *Psychological Assessment, 6*(4), 284–290.

Cicchetti, D. V., & Sparrow, S. S. (1981). Developing criteria for establishing interrater reliability of specific items: Applications to assessment of adaptive behavior. *American Journal of Mental Deficiency, 86*, 127–137.

Cronbach, L. J., & Meehl, P. E. (1955). Construct validity in psychological tests. *Psychological Bulletin, 52*(4), 281–302.

Culbertson, W. C., & Zillmer, E. A. (2005). *Tower of London – Drexel University* (2nd ed.). MHS.

Delis, D. C., Kaplan, E., & Kramer, J. H. (2001). *Delis Kaplan executive function system technical manual*. The Psychological Corporation.

Fastenau, P. S., Bennett, J. M., & Denburg, N. L. (1996). Application of psychometric standards to scoring system evaluation: Is "new" necessarily "improved"? *Journal of Clinical and Experimental Neuropsychology, 18*(3), 462–472.

Franzen, M. D. (1989). *Reliability and validity in neuropsychological assessment*. Plenum Press.

Franzen, M. D. (2000). *Reliability and validity in neurological assessment* (2nd ed.). Kluwer Academic/Plenum Press.

Heaton, R. K., Chelune, G. J., Talley, J. L., Kay, G. G., & Curtis, G. (1993). *Wisconsin card sorting task (WCST) manual, revised and expanded*. Psychological Assessment Resources.

Lineweaver, T. T., & Chelune, G. J. (2003). Use of the WAIS-III and WMS-III in the context of serial assessments: Interpreting reliable and meaningful change. In D. S. Tulsky, D. H. Saklofske, G. J. Chelune, R. K. Heaton, R. Ivnik, R. Bornstein, A. Prifitera, & M. F. Ledbetter (Eds.), *Clinical interpretation of the WAIS-III and WMS-III* (pp. 303–337). Academic.

McGrew, K. S., & Woodcock, R. W. (2001). *Woodcock-Johnson III technical manual*. Riverside Publishing.
Messick, S. (1996). Validity of psychological assessment: Validation of inferences from persons' responses and performances as scientific inquiry into score meaning. *American Psychologist, 50*(9), 741–749.
Mitrushina, M. N., Boone, K. B., Razani, J., & D'Elia, L. F. (2005). *Handbook of normative data for neuropsychological assessment* (2nd ed.). Oxford University Press.
Nevo, B. (1985). Face validity revisited. *Journal of Educational Measurement, 22*, 287–293.
Nunnally, J. C., & Bernstein, I. H. (1994). *Psychometric theory* (3rd ed.). McGraw-Hill.
Psychological Corporation. (2002). *WAIS-III/WMS-III technical manual*. Psychological Corporation.
Rapport, L. J., Brines, D. B., & Axelrod, B. N. (1997). Full scale IQ as a mediator of practice effects: The rich get richer. *The Clinical Neuropsychologist, 11*(4), 375–380.
Reynolds, C. R. (2002). *Comprehensive trail making test*. PRO-ED.
Ruff, R. M., & Hibbard, K. M. (2003). *Ruff neurobehavioral inventory*. Psychological Assessment Resources, Inc.
Sattler, J. M. (2001). *Assessment of children: Cognitive applications* (4th ed.). Jerome M. Sattler Publisher, Inc.
Sjögren, P., Thomsen, A., & Olsen, A. (2000). Impaired neuropsychological performance in chronic nonmalignant pain patients receiving long-term oral opioid therapy. *Journal of Pain and Symptom Management, 19*(2), 100–108.
Stern, R. A., & White, T. (2003). *Neuropsychological assessment battery (NAB)*. Psychological Assessment Resources.
Strauss, E., Sherman, E. M. S., & Spreen, O. (2006). *A compendium of neuropsychological tests* (3rd ed.). Oxford University Press.
Urbina, S. (2004). *Essentials of psychological testing*. Wiley.
Wechsler, D. (2004). *Wechsler intelligence scale for children* (Integrated technical and interpretive manual 4th ed.). San Antonio: The Psychological Corporation.
Wechsler, D., Coalson, D. L., & Raiford, S. E. (2008). *Wechsler adult intelligence scale* (Technical and interpretive manual 4th ed.). San Antonio: NCS Pearson, Inc.
Wechsler, D., Holdnack, J. A., & Drozdick, L. W. (2009). *Wechsler memory scale* (Technical and interpretive manual 4th ed.). San Antonio: NCS Pearson, Inc.
White, T., & Stern, R. A. (2003). *Neuropsychological assessment battery (NAB): Psychometric and technical manual*. Psychological Assessment Resources.
Yun, J., & Ulrich, D. A. (2002). Estimating measurement validity: A tutorial. *Adapted Physical Activity Quarterly, 19*, 32–47.

Chapter 32
Improving Accuracy for Identifying Cognitive Impairment

Grant L. Iverson and Brian L. Brooks

Deficit measurement is the essential task of neuropsychology. The risk, of course, is that we can be so focused on deficit measurement—and so focused on describing the nature and severity of a person's cognitive impairment—that we can underappreciate human diversity and overattribute low or unexpected test scores to brain injury or disease. The North American psychometric tradition has long since attempted to minimize possible misattribution of low test scores through a reliance on the normal curve. However, neuropsychologists know that overly rigid reliance on the normal curve without consideration for normal variability or appreciation for factors that can affect test performance (i.e. demographics, emotional conditions, external incentives, etc.)can result in false positive and false negative attributions of cognitive test performance. Moreover, the normal curve relates to a single test score in relation to a theoretical normal population. Neuropsychologists should never rely on single tests. Instead, we administer numerous tests and we interpret performance in combination, not in isolation. Thus, the principles of normative test score interpretation, applied to *single* test scores, are inherently limited when interpreting performance across a *battery* of tests.

G. L. Iverson (✉)
Department of Physical Medicine and Rehabilitation, Harvard Medical School, Boston, MA, USA

Department of Physical Medicine and Rehabilitation, Spaulding Rehabilitation Hospital, Boston, MA, USA

Schoen Adams Research Institute at Spaulding Rehabilitation, Boston, MA, USA

Mass General for Children Sports Concussion Program, Boston, MA, USA
e-mail: GIverson@mgh.harvard.edu

B. L. Brooks
Alberta Children's Hospital, University of Calgary, Calgary, AB, Canada
e-mail: Brian.brooks@albertahealthservices.ca

M. R. Schoenberg, J. G. Scott (eds.), *The Little Black Book of Neuropsychology*,
https://doi.org/10.1007/978-3-032-07777-6_32

Cognitive impairment can arise from a single cause or it can have a multifactorial etiology. There are a large number of medical, psychiatric and neurological diseases, disorders and conditions that can have an adverse effect on cognition. Clearly, the accurate identification and quantification of cognitive impairment is important in clinical practice, research and in clinical trials. However, comprehensive, psychometrically sophisticated guidelines for identifying and quantifying cognitive impairment across a battery of tests are not clearly delineated in the neuropsychological literature and must clearly take into consideration examinee factors affecting test performance as well as the psychometric properties of each individual test (see previous chapter by Sherman). Considerable psychometric work has been done regarding how to interpret combinations of scores derived from these batteries.

The purpose of this chapter is to provide clinicians with psychometrically sophisticated information that is designed to improve their accuracy for identifying cognitive problems in daily practice. This chapter begins by presenting information on current definitions of cognitive impairment (*Conceptualizing Cognitive Impairment*). In the second section, we describe some of the various classification systems for conceptualizing cognitive impairment (*Classifying Cognitive Impairment*). Fundamental psychometric principles, derived from analyses on co-normed batteries of tests, are illustrated in the third section (*Evaluating Cognitive Impairment: Five Psychometric Principles to Consider*). In the final section, we present new psychometric criteria for identifying cognitive impairment across a battery of neuropsychological measures that adhere to the five psychometric rules (*Identifying Cognitive Impairment: New Psychometric Criteria for Cognitive Disorder NOS*).

Key Points and Chapter Summary

- Cognitive diminishment or impairment can result from a variety of medical, psychiatric and/or neurological conditions.
- There are very few empirically established psychometrically based guidelines for what constitutes mild impairment in cognition.
- Failing to consider fundamental psychometric principles applied to interpreting multiple test scores can readily result in false positive or false negative diagnoses of cognitive impairment.
- Five psychometric principles for interpreting scores: (1) Low scores are relatively common across all test batteries; (2) Low scores depend on where you set your cutoff score; (3) Low scores vary by number of tests administered; (4) Low scores vary by demographic characteristics of the examinee; and (5) Low scores vary by level of intelligence.

Conceptualizing Cognitive Impairment

There is no universally agreed-upon definitive *definition* of cognitive impairment. Establishing a level of cognitive impairment requires multiple sources of convergent information, including input from family members, review of medical records, review of collateral records (e.g., school or employment), interviews with the patient, observations of the patient's behavior, psychological test results and neuropsychological test results. Iverson and colleagues have suggested five categories of cognitive impairment that illustrate a continuum of severity (Iverson et al., 2008a, 2008b). These categories are presented below in Fig. 32.1. These categories reflect

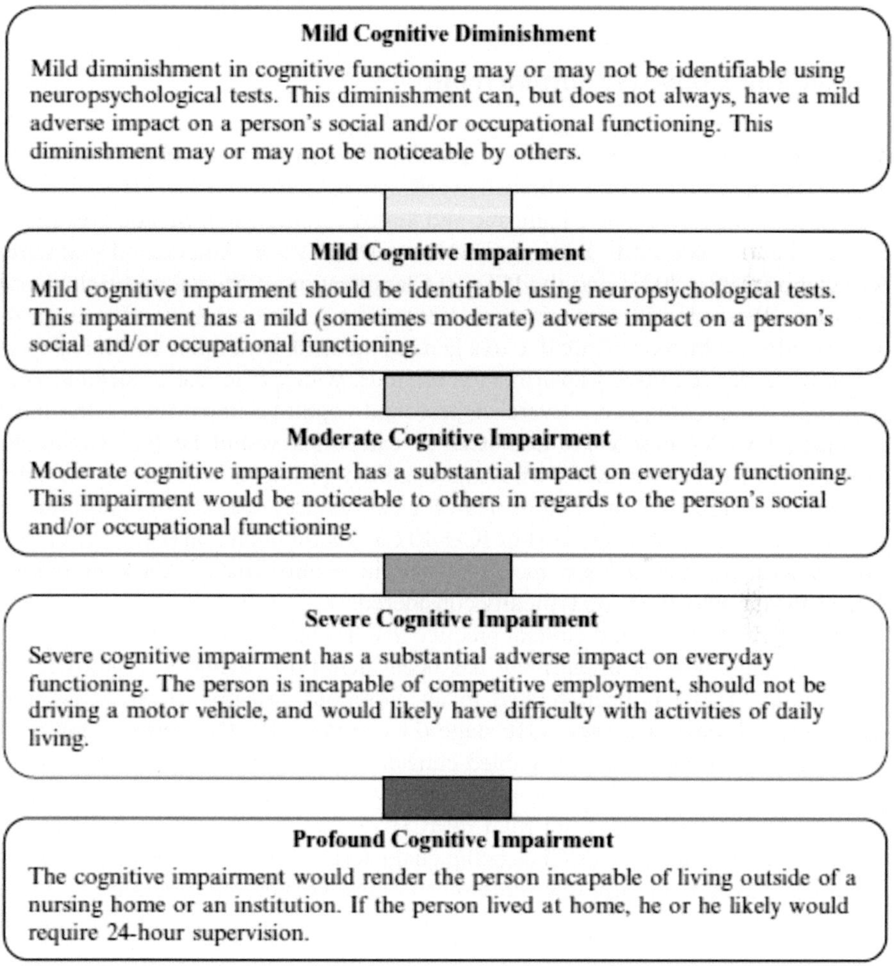

Fig. 32.1 Suggested categories of cognitive impairment along a severity continuum

levels of cognitive impairment in a face valid manner. However, the specific criteria for each level have not been codified or agreed upon.

Neuropsychology, unfortunately, remains far from having uniform psychometric criteria for interpreting the severity of cognitive impairment using neurocognitive tests, nor do we have specific behavioral criteria for quantifying impairment or diminishment in everyday functioning. Research continues to be needed to develop and empirically test criteria for cognitive impairment and impairment in social or occupational functioning. For now, the diagnosis of cognitive impairment, and level of cognitive impairment, is primarily based upon clinical judgment which includes psychometric test performance as well as all other sources of information available to the clinician.

Classifying Cognitive Impairment

In addition to a lack of consensus on defining cognitive impairment, there are no widely accepted, empirically validated *psychometric/statistical criteria* for identifying cognitive disorders. The Diagnostic and Statistical Manual of Mental Disorders, Fourth Edition and Fifth Edition (DSM-IV; DSM-V-TR American Psychiatric Association, 1994, 2023) and the ICD-10 Classification of Mental and Behavioral Disorders (World Health Organization, 1992) offer several categories for diagnosing cognitive problems that are due to a general medical conditions. In clinical situations when the cognitive impairment is obvious, widespread and associated with poor daily functioning (i.e., severe or profound cognitive impairment), the most relevant DSM-IV/DSM-V-TR and ICD-10 categories would be the dementias. However, in clinical situations when the cognitive problems and impact on daily functioning following a medical or neurological disease, disorder or condition are less serious and do not meet DSM or ICD-10 criteria for dementia (i.e., mild cognitive impairment, and perhaps moderate cognitive impairment), then alternative diagnostic classifications are typically considered.

One area of research and clinical practice that has had numerous suggestions for how to define cognitive impairment has been identifying memory impairment in older adults. This has been related to an enormous research effort to identify Alzheimer's disease at a very early stage (i.e., prodromal). One term (along with accompanying criteria) that has gained considerable, but not universal, popularity with clinicians and researchers is mild cognitive impairment (MCI). In particular, this typically refers to amnestic MCI (aMCI).[1] Petersen and colleagues (Petersen et al., 1994, 1999) defined aMCI as being characterized by (1) a subjective memory complaint, (2) an unusually low score on an objective memory measure (based on age only or age and education adjusted normative data), (3) normal general

[1] MCI has been divided into several classifications depending on the type of cognitive impairment. Amnestic MCI (aMCI) is the most commonly studied subtype and refers to impairment with memory.

cognitive functioning, (4) normal activities of daily living and (5) not meeting criteria for dementia. More recent versions of the criteria for aMCI have de-emphasized or dropped the need for a subjective memory complaint. The psychometric criterion for an unusually low score has generally been set at 1.5 SDs below the normative mean for healthy older adults. Of course, this cutoff remains somewhat arbitrary and often researchers might select a psychometric criterion for impairment that ranges anywhere from 1 to 2 SDs below the mean. Even the authors of the recent consensus-based research criteria for probable Alzheimer's disease (Dubois et al., 2007) "have not defined a magnitude of deficit or the comparative norms that should be utilized [for identifying memory impairment]" (p. 742).

The clinical implications for assessing memory functioning in older adults without a solid psychometric foundation are striking. If one assumes that the cutoff score for memory impairment is the fifth percentile, then one accepts a priori that there will be a 5% false positive rate (i.e., 5% of healthy older adults would be falsely diagnosed with MCI). However, that false positive rate applies to a single test score in relation to a theoretical population of healthy older adults. Because a single test score is rarely relied upon, this theoretical false positive rate is not accurate. Clinicians typically administer several tests, which yield multiple test scores. Thus, the false positive rate for having *at least one* low score will be considerably greater than 5%. Moreover, the number of low scores varies by level of intelligence. Those older adults with below average intelligence will have more low scores than those with above average intelligence (Brooks et al., 2007, 2008). These points are illustrated in Fig. 32.2. Notice that, for healthy older adults of average intelligence, 22–38% will have one or more scores ≤fifth percentile across a battery of memory tests. As seen in this figure, the number of low ("abnormal") memory scores in healthy older adults varies considerably by level of intelligence. This will be addressed in more detail later in this chapter.

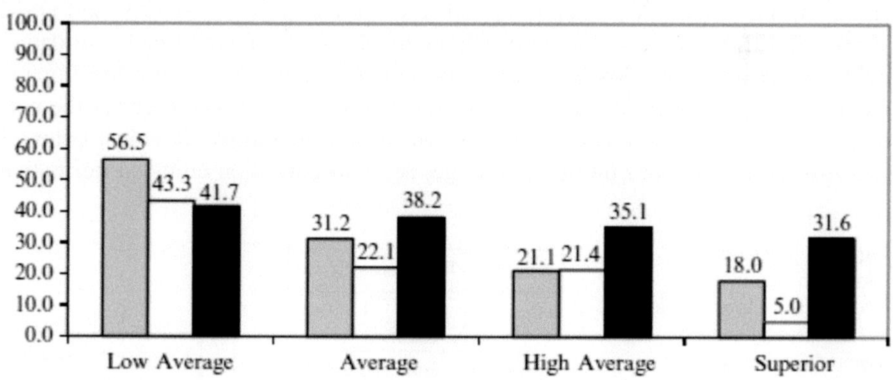

Fig. 32.2 Percent healthy older adults with one or more low memory scores according to the MCI criterion for memory impairment (≤fifth percentile). Note: The NAB memory module consists of four tests that yield 10 demographically adjusted scores. The WMS-III battery consists of four tests that yield 8 age-adjusted (WMS-III age) or demographically adjusted (WMS-III demo) scores

Key Points: Classifying Cognitive Impairment

- There are no universally accepted psychometrically established criteria for cognitive impairment
- Diagnoses using DSM-IV-TR/DSM V-TR or ICD-10 do not contain information about "how to" identify cognitive impairment
- MCI provides a criterion for memory impairment but is subject to false positives when several memory tests are administered and interpreted independently

DSM-IV Cognitive Disorder NOS (Mild Neurocognitive Disorder)

Cognitive disorder NOS (CD-NOS) and Unspecified Neurocognitive disorder (UND) are DSM-IV and DSM-V-TR diagnosis that can be applied to people who have acquired cognitive impairments from an injury, illness or disease. Unfortunately, there are no specific empirically derived, evidence-based criteria for this disorder. CD-NOS/UND can be broken down into two categories, *mild neurocognitive disorder* and *postconcussional disorder*. Our focus in this chapter is on mild neurocognitive disorder. To identify mild neurocognitive disorder, there must be impairment in *at least two domains*, which can include attention or speed of information processing, language, learning and memory, perceptual-motor abilities and/or executive functioning (see Fig. 32.3). These cognitive impairments must be due to a neurological or general medical condition, be considered abnormal or a decline from previous functioning and cause marked psychological distress or impairment in social, occupational or other areas of functioning.

Although the criteria for cognitive disorder NOS/UND have been available to clinicians and researchers since the publication of the DSM-IV in 1994 and DSM V-TR in 2022, there has yet to be psychometrically derived, empirically validated, published criteria, with known sensitivity and specificity, for identifying impairment in these five cognitive domains. Mild Cognitive Impairment requires the person to have *one or more* test scores, in *two or more* cognitive domains, below *1 standard deviation* from the mean on age, sex and education adjusted normative

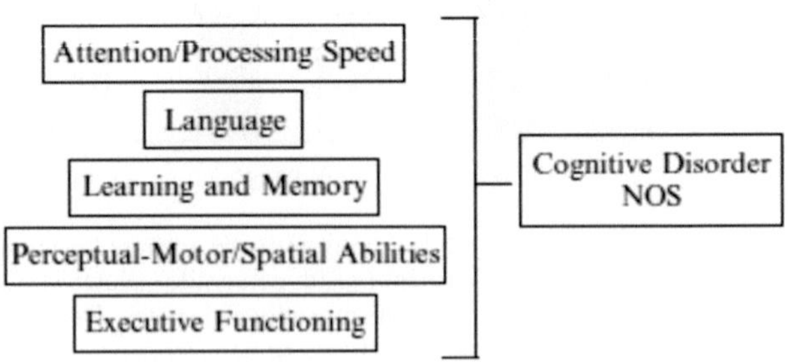

Fig. 32.3 Domains relating to cognitive disorder NOS. Impairment in 2 or more domains is required for diagnosis

data. The seven domains of functioning include: attention/working memory; speed of information processing; verbal/language; memory (learning; recall); abstraction/executive; sensory-perceptual; and motor skills (Antinori et al., 2007).

Clinicians and researchers should note that specific methodological issues can adversely affect diagnostic accuracy of these new consensus-based criteria. We have conducted extensive psychometric analyses on two large databases of healthy adults and found that (1) the more tests that are given, the more likely a person is to have one or more scores fall below 1 SD from the mean, (2) the prevalence of low scores varies by demographics and (3) the prevalence of low scores varies by level of intelligence (see data below). The criteria do not establish the number of tests to be administered and require that a person's performance be considered in regard to his or her age, education and sex (but not intelligence). Thus, diagnostic accuracy can vary based on the number of tests a clinician or researcher chooses to administer. Regarding intelligence, this will result in a substantial number of *false positives* for people with below average intelligence and an increased rate of *false negatives* for people with above average intelligence. The next section elaborates on these fundamental psychometric principles.

Evaluating Cognitive Impairment: Five Psychometric Principles to Consider

Neuropsychologists typically administer numerous tests that can yield dozens of scores. As part of the interpretive procedure, the neuropsychologist must use his or her clinical judgment to consider all of the test scores, medical history, demographics and other information available to the clinician simultaneously and make sense of the patient's performance. Although a low score might be suggestive of an acquired impairment, it is important to consider that having inter-subtest variability and obtaining a low score might be "normal" for that person. Obtaining low scores might be attributable to measurement error (broadly defined), normative sample characteristics (i.e., having healthy people, rather than clinical groups, at the lower end of the distribution), longstanding weaknesses in certain areas, fluctuations in motivation and effort, psychological interference and other situational factors such as inattentiveness, fatigue or minor illness (Binder et al., 2009).

This section introduces and discusses five psychometric principles to consider when evaluating a person for cognitive impairment. Although an understanding of these psychometric principles is invaluable for any clinician, it is important for clinicians to utilize these principles when simultaneously interpreting test scores across a battery of neuropsychological tests.

Principle 1: Low Scores Are Common Across All Test Batteries

Any battery of tests, whether fixed or flexible, will have a certain number of low scores when administered to healthy people (Axelrod & Wall, 2007; Binder et al., 2009; Brooks et al., 2007, 2008; Crawford et al., 2007; Heaton et al., 1991, 2004; Ingraham & Aiken, 1996; Iverson et al., 2008b, 2008c; Palmer et al., 1998; Schretlen et al., 2008). This is because there is a substantial amount of intraindividual variability in the cognitive abilities of healthy people. We use test batteries common to neuropsychology for illustrative purposes; however, this phenomenon is common in all testing scenarios where parametric statistics are used to evaluate performance or a factor that exists on a continuum and is assumed to be distributed in an approximate bell-shaped normal curve with scores varying within a normal population. Figures 32.4 and 32.5 illustrate the first principle that low scores are common across all test batteries. These figures present the prevalence of low scores, using one standard deviation (SD) and ≤fifth percentile as the cutoff scores, in healthy adults on the Neuropsychological Assessment Battery (NAB; Stern & White, 2003), the Expanded Halstead-Reitan Neuropsychological Battery (E-HRNB; Heaton et al., 2004) and the combination of the Wechsler Adult Intelligence Scale—III (WAIS-III; Wechsler, 1997a) and Wechsler Memory Scale—III (WMS-III; Wechsler, 1997b). As seen in Fig. 32.4, the majority of healthy adults have two or more scores

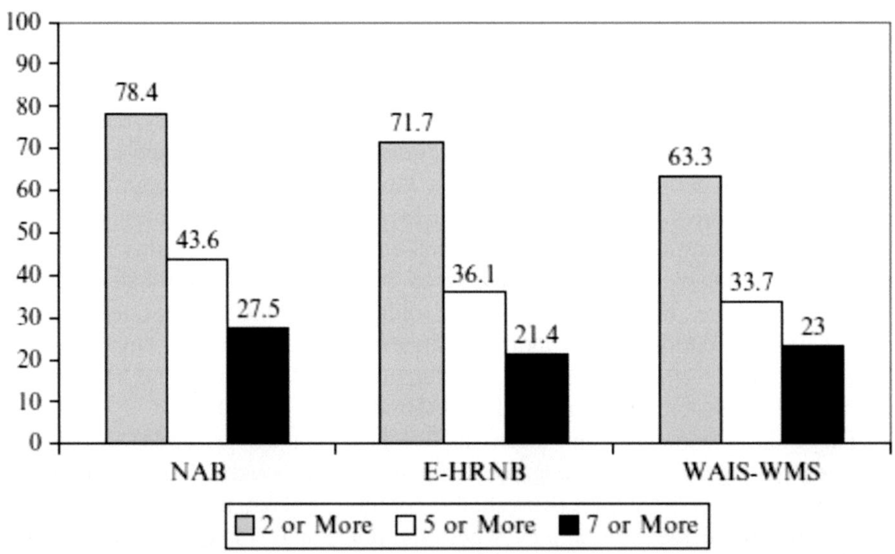

Fig. 32.4 Base rates of low scores across different test batteries: Cutoff <1 SD. *SD* standard deviation, *NAB* Neuropsychological Assessment Battery; *E-HRNB* Expanded Halstead-Reitan Neuropsychological Battery, *WAIS-WMS* Wechsler Adult Intelligence Scale—III and Wechsler Memory Scale—III. The number of scores considered were as follows: NAB = 36, E-HRNB = 25, WAIS-WMS = 20. Bars represent percent of healthy adults from standardization samples who had (1) 2 or more, (2) 5 or more or (3) 7 or more scores below 1SD (i.e., $T < 40$ or SS < 7)

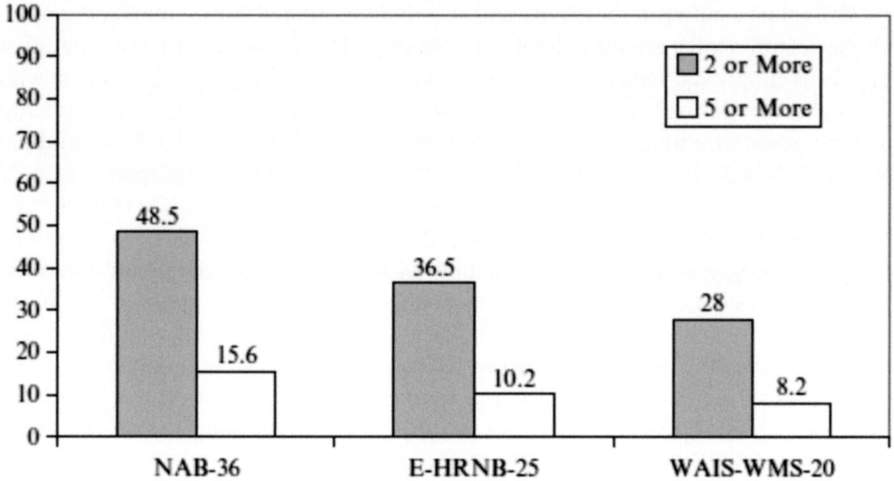

Fig. 32.5 Base rates of low scores across batteries with different numbers of scores being interpreted: Cutoff ≤fifth percentile. *SD* standard deviation. NAB-36 = all 36 scores from the full Neuropsychological Assessment Battery; E-HRNB-25 = 25 scores from the Expanded Halstead-Reitan Neuropsychological Battery; and WAIS-WMS-20 = all 20 primary scores from the Wechsler Adults Intelligence Scale—III and Wechsler Memory Scale—III. Bars represent percent of healthy adults from standardization samples who had (1) 2 or more or (2) 5 or more scores at or below fifth percentile (i.e., $T = 34$ or SS = 5)

below 1SD on all three batteries. Moreover, a substantial percentage have two or more scores ≤fifth percentile on all three batteries (Fig. 32.5).

Key Point: Evaluating cognitive impairment—Principle 1
- Low scores are relatively common in healthy individuals

Principle 2: Low Scores Depend on Where You Set Your Cutoff Score

There is no universal agreement on the definition of a low score. Some neuropsychologists have fixed and consistent definitions of low scores (e.g., 1 SD below the mean, fifth percentile, or 2 SDs below the mean), whereas other neuropsychologists might vary their definition based on the characteristics of the examinee. For example, for a highly educated person, or a person with a superior level of intelligence, the neuropsychologist might choose to interpret some average scores as "low" and some low average scores as "mildly impaired." Both approaches have strengths and weaknesses, psychometrically. The key is to carefully define the psychometric strengths and limitations of the specific approach taken for interpreting neuropsychological tests.

The balance between sensitivity and specificity is related to the cutoff score used. Higher cutoff scores are more likely to correctly identify those who have cognitive problems (improved sensitivity), but they are also more likely to include those who do not have cognitive problems (reduced specificity). This is true when interpreting a single score or multiple scores from a battery. Using data from the NAB and the WAIS-III/WMS-III as examples, Figs. 32.6 and 32.7 illustrate the percentage of healthy people who obtain low scores below four cutoff scores: 1 SD (16th percentile), tenth percentile, fifth percentile and 2 SDs (second percentile). As the cutoff score gets progressively lower, the number of healthy people who would be incorrectly identified (i.e., specificity/false positives) as having cognitive problems declines. For example, having five or more low scores on the NAB would be found in 43.6% of healthy people when using 1SD as the cutoff score but only 5.2% when using 2SD as the cutoff score. Having five or more low scores on the WAIS-III/WMS-III would be found in 33.7% of healthy people when using 1SD as the cutoff score but only 1.9% when using 2SD as the cutoff score.

Key Point: Evaluating Cognitive Impairment—Principle 2

- Different cutoffs can be used to define a low score
- Cutoff scores represent a balance between sensitivity and specificity

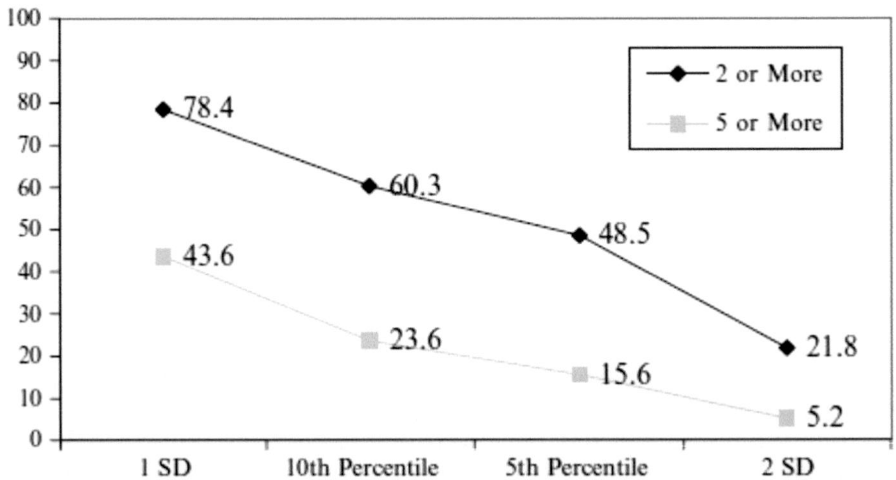

Fig. 32.6 Prevalence of low scores on the NAB across different cutoffs. *SD* standard deviation, *NAB* Neuropsychological Assessment Battery. The 36 primary *T* scores were considered. Each data point represents the percent of healthy adults from the NAB standardization sample who had (1) 2 or more or (2) 5 or more scores below 1 SD (i.e., $T < 40$), below the tenth percentile (i.e., $T < 37$), at or below the fifth percentile (i.e., $T = 34$) or below 2 SDs (i.e., $T < 30$)

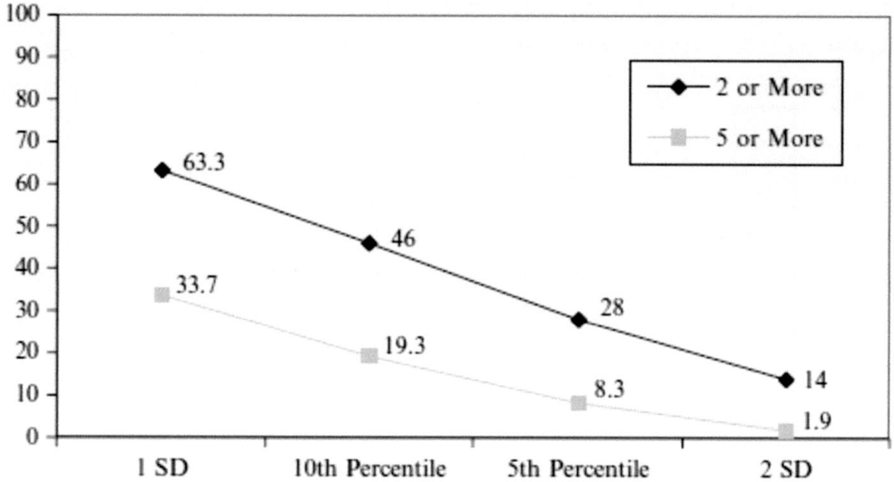

Fig. 32.7 Prevalence of low scores on the WAIS-III/WMS-III across different cutoffs. *SD* standard deviation. WAIS-WMS-20 = all 20 primary scores from the Wechsler Adults Intelligence Scale—III and Wechsler Memory Scale—III. Each data point represents the percent of healthy adults from the WAIS-III/WMS-III standardization sample who had (1) 2 or more or (2) 5 or more scores below 1 SD (i.e., SS < 7), below the tenth percentile (i.e., SS < 6), at or below the fifth percentile (i.e., SS < 5) or below 2 SDs (i.e., SS < 4)

Principle 3: Low Scores Depend on the Number of Tests Administered

Comprehensive neuropsychological evaluations often consist of numerous tests that yield several scores. As an example, the NAB is a 3-h battery that consists of 24 tests, which yield 36 primary scores, five index scores, a summary score and more than 50 secondary scores. As the number of tests administered and interpreted increases, the likelihood of having low scores also increases. Figures 32.8 and 32.9 illustrate this principle using four batteries of varying lengths (i.e., 36 scores from the NAB, 25 scores from the E-HRNB, 20 scores from the WAIS-III/WMS-III and 16 scores from an abbreviated version of the NAB). It should be noted that regardless of which cutoff score is used, the expected number of low scores increases with lengthier test batteries.

Key Point: Evaluating Cognitive Impairment—Principle 3

- The more tests that are administered, and scores interpreted, the more likely it is to find low scores in healthy adults

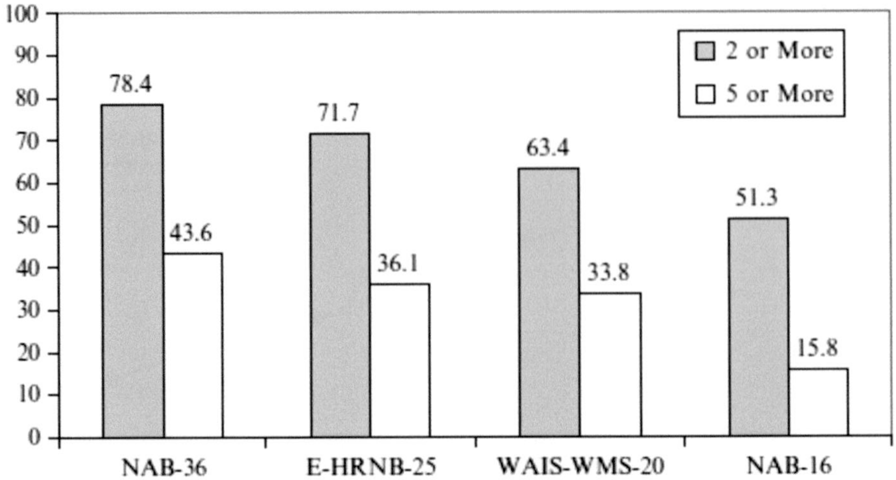

Fig. 32.8 Base rates of low scores across batteries with different numbers of scores being interpreted: Cutoff <1 SD. *SD* standard deviation. NAB-36 = all 36 scores from the full Neuropsychological Assessment Battery; E-HRNB-25 = 25 scores from the Expanded Halstead-Reitan Neuropsychological Battery; WAIS-WMS-20 = all 20 primary scores from the Wechsler Adults Intelligence Scale—III and Wechsler Memory Scale—III; NAB-16 = 16 primary scores from an abbreviated version of the Neuropsychological Assessment Battery. Bars represent percent of healthy adults from standardization samples who had (1) 2 or more or (2) 5 or more scores below 1 SD (i.e., $T < 40$ or $SS < 7$)

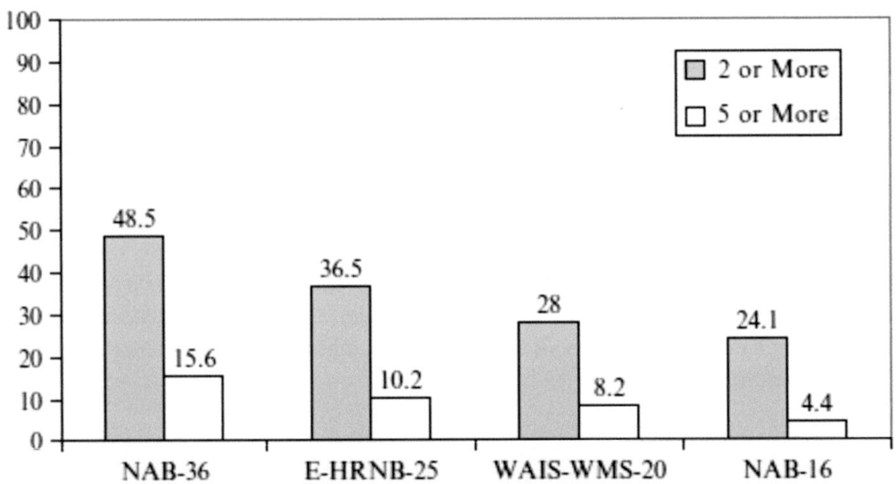

Fig. 32.9 Base rates of low scores across batteries with different numbers of scores being interpreted: Cutoff ≤fifth percentile. *SD* standard deviation. NAB-36 = all 36 scores from the full Neuropsychological Assessment Battery; E-HRNB-25 = 25 scores from the Expanded Halstead-Reitan Neuropsychological Battery; WAIS-WMS-20 = all 20 primary scores from the Wechsler Adults Intelligence Scale—III and Wechsler Memory Scale—III; NAB-16 = 16 primary scores from an abbreviated version of the Neuropsychological Assessment Battery. Bars represent percent of healthy adults from standardization samples who had (1) 2 or more or (2) 5 or more scores at or below fifth percentile (i.e., $T = 34$ or $SS = 5$)

Principle 4: Low Scores Vary by Demographic Characteristics of the Examinee

It is well established that many cognitive abilities vary by demographic characteristics. The impact of age on neuropsychological test performance is well appreciated. For example, performance on tests of memory and processing speed is lower in older adults versus younger adults. As seen in Fig. 32.10, delayed memory for stories (raw score performance) is fairly consistent between the ages of 20 and 55, but then declines in older adults. Thus, virtually all cognitive tests are normed by age.

For some tests, there are sex differences. The literature on sex differences suggests that women perform better on tasks of verbal learning and memory, verbal fluency and processing speed (Beatty et al., 2003; Donders et al., 2001; Herlitz et al., 1997; Norman et al., 2000). Motor dexterity has also been shown to be a strength for women compared to men (Schmidt et al., 2000). In contrast, men tend to perform better on motor speed (Schmidt et al., 2000), some visual-spatial and visual-constructional tasks (Beatty et al., 2003; Collaer & Nelson, 2002; Voyer et al., 1995) and arithmetic reasoning and computations (Geary et al., 2000). As a result of known differences in cognitive abilities, many normative scores for traditional, paper–pencil, neuropsychological measures (e.g., Wechsler Adult Intelligence Scale—III and Wechsler Memory Scale—III demographic norms, Neuropsychological Assessment Battery, Expanded Halstead-Reitan Neuropsychological Battery and California Verbal Learning Test-II) are corrected for gender.

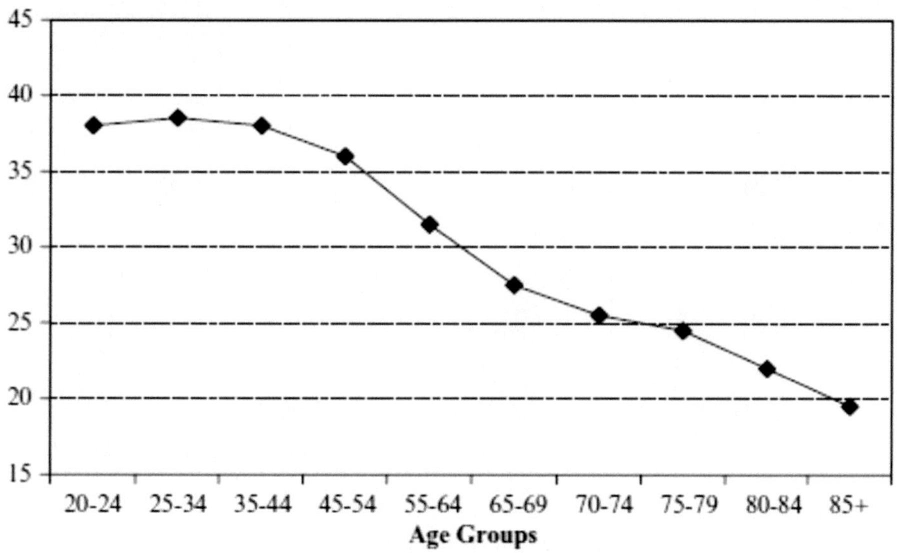

Fig. 32.10 Delayed memory for stories (WRAML-2) by age group. The raw scores corresponding to an age-corrected scaled score of 10 are portrayed for each age group (The data were obtained from Sheslow & Adams, 2003)

Education is an important variable to consider when interpreting cognitive test results (Heaton et al., 2004; Heaton et al., 2003; Ivnik et al., 1996; Morgan et al., 2007; Rosselli & Ardila, 2003; Ryan et al., 2005). It has long been recognized that education is correlated with cognitive test performance. For example, predicted WAIS-III Full Scale IQ scores in Caucasian men, stratified by level of education, are as follows: ≤8 years = 90, 9–11 years = 96, 12 years = 102, 13–15 years = 107, 16 years = 113; and ≥17 years = 118 (The Psychological Corporation, 2001, p. 114). The effects of education and sex on cognitive functioning are illustrated in Fig. 32.11. Normative scores on each test for 35 year olds, adjusted for sex and education, are presented. Higher scores mean *better performance* relative to the normative sample. For example, the Arithmetic subtest of the WAIS-III measures a person's ability to do mental arithmetic. A raw score on this test of 13 was used for all normative comparisons. First, notice the striking effect of education. A raw score of 13 corresponds to a *T* score of 53 for men with 9 years of education (i.e., the 62nd percentile) and 40 for men with 16 years of education (i.e., 16th percentile). Men outperform women on the Arithmetic test; thus, the normative *T* scores for women are higher than the normative *T* scores for men (i.e., a raw score of 13 for women results in a *better* normative score than it does for men). In contrast, women outperform men on Digit Symbol-Coding, a measure of visual-motor processing speed and immediate memory for stories (thus, the same raw score results in a higher normative *T* score for men versus women). Men outperformed women on the Design Construction test, a measure of visual-spatial ability.

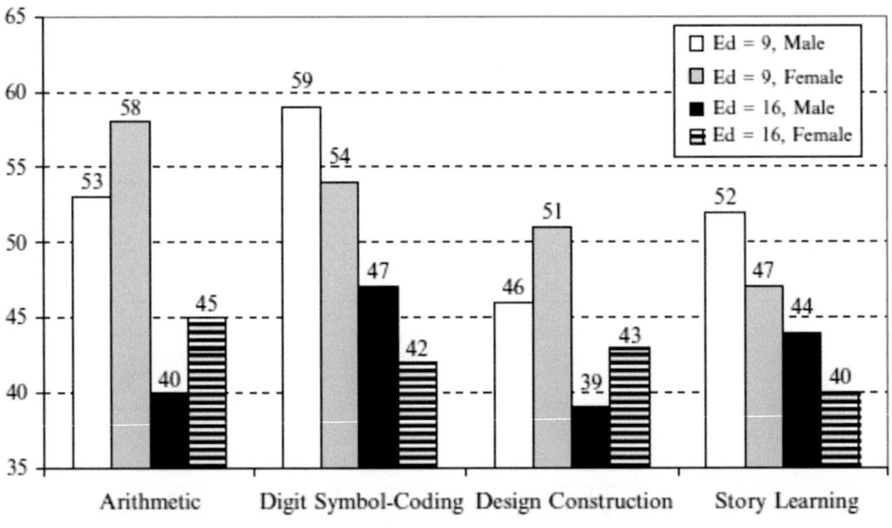

Fig. 32.11 Influence of sex and education on cognitive functioning (normative *T* scores). Normative scores were calculated for 35 year olds based on the following raw scores: WAIS-III Arithmetic = 13, WAIS-III Digit Symbol Coding = 75, NAB Design Construction = 14 and NAB Story Learning Immediate Recall = 61. Education levels of 9 and 16 years were used

Reading ability, as a correlate of both education and intelligence, is also related to neuropsychological test performance. Reading is believed to be relatively resistant to the effects of brain injury and disease (Bright et al., 2002; Maddrey et al., 1996; Strauss et al., 2006); thus, reading test performance has been used to estimate pre-injury or pre-disease cognitive functioning (Bright et al., 2002; Green et al., 2008; Griffin et al., 2002; Paolo et al., 1996). The relation between reading test scores and cognitive functioning is presented in Fig. 32.12.

Researchers working with diverse groups of people, in different settings and in different countries, have repeatedly demonstrated that ethnic groups frequently perform differently on cognitive testing (Ardila, 1995; Brickman et al., 2006; Manly & Echemendia, 2007; O'Bryant et al., 2004). For example, Patton et al. (2003) compared 50 healthy older African-American adults to 50 Caucasians matched on age, education and gender on the Repeatable Battery for the Assessment of Neuropsychological Status (RBANS; Randolph, 1998). The RBANS is a neuropsychological screening battery designed to measure attention/processing speed, expressive language, visual-spatial and constructional abilities, and immediate and delayed memory. The performances of the two groups on the RBANS Index scores are provided in Fig. 32.13. Note that effect sizes ranged from $d = .52$ (Immediate Memory) to $d = .91$ (Total Score).

The practical implication of this study is that ethnic differences are present on neuropsychological tests, both verbal and nonverbal, in people from the same culture who speak the same language. If an elderly African-American was being evaluated for cognitive impairment secondary to Alzheimer's disease, the psychologist might erroneously conclude that the patient was showing frank evidence of memory

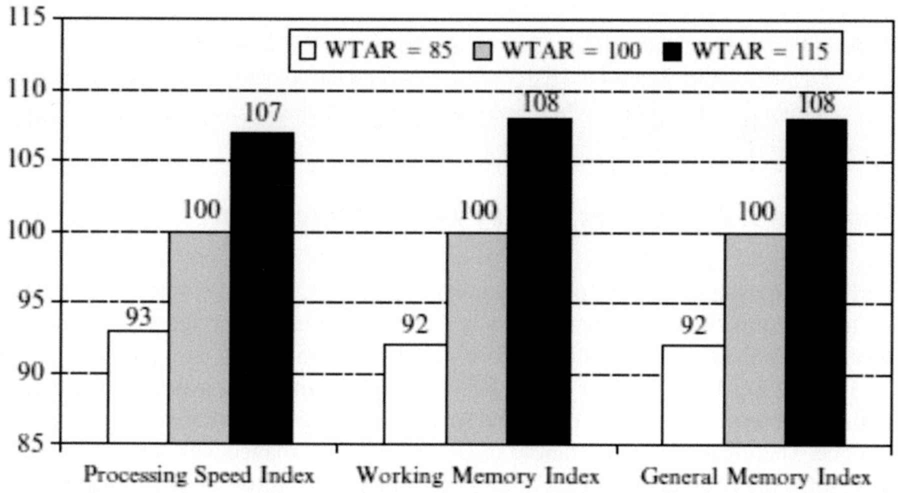

Fig. 32.12 Relation between reading test scores and cognitive functioning in healthy adults. Predicted WAIS-III Processing Speed and WMS-III Working Memory and General Memory Index scores by level of WTAR score

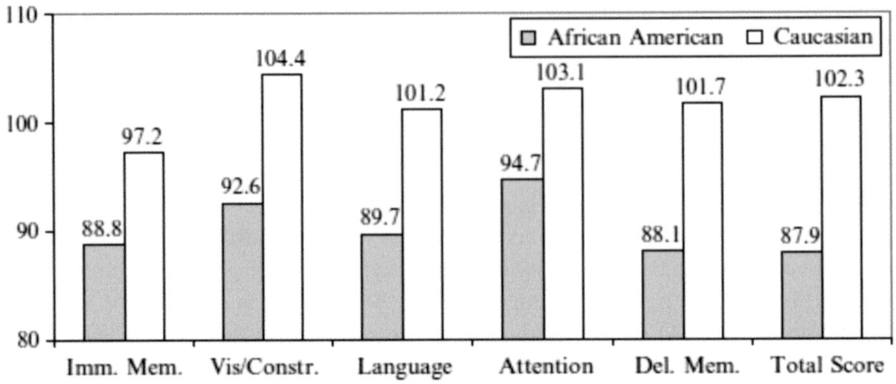

Fig. 32.13 Comparison of healthy African Americans to healthy Caucasians on a neuropsychological screening battery. *Imm. Mem.* Immediate Memory Index, *Vis/Constr.* Visuospatial/Constructional Index, *Del. Mem.* Delayed Memory Index. Values are Index scores with a mean = 100 and standard deviation = 15 (Derived from Patton et al., 2003)

impairment if his or her scores were compared to Caucasian normative data instead of African-American normative data.

The relation between demographic variables and cognitive test performance has clear and compelling implications for research and clinical practice. If the goal of testing is to identify the presence of cognitive impairment, especially a decline attributable to a neurological injury or disease, then diagnostic accuracy will be improved if relevant demographic characteristics are considered in the interpretation of test performance.

Key Point: Evaluating Cognitive Impairment—Principle 4
- Demographic variables (e.g., education and ethnicity) are related to the number of low scores when age-adjusted normative data are used

Principle 5: Low Scores Vary by Level of Intelligence

Perhaps the most often overlooked, yet very important, principle when interpreting multiple scores from a battery of tests is that the number of low scores is related to level of intellectual functioning (Horton, 1999; Steinberg et al., 2005a, 2005b; Tremont et al., 1998; Warner et al., 1987). People with below average intellectual abilities are expected to have more low scores than people with above average intelligence. Therefore, it is important to interpret test performance within the context of a person's intellectual abilities. Figures 32.14 and 32.15 illustrate the fourth principle using performance on the NAB and the WAIS-III/WMS-III that is stratified by level of intelligence (Figs. 32.16 and 32.17). As can be seen, the percentage of healthy people with low scores is greater for those with lesser intelligence.

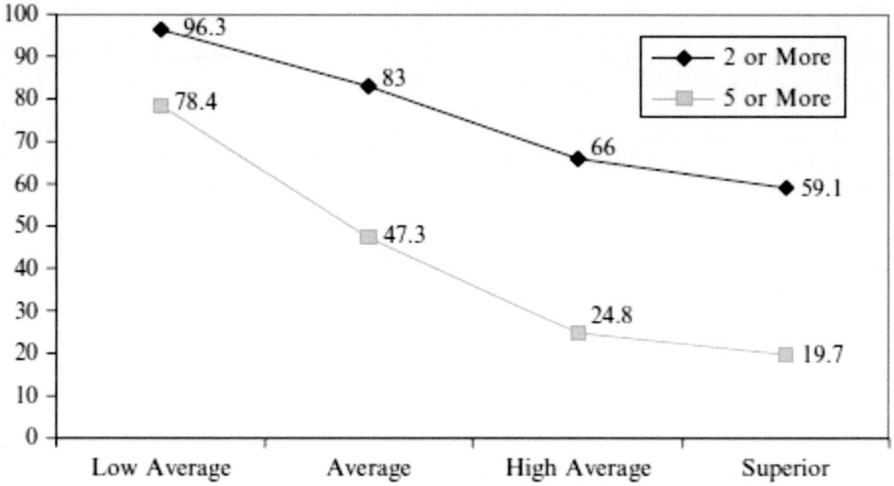

Fig. 32.14 Prevalence of low NAB scores stratified by intelligence (RIST): Cutoff <1 SD. *SD* standard deviation, *NAB* Neuropsychological Assessment Battery. The 36 primary *T* scores were considered. Data points represent the percent of healthy adults from the NAB standardization sample who had (1) 2 or more or (2) 5 or more scores below 1 SD (i.e., $T < 4$ 0). Data are presented for different classifications of intellectual abilities based on RIST Index (i.e., low average, RIST = 80–89; average, RIST = 90–109; high average, RIST = 110–119; and superior, RIST ≥120)

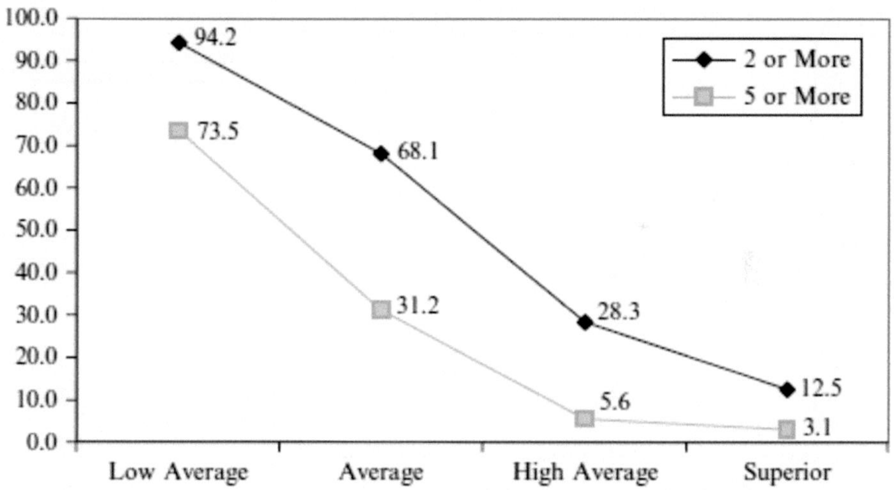

Fig. 32.15 Prevalence of low WAIS-III/WMS-III scores stratified by estimated intelligence (WTAR-Demographics Predicted FSIQ): Cutoff <1 SD. *SD* standard deviation, *WAIS-III* Wechsler Adult Intelligence Scale—Third Edition, *WMS-III* Wechsler Memory Scale—Third Edition. The 20 primary scaled scores from the WAIS-III/WMS-III were considered. Data points represent the percent of healthy adults from the WAIS-III/WMS-III standardization sample who had (1) 2 or more or (2) 5 or more scores at or below the fifth percentile (i.e., SS ≤ 5). Data are presented for different classifications of intellectual abilities based on WTAR-demographics predicted full scale IQ (WTAR-FSIQ; i.e., low average, WTAR-FSIQ = 80–89; average, WTAR-FSIQ = 90–109; high average, WTAR-FSIQ = 110–119; and superior, WTAR-FSIQ ≥120)

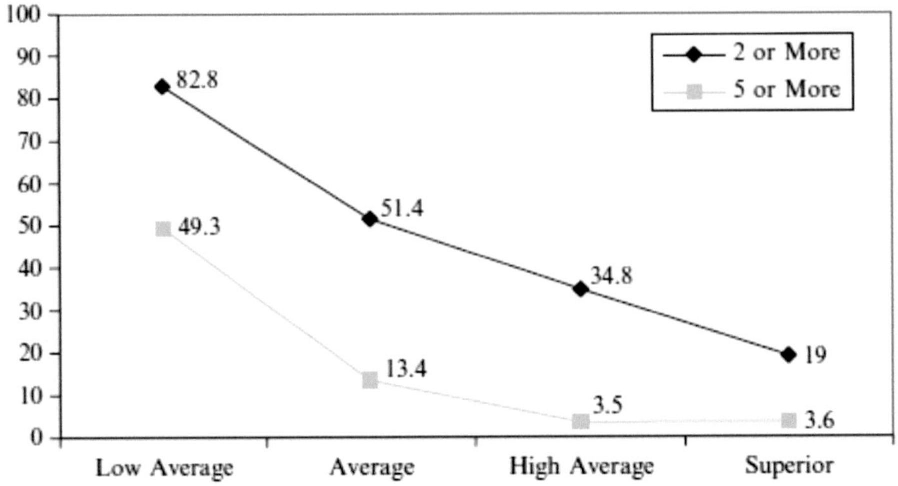

Fig. 32.16 Prevalence of low NAB scores stratified by intelligence (RIST): ≤fifth percentile. *SD* standard deviation, *NAB* Neuropsychological Assessment Battery. The 36 primary *T* scores were considered. Data points represent the percent of healthy adults from the NAB standardization sample who had (1) 2 or more or (2) 5 or more scores at or below the fifth percentile (i.e., $T < 34$). Data are presented for different classifications of intellectual abilities based on RIST Index (i.e., low average, RIST = 80–89; average, RIST = 90–109; high average, RIST = 110–119; and superior, RIST ≥120)

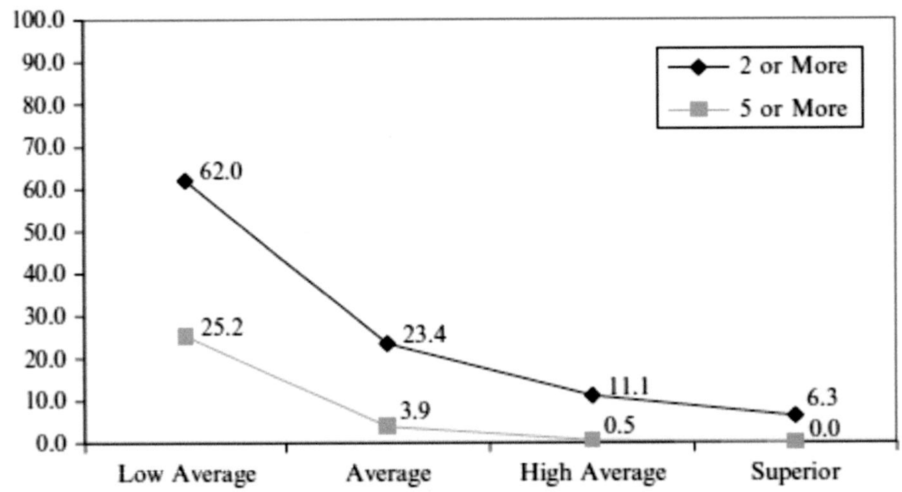

Fig. 32.17 Prevalence of low WAIS-III/WMS-III scores stratified by estimated intelligence (WTAR-Demographics Predicted FSIQ): Cutoff ≤fifth percentile. *SD* standard deviation, *WAIS-III* Wechsler Adult Intelligence Scale—Third Edition, *WMS-III* Wechsler Memory Scale—Third Edition. The 20 primary scaled scores from the WAIS-III/WMS-III were considered. Data points represent the percent of healthy adults from the WAIS-III/WMS-III standardization sample who had (1) 2 or more or (2) 5 or more scores at or below the fifth percentile (i.e., SS ≤ 5). Data are presented for different classifications of intellectual abilities based on WTAR-demographics predicted full scale IQ (WTAR-FSIQ; i.e., low average, WTAR-FSIQ = 80–89; average, WTAR-FSIQ = 90–109; high average, WTAR-FSIQ = 110–119; and superior, WTAR-FSIQ ≥120)

Key Point: Evaluating Cognitive Impairment—Principle 5

- Low scores occur at different rates depending upon the intellectual ability of the individual
- Individuals with lower intellectual ability tend to have more low scores

Identifying Cognitive Impairment: New Psychometric Criteria for Cognitive Disorder NOS

The clinical implications of these five fundamental psychometric principles are obvious. Failing to consider the prevalence of low scores, demographic variables and intelligence carefully and judiciously can result in misdiagnosis or missed diagnosis. For the past 3 years, we have been working on psychometric analyses relating to the base rates of low scores across batteries of neuropsychological tests (Iverson et al., 2008b, 2008c). This work led to the development of new psychometric criteria for the DSM-IV diagnosis Cognitive Disorder NOS (Iverson & Brooks, 2009) using the Neuropsychological Assessment Battery (NAB; Stern & White, 2003). We have attempted to carefully consider the core psychometric principles discussed in this chapter in the development of these psychometric criteria for CD-NOS using the NAB. First, the battery is fixed in number of tests and number of scores that are interpreted (i.e., additional tests can be given, but the fixed number represents the "core" that pertains to the CD-NOS psychometric criteria). Second, the battery covers all the domains of functioning for mild neurocognitive disorder. Third, all tests are co-normed, meaning they were all given to a large normative sample. Fourth, all test scores are presented on a common metric (i.e., *T* scores), and all scores are adjusted for demographic variables (i.e., sex, age and education). Fifth, criteria for impairment are established for different cutoff scores (e.g., 1 SD, tenth percentile and 2 SDs below the mean). Sixth, criteria for impairment in each domain were set with known false positive rates. Finally, the criteria for impairment were stratified by level of intelligence because the entire NAB standardization sample was also administered the Reynolds Intellectual Screening Test (RIST; Reynolds & Kamphaus, 2003), a brief measure of intellectual abilities.

An *abbreviated version of the NAB*, comprised of 15 of the 24 tests, was used to develop the new psychometric criteria. This abbreviated battery requires approximately 2 h to administer. A brief description of the five NAB modules, along with the tests and the 23 primary T scores selected for the development of the CD-NOS criteria, is presented in Table 32.1 (see White and Stern (2003) for additional information about the specific tests).

Development of the criteria involved determining the prevalence of low scores in each domain. All scores within each domain were considered simultaneously, rather than in isolation. The cutoffs used in this study included: <25th percentile; <16th percentile (i.e., <1 SD); <tenth percentile; ≤fifth percentile; and < second percentile (i.e., <2 SDs). For each domain, the number of scores below various cutoffs

Table 32.1 NAB modules and tests used for development of psychometric criteria for CD-NOS

• NAB Attention Module: This module fully assesses "attention and speed of information processing" as described for the DSM-IV mild neurocognitive disorder (e.g., concentration and rapidity of assimilating or analyzing information). All five primary tests are used in the abbreviated battery, but the analyses do not include Numbers & Letter A Speed and Errors).
• NAB Language Module: For the abbreviated NAB, only Oral Production and Naming are used.
• NAB Memory Module: This module measures verbal and visual learning and memory. This clearly covers the memory domain for mild neurocognitive disorder (i.e., "learning or recalling new information"). For the abbreviated NAB, analyses are based on 6 T scores (List Learning A Immediate Recall for 3 Trials; List Learning A Long Delayed Recall; Story Learning Immediate Recall; Story Learning Delayed Recall; Daily Living Memory Immediate Recall; Daily Living Memory Delayed Recall).
• NAB Spatial Module: This module measures perceptual, spatial, constructional and spatial-motor abilities. This is partially related to the DSM-IV category called "perceptual-motor abilities" (e.g., "integrating visual, tactile, or auditory information with motor activities"). For the abbreviated NAB, the Visual Discrimination and Design Construction tests are used.
• NAB Executive Functions Module: Measures different aspects of executive functioning (e.g., planning, abstracting, conceptualizing, judgment and word generativity). This module reasonably covers the "executive functions" domain for mild neurocognitive disorder. For the abbreviated NAB, the Mazes, Categories and Word Generation tests are used.

suggesting the presence of cognitive impairment was determined from frequency distributions. *Possible* impairment is based on having fewer than 20% of healthy adults and *probable* impairment is based on having fewer than 10% of healthy adults obtaining the number of low scores below the given cutoff. In other words, there is a known false positive rate for both possible and probable impairment.

Table 32.2 presents the psychometric criteria, stratified by level of intelligence, for determining possible or probable impairment in each of the five domains from the abbreviated NAB. To use these interpretive tables, there is a three-step procedure: (1) count the number of primary *T* scores in each domain that fall below the five cutoff scores (i.e., 25th, 16th, 10th, fifth, and second percentiles); (2) refer to the appropriate table that corresponds to the person's level of intelligence[2]; and (3) determine if the number of low scores in each cognitive domain is considered *broadly normal*, *possible impairment* or *probable impairment.*

These proposed guidelines, *which were established with a false positive rate of less than 20% for possible cognitive impairment and less than 10% for probable cognitive impairment*, are stratified by level of intellectual abilities. However, it is

[2] We are using the RIST to estimate *current* intellectual abilities. After determining their current RIST score, we combine this information with clinical judgment to estimate premorbid RIST *classification category* (e.g., low average, average, high average or superior). We usually use the obtained RIST as the best estimate of premorbid RIST classification. However, sometimes we might believe that the obtained RIST under-estimates premorbid ability, and thus we might choose one classification higher. An example would be if a person with obvious brain damage obtained a RIST of 109. We might assume that his/her premorbid RIST was more likely to fall in the High Average classification range than in the Average classification range.

Table 32.2 Criteria for possible and probable cognitive impairment by domain

Attention and speed	Psychometric criteria
Low average intelligence (RIST = 80–89)	
Possible impairment	7 scores <25th%; 5 scores <1 SD; 4 scores <10th%; 3 scores ≤5th%
Probable impairment	8 scores <25th%; 6 scores <1 SD; 5 scores <10th%; 2 scores <2nd%
Language	
Possible impairment	2 scores <25th%; 1 score < 2 SD
Probable impairment	2 scores <1 SD
Learning and memory	
Possible impairment	6 scores <25th%; 5 scores <1 SD; 4 score < 10th%; 3 scores ≤5th%
Probable impairment	6 scores <1 SD; 5 scores <10th%; 4 scores ≤5th%; 2 scores <2nd%
Perceptual and spatial	
Possible impairment	2 scores <1 SD; 1 score < 2nd%
Probable impairment	2 scores <10th%
Executive functioning	
Possible impairment	3 scores <25th%; 2 scores <10th%; 1 score < 2nd%
Probable impairment	3 scores <1 SD;; 2 scores ≤5th%
Average intelligence (RIST = 90–109)	
Possible impairment	5 scores <25th%; 3 scores <1 SD; 2 scores <10th%; 1 score < 2nd %
Probable impairment	6 scores <25th%; 4 scores <1 SD; 3 scores <10th%; 2 scores <2nd%
Language	
Possible impairment	1 score < 10th%
Probable impairment	2 scores <25th%; 1 score < 2 SD
Learning and memory	
Possible impairment	3–4 scores <25th%; 2 scores <1 SD; 1 score < 10th%
Probable impairment	5 scores <25th%; 3 scores <1 SD; 2 scores <10th%
Perceptual and spatial	
Possible impairment	1 score < 10th%
Probable impairment	2 scores <25th%
Executive functioning	
Possible impairment	2 scores <25th%; 1 score < 10th%

(continued)

Table 32.2 (continued)

Attention and speed	Psychometric criteria
Probable impairment	3 scores <25th%; 2 scores <1 SD
High average intelligence (RIST = 110–119)	
Possible impairment	4 scores <25th%; 2–3 scores <1 SD; 2 scores <10th%; 1 score ≤ 5th%
Probable impairment	5 scores <25th%; 4 scores <1 SD; 3 scores <10th%; 2 scores ≤5th%; 1 score < 2nd%
Language	
Possible impairment	1 score < 1SD
Probable impairment	2 scores <25th%
Learning and memory	
Possible impairment	3 scores <25th%; 1 score < 10th%
Probable impairment	4 scores <25th%; 2 scores <1 SD
Perceptual and spatial	
Possible impairment	1 score < 1 SD
Probable impairment	2 scores <25th%; 1 score < 10th%
Executive functioning	
Possible impairment	1 score < 1 SD
Probable impairment	2 scores <25th%; 1 score < 10th%
Superior/very superior intelligence (RIST ≥ 120)	
Possible impairment	4 scores <25th%; 3 scores <1 SD;
Probable impairment	6 scores <25th%; 4 scores <1 SD; 2 scores <10th%; 1 score < 2nd%
Language	
Possible impairment	1 score < 1 SD
Probable impairment	2 scores <25th%; 1 score < 10th%
Learning and memory	
Possible impairment	2 scores <25th%; 1 scores <1 SD
Probable impairment	3 scores <25th%; 2 scores <1 SD; 1 score ≤ 5th%
Perceptual and spatial	
Possible impairment	1 score < 25th%
Probable impairment	1 score < 1 SD

(continued)

Table 32.2 (continued)

Attention and speed	Psychometric criteria
Executive functioning	
Possible impairment	1 score < 1 SD
Probable impairment	2 scores <25th%; 1 score < 10th%

Note: Analyses based on subjects between 18 and 79 years of age ($n = 1269$). Produced by special permission of the Publisher, Psychological Assessment Resources, Inc., 16,204 North Florida Avenue, Lutz, Florida 33,549, from the standardization data presented in the Neuropsychological Assessment Battery Psychometric and Technical Manual by Travis White, Ph.D. and Robert A. Stern, Ph.D. Copyright 2001, 2003 by PAR, Inc. Further reproduction is prohibited without permission from PAR, Inc. There are slight variations due to rounding

important to note that the false positive rates are established for each domain *in isolation, not for all domains simultaneously*. We have not determined the criteria, yet, for determining how often a person has two or more "impaired" domains. This work is underway.

The criteria in Table 32.2 can be used to identify widespread diminishment or frank impairment. For example, for adults of average intelligence, having 5 or more scores below average (i.e., below the 25th percentile) in the Attention and Psychomotor Speed domain reflects widespread low performance ("possible impairment"), whereas having 2 scores below the second percentile (i.e., 2 SDs below the mean) reflects circumscribed frank impairment ("probable impairment"). Of course, some patients will show widespread below average performance punctuated by some extremely low scores.

Key Points: Psychometric Criteria for Diagnosing Cognitive Disorder NOS

- Possible cutoff scores include 25th%, 1 SD, 10th%, 5th%, 2nd%
- Number of scores falling below cutoff criteria vary by level of intelligence
- Tables provide base rates of low test scores, in each domain, stratified by intelligence

Case Examples: Patients Treated for Brain Tumors

The new psychometric criteria presented in Table 32.2 allow us to determine whether performance across several measures from a cognitive domain is diminished while still maintaining desired false positive rates. In the tables below, we present case examples of two patients who have been treated for brain tumors and have been evaluated using the abbreviated Neuropsychological Assessment Battery (NAB). These case examples illustrate the use of the psychometric tables for determining the presence of cognitive impairment that would be consistent with cognitive disorder NOS (i.e., Mild Neurocognitive Disorder). The patients' performances on the individual tests comprising the abbreviated NAB are presented in Table 32.3.

Table 32.3 RIST and NAB test data for two brain tumor case examples

	T scores (percentile ranks)	
Domains/tests	Case example 1	Case example 2
RIST index (classification)	High average	Average
Attention and processing speed		
Digits forward	46 (34%)	40 (16%)
Digits backward	52 (58%)	55 (69%)
Dots	58 (79%)	47 (38%)
Numbers and letters A speed	52 (58%)	48 (42%)
Numbers and letters A errors	39 (14%)	27 (1%)
Numbers and letters B efficiency	41 (18%)	32 (4%)
Numbers and letters C efficiency	60 (84%)	35 (7%)
Numbers and letters D efficiency	63 (90%)	36 (8%)
Numbers and letters D disruption	60 (84%)	36 (8%)
Driving scenes	53 (62%)	30 (2%)
Language		
Oral production	48 (42%)	46 (34%)
Naming	55 (69%)	52 (58%)
Learning and memory		
List learning A total immediate	42 (21%)	40 (16%)
List learning A long delay recall	41 (18%)	32 (4%)
Story learning immediate r	59 (82%)	38 (12%)
Story learning delayed recall	57 (76%)	28 (1%)
Daily living memory immediate	42 (21%)	39 (14%)
Daily living memory delayed	45 (31%)	45 (31%)
Perceptual and spatial abilities		
Visual discrimination	61 (86%)	44 (27%)
Design construction	54 (66%)	46 (34%)
Executive functioning		
Mazes	52 (58%)	47 (38%)
Categories	51 (54%)	29 (2%)
Word generation	59 (82%)	40 (16%)

Note: Values represent demographically adjusted *T* scores (percentiles) from the abbreviated NAB

Case Example #1 was a 59-year-old Caucasian woman with 13 years of education. She was diagnosed with metastatic brain tumors (from her cervix), located in her left front-temporal region and her left occipital region. She underwent radiation therapy 14 months before this evaluation. She subsequently underwent chemotherapy for the next 7 months. Her performance on the RIST was high average (RIST Index = 116). Therefore, her performance on each domain is compared to the criteria in Table 32.2. Her performances in the attention, language, spatial and executive functioning domains are considered broadly normal. She has *probable* impairment on the learning and memory module. Thus, she appears to have diminished learning and memory skills. However, she does not appear to meet the psychometric criteria for Cognitive Disorder NOS.

Case Example #2 was a 43-year-old Caucasian man with 14 years of education. He underwent a total resection of a Grade II oligodendroglioma in his right frontal lobe, followed by partial brain radiation therapy and chemotherapy. His surgery was 6.5 years before this evaluation. His performance on the RIST was average (RIST Index = 101). His performance in the language and spatial domains is considered broadly normal. He has *possible* impairment in the executive functioning domain and *probable* impairment in the attention and memory domains. Based on his performance on testing, he meets the psychometric criteria for Cognitive Disorder NOS.

Conclusions

The purpose of this chapter was to provide information for clinicians and researchers that should ultimately improve the accuracy of how we define, conceptualize and measure cognitive impairment in neuropsychology. Five key psychometric principles that should be considered when interpreting a battery of tests are presented in this chapter. These principles include: (1) Low scores are relatively common across all test batteries; (2) Low scores depend on where you set your cutoff score; (3) Low scores vary by number of tests administered; (4) Low scores vary by demographic characteristics of the examinee; and (5) Low scores vary by level of intelligence.

There are clear implications for these principles in day-to-day clinical practice. If a neuropsychologist administers a 3- to 4-h battery of tests, sets the cutoff for impairment at 1SD below the mean (i.e., $T < 40$), then 30–50% of healthy adults will have *five* or *more* low scores. If a more conservative cutoff for impairment on the battery is set at ≤fifth percentile, then 30–50% of healthy adults will have *two* or *more* low scores.

Not surprisingly, the probability of obtaining a low score depends on where you set your cutoff. For example, when considering 36 T scores from the NAB, 44% of healthy adults obtain five or more scores below 1SD and only 5% of healthy adults obtain five or more scores below 2 SD. Similarly, when considering 20 subtest scores from the WAIS-III/WMS-III, 34% have five or more scores below 1SD and only 2% have five or more scores below 2 SD.

The average neuropsychological evaluation might include 20–40 tests that yield 40–60 scores. The more tests that are given, the more likely it is to obtain low scores. For example, if 36 primary T scores are considered across the NAB, then 44% of healthy adults will have five or more scores below 1SD ($T = 39$ or less). If 16 primary *T* scores from the NAB are considered, then 16% of healthy adults will have five or more scores below 1SD.

The failure to consider the demographic characteristics of a patient or research subject can increase the likelihood of a false positive or a false negative diagnosis of cognitive impairment. For example, if test scores are only adjusted for age, then (1) there will be sex differences on some tests, (2) those with less education will perform more poorly than those with more education on some tests and (3) ethnic minorities will perform more poorly than majority culture Caucasians on some tests.

Considering cognitive test performance within the context of intellectual ability can improve a clinician or researcher's ability to accurately identify cognitive impairment. When considering 20 subtest scores from the WAIS-III/WMS-III, 31% of healthy adults of *average* intelligence will have *five or more* low scores (scaled score of 7 or lower) compared to only 5.6% of healthy adults with *high average* intelligence. Therefore, considering pre-injury or pre-disease level of intellectual ability should reduce false negative diagnoses of cognitive impairment in those with higher levels of intelligence and reduce false positive diagnoses in those with lower levels of intelligence.

It is important for clinicians and researchers to (1) have an understanding of these principles and (2) to implement these principles in clinical practice, research programs and clinical trials. It is necessary to apply these principles when developing criteria for cognitive impairment. Failure to appreciate, consider and apply these principles to cognitive assessment will result in decreased diagnostic accuracy. For example, if trying to identify early evidence of cognitive impairment associated with prodromal Alzheimer's disease, failure to consider these principles can result in (1) failure to identify true cognitive diminishment in a Caucasian man of high average intelligence (i.e., a false negative), and (2) misdiagnosing a Hispanic woman with 10 years of education as cognitively impaired when she is not (i.e., a false positive).

We have developed new psychometric criteria for determining the presence of cognitive impairment (Iverson & Brooks, 2009). To the best of our knowledge, this represents the first psychometrically derived and testable guidelines for identifying plausible psychometric criteria for CD-NOS that (1) take into consideration the five psychometric principles, (2) are consistent with the recommendations for cognitive disorder NOS, and (3) are based on fixed number of tests (i.e., an abbreviated version of the NAB) The procedure outlined in this chapter should result in fewer false positive and false negative diagnoses. Of course, additional research is needed to test these criteria in clinical populations with known cognitive impairment.

The guiding principles and research set out in this chapter have important implications for (1) day-to-day clinical practice, (2) the design of research and clinical trials involving cognition and (3) the development of new nosology for cognitive impairment. It is our hope that the next edition of the Diagnostic and Statistical

Manual of Mental Disorders—Fifth Edition (DSM-V) will provide more guidance for the accurate identification of cognitive impairment in patients with medical, psychiatric or neurological conditions.

References

American Psychiatric Association. (1994). *Diagnostic and statistical manual of mental disorders* (4th ed.). American Psychiatric Association.

Antinori, A., Arendt, G., Becker, J. T., Brew, B. J., Byrd, D. A., Cherner, M., et al. (2007). Updated research nosology for HIV-associated neurocognitive disorders. *Neurology, 69*(18), 1789–1799.

Ardila, A. (1995). Directions of research in cross-cultural neuropsychology. *Journal of Clinical and Experimental Neuropsychology, 17*(1), 143–150.

Axelrod, B. N., & Wall, J. R. (2007). Expectancy of impaired neuropsychological test scores in a non-clinical sample. *International Journal of Neuroscience, 117*(11), 1591–1602.

Beatty, W. W., Mold, J. W., & Gontkovsky, S. T. (2003). RBANS performance: Influences of sex and education. *Journal of Clinical and Experimental Neuropsychology, 25*(8), 1065–1069.

Binder, L. M., Iverson, G. L., & Brooks, B. L. (2009). To err is human: "Abnormal" neuropsychological scores and variability are common in healthy adults. *Archives of Clinical Neuropsychology, 24*, 31–46.

Brickman, A. M., Cabo, R., & Manly, J. J. (2006). Ethical issues in cross-cultural neuropsychology. *Applied Neuropsychology, 13*(2), 91–100.

Bright, P., Jaldow, E., & Kopelman, M. D. (2002). The National Adult Reading test as a measure of premorbid intelligence: A comparison with estimates derived from demographic variables. *Journal of the International Neuropsychological Society, 8*(6), 847–854.

Brooks, B. L., Iverson, G. L., Holdnack, J. A., & Feldman, H. H. (2008). The potential for misclassification of mild cognitive impairment: A study of memory scores on the Wechsler Memory Scale-III in healthy older adults. *Journal of the International Neuropsychological Society, 14*(3), 463–478.

Brooks, B. L., Iverson, G. L., & White, T. (2007). Substantial risk of "Accidental MCI" in healthy older adults: Base rates of low memory scores in neuropsychological assessment. *Journal of the International Neuropsychological Society, 13*(3), 490–500.

Collaer, M. L., & Nelson, J. D. (2002). Large visuospatial sex difference in line judgment: Possible role of attentional factors. *Brain and Cognition, 49*(1), 1–12.

Crawford, J. R., Garthwaite, P. H., & Gault, C. B. (2007). Estimating the percentage of the population with abnormally low scores (or abnormally large score differences) on standardized neuropsychological test batteries: A generic method with applications. *Neuropsychology, 21*(4), 419–430.

Donders, J., Zhu, J., & Tulsky, D. (2001). Factor index score patterns in the WAIS-III standardization sample. *Assessment, 8*(2), 193–203.

Dubois, B., Feldman, H. H., Jacova, C., DeKosky, S. T., Barberger-Gateau, P., Cummings, J., et al. (2007). Research criteria for the diagnosis of Alzheimer's disease: Revising the NINCDS-ADRDA criteria – a position paper. *Lancet Neurology, 6*, 734–746.

Geary, D. C., Saults, S. J., Liu, F., & Hoard, M. K. (2000). Sex differences in spatial cognition, computational fluency, and arithmetical reasoning. *Journal of Experimental and Child Psychology, 77*(4), 337–353.

Green, R. E., Melo, B., Christensen, B., Ngo, L. A., Monette, G., & Bradbury, C. (2008). Measuring premorbid IQ in traumatic brain injury: An examination of the validity of the Wechsler Test of Adult Reading (WTAR). *Journal of Clinical and Experimental Neuropsychology, 30*(2), 163–172.

Griffin, S. L., Mindt, M. R., Rankin, E. J., Ritchie, A. J., & Scott, J. G. (2002). Estimating premorbid intelligence: Comparison of traditional and contemporary methods across the intelligence continuum. *Archives of Clinical Neuropsychology, 17*(5), 497–507.

Heaton, R. K., Grant, I., & Matthews, C. G. (1991). *Comprehensive norms for an extended Halstead-Reitan battery: Demographic corrections, research findings, and clinical applications*. Psychological Assessment Resources, Inc.

Heaton, R. K., Miller, S. W., Taylor, M. J., & Grant, I. (2004). *Revised comprehensive norms for an expanded Halstead-Reitan battery: Demographically adjusted neuropsychological norms for African American and Caucasian adults professional manual*. Psychological Assessment Resources.

Heaton, R. K., Taylor, M. J., & Manly, J. (2003). Demographic effects and use of demographically corrected norms with the WAIS-III and WMS-III. In D. S. Tulsky, D. H. Saklofske, G. J. Chelune, R. K. Heaton, R. J. Ivnik, R. Bornstein, A. Prifitera, & M. Ledbetter (Eds.), *Clinical interpretation of the WAIS-III and WMS-III* (pp. 183–210). Academic.

Herlitz, A., Nilsson, L. G., & Backman, L. (1997). Gender differences in episodic memory. *Memory & Cognition, 25*(6), 801–811.

Horton, A. M., Jr. (1999). Above-average intelligence and neuropsychological test score performance. *International Journal of Neuroscience, 99*(1–4), 221–231.

Ingraham, L. J., & Aiken, C. B. (1996). An empirical approach to determining criteria for abnormality in test batteries with multiple measures. *Neuropsychology, 10*, 120–124.

Iverson, G. L., & Brooks, B. L. (2009). New psychometric criteria for DSM-IV cognitive disorder NOS. *Journal of the International Neuropsychological Society*.

Iverson, G. L., Brooks, B. L., & Ashton, V. L. (2008a). Cognitive impairment: Foundations for clinical and forensic practice. In M. P. Duckworth, T. Iezzi, & W. O'Donohue (Eds.), *Motor vehicle collisions: Medical, psychosocial, and legal consequences* (pp. 243–309). Academic.

Iverson, G. L., Brooks, B. L., & Holdnack, J. A. (2008b). Misdiagnosis of cognitive impairment in forensic neuropsychology. In R. L. Heilbronner (Ed.), *Neuropsychology in the courtroom: Expert analysis of reports and testimony* (pp. 243–266). Guilford Press.

Iverson, G. L., Brooks, B. L., White, T., & Stern, R. A. (2008c). Neuropsychological Assessment Battery (NAB): Introduction and advanced interpretation. In A. M. Horton Jr. & D. Wedding (Eds.), *The neuropsychology handbook* (3rd ed., pp. 279–343). Springer.

Ivnik, R. J., Makec, J. F., Smith, G. E., Tangolos, E. G., & Peterson, R. C. (1996). Neuropsychological tests' norms above age 55: COWAT, BNT, MAE Token, WRAT-R Reading, AMNART, STROOP, TMT, and JLO. *The Clinical Neuropsychologist, 10*, 262–278.

Maddrey, A. M., Cullum, C. M., Weiner, M. F., & Filley, C. M. (1996). Premorbid intelligence estimation and level of dementia in Alzheimer's disease. *Journal of the International Neuropsychological Society, 2*(6), 551–555.

Manly, J. J., & Echemendia, R. J. (2007). Race-specific norms: Using the model of hypertension to understand issues of race, culture, and education in neuropsychology. *Archives of Clinical Neuropsychology, 22*(3), 319–325.

Morgan, E. E., Woods, S. P., Scott, J. C., Childers, M., Beck, J. M., Ellis, R. J., et al. (2007). Predictive validity of demographically adjusted normative standards for the HIV dementia scale. *Journal of Clinical and Experimental Neuropsychology, 20*, 1–8.

Norman, M. A., Evans, J. D., Miller, W. S., & Heaton, R. K. (2000). Demographically corrected norms for the California Verbal Learning Test. *Journal of Clinical and Experimental Neuropsychology, 22*(1), 80–94.

O'Bryant, S. E., O'Jile, J. R., & McCaffrey, R. J. (2004). Reporting of demographic variables in neuropsychological research: Trends in the current literature. *The Clinical Neuropsychologist, 18*(2), 229–233.

Palmer, B. W., Boone, K. B., Lesser, I. M., & Wohl, M. A. (1998). Base rates of "impaired" neuropsychological test performance among healthy older adults. *Archives of Clinical Neuropsychology, 13*(6), 503–511.

Paolo, A. M., Ryan, J. J., Troster, A. I., & Hilmer, C. D. (1996). Utility of the Barona demographic equations to estimate premorbid intelligence: Information from the WAIS-R standardization sample. *Journal of Clinical Psychology, 52*(3), 335–343.

Patton, D. E., Duff, K., Schoenberg, M. R., Mold, J., Scott, J. G., & Adams, R. L. (2003). Performance of cognitively normal African Americans on the RBANS in community dwelling older adults. *The Clinical Neuropsychologist, 17*(4), 515–530.

Petersen, R. C., Smith, G. E., Ivnik, R. J., Kokmen, E., & Tangalos, E. G. (1994). Memory function in very early Alzheimer's disease. *Neurology, 44*(5), 867–872.

Petersen, R. C., Smith, G. E., Waring, S. C., Ivnik, R. J., Tangalos, E. G., & Kokmen, E. (1999). Mild cognitive impairment: Clinical characterization and outcome. *Archives of Neurology, 56*(3), 303–308.

Randolph, C. (1998). *Repeatable battery for the assessment of neuropsychological status manual*. The Psychological Corporation.

Reynolds, C. R., & Kamphaus, R. W. (2003). *Reynolds intellectual assessment scales and Reynolds intellectual screening test professional manual*. Psychological Assessment Resources.

Rosselli, M., & Ardila, A. (2003). The impact of culture and education on non-verbal neuropsychological measurements: A critical review. *Brain and Cognition, 52*(3), 326–333.

Ryan, E. L., Baird, R., Mindt, M. R., Byrd, D., Monzones, J., & Bank, S. M. (2005). Neuropsychological impairment in racial/ethnic minorities with HIV infection and low literacy levels: Effects of education and reading level in participant characterization. *Journal of the International Neuropsychological Society, 11*(7), 889–898.

Schmidt, S. L., Oliveira, R. M., Rocha, F. R., & Abreu-Villaca, Y. (2000). Influences of handedness and gender on the grooved pegboard test. *Brain and Cognition, 44*(3), 445–454.

Schretlen, D. J., Testa, S. M., Winicki, J. M., Pearlson, G. D., & Gordon, B. (2008). Frequency and bases of abnormal performance by healthy adults on neuropsychological testing. *Journal of the International Neuropsychological Society, 14*(3), 436–445.

Sheslow, D., & Adams, W. (2003). *Wide range assessment of memory and learning* (Administration and technical manual 2nd ed.). Wilmington: Wide Range, Inc.

Steinberg, B. A., Bieliauskas, L. A., Smith, G. E., & Ivnik, R. J. (2005a). Mayo's Older Americans Normative Studies: Age- and IQ-adjusted norms for the trail-making test, the stroop test, and MAE controlled oral word association test. *The Clinical Neuropsychologist, 19*(3–4), 329–377.

Steinberg, B. A., Bieliauskas, L. A., Smith, G. E., Ivnik, R. J., & Malec, J. F. (2005b). Mayo's Older Americans Normative Studies: Age- and IQ-adjusted norms for the auditory verbal learning test and the visual spatial learning test. *The Clinical Neuropsychologist, 19*(3–4), 464–523.

Stern, R. A., & White, T. (2003). *Neuropsychological assessment battery*. Psychological Assessment Resources.

Strauss, E., Sherman, E. M. S., & Spreen, O. (2006). *A compendium of neuropsychological tests: Administration, norms, and commentary* (3rd ed.). Oxford University Press.

The Psychological Corporation. (2001). *Wechsler test of adult reading manual*. Psychological Corporation.

Tremont, G., Hoffman, R. G., Scott, J. G., & Adams, R. L. (1998). Effect of intellectual level on neuropsychological test performance: A response to Dodrill (1997). *The Clinical Neuropsychologist, 12*, 560–567.

Voyer, D., Voyer, S., & Bryden, M. P. (1995). Magnitude of sex differences in spatial abilities: A meta-analysis and consideration of critical variables. *Psychological Bulletin, 117*(2), 250–270.

Warner, M. H., Ernst, J., Townes, B. D., Peel, J., & Preston, M. (1987). Relationships between IQ and neuropsychological measures in neuropsychiatric populations: Within-laboratory and cross-cultural replications using WAIS and WAIS-R. *Journal of Clinical and Experimental Neuropsychology, 9*(5), 545–562.

Wechsler, D. (1997a). *Wechsler adult intelligence scale* (3rd ed.). Psychological Corporation.

Wechsler, D. (1997b). *Wechsler memory scale* (3rd ed.). The Psychological Corporation.

White, T., & Stern, R. A. (2003). *Neuropsychological assessment battery: Psychometric and technical manual*. Psychological Assessment Resources.

World Health Organization. (1992). *International statistical classification of diseases and related health problems* (10th ed.). World Health Organization.

Index

M. Schoenberg, J. Scott (eds.), *The Little Black Book of Neuropsychology*,
https://doi.org/10.1007/978-3-032-07777-6

MIX
Papier aus verantwortungsvollen Quellen
Paper from responsible sources
FSC® C105338

FSC
www.fsc.org

If you have any concerns about our products,
you can contact us on
ProductSafety@springernature.com

In case Publisher is established outside the EU,
the EU authorized representative is:
Springer Nature Customer Service Center GmbH
Europaplatz 3, 69115 Heidelberg, Germany

Printed by Libri Plureos GmbH
in Hamburg, Germany